Also by Jane Bryant Quinn

EVERYONE'S MONEY BOOK

A HOLE IN THE MARKET

MAKING THE MOST OF YOUR MONEY

COMPLETELY REVISED AND UPDATED FOR THE TWENTY-FIRST CENTURY

Jane Bryant Quinn

Simon & Schuster

SIMON & SCHUSTER
Rockefeller Center
1230 Avenue of the Americas
New York, NY 10020

SIMON & SCHUSTER and colophon are registered trademarks
of Simon & Schuster Inc.

Designed by Levavi & Levavi

Manufactured in the United States of America

1   3   5   7   9   10   8   6   4   2

Library of Congress Cataloging-in-Publication Data
Quinn, Jane Bryant.
Making the most of your money / Jane Bryant Quinn.
p.   cm.
"Completely revised and updated for the twenty-first century."
Includes index.
1. Finance, Personal.   2. Investments.   I. Title.
HG179.Q57   1997
332.024'01—dc21   97-23183   CIP
ISBN 0-684-81176-6

FOR DAVID
and all the joys that money can't buy

Contents

Foreword

My favorite story tells about an ad in the *Financial Times*. It said, "The Clairvoyance Society of Greater London will not meet next Tuesday, because of unforeseen circumstances."

Practically everything is unforeseen. Your future and mine are going to be different from what we expect—maybe better, maybe worse, maybe just *different* in some surprising way.

Still, we have to make plans, if only to give ourselves something to work with when circumstances change. In good years, that means building safety nets: savings, investments, clean credit cards. If something bad happens, we need to know how to retrench until times turn again.

Everything alters: health care, student aid, the securities markets, Social Security, everything. Taxes are changing as I write. New products and services come along. As the sage said, you never step in the same river twice.

This book is built on principles that should survive changes in detail. It's an eight-step system for taking charge of your financial life: learning the fundamentals of money, building a base to keep you and your family safe, and making the kinds of investments that best suit your age and circumstances. Like an Alpine climber, you'll also learn how to stay clipped to a rope so a tumble won't take you down.

Don't hesitate to make your own financial decisions. The chief difference between you and a professional planner is information. This book, I hope, will narrow that gap. You can find the right answers as long as you know what the questions are.

In my dream scheme, you will get a program up and running and then turn to better things—children, friends, social concerns. Money is my business, but I spend as little personal time on it as possible. We need money to live on, but it isn't a life. I hope this book will help you figure that out, too.

JANE BRYANT QUINN
North Salem, N.Y.

STEP 1

BUILDING YOUR BASE

If I could have lunch with anyone, whom would I choose? Shakespeare, for sure. Cleopatra—to see how compelling she really was. Virginia Woolf. The historian Henry Adams. Bill Cosby. (Bill, call me at 212-445-4000.) Archimedes.

Okay, Archimedes isn't someone you would think of right off the bat. But I have a special feeling for the Greek mathematician. Aside from his theoretical work, he constructed ingenious mechanical devices. He showed that great weights could be moved with small effort, provided that the lever was long enough. "Give me a place to stand," he said, "and I will move the world."

Our world could stand a little shove, especially the world of money. Each new generation staggers forward under the weight of old ideas. We "know" too much that isn't true, or isn't true anymore. This is a pressed yet hopeful time (I would explain to Archimedes, over sandwiches). The extravagant eighties are history and the stock-happy nineties nearly so. But what worked in the past doesn't always work in the future. Our minds need moving, as well as our money.

That's a job for a lever. This book was written to help you find a place to stand.

1.

What Archimedes Would Have Done

Where You Stand on the Money Cycle

The finest of all human achievements—
and the most difficult—is merely being reasonable.

All of our deepest beliefs about money are formed in the years when we grow up. We learn the great lessons of our era and set out to put them all to work.

But time is a trickster. Just when you think that you've learned all the rules, some hidden umpire changes the game.

Think about the Depression Kids. Those woeful years left a legacy of fear. Forever after, the generations marked by the thirties saved compulsively. A loan made them feel sick to their stomachs. They took no risks. When the Great Prosperity swelled around them, they mistrusted it. They knew in their hearts it wouldn't last.

Now think about the Inflation Kids, raised in the 1960s and 1970s. They saw in a flash that a dollar saved was a dollar wasted because inflation ate it up. A dollar *borrowed* was a dollar saved. You could use it to buy a car or a stereo before the price increased.

The Inflation Kids felt sorry for the codgers who saved so fruitlessly and lost so much. In the 1970s, the value of fixed savings, pensions, and insurance policies fell apart.

But what do the Inflation Kids—otherwise known as the Baby Boomers —know about money, in their hearts? They, too, are wedded to some of their earliest beliefs. For example, they're waiting for real estate to soar again. They still think it's smart to borrow because inflation—or *something*

—will whisk the repayment burden away. They're wrong, but to think differently goes against their grain. The boomers born later in the cycle replaced real estate with stocks as their dream way of getting rich in a hurry.

The new turn of the wheel is bringing us the Compression Kids, Generation X. They're seeing a very different world. Jobs, chancier than people used to think. Real estate, boring. Wages, not rising very fast. Stocks, paying remarkable returns. As they see it, the rules for living are: save early and often, learn to invest, and let the rising value of stocks carry the burden of debt away.

Can the Inflation Generation change *its* approach to money any better than the Depression Generation could? How soon will the Compression Kids get trapped by the orthodoxies they proclaim today? Can we all find a better place to stand? On the answer to those questions, everything depends.

A CYCLE OF SPENDING AND SAVING

Money comes and goes in your life at different times. Mostly goes, when you're young. Those are the spent years. Maybe the *mis*spent years. But never mind. As you grow older, the urge to save creeps up on you. Here's the typical cycle of wealth:

Ages 20 to 30. You establish credit, buy your first furniture and appliances, take your first auto loan, learn about insurance and taxes. Maybe (here I'm dreaming) you save a little money, in the bank or in company retirement accounts. Retirement accounts are money machines for young people because you have so many years to let them grow untaxed. By the end of the decade, you get married, have a baby, buy a house. (You save for a house the old-fashioned way—by borrowing some of the down payment from your parents.)

Ages 31 to 45. You don't know where your money goes. Bills, bills, bills. College is a freight train headed your way. Maybe (here I'm dreaming again) you start a tuition savings account. Money still dribbles into retirement savings, but only if your company does it for you—by taking it out of your paycheck before you get it to spend. When you're pressed, you open a home-equity line and borrow money against your house. This is a good time to start a business or get more education. Invest in yourself and hope for a payoff.

Ages 46 to 55. You *do* know where your money goes: to good old State U. At the same time, you get the creepy feeling that maybe you won't live forever. You thrash around. You buy books about financial planning. You have an affair. When all else fails, you start to save.

Ages 56 to 65. These are the fat years. You're at the top of your earning power, the kids are gone, the dogs are dead. Twenty percent of your salary can be socked away—which is lucky because you will need extra money for your children's down payments (kids never really go away). Consider long-term-care insurance.

Ages 66 to 75. How golden are these years? As rich as your pension, Social Security, and the income from the money you saved. Start out by living on the first two. Let the income from savings and investments compound for a while, to build a fund for later life.

Ages 76 and Up. Quit saving. Spend, spend, spend! Forget leaving money to your kids—they should have put away more for themselves. Dip into principal to live as comfortably as you deserve. This is what all those years of saving were *for.*

WHEN YOU FALL OFF THE CYCLE

You say you can't find your place on the cycle? That's no surprise. Almost no one lives exactly to order anymore. There are a million ways of getting from birth to death and they all work. If you fall behind financially during any decade, you'll need a plan for catching up.

You Have Your Children in Your 30s. It seemed like a smart idea at the time—diapers tomorrow but never today. No one told you that in your 50s, you'd be paying for college just when you were trying to save for your own retirement. (And even if they told you, you'd never have believed you would ever be that old.) You might have to choose between sending your children to a low-cost college or shortchanging your own future. Maybe your children will have to pay for their education themselves. The moral, for those who can think ahead: save more in your 20s, using the discipline of tax-deferred retirement plans. These plans penalize you for drawing money out, so you're more likely to leave it in.

You Get Divorced and Start Over. Divorce costs you assets and income, with the greater loss usually falling on the woman. She rarely can earn as much money as her ex-husband takes away. For the man, a new wife and new babies might mean that college-tuition bills will arrive in the same mail as the Social Security checks. Unless you're rich or remarry rich, divorce is a decision to cut your standard of living, sometimes permanently.

You Don't Marry. You lack the safety net that a second paycheck provides. On the other hand, there's usually no other mouth to feed. You can start saving and investing earlier than most.

You're Married, with No Children. You've got nothing but money and plenty of it. You are one of the few who *really* can retire early, not just dream about it.

Life Deals You an Accident. A crippling illness. Early widowhood. A child with anguishing medical problems. A family that has always saved can make it through these tragedies. A family in debt to the hilt cannot.

You're Downsized. That's today's euphemism for getting fired. The money in your retirement plan goes for current bills. Your next job pays 20 percent less, with no health insurance or retirement plan. The millennium plays hardball. But you can still secure your future by downscaling your life to match your income. There's honor at every monetary level of life.

You Get the Golden Boot. A forced early retirement. Sometimes you see it coming, sometimes it catches you blindside. You get a consolation prize, in a lump-sum payout or a higher pension for a retiree of your age. But you lose five to ten years of earnings and savings. This risk is the single strongest argument for starting a retirement-savings program young. At your age, a new job will be hard to come by, but you can't afford to retire for real. So it's project work, part-time work, unexpected work like clerking, to pad out your early-retirement check.

Memo to All Workers: Employers don't care that you've worked hard and late, that you haven't been sick in a dozen years, or that every supervisor you've had thinks you're hot stuff. They ask only: What have you done for me lately? Is your job essential to business today? Are your skills the right ones for business tomorrow? Few people *hold* a job anymore. Instead, we have talents that we sell to employers for various projects, some longer term than others. In this kind of world, nothing is more important than continuing education and upgrading skills.

WHO NEEDS WHAT WHEN

The number of financial products on the market today—bank accounts, insurance policies, annuities, mutual funds—I estimate conservatively at two zillion point three ($2.3Z). Most of them nobody needs but buys anyway because some salesperson convinces you to. In fact, you need only a few simple things, matched to your age, your bank balance, and your responsibilities. The rest of this book tells you how to choose them. Here, I offer a general framework for your thinking.

Young and Single. Admit it—you are living your life on hold. Cinderella, waiting for Prince Charming. Peter Pan, not wanting to grow up. You are serious only about your work (or finding work!). Everything else is temporary. There is nothing in your refrigerator and nothing in your bank account. "Wait until I'm married," you say. But what if you don't marry? Or marry late? Looking back, you'll see that you lost ten good years. *Your* future starts now. As a young person you should:

• Establish credit with a low-cost bank card. Practice on one card before getting two. Debt tends to rise to the highest allowable limit. If you're in college, apply for a bank card before you leave. Banks give credit faster to students than to job-seeking young adults. (They count on the parents to save their kids' credit rating by paying off their debts.)

• Get disability insurance coverage. It pays you an income if you're sick or injured and can't work. How will you afford the premiums? By *not* buying life insurance.

• Get health insurance if you don't have a company plan. I know you're immortal, but buy a policy anyway, just in case you should be a teeny-weeny bit mortal and need an operation or a splint. No one wants a charity patient. If you can't afford a policy, maybe your parents will buy it for you. They would probably pay for the splint, so buying your health insurance is really a way of protecting themselves.

• Invest in your own education and training even if it means more student debt. Your earning power is your single greatest asset.

• Start saving money. Put away 10 percent of your earnings. I hear you saying, "I can't do it." So sneak up on it: Start with 5 percent, then move up to 7 percent. You can get to 10 percent within the year. Where should the money go? For starters, part to a bank and part to a retirement plan.

• Start a tax-deferred retirement plan: an Individual Retirement Account or a savings plan through your employer. Put the money into stock-owning mutual funds and leave it there.

• Rent, don't buy an apartment. Condominiums and cooperative apartments may not hold their value. The money you'd spend on a down payment is better invested somewhere else. Buy only when you've definitely put down roots.

• Buy property insurance if you have valuable possessions. You especially need it for business property if you work out of your home. But you don't need it if your apartment is furnished in Modern Attic.

• Make a will unless it's okay for your parents to inherit everything. If you die will-less, that's where your property will probably go.

- Do a power of attorney and a living will (or advanced medical directive). That's basic protection in case you meet with a horrible accident that leaves you alive but not alert. Someone has to act for you, both financially and medically, and you should pick those people yourself.

Older Singles. You might be your own sole support for life, but don't let that scare you into playing your hand too conservatively. Stocks do better than bank accounts or bonds over long periods of time. For financial self-defense, you need:

- A good credit record—good enough for a mortgage or a business loan.
- Enough education and job training to keep your income moving up.
- Good health and disability insurance. The older you get the greater your risk of illness or injury. When you pass 60, consider nursing-home insurance. You don't need any life insurance unless someone depends on your income for support.
- A home of your own. Living will be cheaper and expenses more predictable if you own a house or apartment free and clear when you retire. Keep your homeowners insurance up to date.
- A habit of saving. Try for 15 to 20 percent of your income. No, that's not too much.
- A retirement plan: pension, company tax-deferred savings plan, Individual Retirement Account, Keogh plan, or Simplified Employee Pension for the self-employed. Get more than one plan if you qualify. Fund everything to the max.
- A mix of investments in your retirement plans: some U.S. and foreign stock-owning mutual funds; some Treasuries, tax-exempt municipals, or other bonds.
- An interest beyond your regular job—a pastime or charity. It may open the door to a second career.
- A will, a living will, and a durable power of attorney.
- A good attorney or other surrogate who will manage your money if you can't do it yourself.

Married Couples. You have a lot of responsibilities. Your mate needs security if you die. Children have to be set up, too. After that, the big question is how to handle the family money. You need:

- A cost-sharing system. If you are a two-paycheck couple, will you split the bills or pool your money in one account? If you are a one-paycheck couple, will you start a savings account for the nonearning spouse? Financially speaking, there is no best way, only *your* way.
- Credit cards in the names of both spouses. A wife without joint responsibility for the debt could have her cards yanked if her husband dies or leaves. And vice versa, of course.

• Disability insurance. Every income-earning person needs it, to cover your lost paycheck (and maybe home-health-care bills) if you become too sick or disabled to work.

• Health insurance. Don't go without it, especially between jobs. When you're out of work, you're under a lot of stress, which can lead to accidents and poor health. Working couples should try not to duplicate benefits in their company health plans.

• Life insurance. If your family depends on your income for support, you need life insurance. If your family can get along without your income, you don't. Working couples with no kids may do fine with whatever group term insurance they get from their companies. But you'll need much more coverage if children arrive. Buying insurance on a nonearning spouse is a luxury purchase. Buying it on a child is a waste.

• A will, so that beneficiaries will inherit exactly as much as you intend.

• A power of attorney, so someone can manage your finances if you can't.

• A living will, if you fall into a permanent coma and don't want to spend years on life supports. Also name a surrogate to speak for you, or your living will might be ignored.

• A premarital agreement, if you want to limit what your spouse will collect at divorce or inherit at your death. These agreements are mostly used by people of vastly unequal wealth, the previously divorced who swear that they won't be "burned again," and older people with children from previous marriages to protect. There are postmarital agreements, too, for arrangements you wish you had made earlier.

• Your own home. It should be an acceptable investment if you own it long enough. It's also a form of forced saving and a cheap way to live in retirement, once you own it free and clear. Keep your homeowners insurance up to date.

• Regular savings. Sprinkle 10 percent of every check among ready savings, his-and-hers tax-deferred retirement plans, and college savings. Come to think of it, sprinkle more. You'll never catch up with college costs on a mere 10 percent. Be sure to fund both spouses' retirement plans. Some couples waste a tax deduction by forgetting to fund the plan of a spouse with only modest earnings.

• Job skills. A wife without them is asking for trouble, even if she's home with the kids. Life is not fair. Death or disability occurs. Breadwinners lose their jobs. Not all spouses love each other until the end of time. As the poet said, "Provide, provide."

• Nursing-home insurance, once you pass 60.

Blended Families. Life gets expensive when both bride and groom come with children attached. You need everything that any other married couple does, plus extra protection for stepchildren. Check:

- Whether all the kids are covered by health insurance.
- Whether your will needs changing to include the stepchildren.
- Whether you need trusts to ensure that the children of your former marriages inherit the property they're due.
- Whether all the kids will have enough money for college.

Younger Widows, Widowers, and the Divorced. Maybe you're just plain single again. More likely, there are children to support. It's harder alone. You'll need a substantial safety net:

- Buy as much disability insurance as you can get. If you can't work and can't support your children, the family might break up.
- Don't be without a family health policy for a moment.
- Buy a lot of life insurance if your children's future depends on you. Stick with low-cost term insurance and cancel it when the kids grow up.
- Write a will, especially to name a guardian for your children. Add a living will and a power of attorney.
- Call Social Security. An unmarried child under 18 or 19, or a child disabled before age 22, whose mother or father is dead, can get a monthly Social Security payment on that parent's account. So can a widowed person (including a divorced spouse whose ex-spouse dies) if his or her child is disabled or under 16.
- If you're divorced, report your new status—in writing—to everyone who gave you credit and cancel all joint credit cards. You don't want your ex-spouse's new charges to show up on your personal credit history. (You'll still be responsible for the past debts that you contracted together.)
- If you're widowed, maybe you want to report your new status to credit granters. Then again, maybe you don't. If the card was based on two incomes, or on the income of the spouse who died, you may not be able to keep the card unless you can prove that you're creditworthy. If the family credit history is good and you have an income, the card will doubtless be reissued. But if you have only a small income, it might not be. In that case, nothing in federal law stops you from keeping your old card and keeping mum.
- Find work. Or find better work. Train for a higher-paying job. You can't afford to coast.
- If you collect child support, take out a term insurance policy on your ex-spouse (this should be part of your divorce agreement). The insurance proceeds will make up for your lost child support if he or she dies.
- Save money even at the cost of your standard of living. Maybe you will remarry, but you can't count on it.
- Consider trading down to a smaller house. Keep your homeowners insurance up to date.
- Own a home—your current house or a smaller one—if you're rooted in place. Otherwise, hang loose and rent on a short-term lease. Your next

life may lie somewhere else. Get renters insurance to protect good furniture from fire.

• Take no quick advice about money. Not from your brother. Not from your friends. Above all, not from anyone selling financial products. Salespeople love widows for their ready cash and their presumed dependence on a sympathetic ear. Keep your money in the bank until you've learned something about managing it and know exactly what you want to do.

• Don't automatically turn your life-insurance proceeds into an annuity. Inflation will gradually wipe out the value of a fixed monthly income. You might want to take a lump sum instead, and invest it conservatively.

Older Widows, Widowers, and the Divorced. You have great freedom if your children are grown. Your life can be reconstructed from the ground up. Your checklist includes "cancels" as well as "buys":

• Cancel your life insurance. Use the money to add to your savings and investments.

• Cancel your disability insurance if you have retired and no longer get a paycheck.

• Keep your health insurance. At age 65, get a Medigap policy or join an HMO that will cover what Medicare doesn't.

• Call Social Security. If you worked at least 10 years, you're owed a retirement benefit on your own account, starting as early as 62. Alternatively, you're entitled to benefits based on your spouse's account. You can collect whichever is higher. The widowed are entitled to benefits on their late spouse's account as early as 60 (50 if you're disabled) unless their current earnings are too high. Some other rules:

If you were married for at least 10 years and are now divorced: you're probably eligible for benefits from your ex-spouse's account if (1) you've reached 62, (2) you are not now remarried, and (3) your ex-spouse has also reached age 62 or is receiving Social Security retirement or disability payments.

If you divorced and remarried: you may still get benefits from your ex-spouse's account if (1) your new spouse is receiving Social Security payments *and* (2) your benefits on your new spouse's account would be less than you'd get from your former spouse's account.

If your ex-spouse dies: your benefits can start when you reach 60 (50 if you're disabled). A new wife often worries that Social Security payments to an ex-wife will reduce her own benefits. They won't. Each gets a full payment, as if she were the only wife around. Ditto for husbands collecting on wives' accounts.

• Study up on money management. If you've never handled investments before, this is the moment that nature has chosen for you to learn. In the meantime, keep your money in the bank. Don't give it to anyone else to manage until you've learned a lot about money yourself. You have to be able to follow what your "expert" is doing. Otherwise, your money might be expertly "managed" away.

• Write a will or change your old one. A living will and a power of attorney grow even more urgent as you age. You need someone to speak for you if you become incapable.

• Write to your late spouse's (or ex-spouse's) company immediately after the death or legal separation. Better yet, write in advance. You may be due some employee benefits, including up to 3 years of health insurance at group rates. The employer is supposed to notify you about the health insurance but doesn't always do so. If you don't apply for the policy immediately after losing your coverage as a spouse, you won't be able to get it at all.

• Find work if you need it, perhaps through a temporary help agency.

Sort-of-Married. More than single but less than married, you have only to change the locks to "divorce." You need:

• Separate bank accounts. Contribute to common bills in proportion to earnings. If one of you earns only 30 percent of the total, that person should pay only 30 percent of the expenses. It's not fair to hit him or her for 50 percent.

• Separate property. One buys the lamps, one buys the couch, so that ownership is clear.

• Written agreements for property bought together. What happens to it if you split up? If one of you dies?

• A will, to be sure that the other gets—or doesn't get—what you intend. With no will, everything goes to your family, not to your partner.

• The same health, disability, and living will protection that you'd give yourself as a single person. If you both work, you need no life insurance unless there are children. If you decide that one of you won't work, protect that person with a life insurance policy. In a few jurisdictions, a "domestic partner"—straight, lesbian, or gay—might be covered by the other's employee-benefits plan.

These lists tell you generally what you need. The rest of this book tells you how to get it. As you read, you can construct your own financial plan, chapter by chapter—adding, subtracting, revising, updating—one step at a time.

2.

The Ultimate Wish List

What You've Got and Where You're Going

Need rises with income. What was out of the question when you made $25,000 becomes urgent at $50,000 and indispensable at $80,000.

Your own financial plan starts with a wish list. Write it all down, every single thing. A speedboat. A week in Barbados. State U for two children. Enough money to retire early. Forget that you can't afford it. Maybe you only *think* you can't. The whole reason to have a financial plan is to focus yourself on what matters most and work out a strategy for getting it.

So get out a yellow pad and a pencil and start dreaming. On the left side of the pad, write "What I want." On the right side write "When I want it"—next summer? In three years? 2010? In the middle write "How I get there from here." That middle column is the terra incognita that this book will fill in. You are going to develop some real numbers and a real timetable so you won't still be dreaming five years from now.

Once you've listed all your material wants, stare off into space and think. Even if you can have it all, the cost of getting it might be an extra job, working nights and weekends, working to a later age than you'd intended, or hanging on to a job you hate. Is it worth it? Or would you rather take that speedboat off your wish list?

When reflecting on this question, take another piece of paper and write down your personal goals. Don't kid yourself. If money and status are important, say so. Do you want to write a book by the time you're 30? Start a business? Spend more time with the kids? Move to the country? Become a top officer of your corporation? Change careers? Give more time to charity? All the things you most care about are likely to affect how much money you'll have, which in turn will shape your financial plan. The planning process asks you to set priorities and make trade-offs.

The plan you finally develop may not work—at least, not exactly. Some things may go better than expected, others may go worse. You may fall behind schedule. You may filch money for a new car that should have gone into the education fund.

But the point is, *you'll know it*. You'll see the hole in your kids' tuition account and you'll figure out how to make it up. The reason financial plans succeed is almost stupidly simple. It's their specificity. Instead of vague hopes, you have hard targets—something concrete that you're working toward every year. Once you *see* it, you can get it.

YOUR BASIC SECURITY PACKAGE

Back to your yellow pad. I know you've remembered to list "Barbados vacation." But one or two other things might have slipped your mind, without which your prettier plans might be undone. Here is the basic security package that also has to be on your list:

1. *Life insurance.* Do you have enough? If you die, your spouse or mate needs enough to support himself or herself. Your children need support and education. Part of that money will probably come from the surviving spouse's earnings. You need just enough insurance to cover the rest. For how much life insurance to buy, see Chapter 12.

2. *Disability insurance.* Most people are covered if they die. But what if you fall off a ladder, break your back, and live? That's the risk nobody thinks about (or wants to). You need two levels of disability coverage: (1) for a short illness of 6 to 12 months, during which you'd try to keep your way of life intact, and (2) for a permanent disability, usually requiring a drop in your standard of living. For how large a policy you need, see Chapter 14.

3. *Health insurance.* You probably get it from the company you work for. If not, call an insurance agent, Blue Cross/Blue Shield, or a health maintenance organization. Nursing-home policies are improving rapidly, but they're not yet for younger people. Shop for this coverage when you pass 60. See Chapter 13.

4. *Repaying debt.* It's pointless to save money at 5 percent interest while you're still supporting a Visa card habit at 18 percent. Pay off the Visa first. Often, the best use of savings is to pay off the debts that are costing you more than your savings earn. For ways of saving more money, see Chapter 9.

5. *Owning a home.* How much do you need for a down payment and how will you raise it? The lucky ducks go to the Daddy Bank. Failing that,

you will have to throw every resource you have at the problem. For ways of finding the money for a home of your own, see Chapter 17.

6. *College.* How much will college cost when your children reach 18 and how long do you have to accumulate the money? Four years at the average public college cost around $45,000 in 1997–98 (assuming annual increases of 6 percent). For the average private college, it was $95,000. The most selective and expensive schools topped $120,000. You'll find a list of college savings and investing plans in Chapter 20.

7. *Fun and games.* Put some luxuries on your list. A new kitchen. An RV. A trip to Europe. August at the racetrack. Estimate what they will cost (except for the racetrack, where you'll *make* money, right?) and when you will want them. Chapter 8 tells you how to fit them into your plan.

8. *Retirement savings.* How much will you need to retire on? A younger person hasn't a clue. Too many incalculables exist in the economy and your personal life. Still, you ought to make a start. By your late 40s, the picture should be coming clear. For the book on retirement planning, see Chapter 29.

For your pains, you'll wind up with a daunting list of expenses:

1. The price of more life insurance.
2. The price of a disability policy.
3. The price of health insurance if you don't have a company plan.
4. The extra monthly payments needed to zero out your consumer debts.
5. How much you'll have to save each month for a down payment on a home.
6. The cost of your children's college and the length of time you have to raise the money.
7. The price of anything special you want for yourself, and how long you have to save for it.
8. The amount of savings you'll need for a decent retirement.

Some of you are starting out at the top of this list; others are already partway down. In either case, the total may look unattainable, but I promise it's not. It's like running a marathon: you do one mile at a time until you finish.

FINDING THE MONEY

Winning a lottery would be nice. Maybe you could marry rich. An inheritance is dandy, the drawback being how you get it.

Windfalls aside, there are only three ways of getting the money you need to underwrite a financial plan: culling current income, taking loans, and using the gains from your savings and investments. But everything ultimately springs from income, which sets up your savings and pays off your debts.

No plan will succeed if you live to the brink of your income and beyond. You *must* hold back something for savings and investments. "No way," you say? It takes $50,000 just to pay the grocer? Sure, but only if you build your life that way. Every single one of us can look down the street and see someone living as well as we do on $5,000 less a year than we make. That's $5,000 we could be saving every year and still hold up our heads in the neighborhood. Only by living on less than you make will you ever be able to live on more than you make.

KEEPING SCORE

Start out your plan by figuring your present net worth. Recalculate it once a year. These figures, and the changes in them, will show you a lot of interesting things:

- Whether your debts are under control. Is your indebtedness growing faster than the money you're saving?
- How well you're investing the money you save. Does your investment account generally rise in value? Or are you losing money faster than you're putting it away?
- How much money you could lay your hands on in an emergency. Do you have enough readily salable assets to help you through a bad patch, or are too many of your assets tied up?
- Whether you need more life and disability insurance. What income could you get from your assets compared with how much you need to live on?
- To find your net worth, add up the value of everything you own (your *assets*), figured at what you could reasonably sell each item for. Then subtract everything you owe (your *liabilities*). The remainder is your *net worth*. It's the money you'd have if you converted all of your salable property into cash and paid off your debts. If you owe more than you own, you have a *negative net worth,* and maybe an ulcer. ("I'm going to be a millionaire," a friend of mine who was a gambler used to say. "I'll die owing a million dollars." He came close.)

Your aim is to raise your net worth every year through a combination of new savings, sound investments, and fewer loans.

Just as important, you need a good balance between assets that are tied up, like your house, and assets that can quickly be turned into cash.

Those parts of your net worth that are always on tap are your *quick assets,* like cash, mutual funds, stocks, bonds, and life insurance cash values. You fall back on your quick assets in an emergency.

Those parts that might take a long time to sell are the *slow assets,* like most real estate. Don't load up on slow assets until you have plenty of quick assets on tap.

Some of your net worth is effectively frozen. I'd include here that portion of your home equity against which the bank won't make a loan, an interest in a limited partnership that can't be sold easily, money owed to you at some point in the future, and a lump sum due from your pension plan. Mentally, you might also add a pending inheritance, although it doesn't belong on your personal balance sheet until it's actually yours.

Yet another part of your net worth is *restricted* in that it can be reached only by paying a penalty. This includes most unmatured certificates of deposit, tax-deferred retirement plans, and tax-deferred annuities if you're younger than 59½.

YOUR NET WORTH
Date _____

WHAT YOU OWN (Assets)

	AMOUNT
QUICK ASSETS	
Cash in checking, ready savings, and money-market mutual funds	$ _____
Other mutual funds	_____
Stocks, bonds, government securities, unit trusts	_____
Publicly traded partnerships	_____
Other easily salable investments	_____
Money due you for work you've done	_____
Life insurance cash values	_____
Precious metals	_____
Easily salable personal property: jewelry, silver, cars	_____
RESTRICTED ASSETS	
Certificates of deposit, if they have early-withdrawal penalties	_____
Retirement accounts: IRAs, Keoghs, tax-deferred annuities, company savings accounts, deferred salary	_____
Current worth of your vested pension, if payable in a lump sum	_____
Stock options	_____
SLOW ASSETS	
Your home	_____
Other real estate	_____
Art and antiques	_____
Other valuable personal property: furs, boats, tools, coins	_____
Restricted stock, not readily salable	_____
Limited partnerships, not readily salable	_____
Money owed you in the future	_____
Equity value of a business	_____
TOTAL ASSETS	_____

WHAT YOU OWE (Liabilities)

	Amount	Interest Rate
Current bills outstanding: this month's rent, utilities, medical bills, insurance premiums, etc.	$ ____	
Credit-card debt	____	____
Installment and auto loans	____	____
Life insurance loans	____	____
Home mortgage	____	____
Home-equity loan	____	____
Other mortgages	____	____
Student loans	____	____
Loans against investments, including your margin loans	____	____
Other loans	____	____
Income and real-estate taxes due	____	
Taxes due on your investments if you cash them in	____	
Taxes and penalties due on your retirement accounts, if you cash them in	____	
TOTAL LIABILITIES	____	
NET WORTH (Assets minus liabilities)	____	

When figuring your net worth: (1) You don't have to know the exact value of everything. A ballpark estimate will do. (2) To find out what your bonds and unit trusts are currently worth, ask your stockbroker to price them for you. They will bring more or less than face value, depending on market conditions today. (3) Sherlock Holmes couldn't ferret out the value of limited-partnership shares unless they're traded publicly. Ask your stockbroker whether he can sell them and for how much. If no one is biting, list the shares at zero. When the partnership dissolves, thank the gods for every dollar you get back. (4) In a pinch, you could sell your cars and jewelry. But you won't, so they're not truly part of your usable net worth. You need to know their current value only to keep them well insured.

PATCHING YOUR SAFETY NET

Optimist: "This is the best of all possible worlds."
Pessimist: "That's right."
So far, you've been thinking like an optimist. You're worth more than you thought! Your pencil is flying! Your stock options will pay off your loans and then you'll be on easy street! All it will take is a few more years.

YOUR SURVIVOR'S USABLE CASH
Date _____

ASSETS	
Quick Assets (not counting life-insurance cash values, one of two cars, and personal property)	$ _____
Restricted Assets	_____
Slow Assets (not counting your house and personal property that your spouse would want to keep)	_____
Proceeds from Life Insurance	_____
TOTAL USABLE ASSETS FOR SURVIVOR	_____
LIABILITIES	
Loans Against Insurance Policies	$ _____
Death Costs, including funeral and estate administration, up to 5 percent of assets	_____
Taxes, including final income-tax return and estate taxes, if you're wealthy enough to owe them	
TOTAL	_____
MONEY LEFT FOR SURVIVOR (Usable assets minus liabilities)	$ _____

But what if you don't have a few more years?

Here's where the average plan comes a cropper. How would your family manage if you died? How would you live if you had an accident and couldn't work anymore? There would be some income from your spouse's earnings, Social Security, disability insurance (if you were clever enough to have bought it), and so on. But probably not enough. You'd also have to live on your savings.

To measure the real strength of your position, you have to look at your net worth in another way. How much cash would be available to you or your family if you had to marshal all of your assets to live on?

Start with the figures you just reached and assume three things: (1) you (or your survivor) would not sell your house, one car, and personal property; (2) all other slow assets would be converted to cash; (3) your restricted assets would be freed up for use.

You need a large enough nest egg so that when your savings are combined with other sources of income, your dependents will have enough to meet their expenses. If your savings fall short, fill the gap with more life insurance. If your household depends on two paychecks, make these calculations twice—first assuming that the husband dies, then assuming the death of the wife.

If you think that your family would move to a smaller house at your death, they would net some money from the sale of the house you own now. Add those funds to their assets.

YOUR USABLE CASH, IF YOU'RE DISABLED
Date _____

ASSETS

Quick Assets (except for one car and personal property)	$ _____
Restricted Assets	_____
Slow Assets (not counting your house and any personal property you want to keep)	_____
TOTAL USABLE ASSETS	_____

LIABILITIES

Taxes on funds you withdraw from retirement accounts	$ _____
Uninsured Medical Bills (make a guess)	_____
TOTAL	_____
MONEY ON TAP (Usable assets minus liabilities)	_____

Disability Is Another Story. There's no life insurance payoff, so your usable assets are much smaller. I've shown few liabilities in the table above because you can't predict your lump-sum expenses. Even the size of your uninsured medical bills is a question. You have three ways to prepare for a disability: get a better disability-insurance policy, save more, or invest better.

Use this same calculation for early retirement.

There is one more way of measuring your personal security. Do you have enough quick assets to cover all the bills coming due this year? That would give you a 12-month breathing space if you lost your job. Figure it this way:

1. How much has to be paid on your debts over the next 12 months? Call this your Current Debt: $_____.

2. How large are your quick assets, not counting personal property and life-insurance cash values? Call this your Ready Money: $_____.

3. Your Ready Money should be greater than your Current Debt. If not, you are living with a lot of risk. As time passes, your Ready Money should grow larger and larger than your Current Debt.

ROUNDUP DAY

Once a year sit down with your spouse or mate (if you're single, sit down with yourself) and see where you stand. Go over everything. Are you spending too much? Did you save enough money? Should you change your investments? Did your net worth improve? Do you need more insurance? What financial goal will you shoot for in the next 12 months? What personal purchases would you like to make?

I call this annual accounting Roundup Day. A good time for it is the week between Christmas and New Year's, when things are usually slow. Another good time is the week you do your income taxes, when every money nerve is tingling. Working couples need this day to tally their separate savings and investments. Spouses who don't handle the family money need this day to keep in touch. *Everyone* needs this day to gloat over triumphs, fix mistakes, remember what you're doing, and freshen your resolve.

HOW MUCH IS ENOUGH?

You don't have to get richer every year. At some level of personal security all you need is enough growth to keep your after-tax assets even with inflation. Knowing when to quit and go fishing is just as important as knowing when to keep your shoulder to the wheel.

My job is to help you grow wealthier and more secure. But not everyone is so lucky. Accidents happen. Investments fail. Companies fold. So here's a heretical thought: If your income drops, is that so bad? Is it so terrible to live in a cheaper place with fewer clothes and luxuries? People live happy lives who earn $5,000 less than you, and so do people who earn $5,000 less than they.

I wish you every increase, but if the gods frown there are worse things in life than stepping down.

3.

I Have It Right Here Somewhere

The Right Way to Keep Records

(Don't go away. I'm still looking.)

Okay, I confess.

Sitting here, right now, I can't remember the name of my life insurance company. My husband has both keys to the safe-deposit box in his office but I'm not sure where. In the pile of papers on the floor to the left, I think, there's the booklet explaining the changes in my group health insurance. In short, I am often a slob about my own financial records.

But I am reforming. Writing this chapter has embarrassed me into reorganizing the Quinn family's scattered financial files. And take my word for it: when you finish this kind of job you feel clean, as if you had shined all your shoes and cleaned up the cellar.

With good records:

You Can Find Things. I estimate 84 hours saved per year, right there.

You Can Remember What You Have. Did you sign that power of attorney? Did you fill in the form that lets you take money out of your mutual fund by phone? Now you'll know.

You Can Remember What You Don't Have. No, you didn't sign that power of attorney because you kept misplacing it. Now that you're putting your records together, you'll get it done.

You Can Save Money for Your Heirs. They will be able to find things, too, without paying a lawyer to do detective work for them. They won't shake their heads and mutter, "What a mess."

You Can Feel Terrifically Smart and Well Organized.

You Will Know That If a Ceiling Fell on Your Head This Very Moment, Your Heirs Would Get Every Dime That Was Coming to Them. Sometimes, a deed, contract, or bankbook is hidden away and never found. Ditto mutual fund records, records of small brokerage accounts, and retirement-savings accounts left with a former employer. After several years unclaimed money passes to the state (page 36). Lawyers tell story after story about stumbling across a stray piece of paper that entitled a widow to money that she didn't know anything about. Think of the number of widows who throw those pieces of paper away.

WHERE TO KEEP RECORDS

Invest in a file cabinet. It doesn't have to be steel; cardboard works fine. You can tuck a two-drawer cabinet under a table. Or use it as a table (put a round piece of plywood on top and cover with a cloth). Don't put it in the attic or behind the tennis rackets under the stairs! Unless your cabinet is so handy that you practically trip over it, you'll put off filing your records, which means that your system will fall apart.

Eventually, back tax returns and old bank records will overflow your file drawers. Don't compulsively save everything with your name and a dollar sign on it. Some records can be thrown away (see "What to Keep, What to Toss," page 37). Put beloved old statements that you can't part with into labeled boxes. Keep them in the attic or on a closet shelf.

What? You had a fire? I forgot to tell you: Invest in a fireproof home safe or bank safe-deposit box for records that are a pain in the neck to replace. Throw in pictures of all your clothes and furniture. After a fire you'll have to prove to a fish-eyed insurance investigator that although you lived modestly your possessions were worth a fortune.

A home safe should be rated for fire resistance by the Underwriters Laboratory. You need a class 350 safe, which protects paper documents against high heat for at least half an hour and perhaps up to four. If you keep computer records on floppy disks, you'll need a class 125 safe. An unrated metal box with a lock won't do anything except keep curious children out; in a fire, the heat would scorch to ashes any documents inside.

These safes, incidentally, won't stop a burglar for a moment—they're only for papers. You might as well write the combination on the top to save a thief the trouble of whacking off the lock. To protect valuables at home, you need a much more expensive vault. When you go on vacation, put good jewelry and silver into a safe-deposit box.

Safe-deposit boxes are normally rented from a bank, although they are increasingly being offered by S&Ls and credit unions. Small boxes, for holding papers and a little jewelry, cost around $10 to $50 a year. For a lot of valuables, or your irreplaceable hubcap collection, the bank has larger boxes at a higher price.

Sometimes there's a waiting list, especially for the bigger boxes. As an alternative, you might look at a private vault company. It charges more than banks but is supposed to follow bank security procedures and may even offer 24-hour access—handy for dropping off your diamonds after the ball. If you have something to hide, it will interest you to know that most private vaults let you open an account under a false name (banks require identification). On the downside, private vaults may not provide all the security that customers were promised. Many have gone bankrupt. Personally, I wouldn't go near one.

When you rent a safe-deposit box, you sign a card. The bank or vault will also need the signatures of anyone with access to the box—your spouse, your secretary, a friend. Every time you visit your diamonds or hubcaps you sign again, so that your signature can be checked. It takes two keys to open the box, yours and the bank's. You get two copies of your own key. If you lose one, no problem; it costs maybe $5 to $10 to replace. But it might cost $75 to $100 if you lose both. The bank doesn't keep a copy of your key, so it has to drill into your box and start you out with a brand-new lock.

What to keep in your safe-deposit box depends on how easy it is to enter after you die. About half the states allow your executor free access to the box. Even more states let your spouse in if the two of you owned the box jointly (although other joint owners may be kept out). The rest of the states seal the box until the contents can be inventoried—just in case you were hiding millions in cash. The bank may allow an heir, next of kin, or some other person with legal rights to search a sealed safe-deposit box for a will, insurance policies, or a cemetery deed. In a few states, only the will can be removed immediately.

If all you keep in your safe-deposit box is some jewelry, your marriage license, and old Topps baseball cards, state laws are no problem. Nor are they a problem in the states that don't seal boxes at death. But where boxes are sealed, don't use them for papers that your survivors will need right away. Ask the bank or private vault company what the rules are.

If you and your spouse or mate keep separate boxes, give each other access, just in case something happens. Consider putting a friend's name on the signature card, too, so someone else can enter in an emergency. You don't have to give your friend (known as your deputy) a key, but tell him or her where you keep it.

Don't count on your deputy to clean out the box before the taxman cometh. A deputy's access ends when you die, whether the state seals the box or not. It also ends if you become mentally incapable. With a jointly owned box, access terminates if both joint owners die. So your deputy doesn't have much wiggle room. He or she can get into the box only if you keep all your marbles or if one joint owner stays alive and the box remains unsealed.

If you own a business, get a company safe-deposit box. These boxes are never sealed at death, so you and your spouse can keep your wills and insurance policies there.

Unfortunately, nothing in this world is 100 percent secure, not even safe-deposit boxes. If a thief breaks in, the bank or vault company is not responsible for your losses unless you can prove negligence. Federal deposit insurance isn't responsible, either. It covers only your deposit accounts. But your homeowners or tenants insurance should pay up to the limits of your policy (see page 457). After a theft you have to prove what you kept in the box, which is not always an easy job. Keep receipts, appraisals, and photos, including a photo of your box with the valuables in it.

Tell your heirs where the box is and where you keep the keys. If you keep a home safe, note the combination to the lock in your personal-money file.

YOU DIDN'T LOSE IT, YOU FORGOT IT. NOW WHAT?

Money—billions of dollars of it—gets mislaid in America. People move and don't leave a forwarding address. They forget to give their new address to every institution holding money due them. Sometimes they don't know they're owed some money. Sometimes they get dotty. Maybe they die without leaving the well-organized records that you're about to create, and their heirs can't find all the property.

The federal government is holding an estimated $20 billion worth of uncashed Treasury securities and savings bonds; unclaimed Social Security benefits, civil service retirement checks, tax refunds, veterans' benefits, and refunds for mortgage insurance premiums owed to many homeowners who prepay FHA loans; and property left on federal land. The states hold perhaps $10 billion in unclaimed bank and brokerage accounts; Individual Retirement Accounts and other pension savings; paychecks and dividend checks; refunds from telephone and electric companies that people failed to collect when they moved; uncashed money orders and cashier's checks; unused gift certificates; contents of unclaimed safe-deposit boxes; and life insurance policies that the heirs never knew about.

Every state's unclaimed-property law is a little different. But in general, a bank or other private company, including nonprofits, can't hold dormant funds for more than 3 to 5 years.

Your bank account or mutual fund is considered dormant if you've made no transactions for several years and don't answer mail about the account. Untended savings accounts are especially vulnerable.

Dormant funds held in private hands are eventually transferred ("escheated") to the states. The states list the missing owners in newspaper ads, usually in obscure publications. They may also try to find you through telephone directories, credit bureaus, and motor-vehicle records. Some states try harder than others.

You can reclaim your property no matter how many years have passed (except in New Hampshire, which confiscates money after 3 years). When stocks, bonds, and mutual funds go to the state, they're usually sold after 3 years and the proceeds retained.

To see if you're due any money held by a state, write to the state's unclaimed-property office. Give your full married and maiden names, all addresses you've had in the state, and your Social Security number. Also, write to states where you've previously lived. If your parents or other relatives died at least 5 years ago, write to their states, just in case the family didn't find all the property. Depending on the state, it will take a few weeks or months to check. States often pay interest on reclaimed interest-bearing accounts, like bank deposits, but not on other funds.

For a free list of state unclaimed-property offices, send a self-addressed, stamped, business-size envelope to the Division of State Lands, 775 Summer St. N.E., Salem, OR 97310. Ask for the brochure *Unclaimed Property Information*. On-line, you'll find the list at http://www.intersurf.com/~naupa. That same Web site also lets you hunt for lost money yourself by accessing the states' databases of unclaimed property.

Unfortunately, there's no unclaimed-property office for money held by the federal government, nor do the feds try to track missing owners.

If you're lucky, you'll get a letter from a private tracing service saying it knows where some money is stashed that probably belongs to you. The price of retrieving it usually runs around 30 percent of the recovered funds (the service might ask 50 percent, but you can usually talk it down). People sometimes get sore at these services because they think they charge too much. But if it weren't for their efforts, you wouldn't get any money at all. Call the service if you get such a letter. You can usually negotiate a lower fee. *Never* pay up front (that's not a legitimate request). Pay only when money is produced.

WHAT TO KEEP, WHAT TO TOSS

Clarity, clarity. A filing system should be so logical that anyone who opens the drawers can find exactly what he or she wants. Label every folder, choosing titles that are sensible, not cute. If a financial document doesn't exactly fit into one of the categories you have already, start a new file for it. Keep weeding out documents that don't apply any longer. No sense sending your heirs on wild goose chases.

Your Will

You have one, of course. A good-looking, clever, glowing social success like you wouldn't be so dumb as to go without. The only reason I even put Chapter 6 in this book (it's about writing wills) is that that was the only way to get from Chapter 5 to Chapter 7. Chapter 6. It's on page 100. Just in case.

It is simple and safe to leave the will with your lawyer, keeping a copy for yourself. On your copy, put the lawyer's name, address, and phone number. The drawback—if you see it that way—is that your family might feel forced to use that particular lawyer to handle your estate. They don't have to. They can retrieve the will and pick a different lawyer. If you think that would embarrass them, keep the will yourself.

Keep it somewhere safe and accessible. Maybe in a fireproof home safe. Maybe in a safe-deposit box. Before putting the will into your safe-deposit box, find out from the bank what happens to the box when you die. Is it sealed? Can it be opened instantly to retrieve the will? Can it be opened only in the presence of a tax agent? If there might be some delay, don't put the will in your box—or in your spouse's box, either. The two of you might die together. Put it in someone else's box—your executor's, a family member's, your company box if you own your own business. If none of these solutions make sense, keep it with your lawyer. Whenever you make a new will, destroy the old one along with all copies.

Your Durable Power of Attorney

This is a piece of paper that says, "The named person can act for me, in all matters or in certain matters that I have specified here." The empowered person might be able to manage your money, sell your real estate, or make decisions about your health care.

Put the power of attorney in a fireproof home safe (as long as the person you named knows the combination). Or give it to that person for safekeeping in his or her safe-deposit box (I assume that you trust your deputy; otherwise, you wouldn't have given him or her the power). Don't put this important document into your own safe-deposit box. Your friend can't get into it if you become mentally incapable—which is just when the power of attorney might have to be used. If you own your own business, you could keep the document in the business's box and give your friend access. Keep your copy in your file at home.

The Living Will

This is a piece of paper that says, "If I'm in a permanent coma, pull the plug"—or "don't pull the plug," depending on how you feel about it. Keep your living will in your fireproof home safe where people can find it. Give executed copies to the people who will make these ultimate choices in accordance with your wishes: your spouse or mate, a friend, your doctor (see page 124).

Life Insurance Policies

Keep them in your safe-deposit box only if the bank assures you that, under state law, your beneficiary can get them immediately. Include all correspondence affecting the policy, such as change-of-beneficiary notices or proof that ownership of the policy has been transferred to someone else. Add the name, address, and phone number of your insurance agent.

If your box will be sealed at your death, keep the policies and supporting material in your file cabinet or fireproof home safe. As backup, put the name and address of your insurance company and insurance agent, and your policy number, on the Master List (page 48) that's kept in your safe-deposit box.

In the same file, include a note about any life insurance you have through your employer and how to claim it. Also, file your receipts for mortgage-life and credit-life insurance if you've bought any. These policies pay off your loans if you die. If your executor doesn't know about them, he or she will waste money by paying the debts out of your estate.

You probably have some other forms of coverage that your executor should know about. For example, if you charge a travel ticket to a credit card, it may generate $100,000 or more of life insurance if you die during the trip. You might also be covered for accidental death and dismemberment, whether you travel by plane, train, bus, or ship. Ditto if your accident occurs in an airline terminal or while traveling on public transportation to or from the terminal.

The government will cancel your guaranteed student loans or PLUS loans (Parent Loans for Undergraduate Students) if you die or become permanently disabled.

There may be government benefits if you ever served in the armed forces. Your surviving spouse or minor children should also get a $255 death benefit from Social Security.

Credit-union members sometimes have small life insurance policies linked to their savings accounts.

If you belong to the American Automobile Association, you may be covered if you die in an auto accident. Not all clubs offer this protection, however, and coverage varies according to the type of accident.

Other clubs and organizations may also offer small policies as part of your membership package.

Clues to any payments of this sort should be kept in your life insurance file.

Health and Disability Insurance Policies

You say you have a pain in your side? Your doctor wants your gallbladder out? If you don't get a second opinion and an okay from your insurance company, your health insurance might not pay. Keep the insurance policy, or the booklet explaining it, in your file cabinet. Ditto your disability-income policy. As backup, keep the names of your health-insurance companies, the policy numbers, the phone number of your company's employee-benefits office, or the name of your insurance agent in your home safe or safe-deposit box, as well as on your Master List (page 48). Also, keep the booklets explaining your benefits under Medicare or Medicaid.

If you're arguing with your HMO or insurance company about what should be treated or which bills should be covered, put everything in writing and keep copies. You'll need these records for an appeal or a lawsuit.

Homeowners, Tenants, and Auto Insurance

You usually get a new policy every 6 or 12 months, but don't throw the old ones out. If someone was injured on your property 18 months ago and develops back pains from a previously undiscovered crack in a spinal disk, you'll want to be able to prove that you were insured at the time. Your insurance company should have all the records, but you need backup, just in case. Furthermore, the language of insurance policies changes over the years. It could be important to know exactly what you were covered for when an injury occurred.

Keep current policies in your safe-deposit box. Your insurer can replace them if they're burned, but it might take a week or a month. Also you can't rely on the company's computer to remember all of the special riders you carry.

Keep old policies in a dead file (attic, closet shelf, junk room). State statutes of limitations normally run for 2 or 3 years from the time the medical problem is discovered, so you could be sued for an injury 3 years after it happened. When your liability has expired, you can throw the policies out.

As usual, put the names of these insurance companies, the policy numbers, and the name of your insurance agent in your home safe or safe-deposit box. File information on how to make a claim. If you bought special riders for things like furs, art, jewelry, and silver, include appraisals of their current value or sales slips showing what you paid for them.

Household Inventory

I'm not your mother. I don't care that your room is messy and that you don't write, but you still haven't done your household inventory, and how many times do I have to tell you? I know it's boring. I know that you started out in the living room, put your pencil down while you made some coffee, and never got any further. That's because you were using a pencil. The simple way is to use a camera. Take pictures of every room, every open closet, every open drawer. If you're using a video camera, comment on anything especially valuable. Keep sales slips for expensive purchases. Otherwise, you'll have to compile an inventory of all your possessions from memory if your house burns down. Get appraisals on your antiques, art, rare books, furs, good jewelry, silver, and special collections. Some will need special insurance riders.

Put the appraisals, pictures, and sales slips in your safe-deposit box. If you use a home safe instead, stash copies at a friend's house in case your safe isn't quite as fireproof as promised.

Personal Papers

Anything you need to prove who you are, how long you've been around, and what you've been up to belongs in a fireproof home safe or safe-deposit box. This includes birth certificate, marriage certificate, all documents relating to separation and divorce, military service records, citizenship or adoption papers, diplomas, licenses, passports, permits, union cards, Social Security cards, and family health records such as vaccinations and dates of operations. Keeping an expired passport makes it easier to get a new one. Don't stash your military records before checking with the service to be sure that its dates agree with yours. If the service has them wrong and your survivors don't realize it, they might not get all the benefits they're due. Military service organizations send out newsletters about benefit changes; save them, too.

Tax Records

Yes, I know. You accidentally added the veterinarian's bill to your deductible medical expenses. How long does the IRS have to catch and fine you? Three years, during which time you'd better keep not only your tax return but all supporting data. After that, you're in the clear and can toss the return, unless the vet is the least of it. The government has 6 years to audit you if you underreported your income by more than 25 percent. If it pursues you for fraud, or if you filed no tax return at all, there is no statute of limitations; you can be hit for back taxes anytime.

If you lose your federal returns, you can get copies covering the past 5 (and maybe 6) years. You pay nothing for an IRS transcript covering the past 3 years (a transcript is a computer printout showing what was on the original return). For actual copies of the returns, or returns for earlier years, you're charged $14 each. Make your request on Form 4506. For state returns, ask the state what's available.

Keep the returns that show any investment losses you're carrying forward and tax deductions taken on limited partnerships.

Keep the returns that show any contributions you made to an Individual Retirement Account that were not tax deductible. When you start withdrawing money, you'll need these records to establish how much of each IRA withdrawal is tax exempt. If your heirs don't have these records, they may inadvertently pay taxes on the whole amount.

History buffs keep tax returns for many years because of the personal information in them—like whom you worked for and what you earned.

Nowadays, there's an even bigger reason to keep every single return you file, together with your W-2 forms. Companies don't always keep accurate records of how long you worked and how much you contributed to your retirement plan. You may need your tax returns and W-2s to prove what you're due when you leave your job.

Paycheck Stubs

If you trust your employer to add up your annual earnings correctly (as I do), you can throw your pay stubs away. But sometimes there's special information on them that isn't included on your year-end W-2, such as the number of hours worked. If your union or employer keeps poor records, you may need your pay stubs to prove your eligibility for pension and welfare benefits. The stubs also make it simple to claim unemployment pay. Free-lancers should keep all payment receipts. Clients aren't always good about sending out proper 1099s.

Employee Benefits

They've gotten so complicated that companies often publish them in loose-leaf notebooks. File everything. Keep the annual statements on the status of your pension, profit-sharing, salary-deferral, or retirement-savings plans so you can follow their progress. Keep employment contracts in your home file, safe-deposit box, or the office of the lawyer who negotiated them.

Retirement Plans

Write down the numbers and locations of all your retirement accounts —Keogh plans, Individual Retirement Accounts, Simplified Employee Pensions, 403(b)s, company plans—and put them in the safe-deposit box. Keep the plan documents in your file cabinet along with the annual reports showing how your investments are doing. Keep records of any loans you took against your plans, and loans repaid. An unpaid loan may cost you a tax penalty if you leave the job, and you'll want to be sure that your employer's records are right. Finally, keep withdrawal records. Throw them out when the withdrawals show up on the annual statement of your account.

Bank Records

Some people keep all their canceled checks; others weed them out, keeping only those they might need for tax or insurance purposes. I favor weeding your older checks (starting 3 years back) to keep the paper storage down. But I keep the newer ones. You never know when they'll come in handy. Here are eight good reasons to keep canceled checks:

1. If you want to make a budget, old checks are a road map to what you've been spending.

2. The IRS might disagree with your version of life and ask for proof. Canceled checks can sometimes stand in for receipts in substantiating tax deductions (although usually the IRS wants receipts).

3. Old checks show the names of the people you've done business with and might want to find again.

4. It's easier to collect in full on a property insurance claim if you can show the company what you paid for your rugs, furniture, and other damaged items.

5. Your ex-spouse might claim that you missed some child-support payments. If you didn't, your canceled checks will prove it.

6. You might have to prove to one of your creditors that a bill was paid. For this purpose, keeping checks for 6 months should be enough.

7. If you're one-half of an unmarried couple, and own property jointly, the checks prove what you paid for, which could be important if you split or your mate dies.

Many banks don't return canceled checks anymore. They just send you a statement showing which checks were cashed, which is easier to file.

If you also have loans or certificates of deposit, keep the most recent statements showing their status (old ones can be tossed). When you make new deposits, keep the receipts until the monthly statement comes in so you can check that they were entered correctly. Keep loan agreements and any passbooks for open savings accounts. Keep copies of letters that confirm the instructions you gave about your accounts or CDs. Throw these records out when the loan has been repaid or the account closed. Keep all disclosures you get from the bank about its fees and interest rates so that you can check any changes you question. Note your PIN (personal identification number), lest you forget.

Receipts for Paid Bills

In your file cabinet: Keep receipts for every expense that is tax deductible—ideally, clipped to the check you paid it with. The IRS prefers both if you're ever audited. (Some expenses that aren't deductible on your federal return might still be on your state return.)

In your fireproof safe or safe-deposit box: Keep receipts for high-cost purchases like furs and antiques. They'll prove your claim if you have to dicker with the insurance company after a fire or theft.

In a box on your bureau or desk: Keep receipts for gifts until you know that you won't have to take them back. If you pay in cash, keep the receipt long enough to be sure that the item is in good working order. Throw other receipts out. Your canceled check is normally proof enough of payment.

Medical and Drug Bills

Submit them all to your insurer. They'll be rejected until you have met the annual deductible you owe. But submitting them is a guaranteed way of keeping track.

File copies of all unreimbursed bills. Expenses exceeding 7.5 percent of your adjusted gross income are deductible on your tax return. But you have to be pretty sick, and pretty poorly insured, to qualify for this write-off. If you get no tax deduction, throw the bills away. (The super-cautious keep medical bills for 3 years. If something should change on their tax return that lowers their income—don't ask me what—a borderline miss could turn into a deduction. Also keep any bills that you and your insurer are arguing about.)

Monthly Credit-Card Statements

Check every one as soon as it comes to be sure that every bill is actually yours. A thief needs only your credit-card number and a telephone in order to buy goods and charge them to your account.

Add any statements that show the price of something particularly expensive to your file on homeowners insurance. Keeping the rest of your statements is optional. Personally, I hang on to them for 2 or 3 years. Who knows when an item charged and paid for will erroneously pop up on my bill again? Who knows what will break and need returning—and how else will I remember the name of the store? Who knows when I'll want to look up the name of that great Cajun restaurant in Biloxi? Back bills also help you track your spending and draw up a budget. But if you never use these records, toss them. For tax purposes, you need to keep records only of business purchases.

When you take something back to a store, you'll get a return receipt. Keep it right where you open your mail, to remind you to check that the money was actually credited to your account. Then throw the receipt away.

Deeds, Titles, Title Insurance, Surveys

Records of purchase, property descriptions, and proofs of ownership —including the title to your car—belong in your fireproof home safe or safe-deposit box. Copies are available if you lose the originals, but it's simpler to protect the records you have.

If you inherit property, keep any evidence of what it was worth when you got it. You'll need it to figure the gain when you sell.

File any records of legal proceedings, current tax assessments, and—if you're in a condominium or planned community—rules of the property owners' association. If you rent, file a copy of your lease.

Debts

In the file cabinet: your mortgage, bank-loan records, contracts for installment purchases. No problem if a fire burns them up. Your creditors will remember. They'll even have copies.

But paid-off debts are another story. Get a receipt for the canceled note and keep it in your safe-deposit box. Proof of payment is especially important when you borrow money from an individual. He or she may note the debt in his or her records and forget to erase it. The heirs might ask you (or your survivors) for payment. The receipt shows that you're clean.

Instructions and Warranties

File the operating instructions for any equipment you buy. File warranty information. File maintenance contracts.

Money Owed to You

Keep the note in your home safe or safe-deposit box. Keep the repayment records in your file cabinet. When you get all your money back, cancel the note.

Note any refundable deposits, to the electric company, the phone company, your landlord. When you move, you're entitled to get them back.

Household Help

If you have an employee, keep proof that you paid all applicable taxes: Social Security, unemployment, and any other tax your state requires. Keep a copy of the W-2 you give your employee each January.

Your Phone File

Just to be on the safe side, photocopy your book of friends' addresses and telephone numbers. I lost my book once, unphotocopied. Never again.

Your Computer

BACK UP YOUR FILES!

Investments

Your safe-deposit box is the right place for the following items:

Stocks and other securities. Keep a list of their names, denominations, certificate numbers, and CUSIP numbers (for Committee on Uniform Securities Identification Procedures). If you lose a security, its number gets you a duplicate. (The transfer agent who sent you the security should also have a record of its number.) Take great care with your securities. It's costly and time consuming to replace them (page 659).

Your right to stock options or deferred compensation. These are things your heirs can overlook.

Bonds and Treasury securities. All new U.S. Treasury securities exist only as blips in the mind of a government computer, so you have no actual certificates to store. Many corporate bonds and some municipals are also issued this way. But keep all your purchase records. You may need them to prove your ownership if an interest or principal payment goes astray.

A list of your U.S. Savings Bonds, showing their denominations, serial numbers, and issue dates.

Gold, silver, or platinum bars or coins.

The original prospectus and sales material for any initial public offering you own. If a deal goes bad and was misrepresented, your prospectus could help establish grounds for a lawsuit. Also keep the annual reports that chart the investment's progress.

The names and account numbers of your mutual funds and unit trusts.

What about all the informational material you get from your mutual fund or unit trust? In your file cabinet, keep the original prospectus and sales literature. They tell you what you bought, how to redeem shares, and the services offered to investors. Keep any letters that say the fund has changed its rules. Keep the fund's annual reports. They show its performance compared with the market in general—a valuable history when you're deciding whether to hold or sell. You needn't keep all the interim reports. When you finally sell, dump all but the buy-and-sell records, which you'll need for income-tax purposes.

If you buy individual stocks and bonds, you have three choices: keep the securities in a fireproof safe at home, in a safe-deposit box, or at the brokerage house. If your account is active at all, by all means choose the broker. When you sell, you have to deliver the stock in just 3 business days and that's a nuisance to do by mail. Brokerage firms insure accounts for at least $500,000 and usually much more. But if you trade only occasionally, you might prefer having the securities under your control. For more on this issue, see page 659.

File your brokerage house agreement and annual statements. Keep all confirmations of trades. You have to know exactly when each security was bought and sold, the price, and the commission you paid in order to figure out your income tax. Add up your commissions once a year, to see what you're paying for the account (commissions appear only on your "confirms," not on your annual statement).

Take notes of all conversations you have with your broker. Put all your instructions in writing, including follow-up letters after a phone conversation. Keep copies. If you get into an argument about how the broker handled your account, these records can support your case.

If you're a casual investor, betting your money on someone else's say-so, there's no point cluttering your file drawers with the periodic reports sent by the companies whose stocks you own. But at least read them before tossing them out, or read the company chairman's letter. Maybe you'll learn something. If you're really following the company, you'll keep the most recent reports in your files.

Rental Properties

For reference, keep a couple of years' worth of income and expense records in your current files. Older receipts belong on the shelf with your back tax records.

Business at Home

There you are, in the spare-bedroom-turned-office, trading currency futures for all the parents at your day-care center. You know you can write off your telephone expenses (a separate phone line is best) against the potloads of profits you're making. But what else? For a home-based business, take a lesson from an accountant on how to keep track of income and expenses and what your tax deductions are. For example, you may be able to depreciate that part of the house that serves as your office. You might also write off a portion of what you pay to heat, light, clean, and insure your house (page 139). So you'll need to keep all those bills and canceled checks. Keep current bills in the filing cabinet and old bills with the tax records. Carry a business diary to record tax-deductible expenses for travel, entertainment, supplies, and so on. The IRS gets dark under the eyes when your diary reads as if you composed it just in time to make the audit.

Trust Documents

Keep the originals with your lawyer or in a safe-deposit box. Put copies in your files.

Charities and Gifts

Keep copies of pledges to charities and the letters that acknowledge your contribution. Keep canceled checks showing how much you gave.

Keep the appraisals on donated property. If you do volunteer work, keep track of the miles you drive on the charity's business. They're tax deductible.

Put notes about important gifts to friends and family members in your safe-deposit box if the gifts will affect the size of your estate tax or keep the peace in a squabbling family.

In Case of Death

Keep a last-wishes file. Include the cemetery deed if you have one, material for your obituary (relatives often get things wrong), final instructions about your funeral if it matters to you, and a copy of your living will if you don't want to be kept alive by extraordinary means. Don't bother including an organ donor card; by the time it's found it will be too late. Keep that card in your wallet and tell your doctors and relatives that you want your organs to be used. Also tell your relatives and executor about your living will and last-wishes file, and where to find them. President Franklin D. Roosevelt made detailed notes about how his funeral was to be conducted and put them in the White House safe. They weren't found until after he was buried.

Safe-Deposit-Box Key

Drop it into a toolbox. Keep it with the handkerchiefs. For obscurity— the usual fate of a key to a safe-deposit box—those places are as good as any. In my dreams, however, I see the key resting in your top desk or bureau drawer, labeled, with the bank's name attached (what's the good of a key if your survivors don't know which bank to take it to?). I see a note on your Master List telling everybody where it is. Ditto for the combination to the lock on your home safe.

The Master List of Where Everything Is

Record the results of your masterful filing system on a couple of sheets of paper and leave this Master List in your file for your executor and heirs. If you have a home computer that someone besides you knows how to operate, keep it there, too. Tell your family where to find it so they won't tear the house apart looking for your records. List:
- Your insurance policies and insurance agents.
- Employee benefits and the phone number of the office that handles them.
- Bank accounts and any particular banker you deal with.
- Where to find your safe-deposit box and keys.

- Where you keep your will or living trust, and the name of the lawyer who drew it up.
- Your executor or trustee.
- Where other trust documents are.
- Where all your personal papers are.
- Your brokers or investment advisers—names, addresses, and phone numbers.
- Your accountant.
- Where to find your securities and retirement accounts.
- Where your tax records are.
- What properties you own and where the deeds are.
- Your debts and any money owed you.
- Your Social Security number and that of every family member.

Tell someone where you hide your home safe and give that person the combination to the lock.

Make a list of all your credit cards—account numbers and emergency telephone numbers—in case your wallet is stolen and you have to cancel them.

Photocopy everything in your wallet—ID cards, driver's license, health insurance card, and other items you carry for reference. That makes them easy to replace.

4.

Your Basic Banking

Finding a Bank That Even Your Mother Would Love

Everyone needs a small-town banker.
Especially in a big town.

When you look for a bank, pick a small institution. Or a small branch of a large institution. You get a lot of personal help in a place where you're known, and the smaller the place the sooner you're known. Smaller, independent banks and S&Ls may also charge lower fees than large ones. My small branch:

• Pays my young son's checks when they're written against funds that haven't cleared yet, and waives the fees.

• Answers questions by telephone, free.

• Returns my calls.

• Fixes what's wrong.

• Calls to ask questions if something happens in the account that doesn't look quite right.

• Negotiates interest rates on mortgages and personal loans.

• Looks for ways to say yes.

• Goes to bat for me against the parent company's bureaucracy.

"Aha," you say, "that's only because you write about this stuff." It's not. Only a handful of people operate my branch, and they know their customers—every one of them. The character of the manager is important. The manager sets the tone of any office and mine goes out of the way to please. Not that big banks, or big branches, can't do a good job. Some have created a private-banking division for their big-bucks customers, which amounts to a small bank-within-the-bank. But in general, big banks or branches try harder for corporate customers than for just plain folks. Individuals can't make the personal contacts that grease the wheels when you need a favor done.

Savings and loan associations work the same way: smaller is usually better. S&Ls may charge lower fees and pay higher interest rates than banks. But because of the industry's financial disasters in the 1980s, the number of S&Ls has dwindled. Sooner or later they'll probably all be banks.

On the niceness scale, credit unions are often at the top. Enough of them offer better interest rates and lower banking fees to make it worth your while to take a look. If your employer doesn't offer one, write or call the Credit Union National Association (P.O. Box 431, Madison, WI 53701; 800-358-5710) for the address of your state association. That association, in turn, will give you the names of credit unions that you might be able to join.

Some credit unions offer a limited fare: only checking accounts (known as share-draft accounts), savings deposits, and consumer lending. Others also offer mortgages, credit cards, and stockbrokerage at a discount.

But follow the rules given later in this chapter on judging interest rates and fees. And avoid any credit union that doesn't carry federal deposit insurance. Around 5 percent of them still carry private coverage, which, as previous banking debacles show, can buckle under pressure.

Banklike services can also be had at large brokerage firms through their asset-management accounts (page 660). But those are best used as convenience accounts for investors. For everyday transactions, most people still need a bank.

OPENING AN ACCOUNT

Don't just stop by a bank and wait to see someone who's free. Make an appointment with the person in charge of opening new accounts. That starts you out as a serious client.

Before going to the meeting, pick up the brochures that the bank stocks by the front door, describing its many services. Read them to see what you might want; make a list of questions.

At your meeting, get all your questions answered. And go further than that. Explain to the banker the kind of customer you expect to be. How much money will be flowing through your checking account. How much saving you expect to do. What services you will need. Find out whom to call if you have a question or need some help. Above all, talk about the loans you might want. A home mortgage or home-equity line of credit? Money for real-estate investments or for starting a business? What does the bank offer? What does it take to get a lower interest rate? Bankers love to make loans; that's how they earn their money. They're especially attentive to customers who can help them meet their loan budgets for the year.

Take the measure of the person you're meeting with. Is he or she helpful? Knowledgeable about the bank's products and services? Willing to answer your questions in detail? Ready with good ideas? Interested in getting your business? A banker who starts out gruff, impatient, vague, supercilious, or ill-informed will not improve with time—and what is tolerated in one bank officer will be tolerated in others. Go to a place that makes a better first impression.

Compare the fees and interest rates offered by two or three institutions. They're a statement of business philosophy. High-fee banks are likely to charge even more in the future; low-fee banks are dedicated to holding down overt costs. Banks that pay high interest rates on savings have effectively announced that they'll always be competitive; banks that pay low interest won't be. Those are messages to pay attention to.

If You Do a Substantial Amount of Banking Business, Don't Settle on Just One Bank. Take Two. Different banks have different virtues. Each institution will want to get some of your business from the other, giving you a chance to negotiate lower fees and lower interest rates on loans.

WHICH CHECKING ACCOUNT?

No need to wander through the wilderness, wondering which of half a dozen checking accounts is best. Your choice is simple, because it hangs on a single test: What is the lowest average balance you will leave on deposit every month? If it's small, you'll probably get a checking account that pays no interest. To earn interest, you may have to maintain an average of $1,000 or $2,500 on deposit, depending on the bank. The higher your minimum balance, the higher the interest rate you'll get.

By law, banking institutions must use the *average-daily-balance* method of figuring your minimum balance. This takes the amount you have in your account each day and averages it across the entire month. If you keep $5,000 there for 29 days, and on the thirtieth day write a $5,000 check, that month's average balance would be $4,833. In arriving at your average daily balance, some banks will count both your checking and your savings deposits.

A few small credit unions still gyp customers with *low-balance* accounting, so watch for it. Here, the credit union looks only at the lowest point in your account that month. If you held on to $5,000 for 29 days and then emptied your account, the credit union would call your balance "zero." You would earn no interest. Worse, you might pay a fee for falling below the minimum balance. Fortunately, the law requires low-balance accounting to be phased out.

Besides interest rates and minimum deposits, look at the schedule of fees: monthly fees, fees for each check you write, ATM fees, and others. Don't let your banker's hand be quicker than your eye. A checking account might deliberately carry a low monthly fee or no fee at all in order to make it look cheap to price-shoppers. But the bank might recoup by charging you extra for processing checks or using the ATM machines. A few banks give you free access to ATMs but charge you for using a human teller. Banks are required to give you a full list of fees. Ask for it before opening an account.

You want an account that pays the highest interest rate possible on the average balance you can afford to keep, while not breaking your back with extra fees. So look around. At GoodGuy Bank, your checking deposits might earn $75 a year. At BadGuy Bank, exactly the same account might *cost* $150 even counting your interest earnings. In general, smaller banks charge lower fees and require lower checking-account balances than larger ones. Here's an idea of what's around.

If You Keep a Small Balance and Write Your Account Down Almost to Zero Every Month, Look at:

NO-INTEREST CHECKING. Banks have all kinds of fee schedules, with or without monthly maintenance charges, minimum balances, and charges for every check you write. When there are minimum balances, they generally run between $500 and $1,000, with a fee for falling below the minimum. In any case, no interest is paid on your idle money.

If You Can Maintain a Decent Minimum Balance at All Times, Look at:

INTEREST-PAYING CHECKING. You earn a wee interest rate on your idle balances—at this writing, around 1 to 1.5 percent. That might be a fixed rate or a variable rate set by the bank. But there are usually no check-processing charges or monthly fees. Average minimum balances run in the area of $1,000 to $5,000. If you fall below the minimum or, in some cases, write more than a specified number of checks, fees start to mount.

Some banks "tier" these accounts. The interest you earn, and the fees you pay, vary from month to month, depending on how much money you keep in the bank or how much business you do there.

BUNDLED ACCOUNTS. Your checking account may be "bundled" with other banking services, like free travelers checks, a line of credit at no annual fee, a credit card with a one-year waiver on the fee, discounts on loans, and a quarter-point interest bonus on various savings deposits. You get the whole package for a single low fee or no fee at all.

ASSET-MANAGEMENT ACCOUNTS. These are for active investors who want an easy way to keep track of their cash. They generally combine a money-market account (which doubles as an interest-paying checking account) with a brokerage account and a credit or debit card. With asset management:

• Your cash earns a higher interest rate than you'd get from regular interest-paying checking. Usually it's a money-market rate, although some institutions pay less.

• You can draw on your money with a special checkbook or a debit card (checks may have to be written for a minimum of $250 or more).

• You may get a credit card, which can trigger a loan against any stocks you own.

• A single monthly statement shows all your investment and banking transactions.

• All dividends and interest are automatically reinvested.

• You may get access to your funds through an ATM network.

Some accounts offer an automatic bill-paying service and let you arrange to have your paycheck deposited electronically.

The minimum deposit for asset-management accounts (including the value of your stocks and bonds): $1,000 to as much as $25,000. Annual fees run from zero to $125. Asset-management accounts are offered by a few big banks, brokerage houses, some mutual funds, and a few insurance companies. When you're not with a bank, you may have to wait up to 15 days for the checks to clear.

MONEY MARKET MUTUAL FUNDS. These, too, are normally for investors. Rates of interest change daily but are always higher than those on the banks' interest-paying checking accounts. The funds that offer checking (about half of them do) charge lower fees than banks and zero for falling below the minimum balance. You can arrange to have your paycheck deposited directly. For more on money market funds, see page 187. Most won't cash checks smaller than $100, so they're no good for everyday checking. But at this writing, a couple take checks in any amount. Try Midwest Short Term Government Income Fund in Cincinnati (800-543-8721; $1,000 to start) or FBL Money Market Fund in West Des Moines (800-247-4170; $500 to start). You might want to use your money fund as a small-business checking account.

The drawbacks to using money funds as checking accounts: you may not have access to ATMs, deposited checks will be held up to 15 days before you can draw against them, and you can't get a line of credit.

If You Have a Low Income and Write Only a Few Checks Every Month, Look for:

ECONOMY OR NO-FRILLS CHECKING. These accounts are for people who keep low average balances and write just a few checks a month. There's usually a small monthly fee and, often, access to your account by way of an automated teller machine. The first 10 or 15 checks may be free, with fees of 50 cents or more for each check over the limit (if you write a lot of checks, you should be in regular checking). This simplified service is offered by about half the banks, although it may be restricted to students or the elderly.

If You Sometimes Bounce Checks or Want to Have Instant Credit on Tap, Go for:

OVERDRAFT CHECKING. This lets you write checks for more money than you have in your checking account. At some banks, checks will be covered with funds switched from your savings account. At others, the checks are paid with a loan on which you're charged 10 to 16 percent. Some banks lend only in $50 increments, so if you write a check for $7 more than you have, you'll have to borrow $50 to cover it. Monthly repayments may be deducted from your account automatically.

The right to use overdraft checking may come free or it may cost you $15 to $20 a year plus a fee every time funds are transferred. In either case, you pay interest on the loan amount. The fees ain't cheap, but they're cheaper than bouncing a check.

Free Checking: No bank can advertise that its checking account is free unless it truly is. That means no monthly maintenance fees, no per-check fees, and no fees for falling below the minimum balance. The only allowable charges are those for ATM use, bounced or stopped checks, printing checks, and a few other minor items.

IF YOUR BANK FEES ARE TOO HIGH

Join the crowd. Everyone's screaming. But you may be able to cut your costs. When you opened your checking account, you might have looked only at how much interest you could earn. Now you know that the best account is the one that carries the lowest fees.

To find that account, start by analyzing your recent bank statements. Circle every fee to see how much you're spending each month (it could be as much as $300 a year) and list what all the fees were for. Then make a written summary of the way you use the account. How many checks do you write per month? How often do you use a teller or ATM (and does your bank charge you for it)? How low does your monthly balance go? How many incidental services do you use? How large are your savings deposits there? How much interest have you earned on your interest-paying checking and does it exceed the fees you pay?

Armed with this information, sit down with a bank employee and say that you'd like to find ways of lowering your fees.

• Maybe you have an interest-paying checking account but your balance keeps falling below the required minimum. That might cost you $7 or more each time. You'll save money over the year by choosing no-interest checking with a lower minimum balance.

• Maybe you write so few checks that you can manage on a no-frills account.

- Maybe your fees will drop if you keep more deposits in the bank. If you have a CD somewhere else, move it to this bank when it matures.
- Maybe your bank charges fees for using its ATMs. If so, you'll save money by taking $90 once a week rather than $30 three times a week. Some types of accounts may offer free access to ATMs.
- Maybe you're tapping your account through another bank's ATM. That always costs more than using your own bank's machines. You may even pay twice for the same transaction. One fee goes to the banks and the ATM network, the other fee goes to the owner of the ATM (which may be the bank or an outside company).
- Maybe it costs less to pay by debit card or automatic electronic transfer than to pay by check. Automatic transfers work for any fixed monthly payments: mortgage, rent, auto loan or lease, condo maintenance, life insurance premiums, budgeted utility bills, and regular monthly investments.
- Maybe your bank offers on-line banking from your home computer at a lower price than banking in person or by mail.
- Maybe it's cheaper to have your paycheck deposited electronically or accept a checking-account statement in lieu of canceled checks.
- It's doubtlessly cheaper to switch to a credit union if there's one you can join (page 51).
- For sure, it's cheaper to buy checks from a commercial check printer rather than through your bank. Two to try: Checks in the Mail (800-733-4443) and Current Check Printers (800-533-3973).

Two Final Points: (1) Banks have to tell you at least 30 days in advance when they're raising a fee. But the notice might be written in fine-print Sanskrit, which means that you'll probably throw it away. Prudence dictates that you read all bank notices and get a translation when you don't understand. If you don't bother, check your statements periodically for new fees that you may have missed. (2) *Banks charge wildly different fees!* Yours may be expensive compared with the competition. You might cut your fees in half simply by comparing prices and switching to a cheaper bank. Small banks and credit unions usually charge the least. But a few big banks have eliminated all nuisance fees for customers who keep balances of $2,000 or more.

TEST YOUR BANKER'S IQ

A good banker should be able to answer all seven of the following questions. If you get a blank look—or a gentle drift of oral fog—ask again. You're entitled to a clear and simple statement that makes sense. If you don't understand what the banker is saying, don't blame yourself. Blame the banker, who probably doesn't have all the facts and is covering up. If you had $10 for every "expert" who wasn't, you'd be rich.

1. *Ask:* With interest-paying checking, what does the banking institution pay interest *on?* By law, it must pay on the money that's in your account at the end of each day. That's "day of deposit to day of withdrawal." But some truly pay on each check from the day you put it in. Others pay only on the *collected* balance, which means you get no interest until the check has provisionally cleared. That usually takes one or two days but sometimes more.

Some banks advertise more than one rate, depending on the size of your deposit. They might pay 1.5 percent on balances up to $1,000 and 2.7 percent on larger amounts. But what exactly does that mean? There's a good way and a bad way to figure it.

Say, for example, that you deposit $2,500. You might get 2.7 percent on the whole amount, usually called a *tiered* rate. That's good. Or you might get 1.5 percent on the first $1,000 and 2.7 percent only on the remaining $1,500, usually called a *blended* rate. That's bad. In fact, it's a clip job. Avoid blended rates.

2. *Ask:* What is the penalty for falling below the minimum balance? The fee might exceed the interest that your account is likely to earn. If you can't be sure of maintaining the minimum balance, switch to an account with a lower minimum—for example, a no-interest-paying account.

3. *Ask:* Can the bank *truncate* your checking account? With truncation, you get a monthly list of the checks you wrote but not the canceled checks themselves. If you need a copy of a check to prove that you made a particular payment, the bank might send it to you free or might charge $1 to $5. Most customers like to get canceled checks, but you rarely need them. Truncated accounts are often cheaper; the bank may waive the monthly fee and minimum balance.

4. *Ask:* What fees might you have to pay with this account? You should get a list, including charges for maintaining the account, processing checks, bouncing checks, using an automated teller machine, using a human teller, buying checks printed with your name and address, confirming your current bank balance, buying certified checks, stopping payment on a check, transferring funds by telephone, and depositing checks that turn out to be no good (called *deposit item returned*—see page 59).

5. *Ask:* Will the bank reduce the interest rate on your loans if you keep a checking account there and allow the loan payments to be deducted automatically?

6. *Ask:* If you buy a certificate of deposit or take out a loan, will the bank eliminate the fees it charges for your checking account? Most institutions give their better customers special breaks. Some tie-in deals, however, are not worth having. You might save yourself a quarter point on an auto

loan by taking out a certificate of deposit. But that's no bargain if cheaper auto loans are available somewhere else.

7. *Ask:* When you deposit a check, how long do you have to wait before being able to draw against the funds? By law, your bank has to tell you exactly what the rules are.

HOW FAST WILL YOUR CHECKS CLEAR?

There you stand, like a kid with his nose pressed against a pet-store window. Your money is romping behind the glass and you can't get at it. Any checks you deposit may be held by your bank for a specified number of days.

If you write a check against deposited funds too soon, it will probably bounce. You'll pay $15 to $20 for the error, with some banks charging as much as $30. To bounce-proof your checks, sign up for overdraft checking (page 55). Alternatively, move your account to a friendly bank that will honor checks written against uncollected funds—although you'll probably be charged for the service. A *really* friendly bank will waive the fee.

Under federal law, banking institutions normally *must* give you access to at least $100 of your deposit on the next business day, and *must* clear the rest of your deposit on a specified schedule (with some quirky conditions here and there). All the following limits apply to checks deposited to your account before the bank's cutoff hour—generally, noon for ATM deposits and 2 p.m. for deposits made in person. Add one business day for checks you deposit after the cutoff. The general schedule:

1. One business day for federal, state, and local government checks, electronic payments (like direct deposit of a paycheck or Social Security check), postal money orders, cash, personal checks drawn on the same bank, cashier's checks, and certified checks. To get one-day access, certain checks have to be deposited in person or sometimes on special deposit slips. Ask about this if your timing is critical.

2. Two business days for local checks.

3. Five business days for out-of-town checks.

4. On checks deposited on a business day (not Saturday) in the bank's own ATM: one business day for U.S. Treasury checks; 2 business days for cash, local checks, cashier's checks, and state and local government checks; and 5 business days for out-of-town checks.

5. On checks deposited in an ATM not owned or operated by your bank: 5 business days.

6. On checks you mail to the bank: one business day after receipt by the bank for U.S. Treasury checks; 2 days for cashier's checks, postal money orders, and local checks including the checks of your own state and local governments; 5 days for out-of-town checks.

7. On withdrawing cash against checks you just deposited: The bank can hold certain types of checks an extra day, giving you access to just $400 of the deposit. In practice, however, few banks impose this restriction. The holding periods are usually the same, whether you write checks against your deposit or ask for cash.

At many institutions, most of these rules are irrelevant. They cheerfully offer one-day clearance for almost all checks.

Is a bank ever allowed to hold checks longer than usual? Absolutely. It needs at least some weapons against the risk of fraud. Expect a delay in drawing against deposited checks if:

1. You're a brand-new customer. The bank gets 30 days to take your measure, during which time you might have to wait longer than usual for checks to clear. But on the next business day, even new customers can draw on the first $5,000 of funds from a government, cashier's, or travelers check, or from deposits made electronically. So if you move, transfer your bank account by wire.

2. You repeatedly overdraw your checking account or are redepositing a check that bounced. In this case, a local check can be held for 7 business days and an out-of-town check for 11 business days.

3. You deposit more than $5,000 in checks in a single day. Part of your money will be released on the normal schedule; part can be held up to 6 business days longer.

4. The bank has "reasonable cause" to think something is fishy. This covers such things as suspicion of fraud, suspicion that the account holder is going bankrupt, or concern that the check is too old to cash.

These rules all apply to withdrawals by check or to cash withdrawals through a human teller. Limits are allowed on cash withdrawals through an ATM. Limits on cash withdrawals are always allowed for security reasons, through tellers as well as ATMs.

THE MOST HATED BANK FEE IN AMERICA

It's the fee known in bank jargon as deposit item returned (DIR). You may be charged a DIR when you get a check, deposit it, then learn it bounced. You are blameless. You had no idea the check wouldn't clear. Nevertheless, the bank nicks you for an average of $4.75 to $7.50, with some banks going as high as $10 (large banks charge more than small ones).

In most cases, the checks aren't truly bad. The writer just made a math mistake in his check register, or forgot to enter past checks, or thought his or her paycheck would clear faster than it did. When the check is resubmitted it's usually good. Still, the innocent party pays. If you're hit with a DIR, call your bank and ask it to cancel the charge. Banks sometimes will.

MORE CHECK FACTS

To cash checks at a branch other than your own, get a signature card.

When you endorse a check (that is, sign your name on the back) it becomes as good as money and can be cashed by anyone who finds it. To prevent that, endorse it with instructions: "Pay to the order of Sarah May" or "For deposit only." When accepting an endorsed check from someone else, ask him or her to write "pay to the order of (you)" so that if you lose it neither of you will be out the money.

Endorse checks on the back, at the left-hand end, in the first inch and a half of space. If your signature is anywhere else, the bank may ask you to sign again. Most checks now carry a line to show where your signature goes.

Technically, a check may be good for years. But in practice, the bank might refuse any check that is more than one year old. That is, if the bank notices.

If you write a check and wish you hadn't, call your bank and ask it to stop payment. Your account should be flagged right away, but you have to follow up with written authorization, usually by filing a stop-check form. The cost: $15, on average, but sometimes as much as $30. A stop payment lasts for a limited period of time but can be renewed. If the check slips through, the bank takes responsibility for it. The stop-check form should spell out the rules.

You can arrange for regular, automatic transfers from your checking to your savings account. Interest earned on your certificates of deposit can be deposited into either account.

If someone forges your signature on a check and the bank cashes it, you are entitled to 100 percent reimbursement. It doesn't matter that you failed to report that your checkbook was stolen (although you should have). It doesn't matter that you kept your checks with your credit cards, which carry your signature. In most cases, it is the bank's absolute responsibility to guard against forgery. Some banks blame you and refuse to pay, in which case you should write directly to the bank's president and to its state or federal regulator.

You have a responsibility, too. If you don't report a forgery within 14 days after the bank mailed your statement, and fraudulent checks continue to be cashed by the same person, the later losses are all yours.

Use a *certified* check when the person you're paying wants a guarantee that the check will be good. The bank certifies that the check will be paid by withdrawing the money from your account when the check is issued. A *cashier's* check can be used by people with no checking account. You give the money to the bank and it issues a check on its own account. Banks, S&Ls, money-order companies, and the post office also issue money orders, payable to specific people. Keep all receipts. They're your only proof of payment. File them as if they were canceled checks.

If you have a checking or savings account that you haven't touched for a while, check into its status. Some banks stop paying interest on quiescent accounts. Some even start charging fees. You can usually return to claim an old account, but you won't receive any interest for the years it lay dormant or get back the fees that you were charged.

If your bank accounts lie untouched for 3 to 7 years (and sometimes longer, depending on your state), the money will be turned over to the state treasury. Ditto for property in safe-deposit boxes, certificates of deposit, even property held by the bank in trust. The bank, S&L, or credit union first has to try to reach you by writing to your last known address and putting a notice in the newspaper. The state may have to advertise, too. If you don't show up, the money goes. You (or your heirs) can get it back by going to the state with proof of ownership. But only a few states pay interest on the accounts they've held.

If you owe the bank money and haven't paid, it can generally dip into your other accounts—savings, checking, sometimes even a trust account, depending on the trust document—to satisfy the debt. Some states put modest limits on which accounts can be seized for what. Federal law prevents banks from taking money to satisfy a disputed credit-card bill. But otherwise you are at risk for your own unpaid loans and any loans you co-signed. If you lose your job and foresee a problem paying your mortgage, prudence dictates moving your savings to another bank.

KEEP TRACK OF YOUR DEBIT-CARD SPENDING

Debit cards look like credit cards but they're not. They're plastic checks. When you pay with a debit card, you draw money directly out of your checking account. You *must* enter your debit-card spending in your check register just as if you had cashed a check. Otherwise, you won't know how much money you have left. You might accidentally fall below the minimum balance in your account or even bounce a check. For more on debit cards, see page 225.

BALANCING YOUR CHECKBOOK

Good news: *You don't have to.* The Rockies won't crumble, Gibraltar won't tumble, if you take the bank's word that your balance is right. Personally, I'm not happy unless my checkbook adds up, but that's easy for me to say; I let my husband do it. If you are allergic to arithmetic, here's the minimum you can get away with:

• Enter every deposit and withdrawal on your check register as you go along, not forgetting your dealings with ATMs, direct deposits such as paychecks, bills paid automatically through electronic transfers, and money withdrawn when you paid for something with a debit card. You need a running total so you won't overdraw. Also, you don't want to fall below the minimum balance your account requires.

• When the statement comes in, check every deposit and withdrawal against your check register to be sure there aren't any errors or alterations. If you wait a year or more to report a mistake, the bank might not make good.

• Note each check that was cashed.

• If you have an interest-paying checking account, add the interest the bank paid that month to your checkbook balance. Then subtract all the fees. (These items show on your monthly statement.)

Assuming that nothing feels wildly out of line, it's okay to leave it at that. I don't trust a bank to enter checks correctly but I do trust its addition. (My own addition isn't so hot.) Just don't ask the bank to balance your checkbook. It might charge you $25.

Every 6 months or so, purge your math errors. Take the current balance as reported by your bank, add all new deposits, subtract all uncashed checks, enter the result as the new balance in your checkbook, and start over.

Mind you, I don't recommend that you leave your checkbook a mess. But getting it in balance isn't the end-all of good financial planning.

AUTOMATED TELLER MACHINES

The ATM machine is McBanking at its easiest. You insert a card and punch a few buttons. Instantly, you're in touch with your bank account to confirm your checking-account balance, withdraw or deposit funds, or, at some machines, switch money from one account to another. Thanks to these fast-cash machines, you can get money whenever you want: on your way to work, in the middle of a holiday weekend, late on Sunday night. Banks hook up their ATMs to national networks, so funds are even available if you run short while you're out of town or traveling abroad.

But ATMs are sometimes a nuisance—for example, when they make mistakes. When you ask for $100, only $70 might show up in the drawer. For information on correcting these errors, see page 73.

Around 75 percent of the banks don't charge you for using their own ATMs. The rest charge around 25 cents to $1 per transaction. More than two-thirds of the banks charge if you reach your account through an ATM owned by another institution—maybe 75 cents to $2. The fee is for withdrawals. Deposits are usually free (but not always). You'll probably be charged if all you want is to check the balance in your account.

Most ATMs also accept credit cards. You use them to take out a loan against a line of credit.

If the Big Attraction of ATMs Is Convenience, the Big Risk Is Crime.

When you slip your card into an outdoor ATM, you're a sitting duck for a cruising crook. He knows that you've just picked up some cash. If he has the time, he might force you at knifepoint to tap your account for even more. Then he might steal your car and drive away.

ATM crime is growing, although no one knows by exactly how much. Banks don't like to report it for fear of scaring you away. Also, full disclosure of the risks of using ATMs might give victimized customers stronger grounds for suing the banks to recover their losses. So the bankers keep mum.

Under the Electronic Fund Transfers Act, your bank has to reimburse you for all but $50 of an unauthorized withdrawal, provided that you report the loss immediately. So you're covered if a thief swipes your card and drains your account. You are also covered if you're persuaded by a gun in your back to empty out your account. Some institutions have tried to avoid paying customers in this situation, but the law says you're owed.

It is not at all clear, however, that the bank has any liability for your losses if you're knocked on the head as you're leaving the machine. Customers have sued their banks, but most of the cases are settled out of court. In at least one case, a bank argued successfully that the customer was himself negligent for using a poorly lighted ATM at night. Here's how to play it safe with an ATM:

• Don't use ATMs at night, even if they are located on bank property. A survey by the Bank Administration Institute discovered that most ATM crimes take place between 7 p.m. and midnight, on bank premises.

• Don't use ATMs in isolated areas at any time.

• Don't use ATMs that are badly lit or readily accessible to a quick-hit thief in an automobile.

• Don't be the only person at an ATM.

• Don't use ATMs that are hidden by shrubbery.

• Don't use a drive-up ATM without first locking the car doors.

• Don't use ATMs that lack a permanent surveillance camera that could identify an assailant. (During a Florida lawsuit it was discovered that although a sign at an ATM said the machine was under surveillance, no camera existed.)

• Don't write your personal identification number (PIN) on your ATM card. The PIN tells the bank machine that you're really you. If your card is lost, that number is an open door into your account.

• Don't give your PIN to a stranger. If the stranger claims to be a cop or banker, he's lying. No one but a crook would ask.

FOR FAST, FAST, FAST RELIEF

When you have to get money to someone in a hurry, a check might serve if it's delivered fast. Use a commercial overnight delivery service or the post office's Express Mail. If the recipient has nowhere to cash the check, use one of the following quick-delivery systems:

1. An ATM card. If the recipient has a card, you can put money into his or her U.S. bank account. It can be withdrawn at a cash machine abroad and you'll get the wholesale rate on your currency exchange.

2. Postal money orders sent by Express Mail. But you can count on rapid delivery only within the United States. International money orders are governed by country-to-country agreements and may take 4 to 6 weeks to arrive.

3. Western Union. Call toll-free 800-325-6000 and charge up to $2,000 on your Visa, MasterCard, or Discover card. Or take cash (sometimes a cashier's check is okay) to a local Western Union agent. Some agents, and the 800 service, are available 24 hours a day, 7 days a week. Cash can be transferred within the United States, Puerto Rico, and to more than 100 foreign countries in 15 minutes or less. Funds wired elsewhere usually take at least 2 business days because delivery goes through local banks. The recipient can pick up the money at any Western Union agency. For the address of the closest one, ask the local agent or the 800 operator.

4. The State Department. It's the agency of choice if your son was robbed in Bangladesh. In an emergency it will send cash within 24 hours to any American embassy or consulate for a fee of $15. All you have to do is get the money to the State Department, using Western Union, bank wire, overnight mail, or regular mail. For details, write to the Overseas Citizens Services, Consular Affairs, Room 4800, Department of State, Washington, DC 20520, or call the Citizens Emergency Center, 202-647-5225.

5. Your bank, for big-money transfers within the United States. It can wire money to another bank for pickup the same day or one day later. But mistrust banks for international transfers. Unless the foreign bank pays a lot of attention, a transfer that ought to take a day can take a month.

Ask what identification the recipient will need in order to pick up the money. Usually two proofs are required, like a passport and driver's license with picture attached. Sometimes he or she will also need a code word or authorization number that you furnish.

To Get Extra Money When You're Out of Town: If you run short of cash or travelers checks, or your wallet is stolen, there are several ways to rescue yourself:

1. Get someone at home to send you money, using one of the techniques just described.

2. If you know your Visa or MasterCard number, you can call Western Union at 800-325-6000, charge your card for up to $2,000, and send the money to yourself.

3. If at least one of your cards wasn't stolen (just in case, travelers with two cards should keep them in two different places), you have some choices. Your ATM card will plug into one of the national (and international) ATM networks. You can generally withdraw $200 to $600 a day from your account at home. You might also be able to get a cash advance against your overdraft checking. Transaction fee: usually 75 cents to $2. Many ATM webs have toll-free numbers that you can call to find cash machines wherever you go.

The leading credit cards, such as Visa and MasterCard, and the charge card American Express are also accepted by ATM networks. If you sign up for American Express's Express Cash service, and have a green card, you can use an ATM to tap your bank account for up to $1,000 a week. Gold card holders can get up to $2,500 a week. Fee: 2 percent, with a $2.50 minimum and a $20 maximum. At some ATMs, you can also get American Express travelers checks. Fee: 1 percent.

MasterCard and Visa holders can get loans against their lines of credit through ATMs or banks—domestic and foreign—affiliated with the card's sponsor.

4. Take your checkbook when you travel. Many stores, hotels, and restaurants accept personal checks from tourists. American Express holders can cash personal checks (up to certain limits) at any Amex office, as well as at some hotels and airlines.

WHICH SAVINGS ACCOUNT?

Where you put savings depends on how much you have and what you plan to do with it.

For Only a Small Amount of Money

With less than $200 to $500 or so, you've got problems. Hardly anyone wants your money. Banks might let kids have a small, free savings account. But as an adult, you will probably pay service charges, and they might exceed the interest you earn. Some banks won't pay any interest at all. So instead of growing, your savings account would gradually shrink. One solution: Add that money to your checking account *and don't spend it*. The extra $500 might give you enough to qualify for interest-paying checking. Another solution: try a credit union, which is more likely to accept small savings accounts without charge.

A *statement savings account* might pay interest on small deposits ($100 to $500) and still charge no fees. You don't get a passbook. Instead, you get a statement every month. I like the convenience of statement savings. You don't have to remember where you put the passbook and can usually handle the account through an ATM. At this writing, you earn around 2.5 percent interest. You can take out your money at any time.

A *passbook account* might require a higher minimum balance. Then again, it might not. Everything depends on the bank. Deposits and withdrawals are recorded in the passbook; interest rates run in the area of 2.5 percent.

For Larger Amounts of Money

A *money market deposit account* pays a variable rate of interest—and I do mean variable. The bank has the right to change it at will. In high-rate periods, this account should pay much more than passbook savings; in low-rate periods, it pays about the same. You get unlimited deposits and withdrawals, although withdrawals might have to exceed a certain minimum amount. You're allowed up to 6 preauthorized transactions a month, only 3 of which can be checks to third parties (the others can be automatic bill paying or checks written to yourself). You'll be charged monthly fees if your deposit falls too low.

Money market accounts are a good place for money you're likely to need pretty soon, like rainy-day money, money waiting to be invested somewhere else, money you'll need to live on for the next 6 months, and earmarked money, like a tuition payment due in a few weeks. It is *not* a good place for longer-term savings. It simply doesn't earn enough.

Savers tend to use money market deposit accounts because they're there. But a smarter buy is often a money market mutual fund (page 187). Mutual funds pay around 0.5 percentage points more than bank accounts when interest rates are low and as much as 3 percentage points more when rates are high.

Certificates of deposit commit your money for anywhere from 6 months to 10 years. Some institutions set fixed terms, like one year or 2 years; others let you pick the exact number of days, weeks, or months you want. Normally, the longer the term, the higher the interest rate.

CDs are for money that must be kept safe, like your daughter's tuition for next year, funds that you'll need next year to pay your bills, money you're saving for a new house, some of your retirement money, or all of your savings, until you learn how to invest.

You normally pay a penalty (of one to 6 months' interest, and sometimes more) for withdrawing funds before the term is up. But don't let that scare you out of choosing a CD. If you're forced to break it before maturity and pay the penalty, so be it. That won't be the first bit of money you've frittered away. The chances are, however, that you'll keep your CD for the full term and earn more interest than you'd have gotten from a regular savings account.

TRUTH IN SAVINGS

By federal law, banking institutions all have to figure their interest-rate yields in a standard way. That's disclosed in an *annual percentage yield (APY)*. Always use APY to compare two interest-paying bank accounts. No matter what else the advertisement may say, or how often your deposit compounds, the bank with the highest APY is paying the most on your checking account or savings deposit.

CDs FOR SOPHISTICATES

You can earn the highest possible interest on CDs, without surrendering easy access to your money, by using a simple strategy called *laddering*. Here's how it works, assuming an initial pot of savings of $6,000.

You start out by splitting that money among bank deposits of varying maturities: $1,000 into a money market account, for cash on hand; then $1,000 each into a one-, 2-, 3-, 4-, and 5-year CD (or different maturities, depending on what you find). Normally, the longer the maturity, the higher the interest rate.

One year later, your first CD will mature, paying $1,000 plus interest. If you don't need the cash, reinvest it in a new *5-year* CD, which pays a higher interest rate. You can risk putting money away that long because, in another year, your next CD will mature—once again, giving you cash on hand. If you still don't need the money, it, too, goes into a 5-year CD.

If you do this each time a CD matures, all your money will soon be earning 5-year interest rates. Yet a $1,000 certificate will come due every 12 months, providing ready cash if you need it. Result: you will earn much more on your money without having to tie it all up for five years at a throw. You could stretch out this ladder by using one-, 3-, 5-, 7-, and 9-year CDs.

HIGH-YIELD CERTIFICATES OF DEPOSIT

High-yield CDs pay about one to 2 percentage points more than the national average. Typically, they're offered by strong institutions whose local economies are booming. Quite likely, too much money has been lent and the banks have had to raise interest rates in order to keep on attracting deposits. These economies and institutions may weaken, but that's not your problem. As long as your deposits are federally insured, the CDs are good buys.

You may also get high yields from "virtual" banks on the Internet. Because they have no overhead, their costs can be low and their interest rates high. As long as it's FDIC-insured, you run no risk—but check it out to be sure it's the real thing. An early entrant: Security First Network Bank at http://www.sfnb.com.

A few high-rate institutions are financially troubled. As long as they're operating on their own, your high interest rate is safe, but if they're taken over by the Federal Deposit Insurance Corporation, their attractive CDs may not last very long. The FDIC may sell the insolvent bank to a sound institution, which will cut the old CD rates.

To locate top-yielding, federally insured CDs and bank money-market deposit accounts, subscribe to the publication *100 Highest Yields* (at this writing, $34 for an eight-week trial subscription, from Box 088888, North Palm Beach, FL 33408). It tells you the names, addresses, and latest interest rates of the best-paying institutions in the country. It also publishes Veribanc's safety-and-soundness ratings for those institutions (page 78), so you don't have to worry about dealing with a fly-by-night. All this information is available free on the Internet. Go to http://www.bankrate.com.

To make a long-distance deposit in a high-rate bank or S&L, call the institution that interests you and ask for the person in charge of new accounts. Get the deposit forms and a conditional account number. Fill in the forms and, using the conditional account number, mail the bank a check. You can transfer large amounts of money by wire directly from your present bank.

Alternatively, you can buy insured CDs through one of the major stock-brokerage houses. The minimum investment is generally $1,000; the bank pays the commission, not you. Stockbrokers don't offer the very top-yielders in the country, but their CDs usually pay above average. One hitch: A broker-sold CD can't be cashed in before maturity. If you need the money early, the broker will put it up for sale and try to get you a reasonable price.

Yield-shoppers beware: Advertised high yields are sometimes good for only 30 or 60 days, after which they drop. For a reality check, always compare the annual percentage yield (APY) with that for competing CDs.

DESIGNER CDs

Hungry bankers respond to every fresh scent on the wind. Show them a new market, a new worry, a change in the economic outlook, and they will design a certificate of deposit to match. Not all banks and S&Ls offer exotic CDs; those that do may call them by different names than I have used. But if these ideas interest you, watch for them in the newspaper ads. The better the deal, the larger the minimum deposit the institution may want. Always compare the annual percentage yield (APY) with that being offered by standard CDs of the same term. Sometimes the designer CDs pay less.

No-Penalty CD—if you think you might need some of the money before maturity. You're charged no penalty for early withdrawal of some or all of your funds.

Bump-Up CD—if you expect interest rates to rise. If that indeed happens, the bank will—at your direction—raise the rate you are earning on your CD once or twice during its term.

Step-Up CD—also for people who expect higher rates. This CD pays less now but guarantees higher rates in the future. It's especially important to compare a step-up's APY with that for fixed-rate CDs of the same term. Step-ups offer dazzlingly high yields in, say, their final three months. But *on average* they may pay less than a plain-vanilla CD.

Variable-Rate CD—again, for people who expect higher rates. Your interest rate rises and falls with the general level of rates. Buy it only if there's a guaranteed floor below which the interest rate cannot go.

Anytime CD—if you want your money back on a specific date. The bank will construct a CD that exactly matches the maturity you want.

Relationship CD—if you are trying to lower your banking costs. Buying a CD may entitle you to a lower interest rate on a loan at the same institution, or fewer fees on your checking account.

Tiered CD—if you have substantial savings. The larger your deposit, the higher your interest rate.

Bitter-End CD—if you know you can last for the full term. You get a bonus for keeping your money in the CD for a full five years.

Zero-Coupon CD—if you want to make a gift of money look extra good. You put down a small sum now, at a guaranteed interest rate. It will grow to equal the CD's face value in a given number of years. (Each year's increase in value is taxable, even though you get no cash payout. So zeros are best given to a child or kept in a tax-deferred retirement account.) Always ask for the annual percentage yield and compare it with regular CDs of the same maturity. Some institutions clip you a little on their zeros.

Jumbo CD—if you (or a group of investors) have more than $100,000. Banks pay higher interest rates on large amounts of money. But choose a safe institution. If your bank fails, and the government can't find a buyer for it, your deposits over $100,000 may not be fully reimbursed.

Asset-Linked CD—if you want to speculate a little. CDs have been linked to the stock market, gold, and real estate. Part of your yield may be guaranteed but most of it is hostage to fortune. Furthermore, your CD won't rise by as much as the underlying asset does. You'll get only a portion of the increase.

You're truly gambling with a one-year asset-linked CD because the price of these assets is so volatile in the short run. A five-year investment gives you a better shot at a decent return, but it's still a big risk to take with money that's supposed to be safe. If your bank fails at a moment when your CD shows an investment-linked gain, you'll lose it. Federal deposit insurance normally covers only your guaranteed principal and the guaranteed portion of your return, up to $100,000.

Tax-Deferral CD—if you're chiefly interested in deferring your tax. This 12-month CD is bought at a discount in the current calendar year, to mature next year. No interest is paid until the CD matures, which puts all of your income into the next tax year.

ABSOLUTELY FAKE CDs

Are you looking for higher interest rates than CDs will pay? Some banks and S&Ls sell an instrument called a subordinated debt note, or lobby note. It has also gone by other names, like retail debenture. When you buy it, you are lending money to the institution, unsecured. Lobby notes don't carry federal deposit insurance. If the institution goes broke, your investment will probably be worthless.

The banks and S&Ls that sell these notes may not be in the greatest financial shape. To raise money, they shamelessly peddle "junk notes" to savers who can't evaluate the risk. Not only are you shafted if the institution fails, you are also shafted if it succeeds. The fine print in a lobby note usually allows the bank to redeem it before the full term is up. So you might lose the high interest income you expected.

I say, don't buy. If you're still tempted by these 5- to 20-year wonders, call Veribanc for a financial-soundness rating on your institution (page 78). If it's anything less than three-star (for tops), steer clear. You can get the ratings for the current quarter and for previous ones. If *any* rating falls below three-star, don't buy. In 1989 investors lost $250 million in the lobby notes of the holding company for Lincoln S&L in Irvine, California, whose ratings had been wavering back and forth between high and medium. Later, it turned out that behind its occasional high rating lay some doubtful accounting methods.

WHEN YOUR CD MATURES

When you open a CD, ask the bank what happens when the certificate matures. What instructions do they need on what you want done with the CD's proceeds, and how soon do they need them? Can you give instructions now? All this information will be in your CD contract, but it's important that you understand it exactly.

Each institution handles things a little differently. Normally, there is a short grace period after maturity—maybe 7 to 10 days, but sometimes as little as one day—during which the bank waits to hear from you. Do you want the money moved to another account? Another bank? Invested in another CD? Interest may or may not be paid during this period. If the grace period expires and you haven't told the bank what to do, your money will probably be reinvested in another CD of the same term. If you then decide that you want the cash, you might be able to break the CD without penalty. Then again, you might not.

Banking institutions have to notify you shortly before your CD matures. But keep track of the payment date yourself, just in case there's a slipup. Don't leave your decision to the last minute. The bank might want written instructions and you'll have to allow enough time for them to arrive.

OTHER BANK PRODUCTS

Banks are now urging their customers to buy mutual funds and tax-deferred annuities. They note when your CDs are coming due and call you with a sales pitch. You might visit with someone you think is a banker and never learn that he or she is actually a broker angling to sell you a product and earn a commission. Your friendly teller may have to refer you to these brokers in order to keep his or her job.

At some banks you will get a full and fair explanation of annuities and mutual funds. But don't count on it. All too often, the operation reeks of deceptive sales. How bad is it? *The American Banker,* an industry trade paper, once sent reporters posing as mutual fund customers into ten banks. Reps at eight of those banks "forgot" to mention that mutual funds aren't federally insured; only a few of them disclosed fees; most downplayed the investment risk; some illegally forecast specific (and double-digit) gains; one even suggested that mutual funds were like CDs but with higher yields.

Similar surveys using "mystery shoppers" keep turning up similar results. Some customers don't realize they've bought mutual funds or annuities, don't understand the risks, and find out too late that there's a stiff penalty for withdrawing money before several years have passed. In one case I'm familiar with, a 92-year-old man was sold an annuity with withdrawal fees lasting until he was 99. He thought he was buying a high-rate CD.

According to federal guidelines, banks are supposed to:

• Tell you that mutual funds and annuities aren't backed by the bank or by federal deposit insurance.

• Tell you that the performance of mutual funds and annuities isn't guaranteed.

• Tell you that your interest and principal may be at risk.

• Sell in an area clearly separate from the rest of the bank, with no FDIC signs anywhere near.

• Sell you investments appropriate to your age and financial circumstances.

Industry guidelines add that all sales commissions, surrender charges, and other fees should be fully disclosed.

Should you invest with banks? To help you decide, see Chapter 22 (mutual funds) and page 886 (tax-deferred annuities).

TEST YOUR BANKER'S IQ, AGAIN

1. *Ask:* How often does interest compound? "Compounding" means that the bank adds the interest you earn to your account, and then pays interest on the combined interest and principal. The more often your interest is compounded, the more money you make. Daily or continuous compounding (they're just about the same) yields the most, followed by quarterly, then semiannual, then annual compounding. With "simple" interest there is no compounding at all. What difference does it make? Plenty. At 6 percent interest, compounded daily, your savings are worth 14 percent more after 10 years than if you had earned only simple interest. Compounding is included in the annual percentage yield (APY). At equal rates of interest, an account that compounds daily or continuously will have a higher APY than one that compounds any other way.

2. *Ask:* How often is interest credited to your account? Most banks that compound interest daily do not actually give you the money until the end of the month or the end of the quarter. So then ask: What happens to that last bit of interest if you close your account before the end of the period? Normally, you will lose it even though the bank claims that it's paying you right to the day of withdrawal.

3. *Ask:* What is the annual percentage yield on your savings? This yield takes all kinds of mathematical quirks into consideration, not only interest

COMPOUND INTEREST: THE MAGIC MONEY MACHINE

	A $10,000 DEPOSIT AT 6 PERCENT AFTER:		
COMPOUNDING METHOD	ONE YEAR	FIVE YEARS	TEN YEARS
Daily	$10,618	$13,498	$18,220
Monthly	10,617	13,488	18,194
Quarterly	10,614	13,469	18,140
Semiannually	10,609	13,439	18,061
Annually	10,600	13,382	17,908
Simple interest	10,600	13,000	16,000

SOURCE: Bank Rate Monitor

rate and frequency of compounding but also such technical details as how many days the bank counts as a year. (Some banks use 366 days, others use 365, still others 360. For reasons only Computerman would believe, 360 yields more interest.) The higher the APY, the better the deal.

4. *Ask:* What is the periodic payment rate? That's the rate the bank applies during each compounding period when figuring how much interest you have earned. Knowing it, you can check the bank's calculations to see if it paid you properly. Mistakes are not uncommon. A good bank will give you its periodic payment rate and show you how to use it.

FIXING BANK MISTAKES

Cash. How many times have you cashed a check in a hurry, then walked away without counting the money? Maybe you think the teller is always right. Maybe you are intimidated by the line of grumpy people behind you. But if you count the money at the bank door and find that you're $20 short, you might be stuck. Tellers aren't allowed to hand over extra money on a customer's say-so. After all, you could have slipped the missing $20 into your pocket before you went back to the teller's window.

RULE 1. Always count your money before leaving the window. If you discover an error later, give your name, address, and account number to the manager. If the teller winds up the day with the right amount of extra cash, you'll be reimbursed.

Deposits. Tellers sometimes err when crediting deposits—for example, entering $100 when you actually put in $1,000.

RULE 2. Double-check every transaction for accuracy before leaving the window. What if the teller credits $1,000 to your account when you gave him or her only $100? Don't spend the money. The mistake will be found and in banking, there's no finders keepers.

Automated Teller Machines. ATMs goof, just as people do. They short-change the occasional customer, giving you $70 when you asked for $100. Sometimes they accept cash and checks without crediting them to your account.

RULE 3. Never deposit cash in an ATM. It's impossible to prove how much you put into the envelope, so losses are sometimes hard to recover. Checks are easier to find or replace.

RULE 4. Report mistakes right away. Some banks install telephones next to their ATMs for that purpose, although they may be answered by bank personnel only during banking hours. When you call, leave your name, address, account number, the amount of the loss, and the location of the ATM; then put the same information into a letter. You will have to wait until the accounts are balanced, but if the machine is over by the sum you reported, you will get your money. At the bank's own ATM machines, the error might be fixed at the end of the day. But it will take an extra day or two (and sometimes weeks) if you used an ATM at another bank.

Deposit Slips. It always astonishes me to see the trash baskets near ATMs overflowing with deposit slips. If the deposit is entered wrong, would those customers know it? (I don't remember the exact amounts of all the checks I get.) Withdrawal slips are also dumped—by people who aren't balancing their checkbooks, I guess.

RULE 5. Keep all deposit and withdrawal slips until your bank statement comes in to be sure the transactions were entered right.

Certificates of Deposit. Your bank might automatically renew your CD when it expires even though you told it not to.

RULE 6. Keep a copy of the instructions you gave when you opened the CD, and mark the due date on your calendar. If an error is made, hustle to correct it. Too long a wait may cost you your chance to get your money out.

FEDERAL DEPOSIT INSURANCE

It will pay.

Don't waste your time searching through subclauses, thinking to find a loophole in the coverage. The government will meet every obligation of the deposit insurance fund, period. The S&L bailout of the 1980s is proof of that.

Federally insured money is entirely safe up to $100,000—and more, depending on how the accounts are held. Safe, in a failing bank. Safe, in a bank that pays cockeyed interest rates. Safe, even with a crook or incompetent at the institution's helm. So don't worry, be happy, and collect the highest interest rates that you can find. You get $100,000 worth of deposit insurance for each of the following accounts, or groups of accounts, held in the same financial institution:

1. All the accounts in your name alone, added together, including any accounts in the name of a business you own as sole proprietor.

2. Your share of all retirement plans whose investments you control—including Individual Retirement Accounts, Simplified Employee Pensions, and Keoghs. If you have multiple plans in the bank, the shares are lumped together as if they were a single account.

3. Your share of the retirement fund that your company manages—say, a traditional pension plan or a company-run 401(k). Each person's interest in the fund is normally insured for up to $100,000, assuming that the bank meets certain capital requirements for safety and soundness. If it doesn't, the FDIC insures the fund as a whole for $100,000. That gives each participant much less protection, but so far, this harsh provision of the law has not been applied.

4. Each "in trust for" account or "payable on death" account held for a member of your immediate family—child, spouse, grandchild. There can be multiple owners and multiple beneficiaries, each with his or her own FDIC coverage. For example, if you and your spouse open an account in trust for your three children, you're insured for up to $600,000: $100,000 for each beneficiary of each account owner.

Living trusts and family trusts usually aren't insured separately. Neither are in-trust-for or payable-on-death accounts if the beneficiary is someone other than your child, spouse, or grandchild. Instead, such accounts are added to those held in your sole name.

5. Each account owned by a partnership, corporation, or unincorporated association, such as a union, homeowners association, or fraternal organization. These funds are insured separately from the funds of the principals or the members.

6. Each account you hold jointly with different people.

For insurance purposes, the FDIC splits joint money evenly among the account holders. Each person is individually insured up to the $100,000 limit. For an example of how this works, say you own three joint accounts —one with your spouse for $130,000 and a $60,000 account with each of your two children. Only $100,000 of the first account is insured, so the FDIC assigns $50,000 of coverage to you and $50,000 to your spouse. You're also assigned half ($30,000) of each of the two $60,000 accounts, leaving each child the other half. Your spouse's and children's money falls under the $100,000 umbrella, so their shares are fully insured. But your share totals $110,000. Only $100,000 of that is insured.

The FDIC lumps together all accounts held jointly by the same people, such as a checking and savings account owned by a married couple. Some couples try for double coverage by shuffling the names on the accounts—listing one Husband/Wife (with the husband's Social Security number) and the other Wife/Husband (with the wife's Social Security number). Nice try, but it doesn't work.

If your institution fails, the FDIC has several options for handling your money. Here are the three most common ways:

The First Way. The dead institution is sold to, or merged with, a live one. Both insured and uninsured deposits are transferred to the new institution intact, giving you immediate access to your funds. Your old branch continues to operate, but under a new name. Outstanding checks clear as usual, but the interest rates on your old account aren't guaranteed. High-rate CDs may be knocked down to a market interest rate on 14 days' notice, although some institutions let you keep that high rate until your certificate matures. If you don't like the new terms, you can close your accounts and cash in your CDs without penalty.

The Second Way. No one wants to buy the dead institution, but another bank or S&L takes the insured deposits. All accounts of $100,000 or less are transferred immediately. So are the insured portions of multiple accounts, like pension accounts, held in a single name. Your old branch reopens as a branch of the new institution. Checks clear as usual, but high-rate CDs may be cut back. Dissenters can move their accounts to another institution without penalty. If your bank fails on a Friday (the usual situation), your insured deposits should be available the following Monday, with no break in your interest payments.

As for uninsured deposits, there's no telling how much you'll recover. The failed bank's assets first have to be sold. The proceeds will then be parceled out pro rata among all the uninsured depositors and creditors.

The Third Way. No one wants any part of the dead bank or S&L. The institution fails and stops paying interest. Checks no longer clear. Typically, the bank closes on a Friday and opens on Monday to pay off the insured depositors. If you go in person, you may be able to pick up your money right away. Otherwise, the FDIC will start mailing out payments within a day or two. The majority of accounts clear in the first week. Almost all of them clear within four weeks.

A few accounts, however, face delays. If the institution's records are bad, you may have to prove what your account was worth. Multiple accounts may need sorting out. If you bought a share of a jumbo CD through a stockbroker (page 70), the broker has to show who the CD's owners are.

Any uninsured money stops earning interest and becomes a claim against the assets of the failed bank or S&L. As the assets are sold, the proceeds are distributed to the depositors and creditors on a pro rata basis. Whatever you ultimately recover will be mostly paid the first year, although additional payments may dribble in over the next several years.

Customers should take four precautions: (1) Check each statement to be sure that the bank or S&L has entered all your deposits correctly. (2) Keep copies of pertinent correspondence with the institution and your most recent statements. If the institution's records are in a mess, you may have to prove the size of your holdings. (3) Deposit less than $100,000 so that, even with the interest received, you will never exceed the insured ceiling. Insured depositors always get all of their money back, right away. (4) Ask your bank whether your deposit meets all of the technical qualifications for FDIC coverage.

For further information on deposit insurance, write to the FDIC Division of Compliance and Consumer Affairs, 550 17th St. N.W. (1730 PA), Washington, DC 20429, 800-934-3342; Internet: http://www.fdic.gov/consumer/fdicyid.html.

Never Rely on State or Private Deposit Insurance. This includes the private insurance carried by some credit unions. If just one institution collapses, customers often make a run on other institutions that the fund insures, even the sound ones. That may force them to close, too. The only safe bet is Uncle Sam.

What Happens to Your Loans When Your Bank, S&L, or Credit Union Goes Bust? You keep making the payments to whoever takes over the loan portfolio. In almost all cases, no one can force you to refinance on different terms as long as your payments are up to date.

What happens to an unused credit line? It may be sold to a new institution as is. If no institution buys the credit line, however, it will be terminated.

There's one important exception to the rule that loans in good standing are left alone. If you opened a home-equity line of credit prior to November 7, 1989, it will probably contain a "call" clause, allowing the lender to cancel your loan for any reason. In 1990 the failed Savers Savings Association of Little Rock, Arkansas, called in about 135 home-equity loans, forcing the borrowers to refinance at other institutions.

For anyone behind on a loan, the jig is up. Bad loans often go to the federal deposit insurance fund, which will want a settlement or else.

FINDING A SOUND BANK

Don't rely on corporate financial statements from your own institution. They're always self-serving and may be deceptive. Instead, call the rating service Veribanc in Wakefield, Massachusetts: 800-442-2657. For $10, it will tell you whether the bank or S&L ranks three-star (for tops), two-star, one-star, or no-star for financial soundness. Ratings for additional institutions cost $3 each as long as you ask for them during the same phone call. The fee is charged to your Visa or MasterCard. Veribanc also rates institutions as "green" for good, "yellow" for doubtful, and "red" for lousy. You want a three-star green.

Two problems with Veribanc: (1) Its reports cover only the most recent quarter for which it has data. The situation might have deteriorated since. (2) Crooked institutions dress up their financial statements so that they'll look better than they really are.

Still, you can't hide all traces of a skunk in a rose garden. The telephone operators can give you the previous quarter's rating at no extra charge. Ratings for even earlier quarters are also available. If they're not all three-star, something may be amiss.

Some scamsters sell CDs in banks that don't exist. If you call about a bank that doesn't show up in the regular listings, Veribanc will check a separate "scam database" to see if it's there.

WHAT'S THE SMARTEST WAY OF SETTING UP BANK ACCOUNTS?

Use a convenient bank for your checking account, with acceptable interest rates and well-located ATMs. Keep enough money there to lower the service fees you're charged. But for substantial savings deposits, buy a CD by mail from one of the nation's sound, high-rate institutions. The extra percentage point you earn is worth the stamp.

5.

Poolers, Splitters, and Keepers

Who Should Own the Property— Me? You? Us? Them?

To the question of who should own the property in your household, no answer is right. But then again, no answer is wrong. Who ever said this was going to be easy?

Get out your yellow pad again, and buy some more pencils. Write down all the serious property you have: house, bank accounts, cars, mutual funds, beach house, oil wells, insurance policies, stocks, bonds, gold coins, whatever. Who owns each piece? Whose name is on the deed, title, or purchase order? Whose money bought it? Is it yours alone or is it jointly held? Is that okay, or should it be owned in some other way? You can keep the property or share it. You can give it away. With a trust, you can give it away and still keep it. (Like the economics of the oldest profession in the world: "You get it; you sell it; you still got it.")

Federal estate taxes used to have a bearing on who owned what, but now they matter only if you have a super-high net worth (see page 118). For everyone else, ownership depends on personality and circumstance. Almost every choice has its points.

ONE FOR THE MONEY

Whether never married or formerly married, your singleness defines the rules. You are a *keeper* because you can own everything yourself, no fuss, no muss. All you need is a reliable friend or relative to hold your durable (or springing) power of attorney (page 122) and your health-care proxy (page 124). That person could write checks on your bank account, manage your investments, and deal with your doctors if you were incapable (say, in a coma after the auto accident, God forbid).

That's when you're young. When you age, you may not be quite so independent and sometimes ownership enters in. For example, you might give half of your house to your son and his family if they will live there with you. Or you might put your niece's name on your bank account if she helps you do your taxes and pay your bills. If your son is a good egg and your niece is a doll, co-ownership can work.

But what if your son gets a new job and moves? The house might have to be sold to give him the money to buy a new one. What if he gets divorced? His half of *your* house might have to be divided with *his* ex-wife. What if your nice niece falls for a bounder who persuades her to nip a bit of your money? A co-owner of a bank account can take every penny unless you specifically require both signatures for withdrawal, which, for daily bills, gets tiresome. You can sue a co-owner for withdrawing more than he or she deposited—but the last thing you want, late in life, is to get tangled up in lawsuits with your relatives.

You can escape from a co-owned bank account that you've come to regret just by taking your money out. But it's a lot harder to get back your house once you've given half of it away. With a house, you might also get into a fight over who should live there or how much to spend on repairs.

Then there's the fairness issue. A joint owner with right of survivorship gets the property, regardless of what it says in your will or trust. Say, for example, that your will leaves everything equally to your daughter, Tammis, and son, David. Then you add David to your bank account. He gets every penny of it when you die. You have cut Tammis out. By naming a joint owner, you took your bank account out of your will and Tammis won't be able to touch it. The same is true for anything else you put in joint names with a right of survivorship. The other owner or owners walk away with the prize.

There's a way around this problem: both of you sign a notarized agreement that the joint ownership is for convenience only, not for inheritance (in many states, that's called a convenience account). But this might not work—because the bank pays over to the other owner anyway or David's creditors try to move in on the money. Why run the risk of having to start a lawsuit? Give David a power of attorney to manage your affairs but hang on to the ownership yourself. Or open an *agency account* if your bank offers one. It lets you authorize someone else to write checks on your account without making that person a joint owner.

TWO FOR THE DOUGH

A married couple is a pushmi-pullyu, a two-headed animal with two minds of its own. You have to figure out how to pull together.

When You Both Have Paychecks: *Poolers* put all the money into a common pot. *Splitters* keep their own separate accounts. Which you choose is a matter of soul, not finance. Poolers think that sharing, including financial sharing, is what a marriage is all about. Splitters hold to their own independence within the marriage. The previously married often split but sometimes pool. The first-time married often pool but sometimes split. It's so unpredictable that even your best friend might surprise you. Over time, and if the marriage goes well, splitters usually turn into *spoolers*—splitting some, pooling some, and growing less antsy about who pays for what.

The challenge for poolers is the checkbook and the bank ATM cards. How do you know what's in the bank when both of you draw from the same account? To keep your finances organized, you can:

• Write no checks away from the checkbook. Use credit cards instead, then pay bills by check at the end of the month.

• Use checks backed by carbons. Return all copies to the central checkbook. Use only ATM cards for getting cash. Return the receipts to the central checkbook and enter your withdrawal.

• Faithfully bring back every debit-card receipt, if you use the card to make purchases, and enter the withdrawal.

• Take two or three checks to walk around with. When you use one, enter it into the check register.

• Keep a big balance in the checking account to prevent overdrafts. Or sign up for overdraft checking (page 55).

• Let just one of you handle the bills. The other hangs on to two or three checks and reports whenever one is used. As in *She:* "Honey, I need more checks." *He:* "How's that? You still have two." *She:* "No, I'm out." *He:* "What did you write the last two for?" *She:* "Didn't I tell you?" *He:* "No." *She:* "Oh." It's the only truly romantic system. Once a month you kiss and make up.

Poolers usually have some separate money, probably in pension accounts. There is also something about an inheritance that often resists the impulse to share. But the house, the savings, and the investments are kept routinely in joint names, even if just one of you makes all the investment decisions.

The challenge for splitters lies in keeping track of who pays for what. As in *She:* "I bought the groceries for two weeks running." *He:* "But I got your laundry and paid the sitter." *She:* "But you already owed me two sitters from last month." *He:* "Those sits were short so they just count for one." You never finally kiss and make up because you never figure it out.

For clarity, you can:

• Split all expenses right down the middle, even putting down two credit cards when you eat out. (No kidding. I know a couple that does this.)

• Where earnings are unequal, split expenses accordingly—say, 60 percent him, 40 percent her. Apply these percentages to the income taxes, too.

• Make a list of "his" and "her" household expenses and take turns treating each other to dinners out.

• Toss receipts for cash payments into a box and settle up when the box overflows. Use the same box for "loans" you make to each other.

• Write memos about property bought together, spelling out who owns what percent.

• Keep three checking accounts—his, hers, and ours. Each pays into the "ours" account for common household bills or for the children. (Don't miss the fiendish cleverness of this arrangement. You get the mysteries of separate accounts *plus* the headaches of a joint one. Still, an "ours" account is a practical bill-paying tool for couples who want to keep the rest of their money separate.)

Splitting teaches each person how to handle money and take responsibility for decisions. It also serves couples with different investment styles—say, one a speculator and one a hoarder. Nevertheless, when it comes to major financial decisions, splitters usually make them together. You are still a single financial unit, regardless of how you handle the money.

And then there's the Old Dispensation: The wife's paycheck is "hers" while the husband's is "ours." I hold with this arrangement only if the husband is well paid and the wife is truly earning peanuts. Otherwise, they're in it together and both should pay.

If Only One of You Has a Paycheck: Splitting is Out. Pooling is In. Your basic contract is money-for-services, and everything tends to be jointly owned. If it's all in one name and you divorce, the courts are supposed to treat it as mutual, marital money, although sometimes the homebody gets short shrift. If the husband keeps bank and investment accounts in his own name, the wife should similarly possess her own funds. (It reminds me of what my grandmother used to call "garter money": "Pin two dollars to your garter, dear, and if he reaches for it, take a taxi home.") Here's a fair way for one-paycheck couples to manage if they want separate funds: each year's savings, after the bills are paid, are divided 50/50 between husband and wife.

If Older People Remarry: Your friends will be enchanted, but don't be surprised if your children aren't. It's usually not the "pater" they worry about, but the patrimony. If your new spouse gets your property after your death, he or she is free to cut your children out. Even if you own assets separately, state laws dictate that a surviving spouse should inherit a lot of them.

To prevent this, you need a prenuptial agreement (page 131)—truly important in senior marriages. You agree in advance not to inherit each other's property but to leave most or all of it to your respective children, instead. To provide for each other, you might take out life insurance policies, or make each other the beneficiary of policies you own already. Or you might agree that you each get the income from the other's property for life, with the children getting the principal only after the death of the surviving spouse. A premarital agreement also settles your rights in case of divorce.

If You Owe an Estate Tax: You have a high-class problem. If you're married, you can lower that tax by using bypass trusts (page 120), one in each spouse's will (or in each spouse's living trust). To make bypass trusts work, however, husband and wife have to own property separately, as community property, or as tenants in common without right of survivorship. Bypass trusts can't be funded with property that is jointly owned.

LOVERS AND OTHER ROOMMATES

You are splitters. Each handles personal expenses and you work out a system for paying joint bills. A 50/50 split is fair only if your incomes are roughly equal. If one of you earns two-thirds of your combined income, that person should assume two-thirds of the rent and two-thirds of the grocery bills. Otherwise, the one with the smaller paycheck is subsidizing the other. If there's going to be any subsidy at all, it should be from the richer to the poorer, not the other way around.

Longtime lovers drift toward pooling some of their money. Still, you often live on the tips of your toes, almost ready to run. So for property that is hard to unwind, separate ownership is best.

If you buy a piece of real estate together, do it as tenants in common (page 85). Write an agreement for sharing expenses: how you'll divide the taxes, insurance, and mortgage payments. What happens if one person quits paying his or her share? If the relationship fails, how will you get your money out? Will you put the house on the market and divide the proceeds according to the percentage each person put up? Will one person buy the other out and if so, which? How will you determine the price? A lawyer should draw up these agreements (preferably two lawyers, one for each of you). You'll never think of all the contingencies yourself. You should also have the contractual right to force the sale of the house, if you're having to shoulder more of the cost than you bargained for.

If one of you dies, will his or her share be willed to the other or would a written contract be a safer choice (remember that minds, and wills, can change)?

Ever since the Lee Marvin case in 1979, which raised the possibility of suing for "palimony," that issue has hung over live-in relationships. If, say, the man works and the woman gives up her job to follow him, does she have a right to support if they fall out? Should one partner get some of the money that the other accumulated during their relationship? Denver attorney William Cantwell has been thinking about this problem for a while and offers you his "Wallet Card Non-Marvinizing Agreement," to be signed by both parties to the relationship. It reads like this:

"We have decided to live together beginning on _____. We do not intend that the legal consequences of a common law marriage should arise from this. We have not made any promises to each other about economic matters. We do not intend any economic rights to arise from our relationship. If in the future we decide that any promises of an economic nature should exist between us, we will put them in writing, and only such written promises made by us in a written memorandum signed by us in the future shall have any force between us. Signed at _____ on _____." New York attorney William Zabel adds that the signers generally have to disclose their financial position to each other for such an agreement to hold up in court.

FOUR WAYS TO OWN
PROPERTY TOGETHER

Joint Ownership with Right of Survivorship. The owners (there can be more than two) hold the property together. If one dies, his or her share passes automatically to the other owner (or other owners, usually in equal parts). This form of ownership is for married couples, for any two people who live together and need a convenient household account, and for truly committed unmarried couples. It protects gay couples whose relatives might attack a will. Your contribution to the joint account can be attached by your creditors, but your partner's share can't.

To put something in joint ownership, you list it as such on the deed, title, or other ownership document, specifying "with right of survivorship." That's important. Otherwise, it might be argued that you held the property only as tenants in common (next heading).

Joint ownership isn't an inescapable trap. You can generally get out of it—although not always easily—even if the other owner objects. The ways of doing this vary, depending on your state's laws. When a jointly owned property is sold, the proceeds are normally divided equally. If you all agree, however, you can make an unequal division (gift taxes might be due if one owner gives the others part or all of his share).

Tenancy in Common. This is a good way to own a beach house or snowblower with a friend. Married couples use this method when they want to leave their share of a co-owned property in trust. So do unmarried couples who can imagine an end to their relationship.

Each tenant in common has a share in the property, although not necessarily an equal share. You can sell or give away your share at any time. In the case of a house owned in common, for example, your partner could sell his piece to his brother and suddenly you would have a new roommate. If the owners fall out, one might buy the other's share. Or one could file a partition lawsuit that might force the property to be sold.

You can pass your share to anyone at death; it doesn't automatically go to the other owners. If you die without a will, your share of the property will be distributed to your relatives, according to state law.

Tenancy by the Entirety. This arrangement, for married couples only, must be established in writing (a properly worded deed will do it) and is recognized by twenty states. It's similar to property owned jointly with the right of survivorship but gives each of the owners more protection. Neither of you can divide the property without the other's consent. In many cases, it's protected against one spouse's creditors (assuming that only one spouse signed the debt). If you divorce, it's automatically split 50/50.

Community Property. Nine states (Arizona, California, Idaho, Louisiana, Nevada, New Mexico, Texas, Washington, and Wisconsin) have community property rules for married couples. They declare that property acquired by either spouse, from money earned during the marriage, is owned by both, regardless of whose name is on it. This rule affects anyone who ever lived in a community property state. Even if you move away, your community property keeps its character. It is always 50 percent owned by each spouse (although, as a practical matter, these ownership rights can be lost if you don't document them when you move to a noncommunity property state). The portion of a private pension earned during a marriage is usually community property, but Social Security isn't.

During life it is hard to dispose of your half of the community property without the other's consent. At death, however, you can generally leave it to whomever you want; it doesn't have to go to your spouse. Unlike jointly owned property, community property goes through probate (that is, unless you hold it in trust or use some other probate-avoiding mechanism allowed by your state).

All the states have slightly different rules about what is not community property. They generally exempt inheritances, gifts, and property acquired before marriage. Most (but not all) states exempt property acquired before moving to the state. However, to stay solely yours, separate property has to be kept apart from the property you own together. If you inherit money and want to maintain sole ownership, put it into a bank account or other investment in your own name. If you mix separate property with community property, it may join the community whether you mean it to or not.

You can get out of community property if you'd rather hold your assets in some other way. Each state runs its own escape routes. For example, you might make a gift of your community property interest to your spouse. You might sign an agreement specifying what is community property and what isn't. In most of the states (but not all), you can annul the community property rule with a premarital or postmarital agreement. Noncommunity property can be owned separately or jointly, as you prefer.

WHY MOST MARRIEDS LOVE JOINT OWNERSHIP

1. It makes marriage a partnership, share and share alike.
2. When one of you dies, the other automatically gets the goods. No doubts, no delays, no tears, no probate.
3. The other owner can't wheel and deal the money away. As a practical matter, most joint property cannot be sold or borrowed against unless both of you sign.

This applies especially to real estate and securities registered in your personal names. Securities held in the name of a brokerage house ("street names"—page 659) are another story. It normally takes only one of you to buy and sell, even if the account is jointly owned. Similarly, mutual funds usually allow either of you to make telephone switches. But be it a mutual fund or a brokerage account, neither of you should be able to take the money and run. A check for the proceeds of any sale will be issued in joint names. (This doesn't prevent some spouses from forging the other's signature!)

Your most vulnerable property is a jointly owned bank account, which your spouse can easily clean out.

4. In divorce, you are a more formidable force. Under state laws, the marital assets are supposed to be divided fairly, without regard to who holds title. But possession might still be seven-tenths of the law. If you hold the property, or at least have your name on it, your bargaining position is stronger than if you don't.
5. Out-of-state property passes to the other owner, without probate in that state. This saves your survivor some time and money.
6. Say there's a debt that you're not responsible for, like a judgment levied against your spouse. If he or she dies, those creditors usually can't collect a dime from joint property. During your spouse's lifetime, however, joint property is vulnerable—to what extent depends on the laws of your state. You get the most protection in a tenancy by the entirety (page 85).

WHY SOME MARRIEDS HATE
JOINT OWNERSHIP

1. If one of you splits, he or she can clean out the bank accounts and safe-deposit box. You can file a lawsuit to get back what's yours, but the effort might cost more than it's worth.

2. Some investments can't be sold if one of you is too sick or senile to sign the papers, or too sore to cooperate. A durable power of attorney solves the first two problems. The third is all yours.

3. You can't set up a bypass trust to reduce your estate taxes if your property is jointly owned with a right of survivorship. So if you're wealthy, this form of ownership costs you money. (However, joint property can be "disclaimed" into a bypass trust. You disclaim an inheritance when you refuse to accept it. If you're disclaiming for tax purposes, federal law gives you nine months to decide. The inheritance then passes to the next person or people in line, perhaps in trust.)

4. Your kids might lose money if you marry more than once. Say you put all your property in joint names with a new spouse, and die. That spouse gets everything, and can cut out the children of your previous marriage. Not that such an awful thing will actually happen, but it could.

5. Joint property can be tied up for a long time in divorce because it often can't be sold until both spouses agree to sign. Separate property can be sold anytime you want unless a judge ties it up during a contested divorce.

6. In community property states, you'll save taxes by choosing community ownership rather than joint ownership. When an owner dies, any taxable capital gains on the property are erased. This applies to only one-half of joint property but all of community property.

JOINT PROPERTY FOR UNMARRIEDS?

The Weak Case in Favor

1. It passes automatically to the other without a will and without probate. This is a strong case only for committed couples—gay couples, for example, whose families disapprove of the relationship and might challenge a will. A carefully drawn will usually can't be broken, however, except by a surviving spouse who wasn't left the share of the property required by state law.

2. It's a sign of good faith.

3. It's convenient. A mother and daughter living together may want a joint account for household bills.

The Strong Case Against

1. If you want to take your property out of joint names and the other person refuses, you may have the devil's own time getting it back. Only bank accounts are simple to reclaim. You just take the money out (unless . . .

2. . . . the other person got there first). Either owner can empty a joint bank account. You'd have to sue to get your money back.

3. You might need both signatures to sell an investment or to cash a check for the proceeds of a sale. What if your ex-mate gets sore or leaves town?

4. Say you put your investments in joint names with your son, who manages them for you. His business goes broke. *His* half of *your* property could be attached to pay his debts. (He can manage your money just as well with a power of attorney or through a trust.)

5. Assume the same story as in item 4, only your son gets divorced. Part of your property might go to his ex-wife.

6. Same story, only you have two sons. When you die, Son One inherits your investments and Son Two gets nothing. Joint property usually goes to the surviving joint owner, cutting other beneficiaries out. (A few states might allow you to designate that your joint account goes half to Son One and half to Son Two or your other beneficiaries.)

7. The relationship might end but not joint ownership. For example, say that you and a boyfriend own a house together. Even if the boyfriend buys you out, you're still on the mortgage and are fully responsible for the debt. Only the lender can release you and the lender may refuse to do so. If your boyfriend (*ex*-boyfriend) quits paying the mortgage without your knowledge, the default will show up on your credit report. Ditto any liens that your ex's creditors put on the house. If the bank comes after you for the mortgage payments, you'll be supporting your ex-boyfriend's real-estate investment and getting nothing in return (unless a written agreement allows you to force the sale of the house to recover the money you put up).

8. If you're rich enough to owe federal gift and estate taxes (page 118), you can trigger a tax liability when: (1) Stocks or real estate go into joint names and the owner doesn't pay for his or her half share. (2) The noncontributing owner takes money out of a joint bank account or U.S. Savings Bonds. (3) One of you dies. All joint property is taxed in the estate of the first owner to die, except for anything that the survivor can prove he or she paid for. (These rules, incidentally, apply only to joint owners who aren't married. Married couples can give, or leave, each other property without paying federal gift or estate taxes. You can also give away $10,000 annually, tax free—$20,000 for gifts made with a spouse—to each of as many people as you want.)

In Either Case . . .

Own Your Cars Separately. If you cause an accident and are hit with a judgment that exceeds your insurance, your other property can be attached —and so can the property of the car's joint owners. If you own the car alone, no one else will be affected.

SHOULD YOUR KID OWN IT?

Sure. A kid is still a walking tax shelter, assuming that his or her bracket is lower than yours. Money put into a child's name will be worth more, after tax, than if you keep it in yours.

How much income can be tax sheltered? That depends on when you read this. The amounts are indexed to inflation, so they'll probably rise each year. Here's the general concept, using income limits for 1997:

For a child under 14: (1) Up to $650 of the child's unearned income (from sources like interest and dividends) passes tax free. (2) The next $650 in unearned income is taxed in the child's own bracket, probably only 15 percent. So the family gets a tax break on up to $1,300 a year. That's roughly the return on $22,000 invested in a 6 percent certificate of deposit, or $43,000 invested in stocks that pay 3 percent dividends. (3) Any unearned income over $1,300 is taxed in the parents' highest bracket.

These income levels may increase in future years. Check a recent tax guide for the latest dope.

Once the child reaches 14, all the unearned income is taxed in his or her bracket. At that point you might shift even more of your savings into the child's name.

But any gift has to pass through these four wickets:

1. You won't need the property back. This isn't Ping-Pong. Whatever you give your child is his or hers to keep.

2. You have the sort of kid who won't take the money and blow it. At age 18 or 21, depending on state law, the property belongs to the child unless it's protected by a trust or some other alternative, like a family limited partnership (ask a lawyer about that one).

3. The tax savings are worth the loss of flexibility. In 1997, a gift to a child under 14 might save $417 a year if you were in the 39.6 percent tax bracket and $267 a year if you were in the 28 percent bracket.

4. You think that your child won't be eligible for much college aid. Eligible students get larger grants or loans if the savings are in the parent's name rather than the child's name (see page 535).

There are better and worse ways of giving money and property to a child under 18. Here are your choices:

1. *Outright ownership.* You hand the money to the child with a ribbon around it. That's okay for a $100 birthday present or a $50 savings bond at a bar mitzvah, but not for larger sums. Sometimes access is too easy: the child can pillage bank accounts or savings bonds whenever he or she wants. With stocks and real estate, on the other hand, access is too strict: it's tough, sometimes impossible, for your son or daughter to sell the property while underage. If the stock market crashes, you can only sit there and weep.

Some people think they have given money to a child by opening a bank account in trust for him or her. Not so. You still own the money and pay taxes on the interest. It doesn't pass to the child until you die.

2. *Joint property.* Forget it. Putting property in joint names with a child is even worse than giving it outright. You can't sell the whole property without the child's consent. If the child is underage, he or she usually can't give consent without the agreement of a court-appointed guardian. You still owe taxes on at least part of the income. If you die rich enough to owe estate taxes, the entire property can be taxed in your estate (depending on your state). The only joint property that you can liquidate easily is a joint bank account. But that doesn't even count as a gift, or save you taxes, unless the child withdraws the money.

3. *Uniform Transfers to Minors Act.* In the states that have passed it, UTMA is the ticket. Use it for anything more than a nominal gift. Cash, stocks, mutual funds, bonds, real estate, and perhaps even insurance policies can be given to an adult acting as custodian for the child.

The custodian—typically your spouse, the child's parent, or some other close relative—manages the money and can spend it on things like college tuition. Most states require the remaining money to be distributed to the child at age 18 or 21, although some have extended the time period.

States without UTMA have the older but similar Uniform Gifts to Minors Act (UGMA). With UGMA, however, you can't transfer real estate or other complex types of property. At 18 or 21, depending on state law, the child gets the money free and clear.

Gifts under UTMA or UGMA pass with no muss and no fuss. Your bank, stockbroker, or insurance agent can give you the papers and tell you where to sign. In fact, it's almost too easy. Without legal advice, you might make a gift that you'll regret.

Don't name yourself custodian. If you do, and die before the child becomes a legal adult, the money will be included in your taxable estate just as if you hadn't given it away.

4. *Trusts.* To give a child a large sum of money, see a lawyer experienced in trusts. A trust can do almost anything you want it to: accumulate the income or pay it out, pay out income but not principal, hand over the money at whatever age you think your child will be grown up (no, don't wait until 50; if the child doesn't grow up earlier, he or she never will).

Don't use trust income for the child's support, and be sure that the trust so specifies. Support is your legal obligation. If the trust picks up your obligation—by paying for your child's food and clothing—that income can be taxed back to you.

So here's the big question for well-to-do parents: Can trust income be used to pay for private school or college? In divorce courts, education is increasingly considered a legal obligation for parents with money. But so far, there has been no tax attack on the many trusts that pay school and college bills. Parents should not sign a contract to pay tuition if a trust is involved. However, it's okay for them to sign as trustee.

SHOULD A TRUST OWN IT?

Maybe. A lot of people set up living trusts, principally to avoid probate. But probate isn't always a black hole (page 97). Take a look at the uses of trusts, discussed next, and ask yourself which of them really matter to you, or matter enough to pay for a trust and keep up with the paperwork.

A *revocable living trust* is not unlike a mirror maze in a funhouse where you see yourself in every glass. When you set up the trust, you can give some or all of your property to yourself *as trustee*. You no longer own it; it's owned by your trustee, who happens to be you. (I told you this was done with mirrors.) Some states require at least one other trustee. You and your spouse or mate can be co-trustees or you can name an outside trustee.

As trustee, you run the money just as if you still owned it in the old-fashioned way. You can invest the money as you like, use income and principal, leave the money to whomever you want, change beneficiaries at will, even revoke the trust altogether. You name one or more *successor trustees* to manage the money if you become incapable and distribute the assets when you die.

If someone other than you is trustee and he or she won't follow orders, you can fire that person and install someone else if the trust document allows it. As long as you're competent, you're completely in charge.

All your probatable property has to be put into the name of the trust. *You* will no longer own your home; instead, you'll hold it as "Len F. Jordan, trustee of the Jordan Family Trust dated February 5, 1997." Ditto for your securities, business interests, cars, and most other assets.

When you buy additional property, like a new house or more mutual fund shares, they also have to be bought in the name of the trust. Checks for these purchases have to be signed "Len F. Jordan trustee (etc.)" and be issued from the trust's bank account. You report your trust's taxable income on your regular Form 1040. Los Angeles attorney Charles A. Collier Jr. suggests that you set up a bank account outside your trust for routine bills and transfer money to it as needed. An outside account lets you pay bills without involving your trust. It also saves you from having to disclose the language of your trust to banks or other sources of credit. As long as the sum in the account is nominal, it shouldn't trigger probate.

Any property not held in trust can't be distributed by your successor trustee after you die. It goes through probate instead, to be handled under the terms of your will. Your will, however, can say that the property should be added to the trust. To simplify matters, your successor trustee and the executor under your will should be the same person.

Many people start a trust on a salesperson's say-so but never deed their property to it. That's a total waste of money. It's the same as having no trust at all.

Why You Might Want a Living Trust:

1. *To avoid probate.* Property in trust goes directly to the beneficiaries when you die, without pausing in the probate court. A trustee can often distribute the inheritance faster than if it had been left by will (although distribution can be delayed for reasons other than probate; deeds still have to change hands, assets valued, and tax forms filled in). For more on probate, see page 97. To compare trusts with wills, see page 125. As far as specific inheritances are concerned, you can make exactly the same provisions whether you leave your property by trust or by will.

2. *To have someone reliably on tap to handle your money if you're incapacitated.* You might be ill. You might have grown permanently vague. The easiest way around this problem is to give someone a durable power of attorney. Many states have laws requiring banks to accept a durable power, as long as it's worded properly. Nevertheless, some retrograde insurers and brokers might refuse it. That's where the trust comes in. They can't refuse someone who succeeds you as trustee of your living trust.

The trust should specify when your trustee can move to take over your affairs. Give yourself a lot of latitude; you should be free to throw money at a gigolo, retreat to an ashram, or hunt for gold in Alaska. The law lets you waste your assets however you like, as long as you *know* that you may be doing something dumb. Only when your mental capacity goes, as determined by independent doctors, should your trustee be empowered to act.

3. *To handle real properties out of state.* Your will has to be probated in every state where you hold real estate unless you hold it in joint names or in trust.

4. *To handle closely held business interests, rental real estate, large stock portfolios, or other complex properties.* A knowledgeable trustee can keep all your business interests functioning smoothly until they're sold or otherwise disposed of. The trustee can also manage the property if you're disabled or on vacation for an extended period of time.

5. *To test the ability of a professional money manager.* If you don't feel good about running money yourself, or don't have the time for it, an investment-management firm or bank trust department will handle it for you. The bank can act simply as a money manager while you remain trustee —usually the best arrangement. Or you can name the bank trustee.

Banks take almost any sum of money. Amounts exceeding $150,000 to $300,000 can be managed individually, if that's what you want. Smaller amounts (and larger ones, too) can go into pooled accounts that work like mutual funds. Make sure that your arrangement allows you to switch to a different money manager if you don't like the personal treatment you get or the investment results.

6. *To defend against relatives who might challenge your will.* Trusts can be challenged, too, but they're generally harder to break than wills. Among other reasons, all the relatives needn't be notified of the terms of the trust. Still, a judge might overturn a change of beneficiary if you were senile when you dictated the new name. Some states allow you to use living trusts to disinherit spouses who would normally be entitled to a substantial portion of your estate. Disinheriting a spouse is contrary to public policy, not to mention dadgummed mean, but it's done.

7. *To keep matters private.* Wills are public documents and therefore, in many states, so is the inventory of your estate. Trusts are normally private.

8. *To try to avoid creditors.* In some states, funds in a living trust that haven't been pledged to secure a debt might not be available to pay your creditors after your death. But this common-law protection is crumbling. For the best protection against creditors after death, use tenancy by the entirety (page 85).

9. *To simplify the process of leaving money to young children.* Your will can set up a trust for your minor children, but it's under the supervision of a court. Living trusts escape that scrutiny (although you have to trust the trustee).

Living Trusts Don't Save Taxes: They're not unique vehicles for cutting your income taxes or estate taxes. Many people erroneously think they are because a living trust lawyer or salesperson told them so. But as long as you control the property, it will be income-taxed to you and treated as part of your taxable estate. Your living trust can contain other trusts that reduce or eliminate estate taxes. But those tax-avoiding trusts can be put in wills, too (page 116). In short, living trusts have no significant tax advantages.

LIVING TRUSTS PROBABLY WON'T SAVE MONEY . . .

. . . in jurisdictions with reformed and speedy probate procedures, such as those under the Uniform Probate Code (page 97). When you prepare a living trust you also have to prepare a will to handle anything that, accidentally or on purpose, gets left out of the trust. That normally costs more than preparing a will alone. Also, all your property has to be deeded over to the trust—more paperwork for a lawyer to handle. After death, living trusts cost less to administer, but often not a lot less, in states with enlightened probate procedures. The costs and the savings may balance out.

LIVING TRUSTS PROBABLY WILL SAVE MONEY . . .

. . . as well as time and aggravation, in jurisdictions where the probate courts deserve to be shot. Happily, their numbers are shrinking. A lawyer who's a friend can tell you about the local courts. Or call or visit the court clerk and ask, (1) Are there simplified probate procedures? (2) What are they? (3) To what kinds of estates do they apply? Even a state plagued with delays may have some streamlined jurisdictions.

In states with complex procedures, you don't need a trust if each piece of property goes to a named beneficiary (page 103). In states that set maximums on how much a probate lawyer can charge, you can often negotiate a much lower fee.

MORE LIVING TRUST FACTS

The states have different rules and taxes affecting trusts, so see a lawyer if you move. Your trust document should specifically allow for a change of state so the laws that govern the trust can change, too. Otherwise, the laws (and taxes) of your former state apply unless you get a court order allowing a change.

There's a lot of legwork involved in transferring property into a trust. Your lawyer will prepare the new deed for your real property, as well as transfer letters for assets held by your bank, broker, and other financial connections. But you'll have to follow up.

Don't make the trust the beneficiary of your 401(k) or Individual Retirement Account. If you died, that whole sum of money would go into the trust and be taxed right away. By contrast, a spouse or other individual beneficiary can roll the 401(k) into an IRA and take payments over many years. That spreads the taxes out.

You can name the trust beneficiary of your life insurance policy. The proceeds would then go into the trust to be distributed as you directed. Before doing this, however, married people should ensure that a surviving spouse will have plenty of ready cash in case there's a delay in getting the trust paid out.

Your trust should define what it means to be disabled, requiring a successor trustee to handle your affairs. For example: "I shall be deemed to be disabled when two physicians licensed to practice medicine in my state sign a paper stating that I am disabled and unable to handle my financial affairs." The same language can be used to determine when your disability has passed.

To change the terms of a living trust, you prepare a written amendment. Don't scratch in the changes on the trust document; they won't be accepted. In some states, the amendment has to be signed and, maybe, witnessed just like a will. But in most states, a notarized signature will do.

A married couple should ask an experienced estate-planning lawyer (not a lawyer or insurance agent who's hard-selling trusts) whether they need one trust or two. In community property states, it's common to have a single trust document for all the property; each spouse's separate property interests are segregated within the trust; at the death of the first spouse, the trust divides into multiple trusts. In other states, dual trusts are more common. With a single trust, you both may have to agree on changing the beneficiaries or other terms of the trust unless the document specifically permits only one of you to act. Ditto with investment decisions. Ditto the decision to withdraw your property from the trust, or revoke it, if you split. In some cases, joint trusts create strange tax consequences that you need an expert to expound.

To revoke a living trust, you have to retitle all the trust property in some other name. It's legwork, legwork all over again.

If a couple's joint trust is revoked, the assets might be distributed 50/50 unless the trust document provides for a specific uneven split. If one of you puts in 70 percent of the assets and the other puts in 30 percent, you might want to provide for a 70/30 split in case of dissolution.

If you have an individual trust naming your spouse as beneficiary, and you separate or divorce, remove the spouse's name immediately. If you die, a separated spouse can inherit; in some states, so can a divorced spouse. (By contrast, a divorced spouse generally cannot inherit under your will, even if he or she is still named as beneficiary.)

You normally need a will to appoint a guardian of your minor children. State law might allow you to use some other document, but check with a lawyer to see if a living trust will meet the requirements. It may not.

If your trust owns a certificate of deposit and it matures, the payment must be made into a bank account opened in the name of the trust. Ditto for any proceeds from the sale of real estate or securities.

A successor trustee who takes over from you must distribute the income and principal as the trust requires. You can give your trustee the discretion to distribute unequally among the named beneficiaries if that seems like the right thing to do.

All the trust's property doesn't have to be distributed right away. You can instruct the trustee to hold property until your children are older, or distribute just the income, or distribute property to some beneficiaries and not to others. Whatever you want.

Check "More Will Facts," page 113. Many of those rules apply to trusts, too.

For a discussion of wills vs. living trusts, see page 125.

CHOOSING A TRUSTEE

If you go for a trust, your toughest decision will be choosing an outside trustee. Someone has to be ready to step in if you or your spouse can no longer serve.

A dependable grown child will see to your welfare but might have bad financial or investment judgment.

A business associate or lawyer might be good at managing your money but help himself to it.

A bank or brokerage house has investment experience, won't skip out or steal, and will handle the paperwork. But it's expensive and it may not knock itself out to keep you happy.

Co-trustees often work well—a family member and a bank or investment adviser. But again, you pay.

In the end, you can only go for integrity and intelligence and keep your fingers crossed. And, of course, provide a method for kicking out a trustee whom the family doesn't like. (For more on this subject, see page 118.)

Don't Try to Save Money by Setting Up a Trust Without Using an Experienced Lawyer. Books with tear-out forms for doing trusts, or do-it-yourself computer programs, are not your friend. You might misunderstand the instructions, which are complicated and often incomplete. You might fill in ambiguous forms ambiguously. Without your knowing it, the forms may be unsuited to your purpose. You might miss an important angle that specifically affects your family. You might be working with a defective or out-of-date book. You might think you've put property into trust when you haven't because you didn't transfer the title to yourself *as trustee.* You risk making the same kinds of errors with bequests that are made with homemade wills (page 106). I beg you to see an experienced tax and estate-planning lawyer. I am down on my knees. If it's worth avoiding probate, it's worth doing the job right.

If you insist on doing the job, consider *Make Your Own Living Trust* ($21.95) or the software *Living Trust Maker* ($79.95), from Nolo Press, 950 Parker St., Berkeley, CA 94710. Helpful as these are, I wouldn't touch them myself.

THE POOR MAN'S LIVING TRUST

This is the *durable power of attorney* (page 122). You name someone to manage your affairs if you become incapable, without bothering to set up a trust. But check with all the institutions you do business with: bank, broker, insurance company. Some will want the power written on their own form, or will have other antiquated rules.

Another approach to the incapacity problem is to set up a "standby" living trust containing only a token amount of property. If you ever become mentally incompetent, the person holding your durable power of attorney could activate the trust, put the rest of your property into it (if the durable power so authorized), and arrange for it to be properly managed.

ACCOUNTS "IN TRUST FOR" OR PAYABLE ON DEATH

These are the simplest living trusts. At banking institutions, you register the savings account "in trust for" or "payable on death" to one or more beneficiaries. In twenty-five states, you can do the same with stockbrokerage accounts or mutual fund shares; these accounts are referred to as "transferable on death." In all cases, control stays with you—to change the investments, change the beneficiary, even cancel the trust by taking every penny out. You haven't made a gift, so the income is still taxable to you. The beneficiary can't touch the money until you die. But at death, the account passes directly to the beneficiary without going through probate.

One possible drawback: when you die, the beneficiary gets the money immediately, ready or not. So don't put a big bank account or any securities account in trust for a minor child (see page 89).

DOES PROBATE REALLY MATTER?

Hardly anyone is noticing. But for the average person, passing property to new owners at death is not always the struggle it used to be. So avoiding probate doesn't matter as much.

Probate means "prove." It's the system that assures that your will is valid and that your property passes to the person who is supposed to get it. Scandals have swirled around the process. Survivors have sometimes waited years for their money while judges dithered and greedy lawyers bled the estate.

In recent years, however, many states have passed probate-simplification laws,* especially for small estates or estates in which everything passes to the spouse. There may also be speedy procedures for estates

---

* Here are the states that, at this writing, have instituted the Uniform Probate Code or similar forms of simplified probate procedures: Alabama, Alaska, Arizona, Colorado, Georgia, Hawaii, Idaho, Illinois, Indiana, Maine, Michigan, Minnesota, Missouri, Montana, Nebraska, New Jersey, New Mexico, North Dakota, Pennsylvania, South Carolina, South Dakota, Texas, Utah, Washington, Wisconsin.

that aren't contested. Odds and ends of personal property, including a car, rarely have to go through probate. They're divided as your will directs or by private agreement among your heirs. Families can handle the paperwork themselves; they just go to the probate court and let the clerk tell them what to do. Or a lawyer can handle it for you. With simplified procedures —meaning little or no court oversight—the lawyer shouldn't charge too much (show the lawyer this sentence!).

There Are Three Main Ways of Avoiding Probate: (1) putting property into joint names with right of survivorship; (2) naming a beneficiary for a particular piece of property, like a life insurance policy, bank account, securities account, house, or retirement account; (3) putting property in trust. Each method runs risks. The joint owner might take your money and run, or die a week after you do, leaving the assets to be probated in his or her estate. Naming individual beneficiaries for each of your properties might accidentally leave one of your children less money than another. Do-it-yourself trusts might not work out. Lawyer-drawn trusts need, well, a lawyer. When there's a trustee involved, it can be a bit more complicated to sell stocks or real estate than when there isn't.

Even with a trust, it can take a year or more to settle an estate. That's because actual probate—court procedure—often isn't the problem. The delays arise when you try to get property appraised, get ownership transferred into new names, and complete the final tax forms—all of which have to be done whether there's a trust or not.

THEY'RE OUT TO GET YOU

Squadrons of insurance agents are knocking on doors all over the country, using high-pressure tactics to sell one-size-fits-all trusts, at too high a price, to people who often do not need them. Battalions of lawyers are holding seminars, especially in retirement areas, claiming that trusts will solve all life's problems, up to curing the common cold. They're telling you lies. Typically, they lead you to think that probate costs tens of thousands of dollars more than trusts (in fact, probate can be cheaper than the trusts these phonies sell); that only trusts can lower your estate taxes (not true; there's no tax advantage to trusts over wills); and that if you became incompetent, only a trust would save your family from an embarrassing court procedure to appoint a guardian (you can prepare for this with a durable power of attorney instead of a trust).

For a true comparison of wills and trusts, see page 125. If you decide that you do want a trust, don't buy it from one of these slick salespeople. You're likely to get a shoddy product that doesn't meet your family's particular needs—and you'll be overcharged, to boot. Go to a lawyer experienced in both wills and trusts, who'll examine all your assets, question you closely about your family's needs, and draw up the best document to serve them.

Don't Decide on a Living Trust Out of Fear. Many of the stories you hear about being "tied up in probate" involve disputed property, delays by banks and brokers in getting the title changed, or disputes with insurance companies over old policies—none of which have anything to do with the courts. It may also have taken a lot of time to find all the property if the deceased didn't keep good records. You'd face exactly the same problems and delays if the assets were in living trusts (especially as people may forget to transfer all their assets to the trust). Sometimes the probate courts are indeed the baddies, but often they're not. Don't waste money on a trust before finding out.

6.

Willing Makes It So

Wills and Trusts—For Everything You Can't Take with You

The three immutable facts: You own stuff. You will die. Someone will get that stuff.

*E*veryone has a will. If you don't write your own or put everything into joint ownership, you get the universal will that your state wrote for you. The state means well but it's not too clever, brooks no appeal, and makes no exceptions to its rules. All your nearest relatives get a piece of your property, but no one else does—and no one gets more than the state-allotted share, even if it's unfair. Depending on the state, a spouse can get the short end of the stick.

The tangled tales from probate court would tantalize the brothers Grimm. Yet many people who know better still don't write wills or living trusts and are not moved by the mess they're likely to leave behind. Maybe they don't intend to die. Neither do I, but I have a will anyway, just in case.

While I'm here on my soapbox, let me also nag at those of you whose wills or trusts are out of date. Old wills, written before your income went up or before family members married, divorced, or died, can wreak just as much havoc as no will at all.

Making a will is so engrossing that it beats me why anyone has to be dragged to it. You imagine their gratitude as you assign your jewelry to Barbara and your antique clock to Jeff. You feel like God; you arrange everything.

I've heard plenty of excuses for not writing a will. To answer some of them: You can write a will even though your financial affairs are a mess. You don't have to have your property appraised. Neither the witnesses to the will nor the beneficiaries have any right to know what is in it. Your property isn't locked up in any way. You can change things as often as you want. You won't suddenly drop dead.

WITHOUT A WILL . . .

- Depending on state law, not all of the property may go to your spouse.
- Your grown children may get some of the money that was meant for your spouse, leaving your spouse with too little to live on.
- Adopted children might get nothing.
- A court will choose your minor children's guardian.
- Stepchildren get nothing.
- Neither do your friends or your live-in mate.
- Your family might battle in the courts.
- A fight might break out among your relatives over who is the guardian of the children and who controls their inheritance.
- There probably won't be a trust to take care of your young children's money.
- Part of the money that you meant for your spouse may go to your young kids. Your spouse, as guardian, can use it only for their support. The court will have to approve certain expenditures and may require an annual accounting.
- Part of the family might be cut off from the family business.
- You can't leave your favorite things to your favorite people.
- The state bends over backward to keep money safe for young children, then hands it all over to them when they reach majority, usually age 18. If they're not ready for the responsibility, too bad.
- You can't leave a contribution to a church or charity.
- A closely held business will have to be sold fast because the estate might not be permitted to run it.
- Your retarded or handicapped child may inherit money, disqualifying him or her from government aid.
- Everyone will be sore at you.

If you're married, wills sometimes seem to be beside the point. You simply put all the property into joint names so that your spouse will inherit. But what if you die together in an accident? Who gets the property then, and how are any children taken care of? You wouldn't go out at night and leave your youngsters without a babysitter. Why would you go out forever and leave them without a guardian? If you have no children and the wife

If You're	And Die Without a Will, Your Property Will Go
Unmarried, no children, parents living	To your parents. In some states, they split it with your brothers and sisters.
Unmarried, no children, parents dead	To your brothers and sisters; if you were an only child, to other next of kin.
Unmarried, with children	To your children, but probably not to stepchildren. The court appoints a guardian for your minor children and their funds.
Unmarried, no relatives	To the state.
Married, with children	Depending on the state and the size of the estate, all to the surviving spouse, or part to the spouse, part to the children. The spouse may get one-third to one-half of your separately owned property, part or all of the community property, and all of the joint property you held together.
Married, without children	Depending on the state and the size of the estate, all to the surviving spouse, or part to the spouse, part to your parents, and perhaps even part to your siblings. The spouse may get one-half of your separately owned property, part or all of the community property, and all of the joint property.

dies five days before the husband, everything may pass to his relatives, leaving hers out, and vice versa (the exact number of days depends on state law or what it says in the will). If you die together and are worth more than the estate-tax exemption (page 118) as a couple, your estates will owe federal taxes that could have been avoided if you'd drawn a will with the proper trust (page 120).

Single people may not care that everything goes to their parents. But it takes a will or trust to include a friend, a roommate, a charity, or, in most states, a sibling. A will is especially important for live-in couples, straight or gay. If your parents hate your way of life, they may vent their anger on the survivor, seizing property he or she ought to have.

Innocents think that even without a will, property passes to the person who most ought to own it. How mistaken they are! What's "right" under state law may be all wrong for your family and friends. Laws vary, but the following table gives you a general idea of what could happen if you die *intestate* (will-less).

WHAT PASSES BY WILL?

One bright spot, for the families of will truants, is that so little nowadays may be covered by a will. A will dictates only what happens to property that you own individually (including your half of community property and property held as tenants in common) *and* that does not have a named beneficiary. If there's a named beneficiary, it will get to its rightful new owner without the intercession of your will. For example:

• All joint property with rights of survivorship automatically goes to the other owner or owners.

• Property disposed of by contract goes to the person named.

• So does property with a named beneficiary, like life insurance, retirement accounts, U.S. Savings Bonds, tax-deferred annuities, and bank accounts in trust for others.

• Property put into a revocable living trust goes to the beneficiaries of the trust.

• The usual sort of personal property that we all own—the clock, the sugar bowl, the TV set—is usually divided by private agreement without a will, assuming that no one in the family lodges a formal protest. Many states even let you transfer title to an automobile without cranking up the probate machine.

To a surprising degree, we are seeing the rise of what Yale Law School professor John Langbein calls "the nonprobate estate" ("probate estate" meaning anything covered by your will). By accident or on purpose, people are leaving their probate estates almost dry. If most of your assets pass outside your will, your state might not require probate for the small amount of personal property that remains.

Some people go out of their way to avoid probate by using named beneficiaries or living trusts (for the pros and cons, see page 92). Others find it simpler to handle everything by will. If you choose a will, pay attention to the names you put on your property. It's easy to take actions that seem sensible at the time but that frustrate your true intent.

For example, you might say in your will, "Divide my estate equally between my beloved children, Ellen and Bob." Later, you put Ellen's name on your bank account so that she can help you pay your bills. When you die, the account will probably go to Ellen. Too bad for Bob. (Instead of using joint ownership, give Ellen your power of attorney. That frees her to write checks for you. On your death the remaining money will still be split between Ellen and Bob.)

Or your will might order that your Individual Retirement Account be paid to your brother and sister. But what if, when you started the IRA, you named only your brother as beneficiary? He'll get the money. Your sister is cut out. You should have told your IRA trustee (the mutual fund, bank, or brokerage house that holds the account) to change the beneficiary on the IRA documents.

Or your will might set up an estate-tax-saving trust to hold, say, $1 million of your assets. But your major asset is your mansion, which you keep in joint names with your spouse. You also have a life insurance policy, naming your spouse as beneficiary. When you die, your spouse gets the mansion and the life insurance. There may not be enough in your probate estate to fund the trust. Several thousand dollars' worth of estate planning will have gone down the drain, along with the tax savings you'd hoped for. You should have kept at least $1 million in your separate name, or named your estate the beneficiary of your life insurance.

The lawyer who prepares your will should quiz you about all the assets you own to see how they're held, what they're worth, and whether you have named beneficiaries. You may be advised to change the beneficiaries of insurance policies and retirement plans to make the will work the way you want. If you write your own will, these complicated ownership questions will be entirely in your hands. If you slip up, you may leave some beloved family members less than you intended.

If Virtually All of Your Property Is Disposed Of in Other Ways, Why Bother with a Will? Several reasons:
- To name a guardian or conservator for your minor children.
- To name a trustee to protect your children's inheritances until they can manage their own affairs.
- To dispose of property you didn't expect to own. This especially affects married couples. Say that a husband with no will inherits from his wife. If he himself dies soon thereafter (perhaps because they were both in the same auto accident), the property and the children will be left in the arms of the state.
- To dispose of any property you get after your death. You actually can get rich posthumously. For example, if you die in an accident, a jury might bring in a big judgment payable to your estate.
- To avoid fierce family arguments over who gets the beloved painting of Uncle Rick.
- To avoid all the problems of joint ownership and named beneficiaries (page 103).
- To dispose of your half of jointly owned property if both you and the other owner die in the same accident.
- To make sure that your probate-avoiding tactics work. If you set up a living trust, you need a so-called pour-over will. It guarantees that any property you forgot, or that comes to you after your death, will be added to your trust.

DO YOU NEED A LAWYER?

Strictly speaking, no. You can draw your own will. But a lawyer who represents himself is said to have a fool for a client. I think the same about people who handwrite their wills and stick them in desk drawers.

Centuries of tradition and legal precedent stand behind the formalities of wills. The words are precise (if often legalistic) to avoid ambiguity. The procedures are as orderly as a ballet, to make it irrefutably plain that these indeed are your intentions. Homemade documents—clear to you—may be so vague to others that your heirs have to get a reading in court. The will may even be thrown out and your property distributed according to state law. Books and computer programs exist that guide you through writing a valid will, but they take a lot of time and study. A lawyer shouldn't charge more than $300 or so for a very simple will (although you can pay in the thousands for a document that is complex).

Here's why you need an attorney:

To Say Exactly What You Mean. If you leave money to "Ada and her children," do you mean "Ada, if living, and if not, to her children"? Or do you mean, "divided in equal parts among Ada and her children"? Or "one-half to Ada and one-half to her children"? Who knows? Depending on the state, Ada and her children may become joint owners, or Ada may get the income from the property for life, or Ada may be able to occupy the land for life, with the children inheriting it after her death.

To Advise You on How to Hold Your Property—jointly? individually? in trust?

To See That the Names on the Property Agree with Legacies in Your Will. Here's where many estates get fouled up. Your will says one thing but the names on your property say another. For example, take a will that divides the property equally among three children. For help with money management, however, the parent put one child's name on the securities account. That child gets the whole account *plus* one-third of everything else. The other children are shortchanged.

To Clue You In on Your State's Weird Inheritance Laws. For example, if you leave someone a house with a mortgage on it, your estate might have to pay off the loan unless you specifically indicate it shouldn't. If your daughter witnesses the will, she may not be able to inherit.

To Reduce Federal Death Taxes if your estate is larger than the federal estate-tax exemption (see page 118). Even smaller estates may be subject to death taxes at the state level.

To See That Your Heirs Are Not Robbed of Their Share of Your Closely Held Business. Unless someone agrees, in writing, to buy out your interest, the business may be worthless to the family you leave behind.

To Ask Questions That Might Not Occur to You. For example, do you want your executor to post a bond to ensure that he or she won't misappropriate the assets? If you named a family member executor, you will probably want to spare the expense. But your will must specify that no bond is needed.

And another example: If one of your adult children dies before you do, who should inherit his or her share of your property? It would normally go to your child's children (your grandchildren). You'd have to make a specific bequest if you wanted some money to go somewhere else—perhaps to your late child's spouse. If your will happens to leave your property to your "surviving children," and one child dies before you do, that child's children could be cut out, even if that weren't your intent.

To Make Your Will Challenge-Proof. All the formalities have to be followed. You need the right number of witnesses, all of whom can testify that you knew you were signing your will, that you were competent to do so, and that the signature on the will is yours.

HOMEMADE WILLS

You don't believe me. You think you're smarter than a lawyer and don't see why you should pay him or her to complicate your life. So . . .

You Handwrite a Will, Sign It, Date It, Leave It Unwitnessed, and Put It in Your Desk Drawer. Is it valid? Yes, in about thirty states; no, in the rest. The bad news for lawyerphobes is that you have to ask a lawyer what your state allows. Some require that every word be handwritten; others might accept your handwriting on preprinted will forms. Even if the will is good, its terms may be fuzzy. That won't matter as long as your heirs agree on where you wanted your money to go. But if they disagree, your "will" could set off a terrible fight. People who boast that they've done their own wills wouldn't be so smug if they saw what often happened to them later.

You Type a Will, Sign It, Date It, and Put It in Your Desk Drawer. At this writing, it's invalid in all but three states (Montana, South Dakota, and Colorado), and it's not even foolproof there. It is not considered a handwritten will. To validate it, you need the signatures of the right number of witnesses. And both you and the witnesses have to follow certain procedures, required by your state, for creating a valid will.

You Get Witnesses. You must be sure to follow the rules. The witnesses may have to see you sign, or hear you acknowledge your signature to them.

You may have to tell the witnesses that this is your will. You may have to see the witnesses sign, or they may have to sign in the presence of one another. Some states and courts will accept a will with minor technical flaws as long as no one challenges it. But others won't, and there's no way you can tell in advance. Who witnesses the will may also be critical. Many states put limits on what a witness can inherit. A few states don't let a witness inherit anything.

You Fill In the Standard Do-It-Yourself Will Form That a Few States Provide. These forms are fine, in theory, for simple wills ("everything to my spouse" or "everything to my child"). But they don't allow for many choices. Like a typed will, they need witnesses. If you misinterpret the instructions and make a mistake in getting the will witnessed, it probably won't be valid.

You Tell People, Orally, What You Want. That's a valid will only if you're in imminent danger of death, not much property is involved, and several witnesses hear you. Some states allow only servicemen in combat to have oral wills. If you survive longer than a certain period, your oral will evaporates.

You Videotape Yourself Reciting Your Bequests. You do *not* have a will. The tape has no formal standing in law. A videotape of you signing the will, however, can prevent unhappy relatives from charging that you were too woolly to make decisions.

You Get a Book on How to Write Your Own Will and Follow Directions. If you're patient, and you read the directions carefully, and there aren't too many mistakes in the book, and your affairs are truly simple, maybe it will work. Daredevils might consider *Nolo's Simple Will Book* by Denis Clifford, at this writing $17.95. It's available in many bookstores or directly from Nolo Press, 950 Parker St., Berkeley, CA 94710. Nolo also has a software program, *Willmaker,* $67.75.

But even with guidance, you're better off not writing your own. In simple situations, the cost of a lawyer is surprisingly small and worth every penny. If your situation is more complex, look for a tax-planning lawyer who has actually handled estates. The more a lawyer sees of what can happen in a family after a death, the more sensitive he or she becomes to how exact a will has to be.

JOINT WILLS

This is a single will for two people, usually a husband and wife. They might each leave all the property to the other, and to the children equally when the second spouse dies.

I believe in sharing secrets, sharing beds, and sharing property—but not in sharing wills. Don't do it. A joint will can be hard to change without the consent of your spouse. The surviving spouse might not be able to change it after the first spouse dies. And it might not qualify for the marital deduction (page 120)—a tax disaster, for people wealthy enough to owe estate taxes.

NAMING AN EXECUTOR

The executor—or, in many states, personal representative—sees that your will is carried out. It's a tiresome, detailed, time-consuming, thankless job. You're doing no favors for the person you name. All the property has to be tracked down and assembled (no easy job if you didn't keep good records). Creditors notified. Heirs dealt with tactfully. Arguments settled. Bills and taxes paid. Property appraised and distributed or sold. Life insurance claimed if it's payable to the estate. Investments managed until they can be distributed to their new owners. Final accounting to be made, to the heirs and, perhaps, to the courts.

The executor usually works with a lawyer, so you don't need an expert in estate law or high finance. You need virtues that are much harder to find. An executor has to be willing, reliable, well organized, honest, responsible about money, fair-minded, and sensitive to the worries of the heirs. The usual practice is to ask an able heir (or friend) to do the job. If you name a professional executor—a bank or a lawyer—include a family member as co-executor, just to keep things moving along. Get permission before putting down someone's name. If money is misspent or errors made, the executor can be held personally responsible.

A friend or family member usually doesn't ask for compensation. But you should specify this in the will; otherwise, they may claim the commission allowed by law, even though you expected them to serve for nothing. (In large estates, it may be cheaper for a family member to take a commission than to take the same amount of money as an inheritance. The income tax on the commission may be lower than the death tax on the net estate.)

When banks or attorneys are executors, however, they may charge, and charge, and charge—sometimes by the hour, sometimes a fixed fee, sometimes a percentage of the assets in the estate that goes to probate. Your estate will pay less if you keep the executorship at home and let your family hire a lawyer by the hour or by the job. (Executors should shop lawyers, asking more than one what they'll charge; like any other businesspeople, lawyers cut fees for jobs they want and that they know are up for bid.)

In a state with simplified probate laws (page 97), legal fees will be lower because there are fewer court procedures. Your family may not even need an attorney. The job may be easy enough to do themselves. They should go to the courthouse and ask the clerk of the probate court what's involved, or have a onetime conference with a knowledgeable lawyer. Very small estates might not have to go through probate at all.

WHO GETS THE ANDIRONS?

"How nice. Mommy Dearest left me a nice, round $1 million . . . but what did you say? Sandy took the andirons? They were supposed to be mine! I'll sue!"

And so it goes. Personal property usually goes to a surviving spouse. If there is none, it's often divided equally among your heirs, leaving it to them to decide exactly who gets what. Or it's lumped together and left to your main beneficiary, who divides it among the family members. If your heirs fall out, money may not be the issue. They're more likely to fight about all the things that can't be split—the grandfather's clock, the opal earrings, the china, the antique pool table.

To avoid this, you can make named bequests—the andirons to Sandy, the feather boa to Sarah. The easiest way is to put your desires in a separate letter attached to your will. You can then change your mind about the andirons without having to reexecute the will itself. In some states this letter has the force of law *if* your will states that you'll leave a letter and *if* the letter is properly written (for example, it should be signed, dated, and say specifically that you want these particular people to get these particular items). In other states, you're simply depending on your family and executor to cooperate.

The letter might also tell your heirs which items are of special value. If you collect Batman comics or Japanese netsuke, leave the name of a dealer who might buy them back. Guns should be left to a person who can possess them lawfully.

If you carry insurance on special items, such as a gun collection or an antique car, ask your insurer to make it available to an heir for a certain period. Then state in your will that the policy follows the gift. This protects the valuables from the time you die to the time the heir collects them and gets insurance of his or her own.

Pets—or "heirdales," as rich dogs are called by Lawrence Waggoner of the University of Michigan Law School—are not allowed to inherit. You can leave a trust for their upkeep as long as the trustee is willing to carry out its terms. But in many states, the trust isn't enforceable if the trustee you name doesn't want to bother. So settle with your Good Samaritan in advance.

SETTLING SHARES

Unequal shares, to people who feel that they ought to be equals, become an eternal thorn in the side. Aunt Emily's last revenge on an irritating nephew is to leave him only $1,000 while his brother gets $2,000.

For the sake of family relations, equal shares are politic—with a few exceptions. If you've already put two kids through college and have one to go, that child deserves something extra for his education. He shouldn't have to spend his inheritance on a college degree that, for everyone else, was financed out of family funds. If one daughter married in state, the other should be able to afford the same. If one adult child is rich and the other poor, you might all agree to help the one who really needs it (although beware of divorce; a rich child may be suddenly poor if his or her marriage breaks up).

Don't keep your kids in the dark about the will. Explain the provisions, by letter or in a tape—especially if you've left them unequal shares. You want them to understand your reasoning, to avoid bitterness and deflect a challenge to the will.

PICKING A GUARDIAN

If you and your spouse both die, who better than Grandma to look after the minor children? The answer to that question is: practically anyone you can think of. Grandma paid her dues. She shouldn't have to gear up for child rearing all over again. Furthermore, if your parents are named guardians, you are setting up your children to lose a mom and dad all over again.

A brother or sister is a better choice. So is an older, married child or a close friend who shares your values and way of life. Of course, the guardian should be willing to undertake the job. If you name a friend instead of a family member, spell out your reasons in your will. The family might challenge your choice and you want the court to understand your thinking.

If your children are old enough to understand the question, ask them where they'd like to live if anything happened to you—and let them in on what you decide. Don't be afraid to raise the issue. Children are often better able to cope with thoughts of dying than adults—maybe because to them death seems so remote. The older the child, the more important that he or she be part of the decision.

Besides a guardian for your children, you need a protector of their inheritance. Usually, the same person does both. But if your loving brother is an airhead about money, pick someone else to look after the child's property. You don't need a financial genius, just a conscientious person with common sense who knows how to get good investment advice. Leave enough money—if not in property then in life insurance—so that your child can be properly raised and educated. You don't want him or her to be a financial burden on the guardian.

If you're divorced, the guardianship of the children normally goes to your ex-spouse as long as he or she wants it. A court will step in only if the parent is clearly unfit (say, a drug addict) or has legally abandoned the child. If you don't think your ex-spouse is interested, name someone else and explain in your will why you made that choice. Your ex-spouse still gets first crack. But your candidate should come in ahead of all other contenders. As far as the children's money is concerned, you don't have to name your ex-spouse the protector of that if you think he or she is financially irresponsible. But the keeper of the children's money should be able to get along with your ex, and should willingly dole out money that the children need.

If you're putting off naming a guardian, consider this sad story. In 1995 four people battled for the guardianship of a toddler whose parents were killed in a boat explosion. The contenders: an uncle, an aunt, a cousin, and a friend. Part of the child's attraction: a potential multimillion-dollar wrongful death settlement from the boat company. Too bad the parents hadn't picked a guardian themselves.

WAYS TO LEAVE MONEY TO YOUNG CHILDREN

1. *Name a legal guardian for the children's funds.* State law determines what can be spent on the children and what investments can be made. The guardian makes an annual accounting to the court. When the child comes of age—at 18 or 21, depending on your state—he or she gets the money.

2. *Use the Uniform Gifts to Minors Act (UGMA).* In many states, you have to make the gift during your lifetime rather than by will. The funds are left to an adult who acts as custodian for the child. The law determines how the money can be spent and invested. A custodian may have more flexibility in handling money than a guardian does. The funds go to the child when he or she comes of age, usually at 18.

3. *Use the Uniform Transfers to Minors Act (UTMA) if your state has adopted it.* UTMA allows transfers by will, as well as gifts during your lifetime. The custodian can hold the assets until the child is 18 or 21 (higher, in some states).

4. *Leave the money in a trust that your will establishes.* This is the best solution for sums over $20,000 or so. It's also best for property that starts small but will grow substantially over the years. Your trustee—a relative,

friend, attorney, or bank—manages the inheritance and pays it to the child according to your instructions. He or she can dole out income and principal as needed for the child's education and living expenses. The remainder is turned over to the child at the age you set—maybe 30 or 40. You can provide that the child gets the money all at once or in installments—say, at ages 25, 30, 35, and 40. The trustee can be told to withhold payments if it seems to be in the child's best interest. (Do you want the child to inherit if he or she has just joined a religious cult and will give it every penny?) You might make the child co-trustee at, say, age 23. That allows him or her to share in investment decisions without yet having to handle the money alone.

Set up a single trust for all the children. If one child has big medical bills, they can be paid out of common funds without pillaging that child's basic inheritance. Typically, the document will provide for all the money to stay in trust until the youngest child reaches, say, 25. Then the trust dissolves and everyone gets his or her appointed share. (At your death, however, a nominal payment might be made to the older children; if the children are quite a bit older, they may get a larger disbursement).

LEAVING PROPERTY TO A LOVER

Since families often hate these relationships—especially gay ones—the loving couple can't be too careful. After the death of one, the parents might make a strong effort to carry everything away. If you want your mate to get your money, you need a will. And spell out, specifically, why you chose your lover to inherit rather than your family. "Mickey, who has lived with me faithfully for seven years. . . ."

HOW TO RUIN A RELATIONSHIP

Your nieces, Kathy and Martha, love your antique grandfather's clock, so you leave it to both of them. Your 1957 black Thunderbird with tailfins goes to your two grandsons. Three of your children inherit the beach house.

Is this generosity? Will it bring the new owners together in an orgy of sharing? Not likely. You may have created a monster that will eat your family up. Your nieces, once in perfect sympathy, may well fall out over whose time it is.

Few people can reach perfect accord over what to do with mutually owned property. Their personal and financial situations are different. So are their attitudes. If Martha moves to a distant state and takes the clock with her, how does Kathy get her share back? If your older grandson is a demon driver and wrecks the car, can the younger one force him to put it back into prime condition? What if the beach house needs a new roof but one of the owners can't afford to pay? What if one owner wants to sell?

Anything that can't be divided should either be left to one person or sold and the proceeds split.

MORE WILL FACTS

Execute only one copy of your will. If you sign more, the court will hold up probate until they're all found. For extras, make photocopies.

Have your will checked when you move to a new state. A properly signed and witnessed will is usually valid everywhere. But ownership rights differ from state to state, which might make a difference in how your property is held.

Two ways to cancel a will: (1) The only sure way is to make a new one, specifically revoking all wills and codicils that have come before. (2) You can tear up your old will. But do so in the presence of several witnesses (*young* witnesses, who shouldn't die before you do) and say specifically that this will is no longer valid. Otherwise, an heir might argue successfully that your executed will is merely missing. A photocopy in the lawyer's keeping might then be accepted as a valid will, even though you meant to revoke it.

The *only* way to make a small change in a will is to execute a formal *codicil,* amending it. Don't ink out an old provision or insert a new one. In a few states and with some provisions, that might work; in most, it doesn't. Any change should be signed, dated, and witnessed according to your state's procedures. Otherwise, the court will ignore the change or revoke the entire provision. Extensive changes might invalidate the entire will.

Say you leave your spouse money, get divorced, and die before you change your will. Does the ex-spouse collect? Generally, no. The rest of the will is usually valid but your ex-spouse will be cut out. However, exceptions exist, so change your will as soon as the divorce negotiations get under way. If you don't change your will, and die when you're legally separated but not divorced, your spouse *will* collect. Even if you do change your will, your spouse will collect his or her legal share (page 114) if you haven't yet divorced.

If you're getting divorced, *immediately* drop your spouse as beneficiary on your life-insurance policy, employee-benefit plan, IRAs, Keogh, 401(k), and revocable trust. If you don't, and die, most states allow your ex-spouse to collect even if you have married again.

Say you leave half of your property to "my dear children, Justin and

Matthew." Then Heather is born, but you die before specifically including her in your will. Is she disinherited? No, but how much she gets will depend on your state. She might get exactly what the other children do. Or she might be given what she'd have received if you had died without a will—which could be more, or less, than the other children inherit. The same is true for an adopted child, but not a stepchild. Unless specifically mentioned, a stepchild is out.

Say you get married but your will still leaves everything to your pals. Is your spouse disinherited? No. State law dictates that he or she get at least something from your estate. But it may not be as much as you want. Moral: execute a new will on the way out of church.

Say you get married and regret it. Your will leaves nothing to your spouse. Tough luck. Your spouse still collects something. His or her minimal inheritance depends on state law. For short marriages, it might be $50,000; for long ones, half of all of the marital assets. It might be one-third to one-half of the late spouse's assets. It might be the spouse's own share of the community property. The spouse gets taken care of first. The bequests to the rest of the heirs are reduced proportionately.

A spouse won't inherit, however, if you both signed a valid premarital contract to that effect, exerting no unfair pressure to sign and disclosing all assets. You can write a postmarital contract, too (page 133).

When leaving money to charity, check that you have the legal name and address. Many charities have similar names and might mount a fight over the bequest. Name an alternative charity in case the first one is out of business or no longer qualifies as a tax-deductible recipient.

If your estate will owe taxes, consider directing that people who receive small cash gifts and items of personal property inherit free of tax. All the taxes will then be paid from the balance of the estate.

If you own homes in more than one state, establish one of them as your legal residence (by voting there, paying taxes there, listing that address on your credit cards, getting a driver's license in that state, and so on). Otherwise, both states might try to tax your estate. Real estate, such as a vacation home, is taxed in the state where it's located.

You can disinherit a child in every state except Louisiana. Your will should state specifically that you are leaving that child no money, or leaving a nominal sum like one dollar.

Small bequests are usually stated in dollar amounts, like "$1,000 for my friend Diane, if she survives me. . . ." But it's generally better to state major bequests in percentage terms rather than in dollar amounts. Consider what might happen if you leave $30,000 to each of three nieces and the remainder to charity, expecting the charity to get a large share. If the stock market crashes and your estate winds up with only $90,000, your nieces will get theirs and the charity will get nothing. So instead, say "40 percent for the charity and 20 percent for each of my nieces."

Your will can forgive debts. In a community property state, however, you may be able to forgive only half of the debt. Your spouse would have to forgive the other half.

Some reasons to change your will: (1) a big rise or fall in your net worth; (2) a new child, by birth, adoption, or marriage; (3) marriage, separation, or divorce; (4) a child's marriage, separation, or divorce; (5) a child's college graduation; (6) the death or disability of an heir; (7) an illness in the family that may go on for life; (8) changing financial circumstances in your family or a child's family; (9) a change in the property or inheritance laws.

Are you holding investment real estate? If your heirs aren't capable of managing real estate, leave a letter for the executor giving all the details about the investment, what it should be worth, and who is most qualified to sell it.

If estate taxes will be due, and your estate is made up mostly of illiquid real estate, leave enough life insurance to cover the bill. When considering how large a policy to buy, remember that the policy itself may increase the value of the estate (although there are ways of getting it out of your estate —page 119).

Are you holding old tax shelters, such as partnerships invested in real estate or oil drilling? Large payments may be due for several years into the future—payments that your spouse or other heirs could not meet. The units may be taxable but not salable. If you manage to sell, the accumulated tax liability may be greater than the shelter's current value. Examine your exposure and leave extra life insurance if necessary.

Does your net worth depend on a closely held business? Get buyout agreements with your partners, enough life insurance to cover estate taxes, and agreements to protect your family's interests. Otherwise, the business might prosper while your heirs get nary a penny.

If you're married and made your will before September 13, 1981, revise it. Under current law, no gift or estate taxes are due on property left to a spouse. But wills drawn before that 1981 date may be subject to an older law, which could leave some of the money open to tax.

All of your property doesn't have to be distributed right away. You can set up trusts in your will and instruct the trustee to hold the property until your children are older, distribute just the trust income, or distribute property to some beneficiaries and not to others. Whatever you want.

Five grounds for challenging a will: (1) a procedural flaw, like an unwitnessed change in the text; (2) too young (the will was made when the person was still a minor); (3) undue influence or duress (the will was signed under pressure); (4) fraud (the person thought he or she was signing a letter or contract rather than a will); (5) mental incapacity (the person was too senile to have made or changed his or her will). But you have to raise your objection quickly. If you miss the deadline set by your state, you won't be allowed to make your case.

SEXISM AND WILLS

It lingers on. Fathers may leave less to their daughters than to their sons. Daughters may be shut out of the family business. Wives may not be consulted on the will. Money for a wife or daughter may be left in trust, forcing them to live on a trustee's dole for the rest of their lives. The wife might even have agreed to the trust because she took no interest in investing while her husband was alive. But when a wife becomes a widow, things change. She often discovers the lovely little secret that conservative money management isn't hard. She may come to resent her infantile dependency on a trustee or bank trust department.

In the case of a longtime marriage, especially a first marriage, all questions about what happens to the money when the husband dies should be resolved on the side of the widow's freedom to act. The husband should add a trust to his will only to minimize estate taxes, not to "protect" his wife from making her own decisions about her money. If she decides that she'd rather not, she can give it to a bank trust department herself. But the issues may be different with second marriages, especially second marriages later in life. Each spouse may want to leave money in trust for the children of a former marriage.

WILLS THAT LEAVE MONEY IN TRUST

A *testamentary trust* is set up by your will. Instead of leaving money directly to the beneficiary, you leave it in trust, to be managed by a trustee. Funds can be paid out for various purposes. At some point, the trust dissolves and the money is distributed.

A Trust Can Hold Money Until a Child Grows Up (page 111). But don't be a dead hand from the grave, holding on to the child's inheritance for years. By the time they're 30 or 35, the children should be able to get the money and take their chances (except in unusual conditions, like drug addiction or a pending divorce).

A Trust Can Save Estate Taxes. If your net worth exceeds the federal estate-tax exemption (page 118), talk to a lawyer about how to cut the tax. There may be state death taxes due on even smaller sums. Trusts are just one solution. Often, you can cut taxes without using a trust (page 118).

A Trust Can Manage Money Left to a Spouse. A trustee runs the money. The spouse receives the income and, if needed, payments out of principal.

When the spouse dies, the remaining money goes to whoever is named. A family member, bank, or investment adviser is generally the trustee. The spouse should be able to change trustees if the relationship isn't working. But don't lock up *all* of a widow's money in trust. Maybe she didn't take much interest in investing while her husband was alive, but in widowhood she might turn into a demon money manager. I've seen it happen. Leave her free to run at least part of her funds as she pleases.

A Trust Can Provide for Retarded or Handicapped Children. State and federal programs cover basic medical and residential care, but only if the child has almost no money. This presents parents with a dilemma: Money left to the handicapped child will be consumed by the institution. But without that money, the child will get only bare-bones support.

Middle-income parents may feel that they have little choice. They leave their modest assets to their healthy children and let the handicapped one get government aid. In this case, you should specifically disinherit the handicapped child (and tell your relatives to do likewise). Your healthy children should be willing to provide any extra comforts that their institutionalized sibling needs.

Higher-income parents, however, might set up a trust, often funded by life insurance. The handicapped child (possessing little or no money) can qualify for government aid while the trust supplies extra maintenance and support. But the wording is critical to ensure that the government can't break the trust (words like "health," "welfare," and "support" are no-nos). For advice on getting a well-drafted trust, call your state or local Association for Retarded Citizens. Ask for the names of lawyers experienced in your state's public-assistance laws. For the booklet *How to Provide for Their Future*, send $10 to the Association for Retarded Citizens, P.O. Box 1047, Arlington, TX 76004.

A Trust Can Assure That the Children of a Prior Marriage Will Inherit. If you leave all your money to a second spouse, he or she can do absolutely anything with it. For example, your spouse can leave it all to charity, cutting your children out. A trust prevents this. You can give your second spouse an income for life while guaranteeing that your children will ultimately inherit the principal.

Whatever you do, don't lock your heirs into an estate planner's prison. It's not worth saving the taxes if your trust will completely inhibit your family's freedom to act.

CHOOSING A TRUSTEE

The average trust does just fine with an individual trustee—a family member, friend, lawyer, or business associate. His or her powers are outlined in your will or in the trust document. Fundamentally, you want the trustee to do what you would have done, had you been alive. So you really have to believe in this person's morals and motives—and the morals and motives of a successor, if he or she should die.

Give your trustee wide latitude. You don't know what's going to happen ten or twenty years hence and shouldn't try to guess. Write a letter to all the trustees (including successor trustees), with copies to all beneficiaries, explaining what you want the trust to accomplish and what the money can be distributed for. That way everyone understands exactly what you have in mind.

Your risk is that the trustee will slip. His or her judgment may go. The trustee may steal, or disapprove of one of your children and deny that child funds, or grow senile, or become disabled. Your will or trust document should provide for a substitute if the family demands it or when the trustee passes a certain age.

The alternative to a friend or relative is a bank or trust company. There you get a professional money manager and experienced estate administrator, which won't move away and won't steal. If your family hates its trust officer, it can ask the bank for another one. But this choice has some drawbacks, too. The bank charges money. It takes only larger trusts for personal management (generally, $150,000 and up). It is often too busy to take an interest in the family, although this can be solved by naming your spouse or another relative co-trustee.

Always put an escape clause in the document so your heirs (or their guardian, if they're minors) have the option of moving the trust to another bank or trust company. The new trustee shouldn't be related or beholden to any person with the power of removing him or her.

Sometimes trusts can be divided if it makes sense to have more than one pool of assets.

AVOIDING TAXES

The amount exempt from federal estate taxes rises gradually between now and 2006. Over each year's limit, tax rates start at 37 percent. Top rate: 55 percent on taxable transfers over $3 million (with an effective rate of 60 percent on transfers between $10 and $21.2 million). Some states also levy death taxes, often on amounts smaller than the federal exemption.

Here's what's exempt from federal tax:

Year	Amount You Can Transfer Estate-Tax Free
1997	$ 600,000
1998	625,000
1999	650,000
2000–01	675,000
2002–03	700,000
2004	850,000
2005	950,000
2006 and thereafter	1,000,000

It takes a lawyer to cut your tax bill without mishap. Among his or her bag of tricks:

1. *Make gifts while you're alive.* Up to $10,000 a year can go to each of as many people as you like, tax free. (That sum includes small gifts like $50 at Christmas.) If your spouse joins in the gift, you can give up to $20,000— even if it's all your money (the gift exemption is indexed starting in 1999). Larger gifts will eat into your federal estate-tax exemption and may even trigger taxes. But in most cases, no payment is due until after you die. The rule is: a gift is taxable only if its value, when added to the value of your estate at death, turns out to exceed the current estate-tax exemption. Even if the gift will lead to taxes, the cost may be worth it. If you give, say, $30,000 worth of stock, the gains will accumulate in the recipient's name instead of yours, saving you income taxes and maybe even estate taxes.

2. *Give away your life insurance policy*—to your spouse, your child, or an irrevocable trust. That takes the proceeds out of your estate (unless you die within three years of making the gift; then the proceeds, and taxes, come back). You can even continue paying the premiums, although if you do they could become a taxable gift to the new owner. (To minimize the gift, use what's called a Crummey power. I'll leave it to your lawyer to explain that one.) Alternatively, the new owner can pay the premiums.

The new owner can change the beneficiary, withdraw the cash value, or even cancel the policy. If you give the policy to your spouse and then divorce, tough luck.

If your spouse owns the policy, his or her will should leave it to the children or another beneficiary. Otherwise, if your spouse dies before you do, the policy might come right back to your estate. If your spouse leaves the policy to your children in trust and you're the trustee, it could also be taxed in your estate. (You see why I told you to see a lawyer.)

If your spouse owns the policy, he or she should be named beneficiary. If you make the children the beneficiaries and you die, the IRS may say that your spouse made the children a taxable gift of the insurance proceeds.

To give away an individual policy, ask the insurance company for an *assignment form*. You can also give away a group policy that you hold through your employer. Term policies, in particular, make terrific gifts because there's no cash value, so no gift tax can be imposed.

3. *Marry.* No estate tax is levied on property given or bequeathed to a spouse. When the spouse dies, any money exceeding the estate-tax exemption can be taxed in the spouse's estate when he or she dies unless, of course, the spouse remarries and passes the tax deferral on.

To avoid a tax when the surviving spouse dies, the wills of married couples should create his-and-her trusts (sometimes known as *credit-shelter trusts,* or *bypass trusts*, because they bypass estate taxes). These trusts can each hold assets worth up to the current estate-tax exemption (page 118). That money generally goes to the children, although the spouse can have some or all of the income from the trust and access to the principal for life. The children can also be given some or all of the income. Here's how this strategy usually plays out if the husband dies first and the law exempts $1 million from tax (reverse it if the wife dies first):

a. The husband dies.

b. Up to $1 million of his assets go into a bypass trust for the children and the wife. This money passes estate-tax free because it's protected by the husband's estate-tax credit.

c. The wife gets the income from the trust for life, *plus* the right to receive funds directly from the principal if needed. That's a key point. She always has access to all of the money. It's never locked away from her. Each year she can take $5,000 from principal or 5 percent of the value of the trust without asking the trustee (and without paying any tax). If she wants even more of the principal, the trustee has to agree. But that shouldn't be a problem as long as the husband names a sympathetic trustee and makes it clear that his wife should be given whatever she wants. The trust document should broadly provide that the money be used for her happiness and general welfare.

d. After benefiting from the trust for many years, the wife dies. All the remaining money in trust is distributed to the children, tax free.

e. The wife leaves the children another $1 million, sheltered by her own estate-tax credit.

f. A total of $2 million (or more, if the value of the first trust has grown) has been left to the kids tax free. That's at least twice the amount that the kids could otherwise get untaxed.

For this to work, each spouse has to have enough assets to fund a trust —held in his or her separate name, in both names as community property, or as tenants in common without rights of survivorship. If you own everything jointly, your tax-saving trust won't work. If your house is a substantial part of your net worth, consider owning it as tenants in common (page 85). Your half of the house (or the spouse's half) can then become part of the trust.

But don't put Individual Retirement Accounts or other tax-deferred retirement savings into a bypass trust. If you do, your spouse loses the right to stretch out the payments over his or her lifetime. Instead, the money is all received—and taxed—at once.

What if you're worth just a little over $1 million and don't want to decide in advance whether to put money into a trust? Your spouse can assess the situation after your death and, if it seems smart, disclaim (refuse) any part of the inheritance. Your will can provide that any disclaimed money would go into a trust. A beneficiary has a limited period of time within which to disclaim—9 months from the date of death for federal tax purposes; longer, in some states, if you want to disclaim for reasons other than saving tax.

What if you're in a second marriage and your spouse is about the same age as your children? Give them some money when you die. Otherwise, they may never see it.

4. *Disclaim.* Let's say that your uncle Joshua died and left you some money. But you're well off and your son in college is next in line to inherit. You can say no to the bequest, letting it go directly to your son. That saves your estate from paying taxes on that money when you die. A spouse might want to disclaim a payout from a late spouse's 401(k) plan and let the money go directly to the children if they're the alternate beneficiaries.

5. *Give money to charity.* Money given—or left—to charity reduces your estate, hence your estate tax. See page 125 for information about charitable trusts.

6. *Start a family limited partnership.* This arrangement lets parents and children, as well as other relatives, own assets together. Over time you gradually raise the children's stake in the assets. The earlier they possess them, the more of the assets' capital appreciation will be moved out of the parents' estates. That will lower their tax. Typically, the parents are the general partners, which gives them the right to make decisions about the assets. The children are limited partners with no voice in management. They sign buy-sell agreements so the other partners can buy them out if they want to quit. (Those shares are *theirs,* by the way. The parents can't take the assets back.) Family limited partnerships are usually used to hold business interests and real estate. A couple needn't go to this trouble, however, if their joint estate will probably be worth less than the federal estate-tax exemption. Certain family businesses get a $1.3 million estate-tax exemption.

A Last Word: It isn't graven in stone that you have to avoid estate taxes for the sake of your heirs. You come first. Don't give away so much property, or put so much in trust, that you or your spouse will become dependent on others, even if they're your own children. And *don't* undertake your own tax planning. To explain all these concepts, I have made a meadow out of what is actually a briar patch. Only an experienced estate-planning attorney can walk you through unscratched.

WHEN ARE INHERITANCES PAID?

Probate can go quickly when your lawyer hustles, the courts are efficient, there aren't a lot of distant heirs to notify, and no one challenges the will. A will might be admitted to probate in anything from a couple of days to a couple of weeks and declared valid almost immediately. A surviving spouse can generally start taking modest sums from the estate right away in order to meet living expenses. Life insurance is paid out pronto. So is jointly owned property, in most cases. If you wait for months before anything happens, it means either that your lawyer isn't paying much attention or that you had the bad luck to land in a lousy court.

Some executors start distributing the property without delay. Others prefer to wait for 4 to 12 months, which is the time generally allowed for creditors to file claims against the estate. Stocks, cars, and bank accounts can be distributed as quickly as title can be passed. Other property—real estate, for example—takes longer to transfer because of the paperwork or the need to sell at a reasonable price. Valuable personal property often can't be divided until it's appraised, unless all the beneficiaries agree on who gets what.

Executors usually hold back a little money until the final tax return is accepted (if there's a deficiency the executor is personally responsible). The average estate might be fully distributed in 6 months to a year. Large estates can take several years—not because probate delays things but because the property is complex. It would take just as long to distribute it from a living trust. In some states, trustees as well as executors are liable for unpaid bills and taxes, so they're careful to get these obligations paid before distributing all the money to heirs.

GRANTING THE POWER, DURABLY

Everyone needs a backup—a person to act for you if you're away, if you're sick, if you get hit by a car and can't function for a while, or if you grow senile. That means giving someone—a spouse, mate, parent, adult child, or trusted friend—your power of attorney. A lawyer can get this document together in a jiffy. It's probably in his word processor and just needs printing out. Young people need a power of attorney as well as the old.

Limited powers of attorney grant narrow rights, such as: "Christopher can write checks on my bank account to pay my bills while I'm out of the country for six months." *Ordinary* powers of attorney give broader powers over your finances. But both limited and ordinary powers expire if you become mentally disabled, however, which is exactly when you need the help the most.

So protect yourself against doomsday by asking a lawyer to draw up a *durable* power of attorney. It lets someone act for you if you're judged senile or mentally disabled, if you fall into a coma, or if illness or accident damages your brain. A durable power lasts while other powers don't. As long as you are mentally capable, you can revoke a durable power whenever you like.

The person who holds your power of attorney could, theoretically, exercise it at any time, even if you're healthy. He or she could sell your investments and clean out your bank account. But that's not as easy as it sounds. Banks and brokers normally check on what has happened to you before accepting a power of attorney. Besides, you wouldn't give the power to someone you didn't trust.

Be sure to execute copies of the durable power—maybe even 10 or more. Some institutions want an original for their files (photocopies won't do) before they'll cooperate with the attorney-in-fact.

In many states, you have to execute new durable powers every 4 or 5 years to show that your intention holds. Insurance companies and financial institutions probably won't honor an old power. A few won't honor any durable power of attorney at all, or any power more than 6 months old, or any power not written on their own forms. In my view, that's harassment, but they sometimes do it and you might be stuck. *Always* ask your bank, broker, or insurance company what its policy is, so you'll know for sure that the power you've signed is going to work. If your bank or broker won't accept the power you show them with the provisions you want, move your money somewhere else. The heck with them. If they dig in their heels when you're too senile to make decisions, your attorney-in-fact will have to apply to the court for a guardianship. No institution can refuse to obey a court-appointed guardian, but it's outrageous that any should push the issue this far. Fortunately, few do.

To protect yourself against recalcitrant institutions, set up a living trust with little or no money in it; then create a durable power of attorney, giving your attorney-in-fact the right to move your assets into the trust. If a bank or brokerage house makes a pain of itself, your agent can move that property into the trust and exercise his or her power as trustee. The institution will have to obey.

If you'd rather not trust anyone until you absolutely have to, write a *springing* power of attorney. It doesn't take effect unless you become mentally incapacitated and the document defines exactly what that means. For example: "I shall be deemed to be disabled when two physicians licensed to practice medicine in my state sign a paper stating that I am disabled and unable to handle my financial affairs." The same language can be used to determine when your disability has passed. Execute multiple copies of the springing power, too.

How do you cancel a durable power of attorney? Tell the person holding it that he or she is out; get all signed copies of the power back; destroy the copies, preferably in front of witnesses; where there are duplicates, write to the institutions holding your money telling them not to accept that person as your agent.

A LIVING WILL AND HEALTH-CARE PROXY

Anyone who has seen a dying or permanently comatose person hooked up fruitlessly—sometimes painfully—to life-support machines understands the issue of the right to die. Many of those attached to respirators and food-and-water tubes, without hope of recovery, have been forced to it by state law or custom, or because no one is authorized to pull the plug. Such supports can be merely death-delaying rather than truly life-sustaining. Maintaining a permanently comatose person can also strip the family finances bare.

Your best hope of avoiding this fate yourself is to write an *advance directive*. It includes a living will dictating the kind of treatment you want if you cannot speak for yourself and a health-care proxy or durable health-care power of attorney naming an agent to see that your wishes are carried out. An agent may also be named in a living will but can usually act only in accordance with the will's specific terms. The proxy confers broader powers to make decisions, although the ability to withhold or withdraw life support varies from state to state. Lawyers advise that you name two stand-ins to act for you in case one isn't around when critical decisions have to be made. To avoid inaction or delay, either one should be able to act alone.

All states but three recommend specific living-will language; in the remaining three (Massachusetts, Michigan, and New York), you should look for a form that fully documents your end-of-life wishes, especially as to withholding or withdrawing treatment, food-and-water tubes, and a respirator. If you spend time in more than one state, write an advance directive in each. It's not clear that one state (or the local doctors or hospital) will honor a directive executed under another state's laws.

Even with a living will, your wishes might not be carried out. A son might say, "I don't care what my father thought he wanted, go ahead and treat him," and the doctor probably would. Your best hope of avoiding this is to talk with everyone in a position to influence your treatment: spouse, children, siblings, doctors, and the person or people named in your health-care proxy. Discuss exactly what you'd expect, under different circumstances. Let them ask you hypothetical questions about your end-of-life care.

What happens if you fall into a permanent coma or painful terminal illness without having written a living will? In twenty-five states and Washington, D.C., written legislation permits family members or a legal guardian to "stand in the patient's shoes" to make the life-or-death decision that the patient would probably make were he or she able to do so. Case-by-case court decisions or understanding doctors may lead to the same result in other states, although you can't count on it. The issue may have to go to a hospital ethics committee, which could put families through a difficult question-and-answer session. In Michigan, Missouri, and New York, no surrogate decisions can be accepted unless there's clear and convincing evidence that the patient—while still functioning—expressed a wish not to be artificially kept alive.

An advance directive is the clearest expression of your intent. You can often get your state's form free from a hospital or the department of health. The lawyer who drafts your regular will or living trust may include it as part of the package. Or send $3.50 to Choice in Dying, Suite 1001, 200 Varick St., New York, NY 10014, asking for documents specific to the state you want. Choice in Dying's documents are free on its Web site, http://www.choices.org. It will also answer questions (call 800-989-WILL) and provide educational materials.

WILLS VS. LIVING TRUSTS

A huge industry exists in America peddling the false idea that everyone needs a living trust. Trusts are flogged via seminars and cold-call telemarketing by lawyers, insurance agents, and financial planners, all of whom will make a few bucks (in fact, more than a few) if you set one up. Deceptive selling is widespread. Many people believe, for example, that only living trusts will lower your estate taxes when, in fact, you can get exactly the same savings from wills.

In some circumstances, living trusts are dream machines; in others, a waste of money. For the details on living trusts, see page 91. There is a checklist on page 126 to help you decide whether wills or trusts are best for you. Read the footnotes carefully; the answers you seek aren't simple ones.

CHARITABLE TRUSTS

If the tax code didn't exist, America's charities would have to invent it. Generous donors start with a personal sense of mission, but it doesn't hurt that gifts for good works are, within limits, written off on your tax return.

Planned giving is especially appealing. It's a six-step program for making gifts and strengthening your retirement income, too. Here's how it works: (1) You donate cash savings to the charity, or stocks or land that have appreciated in value. (2) You win substantial tax breaks. (3) The

WHICH TO CHOOSE: A WILL OR A LIVING TRUST?

OBJECTIVE	WILL	LIVING TRUST
Save estate taxes	Yes	Yes
Save income taxes	Barely[1]	No[1]
Make charitable gifts, directly or in trust	Yes	Yes
Make annual $10,000 tax-free gifts (indexed starting in 1999)	Yes[2]	Usually[3]
Save money up front	Yes	No[4]
Save costs at death	No[5]	Yes
Clear the way for speedy distribution of property after death	Often[6]	Yes
Actual speedy distribution of property	Sometimes[7]	Sometimes[7]
Keep your affairs private	Sometimes[8]	Usually[9]
Provide for continuous management of small business interests	No[10]	Yes
Provide for continuous money management after your death	No[10]	Yes
Duck your creditors	No	Sometimes[11]
Provide for your money to be managed if you become incapable	Usually[12]	Yes
Provide for personal matters to be handled if you become incapable	Yes[12]	No[13]
Stop a challenge to your bequests	No[14]	No[15]
Avoid out-of-state probate	No[16]	Yes
Avoid paperwork	No[16]	No[17]

[1] Probate estates get a $600 income-tax exemption, can choose a fiscal year that defers taxes, and can deduct income set aside for future distribution to a charity. A living trust gets only a $100 exemption, must use a calendar year, and gets the charitable deduction only when the gift is made. It offers no income-tax benefits that can't be matched by a will.

[2] The will itself doesn't do this because you can make gifts only while alive. But the will is no hindrance to making gifts.

[3] Gifts made from trusts within 3 years of death might be included in your estate unless you use so-called Crummey powers (for which, see a lawyer).

[4] It costs more to set up living trusts than to prepare wills—maybe by $500 or so. Trusts require a backup will plus the paperwork for transferring property into the trust and setting up the trust's books. Trusts also raise the cost of preparing your annual tax returns.

[5] Probate usually costs more because of court expenses, but not necessarily a lot more—perhaps just a few hundred dollars. In some states, money-grubbing lawyers and antique court practices do indeed run up the fee. In many other states, however, especially those that have adopted the Uniform Probate Code, streamlined probate procedures let the family settle many estates with zero legal costs. If you consult a lawyer about transferring property into new names and preparing tax forms, it shouldn't matter whether the property is in trust or in an estate: your bill should be the same.

[6] Executors of wills have to wait until their formal appointment, which takes anywhere from 3 days to 3 weeks or more, depending on the court. After that, distributions can begin. Trustees don't have to wait at all.

[7] Executors usually wait until the debts are assessed, bills paid, and taxes wound up, although adequate amounts may be distributed promptly to a spouse or a child needing cash. It's the same for trustees in states where trusts are liable for debts. In other states, trustees may act more quickly; that is, they may try. To get property into the names of new owners takes the same length of time, whether it's being distributed from a trust or a probate estate. When people speak of being "tied up in probate," they often mean that it's taking forever to get title to what they've inherited. That's the fault of the bank or broker responsible for making the name change, or of a dilatory executor, not of the probate court. A trustee can be dilatory, too.

[8] With probate estates, many states require that an inventory of the assets and debts be filed with the court. Others don't. Few of us have to worry about nosy neighbors running down to the courthouse. But this may be an issue for people in the limelight or business owners who don't want their competitors to know their true financial position. Trusts normally don't have to file an inventory.

[9] Unless the trust is contested. If real property is added to a trust, the title company might require the trust instrument to be publicly recorded.

[10] Trusts set up in wills can handle or distribute business interests and provide continuous money management for such purposes as dispensing income to spouses or disabled children. But the trustee has to be appointed by the will and then get geared up to act (unless he or she has already been handling your affairs via a durable power of attorney). Trustees of living trusts are already on the job, although they too will have to get geared up unless they've been acting for you already.

[11] This is a pretty inglorious intent, but in some states, unpaid creditors can't attach the assets in a living trust. In other states, they can. They can definitely go after assets in a probate estate. The executor can be personally responsible for unpaid bills. One reason for delay in distributing probate assets is that the executor wants to be sure that all the estate's bills are paid.

[12] The will itself doesn't do this but it's no hindrance. Your lawyer usually arranges for money management as part of the will-writing process. You'll sign a durable power of attorney naming someone to act for you ("attorney-in-fact") if you're too sick or senile to act for yourself. Some banks, insurers, and brokerage houses are a pain about powers of attorney. They won't recognize them unless they're written on the institution's forms (or on forms legislated by the state). Trustees, by contrast, can't be denied. One wrinkle is that, with a living trust, incapacity has to be confirmed (maybe by a doctor; the trust will specify the rules). Attorneys-in-fact are empowered to act without this step. Assured continuity of management is especially important for people with no family member to handle their affairs.

[13] A trustee can't deal with questions involving Medicare, Medicaid, retirement-plan transactions, family matters, and tax matters, and can't go into the safe-deposit box unless his or her name is on the signature card. All these things can be done, however, by an attorney-in-fact under the durable power of attorney prepared with wills. Neither attorneys-in-fact nor trustees can normally make gifts of your property unless the documents specifically allow it. In some states, the attorney-in-fact can make annual gifts if you previously established the pattern.

[14] Wills are broken for technical errors or because you're shown to have been too ga-ga to know what you were doing. But you can include a no-contest clause, removing a bequest from anyone who challenges your will.

[15] Technical errors in trusts rarely sink them completely. And because living trusts are typically in effect for some time before your death, it's hard to prove you were incompetent when you set them up. In some states, you can include a no-contest clause, removing a bequest from anyone who challenges your trust. The legal period for filing claims against a trust may be longer than for a will.

[16] Property you own in another state will undergo probate there unless it's jointly owned or in trust.

[17] It will take a lot of personal effort to get your assets transferred into your living trust (unless you have your lawyer do it, which runs up your fees). Banks, brokers, and other institutions may demand a copy of the trust to be sure they're dealing with a legitimate representative (you shouldn't have to produce the whole trust; your lawyer will normally prepare an abstract showing the first page of the trust, the signature page, and the pages that list the trustees and enumerate their powers). You'll have to transact business in the trust's name, which sometimes gets complicated. At death, both trustee and executor must, among other things, gather information about the assets, get real property appraised, value closely held business interests, round up and pay all outstanding bills, decide whether assets should be sold, transfer assets into new names, decide when assets should be distributed, make a final accounting to beneficiaries, and file final tax returns. Executors face the extra step of filing the will with the court and complying with any other court rules.

charity invests your money for growth. (4) Now or in the future, the charity starts paying you (and perhaps your spouse or another person) a lifetime income. (5) When the last beneficiary dies, the charity gets the remaining money. (6) If you want, you can replace some of the money you gave away by using your tax savings to help buy life insurance to leave to your kids.

These gifts are irrevocable. You cannot get your principal back. But you'll enjoy the following tax savings:

• *You sidestep the capital gains tax on appreciated property.* Say, for example, that you made a huge profit in stocks or land but now want to switch to a more conservative income investment. If you sell, the federal tax forceps will extract a protion of the gain. But if you give the asset to a charitable trust and the trust sells, it generally pays no tax. It can reinvest all the money and use it to pay you an income for life.

• *You create an immediate tax write-off.* The size of this deduction depends, among other things, on your age and the amount of income you want to receive.

• *You lower your estate taxes.* A charitable gift reduces the size of your estate, saving federal taxes if your net worth exceeds the federal estate-tax exemption.

A complex Rubik's Cube estate requires the expensive services of lawyers, accountants, trust companies, money managers, and expert insurance planners. But for gifts on a more modest scale, the charity can do most of the work and will usually absorb the expense. When you cast your bread upon the waters, here are the ways to guarantee that you'll get some of it back:

The Charity's Pooled-Income Fund, for donors seeking conservative growth. It's similar to a mutual fund and pays you a pro rata share of its earnings, so your income fluctuates but could rise. Minimum investment: usually around $5,000 to $10,000.

A Gift Annuity, favored by older retirees. It pays a fixed income, guaranteed for life and partly tax free. The size of your payout depends on your age. The older you are the bigger your check.

A Deferred Gift Annuity, favored by younger and middle-aged donors. The gift grows in value for several years before the fixed payments start.

A Charitable Remainder Annuity Trust also pays a fixed income. Minimum investment: usually $50,000. Payouts can be higher than with gift annuities, but if the trust runs out of money your income stops, whereas gift annuities always pay.

A Charitable Remainder Unitrust—chief object of affection for inventive lawyers and donors alike. Minimum: usually $50,000. Your income varies, depending on how the investment grows. Payout rates are based on the trust's entire market value, running from 5 to about 8 percent. Savvy investors choose the lower number. It gives them the largest tax write-off plus bigger payouts over time because more money stays in the trust to grow.

A Spigot Trust—star of the show. Minimum: usually $50,000, invested in a tax-deferred variable annuity. This unitrust lets you turn your income on and off. For example, you might forgo payments in the early years while the trust's investments build. Later on you can withdraw extra money to make up for the years you missed. By law, the trust pays out only income, not principal. But in most states, your trust can define income broadly to include your capital gains. Spigots can help fund a wedding, add to a retirement plan, or pay future income to a child.

One warning about a unitrust: Your actual payout depends on its annual investment performance. Take a $50,000 unitrust with a 5 percent payout to the donor that invested in Standard & Poor's 500-stock index from 1969 to 1994. Projecting average annual performance (10.52 percent), you might expect to receive a total income of $95,400. But *actual* performance—some good years, some bad—yielded a total income of only $72,700. As the poet said, everything depends. All that's certain are your tax savings and the pleasure gained from your charitable act. For a true giver, just the latter is enough.

THE WRITER'S MALPRACTICE AVOIDANCE PARAGRAPH

Writers are licensed only by the First Amendment. We can be as pigheaded and opinionated as the vocabulary allows, but we don't practice law. This chapter should give you a general understanding of wills, living trusts, and estate planning. But in practice, the field is pocked with traps that you've never heard of and wouldn't believe if you did. So when I write "see a lawyer" I really mean *see a lawyer*. That's the only way to do this right.

7.

All in the Family

Eleven Checklists for Life's Milestones

Learn from the mistakes of others. You won't live long enough to make them all yourself.

A PREMARITAL CHECKLIST

1. *Talk money.* It's the last taboo. Get a loaf of bread, a jug of wine, and your net worth statement, and make an afternoon of it. What does each of you earn? What do you own? What do you owe? Are there any other sources of income, like a trust? After the marriage, will one spouse quit work? How about after a baby is born? In a two-paycheck marriage, who pays for what (see page 81)? Will you invest separately or together? One bank account or two? Has either of you ever gone bankrupt? Full disclosure is in order. You might bring a copy of your credit history and maybe a second jug of wine.

2. *Talk debt.* How do you feel about it? If one of you has a black belt in credit-card shopping while the other only wants to pay cash, there may be trouble ahead. You're both liable for any bills run up on a jointly held credit card. In the nine community property states (page 85), you're generally responsible for all the debts of the marriage, even those racked up on a separate card.

3. *Talk life insurance.* Who needs it and how much (page 278)? You may have some automatic coverage from your company. If you die, is that enough to support your spouse? If not, buy more coverage right after

the wedding. Two-paycheck professional couples may not need extra life insurance until they buy a house or have a baby because each would be self-supporting if the other one died.

4. *Talk health insurance.* Will you keep separate policies (if you're both lucky enough to have them) or should you consolidate? What maternity benefits are paid if there's an unplanned pregnancy? At some companies, one spouse can drop health insurance entirely and choose another benefit instead.

An older couple might choose to buy long-term-care insurance in case one has to enter a nursing home. That way the other's assets won't be depleted to cover the bills.

5. *Talk savings.* Be idealistic; assume that you'll have some. How much can you put away each year and how will you do it? Go for automatic payroll deduction if your company provides it. Fund to the max any retirement plan where the company matches the contributions you make.

6. *Talk commitments.* Does one of you have an aging parent to care for? Is one of you paying alimony and child support? Does one of you want to go back to school? These will all become joint responsibilities, so walk in with your eyes open. An older man marrying a younger woman will probably have to postpone his retirement. That younger woman can expect to nurse him through his last illness and spend many years a widow.

7. *Talk houses.* If you each own a house or condominium, where will you live? If you don't have a house, do you want one and how do you think you might raise the down payment?

8. *Talk name.* Women (and men) can keep their last name or change it. If you make a change, tell Social Security, all your creditors, and anyone else you do business with. If you don't, just leave things as they are. No law requires a Mr. and Mrs. to have the same name. But a Mrs. with her maiden name should check her Social Security account every 3 or 4 years (page 902) to be sure each year's earnings were credited. Sometimes the IRS fails to pick up your maiden name from the joint tax return and your Social Security credits fall into a black hole.

9. *Talk education.* Say the woman agrees to put the man through medical school if he will then put her through law school. Will he put his promise in writing?

10. *Talk prenuptial agreement.* On the other hand, don't. Lawyers adore these contracts because they simplify divorce, but they're often the enemy of love.

The purpose of most prenups is pretty obvious: one spouse wants to guarantee that, in case of death or divorce, the other spouse doesn't get his or her money, or doesn't get a full spouse's portion. In bad prenups, one plays the bully, the other plays the martyr, and then they wonder why their honeymoon isn't a joy. A few agreements are signed on the eve of the wedding, under the threat that the bully won't show. The other should always call the bluff. Better to learn the bad news now than to start a marriage with a mortal wound. A nice way of putting it is, "I'm sorry, but I couldn't sign an agreement that's unfair to me and to our future children." And who knows? Maybe the bully will repent.

Don't try to write the prenup yourselves. It's too important for amateurs. You each need a lawyer to advise you on every proposal's pros and cons; one lawyer can't ethically help you both. Experienced lawyers will know ways of melding clashing interests. In a second marriage, for example, what if a wealthy groom wants all his property to go to his kids while the bride wants her kids to get at least something out of the relationship? One solution: the husband could buy a life insurance policy on his wife, payable to the wife's children. Another important issue is the retirement account. By law, one spouse has a right to the other's non-IRA retirement benefits. That right can be waived but not before marriage. In the prenup, you'd agree to sign the right waivers after the marriage.

Prenups are dandy arrangements when:

- Both parties want them and both parties think they're fair.
- Both parties have enough income to live comfortably on their own.
- Both parties want to preserve their own wealth for the children of their previous marriages.
- You have a closely held business and don't want to lose part of it in divorce.
- The spouse in the weaker financial position is guaranteed a decent settlement.
- Neither spouse is left high and dry, without an income from any source.
- If you do decide on a one-sided deal, it self-destructs or phases out after the marriage has lasted a certain number of years.
- The agreement covers only money, not where to live or who washes the dishes.

You have to disclose all your assets, understand all the consequences, and sign the prenup freely, without being forced. If those conditions aren't met, the prenup means nothing. If they are met, a prenup is almost impossible to break.

A POSTMARITAL CHECKLIST

1. *Change the beneficiary on existing contracts if you want your spouse to inherit.* Do this for life insurance, pension plans, annuities, living trusts, and Individual Retirement Accounts.

2. *Redo your will.* Or make one.

3. *Set up a joint financial file* (see Chapter 3). You each should know where the other's personal records are.

4. *Consider a joint bank account.* It's useful for household expenses, even if you keep separate his-and-hers accounts for personal spending (page 81).

5. *Give each other a durable power of attorney.* That lets each of you act for the other in an emergency (page 122). Also, consider giving your spouse the right to make medical decisions for you if you're in a coma.

6. *At some point in the future, you might want a postmarital agreement.* It suits a few circumstances, like the couple with children from earlier marriages who couldn't afford to leave them separate property when the new marriage started. Or the person who starts a successful business and wants to be sure of retaining all the stock even if the marriage blows up (the other spouse could give up his or her stock rights in exchange for cash).

A NEW-BABY CHECKLIST

Before Your Pregnancy

1. *Check your medical insurance.* You may have been covered for pregnancy from the day you (or your husband) were hired. Then again, you may not be. You need to find out what your plan will pay. An HMO typically covers most of the cost of a routine birth. Other plans pay the "reasonable and customary" charge in your area, minus the deductible. If your doctor charges more than the plan deems "reasonable," it comes out of your pocket.

2. *Check your other employee benefits.* You may find some gems. For example, if your company employs 15 or more people and covers its workers with disability insurance, pregnancy will be treated as a disability. You might get payments for 90 days or more if your pregnancy is troubled and you have to stay home.

You and your spouse are also entitled to at least 12 weeks of unpaid family leave if you work for a company with 50 or more employees in the local office, have been there for at least 12 months, and work at least 1,250 hours a year. Some states allow even more leave and mandate it for smaller companies. You keep your group-health and disability coverage while you're gone, although it's up to your employer whether to continue your group life insurance, accrued vacation time, and other benefits.

When you return to work, you get your old job back or an equivalent job with the same pay, benefits, and terms of employment, including seniority. That is, unless you're in the top 10 percent of your company's pay range. In that case, your job doesn't have to be held, although companies will doubtlessly accommodate a valuable executive. While you're home, by the way, no additional seniority or pension credits build.

You can take family leave not only for newborns but also when you adopt a child, accept a new child in foster care, or have to nurse a close relative.

3. *Save money.* In most cases, you'll have to pay part of the medical bill yourself. Even if you don't, most insurance policies don't pay a dime until after the baby is born. Your doctor, however, might require you to pay as you grow. Some insurers offer interim payments to consumers in these situations.

If your company offers a flexible-spending account, put away some money toward the pregnancy bills. That's a way of getting a tax deduction for your share of the medical expenses.

During Your Pregnancy

1. *Buy more life insurance.* That's not just a baby you're getting, it's bicycles, braces, and a college tuition bill.

2. *Obey your health plan's provisions.* You might be required to attend prenatal classes or join a maternity managed-care program. If you don't, your insurer might pay less of the bill. You may also have to get special permission for certain procedures such as amniocentesis or ultrasound (or else pay for them yourself).

3. *Find out what your health plan pays for routine births,* then ask your doctor if he or she will charge no more than that amount. Usually not, but you just might be surprised.

4. *Call the hospitals in the area and make an appointment to see the birthing facilities* (that is, if you're not in an HMO that requires you to use a certain hospital). There's a lot of competition for maternity business. Some hospitals offer package plans: bedroomlike birthing rooms, prenatal exercise classes, and a candlelit meal with your spouse.

5. *Find out how long your insurer will let you stay in the hospital.* Normally, it's 2 days for a routine birth and 4 days for a cesarean. Any extra days are on your tab unless your health plan agrees that you need to be in the hospital longer.

6. *Think carefully before choosing a separate birthing center instead of a hospital's birthing rooms.* Centers may charge half the price and are great for women with normal deliveries. But they have no high-tech operating rooms or intensive-care facilities. If something suddenly goes wrong, you're zipped to a hospital, but how long is the ride? Ten minutes? Fifteen? That's not good enough.

Take my friend Judy, whose second baby got into trouble at the very last minute. Her doctor slammed her wheeled bed into the operating room and did a cesarean in two minutes flat. Being in a hospital saved her baby's life. Or take my friend Angela. Right after the normal delivery of her third baby she started to hemorrhage. She might not be alive today if, five minutes later, she hadn't been in the operating room, stanched and sewn up. Some birthing centers are built right into hospitals, which is another matter. But if you're a few minutes away and something goes wrong, the lives of mother and baby are on the line.

7. *Women with paying jobs should be frank with their companies about what happens next.* Some new mothers go right back to work within a few weeks. Some want part-time jobs while their children are small. Some aren't yet sure what they want. It's not fair to your boss to delay a decision or keep mum about what your plans really are. If you'll want a part-time schedule for two or three years, be up front about it. A growing number of companies make such deals with valuable employees.

8. *Write a will or update the will you have.* You'll need a guardian, both for the child and for the child's inheritance. Otherwise, the court might put a stranger in charge of the money—and who knows how honest that stranger will be?

After the Birth

1. *Notify your health plan of the new arrival within 30 days.* Otherwise, the baby might not be covered on your family plan. If you have an individual health plan, you'll have to buy family coverage. If your baby is diagnosed with a serious illness and wasn't signed up for your family plan in time, the plan may reject the child.

2. *Be sure you'll have family health insurance if the mother quits work.* If the mother carried the family coverage on her company plan, and the father has no company plan of his own, ask about COBRA benefits. When a company has at least 20 employees, a worker who leaves can keep that group health plan for up to 18 months at his or her expense (29 months if the worker or a dependent is disabled). But you get this insurance only if you ask for it within 60 days of leaving your job, so don't miss the deadline.

If it's unlikely that the father will acquire a company plan, start shopping immediately for separate family coverage. You'll want to buy it while you're all insurable. If, God forbid, one of you falls sick, you might not qualify for coverage once your COBRA benefits run out.

3. *Start saving for college.* It's not a moment too soon.

A DAY-CARE CHECKLIST

1. *Don't kid yourself about the cost.* Children aren't cheap at any age. Working parents might pay 10 to 20 percent of their income for day care, with infant care the most expensive and hardest to come by.

2. *See what your company has to offer.* Some companies run an information service about the day-care centers in town. Some subsidize places for employees' children. Some provide flexible employee benefits, with day care as an option. Some help with emergency care when your regular sitter calls in sick. A few even run a center of their own. If your company has its head in the sand about child care, form a committee, find out what forward-looking companies are doing (your public library can help), and make a proposal to management.

3. *If your company's flexible-benefits plan includes day care, take it.* You're one of the lucky ones. Part of your pretax salary (up to $5,000) goes into a special day-care account. The company often contributes, too. That account is then used to pay the babysitter's bills. This is the cheapest way of paying for day care because you are using pretax dollars.

4. *If both parents work and you have no flexible-benefits plan, use the child-care credit on your income-tax return.* You can also claim the credit if you're a full-time student or incapacitated. You subtract from your income taxes a portion of your child-care expenses: day care, babysitters, day camp, even the price of room and board at boarding school. Tax credits are normally available for the care of children under 13. But there's an exception. If you have a company flexible-benefits plan (item 3), you have to choose between it and the income-tax credit. You can't use both. For most people, the flexible-benefits plan is better.

5. *Here are your day-care choices, ranked by cost:*
- Your own full-time housekeeper or nanny. Sleep-in help costs about the same as someone who works from nine to five. Besides salary, plan on paying for health insurance, half or all of the Social Security tax, unemployment taxes, worker's compensation in some states, and a paid vacation.
- Day-care centers. They cater principally to toddlers and up.
- Family day care. This describes the neighborhood mother who takes care of several children in her own home. Infants are more likely to be accepted here.
- After-school care for older children. You might find it at day-care centers or in the neighborhood. You should pay no more than half the cost of full-time care.
- Grandma. But give her a break if you can. She has already raised one set of children. Why should she be saddled with another?

6. *Some things to look for in a day-care center or a family day-care home:* a state license if one is required; a stable workforce; clean, happy children; plenty of clean, appropriate toys; a safe place to play, indoors and out; an organized daily child-care plan; friendly people; at least one adult for every 4 infants and one adult for every 6 toddlers; references, so you can ask other parents how they like the center; organized games rather than care-by-TV; after-hours care, if necessary; a connection with a doctor or nurse for medical emergencies; your own child's attitude—does he or she seem to be having fun?

7. *Be prepared for the taxes owed on a nanny's wages.* You don't have to withhold income taxes if you'd rather not, but you MUST pay Social Security and Medicare taxes for every employee to whom you paid cash wages of $1,000 or more. Of the 15.3 percent due, you owe half. The other half is deducted from the nanny's wages. If you pay both halves, the nanny's half must be added to her taxable income for the year. At the end of the year, the nanny gets a W-2 form showing wages earned and Social Security taxes paid.

You also owe federal unemployment taxes if you pay an employee more than $1,000 in a calendar quarter.

All these taxes are paid annually as part of your personal tax return. To be sure you have the money by April 15, ask your own employer to increase your tax withholding. If you're self-employed, increase your quarterly estimated tax payments.

If you don't pay these taxes, it might become a public issue if you're ever a candidate for a cushy political job. Even if you're not, your nanny might rat on you to the IRS.

Ask your state about its own nanny taxes, for workers' compensation and the unemployment fund. These taxes might have to be paid quarterly. You also must pay quarterly if you withhold federal income taxes from an employee's wage.

A CHECKLIST FOR STARTING A BUSINESS AT HOME

1. *A good accountant is a must.* You need to know how to keep your books, what's tax deductible, and what employee benefits your business can legitimately pay for.

2. *Open a business bank account.* Mixing your business with your personal money makes it harder to track your business profits and to do your tax returns.

3. *Get a separate business telephone.* If you're not there, let the call jump to an answering machine or answering service (it's not professional for your kids to answer). Turn down the ringer when you "leave the office." A surprising number of people today leave orders at midnight, expecting to reach a machine. The entire cost of this telephone is tax deductible.

If your home phone is also your business phone, you cannot deduct the standard cost of the first line into the house—only the added business costs, such as call waiting and business-related long-distance calls. You'll also have to document your business use of the telephone.

4. *Get a vendor number from your state* (in most cases, you apply to your state's retail sales tax division). That enables you to buy goods wholesale instead of retail, which is a huge moneysaver. On goods bought for resale, you often pay no sales tax (check the rules of your state).

5. *Apply for a merchant card,* which lets you take customers' credit cards when you make a sale. Banks normally don't give merchant cards to home-based businesses unless they have a long track record. But you may be able to qualify after a year or two through membership in a home-business organization. For a list of such organizations and the services they provide, send $6 to Barbara Brabec, consultant and author of *Homemade Money,* P.O. Box 2137, Naperville, IL 60567.

6. *Prospect for health insurance.* If you're not covered through a spouse and can't find an affordable policy, turn to Barbara Brabec again. She has a $6 list of small-business organizations through which you might be able to buy coverage.

Another angle is to hire your spouse, then set up a tax-deductible medical reimbursement plan (your accountant does it for you). The plan can't include you directly, it's only for your employees and their dependents. You get coverage as a dependent of your employee/spouse. With this plan, you don't have to buy insurance. Instead, your business reimburses —and tax-deducts—your employees' out-of-pocket medical, dental, and psychiatric expenses. That includes any health-insurance premiums you pay, the deductible and co-payments in a group plan, and any bills not covered by insurance. If you have employees other than your spouse, the plan has to cover them, too. This works for all types of small-business arrangements except S Corporations.

7. *Check your business-insurance coverage.* You probably have inventory and business equipment to protect; you're also potentially liable if a client is injured on your property or by using your product. For a craft business, your basic homeowners policy may be enough. If you have a lot of computer equipment, you might add a rider that raises the basic coverage limit. There are separate policies for more elaborate business needs including liability coverage.

8. *Check your local zoning.* Some neighborhoods or apartment houses don't allow any home businesses, no matter how unobtrusive. Others rule out businesses that put up signs or attract traffic. If you're out of compliance, it takes only one unpleasant neighbor to shut you down—so keep quiet about your home office if you don't have to troll for customers locally. If your business isn't a nuisance and your neighbors support you, you can ask for an exception (a variance), even where the law is against you. But you might not win.

9. *Get a separate business computer* with software to track your orders and expenses. If you mix home and business use, you'll have to document the time you spend on business and write off only that portion of the computer's cost. You also don't want your kids and their friends playing with the machine that you use for business, just in case one of them is accident prone.

10. *Find out what business licenses you'll need.* Also check your business tax obligations. You'll have to make estimated quarterly income-tax payments, including the Social Security/Medicare tax on the self-employed.

11. *Keep careful records of your direct business expenses,* including equipment, business-magazine subscriptions, advertising, office supplies, the wholesale cost of any products you resell, employee wages (including wages paid to your spouse and kids), office furniture, business travel, a business car, and business entertainment. Your business driving is deductible at a flat rate per mile plus parking and tolls, but you have to document the miles driven. That means a driver's diary showing the date, purpose, and mileage of each business trip. You can also deduct a portion of your car-loan interest.

If your expenses exceed the income from your business, as they doubtlessly will at first, you can write off those costs against income you have from another job or your spouse's job. That lowers your total taxable income, hence cuts your tax. Your home business becomes a tax shelter.

As a general rule, however, your business has to turn a profit in 3 years out of the first 5. If it doesn't and you're audited, the IRS will probably rule that it's not a real business, it's just a hobby (although you might be given a grace period if you're seriously trying to make a go of it).

With a hobby-business, you can still deduct expenses up to the amount of your net business income. But you're not allowed to tax-deduct additional losses, so your tax shelter goes bye-bye. What's more, all prior tax-shelter deductions will be disallowed. You'll owe back taxes, interest, and penalties. The best way out of this squeeze is to close your unprofitable business. That usually leaves you with most of your past deductions, although you have to repay any write-offs you took for accelerated depreciation. Start-up businesses probably shouldn't take accelerated depreciation, just in case.

12. *Set up a deductible home office.* It can be a room or a portion of a room, but it must be used exclusively and regularly as your primary place of business. Otherwise, it won't qualify for a tax deduction. There's zero write-off for an office that doubles as the dining-room table.

The size of the deduction depends on the percentage of floor space used. If your office takes up, say, 10 percent of your house, you can write off 10 percent of your mortgage interest or rent, homeowners insurance, home maintenance such as housepainting, and the bills for heat, electricity, trash removal, and a home security system. You can also depreciate your office space.

There's a limit, however. Most home-office write-offs can't exceed your net business income. So you get zip if you're running at a loss (the exception: you're allowed full write-offs for real-estate taxes and mortgage interest). Unused home-office deductions can be carried forward and deducted against profits in the future. For more on taxes, call the IRS at 800-TAX-FORM and ask for the free publication #587, *Business Use of Your Home.* Some other useful IRS publications: #334 (on small business), #463 (on travel and entertainment), #535 (on business expenses), and #917 (on auto expenses).

13. *Don't try to tax-deduct your vacations.* Only business trips are deductible. It's legit to combine a business trip with a vacation. To deduct the cost of travel, however, you have to document that the trip's primary purpose was business. Visiting suppliers for a day or having a couple of job interviews is not enough to turn a week's vacation into a business trip. At best, it lets you deduct one day of hotel bills, meals, and some taxi fares. Business conventions are deductible, however, even if you spend the afternoons on the golf course. To tax-deduct a spouse who accompanies you on any trip, he or she has to be an employee of the business and have a legitimate business reason for being there.

14. *Hire a babysitter, even if for only half a day.* A lot of women start a business at home so that they can be with their children. But you can't keep your customers and a three-year-old happy at the same time. Homeworkers often need child care, just as office workers do. And speaking of kids, tell your spouse not to interrupt you unless the house is on fire.

15. *Hire your older kids* and pay them tax-deductible wages instead of an allowance. No Social Security taxes are owed if they're under 18 and your business isn't incorporated. If their wages are low enough, they won't owe income taxes, either. But they have to do real work and be treated as real employees. That means preparing W-4 forms for tax withholding even if you don't withhold, filing quarterly 941 forms showing wages paid to family employees; and issuing annual W-2 forms. Otherwise, their wages may be disallowed on audit.

16. *Set up a retirement plan.* Every year you can put up to $2,000 of your earnings into a tax-deductible Individual Retirement Account. If you hire your spouse to keep the books or do other part-time work, he or she can start an IRA, too. For that matter, even the kids who work in your business can start IRAs to help tax-shelter the money they've earned (although they'd also want some pocket money, too). If your business gets bigger, you might start a Simplified Employee Pension (page 862) or Keogh plan (page 863), which would let you put even more money away. These plans are available through banks, brokers, and mutual funds.

17. *Avoid the prepackaged businesses that are flogged in get-rich seminars and on cable TV.* The promoters tend to overcharge for the books, manuals, and computers they sell you. And they overstate your chance of success. They may also encourage you to tax-deduct personal expenses, which could lead to a nasty audit. Your best shot is a business that grows out of a past job or hobby you like and are good at, and where you can make the professional contacts you're going to need.

A CHECKLIST FOR KIDS' ALLOWANCES

When parents teach their children about money, their questions center on technique. When should an allowance be paid? What should I let my kids do with their savings? Should I pay them for doing chores around the house?

But technique isn't nearly as important as the values you communicate. All your cash transactions with your kids tell them what you feel about money. If you're uncomfortable talking about it, your children may not learn what you intend.

There's no right or wrong way of teaching children good values and sound financial habits. Different families make different choices, and they all work. What's most important is for parents to agree. Only then can they send consistent messages to their children. Here are some ideas for you to play with:

1. *Pay allowances early, starting as young as 6 or 7.* How large should the payment be? Large enough for your children to think they have money to squander, but not so much that you'll be upset when they do. Surveys show that children who get no allowances receive roughly as much money from their parents as children who do. But those on a regular paycheck learn more about managing money.

2. *Tie allowances to a budget.* Ask your children to estimate what they'll be buying and set the payment accordingly. Don't underestimate their cost of living. Sodas are a lot more expensive than when you were a kid.

3. *Many parents tie allowances to chores.* Some put price tags on specific jobs and pay for performance every week. Some provide basic pay plus extra money for doing certain nasty chores, like taking out garbage. Some give weekly pay with a side agreement on what the child is expected to do. Your choice will depend on your principal goal. Are you teaching your children to manage money? Or is the objective to show them that they don't get something for nothing?

4. *Consider a three-tier system for allocating your children's cash—* one jar for spending money, one for savings, one for church or charities. Savings work best when a child has a specific objective, such as a jacket that costs more than you're willing to pay. Consider paying "interest" on the money by adding a nickel for every dollar left in the savings jar each week. As for charities, many families tithe, putting 10 percent of their income toward good causes. Children should be encouraged to choose a cause of their own.

5. *Treat the supermarket as a school.* Give the kids a grocery cart, a list, and $20 and see how far they can make their money stretch. Send them searching the aisles for goods that you have cents-off coupons for. Ask them to pick the best buys.

6. *Don't lie to your kids.* Make a clear distinction between what you can't afford and what you don't think is worth paying for. If they still want it, let them save for it. If it violates your principles, just say no.

7. *By their mid-teens, start giving your kids a sense of what life is like by having them pay the family bills for two or three months.* Sit down

together with the bills and show them how to write the checks for the light, heat, mortgage, rent, phone, water, and credit cards. They'll find it instructive to see how fast the bank balance drops.

A CHECKLIST FOR LIVE-IN LOVERS

1. *Keep all property separate at the start.* You don't know how long this relationship will last. If one of you is wealthy, sign a non-Marvinizing agreement (page 84) to avoid demands for palimony if you break up.

2. *Decide how to divide the household bills.* Typically, you'd contribute according to your income. If you provide 40 percent of the mutual income, you'd pay 40 percent of the household expenses.

3. *If you buy a house together, agree—in writing—what happens if you separate.* Do you sell the house and split the proceeds? Does one partner buy the other out, and who sets the price? Even if you sell to your partner, the bank can keep you on the mortgage, so you're liable if your partner fails to make the monthly payments. For more on this, see page 88.

4. *See if your employer gives health benefits to domestic partners.* Most don't, but the number that do increases every year. To qualify your partner, however, you might have to agree to be financially responsible for him or her—raising the palimony risk. You may also owe taxes on your partner's benefits.

5. *If you want to leave property to your partner, have a lawyer draw up a will or living trust.* This is no time for a do-it-yourself document, especially if your parents hate the relationship. A will or trust you write yourself is often easy to attack. If a court knocks your partner out (or if there's no will or trust at all), your property goes to your parents or other close relatives.

While you're getting a will, get a durable power of attorney so your partner can act for you in an emergency. You'll also want a health-care proxy (page 124), allowing your partner to deal with your doctors if you're in a coma.

6. *If you adopt a child together, who will be financially responsible?* Sign an agreement that you both will pay. Both parents are always responsible for their children under the law, but if one of you walks out, a legal agreement can make it easier to collect child support. You definitely need an agreement if there's only one parent (for example, if one of a lesbian couple went to a sperm bank). Otherwise, your partner could walk out, leaving you on the hook and the child in a hole. If your partner wants to keep your child if you die, he or she may have to adopt. Otherwise, the court may give the child to someone else, even though you named your partner the guardian in your will.

A CHECKLIST FOR PEOPLE WHO MIGHT BE LAID OFF, BUT THEN AGAIN MIGHT NOT

1. *Secure your home.* Be sure to refinance when interest rates fall to minimize your monthly mortgage payment. And consider taking a 30-year loan for its flexibility. To some borrowers, that's surprising advice. A 15-year loan costs a lot less because of its lower interest rate and because you'll repay it in half the time. But you're locked into higher monthly payments —not a good idea if your job is at risk. So follow this strategy instead: Take a 30-year loan; make larger monthly payments than the bank requires (in fact, pay as if you had actually taken a 15-year loan); if you keep your job, you'll get rid of the mortgage early; if you lose your job, you can cut your monthly payment to the minimum level that the 30-year loan requires.

2. *Secure your life insurance.* Your company may give you up to $50,000 of free term insurance, plus the option of buying more through payroll deduction. But you generally can't take that policy with you when you leave your job. If you should become uninsurable, you'd be stuck with converting your company policy into an individual one—and believe me, that doesn't come cheap. It's smarter not to buy extra coverage through payroll deduction. Use that money to buy insurance outside the company, which gives you a policy you can keep no matter where you work. The outside policy might even cost you less.

3. *Your consumer and home-equity credit.* Open a home-equity line of credit if you have home equity, but don't borrow against it. This will become your safety net if you're fired and need quick cash. If you already have consumer debt, start a ferocious plan to get rid of it. You don't want to face stiff home-equity and credit-card payments if you're out of work.

4. *Your ready savings.* The rule of thumb calls for having 3 to 6 months' worth of living expenses in the bank. But that can be dumb if you're also carrying credit card debt. Say that your debt costs you 16 percent while your savings earn only 3 percent. You're losing 13 percent a year. Clear out your savings account and use it to pay down that expensive debt. Then keep your credit cards and home-equity lines clean. If you're fired, you can always draw on your credit lines again. *Those* are your true emergency funds. You should be safe if you've arranged for 6 to 12 months' worth of guaranteed borrowing power.

5. *Your retirement savings.* Keep on putting money into your 401(k) or 403(b) account. Retirement contributions reduce your taxes, give you hope for the future, and may attract company matching funds. In order of importance, funding your tax-deferred retirement plan comes even before paying down consumer debt. If you leave your job, take your 403(b) plan with you. Your 401(k) can be rolled into an Individual Retirement

Account. You can borrow against the 403(b), if the plan allows it, or make withdrawals from your IRA (paying taxes and a 10 percent penalty if you're under 59½).

You can borrow against your 401(k) while you're still at work, but don't do so if your job is at risk. When you leave the company, loans generally have to be repaid immediately. If you don't have the cash (or can't borrow it), the loan will be treated as a withdrawal, subject to taxes and penalties.

6. *Your spending.* Look for ways to cut back before a job loss or salary reduction forces your income down. Living on 10 percent less than you make isn't downward mobility, it's common sense. For help on financial planning after you've lost your job, see page 173.

AN ELDER-CARE CHECKLIST

1. *Don't swoop down on a capable parent.* Most older people are perfectly able to manage themselves. In fact, their finances may be in better shape than yours. When help is truly needed, don't go overboard. It might be enough to find a good home health service or make a suggestion about certificates of deposit. Respect your parents' wishes; don't push them around. If your parent loses track of the bills, however, or worries obsessively about money, don't hesitate to take more responsibility. When one parent dies, keep an eye on how the other handles the finances. Find out where your parent keeps all the financial records in case you have to step in fast.

2. *Don't miss any tax write-offs.* If you support (or help support) a parent, you may be entitled to a dependency exemption. If you have to hire help to take care of your parent so that you can go to work, you get the tax credit for dependent care (it's the same as the child-care credit).

3. *Check your employee benefits.* If your company employs 50 or more people in the local area, the same law that gives new parents family leave (page 133) gives you time off from the job to care for a parent who has a serious health condition. If there's a flexible-benefits plan, you can generally arrange to pay for elder care with pretax dollars (it works like child care; see page 136). A few companies even offer elder-care consultations as an employee benefit.

4. *Call the Eldercare Locator:* 800-677-1116, sponsored by the U.S. Administration on Aging and several nonprofit senior-citizen groups. The locator sends you to a community agency, which tells you how to locate elder-care services such as adult day care, senior-citizen lunch groups, home-delivered meals, home health care, chore services, financial aid, legal services, hospice programs, and transportation. The local agency may also be able to find you a care manager, who will visit your parent, assess any health and homemaking needs, and suggest services that can help. There may be a waiting list for assessments, but give it a try.

Also try the Office for the Aging in the capital of the state where your parent lives. It will refer you to a local Area Agency on Aging or other assistance agency for free booklets and advice. For other local organizations, check the Yellow Pages under "Elderly" or under your city's government listings.

Don't fail to send for the free *Caregivers Resource Kit* (D15267), American Association of Retired Persons Fulfillment—EEO1046, 601 E St. N.W., Washington, DC 20049. Among other things, it contains the valuable booklet *Miles Away and Still Caring.*

5. *Square away the finances.* If you're going to handle your parent's money, you'll need a durable power of attorney (page 122) and the authority to write checks on his or her account (page 122). Or perhaps you might become the trustee of your parent's living trust. Arrange for the bills to be sent to your address, or for the bank to pay regular bills automatically. Arrange for the pension and Social Security checks to be paid directly into your parent's bank account. Reorganize the investments to produce maximum income with minimum risk. Find all the financial documents—like stocks, deeds, life insurance policies; and personal documents—birth certificate, marriage license, and military discharge papers. Cancel the life insurance policy if it's no longer needed. See to the income taxes and get your parent an up-to-date will. These matters are best settled while your parent is sound of mind. If confusion ever descends, so may suspicion about money and an instinct to shut you out.

6. *Make a safety check of your parent's house.* Are the lights bright enough (older people need extra illumination). Can you get rid of throw rugs? Should the doorsills be removed (they're a major cause of falls)? Does your parent need a stool in the tub, a higher toilet seat, a stair elevator?

7. *See to your parent's health.* Make sure that he or she eats. Help arrange regular medical checkups. If you can, see that the doctor's orders for taking pills and other medications are carried out. If your parent moves slowly, suffers pain, or forgets things, don't write it off as "old age." Many such problems can be corrected.

8. *Deal with Medicare.* This is a kindness that will qualify you for sainthood. Doctors and other providers of medical services submit your parent's Medicare claims. But if your parent will pay part of the bill, it's important to see that the claim was properly paid. You always have the right of appeal when Medicare rejects a bill, but the process is aggravating and time consuming. Sometimes the doctor or hospital makes an error when a bill is submitted, and when you call the hospital the billing office may blandly deny it. I've known of cases when it took a call to a congressman's office before Medicare would pay attention. If your parent is in a Medicare HMO, make sure he or she is getting enough treatment, especially for chronic illnesses.

To back up Medicare, be sure that your parent has a single, comprehensive Medigap policy if needed (page 395). Cancel any duplicate policies. Seniors with low incomes and few assets qualify for Medicaid.

9. *Shoot down the scams.* The elderly are to crooks as meat is to hyenas. Some older people will send money to every "charity" that asks, buy a dozen worthless health-insurance policies, and fall for any quick-buck or free-gift scheme that comes along. Work with your parent to solve the problem. Maybe you or a neighbor can help your parent go over the mail. Maybe your parent will agree not to make a donation or spend more than $500 without telling you. Maybe you should handle the checking account.

10. *Get help from willing neighbors.* Line up a teenager to mow the lawn, weed the garden, and shovel snow. Line up a neighbor to check on your parent if he or she doesn't answer the phone when you call. Line up someone to run the little errands that you can't if you live far away. Offer to pay a caregiver who will drop in, shop, do a wash, and fix a meal.

11. *Make a list for yourself of your parent's current support system—* doctor, lawyer, banker, broker or planner, insurance agent, church or temple, neighbors, friends.

12. *Consider a private care manager.* This new and rapidly growing field is peopled with nurses, social workers, psychologists, and self-styled gerontologists. For a fee in the $150 to $350 range, they'll visit your parent and make a report. For additional fees (perhaps $50 to $125 an hour), they'll find home health workers, recommend nursing homes, pay regular visits, and handle emergencies. Your first stop for referrals: local nursing homes, doctors, and hospital social-service offices. Second stop: the National Association of Professional Geriatric Care Managers, 1604 N. Country Club Rd., Tucson, AZ 85716, (520) 881-8008. Send a self-addressed, stamped, business-size envelope and you'll get a free list of members in your area. NAPGCM members pay $25 to join and have to meet certain professional standards. Third stop: Children of Aging Parents, 2761 Trenton Rd., Levittown, PA 19056. For the names of care managers in your state, send CAP $2 plus a self-addressed, stamped envelope.

Warning: This field is totally unregulated. So talk to the care manager in person and check every claim on the résumé to see if it's true. Interview at least three of the care manager's clients, get a written plan of action for your parent, nail down costs, and don't choose anyone who rubs you wrong.

13. *Don't shrink from the nursing-home decision.* This may be your best option if your parent can't manage alone, can't afford a companion, can't find a home-sharing arrangement, and—for any number of reasons— can't move in with a family member. Make the same decision for a parent who already lives with you if his or her physical or mental problems exceed your ability to cope. Nursing homes are not snake pits. Although some are indeed mediocre, you'll also find some excellent places where the patients are clean, cheerful, mentally and physically active, and watched over by caring staffs. Ask a doctor, nurse, or the social-service worker at a hospital

for recommendations and visit them all. Don't feel guilty about it! Many parents who fight the idea find a nursing home congenial once they've settled in and made some friends. And even if they don't, some things can't be helped.

14. *Bring up the question of a living will and health-care proxy* (page 124). What is your parent's opinion about artificial life supports if he or she is terminally ill?

15. *Collect information for the obituary.* Many families put out wrong information because they're hazy on the details of their parents' lives.

A DIVORCE CHECKLIST

1. *Follow the money.* Modern divorce is not about who's the meanest or who slept where. It's mainly about children and money—how to split up any property and what to allocate for alimony and child support. The financial division won't be fair unless all the income and property is on the table.

If you don't know much about your spouse's finances and fear that he or she won't pay, go ahead and snoop. Any financial document can be a clue to income, assets, and debts. Look for:

• Your spouse's payroll stubs. They show whether money is being deducted for savings and retirement accounts.

• Current statements for any retirement plan held by your spouse: Individual Retirement Account, Simplified Employee Pension, Keogh plan, 403(b), 401(k), and company pension and profit-sharing.

• The most recent state and federal income-tax returns. Try for returns from at least the past 5 years. If you can't find copies, get them from the IRS or the state tax office. You have an absolute right to copies if you filed a joint return. There's no charge for an IRS transcript of your returns for the past 3 years (that's a computer printout showing what was on the original return). For actual copies of the returns, or returns for the 2 earlier years, you're charged $14 each. Make your request on Form 4506.

• A copy of all financial statements filed for all recent mortgages or business loans. Again, you have an absolute right to copies of anything you co-signed. If you don't want to mention divorce, you can tell the lenders that you're updating your personal financial statement and have lost the original.

• Copies of appraisals on the house, furnishings, and jewelry, done for insurance purposes.

• Deeds, bank statements, check registers, loan documents, credit-card statements, mutual fund reports, statements from stockbrokers, statements of employee benefits, insurance policies. These not only document assets, they also help establish your marital standard of living.

• A copy of your credit report, which will show transactions on jointly held accounts. Some credit bureaus will also send your spouse's report, so you can look for separate accounts. But don't ask to have your spouse's report sent to a different address; the credit bureau won't do it.

• A list of all your debts, secured and unsecured. They, too, need to be divided. Even if your spouse takes them as his or her obligations, however, you may remain liable to the lender for payment (page 217).

Each spouse should have a copy of all these financial records. Neither one of you should spirit them away. If one of you plays nasty, so will the other. You'll throw away money on court battles and wind up testing the limits of your mutual capacity to hurt.

2. *Hire an investigative accountant if your spouse owns a business or you believe that he or she is hiding assets.* Wholly owned businesses are especially notorious for shielding income and assets from public view. One accountant who specializes in divorce cases says that underreporting deprives spouses (usually wives) of 20 to 50 percent of their rightful share of property and support. You need someone with a well-developed sense of the absurd to examine your spouse's business tax returns and to press for documents that show more fully what the business earns. (Sorry, but you've nothing to gain by vindictively calling the IRS. If your spouse underreported personal income, and you signed the joint income-tax return and benefited from the tax evasion, the IRS generally holds you equally liable for the taxes owed. There's something called the innocent spouse rule, but it's rarely applied.)

If you worked in your spouse's business—even if unpaid—document what you did and the hours you worked. If your relatives helped your spouse get started, prepare to prove it. While you're working there, try for a fancy title, like vice president. Evidence of your contribution and position may raise the payout you receive. In many states, however, any ownership interest you get in the business as part of the divorce wipes out separate payment for unpaid work.

3. *Protect your flanks.* You'll need personal money to tide yourself over the months it takes to reach a settlement, so start putting part of each paycheck into a separate account. You might move half of the cash in a joint bank account into your separate name. But don't be greedy. Take only your share, explain what you've done, and take over part of the bills. Once the divorce is under way, disclose exactly what assets you have.

Next, tell your stockbroker and mutual fund companies, in writing, not to sell jointly owned investments unless your signature is on the order. Tell the banks that your signature is needed for withdrawals from your joint accounts. Tear up any power of attorney that gives your spouse power over your assets, and tell your banks and brokers, in writing, not to accept any copies. Consider destroying any health-care proxy (page 124) that gives your spouse the right to make medical decisions for you, and putting that power in other hands. Open your own safe-deposit box and keep your valuables there. Don't co-sign any new loans with your spouse.

Photocopy the latest credit-card bills so it's easy to tell who's responsible for any future spending.

Write to your creditors and close joint home-equity credit lines and credit-card accounts (registered mail, return receipt requested). Also state that you won't be responsible for future debts added to the card. Tell your spouse what you're doing, by the way; it's bad form to leave him or her with a card that some clerk at a cash register will confiscate. Closing the cards is normally in both spouse's interest unless it leaves one of you without credit.

If you alone signed the credit-card application, making your spouse an authorized user, you can cancel your spouse's card while keeping yours intact. If you both signed, however, the account will be closed and you'll both have to apply for credit all over again. If one spouse doesn't qualify for unsecured credit, he or she should apply for a secured card (page 223).

When an account is closed, some creditors may require that any existing debt be paid in full. If you don't have the cash, you and your spouse could divide the joint credit-card balances and transfer them to your separate cards. If debt is left in a closed joint account, you're both responsible for paying it—on time and in full.

When you decide on who should pay the mortgage and the auto loans, ask the lender to transfer the debt into that spouse's name alone. There's no guarantee, however, that the lender—especially a mortgage lender—will agree. If you can't move the debt or refinance it into a separate name, you'll both remain responsible for it. If neither of you pays, it will be a blot on both your credit reports.

Start a child-care diary, noting which of you fills the children's various daily needs. It may be helpful in a custody battle—although that kind of warfare hurts the children above all.

If you have no income of your own, you're at a disadvantage. Every nonworking spouse needs personal savings for emergencies like this. You might be able to stake yourself by pulling cash from a credit card or home-equity line of credit. But don't be surprised if your spouse refuses to make monthly payments on those loans. You're better off applying to the court for temporary support. Be prepared for a fight if yours is a difficult divorce. Temporary-support hearings can be as intense as a full trial.

4. *Count on a reasonable share of the reported property if there is any.* In community property states, the assets of the marriage are normally divided in half. Spouses fight over which those assets are and what they're worth. In other states, the division turns on the length of the marriage and each spouse's contribution, professionally or in the home. The law calls for "equitable" division regardless of fault; in practice, that comes pretty close to equal division. Inheritances and assets owned before marriage usually

stay with the spouse they came with. The same may be true for rents and profits from premarital assets as long as they haven't been mixed with marital assets. Unwinding such assets is tricky. You need an expert.

5. *Don't forget the pension.* In many marriages, the only assets are the house and the pension or retirement savings. Spouses are generally entitled to a share of each, although not necessarily a half share. When you both have retirement savings, both plans—his and hers—will be on the table. Your lawyer should call in an expert to check the value of the pension, propose the best method of division, and be sure the rules are followed. If you can get only a future allocation from the pension plan, not a current payout, you might prefer to take property of equivalent worth. Here's what you generally can expect:

• Individual Retirement Accounts and Simplified Employee Pensions are divisible at the time of divorce, with a written agreement or court order. Your portion can be transferred into an IRA in your own name, with no current taxes due. You can tap the IRA for instant cash, but that triggers income taxes plus a 10 percent tax penalty if you're under $59\frac{1}{2}$.

• Company 401(k) plans, including the employer's contribution, are generally divisible right away. You may take any payout option the plan offers: a lifetime annuity, payment over 10 or 20 years, or a lump-sum distribution. If you cash out right away, you'll owe income taxes but no 10 percent penalty. If you want to keep the tax deferral, you can roll the lump sum into an IRA, but any later withdrawals are subject to the 10 percent penalty. Attorney Marcia Fidis of Pasternak & Fidis advises that you figure out how much cash you'll need from the plan, take that immediately, and roll the rest into an IRA.

Alternatively, you can keep your portion of the money in your ex's 401(k) in your name and invested in the plan's mutual funds. If you want the money later you can usually take it, subject to the 10 percent penalty. Some plans make you wait for payout until your ex leaves the job or reaches age 50. Check all the rules before deciding.

The same rules that apply to 401(k)s also apply to your company's profit-sharing plan, if there is one.

• 403(b) retirement plans, typically held by teachers and employees of nonprofit institutions, can also be formally split as part of the divorce agreement. But they're not rolled into IRAs. Whether you can tap the money (paying taxes and, maybe, penalties) depends on the plan, the investments, and your age. Your lawyer should contact the plan's custodian to find out what your options are.

• Traditional pensions, known as defined-benefit plans, generally won't pay until your ex reaches retirement age—typically, 55 and up. At that point, payouts are possible even though your ex is still at work. The pension might be payable in a lump sum, which can be rolled into an IRA. More often, it's paid as a monthly income for life. Your checks come directly from the plan. They don't pass through your ex's hands. Some of the smaller defined-benefit plans may give you a lump sum at divorce.

• Non-IRA plans for the self-employed or partnerships, commonly called Keoghs, follow the rules for 401(k)s or for traditional pensions, depending on the type of Keogh.

To nail down a share of a 401(k), 403(b), profit-sharing, or pension plan, you need something called a qualified domestic relations order (QDRO), issued by the court. (The order has slightly different names if it's served on a federal civil service or military pension plan.) It spells out exactly what you will get. Well-drawn orders also state how the payment will be figured (including whether you get interest on the amount) and what you get if your ex should die. A QDRO must be approved by the pension-plan administrator as well as the court, to be sure that it follows all the plan's rules. If it doesn't, the plan will not pay, no matter what the divorce agreement says. Be sure that the QDRO is signed at divorce. Otherwise, your rights might be jeopardized.

The QDRO makes you a plan beneficiary. Well in advance of the divorce, your lawyer should get you a summary of how the plan works along with a current benefit statement. After the QDRO is delivered to the plan administrator, you should start getting annual statements. Unfortunately, plans often don't send the statements to ex-spouses. Try to get your name on the list when the QDRO is approved. Otherwise, send a certified letter to the plan administrator, citing your right to information under ERISA (the pension law) Section 105. (Federal pension plans aren't covered by ERISA.)

If your spouse has stock options, an excess-benefits plan, a supplemental-benefits plan, or any other "nonqualified" plan, negotiate for a share of it, too. (A plan is nonqualified when the company makes no current payment but promises the full benefit when the employee—usually an executive—dies, retires, or leaves the job.) But you can't get your share of these valuable plans directly from the company because they don't have to follow the QDRO rules. The divorce agreement has to call for your ex to pay you these benefits when he or she receives them.

6. *Don't forget the professional degree.* Remember the Ph.T. (Putting Hubby Through)? If the wife worked in order to get her spouse through medical or law school, she may, in some states, be entitled to share in the income likely to be produced by that degree. And vice versa, in case of a Pw.T. But you may have to show actual dollars spent, such as a co-signed student loan. Alternatively, the court may take your whole marital history into consideration when awarding support, without focusing on who did what for whom.

7. *Don't expect permanent alimony.* Spouses with decent paychecks get no alimony. Spouses with tiny paychecks or none at all may get only temporary support while they go back to school or learn a job skill. This can be tragically unfair to middle-aged homemakers, who will probably

have a hard time finding well-paid work. If the marriage lasted more than 10 years, however, the court may order alimony when the other spouse can afford to pay. In several states, older women with long-term marriages have a right to support for life. Even so, the wife's standard of living usually falls after a divorce while, over time, the husband's improves. (Increasingly, a dependent husband gets temporary or permanent alimony from an employed wife, but bias against male dependents still prevails in many courts.)

8. *Parents without custody should expect generous child-visitation rights.* Both courts and lawyers have grown more sensitive to the rights of noncustodial parents, typically fathers. Custody of young children still tends to go to the mother, by family agreement. But fathers are pursuing and winning more cases, especially if the mother wants to move to another state. Mothers who will put their children in day care while they work also have weaker claims, as do mothers with low incomes and gay and lesbian parents (although many states now bar discrimination based on sexual preference).

9. *Parents with custody shouldn't have to settle for nominal child support.* Federally mandated child-support guidelines direct how much of a parent's income has to go toward maintaining the children. Some states look only at the income of the noncustodial parent, others look at the parents' combined incomes. If your current award is below the guidelines, you can get it raised.

In one interesting twist, a mother with a job who decides to quit and stay home with her children may not be able to get extra child support. The court may base her expected financial contribution on what she could have earned had she stayed at work. Her ex-husband wouldn't have to pay more just because she decided to give more time to the kids.

You might try to negotiate cost-of-living adjustments (COLAs) for long-term child-support payments, so your children's standard of living won't fall. If you don't have a COLA in your divorce agreement, ask your state's Child Support Enforcement agency about getting the payments raised to today's guideline levels. You should find the phone number under the state or county listings for social-service agencies.

What if your ex doesn't pay? Call the state Child Support Enforcement agency. The state can also help you trace a parent who skipped. To apply for help will cost you zero to $25. If you're not on welfare, states may charge a modest amount for their legal services, based on your ability to pay.

All states will enforce a court order to withhold child-support payments (and sometimes alimony) from a parent's paycheck. They can tap your ex-spouse's state and federal income-tax refunds. Some states will even order a spouse to pay through a court trustee to simplify collection. The process of obtaining an order, however, is often slow. It's especially hard to nail a parent who deliberately moves around.

Even if your ex doesn't pay, you're not allowed to withhold visiting rights. Conversely, the law doesn't allow you to withhold payments if your ex is making it tough for you to see the kids. Custody and support are two separate parts of the agreement.

How well these rules work depends on where you live. Some states have terrific child-support procedures and a large enough staff to keep up with all the new cases coming in. Many other states, however, are desultory and understaffed. Nevertheless, try the public child-support office before paying the large sum that a private lawyer would want.

The government publishes a free *Handbook on Child Support Enforcement*. Get it from the Office of Child Support Enforcement, 370 L'Enfant Promenade S.W., Washington, DC 20447.

An organization that helps women collect their child-support awards is the Association for Children for Enforcement of Support, 2260 Upton Ave., Toledo, OH 43606 (or call 800-537-7072). ACES will work with you directly or put you in touch with a local chapter. It publishes a booklet called *How to Collect Child Support,* which, at this writing, costs $9.39.

You're most apt to collect your child support if you're on good terms with your ex-spouse and he or she sees the children regularly. In most states, it's still hard to get money from a spouse who's determined to resist.

The courts generally won't adjust an alimony award unless there's a major change in circumstances (some agreements state that alimony can't be modified). Property settlements usually are cast in stone unless you can prove that they were obtained through fraud or duress.

10. *Reach an agreement on who pays for college.* Child support stops at 18 unless the parents agree to continue. Some dependent wives elect not to give up other financial support in exchange for a college agreement, trusting the husband to see that the kids get a good education. But be sure to plan for the tax deduction for college-loan interest (page 544).

When it comes to awarding financial aid, schools generally ignore what the court papers say. State colleges and universities tend to base awards on the income of the custodial parent (and stepparent, if there is one). By contrast, most private colleges and universities base financial aid on both parents' incomes (including stepparents), regardless of whom the child lives with.

11. *Don't borrow against your house if your marriage isn't going well.* Your house is often your major asset. What happens if a wife (for example) agrees to sign for a home-equity line of credit and her husband (for example) takes the money and spends it? Her share of the home equity has been eaten up and she might not be able to get it back. In a case like this, the judge should order the husband to repay, but you can't assume that's going to happen. Take big loans only if you're sure that you'll both be there to pay them off. If the marriage looks shaky, you'd be smart to freeze or cancel the credit line. Either one of you can usually do so unilaterally.

12. *Don't hit below the belt.* Don't cancel all the joint credit cards unless your spouse has a card of his or her own (or can qualify for a new one). Assure your spouse that, during the divorce negotiation, you'll continue to cover the household bills that you've always paid. Don't hide or destroy financial records. Don't hijack valuables out of the house and claim they've been lost. Don't steal money. Integrity not only facilitates divorce, it also helps the children recover. Remember that divorce, unlike marriage, really does last until death do you part.

13. *Hire a lawyer who believes in settlement.* A peaceful solution can keep you out of court, hold down your costs, and leave your relationship reasonably cordial. When looking for a lawyer, talk to friends who have been divorced for a while and have some perspective on what they went through. Meet with the lawyer before you proceed. It's important to like the person who represents you.

Don't hire a "bomber" who gets his or her kicks by hanging up your spouse by the thumbs. It may feel good at first but, in the long run, will hang you, too. Bomber tactics lengthen the negotiation, tempt you into dishonorable acts, ruin any hope of an amicable relationship after the divorce, and fatten the lawyers' bills. Don't hire a bomber even if your spouse has one; they'll play well-rehearsed war games at your expense. Just be sure that your own lawyer is familiar with divorces. Bombers eat general practitioners and corporate lawyers for lunch, but experienced divorce lawyers can hold their own.

The same lawyer should never represent you both. In theory, this could work if the split is amicable, both parties can support themselves comfortably, you're in perfect agreement about who gets what property, and no children are involved. Even so, most lawyers would think it unethical. You each need separate representation.

What raises the price of divorce is arguments. The more you quarrel over property, the more you struggle over payments, custody, and visiting rights, the more you delay, prevaricate, and punish each other, the more you'll pay. You'll wind up spending your kids' college educations on lawyers' fees. Try to put together some ground rules for conduct even before you see your lawyers.

Special mediation services exist to help resolve differences between you and your spouse. If you use one, see a lawyer first, so you'll know your legal rights and the tax issues involved. You should also check in with the lawyer before major agreements are reached. Mediation-cum-legal-advice should be cheaper than letting your lawyers do all the work. But beware the mediator who strong-arms an agreement by beating on the more compliant spouse. If you agree to a poor or misguided settlement, it may be too late or too difficult to start negotiating again.

14. *Get good tax advice if there's a lot of money at stake.* You need to know what's deductible and what's not, and what the after-tax value of

your settlement is. For example, if you accept highly appreciated stock, you'll pay taxes when you convert it to cash, so it's not worth as much as you thought. The same could be true of your home. If you sell at a profit, and lived there for fewer than 2 of the past 5 years, you're taxed on the gain. Ditto if your profit exceeds $250,000 (if single) or $500,000 (if married), no matter how long you owned.

15. *Get financial planning advice right from the start.* How much will you need to support yourself? Do you really want the house, or is the mortgage and maintenance too much for you to carry? Is your spouse proposing that you get the risky investments while he or she keeps the safe ones? Can you live on the settlement that's proposed, not just this year but 10 or 20 years from now? A good financial planner can help you think through these and other issues during the negotiation.

16. *If you work for the federal government, get an attorney familiar with its benefits.* Ex-military, foreign service, and civil service spouses qualify for a variety of benefits, depending on how their divorce is structured.

17. *Do it yourself, with help.* In some states, lawyers have published do-it-yourself divorce guides. They work best for working couples who are ending their marriage politely, with minimal assets and no children to consider. But before you make the settlement final, pay a visit to a lawyer just to be sure that you haven't overlooked anything important.

18. *Don't lose your health benefits.* Wives are no longer dropped automatically from their husbands' company health plans, and vice versa. If the company employs at least 20 people, you can stay in your ex-spouse's group plan, at your expense, for up to 3 years. This is called your COBRA benefit. To arrange it, notify the employee-benefits office, in writing, within 60 days of your legal separation or divorce. If you can't afford the premiums, you might try to get your spouse to pay as part of the divorce agreement. You normally lose COBRA coverage if you remarry and come under your new spouse's insurance, or get a job that covers you with another plan. Your ex's plan would have to keep you only if you're ill and there's a waiting period before the new plan covers your preexisting conditions.

19. *Get life insurance on your spouse for as long as alimony or child-support payments are due.* You need an inexpensive term-insurance policy that runs out when the obligation does. To be sure that the policy stays in force and that you're the beneficiary, own it yourself and make the premium payments. Your spouse can reimburse you through regular support payments (put this in the divorce agreement).

20. *Collect all your Social Security benefits.* That you're divorced doesn't cut you loose. You are generally entitled to benefits on your ex-spouse's account as long as the marriage lasted for at least 10 years. Social Security looks first to your own account to see how high your personal benefits are. If you'd collect more as an ex-spouse, that's what you'll get. Here's when you can stake a claim on your ex's account:

a. For retirement benefits: (1) You're at least 62 and haven't remarried. (2) Your ex-spouse is also on Social Security. (3) If your ex is eligible for benefits but not collecting them, you can still collect as long as you've been divorced for at least 2 years.

b. For survivor's benefits, after your ex-spouse's death: (1) You're 60 or older and haven't remarried. (2) You're any age, unmarried, and caring for the deceased worker's child who is disabled or under 16. In this case, you can collect even if you were married for less than 10 years. (3) You remarried after age 60 but are entitled to a better Social Security benefit from your ex-spouse's account than from the account of your new spouse.

c. For disability benefits: (1) You're at least 50 and unmarried, and your ex-spouse is dead. (2) You're permanently and totally disabled under Social Security's hard-nosed rules. (3) You remarried, but did so after age 50 and after becoming disabled. In this case, you can still collect from your ex's account if that payment is more than you'd get from the account of your new spouse.

What if your ex-spouse remarries? Both you and the new spouse are eligible for exactly the same benefits. Neither of you takes one dime away from the other.

21. *Don't take a note from your spouse for money owed if you can help it.* If there's no option, see that it pays a competitive interest rate and is guaranteed by a performance bond or a lien against property. You need some easy way to collect in case he or she declines to pay.

22. *Don't challenge a premarital or postmarital agreement* unless you can truly show that you were bullied or defrauded into signing and harassed into keeping silent about it; or that, by failing to disclose some significant assets, your spouse led you to a wrong decision. Judges are reluctant to revoke these contracts except for a very good reason. It usually does no good merely to argue that the contract is "unfair." Presumably, you knew that when you signed it.

23. *Change your beneficiaries.* As soon as you separate, take your spouse's name off your savings account, brokerage account, retirement accounts, pension plan, will, and living trust. Whether to change your life insurance depends on whether you expect the insurance policy to be included as part of the financial settlement.

24. *Do it right the first time.* Except for alimony and child support, divorce agreements usually can't be reopened unless you both agree.

A CHECKLIST FOR NEW WIDOWS AND WIDOWERS

1. Get multiple, certified copies of the death certificate—perhaps 20 or more. This chore is usually handled by the funeral director. You'll need the

copies for claiming insurance proceeds and Social Security benefits, and for transferring property into new names.

2. Inventory the safe-deposit box.

3. Find the will and any trusts. Decide whether to handle the estate yourself or to hire a lawyer to help. If there's an outside trustee, talk to that person about how the assets should be managed.

4. Find any life insurance, including company insurance, and put in a claim immediately. An insurance agent or lawyer can help, or call the insurer for instructions. Don't make an irrevocable decision about how to handle the policy's proceeds until you've had time to think about your financial affairs (page 322).

5. If you're covered under your spouse's company health insurance, find out immediately about keeping the policy. Under the so-called COBRA rules, most companies that employ at least 20 people have to keep you in the plan, at your expense, for up to 3 years (page 386). But you *must* notify the company, in writing, within 30 days of your spouse's death. When you hear from the health insurer, you must say yes to the policy within 60 days. If you're not protected by COBRA, you may be able to convert the group policy into individual coverage. If you pay for your own family health insurance, tell the insurer that your spouse is dead. Your insurance premium will drop.

6. Find the rest of the assets—deeds, securities, bank accounts, contracts, partnerships, retirement accounts, annuities, deferred salary, stock options from previous employers, money lent to a third party. And the liabilities—mortgages, personal debts, business debts. Go through the checkbooks and bank statements for clues to property you didn't know about.

7. Pay all bills on time if they relate to your personal life. You don't want to lose your good-credit history or have a credit card withdrawn. Business bills should go to the person handling that side of the estate.

8. Claim any benefits you're entitled to: Social Security (page 901), railroad retirement, civil service, veterans, travel-accident insurance.

9. Write to your spouse's employer to see how much money is due. There may be company life insurance, deferred salary, stock options, retirement funds, commissions, a bonus, or accrued vacation pay. Labor unions may pay benefits, too. If your spouse died from a work-related injury or disease, you may be entitled to payments from workers' compensation.

10. Inspect all your spouse's papers and don't throw anything away. They may relate to assets or liabilities you knew nothing about. If the papers were in disarray, promise yourself that when you die your family will find everything in order.

11. If your spouse owned a business, be sure the administration is in competent hands. Consult with the business's attorney and accountant.

12. If your spouse died in an accident, talk to a lawyer about whether you have a legitimate claim for wrongful death.

13. Reconsider your will or living trust, or draw one if you haven't. Give someone your durable power of attorney (page 122) and your health-care proxy (page 124).

14. *Make no irrevocable decisions!* Don't sell the house, change your investments, invest in a business, or give your insurance proceeds to a financial planner to manage. Keep your cash in a bank and your hands in your pockets until the emotional storm has passed. You'll make better decisions once you've had time to assess your situation.

STEP 2
FINDING THE MONEY

Most people don't come to financial planning until they have some extra money. They start with the question, How should I invest?

You should start earlier. The right question is, How will I get the money that I will then wonder how to invest? You need a way to acquire cash.

You can win your kitty in a lottery. You can hope to marry well. You can wait for the ground to open before you and a delicate hand to thrust $100,000 into your waiting wallet. Or you can cull the money from what you earn. Save it or borrow it. You are the source. If you do something you'll have something. If you do nothing . . . (finish the sentence yourself).

The earlier this idea hits you, the wealthier you can be. Time is as much a money machine as earning power. Funds put away when you're 25 are worth far more than funds put away at 40, which in turn are worth more than funds put away at 55. So don't just sit there. Read.

8.

A Spending Plan
That Works

How to Take Charge of
Your Money—At Last

*If all of us had every dime that we've wasted in our lives,
we'd be a nation of millionaires.*

Make yourself a spending plan. Not for discipline, not for tidiness, not because your mother told you to. Make it for your own sake. That's the only way to coerce your money into doing what you really want. I've lived with spending plans and I've lived without. I come back to them every time I'm in a pinch.

A Spending Plan Always Works. It captures the cash that slips through your fingers, unnoticed, every day. It discriminates between what's important to have and what you buy because it's there. It rescues you when your income falls short. It lets you save money painlessly, and that's the truth.

A plan is an active strategy for getting wherever you want to go. It starts with a general idea: "I want to live better." "I want to get out of debt." "I want to invest more." "I want to retire early." Then it breaks up that dream into small, specific, everyday actions that you can accomplish one by one.

Plans always have to be written down. And they need simple measuring posts to show how you're doing. Imaginary plans that you follow in your head will always be no more than that: a walking dream. They won't get you anywhere.

To start, take this test: Write down where your money went last month. Don't do it from memory; use your checkbook for reference.

Compare the result with your take-home pay. Odds are that you can't account for all the money. In fact, there will probably be a substantial gap between what you earned and what you can remember spending—money that seems to have gone up in smoke. Some of it did.

Here's another test: Of all the things you bought last month, how many could have been put off for 30 days without doing any harm? And then put off for another 30 days? You probably could have postponed quite a bit. In fact, now that you think of it, some of what you bought may not be worth the debt you're carrying.

Now the final test: How inviolate, really, is your "fixed-expense" list? Can you cut your taxes, pay less for insurance, refinance your mortgage to get lower payments, find a cheaper apartment, sell your second car? (Spending $15 on taxis every working day might cost $3,600 a year—a fraction of the price of owning, insuring, gassing, and repairing an automobile. And think of the savings if you took a bus.) If you paid off more debt, you would reduce your interest payments, giving you more cash in hand.

I am not advising that you lower your standard of living. Good financial planning starts from where you are and makes things better. On the other hand, neither should you feel locked into your current way of life, no matter how immutable the bills may seem. There are, as a science fiction writer would say, *alternative realities*. And you are going to find them.

Truth in authoring compels me to say that this process carries another name. An awful name. *Budgeting*, the dreaded B word, smelling of shortages, self-denial, and regret. A budget seemed to say, "I can't afford the things I want," and on that depressing thought good intentions usually founder.

A spending plan, on the other hand, says, "You can get what you want just by figuring out how to do it." It's a positive step that allows for choices and new ideas. It puts you in control.

SEVENTEEN REASONS TO HAVE A SPENDING PLAN

1. To find out what you're spending money on. Few of us know.
2. To extract more money for savings and investments.
3. To figure out how to quit a job, move, build a house, have a baby.
4. To get out of debt.
5. To show the spouse who doesn't pay the bills where the money goes.
6. To live on your income.
7. To prepare for big expenses like college, a new house, a major vacation, a facelift (that's probably not covered by your HMO!).

8. To retool your life after losing a job or a spouse, or becoming too sick to work.

9. To keep money from slipping through your fingers.

10. To determine the minimum income you can live on, so you can handle a cut in earnings, erratic paychecks, a divorce, a period of retraining for a different job, early retirement.

11. To know how you'll handle unexpected expenses.

12. To be able to buy what you want.

13. To prepare for harder times.

14. To make the best use of the money you get in better times.

15. To get the whole family pulling in the same direction.

16. To put a tool in your hands that can change your life.

17. To put your new financial plan into action. Which plan? The one you're developing as you read this book.

THREE REASONS NOT TO HAVE A PLAN

1. You're rich enough to buy anything you want and still have plenty of money left over.

2. I forgot the other two.

A FREE LIST OF EXCUSES FOR DUCKING THIS JOB

1. *Making a spending plan takes too much time.* (It will take no more than a weekend of thinking, research, and erasing what you just wrote down, followed by a few minutes every day for a month or so. In the beginning, you'll spend an hour or two, once a month, to see how you're doing. After that, it's just as easy as spending money without a plan.)

2. *I won't keep it up.* (But you might. Most people do, once they decide they want better control of their money, because this is the only way to get it. As soon as your plan is up and running, there's not a lot more to do.)

3. *I don't want to live in a straitjacket.* (You won't. Your plan will move and breathe. If it pinches, you can change it. It will always include a provision for buying some of the things you really like, so you won't feel deprived.)

4. *I hate arithmetic.* (So do I. So what?)

5. *None of my friends do it.* (Too bad for them.)

6. *I budget in my head.* (And all your good intentions run out your ears. You're sure that you have an extra $55 this month for a turtleneck sweater. Then you discover that you can't pay the dentist. Besides, I'm not asking you to budget. I'm asking you to *plan*.)

7. *I'm too tired, too young, too old, too busy, too poor, not poor enough*. My husband, wife, daughter, parakeet won't cooperate. It won't work, can't work, would drive me bananas if it really did work. I'm too dumb, too smart, too short, too tall, too fat, and can't give up smoking. (You can always think of reasons not to take charge of your life. But if you don't mean to change, why did you waste your money by buying this book?)

HOW TO BEGIN

Write down all your cash expenditures every day for a month. And I mean *everything*. Carry a notebook in your pocket or purse so that no expense will slip away. Start with "Monday, April 8" and go on to "Tuesday, April 9." Day by day by day.

Some things may seem too trivial to bother with. Coffee, newspapers, flowers, an apple. But look at it this way: If you saved $5 every day for a year you'd have $1,825. That would nearly fund an Individual Retirement Account or give you two nice weeks in Maui watching whales. Small expenses are not trivial.

During this month make no effort to change your spending habits. You're simply taking a snapshot of how you live now.

Take one weekend to go through your checkbooks and itemized bank card statements for the past 6 months. Write down the size of your regular monthly bills: utilities, mortgage, rent, car payments, day care. On another sheet, write down your intermittent expenses: clothing, life insurance payments, birthday presents, car repairs, dentist bills.

Some spending is hard to reconstruct. Maybe you've been throwing out old credit-card bills. Maybe you haven't been noting on your checks exactly what the money was for. When your records are bad, it might take 2 or 3 months to learn where all the money goes.

Once you've got the information, organize it into categories, showing how much you spend every month. Laundry. Groceries. Drinks. Books. Cosmetics. Gasoline. Bus fare. Credit-card debt. Tennis. Haircuts. Restaurants. Pets. Children's clothes. Your clothes. Doctors. Real-estate taxes. Movies. The more precise the better. You need a detailed picture as a starting point.

Construct a chart of how you spent your money, month by month, over the past 6 months. Assume that the walking-around expenses that you recorded in your notebook will always be the same.

Now write down your monthly income, minus federal, state, and local income taxes, Social Security taxes, and any other automatic deductions due to employment, such as union dues. Include all your income: wages, annuities, pensions, dividends, interest, rents, everything.

Compare your spending with your income and don't panic if you're in the red. That's what a spending plan will fix.

The snapshot you took may surprise you.

Many people learn that, except for credit-card repayments, they are spending less than they earn. They're short of money only because they are doing battle with old debt. Once they pay it off, they'll have a substantial sum to invest.

Others are astonished at how much they are spending on particular items—health clubs, books, fast-food restaurants, beauty salons, tools, fishing. You must spend money on yourself; otherwise your spending plan will be too disheartening to stick with. But maybe you can pick one thing and cut down on others. Exercise with weights at home, use your library card, make your own hamburgers, ski cross-country instead of downhill. That frees up cash for something else.

It is not unusual to discover that you are better off than you thought. Fear often arises from ignorance. Once you take an organized look at your situation, you might see that your worries have no basis in fact.

On the other hand, if you really are in trouble, you'll learn by how much.

Above all, you'll finally find out where the money goes because most of us don't have a clue. With that snapshot as a guide, you are ready to channel some of your spending in new directions.

WHAT DO YOU REALLY WANT?

First, you want to know what you're redirecting your spending *for.* What do you want from your money that you're not getting now?

Maybe you need to be out of debt. Maybe you need college money, for your children or yourself. Maybe you want to build a rainy-day fund or save for a down payment on a house. Maybe you want to get serious about a retirement fund.

Your goal won't always be the same. The important thing right now is to focus on a limited and specific objective that you can achieve.

Write it down at the top of your spending plan. "Goal: Save an extra $100 a month." Or, "Goal: Put an extra $100 a month toward paying off the Visa card." Take that money right off the top of every paycheck. Then rearrange the rest of your spending to fit within the income that's left.

DRAWING YOUR PLAN

The plan (page 166) will look very much like a b----t, but it differs in four ways:

First, you enter your current goal at the top of the page. That will be funded every month before you pay any other bills. Don't even give it a moment's thought. Set the money aside, and then start to juggle. Just having that goal transforms a b----t into a plan.

Second, start a column called Current Spending. Here, you write down what you've been spending in every category. This is your benchmark—the money habits you have now, which you want to change.

Third comes your Spending Plan. Play with your income and expenses and write down where you'd like the money to go.

Fourth comes the payoff—the column called Actual. Once a month enter what you actually spent in each category. If you're spending more than you planned for telephone bills or sports, you may have to strengthen your resolve. On the other hand, maybe your telephone goal was unrealistic and should be changed. After several months you'll arrive at a plan you can live with. Then it becomes a habit.

Some Technical Matters

Start with a 6-month plan to see how it works. One year is too long for someone just learning where the money goes.

Make your categories specific. For example, instead of lumping all your medical expenses together, create separate columns for Doctor, Dentist, Therapist, Medicines, Veterinarian. Instead of Utilities, write Water, Electricity, Heat, Telephone.

To cut spending, squeeze a little something out of every category rather than slashing just one or two. Even if you're trimming just $10 or $20, that's money you'll have for something else. Don't eliminate categories; in most cases, you'll be kidding yourself. Above all, don't wipe out all the things that make you the happiest. You need to get some fun from your money, to have the incentive to carry on. Every member of your family also needs a personal playpen.

It helps to enter your spending at least weekly so you won't lose track. Subtract each week's expenses from the budgeted monthly amounts so you'll know how much you have left. At the end of the month, carry forward to the next month the money unspent in any category. For example, if you budgeted $100 for entertainment and spent only $80, start out next month with $120. If any category gets bigger and bigger each month, cut back your targeted spending there and add the funds somewhere else. If most categories come in on target but a couple always fall behind, go over your budget again and trim.

The categories in the sample Spending Plan on page 166 are just a suggestion; most plans contain many more.

When a bill is paid quarterly, budget for one-third of it every month. For the first two months, that money stays in your checking account; in the third, you'll have enough for the payment. If you're an irrepressible

SPENDING PLAN

Month _____, 19 _

Total income _____

Special goal _____

Reserve fund _____

Expenses	Current Spending	Spending Plan	Actual				Total
			Wk. 1	Wk. 2	Wk. 3	Wk. 4	
Savings							
Mortgage/rent							
Heat/light/water							
Telephone							
Life insurance							
Health insurance							
Disability insurance							
Homeowners insurance							
Auto insurance							
Auto loan							
Credit-card payments							
Back bills							
School/college							
Child care/support							
Groceries/drinks							
Clothing							
Doctor/dentist							
Veterinarian							
Gasoline							
Bus/subway/taxi							
Restaurants							
Entertainment							
Sports/pastimes							
Books/magazines							
Repairs/upkeep							
Housecleaning							
Personal care							
Laundry							
Contributions							
Furniture							
Birthdays/holidays							
Vacation							
Walking-around money							
TOTALS							

spender, write a monthly check for one-third of each quarterly bill and deposit it in your savings account. Or subtract one-third of the cost from your check register every month without actually writing a check. If you don't see the money, you won't spend it (I hope).

Handle clothing the same way. Budget a certain amount every month and let it build up. Some months you'll exceed your plan, but over a year it should even out.

Unexpected expenses, like car repairs or an operation for a sick dog, should be listed in their proper categories so you'll know how much you've spent. But you cannot specifically budget for them. Instead, put some money for these bills into a modest reserve fund every month.

You will have some bothersome spending overruns. Don't quit; just try again. Spending plans don't prohibit splurges. They merely show you—graphically—that for every extra purchase you make, you have to cut spending in another category or go further into debt. We're talking *choice*. It may take awhile for your real desires to overcome your trivial ones.

Add up your spending every month to see how you're doing. Juggle the categories; some will be high, others will be low. But it shouldn't take long to develop a framework. If you overspend in one area in April, you'll have to find a place to compensate in May.

SPENDING PLANS FOR WORKING COUPLES

Some couples pool their money. A single, unified spending plan is all they need.

Other couples keep their paychecks separate. They might need three plans: one each for husband and wife to keep track of their personal expenses and set their personal saving and spending goals, and one for shared household expenses, to which each contributes.

CAN ANYONE LOVE A DECIMAL POINT?

Some people love keeping records to the penny, and may the God of the Green Eyeshade be with them. Others manage quite nicely by rounding off. Rounding off a lot. A lucky few don't even care if the columns add up as long as they're (probably) not too far wrong.

Keep your accounts however it suits you. The objective is mainly to *keep accounts*. You'll learn more from setting up detailed budget categories than you will from struggling over the math.

WAYS TO SHIFT SPENDING

To get more money for something you want, you have to spend less on something else. That's all there is to it. You can climb the highest mountain, consult the wisest wizard, and you'll get the same answer.

You can borrow the money, but then you'll have even less to spend because there's another loan to repay. That's like having another mouth to feed. Too many mouths, and pretty soon you are really poor.

Everyone finds different ways to save. But here are some surefire places to look:

Bury your credit cards. Charge nothing. Interest payments will then melt away. (Okay, charge *something,* but not much.)

Declare a new-clothes moratorium until you have your present wardrobe paid for.

Quit smoking. You'll save on cigarettes, life insurance, doctor bills, breath sweeteners, and soap to rub off the yellow stains.

Drink wine instead of hard liquor. Cheap wine.

Rent, don't buy, things you rarely use. Or split the cost with a neighbor (even-steven on the snowblower and all repairs).

Buy toilet paper labeled Toilet Paper. Buy peanut butter labeled Peanut Butter. If you hate the generic stuff switch back to the higher-priced brand names, but try the cheap ones first.

Shop with a list and stick to it. No impulse purchases, unless . . .

. . . unless there's a terrific sale. Then buy by the carton. You say you can't be bothered saving $6.25 on tuna fish in bulk? Do you realize that you need $250 in the bank to *earn* $6.25?

Own an economy car. It runs on economy gas, with economy insurance and economy repairs. Make that a *used* economy car.

Use up your savings to get out of debt. Only losers pay 18 percent on their credit cards so they can keep earning 5 percent on their bank accounts.

Never pass up a garage sale. (But pass up most of what's there. It's hard to believe what people buy at garage sales and then chuck into their own garages.)

Don't trust any bills, especially those that are computer-generated. If you take the time to check for errors, you'll find a lot of overcharges.

Stop subscribing to magazines you don't read. That not only saves you money, it also saves the space next to your bed or chair where they pile up.

Refinance any high-rate loan. But use home-equity loans to eliminate credit-card bills only if you're swearing off your credit card. Otherwise, you'll run up your credit cards again, winding up with two debts where there used to be one.

Serve punch and hors d'oeuvres at parties rather than drinks and dinner. People drink less punch because the cups get sticky.

Learn to love your neighbors. With them, you can pool services like babysitting and transportation. You can even swap skills: you do my taxes, I'll paint your garage.

Track down all local resale shops, discount centers, and factory outlets.

Vacation at off-season rates. The sun is just as hot the week before Memorial Day as the week after.

Sell something that's expensive to keep, like a second car that you don't use regularly to drive to work.

Call your mother in the evening, at cheap rates. Better yet, write, don't call. Or don't write. Maybe she'll call you.

Go to the movies instead of buying a VCR. If you already own a VCR, rent videos instead of going to the movies. Or get a library card and borrow videos.

Maintain your car properly so you can keep it longer.

Eat more meals at home.

Ask your doctor to write prescriptions for generic drugs.

Look for cheaper insurance. You can probably find a company that charges less than you're paying now. Take a larger deductible on your fire and auto coverage. Cancel collision insurance on an old car.

Make your own gifts. Or perform a personal service instead of purchasing a *thing*.

Look for cheap entertainment. Museums. The zoo. Parks. Walks. Library books. Picnics. Parades. Friends.

Do your own home repair, car repair, sewing, painting. I reupholstered a chair in my Attic Furniture days and it came out fine.

Pay cash for gasoline instead of using a credit card. You might save up to 5 cents a gallon at many service stations.

Eat more meatless meals. They're good for you.

Switch to lower-watt bulbs in all but your reading lamps.

Exercise at home instead of at a health club. Or join a Y.

Shift your credit-card balances to a lower-rate card, then use the interest savings to pay down the debt.

Clip cents-off coupons. There's no point throwing them out with the trash.

E-mail your friends and your kids instead of calling long-distance.

Join a home-swap network for cheaper family vacations.

Find new uses for things instead of throwing them out. Start seedlings in the cutoff bottoms of milk cartons. Twist newspapers into cylinders for kindling. Maintain a useless-objects shelf for items that might be reclaimed someday. The handier you are, the more money you'll save.

When you think you're at rock bottom, with all of the air sucked out of your budget, go back for one more try.

• • •

BUT . . . none of these ways to use money are right or wrong. Your spending reflects your values, just as my spending reflects mine. There's no ideal budget or ideal percentage of income to put toward this or that. Your goal is to live within your income *your* way.

WHEN ALL THIS TALK FALLS ON DEAF EARS

Maybe you don't budget because you think you're okay. Every month you meet all your bills and even have some dinners out. But then a big expense comes along, like a vacation, and you don't have the money to pay for it. So you put it on a credit card and, bit by bit, your debt builds up.

You aren't saving money because you can't resist spending what's in your checking account. And you can't bear to rein yourself in by writing down every little expense. Ugh, ugh. For you, the best strategy is to spirit some cash out of sight (unseen means unspent). Do it by setting up three accounts:

1. *Create a retirement investment account.* If you're lucky, your employer will deduct money from every paycheck automatically. Second choice: Have your bank deduct money every month from your checking account and ship it to a mutual fund. There, you can invest it in an Individual Retirement Account, Keogh plan, or ordinary investment account. Third and worst choice: write your own check to a mutual fund each month. (Maybe writing your own checks will work, but you know from experience that any money in your checking account will often be spent on other things.)

2. *Create a big-bill account* at a money-market mutual fund or a bank money-market account. This is for bills that turn up now and then, like quarterly life-insurance premiums, vacations, estimated taxes, Christmas presents, household repairs. Go through your checkbook for the past 6 to 12 months to gauge what you're spending annually on these things. Then divide the total by the number of paychecks you get every year (by 12 if you're paid monthly, 26 if you're paid biweekly). Write a check for that amount every time you're paid and immediately deposit it into your big-bill account. When those bills come in, you'll have the money to cover them. This takes some fine tuning but works well. It's the closest to true budgeting you'll have to do.

3. *Keep a checking account at a bank, S&L, or credit union.* Your paychecks go into this account. Your deposits into the big-bill account are taken right out, along with any automatic investments in a mutual fund. Everything left is yours to spend on your regular household bills. You won't need a budget for this money. You'll continue your old habit of spending

everything that you see in your checking account—and surprisingly, you'll still pay all your bills and have dinners out. Try it and see. What's going into the other accounts is money that used to be wasted on things you can do without.

WHEN THERE REALLY IS *NO MONEY*

When you're truly living on a wing and a prayer, it is fruitless to look for meaningful budget cuts. You'll have to increase your income in some way. A second job. A better job. A session of night school, to qualify for a different line of work. A sideline business run from home.

If those routes aren't practical, try for a job with better employee benefits. A company puts money into your pocket by paying most of your doctor bills as surely as it does by giving you a raise.

HOW LONG, OH LORD?

Keep up your monthly budget for as long as it takes to get more from your money. By then, you should know how to do it without always putting pencil to paper.

As your goals change, however, you may need new spending plans to achieve them.

Your first year's aim might be quite modest: "Reduce by half my credit-card debt," achieved by doubling payments every month. Having succeeded, you'll get more ambitious: "Carry no debt and build a cash-reserve fund." Then you'll move on to: "Save 10 percent of my income."

Along the way you'll have mini-goals, like: "Buy a VCR." "Spend a long weekend in New York and go to the theater." Write these goals down, allocate money to them, and check them off as you succeed.

Sometimes you force a goal on yourself—for example, by buying a house. Meeting your mortgage payments then becomes your first priority. All the rest of your spending shrinks.

Once you've got a plan that works, there may be no reason for keeping monthly accounts. Start over again, however, if:

- Something changes in your life.
- You begin to feel that you're losing track.
- You notice that you can't meet expenses without putting down a credit card and stretching out payments. That means you're spending more than you earn.

SPECIAL PROBLEMS WITH IRREGULAR INCOMES

Neat monthly spending plans may sound hopeless to people without a regular paycheck: freelancers, project workers, consultants, small-business owners. But you can do it easily. Start with the premise that your *total* income is more predictable than when your paychecks will arrive. And budget this way:

Estimate, conservatively, what you're likely to earn this year; estimate monthly income by dividing by 12. Using that income, develop a regular monthly budget. Whenever a fee comes in, put it in the bank and spend it according to your budget. If there's money left over, leave it alone; it might be a while before another check comes in.

If you fall short, you might have to dip into overdraft checking or run up some debt on your credit cards. If this happens more than once, reconsider your basic budget. You may be living higher than you can afford. When another check comes in, your first priority should be getting rid of that debt. Then build a reserve fund of 3 to 6 months' living expenses in a bank or money-market mutual fund. With a fully funded reserve, you can start putting extra money into personal consumption and longer-term savings and investments. You also need at least 3 months' reserve in your business account. When you're flush, try to set up a home-equity line of credit, also for emergency cash.

If, after a few months, it appears that your income will fall short for the year as a whole, revise your spending plan downward. If you're doing better than expected, revise it upward. Whenever you dip into your reserves, replace that money before doing extra spending of any kind.

Many workers with regular paychecks also have irregular total incomes because part of their pay comes from bonuses or incentive plans. In this case, draw a budget based on the pay that's guaranteed. Your bonus can pay for next year's extras—additional investments, a vacation, a new living-room rug. Don't count on a bonus for *this* year's extras. You might not get as big a payout as you hoped.

All workers with irregular incomes should hold their fixed expenses down. This year might rain money. But if you move into a bigger house, you might not be able to keep up the mortgage in a drought.

PLANNING WHEN TAXES AREN'T WITHHELD

People paid by fee, with no income taxes withheld, are true heroes if they make it to April 15 without spending any of their tax money. You have to pay estimated taxes every quarter. But it's all too easy to fall behind. If you're too far behind, you'll owe a penalty on top of the tax.

How to solve this problem? Look at last year's tax return to see what percentage of your total income went for taxes. Take that percentage off the top of every check you get. Earmark it for the government and tuck it into a savings account. Only your net spendable income, after taxes, should land in your checking account.

PLANNING FOR A RAISE

Will you gross an extra $2,000 this year? If you spend it all, you'll be worse off than you were before. A $2,000 raise may leave only around $1,200 in the bank after state and local income and Social Security taxes. Spending the gross puts you into debt—which is why so many people feel poorer and poorer as their incomes rise.

Anyone allergic to saving money should regard a raise as a Main Chance. Just pretend it didn't happen. Keep on living the way you did before and put that extra money in the bank. Or buy one thing and save what's left. Many companies these days give bonuses instead of raises. That's an easy chunk of money to save (if you haven't spent it in advance).

PLANNING AFTER THE PINK SLIP COMES

At first, you may panic—especially if you've never lost a job before. You're spending every penny you make. How can you live on a nickel less? This very month the bank will foreclose. Your creditors will cart off your furniture. You'll join the homeless. Your children will have to live on a grate.

Not so. You have far more financial resilience than you imagine. Here's what to do:

1. *Find out how your ex-employer can help.* A firm that employs 20 people or more has to offer to keep you in the group health plan for up to 18 months, at your expense. You generally have 60 days to decide, from the day you're notified about the option. By all means sign up unless you can be insured immediately under a spouse's plan. Also, ask for your severance check to be paid in monthly installments; if you take it all at once, your tax bracket might jump. Consider leaving your 401(k) with the company, as long as you can tap it anytime you want. You have troubles enough without fretting over finding a place to invest those funds. You can move the money later, when your life is more settled and you're able to make long-term decisions again.

2. *Draw up a bare-bones spending plan.* Cover the mortgage, car loan, utilities, gasoline, food, life and health insurance, the minimum on credit-card bills, and the expenses of looking for another job. At first, budget only for these. Put all other bills aside. Job-hunting expenses, by the way, can include your golf-club membership; it's important to keep up all of your social and business contacts. If you couldn't continue your company's health insurance plan, ask your insurance agent for a low-cost, short-term policy. If you carried your life insurance through your ex-employer, buy some low-cost term coverage. Your family can't afford to have you go without.

3. *Add up what remains of your regular income*—a second paycheck in the family, union benefits, interest from savings, dividends, unemployment insurance. Don't reject unemployment payments. Many white-collar workers are ashamed or afraid of standing in unemployment lines. But times have changed. Whole echelons of middle management have been laid off. Your ex-employer pays taxes to assure that you get some financial support between jobs, and you should take every nickel due. You'll find your peers in line behind you.

4. *Compare your remaining monthly income with your bare-bones spending plan.* If you can cover your basic bills, you're in good shape. If not, write down how much more money you're going to need each month.

5. *Add up all your lump sums of money, not counting tax-deferred retirement accounts:* a final paycheck due from your company, severance pay, savings, investments. A portion of this cash reserve can be used each month to fill the gap in your spending plan. Your goal, at this point, is to find a way to cover your essential bills for at least 9 months, and longer if you think that your job hunt will be a tough one. If you have to sell stocks or mutual fund shares, dump those with losses or small capital gains (for how to specify these shares, see page 637). Hang on to those with big capital gains to avoid the tax you'd owe on the profits.

6. *If you have enough income left over,* after covering bare-bones expenses, allocate it to other expenses.

7. *Try to reduce those expenses that look immutable but might not be.* For example, if your child is in day care, private school, or college, tell the school about your financial emergency. You'll rarely get a moratorium on payments, but you might be offered more scholarship aid or a low-interest loan. Take the same approach to any other service that you feel should not be interrupted, like dental procedures or children's music lessons.

8. *If you need more cash, borrow it.* Take loans against your credit cards, home-equity line of credit, securities, and insurance policies. But don't clean yourself out. You may need some money to relocate.

9. *Don't take cash out of retirement accounts unless absolutely necessary.* Ideally, you will leave your 401(k) with your employer for now, so it can be managed efficiently. Or you'll roll the money into an Individual

Retirement Account to avoid current taxes and penalties and keep your investment building up. But you might not have the luxury of keeping retirement savings whole.

If you have to make withdrawals from a tax-deferred plan, you'll owe income taxes on what you take. There's also a 10 percent tax penalty in the following situations: on withdrawals from an IRA if you're younger than 59½, and on withdrawals from a 401(k) or 403(b) if you left the company when you were younger than 55.

You can duck the 10 percent IRA penalty by setting up a withdrawal plan that will pay you a steady monthly income based on your life expectancy (see page 1025). The withdrawals must continue for at least 5 years *and* until you reach 59½. After that, you can stop and let your IRA build up again. But avoid this deal if you expect to be reemployed soon. You don't want to be locked into monthly withdrawals for years after it's necessary.

Best advice for handling your tax-deferred plan while you're unemployed: Move a portion of your investments out of stocks and bonds and into the plan's money market mutual fund. You don't want to risk losing money in the market if you might need this cash to pay your bills. If you do have to tap your retirement account, draw from the money market fund and take only as much as you need each month. That holds down taxes and penalties. When you get a job again, you can put what's left of your money market investment back into stocks and bonds.

If you know for sure that you're going to need some of the money in your 401(k) or 403(b), and you're between 55 and 59½, you might as well take it out of the plan immediately. That avoids the 10 percent penalty. If you roll your 401(k) into an IRA and then take some money out, the penalty is due.

10. *Do not pay what you can't afford to pay!* That sounds obvious, but it's a basic rule of survival that laid-off workers violate all the time.

Don't use your severance check to pay off your credit-card debts; conserve that cash and pay only the minimum each month. Make no payments on postponable bills if doing so means that you'll run out of money within a few months. Write to your doctor that you'll pay in the future with interest. Let the school tax slide and accept the late-payment penalty.

At the start, keep current with your credit cards and mortgage in order to keep your credit history clean. Some employers check the record when they vet you for a job.

But if months drag on with no sign of work, you'll have to reconsider your credit-card expenses, too. Slow pay hurts your credit rating, but it's far more important to conserve your savings in order to keep the lights on, the telephone working, gas in the car, and food on the table.

When you don't pay, however, you must tell your creditors what you're doing. Write each one a letter explaining that you have been laid off and cannot currently cover your bill. But say that you will, absolutely, resume making payments in full (including interest and late charges) when you get work. Another approach is to say that you will pay $5 or $10 a month as a token of your good faith. You might also add a note to your credit file explaining that unemployment has temporarily hindered your ability to pay.

Many creditors will take this deal. If they don't respond, or if only their computers respond by sending another bill, set up a telephone appointment to discuss your debt (or a personal appointment, if you live nearby).

If you don't find work in a couple of months, write or call again. This keeps the creditors informed and reassures them that you're not going to skip.

Hold to your position even if your creditors bluster, threaten to ruin your credit rating, or claim that they'll sue. Keep on explaining your situation in reasonable language. Say that you're out of work; say that you'll pay eventually; say that you can't pay now or can pay only $10 a month. Don't cave in, even if your account is turned over to a bill collector. Your main priorities are to husband cash, hold your life together, and keep your job search going. When you find a job, and you will, you can work out a repayment plan.

It's tough to write those letters and make those appointments. You'd rather keep your joblessness—and your cashlessness—a secret. But by coming clean instead of hiding, you stand a better chance of getting your creditors to lay off.

11. *If 3 months pass without a job nibble,* talk to the bank that holds your mortgage. You'll probably be expected to take a home-equity loan, using the proceeds to keep your mortgage current. If you're low on equity, however, the bank might agree to accept only interest payments for a few months, letting the principal coast. Or it might renegotiate your mortgage. This will take a personal visit but it often works. All banks can offer you these deals even though your mortgage has been sold to an outside investor. Those investors have forbearance procedures to avoid unnecessary foreclosures.

12. *Try to bring in some extra income.* Sign up with a temporary-help agency. Pitch for consulting jobs. Accept project work and temporary-executive spots (sometimes they lead to full-time jobs). Advertise your services in the neighborhood: typing, carpentry, accounting, day care. If your spouse doesn't work, now is the time for him or her to start. Ask your teenagers to pitch in with after-school jobs.

13. *There's no item 13 on this list.* It's unlucky, and you need all the luck you can get.

14. *Be cautious about starting or buying a business.* With your severance and 401(k) plan in hand, you might buy a franchise or start your own small business. But the failure rate is high and you could lose the last stake you'll ever have. Work in the business for a year before deciding whether

to buy. Or investigate it exhaustively by visiting outlets—or similar businesses—over a wide geographical area.

15. *If you don't find work and see that your money won't last,* it's time to rethink your life from the ground up. Look for cheaper housing. Move to an area where living costs are lower. Consider jobs at a much lower salary. Tell your children they'll have to leave college for a while or transfer to a school they can pay for entirely with their earnings and student loans.

Reach these decisions before you start borrowing from relatives. My reasoning here is tactical, not moral. Your relatives are normally your ace in the hole, the only people who might help you finance a new start in life. So try to tap them last, not first.

PLANNING FOR INFLATION AND DEFLATION

You can't. The effects are too unpredictable to be built into a spending plan. That's why budgets do best on a 6-month cycle; you can look at your actual spending and adjust.

SPENDING AND YOUR FINANCIAL PLAN

A spending plan is the visible evidence of financial planning at work. The other chapters of this book will help you make strategic choices. The spending plan executes them.

9.

Saving More Money

Patented, Painless Ways to Save and Where to Save It

The 1980s worshiped spending. The 1990s reconsidered.
The twenty-first century will belong to the saver.

It seems like only yesterday that savers were dorks. They kept piggy banks. They drove last year's cars. They fished in their change purses for nickels while the superstars flashed credit cards.

Today, values have changed. The new object of veneration is not money on the hoof but money in the bank—and the dorks have it. The more you save the freer you get because time is on the saver's side. Compound interest floats all boats.

Like most people who make their own money, I started out living paycheck to paycheck. I could cover my bills (most of the time). But I "knew" that I couldn't afford to save so I didn't bother. Even had I bothered, my small $20 or so a week wouldn't have seemed worth the effort.

Some years (and many lost $20s) later, I learned I was wrong. Anyone can put money aside, at any level of income. You just have to *do* it. Of all of the New Era's new virtues—daily jogging, eating bran, quitting smoking—saving money is the simplest and the least demanding of your time and attention. Savers can lie in a hammock all day eating Mars Bars and still feel good about themselves. As for the value of a tiny $20 a week, take a look at the table on page 183.

A financial plan is grounded in savings. That's how you get enough money to pay off your debts and accumulate an investment fund.

How much should you save? The answer comes from ancient times.

You tithe. It was learned generations ago—and is still true—that most people can save up to 10 percent of their incomes *and hardly notice.* I can't tell you why it works, only that it does. Maybe tithing just collects the money that otherwise goes up in smoke (it's 9 a.m.; do you know where yesterday's $10 is?). On a $30,000 paycheck, you can save $250 a month, $3,000 a year. On $60,000, shoot for $500 a month, $6,000 a year. On $100,000, save $833 a month, $10,000 a year.

I hear you, I hear you. You say you can't do it. Your rent is too high, your bills are too large, your needs are too great, your credit lines are too long. None of those things is actually an impediment, but it will take you awhile to see it. So start by saving only 5 percent of your income. Take that money off the top of every paycheck and live on what's left. What will happen to that pile of monthly bills once you start putting 5 percent aside? They will be paid! You'll still go to the movies and put gas in your car. Your standard of living will be unchanged. Those savings pick up dollars that leak through your fingers unseen. The rest of your life goes on exactly as before.

You say you don't believe me? Fine. Try it and prove me wrong. When you find out it works, raise your savings to 7 percent. I predict that you'll be at 10 percent within the year.

If you're already tithing to your future, take a moment to feel superior. What's life without a touch of smug?

WHAT ARE YOU SAVING MONEY *FOR?*

A savings account isn't something to hang on the wall and stare at, like a Rembrandt. You're not hoarding. You're preparing to use your money in a different way.

Refer, please, to your Spending Plan (Chapter 8). It says that your current goal is to pay down debt. Or 3 months' living expenses in the bank. Or $2,000 more in a college account this year. Or $5,000 for long-term investments. Or $1,000 to play the slots in Vegas, where you'll *really* make some money. Tithing, or semitithing, is how you're going to raise your stake.

Here's how to accomplish it:

First, write down how much you're going to save (5 or 10 percent of each paycheck).

Second, write down how long it will take to reach your goal. At $250 a month, you'll have your college account in 8 months. You'll have a college account *and* Las Vegas in 12 months. (Tip: It's easier to save $59 a week than $250 a month. The smaller sum sounds more doable, even though it comes to the same in the end.)

Third, note each future $250 (or $59) payment on your calendar and check off every one you make. That may sound hokey but it's a strong motivational tool. Every time you turn to a new week or new month, there's a written reminder to keep up your resolve. Saving money is easier if you see it climb toward a specific end. It's like polishing the car. You feel that you've accomplished something.

Fourth, when you've reached your goal give yourself a little present. Then start the process all over again.

SHOULD YOU BUILD UP A BANK ACCOUNT INSTEAD OF PAYING OFF DEBT?

No, no, and again, no. Repeat after me: *paying off debt is a form of saving*. In fact, debt repayment is one of the most lucrative ways to save. It's nuts to keep money in the bank at 4 percent interest while carrying credit-card debt at 18 percent. You are losing 14 percent a year on that deal (the 18 percent cost of the debt minus the 4 percent earned on the bank account). Take most of your money out of the bank and reduce the debt. If you need quick cash, you can borrow against your card again, and in the meantime, you're saving yourself a mountain of interest. (Just be sure that you choose a credit card that doesn't charge extra for cash advances—page 215.)

Using savings to pay off debt is one of the simplest, fastest ways of setting your finances aright. It's also a fabulous use of your money. Your return on investment equals the interest rate on the debt. When you make an extra payment on your 18 percent credit card, for example, you're getting an 18 percent return, guaranteed. No other investment can offer the same.

You may find it hard to accept this truth. Money in the bank is so comforting. Haven't you read that everyone should keep 3 to 6 months' worth of expenses in an emergency savings account? Hardly anybody does, but the books all say that's the right thing.

Not this book—at least, not while you carry debt. You do indeed need 3 to 6 months' worth of expenses on tap in case of illness, job loss, or other emergency. A year's worth of expenses would be even better. But you can protect yourself nearly as well with 12 months' worth of borrowing power, on credit cards or a home-equity line. (I say "nearly" because borrowing builds up an obligation while taking money from savings doesn't.)

For mathematical proof that this strategy works, assume that you have $1,000 in the bank earning 4 percent, a $1,000 credit-card debt at 18 percent, and no extra fee for taking a cash advance. Here's your position, under various scenarios:

First, assume that no emergency comes up. You might:

• Leave your $1,000 in the bank. Your savings and debt together will cost you a hefty 14 percent a year.

• Use your $1,000 to pay off the debt. Instantly, you've *earned* 14 percent (the 18 percent you gained by eliminating debt minus the 4 percent you lost by giving up the savings account).

Second, assume that a $1,000 emergency comes up. You might:

- Take the $1,000 you left in the bank. Your cost: 18 percent (the price of not using that $1,000 to reduce your debt).
- If you already used the $1,000 to cut your credit-card debt, borrow that $1,000 against the credit card again. This, too, costs you 18 percent. But you saved a lot of interest during the time that your debt was reduced.
- Leave your $1,000 in the bank and borrow $1,000 more on your credit cards. This is an expensive choice. It costs you a net $320 in interest, compared with $180 had your savings been used to lower your debt.

The same mathematics applies to prepaying your mortgage. Clean out your savings and use the money to reduce your mortgage debt (or make larger mortgage payments each month in lieu of savings). Just be sure that you have a substantial home-equity line of credit in case you lose your job and have to borrow to stay afloat.

You'll probably want to keep a little quick cash in the bank, especially if your credit cards charge extra for cash advances. But don't try to build a larger account until your debts are paid off.

Here's another version of the saving-vs.-borrowing question: "I need a new gallimawhatsis. I have enough money in the bank to pay cash. Should I use that money or take a loan instead?" One argument favors the loan: you will be forced to repay the money, whereas no one will grump if you leave a hole in your savings account. But a better argument favors cash: Taking money from savings is the cheapest way to buy. Once you've made the purchase, make regular payments into your savings account (just as you'd have made regular payments on the loan) to replace the money you took out. As long as you're capable of saving more money, you don't have to worry about using it from time to time.

But I'd vote differently if your savings cache came from an inheritance, a life insurance payoff, or a lottery ticket, *and* you've never been able to save by yourself. In that case, consider the loan. Preserve that precious windfall for college tuition or your old age. The interest you pay, unnecessarily, is the price of lacking discipline.

For a personal calculator showing exactly how much you'd save by raiding your bank account to pay off your debts, dial up the Internet: http://www.financenter.com.

SAVING VS. INVESTING

Savings are, by definition, *safe*. You can turn your back and they won't escape. When the market crashes, they're unalarmed. Every time you look, they've earned more interest. You're never going to lose a dime.

Investments, by contrast, put your money at risk. Good investments yield much more than savings over the long run. But you have to put up with occasional losses, too.

Savings Will Not Make You Rich. Only canny investments do that. The role of savings is to keep you from becoming poor. They're your security. Your base. They preserve your purchasing power. With enough savings tucked into your jeans, you can afford to take chances with the rest of your money, and with your life.

Should You Invest Rather Than Pay Down Debt? That depends. Use any spare money to reduce debt if you're paying a higher interest rate than your investments could earn after tax. But invest if that will net more than you're paying on debt. In general, you'd first put the maximum amount into a tax-deferred retirement account (page 842). Next, you'd pay off credit-card and other consumer debt. Whether your third step should be to prepay your mortgage depends on its after-tax cost compared with the gains you might make on investments that aren't tax deferred.

THE BEST YEARS OF YOUR LIFE . . .

. . . are when you're young. At least, they're the best years for saving money. The sooner you start, the more time your savings have to compound.

Typically, young people turn a deaf ear. "I'm too broke," they say. "I'll save when I'm older." But later money won't earn you nearly the return that early money pays.

Take a look at the startling table that follows, prepared by Professor Emeritus Richard L. D. Morse of Kansas State University, who knows more about savings-account interest than anyone else in the country.

The Early Saver deposits $1,000 a year for 15 years, at 5 percent compounded daily. Then she stops. Having put in a total of $15,000, she leaves her stash alone to build.

All during that time, the Late Saver doesn't darken a bank door. In the sixteenth year he gets religion and starts saving $1,000 a year, also at 5 percent. Forty years later, he has put up a total of $40,000. But he hasn't caught up with the Early Saver—and never will! He can go on depositing $1,000 a year until the third millennium. At 5 percent interest, the Early Saver (although still depositing no more money) will pull further ahead of the Late Saver every year.

HOW LONG DOES IT TAKE
TO DOUBLE YOUR MONEY?

For a close estimate, use the rule of 72s. Divide 72 by the yield you expect to earn. The result is how long it will take for your money to double.

	EARLY SAVER *Depositing $1,000* *a year at 5%*	LATE SAVER *Depositing nothing*
Year 1	$ 1,051	0
Year 5	5,824	0
Year 10	13,301	0
Year 15	22,903	0
	Depositing nothing *but building at 5%*	*Depositing $1,000* *a year at 5%*
Year 16	$ 24,077	$ 1,051
Year 20	29,407	5,824
Year 25	37,758	13,301
Year 30	48,482	22,902
Year 35	62,251	35,230
Year 40	79,931	51,060
Year 45	102,631	71,384
Year 50	131,779	97,482
Year 55	169,205	130,990

SOURCE: Richard L. D. Morse

At 5 percent, your money will double in roughly 14.4 years. At 8 percent, it takes 9 years.

TWENTY-ONE PATENTED PAINLESS WAYS TO SAVE . . .

1. Pay yourself first. That's the oldest financial advice in the world, and one of those things you can't improve on. Take a slice of savings off the top of every paycheck before paying any of your bills. If you pay your bills first and save what's left, you'll always be broke because there is never anything left.

2. Bill yourself first. Keep stamped envelopes, addressed to your bank, in the same drawer as your bills. Send the bank a fixed check every month, as if it were just as pressing as keeping the mortgage current. In point of fact, it is. If you're paid irregularly, send a fixed percentage of every paycheck.

3. Get someone else to save for you (Part One). Your bank or S&L might transfer a fixed sum of money every month from your checking account into savings or a mutual fund. Enter each transfer in your checkbook so you won't accidentally overdraw.

4. Get someone else to save for you (Part Two). You'll never find a better savings machine than your company's payroll deduction plan. A fixed amount of money is taken out of every paycheck so the cash never

hits your checking account. What you don't see, you don't miss—and you don't spend. Depending on the company, there may be deductions for retirement plans and for other types of accounts.

5. Do coupons turn you on? Create your own Christmas Club or Vacation Club. Decide how much money you want 12 months from now, divide it into 12 equal payments, and make "coupons" to remind you to keep up the monthly deposits. Or make 52 coupons for weekly payments. You could call it a Down-Payment-on-a-First-Home Club or an I'll-Send-Junior-to-College-If-It-Kills-Me Club.

6. Save all dividends and interest when you don't need this money to live on. If you have a mutual fund, arrange for all dividends to be reinvested automatically. If you keep stocks with a stockbroker, have the payments swept into a money-market fund for reinvestment.

7. Don't spend your next raise. Put the extra money away, even if it's just $20 a week. The more money you earn, the more of it you should set aside. Toward late middle age, you should be saving 15 to 20 percent of your income, at least.

8. Quit spending your year-end bonus in advance. Save it instead. At the very least, quit spending more than your bonus.

9. Save all gifts you get in cash, even small ones. *Nothing* is too small to save.

10. Pay off your mortgage faster by doubling up on principal payments every month. You'll build equity sooner, which is a form of saving. You'll also spend much less on interest payments.

11. Quit buying books (except, of course, for this one, which no prudent saver should be without!). Get a library card, instead.

12. Refinance your credit-card, auto, or other high-interest loans at a lower interest rate. You might shift your credit-card balances to a cheaper card. If you're disciplined, transfer the debts to a home-equity line of credit; the interest is tax deductible if you itemize deductions (page 249). Use the money you're saving on interest payments to reduce your debts even faster.

13. Don't trade in your car as soon as the loan is paid off. Make repairs, if you have to, and keep it for a year or two longer. Save the money you were spending on monthly car payments.

14. Pay cash for everything. You will spend less because it's harder to part with cash than to put down a credit card.

15. Take $5 out of your wallet every day and put it in a coffee can. That's $1,825 a year—almost enough to fund an Individual Retirement Account in full.

16. Take a part-time job and save all the income.

17. Let the government withhold extra tax money from your paycheck, and save the refund.

18. Pay off your credit cards, then save the money you're no longer spending on interest charges.

19. Trim your spending by 5 percent, then trim it by another 5 percent.

20. Think about buying cash-value life insurance. Your payments go partly for life insurance and partly into a savings fund. This can be a pretty poor route to thrift (see page 296). I suggest it only for high-income people or people who cannot save money any other way.

21. Save early and often. The sooner you put some money away, the longer it has to fatten on compound interest. Saving money *young* is a painless way of saving *more*.

. . . PLUS SEVEN TAX-BLESSED WAYS OF RAISING RETIREMENT MONEY

1. Join the company retirement-savings plan. Your basic contribution escapes current taxes and will accumulate tax deferred. What's more, these plans often *give away money free*. The company matches your contribution —say, $1 for every $2 you put up. That's a 50 percent return on investment, instantly and at no risk. There's no better investment deal in the entire U.S. of A. You may also be able to add a nondeductible contribution that can accumulate tax deferred.

2. Join your company's stock-purchase plan. You run the risk that the stock will fall. But over long periods your investment should do better than a savings account. (One warning: Don't let too much of your net worth accumulate here. It's risky to bet your future principally on one stock. From time to time sell some of the stock and diversify into other investments.)

3. Sign up for an Individual Retirement Account. Make monthly payments so you won't have to scramble for money when the deadline for contributions looms. For more on IRAs, see page 867.

4. Don't spend the lump-sum distribution you may get from your retirement plan when you leave the company, even if it's small. You generally have three investment choices: leave it in your ex-employer's plan, roll it into an Individual Retirement Account, or roll it into your new employer's retirement plan.

5. If it takes a contribution to join your company's pension plan, make it—even if you're young. If you leave early, you'll get your money back plus everything your money earned. If you last at least 3 to 5 years, you'll walk away with the company's contributions, too. (With some plans, you have to work 7 years to get the full company contribution.)

6. Start a tax-deferred Simplified Employee Pension or Keogh plan if you're self-employed or earn self-employment money by moonlighting (page 862).

7. Consider a tax-deferred annuity if it has a good investment record— but only if you'll hold the investment for at least 20 years (page 887). There's more on this subject in Chapter 29.

WHAT YOUR SAVINGS HAVE TO EARN

Say that inflation is running at around 3 percent. And say that you're earning 5 percent in a savings deposit. What's the effective return on your money after state and federal taxes? Probably pretty close to zero—either just above it or just below, depending on your tax bracket. You may have preserved your purchasing power but you haven't increased it, or not by much.

I'm not knocking a breakeven result. The basic job of a bond or a bank account is to keep you from falling behind. But you won't achieve even this much protection unless you avoid low-rate deposits.

The table below gives you some guidelines. Find the current inflation rate at the left, then look across to the column showing your federal income-tax bracket. Take the interest rate shown and up it a little to compensate for state and local taxes. That's the minimum rate that your money has to earn to keep the value of your savings from eroding.

WHERE TO KEEP YOUR SAVINGS

Don't automatically think "bank." That's only one of many choices. To find the right place to keep your savings, start with what you want from your money and work back. You need: (1) at least the breakeven yield that you've just found, and (2) access to the money when you need it *but not a day sooner.* Funds you won't want until next year can be invested differently—and more profitably—from funds you're going to use next week.

AT THIS RATE OF INFLATION	YOU NEED TO EARN THIS RATE OF INTEREST TO BREAK EVEN IN THE FOLLOWING TAX BRACKETS				
	15%	28%	31%	36%	39.6%
1%	1.20%	1.39%	1.49%	1.56%	1.66%
2%	2.35	2.78	2.90	3.13	3.31
3%	3.53	4.17	4.35	4.69	4.97
4%	4.71	5.56	5.80	6.25	6.62
5%	5.88	6.94	7.25	7.81	8.28
6%	7.06	8.33	8.70	9.38	9.93
7%	8.24	9.72	10.14	10.94	11.59
8%	9.41	11.11	11.59	12.50	13.25
9%	10.59	12.50	13.04	14.06	14.90
10%	11.76	13.89	14.49	15.63	16.56

SOURCE: David Kahn, Goldstein Golub Kessler & Co.

For Savings You'll Need Immediately

(And I mean right now. Or a week from Friday. Within 3 months, at the very most.)

Hold this part of your cash cache to a minimum because ready money earns less interest than money invested for longer terms. I'd include only:

1. Funds that you know will be spent very soon, like a down payment on a car you'll buy this month.

2. Your permanent floating emergency fund, if you have one (page 180). Don't let this fund get too large. Keeping $5,000 in a passbook account—just in case the house should burn, the world explode, or your hair drop out—is dumb. Into the dailiness of life, alarming emergencies rarely fall. If one does, you can always retrieve your money from wherever you stashed it. A quick-cash fund of one month's earnings should be plenty. Savings do better when stored at higher rates of return or used to reduce debt.

3. Money waiting to be invested in stocks, bonds, or real estate.

Here's where your short-term money can be kept:

Money Market Deposit Accounts at Banks. They're handy, they're easy, they're government insured. You earn a floating interest rate that is loosely tied to the general level of market rates. (And I mean loosely. When other interest rates go up, banks are slow to raise the rate on money market accounts. But they drop rates enthusiastically when other interest rates go down.) You can take out money whenever you want, although only 6 transactions a month can be with third parties (only 3 of them by check). Minimum balances fall in the area of $500 to $2,500. You'll pay a penalty if your account drops below the minimum.

Ready access, however, has its price. The interest rate paid on the average money market account rarely meets the breakeven test. Your savings may lose value after counting inflation and taxes. If the bank charges fees, you'll lose even more. The only way to maintain your money's purchasing power is to search out an institution that pays especially high interest rates on money market deposits. (Do it by checking *100 Highest Yields*, page 68.)

Passbook Accounts. These pay even less than money market accounts. Skip them, unless you're below the minimum for a money market account.

Taxable Money Market Mutual Funds. Money funds offer a somewhat better chance of breaking even. Even after management fees, the average fund pays around 0.5 percentage points more than the average bank money market account when interest rates are low and as much as 3 percentage points more when rates are high.

Your cash is kept in safe investments that earn taxable, short-term interest. The Securities and Exchange Commission limits taxable money-fund investments largely to U.S. Treasury securities, insured bank certificates of deposit, and top-grade commercial paper (short-term loans to creditworthy corporations). Up to 5 percent of the portfolio can go into second-tier commercial paper. All these investments usually mature within a brief time—a day, a week, 3 months, 6 months.

Money market mutual funds are all worth $1 a share, no more, no less. They generally credit you with dividends daily (and pay them monthly), passing along whatever the fund is currently earning. Your minimum investment: $5,000 to $1,000 but sometimes less. You can write an unlimited number of checks on the fund, generally for a minimum of $250 or $500. A few process $100 checks (and a couple process them in any amount—page 54), in which case, consider using the fund as an interest-paying checking account. You pay no penalties for low deposits, although many funds will cash out your shares if your balance falls below a certain minimum, like $500 or so.

Money funds, including the money funds sold by banks, don't carry federal deposit insurance (only the bank's money market deposit accounts, page 187, are FDIC insured). So although the funds are extremely safe they're not *perfectly* safe. In any market crunch, there are always a handful of dumb (or unlucky) money managers who miss a trick and risk a loss.

In 1979 a fund got into trouble by gambling on longer-term investments, like 2-year maturities. Interest rates rose and the fund lost some money. Its shareholders were institutions; individuals weren't affected.

In 1989 and 1990 some corporations defaulted on their commercial paper—a potential loss to a few money funds. Fortunately, they all belonged to solvent financial-services organizations, which dipped into their pockets to make investors whole.

In 1994 a sharp rise in interest rates damaged a handful of funds invested in the riskiest sort of derivatives (page 749). But again, the fund sponsors rode to the rescue so no investors lost any money.

Some investors seek safety in money funds that invest only in U.S. Treasury bills and buy no Treasury derivatives. Treasury funds yield 0.25 to 0.5 percentage points less than funds that also buy corporate securities, so you're giving up $12.50 to $25 a year on a $5,000 investment. In my opinion, the money funds with broader investment policies, and sponsored by major financial organizations, are safe enough.

If you're investing outside a tax-deferred account, however, Treasury funds offer a tax advantage that may make up for their lower yields. Virtually all states exempt the dividends they pay from state and local tax. In high-tax states like California, Massachusetts, and New York, they may net more than a fund invested in corporates, especially if the Treasury fund has low expenses.

"U.S. Government" money market funds include a mix of government securities, only some of which are state-tax exempt. Your fund should tell you what's reportable in your state.

Regardless of the type of fund you're interested in, don't break your neck hunting for the highest payer. There's always a different name at the top of the list, depending on each fund's holdings and how fast it responds to daily changes in interest rates. If a fund stays at the top of the list, it's probably buying riskier securities.

I'd use six criteria in choosing a fund:

1. Are its expenses low? You'll find the answer in the prospectus, in the table that shows all the fees and expenses. Managers who charge 0.5 percent of assets or less have a good shot at being top performers. Fees of one percent or more usually mark the funds that do the worst. Some funds with low expense ratios levy separate service charges, like $2 per check or $5 per telephone transfer. If those fees were figured into the expense ratio, the fund would show a slightly higher cost. Some funds are temporarily waiving fees. For now, they flash an especially high yield. But when the fees start, your yield will drop. In general, large money funds are more cost efficient than small ones.

2. Does it fit your purse? You should have no problem meeting the fund's minimum balance and check-writing rules.

3. Is it handy? If you work with a particular stockbrokerage firm, you'll probably use the firm's own money fund as a place to park cash awaiting investment. If you hold stock or bond mutual funds, you'll choose that company's money fund. The fund should have plenty of telephone lines so you don't often get a busy signal.

4. What's the fund's average maturity—meaning, how long does it take for its average investment to come due? The shorter the term, the less risk the fund takes. Under SEC rules, average maturity generally can't exceed 90 days. Most funds post even shorter terms. The average maturities for all the funds are printed on Thursdays in *The Wall Street Journal* and most other newspapers.

5. Does the fund belong to a major financial organization—a mutual fund group, a large brokerage house, an insurance company? This is your equivalent of deposit insurance. So far, money-fund sponsors have always paid for their mistakes rather than saddle their shareholders with a loss. A fund without major sponsorship might not be able to cover a major error's cost.

6. Are you comfortable with the fund's investment policies? Safety is the watchword here, but that means different things to different people. You might want a fund that buys only Treasury bills. In a broader-based fund, you might want certificates of deposit only from the soundest banks

and commercial paper only from companies rated "P-1" by Moody's rating service or "A-1" by Standard & Poor's. Or you might accept a foray into second-tier "P-2" or "A-2" commercial paper in return for a marginally higher yield.

As for derivatives, some of them aren't particularly dangerous. Others can lose an unexpected amount of value when interest rates decline. After the 1994 debacle the SEC warned funds off the riskier derivatives—the "floaters" (adjustable-rate derivatives) and "structured notes."

How do you find out what a money fund buys? Only one way. Read the prospectus. If it discloses no policy on derivatives, call the fund and ask about it. The best answer is, "No derivatives at all." You can also look for derivatives in the fund's latest annual report.

Funds that consistently pay higher yields than the competition are often the ones taking higher risks. And why would you take a risk at all? On $5,000, the difference between 3.5 and 3.1 percent comes to $20 a year. Big deal. If you've got $5 million, that 0.4 percent is worth a tidy $20,000—but short of that, why mess around?

Tax-Exempt Money Market Funds. Some people will do anything to beat Uncle Sam out of a few bucks, even if it costs them money. Take the knee-jerk popularity of tax-exempt money market funds. Half the people in them would probably do better in a taxable fund, but they've never even checked it out.

Look at a tax-free fund only if: (1) you are in a high federal tax bracket (31 percent and up), or (2) you're in the next-highest bracket (28 percent), live in a highly taxed state, and get a fund that's exempt from state and local taxes.

Here's how to figure whether you'll net more money from a tax-exempt fund: Subtract your tax bracket from 1.00. Divide the result into the current yield of the tax-exempt fund you're looking at. The result is your breakeven point. If you can find a taxable fund paying more than the breakeven point, buy it.

For example, say you're in the 28 percent bracket and are considering a tax-free fund yielding 3.5 percent. Subtracting 0.28 from 1.00 gives you 0.72. Dividing that into 3.5 gives you 4.86. A taxable fund paying more than 4.86 percent will yield you more, after federal taxes, than the tax-free fund.

Where can you find a money market mutual fund? All the major mutual-fund groups sell them, and so do stockbrokers. You can check their names and current yields in *The Wall Street Journal* and *Barron's* magazine for investors. For investment information on 280 money funds, as well as other mutual funds, get the excellent *Handbook for No-Load Fund Investors* (at this writing, $45 from The No-Load Fund Investor, P.O. Box 318, Irvington-on-Hudson, NY 10533).

For Money You'll Need for Sure in 6 Months to 4 Years

Here, I count everything from college tuition due next fall to the down payment on the house you hope to buy the year after next. You can't risk losing a penny of it so you can't afford to play around. On the other hand, neither should these funds nap in a low-interest savings account. By choosing a guaranteed investment that pays a higher interest rate, you'll pile up savings faster.

Most of you will agree with me about 6-month money. But 4 years sounds a lot further away. Why not invest in stocks for growth? Here is my argument against: Stock prices rise and fall. For money you need, it's the "fall" you have to worry about. If you have the bad luck to invest just before stocks go into a decline, you'll lose some of your principal—which could be disastrous if that money is needed to pay a specific bill. Since 1929 it has taken investors an average of nearly 3.5 years to get even again after a major stock-market drop, assuming that dividends were reinvested. So that's the time period to be careful about.

If you're more adventurous, you might decide to keep only 2-year money totally safe. Since World War II the average stock-market recovery took just under 2 years. Still, the lengthiest bear market, which started in 1972, took just over 3.5 years to come back.

Certificates of Deposit. With a CD, you put your money in a bank, savings and loan, or credit union for a fixed term. You normally earn a higher interest rate than you would in passbook savings or a money-market account.

Some people hate CDs because they feel that their money is locked away. But it's not. You can break into a certificate anytime you want before maturity. The worst that can happen is that you'll pay an interest penalty. Big deal. That's nothing, compared with the interest you lose by keeping too much money in a low-interest savings account. If you balance risk and reward, CDs are a shoo-in. Most savers will *not* face an emergency need for cash. You'll hold your CD to maturity and earn more interest along the way.

Institutions may offer standard terms for CDs, like 6, 12, or 30 months. Some let you pick whatever term you like. Normally, the longer the term, the more interest you earn. For the many varieties of certificates of deposit, and how to get higher interest through "laddering," see page 67.

U.S. Treasury Securities. A Treasury security is the fruit of federal deficit spending. When the government spends more money than it collects in taxes, it has to borrow to make up the difference—and it borrows from you, by selling you Treasuries. You are actually lending money to Uncle Sam for a fixed period, earning interest all the while.

It takes a little more effort to buy a Treasury than a certificate of deposit. Instead of walking into a bank or S&L, you have to visit, or write to, the nearest Federal Reserve bank or branch (the banks are listed on page 204) and: (1) get information about buying Treasuries, (2) read the directions, (3) fill in a form, and (4) send in a certified check. The job is not exactly a brain-buster, and there are no charges to pay when you buy from the Fed. Still, I can hear some of you groaning. If this sounds like too much work, a bank or a stockbroker will buy Treasuries for you, for a fee.

What's your reward for becoming a Treasury investor? An instant break on your income taxes. The interest you earn on U.S. Treasury securities—while taxed at the federal level—cannot be taxed by states and cities. So you might earn a higher after-tax return than you'd get from the average certificate of deposit.

The yield on a Treasury security is set through public auction, by the big institutions that put in bids. When you buy directly from the Federal Reserve, you piggyback on what the institutions pay. A phone call to the nearest Fed gets you the most recent auction prices and yields (there's usually a 24-hour prerecorded announcement). Which Treasuries to buy depends on when you'll want the money.

Treasury Bills mature in 3 months, 6 months, or one year. Minimum investment: $10,000, plus $5,000 increments. You send the Fed a certified check. Immediately after the auction you get a "discount" payment back, representing the difference between the face value of the bill and the lower auction price. At maturity, you're paid the face value. Your profit is the difference between the two.

For example, say you send $10,000 for a one-year bill that sells for $9,500. The Treasury sends you $500 back. At maturity, your T-bill pays $10,000, yielding a $500 profit.

There are two ways of measuring your return on investment. The newspaper stories generally highlight the "discount rate," which compares your profit ($500) with the bill's face value ($10,000). By this measure, you've earned 5 percent.

But that understates what you've really earned. After all, you didn't put up the full $10,000. In this example, you invested only $9,500. A $500 return on $9,500 comes to about 5.3 percent. That's called the coupon-equivalent yield, and is the true measure of your return. Use it to compare the profit in Treasury bills with what you might get from alternative investments, like bonds and CDs. You'll find the coupon-equivalent yields in the newspaper tables reporting the outcomes of Treasury auctions. Often, they're given in the newspaper stories, too.

T-bills let you play income-tax games. If you buy a security today that matures in the next calendar year, your interest income falls into that year, so you have deferred the tax you owe. Note that your taxable profit is not the discount check that the Treasury sends you right away. It's the profit you make when the bill matures.

Treasury Notes mature in 2, 3, 4, 5, 7, or 10 years. Minimum investment: $5,000 for 2- and 3-year notes, plus $5,000 increments; or $1,000 for longer terms, plus $1,000 increments. Different maturities are auctioned at different times—all of which the Fed will be glad to fill you in on. You send in a check for the face amount of the notes you want. Immediately after the auction, you will usually get a few dollars back because the notes sold for a hair less than their face value. Only one yield is reported (there's no coupon-equivalent yield to worry about, as with Treasury bills). Interest is paid on your full investment twice a year.

When choosing Treasury notes, pick a maturity that coincides with the date you'll want to use the money. For information on buying Treasuries, see page 203.

Treasury Bonds have the longest maturities, generally up to 30 years. Minimum investment: $1,000, with $1,000 increments. They're auctioned in the same way as Treasury notes, with interest payable twice a year. I mention them here only to be orderly. Conventional long-term Treasuries aren't the right place for savings you might have to tap. If you sell them before maturity, you'll be exposed to the hard, cold winds of the open market, where your bond might bring less than you originally paid. The newer inflation-indexed Treasuries keep your principal safe, but they pay a smaller current income than conventional Treasuries do. For ways to use long-term Treasury bonds, see page 759.

Zero-Coupon Treasuries can be good ways to save over 4 years. Just be sure that the bond will actually mature in that span of time. You may lose money if you have to sell a zero before maturity.

The "coupon" is the interest rate, so "zero coupon" means that no interest is paid currently on these bonds. Instead, you buy for less than the bond's face value. Every year the interest builds up within the bond, until it reaches face value at maturity. For example, you might pay $729 (before sales commissions) for a zero that will be worth $1,000 in 5 years. That's an annual compound yield of 6.47 percent.

What's nice about zeros is that they reinvest your interest at the same rate that you're earning on the bond itself. With the zero just discussed, for example, you earn 6.47 percent on every interest payment. With other bonds, you're paid in cash and have to reinvest the money yourself. Small payments (if not spent) will probably land in a bank account or money market fund, where they'll generally earn much less than the bond is paying.

What's bad about zeros is that you're taxed every year on the interest that builds up, even though you don't physically receive the money. To avoid the tax, buy a zero in a tax-deferred retirement account. Or give the zero to a child who owes no taxes.

A 4-year zero-coupon Treasury is a reasonable bet for your teenager's education fund. Buy one when the child is 14 years old, to cash in when he or she reaches 18. Your money is safe and the earnings should compound at a reasonable rate of interest. (For younger children, don't buy zeros, buy stock-owning mutual funds—see page 556.)

Zero-coupon Treasuries are bought through stockbrokers. But some firms clip you for a higher price than you should pay. They trap you by quoting a dollar figure—"only $729 for these bonds"—without telling you what the bonds are priced to yield. That might saddle you with an unfairly low rate of return.

A smart investor buys through a discount broker. Ask for both the dollar price and the *net yield to maturity after sales charges*, which is what the bond pays over its full term.

Long-term zeros are another story. Like other 20- and 30-year nonindexed Treasury bonds, they're generally wrong for short-term savers. Zeros lose value faster than other bonds do, which can hurt you if you have to sell before maturity. For more on zeros, see page 779.

For Money You Won't Need for 5 Years or More

Risk a majority of it in the stock market or other growth investment (perhaps real estate if you're holding for 10 years or more). Otherwise, you'll never get ahead of inflation and taxes.

But you might want to keep even some of your long-term money absolutely safe. For this purpose, two suggestions:

1. Five-Year Certificates of Deposit or Treasury Notes, Continually Reinvested. They should roughly preserve your purchasing power, provided that you reinvest all of the interest as well as the principal. You're buying for only 5 years at a time, so you'll probably be able to hold each note until maturity. That's important. You might lose money if you have to sell before maturity.

You can "ladder" Treasury bills and notes just the way you do certificates of deposit (explained on page 755). The traditional ladder, however, requires that you buy some shorter-term Treasuries, which are expensive. For small investors, I'd suggest the following Treasury ladder, built from the notes that cost only $1,000 each:

Buy a 5-year Treasury note this year, another one next year, a third one the year after, and so on for 5 years. When your first note matures, use the cash if you need it. If not, reinvest the money for another 5 years. The following year you have the same choice—use the cash or reinvest it in another 5-year note. And so on and so on. You'll have ready access to some of your money every year without the need to sell a note before maturity. Yet all of your savings will eventually earn interest at the 5-year rate instead of the lower one-year rate.

2. U.S. Savings Bonds. Savings bonds, although issued by the U.S. Treasury, are not what investors know as Treasury securities. Treasuries pay competitive interest rates and can be bought and sold on the open market. Savings bonds don't and can't. They're a special type of bond, sold principally to small investors. You pay no fees to buy or sell. You cannot lose money on savings bonds, regardless of general market conditions.

All newly issued Series EE bonds pay a floating interest rate—90 percent of the rate on 5-year Treasury securities, averaged over the past 6 months. The rate on savings bonds changes every May 1 and November 1. Interest is compounded semiannually and credited monthly.

If you sell within the first 17 years, you'll get whatever the bonds have earned for you since the month you bought. You get the same if you sell after holding 17 years or more, but with this guarantee: after that length of time, your EE-bond investment will—at minimum—double in value. That gives super-long-term holders a base rate of 4.1 percent, and higher if long-term interest rates stay above that level. For a recorded announcement of current savings-bond interest rates, call toll-free 800-US-BONDS.

Obviously, you can earn 10 percent more interest by buying regular 5-year Treasuries. For many investors, that's a better choice. But savings bonds have some special virtues:

1. You can earn these rates on a very small amount of money. The cheapest bond costs $25 ($50 if you buy through payroll deduction).

2. You can tax-defer the interest until the bonds are finally cashed in or until they reach their final maturity date, whichever comes first.

3. You receive no money until redemption, so you can't go out and spend the interest. In this respect, savings bonds (as well as zero-coupon bonds) force you to save.

4. If you bought savings bonds after December 31, 1989, and use the proceeds to cover tuition for qualified higher education, you might pay no income tax on the interest you earn (page 565).

Series EE bonds sell at a 50 percent discount from face value. The $100 bond costs $50; the $500 bond costs $250. Each month's interest is added to the bond's redemption value. You must hold the bond for at least 6 months. After that, you may cash it in whenever it suits you. As with other Treasury securities, you owe only federal income taxes on the interest you earn, no state and local income taxes. There's a 3-month interest penalty on bonds redeemed within the first 5 years.

Savings Bond Maturities. Here's a subject that's widely misunderstood. Unlike certificates of deposit, savings bonds do not have to be held to a particular maturity date. You redeem them at your convenience, receiving whatever they're worth at the time.

This misunderstanding arises because of the way bonds are sold. You buy at a 50 percent discount, paying $50 for a $100 bond. So you naturally think that you have to hold until your bond is worth $100. Not so. You have no idea when it will be worth $100 because that depends on what happens to interest rates. At the very worst, you'd get $100 after 17 years because that's your government guarantee. But the bond might reach $100 in value sooner than that. In any event, none of this matters. You just cash in the bond when you need the money and will get all your principal plus any interest due. You do not have to hold for 17 years.

Here are the maturities of savings bonds and what they mean:

1. *Original maturity.* This is the maximum time it will take for a bond to reach its face value. For newly issued bonds, that's 17 years (even though they may actually reach face value sooner).

2. *First extended maturity.* This lasts for 10 years after the original maturity date.

3. *Additional extended maturities.* In recent years, there has been only one, but there can be several. These last for 10 years or less, paying interest all the while.

4. *Final maturity.* This is the date after which the bond will no longer earn interest. On newly issued bonds, the final maturity—printed on the face of the bond—is 30 years away. Here are the final maturity dates for all other bonds (note that the older of these are no longer earning interest): Series E bonds issued earlier than December 1965—40 years after their issue date; Series E and EE bonds and Freedom Shares issued after November 1965—30 years after their issue date; Series H bonds issued between 1959 and 1979—30 years after their issue date; Series HH bonds issued since 1980—20 years after their issue date.

Don't hang on to old savings bonds that aren't paying interest anymore! Cash them in and get the money. Ask older family members whether they have any E bonds stashed away, and check the dates. When an E or EE bond reaches its final maturity, all the unreported interest becomes taxable even if you don't turn it in—that is, unless you exchange it for an HH bond (page 201). And you have only one year in which to make that HH-bond exchange.

SOME ANGLES TO
SAVINGS BOND INVESTMENTS

✔ Savings bonds are usually an improvement on passbook accounts, money market deposit accounts, and money market mutual funds, provided that you can hold for at least 6 months. But if you have the minimum investment required, Treasury securities and high-rate CDs yield more.

✔ You can buy EE bonds through most commercial banks, many S&Ls, and some credit unions (if your own institution doesn't sell them, call around); through a payroll-deduction plan at work; or through a Federal Reserve bank (page 204). You'll receive the bond by mail in about 3 weeks. If you're buying for Christmas or a birthday next week, the bank may provide you with a gift certificate.

The same institutions exchange E or EE bonds for HH bonds. HH bonds cannot be bought directly.

✔ Bonds earn interest from the issue date, which is always the first day of the month you bought. If you buy a bond on the last day of the month, it will be backdated to the first day. Interest on older EE bonds— those bought prior to May 1, 1997—is normally credited every 6 months. You earn more money by cashing them just after the crediting date rather than just before. To learn that date, get the Treasury's table of Interest Accrual Dates, free from the U.S. Savings Bond Marketing Office (address on page 201). You can also get free Tables of Redemption Values for Accrual Type Securities, showing current values for $25 Series E bonds and Savings Notes and $50 Series EE bonds (ask for the one you want). Happily, new bonds credit interest monthly, so new buyers don't have to bother with all this.

✔ An individual can invest up to $15,000 in a calendar year ($30,000 face value). Two co-owners can invest up to $30,000 ($60,000 face value).

✔ You can redeem just part of a bond if its face value is at least $50 for Series E bonds, $100 for Series EE, or $1,000 for Series H or HH. For example, a bond worth $1,000, with an accrued value of $700, can be turned in for $700 in cash and $300 in bonds. The new bonds will have the same issue date as the old one did.

✔ If you buy a savings bond in your own name, you control it completely. If you name a beneficiary on an EE bond, you can change the beneficiary whenever you want just by filling in Form PD 4000 (available from the government, page 199, and from many of the agents who issue savings bonds). The rules are different for the older, Series E bonds. With them, the beneficiary has to agree to being removed, by signing Form PD 4000.

✔ If you buy a savings bond in joint names, both owners have to agree to any changes. But either one of you can cash in the bond and the other doesn't have to know. Whoever holds it, controls it.

✔ The person whose money bought the bond is called the principal co-owner, and all the income should be taxed to him or her. If both of you contributed, there is no principal co-owner and taxes should be allocated according to what percent each of you paid. As a practical matter, however, the tax is usually paid by the person who redeems the bond.

✔ If the bond is a gift, the interest is taxed to the person receiving it. Technically, others should sometimes pay. For example, the interest is taxable to you if you buy a bond as a gift for a child and name yourself co-owner. Nevertheless, if the child grows up and redeems the bond, the 1099 will be issued in the child's name.

✔ The interest earned on savings bonds is normally tax deferred. But children who own bonds and are in low (or zero) brackets should not defer. Report the interest now, when little or no tax will be due, rather than wait until the child grows up. To get this easy tax break on bonds bought this year: File a return for the child showing how much the EE bonds gained in value (your bank, S&L, or credit union may have this information; or write, call, or dial up on the Internet the Bureau of the Public Debt, address page 201). No more tax returns have to be filed for those particular bonds as long as the child owes no tax. In any year the child does owe a tax, the return will have to show that year's gain in the EE bonds' value.

What if your child deferred income taxes in the past and now wants to pay them currently? In the year you switch, all past gains must be reported.

What if the child has been paying taxes currently and now wants to defer (deferral is smart for children who have enough unearned income to owe a kiddie tax—page 89)? File Form 3115, Application for Change in Accounting Method, with the child's tax return for the year you want the change to start.

Keep copies of all the child's tax returns. When the bonds are cashed in, you (or your child) must be prepared to prove which gains were previously reported. Otherwise, the IRS might conclude that the child owes taxes on all of the profits.

✔ Bonds may be held by the trustee of your trust. But the trust can't be co-owner or beneficiary.

✔ What if you die holding savings bonds? Your executor or trustee has two tax choices:

1. All the income to date can be reported on your final tax return, and the taxes paid. The beneficiary who receives the bonds should then be taxed only on the income earned from that point on. To avoid being taxed on the full amount at redemption, however, the beneficiary must have a copy of the tax return to prove how much was previously paid.

2. The bonds can be passed to the beneficiary as is, with all the tax deferred. When the beneficiary redeems, he or she pays the entire tax.

✔ When one owner dies, a co-owner takes over the bonds automatically. But they should be reissued in the surviving owner's name (or in the name of the surviving owner—named first—plus a new co-owner). If you inherit a savings bond that was issued to someone else, you can also have it reissued in your name (or in your name plus a co-owner).

On reissue, the bond's final maturity remains the same, interest accumulates as usual, and no taxes are due. However, you can't have a bond reissued if it's close to its final maturity. Such bonds must be redeemed.

To redeem a bond or have it reissued in a new name, a beneficiary has to produce a death certificate. A co-owner can redeem without a death certificate but will need it for reissue.

If you inherit a bond and die without having the former owner's name removed, your heirs will have to produce two death certificates—yours and the former owner's—before they can redeem the bonds.

Co-owners can redeem their bonds at any bank that handles that business. If you inherited someone else's bond, however, you have to redeem through a Federal Reserve bank or the Bureau of the Public Debt (page 201).

✔ If you die without a will, your family will have to suffer a mess of paperwork (Form PD 5336) before your savings bonds can be passed to a new owner. So don't.

✔ If you co-own bonds that cannot be found after the other owner's death, file a lost-bond claim with the Bureau of the Public Debt and have them reissued. You may discover that the previous owner cashed them without telling you.

✔ For a reissue form (PD 4000), ask a commercial bank that handles savings bond sales or call the nearest regional Federal Reserve bank or branch. The forms are fairly simple. If you have a question, call the nearest Fed. Your bank might also help you—sometimes free, sometimes for a fee. For the five Feds that handle reissue, see page 200.

✔ What if you want to give away a savings bond, and have it reissued in the name of your spouse, child, or blood relative? Suppress the thought. You'll owe income taxes currently on the accumulated interest even though that interest won't actually be paid out. Years later, when the recipient redeems the bond, all the interest will be taxable unless he or she can prove that part of the tax was already paid. These rules also apply if you're the bond's principal co-owner (listed first on the bond's face) and want to reissue it solely in the name of the other owner. There's no tax, however, if you are merely removing the second co-owner's name or reissuing the bond in the name of your trustee.

✔ What if you marry and change your name? You don't have to get your savings bonds reissued. When you cash them in, just sign the bond with both your maiden name and your married name.

✔ What if you buy a bond and it comes with your name spelled wrong or the wrong date on it? Don't fix it yourself. You cannot redeem a bond that has been altered. Return it to the place that issued it and get the error fixed.

✔ You're not allowed to borrow against your savings bonds.

✔ If you lose a bond it's easy to replace as long as you know its face value (denomination), issue date, registration number, and the name or names in which it was issued, their addresses, and their Social Security numbers. Photocopy each bond you own or list the critical information. Keep these records in your safe-deposit box or fireproof home safe.

The Federal Reserve banks or branches that handle requests to reissue a savings bond in another name:

Federal Reserve Bank
Buffalo Branch
P.O. Box 961
Buffalo, NY 14240
(716) 849-5165
http://www.ny.frb.org

Federal Reserve Bank
Pittsburgh Branch
P.O. Box 867
Pittsburgh, PA 15230
(412) 261-7900
http://www.clev.frb.org

Federal Reserve Bank of Richmond
P.O. Box 27622
Richmond, VA 23261
(804) 697-8370
http://www.rich.frb.org

Federal Reserve Bank of Minneapolis
250 Marquette Ave.
Minneapolis, MN 55401
(612) 343-5300
http://woodrow.mpls.frb.fed.us

Federal Reserve Bank of Kansas City
P.O. Box 419440
Kansas City, MO 64198
(816) 881-2919
http://www.frbkc.org

If you don't keep good records, the Treasury may be able to trace the bond for you, especially if it was issued since January 1974. All those savings bonds have Social Security numbers on them. What's lost can be found if the Treasury knows the Social Security number of the first owner named on the bond.

Older bonds sometimes carry Social Security numbers, too. If not, the Treasury can't hope to trace ownership unless it knows the bond's serial number or the name on the bond and that person's address when it was bought.

A lost bond can be replaced at no cost to you. If you're replacing a partly burned or mutilated bond, send the Bureau of the Public Debt (page 201) the remains. The form used for replacement is PD 1048, available from many commercial banks, a regional Federal Reserve bank or branch (see above), and the Bureau of the Public Debt. Replacement takes anywhere from 8 to 24 weeks.

If you replace a bond and the original turns up, it must be surrendered for cancellation. The government won't let you cash the same bond twice. If you try, you'll find out that Big Brother knows.

✔ If you're in a payroll-deduction plan, you can buy fractions of bonds. For example, you might have $25 taken from every paycheck and credited toward the $50 cost of a $100 bond. After two payments you should be issued your bond. Arrange to have the bonds mailed to you and check that the amounts are right. Your only proof of purchase is normally the deduction shown on your pay stub—and it's up to you to check that you received what you paid for. To simplify the job, buy a full bond with each deduction, rather than a fraction of a bond. If your bonds don't arrive or you get the wrong denominations, query your payroll department, which should initiate a claims procedure.

✔ Any bank authorized to sell EE bonds can also cash them in for you, although some redemptions, like those by a guardian or trustee, have to be handled directly by the government. Try to redeem at a place you're known, such as your own bank. If you're not known, you will need documentary identification—a picture driver's license, an employee card with your picture on it—and may be limited to redeeming only $1,000 worth of bonds.

✔ Your accumulated bond interest becomes taxable when you cash the bonds in. So if possible, don't redeem them in a high-earning, preretirement year. Wait until well after you retire, when your income may have dropped.

✔ You can't rely on banks to answer your questions on savings bonds correctly, even if they handle them. The program is complex and the clerks may not be fully trained. You should get information brochures and research the bonds yourself.

✔ For a good, free guide, write for *The Savings Bonds Question & Answer Book*, Department of the Treasury, U.S. Savings Bond Marketing Office, Washington, DC 20226. The Bureau of the Public Debt answers questions, handles problems, and mails out forms. Call 304-480-6112 or send a postcard to the Bureau of the Public Debt, U.S. Savings Bond Operations Office, P.O. Box 1328, Parkersburg, WV 26106. For a lot more info about your bonds, including a calculator for computing your bonds' redemption values, visit the Web site: http://www.ustreas.gov/treasury/bureaus.

For a valuable reference book, get *U.S. Savings Bonds* by Daniel J. Pederson, $24.95, from TSBI Publishing, P.O. Box 9249, Detroit, MI 48209, or call 800-927-1901. For a fee, both Pederson and Union Information Services (see next paragraph) will dig out the current rates, interest-crediting dates, current worth, and maturity dates of every savings bond you own (some of the government's tables on these subjects are impenetrable).

You can manage your bond investments yourself with a software program called *The United States Savings Bond Consultant, Manager Version*: $64.90, including shipping, from Union Information Services, 1540 Route #38, Suite #307, Wall, NJ 07719 or call 800-717-BOND. To receive information about bonds by phone, call UIS at 900-225-5426 and have your bond's series, denomination, and issue date handy. Calls cost 95 cents a minute.

Inflation-Protection Savings Bonds. Watch for a new type of savings bond whose return is linked to the rise in the consumer price index. At this writing, the details haven't been released. In concept, they'll work like the inflation-indexed Treasury bonds introduced in 1997 (page 193).

HH Bonds: The Case Against. You can tax-defer your gains on Series E and EE bonds by exchanging them for HH bonds. HH bonds pay out taxable interest every 6 months.

But HH bonds are a lousy deal. For 10 long years they won't pay more than the guaranteed interest rate on the day they were issued—currently only 4 percent. A new rate will be set for the subsequent 10 years, but you can't expect a better deal as long as market rates stay low. Here are two alternatives to HH bonds:

1. Best choice for government-insured income, in most tax brackets: Cash in all your E and EE bonds, pay the tax, and buy a 10-year Treasury bond (page 762). You'll get a much higher income than HH bonds pay. You'll also be left with more principal, after tax, when the bonds mature. Savers often hate to do this because paying taxes makes them break out in a rash. But that allergy deprives them of extra money to live on.

If cashing in all the bonds at once will raise your tax bracket, cash them over two years—say, some in December and some in January.

2. Best choice in the top tax bracket and second-best for everyone else: Hang on to your E and EE bonds. For income, cash in a portion of them every year. By cashing in 4 percent of your bonds' face value, you'd get the same income HH bonds would pay but with this advantage: cashed-in E and EE bonds are only partly taxable (part is income but part is a return of your original investment). HH-bond interest is taxable in full. For a higher income, cash in enough E and EE bonds to equal what you might have received by switching to Treasury bonds.

When cashing in bonds, be sure you know how much they currently earn. Each bond is paying anywhere from 4 to 6 percent, depending on when it was bought. By selectively cashing in low-rate bonds, you get a steady income without giving up your higher-rate bonds. Over the years, this strategy earns you more.

When might HH bonds make sense? When your E or EE bonds have reached final maturity (so they're not paying interest anymore) and you don't want to buy Treasury securities. HH bonds will pay more than if you redeemed your Es and EEs, paid the tax, and put the proceeds in a pass-book account. They might also net more than Treasuries if you're going from a high tax bracket to a low one.

You might prefer savings bonds for their liquidity. You can sell an EE or HH at any time and get the full price. If you sell a Treasury bond before maturity, you get either less or more than you paid, depending on market conditions at the time.

A Tip on Older Savings Bonds, Bought Prior to May 1, 1995: These bonds have interest-rate guarantees ranging from 4 to 6 percent. Don't cash in an older bond without ascertaining its guarantee. It may be earning more than any other fixed-income investment you own. To check the guarantee, send a postcard for the free Table of Guaranteed Minimum Rates and Original Maturity Periods, free from the Bureau of the Public Debt (page 201).

HOW TO BUY TREASURIES

There's no such thing as a physical Treasury certificate anymore. Your purchase is recorded. You get a statement. But you don't get the thing itself to hold in your hand because there is no "thing itself." A Treasury certificate has become a concept in the mind and a byte in the computer.

You can buy Treasuries through a Federal Reserve bank or branch (page 204), or through a commercial bank or stockbroker. Which one to choose depends on the kind of investor you are.

Savers: Buy Through the Fed

Every penny you earn in yield is yours to keep because you pay no fees or commissions on securities held to maturity. All your transactions are handled free. There's almost no paperwork because everything is accomplished electronically.

Under a system called Treasury Direct, you open an account with the Federal Reserve, which keeps track of all your transactions. To buy, you mail in a "tender" form, along with a certified check or authorization for the Fed to subtract the payment from your bank account. Your interest earnings are paid electronically into your bank or mutual-fund account. When your securities mature, you can reinvest by Touch-Tone phone or have the principal forwarded to your account.

To sell prior to maturity, you mail a form to the Chicago Federal Reserve Bank (page 204), which will get three price quotes from dealers and sell for you at the highest bid. Fee for this service: $34.

The Fed will send you information on Treasury Direct. Or dial up Treasury Direct on the U.S. Bureau of the Public Debt's Web site, http://www.publicdebt.treas.gov. When you open an account, you'll be asked for your bank's nine-digit American Bankers Association Routing Transit Number. That's the number on the bottom of any check or deposit slip. At this writing, plans are afoot to let you buy by phone or Web.

Speculators: Buy Through Banks or Stockbrokers

A speculator buys and sells long-term Treasury bonds, hoping to earn a profit from changes in interest rates. This means selling securities before they mature, and at a moment's notice. Only commercial banks or stockbrokerage firms do that. They also let you order by phone and will lend you

FEDERAL RESERVE BANKS

600 Atlantic Avenue
Boston, MA 02106
(617) 973-3000
http://www.bos.frb.org

33 Liberty Street
Federal Reserve P.O. Station
New York, NY 10045
(212) 720-5000
http://www.ny.frb.org

Ten Independence Mall
P.O. Box 66
Philadelphia, PA 19108
(215) 574-6000
http://www.phil.frb.org

1455 East Sixth Street
P.O. Box 6387
Cleveland, OH 44101
(216) 579-2000
http://www.clev.frb.org

701 East Byrd Street
P.O. Box 27622
Richmond, VA 23261
(804) 697-8000
http://www.rich.frb.org

104 Marietta Street, N.W.
Atlanta, GA 30303
(404) 521-8500
http://www.frbatlanta.org

230 South LaSalle Street
P.O. Box 834
Chicago, IL 60690
(312) 322-5322
http://www.frbchi.org

411 Locust Street
P.O. Box 442
St. Louis, MO 63166
(314) 444-8444
http://www.stls.frb.org

250 Marquette Avenue
Minneapolis, MN 55401
(612) 340-2345
http://woodrow.mpls.frb.fed.us

925 Grand Boulevard
Kansas City, MO 64198
(816) 881-2000
http://www.frbkc.org

2200 North Pearl Street
P.O. Box 655906
Dallas, TX 75265
(214) 922-6000
http://www.dallasfed.org

101 Market Street
P.O. Box 7702
San Francisco, CA 94120
(415) 974-2000
http://www.frbsf.org

money against your securities. Sales commissions: a minimum of $15 to $60 every time you buy or sell.

It makes no sense at all to use brokerage firms for small orders of short-term Treasury securities. The commission might slash your yield by half a percent on a one-year, $10,000 T-bill. On larger purchases or on longer-term securities, however, brokerage fees don't take such a big bite.

SHOULD YOU BUY A MUTUAL FUND THAT INVESTS ONLY IN TREASURIES?

If you're a saver, no.

Savers need a sure thing. You want to earn interest while keeping your capital absolutely safe. Treasuries do that for you, as long as you own them individually and hold them to maturity.

Buying a mutual fund that invests in Treasuries introduces risk. Maybe you'll make money; then again, maybe you'll lose it. The value of your mutual fund will rise and fall along with changes in interest rates.

That's okay for investors who know what they're doing (to find out what you're doing, see Chapter 25). But hard-core savers should stay away. Funds aren't for people who'll have palpitations if their investment loses value, even temporarily. If you don't have the $10,000 for an individual Treasury bill, and don't want to put your $1,000 into a Treasury note lasting 4 years or more, put the money into a certificate of deposit.

SAVING MONEY IN A LIFE INSURANCE POLICY

When you buy cash-value life insurance, you buy a kind of savings account that builds up over many years. But there are two fatal drawbacks to this form of savings: (1) Very little money normally accumulates in the early years. (2) To get at your money, you generally have to borrow it, paying interest as you go. If you choose the money-fund option in a variable-life policy, the annual fees will virtually wipe out your yield. I'm all for good insurance, and a cash-value policy may be exactly what you want (page 296). But if savings are your primary interest, most people look somewhere else.

WHERE ELSE NOT TO KEEP CASH

Don't opt for the guaranteed savings options inside a variable annuity (page 896) or a brokerage-firm wrap account (page 667). The annual fees eat up your yield.

WHEN TO STOP SAVING

When you're young, you have to learn how to save. When you're old, you have to learn how to stop. Many older people live on the edge of poverty because they're afraid to spend the money they have so carefully put aside.

But past a certain age it's time to spend your children's inheritance, to give yourself the decent retirement you deserve. In Chapter 30, you'll find guidelines on how to spend your money without running out.

10.
Kicking the Credit-Card Habit

Learning to Live Without Consumer Debt

The new macho for the 1990s is canceling your credit cards. It says that you have money enough not to take plastic seriously.

Why do you need a fistful of credit cards? They're heavy. They make your wallet bulge. They cost money. You can't remember how much you've charged on them. Now that even the hoi polloi carry gold cards, prestige lies in flashing a plain-vanilla card. For an even bigger thrill, pay cash.

As a status symbol, the credit card is finished. It's now just a transactions workhorse, and having too many of them says you're dumb. Assuming, as I do, that you want to get out of debt and build some savings, plastic ought to serve a single purpose: convenience. You put it down instead of writing a check or paying cash. At the end of the month, you pay the bill. The *whole* bill.

Not that you're perfect. You'll still stretch the occasional bill over two or three months—maybe at Christmas or after a vacation. But your goal is never to charge any more than you can easily repay. For the twenty-first century, debt is Out.

HOW TO GET RID OF CONSUMER DEBT

It's so simple that I'm almost embarrassed to mention it.
Don't borrow anymore.

That's all there is to it.

Say to yourself, "Today, I am not going to put down a charge card for anything." When you buy something, pay cash or write a check.

Tomorrow, say the same thing: "I am not going to put down a charge card for anything. I am not even going to borrow $10 from a friend." Take it slowly, one day at a time. It's like stopping smoking. You'll be nervous at first; you won't see how it's possible to live; you'll suffer relapses and sneak a new debt or two. But when you get up every morning, renew your pledge. To make it easier, quit carrying credit cards.

I hear you saying, "I can't get along without a credit card." Of course you can. You can pay by check or debit card. On trips, you can use travelers checks. You may have to show a credit card to rent a car. But when you bring the car back, pay the bill by personal check or travelers check. (If the rental agent won't take your personal check, pay by card and immediately make out a check to the credit-card issuer; pay this bill the moment it arrives.)

If you object that you can't pay by check because you don't have enough money in the bank, you're missing my point. When you don't have the money in the bank, don't buy. If you find that you have to put down plastic, use an American Express card. It's not a credit card. You have to pay your bill in full by the end of the month.

Once you stop using credit cards, three things will happen:

1. You will buy less—and whatever you do buy will probably be a less expensive model or make. Studies have found that people spend more when they pay with plastic because it doesn't feel like real money. When it *is* real money, you're more sensible.

2. Your total debt will shrink rapidly. By paying off back bills and not adding new ones, you leave yourself pots of extra money to apply to debt reduction. You're also paying less interest, a big saving right there.

3. You will grow incredibly smug. You're the first on your block to get out of debt. Others will follow, but you'll be the first.

I'm not against credit cards. They're easy to use. They're handy. If your card has a low annual fee and a 25-day, interest-free grace period for paying your bills, you're getting monthly loans for practically nothing. What I'm against is buying more on your credit cards than you can pay for at the end of the month.

Once you've fought your way out of debt you can start using credit cards again, but only for the convenience of not carrying cash. Your days of debt are done. A big expense may sometimes drive you over the limit. A stereo. A llama. A hot-air balloon. Whenever you limp home, back in debt, recite your mantra: "From now on, I'm not going to put down a charge card for anything." Stick with it until you're free again.

REHAB, IN SEVEN STEPS

1. List each of your loans: how much you owe (most people don't know), the minimum monthly payment, the gross interest rate, and the rate after tax (the interest on home-equity loans is tax deductible if you itemize on your returns, but not the interest on most other loans). Note any service fees you're charged for carrying small balances. Total it up.

2. Restructure your debt to reduce the interest cost. You can transfer credit-card balances to lower-rate cards (some cards charge a 2 percent cash-advance fee but many don't). Or consolidate consumer loans on a credit-union loan or home-equity line of credit, provided that you won't run up your credit cards all over again. If you ask, the lender may lower the rate and the annual fee—especially if you're threatening to cancel the card.

3. Make one-shot reductions in your loan balances. You might run a yard sale and use all the proceeds to pay off debt. Or sell off a few shares of stock you inherited. Or use your savings, if you have any. It's smarter to chop debt than to hoard a low-rate savings account. (But keep on adding to your retirement account because those contributions lower your tax.)

4. Pay the monthly minimums on your lower-rate loans while putting the rest of your available money toward the highest-rate loan. The size of the loan doesn't matter, only the size of the interest rate. The faster you knock off high-rate debt, the faster your burden will decline.

5. Increase your monthly debt-reduction budget even if it's only by a small amount. Small amounts make an enormous difference. Say that you owe $3,000 at 18 percent interest, on which you're paying the bare minimum: 2 percent of the balance each month. You start out at $60 a month and pay a little less each time. On this schedule, it will take 30 years and 10 months to get out of debt. If you add just $15 to each of your payments, you'll be out of debt in 5 years and 3 months, saving an enormous $5,759 in interest. (A lot of people find this calculation, and others like it, too astonishing to be true. But it *is* true. Honest.)

6. Keep on paying the same amount each month, even though your loan balance goes down. The faster you pay off principal, the more interest you save and the faster your total debt declines. Once you've erased the highest-rate loan, start on the next highest—still paying the same fixed amount. For help and motivation, try the Debt Zapper, $15 from Bankcard Holders of America, 524 Branch Dr., Salem, VA 24153. This service calculates the most efficient way to get rid of your debts and gives you a monthly repayment schedule for each.

7. Work your way down the list, debt by debt. To keep yourself motivated, you have to take pleasure in the process. Post your payment schedule on the refrigerator and check each one off. Or give yourself a quarterly reward for staying on the wagon.

WHAT'S THE BEST CREDIT CARD?

Credit cards aren't the problem. The problem is excessive debt. Paying with plastic is an enormous convenience, but which one is best depends on how you typically pay.

When you don't carry debt, the Best Credit Card has no annual fee or only a small one—no more than $10. And it offers a 25-day grace period, during which time no interest is charged on the money you owe. That's all. You don't give two hoots what the interest rate is. The bank could charge 30 percent and it wouldn't matter because you'll never (almost never) have to pay it. You are getting your monthly credit virtually free.

Unreconstructed debtors need a different kind of card. For you, the annual fee doesn't matter. Neither does the grace period, since you'll never use it. Your Best Credit Card has the lowest possible interest rate because you are always rolling over debt.

Many of us have a foot in both camps—sometimes staying ahead, sometimes falling behind. This suggests owning two credit cards: (1) *a convenience card*, with no or low fees and a grace period, for bills that you know you can cover at the end of the month. Buy all perishables, like restaurant meals and gasoline, with this card, and all other items you know you can pay for immediately; (2) *a low-interest card*, for major purchases that will take months to pay for. Go for an interest rate in the area of 12 to 15 percent (top credit risks can get even less). Charge only items that will last a long time because those are the only ones worth paying interest for.

VARIABLES, TEASERS, AND FUZZIES

More than 80 percent of cards today charge variable interest rates on your revolving balances. Typically, you pay a fixed number of percentage points over the bank's prime rate (the prime is the benchmark lending rate). For example, you might pay prime plus 7.5 points. That's 15.5 percent with the prime at 8 percent, and 17.5 percent with the prime at 10 percent. About half the banks adjust card rates monthly, the other half do it quarterly. The higher rates go, the wider the gap between high- and low-rate cards. When interest rates rise, you can hold down your monthly payments by reducing debt.

One warning: When the prime rate falls, your credit-card rate may not fall commensurately. Many cards impose minimum rates and set them high, so your cost can rise but never fall by very much (if it falls at all). Look for this gyp in the fine print, and pass these cards by.

Teasers are the super-low rates that card issuers dangle when they're trying to sign you up. They last no longer than a few months, then jump up to the standard rate. Sometimes they cover only balances transferred from another card, not new purchases. When you're choosing a card, the standard rate is the one to evaluate. Your best long-term bet: a low-rate card, even if it lacks a spiffy introductory offer.

Fuzzies are cards you have to accept without knowing all the terms. The credit-card mailing promises you a rate "as low as [say] 7.9 percent" but "subject to credit history." Surprise, surprise, your history may not be good enough. When you get the card, it may cost you more than 7.9 percent. It may also have a lower credit limit than you expected. But you've now got the card, and probably won't bother to cancel it.

FINDING A LOW-RATE CARD

Low-rate credit cards—charging 3 to 5 percentage points over the prime rate or less—are generally offered by institutions that don't offer much in the way of rebates or rewards (page 211). They look for the very best credit risks. According to Bankcard Holders of America, that's applicants who: (1) carry a reasonable amount of debt relative to their incomes —no more than 40 percent tops, including the mortgage; (2) always pay on time; (3) have at least two active accounts that have been in use for a year or more; (4) use only part of the available credit, with balances on no more than four accounts; (5) have worked at the same company, and lived in the same place, for a couple of years; (6) had no credit problems in the past; (7) are U.S. citizens; and (8) haven't opened another credit line recently.

The last point—no new credit lately—eliminates a lot of people who think of themselves as good credit risks. Here's why:

Whenever you apply for credit, the lender inquires about your payment history. That inquiry shows on your credit report. If you have just refinanced your house at one bank and applied for a new credit card at another one, your credit report will show that two lenders asked about you. The report doesn't say whether they accepted you or turned you down, only that they asked.

But that makes a low-rate lender's computer a tad suspicious. It will assume that you're suddenly loading up on credit, for purposes it doesn't care to analyze. It will reject you rather than take the risk.

So you need a strategic plan for getting a low-rate card. First, pay down your current debts. Second, let at least a year go by without applying for any new loans or accepting a higher credit limit on your current cards. Third, cancel the credit cards you're not currently using by writing to the creditor. Get a copy of your credit report (page 234) to be sure that the creditor obeyed. (Your canceled cards will still show on your report because they're part of your history, but the accounts should be shown as closed.) Then try again for the low-rate card you want. Some national banks have low-rate cards. More often, you'll find them at local banks, S&Ls, or credit unions.

A handful of small banks offer super-low rates, at 2 percentage points or less over the prime. They generally charge annual fees in the $25 range and provide low credit lines.

If you can't land a low-rate card, move to the next level: 6 or 7 percentage points over prime. Many big banks offer these rates and mail applications nationally. You needn't be squeaky clean to qualify. Anyone with a decent credit history should be able to get one.

Now we come to the cards that charge 8 percentage points or more over prime. They take practically everybody with a heartbeat and a mailbox. Good credit risks shouldn't bother with these high-rate cards because they can do better. Why do so many people take them anyway? Because they're lazy. It's easier to sign an application that you get in the mail than to hunt around for a cheaper card.

But credit-card hunting isn't hard. A couple of organizations publish lists of banks with likely cards. Try RAM Research, P.O. Box 1700, Frederick, MD 21702 (800-344-7714)—$5 for its latest issue of *CardTrak*, a list of the best deals in low-rate cards, no-fee cards, rewards cards (see below), and secured cards (page 223); free on the Internet at http://www.cardtrak.com. Or Bankcard Holders of America, 524 Branch Dr., Salem, VA 24153—$4 for a *Low-Rate, No-Fee Credit Card List.*

Another possibility: Instead of switching to a new card, ask your current bank to lower your interest rate, waive your annual fee, or both. It almost certainly will if you pay on time, charge at least $3,000 a year, and carry a balance of at least $2,000. You might also win a lower fee from American Express if you use the card a lot.

REWARDS CARDS

Use your credit card, win a prize! Prize jerk, I'd say, unless you handle your balances exactly right.

Rewards cards offer you cash rebates, frequent-flier miles, discounts on goods and services, interest-rate reductions, and other goodies pegged to the volume of charges you put on the card. You might also win points for transferring unpaid balances from another card or carrying balances instead of paying in full at the end of the month. (The card industry loves debtors best because most of its profits come from the interest charged.)

Your prizes are worth about one to 2 percent of the sum you charge. To earn them, you're probably paying 2 or 3 percentage points more in interest than competing cards charge plus much higher annual fees (surely you didn't think that all those "gifts" were free?). Rewards cards can be dandy as long as you: (1) Charge a large sum—enough to earn back the annual fee. For example, if the card costs $50, and the average frequent-flier mile is worth 2 cents, you have to charge $2,500 a year just to break even. (2) Always pay the full bill at the end of the month or transfer each month's unpaid balances to a lower-rate credit card. Otherwise, you're a loser. You're paying more than your prizes are worth.

For a list of the leading rewards cards and a cost-benefit analysis, send $5 for the *Rebate/Frequent-Flyer Guide,* Bankcard Holders of America, 524 Branch Dr., Salem, VA 24153. Warning: The issuers can change their rewards without warning, leaving you with an even less valuable card.

HOW TO BE A CONVENIENCE USER

More shoppers are twigging onto the credit-card game. They're using their cards to buy everything in sight, then paying the full bill at the end of the month. That gives them all the convenience of plastic and none of the cost. They're even saving on ATM fees because they use so much less cash.

To be a convenience user, get a card with no annual fee and a 25- or 30-day grace period before interest is charged on new purchases. Pay every bill in full. To be sure that you can, deduct every purchase from your checking-account balance as you go along, so you won't overspend your account. For you, rebates and frequent-flier miles are pure profit. If the card issuer decides to impose a fee on convenience users, protest with all your might. If that doesn't work, say ta-ta and choose another card.

WHY ARE YOU SO POPULAR?

Your mail is full of letters from bankers begging you to take a new "prescreened" credit card. It's not your good looks that attract them. It's not even your income. It's your gorgeous pile of debt.

These banks buy lists of names from credit bureaus. They typically want people who have no more than five or six credit cards already, are carrying debt on most of them, and pay their bills on time. You may be choking on your debts. You may be paying just the minimum on every single card you have. You may be taking cash from one card to pay off another. That doesn't matter. As long as you're not a late payer, these banks want to reel you in. Some even go after people who have ten cards or more. They'll tempt you with credit lines of $1,000 to $10,000 on which they charge 18 to 22 percent.

Spendaholics imagine that as long as the bankers keep offering them credit, they must not be too deeply in debt. They think that the credit machine will flash *tilt* when they have finally gone too far. That's an illusion. Banks that charge high interest rates find it profitable to give cards even to spendaholics. A certain percentage of defaults is built right into the rate they charge. If you go broke that's your lookout, not theirs.

WHAT'S HAPPENING TO CREDIT-CARD PRICES

They're shooting the moon. You may not notice because the trend is toward lower or zero annual fees. To make up for cutting that cost, however, credit cards now rival checking accounts in the number and creativity of the fees they carry.

For example, many card issuers are (1) cutting out grace periods, so you pay interest from the time you make each purchase; (2) starting the interest clock from the day you make the purchase instead of the day the purchase is posted to your account; (3) imposing late-payment fees—commonly $15 at this writing and as much as $25; (4) imposing late fees for payments as little as one to 15 days late, as opposed to the traditional 30 days; (5) imposing $15 fees for exceeding your credit limit; (6) charging $20 to $30 for bouncing a check; (7) raising your interest rate by 3 to 10 percentage points for a year or more if you pay late or exceed your credit limit; (8) imposing a similar interest-rate penalty if your credit report shows that you're not as good a risk as you used to be; (9) charging you for inquiring about your credit limit; (10) compounding your loan interest daily instead of the traditional monthly (check the disclosure for the phrase *daily periodic rate* as opposed to a *monthly* periodic rate); (11) slamming you by adding extras to your account that you didn't agree to buy—for example, credit-life insurance or catalogue shopping; (12) charging fees if you don't carry a balance on your card or don't use your card enough.

Check for these fees before agreeing to buy a card. I wouldn't have one that had the right to raise my rate unexpectedly. If you get a new cardholder agreement in the mail, read it over carefully, even if you need a magnifying glass. The bank may have kicked up a number of fees. You might want to switch your debt to a lower-cost card. If your rate goes up, seventeen states allow you to pay off the debt at the former interest rate if you notify the bank in writing and quit using the card.

As cards grow more expensive and the interest-free grace period vanishes, convenience users might think about switching to debit cards (page 225).

If you have a lot of credit cards, save yourself money by canceling all but two or three. And ask yourself whether you really need a gold card. They cost more and come with perks that you may not use. But you may like their higher credit lines.

A few cards peddle gimmicks for an extra $20 to $35 a year—things like extended warranties for certain products purchased with the card, travel rebates if you book through a certain travel agent, rental-car collision insurance (although you may already have it in your auto policy), baggage insurance, discount catalogue shopping. Maybe you'll find these enhancements worth it, but maybe not. They may be added to gold cards at no extra cost.

WHAT YOU'LL LEARN IF YOU READ THE DISCLOSURE BOX ON THE CREDIT-CARD OFFER

Read the disclosures? Is Quinn nuts? All that stupid fine print and sentences written by Philadelphia lawyers?

I know what you mean. But if you read slowly, the sentences almost parse. The disclosures tell you pretty quickly which cards are worth getting and which are pickpockets in disguise. There's a disclosure box on the back of every credit-card application. Here's what to look for:

• *The interest rate.* Personally, I like plain-vanilla low-rate cards. But the fad today is for low "introductory" rates followed by higher rates. Check to see how soon you'll be raised and what that higher rate will be. Your regular rate is usually couched as "the prime rate plus X percentage points," but do you know where the prime rate is? At this writing, rates of 17 percent and higher aren't competitive for people of average credit risk. Some cards peg their rates to LIBOR (the London InterBank Offered Rate), which greatly confuses card users. Forget about LIBOR. Go with a rate that's easier to understand.

A few cards are starting to levy penalty rates on people whose accounts are no longer "in good standing" (page 222), probably because a payment was late. You'll see a lot more of this in the future. Your interest rate may be pegged to your credit score (page 219).

• *The grace period.* Most cards give you 25 days before charging interest if you're not carrying any unpaid balances. Some give you 30. But others have cut back to 20 or 15 days. A few have no grace period at all, charging you interest all the time on everything you buy. On most cards there's also no grace period for cash advances, nor for new purchases if you're carrying forward a debt from the previous month.

• *The annual fee.* Convenience users seek out no-fee cards. But sometimes the fee is waived for the first year only, or waived only if you charge a substantial amount. Unless you're a big spender, the rewards cards aren't worth their annual fees (page 211). Your fee might be cut or eliminated if you call and ask, especially if you habitually carry a balance. Banks like customers who pay interest.

- *Other fees.* The disclosure should lay out all your fees, but may not explain them in full. For example, you probably won't be told exactly when late charges are assessed.

- *The cash advance.* What you're looking for here is the cost of borrowing cash. Some cards charge a onetime cash-advance fee plus a much higher interest rate than the standard rate that's applied to purchases (page 214). Other cards have no fee and charge the same rate for everything.

You *must* hunt down the latter type if your strategy is to use your spare cash to pay off debts rather than build a savings account (page 208). In an emergency you'll have to get cash from your card, and you don't want it to cost too much. Unfortunately, the disclosure box may show only the cash-advance fee. If no interest rate is specified for cash advances, call the issuer and ask for it. Don't assume it's the same as the card's standard rate.

You can use cash advances to pay off balances on other credit cards. In this case, you're usually charged the standard rate and no cash-advance fee —but check in advance.

- *How interest is calculated on unpaid balances.* Most cards use the *average daily balance.* That averages each day's debt and charges you interest on it. The calculation you don't want is known as *two-cycle billing.* It effectively charges you an extra month's interest the first month you carry a balance on the card. This makes almost no difference to people who always carry a balance, but it's costly to people who alternate between carrying a balance and paying in full. You could be charged as much as 4 extra months' interest a year. Dean Witter's Discover card uses two-cycle billing; First USA uses it for some accounts. Expect to see more of it as issuers scramble for greater profits.

The disclosure will also tell you whether your loan interest is being compounded daily or monthly (the latter is a little cheaper).

The Cardholder Agreement. Once you've signed up for the card, you'll get the full cardholder agreement laying out all the terms that the early disclosure didn't mention. Hardly anyone reads this agreement. But if you protest a fee, expect the issuer to tell you that it's in the contract.

YOUR CREDIT-CARD FACT SHEET

- Visa, MasterCard, Discover, Universal Card, and American Express's Optima are revolving-credit cards. You can charge up to a certain limit and carry most of the debt forward from one month to the next.
- Department-store cards work like Visa and MasterCard, but may have a lower credit limit and a higher interest rate. It usually pays to use your bank card instead of the store's own charge card.

When you shop, you may be offered 10 percent off on that day's purchases if you'll apply for the store's own card. Don't do it unless you'll really use it. Otherwise, you're just adding a credit line that makes you look vulnerable to debt. Such a perception could keep you from qualifying for a lower-rate card.

• American Express's green-and-gold cards, Carte Blanche, and Diners Club are charge cards. You pay the full bill at the end of each month, although some credit is allowed. For example, you can stretch out payments on airline tickets charged to American Express.

As a practical matter, you probably don't need charge cards. They carry higher annual fees than credit cards do, and are accepted in fewer places. They impose a discipline: you must pay them off, so you can't run up interest charges. But disciplined users of credit cards do just as well.

• Oil-company cards usually require you to pay each monthly bill in full. But some let you stretch out payments for tires or car repairs.

• No central organization sets the interest rates and charges on MasterCard and Visa cards. Each issuing bank determines its own prices, so costs vary widely. There are wonderful cards and rotten cards, depending on the deal. By contrast, all of the cards from a charge-card company cost the same.

• Card issuers have quietly lowered minimum monthly payments to 2 percent of your balance or less. Some require as little as 1.7 percent. That stretches out your payment over more than 30 years, at an enormous interest cost. Pay more than the minimum or you'll never get out of debt.

• Some cards require that you take a cash advance when you first sign up, so you start out with a $2,000 debt. Avoid them.

• "Prescreened" cards often dangle a handsome credit limit in front of you—maybe "as much as" $10,000. But those are three little wiggle words. Once you say yes, the issuer will recheck your credit report. The card you get in the mail may have a lower credit limit and a higher interest rate than the lender originally promised. Best advice: send it back.

• Having too many credit cards will prevent you from getting other loans, even if all your payments are up to date. That's because each of your cards has a line of credit that you could borrow against at any time. A lender will ask: Could you carry your debts if you borrowed against every card to the max? If not, you'll be denied another loan. How do lenders know how big your credit lines are? They check your credit report at the credit bureau.

• You can become a prisoner of the cards you have. That happens if you let lenders shower you with larger credit lines. Even if you don't use the line, all that credit may deter other card issuers from accepting your application, especially for a low-rate card.

• Ask the issuer of your lowest-rate card how to use its credit line to pay off balances on other cards. Some ask for the list of your debts and handle the payoffs themselves. Some accept telephone requests. Some send you a "convenience check" or a pack of them. Before you act, check on the interest rate and fees.

• You say that you canceled the credit cards that you don't use. Have you looked to see if the cancellation took? Some lenders keep on reporting you as a cardholder even after you drop them. There's only one way to find out. Get a copy of your credit report (page 234) and look. If the card isn't shown as closed (using a designation such as "paid satisfied" or "closed by the customer"), call your former creditor and find out what it takes to get your name off its files. Then follow through in writing.

• Are you tempted by a "tax-deductible" credit card? Normally, interest paid on credit-card debt isn't tax deductible. In this case it is, because the card is linked to your home equity. Every time you make a purchase you are taking a tiny second mortgage, and mortgage interest can be written off. Home-equity cards are okay if you always pay off your bill at the end of the month. But if you let your indebtedness rise, you'll be spending your equity at the mall: trading a house for a blouse.

• You might be offered a bank card that carries the name of your college, your union, or a favored charity. My question: Has the group bargained for the best deal for its members, or has it taken the best deal for itself? Most organizations think "me first." They get perhaps 0.5 percent of whatever you charge on the card, or 25 cents per transaction, or a bounty for everyone who signs up. You'll pay the price, in a higher rate or fee. Accept a bank card only on competitive terms. If you want to support your college or a charity, give money directly and take a tax deduction.

• You are not responsible for your spouse's debts that occurred before the marriage, or occurred during the marriage for purposes unrelated to it. For example, you wouldn't have to pay if your spouse sneaked off to Las Vegas and put the trip on his or her personal credit card. But you're generally responsible for marital debts that are considered "necessaries," or purchases made by one spouse as "agent" for the other. You're also responsible if you co-signed the debt or the credit card (including the credit card used for the Vegas trip).

• Credit-card registration services keep a list of all your cards and will notify the issuers if you lose your wallet or change your address. Is this service really worth the $39 or so you're charged? Maybe so if your wallet is stuffed with twenty cards. Probably not if you carry just a couple. You can keep a list of your cards (or photocopy them) and call the issuers yourself. To make themselves seem more valuable, these services are adding extras like free copies of your credit report.

• Do you plan to pay for an ongoing service by having the company debit your bank account automatically? Consider giving the company your credit-card number, instead. If there's a dispute and you cancel the service, automatic debits may take awhile to stop. But you can get credit-card payments reversed by reporting them as an unauthorized charge (page 228).

• Don't jump at a creditor's offer to let you skip a month of payments. All you're doing is running up extra interest charges.

• If you marry and change your name, change it on your credit cards, too. Always use the same name when you apply for credit in order to keep your credit history all together.

• If you're carrying unpaid balances, send in your payment as soon as you get the bill. That saves you a little interest if your lender computes interest charges daily.

• You think you're paying the stated rate on your credit card? Guess again. After monthly compounding, an 18 percent card actually costs you 19.65 percent. You might also have no grace period, daily instead of monthly compounding, and two-cycle billing. A study by Bankcard Holders of America found that a so-called 18 percent card could cost anywhere from $66 to $196 in finance charges, depending on how the interest was figured.

• Would you believe "zero percent financing"? In most cases, you shouldn't. A store may offer you zero percent on furniture or appliances if you pay by a certain date, usually within 6 months. But (1) the financing price is probably built into the item's cost; (2) if you don't pay within the stated time, the store might charge you 22 percent from the date of purchase.

• Don't buy credit-card life insurance to pay off the balance if you die unless it's the only coverage you can get. It's dreadfully expensive for the benefit you receive. Ditto credit-card disability and unemployment insurance, which offer very limited protection (page 274).

• When you pay with a Visa, MasterCard, or American Express card, you shouldn't have to present any identification. The merchant will check the validity of the card, electronically or by telephone, and check the signature on the card against the way you sign the bill. You can be asked for ID if you've forgotten to sign the card, or asked for your address if you order by telephone. Otherwise, you shouldn't have to prove anything. The card companies all guarantee payment on cards that have been properly checked.

At any rate, those are the rules. Some merchants do check and it's hard to override them. There are exceptions for suspicious circumstances, which some merchants stretch. Ill-trained bank-card personnel may tell you, erroneously, that merchants can do whatever they want. If a merchant insisted on your ID, report the incident to: MasterCard International, Radio City Station, P.O. Box 1288, New York, NY 10101; Visa, P.O. Box 8999, San Francisco, CA 94128; or American Express at 800-YES-CARD. Merchants that take Discover cards can check IDs at will.

• If you don't want the credit bureaus to sell your name to direct-market companies, write and tell them so. They have to take your name off the list. You have to write to just one of the three major bureaus; it spreads the word to the other two.

• Here's a useful tip from a reader. "While on a trip, I started having trouble with my ATM card. At first it worked erratically in the ATM machines, then not at all. It turned out that I had a magnetic clasp on my billfold which demagnetized my card. I had never heard of that." Neither had I, but now all the other readers will!

WHAT MAKES YOU CREDITWORTHY?

Lenders build computer models to define the kinds of borrowers who repay their debts. You're given points for various conditions of your life, such as how many years you've been in the workforce, how long you've used credit cards, and how steadily you pay. It doesn't matter if some items tally low as long as others come in high. If you accumulate enough points —known as your credit score—you qualify for a card.

You can't find out your score. It's released only to people who inquire about you. The most commonly used system puts your number anywhere from 300 ("bounce the bum") to 800 ("borrow money from us, *please*"). Scores change as new information comes in.

Each lender skews its credit-scoring system to approve the kinds of customers it wants. When you apply for a credit card or loan, a computer dials up your score to see if it makes that particular lender's cut. High-rate lenders accept lower scores than low-rate lenders do. But you're the ideal applicant everywhere if:

- You have held your job for a while (you probably aren't going to be fired, although that's hardly a certainty anymore).
- You own your home (owners are less transient than renters).
- You've lived in your home or rented your current apartment for a while (proving that you can handle the payments).
- You hold just a few credit cards and always pay on time (you may rate more highly for managing four cards than just one).
- You carry balances on your card rather than paying in full each month (card companies love debtors best).
- You have reasonable debts and credit lines compared with your income (high incomes aren't required, just evidence that you live within your means or not far beyond it).
- You haven't recently applied for other credit or run up new debt on the cards you have.
- You carry more bank cards than department-store or retail cards.
- You've led a spotless credit life: no delinquencies, no charge-offs, no liens, no bankruptcy.
- You work in a field considered steady (teachers are more desirable than farm owners because farms can go bust; doctors are more desirable than lawyers because lawyers worry less about being sued).

Not all this information can be gleaned from a credit file. Banks that mass-mail "preapproved" cards don't know that you were recently fired or that you took a new job last year at a cut in pay. They can't tell if you're scrambling to pay the minimum on your present debt or if you're paying the minimum by choice. So you may be offered far more credit than you can handle. That doesn't bother banks that charge high interest rates; they make money even if you default. But why should you take a high-rate card if you're a good credit risk? Throw out those mass mailings and apply instead to a lower-interest bank.

If you're turned down for credit, lenders have to say why. The letter might list several items you scored low on; none is the deciding factor and some may be incomprehensible (how would you interpret the following explanation: "recently active or lack of bank, retail, or finance accounts"?). If just one of your low-scoring items had been higher, you might have been lifted above the line. At a local bank, you can speak to a credit manager personally to find out how to improve your score. At a bank that mails applications nationally, forget it.

Sometimes you can get the decision reversed (at a local bank, at least) by explaining the circumstances. Did your credit report show a recent inquiry by another lender? Maybe you were refinancing a mortgage at a lower interest rate. Have you lived at your address for only two months? Maybe you just got a new job and a big promotion. Does your credit history show an unpaid bill? Maybe there was a dispute and you haven't yet filed your side of the story with the credit bureau, or you filed but the creditor ignored it. Computers don't care if you have an excuse.

I believe reversals to be rare. If you're turned down for credit, your wisest course is to wait 6 months, then try again. And next time apply for one of the nationally distributed, higher-rate bank cards that accept people whose credit scores are less than sterling. After all, you can always pay your bills in full and never trigger the interest rate, right? Right?

If you've just moved, keep on using the bank cards you have already. This isn't the moment to apply for a card with a lower rate. Don't ask for new credit (except, perhaps, a department store charge) until you have been at your new job and new address for a year.

Don't Apply for a Lot of Credit at Once. Every time a potential lender pulls your credit history that "inquiry" shows on your record. Some lenders automatically turn down anyone with two or three inquiries—say, for a mortgage and a credit card—over a short period of time. Apply for just one card and build a good credit history on it. Then apply for a second (following the strategy of owning two different types of cards—page 209). After that, get another card only if it's better than one you already have. Don't keep too many cards.

New Uses for Your Credit Score. When you get instant credit at a department store or instant approval for an auto loan, the lender is dialing up your credit score. It's increasingly being used to judge mortgage applications, approve small-business loans, and check on job applicants. A number of insurers even check your score before selling you a homeowners or auto insurance policy. Low scores, they say, indicate people who might make insurance claims. Who knows where scoring will spread next? More than ever, you need to keep your nose clean and periodically check the accuracy of your credit report.

HOW TO GET YOUR FIRST CREDIT CARD

If you're in college, you'll be bombarded with credit-card offers. It's smart to take one (and use the card prudently, of course). Young students can get cards even though they have no income or credit records. Issuers tacitly assume that if they can't pay, their parents will. Once students leave school, however, that presumption vanishes. So they should grab a card—and start a credit history—while they still get the benefit of the doubt. *Don't put more on the card than you can pay for!* Otherwise, you'll start out in life with wrecked credit and a mountain of student loans.

Sometimes parents are asked to co-sign their student's card. Assuming that you trust the child, go ahead and do it. Credit cards can help kids out of a jam, like a car breakdown on the way home from college. They're accepted in places where a personal check might not be. Once children are well established, they can cancel the co-signed card and get one entirely on their own. Any debt on the old card should either be paid off or transferred to the new one.

If you don't have the college-student advantage, start your credit life with a checking account at a bank or S&L. After a few months, apply for a Visa or MasterCard. If you're turned down, make an appointment with the credit-card manager and ask what you have to do to qualify. Then do it.

If you've had a steady job and address for a few months, go to a major retailer (one that will report your payment history to a credit bureau) and apply for a charge account. At the start, you'll be given a low line of credit, but that doesn't matter. Once you prove your reliability, you'll be able to charge more.

What if you're a widow whose credit history and credit cards were all in your late husband's name? This problem occurs much less than it used to; all credit held jointly is now reported in both spouses' names (page 239). You might have a credit history without knowing it, so check and see (page 233).

If you don't, however, start with the bank where you've always done business. Instead of applying for a card and letting the computer turn you down, make a personal appointment with the credit manager. Explain that you have no formal credit history, show your late husband's history (the credit bureau will send you a copy), show your income and assets, and make the case (if true) that you always paid the bills. Make the same case at the stores where you've always charged. You should have put your husband's credit history into your name before he died, but many creditors will extend you that courtesy posthumously. If you're turned down by one credit granter, don't assume that you're dead meat. Every lender has its own rules.

WHAT HAPPENS IF YOU CAN'T PAY YOUR BILLS?

Every lender has different rules for handling delinquents, but here are some general answers:

• *What if I pay late on my credit cards?* Each statement will carry a late fee in the $10 to $20 range. You may be reported to the credit bureau as slow paying if you haven't paid within 30 days. Other lenders wait 60 days. An occasional late check won't hurt your retail credit. But when you apply for a mortgage, the lender may demand an explanation for any late payment within the past 2 years.

• *What if I miss a payment?* After the first month, you'll get a letter or phone call from the bank. At that point, or one month later, your charge privileges will be suspended. New cards are suspended more quickly than older ones. If you try to use the card, it will be rejected at the cash register.

• *Will the lender restructure my debt?* Sometimes, if your problem appears to be temporary and not of your making. Banks understand sudden unemployment but have no sympathy for people who spend themselves into oblivion. If you think your cash shortage won't last long, talk to the bank *before* your payments start falling behind. On personal loans, you might get a break on the interest rate. On credit cards, you might get away with lower payments, or no payments, for a few months. If you're truly desperate, the bank might settle for less—say, 50 or 70 cents on the dollar for unsecured credit. Skipped payments are usually reported to the credit bureaus, but at least you won't be dunned. Banks don't always offer a hand. Still, you might as well ask.

• *If my credit card is suspended, can I get it back?* Usually yes, as long as you pay enough to bring your card up to date. But if you miss two payments, some issuers will raise your interest rate for a year. If you rack up two or three 60-day payment gaps, or don't pay for 3 months or more, your account will probably be revoked. You might still recover your card by making back payments. But the bank may reduce your credit limit, perhaps leaving you too little credit for business travel.

After 3 to 6 months of skipped payments (each bank has its own rules), your account will be reported to the credit bureau as a charge-off—

meaning no pay. Even if you eventually repay, that lender is unlikely to restore your card. When you think you can pass a credit review, go to a different lender.

• *Why bother repaying if I already have a charge-off on my credit record?* You can't remove this credit blot by bringing your account up to date. It will stay there for 7 years, warning other creditors to beware. But the record will also show if you eventually paid (check your credit report to be sure). Making payments gives you a better shot at new credit than if you let the delinquency stand.

• *Will the lender sue?* That depends on how much you owe, what assets you have, and where you live. Some states make it easier than others for a creditor to win a lawsuit and collect. The cost of filing suit is also an issue; one county might charge $45 and another $140. One bank might sue for as little as $500 in a pro-creditor state if you have assets and the cost of the lawsuit is less than it hopes to recoup. At another bank, the lawsuit trigger might be $1,000.

• *Can I keep the one or two credit cards that are up to date even though I've stopped paying others?* That depends on how lucky you are. Some lenders check a random sample of its customers' credit reports every month. Other lenders review them annually when a customer's card is renewed. If the bank finds out that you're seriously delinquent on other bills, it will suspend your card even though you're making payments on time. You probably won't get your charge privileges back until you can bring all your debts up to date.

• *If my credit cards are taken away, what should I do?* Start a repayment plan, perhaps through a local office of the Consumer Credit Counseling Service (for an office near you, call 800-388-CCCS). The initial consultation is free.

CREDIT CARDS FOR PEOPLE WHO CAN'T GET CREDIT

Did you once embarrass yourself by not paying your bills? Are you an ex-bankrupt? Have you no credit history? Are you a bartender (bartenders' jobs are considered unstable)?

You need a secured card. You make a cash deposit into an interest-earning savings account. In return, the bank gives you a Visa or MasterCard. The card's credit limit will typically be 100 percent of the money you've left on deposit. If you deposit $500, for example, you can charge $500 worth of goods. Most secured cards charge 18 to 22 percent interest on unpaid balances, plus annual fees. If you make timely payments, you can graduate to a regular credit card. If you don't pay on time, your cash deposit can be seized to cover the debt.

Ask your own bank or credit union about a secured card. Many lenders provide them, even when they don't advertise the fact. If not, get the *Secured Credit Card Report,* reviewing some 50 cards, $10 from RAM Research, Box 1700, Frederick, MD 21702 (800-874-8999); on the Net, http://www.cardtrak.com. Or the *Secured Credit Card* list of 15 cards, $4 from Bankcard Holders of America, 524 Branch Dr., Salem, VA 24153. Both list all the cards' costs and tell you who qualifies.

Not everyone can get a secured card. Different lenders have different requirements. You'll need a certain minimum income (often $12,000 but sometimes less), no federal tax liens, a job, a verifiable address and phone number, no current credit problems, and a clean record for a certain number of months. If you went bankrupt, the proceedings may have to be 6 to 12 months behind you. Secured cards are for reformed spendaholics, not for those who are still hitting the plastic. Some lenders specialize in people with no credit histories; these cards cost less than those that also take people with poor credit histories. A few issuers also offer a secured small-business card.

Once you get a secured card, use it. Run up some debt and take several months to pay it down. This costs you extra interest but is the fastest way to establish yourself as creditworthy. If you have the money, open two secured-card accounts.

Those who haven't had credit before might qualify for other loans after 12 to 18 months. Those with a poor credit history might have to wait up to 3 years, depending on what the problem was. Bankrupts generally wait the longest.

Don't Answer the Ads You See In Newspapers Reading "Get a Visa Card, $25. Bad Credit, Bankrupt—No Problem." Nonsense. It's always a problem. You'll pay $25 and may not get a card because your credit is too poor even for secured lenders. The people who place these ads may send you an application for the card of a respectable bank. But the bank didn't hire them as agents and has no obligation to accept you. If you're turned down, you may find it hard to get your $25 back.

While I'm at it, let me also warn you about 900 numbers. Banks that offer secured cards have toll-free 800 numbers. With a 900-number toll call, you're paying an intermediary for something you can do for free.

Don't Answer Ads Promising "Gold Cards" to All Comers. These aren't gold Visa or MasterCards. They're cards that you can use only to purchase goods from an overpriced catalogue. The ads claim that they'll help you reestablish credit, but don't believe it. The catalogue companies don't report regularly to credit bureaus and the major credit grantors ignore them. You'll just run up more debts buying catalogue goods.

RETAIL DEBIT CARDS

You'll soon be carrying one of these, if you aren't already. A debit card is the electronic equivalent of a check—for when you want to pay cash instead of using credit.

Your ATM (automated teller machine) card is a debit card. It "debits"— withdraws—money from your bank account. It becomes a *retail* debit card when you can also use it to buy goods. When you pay with that card, you are telling the bank to take money directly out of your account and give it to the store.

These cards come in two types:

First, there's the basic ATM card—accepted by a growing number of supermarkets, gas stations, and convenience stores. You slip the card into a terminal. After the clerk adds up your purchases, you punch in your personal identification number (PIN) and zap the payment out of your account. When you use a debit card at certain gas stations, you get the 3- to 5-cent discount sometimes given to customers who pay cash.

Second, there is the ATM card with a Visa or MasterCard logo on it. It can be used in any store or restaurant, anywhere in the world, which also takes the credit card (although it might not be accepted by a rental-car agency). There are no terminals and, for retail use, no PINs. You use the card just the way you would a credit card. In fact, the clerk probably can't tell the difference. Only when the transaction reaches your bank does it register as a debit.

You can also get this type of card by opening a cash-management account at some of the major stockbrokerage houses. You would then keep your cash in the broker's money market mutual fund instead of a bank. Whenever you used the debit card, payment would be made from the money-fund account.

Many consumers don't see much use for a debit card. If you want to pay cash, you can always use greenbacks or write a check. You can even put down a credit card and pay at the end of the month, before running up any interest charges. But as more people struggle to get their spending under control, the convenience of debiting will grow more apparent.

WHEN YOU'D USE A DEBIT CARD:

1. You're swearing off credit cards but want the convenience of paying with plastic.

2. You don't want to bother carrying your checkbook or hauling out identification to get your check approved.

3. You're married, with a joint checking account. Debit cards eliminate the need to juggle two checkbooks or carry loose checks.

4. You need a fallback when you're short of cash. With a debit card, you don't have to go to the ATM so often.

5. You don't want to run the risk of paying interest on your purchases —as you might if you paid with a credit card and couldn't cover the full bill at the end of the month.

6. You want a plastic way of making small purchases without adding them to your credit card and triggering extra interest that month.

7. You're learning financial discipline. Debit cards don't let you spend any more money than you have in the bank. (A few debit cards give you access to loans if you overdraw. Resist.)

What about the float? When you write a check, you have a couple of days before it clears, during which time your funds can still earn interest. There is no float at all when you pay by inserting an ATM card into a terminal. However, the ATM cards with Visa or MasterCard logos allow a float ranging from one day to more than a week, depending on how fast the merchants put in for payment. The smaller the merchant, the longer it may take for your debit to clear.

THE DOWNSIDE OF USING DEBIT CARDS:

1. Banks are adding more fees. You might pay $12 to $15 annually, and perhaps a transaction fee every time you make a debit. A no-fee credit card is cheaper as long as you don't run up a balance.

2. If your wallet is stolen, you *must* report losing your debit card immediately. There's no law imposing a $50 limit on losses as there is with a credit card (page 228). But MasterCard offers zero liability if you report the loss within one business day of discovering it, and a $50 limit thereafter. With Visa, it's two business days and $50 thereafter.

3. If a thief empties your bank account, you might bounce some checks. That could create a late payment in one of your credit-card accounts and a blotch on your credit record.

4. Payments by debit card don't help you build a credit record (although you're probably using a credit card, too, which keeps your record up to date).

5. You can't stop a transaction the way you can stop a check.

6. If you buy something that's defective and pay by debit card, you have no leverage when you ask for your money back. By contrast, if you pay by credit card you might be able to rescind the payment (page 229).

Don't Mix Up Your Debit and Credit Cards. Your bank might mail you an unsolicited ATM card that's also a retail debit card. These cards are being widely distributed to creditworthy customers under various names: Cash Card, Pocket Check, Check Card, Convenience Card. But if you're not familiar with them, and don't read the flyer the bank sent, you might mistake your new debit card for a Visa or MasterCard credit card. Banks haven't been doing nearly enough to explain the difference.

When you overspend with a credit card, the banks love you and charge you interest on the unpaid balance. But if you overspend with a debit card, thinking it's a credit card, you will unknowingly be draining all the cash from your account. Once you've drained it dry, here's what will happen: (1) The next time you put down the debit card it won't go through because you don't have enough cash to pay. (2) When you write your usual checks on the account they'll bounce, because you've already spent the money with your debit card. For every check you bounce, the bank might charge $15 or so. The merchant who took the bad check might also charge a fee. You can lower these risks by attaching overdraft checking to your account (page 55).

Every time you use your debit card, you should enter the amount in your check register and subtract it from your balance. That way you'll know how much cash you have left.

SMARTCARDS

The next piece of plastic the banks want you to keep in your wallet is a smartcard. They come in several varieties and most aren't yet ready for mass distribution, but, at this writing, pilot projects are forging ahead.

Promoters of smartcards make the assumption that you hate to carry cash. You don't like fishing for bills and coins to buy a newspaper or a soda. You'd rather put down plastic instead.

This plastic card has money on it, embedded in a computer chip. A $20 card, for example, will give you $20 in spending power. If you buy a 75-cent newspaper, the seller will put your card in a special terminal and drain off 75 cents. No identification or signature is required.

You now have a card with $19.25 left on it. After spending $1 on a soda, the value of your card goes down to $18.25. If you forget how much you have, you can check it with a little portable card reader. Some readers might also list the last five things you've bought.

If every merchant, street vendor, taxi driver, and bus accepted smartcards, you wouldn't have to carry cash. To some, that would be a huge convenience; to others, it's a shrug. If some merchants took smartcards and others didn't, however, you'd have to carry both.

Smartcards come in three varieties, some of them more flexible than others:

• *A prepaid, disposable single-purpose card.* Telephone cards are a good example. You pay $10 or $20 for a card, dial an 800 number, give the number of your card, and then make your telephone call. Minute by minute, the cost of the call is deducted from the value of the card. When you've drained all the money out of the card, you throw it out.

• *A prepaid, disposable bank card.* You buy the card at a bank and can use it at any store that has a terminal.

• *A reloadable card.* When your money runs out, you can take it to the bank, an ATM, or a special kiosk and load it up again. A reloadable card could also serve as your credit card, retail debit card, or ATM card.

What's in it for the bank? Eventually (although not at first), the bank will charge you for the card. There might be a fee when you accessed the ATM to load it up. The merchant would also pay a fee in return for getting what is presumably a more secure transaction.

What's in it for you? Convenience, maybe. Putting down a card is a tad quicker than pulling out cash. You always have the equivalent of exact change. You wouldn't have to count your change (but you'd have to use the card reader to be sure the merchant's terminal deducted the right amount). You might also use the card to make small purchases over the Internet.

For a while, the smartcards probably won't have any more than $100 on them and the limit might be lower than that. So they're strictly for walking-around money. You'd still need your credit card, debit card, or checkbook for more serious shopping.

If the card malfunctions—say, it registers $14 when you're sure you were carrying $36—the bank can check the balance on the computer chip. But if you lose the card, it's just like losing cash. You're out the money.

YOUR RIGHTS WHEN YOU PAY . . .

. . . With a Credit Card

Unauthorized Use: Here's what you have to pay if your credit card is stolen and charges are run up: *Nothing* if you reported the loss to the bank before a fraudulent charge occurred. *Up to $50* for charges run up before the theft was reported to the card issuer—and banks often waive even that small fee. *Nothing* if you still have your card but your number was used fraudulently—for example, in a mail-order transaction or a transaction over the Internet. This covers both business and consumer transactions.

Billing Errors: You're fully protected against consumer billing errors. If you've already paid an erroneous bill, you'll get your money back. Check all your bills for the following common mistakes:
- You get someone else's bills.
- You're billed for something you didn't buy.
- You paid the bill and shouldn't have been charged any interest.
- An item you returned was never credited to your account.
- When the store finds its mistake, it doesn't rescind the interest you were charged.
- You're not charged for an item you bought (that's an honesty test; would you tell?).
- You're charged twice for the same purchase (*now* would you tell?).

- The bill was mailed to your old address and by the time you got it finance charges were due (but you have to have given the lender the correct address at least 20 days before the end of the billing period).
- Your bill was mailed too late to reach you before the clock started running on finance charges.
- The item you ordered arrived broken and hasn't been replaced, but the bills (and finance charges) keep coming.
- The goods never came.
- The goods came but in the wrong color or quantity, and you sent them back.
- You refused to accept the goods on delivery.
- The bill contains an arithmetic error.
- An unauthorized person used your card.

Many credit-card bills don't include copies of your receipts. Instead, you get a simple list of purchases, with the stores sometimes shown under a corporate name you're not familiar with. Keep all receipts until the bills come in. That makes it easier to find mistakes.

To solve a billing error under the Fair Credit Billing Act, notify the credit-card issuer *immediately and in writing* that a problem exists. A phone call won't preserve your rights.

The card issuer has to receive your letter within 60 days of the date your credit-card statement was mailed. Send the letter to the address designated for billing errors, not the address where you pay your bills. Keep a copy of the letter. For safety, use registered mail with a return receipt requested, and keep a copy.

Give your name, address, and account number, a concise description of what's wrong (with copies of supporting documents), the date of the error, and the dollar amount in dispute. Just give the facts; don't moan and groan all over the page.

The card issuer has to acknowledge your letter within 30 days of receiving it, and resolve the problem within 90 days. In the meantime, you can withhold payment for the item and the creditor can't report you as delinquent. Any other charges on your bill, however, must be paid as usual.

If you turn out to be right, the disputed charge and any finance charges related to it will be taken off your bill. If the merchant claims the charge was valid, you can ask for supporting documents. If the merchant supplies them and you still disagree, you have three choices:

1. Pay the bill, including any late charges. This keeps a black mark off your credit record. You can sue the merchant for recompense.

2. Don't pay, be reported as delinquent to the credit bureau, and risk being sued by the card issuer. Send a statement of your side of the story to the credit bureau, to be included in your file.

3. Don't pay, assert that you received defective goods or services, and ask your credit-card issuer to rescind the charge. If the issuer agrees that

you were taken advantage of, it will charge the payment back to the merchant's bank and you won't be reported as delinquent. This strategy will succeed, however, only if you meet all of the qualifications listed next.

Defective Goods: You might not have to pay if you received, and returned, consumer goods or services that weren't what you ordered, came too late to be useful, or were defective in some way. You're also protected if you never received the goods but were charged for them anyway. To go this route, however, you have to meet the following tests:

• You used a credit card issued by the same store you're having the dispute with, *or* . . .

• You used a bank card like Visa or MasterCard, or a charge card like American Express. In this case, the item in dispute must cost more than $50. You also had to have bought it in your home state or, if not, then within 100 miles of your mailing address. (Some card issuers typically waive the 100-mile rule.)

• You purchased by phone, mail order, or the Internet from a company that advertises in-state or sent material (such as a catalogue) to you there. Whether these transactions occur in-state depends on state law, but they normally do.

• You made a good-faith effort, in writing, to resolve the issue with the merchant (unless the merchant is out of business). Keep copies of all correspondence with the merchant, including follow-up notes sent to confirm a phone conversation. Best advice: follow the rules prescribed by the Fair Credit Billing Act, page 229.

• You're complaining about a consumer purchase, not a purchase for use in a business.

• You haven't yet paid for the item, or haven't paid in full. Banks can erase outstanding bills, but they don't retrieve cash from the merchant's bank account.

Make your claim in writing (not by phone), supported by evidence that you tried and failed to resolve the dispute. The card issuer must investigate. Until the argument is resolved, the issuer cannot close your account or report you as delinquent, although it can note on your credit report that the payment is in dispute.

You're allowed to withhold payment only on that one transaction. Keep making payments on anything else charged to the card.

If the card issuer takes your side in the dispute, it will charge the disputed payment back to the merchant's bank. The unpaid amount, plus any finance charges, will be removed from your account. But you won't recover any money you already paid.

If the card issuer concludes that the fault is yours, it may report you as delinquent, turn the bill over to a collection agency, or sue. You, in turn, may assert any consumer rights you have.

...With a Cash-Advance Check Written Against a Credit Card

You get full protection against unauthorized use and billing errors. But you can't force a chargeback if you received defective goods or services.

...With a Debit Card

Unauthorized Use: If fraudulent charges are run up, here's what federal law says you owe: *Up to $50* as long as you tell the bank about the loss within 2 business days of discovering it. *Up to $500* if you let 3 to 60 days go by before reporting the problem. If you wait more than 60 days after getting a statement showing the fraudulent charges, you'll generally owe *$50 plus everything charged to the card from 61 days on.* Only a few states put lower limits on how much you can lose. MasterCard and Visa limit your loss to $50, and many banks don't even charge that.

A thief needs your PIN to use the card to withdraw cash. But using it as a retail card, he or she can shop up to the limit of your bank account plus any credit line the card will access. If you lose a card linked to a brokerage account, the thief can spend all the cash you're holding there, plus the value of your margin account (that's up to half the value of your stocks and stock-owning mutual funds, and even more for bonds).

Billing Errors: You get roughly the same protection that you would with a credit card.

Defective Goods: Your level of protection depends on which card you have. With a Visa or MasterCard debit card, the bank will give you chargeback protection. With another debit card, it won't.

...With a Check

If a thief cashes one of your checks, and you sign an affidavit of forgery, the bank will pay. So you're fully protected.

If you regret your purchase, you can ask the bank to stop the check. You'll have to follow up your telephone call with a written stop-check order. If the check slips through anyway, it's the bank's responsibility.

YOUR CREDIT HISTORY

Here's what shows up on a typical credit report:

1. Your name and the variations you've used on credit applications, current and previous addresses, Social Security number, year of birth,

current and previous employers, and the name of your spouse, if you have one.

2. Your bank cards, charge accounts, and home-equity lines and how long you've had them; probably, your first mortgage, too.

3. The date of your last payment.

4. The top that you're allowed to charge.

5. The current amount owed on each credit line, and the largest amount that you've ever owed to that particular creditor.

6. Whether your payments are up to date (creditors pay more attention to the past 2 years than to your previous history).

7. The amount that's past due.

8. The type of loan or account, and its terms.

9. The latest you ever paid on that account and how many times you've been delinquent.

10. Any special problems with your account—for example, that goods were repossessed or that a bill collector had to be called in.

11. Court actions such as liens, judgments awarded to creditors, bankruptcies, foreclosures, and, in some states, delinquent child-support payments.

12. Your legal relationship to the account: Are you jointly responsible? Individually responsible? A co-signer? Who else is responsible for paying?

13. Past accounts, paid in full but now closed.

14. Whether you've put a statement on the record in a dispute with the lender.

15. The names of the companies that have looked at your account. Your copy of the report includes companies that decided to send you promotional mailings in the past year, current creditors who are monitoring your report, companies that vetted your report for employment purposes during the past 2 years, and companies checking you out because you solicited credit. All these are for your eyes only. Companies checking you for credit see only the inquiries from other potential credit granters made in the past 2 years.

A credit bureau may know what you do for a living but not how much money you make. It doesn't know if you're divorced or have nine kids or drink, or what color you are and whether you just had a heart bypass. It does not make credit decisions. It simply reports your payment history and credit score to lenders who are thinking about giving you money. The lenders make their own judgments about whether to take you on. One lender may love you and give you a huge credit line; another one may turn you down.

Most people have good credit. All you need is a steady job with a history of paying bills approximately on time. Your credit won't be ruined if you sometimes pay late. You can even go through a rough patch—getting stiff overdue notices—without damaging your basic creditworthiness. It's not smart to apply for new credit at a time when you're behind. But once you've caught up, you'll be back in most lenders' good graces.

Here are the few things that lenders *don't* like to see:

- You already have a lot of credit cards, with large credit lines and a lot of debt.
- You had to be chased for payment by a collection agency.
- You were sued for money owed.
- There's a lien on your property.
- A creditor closed one of your accounts.
- You went bankrupt.
- You have been applying for a lot of credit lately. (Maybe you're in trouble? Maybe you're going to charge up a storm and go bankrupt?)

Negative credit information, including the history of closed accounts, stays in your file for 7 years. Positive information can be reported indefinitely. "Wage-earner plans" (Chapter 13 under the Bankruptcy Code, page 243) may be wiped out after 7 years, but straight bankruptcies will weigh down your record for up to 10 years.

Money Secrets That Credit Bureaus Don't Know About

Most people assume that credit bureaus know all the shabby little secrets of their financial lives. But if you look at your credit report, you'll see things missing. Small shops usually don't report their charge-account customers to credit bureaus. Neither do some small banks, S&Ls, and credit unions. Neither do doctors, most hospitals, and utility companies (although you'll be found out if they give your account to a bill collector who reports). Home-equity lines of credit are reported, but first mortgages and traditional second mortgages are coming on-line more slowly. As for your payment history, it may look better than it really is. Some lenders consider payment within 60 days satisfactory and give it the same top rating that other lenders reserve for 30-day payments.

Checking Up on Your Credit Report

Where do credit bureaus get their information? Either from your creditors, who report your payment history on computer tape, or from their connections at courthouses, where lawsuits are tracked. If their informants are wrong, there will be a mistake in your credit report. Mistakes might also be made by the bureau itself.

A minor error makes no difference as long as it doesn't prevent you from getting credit. But you never know what's going to be minor. Take a single, erroneous "slow-pay" report. A lender that charges 21 percent might overlook it; one that charges 12 percent might turn you down. A major mistake, like showing a tax lien against you that belongs to someone else of the same name, will cut you off from credit during the months it takes to straighten out the mess.

Normally, you report a mistake to your creditor, who will send a correction to the credit bureaus it uses. The credit bureau will also accept certain evidence from you directly—for example, canceled checks proving that a debt was paid, or a receipt showing that a disputed item was indeed returned.

You can't sue a creditor for making a mistake. Lawsuits will be possible, however, if the creditor doesn't correct a mistake or reinserts erroneous data in your file. Creditors also have to report, and your credit history has to show, when an account is in dispute and if you closed an account voluntarily.

Get a Copy of Your Credit History and Check It for Accuracy. All credit bureaus give you a free report if you ask for it within 60 days of being turned down for credit, an apartment, insurance, or a job based on something the report says. The turndown letters will tell you where to write or call. You also get a free report if you live in Georgia, Massachusetts, Maryland, or Vermont; if you're a victim of fraud; if you're on welfare; and if you're unemployed and looking for work.

Otherwise, the bureaus charge up to $8 for a report, depending on your state. To get a copy of your report, call or check the bureau's Web site to find out what identifying information you have to send. You may be asked to supply your full name (including Jr., Sr., II), Social Security number, current and previous addresses within the past 2 or 5 years, birthday, current employer, phone number, and signature. If you find a mistake on one credit report, call the other two bureaus, too. You might have a file in each, and they don't always share corrections.

The three major bureaus: Equifax Information Service Center, P.O. Box 740241, Atlanta, GA 30374 (800-685-1111 or http://www.equifax.com); Experian Consumer Assistance (formerly TRW), P.O. Box 2104, Allen, TX 75013 (800-682-7654; http://www.experian.com); and Trans Union Corp., Consumer Disclosure Center, P.O. Box 390, Springfield, PA 19064 (316-634-8440, for requesting a copy of your credit report when you're just checking; 800-916-8800 if you've been turned down for credit; or http://www.tuc.com).

Some bureaus will send you your spouse's record; others require his or her express consent. The spouse's record goes to the address shown on the credit file, so you can't spy on a spouse who has changed his or her address.

If You Find Yourself in Any of the Following Five Situations, It's Especially Important That You Check Your Credit Report and Fix Any Mistakes:

1. You are applying for an important loan, like a mortgage. An inaccurate credit history might keep you from getting it.

Married people should ask for reports listed under their personal names and Social Security numbers (Bill and Laurie Smith, not Mr. and Mrs. Bill

Smith). If you just use one name (the Mr. and Mrs.), you'll get only one credit report. Lenders will look at both. There's no such thing as a joint report covering both of you. Transactions arising from joint accounts are reported twice, once to the husband's account, once to the wife's.

2. You are separating from your spouse and want his or her new transactions off your personal credit record.

Write to all your creditors, closing joint accounts and asking for a new account in your name alone (tell your spouse you're doing it so that he or she can write for a personal card at the same time; it's vindictive to leave a spouse with an invalid card). Three months later, get a copy of your credit report. It should show your joint accounts as closed. If it doesn't, tell each of the bureaus that the joint accounts are listed in error. At the same time, go back to the creditors and demand a correction.

The closed accounts will remain on your report as part of your credit history. And you're both still responsible for any debt you contracted jointly. If neither of you pays, the blot will show up on both your reports. For this reason, it's safer to move all joint debt to separate cards (page 240).

3. You've paid off a court judgment against you for money owed. Your credit report may carry the judgment. You want to be sure that the record shows the judgment paid.

4. You've had a dispute with a store and refused to pay a bill. You and the store cannot reach agreement so you're reported as delinquent.

You are entitled to put a 100-word explanation into your credit report. Call each of the three bureaus in case they all have files on you. The report will summarize your side of the story or list the type of dispute by code number. Warning: This procedure may help in face-to-face credit situations —say, if you've applied for a mortgage or a personal loan and can tell the lender more about the dispute. But if you apply for a credit card and are checked by computer, your explanation will normally be ignored. If the issue gets resolved, or 7 years pass, be sure to remove the explanation.

5. You have been harmed (turned down for credit, rejected for insurance or a job) based on information in a credit report. The lender has to tell you the name and address of the bureau it used. That bureau will send you a free copy of your report as long as you ask for it within 60 days, plus the names of everyone who got the report in the past 6 months, plus the form for challenging erroneous information.

To Fix Mistakes

Note the errors on the form you get from the credit bureau, make a copy, and mail back the original. The bureau must check the disputed information. If it can't be verified within a reasonable time (around 25 days), it should be deleted. Request a report from all three major bureaus (Equifax, Experian, Trans Union); they may share the identical mistake.

If your creditor verifies the report, write (don't call), explain why the money isn't owed, enclose copies of any proof you have, and ask for a correction.

When your name is cleared, check your report at each of the three major credit bureaus—and ask those bureaus to send fresh reports to the smaller bureaus they sell information to. Sometimes this job is only a headache. Sometimes it's a nightmare.

If any correction is made in your credit report, the credit bureau has to send a corrected copy to any creditor who received it in the past 6 months and any employer who received it within the past 2 years.

The Credit Nightmare: Identity Theft

Did you know that the credit bureaus are selling your name, address, and other identifying information—sometimes even your Social Security number? They sell it to banks that want to send you credit cards, catalogue retailers, insurance marketers, and other direct mailers.

Maybe you like getting catalogues and credit-card solicitations, so it doesn't bother you to have your name on these lists. But it should. A form of theft called identity theft is spreading fast, and you're exposed if your name is on these credit-card marketing lists.

Identity thieves masquerade as you. They open fraudulent accounts in your name, or change the address on your credit cards and take over accounts you already have. They run up huge bills and leave you with the mess. Creditors may not believe you when you say that you didn't use that card. Bill collectors may dun you. Liens may pile up on your property. Because of your apparent debts, you may lose your access to credit, be rejected for jobs and apartments, even be subject to arrest.

One way the thieves operate is to steal credit-card offers from your mailbox or place of business. They apply in your name but with a different address. The credit card and all subsequent statements will be sent to that false address. They sometimes get the card even if they give a wrong Social Security number. You'll know nothing about it until you get the first dunning phone call.

Credit-card mailers have to disclose that they got your name from a credit bureau and tell you how to get off the list. You can do that right now by telling the three major credit bureaus to quit selling your name. Call Experian at 800-353-0809 and Trans Union at 800-680-7293. Write to Equifax at Equifax Options, P.O. Box 740123, Atlanta, Georgia 30374.

But believe it or not, you can take your name only off the lists drawn from personal credit information, which are sold for credit-card solicitations. Credit bureaus can continue to sell so-called header information (the identifying items at the top, or head, of your credit report, such as name, address, and even Social Security number), whether you approve or not.

Improving Your Credit History

Here are the only legitimate ways of doing it:

- Start paying all your bills on time.
- Pay off back bills. They don't go away.
- Reduce the monthly payments you owe (including your mortgage) to less than 40 percent of your gross monthly income.
- Fix any mistakes on your credit record.
- Cancel any credit cards you're not using. (The accounts will not actually be taken off your credit history, but they should be shown as closed.)
- Give the credit bureau a reason for any black mark on your record, like several bills 3 months past due 2 years ago. Explain what happened and point out that these accounts are now up to date. Your explanation becomes part of your file.
- Be sure that the credit bureau has removed any data older than 7 years and bankruptcies older than 10 years. This should happen automatically, but sometimes credit bureaus slip up.
- Don't waste your time trying to add good accounts that don't normally report to the credit bureau. Some bureaus won't take them; some will, but charge you $2 to $5. The information isn't useful because it won't be updated regularly. Potential creditors may reject reports from lenders who don't belong to the credit bureau for fear that some of those accounts are fraudulent.

Credit-Repair Firms

Don't give them a nickel. Their ads imply that they can wave a wand over a bad credit history and bring you out smelling like a rose. They can't. If there are errors in your record, you can fix them yourself (page 235). True information cannot legally be removed.

Some credit repairers harass credit bureaus, challenging even items that are correct. Their strategy is to question more items in your record than the bureau can verify within the time limit, so it will have to expunge derogatory facts. But credit bureaus are resisting. They don't have to follow up on frivolous challenges. They might not deal with a particular credit clinic at all. Under the law, clinics aren't allowed to charge you until they've delivered the goods. If you pay up front, you're waving bye-bye to your cash.

Incidentally, you can't get rid of a bad credit report by moving. The big bureaus are national. Your record follows you everywhere.

If Manic Overspending Got You into Trouble, a Rotten Credit History Actually Does You a Favor. It stops you from getting any deeper into debt. Once you quit borrowing more than you can repay, your credit history will gradually repair itself.

How long that takes depends on why you fell behind. Lenders are not gentle to the middle-class deadbeat who charges too much, then has to be wrestled to the mat for payment. They look more kindly on people whose money troubles were at least partly beyond their control—unemployment, uninsured illness, and divorce being the most acceptable excuses.

If you've straightened out, and *if* you had an excuse, and *if* you're dealing with a local lender to whom you can explain yourself (or a secured-card lender, page 223), you might start getting your credit back in 6 months to a year.

You can generally get an auto loan with bad credit behind you as long as it's *behind* you. Lenders take the chance because they can repossess if you don't pay. But you might have to put down 50 percent of the price in cash. As for a mortgage, increasing numbers of lenders will take you on, at a much higher interest rate. But you will have to put more money down. Suggestion: Ask a mortgage broker to look for a mortgage for you.

One exception to this happy ending is the bankrupt. Lenders like to see people fight their way out of debt. They hate bankruptcies. If you have a steady job and roots in the community you might get short-term credit, like an auto loan, after a year or so. In 6 months to a year, a secured card is usually an option. Finance companies will talk to you, at a price. Some bankrupts carry a paid-up bank card with them through bankruptcy, which works as long as the creditor doesn't check your credit history. But it will take longer to get a large credit line or a normal mortgage, lest you fall behind again. You might even have difficulty renting an apartment or going into business. That's something the bankruptcy lawyer might not have made absolutely clear.

Don't expect a lender to suggest that you might be borrowing too much. *You* have to decide. Lenders do take a general look at your balance sheet and outstanding credit lines, and turn down people who are obviously overloaded. But the only way they make money is to make more loans. So they'll cheerfully take you right to the brink and sometimes beyond. They charge a high enough interest rate to cover a certain number of defaults, so going broke is your worry, not theirs.

Investigative Reports

When you apply for a big life insurance policy, the insurer wants to know more than whether you pay your bills. It will wonder whether you've told the truth about where you work, whether you've ever been caught driving drunk, and whether your hobby is skydiving. So it will turn to one of the bureaus that specialize in gathering personal information. Some employers do the same. You give permission for the investigation when you sign the insurance or job-application form.

Who is the chief source of information for this type of report? Usually you. The investigator calls you up and asks you some questions. Your neighbors may also be called, or a former employer. The interviewer has to identify himself and his purpose. Before answering, write down the interviewer's name and get a place to call to check up on him.

These reports are not kept very long because the information goes stale. They may be junked after just 90 days (although they'll stay in storage for 6 months, in case a consumer requests disclosure). If you're turned down for insurance or charged more than the basic rate, based on information in an investigative report, you have a right to see and challenge it. The bureau can withhold just two things: (1) the names of the people who gave the information, and (2) the nature of any medical information that may have been given directly to the insurer or potential employer, without being copied into the bureau's files.

CREDIT DISCRIMINATION

You can't be denied credit solely on the basis of color, race, religion, sex, age, marital status, national origin, or the fact that you're on welfare. If you *are* turned down for a loan or a bank card, it is probably because:

1. You don't have enough income.
2. You don't have a steady job history.
3. Your debts are too large relative to your income.
4. You don't have a credit history.

Wives and Credit

Many married women apply for credit based entirely on their own incomes and think it's pure discrimination if they're turned down. It's probably not. They simply haven't focused on how large their debts really are.

Take a wife who co-signs a mortgage with her husband. If he skips out, that obligation becomes hers. It would probably overwhelm her resources.

She doesn't think about that debt as long as she's well married, but her creditors do. If she tries to get credit based on her income alone, the lender will set off that mortgage against her paycheck and conclude that she can't carry any more loans. The same would be true for a married man who couldn't meet the mortgage payments were it not for the salary of his wife.

Learning this, some married women wonder how they will ever get credit "in their own name." But they don't understand what that phrase means. You *have* credit in your own name as long as the accounts you hold with your husband were applied for jointly. They'll be reported in your name at the credit bureau as well as his—Hallee Jones, not Mrs. Elias Jones. How do you tell? Your name is on the credit card.

That's all there is to it. It doesn't matter whether the loan or the credit card is supported by your income, both your incomes, or your husband's income alone. As long as it's reported under your personal name rather than your Mrs., it is your credit.

Married couples usually apply for credit jointly in order to get the benefit of both incomes. When a married person applies separately, it's usually for a business loan. A bank can ask you for a co-signer, but it can't demand that the co-signer be your spouse. What if your spouse has an interest in the property you're putting up as collateral? The lender can require the spouse to sign a waiver allowing the property to be seized if you don't pay, but that's different from co-signing the loan itself. As a practical matter, however, your spouse is usually your best co-signer.

If you're widowed or divorced and your credit cards were granted partly on the strength of your spouse's income, the lender can require you to show that you're still creditworthy. You may have to reapply for credit, showing your current level of income and debt. While you're being re-checked, your credit cannot be revoked unless you fail to pay your bills. If you're too distraught at the time of the crisis to open the mail and write checks, find someone who can do that for you.

Often, widows just keep on using their cards. Nobody finds out and nobody kicks. Obviously, lenders would rather you confessed that you're now single (and some may put a clause in your credit-card contract requiring it). But nothing in federal law stops you from keeping mum.

The divorced can't help revealing their status when they close joint accounts and ask for new cards in their own name. If your payment record has been good, creditors will generally issue you a card without question. But they're entitled to put you through a credit check all over again. The lender must consider alimony as part of your regular income unless there's evidence that it's not being paid.

On a marital card, a spouse can be either *jointly responsible* for the debt or an *authorized user,* with the other spouse solely responsible for payment. You normally want to be jointly responsible. That puts you in a stronger position if you ever have to apply for credit on your own. How do you find out what your status is? The easiest way is to get a copy of your credit report, which will tell you who's responsible for each account. How do you change your status? Write to the lender and request it.

It's important to understand, however, that the lender doesn't have to make you jointly responsible. The law requires only that the account be reported in each spouse's name. To raise your status, you and your spouse may have to reapply for credit jointly, and you might have to show that you have an income (although usually not).

Any account opened with your spouse since June 1, 1977, will be reported in both your names, whether you're jointly responsible or not. But wives whose accounts were opened earlier may find all the credit reported only in their husband's name. To change that, you have to write to the store or the bank and ask that your name be put on the credit file, too. You'll normally get a form to sign. If it's an "authorized user" form, write back to the card issuer and ask how you can become jointly responsible, although, in some cases, you won't want to be.

If your spouse is a deadbeat, his or her bad habits will taint your own creditworthiness unless you can show that you lead a more responsible life. One possible way to do this: get a bank card or store charge in your name (a friend or a parent may have to co-sign it), keep it solely for your own use, and keep the bills up to date. You can show that account as proof of your personal reliability. Similarly, buy a car yourself (or with a co-signer) and make all the payments on it. It will show on your credit history as your own debt. Finally, don't co-sign any of your spouse's loans or credit cards. If circumstances allow it, you should cancel the cards and credit lines that you've co-signed already.

Older People and Credit

Older people often feel that they're being discriminated against. More likely, it's that their clean lifestyle doesn't fit the profile of a good credit risk. Here are several eye-opening cases that were supplied to me by the American Association of Retired Persons:

• Ray G., age 71, retired businessman, was refused a Visa card because of his "limited credit experience." His mistake: when he retired, he paid up everything, dropped all his credit cards, and started living on cash. Six years later, when he wanted a credit card to travel with, he no longer had sufficient credit history.

• Martin K. couldn't get a Discover card because he had too many other cards. That made him sore because nine of his cards he never used, but how was the lender to know that? If you have accumulated a lot of cards over the years, get rid of all but two or three of them.

• Evelyn L., 75 and widowed, was turned down for a card because she had no credit history. She had always paid cash for everything, a way of life handed down to her by her parents. In old age, she wanted a credit card for catalogue shopping but couldn't get one.

The moral of these stories is to get a card when you're young, working, and laden with debt—the very customer the lenders want. Keep that card for when you retire or are widowed, even if you don't use it. The time may come when you'll want it again, and it's hard to recover your credit once you've given it up.

None of the turndowns just cited were illegal. They were all based on legitimate credit criteria. But consider the following stories:

• Marjorie W., 68, bought a travel trailer on an installment contract. Later, the dealer called and canceled because the finance company wouldn't lend more than $6,000 to someone over 65.

• Robert M., 72, was denied a loan because his bank wouldn't lend to anyone over 70.

• Martha P., 71, was rejected by a finance company because she didn't qualify for credit-life insurance.

All of these lenders broke the law. You cannot be turned down for credit solely on the basis of age. Nor can a lender set different terms for older people than for younger people in the same situation. A lender is allowed to consider age only if it makes a proven difference to creditworthiness. For example, if a 75-year-old applies for a 30-year mortgage, a bank might legitimately ask about his or her future cash flow or request a larger down payment. But the senior can't be turned down if the loan would be granted to a younger person with the same income and assets.

What can an older person do if he or she has no credit history? Ask your bank for a card with a low credit limit. Ask a store where you shop for a charge account. It may take a personal visit but it's worth it. Or get a secured card (page 223).

IF YOU CAN'T PAY YOUR BILLS

Don't hide. Don't cry. Don't shove unopened bills into a drawer. Don't have your cousin tell the bank that you've gone to Sicily for the summer. That won't help. Someone will find you—probably a bill collector—and you'll be in more trouble than you were before.

What's your biggest problem when you can't pay your bills? Money, you say. I say it's fear. You're sure that everyone will point and sneer. Your son will be kicked out of Boy Scouts. The police will hang you up by your thumbs. *But nothing like that is going to happen.* You're not Jack the Ripper. You don't beat up babies or set fire to cats. All you did wrong was to buy more things than you can pay for right away. That's an error in judgment but not a sin. You will pay eventually and your errors will be forgiven.

If you can't pay your bills, write a letter to your creditors and tell them so. For a really big bill, like a mortgage, make an appointment to see someone in the credit department. Don't slump in like a bankrupt. Approach the interview like a businessperson with a problem to solve.

To do this you need: (1) a spending plan showing how much money you need to live on (page 161); (2) a repayment plan showing how much you can spread among your creditors every month; (3) a specific offer for each creditor, as in, "I will pay you $50 a month and clear up this bill in 10 months." If your situation is dire, offer your unsecured creditors a settlement—say, 50 cents on the dollar.

Each creditor will want more. But if you hold firm—and keep making the payments you've decided on—they will eventually accept the deal. If someone threatens to sue, don't ruin your rehabilitation plan by trying to accommodate him. Keep on talking, keep making your payments, even go to court. No judge will order you to pay more than you can afford, and your creditors know it. Your strengths are three: the lender would rather stretch out payments than repossess, it's cheaper to talk than to hire a debt collector, and the interest you pay is compensation for the delay.

If you can't handle these negotiations yourself, or if you're such a spendaholic that you find yourself hurtling toward bankruptcy, nonprofit credit counselors can help. Counselors give you moral support. They help you develop a bud--t, er, I mean, a spending plan. They talk to your creditors and get them to accept smaller payments. Many lenders will direct you to credit counselors rather than accept the spending plan that you drew up.

Nonprofit counselors charge modest fees. Their basic budget consultation is often free and may be all the help you need. If you enter a formal debt-repayment plan, they charge perhaps $10 to $50 a month, and zero for clients with low incomes. They normally handle only personal debts, not business debts. Their plans may cover only unsecured consumer debts such as credit-card bills, not secured debt such as mortgages and car payments (although some offices will negotiate lower payments on mortgages, too). For the name of a nonprofit counseling agency, ask your city's department of social services; the debt-collection office of your bank, credit union, or a major department store; the Consumer Credit Counseling Service (call 800-338-CCCS for an office near you); or Family Service America, 11700 West Lake Park Dr., Milwaukee, WI 53224. Although the FSA has affiliates all over the country, not all of them offer credit counseling.

Don't be afraid to ask for help. Thousands of people share your problem. Counselors and credit managers have seen it all and consider it their job to haul you out of the pit.

Do *not* pay a lawyer or firm that offers to straighten out your debts in return for a percentage of what you owe. You can't afford it and it won't work. Call the CCCS or FSA instead.

If negotiation doesn't solve the problem, consider Chapter 13 of the Bankruptcy Code, formerly known as the wage-earner plan. It stops your creditors from hounding you and lets you keep your property while you start on a formal, court-approved plan to pay at least part of your debts over 3 to 5 years.

If even that's too tough, go for Chapter 7, straight bankruptcy. Most of your debts will be canceled, although you may have to give up some of your property to repay creditors. Get good legal advice. It's risky to read a book and try to do it yourself because you might miss something of advantage to you.

Certain debts normally cannot be discharged in bankruptcy, although there are some exceptions to the rules. These debts include recent student loans, child support, alimony, most taxes, loans you didn't mention on your bankruptcy petition, loans granted on the basis of untrue financial statements, and court judgments for certain damages, such as an accident you caused while driving drunk. You also can't get out of consumer loans over $500 owed to a single creditor and incurred for luxury goods and services within 40 days of a bankruptcy filing (that's the "no-last-minute-BMWs" rule); or cash advances for more than $1,000 from an open-ended credit plan taken within 20 days of the filing (the "no-last-minute-Caribbean-vacation" rule).

Chapter 7 bankruptcy is the hardest for lenders to forget. It hangs around on your credit record for a decade.

HOW TO TELL YOU'RE IN TROUBLE

Quit buying on credit if:

1. You can afford to pay only the minimum on your credit cards every month, and even that's a stretch.

2. You have to charge purchases that you used to pay for in cash.

3. You took a debt-consolidation loan and now you're running up fresh debts.

4. You can't save a dime.

5. You look forward to the junk mail, hoping that a new bank will be careless enough to offer you a credit card.

6. You're taking cash advances from one card in order to make payments on another.

7. You can't pay your basic bills on time.

8. You're being dunned.

9. You get turned down for credit.

10. You don't even want some of the things you buy.

11. Your friends can't figure out how you manage to live so well.

12. Without overtime or moonlighting, you'd lose your house, your car, and your kids.

13. You're taking cash advances for daily expenses like food and rent.

14. You borrow $50 from the guy in the next office until the end of the week. You borrow $500 from your brother.

15. You don't open an envelope that you know contains a bill.

16. When you buy on credit, you always choose the longest time period to repay.

17. You never pay off your credit cards completely.

18. You put off paying by fiddling your creditors—putting the bill for the dentist in the envelope addressed to the doctor, and vice versa.

19. You bounce checks.

20. You don't know exactly how much you owe.

21. You get scared about money in the middle of the night.

22. You don't dare tell your mother. Or your spouse. Or, sometimes, yourself.

Credit-card issuers have developed sophisticated systems for identifying borrowers who are likely to default. They call it behavior scoring. Here are six of the warning signals that creditors look for:

1. You pay only the bare minimum every month and never more than the minimum.

2. You make partial payments.

3. You started falling behind on your payments soon after opening an account.

4. You have taken the maximum cash advance.

5. Your account balance always grows; you can't ever seem to pay it off.

6. You have periodic bouts of late payment.

If this describes you, your number-one job is to get out of debt. Only then can you start getting rich.

11.

When to Hock the Farm

All the Best Ways to Borrow Money to Invest

The rich didn't get that way by saving pennies. That's only what they tell their biographers. They made their fortunes on borrowed money.

Don't borrow to spend. Occasional debt on a credit card never hurt anybody, but permanent indebtedness to support an implacable spending habit is a staggering waste. A loser's game. At 18 percent interest, you are overpaying for everything by nearly one-fifth. Why would you want to throw that much money away? You're living rich while growing poor.

But don't be shy about borrowing to invest. That's how people get rich. They use OPM—Other People's Money—to build something of value for themselves. Here are the classic steps to wealth: First, shed consumer debt. Second, build assets—through homeownership, saving money, and investing. Third, borrow prudently against some of those assets to invest for even more net worth.

WHAT IS INVESTMENT DEBT?

Investment debt is money you borrow to acquire an asset that, with luck, might rise in price. You're gambling that the price increase will more than cover the loan's cost. You hope to be left with a profit after selling the asset and paying off the loan.

A mortgage is the most ubiquitous form of investment debt. A college loan comes second; an education is an investment because it builds your earning power or the earning power of your children. A loan to start or buy into a business can multiply your money many times if the business succeeds. A car loan supports both your earning power (you drive to work) and your investment program (by buying a car with borrowed money instead of cash, you're left with more earnings to stash in a tax-deferred retirement account). Even a debt-consolidation loan is worthwhile if it lowers the interest you have to pay.

The critical test of any loan is that the money you borrow not disappear. It should be used in some way to maintain and improve your wealth.

HOW MUCH INVESTMENT DEBT CAN YOU AFFORD?

When You Borrow for Investment . . .

1. *You can afford any debt that will support itself.* Can you rent out a duplex for enough to cover the costs? If so, and you like being a landlord, go ahead.

2. *You can afford any debt that you can easily repay out of personal earnings.* If your job is secure, up to 40 percent of your income can be committed to monthly repayments, including mortgage repayments. When you borrow against your salary, however, you should generally be making a *liquid* investment—that is, an investment that's instantly salable at the current market price. If your income drops and you're pressed for cash, you can dump the investment and eliminate the debt. Mutual funds are liquid. Second homes aren't. When you finance a second home out of earnings, you should either be dead sure of your job or have enough savings to carry the mortgage for a year or two if your income falls.

3. *You can go into debt to make an illiquid investment as long as you have a substantial amount of liquid securities or money in the bank.* Say, for example, that you borrow to buy a piece of land that you intend to subdivide and sell as separate building lots. Then you lose your job. The land may not be salable except at a giveaway price. But your lender (that stone-hearted bean counter) thinks you should keep on making monthly payments. How will you manage? No sweat, as long as you have a lot of cash or stocks that you can liquidate. If you don't, never finance an investment like this. You'll be playing dice with your solvency.

THE MONEY STORES

When you want a loan, don't put on the sackcloth of a mendicant and approach your banker on bended knee. You are a *customer* in a *money store.* Everyone wants your business if you're a good credit risk. You can negotiate terms just the way you negotiate a new-car price. Bankers expect borrowers to be choosy and are astounded when they're not.

In any city, the most costly lender may charge anywhere from 2 to 6 percentage points more than the cheapest one. A poor credit risk may have to accept those terms; a good one doesn't.

Your search for a loan might start with a credit union, if you can find one to join (page 51). After that, look at S&Ls, then at banks. In general, smaller institutions charge lower rates and fewer fees than large ones, and may be more willing to negotiate. Always make an appointment to see a loan officer, don't just wander in off the street. Innocents wander; smarties prearrange.

Make a list of the things you want to know: annual percentage rate, fees, down payment, repayment schedule. Ask: "Is that the best you can do?" "Will you cut half a point off the interest rate?" "Will you lower the points I have to pay up front?" If it's a big personal loan, ask: "Can I borrow at the prime lending rate [that's the bank's benchmark rate]? "Then say, "Thanks very much, I'll think it over," and leave.

Repeat the scene with one or two more lenders. If your favorite bank has a higher interest rate than the others, tell it what the competition is doing. If it wants your business, it will come down. You'll get the best rate if you have at least two banks bidding for the loan.

Go to the major consumer-loan companies, too. They can be competitive for large home-equity lines of credit.

Finance companies, however, generally charge higher interest rates and fees than the competition. They may also want your house as collateral, even for very small loans. If you take a series of small loans, you'll find fee piled on fee, making borrowing hugely expensive. Use a finance company only if you *must* have credit and can't borrow anywhere else. If you already have a finance-company loan, try to pay it off with a lower-rate loan from a credit union or bank.

BORROWING AGAINST YOUR HOUSE

It may sound uncharacteristically wild of me to suggest your home as a source of risk capital, but that is the only source that many of us have. If you think you can profit by borrowing money against your home, it's worth a try. But *only* if you can comfortably carry the larger mortgage; and *only* if you're sure of your job; and *only* if you've applied the rules of sound investing (Chapter 21); and *only* if you expect the investment to appreciate by more than your net interest cost; and *only* if you wouldn't be devastated if the deal flopped.

You borrow against your "equity," which is the difference between the value of your home and the mortgages you carry. It's the cash you'd realize if you sold the house and repaid the bank.

Generally speaking, people feel more comfortable tapping their homes for real-estate investments than for stocks. For example, you might use your equity to finance a rental property. Homes are also a good source of college money—an investment in future earning power.

But there's nothing wrong with carrying a larger mortgage in order to be invested in stocks as long as your mortgage interest rate is 10 percent or less. Put another way, I wouldn't sell my stocks in order to minimize my mortgage. Stocks should earn more than 10 percent over the long run (although not necessarily over the short run). In an emergency, you could always sell the stocks to reduce the loan.

Second Mortgages: A Traditional Loan vs. a Home-Equity Line

The loan of choice today is a second mortgage, also called a second trust, which pledges your house as collateral. Pretty soon it will be standard issue, like a car loan or blue jeans. Some lenders also give second mortgages on condominiums and mobile homes.

It's a child of the tax laws. You can tax-deduct the interest on second mortgages up to $100,000 (although the loan can't exceed your home's fair market value). By contrast, you get no deduction at all for interest paid on auto loans, many student loans (page 544), credit-card debt, and personal loans. You can save money by skipping those loans and putting your house in hock instead.

A traditional second mortgage works just like a first. You borrow a lump sum of money and pay back over a fixed term, usually 7 to 15 years. The interest rate may be fixed or variable. Marginal credit risks should try for a Title I home-improvement loan insured by the Federal Housing Administration (FHA) and offered by a limited number of banks. For a brochure and the names of FHA lenders in your area, call 800-733-4663.

Borrowers, however, have fallen in love with a different kind of second mortgage—the home-equity line of credit. It's a loan tailor-made for our self-service times. Instead of borrowing a fixed amount of money, you arrange for a fixed amount of borrowing power (minimum: $5,000 to $10,000; maximum: $100,000 to $250,000), available over the next 5 to 10 years. During that time you can take a loan anytime you want, with no further approval from the bank.

Different lenders provide different ways of accessing your credit. You might use a special check, put down a credit or debit card, attach the credit line to your regular checking account, or make a phone call asking that funds be transferred into your account. The minimum loan is usually $250 to $500. You pay interest only on the money that you actually use, at a variable rate.

How fast you repay is often up to you. Depending on the lender, you can generally choose to: (1) Pay interest and a portion of the principal each month, erasing the loan over 5 to 20 years. (2) Pay only the interest for 5 to 7 years. After that, you might renegotiate the loan terms, continuing to pay interest only. Or you might start paying down the principal. (3) Pay substantial amounts each month to clear up the loan as fast as you can. If this is your plan, get a loan without prepayment penalties. Some lenders charge extra for prepayments during the first 3 to 5 years. Whichever method you choose, the loan is payable in full when the house is sold.

Home-equity lines are offered by commercial banks, mortgage banks, S&Ls, credit unions, consumer-credit companies, finance companies, even some large brokerage houses. Credit unions often have the best terms. Finance companies have the worst.

Should You Take a Home-Equity Line or a Traditional Second Mortgage?

A traditional second mortgage is all discipline. Your monthly payments are usually fixed, so the loan won't cost more when interest rates rise. You cannot easily add to the loan—no temptation there. It's a good way to borrow for a single purpose, like redoing the kitchen. It's the right loan for people on limited budgets. And it's a good defensive loan in a shaky marriage. The money goes toward something you both want and there's no other borrowing power on tap. This loan is the wrong choice, however, if you want the opportunity to keep borrowing more.

For multiple loans, go for a home-equity line of credit. Once you've opened the line, you can borrow against it whenever you want. So it's the right choice for meeting a series of needs, like college tuition for the next four years. Most lenders charge variable interest rates—typically, one to 3 percentage points over the prime interest rate. So your monthly payments can rise and fall. This loan is safest for people with comfortable incomes who won't faint when rates go up.

Which is cheaper, a traditional second mortgage or a home-equity loan? That's hard to tell. You can't necessarily compare their annual percentage rates of interest (APRs) because they're figured differently.

On a fixed-term second mortgage, all the financing fees are considered part of the APR. They aren't counted, however, on a home-equity loan. If the home-equity lender charges no fees, the APR tells you the loan's true cost. Where fees are charged, however, the effective rate is higher than the lender says.

In general, both the interest rates and closing costs on fixed-term second mortgages are higher than on lines of credit. But not always. To compare these loans, list all their costs: their interest rates, any financing fees (application fees, points, and loan-origination fees), and any service fees (for title search, survey, appraisal, credit check, legal work, and so on). Many home-equity lines charge nothing up front, but typically levy annual fees of anywhere from $20 to $75. Loans with high up-front fees may not be worth their cost.

Should You Take a Home-Equity Loan or an Auto Loan? Unfortunately, you can't necessarily compare their annual percentage rates of interest to see which deal is better. Up-front fees are figured into the APR for the auto loan but not for the home-equity loan. The comparison is fair only if the home-equity lender doesn't charge any fees. Otherwise, that loan costs a little more than it appears.

The auto loan might be cheaper if you can get a super-low-cost promotional loan. Otherwise, the home-equity loan should be cheaper because you can tax-deduct the interest.

Should You Take a Home-Equity Loan to Pay Off Your Credit-Card Debt? I can think of two reasons to say yes and four to say no. First, the positives:

It's almost always smart to substitute low-cost debt for high-cost debt, and home-equity loans cost less. The money you save can be used to reduce your home-equity debt or to raise the amount you contribute to a tax-deferred retirement account.

Furthermore, home-equity interest is tax deductible on loans up to $100,000 if you itemize deductions. There's no tax write-off for credit-card interest. (There's also no write-off for home-equity interest if you use the standard deduction.)

Now the negatives:

Most credit-card debts are paid off within about 15 months. That holds down the interest bill. On home-equity lines, however, loans usually linger much longer. Some people treat them as permanent debt to be paid off when the house is sold. So despite the lower interest rate, a home-equity loan might cost you more.

You might borrow against your home to clean up your credit-card debt, then run up your credit cards all over again. That gives you double the debt you used to have.

With so much home equity at your fingertips, you might shop up a storm. Your home value could vanish in a mad afternoon at the mall.

When you don't repay your credit-card debt, the lender duns you and may sue. At worst, this ruins your credit record. But if you don't repay home-equity debt, you are foreclosed. For this reason, you shouldn't pile all your consumer loans onto your house, regardless of the tax advantage. In an emergency, you need some loans you can duck.

Bottom line: It's fine to refinance non-tax-deductible consumer debt with a home-equity loan *if* you pay it off fast and resist new debt. Otherwise, forget it. To spendaholics, home-equity lines are a doomsday machine.

Should You Borrow If You Plan to Move? This is the downside nobody thinks about. When you sell your house, you have to pay off your first mortgage and the home-equity loan. That leaves you less cash to put down on your next home and may stop you from trading up. If you think you'll move in 4 or 5 years, buy your car with a separate auto loan and leave your home equity alone.

Should You Agree to a Home-Equity Line If Your Marriage Is in Trouble?
Absolutely not. And tell the bank, in writing, to freeze any lines you already have. When you're married, it takes only one signature to originate a home-equity loan. One spouse could borrow up to the limit of the line and spend the money, yet you're both responsible for the debt. A divorce-court judge ought to tell the spouse who took the money to pay it back, but you can't count on that.

How to Use Home-Equity Lines

1. *Don't open a larger credit line than you really need.*
If you apply for a credit card, the lender will check your credit report to see how much borrowing power you have already. A large, unused home-equity line shows that you could add substantially to your debts. As a result, you may be turned down for a low-rate card that you particularly want.

Some lenders charge a percentage point for granting the line—and it's one percent of the whole line, not just the amount you borrow. That's $100 for a $10,000 line but $500 for a $50,000 line. Look first for a lender who charges less up front. If you don't qualify for less expensive credit, take the smallest line you need. If you want more money later, you can probably increase the line for a modest fee. You can decrease the size of your line just by sending the lender a letter.

2. *Don't overborrow.* Banks usually lend a maximum of 70 to 85 percent of the value of your house, minus the amount remaining on your first mortgage. On a $200,000 house with a $120,000 first mortgage, for example, you could get $20,000 to $50,000 more. A few lenders let you borrow up to 100 percent of equity; in this example, that would give you access to $80,000 more.

If your income seems too low to carry so large a debt, the bank will lend less. But some lenders stretch you right to the edge of your income and beyond. It's up to you to say, "enough."

3. *Compare prices before deciding on a lender.* On variable-rate loans, the interest rate usually floats one to 3 percentage points above the prime lending rate. You'll save money by shopping for a narrow spread. (The spread is the difference between the two rates.) Many lenders give you a cheap rate for the first 6 or 12 months, then raise it later.

A majority of lenders charge no up-front closing costs, so there's normally no reason to pay points, application fees, and other charges. Costs rise, however, if you borrow 90 or 100 percent of your equity.

Many lenders charge an annual fee. There may also be transaction fees or fees for closing your credit line within the first year. Ask about them.

Not many lenders offer fixed-rate home-equity lines. When they do, they generally fix the rate for only 5 years or so, and then are free to put it up. Such lines cost about 0.5 percentage points more at the start than variables do. Some lenders will give you a onetime rate cut if the general level of rates declines.

4. *Check the cap*. There's a limit to how high your interest rate can rise, over the life of the loan. The usual cap: 5 or 6 percentage points more than the rate you started with. If you opened your home-equity line before lifetime caps were required (December 8, 1987), you have no high-inflation protection. Ask your lender to add a cap to your agreement. That's easier than opening a new line somewhere else.

Many lenders have introduced an annual cap. That typically prevents your rate from rising more than 2 percentage points in a single year.

Where there's a ceiling there's sometimes a floor. Your rate might not be allowed to drop lower than 6 or 8 percent. But if the general level of rates goes much further down, you can usually refinance. Some home-equity lines have prepayment penalties.

5. *Read the fine print*. Lenders choose tiny type for information that they don't care if you overlook. So do yourself a favor: put on your glasses and read through the loan agreement.

You'll probably learn that your credit line can be reduced or frozen if: (1) you don't pass continuing credit checks, (2) the value of your house goes down, or (3) interest rates have risen above the cap. You'll learn when and how your interest rate adjusts, what all the fees are, when your credit line expires, all the repayment terms, and whether you'll face a single large payment when the loan ultimately falls due. On credit lines opened before November 7, 1989, the lender can change all the terms at will—raising fees, changing the way interest rates are calculated, changing the monthly amounts you repay. On credit lines opened since then, however, most of the terms are guaranteed.

When you open a home-equity line of credit, you're supposed to get a government-mandated brochure telling you what to ask the lender. Get answers to every question on the list.

6. *Repay early and often*. Lenders encourage you to take 10 or 20 years to repay. But stretching out your loans over that length of time is a sucker's game. If you use your home-equity credit line to buy a new car every three years, and make only the minimum payments, you could find yourself paying for your present car plus the four previous ones all at once. That's a lot of money down the drain.

Fit your payment schedule to the purchase. Get rid of a debt-consolidation loan in a year and a half. Clean up an auto loan in 3 to 4 years. Don't let a home-improvement loan hang around for more than 7 years. Reduce a loan that is carrying a successful investment so you'll have the equity to make more investments.

7. *Beware the call clause.* Lenders reserve the right to "call," or force you to repay, a home-equity loan that might be in trouble. This could happen if you miss some payments, or if you endanger the bank's interest in the house, perhaps by being unable to keep it in good repair. Exactly what can trigger a call will be outlined in your loan agreement. The moral: Back up your home-equity loans with liquid investments. You should be prepared to make 6 months of payments, even if you're out of work.

8. *Don't bet against the real-estate market.* If house prices are getting beaten up in your community, stay away from home-equity loans. If you have a big loan and need to move, you might spend your entire equity paying off your mortgages and covering the real-estate broker's commission. You'd have little or nothing to put down on another house.

It's Okay to Borrow Against Your House When:

You put no consumables, like parties or clothes, on the credit line. Put these on a credit card and pay them off in the same month.

You use the line to consolidate expensive credit-card debt and repay the loan fast.

You use it for unavoidable consumer debt, like buying a car, and repay it fast.

You use it for major investments—education, home improvements, buying property or stocks. These investments should yield more than the cost of the loan.

You don't run up other loans on top of those on your home-equity line.

You can handle the payments comfortably. If your income drops, you can sell assets to repay the loan.

You have other sources of cash to help make a down payment on a new house if you move.

You hate and fear home-equity lines. You worry when you use them. You treat them like time bombs.

It's Wrong to Borrow Against Your House When:

You love home-equity lines. They're mother's milk. You feel wealthy when you use them.

You borrow to support your consumer-spending habit.

You will stretch out the loans for many years, paying jillions in interest.

You think of the loan as a permanent debt, not to be repaid until you sell your house.

Your job is shaky.

You're borrowing to make an investment but have chosen rotten investments in the past.

You'd be left with so little equity that, if you sold your house and repaid all the loans, you couldn't afford the down payment on a new house.

You will need your home equity pretty soon to pay for college.

You can't repay if your income drops, except by selling the house.

Home values in your area are going down.

Refinancing Your House

When you refinance, you get a new first mortgage and use the proceeds to pay off the old one. If your house has risen in value, you can take a larger mortgage than you had before and use the extra money for other investments.

If you're going to tap your house for funds, you have two ways to do it: refinance with a larger first mortgage or add a second mortgage, either a fixed-term loan or a home-equity line of credit. To choose, compare the following:

Up-Front Costs. Refinancing usually carries higher up-front costs. Fees run in the area of one to 2 percent of the mortgage amount, although your own lender may do the job for less.

Interest Rate. The rate will be lower on a refinanced first mortgage but that doesn't necessarily make it cheaper. Compare the monthly payment on a refinanced loan with the monthly cost of keeping your old mortgage and adding a home-equity loan.

Flexibility. You can't beat a home-equity line. You borrow periodically rather than in a big lump sum and pay interest only on the money you actually take.

Term. When you refinance, you start your primary mortgage from scratch, with payments typically lasting for 15 or 30 years. Home-equity loans usually run for shorter terms, so you pay less interest in the long run.

Risk. How fast and how high could your monthly payments rise, if interest rates go up? Your risk is higher with home-equity lines. Minimum monthly payments change immediately, and rates can run higher than on first mortgages.

What You Can Tax-Deduct on a Refinancing

1. Deduct interest on any new mortgage loan that equals your old loan plus up to $100,000.

2. Deduct interest on any new loan that equals your old loan plus the cost of a home improvement (if you are borrowing to finance that home improvement) plus $100,000.

Both of these rules apply to your primary house and to one vacation house. A cabin, condominium, mobile home, even a sleep-in boat can count as a house.

Both of these rules are also subject to a cap. You can't deduct mortgage interest on loans higher than $1.1 million on your regular house and vacation house, combined. If you borrow more, however, and use the extra money to start a business or make investments, the interest may be deductible as business or investment interest. (Mortgages acquired on or before October 13, 1987, are still fully deductible even if they exceed the $1.1 million cap.)

3. Up-front points paid to the lender when you refinance normally have to be deducted over the life of the loan. With this exception: if part of the loan is used to improve your principal home, you get an immediate write-off for the points attributable to that portion of the loan.

BORROWING AGAINST YOUR CASH-VALUE LIFE INSURANCE

You don't take cash directly from your insurance policy. You borrow *against* your cash values, using them as collateral. The money stashed in your policy keeps on earning interest. But an amount equal to your loan may earn interest at a lower rate.

That loss of interest raises the cost of your loan, so you're paying more than you realize. Instead of the 6 percent or so that your policy states, your actual loan rate can be 8 or 9 percent.

To see how to figure the true rate of interest on a loan against a universal-life insurance policy, see the table that follows. The footnotes show you how to adjust for loans against whole life or variable life policies.

No matter what the agent claims, the cost of a life insurance loan is typically about the same as a home-equity loan or a margin loan against the value of your stocks or mutual funds. Policy loans, however, aren't tax deductible.

Borrowers normally don't pay the interest out of pocket (although they could). Instead, they add each year's interest to the loan.

The policy's death benefit will be reduced by the loan amount. Say, for example, that you have a $100,000 policy and borrow $30,000. Initially, that leaves $70,000 for your heirs. Each year the cash value will rise by the premiums you pay and the interest your money earns, but decline by the insurance charges and the unpaid interest on the loan. If you keep that loan for many years, or increase your borrowing, you may tear the policy apart. The net cash value may decline to the point where it can't support the policy anymore. You'll have to start repaying the loan or let the policy lapse. If the policy lapses, you'll generally owe taxes on the amount by which your loan exceeded the premiums you paid. The tax bill can be a shocker if the loan was large.

FIGURING THE TRUE RATE OF INTEREST ON A
UNIVERSAL-LIFE INSURANCE POLICY LOAN

The Method	An Example
1. Find out the stated loan interest rate that the policy guarantees.	Your policy loan rate is 6 percent.
2. Find out what rate of interest the insurance company currently pays on your cash values. Typically, you're earning about the same as you would on a Treasury bond.	Your company credits 6.25 percent on cash values.
3. Find out what interest rate the company pays on any cash values you borrow against. It will usually be the policy's minimum rate, say, 4 percent.	If you borrow $5,000, the insurer credits $5,000 of your cash values with an interest rate of only 4 percent.
4. Subtract the reduced rate of interest earned on the cash you're using as collateral from the interest the insurer pays when you haven't borrowed (item 2). The difference shows you how much interest you are losing.	You are earning 4 percent on $5,000 in cash values, instead of 6.25 percent. That's a 2.25 percent loss.
5. Your true borrowing cost is the stated rate of loan interest plus the interest lost on your cash values.	Your $5,000 loan costs 6 percent plus the 2.25 percent loss of interest —8.25 percent in all.
6. *The agent might say that your loan's "true cost" is the difference between the loan interest you pay and the interest your cash value earns.*	*The "true cost" is said to be 2 percent—the 6 percent loan rate minus the 4 percent the insurer is still crediting to your policy.*
7. THAT'S PURE BALONEY.	*The true rate is 8.25 percent, as explained.*

FOR WHOLE LIFE POLICIES: Find out what the policy's dividend will be if you borrow and if you don't. You can get this information from an agent or from the insurance company. Add the difference between those two dividends to the amount of interest you'll pay to get your true borrowing cost. Divide the cost by the size of the loan to get the percentage rate. You'll have to do that every year. If your dividend will remain unchanged, then the policy loan rate is indeed your cost. Old whole-life policies (roughly, those issued prior to 1980) charge a loan rate of 5 to 6 percent. Newer policies may charge 8 percent or a variable rate.

FOR VARIABLE LIFE POLICIES: An amount equal to your loan is transferred out of your separate investment account and into the insurer's general account. Find out the difference between what you pay on the loan and what your cash will earn in the general account. Add that to the policy loan rate to get your true borrowing cost.

Ask your insurance company or agent for a computer-generated policy illustration showing what may happen to your cash values and death benefit over the next 30 years with and without the loan. That tells you whether your policy can last and how much you'll leave for your beneficiaries, assuming current interest rates. Get a new illustration from time to time.

If you borrow to invest, and the investment earns less than the true rate of interest you're paying on the policy loan, you've made a mistake. Counting both the investment and what remains of the policy, your heirs will get less than if you had left the policy alone.

It often doesn't occur to people to repay their policy loans. That's another mistake. You improve your financial position by taking a lower-earning asset (say, a 5 percent bank account or 6 percent bond) and using it to repay an 8 or 9 percent policy loan. Repaying is the financial equivalent of investing, tax-free and risk-free, at the effective policy-loan rate.

If you do tap a universal policy for funds, leave enough money there to be sure your insurance will stay in force for the rest of your life. If you take out too much, the policy may expire before you do. Your insurance company or agent can tell you where the withdrawal limits lie. As usual, the policy's death benefit will be reduced by the amount you withdraw.

For more on cash-value policies, including the question of whether to take withdrawals instead of loans, see page 296.

BORROWING AGAINST CERTIFICATES OF DEPOSIT

The bank will lend you money against your CDs. But do you really want that loan? Would it be smarter to cancel the CD, pay the early-withdrawal penalty, and use your own money for whatever you want to buy?

To answer this question, use your hand-held calculator and your common sense. Figure out how much interest you'd pay on the loan; compare it with the money you'd lose by cashing in the CD (you'd lose your after-tax interest rate plus the early-withdrawal penalty). Then . . .

• Take the loan if it costs less than cashing in the CD.

• Break the CD if it earns less than you'd pay for the loan (which is usually the case).

• Take a loan that costs more if the CD is from an inheritance and you'd never be able to save such a sum yourself.

Loans against CDs aren't as cheap as the banks make them out to be. Say that you borrow at 9 percent while your CD is earning 6 percent. Your banker might say that you're paying only 3 percent "real"—and claim that's a better deal than, say, an 8 percent promotional loan from an auto dealer. Not true, not true. To prove it, apply the banker's "logic" to the auto loan. If you keep the 6 percent CD and pay the car dealer 8 percent, you're paying only 2 percent "real." So the auto loan still costs less.

To find the cheapest loan, ignore net-cost gimmicks and compare each loan's annual percentage rate. The lower the APR, the less it costs. If you use the cash in your CD to reduce or eliminate the loan, that's the cheapest strategy of all.

BORROWING AGAINST STOCKS, BONDS, AND MUTUAL FUNDS

Loans against securities are called margin loans. You usually borrow from a stockbroker, although banks are in this business, too. You can borrow up to 50 percent of the value of stocks listed on a stock exchange, well-diversified mutual funds, some over-the-counter stocks ("over-the-counter" means they aren't sold on formal exchanges—page 711), and listed convertible bonds; up to 75 percent of the value of listed corporate bonds; up to 85 percent on municipal bonds; and up to 95 percent on Treasury securities. Your brokerage firm may set its own limit at something less than these maximum amounts. You generally need an account with a discount stockbroker to borrow against no-load mutual funds (those are funds with no up-front sales charges).

Margin loans are usually used to buy securities. With just $10,000 cash, you can borrow enough money to buy up to $20,000 worth of listed stocks or $200,000 worth of U.S. government bonds.

But you can borrow against your securities for other purposes, too. Interest rates run 0.5 to 2.5 percentage points over the broker call rate, which is what banks charge brokers for their money. You don't have to make any loan repayments. The interest compounds in your brokerage account, payable when the securities are sold.

There are two major risks with margin loans:

1. Interest charges and sales commissions can easily eat up any profit you make on your securities.

2. If your stocks drop too far in price, the broker will ask for more collateral in the form of cash or securities. That's what's known as a *margin call*. If you don't have the money, some of your securities will be sold to cover the debt. You usually get a margin call if the value of your interest in the securities, net of the debt, shrinks to 30 or 25 percent of the market price.

Thousands of Investors Take Margin Loans Without Knowing What They've Done. Here's how that happens:

The monthly statement from your broker may show, in one corner, your "borrowing power." The broker encourages you to use the money to buy a car or take a vacation. (The firm earns a nice piece of change on these loans.) He or she forgets to tell you that it's not an ordinary loan. Suddenly the market drops and you get a margin call. You have to repay part of what you borrowed or lose some of your securities. But you've spent the money and haven't got any extra cash, so you have to sell some of your stocks.

There goes some retirement money down the drain.

If you borrow from your broker, don't do it for spending money. Borrow only to buy more securities in hopes of increasing your net worth, and don't hold the margin loan for long.

Loan Costs Can Demolish Your Profits. After paying loan interest and brokerage commissions, you might earn less on a margined investment than if you hadn't borrowed at all. This true story is best told by example.

Say that you have $5,000 to spend on a $50 stock. You can buy 100 shares for cash. Or you can buy 200 shares, putting up $5,000 and borrowing another $5,000 from your stockbroker. If the share price rises by $5, the cash investor grosses $500, or 10 percent. The margin investor makes $1,000, grossing 20 percent on his or her original $5,000. Wow. Gimme a loan.

But what if you hold your margined position for a year? You'd pay $490 on a loan that charged 9.8 percent interest. You paid your broker maybe $200 in sales commissions (twice the commission than if you hadn't bought on margin). That's $690 in costs, subtracted from your $1,000 profit, for a net gain of $310—a 6.2 percent return. Compare that with the unmargined investment: a $500 profit minus $100 in sales commissions for a $400 gain —a fatter, 8 percent return. So maybe the loan isn't such a hot idea. For it to work you need either large gains or fast ones, so you don't have to hold the margined position very long.

On the downside, margin loans are poison. Still using the same example, assume that the share price drops by $5. The cash investor loses 10 percent but the margin investor loses 20 percent plus the extra commission and interest expenses. If the price drops by $12 a share, the margin buyer has to put up more money or be partly sold out.

Do You Really Want to Borrow Against Your Securities?

Yes, if you're a proven success as an investor and will use those loans to compound your winnings. *Yes,* if you're able, temperamentally, to sell losing stocks quickly. *Yes,* if you know the cost of your loan and will balance it carefully against your potential for profit.

No, if you're a new or uncertain investor, because you'll probably go wrong. *No,* if you're a long-term investor rather than a quick trader. *No,* if it wouldn't occur to you to borrow unless your stockbroker suggested it. *No,* if you're borrowing to take a vacation or buy a car—that simply consumes the investments that you are laboring so hard to build. *No,* if you're dabbling in mysterious investments that you only faintly understand. Some of the biggest losses in the Crash of '87 were taken by investors who borrowed against stocks to pyramid stock-index options. They didn't have a clue what they were doing. Many wound up losing far more money than they invested.

BORROWING AGAINST YOUR SMILE

Collateral is property you put up to guarantee or *secure* a loan. Stocks, certificates of deposit, automobiles, and real estate all can be used as collateral. The lender will grab them if you don't pay.

An *unsecured* loan is given on the strength of your paycheck and credit history. If you don't pay, the lender can only sue. The interest rate is higher than on secured loans and the repayment period often shorter.

The commonest unsecured loans are the lines of credit tied to your credit cards or checking account. The lender gives you the right to borrow up to a certain amount—maybe $1,500 to $15,000—whenever you want. You get the money by writing a check for more than you have in your account or by slipping your card into an automated teller machine.

Your interest rate is the same as, or higher than, the rate on the unpaid balance on your credit card. There may also be a transaction fee. Some banks lend money only in multiples of $50 or $100, so if you write an overdraft for $105 you might find that you've had to borrow $150 or $200. You are rarely pressed to eliminate the debt, beyond a minimum monthly payment. The bank has you just where it wants you: in hock. Credit-card advances or overdraft checking are handy for sudden emergencies, but clear up these expensive loans as fast as you can.

If you need a larger sum of money for a short period of time—say, to pay your taxes—your bank might give you a 3-month loan at a lower rate than you'd pay for overdraft checking. This loan can usually be renewed a couple of times. The warmer your relationship with your banker, and the more accounts you keep there, the easier these loans are to get. That's one reason I recommend a small bank or branch. It's simpler to get to know the people in charge.

If you have a good salary and a high net worth, you might qualify for "personal banking." Someone is assigned to your account and it's his or her job to make you happy. Whatever you need—loans, brokerage services, certificates of deposit, Treasury securities—your personal banker makes it work. Interest rates are negotiable. High-income clients can usually get a better deal than anyone else because they bring the bank more business.

How much you can borrow unsecured depends on your salary and the value of your assets, such as savings, investments, and real estate. It's not illegal to puff your net worth a bit by taking an optimistic view of the value of your house. But if you borrow more than you can handle, you're the loser in the end.

BORROWING AGAINST YOUR RETIREMENT FUNDS

It's a lousy idea to borrow against your retirement funds for spending money. But borrowing to make an investment (a solid, well-considered investment) can be pretty smart. Stocks and bonds are usually available within the plan. But you might want to borrow to buy real estate or invest in a business.

A loan from a retirement plan does not necessarily deplete your assets. Sometimes it enlarges them. Follow me through an optimal transaction and I'll show you how:

1. You borrow money from your retirement plan and invest it.

2. You pay interest on the loan, at one to 3 percentage points over the prime rate. That interest payment usually goes right into your own retirement account, so you're paying interest to yourself instead of a bank. If your retirement fund had been earning 7 percent on the money you borrowed, and you pay 10 percent on the loan, your account has just picked up an extra 3 percentage points.

3. You repay most loans over 5 years, in regular monthly or quarterly amounts. As I see it, that's a form of forced saving. If you borrow to buy a principal residence, your monthly payments are amortized over 10 to 30 years, depending on the plan. Loan repayments are usually deducted automatically from your paycheck.

4. Your retirement fund gets its money back plus interest. Meanwhile, the money you borrowed is (one hopes) prospering in your outside investment. It has to earn at least enough to cover the extra income taxes this loan will cost.

Your Tax Cost. One drawback to loans against retirement plans is the extra tax you pay. The loan interest normally isn't tax deductible. Neither is the money you use to repay principal. So that money is taxed twice—once when you earn it and use it to make loan repayments into the plan, and again when you retire and take it out of the plan. Put another way, you put after-tax money into the plan and it's taxed again when you take it out.

Loan interest would be deductible only if it meets the following two tests: (1) you borrow your employer's contributions, not yours (the employer would have to segregate these funds, and few do); and (2) the money is used for a deductible purpose, such as running your small business or making an investment (page 264).

Your Investment Cost. Sometimes your retirement plan is earning more than the interest charged on loans. Then, the loan creates a loss. For example, say your retirement investments yield 12 percent but you'd pay only 10 percent if you borrowed the money out. That's a 2 percentage point loss, which would compound over time. The loan's true cost becomes 12 percent (the 10 percent loan rate plus the 2-point drop in yield). You might find a bank that charges less.

It's unlikely, however, that all of your plan's investments earn the same high rate of return. If you borrow, you can arrange for the loan to come from the lowest-earning assets.

Borrowing from Your Plan Makes Sense as Long as:

• The plan charges a lower interest rate than you could get at a bank, counting both the direct loan rate and any loss your plan takes by lending to you rather than making other investments. A home-equity loan will almost always be better than a retirement-plan loan because interest on home-equity loans is tax deductible.

• You pay a higher interest rate on the loan than your pension was earning on its investments. That way you are adding assets to your plan.

• Your outside investment earns enough to cover its tax cost, plus something extra to compensate you for the risk you took.

• You'll be with the company long enough to repay the loan. If you quit or are fired, a few companies let you continue the payments as scheduled. More likely, you'll have to repay the loan immediately. If you don't, it's treated as a withdrawal. You'll owe income taxes on the remaining loan amount plus a 10 percent penalty if you're younger than $59\frac{1}{2}$. Retirees may be allowed to repay on the original schedule, even if others aren't.

Should You Borrow with a Credit Card? Credit cards linked to 401(k)s are so new that few employers offer them. A bank runs the program. When you buy something with this credit card you are taking a loan from your retirement plan.

It's quicker to borrow this way than to apply directly to the plan, and you can borrow in smaller amounts. But you'll pay a higher interest rate, and part of it goes to the bank instead of into your 401(k) account. Furthermore, your monthly payments can't be deducted from your wages; you will have to pay by check. If you default, the lapse goes on your credit report and the remaining loan is treated as a taxable withdrawal from the plan. Bottom line: 401(k) cards don't seem to be worth their cost or their risk.

Here's How Much You Can Borrow from the Plan: (1) Up to 50 percent of the assets in your company savings or profit-sharing plan or $50,000, whichever is smaller. If you borrow any more, it will be treated as a taxable withdrawal. (2) If your plan is worth less than $20,000, you may be able to borrow up to $10,000 as long as the loan is adequately secured.

With Keogh plans, you can borrow if you're an employee but not if you own the business or are self-employed. With Individual Retirement Accounts, you cannot borrow at all.

For more on retirement accounts, see Chapter 29.

YOUR TAX DEDUCTION ON LOANS FOR INVESTMENT

You're going to hate this. The deduction is so complicated that it makes no sense for me to try to explain it. For the gory details, ask an accountant or get a current tax guide. I'll just give you the gist.

If you take out a loan to make an investment, the interest is deductible to the extent that you have net taxable income from investments (after deducting your expenses).

Say, for example, that you collect a net of $1,500 in dividends and interest. That allows you to write off $1,500 of interest paid on loans that were taken to make investments. If you pay more investment-loan interest than you receive in investment income, the extra can be carried forward and deducted in future years.

Answers to Some of Your Other Tax Questions

What if you borrow money and do two things with the proceeds: buy some stocks and buy a car? The interest on the money used to buy stocks falls under the investment rule—deductible, to the extent that you have net investment income. The interest on the money used to buy the car falls under the consumer-loan rule—not deductible at all. Are you still with me? If not, call a tax preparer.

What if you borrow against your house? The interest is fully deductible as mortgage interest as long as you stay within the loan limits (page 249). The interest on larger loans can be deducted as investment interest if you make investments with the money.

What if you borrow to buy tax-exempt municipals? The interest on such loans is never deductible.

What if you borrow to fund an Individual Retirement Account? No interest deduction is allowed.

What if you borrow to buy investment real estate? The interest is deductible against your rents, as well as against income from limited partnerships and other tax-shelter investments (check the tax guides for the "passive activity" rules). If you have a vacation home that you rent out, larger amounts of interest are sometimes deductible (see page 512).

What if you borrow to start or enlarge your own business? All the interest is deductible as a business expense.

What if you borrow from your retirement-savings plan? You get no tax deduction for interest on any part of an unsecured loan attributable to your own pretax contributions plus the money your contributions earned, or for money commingled with money your employer put in. But you do get a write-off if you borrow for a deductible purpose and take money the employer contributed. See if you can specify that those are the funds you want. Some companies let you put up home equity as collateral, which makes the interest on any loan deductible.

What if you contributed after-tax money to your company plan? You can borrow against it, for a deductible purpose, and get the write-off.

What if you borrow from your retirement-savings plan to buy a principal residence? The interest is deductible only if you put up your house as collateral for the loan. Some company plans let you do this, others don't.

What if you're a key employee of the business (generally, owners and officers) and borrow from the company savings plan? You get no interest deduction, no matter what you invest in.

Here's How to Assure That You Get Your Proper Interest Deductions. When you borrow money for more than one purpose, don't put all the loan proceeds into the same bank account. Keep separate checking accounts for personal borrowing (which is nondeductible), business borrowing, and investment borrowing.

Say, for example, that you take a $30,000 bank loan to buy a car, a computer for your business, and some stock. Put $18,000 for the car into your regular personal account, $2,000 for the computer into your business account, and $10,000 for the stock into an investment account. That makes it clear how much interest is deductible on each part of the loan.

Don't Put All the Loan Proceeds into Your Personal Checking Account. If you do, and wait more than 15 days to buy your business computer or make an investment, some of the loan may be treated as funding your normal living expenses. That will reduce your loan-interest deduction.

I'll stop here. The actual rules are even more complicated than I've suggested. It's madness to have to pay for extra bank accounts just to keep track of your tax deductions. Even thinking about it can drive you nuts.

AUTO LOANS

Car dealers love you when cars aren't selling well. On certain models, they'll offer the lowest interest rate on the block—as little as zero to 5 percent on 2-year loans. But when dealers are fat, their interest rates rise. Then, the best deal might be a home-equity loan.

Always compare the two types of loans after tax. You can deduct the interest on a home-equity loan if you itemize on your tax return. But on auto loans from any other source, there's no potential write-off at all. For an on-line financial calculator comparing different ways of financing a car, go to http://www.financenter.com.

If you don't want to borrow against your house (or don't own a house), look first to a credit union, followed by S&Ls and banks. Some banks give you a discount of up to one percentage point if you keep other accounts there. To compete, some auto dealers cut the rate by around 0.5 percentage points for customers with top credit ratings.

Auto loans come with fixed interest rates or variable rates. Consider a variable only if you can get it for at least one percentage point less than the cheapest fixed-rate loan around. You deserve a lower payment for shouldering the risk that rates will rise. A variable loan will be cheaper if interest rates decline, stay level, or rise just a little bit. But these loans have no caps, or high caps, so you'd be hurt if rates took a sudden jump and remained on that new plateau.

If you do choose a variable loan and interest rates rise, one of two things will happen: (1) Your monthly payments will go up, but probably not by very much. On a $10,000, 4-year, 8.5 percent loan, an increase to 10 percent would cost you an extra $7 a month. (2) Your payments will stay level but the term of your loan will be extended. Taking this same example and assuming that the rate rose after the first 12 months, you'd owe an extra 1.2 months' worth of payments.

Many lenders are adding up-front fees that raise the effective cost of your loan. Compare each loan's annual percentage rate (APR) to see which is cheapest. Rates can vary by 3 or 4 percentage points within the same metropolitan area.

When you borrow through a car dealer, you usually need a 10 to 20 percent down payment, which can often be covered by the value of the car you trade in. If you don't have the down payment, try a bank or credit union. Many of them lend 100 percent of the car price, although such a loan may cost an extra one percent interest.

Auto Loans for Poorer Risks. You're no longer poison if your credit history shows a bad patch, you're currently unemployed, or you've already borrowed a heap of money. Instead, you're a "subprime borrower." Lenders are willing to consider your business.

A few credit unions give subprime loans; banks are also edging into the market. But at this writing, your best source is an auto dealer. You'll pay a higher rate of interest than prime borrowers do, you may not be able to bargain the car price quite as far down, and there may be a higher down payment. But you'll get a loan. After a year, recheck your credit. If you've paid all your bills on time and are steadily employed, you may be able to refinance at a lower rate.

Now for the Nub of Your Decision: How Many Years Will You Carry the Loan? The longer the term, the lower the monthly payment and the easier it is to buy today's expensive cars. Auto-finance companies let you borrow for up to 5 years. Some banks and auto dealers offer 6- or 7-year loans on luxury cars. On a $20,000 loan at 8.5 percent, you pay $63 less a month by stretching the loan to 6 years instead of holding it down to 4. The downside is that the longer-term loan costs you an extra $1,941 in interest.

To hardened spenders, interest costs are a yawn. So I'll give long-term borrowers something else to worry about. (What good is a personal-finance book that doesn't give readers something to worry about?)

A Long-Term Auto Loan May Prevent You from Trading In Your Car as Soon as You'd Like. Why? Because you're "upside down"—the industry's term for owing more than the car is worth.

Most auto loans are upside down in the first year or three. But then they straighten up. Gradually you build equity value. That equity gives you a trade-in allowance when you buy a new car.

But long-term loans may be upside down for 4 or 5 years, so there's nothing to trade with. Your car's net value is less than zero.

If you paint yourself into this corner and want a new car, you have three choices:

1. Find the cash to repay your old loan and make a down payment on a new car. Your savings take a hit, but your debts don't balloon.

2. Refinance your remaining loan and borrow even more to buy a new car. That means you'll be carrying two auto loans instead of one.

3. Repair your old car. Keep on driving it until it's paid for. This choice gets my vote every time. If you feel trapped—well, now you've learned something about long-term car loans.

No Car Should Be Financed Over More Years Than You Expect to Keep It. If you'll turn it in after four years, get a 4-year loan. Even better, get a 3-year loan. You'll save on interest payments and drive the last year "free."

You'll need personal discipline to follow this rule if you finance with a home-equity loan. Your banker—no slouch when it comes to collecting interest payments—may let you stretch the loan over 10 or 15 years. But what if you want a new car 3 years from now? No problem. You just borrow against your home equity again. And borrow again, 3 years after that. At that point, you'd be paying for your present car plus two old cars you no longer drive. That's a never-ending spiral down. To avoid it, find out what it takes to repay your car loan over 3 or 4 years and repay your home-equity loan at that rate.

If you do take a 6-year auto loan, prepare to drive your car for the full term. Keep it tuned up, with the brakes lined and the oil changed. Do what it says in the owner's manual. Make small repairs as they come along.

Swallow a big repair if you have to. Your car can run, reliably, for 100,000 miles or more.

Financing a Used Car

A used-car loan costs more than a new-car loan by a couple of percentage points. That makes a home-equity loan look even better as a financing tool—always assuming that you'll hustle to pay it off. Like a new car, a used car should be financed over the number of years you expect to drive it. If you don't own a house, or have no spare equity in your home, start your search for a car loan with a credit union (see page 51 for information on how you might join one).

Pay Cash or Take Out a Loan?

It's cheaper to pay cash. But many auto dealers (who make money on car loans) have come up with a clever, computerized gimmick to bamboozle customers into thinking that loans are a better deal.

For example, say you have $10,000. You can put it into a certificate of deposit earning 6 percent interest or use it toward buying a new car. The dealer may argue that it's smarter to choose the CD and take out an 8.5 percent auto loan.

Here's the dealer's four-step "proof":

1. If you leave your $10,000 in the bank for 4 years, you'll earn $2,712 in interest, pretax.

2. A 4-year, $10,000 auto loan will cost $1,832 in interest (the interest is less than you think because it's paid on a declining balance).

3. So by keeping the CD and taking the loan, you're $880 ahead. (You're only $121 ahead after federal taxes in the 28 percent bracket, but the loan may still look good to people who hate to part with savings.)

4. Furthermore, the dealer croons, debtors do even better when the loan's term is up. Say the car is worth $5,000 at trade-in. That's all the cash the buyer has in hand. But the borrower supposedly gets an amazing $15,880—adding together $5,000 from the trade-in, the $880 gain in interest, plus the $10,000 still in the bank.

Before you decide that the road to riches is paved with auto loans, sit back and think a minute. There's something the dealer overlooked. Where does the money come from to repay the loan?

If you take the monthly payments out of your bank account, your savings will be wiped out before the loan is entirely repaid.

If you make the monthly payments out of earnings, you'll be giving up $11,832 that you could have saved or invested. Either way, the loan costs you more.

So pay cash. Then take the equivalent of the monthly payment, which you're *not* spending on the auto loan, and use it to replenish your savings. At the end of the term, you'll have your car and more than $10,000 back.

I'd vote for the loan only if your fat savings account was a windfall—a gift, an inheritance, a winning lottery ticket—that you'd never be able to replace.

Should You Lease Instead of Buy?

For the poor of pocketbook but rich in taste, auto leasing is hard to beat. You can drive out of a dealer's lot on four of his classiest wheels for a small up-front deposit and lower monthly payments than you'd owe on most auto loans. But leasing isn't for everyone.

You Shouldn't Lease If:

• You want to save money. Most leases don't.

• You expect to keep your car for many years. If you lease for a while, then buy when the lease runs out, you'll usually pay more than if you purchased the car up front. This isn't always true, but it's true often enough.

• You hate monthly payments. Loan payments eventually stop but lease payments never do. It's like burying your grandfather in a rented suit.

• You'll want to trade in the car before the lease is up. A majority of leases have no prepayment penalty. But the balance due on the lease contract may be substantial.

But Consider a Lease If:

• You have no car to trade in and not enough cash for a down payment (although some banks now give no-down-payment loans).

• You have the down payment but can put it to work earning more than 10 percent a year, says Randall McCathren of Bank Lease Consultants in Nashville. (You earn more than 10 percent on your money just by paying off credit-card debt that is costing at least that much in interest.)

• You want lower monthly payments.

• You want a more expensive car than you could otherwise afford.

• You're trading in your car in the fourth year of a 6-year auto loan and owe more than the car is worth. You can't afford to pay off your old loan and make a down payment on a new car, too.

• You want to drive a new car every 2 to 4 years and don't mind having permanent monthly car payments.

• You make plenty of money and want someone else to worry about keeping your car in good repair. For an extra fee ($25 a month and up), the lessor will do all the maintenance and lend you a car to drive while yours is in the shop.

• You're looking for business tax breaks. Business use of your car is deductible whether you lease or own. But because of quirks in the tax law, lessees can write off more of the cost of the car than owners can. Leasing also bypasses your state's sales tax, which can be a substantial saving.

Is Leasing Always More Expensive Than Buying? Usually but not always. Here are two circumstances when leasing is cheaper:

1. It's cheaper to lease when the automaker subsidizes the transaction. The effective interest rate in the lease is less than you'd pay for an auto loan.

Unfortunately, you can't easily tell when a lease is being subsidized. The interest rate doesn't show in the leasing contract. But the dealer can calculate it for you accurately if your lease lets you purchase the car at the end of the term for a guaranteed (or "residual") value.

2. It's cheaper to lease when the car's market price, at the end of the lease, is lower than the purchase price that the lessor guaranteed *and* if the lessor will let you buy at that lower price. If the lessor won't agree, you can walk away from the lease and buy a similar car—at market price—that came off someone else's lease. Unfortunately, there's no way to know in advance when these bargains might occur.

The leasing process is pretty simple. You typically make one month's payment up front, plus a refundable deposit roughly equal to one month's payment, and drive away. On low-cost leases, the dealer may want a down payment, too—usually 10 percent.

On a *closed-end lease,* your basic costs are fixed. At the end of the term, you can usually buy the car you've been driving at a guaranteed price or turn in your keys and get a new one. In some cases, you can lease it again. Almost all consumer leases are closed-end.

On an *open-end lease,* which should cost less per month, your final cost depends on the car's resale value. If it sells for more than the lessor expected, you may get a refund. If it sells for less, you pay the difference (although you normally cannot be charged more than three times the monthly payment).

On both types of leases, you buy your own auto insurance and are responsible for general maintenance. You have to make engine repairs and keep the body in good shape. You'll generally owe an extra 8 to 15 cents a mile for driving more than 12,000 miles a year. (Watch this excess mileage charge; some lessors hit you for 20 cents.) There are extra charges for excessive wear and tear, like cracked glass, lost trim, bald tires, torn seats, and deep dents (look for an itemized list in the lease). The lessor decides how much wear is excessive and generally will not overreach. If you get sore, he loses your business.

Don't Lease the Car for a Longer Period Than You Expect to Drive It. Some drivers go for 5-year leases because of the super-low monthly payments. The dealer might even say there's no problem breaking the lease if you want to switch to a brand-new car. But there *is* a problem. You generally face an "early termination deficiency" for the depreciation that you haven't paid for yet. It could be $150, it could be $2,000 or more. The dealer might be able to roll the debt into your next lease, but not always.

The formula for fixing your deficiency will be printed in your contract, probably in Sanskrit. So ask the dealer to tell you exactly how much you'd owe at the end of each year if you decided to quit the lease. To avoid that cost, plan to drive the car for the lease's full term.

What happens if your leased car is stolen or wrecked? That's usually counted as an early termination. Your auto insurance will cover the car's market value. But money will still be owed on the lease. Major lessors now provide *gap insurance*, which covers your portion of the loss. Don't drive away without it.

Check the Lease's Fine Print If You Think That You Might Move Out of State. A few lessors charge an extra $10 a month if you do. A few make you convert the lease to a loan. Tell the dealer you want a national lessor who doesn't care where you live.

Tips for Getting the Cheapest Lease:

1. When you start talking lease, the dealer will offer you "$X a month." That's usually based on the car's full list price, which is more than you ought to pay. Before talking monthly payments, bargain down the price of the car. A lower car price gives you a lower lease price, too. To be sure you're getting that lower price, check the car's "capitalized cost" (page 272).

2. You can lower the lease cost by making a down payment up front. (But a smarter use of that money may be to lower your credit-card debts. Cards ding you for higher finance costs than you pay in the lease.)

3. Negotiate all the fees in the lease, such as the "acquisition fee" for acquiring the car or the "disposition fee" for selling it. They're not fixed in stone. You'll get the best price if you're bargaining with two dealers at once.

4. If you'll drive more than the standard 12,000 miles a year that leases usually allow, buy excess mileage in advance. For example, you might arrange to drive the car for 15,000 miles. That's cheaper than paying for an extra 3,000 miles when you turn the car in.

5. A growing number of credit unions offer cheap leases to their members.

6. Lessors are now required to make standard disclosures on their leases. That makes it easy to compare one lease with another, to see which offers the better terms. *Always* comparison shop.

7. At the end of the lease, find out if the market price of the car is substantially higher than the value that the lessor guaranteed. If so, don't

turn the car over to the dealer and lease a new one. Instead, buy the car, resell it yourself, and roll your profits into a new lease.

8. Sometimes you're offered a chance to extend your lease for another two or three years. Compare this with the cost of leasing a new car. When there are factory-subsidized deals, the new car may be cheaper.

Leasing a Used Car. Er, I mean a *pre-owned* car, which is the idiom that dealers prefer. Originally, lessors offered only luxury cars. But now they'll lease almost any car that's no more than one to 3 years old and hasn't been driven more than 15,000 to 45,000 miles. Formerly, used cars came with 30-day limited warranties, at best. Today's cream puffs are often "certified" by the manufacturer as being completely reconditioned. They also come with one- or 2-year limited warranties.

But compare the price with the cost of leasing the same car new. A used-car lease may save you only $20 to $50 a month, which might tip you toward leasing a new car instead.

Dirty Tricks Some Lessors Play

1. You bargain down the car price, give the dealer your old car, and make a down payment. But the dealer still bases the lease on the new car's list price. If this happens, all the money you put toward the new car has effectively been stolen. To protect yourself, check the lease for the car's "capitalized cost." That should reflect the list price, minus the discount you negotiated, minus the value of any car you traded in, minus any rebate the dealer offers, minus your down payment, plus taxes and such incidentals as fees, rustproofing, and maintenance agreements. The lessor is required to itemize all this if you ask. Your lease payments are based on the capitalized cost.

2. You intend to buy a car, but after the negotiation the dealer gives you a lease to sign instead. You're told it's a special, low-priced deal. You don't notice it's a lease because the salesperson's hand covers up the heading on the contract. The lease is based on a high car price. When you discover the deception and protest, the salesperson claims that you always knew you were leasing the car. To avoid this, hold the documents in your hand and read them before signing.

3. You're attracted to a lease with an especially low monthly cost. But it's cheap only because the allowable mileage is low: You might be buying just 10,000 miles a year. If you drive another 5,000 miles on a 4-year lease, you might owe $3,000 when you turn the car in. To avoid this, estimate realistically how much you drive and cover it in advance. A 10,000-mile allowance gives you only 27 miles a day. A 12,000-mile allowance gives you almost 32 miles. A 15,000-mile allowance gives you 41 miles. If you're faced with a big mileage bill at the end of the lease, it may be smarter to buy the car instead of turning it in.

4. You're overcharged for wear and tear. When you turn the car in, the dealer says "no problem." But after it's been wholesaled you get a large bill. If you don't pay, it goes on your credit history. To avoid this, check the lease before turning the car in, to see what damage you're responsible for. Get it repaired yourself. Or have the dealer inspect the car, draw up a "condition report," and estimate the damage cost before you turn in the keys. It may be cheaper to buy the car, get it fixed, and drive it a while longer.

What's the Cheapest Lease? When comparing leases, shoppers usually look only at the monthly payment. That works *if* you'll keep the lease for its full term and *if,* at the end of the lease, you turn in the car and lease a new one. Given two comparable leases for the same car (with the same down payment and mileage allowance), the best deal is the one with the lower monthly cost.

If you plan to buy the car at the end of the lease, however, add up all the monthly payments plus the end-of-lease purchase price. The car with the lower total cost is the better deal.

HOW TO LOWER YOUR INTEREST CHARGES

1. *Pick the right type of interest rate.* Variable-rate loans should be cheaper than fixed-rate loans if you hold for many years. You start out with lower payments, which save money right there. Payments go up when interest rates do, so you have to be able to afford the increase. But rates generally don't rise for much more than a year or two at a clip. After that they decline and your loan payments shrink.

If deflation lies ahead, a variable-rate loan will be especially cheap. But rising inflation remains a risk. To guard against it, your loan should carry an interest-rate cap to keep your rate from rising by more than 5 percentage points.

2. *Pick the right lender.* Credit unions often charge less than S&Ls, which often charge less than banks. Competing lenders may be 2 or 3 percentage points apart in rates, which is discoverable only by people who price-shop. You might get a lower rate if you open a certificate of deposit or a checking account with the lending institution.

3. *Pick the right loan.* Home-equity loans cost less than credit-card debt (if you repay swiftly). Auto loans cost less than personal loans. Short-term personal loans, for 3 or 6 months, sometimes go for a point over the prime lending rate. Tell your banker how much money you want and when you'll pay it back. Then ask how cheaply the deal can be done.

4. *Pick the right annual percentage rate (APR)*. Don't look only at the interest rate. Look at the APR, which usually counts up-front fees as well as the interest itself. Only home-equity loans have a misleading APR (page 250).

5. *Pick the right time period*. The longer the term, the more expensive the loan, because you make so many more payments. If you're doing something constructive with the money, like holding an appreciating piece of land, never mind the longer term. But on depreciating assets like a car, keep the term as short as possible.

6. *Put on the squeeze*. Many borrowers don't realize that lenders compete. If Bank A will give you an adjustable-rate mortgage at 8.1 percent in the first year, and you tell that to Bank B, dear old Bank B may counter with 7.9 percent. It happens a lot, but only to borrowers who price-shop. If you're borrowing a lot of money, you might get a quarter point off your interest rate just by asking for it.

7. *Avoid traditional installment loans*. They're often front-end-loaded. You pay more of the interest in the early months than you do in the later ones, which penalizes you if you pay off your loan ahead of time.

The better loans charge the same amount of interest every month. Given two loans with the same annual percentage rate, the one with equal interest payments will cost less over the life of the loan than the one with front-end loading.

How can you tell if you're offered a front-end-loaded loan? Your installment-loan agreement will say that interest is figured by the "rule of 78s." Retailers may offer only front-loaded loans. But at a bank, you should be able to get a loan with level interest payments if you ask for it.

8. *Don't buy credit-life, disability, or unemployment insurance from the lender*. These policies cover your minimum monthly payments for a certain length of time if you're disabled or unemployed. If you die, they pay the debt in full.

In some states—for example, New York, Maine, and Vermont—regulators hold the cost to what consumer experts say is a reasonable level. Other states are way out of line. There are also limitations on when, and how much, the disability and unemployment policies pay.

The price of credit insurance is usually rolled right into your loan, so you wind up borrowing—and paying interest on—your insurance premiums. It's a costly system, which often enriches the loan officer personally. At some banks, he or she earns commissions on the sales.

Best advice: Cover debt payoff with regular term life insurance rather than with credit-life (unless your health prevents you from buying low-cost term). Forget disability or unemployment coverage because they typically pay so little. Sometimes the lender adds this coverage automatically and asks you to sign. That's called sliding the policy. The lender hopes you'll say okay just because the paperwork is done. But don't submit to that kind of pressure. By law, this insurance is optional. Tell the lender to redo the contract, leaving the insurance out.

YOUR PERSONAL FINANCIAL STATEMENT

For a big loan, a lender wants a financial statement and, often, a copy of your income-tax return. What do you earn? What's the value of your house, your other real estate, your savings accounts, your stocks? How much do you owe? Put down everything you can think of, including any bonuses due. How much you can borrow depends a lot on what you're worth.

IF YOU'RE TURNED DOWN FOR CREDIT

Lenders have to say *why* they turned you down. If it's because of something they saw in your credit report, get a copy of the report and check it for errors (page 234). If it's because your credit score is too low (page 219), there's no easy fix. But the turndown letter should mention some things that weighed against you, which, over time, you might be able to fix. If the lender is local, make a date to talk. There might be something you can do immediately.

Never give up. If one lender won't take you, another one might. Lenders that charge higher interest rates take borrowers with lower credit scores.

CO-SIGNERS

A *co-signer* is best defined as a saint, an idiot, or a parent. If your child can't get an auto loan, credit card, or apartment lease based on his or her credit alone, you might be asked to co-sign the application.

The moment you do, that loan is just as much yours as his. Its payment history goes on your credit report. If your kid doesn't pay the bills on time, your credit record shares the black mark. If the child defaults, you are shown as having defaulted, too—a sin that will put you in credit hell for seven long years. It does no good to argue that you didn't know your child wasn't making payments. You're expected to keep track.

You're liable for every nickel of a debt you co-sign. The lender may not even bother pursuing the original debtor or collecting the security that the debtor pledged. As co-signer, you can be asked for the money immediately, in cash. Many children can be trusted not to wreck your credit report, but others can't. To them, even a saint might say no.

If you say yes, tell your child or other co-signee about the risk you're going to run. He or she may not realize that the payments will show on your credit report. Ask to be told immediately if the debtor can't pay. And don't yell about it or the child might be afraid to say.

If you find out too late that the loan is in delinquency, take over the payments immediately. Then contact each of the three major credit bureaus (page 234) to see if you have a credit file there. If so, add a statement to your record explaining why the loan was late.

Credit-card issuers ignore the personal statements in credit reports. But if you apply for a mortgage or a personal loan, the lender will see the explanation and give you a chance to make your case.

DOOMSDAY

What if the world falls apart? Your income drops, your spouse gets fired, you can't pay your bills, your children are crying, and you have to give away the dog? With all these overhanging risks, isn't it dangerous to borrow to invest?

Not if you follow sound principles. First, make suitable investments (Chapter 21). Second, construct an escape hatch for yourself.

To save yourself if hard times strike, your investments should meet one or more of the following tests:

1. They must be liquid, meaning they can easily be sold to pay off your debt. Mutual funds are liquid. Vacant lots are not.

2. If not liquid, your investments should yield enough income to carry themselves. If you buy a condominium, your tenant's rent should cover the mortgage, taxes, monthly maintenance, insurance, and other expenses, plus 5 to 10 percent for emergencies. That saves you from having to unload the condo at a give-away price if your personal earnings drop.

3. Any investment that is not liquid and not yielding enough income should be backstopped by liquid investments. For example, if you buy a rental property that isn't covering its costs, you should have enough money in mutual funds or in the bank to support the property and cover your living expenses for 12 months. If you don't have this much liquidity, don't make such investments. They're too risky for you.

4. The value of your investment shouldn't fall below the size of the debt that's carrying it. If its price declines, put it on the market while you're still ahead. Sell it as soon as you can, and pay off your loan.

Debt isn't a free pass to the high life. Overused, it can bankrupt you. But well used, debt is *the* building block of wealth.

STEP 3
YOUR SAFETY NET

Insurance is a protection racket. Everyone hates to pay the price.

But until you are well enough insured, you might as well have no assets at all. Everything you own is a hostage to fortune. Sickness or accident could leave you a pauper.

I know. I hear you. It's never going to happen to you.

The funny thing is, I've never met anyone "it" was going to happen to. So who are all those people in the hospitals, the wheelchairs, the funeral homes? Who are those stunned families staring at smoking ruins? Visitors from Mars?

A classic story for personal-finance reporters is the interview with some unfortunate souls who found out what "it" really feels like. They deliver a lecture that might be generically entitled "What You Should Do Right Now So You Won't End Up a Wreck Like Me."

Here is that lecture.

12.

The Money on Your Life

What Kind of Life Insurance?
How Much Is Enough?

*Life insurance is full of more angles than a hardware store.
Maybe that's why grieving widows are handed small checks
when they could have been handed large ones.*

Here is the single most important thing to know about life insurance. *It is not for you!* It's for the people you'll leave behind. You pay for it; they use it. Wear that principle like an amulet, to ward off nonsense. If you're not leaving anyone behind—and don't want to leave a special bequest to a charity—you don't need life insurance.

The second rule is to *keep it simple*. Life insurance can be numbingly complicated. Clients often turn off their brains and surrender their judgment to the very agent or planner who brought on their coma in the first place. Clean and easy policies are the surest. Fancy tax-dodging deals make money for the agent but may not reliably do the job you want.

The third rule: *Be a cheapskate*. If you want to show off your spending power, do it in a way that counts—like, say, 10 carats. Buy the lowest-cost life insurance policy you can find (from an agent who isn't kidding you about the price—page 291).

For most people, the coverage that best fills the bill is plain-vanilla *term insurance*. It's cheap and simple, with nothing in it for you but the knowledge that you've done the right thing. Term insurance pays off if you die prematurely. That's all. No gimmicks, no tax games, no investment values. Just a check—and a large one—paid to the people who depend on you.

All other forms of coverage—known generally as *cash-value insurance* —contain a savings or investment element that raises your out-of-pocket outlay. One of these policies might be a reasonable place to invest some of your long-term money if you can also afford all the coverage you need. Most of us can't. In any event, whether to invest through life insurance is an entirely separate decision from whether to have death protection at all and if so, how much.

WHO NEEDS LIFE INSURANCE?

1. *You're young, single, with no dependents.* Forget life insurance. Buy disability coverage (page 415) and add to your investments instead.

Ignore an insurance agent who advises you to buy cash-value coverage because premiums are lower for the young. If you don't need insurance, you'd be wasting your money. It's like buying a tennis racket just in case, ten years from now, you might want to learn the game.

Besides, insurance premiums rise so slowly that waiting doesn't matter much. If you buy a $100,000 term policy at age 40 instead of 30, you might pay an extra $27 that year. Big deal. A cash-value policy might cost you an extra $550 or so. If you skip the insurance and bank the money you don't spend, those accumulated savings will probably cover the higher premiums you might pay in the future if you should ever need a policy.

An agent might also argue, "Buy now just in case you develop a dread disease, become uninsurable, and then discover a need for insurance." You might just as easily marry a zillionaire and not need life insurance at all. The odds of either are small. One exception: You might want to buy cash-value coverage if you're at risk of getting AIDS or another serious illness and know that you're lousy at saving money. Many insurers let you withdraw part of your policy's face value if you become terminally ill; alternatively, you may be able to sell the policy for 50 to 70 percent of face value (page 338). So for you, insurance is like a big savings account.

2. *You're older and single, with no dependents.* Maybe you never married. Maybe you're a widow whose children have left home. You need no insurance. If you do have coverage, investigate what it's earning (page 314) and ask yourself whether you'd rather have ready money than cash building up inside an insurance policy. Your beneficiaries might prefer that you keep the policy. But if you need more income to live on, cancel it and save the cost of the premium. Put the cash value, if any, into savings or investments.

3. *You're single, with dependents.* What happens to those dependents if you die? If you're a divorced parent, and the children would go to the other parent, you may not need life insurance if the other parent can afford to take care of them. If not, keep the policy for the children's education

and support (your lawyer, financial planner, or insurance agent can help you make sure that the money goes to the kids, not to your ex, perhaps by leaving the proceeds in trust for them). Keep the policy, too, if the children will go to one of your relatives. They shouldn't arrive like beggars, cup in hand. You may also need life insurance if you're supporting an elderly parent.

4. *You're a DINK—a double-income couple with no kids.* You might not need insurance. Each spouse could be self-supporting if the other died. Buy coverage only to keep the other from sinking to an unacceptable standard of living.

5. *You're an OINK—a one-income couple with no kids.* The working spouse probably needs life insurance if you want to preserve your current standard of living for the spouse at home.

6. *You're married, with young children.* You need insurance, a lot of it. Those kids have to be raised and educated, and it's not cheap. But you probably need the coverage only until they're on their own. Then this portion of your insurance can be canceled.

7. *You had kids at an older age.* You need insurance, just as a young parent does, and it will have to last into your 60s or 70s. Go for term insurance to get all the coverage you need. Take special pains to find an inexpensive policy (page 291), checking the premiums both for your present age and for later ages. But include some cash-value coverage to carry you into your 70s and beyond. Another option: buy term from a company that offers good cash-value policies, and convert to cash-value later when you've a better fix on what you need.

8. *You're a wife, with kids, who doesn't work.* Insurance on your life is generally misguided. You have no income that has to be replaced. You and the children will be more secure if your husband fully insures himself and uses any extra money to add to savings and investments. People who favor housewife insurance say that husbands need these payouts to cover the cost of day care and housecleaning when they're alone. That's fine, but *only if* you have small children, your husband truly couldn't afford the expense (remember: he's saving money by not having your expenses anymore), and he carries enough insurance on his own life to cover you and the kids in full. Full insurance on a breadwinner is rare, especially in families that can't afford day care. So I continue to believe that housewife insurance should be a low priority. (Ditto insurance on a husband who is supported by his wife.)

9. *You're retired.* You need insurance only if your retirement planning failed and your spouse couldn't live on the Social Security, pension, and savings that you'll leave behind. If your spouse dies and you're short of money, cancel the coverage, which saves you the cost of the premium. Keep a cash-value policy, however, if you have enough money to live on and want to leave a larger estate for a charity or your kids. If you're short

of money, consider borrowing from the policy's cash value, especially if canceling it would create a tax liability (page 320).

10. *You're a kid.* Insurance on a child is a waste of money. What secures a child's future is life insurance on the parents and a college-savings fund. Some parents are persuaded to save for college in a cash-value, kid-insurance policy. But the cost of the needless life insurance slashes your return on investment (page 564). For a far larger college fund, put the money into a stock-owning mutual fund instead, arranging for automatic monthly contributions from your bank account.

11. *You're a college student.* I can think of only one reason to have life insurance: You plan to repay your parents for the money they're spending on your education. Otherwise, coverage is a waste of money.

12. *You own a business.* Either you or the company will doubtless need a policy on your life. For sole owners, the impetus may be to cover the debts they signed personally or to pay estate taxes. (You may want a trust to own the policy, to hold down taxes by keeping the proceeds out of your estate.) A co-owner may want to be able to buy his or her partner's share of the business if the partner dies or becomes disabled. Ditto a key employee, who could buy the business with the proceeds of a policy on the owner's life. Talk to your lawyer about a buy/sell agreement funded by life and disability insurance. Don't leave your spouse and kids to a partner's tender mercies, no matter how friendly you are now. The business might never make a cash distribution or declare a dividend, and your family wouldn't get a dime.

13. *You're rich.* Life insurance can help pay your estate taxes. On the other hand, you're so rich that taxes can be paid out of your investments. On the third hand, your investments may be illiquid (real estate, a small business), so your estate will need the insurance to provide ready cash. On the fourth hand, you want to leave an even larger estate than the one you have. Take your pick. To keep the insurance proceeds out of your estate (lest they raise your taxes even more), put the policy into an irrevocable trust.

14. *Your job is covered by Social Security.* You automatically have "free" insurance that covers an older spouse, a spouse caring for young children, your children, even parents you support (see page 284). Don't forget about this when estimating how much more coverage you should buy.

HOW MUCH INSURANCE?

If you need it at all, you probably need plenty—almost certainly more than you have now. And you can afford it. Low-cost term insurance can be slipped into almost any spending plan.

In fact, buying it is the easy part. The hard part is knowing what kind and how much to buy.

I've seen rules of thumb about how much life insurance you need: three times income, five times income, ten times income, depending on how heavy the thumb. None of them is accurate because so much depends on how old you are, whether you have children, what your spouse earns, and how much money you've saved.

If you want to make it simple, however, the Consumer Federation of America (CFA) recommends six to eight times income for a married couple with two small children. That sum includes any group insurance you get at work as well as Social Security survivor's benefits. It assumes that, if a parent dies, the policy's proceeds will be invested conservatively, and that the surviving family will spend both income and principal. It doesn't include a specific college fund.

When only one parent works, he or she should carry all the coverage. When both parents work, split the coverage proportionately: if the wife earns 40 percent of the family income, she should carry 40 percent of the coverage, leaving the remaining 60 percent to the husband. The cheapest way to cover the lower earner may be through a rider on the policy of the higher earner.

On the following page is another shortcut—one that takes a little calculating. It calls for more insurance than CFA does, mainly because it includes a college fund.

Nevertheless, these quick solutions can't help being wide of the mark. You might buy too much insurance for your particular needs—and why pay one nickel more than you have to? Or you might buy too little, leaving your family at risk.

For a true fix on your insurance needs, turn to Appendix 1, page 970, for The Best Life Insurance Planner You Will Ever Find. You will be following a system used by top professionals in the field of financial planning. In no other place have I seen this sophisticated calculation broken down into orderly steps for individuals working out plans on paper rather than on a computer.

So take advantage of it. You're aiming for just enough coverage to fill the gap between your family's expenses and their other sources of income —no more, no less. Getting the right answer takes a little work, but that's why God made yellow pads.

YOUR SOCIAL SECURITY INSURANCE

Most people think of Social Security purely as a retirement plan. But your payroll tax also pays for life insurance and disability coverage. There's a lump-sum death benefit of $255, plus monthly payments to dependents.

THE QUICK-FIX INSURANCE PLANNER

IF YOU DIE	YOUR MONEY	MY EXAMPLE
1. Your family's annual cost of living	$ _____	$ 65,000
2. Your family's annual income from:		
• Social Security*	$ _____	$ 12,000
• Spouse's earnings	$ _____	$ 30,000
• Other (except income from investments)	$ _____	0
TOTAL	$ _____	$ 42,000
3. Your family's investment income:		
• Your investment capital, from page 28	$ _____	$100,000
• Multiply by what your capital might earn pretax: 5%? 7%? 9%?	× _____	7%
RESULT: your family's annual income from current savings	$ _____	$ 7,000
4. Your family's annual budget gap: the totals in steps 2 and 3 subtracted from line 1	$ _____	$ 16,000
5. To fill that budget gap:		
• Turn to the table on page 1025 to estimate your spouse's life expectancy.	___ years	45
• Turn to the table on page 914† and find the column that shows what you think your money can earn (the same percentage you used in step 3).	___ %	7%
• Looking down that column, find your spouse's life expectancy or something close to it. Look across to the left to see what percent of capital your spouse can withdraw annually to make the money last a lifetime.	___ %	4.8%
• Divide line 4 by the percent your spouse will withdraw annually.		
RESULT: the additional money needed for living expenses	$ _____	$333,333
6. College fund for the children (page 521)	$ _____	$100,000
7. TOTAL LIFE INSURANCE NEEDED	$ _____	$433,333

* For two small children. This drops to zero when the children pass age 18 or 19.
† Assuming a 3 percent inflation rate. For other inflation rates, see page 1015.

To find out how much your family would get, see page 902. Here's who could collect on your Social Security account after your death:

1. Surviving spouses age 60 and up and disabled spouses 50 and up. Ditto divorced spouses of the same age if the marriage lasted at least 10 years. A spouse or divorced spouse who remarries can still collect on the first spouse's account if that's a better deal than the new spouse's account.

2. Unremarried surviving spouses caring for your child who is under 16 or was disabled before age 22. Unremarried divorced spouses, too, regardless of how long the marriage lasted.

3. Unmarried dependent children under 18, or under 19 if still in secondary school.

4. Parents 62 and older who got at least half their support from you.

THE GREAT DEBATE: TERM INSURANCE VS. CASH-VALUE COVERAGE

Term Insurance is pure protection, like fire insurance or auto insurance. Its sole function is to support your family if you die. You get far more coverage for your money than you do from cash-value insurance, so it's the right kind of policy for anyone with an average income and family responsibilities.

The cost of term coverage rises gradually as you age. Once you reach your late 60s or early 70s, you probably won't want to carry this kind of policy anymore. With any luck, you will not need it. Your savings, pension, and Social Security will support any remaining dependents if you die. If you suspect that's not going to happen, you can switch to some cash-value coverage in your 50s or 60s.

Cash-Value Insurance comes in two parts: (1) an insurance policy and (2) a savings or investment account. You pay a large premium compared with the premium for term insurance. Most of the extra money goes into savings, which build up tax free or tax deferred.

If you die, the insurance company uses those savings to pay part of your death benefit. As the years go by, your mounting savings normally cover more and more of the policy's face value, leaving the insurer liable for less and less.

Because the insurer's risk declines (and because it can draw on the money it earns by investing your cash value), it doesn't have to raise your rates as you get older. You pay more at the start for a cash-value policy than you'd pay for term. But in a properly funded policy, the premiums stay level for life. These are the only policies that most people can afford to carry into their 80s, if they'll need insurance that long.

The cash tucked into your policy is always yours to use. You can borrow against it, just as you'd borrow against a bank certificate of deposit. The loan is subtracted from the policy's proceeds if you die. If you cancel the policy, you can put the cash value (net of surrender charges) into your pocket.

Because of the higher premiums on cash-value coverage, wage-earners usually can't buy as much of it as they need. That's why term coverage is usually the better choice. With it, you can afford to protect your family in full. Furthermore, by the time you're old, the purchasing power of a cash-value policy with a level death benefit will have shrunk greatly, so it's not necessarily the long-term boon that it seems now.

Nevertheless, higher-income people who can afford plenty of insurance might consider certain cash-value policies as a long-term investment (see page 314).

ALL ABOUT TERM INSURANCE

For total family protection, the term-ites are right. To get the large amount of insurance you probably need, pure term is the answer.

How Much Cheaper Is Term Insurance?

The table that follows shows dramatically how much more coverage you get for your money with term insurance. I've used the policies of Northwestern Mutual Life, which offers good consumer values. Prices are for $100,000 in coverage on a healthy nonsmoking male. Premiums on term insurance rise every year: if you buy for $133 a year at 30, you'll probably

YEARLY PREMIUMS FOR A $100,000 POLICY*

Age	Annually Renewable Term Insurance	Blended Term and Whole Life †	Whole Life Insurance
30	$ 133	$ 728	$1,124
35	137	913	1,351
40	159	1,167	1,656
45	204	1,513	2,063
50	262	1,975	2,439
55	354	2,606	3,026
60	591	3,464	3,913
65	1,105	4,653	5.257

* Includes an $84 policy fee. The specific policies are from Northwestern Mutual Life: Term to Age 70, Adjustable CompLife, and Select 100 Life.
† Initially, 60% term, 40% whole life.

be spending $262 at 50 (although premiums aren't guaranteed). With whole life and blends, by contrast, your premiums are fixed. A blend bought for $728 at 30 still costs you $728 at 50.

Cash-value coverage has its place and blends are a particularly savvy way of buying it. But for what's most affordable at any given age, straight term insurance wins hands down.

Employee Term Insurance

Increasingly, life insurance is being sold through the workplace—and it's often a good deal. Employers may provide a certain amount of coverage free. Employees are offered the chance to buy more, paying the premiums through payroll deduction. You may get group coverage, open to everyone regardless of health; or individual coverage, for which you have to take a health exam.

Before loading up on term insurance in the workplace, however, do two things:

• Check the price against the list on page 285 and what you can get through a price-quote service. Policies bought elsewhere may be quite a bit cheaper.

• Find out what happens if you leave your job. "Group individual" policies can follow you wherever you go, and at no increase in premium. With true group coverage, however, you'd have to convert to an individual policy (usually cash-value, rarely term). You can do so regardless of health, so conversion attracts people who can't get good coverage somewhere else. For that very reason, however, the premiums are high and the benefits often limited. You don't want to get stuck with this as your only option. If you can't get individual coverage, don't buy your life insurance at work. Buy from an outside insurer instead.

Note that any free group insurance given to workers or retirees generally can be reduced or eliminated by the company. Benefits are not guaranteed. It's reasonable to expect a payoff, but don't stake your spouse's future on it. By the time retirement comes, you should have enough savings, pension income, and Social Security so that the proceeds from a company-paid life insurance policy will be frosting on the cake.

Other Group-Term Coverage

Apply a sniff test to group coverage offered by trade groups, professional associations, alumni associations, and fraternal orders. Sometimes it's good; sometimes it's not. Professional associations often slant their coverage toward younger people, offering them much better rates, relatively speaking, than older people get. If you're middle-aged, in good health, and don't smoke, you should be able to find a cheaper policy elsewhere. Check the rates your association offers against what you can get through a quote service (page 291).

Be sure you can take your policy with you if you resign from the group, regardless of your health at the time. If you can't, buy your coverage somewhere else. Also, check that your term policy is convertible into cash-value coverage if you should ever want it.

Individual Term-Insurance Policies

Plain-vanilla term insurance is good, reliable, and cheap. You can afford to buy your family a huge benefit as a hedge against your death. Term policies cost more out of pocket as you get older. When you reach your late 60s or early 70s, you will probably want to cancel out. But your policy will have done its job if it protected your spouse and children during the years they needed it. If your health is good, you'll be able to find well-priced term coverage even at later ages.

Life insurance agents are perfectly willing to sell term insurance, but they'll generally press you to buy cash-value coverage, too. They've been taught (and believe) that cash-value should lie at the core of any insurance plan. Conveniently, they earn higher (much higher) commissions for selling it. Many agents will push it even when it leaves your family poorly protected. Here are some answers to their silky arguments against term insurance.

WHAT TO THINK WHEN THE LIFE INSURANCE AGENT SAYS . . .

"Term premiums are wasted because you have nothing to show for them in the end." Wrong. You've had years of protection, and that's what you paid for. Would you say that you've wasted the money you've paid for fire insurance because your house didn't burn down?

"Term is like renting. Cash-value is like buying." And some things it's smarter to rent, like life insurance.

"Term insurance is an illusion. Hardly anyone collects on it." Hardly anyone collects on fire insurance, either. Term insurance is *meant* to be canceled when the need for protection no longer exists. When you think about "collecting" on your own life insurance, you are thinking, What's in it for me?—and that's the thought that leads you wrong.

"You will need permanent life insurance eventually, so you might as well buy it now." Any life insurance policy, including term insurance, is "permanent" if it lasts until you die. If the agent means, "You will always need life insurance until you die of old age," the answer is "nonsense." An

insurance policy replaces earnings if you die prematurely. When you retire, you have no paycheck to replace. You'll be living on your pension, your savings, and Social Security—all of which can continue to pay your spouse after you die.

You will need life insurance into old age only if: (1) You plan to work until you drop *and* you expect that your spouse or children will always depend on that income. (2) You don't expect to leave your spouse enough income to live on from your pension, savings, and Social Security. (3) You're worth a lot of money and will need insurance to cover the estate taxes. (4) You want to leave extra money to your children or a charity. (For a discussion of using life insurance to replace a pension, see page 337.)

"You should start converting your term insurance into a permanent policy so you'll never be without protection." Same answer.

"You will need insurance in middle age to protect your family. Term insurance is too expensive then." If you use one of the price-quote services on page 292, you can find reasonably priced term insurance even in your 60s or 70s.

"Cash-value policies force you to save for old age." Here again, the agent wants you to think, What's in it for me? By putting yourself first, you put your spouse and children last. The rule is: protection first, savings later. If you can afford all the term insurance you need, and will have some money left over, *then* think about whether you want to use a life insurance policy as a piggy bank.

"I can sell you paid-up insurance. At age 60, you'll have a permanent policy with no more premiums due." Even if true, so what? This kind of coverage costs you larger-than-usual premiums in the early years. You're prepaying for something you may not need. And at 60, you may discover that the premiums don't end as promised. The agent may have steered you wrong (page 333).

"Buy term, but add a small cash-value policy just in case you'll need it later." And what will that "valuable" policy be worth when you're old? At 3 percent inflation, a $50,000 death benefit bought today will have a purchasing power of about $20,600 in 30 years. That won't keep the wolf from the door unless your need for insurance drops. Even policies that pay a rising death benefit may not grow fast enough to hold even with inflation. A surer approach is to buy more term insurance as you go along and build up investments on the side. If you eventually decide that you need cash-value coverage, you can acquire it in middle age. Those with health problems can convert to cash-value from their current term insurance (be sure you have a conversion option—page 289). The healthy can check out the policies of several insurers. At 45, a $100,000 cash-value policy might cost $125 a month.

"Since you can afford all the insurance you need, think about using a cash-value policy for tax-sheltered savings or to build a larger estate." This

is the only legitimate argument. And it's legit only for a cash-value policy with low costs and a genuinely competitive return (page 314).

TYPES OF TERM

There's *annually renewable term*—renewable every year without a health exam. Initially, it's the cheapest. Every year your premium goes up, but not by very much. A $100,000 policy might cost a nonsmoking woman $4 more at age 36 than at 35 and $19 more at 56 than at 55.

And there's *level-premium term*—your premiums stay the same for 5, 10, 15, or 20 years, or until a specific age such as 65. Initially, level-premium term costs more than annually renewable term, but over the entire period it usually costs less. Still, read the fine print. Some 10- to 20-year policies guarantee rates only for the first 5 years, in which case you don't know exactly what you'll ultimately pay.

In general, however, the overall cost of level-premium term is so appealing that buyers often look no further. But listen up. Please. I'm yelling in your ear! You run a big risk when the term runs out and you want to renew. The insurer lets you switch to another policy (usually, annually renewable term), regardless of health. But the premiums will be shockingly high. To get decent rates, you have to pass a new health exam ("reentry" —page 358). If you can't, and you still need life insurance, you're stuck with whatever premium the company wants to charge.

Before buying level-premium term, find out what you'll have to pay at renewal if you can't pass the physical. Compare that with what you'd pay, at that age, for an annually renewable policy bought today. (Example, for a 30-year-old buyer: If you choose 20-year term today, what will you pay to renew at 50 if your health is poor? Alternatively, if you choose annually renewable term today, what will you pay when you're 50, regardless of health?) You'll discover that, for those whose health deteriorates, annually renewable term is far less expensive.

Safest strategy: Buy level-premium term only if you won't need it when it expires. For example, you might choose a 20-year policy to protect your young children against your death, then let it go. These policies become too expensive if you're not in good health at the end of the term. To protect a dependent for a longer period of time, choose annually renewable term.

If you've already chosen level-premium term and get stuck with a high renewal premium, see if it makes sense to convert to the company's cash-value policy instead.

When You Buy Term Insurance . . .

Make It Convertible. Your term policy should be convertible into cash-value coverage—at standard rates and without a health exam—right up to

65. That gives you a chance to continue your policy into old age, even if your health deteriorates. The lowest-cost policies may provide conversion rights only for the first 5 years. But you don't know what the future will bring, so it's worth paying extra for a longer conversion option.

Your agent may encourage you to convert when you're young. Don't do it unless there's a very good reason. What might that be? (1) You plan to work well into older age and someone (a spouse, a teenager) will depend on those earnings. (2) You have a disabled child and want to leave plenty of money for his or her care. (3) You got rich and want money to pay the estate taxes.

If you do decide that you need cash-value coverage, don't automatically convert the term policy you have. If you're insurable, you might find less expensive coverage through another company (page 295). Your 50s are good years for making the switch.

Make It a Nonsmoker Policy. Save money. Quit smoking. Nonsmokers live longer than smokers (memo to the Tobacco Institute: Can I get you an actuary?) and pay 40 to 60 percent less for their term insurance. To most insurers, you're a nonsmoker if you've avoided the weed for one to 2 years.

Look at the Premium Guarantees. Most level-premium policies guarantee your premiums for the full term, then can charge what they want. Most annually renewable policies guarantee premiums in the early years but reserve the right to raise them later. If two annually renewable policies charge the same, but one guarantees low premiums for more years than the other, take it.

Tell the Whole Truth. Don't misspeak on your application or let the insurance agent misspeak for you. Insurers can test your honesty with a medical exam or by checking your medical history with the Medical Information Bureau (page 412). What happens if a deception slips through (for example, you don't confess that you smoke cigarettes)? If you die during the first 2 years that you hold the policy, the company will routinely check your application against your medical records. It may even assign an investigator. If it finds a misstatement that would have affected how your application was handled, it may cancel your coverage posthumously. Your beneficiaries will get back all the premiums you paid but will lose the large lump sum you intended them to have.

Will the Real "Low-Cost" Term Policy Please Stand Up?

Some policies are cheap in the early years but get more expensive (relative to other term policies) when you've held them awhile. Other policies cost more at first but relatively less by the tenth or fifteenth year. Which type to buy?

1. Pick the first kind if you'll want insurance only for 5 years or so.

2. Pick the first kind if you'll shop for a new insurance company every 5 years. When its rates get too high, you can hop to a lower-cost insurer. (But if you've become uninsurable—a remote possibility—you'll be locked into the policy you already have.)

3. Pick the second kind if you want to keep the policy for more than 5 years.

How to Find Cheap Term Insurance

Ask a computerized price-quote service to find cheap term insurance for you. Your age and health status is run through a data bank. Out comes a list of at least five policies to consider, along with brief policy descriptions and the insurers' safety ratings (the quote services offer only higher-rated companies).

The policies won't necessarily be America's cheapest, only the cheapest of those that the quote service follows or does business with. If you check with two or three of these services, however, you'll get a pretty good list to pick from.

Every 5 years run yourself through the computers again. If you stay in good health, you'll probably find something cheaper every time. I found my own low-cost term policy here and wouldn't dream of shopping any other way.

The first company on the list, Insurance Information, Inc., charges for the information but sells no insurance. The other services, offered by life insurance agents, provide quotes free. If you like what you see, the agent will buy the policy for you and earn the commission. But there's no obligation and no salesperson will call. One caveat: Quote services that also sell insurance exclude companies that write policies only through their own agents or personnel. They won't quote you the term policies of Northwestern Mutual Life (highly competitive for people in excellent health) or USAA Life (try it for face amounts of $100,000 or less). A second caveat: don't deal with a service that sells you term insurance, then tries to talk you into buying cash-value coverage, too.

When you call one of these services, a representative asks you your age, health status, profession, hobbies (do you rock-climb?), how much insurance you want, and whether you prefer level-premium term or annually renewable term. Based on your answers to the personal questions, you'll be quoted a super-preferred, preferred, standard, or substandard rate. Your actual rate, however, will depend on the outcome of a medical exam. If you're bumped from preferred down to standard rates, call the quote services again and ask for a list of their best standard-rate policies.

You should also get a second round of quotes if you don't act on the first ones right away. There's fierce competition in this market. A cheaper policy might pop up.

Insurance Information, Inc., of Hyannis, Massachusetts (800-472-5800). For $50, it will send you the names and phone numbers of the 5 insurance companies (out of some 500 it monitors) that offer the lowest term rates for someone in your circumstances. Your $50 will be refunded if you don't find a policy more than $50 cheaper than the one you have now. When you call the insurance company, you'll be directed to a local agent.

LifeRates of America, Newtown, Pennsylvania (800-457-2837), monitors some 200 companies.

MasterQuote in Chicago (800-337-5433) monitors 300 companies. For applications on the Web: http://www.masterquote.com.

Quotesmith of Darien, Illinois (800-431-1147), monitors around 150 companies. For instant quotes, policy descriptions, and insurance applications on the Web: http://www.quotesmith.com.

SelectQuote of San Francisco (800-343-1985) follows 18 companies.

TermQuote of Dayton, Ohio (800-444-TERM), has about 25 companies in its database at any one time.

Jack White of San Diego (800-233-3411) has a database of some 350 companies including the low-loads (page 312).

Wholesale Insurance Network (WIN) of Tampa, Florida (800-808-5810), is good for low-load term and cash-value policies (page 313). Ask about term rates offered by Federal Home Life.

At this writing, banks are starting to offer quote services, too. They're going to spread like measles. Except for WIN, however, these services should be used only for term insurance. Cash-value policies require a very different kind of shopping.

Warning: Most of the low-cost policies that the services quote will be level-premium "reentry" term (page 289). Their renewal rate is good only for people in good health. If you expect to keep the policy beyond the guaranteed term, ask what you'd pay if you're not in good health. Better yet, ask the service to give you the rates only for annually renewable term, which doesn't cost more if your health deteriorates.

In theory, there's a second way of finding cheap life insurance: check the policy's "interest-adjusted net payment index," and compare it with the index number on competing policies. But I say *forgeddaboudit.* As a practical matter, these indexes don't work. Call a quote service instead.

Savings Bank Insurance

You can buy term life insurance at many savings banks in:
• Massachusetts—up to $1 million. Highly rated whole life insurance is available, too. The Savings Bank Life Insurance Company of Massachusetts also does business in New Hampshire and Rhode Island (residents can phone 888-GET-SBLI) and plans to move into other states. Thanks to low

expenses and good mortality experience, premiums are pretty low. At this writing, rates are also unisex: men pay the same as women even though they have shorter life spans. So male rates are especially attractive. Rates for young women are generally okay, but women over 40 or so can probably do better somewhere else. (At some point in the future, the Massachusetts SBLI may drop unisex pricing.)

• New York—up to $500,000 at banks with group policies for customers. You can buy whole life insurance, too. You qualify only if you live or work in the state. Term rates start low but rise rapidly.

• Connecticut—up to $200,000 at banks that offer a group policy to their customers, plus another $100,000 in an individual policy. You qualify if you live or work in the state. Term rates in this state have not been competitive, but check to see if they've improved.

Mortgage-Life Insurance

Do you want to leave your survivors a house free and clear? If so, get enough coverage to repay the mortgage as well as pay all the rest of your family's expenses. There are two ways to go.

1. Buy mortgage-life insurance from the lender. It's a term policy whose cost can be bundled into your monthly mortgage payment. If you die, the proceeds pay off your loan.

Sound good so far? Now watch me trash it. First, this coverage can be shockingly expensive. Second, it locks your survivors into using the policy to pay off the mortgage loan. Maybe they'd rather use the money for something else. Mortgage-life is worth considering only for smokers and people in poor health who can't get life insurance elsewhere at standard rates. (And even then, compare prices before settling for the lender's policy.)

2. The better choice is regular term insurance, which is generally cheaper than what the lender has to sell. With "decreasing term," the policy's face value declines right along with the mortgage. The price of these policies, however, tends to be high. As an alternative, take level-premium term for a period lasting at least as long as the mortgage will. Some insurers let you simulate decreasing-term by reducing the policy's face amount from time to time. If you die, the proceeds go to your survivors, not to the lender. They decide what to do with the money. Maybe they'd rather keep on making mortgage payments and use the insurance money for savings or investments.

Credit-Life Insurance

Like mortgage insurance, it's offered by a lender. And it's overpriced in many states, especially for younger people and those in good health.

Credit-life may be offered in tandem with a car loan, personal loan, installment loan, credit card, or home-equity line of credit. It's generally, but not always, packaged with credit-disability insurance. Credit-card companies often include unemployment insurance (page 274). It's against the law to pressure you into buying this coverage, although lenders may try (they make a lot of money selling credit-life). If you want your debts paid off at your death, skip these high-priced bits of credit insurance and buy more term insurance instead.

I make two exceptions:

1. Credit-life, when sold by credit unions, is reasonably priced. Their credit-disability coverage, however, can be high.

2. If you're otherwise uninsurable, credit-life sold by any institution is worth the price. There's no health exam, although a few simple health questions may be asked and the insurer might require that you be actively at work. In some states, credit-life insurers can refuse to pay if, within 6 months of the policy's start-up date, you die from an illness that was treated or diagnosed in the 6 months before you bought. Some insurers collect medical information from people taking out policies larger than $20,000 to $25,000. Payment can be denied if you hide your true physical condition and die within 2 years.

Miscellaneous Insurance

Keep a note in your life insurance file if you qualify for any of the following payments so that your survivors will know where there's money to collect:

1. Credit unions sometimes provide a small amount of free insurance —on the order of $2,000 in coverage for a $2,000 account.

2. If you charge a travel ticket to a credit card, it may generate $100,000 or more of free life insurance. You might be covered for accidental death and dismemberment, whether you travel by plane, train, bus, or ship. Ditto, if your accident occurs in an airline terminal or while traveling on public transportation to and from the terminal.

3. If you belong to the American Automobile Association, your membership fee may include a small amount of life insurance for members who die in auto accidents.

4. You might have bought some credit-life insurance when you took out a loan. I don't recommend it except at credit unions (see above). But if you do buy, note it in your file so the money won't be wasted.

5. Employers may provide up to $50,000 worth of free life insurance.

6. Some retirement systems also provide benefits.

YOU'RE GETTING OLDER—DO YOU STILL WANT TERM?

At some point, you'll ask yourself, What now? Should you keep your term policy even though it's getting more expensive; should you drop it; or should you switch to cash-value coverage?

Your insurance agent will typically urge you to switch to a cash-value policy—and the sooner the better, from his or her point of view. Cash-value premiums will be higher than what you're currently paying for term, so you might have to cut back on coverage. But that's not so bad if your kids are mostly grown. A properly structured cash-value policy will last you for the rest of your life.

The real question is, do you need coverage for life? Every policyholder will answer differently.

If your term policy was bought to ensure your children's support and education, you can cancel it as soon as the kids are on their own. Even a breadwinner whose kids won't finish school until he or she is 65 might find it cheaper to stick with term.

If the insurance protects a spouse, take a close look at whether the spouse still needs it. You can do without if your spouse is self-supporting or if your pension, Social Security, and savings can provide an income for life. If you're building investments at a satisfactory rate, you might keep your term policy until you're 65 or 70 and cancel it then.

If you decide that term insurance remains the right choice, shop for a cheaper policy every 5 years, as long as you remain insurable. Different insurance companies offer better rates at later ages. Just be sure that policy gives you the right to convert to cash-value coverage, with no medical exam, up to 65 or even 75, should the need arise.

There are several good reasons to convert to cash-value coverage. Maybe you have a mentally or physically handicapped child who will never be self-supporting. Maybe you haven't saved enough to leave a decent income for a dependent spouse. Maybe you started your own business, which has tied up your assets.

You might also consider cash-value coverage if you owe federal estate taxes (page 119). If your assets are illiquid—for example, tied up in real estate—life insurance is essential. Your heirs will need cash from the policy to pay the tax. If your assets are liquid, however, insurance is optional. Your estate could sell some securities to pay the tax. You'd buy the insurance only if you wanted to leave extra money to the kids.

If you're earning a big salary, you might want to use cash-value insurance as an investment. Your earnings build up tax deferred; at death, they pass to your beneficiaries tax-free.

Don't automatically convert from term to cash-value with the same insurance company. If you're in good health, other insurers may offer you a better deal.

ALL ABOUT CASH-VALUE INSURANCE

The premium you pay for a cash-value policy is divided three ways. Part of it pays for insurance coverage. Part covers the insurer's expenses. Part goes into a tax-protected savings fund. This kind of coverage has two main appeals:

First, you can hold the policy's premiums level so it stays affordable (or reasonably so) right into old age. You'll want coverage in old age if: (1) you expect to be working and have a spouse or handicapped child who'll depend on your income; (2) your pension doesn't provide a cost-of-living increase, and your savings aren't large enough to protect your spouse against rising costs; (3) you want to leave your family or a charity a sizable pot of money free of tax (although the charity may do better if you give it the premiums, instead); (4) your estate will owe death taxes and you want them paid out of life insurance proceeds. Large term policies grow impossibly expensive in late old age if, indeed, you can buy them at all.

The second reason for buying cash-value insurance is the tax-protected investment it offers. In old age, you can either borrow against that money tax-free or surrender the policy and pocket the proceeds after any tax.

Here's the big question: Do you want to put your investment funds into cash-value life insurance? Are the returns high enough? Or should you buy only term insurance and invest your money somewhere else?

This used to be a no-brainer: Buy cheap term insurance and invest elsewhere. And you still should if your separate investment account is tax deductible and tax deferred. Term insurance plus a company tax-deferred savings plan or deductible Individual Retirement Account will beat cash-value policies that make comparable investments.

But *some* policies from *some* companies for *some* people can be good investments if you play them right. I repeat that you must be able to afford enough insurance to protect your family, which usually means term coverage. But assuming that necessity is met, some cash-value policies can be an interesting buy.

Two important points: (1) You must choose carefully. Many of the advertised yields are deceptive. Your cash value may be earning far less than you think. (2) If interest rates fall, your policy won't build the value you expected, as thousands of policyholders have learned to their regret. So you have to have a contingency plan right from the start.

You also have to be able to understand the insurance policy illustrations —those columns of figures the agent gives you purporting to show how much money your policy could earn over the next 30 to 50 years. For the truth about policy illustrations, see page 309.

There are four kinds of cash-value policies: traditional whole life, "blended" (mixed whole life and term), universal life, and variable universal life. Here's the scoop on all of them.

Traditional Whole Life Insurance

Call these policies "no surprises" when used in a traditional way. You pay a fixed premium every year up to age 95 or 100. The premium may be level or it may rise after a certain number of years, but you know exactly what you'll owe. You can choose to pay larger premiums up front so the policy will be paid in full by a certain age—and that result can be guaranteed (although sometimes it's not: see "vanishing premium," page 298). You earn guaranteed interest on your cash values, plus an annual dividend (although its size is not guaranteed). You know for sure that when you die, your beneficiaries will get at least the policy's face value. You can increase the policy's face value every year by using your dividends to buy more insurance.

What percentage return will you earn on the money you invest in a whole life policy? Beats me. The insurance company usually doesn't reveal how much of each premium goes to cover the cost of insurance and overhead expenses, so you can't tell what you're earning on the rest of your funds. Generally speaking, your policy will earn little or nothing in the first year or two and small amounts in the years immediately thereafter. Over 20 years, however, good whole life insurance will earn as much as a quality corporate bond, tax deferred. If you hold until death, the gains are entirely tax-free.

Dividends are declared once a year, on your policy's anniversary date. If you surrender the policy before that date, you'll lose your share of that year's dividend.

Two problems with whole life, both related to the lack of honest price disclosure in the life insurance industry:

PROBLEM ONE. The insurance company may indeed "reveal" what it pays on your policy's cash values, but there are several smarmy ways of making your yield look higher than it really is. To take one example, you're typically told the gross dividend rate before the company deducts your costs. A policy claiming an 8 percent yield might actually be earning a net of only 4 percent. "We have plenty of examples of this sort," reports insurance professor Harold Skipper of Georgia State University.

Agents opposed to whole life insurance use counterdeceptions of their own. Joseph Belth, insurance professor emeritus of Indiana University and author of *Life Insurance: A Consumer's Handbook*, tells of a policy whose insurance portion was said—by a deceptive agent—to be overpriced at $173.60 per $1,000 worth of coverage, when the true cost was more like $8.93.

Deception is possible in insurance sales because you cannot easily figure out the yield yourself. Still, you don't have to swallow whatever the agent or insurer dishes out. Get an independent opinion of the policy's investment value from the Consumer Federation of America (for details on this excellent service, see page 313).

PROBLEM TWO. You will be docked if you cancel the policy. Surrender charges in the early years can slash your return to a number too low to mention in polite company. ("Oh, c'mon, say it," urges New York fee-only life insurance adviser Glenn Daily.* "You can lose 100 percent of the money you put up.") The surrender charge, like other expenses, is not disclosed. Low-load policies are an exception (page 312). There, you get most or all of your money back. Buyers of blended policies (page 299) also get back a decent percentage of their investment.

PROBLEM THREE. You might buy a policy that you think will be paid in full after a certain number of years. After that, no more payments are supposedly due (the premiums are said to "vanish"). When that time comes, however, the agent says, "Oops, you owe us for a few years more." To be sure that your premiums really will vanish, ask the agent for a computerized policy illustration. The column labeled Guaranteed Values should show the insurance lasting for life (for more on this, see "paid-up policies," page 320).

PROBLEM FOUR. Many insurers currently pay higher dividends than the market can sustain. That's fine for now. But as part of the sale, the agent will show you a policy illustration with today's high dividends projected 20 and 30 years into the future. That paints far too rosy a picture. Be sure the projection also shows what happens if the dividends drop (see page 310).

Who Might Buy. Whole life policies are for people who want certainty in their plans. You can pay your money, get a guaranteed death benefit, and accumulate cash value. The premium normally stays the same throughout your life. The cash value gives you an extra source of retirement money, just in case. If you want to quit paying premiums, you can use the cash value to buy a smaller "paid-up" policy, on which no more premiums are due. For several years, whole life policies were eclipsed by the dazzle of universal life (page 300), which appeared to offer higher returns. But when interest rates fell, those returns turned out to be a mirage. Among policies sold by agents, as opposed to low-loads (page 312), whole life policies from mutual insurance companies have generally been the better buy. (A mutual company is owned by its policyholders and has "mutual" in its name.)

A terrific insurance bonus: You can use your whole life dividends to buy "paid-up additions." These are tiny, paid-up policies added to your basic policy. They raise your cash value and guaranteed death benefit every

---

* Daily's booklet, *Life Insurance Sense and Nonsense, for people who don't mind a little complexity,* is available for $12 from the author at 212-249-9882.

year—a valuable inflation hedge. This is also a highly efficient way of insuring yourself. The agent earns no commission on each addition, so all of your dividend dollars go for family protection.

Blended Policies—Combining Whole Life and Term

Blends are the cherished little secret of consumers in the know. They let you buy coverage at a much lower cost than you'd pay for traditional whole life.

But agents earn lower commissions when they sell a blend, so they don't go out of their way to offer one. Some agents might not even know a lot about the product. It's usually sold to customers of fee-only insurance advisers, or to buyers of large cash-value policies who have a couple of agents competing for their business. But anyone who knows the product and hunts for an agent who will sell it can get a blend. It's available from many first-class companies, including Northwestern Mutual Life and Guardian Mutual Life. The average buyer, however, may do better with a low-load product (page 312), so check out both types out. Here's how blends work:

Say you need $400,000 in coverage. The blend might contain $240,000 worth of whole life insurance and $160,000 worth of term, although this division won't be obvious to you. Every year the policy's dividends go toward buying more whole life coverage ("paid-up additions"), which gradually replaces the term insurance. You can also buy paid-up additions with part of your premium. You pay the full sales commission on the term and whole life pieces. But the agent earns very little on the paid-up additions portion, which translates into savings for you.

You lower your insurance costs in one of two ways, depending on what you want to achieve:

1. *The blend can lower your premium*—the most popular choice. When agents compete for your business they usually do so by showing how little you have to pay for a large amount of coverage. This type of blend builds lower cash value in the policy's early years but catches up in the later years.

When you lower your premium, however, blends carry a risk. You're counting on getting large enough dividends to replace the term insurance on schedule. If interest rates fall or term insurance costs rise, your dividends won't do the job and your policy will gradually unravel. To save it, you'd have to increase your premiums or pay them for more years than you intended.

To avoid this risk, buyers who want to save money up front shouldn't cut their premium very far—say, no more than 10 percent below what they'd pay for straight whole life.

2. *The blend can build cash value faster than usual*—another way of lowering costs. You pay the same premium as you would for whole life insurance, but less of your money is siphoned off in sales commissions and those savings go directly into your policy. This approach makes good sense for investors who want a higher tax-deferred retirement fund.

For the best buy in blends, tell the agent you'll pay the full whole life premium (or close to it) for a mix that contains the largest possible amount of term. That puts the maximum amount of money at work for you. By paying the full premium, you also eliminate policy risk.

With blends, your death benefit generally stays the same for life, so inflation erodes its purchasing power. With straight whole life policies, by contrast, death benefits can rise.

Who Might Buy. People who will need insurance into old age and want a lower fixed premium. People who will have a decreasing need for insurance as they age, so they're not alarmed by the decline in purchasing power. People seeking more cash value for each premium dollar they put up. But don't buy until you've checked out the low-loads. They build cash value even faster than blends.

Universal Life Insurance

These policies are flexible. You decide how much premium to pay, subject to specified minimums and maximums. If you put in enough, your policy lasts for life and builds substantial cash values. If you put in too little, however, your policy will eventually lapse. Your choice of premium dictates the result.

So how do you choose?

1. The insurance agent may recommend a "target" or "guideline" premium pegged to the highest percentage commission he or she can earn. From your point of view, this is a worthwhile choice. It guarantees that your coverage will last for life.

2. You can put in additional money if you're using the policy as a tax-protected investment.

3. If you're watching every dollar, you can put in a little less and still have a policy that's reasonably safe. The target premium is typically a bit higher than necessary.

4. You can pay a lot less if money is tight. But in this case, you'll have to pay more in the later years to keep the policy alive.

5. You can vary the size of your premiums, paying more this month, then skipping the next 3 months. In theory, that's an advantage; in practice, maybe not, if it leads to a policy starved for cash.

What happens if, in any month, you don't pay a high enough premium to cover the current cost of your insurance protection? The insurer will take the missing payment out of your policy's cash value. If you consistently pay too little, your cash value declines and the policy will eventually collapse (page 303).

To be sure that doesn't happen, here's the suggestion of James Hunt, consulting actuary for the Consumer Federation of America: Pay whatever premium will cause the policy's cash surrender value to equal its face amount by age 100. The company or agent can easily figure this out for you. The calculation should assume that the policy earns 5 percent interest and that today's insurance charges will stay the same. Here's a countersuggestion from fee-only life insurance adviser Glenn Daily: pay the target premium and relax.

One type of universal policy—interest-sensitive whole life—offers premiums that are fixed, or fixed for a certain period. Its required premium guarantees coverage for life.

You can also choose how large a death benefit you want your premium to buy. You have two options:

Option A: Your death benefit generally stays level. Your policy's earnings go into extra cash value. This option gives you more coverage now for the money you put up.

Option B: Your death benefit rises. Your beneficiaries get the policy's face value plus the cash value, which normally goes up every year. You get a bit less coverage for a given amount of premium, but you gain an inflation hedge. If you dump extra money into an Option B policy, those funds will earn a tax-deferred return and go to your family tax-free at death (low-load policies, page 312, offer the most efficient investment option).

Option B gets expensive at later ages. Your premium may have to go up. If you start with Option B, to give yourself an inflation hedge when your family is young, consider switching later to Option A. If you start with A, however, and want to switch to B, you'll have to pass a medical exam because Option B increases your coverage.

In either case, your family will get no less than the policy's face value, provided that the insurance remains in force.

You can take money out of a universal life policy without borrowing against it. Instead, you make a "partial withdrawal," usually paying a $25 fee. Ask the insurance company whether any part of the withdrawal is taxable. The answer depends on actuarial calculations. There also may be surrender charges. For deciding between loans and partial withdrawals, see page 320.

You'll pay substantial surrender charges if you drop the policy before 10 to 20 years have passed. For that reason, you should ignore the column in your policy illustration labeled Policy Values (or perhaps Account Values, Accumulation Values, or even Cash Value). Those aren't usable values at all as long as there's a surrender charge. If you cash in the policy or borrow against it, you'll get the policy value *minus* the surrender charge, which is usually large. For you, the column in the illustration that really matters is the one labeled Surrender Value.

Unlike most traditional whole life insurance, universal policies disclose the interest rate that you're earning on your policy's cash value. Sometimes rates are guaranteed for a year; sometimes they change more frequently. You get an annual statement showing how much interest you earned, how much was withdrawn from your policy to cover costs, and how much your savings fund increased.

But universal life comes with problems just as whole life does.

PROBLEM ONE. The advertised yield tells you next to nothing! You may be credited with high interest on your life insurance savings. To compensate, however, the insurer may charge extra for expenses and for the insurance portion of the policy, so your net yield is lower than you think. A policy with lower advertised rates and much lower expenses would give you a higher return in the long run.

Furthermore, these interest rates aren't guaranteed. Actual rates will be lower, or higher, than the insurance company projects. In recent years they've been substantially lower and thousands of policies have failed (page 303). Rates paid on cash values usually change every year. You are guaranteed only the company's minimum, typically 4 percent.

Never compare the iffy advertised interest rates on life insurance savings with the guaranteed interest rates on bonds or bank accounts. They don't compute. You can't even compare one insurer's interest rates with another's because the companies subtract different amounts from your cash value to cover their costs. If you're thinking about buying a universal life policy (or any other form of cash-value insurance) write or call the Consumer Federation of America (page 314) for an analysis of what the policy might really earn.

PROBLEM TWO. In most cases, you lose most or all of your money if you cancel the policy early (page 322). Unlike whole life, however, universal life discloses how much you will lose. Low-load policies are an exception to this rule (page 312). They give you most or all of your money back.

PROBLEM THREE. You may mistake the premium you pay for the policy's cost. The cost is the expense of insuring you every year plus the company's overhead and profit. The premium is merely the money that you choose to put in. At the start, your premium may indeed cover all your costs. If costs rise, however, your premium may be too low. Some agents deliberately suggest a low premium to make the policy look low-cost compared with others on the market. This is a sham. Too low a premium sets you up for rising premiums in the future.

PROBLEM FOUR. You can kid yourself that your universal policy is providing you with enough savings and insurance when it's really not.

When interest rates fall, your cash value will not build up as fast as the agent projected. You might coast along, faithfully paying the premium you had bargained for, not knowing that it's no longer enough.

The shortfall will be subtracted from your policy's cash value. But that can't go on forever. To keep the policy going, you'd have to raise the premium you pay, pay premiums for many years longer than you anticipated, or accept a lower amount of insurance. If you don't, the cash value will shrink to the point where it no longer covers the policy's cost and your life insurance will lapse. In the worst case, you won't discover the problem until you've retired, when you no longer have the income to pay a substantially higher cost.

PROBLEM FIVE. You now know that if interest rates fall, the cost of your policy goes up. But the cost of your policy can rise in other ways less easy to spot. For example, the insurer can increase the "mortality charge" that's subtracted from your premium. On paper, you're still earning top-market interest rates; in practice, the insurer is draining some of your earnings away. Your cash value might fall, meaning that your policy has begun the spiral down.

A good insurance agent will track your policy and keep you informed of what's happening. If you have to increase your premiums, he or she will tell you so.

Slimy or incompetent agents won't be so forthcoming. Sometimes they don't understand the policies they've sold; sometimes they spend so much time finding new customers that they don't have time for old ones; sometimes they don't want to tell you that your policy is in trouble; sometimes they've left the business and couldn't care less.

Anyone with a Universal Policy Should:

• Pay the full premium needed to secure the policy for life even if interest rates decline (page 300). If you can't afford it, at least pay enough to keep the policy going under current interest rates. If you can't afford that, universal life is not for you. Your policy will eventually lapse, costing you all the money you put in and leaving your family without protection. You'd be better off with term insurance from the start.

• Call your insurance agent when interest rates fall to see if you ought to raise your premiums.

• Check the annual statement that the insurance company sends you. At the end, you may find a sentence disclosing how many years your policy will remain in force if you (1) pay no more premiums or (2) keep paying premiums at the originally scheduled rate. If the policy will obviously lapse before you do, call your agent to see what your options are. If you can't find that disclosure on your annual statement, call your agent and ask for it. Don't dally, and accept no excuses. You *must find out* if your insurance is running down!

• Ask the agent or company for an "in-force" or "current" illustration. It shows what will happen to your cash value and death benefit over the next 30 years or so if interest rates and your premium payments stay the same. Check the illustration to see if it shows your cash value falling in some future year. That means you're not paying high enough premiums to keep the policy going. Shrinking cash values should always be treated as a red alert.

• Send an in-force illustration to the Consumer Federation of America for analysis (page 314). Don't add more money to your policy until you find out whether you're earning a decent return. If you're not, reduce or cancel the coverage. Buy term insurance or a truly competitive cash-value policy instead. If you are indeed earning an acceptable return (odds are you are), ask the agent or company what size premium you should pay to keep the policy in force to age 95 or 100.

• Don't be lulled by the policy's guarantees. There's a guaranteed 4 percent interest rate but no guarantee that that's what the policy will yield after expenses. There's a guaranteed death benefit while the policy is in force, but if the cash value sinks there's also no guarantee that the policy won't expire.

• Some people invest extra money in their universal life insurance for the tax-protected return. This introduces a new complication. Too large an investment will turn your policy into something called a modified endowment contract. Loans and withdrawals against modified endowments create taxable income plus a 10 percent penalty if you're under age 59½ and not disabled. Ask your insurance agent how much you can safely invest without running into tax complications.

Who Might Be in Trouble with an Older Universal Life Policy Right Now: (1) Anyone who bought when interest rates were higher, yet isn't paying a higher annual premium. (2) Anyone with a loan on a policy, or who has taken a withdrawal. (3) Anyone who has skipped premiums, or is paying less than originally planned. (4) Anyone who paid an unusually low premium to be able to afford additional insurance. (5) Anyone who bought with a single lump sum and hasn't added money since.

What to Do. Call your agent. If he or she is no longer in business, get someone else in that same office. Ask: If I continue to pay premiums at my current rate, how long will the policy last? If it won't last for life, how much more do I have to pay? How much more would I have to pay if interest rates declined by one percentage point? How about 2 percentage points? Would my policy work out if I switched from a rising death benefit (Option B) to a level death benefit (Option A—page 301)? Would my policy work out if I repaid the loan? If I can't pay a higher premium, how much would my policy have to shrink to produce a level of coverage that my current premium could support? Unless you're in poor health, it's better to reduce your policy's face amount than to keep pouring money into a larger policy that will eventually lapse (*warning:* reducing the face value sometimes triggers a surrender charge).

Finally, get a new policy illustration showing what your cash value and death benefit is currently projected to be 20 and 30 years ahead. If you thought your cash value would rise to $300,000 and it now looks more like $225,000, you've been warned in advance. Update your illustration every 3 years. Insurers sometimes wait awhile before passing on interest-rate declines.

Yet another warning: You may be advised to switch to another policy. That's often the agent's self-interest talking; he or she wants to earn a commission. Switching is almost always wrong (page 326).

Who Might Buy. Look at universal life if you want the flexibility of deciding how much money to invest. But monitor the cash value to be sure it's large enough to keep the policy in force. You shouldn't buy unless you *will* check your coverage once a year and *can* afford to pay more if needed. Financial planners also like to work with universal life because it gives their clients more choices as their circumstances change. Regarding policy performance, the average universal should do as well as average whole life. Low-load universal should do as well as whole life sold by quality mutual companies.

Variable Universal Life Insurance

A variable policy ties your death benefit and cash value to the investment performance of stocks, bonds, or money market securities. You can vary the premiums you pay, just as you do with regular universal life. What's different is that you get to choose what your policy will be invested in. You're offered a handful of mutual funds; you pick one (or several) and can move your money among them at will. What rings buyers' bells is the chance to invest in stocks. The assets behind other life-insurance policies are invested mainly in mortgages and bonds. Variable policies give you a shot at higher growth.

When your investments do well, your cash value rises. If you chose Option B for policy earnings (page 301), your death benefit rises, too. When your investments do badly, however, your cash value falls. Your death benefit also falls unless you add more money to the policy—in a lump sum or in higher premium payments. (Under Option A, your death benefit may rise or fall in the future but not right away.)

Some policies offer a guaranteed minimum death benefit, usually for a limited number of years, to keep the policy from lapsing if the stock market drops soon after you buy. This feature usually involves an extra cost.

Your cash values, however, are never guaranteed. In good markets, they'll rise; in bad ones, they'll fall.

Over 20 or 30 years, you assume, the value of your policy has nowhere to go but up. But how far up? Not as much as you might think. That's because of the policy's costs. The internal charges levied against variable policies tend to be higher than on other forms of cash-value coverage.

Take one typical contract earning 10.2 percent on its cash value, analyzed by consulting actuary James Hunt. After 5 years the policyholder had a negative investment return (− 8.7 percent), principally due to the up-front sales charge. After 10 years the policy still returned a net of just 4.8 percent; after 15 years, 6.6 percent; after 20 years, 7.3 percent. These policies don't reward you for the investment risk you take.

Furthermore, your results depend on the pattern of market performance, which few investors realize. You think, "Stocks will average 10 percent," and get a policy illustration based on that assumption. But markets do better in some years and worse in others. In the down years, your policy's expenses will amount to a larger percentage of its cash value. So your policy may lag even though, on paper, your fund yields an average of 10 percent. If the stock market does badly late in the policy's life, you might have to add some money to keep the policy intact. "Die on a stock-market uptick," says the wisecracking insurance professor Joseph Belth.

If you're trying to decide between variable life and universal life, get illustrations that project their cash value for the next 20 years. They may not perform as differently as you might think.

How to Invest with Variable Universal Life:

• Don't minimize your premiums. That raises the odds that you'll have to pay higher premiums later. If you can't afford them, your investment will be at risk. All the caveats that apply to regular universal life (page 302) apply to the variable version, too.

• Low- and medium-yield investments are a waste of money even if you use them for only part of your policy's cash value. Money market returns have virtually no chance of raising your death benefit after subtracting costs. Bond funds yield about what you'd get from regular life insurance, so you'd get nothing in return for paying a variable policy's higher cost.

• If you're going to bet on variable universal life, go all the way. Put your money (or most of it) in a pure stock fund and leave it there. Don't even bother with an asset-allocation fund, which switches your money from one type of investment to another. If you don't want to hold stocks for the long term, don't buy variable insurance.

• Buy this insurance only in large amounts. The insurer might levy $5 or $6 a month in fees, in addition to all its other costs. That batters investments of just $50 or $100 a month. Costs are more reasonable if you're investing $500 a month. Before signing up, make a list of all costs (they're buried in various places in the prospectus and the agent may not remember them all). There are substantial surrender costs if you give up the policy before 10 to 15 years have passed.

- You can use the policy's earnings to build either the maximum cash value or the maximum death benefit, just as with regular universal life (see Options A and B, page 301).

Who Might Buy. A gambler, dreamer, or persistent investor who *really will* hold stocks for the long term, even if the market drops. If you chicken out and switch to bonds after a decline, your losses will be hard to recoup and your policy will cost you more. Because of a variable policy's extra costs, you need superior stock-market returns, over a long holding period, for this investment to do better than other forms of cash-value insurance. If you plan to hold for 20 years or so, you have a shot.

IT CAN'T BE SAID OFTEN ENOUGH! UNLESS YOU BUY GUARAN-TEED WHOLE LIFE INSURANCE, OR PAY THE "TARGET" PREMIUM ON UNIVERSAL LIFE, YOUR "PERMANENT INSURANCE" MIGHT LAPSE WHEN YOU'RE 60, 70, OR 80, LEAVING YOU WITHOUT THE COVERAGE THAT YOU SPENT YOUR YOUTH PAYING FOR. Find out *now* how long your current policy is actually going to last! Call your agent or insurance company for a current illustration. Check the end of your most recent annual statement, where a universal policy's lapse date may be disclosed. Check your policy's viability with the Consumer Federation of America (page 314).

SECOND-TO-DIE INSURANCE

These policies are for well-to-do married couples who want extra cash to cover the death tax. No tax is generally due when the first spouse dies because the second spouse inherits. It's only when the second spouse dies that the government takes its cut.

Enter second-to-die insurance. It insures both lives but pays off only at the second death. The premium is lower than if you bought separate cash-value policies, one for each.

This policy should probably be transferred into an irrevocable trust so as not to be taxed in your estate. After the second death the life insurance pays off; the trust uses the proceeds to buy assets from the estate; that provides the estate with the money it needs to pay the death tax. Don't rely on an insurance agent to structure this arrangement for you. See a tax attorney who specializes in estate planning.

Before buying, check what will happen to your insurance if interest rates fall. Agents often compete for your business by proposing that you pay aggressively low premiums. But if the policy's expenses rise, or interest rates fall, those premiums won't keep your policy going for life. You might end up at 85 needing to pay $100,000 to keep a $1 million policy in force.

For safety, these policies should be overfunded rather than marginally funded. Recommendation: Your annual premium should be high enough to fund a cash-surrender value equal to the policy's face value when the younger insured reaches age 100. Run this illustration at a conservative rate of interest—say, 5 percent.

Also, look at your options if you get divorced or if tax laws change. You should be able to split this policy in two, if you're in poor health, without having to pass a health exam or pay sales commissions on two new policies. There may be taxes and fees, however, and some companies impose a surrender charge on the original policy. If you're insurable, it's usually better to cash in the policy and make other insurance arrangements.

Big premiums are usually involved in second-to-die insurance. You should be looking at low-loads (page 312) and well-funded blends (page 299) that provide the safe level of premiums you want at a lower sales cost.

FIRST-TO-DIE INSURANCE

A couple might prefer a joint cash-value policy that pays on the first death rather than the second. The surviving spouse gets the payout right away. Joint coverage can be cheaper than carrying two separate policies, although if you use a low-load insurer (page 312), separate policies may be cheaper. At this writing, first-to-die is pretty new and not sold by many companies. Insurance advisers are still evaluating it.

You should be able to split the policy at divorce without having to pass a health exam and without paying sales commissions on two new policies. But you might prefer to buy two new policies. See the discussion under second-to-die, page 307.

A SIMPLE WAY THROUGH THE REST OF THIS CHAPTER

Skip directly to page 312, where you'll find the names of two fine, high-value, low-cost insurance companies. You can buy them yourself, by telephone. They're blue chips. What else do you really need to know?

Between this page and that you'll find a lot of detail about why it's so hard to analyze an insurance proposal and how an insurance agent can lead you down the garden path.

There are many reliable insurance companies with useful products. But there are high-cost and low-cost policies, good agents and agents who mislead, appropriate and inappropriate policies for someone in your circumstances—and even with help, the average buyer can't tell the difference. You'll simplify your life by choosing policies known to be good.

CAN YOU TRUST COMPUTER-GENERATED LIFE INSURANCE PROPOSALS?

No. Not for a minute, for cash-value policies. Illustrations for term policies are usually pretty clear. And some cash-value illustrations are reasonably honest. But most are strictly GIGO—"garbage in, garbage out." Their neat rows of columns pretend to show what your policy will be worth 20 years or more into the future. But illustrations can be shamelessly manipulated to make a cash-value policy look less expensive than it really is.

Their sins are impossible for a layman to spot. Depending on whether you're looking at whole life or universal life, the projection might:

• Lower your apparent cost by assuming longer average life spans in the future. If life spans don't actually drop that much, your cost of insurance will rise, but by then you may be locked into the policy by poor health or large surrender charges.

• Assume that the current dividend scale on your whole life insurance will stay the same. More likely, it is going to fall.

• Show that your out-of-pocket premium cost will stop after a certain number of years when it may not.

• Tout a "guaranteed" future bonus on universal life, which isn't a true bonus at all. The insurer gets the money to "pay" you by lowering your policy's interest rate.

• Project future cash values for a preferred health risk when you're actually a standard risk. Standard risks pay higher insurance costs, so your cash values won't be as high as the illustration shows.

Some states and many major insurers have adopted the rules for whole life and universal life illustrations approved by the National Association of Insurance Commissioners (NAIC). They may diminish some of the distortions I listed, but will mislead you in other ways. For example, they might:

• Raise the projected cash value on universal life by assuming you'll hold the policy for 15 years and qualify for an interest or premium bonus.

• Reduce your projected premium costs by assuming you'll pay them annually when, in fact, you'll pay them monthly. For monthly payments by check, some whole life insurers charge interest rates of an undisclosed 17 percent or more, even if the payments are debited automatically from your checking account. One well-known offender: Metropolitan Life.

• Throw in some extra cash value in years 5, 10, 15, and 20, which buyers often use for comparison shopping. The years between, however, may be undernourished.

• Dazzle you with a high rate of interest paid on the cash values in universal life while charging a super-high price for the underlying insurance. That leaves you with a low return on investment, after costs.

Some insurers do none of these things, *but you can't tell the better illustrations from the awful ones!* So what is a buyer to do?

1. If you're using the illustrations to compare one policy with another, look only at the first 10 policy years. Long-term comparisons are fruitless because the assumptions behind the projections can be so different. When an agent brags that his or her policy accumulates more cash 20 years or more in the future, assume that statement to be false no matter what the printout shows. But an illustration does one good thing: it shows you how much money you'll lose if you quit the policy in the first few years after purchase.

2. Look for a written explanation of the policy. It should give you a fairly clear idea of what you're buying.

3. Be sure you have all the pages of the illustration. A seven-page illustration, for example, should be numbered "1 of 7," "2 of 7," and so on. Some agents give you the pages they like but not the pages they don't like. Also check that the illustration reflects your age, the premium you're paying, your payment method (monthly, quarterly, annually), and your health classification.

4. If you're looking at whole life insurance, be sure the illustration applies the policy dividends in the way you want (see page 297 for dividend options). If you're looking at universal life, you can choose Option A—the policy's earnings raise your cash value; or Option B—the earnings raise your death benefit (page 301).

5. Check what the policy guarantees and what it doesn't. Illustrations complying with the NAIC rules will show you: (1) the guaranteed minimum death benefit and surrender value; (2) for whole life, the death benefit and surrender value if the policy's dividend scale remains unchanged; (3) for universal life, the death benefit and surrender value if the policy's current interest rate, mortality charges, and expenses remain unchanged; (4) the death benefit and surrender value if there's a 50 percent drop in the policy's dividends or other current assumptions.

If the illustration doesn't provide all this information, consider not doing business with the company. Honest companies should follow the NAIC rules voluntarily, even if their state doesn't require it. (Even under the rules, however, some insurers continue to mislead.)

6. Understand that the illustration is only a hypothetical projection. It's not an "actuarial study," as some deceptive agents say. You may wind up with less, or more, cash value and death benefit than the agent originally displayed. Your actual result depends on future investment returns, future policy costs, and your own future premiums. At this writing, it is more likely than not that cash-value policies will deliver less than the illustrations show.

7. Check the columns of figures showing the policy's projected cash values. Is there anyplace where the numbers decline? Declining cash values (unless followed by rising cash values) mean that the policy will slowly run out of money. You'll have to raise your premium to be sure that your coverage will last.

8. Check the columns of figures for zeros or blanks. They tell you two critical things:

Thing one—any zeros in the column showing your future premium payments. They're commonly found in so-called vanishing premium policies (page 298). You're supposed to pay premiums for a limited number of years. After that, there are zeros in the payment column, meaning that no further premiums are owed. Under NAIC rules, zeros or blanks cannot be used unless the insurer *guarantees* that your payments will stop. If changing conditions might cause your payments to continue, the zeros should have an asterisk and a footnote disclosing that fact. Always ask the agent if the zero is for real.

Thing two—any zeros in the columns that project your future death benefit and cash value. Their meaning is simple. They show that, in those years, your policy will have lapsed, collapsed, exploded, gone up in smoke, given up the ghost. There's no more insurance. In the plan proposed, you're not paying a high enough premium to keep the policy going.

9. A universal life illustration may show an "account value" (also called accumulation value or, more deceptively, cash value). But that's not usable money. It's subject to a surrender charge. Only the "surrender value" is usable, but you get it only if you cash in the policy or borrow against it.

Finally, be suspicious of any policy with especially low premiums or high interest rates. There is almost certainly something wrong.

WHAT YOU SHOULD KNOW ABOUT SELLING EXPENSES

The expenses of selling the policy—also called loads—are deducted from the premiums you pay. Some deductions are direct, such as a fixed percent of each premium. Some are indirect, such as surrender charges if you quit. Most policies charge both.

For agent-sold cash-value policies, sales expenses normally run from 50 percent to more than 100 percent of your first-year premium, and 5 to 10 percent of your renewal premiums for many years. That load covers the salesperson's commission, a percentage payment to the manager of the sales office, an override for office and training expenses, fringe benefits for agents, and other marketing costs.

A few universal policies have no front-end load, only a back-end load or surrender charge, which you pay if you drop the insurance within the first 15 or 20 years. An agent might call this no-load insurance. It is not. The agent gets an up-front commission, paid by the insurance company. The company recoups its cost by charging higher policy expenses or paying lower interest rates on your cash values.

Sales expenses for low-loads (page 312) come out of the policy itself rather than being deducted from your premium up front. They usually come to less than 20 percent of your first-year premium and 2 to 3 percent of subsequent premiums.

On Loaded Universal Life, Some Insurers Let the Agents Decide the Sales Commission. Guess What They Decide? They can charge you a high commission (giving you skinnier cash values) or a low commission (giving you fatter cash values). The low commission is definitely better for consumers, but in most cases you'll never know you had a choice. It's offered only to customers who ask for it, or to win the business of someone who's shopping around.

To test whether a company has a secret low-commission policy, tell the agent that you want the following: a first-year policy surrender value (cash value minus surrender charge) in the neighborhood of 50 percent of the annual target premium for universal life plus 100 percent of whatever extra money you put in. If he or she says it's not possible, say you're sorry and walk away. Look at low-load policies instead.

THE LOW-LOAD SOLUTION

Low-load insurance—a small but growing industry—doesn't sell through agents and pays no overt sales commissions. Some selling expenses are built into the policy but they're generally modest—usually less than 20 percent of your first-year premium and 2 to 3 percent of subsequent premiums.

Low-loads save the most money for buyers of cash-value coverage. By eliminating sales commissions, the insurer can offer you lower premiums, higher death benefits, and/or higher cash values. Virtually all of your premium payments flow into the policy's cash value, which builds up your investment faster. If you cancel a low-load early, you'll get virtually all of your money back. (Contrast this with the pittance you get after quitting an agent-sold policy early.)

An agent may tout a competing policy that appears to build higher cash values than the low-loads do. But remember GIGO (page 309)! The illustration may be full of gimmicks that you'll never be able to find. In the real world, the low-loads should beat the agent-sold high-load over short periods like 5 to 10 years. Over 20 years, it's anybody's guess, but to win, high-load policies need to earn significantly higher investment returns. Why pay a sales commission to find out if they really can? You might not even keep your insurance for 20 years, although you mean to now.

How to Buy Low-Loads. Two low-loads sell by telephone directly to the public. Call USAA Life* in San Antonio (800-531-8000) or Veritas Insurance Marketing Corp. in Houston (800-552-3553), a subsidiary of Ameritas Life in Lincoln, Nebraska.

---

* For auto and homeowners coverage, USAA insures only military officers, certain enlisted personnel, and a few other groups. But anyone can apply for its life insurance and annuities.

That's the recommendation of the Consumer Federation of America. CFA likes both companies' universal life insurance (although USAA's policy is less competitive for older people). Veritas also offers good buys in variable life and second-to-die insurance. USAA's whole life is a "best buy" for people who can afford the relatively high premiums (premiums are high but so is cash value, and costs are low, so you come out well). There are no surrender charges at Veritas or on USAA's universal policy. If you cancel these policies in the first couple of years, you should get most or all of your money back. USAA builds a modest surrender cost into its whole life policy in the early years.

Best bet: Ask both Veritas and USAA for a universal life proposal showing the same death benefit and the same premium. The policy with the better cash surrender values, over 10 to 15 years, is the better deal. *Warning:* Ameritas also sells full-commission products through insurance agents, so be sure you don't buy one by mistake. They're more expensive because of the sales load you pay.

To find out about the low-load policies of nine other insurers, call the Wholesale Insurance Network (WIN) in Tampa, Florida (800-808-5810). Tell a WIN representative your age, whether you smoke, your general medical condition, how much coverage you want, what type of policy you need, and what state you live in. Based on that interview, WIN will send you free quotes from at least two insurance companies, application forms, computer illustrations of how the policies work, and some basic information about the companies. You can get a free worksheet to help you decide how much coverage to buy (or see page 283). You can also fax WIN a proposal from an insurance agent to see if one of its low-load companies can beat it (fax: 800-424-0909).

If you like a policy WIN suggests, the insurer will arrange for a medical exam (no salesperson will call). If you turn out to have a health problem that you didn't mention before, you'll have to pay more than the original quote.

WIN cheerfully answers basic insurance questions by phone. But if life insurance remains a mystery to you (even after reading the previous pages!), or you need complex estate-planning advice, WIN will refer you to a fee-only insurance adviser or financial planner. That person will help you choose appropriate low-load insurance for a fee that's generally less than you'd pay in sales commissions.

WIN offers policies in all states but Oregon. There, a monopolistic agent-protection law keeps out all low-loads except those sold by USAA.

YOUR ONE-STOP LIFE INSURANCE ANALYZER

Rely on the Consumer Federation of America (CFA). That's the only place I know where you can get an unbiased analysis of cash-value life insurance at a reasonable cost. It evaluates any proposal you get from a life insurance agent or company, be it a proposal to buy a new policy or to replace or restructure one you already have. It also tells you what your present policy earns and what it's projected to earn in the future.

That knowledge is power. You'll know whether your present policy should be replaced, whether it's better to invest outside the policy or add more money to its tax-protected cash value, and which of two competing policies makes more sense. You will also get a handwritten note from CFA's consulting life insurance actuary, James Hunt, giving his opinion of your policy and—if appropriate—suggesting a better choice.

Send your request directly to James Hunt, 8 Tahanto St., Concord, NH 03301. Make out the check to the CFA Insurance Group. At this writing, you pay $40 for the first analysis and $30 for each additional analysis asked for in the same letter. He charges $75 if the policy is second-to-die (page 307). Don't send the policy itself. Send a stamped, self-addressed envelope, your evening telephone number, and the following information:

For a New Cash-Value Policy. Send the computerized policy illustration you should have received from the life insurance agent (if you don't have an illustration, get one). It should show your age, sex, smoking status, the policy's face amount, annual premium, and the projected cash values and death benefits, year by year, for at least 20 years. If possible, send a proposal without any riders for such things as disability or accidental death. Alternatively, show the cost of such riders separately. The agent can do that for you.

For a Cash-Value Policy You Already Own. Send an "in-force" or "current" illustration, which the company or agent can get easily. It shows your policy's future cash values and death benefits, based on current dividends or investment returns and costs. Hunt also needs the separate cost of any riders. It should be broken out on your policy illustration, the cover page of your insurance policy, or the most recent annual policy report that your insurance company sent. Hunt can also work with the original policy illustration or the original Statement of Policy Cost and Benefit Information if the policy is no more than 2 or 3 years old.

For further information on the service, call the Consumer Federation of America at 202-387-0087. Hunt has also written an excellent book for CFA called *Taking the Bite Out of Insurance*, $15.

SHOULD YOU INVEST IN CASH-VALUE INSURANCE?

Consider It, If . . .

1. You have used up all the tax-deductible, tax-deferred savings available to you. Company retirement-savings plans, deferred compensation,

Keogh plans, and deductible Individual Retirement Accounts are better deals than cash-value insurance. So is the Roth IRA (page 868).

2. You don't expect to need the savings in your life insurance policy for a long time—at least 15 years and often more. That's how long it usually takes for an agent-sold policy to earn a decent return. Low-loads can earn a decent return in about 10 years. (Some 50 percent of policies are dropped within 10 years and 75 percent within 20 years, which makes most of the agent-sold policies money losers.)

3. You can afford all the insurance protection that your family needs.

4. You are content to earn annual tax-protected returns similar to those paid by quality corporate bonds or longer-term certificates of deposit. If you reach for higher returns by buying stock-owning variable life, you must be prepared to hold for the 15-plus years it could take for this strategy to work.

5. You'll buy a low-load product, or have the agent-sold policy analyzed by the Consumer Federation of America before you start pouring money into it.

An Investment Q&A

Question: What's a better retirement-savings strategy, good cash-value insurance or term insurance plus a tax-deferred annuity (page 886)? *Answer:* Good cash-value insurance. Both investments give you insurance and tax-deferred savings. But taxes are owed on earnings withdrawn from the annuity, either before or after death. With life insurance, by contrast, money can be borrowed or withdrawn untaxed. No taxes are ever due on the policy if you keep it until you die.

Question: What's a better long-term investment, good cash-value insurance that pays a tax-protected rate of interest or term insurance plus a no-load (no sales charge) mutual fund invested in stocks? *Answer:* Probably term insurance plus a mutual fund, assuming that you pick a good fund. Over long holding periods—10 to 15 years and more—stocks outdo fixed-rate investments. You get some tax deferral from mutual funds, too, simply by not selling them.

Question: What's a better investment, variable universal life insurance invested solely in stocks or term insurance plus a no-load mutual fund? *Answer:* In both the short and medium term, term insurance plus a mutual fund. The heavy costs of variable life drag down its yield. In the long term (15 to 20 years), the variable insurance has a shot at doing better because of the tax deferral. But it's a gamble. The higher your income-tax rate, the more attractive the life insurance option.

Question: What's a better 10-year investment, good cash-value insurance or term insurance plus a 10-year bond or certificate of deposit? *Answer:* Compared with the average insurance policy, term insurance plus the bond or CD. Over short holding periods, the expenses built into cash-value insurance reduce its return. Over longer periods, however, good cash-value insurance should outperform because its return is tax-protected. *Exception:* A low-load universal policy, with minimal sales expenses, should beat term insurance plus a CD even over the shorter 10-year period.

Question: What's the better investment, good cash-value insurance or term insurance plus a tax-deductible Individual Retirement Account? *Answer:* Term plus the IRA. Ditto for term insurance plus other tax-deductible retirement accounts. Life insurance tax-defers the earnings in the policy but you can't deduct the money you spend on the policy itself.

SINGLE-PREMIUM LIFE: A GREAT INVESTMENT FOR SOME PEOPLE

You are exactly the right person for a single-premium cash-value life policy if you (1) are over age 59½ (or soon to be), (2) are well fixed financially, (3) want to leave even more money to your beneficiaries, but (4) want a fallback in case you should need extra cash. If you nodded your way through all four points, read on.

You might think of this deal as a tax-deferred annuity wrapped in a life insurance shell. You put up a lump sum of money—as little as $5,000 but more often $20,000 to $50,000. You get insurance plus a large pool of cash values, the amount depending on the company and your age. Most true single-premium policies are universal life, so you have to put in a substantial premium relative to the death benefit to be sure it works.

With straight universal life, your investment will earn interest at a rate fixed by the insurance company, usually changing once a year. That rate ought to compete with longer-term bank certificates of deposit. With universal variable life, you pick your own investments, choosing from stocks, bonds, and money market funds.

If you bought a single-premium policy before June 21, 1988, congratulations. You can use your investment profits without paying any taxes on them, just by borrowing against the cash value. If you ever cancel the policy, however, taxes will fall due.

The free-borrowing loophole was closed for newer single-premium policies, also known as modified endowment contracts. On those issued since June 21, 1988, any loans or withdrawals up to the amount of money that the policy has earned must be treated as taxable income. If you are under age 59½ and not disabled, you also pay a 10 percent penalty on any earnings you borrow or withdraw.

Still, these are good investments for people who don't expect to borrow against them or withdraw any funds. The cash in the policy grows tax deferred (tax-free, if you hold until death). If you find you need some of this money, and have to withdraw it and pay a tax, so what? You are probably still leaving more for your heirs than if your investment had slept in a certificate of deposit.

Warning: Some companies are trying to re-create the old-style single-premium policy by combining it with a freestanding tax-deferred annuity. You pay a single premium. Part of your money goes for life insurance, the rest goes into the annuity. Over the next 6 years the annuity pays your life-insurance premiums. After that, you have a "paid-up" policy. You can borrow against it anytime you want, with no taxes due, because you didn't pay for it all at once. The drawbacks: (1) You owe taxes on the annuity interest every year; (2) the policy is not truly paid up (at some point, you might have to put in more money to keep it alive); (3) you're buying a whole life policy that pays the agent a high sales commission; and (4) the government may rain on your parade at any time. This policy attracts people who will waste their money on practically anything if they see a tax angle to it.

RIDERS TO YOUR POLICY

A rider is a policy benefit that you purchase separately. Here are the most common ones.

Waiver of Premium—pays your insurance premiums if, before a certain age (usually 65), you've been totally disabled for 6 months. It's a worthwhile buy unless you have ample coverage from a separate disability-income policy (page 415). Ask what the insurer means by "disabled." Typically, the rider is triggered only if you can't handle any work at all.

Accidental Death Benefit—pays off in the unlikely case that you die in an accident. People buy it like a lottery ticket, but it's not worth the price.

Cost of Living—raises your death benefit annually in tandem with the Consumer Price Index, without your having to take a health exam. Where there's a charge for the rider it's a waste of money, in the opinion of the Consumer Federation of America. For better protection, buy paid-up additions (with whole life) or take Option B (with universal life).

Guaranteed Insurability—lets you buy more insurance, at standard rates, without taking a health exam. You have to buy certain amounts at certain ages; if you skip a buying opportunity, you don't get it back. This rider is generally available only to people under 40, and usually with cash-value policies (not term insurance). It becomes valuable only if (1) your health gets so bad that you can't buy normal coverage *and* (2) you think you might need substantially larger amounts of life insurance. CFA advises you to forget the guaranteed-insurability option. If you expect to need more coverage, buy it now in the form of extra term insurance.

Term Insurance—attached as a rider to a cash-value policy, to provide extra coverage for you or your spouse. Some riders are expensive, others aren't. Check their rates against the term prices on page 285.

SIX WAYS OF HANDLING INSURANCE POLICY DIVIDENDS

You get dividends with whole life insurance, rarely with term insurance or universal life. Use your dividends to . . .

1. Buy small "paid-up" additions to your whole life policy. This is my favorite use of dividends for people with families to protect. The paid-up additions give you extra insurance without deducting any sales charges. There's no medical exam, so your coverage can grow even if your health declines.

2. Take the money in cash. It's not taxed unless you have a modified endowment policy or in the unlikely event that the dividends you take in cash exceed the premiums you paid.

3. Reduce your annual premium.

4. Buy extra term insurance, good for one year. Only a few companies offer this option. You have to weigh the value of buying with pretax dollars against the policy's cost. It may be cheaper to buy your term from another insurer.

5. Reduce your policy loan.

6. Open a savings (or "accumulation") account with the insurance company, where your dividends will accumulate and earn interest. You can use this money whenever you want (although you can't always get it fast). At your death, it passes to your beneficiaries. The dividends aren't taxable but the interest is. Because of the taxes, this is generally a poor choice. Some agents suggest it, however, for a devious reason. They plan to call you in a few years and persuade you to use this money to buy more insurance. What a bum deal! If you simply buy paid-up additions (strategy #1), you avoid any taxes, eliminate sales commissions, get more insurance to leave to your family, and earn more on the money you invest.

PAYING PREMIUMS

It's cheapest to pay whole life premiums annually. Next best is usually monthly payments drawn automatically from your bank account. You can also pay quarterly or semiannually. When you don't pay annually, however, you pay an undisclosed interest charge, typically running from 8 to 18 percent (and occasionally higher).

You pay into universal policies anytime you want, with no effective interest charge. Sometimes, however, there's a processing fee of up to $2 for every payment, which punishes you for making a lot of small payments.

WHAT HAPPENS IF YOU QUIT PAYING PREMIUMS?

With whole life, there are two possibilities. (1) When you buy the policy, you arrange for an automatic loan provision. If premiums aren't paid, the money is borrowed from the cash value, keeping your coverage in force. When the loan limit is reached, your policy lapses. You may or may not get a bit of money back. (2) If there's no automatic loan provision, your insurance stays in force for 31 days after the date the unpaid premium was due. If you die during that period, your survivors get the full payoff minus the missing premium. After 31 days, the policy lapses. The company sends you a check for its cash-surrender value.

With universal life, the insurer automatically takes money from cash value to cover the unpaid premiums. You're insured until your cash value has been used up.

When cash-value policies lapse, it's possible that you may owe a tax (page 340).

INCONTESTABILITY

Once you've held your life insurance policy for 2 years, it's generally impregnable. Your survivors get the payoff, even if you made misstatements on your application.

If you misstated your age, the payout will be adjusted to reflect how old you really were. Tell your beneficiaries where to find proof of your age in case a mistake is made on your death certificate.

SUICIDE

Your survivors get no payoff if you kill yourself within 2 years after taking out the policy (the exact time limit depends on the policy and state law). The insurer merely pays your premiums back, sometimes with interest. But after that, you can swallow poison or jump out a window and your survivors will collect in full. Aren't you glad you asked?

PAID-UP POLICIES

A "paid-up" policy is (1) cash-value coverage (2) *guaranteed* to last for the rest of your life (3) with no further premiums due in cash. This idea appeals to many people. They'd like to quit paying premiums when they retire or when they start sending their children to college. To reach this blissful state, they pay extra-large premiums for 10 or 15 years and then stop. From that point on, a true paid-up policy carries itself. All further premiums come from the policy's own dividends, earnings, or cash values.

But how certain is your policy's paid-upness? With both whole life and universal life, you can get a rock-solid guarantee but only by paying a high enough premium while you're building the policy up.

Many buyers *think* they're paying enough. Your agent may say that your premiums will "vanish" after a certain year. But if interest rates fall, all that vanishes will be your insurance agent's promise. With whole life, you'll have to keep paying premiums or else your policy will lapse. With universal life, you can stop paying premiums but because your policy is underfunded, it may collapse before you die. (For more on vanishing premium scams, see page 333.)

To avoid this problem, tell the agent that you want to fund the policy right up to the guaranteed level.

So that's how to achieve paid-upness. My question is, why would you want to? It feels good psychologically, but financially, it's dumb to pay current expenses (your premiums) with tax-sheltered dollars (your policy's dividends and earnings). You're also suppressing the growth of your policy's death benefit and cash value. The death benefit might actually decline.

Taxwise investors, who own attractive policies, pay premiums out of cash savings and let their insurance savings grow. If you need extra money in retirement, you can always borrow against your accumulated cash value.

POLICY LOANS

You can borrow from the insurance company, using the cash value of your insurance policy as collateral. If you die without repaying the loan, the loan proceeds and all the compounded interest are deducted from the death benefit. So your survivors get less.

Life insurance loans are often said to be cheap, cheap, cheap. But that's usually not true. For the scoop on the true cost of policy loans, see page 321.

Universal policies give you the option of taking money directly out of the cash value rather than borrowing against it. There's a fee—maybe $25 —and often a partial surrender charge. Your death benefit is reduced by the amount withdrawn, but you save yourself the loan interest cost.

Withdrawals make sense if you don't expect to repay the money. You can probably take a substantial amount before incurring income taxes (check with your agent or company on this and other tax effects). But be sure you don't withdraw too much. You need enough cash in the policy to keep it from falling apart (page 300). If you eventually decide that you want to put the money back into the policy's cash value, you'll have to pay a sales commission.

If you think you will repay the money, take a loan. Loans avoid the partial surrender charge. There's also no sales commission on repayments. With universal policies, you can use your premiums to repay the loan.

Borrowing When Your Insurance Company Is Shaky. Borrow, borrow, borrow every dime you can before the regulators move in. In every insurance-company collapse so far, policyholders had their cash values slashed but no one tried to collect on any outstanding loans. There's a risk that attitude might change. But so far, loans have proven to be a way of getting your capital out.

Why You Should Repay an Insurance Policy Loan. Many people don't. It sits there for years, costing increasingly more interest. You may even lose track of the size of your debt. When you die, however, your family will learn how much you owe. The loan plus the interest will be subtracted from the death benefit they get.

It's smart to repay a policy loan, especially if the loan keeps you from earning higher dividends or interest on part of your policy's cash value (page 295). The money you put back will earn that higher rate tax-free, which is more than it earns in a taxable bank certificate of deposit. When you die, all that money returns to your heirs and you've saved them a lot of interest expense. People don't think of switching their CD money into their policies, but it's a sound strategy today. If you own a whole life policy, you can use its dividends to pay down the loan.

If you own a universal policy and can't repay the loan, restructure it. Create a smaller policy—smaller death benefit, smaller cash value, no debt—and save yourself the future interest payments. One exception to this advice: you wouldn't want to restructure if you're liable for a large surrender charge.

Here are the rules on tax-deducting the interest you pay on life insurance loans:

• If you let the interest compound inside the policy instead of paying it out of pocket, it's not tax deductible.

• If you pay the interest out of pocket and use the loan for college or consumer purchases, it's not deductible.

• If you pay the interest and use the proceeds to make other investments, you can deduct the interest to the extent that you have net taxable income from investments.

• If you pay the interest and use the money in an unincorporated business in which you're actively involved, it's deductible as a business expense. If you have a regular corporation, it's treated as investment interest.

• If your corporation owns the policy and borrows against it, loan interest is deductible within limits (check with your accountant).

• If you have a modified endowment contract (page 341), your loan (as well as any withdrawals or use of your policy as collateral) creates taxable income up to the amount that the policy has earned. You'll also owe a 10 percent penalty unless you're over age 59½ or disabled.

QUITTING

If you cancel a cash-value policy that you've had awhile, you'll get some money back. There are four things you can do with it:

1. Put the cash in your pocket. You'll owe income taxes on any gains (page 341).

2. Restructure it into a smaller, paid-up insurance policy. It can sit there for life without your putting any more money in. This is an excellent option if you want to stop paying premiums while retaining your insurance-policy investment.

3. Convert the policy to term insurance. You'll be covered for as long as the money lasts. The price of this "extended term" option is usually high, so choose it only if you're ill and think you won't outlive the benefit. Otherwise, buy a new term policy from a low-cost company.

4. Exchange it (in a tax-free "Section 1035" exchange) for a tax-deferred annuity. If you paid more into the policy than you're getting back, your insurance investment shows a loss. You should be able to transfer that loss directly to the annuity, where it can be used to tax-shelter some future investment gains. To see that this happens, ask the insurer, "What is my investment in the contract?" After the exchange, ask the annuity company, "What value for my annuity do you show on your books?" Both numbers should be the same. *Warning:* Sometimes the annuity company mistakenly enters your investment as zero. If that happens, you will be taxed on everything you withdraw, including your original principal.

If you have a taxable gain on your insurance investment, exchanging it for an annuity postpones the tax.

COLLECTING

When cashing in a policy or collecting its death benefit, there are usually four ways of taking the money. Don't lock your beneficiary into any of these options in advance. You can't predict which one will work out the best.

1. *A lump sum.* This is best for small payments, for money you'll put in your checking account (if your bank pays more interest than the insurer does—see item number 2), and for people who want to invest the proceeds themselves.

2. *Interest only.* You park the proceeds with the insurer in an interest-paying account. That's a good place for money you're still deciding what to do with, provided that the insurer pays more interest than you'd earn in a bank or money market mutual fund. (Some insurers rush you a checkbook so you can pay bills with the proceeds immediately. If you accept, however, you might not get much interest on your policy proceeds.)

3. *Installment payments.* The insurance company pays you in regular installments of interest and principal. You can arrange for a fixed amount per month or for payments over a fixed period. You'll want a competitive rate of interest and the right to change the size of the payments when it suits you.

4. *A life annuity.* This method of payment guarantees you (or you plus a spouse or partner) a fixed and guaranteed monthly income for life. You can also arrange for payments to go to a beneficiary if you die before a certain number of years have elapsed (typically 10). But inflation will wear down fixed payments that last for much more than 10 years. So you wouldn't want the bulk of your money in an annuity unless you're, say, over 75. Nor would you choose an annuity if you're in poor health because you might not live long enough to collect very much.

You might want an annuity, however, if you've cashed in a policy that contains a large taxable gain. The annuity spreads the gain—and the taxes—into the future. For more on annuities, see page 886.

Best tip on this page: Before converting your insurance proceeds into an annuity with the same insurance company, check what other insurers are offering. Some companies pay much more per month than others (page 342). You might raise your income by taking your payout in a lump sum and buying an annuity from someone else. If you buy from the company that wrote the life insurance policy, check that your monthly payment is fully guaranteed. Some companies guarantee only a minimum payment, with the rest of your income linked to the size of the company's dividend.

RATING YOU FOR RISK

You don't smoke? Good news. You will live longer and will get a break on your life insurance rates. At some insurance companies, nonsmokers are further divided into preferred and nonpreferred risks. Preferred nonsmokers pay the least. Some term insurers break down the top group even further, into preferred and super-preferred—based on careful medical testing and family history. There are also preferred and standard smokers. Next step for accepting or rejecting applicants: genetic testing, unless Congress outlaws it (it has been outlawed for limited types of health insurance but not for life insurance). And the step after that? Only immortals need apply?

Obviously, risk categories aren't as clear as they used to be. You may make the best class at one insurer but only the second-best class at another. But the second-best class might be called "preferred," leading you to believe that you're getting the lowest rate.

So find out exactly what categories the company has and where you stand. If you're in good health, and are rated "standard" instead of "preferred," resist, resist. These classifications are idiosyncratic and vary a lot from one insurer to another. Shoppers using an agent should ask him or her to try different companies. Sometimes the first company will move you up in class to close the deal. If you're buying term insurance through a quote service, check with several of the companies on your best-buy list. You have options when you're truly in good shape.

You will and should pay more, however, if you've recovered from cancer, a heart attack, or other serious health problems, manifested various mild but chronic conditions, come from a family that has a history of disease, or go skydiving on weekends. You're what the industry calls a rated risk. People with HIV or recent cancer or heart problems probably won't be able to get insurance at all.

Most companies nowadays put every applicant through a blood and urine test. Besides disease, they look for hard drugs, liver damage that can reveal a problem drinker, and nicotine in the blood of people claiming not to smoke. If your condition is suspect, they may order more tests. They also check your reported medical history at the Medical Information Bureau.

Here's What to Do If You're a Rated Risk:

1. Challenge any data you think is wrong. There may be an error in your file at the Medical Information Bureau (MIB) (page 412). The insurer has to tell you if you're turned down for coverage or charged a higher premium due to something on your MIB report. If you write to MIB within 30 days, you're entitled to a free summary of your report.

2. Don't meekly accept a higher premium on an individual policy. Shop around. One company might quote a high price to a person with high blood pressure. Another, believing that the condition is under control, might give that same person a standard rate. Most quality companies have several reinsurance outlets to which they'll refer your case for quotes. Ask whether this was done and what kind of rating you received.

One warning: Some insurers specialize in writing standard-rate policies for people with medical problems. But they're often expensive. You might pay less for a "rated" policy from a quality insurer.

3. Don't work with the captive insurance agent of a single company. He or she will rarely get you the best price. Go to an independent agent. In

fact, go to two. They typically work with different companies. If each of them knows that someone else is bidding for the business, they'll both work a little harder for you.

4. Look for trade or professional groups you can join. There's usually a medical questionnaire, but you may be charged less than you would for an individual policy.

5. Try to buy extra coverage through your employer.

6. If your health has improved, shop around again for coverage. A person who had a stroke five years ago, with no further symptoms or recurrence, might get a new policy at a standard rate. The same might be true five years after a heart attack, or after being cured of certain types of cancer.

7. You may have access to credit-life insurance as long as you're not on your deathbed. You might, for example, buy a car on credit and insure the loan. If you die, the insurance company will pay. But credit-life policies are growing more restrictive, so don't buy without checking the health requirement and the limitations on payment (page 293).

8. If you can't get normal insurance, even at a higher price, look at no-turndown, "guaranteed-issue" policies that take all comers. You can sometimes buy up to $25,000 in coverage just by signing a check. But don't expect a terrific deal. These policies are priced to include the obese, people with HIV, and other uninsurables, so they're hugely expensive for the benefit you get. What's more, you have to live for a while before your beneficiary can collect in full. If you die within 2 years of purchase, some policies merely repay your premiums plus interest (unless you die in an accident). Other policies pay graded benefits: 10 to 30 percent of the death benefit if you die in the first year, 25 to 60 percent in the second year, and full payment from the third or fourth year on.

Small burial policies are sometimes touted to seniors at, say, $10 a month. That buys maybe $1,000 in coverage for a 65-year-old, and less as you get older. At age 70, your coverage might drop to $700. By 71, you'd have paid a total of $720 for coverage worth only $700. After that, every month you keep that foolish policy, you're losing money.

Healthy People Should Stay Away From No-Turndown Insurance. You may be tempted by a flyer you get in the mail or an ad you see on TV: instant coverage for a mere $6.95 a month. Don't respond. The same money can buy you better coverage somewhere else.

WOMEN AND RISK

On average, women live longer than men, so they get lower life insurance rates. But how much lower? Some insurers charge close to the male rate, others charge quite a bit less. Most insurance is sold to men, so it's hard to know how well an agent knows what's available for women. You have to do a lot of shopping around, especially if you're 40 and up.

Montana is a special case. It has unisex rules that average women's rates with men's. As a result, women pay more than they'd normally have to for life insurance (although less for health and disability insurance). You can buy cheaper life coverage out of state, but only from companies not licensed to do business in Montana. That diminishes your consumer protection.

Life insurance bought through employers also carries unisex rates. Women will probably do better with a quote service (for term and low-load cash-value, page 292) or an insurance agent.

SHOULD YOU SWITCH POLICIES?

This is one of the hottest arguments in life insurance today. When you switch policies—the industry calls it replacement—you pay the sales commission and other expenses all over again. That's dandy for the agent but a downer for you because the commission comes out of your tax-protected cash value. Your new policy has to pay much higher interest or dividends than your old one did just to bring your investment back to where it was before the switch. Don't replace a policy without asking the Consumer Federation of America for its unbiased view of how the new and the old plans compare (page 342).

In general, six types of switching are going on:

SWITCH ONE. You have a modest cash-value policy and trade it in for a larger amount of term insurance. This may make sense for families that need more coverage but can't afford it unless they give their old policy up. But term insurance doesn't cost very much at younger ages. You can probably keep the old policy and add term on the side. Two good reasons for keeping the policy you've got: (1) It will probably earn a decent tax-protected return (unless it's a midget, in the $5,000 range); (2) you may need coverage in old age, when your term insurance will have lapsed. If you use whole life dividends to buy additional, paid-up insurance, your family can count on a higher payout every year. Another alternative to selling: turn the whole life insurance into a smaller, paid-up policy. You'll owe no more premiums and its cash value will continue to build tax free (page 320).

SWITCH TWO. You have a cash-value policy and trade it in for term insurance plus a mutual fund. That can be a wise choice if it means you'll buy funds, especially stock funds, through a tax-deferred retirement plan such as a 401(k). If you're investing outside a retirement plan, however, everything depends on the fund you pick. A good stock fund should outperform most insurance policies, but a bond fund probably won't. Even for the stock fund to work, you have to make regular investments over 15 or 20 years, so sign up for the fund's automatic monthly investment plan. If you abandon the plan, you'd have been better served by keeping the cash-value insurance.

I have to say a special word about agents from Primerica, a subsidiary of the Travelers Group, who specialize in Switch Twos. In the past they've been fined for making misleading statements to get you on board. For example, they may convince you that you have a worthless cash-value policy by leaving out dividends when projecting its future value. They may also claim, falsely, that you lose your cash value when you die; in fact, your family gets it when you buy universal life and choose Option B (page 301). In whole life policies, the value of the cash buildup is included in the price you pay. These Primerica agents probably aren't deliberately taking you for a ride. They're often part-timers who don't know a lot about life insurance and haven't been well trained. Their concept—buy term insurance and invest in mutual funds—may be right for you as long as you don't give up a good existing policy to do it. But there's something wrong when a company has been known to mislead. If you do choose this concept, you can find cheaper term insurance somewhere else and mutual funds without Primerica's sales charges. Before even considering a mutual fund, put the maximum into any tax-deferred retirement account you're eligible for.

SWITCH THREE. You have a term insurance policy and find another one with a much lower premium. This is a no-brainer. Switch. In fact, you should check term insurance rates every 3 to 5 years to find cheaper coverage. Companies with low rates for young people may not be the best for the middle-aged.

SWITCH FOUR. You have an older cash-value policy and your agent suggests that you switch to a newer and "better" one. He or she may be churning (page 333). Universal, variable, or dividend-paying whole life coverage usually shouldn't be replaced. If you need a larger policy, add coverage rather than giving up the policy you have. Here are the only candidates for possible change:

• Nondividend-paying whole life policies 12 years old or more that you know for sure have a poor return.

• Some older dividend policies from faithless companies. Longtime policyholders might earn lower rates of interest than new buyers get. The better policies have updated their dividends to give their older customers a better shake.

• Several small policies. You might (just *might*) get a better return by consolidating them into one large policy.

• Certain paid-up policies, especially if they pay no dividends. They may contain enough cash to buy a new paid-up policy for the same face value, with some money left over for an outside investment.

• A policy that's greatly overpriced, according to an evaluation by the Consumer Federation of America. You might get higher cash values and better performance by switching to a low-load policy.

• Policies in a shaky insurance company. You can swap to another company's policy in a tax-free exchange. But don't jump too quickly. Agents bad-mouth companies with falling safety-and-soundness ratings, but almost all of them recover.

SWITCH FIVE. You have been paying your premiums with money borrowed against your policy's cash value. What should you do with that policy, which is costing you interest every year?

1. You can die. Not recommended.

2. You can pay off the loan. If you can't pay it quickly, pay your premiums out of pocket and use each year's dividends to reduce your loan. The money paid into the policy may earn a competitive, tax-protected interest rate.

3. You can Switch Five. Swap to another policy in the same company or in a different company. It might offer the same face value but a lower cash value and lower loan. Or a lower face value and no loan at all. Swaps are normally tax free under tax-code section 1035. The IRS hasn't ruled on whether taxable income is created when a swap reduces or eliminates a loan.

4. Cancel the policy. If the money you receive, plus any policy loans you've taken, exceeds the premiums you paid, you'll owe income taxes on that excess amount. You could use the net proceeds to buy a substantial term-insurance policy covering the years of your family's highest need.

SWITCH SIX. You bought what you thought was a tax-deferred retirement-savings account but it turned out to be life insurance. If you cancel and buy a tax-deferred annuity, you get only a smidgen of your money back. Possible solution: exchange your policy for a low-cost annuity (page 886) in a tax-free 1035 exchange. You've taken a loss, but that loss can probably be carried over to your annuity, where you can use it to tax-shelter gains of an equivalent amount. Ask the annuity company if this is permitted, or consult a tax adviser. The IRS hasn't ruled on it yet.

Approach with Caution Any Comparisons Shown You by Agents Who Want You to Switch. There are a dozen ways to mislead you, and laypersons can't possibly spot the lie. Every day unprincipled agents churn the assets in somebody's insurance policy in order to earn a sales commission. So-called principled agents do, too, claiming they're doing a good deed by getting you extra life insurance. But they're raiding your cash values, which may be earning an attractive yield. Too many Americans are innocently turning in policies they should keep.

When you're replacing one policy with another, that fact should be marked on your new-policy application. Check to see that it is. If it isn't, assume that the sale is in some way disreputable. Otherwise, the agent wouldn't be hiding it from the company.

If the agent proposes to switch you to a new insurer, ask him or her to complete the Replacement Questionnaire (RQ) developed by the American Society of CLU & ChFC (that means Certified Life Underwriters and Chartered Financial Consultants—a.k.a. insurance agents) in Bryn Mawr, Pennsylvania. The RQ discloses what you gain and lose from a switch, which will help you decide. To get a free copy of the RQ, call the American Society at 800-392-6900. Be sure to ask for the Question and Answer pages that explain the RQ's purpose and list the specific questions the agent should be asked.

While you're on the phone, also ask for a free Life Insurance Illustration Questionnaire (IQ) or Variable Life Insurance Questionnaire (VIQ), depending on which type of policy you have or are thinking of buying. These forms provide basic information about the policies in question and are required for completing the all-important RQ in full.

If your agent can't figure out the RQ, IQ, or VIQ, or won't answer all the questions and explain to you clearly what they mean, you're dealing with either a dummy or a dastard. In that case, put the switch on hold. If you do get completed documents, keep them with your insurance records. If something goes wrong, they may be irrefutable proof that you were misled.

You might also show the switch proposal, along with the answers to the various questionnaires, to your current company, which will be happy to tell you anything that's wrong. Does the new plan offer lower premiums? (Maybe that's temporary.) Higher cash value? (Maybe the illustration was skewed.) Higher dividend rates? (But it may take years for the new policy to equal the cash value you have now.) Rising death benefits? No more premiums? (Your old company can arrange that, too.) Let the competing agents pick each other's proposals apart. Only problem: They might both blow sand in your eyes. So maybe you'd better ask the Consumer Federation of America instead (page 314).

What's the Best Way to Make a Switch? If you might owe income taxes on a policy you drop (because its cash value is larger than the premiums you've paid—page 340), don't cancel it outright. Instead, do a tax-free 1035 exchange. You can swap one policy for another, or swap from life insurance into a tax-deferred annuity. The agent or company will show you how. You can also swap a loss from one policy to another.

FINDING A LIFE INSURANCE AGENT

This subject makes my heart sink. Yes, there are many splendid life insurance agents in the United States. And yes, they can do wonderful work for you.

It's just that when I interview agents in the course of writing articles, I run into a lot of problems. Some agents don't know a lot about their policies and bluff. Some agents have been trained to mislead and are too thick to know it. Some agents know it and don't care. Some agents say they'll shop the market for you and don't. Some agents resist new information and ideas. Some agents assume that everyone needs to buy something, which isn't true. Some agents mean well but are sincerely and honestly wrong. Some agents have blind spots. Some agents will say anything to close a sale. (Sales commissions run from about 50 percent to more than 100 percent of your first premium, plus 5 to 10 percent of your renewal premiums, and maybe a bonus trip to Hawaii.)

On the other hand, some agents study for years to become technically competent, search out the best policies and strategies, care deeply about the ethics of their business, go to bat for you with the company, solve problems that have been pressing on you, encourage you to buy only what you need, keep your life insurance program up to date, research your questions to find the best answers, and help you squeeze the most out of every dollar you invest—for example, by selling you blends (page 299).

I don't know how to find one of these smart, straightforward insurance agents. You ask around. You interview. You try the following techniques to light a lamp against the dark:

1. **Find your agent yourself.** Don't take someone who cold-calls with a proposal, or comes with a reference from a friend that he or she just sold a policy to, or "happens" to bump into you on the street. There's small chance that these prospecting agents will be the smartest ones. Instead, ask your friends, business associates, accountant, banker, and lawyer who they think are the best life insurance agents in your community and why. Emphasize that you want competence and experience first. Agents with a Chartered Life Underwriter (CLU) designation have given the field more serious study than other agents.

2. **Draw up a short list of agents and make appointments to see them.** Take the questions you'd like to ask. You want full-time agents, in business for at least 5 years, who represent large, high-quality companies (10 consecutive years of top ratings from the insurance-rating services, page 342). CLUs are best. Younger agents should be working on their CLUs, with some of the ten CLU exams behind them. Ask about their histories—where they went to school, why they're selling insurance, where they previously worked.

Also ask: Do they do business with a primary insurance company? If so, what do they think of placing business somewhere else (if they generally don't, you'll have limited policy choices)? What kinds of policies do they like and why? How often do they attend continuing-education seminars or, better yet, do they teach them? How do they develop an insurance proposal? What roles do they think life insurance should play in a financial plan? What system do they have for keeping policies up to date, and who would service the business if they suddenly died? How are they paid—fees, sales commission, bonus compensation, trips and other rewards for achieving high sales? (Tell the agents that you expect to be told what they'll earn on the proposals they make to you.) How do they feel about policies that reduce commissions—specifically, blends (page 299). What are the names of two or three clients you could talk to? If the agent resents any of these questions, move on to the next name on your list.

While you're there, by the way, notice if the agent asked about you—your situation, your attitude toward insurance, what you're looking for. This should be a two-way interview.

3. Check up on what you've heard. Talk to the clients: Are they happy about everything? Any tips on working with the agent? If the agent sells variable life, he or she should have an employment and complaint file at the Central Registration Depository run by the National Association of Securities Dealers. Call your state securities regulator to find out what that file says (for the telephone number in your state, call the North American Securities Administrators Association at 202-737-0900). If the agent told you anything false about his or her past, bail out.

4. In the end, you'll pick an agent who feels right to you, but the conversation you instigated will, subtly, help you choose.

When you present yourself as a client, write down your general objectives and your attitude toward investments. Keep notes of your conversations with the agent and copies of all correspondence. Ask that all proposals be in writing, including any assertions about the policy that the agent makes. Keep all sales literature and all policy illustrations. If something goes wrong, this paper trail may help you get your money back.

Many financial planners also sell life insurance. All the caveats about insurance agents apply to planners, too.

Increasingly, employees can buy cash-value insurance at work. Apply the same tests to this coverage as you would to employee term insurance (page 286).

FINDING A FEE-PAID INSURANCE ADVISER

There aren't a lot of independent insurance advisers, but they're treasures when you come across them. Some are *fee-only:* they recommend only low-load policies and are compensated entirely by fees. Others are *fee-based:* they recommend low-loads and charge fees but also sell a few (just a few!) loaded policies, subtracting the sales commission from the fee the client pays. Typical fee: $100 to $250 an hour. That may sound pretty stiff but it's usually a bargain for people who need cash-value coverage.

Insurance agents often earn more in sales commissions than advisers collect in fees.

Let's say you're buying a universal life policy, paying $200 a month—$2,400 a year. An adviser might charge $1,250 ($250 an hour) for evaluating your need and setting you up with the right kind of low-load policy. The agent, by contrast, might take $2,400 in commissions and other expenses, plus $120 a year over the next nine years—nearly triple the adviser's fee. You don't notice how much you've paid the agent; it's tucked into the premium you pay. But it's clearly visible in your new policy's cash value. The agent-sold policy is probably worth zero the first year and $250 the second. By contrast the low-load policy could be worth around $2,300 the first year and $4,700 the second. After deducting the adviser's fee, you are still way ahead. Fee-only advisers can also be more objective about your needs because they get paid whether you buy something or not.

Fee-based advisers still have a conflict of interest—noticeable if they urge you to buy a load policy as well as a low-load.

Tax attorneys and accounting firms may know of fee-paid insurance advisers who practice locally. Or get a reference from the Wholesale Insurance Network (page 313). When you interview advisers, ask the same questions you'd ask of an insurance agent (page 330). Think twice about dealing with a fee-only planner who charges one percent of the policy's face value. That may be too high. It may also tempt the planner to recommend larger policies than necessary. Fee-only advisers should have *no* financial interest in the customer's insurance decision.

Warning: Plenty of insurance agents have their business cards reprinted to read "financial planner," "insurance adviser," or "actuarial consultant." They may present themselves as "fee-based," when most of their income actually comes from sales commissions. They may even duck the word "insurance" and falsely sell their policies as college- or retirement-savings plans. If your "adviser's" proposal shows a policy with little or no cash value in the first and second year, and you're told, "Congratulations, I'm reducing your fee," he or she is most certainly not a fee-paid planner. You've got a plain old commissioned salesperson pulling the wool over your eyes.

ROTTEN GAMES SOME AGENTS PLAY

In recent years, some of the country's largest insurers—including Metropolitan Life and Prudential Insurance—paid huge fines because some of their agents sold cash-value life insurance in a deceptive way. They did it to earn sales commissions and didn't give a fig for the people whose financial security they wrecked. Nevertheless, throughout the insurance industry, these practices continue. You might run into the following schemes at almost any insurance company:

Churning (or Deceptive Replacement). You have a cash-value policy. A new agent calls and suggests a free policy review. Or your old agent calls with a "routine update." Surprise, surprise—the agent finds that your policy should be replaced with one that he or she claims is better. When you replace, however, you pay the sales commission all over again. You also wind up with less cash value than you had before. Existing policies should almost never be replaced (page 326).

Piggybacking. You're especially vulnerable to piggybacking if you have a small policy with a relatively high cash value. An agent calls and says, "Would you like more insurance for the same premium you're paying now?" Sure you would. But the agent is lying. The cost of the additional insurance is borrowed out of your policy's cash value. Your cash value is further reduced by the commission the agent earns.

In a variant of this fraud, the agent says, "Would you like a second policy at a low bargain price?" If you say yes, you'll be paying full price but in a hidden way. The few extra dollars you pay per month cover only part of the new premium due. The rest comes from loans against your original policy's cash value.

If you notice the loans on your annual statement, your agent may tell you it's a mistake. But it's no mistake. Eventually, the policy's cash value will run out. At that point you'll lose your coverage unless you can start repaying your loan and/or increase—substantially—the regular premium you pay. If you complain to the insurer, the agent will claim that you knew exactly what you were doing.

Windowing. Agents get away with piggybacking because you signed a form agreeing to the policy loans. But maybe you didn't. The agent may have held your signature up to a window and traced it onto the loan-permission form. Or you might have signed a form in blank that the agent passed off as routine paperwork.

Vanishing Premium. You buy a whole life or universal life policy that you believe will be paid up in a certain number of years. To achieve this, you pay a larger-than-normal premium. Once you've built up a certain amount of cash value, you don't pay any more cash out of pocket. The policy's dividends or earnings are supposed to pay the premiums until you die.

But the agent "forgets" to tell you that if interest rates drop, the cash value won't grow large enough to do the job. To keep the whole life insurance, you'd have to pay premiums for many years more—a serious problem if you're retired and don't have much income to spare. With the universal life, you can indeed stop paying premiums on the target date but will probably have to resume in the future.

In a variant of this scheme, the agent might sell you a policy that lasts only to age 90. That lowers the premium payments to something you can afford but wipes out your life insurance if you live to a later age.

A good agent will explain how paid-up policies work (page 320) and whether you're running any risks. If there's a problem, he or she will alert you early so you can adjust your plan. A bad agent lets your insurance planning fall apart.

Retirement-Plan Scam. The agent approaches you with a so-called tax-deferred retirement plan. It may have a name that sounds like Individual Retirement Account—for example, "individual retirement benefit." The agent speaks of "deposits" or "contributions" and the tax-deferred buildup in your "savings plan." He or she may mention in passing that some death benefits are involved, but you get the idea that they're marginal. You think you're buying a tax-deferred annuity when, in fact, it's a straight cash-value life insurance policy. If you need retirement savings but don't need insurance, this purchase wastes your money. What's more, the whole sales presentation is illegal—illegal not to disclose that you're buying life insurance; illegal to pretend that your payments are contributions to a retirement account. If you have all this in writing, you ought to be able to get your money back.

Nursing-Home-Insurance Scam. See above. It's the same subterfuge under a different name. Older people are cheated into buying life insurance, thinking they're buying a policy to cover nursing-home expenses. The policy may indeed cover some of those costs, but the buyers are also paying for life insurance that they didn't need. They'd get much more protection from a pure long-term-care policy.

College-Savings Scam. See above. Same cheat, only this time the policy is presented as a college-savings account.

Pension Destruction, cynically called pension maximization. See page 923.

Web Scams. Rogue agents can create fancy home pages on the Internet and sell you anything they want. They might offer worthless insurance or insurance that doesn't exist, peddled from an offshore island beyond U.S. law. Their policies might not be licensed for sale in your state; the agents might not be licensed, either; if you buy and the insurer fails, you might not be covered by your state's guaranty fund. The Internet makes it harder for regulators to keep the bad guys out. Many legitimate companies and agents will also be selling on the Net, but don't send them any money unless you've established their legitimacy.

• • •

How can you protect yourself, with all these bandits on the prowl? Ask any agent who makes a policy proposal to make it in writing. Most misrepresentations are oral, hence deniable by the salesperson. A written document should reduce outrageous claims and preserve your legal rights. The letter should address the particular need the insurance is supposed to fill, describe the policy in full, explain how dividends will be used, state whether cash values will be used to cover premiums, explain the uncertainties of a vanishing premium plan, and say whether or not the insurance is guaranteed to last to 95 or 100. If the agent is replacing a policy, state laws require that the agent disclose the pros and cons. Enlarging the policy you have and using its cash value to fund another policy are forms of replacement that also trigger the disclosure laws. Keep all this material, including the notes you took during any conversation with the agent. If your policy goes wrong, it may help you get your money back.

In addition, don't sign any form that contains blanks or has boxes that are left unchecked. Always read the annual policy statement you get from the insurance company. Assume it's right, no matter what the agent says. If the agent claims it's wrong, write directly to the company president and be sure to keep a copy of your letter. Send a copy of your statement, report what the agent said about it, and ask for an explanation. You should get some action fast. (For the president's name, check your library, call the company's headquarters, or see if it has a home page on the Internet.)

You should also report any problems to your state insurance department, located in the state capital. If you can't find the number in the phone book, the information operator can help. States differ greatly in their response to consumer complaints, but it can't hurt to call and it might help.

How to Get Your Money Back If You've Been Scammed:

First, you need proof. Here are six ways to get it:

1. Check your original application, which should be in the back of your policy. One question reads, roughly, "Do you intend to borrow against, surrender, or discontinue any existing insurance," or "Is this replacement insurance?" If the agent said no, when in fact you gave up a policy or borrowed from your present insurance to finance additional coverage, that's fraud.

Your own bank and tax records can help prove that a replacement occurred. For example, the agent may have canceled Policy A, sent you a check, then had you write a new check for Policy B. (In some cases, canceling Policy A creates an income-tax liability. You can avoid it by using a tax-free rollover to Policy B. But that discloses the replacement. Agents trying to hide it will handle the transaction in cash.)

2. Check the policy illustration—the pages with columns of numbers showing how the policy works. There are two possible deceptions here:

First, the agent may have illustrated a policy for a healthy ("preferred") nonsmoker. But you might be a smoker or have a health problem that caused you to be a "standard," "rated," or "special" risk. If so, you're paying more for the insurance than the illustration assumes, so your policy can't accumulate as much money as you think.

Second, the pages should be numbered "page 1 of 4," "page 2 of 4," and so on. Or the illustration might say "not valid without footnotes." But the agent may not have given you all the pages or footnotes—usually to hide a required disclosure.

3. Check the sales material if you still have it. Was the sales proposal enclosed in a retirement-plan or college-plan binder? Was the policy called an investment rather than life insurance? Were your premiums called contributions or deposits? That's evidence of illegal deception.

4. Were you presented with official insurance-company sales material or material the agent embellished? Official company material will have a control number on the bottom of each page or on the back. Either way, you have a case, but company-wide deceptions could be a class-action case.

5. Write to the customer service or customer relations office of the insurance company for a copy of the "agent's report" which accompanied your application for insurance. The agent may have falsely said your policy wasn't a replacement.

If you were piggybacked, ask for a copy of the withdrawal and loan history on your older policy or policies, and payment history on your new one. They will show payments matching up.

6. If you didn't realize that loans were being taken against your policies, ask the insurer for a copy of the loan-authorization document. Check the signature carefully. The agent may have forged it by tracing your signature from another document. You might also have signed the form in blank for another purpose, not knowing that the agent planned to check the box authorizing loans. There may be a difference between your handwriting and the writing on the rest of the form.

When you write to the company, send copies of your evidence, not the originals. Send a copy of that letter to the state insurance department.

Even with evidence, a company might blow you off if you write yourself. Best advice: get a lawyer, competent financial planner, or honest insurance agent to write for you. Insurers listen harder when they know you've got muscle on your side. Be cautious about the agent or planner you choose, however. Some will look at your problem, shake their heads, and advise you to dump the policy. If you do, you've been churned all over again.

If you've been ripped off, what should you ask for? If you were churned from one policy to another within the same company, ask for your original policy back, with all loans canceled and all past dividends credited. Ditto if you were piggybacked. Victims of investment scams should ask for their money back plus interest so they can invest in something else.

Vanishing premium schemes are harder to fix. Insurance companies won't let your policy vanish on the schedule you accepted unless you have hard evidence that the agent gave you a guarantee (for example, maybe the agent wrote on your policy illustration "paid up in X years"). You'll probably grind your teeth and keep on paying. Many of these policies provide high tax-protected returns on policies held for 10 years or more. Try to restructure them if you can't pay the full premium. Ditto if you were churned into another insurance company, which makes it impossible to restore what you formerly had.

THE "PRIVATE PENSION PLAN"

Should you buy a universal life policy for retirement savings, even if you don't need the insurance? For sure, say many insurance agents, who'd sell to a corpse if it had any money.

Their rationale for the so-called private pension plan goes like this: The cash in a life insurance policy builds up tax deferred. You can take a certain amount of money tax-free at retirement. After that, you can start taking tax-free loans to supplement your other retirement income. When you die, your heirs get any remaining benefits tax-free. The tax advantage more than offsets the money you paid for the unnecessary life insurance. And the agents have policy illustrations (garbage-in, garbage-out illustrations) to prove it.

As you might have guessed, this neat little summary fails to consider several things:

1. If you don't buy insurance, what would you do with the money instead? Would you put it into a tax-deductible company retirement plan, where the company matches your contribution? If so, that's a deal absolutely nothing can beat. If the agent gives you an illustration showing that life insurance is better, the illustration probably leaves out the company match.

What if your company doesn't match your contribution? It's still smarter to fatten your retirement plan than to buy a life insurance policy, given comparable investments. On the surface, this doesn't seem to be so. You have to pay taxes when you take savings out of a retirement plan while insurance cash values can be taken or borrowed tax-free. In real life, however, it's dangerous to use any more than 70 percent of your policy cash values (see item 3), while every scrap of your retirement-plan money is on tap.

2. If you buy the insurance, will you invest the maximum annual premium to build up the highest possible cash value? If not, this scheme will probably blow up in your face. To make the sale, the agent might quote you a lower annual premium rate, counting on policy dividends or earnings to build the necessary cash values. But if interest rates fall, your cash value

will build more slowly than planned and might even start to decline. Your "private pension" would gradually erode unless you put substantially more money into the policy. If you decided not to, the cash value might decline so far that the policy would lapse. You'd have paid for insurance you didn't need and lost your "private pension," too.

3. Do you understand the implication of the loans? Once you've borrowed substantial amounts from your insurance cash values to provide yourself with a tax-free retirement income, you're locked into keeping that policy for life (or another policy taken in a tax-free 1035 exchange). If you drop the insurance, part of the money you've borrowed will become taxable income. Your tax bill could be large—maybe more than you could afford to pay. The same thing would happen if you borrowed so much that the policy eventually lapsed. To be on the safe side, you should borrow no more than 70 percent of the cash value, which may mean no more borrowing from about age 80 on. At that point, you'd still have to pay your annual premiums but your "tax-free income" would end. A straight savings plan, by contrast, could be tapped until any age—and with no premiums to pay.

When illustrated on paper, a "private pension" can be made to look better than an Individual Retirement Account. But real life has hijacked a lot of life insurance tax-avoidance schemes. This is a risky program that could ruin your finances in the end.

INSURANCE ALIVE

It's a pity that the only way to collect on your life insurance is to die. Such a pity that the industry has come up with a product that pays off while you're still alive.

It's a "living benefits" provision. Some insurers let you withdraw part of your policy's face value if you're struck by one of half a dozen dread diseases (stroke, terminal cancer, AIDS, Alzheimer's, heart attack, kidney failure) or dread operations (cardiac bypass, organ transplant). Others pay if you're diagnosed as having only 6 to 12 months to live. Yet others supply monthly benefits for the rest of your life if you enter a nursing home. This is not a policy loan. You receive actual, tax-free death benefits in advance —either part of the policy or almost all of it, depending on what your insurer allows. When you die, your beneficiary gets whatever is left.

Living benefits are available with many cash-value policies, some term policies, even some group policies. Some insurers add these benefits to every new policy sold, at no extra charge; some have applied them to old policies retroactively; some charge nothing extra but require you to ask for the benefits when you buy; some charge for the benefits separately; some charge nothing up front but impose a fee when the payout is taken. Many people don't even know that they have living benefits in their policies.

Who might be interested? (1) Those at risk for AIDS or for getting a fatal disease that runs in the family. (2) The middle-aged who worry about serious illnesses. (3) A small business that could use the policy to buy out a partner who's terminally ill. (4) Older people concerned about nursing-home expenses. A nursing-home living-benefits rider is cheaper than buying separate nursing-home insurance, but doesn't deliver the same level of benefits.

The drawback to living benefits is that you can't use the same life-insurance dollar twice. If you draw out money for the cost of a final illness, the policy will pay less to your surviving spouse. On the other hand, your spouse would have had to pay most of those bills anyway. You might need a larger policy if you want it to hedge against the risk of a lingering illness.

If you don't need life insurance (because you have no dependents), you don't buy it just for living-benefits life. One exception: Those at risk of getting AIDS. New drugs have made AIDS more survivable, but not everyone can afford them nor can you be sure they'll work. If you become terminally ill, you can use living benefits or sell your policy to a viatical company. If you don't, you can use the cash value for retirement.

VIATICAL SALES

A viatical company buys life insurance policies from the terminally ill, paying a discount from face value. The word comes from *viaticum*, the communion given to Christians who are dying or in danger of death. End-stage cancer patients and people with full-blown AIDS use these settlements most. A $100,000 policy might garner a cancer patient $60,000 to $80,000, tax-free.

The company, or the investors in a viatical policy, prefer dealing with people who, in a doctor's opinion, have less than a year to live. Some buyers accept patients with as much as 5 years to live, but the longer the probable life span, the less money the patient is going to get. At death, the investors collect the insurance proceeds.

Three important points if you're thinking about selling your policy: (1) You might receive so much money that you're disqualified from Medicaid and other government programs for low-income people. (2) You can sell just a portion of your policy, keeping the rest of it for your heirs. You can also keep the benefit paid for accidental death. (3) Different companies offer different prices, so you should shop diligently. Take the time to fill out several applications. Many thousands of dollars ride in the balance. There are two viatical associations, each of which will send you a free list of members: the Viatical Association of America in Washington, D.C., whose companies buy policies directly from sellers (800-842-9811 or 202-429-5129); and the National Viatical Association in Waco, Texas, which includes direct buyers and brokers (800-741-9465). Brokers shop the policy for you

—"free," they say, because the buyers pay the commission. But that cost reduces the payout you get. (For investing in viaticals, see page 785).

RAISING MONEY FOR THE TERMINALLY ILL

Don't turn immediately to your life insurance to cover household bills, home health expenses, and hospital care. At the start, there are better places to look.

Your first step should be to preserve any medical coverage you have. If you're insured at the job, and your company employs at least 20 people, you can continue the policy for 18 months at your expense. Second, turn to your disability-income policy (you bought one, of course). Third, apply for Social Security disability benefits. Fourth, sell assets that won't be of use to your heirs. If you're single and dying, for example, there's no point holding on to your investments. If you're married, you might still have to sell some investments in order to pay the bills. Fifth, use savings. Sixth, single people might take credit-card and home-equity loans, to be repaid from their remaining assets when they die. This is riskier for married people, who'd be leaving their spouses with extra debt. Seventh, see if your income is low enough to qualify you for Medicaid. Eighth, borrow against the policy or take living benefits. Some viatical companies will even lend against term insurance. A loan or a low withdrawal will leave some insurance for your family. A high withdrawal will probably net you more than you'd get from a viatical sale. Ninth and last, sell your insurance policy to a viatical company, accepting a discount from face value.

INSURANCE AND TAXES

Here's everything you didn't want to know about the taxes due on your life insurance.

The dividends paid on whole life policies come tax-free. If you reinvest them in more insurance (paid-up additions—page 298), they also accumulate tax-free. If you hold the dividends in a separate savings account, however, the interest they earn is taxable.

The interest or earnings credited to your cash values in universal life policies is tax-free.

If you withdraw dividends from whole life policies or interest from universal life, it's generally not taxed until it exceeds the premiums you've paid. Check on this before taking any money out.

You pay no taxes on money borrowed against virtually all policies on which you pay regular premiums. Partial withdrawals from universal policies may be taxable, however (page 301). Ask your agent or company about it.

Single-premium policies issued after June 20, 1988, as well as other policies that allow a fast cash buildup, are a special case. They're known as modified endowment policies. If you own one, you owe income taxes on loans you take against the policy up to the amount that the policy has earned. Ditto for any money received when pledging your policy as collateral. You owe a further 10 percent penalty on loans or withdrawals made before age 59½ unless you're totally disabled. In that case, you owe taxes but no penalty.

Beneficiaries pay no income tax on the policy proceeds they receive.

Any policy you own at death is part of your taxable estate. But the estate will not owe a federal death tax on the policy's proceeds if you're worth less than the current estate-tax exemption (page 118) or your estate is going to your spouse. State inheritance taxes may be due on smaller estates.

Normally, no estate taxes are due if, before you died, you gave the policy to someone else, like your children or a trust. If you die within 3 years of making the gift, however, the policy proceeds will still be counted as part of the taxable estate.

If you cash in the policy, you'll owe income taxes only on that portion of the payout (plus loans and loan interest) that exceeds all the premiums you paid minus any dividends not used to buy more insurance. So the money you earn on your insurance cash values is tax sheltered by the premiums you pay. If you cash in a variable insurance policy, it is treated the same way; you get some tax shelter but lose any special treatment given capital gains. Always ask about your policy's tax status before you surrender it.

You can transfer gains and losses to a new policy or a tax-deferred annuity tax-free (page 886).

STICK WITH SAFE COMPANIES

Buying life insurance is an act of faith. When you die—in 30 or 40 or 50 years—you expect some young kid, not yet born, to process your claim and send your family a check.

In general, that's been a good bet. But several insurers failed in the 1980s, including some big ones. What would happen if yours failed next?

• Your policies might be bought by another insurance company. Your death benefit would be safe, but your premiums could rise, you might lose some cash value, those cash values might not accumulate as fast as they did before, and it might be years before you could draw them out without penalty.

- If no other insurer buys your policy, you're protected—in whole or in part—by a state guaranty fund. It normally (but not always) pays death claims immediately and continues to make full payments to people currently receiving monthly annuity payments.

Not all states pay the same amount, however, and no state covers large claims. In general, the guaranty funds cap payments on individual policies at $100,000 for cash values or annuities, $300,000 for death benefits, and $300,000 for all claims combined. In a major bankruptcy, even these claims may not be paid right away because the guaranty funds don't have enough money. Your cash value could be frozen and some claims not paid, while the industry arranges a bailout. Dividends may be slashed or eliminated. The policy's internal expenses may soar.

- Not all guaranty funds cover the same things. They have different rules for covering out-of-state policyholders; different rules about people who move to the state and hold policies from companies not licensed there; different rules for annuitants; different rules about covering guaranteed investment contracts held in company retirement plans. How well you're protected depends on where you live.

- Even if your insurance company doesn't fail, a weak balance sheet could mean lower dividends and skimpier cash values in the years ahead. Cash-value investors might not get the returns they expected. Term-policy buyers might have to pay more for their coverage.

So buy only from a company with good-quality ratings from at least three of the five insurance-rating companies and no mediocre ratings. Almost every insurer will have a rating from A.M. Best, Standard & Poor's, and Weiss Research. Around 150 to 200 will also be rated by Moody's or Duff & Phelps. In general, A.M. Best is considered the easiest marker, followed by Duff & Phelps, then Standard & Poor's, then Moody's, then Weiss.

If a company has a good Best's rating but a zinger from Moody's, its agents may disseminate only the first. So here's how you can check all of an insurer's safety ratings yourself:

1. Ask the insurance company, directly, what the raters have said, mentioning each rating company by name. Unfortunately, you can't depend on the company to disclose mediocre ratings, either, but give it a shot.

2. Send for the special ratings issue of *The Insurance Forum,* P.O. Box 245-J, Ellettsville, IN 47429 ($15, at this writing). It shows each insurer's rating from every company except A.M. Best (Best won't let the *Forum* publish them). The *Forum* also explains the meaning of each rating, notes all cases where the raters disagree, publishes a Watch List of insurers that you might reasonably have some concerns about, and gives you three lists of companies with high safety ratings—one for *super*-conservative customers, one for the *very* conservative, one for the *merely* conservative.

Here are the ratings the *Forum*'s editor, Joseph Belth, calls "high": For super-conservative investors, A + + from A.M. Best, AA + and better from

S&P, Aa2 and better from Moody's, AAA from Duff & Phelps, B+ and better from Weiss. For the very conservative, A+ or better from A.M. Best, AAq and better from S&P, Aa3 and better from Moody's, AA+ and better from Duff & Phelps, B and better from Weiss. For conservative investors, A+ and better from A.M. Best, AA− and better from S&P, Aa1 and better from Moody's, AA and better from Duff & Phelps, B− and better from Weiss.

3. Call the rating services directly. Here's what you'll get: At Standard & Poor's, free ratings on up to five companies per call (212-208-1527). At Duff & Phelps, free ratings on up to five companies per phone call, $25 for a written report (312-368-3198). At Moody's, free ratings on up to three companies per call (212-553-0377). At Weiss, $15 for a rating by phone, $25 for a one-page report, $45 for a more detailed report (800-289-9222). At A.M. Best, $4.95 for each telephone rating and $15 for a written report (800-424-BEST to bill it to your credit card, 900-555-BEST [a $2.95 call] to bill it to your telephone). Best's is an automated system, so you'll need the insurer's exact name. When might you want a rater's written report? When the insurance company has less-than-top ratings and the agent tries to reassure you by quoting something favorable from the report. Agents are notorious for quoting the good things and burying the bad ones.

It's not enough to know that an insurer is rated, say, A+. You need to know how high A+ is in that particular rater's system. At Weiss, for example, A+ is the very top rating. At A.M. Best, it's the second rating down. At Standard & Poor's, it's the fifth rating down ("good," not "excellent"). When you telephone, every rater except A.M. Best has a human being on the line to explain the rating to you. You'll find each company's ratings (except for the lowest) ranked by relative strength in the box on this page.

THE INSURANCE RATING SYSTEMS*

Rank Number	A.M. Best	S&P	Moody's	Duff & Phelps	Weiss
1	A++	AAA,AAAq	Aaa	AAA	A+
2	A±	AA+	Aa1	AA+	A
3	A	AA,AAq	Aa2	AA	A−
4	A−	AA−	Aa3	AA−	B+
5	B++	A+	A1	A+	B
6	B+	A,Aq	A2	A	B−
7	B	A−	A3	A−	C+
8	B−	BBB+	Baa1	BBB+	C
9	C++	BBB,BBBq	Baa2	BBB	C−
10	C+	BBB−	Baa3	BBB−	D+†
11	C	BB+†	Ba1†	BB+†	D

* Lowest ratings not included. The ratings in each rank are not necessarily equivalent to each other.
† At this rating and below, *The Insurance Forum* puts the insurance company on its Watch List.

Should you reject a company with less than top ratings? Not necessarily. Of some 1,700 insurers in America, only a handful have ever failed. The second-tier companies aren't as financially strong as the companies in the top tier, but they're a long way from going broke.

If your company slips in the ratings, then slips again, ask for a written explanation. It's costly to swap policies, but at some point you might decide that you're willing to pay the price.

Here's a real shocker: You may have no control over which insurer ultimately owns your insurance policy or annuity. You might shop diligently for a blue-chip company, but in many states that company can transfer your policy to any insurer it wants without your permission. Some policyholders have been transferred to companies that ultimately failed.

If you get a letter saying that your policy is being transferred, check the new company's safety rating. If it's not up to snuff, write a letter to your present company saying, "I won't go." Some insurers disclose that you have this option, others don't. If your insurer tells you no option exists, call your state's insurance commission and complain. You could also transfer your business to a better company through a tax-free exchange, but that will cost you a new sales commission.

To minimize the risk of having your policy handed around, buy from a mutual insurance company (it has "mutual" in its name and is owned by its policyholders).

WHEN ALL IS SAID AND DONE, HOW WOULD I BUY LIFE INSURANCE?

I'd start with low-cost term insurance, expecting to cancel it when I retire or when my kids are grown and my spouse is self-supporting. I'd find the insurer through a telephone-quote service.

If I had some employee coverage, a small cash-value policy, and a family, I would hastily buy more term insurance to protect them.

I'd build up investments somewhere else—in retirement funds, stock-owning mutual funds, Treasury securities, and real estate—to guarantee my security.

I would buy no life insurance on any of my children.

If it seemed that I might need insurance after 65, I'd look at the cash-value policies sold by USAA or Ameritas Life.

If I decided to get fancy and invest in insurance, or buy insurance to pay estate taxes, I'd consider using a fee-only insurance planner.

If I had a universal policy, I'd check it every year to see if I'd been putting enough money in.

If I knew I'd hold a cash-value policy for 20 years or more, I'd look at low-load variable.

If I wondered how my policy was really doing, I'd have its rate of return checked by the Consumer Federation of America.

I'd pay the premiums on my life-insurance policy even in hard times. I owe it to the people who depend on me.

13.

The Health Insurance Lottery

Learning to Live with Rationing

You're paying more, getting less, and sore about it. More people every year slip into the limbo of the uninsured.

When it comes to decent medical coverage, Americans are cleanly divided into haves and have-nots. The haves work for companies that pay a substantial portion of their medical-insurance costs. The have-nots have to buy their own.

As neatly as dominoes, the have-nots are divided, too. They can either afford decent coverage or they can't. Anyone who can't should at least try to insure against major illnesses. You're dreaming if you think that the uninsured get equal care, especially if you're seriously or chronically ill.

The plans themselves, be they corporate or individual, either let you choose your own medical treatment or they don't. If not, you'll lose access to certain doctors, hospitals, treatments, and prescription drugs unless you pay for them yourself.

There's one last division—this one among the haves who are covered by employer plans. Your company either puts a high value on finding quality medical care or it doesn't. Employers *say* that they choose the best managed-health plans, but they may be kidding themselves and you. In many cases, their primary aim is to find the plan that costs the least.

The switch to managed care was inevitable. Neither individuals nor employers could afford the old system's galloping increases in cost. The modern medical system, and the rationing it imposes, works fine for some but not for everyone.

MODERN MEDICAL CARE: WHAT YOU'VE GAINED

This subject, along with female orchestra conductors and Herbert Hoover's best jokes, would make one of the world's smallest books. Managed-care plans save money compared with traditional fee-for-service plans. They dole out more insured services to healthy people: annual physicals, well-baby care, mammograms, vision and dental checkups. They're rooting out waste in the medical system. Their preventive care catches problems early, when they're easier to treat. What's more . . . mmmmm, er, . . . I've run out.

WHAT YOU'VE LOST

• You're less likely to have an insurance plan that is almost entirely company-paid.

• You're less likely to get company-paid benefits for your spouse and children.

• You probably have a limited choice of employee plans—meaning a limited choice of doctors and hospitals you can go to. More than half the time, workers have no choice at all.

• What's good for the goose (you) is unacceptable to the gander (the boss). Top executives often get cushy plans, offering every medical choice and mostly at company expense.

• Fewer employers cover part-timers, even permanent part-timers.

• You're paying a higher percentage of the group-plan insurance premium than you did in the early 1990s, and more cash out of pocket toward your bills.

• Plans that let you see a doctor outside the network are charging you more for it. They also charge more for any treatment that doctor prescribes. As a practical matter, you may find outside specialists too expensive to see.

• If you change jobs, you'll probably have to change medical plans. That often means finding new doctors, even if you're in the middle of a course of treatment. You may also have to change doctors because your company switched insurers. With patients switching around so much, it's easier for doctors to make mistakes.

• If you're retired, you're less apt to have a company-paid Medigap plan to pick up the bills that Medicare doesn't. If you're lucky enough to have one, you're paying more for it.

• In most states, individual health insurance is tougher to get. The policies cost more than they used to, yet require you to pay more out of pocket toward your bills. A few states require insurers to accept everyone, but there aren't many carriers to choose from and premiums are high.

- If you're in a managed-care plan, you can't be sure that you're always getting the best treatment for your illness. The plan may limit your access to the best specialists, limit some types of ordinary care, treat the illnesses of older people less aggressively, or refuse you a particular brand of drug that's most effective for you.

- You may have to leave the hospital in 24 hours or less, even if you've had major surgery. You can stay longer but your plan won't pay for it.

- Insured coverage for mental illness is being sharply curtailed. You might get just a handful of visits, a prescription for antidepressant pills, and referral to a self-help group.

- You pay more for individual coverage if you're in certain unacceptable jobs. Depending on the insurer, this might include housepainters, dancers, fishermen, musicians, and a host of others. In a few states, you can't get coverage at all. This was always true, but insurers are getting tighter than ever.

- You can't get individual coverage at regular rates if the tiniest thing is wrong with you. Ditto if you seek family coverage and one of your family members isn't in tip-top health. Insurers have always charged health risks more, but now they're taking no chances at all.

- Confidentiality is out the window. The doctor has to discuss your case with the insurer—including your personal, mental problems—to get authorization for continued care.

- Studies show that two groups don't do as well under managed care as under traditional plans: sick people who are old or poor. Younger people, people with more money, and people less ill do equally well in both types of plans. You, personally, may be just fine. But overall, the quality of American health care has declined.

- More Americans than ever are now uninsured. At this writing, their number exceeds 40 million at any one time. A majority work full-time or are the dependents of full-time workers. Around one-fifth work part-time. They usually hold lower- or lower-middle-income jobs, meaning they'll find it hard to pay their own doctor bills. They're almost all under 65 (older people have government health insurance).

HOW MUCH WILL HEALTH INSURANCE COST?

You'll pay a small fortune if you have to buy an individual policy. Premiums may start at $150 to $350 a month. Family coverage starts at $350 and runs up. You'll pay more as you age, and even more as your group of policies experiences more claims (page 363). Every year another half-million people join the ranks of the uninsured, usually because coverage costs more than they're willing or able to pay. Insured America stonily averts its eyes.

Employer-subsidized insurance is something else. You may be offered a choice of plans, some of them cheaper than the others. Whatever is on the company menu, you ought to find something you *can* afford. For typical costs and a discussion of the types of plans, see page 354.

When adding up what you'll pay out of pocket, in employer or individual plans, here's what to look for:

1. *The premium*—what you pay each month. Plans that cover your spouse and children cost more than individual plans. Employers typically subsidize part or all of your coverage, and often pay something toward the cost of insuring your children and spouse. The rest of the cost you pay yourself.

2. *The deductible*—how much you pay in a single year before the insurance plan kicks in. In employer plans, deductibles range from zero, for some health maintenance organizations (HMOs), to more than $600 for traditional fee-for-service family plans. Affordable individual plans have deductibles of $1,000 and up. The higher the deductible, the lower your cost.

3. *The co-payment, or "co-insurance"*—the amount you pay toward each medical service. Some co-payments are small. They might run $5 or $10 for every doctor visit at an HMO. But when HMO members go to doctors outside the network, they might pay 30 to 50 percent of the bill (page 365), up to a specified annual cap. On individual insurance, a typical co-pay is 20 percent.

4. *The annual cap*—the most you have to pay out of pocket in any year for your covered medical bills. It typically runs in the $2,500 to $3,000 range. Once you've spent that much, your plan pays your covered expenses in full. There are often two caps for HMO members: one if you see only doctors in the network and a higher one if you go outside the network. Some health plans have no annual cap; avoid them if you can.

5. *The lifetime cap*—how much the plan will pay in all. You should be covered for at least $1 million in total bills over your lifetime. With a deeply disabling illness or accident, however, you could blow through $1 million pretty fast. Some plans have lifetime limits for certain treatments or conditions. A small but growing number of plans set no ceilings at all.

6. *The annual limits*—plans often restrict what they'll pay for certain services. For example, there may be a dollar cap on dental bills or a max of 10 visits to a chiropractor. Anything more you pay yourself.

7. *The services not covered*—things you have to pay yourself. Every plan has a list of what's not covered. Some typical examples: cosmetic surgery, routine physicals, hearing aids, infertility treatments, rehabilitation therapy lasting more than 2 months, dental care, or experimental proce-

dures (the insurer gets to decide what's experimental). For the rules on covering preexisting conditions, see page 352. Some illnesses are excluded, period.

8. *The cost of choice*—relevant to managed-care plans. They have an approved list of doctors you're allowed to see. You might occasionally be referred to someone outside the plan. Otherwise, going outside the network will cost you a higher percentage of the bill—perhaps even all of it.

9. *The gender cost*—especially relevant to women. Younger women (under 45 or 50) typically have more claims than younger men, so they usually pay more for health insurance. All employer plans and many group plans sold by associations, however, charge unisex rates. There, women get a better break.

Please, Doc, Be Reasonable. Insurers draw up lists of the "usual and customary" charges for various medical services. That's the maximum they'll pay, even if your doctor charges more.

This rule can run up your out-of-pocket costs unexpectedly. As an example, say your insurer pays 70 percent of each doctor bill. The doc thumps your chest and charges $500. You figure the plan will pay $350, leaving $150 for you. But your plan may say, "No, for chest-thumping $300 is the usual fee." You're paid 70 percent of $300, or $210. The remaining $280 is all yours. What's more, that excess payment isn't counted toward your annual deductible. Ask your doctor if he or she will accept the insurer's version of what the fee should be. Some do—and should. Only around 20 to 25 percent of fees fall above the norm.

WHAT YOUR POLICY SHOULD COVER

Don't ever assume that everything is covered. It isn't. Inexpensive policies don't pay much at all, no matter what the advertising says. You need a comprehensive, major medical health insurance plan, either a traditional plan or an HMO. Here's what they both should cover:

• *The cost of basic hospital services.* This includes a semiprivate room, board, emergency room, nurses, intensive care, medicines, ambulance services, X-rays, and lab tests. If you take a private room, the extra cost is generally yours (unless your plan determines that it's medically necessary).

• *The cost of surgery,* including surgeons, assistant surgeons, anesthesiologists, and outpatient surgery, that are "usual and customary" for that area. If your doctor charges more, you pay the difference. You'll face no extra charge if your surgeon is part of your HMO.

Some policies pay a specified dollar amount for each type of surgical procedure, which is usually well below the doctor's actual fee. In this case, you will almost certainly have to pay more out of pocket.

• *The cost of outpatient care.* Take a good look at this section of your policy. Many procedures that used to require hospitalization are now "cut and run." To prevent infections and other ill effects, your policy should provide good home health support.

• *Part of the bill for home health care* that is ordered by your doctor.

• *Good coverage for children,* including stepchildren and foster children if you're responsible for their support. Check how long they can stay on your policy. Typically, they're covered up to age 19 if they're not full-time students and anywhere between age 21 to 25 if they are. Even after that, they may be able to stay in the plan at your expense. Children with mental or physical handicaps who can't support themselves should be covered permanently, as long as the disability occurred while they were still insured.

Children generally lose coverage if they marry. When they become ineligible, however, they may have the option of remaining in the plan at your (or their) expense—temporarily or permanently.

Find out what happens if the child goes to school part-time or drops out for a year (see page 362 for more on student policies). Notify your insurer or plan sponsor in writing if you're responsible for children who live elsewhere—for example, children who live with a former spouse.

• *Care for an infant from the moment it is born.* To get the child on your group health plan, you generally have to tell the insurer about the birth within 30 days. All group plans and most individual plans provide the infant with major medical coverage from the moment it's born. But they may not cover therapy for all birth defects.

• *Most doctor bills,* in full or in part. But the plan will cover only "usual and customary" charges, and the insurer decides (page 350).

• *Part of the bill for convalescing in a nursing home* after you've been in the hospital.

• *Part of the cost of prescription drugs.*

• *Part of the treatment for mental problems, drug abuse, and alcohol abuse,* although many plans are paring this coverage to the bone or subjecting it to strict oversight.

• *Most of the cost of incidental expenses:* physical therapy, oxygen, medical devices, and so on.

• *Part of the cost of oral surgery*—for example, for impacted teeth. But dental surgery usually isn't covered except under a separate dental plan.

Don't Accept a Simple Sales Brochure. HMOs, in particular, may airily say, "Everything is covered," and let you find out later what's not. Get a copy of the contract, showing exactly what's insured and how much of the bill you're expected to pay.

PREEXISTING CONDITIONS

In general, a "preexisting condition" is a problem that was diagnosed or treated—or was manifestly obvious—during the 3- or 6-month period before you bought the policy. The shorter the period, the better the policy.

If you have such an illness, or someone in your family does, it's important to know when the plan will start paying the bills.

Group policies: Health plans can impose a waiting period before any benefits start. Generous plans start your coverage right away or within 30 days. Others may impose longer waits.

Preexisting conditions have to be covered as soon as other benefits begin, if you previously had health insurance for at least 12 months and sign up for the health plan as soon as you join the company. Your previous insurer will give you a Certificate of Coverage, showing how long you've been insured. If you were covered for less than 12 months, the group plan can wait before covering preexisting conditions, but in any case no longer than 12 months. (Those periods can stretch to 18 months if you didn't join the health plan right away.)

Maternity benefits, however, always start when general benefits do; so do benefits for newborns and children placed in your home pending adoption.

To come under this federal law, groups need at least two employees. Group plans sold by associations are covered, too.

Plans can impose longer waiting periods or refuse to cover preexisting conditions if you previously had no health insurance. You're defined as having no insurance if you lacked coverage during the previous 63 days.

Around 18 states give various forms of protection to sole proprietors and the self-employed, ruling that they're "groups" of one.

No health plan guarantees coverage for everything. Insurers can exclude certain illnesses or cap payments for them, even after the waiting period, provided that they treat everyone alike.

Individual policies: If you previously had 18 months of coverage, most recently under a group health plan, and you're not currently eligible for a group or government health plan, you're entitled to buy a new individual policy that includes preexisting conditions, including pregnancy. Coverage starts on your policy's effective date. You purchase the plan through an individual insurer or a special high-risk pool and it ain't cheap.

Without that previous insurance, however, you're not entitled to coverage for preexisting conditions in most states—and that means trouble. Health screening can be astoundingly rigorous. The insurer might: (1) Refuse to cover a particular condition for a certain period of time. If little Eric has had two sinus infections this year, future infections might not be insured until he has been symptom-free for 12 months. (2) Refuse to cover a specific condition permanently. Two sinus infections might rule out that ailment for any coverage, ever. (3) Charge you more money. Mild high blood pressure, for example, will cause your premium to soar. (4) Reject you entirely. People who have had, say, diabetes, heart disease, or epilepsy probably will be turned down. You might not even get coverage if you've ever had psychological care, including—would you believe it?—marriage counseling.

Health underwriting is getting tighter every year. If you're financially capable of buying insurance, do so now, before higher barriers go up.

A handful of states require insurers to accept everyone, regardless of health. A few even prevent them from charging the sick a substantially higher premium. Both these rules are a godsend to people who otherwise couldn't get any coverage at all. But they raise average premiums, deductibles, and co-payments for the healthy, perhaps forcing some of them to go uninsured.

Dependents: The rules on preexisting conditions apply equally to your spouse and children. For example, say you divorce and your ex-spouse has a health problem. If your ex was previously in your health plan, he or she has the same right to future coverage as you.

General Health. Except for preexisting conditions, you're generally covered in group or individual plans as soon as you buy or within 30 to 90 days. With individual plans, however, your coverage may be canceled within the first year or two if the insurer discovers that you misrepresented, in a significant way, your state of health (page 412). The same is true for members of employee or association plans who don't sign up for coverage the first time they're eligible.

The Federal Nondiscrimination Rules. These apply to group plans but not to individual plans. Group plans cannot reject you on grounds of poor health, medical history, a history of domestic violence, too many previous claims, or disability. However, they can exclude specific medical problems, such as internal cancer. Or they might cap the payments allowed for specific illnesses.

Some states apply similar nondiscrimination rules to individual health-insurance policies, but many don't.

Genetic Testing. Some twenty states prevent health insurers from denying coverage, or raising their price, to people who carry a gene that suggests they'll contract a specific disease. But that leaves thirty more. Cases exist of insurers who refused to pay for breast-cancer treatments, arguing that the cancer gene was an uninsured "preexisting condition." By all means get tested if you're at high risk for any illness that's curable if caught in time. But do it at a place that will preserve your anonymity. Before telling your doctor the test results, ask if he or she insists on putting everything into your written record. If the answer is yes, keep your mouth shut and shop for another doctor. Despite the results of your test, you might never develop breast cancer, but the test itself might seal you off from future coverage.

Under the federal law requiring portable benefits (page 356), genetic information can't be considered a preexisting condition if an actual illness hasn't developed. But that applies only to people switching from group health plans to other insurance. At this writing, several proposals exist to extend the prohibition to health insurance in general.

COMPANY PLANS

Companies are increasingly dividing into *generous* and *ungenerous* employers. They have employee health plans but differ in the sweep of benefits they offer. Generous companies usually give you a choice of plans, including an HMO and something close to traditional fee-for-service. They also cover much of the cost. Ungenerous companies (or companies that believe they can't afford good plans) give you little or no choice and require you to pay a higher percentage of the cost.

When small companies have plans, they often fall into the ungenerous camp—sometimes by choice, sometimes by necessity. Small companies pay more per person for coverage and may not have access to the same benefits offered to larger groups. Very small companies typically offer no health insurance at all.

Multiple Employer Welfare Arrangements (MEWAs): These plans are established by trade associations and other entities and offered to small-employer groups. The employers themselves are supposed to pay the medical bills. If there's an insurance company involved, it is only administering the plan. In the past, some MEWAs have set premiums too low to cover future claims. If they fail, you're stuck with any outstanding medical bills (MEWAs may not be covered by state insurance guaranty funds—page 413).

Watch for Changes in the Rules. You have to be notified within 2 or 3 months if your group plan drops or modifies a benefit or changes an administrative procedure. Read all mail from your plan and keep benefit info on file.

If Both Husband and Wife Have Employee Plans and you don't have children, you each may pay little or nothing for your own health insurance. Your costs start to rise, however, when you have dependents to insure.

Family benefits typically cost around three times the individual premium. In most cases, you'll buy only the better plan after comparing their costs and benefits point by point. The other spouse would take no family benefits. (Memo to the other spouse: find out how to acquire those benefits if you're divorced or your spouse dies.)

In rare instances, couples see value in buying two family plans—because premiums are low and the children (and spouse) can be covered by both simultaneously. You don't get paid for the same bill twice, but the bills not paid by one spouse's plan, including the deductible, may be picked up by the other plan. Where plans coordinate benefits, however, there's usually no value in doubling up.

You're in clover if at least one spouse has a "cafeteria plan." That lets you pick what you want from a long list of employee benefits. One of you might choose family health insurance while the other takes extra savings or child care.

Consider a "flexible spending account" if your employer offers one. You divert pretax money into the account and use it to pay your uninsured bills, including the deductibles and co-payments on your insurance plan. If you're in an HMO, you can use it for doctors outside the HMO network. There's one risk. Any money left in the account at the end of the year reverts to the company, by law. So don't deposit anything more than you're sure you'll use. If you deposited too much, look for things to buy: prescription sunglasses, a supply of prescription drugs, dental work. Your company will tell you what federal tax law accepts as a qualified medical expense.

If your company plan has a lifetime cap of $500,000, you're underinsured. Look into the cost of buying an individual plan with a high deductible—say $25,000—but a lifetime cap of $1 million or more. This type of insurance may not cost very much and buys a lot of peace of mind. Alternatively, petition your company to raise its maximum.

LEAVING YOUR COMPANY

If You Leave Your Job, Don't Come Under a New Employee Group Plan, and Your Company Employs 20 People or More: You can keep your old plan for a while at your own expense. This is known as a COBRA benefit because it was created by the Consolidated Omnibus Budget Reconciliation Act of 1985. To get it, you generally have to apply within 60 days of being notified about the option. You're allowed up to 18 months of continued coverage if you quit, are laid off, have your hours reduced to something less than the coverage threshold, or even if you are fired (as long as the firing wasn't for "gross misconduct," whatever that is). You pay the group health premium (either family or individual) plus 2 percent. If you chose an expensive company plan and now would prefer a cheaper option, you have the same right to switch that current employees have. Newborns and newly adopted children can always be added to COBRA family coverage as long as you notify the plan in time (usually within 30 days).

COBRA lapses early if you find a new job that covers you with group health insurance. Don't let COBRA go, however, until your new policy's waiting periods expire. You can also continue to call on COBRA if it covers an illness that your new policy excludes.

If you leave your job because you're totally disabled, you can keep the group plan for up to 29 months. These rights also click in if you go on COBRA and are disabled within 60 days. Disability protection doesn't come cheap, however. After the first 18 months, you can be charged as much as 50 percent above the normal group health premium. If you go on Social Security disability and you're under 65, you're eligible for Medicare. But you may or may not have guaranteed access to Medigap coverage, depending on your state. You can get Medigap, however, at 65.

If You Work for a Company with Fewer Than 20 Employees: You're not covered by COBRA. A few states, however, require the plan to keep you for 3 to 18 months. Alternatively, the plan may be convertible into individual coverage. If it's an HMO, the conversion plan may be pretty good. If it's a traditional plan, conversion may be hugely expensive and provide you with limited benefits. Still, that's a better option than a state risk pool if you're otherwise uninsurable.

COBRA also doesn't cover group plans established for members of an association (although it may cover that association's direct employees).

But any group-plan member—in an association, small firm, or large firm—has portability rights.

Your Portability Rights When You Move to a New Group Health Plan. See page 352 for your right to continuing coverage for preexisting illnesses. If you leave a group plan and won't join a new one right away, be sure to buy COBRA, if you're eligible, or buy an interim individual policy, even though its cost is high. Both preserve your right to future coverage. If you go for more than 63 days without health insurance, your next employer can refuse to cover preexisting conditions for as much as 12 months.

Your Portability Rights When You Leave a Group Plan and Don't Have Another One to Join. This applies to people who retire early, start their own businesses or join companies that don't provide medical benefits. You're often guaranteed access to an individual policy when COBRA runs out (or as soon as you leave the company, if you don't qualify for COBRA)—for details, see page 386.

There's one little problem: You have to pay for the policy yourself. At this writing, family coverage normally costs around $4,000 to $5,000. Policies offered under the portability rules might cost even more. If the average worker had that kind of money, there wouldn't be 40 million uninsured.

In the following cases, you might *not* be guaranteed the right to portable coverage: you haven't had 18 months of coverage, most recently in a group plan; you've been without group health insurance for more than 63 days; you want to switch from one individual policy to another.

IF YOU'RE BUYING YOUR OWN INSURANCE . . .

My condolences. Good health insurance does not exist at a decent price, especially when you have a family. And in recent years, insurers have hired Abominable No-Men to choose the health risks they'll insure. Someday the tragedy of the uninsured and underinsured will surely spark a political revolt.

You must make every sacrifice to buy health insurance. I've heard too many stories about families wiped out by a breadwinner's cancer, a newborn's deformity, a paralyzing automobile accident. And please, apply for coverage while you and your family are still in good health! If you wait and develop an ailment of some sort, you'll pay more for your coverage—if you can find it at all (page 384). You cannot believe how hard it is to get general health insurance today, even if your health problem doesn't amount to very much.

Once you've got a policy, it's guaranteed renewable. The insurer can't cancel it unless you fail to pay premiums, you leave the association through which you carried the coverage, or the insurer quits doing business in your area. Your premiums will rise every year or so, in line with your increasing age and the general rise in medical costs. These hikes will apply to all of the company's policies in a specific class, not just to yours. So you can't be singled out if you make a lot of claims.

Don't Go Bare If You Can Possibly Avoid It. Doctors usually give the uninsured a price break in an emergency, but you may not be able to afford even that. They're much less willing to help with expensive or long-lasting illnesses. Studies show that the uninsured use doctors less than the insured (putting off care they need), aren't screened for breast or cervical cancer, don't get continuous treatment for chronic conditions, go to the hospital sicker, and are more likely to die when their illness is serious.

The Best Buys and the Cheapest Ways In

• *Buy group insurance from an association.* Many organizations—professional groups, trade groups, even political action and social responsibility groups—offer health insurance to members. Group coverage generally costs less than individual coverage, but not always. Compare both the price and the benefits with what you can get on the individual market.

You'll have to answer some health questions for both yourself and your dependents. All members of the group have to be accepted. But the policy may exclude certain serious or chronic illnesses, or limit how much is paid for them.

There are some drawbacks to association health insurance:

First, the policy may be canceled. Usually, the association finds another insurer but sometimes it doesn't. The new insurer generally picks up all the old policyholders, but it doesn't have to. Individual policies, by contrast, normally aren't canceled.

Second, the price of group insurance may climb steeply from year to year. Most state regulators don't review rate increases in advance as they do for individual coverage.

Third, some group insurers "death spiral" their policies (page 363). Every year rates rise by a large amount. Healthy members are offered new policies at lower rates while sicker members are stuck with the policy they have. If you're among the stuck, your policy will keep getting more and more expensive. Eventually, you may be forced out—and at that point, no other insurer will touch you. So don't join a group plan that offers nifty new "reentry" rates every year. If you can't take advantage of them, you'll be sunk.

Finally, be suspicious of pitches for group policies that arrive unsolicited in the mail. They sound terrific up front but are probably riddled with unfair exclusions.

Ask what happens if you leave the association. Sometimes you can keep the plan with no change in premium, sometimes you can convert to a more limited plan, sometimes you'll have to abandon the coverage entirely.

• *See if any local HMOs sell to individuals.* Most take only group plans but you might get lucky. HMOs are generally cheaper than traditional plans.

• *Get comparative price quotes.* An insurance agent can shop most companies for you. But insurers like State Farm, Blue Cross, and some HMOs sell only through their own agents, so you have to make those calls yourself. But don't shop for price alone. Sometimes plans have low premiums because they limit the benefits they offer. Others hold down costs by attracting healthier people, then death-spiral them—page 363. Yet others may make it hard to get expensive services or work with lower-quality doctors and hospitals. In a health plan, go for quality first.

• *Look for unisex rates* if you're a woman under 50. Younger women generally pay more for their coverage than men. But some groups charge men and women the same.

• *Create your own group insurance.* If you're self-employed or a business owner and have at least one employee, you can generally buy at group rates. You may also qualify for HMOs that don't take individual policyholders. In some states, you can buy at group rates even with no employees.

Be warned: Some insurers lure you with first-year bargain rates, then sock you with huge increases. You can switch to a lower-cost insurer as long as you and your workers remain in good health. But switching may require you to use a different set of doctors. Furthermore, if someone in your family or company gets sick, you'll face high premiums everywhere.

You're better off with a health plan that charges more to start with if its rate increases are less steep. Ask the agent to show you—in black and white—what has happened to that insurer's prices in the past (trust but verify!). Ask other small-business owners what their experience has been.

For a list of organizations that offer some form of health insurance to home businesses, send $6 to Barbara Brabec, author of *Homemade Money*, at P.O. Box 2137, Naperville, IL 60567.

- *Take a big deductible.* The more small bills you cover yourself, the less your health-insurance costs. In some states, individual policies are routinely sold with deductibles of $2,500 or more. You might take a $10,000 or $25,000 deductible, to be covered only for true catastrophes. These can save you from bankruptcy if you, your spouse, or a child develops a costly illness—and that's what matters most.
- *Take a big co-pay.* Premiums are lower if you pay 50 percent of every medical bill than if you pay only 20 percent. But get a policy that caps the total you have to pay each year. Otherwise, these expenses might run away with you.
- *Quit smoking.* Most insurers charge nonsmokers less.
- *Check out Blue Cross and Blue Shield.* The first covers hospital bills, the second covers doctor bills. They're sometimes cheaper than other private insurance companies. Where their price is lower, however, their coverage may not be as good. Get a price quote and list of benefits from the Blues, then ask an insurance agent if he or she can beat it.
- *Share the cost with the insurer.* A policy that pays only 80 percent of certain hospital and doctor bills costs less than one that pays 90 percent. Typically, you'd pay 20 percent up to a ceiling, like $2,500. After that, the policy would pay in full. Policies without ceilings, however, leave you vulnerable to huge bills.
- *Improve your health status.* The insurer may charge you extra because you smoke or are overweight. If you quit smoking, lose weight, and pester the insurer, you may be dropped to a lower-risk category where insurance costs less.
- *Consider hospital/surgical coverage.* It's much cheaper than comprehensive coverage because it insures only hospital bills and the various costs of surgery, not your regular doctor bills or bills for the care of chronic conditions. Each procedure may be insured for a fixed fee, which won't rise with inflation. It almost certainly will not cover your full bill. I'd rather have major medical insurance with a big deductible. Still, these policies are better than nothing. If you buy one, be sure that it covers outpatient surgery, which is increasingly used today.

- *Shop everywhere if you're in poor health or someone in your family is.* Insurers put every applicant through certain medical tests. Besides disease, they may look for addictive drugs, liver damage that can reveal a problem drinker, and nicotine in the blood of people claiming not to smoke. If your condition is suspect, they may order more tests. They also check your reported medical history at the Medical Information Bureau (page 412). If you're something less than a top risk, ask your agent to show you proposals from several insurers. Some will cut you a better deal than others.

- *Send all medical bills to your insurer,* even though they're below the deductible. Your coverage will click in as soon as the bills you report exceed the limit. If you don't send in bills, you may accidentally pay more than you ought. The deductible should be levied only once a year. If you have a family policy, the deductible should be satisfied by the bills of just two or three of you. And by the way, file bills on time. Most insurers won't pay if you file 18 or 24 months late.

- *Buy short-term coverage.* Some college alumni plans offer short-term policies to new graduates to carry them over from school to work. They're also good for students who drop out of school for a while and will lose coverage on their parents' plan. Short-term health insurance typically lasts for 6 or 12 months and may not insure preexisting conditions, pregnancy, substance abuse, illness while you're traveling abroad, or mental health. If you're allowed to renew, any ongoing health problem may be classified as a preexisting condition and ruled out.

- *See if your state allows bare-bones plans.* Stripped-down policies may be available to small groups and sometimes to individuals, too. You get fewer benefits but you save on premiums. An insurance agent will know if there's something like this around.

- *Talk to your parents.* Young people in low-paying jobs have a hard time paying their rent, let alone their health insurance. Feeling immortal, they often go without. Parents shouldn't let that happen. If your child got sick or had a terrible accident, you would raid your savings account to help. So buying your kid a health insurance policy protects your own financial plan.

- *Ask about Medicaid.* States pay the medical bills for people with very low incomes.

- *Follow the rules.* You generally need preauthorization for elective surgery. If you have emergency surgery, it may have to be reported to the insurer within a day. You may need special approval for expensive treatments or an extra day in the hospital. If you don't follow all the rules, you may have to pay the bill yourself.

MEDICAL SAVINGS ACCOUNTS

If you qualify, there's a way of paying for some of your health expenses tax free. You sign up for a medical savings account (MSA). At this writing, MSAs are generally available to people who are self-employed or work for companies that have 50 or fewer employees and offer no group health insurance. You can set up an MSA yourself or your company can provide it. You may find it expensive, however, compared with an individual major-medical plan or group insurance bought through an association. Here's how MSAs work:

1. You buy a health insurance policy with a high upfront deductible. In 1997, the deductible could be as much as $2,250 for an individual plan and $4,500 for a family plan, indexed to inflation (the deductible is the amount you pay for medical bills before your policy kicks in). You also may owe a percentage of each medical bill. But there's a cap on how much you have to pay for covered illnesses. For individual plans, you can't be asked to pay any more than $3,000 a year; for family plans, no more than $5,500.

2. You start a tax-deductible medical savings account. Every year you can deposit up to 65 percent of the deductible for an individual plan or 75 percent for a family plan. The money is held by a custodian—usually the insurer or a bank. You earn tax-deferred interest on the money (some custodians let you invest in mutual funds).

Alternately, your employer can deposit money on your behalf—in which case, it's free of Social Security tax. If your employer deposits less than the maximum, however, you can't top it up.

3. Whenever you have a medical expense, you can write an MSA check to cover it. Some MSAs let you pay by debit card. Any money not spent within the year carries forward to future years.

4. You can use your tax-free MSA for expenses not covered by your insurance, such as eyeglasses and vanity cosmetic surgery. But the money you spend on uninsured expenses doesn't count toward your deductible.

Two other kinds of expenditure also don't count toward your deductible: any portion of a doctor's bill the insurer deems unreasonably high; and any part of a bill from a nonnetwork doctor, if you're in a managed-care MSA.

Ask how your plan keeps track of the bills that count toward your deductible. You may have to keep the records yourself.

5. You're allowed to use MSA money for nonmedical expenses. When that happens, however, you're supposed to report the expenditure as taxable income. You also owe a 15 percent penalty if you're under 65. Talk about a loophole. Some people will spend their tax-free money on nonmedical expenses, and who will know? There's no 1099 reporting. You're subject to IRS audit, but audits are rare.

MSAs can be dandy for healthy people with plenty of money. You might even pay small medical bills out of pocket, to let more of your saving accumulate, tax deferred. The plans are risky, however, for people on tight budgets. You get high-deductible insurance to protect you from catastrophic medical bills. But the savings part is another matter. What if you can't afford to save the full MSA sum every year? What if you save it, then need the MSA money for a nonmedical emergency? There's a stiff penalty on withdrawals.

If you have an MSA and take a job with a company where MSAs aren't allowed, you'll no longer be able to use your MSA tax free. Nevertheless, the money could build until retirement, tax deferred.

Small employers interested in offering MSAs as a form of employee health insurance should call the Employers Council on Flexible Compensation in Washington, D.C. (202-659-4300). It may be able to tell you which insurers offer MSAs in your state.

STUDENT PLANS

Students who aren't on their parents' health insurance plan can often buy coverage through the college or university at a reasonable price. Students also need a plan if they're away at school and the parental HMO won't cover out-of-town expenses.

But benefits are limited. For example, preexisting conditions might not be covered for a year or two, major medical insurance may be capped at $25,000, and the policy will probably exclude the hazards of youth, such as injuries sustained while stoned or drunk. Student policies are cheap because they're for the typical kinds of problems handled by the student health center. If you want more protection, consider buying it separately. Parents may be able to put their child on COBRA (page 386). Some company plans will keep your child even after COBRA expires, at your expense.

Be sure you know what happens when the student is temporarily out of school. There's typically a fee for continuing coverage during the summer vacation or any semester that the student takes off. If you drop the coverage over the summer and start it again in the fall, the limit on preexisting conditions starts all over again. If the student has developed a chronic condition, the plan might not accept him or her at all.

MATERNITY BENEFITS

A few states require that all individual policies include maternity benefits. But most policies exclude it unless you purchase a special rider. This rider is expensive. You might come out ahead by banking the extra premium and handling the bill yourself. If you do want maternity benefits, you may have to sign up when you first take the policy out, although some insurers allow you to purchase it later. If you have a baby within a year or two after buying the policy, you may be paid a reduced amount or nothing at all.

You do need insurance for complications of pregnancy, including Caesarean sections. But that's normally included in your basic policy even if you don't buy maternity coverage. Ask about it.

Group plans cover maternity costs in the same way they cover other medical procedures. There may be a fee schedule. More likely, the plan will pay a high percentage of the cost.

THE DEATH SPIRAL

Buyers of individual or small-group coverage may run into an odious method of pricing health insurance. It's known, appropriately, as the death spiral and could cost you your health insurance when you need it most. Here's how it works:

You buy a health insurance policy, carefully checking to be sure that it's guaranteed renewable. You've now joined a specific pool of people who are sharing risks. Most members are healthy and make few claims. Their premiums more than offset the payments made to members who are sick. A constant infusion of new, healthy members makes the pool work.

But most health insurers don't keep these pools open to new blood. After 12 to 36 months they may close your pool and start a new one, issued on a new policy form. As the people in your pool age, the number and size of their claims go up. Your insurer shows this "bad experience" to the state insurance regulator, who may approve premium increases over and over again.

Pretty soon, your pool's healthy members start dropping out. They switch to newer, cheaper pools, offered by that same insurer or by some other insurance company. That's when the death spiral begins. The members left behind are in poorer health, which drives up your premiums even more. Slowly, the sicker people leave, too, because they can't afford the price.

As long as you and your family remain in excellent health, you can jump to cheaper policies. But someday one of you may fall ill, and that's when your personal death spiral starts.

There are two other ways an insurer might play this game. If it's insuring an association, it might offer new, low-cost coverage to the healthier members every year, leaving sicker members in older policies whose rates will soar. Or it might maintain several risk pools and move all its higher-risk people into the same pool.

I can't give you six easy tips for avoiding this crime against the public.

It can only be stopped by state regulators. Your best hint of trouble is the policy's price. Given similar benefits, the lowest-cost policy is apt to start death-spiraling first.

LEARNING TO LIVE WITH MANAGED CARE

You've probably got it. If you haven't, you will. Like the common cold, managed care has become an embedded part of life. HMOs cost less than traditional plans and in today's high-cost health-care world, that's a relief. Millions of members are happy with them.

This new system, however, is still under construction, so the plans we have now are different from what we'll eventually get. Rules are changing rapidly, so read the newspapers and keep in touch. Tension is rising between the forces of medical rationing, led by a concern for cost, and an incipient public rebellion against HMOs that go too far. In the second half of the twentieth century, people fought for consumer and environmental rights. In the twenty-first century, they'll be marching for patients' rights.

Types of Managed Care

All managed-care programs limit your medical choice in some way. You're expected to use a specified network of doctors and follow a particular set of rules. You'll typically have a "primary-care" doctor who controls your medical treatment. If you're sick, that's the doctor you see or call first. He or she decides whether to refer you to a specialist, probably another doctor in the network. If you go to a specialist on your own, the plan will refuse to cover part or all of the bill—a limiting factor in itself.

HMOs save money by practicing an abstemious sort of medicine—fewer diagnostic tests than traditional plans pay for, fewer visits to specialists, fewer and shorter hospital stays. Maybe that's exactly the right amount of treatment. HMOs seek quality plus efficiency. Studies show that, on average, working-age people do just as well in HMOs as in traditional fee-for-service plans. Sometimes, however, limited medicine isn't enough. Among the chronically ill, for example, older people and the sickest poor tend to fare poorly in HMOs.

HMOs do offer extra preventive services, such as annual physicals, immunizations, well-baby care, PAP smears, and mammograms. You might also get eyeglasses, dental care, and prescription drugs, sometimes for an extra premium.

Most HMO care goes swimmingly. But because HMOs refuse treatment more often than traditional plans do, you may find yourself doing battle from time to time. If you're too sick, a family member may have to fight on your behalf. You get the most from an HMO when you're aggressive and determined. It's also essential to know the rules and how to formulate appeals—page 371. (One of my friends, however, who was just diagnosed with Parkinson's disease, says, "You may think you know the rules, but when you get really sick you may find out the rules aren't what you thought.")

Here are the general types of plans around today:

Health Maintenance Organizations (HMOs). These plans exercise the most control. Sometimes they run a medical center staffed by a specific medical group or salaried doctors, nurses, technicians, and therapists. More often, they pay fees to networks of doctors and medical groups, who see HMO patients in their own offices. You use specific hospitals that treat the plan's patients at a discount. Participating doctors have to follow the HMO's treatment guidelines. There are rarely claim forms to fill in; you're billed for your share of the cost, if any. The plan pays nothing for treatment it doesn't authorize, except in medical emergencies.

Point-of-Service HMOs (POSs). These are the most rapidly growing form of HMO. They let you go outside the network to seek treatment not authorized by your primary doctor. But if you do, the HMO will pay only part of the bill—say, 50 to 80 percent. You'll have to submit a claim form and, perhaps, argue with the plan about what's a "usual and customary" fee (page 350). Patients generally use outside doctors only for especially difficult illnesses, so your share of the fee may add up to big bucks.

Preferred Provider Organizations (PPOs). These networks of doctors and hospitals sign up with employers and insurers to treat patients at a discount. You don't have to go through a primary doctor. You may see any doctor, inside or outside the plan, whenever you want. When you go outside, however, you'll pay a higher portion of the cost.

Traditional Plans Impose Some Limits, Too. You can see any doctor, anytime. But you may need permission from the insurer for nonemergency surgery and may have to get a second opinion before the cut. There are usually limits imposed on any hospital stay. How sternly your case will be reviewed depends on your employer. Some companies say "go easy," others say, "hang tough."

Which Plan Can You Get? HMOs, PPOs, and POSs are often limited to groups, such as employees of a certain company or members of a certain association. Only about a quarter of them accept individual members. Individuals 65 and up may have access to a Medicare HMO (page 377). Otherwise, you'll have to take a traditional plan—the most expensive of the lot. For typical employee costs, see the following table:

WHAT EMPLOYEES MIGHT PAY FOR COMPANY PLANS

Plan costs vary widely, but here's a rough average of what workers paid in 1996. Employee contributions and other expenses were expected to rise, especially at for-profit HMOs and traditional fee-for-service plans. In a minority of plans, the employer pays the premium in full.

	TRADITIONAL PLAN	HMO	PPO*	POS*
Monthly payroll deduction				
Individual:	$ 30	$ 40	$ 35	$ 40
Family:	115	145	120	120
Deductible				
Individual:	$ 260	0	$ 160†	$ 60‡
Family:	580	0	N/A	N/A
Co-payment				
You pay:	20% of the bill	$10 per visit	10% of the bill	10% of the bill**
Annual cap				
Individual:	$2,000	0	$1,000	$2,000
Family:	N/A	0	N/A	N/A

* For in-network doctors.
† Out-of-network: $290.
‡ Out-of-network: $320.
** Out-of-network: 20% of the bill.
SOURCE: KPMG Peat Marwick

QUESTIONS TO ASK ABOUT MANAGED CARE

Sometimes you can choose a plan yourself. Sometimes your employer picks the plan for you, in which case you need to know its rules. When I say HMO in the discussion, I mean any of the limiting plans: HMOs, PPOs, and POSs. For a list of the costs to ask about, see page 349. For judging the quality of a plan, see page 374. Additional questions you need answers to:

• *Which doctors can you choose?* An HMO can't be any better than the doctors it uses. See if you recognize the doctors on the list. You're generally allowed to change primary-care doctors if you don't like the one you started with. If you want a particular primary-care doctor, however, find out if he or she is accepting new patients. Some are booked up. Some are deliberately turning down patients from that particular plan, perhaps because the plan is difficult to deal with. Note this, however: A wide choice of doctors isn't necessarily best. Plans with high-quality reputations are often those with a central clinic and a closely knit group of salaried doctors working together to find the best treatment for each disease.

• *Will the doctor treat by phone?* You shouldn't have to see the doctor for minor illnesses that you're susceptible to, such as certain types of infections.

• *What happens nights and weekends?* Can you reach your primary doctor or will you be served by whoever is on duty then? There should be emergency phone lines and convenient urgent-care centers for treatment.

• *Does your primary doctor take patients from several HMOs?* If not, you may have to switch doctors if you change your job. This is one of the more aggravating aspects of today's medical system. Different employees offer different plans. A job switch may require everyone in your family to develop new medical relationships from scratch even if they're in the middle of a course of treatment.

• *How easy is it to see a specialist?* Usually, you have to see your primary-care doctor first and let him or her try to assess the problem. If not, a specialist may be ordered. Some primary docs will skip this step and refer you to a specialist by phone—a big time-saver. A few HMOs even let you see specialists in the plan without prior permission. But the specialist may have to get an okay from your primary doctor before prescribing a course of treatment. Otherwise, you may have to pay a fee.

• *Which specialists can you see?* Surveys show that most patients think they are given sufficient access to specialists. But you're usually limited to those in the plan who may or may not be the top people locally. New HMOs—say, those less than 10 years old—are especially apt to have subpar specialist lists.

Some HMOs let you seek out the doctors with national reputations. Others, however, may tell you to use a less expensive surgeon who may not have much experience in the type of operation you need. There are appeals procedures (page 371), but it may take weeks to resolve your case and you may be in no condition to wait. Cutting-edge treatments may not be approved at all, if the HMO declares them to be "experimental."

• *To what extent does the HMO limit the drugs your doctor can prescribe?* HMOs have "formularies"—lists of drugs its doctors are allowed to prescribe. Some lists are broad, some are sharply limited. Some switch from one name-brand drug to another, if that manufacturer will give them special discounts. Some drug manufacturers contract to handle an HMO's prescription business and kick competing drugs off the list. But drugs aren't necessarily interchangeable—especially brand-name drugs. If you're on a maintenance drug, ask if it's on the HMO's list. If not, what will the health plan do? Some let you use your present drug, although your doctor will have to make a case for it. Some force you to switch to another drug that may be less effective for you or have unpleasant side effects. In the tougher

HMOs, doctors will occasionally fight for a change of drugs—but not too often, or they risk getting dropped by the plan.

• *Which hospitals are on the list and do you have a choice?* HMOs will generally list the best hospitals in the area. But they don't necessarily let you go there. The best may be reserved for more serious illnesses; otherwise, you may be sent to a less costly place. Find out if you have access to a major medical center if you or a family member needs unusually complex surgery. If you have to travel because the HMO picked a center far away, will it help with travel costs?

• *How convenient are the doctors, hospitals, physical therapy centers, pharmacies, and other services?* You don't want to have to drive to the other side of town when there are perfectly good services nearby.

• *What if you're traveling and get sick?* HMOs cover emergency screening and stabilization provided by non-network doctors and hospitals. Once you've been stabilized, however, they have to call the HMO, generally within 24 or 48 hours. If they treat you further without getting permission, the HMO probably won't pay. Carry your HMO card in your wallet just in case you've been knocked out!

A murkier question is how the HMO handles urgent but nonemergency care. What if you're visiting your mother for a weekend and your son gets a terrible earache? What if you're on a business trip and wake up with chills, a high fever, and sick stomach? The standard HMO advice: call your plan before leaving town and run through your itinerary. Big HMOs have affiliated doctors in other cities or guest privileges at other HMOs. Blue Cross/Blue Shield launched a national network in 1996 and started adding international hospitals in 1997. As long as you call a preapproved medical group, your HMO will cover your bill.

But what if you don't call before each and every trip (and who would)? You must call the plan from wherever you are and describe your symptoms to the person staffing the medical-advice line. Based on what you say, you'll be told to go to a local clinic, call a local HMO, or take two aspirin and see your doctor when you come home. If you see a local doctor without permission, it's on your nickel.

• *What if you spend part of each year at a second home?* Unless the HMO has affiliates in both places, that plan is not for you.

• *What's an emergency and who decides?* If you think you're in a situation that threatens your life or health, you can rush to the nearest emergency room even when it isn't part of your HMO. But what if the pain in your chest turns out to be indigestion rather than a heart attack? HMOs are supposed to pay for out-of-network care if a prudent person might reasonably believe that there was a need for immediate medical treatment. With perfect hindsight, however, the HMO may reject the bill—a pretty cynical way of saving money. Some states have passed the "prudent person" standard into law.

When you call the HMO, by the way, note the time of the call and the name of the person you spoke to. Some HMOs have denied payment because they said that the patient never called.

• *How does the HMO handle preexisting conditions?* Find out if you're covered right away for ailments that you and your family have recently had. There may or may not be a waiting period. Those with chronic illnesses or disabilities should ask who the specialists are and how the illness will be handled. If you need medical equipment, see what's covered and how often it can be upgraded or changed—for example, new wheelchairs for a growing child. Ask if any illnesses are excluded from coverage completely.

• *What is the HMO's policy on super-expensive treatments, like organ transplants and bone-marrow transplants for breast cancer?* There's usually a wishy-washy assurance that they're covered if appropriate. You can't be sure what's "appropriate" until you're actually there. HMOs won't pay for treatments considered "experimental," but there's a lot of discussion about what that means. At some HMOs, it's anything new or any treatment not commonly used, even if it might be exactly right for you. A doctor you trust may be able to tell you how the HMO behaves.

• *What does the HMO pay for mental illness and substance abuse?* Here's where all plans are radically cutting back—traditional fee-for-service plans, too. But mental health professionals say that HMOs are especially tight. Patients with serious problems may be granted no more than a handful of visits to a psychologist or psychiatrist. If you or your child has a drug or alcohol problem, you may be allowed only 7 days in a treatment program.

• *Do you have all this information in writing?* What salespeople say over the phone may be different from the plan's actual rules. But the rules rule every time.

For a free copy of *Managed Care: An AARP Guide* (Stock #D15595), write to the American Association of Retired Persons, Fulfillment EEO1153, 601 E St. N.W., Washington, DC 20049.

HOW IS YOUR DOCTOR PAID?

Patients never used to think about this. In traditional plans, where doctors earn fees for services, patients feel sure that they're hearing about every treatment possible. If anything, they might be offered treatment beyond what they really need. In most HMOs, however, compensation matters a lot. Your doctor typically gets paid more for treating you less. The HMO may:

• Pay doctors a salary, then give them a modest bonus at year-end. This particular method of HMO payment keeps the doctor on your side. He or she gets paid the same, no matter what treatment is proposed.

• Pay a fixed "capitation" fee—say, $12 or $18 a month—for every primary-care patient on the doctor's or medical group's books. Healthy patients yield profits; patients with illnesses are generally treated at a loss. Capitation is more critical to small practices, where a handful of really sick patients can break the bank. Large practices are in a position to balance the risks (although individual doctors may still be warned if they refer too many patients to specialists—regardless of the patient's needs). Much depends on the size of the capitation fee. An adequate fee should cover the treatments your doctor thinks you need. Inadequate fees force docs to take short cuts, like it or not. The fewer sick patients doctors have, or the fewer expensive treatments they authorize, the more money they will make. Doctors with mixed practices—some HMO patients, some on fee-for-service plans—may use fee-paying patients to make up for stingy HMO fees. Even if fee-payers have an illness diagnosable by phone, the doctor might say, "Come into the office," just to be able to charge for a visit.

• Pay discounted fees for services plus a bonus based on profits, on money saved, or on meeting certain treatment goals.

• Allocate doctors an annual lump sum from which they write checks for all their patients' medical costs, even the hospital bills. Anything left over is what the doctor earns for the year. Talk about conflict of interest!

• Pay the doctors a fee for every service. But 15 to 20 percent of each fee may be withheld. At the end of the year, the docs get all or part of their "withhold," depending on how well they held down costs—say, by limiting the number of patients sent to the hospital or cutting down on diagnostic tests.

There's no research on whether these treatment-based payment plans change the way doctors order care. But if traditional fee-for-service plans tempt doctors to overtreat, then HMOs must be tempting them to undertreat. There's an incentive *not* to hospitalize you, *not* to send you to a specialist, *not* to prescribe an expensive drug, *not* to order diagnostic tests —in fact, not to accept you as a patient at all if your illness is obviously going to cost a lot.

Every doctor (well, *almost* every doctor) tries to do the best by his or her patients. Minimal treatment may be exactly what you need. By considering cost, your doctor may even discover new procedures that you yourself find simpler and more effective. But when docs are paid more for treating less, patients don't always get the best advice or hear about the newest treatments, especially if they have a serious, chronic, or disabling illness. Patients are trying to learn more about their illnesses today (witness the discussion groups on the Internet), partly as a check on what their doctors say.

Always Ask Your HMO or Your Doctor to Disclose How Payment Is Made. You're subtly suggesting that you're prepared to charge self-interest if the

HMO is slow to treat a serious medical problem. In HMO-land, that's a hint that can help.

WHO DECIDES WHAT YOUR DOCTOR CAN DO?

Ideally, you and your doctor decide on the best course of treatment after considering all the alternatives. And it's still that way at the HMOs where practicing physicians have a big say.

But it's different at other HMOs, and the risk is greatest at those that operate for profit and whose shares trade on a stock exchange. There, the medical panels that set treatment rules may be less flexible. Low-cost treatments may have to be tried first, even when your doctor doubts they're going to work. You may be required to use a generic drug even if, in your case, the brand-name version is more effective or has fewer side effects. HMO panels may reject the treatment your doctor thinks is best. You may not even hear about all your medical options. If your doctor presses too often for treatments the HMO opposes or prescription drugs not on its list, he or she may be dropped from the plan—and for doctors, that's financial suicide. They're learning not to rock the boat.

None of this affects patients with run-of-the-mill illnesses. But it adds to the anxiety of patients who are chronically or seriously ill. The odds are that you'll get the best treatment possible. Still, it might be worth paying for a second, non-HMO opinion to assure yourself that you know all the alternatives. Some doctors say that their HMOs don't let them practice medicine as thoroughly as they would like.

This Is Rationing and It's Going to Get Worse. Under the old system, America rationed care by price and luck. Those who couldn't afford health insurance got poor care; those with personal or employee coverage got whatever treatment they wanted, without much concern for cost. Health care today is still rationed by price in that coverage is more expensive than ever. But it's also rationed for the insured. They get only the benefits that their insurers and employers are willing to pay for.

APPEALING A DECISION WITH THE DECK STACKED AGAINST YOU

Every HMO has an appeals procedure for patients who have been turned down for a particular treatment. You must appeal before you're allowed to go to court. But if you're in an employee plan, the pitfalls will astonish you.

1. You're generally given a brochure about the basic appeals procedures. But you rarely know exactly why you were turned down. You *think* you know—for example, you're told the treatment is "experimental," hence not covered by the plan. But what does "experimental" mean? There may be no specific definition; it means what the HMO says it means in any particular case. When you ask for the HMO's full, official definition (as you must, when preparing your argument), you might find it so broad that many accepted treatments could be called "experimental" if the HMO so chose.

2. You often don't know the case against you. The HMO will investigate the procedure you want, but you generally won't get the report, so you can't challenge it for thoroughness and accuracy. The investigator may not even be an expert in your particular disease.

3. When you enter the hearing, you don't know exactly what you have to prove. Typically, you bring information from the doctor who will supply the treatment, medical articles, and perhaps a second opinion from another doctor. But let's face it: You're appealing to the same bunch that turned you down before. And you won't know how to use the plan's own treatment rules to make your case.

4. If you're turned down again, you can sue in court if you believe the treatment you need is covered under the plan. But if you're in an employee HMO, you have almost no chance of winning. Under the law, the court can consider only one thing: Did the plan make a reasonable decision *based on the information before it at the time?* Maybe there's plenty of research to support your side, but you didn't know how to find it; maybe the HMO didn't make a thorough investigation. Tough luck. No new evidence is admissible in court—even when the HMO is obviously wrong! Under such a law, the HMO has no incentive to rethink an expensive treatment it doesn't want to pay for. And it certainly isn't going to tell you the consequences of arguing your case without professional advice.

5. In court, the law gives employee health plans extraordinary rights. Any vague language in the contract or general words like "experimental" can be interpreted by the HMO in almost any way that's plausible. Ambiguity must be resolved on the side of the insurer. By contrast, in individual health-insurance contracts, ambiguity must be resolved on the consumer's side.

What to Do When Appealing to the HMO.

• Pay a medical expert to advise you—*before* the appeal—on how to assemble evidence. Assume there will be a biased report on the other side. The expert's job is to overcome it.

• Demand the actual language from the plan's master document on which the HMO based its decision to turn you down (the language in your plan handbook is only a summary). If the wording is vague, demand the specific definition the HMO relied on—for example, what does "experimental" mean? You may find the language so broad that it can mean whatever the HMO wants it to mean.

- Demand the credentials of the people who are investigating your case (you'll want to challenge the expertise of, say, a pediatrician asked to evaluate a cancer treatment). Demand his or her final report so you can look for inaccuracies and holes.

- Demand any reports the HMO gets from third-party experts, as well as their credentials. In most jurisdictions, you're entitled to know the full case against you—but the HMO might not want to tell. In some states, you are *not* entitled to know, believe it or not.

- You need to rebut the HMO point by point, and your documentation should be overwhelming—medical papers, proof of how often the treatment is used in your kind of case, proof of its efficacy, proof that it's the best possible treatment in your case, several supporting witnesses. Remember: if you go to court, the evidence presented during your appeal is the only information you'll be allowed to submit.

- Pay a lawyer to advise you. Even better, have the lawyer come to the hearing and plead your case.

- Follow all the appeal rules. Handle everything in writing, keeping copies for yourself so you'll be able to prove what you said and did. If you have a telephone conversation about the problem, note when the call came, the person you spoke with, and what was said.

If the plan says no again, many patients stop. In life-threatening situations, they pay for the treatment themselves if they can dredge up the money. Or their condition gets so bad the HMO finally acts. Or they die. The patient or family may sue to recover any money they spent themselves. But you can use only the record you made during the HMO appeal, which may or may not be sufficient. You can see in a flash how cruel these rules are. The patient's family may rush the appeal because the condition is critical. When they later sue for payment, their hasty presentation will probably prevent them from getting their money back, even if they were in the right.

In less critical situations—for example, getting a larger wheelchair for a growing child from a plan that says it will provide just one—persistence may pay off. Dig deeply into the language of the plan. Call, write, submit opinions from outside doctors, have a lawyer write, referring specifically to the section of the plan you think applies. The meek may inherit the earth, as the scriptures say, but they won't get anywhere with their HMO. You have to be a pain in the tail. Your objective is to show that the contract does indeed cover the treatment or medical equipment your doctor says you need. When it's an employee plan, your state insurance department usually won't intervene (although some do). But do complain to your company. Some consumers get lucky by writing to a newspaper or television reporter who covers consumer or health-care issues, or to their state representative. If you make a good case and the treatment doesn't cost you a lot, you may eventually win. You'll come out of the experience with a better understanding of where health rationing is headed.

The Back Channel. Go to your company employee-benefits office and pound the table. See the company president if you can, or write an internal memo. Rally other employees round. If your company represents enough business for the HMO, the HMO will usually do what it's told.

Can You Sue an HMO for Malpractice if stingy medical treatment led to death or permanent disability? In many states, no, if the HMO is part of an employer plan. You can sue the doctors. But HMOs can normally be sued only in federal court and for just one thing: mistakes in deciding whether the plan should pay a particular medical bill. If you win such a case, all you get is the cost of the benefit you erroneously had to pay yourself. For example, say your late wife was sick and the HMO wouldn't authorize a blood test. She gets sicker, you pay for the test yourself, and it reveals a disease that has now progressed too far to treat. You can sue only to recover the $150 you paid for the test plus, if you're lucky, "reasonable" attorney's fees. You cannot bring a malpractice suit. You cannot get damages for negligence, bad faith, or wrongful death. What's more, your burden of proof is higher than for malpractice suits. Justice aside, alas, these cases are rarely worth bringing at all.

There are exceptions. You can sue if you joined the HMO as an individual rather than as part of an employee group. Ditto if you're in an employer plan offered by a state government, church, or church-related group. A different law, which is more patient-friendly, covers federal employees. Members of Congress, who passed the law limiting your rights, are themselves free to sue for malpractice, bad faith, and other damages. Hmmmmm.

At this writing, a few courts have started to allow malpractice suits by others, too. If you've been injured because an HMO declined or delayed a treatment your doctor said you should have, ask a lawyer whether malpractice suits are available in your state.

Some Health Plans Require That Disputes Be Settled by Arbitration. That's faster and cheaper than bringing a lawsuit and can produce a fair award. But the way the panels are constructed generally favors the HMOs. Get a medical adviser and a lawyer to help with your arbitration, too.

At this writing, New Jersey has just set up an independent appeals panel for patients who are fighting their HMOs for additional treatment. Only experience will show if this actually helps.

HOW GOOD IS YOUR HMO?

Some people can choose among several HMOs. Some have only the plan their employer provides. But how do you or your employer decide which one to use?

When your company chooses, it's looking for a low price and good patient services. When you choose yourself, you also look at the names of the doctors in the plan and what it would cost to seek treatment outside the HMO.

Sad to say, there's no reliable way of telling how well an HMO (or any medical plan) does its central job, which is to cure the sick. You get assurances of good care but no proof. An effort is currently under way to develop standardized treatment measures. Until they're widely available, here are the next-best things to look for:

• Consider an HMO that operates out of a single site and has doctors on staff. These tend to have good reputations for quality.

• Get a plan that's accredited by the National Committee for Quality Assurance (NCQA). It inspects HMOs and approves those that meet certain levels of service and care. In early 1997, however, only 18 percent of all managed-care plans had received full accreditation, 17 percent had temporary accreditation of some kind, and 4 percent had flunked. Nearly 50 percent hadn't bothered to apply and are getting business anyway, from employers who don't insist on the highest quality standards. If you're offered only an unaccredited HMO, make a stink. You can check accreditation on the Web at http://www.ncqa.org.

• Look for a patient-satisfaction survey prepared by an independent organization. One such is the survey published in the excellent *Consumer's Guide to Health Plans*, at this writing $12 from Consumers' Checkbook, 733 15th St. N.W., Suite 820, Washington, DC 20005. It covers only HMOs, not PPOs, and not all HMOs participate. Some large ones and many small ones are among the missing (not too smart, in my opinion). But you'll find a lot of useful consumer information about some 300 HMOs. Avoid the plans with the lowest scores and high disenrollment rates.

Many HMOs do their own patient surveys, or pay to have them done. Treat this data as entirely self-serving.

• See if you know any of the doctors in the plan. If so, schedule half an hour of consultation to discuss the HMO. One big question to ask: Will I get the same treatment under the HMO as I would under some other plan? The HMO will have rules about treatments and prescription drugs that may be different from what the doctor would normally order.

• A typical piece of advice is to look for HMOs whose doctor roster is 80 percent "board certified." Such a doctor has had extra training in his or her specialty and passed a tough exam established by the American Board of Medical Specialties (ABMS). Certification doesn't guarantee competence, however. Newer doctors, still qualifying for their boards, may be just as good or better. Still, it's a baseline test. (There are other "boards" that admit doctors with little or no testing. Your HMO should count only ABMS boards.)

• Get on the Web to research the latest and best treatments for your disease. You can't be sure that your HMO doctor will tell you about cutting-edge procedures that your HMO doesn't want to authorize. So the goal is to find them yourself, then push the HMO to consider them. One place to start: http://infonet.welch.jhu.edu/advocacy.html—a list of patient-advocacy organizations compiled by Johns Hopkins University.

• Avoid new HMOs. They need time to test their treatment methods and line up decent rosters of doctors.

• Watch for new developments. In 1997, the Health Care Financing Administration, which administers Medicare, ordered Medicare HMOs to start collecting various types of quality data, which it intends to publish. Other organizations are working on measures of how sick people fare. In the years ahead, some kind of health-care rating system should emerge.

• Learn to rely on objective tests! People often ask their friends to recommend doctors, but what do most of us know about our doctors' real medical talents? We judge them by their caring attitude, their accessibility, and their skill in building trust. But other doctors may be smarter, with better diagnostic skills and cleverer ideas for treatment. As the industry starts to develop credible health-care measures, consumers should look to them first when selecting a doctor or an HMO.

• Press your employer for information. It picked the HMO for you or picked a couple for you to choose between. As part of the deal, your employer should require the HMO to offer *independent* patient-satisfaction surveys, participate in quality surveys and disclose the results, and provide booklets explaining what's covered, your appeal rights, and what everything costs.

State Quality Rules. When cost control gets so tight that patients feel deprived of care, they often scream to their legislators, who pass a law. Many states now require: (1) access to certain specialists, such as gynecologists, without going through your primary doctor; (2) the right to choose certain specialists as your primary doctor; (3) payment for treatment in the emergency room of a hospital not affiliated with the HMO if you reasonably believed that immediate treatment was needed; (4) free speech for doctors so they can tell you about costly treatments the HMO might be reluctant to authorize; (5) hospital stays for mastectomy patients so your insurer can't send you home right after the operation; (6) bone-marrow transplants for women with advanced breast cancer so the HMO can't ban them as "experimental" procedures (most HMOs cover these now, mainly because one patient's survivors won a giant lawsuit). Federal law requires HMOs to allow newborns and their mothers to stay in the hospital for up to 48 hours for normal births and 96 hours for cesareans. These rules all apply to traditional fee-for-service plans, too.

The more voters complain, the more such laws are going to be passed. Mandates may raise costs but patients won't let health plans take too much away.

HMOs WHEN YOU'RE 65 OR OLDER

Some HMOs sign up with Medicare to cover all of your medical costs. Financially, it's a good deal. Medicare HMOs give you Medicare Parts A and B (for hospitalization and doctor bills) plus coverage for all Medicare co-payments and deductibles. Sometimes they add extra benefits, such as annual physicals, eyeglasses, dental coverage, and cut-rate prices on prescription drugs. Around 14 percent of Medicare beneficiaries have joined HMOs and the portion is rising every year.

You continue to pay Part B Medicare premiums (in 1997, $43.80 a month). But you don't have to buy a Medigap policy to plug the holes in Medicare (page 395). The HMO is your Medigap.

Most Medicare HMOs charge zero premiums. A few charge between $10 and $60 a month. There might also be co-payments for every doctor visit, in the range of $5 or $10. Extra benefits may be available for a higher price.

There's no paperwork as long as you stick with the doctors in the network. Medicare pays your HMO directly.

Not every area has a Medicare HMO. To find one (if its aggressive sales efforts haven't yet found *you*), call your local Social Security office or Area Agency on Aging. The AAA should be in the Yellow Pages. If not, call the Eldercare Locator (page 144).

To take advantage of a Medicare HMO, you normally have to live in the area full-time. If you join one in Texas but spend four months a year in Maine, none of your Maine doctor bills will be covered, either by Medicare or by the HMO. Medicare pays for non-HMO care only if you are temporarily out of town for up to 90 days and urgently need to see a doctor. Some HMOs have federally approved affiliates in other cities. If you luck into one near your second home and register with it properly, Medicare will pay for treatment the affiliate gives.

Medicare HMOs must accept almost anyone who applies, without preconditions and regardless of health. The only exceptions: people with kidney failure or in hospice care. Recruiting efforts, however, are often targeted at healthy seniors, not the sick. (You can also be turned down if the HMO is not currently accepting new members.)

Thousands of older people are grateful for their money-saving Medicare

HMOs and satisfied with the treatment they provide. They're an especially good deal for lower- or middle-income people who can't afford a lot of medical bills and who aren't seriously or chronically ill.

But these plans aren't always peaches and cream. Read the section on HMOs (page 364). Then consider the following risks that face older people in particular.

RISKS IN MEDICARE HMOs

1. Studies show that older people who are chronically ill might not be as well taken care of in HMOs as they are in traditional plans. Don't sign up for an HMO before talking with some of its older members, especially those with long-term illnesses. You may find that all is well, but check.

2. You're locked into choosing a primary-care doctor from the HMO's list. You normally have to see its specialists, too. The doctors are doubtlessly fine, but some salespeople don't explain this point. If you see another doctor without the HMO's permission, neither the HMO nor Medicare will pay. A point-of-service HMO lets you see other doctors, but you still may need permission and will have to pay a significant portion of the cost—maybe 20 or 30 percent. Such visits would be cheaper under straight Medicare plus Medigap insurance. Choose an HMO only if you'll stay inside the network.

3. You may decide on an HMO because your doctor is on its list. But its rules may require your doctor to handle your treatment differently. For example, you may not be able to get the same drugs you're using now. Discuss this with your doctor before making the switch.

4. Medicare HMOs have a special appeals process that can go all the way to the federal government. By law, you're supposed to be given a statement about your appeal rights if you're denied a prescription drug, therapy, or medical service that your doctor thinks you need. Most complaints are supposed to be resolved within 72 hours, especially those that affect your immediate life and health. But sometimes it takes a couple of months. The HMO may or may not tell you precisely why you were denied, how to press a claim, and what evidence you'll have to show. If you're ill and have no one to speak for you, you may lose coverage you need and deserve. For more on HMO appeals, see page 371.

5. If you switch to an HMO and hate it, you can switch back to regular Medicare (Parts A and B) at the end of any month. Simply notify the HMO in writing (certified mail is safest; keep a copy of the letter) or complete HCFA Form 566 at your local Social Security office. Starting in 2002, however, you'll have to stay in the HMO for at least 6 months before moving out. In 2003 and thereafter, you'll be locked in for 9 months at a time (although you get to switch if you move to another town).

At this writing, consumers who go from an HMO back to traditional Medicare can't automatically buy a private Medigap policy (page 395). You can buy one if you're in good health (probably with a 3- to 6-month waiting period for preexisting conditions). If your health is mediocre, however, insurers usually turn you down. Cautious consumers who join HMOs have been holding on to their Medigap plans a few months. That way they lose nothing if they decide to disenroll. Starting in July 1998, however, a consumer who joins a managed-care plan and regrets it will have a limited period to buy a new Medigap policy, regardless of health (page 395).

If you do disenroll, it may take a month or more for Medicare's computers to catch up with your move. Assuming that you see a doctor during that time, Medicare might refuse to pay in the mistaken belief that you still belong to the HMO. Don't pop a blood vessel. Simply resubmit the claim, along with a letter saying you left the HMO and a copy of the form showing your disenrollment date.

6. If your HMO goes bankrupt, leaving some of your medical bills unpaid, you may or may not be covered by the state guaranty fund. Doctors and hospitals aren't supposed to dun you for payments owed by your HMO, but you never can tell. You may also be at risk if the HMO loses its Medicare contract, as some have. So sign up only with an HMO that has been with Medicare for several years and has a good safety-and-soundness rating (page 343—Weiss is the only firm that rates large numbers of HMOs).

7. Congress is cutting back on payments to Medicare HMOs. This portends higher premiums to members and fewer free services in the future. But they'll probably still be cheaper than Medicare plus Medigap insurance.

NEW MEDICARE OPTIONS

Congress has provided a range of new Medicare choices which, at this writing, haven't yet been worked out. In general, however, Medicare will pay each plan an annual dollar amount per member, with payments varying by age, sex, where the plan is located, and (in 2000) how healthy plan members are. Members will continue paying Medicare Part B. If your plan failed, you'd switch to another Medicare plan and wouldn't owe any covered bills that were left unpaid. Here's what's under development:

1. Preferred Provider Organizations (PPOs). You're covered for the usual Medicare amounts if you visit doctors in the network. If you go outside the network, there's an extra charge that you'll have to pay yourself.

2. Provider Sponsored Organizations (PSOs). A PSO is a form of HMO or PPO, but organized by doctors and hospitals rather than insurance companies.

3. Private fee-for-service plans—for people of wealth. The plans may charge premiums on top of Medicare Part B. You can go to any doctor who

accepts the plan's fees. There may or may not be an overlay of managed care. Among other things, these plans should allow for more diagnostic tests, cutting-edge medical procedures, and psychiatric care. The plans will set fees for doctors, hospitals, and other providers. Those fees will be higher than Medicare's; you can also be hit for an extra 15 percent on any bill (including the hospital charge). The plans have to disclose in advance what the extra costs might be.

4. Once a year, Medicare enrollees will get a list of all their options, including costs and benefits. You'll be able to switch to any plan you want, regardless of health.

5. At any time, you can contract for a particular doctor's services, at whatever fee the doctor wants to charge. No bills are submitted to Medicare. You pay everything yourself or through a private insurance company. Many top specialists may choose to practice this way, leaving them beyond the reach of the average patient. Doctors who write private contracts aren't allowed to participate in Medicare.

6. Starting in 1999, there's a special Medicare-linked insurance plan called a medical savings account (MSA). You sign up for private health insurance with an annual deductible of as much as $6,000. You also get an MSA account.

Each year, Medicare will pay the same sum into that account as it would for any other plan. Part of the payment will cover your private health-insurance premium. The rest is yours to use, tax free, to pay medical bills, including bills not covered under Medicare. Anything not spent earns interest tax deferred.

You're responsible for up to $6,000 in bills that Medicare would have covered, and some or all of the Medicare deductibles, too. After that, your private insurer gives you the equivalent of Medicare coverage (or better). One warning: your doctors can charge higher fees than Medicare allows.

Who might want to try a Medicare MSA? Healthy seniors with plenty of cash. If your actual medical expenses are small compared with what Medicare pays you each year, you'll accumulate a healthy tax-favored savings account. You can let it build toward future medical expenses (all tax free). Or you can use part of the money for other purposes (in which case you're taxed on what you withdraw). If you contract a serious illness, you can return to traditional Medicare the following year—keeping any MSA money you haven't spent. You could even hold off on expensive elective surgery, like a hip replacement, until you're back under Medicare's umbrella.

You will not want an MSA if: (1) You're spending substantial amounts of money on medical bills each year. Traditional Medicare or a Medicare HMO will cost you less. (2) You're healthy but living on a tight budget. You can't afford to pay $6,000 or more in a year that illness strikes. (When you're in a Medicare MSA, you're not allowed to buy Medigap coverage.)

If a salesperson approaches you touting "tax free Medicare income," he or she is selling MSAs. Get a list of all the expenses you'll be responsible for. Not many seniors can afford this risk.

SOME SALESPEOPLE FOR MEDICARE HMOs OUGHT TO BE ARRESTED

They launch themselves onto the elderly with only sales commissions in mind. Patients sign up without understanding the rules, especially the lock-in provision that requires them to see only HMO doctors.

If you think that you (or an elderly parent) were deceived by an HMO salesperson, complain to your local Social Security office. If you signed up for the HMO but never truly used its services, and can show that you didn't understand the lock-in provision, the government might decide that you were never actually a member. In that case, your back medical bills will all be paid, just as if you had never signed up. This process is called retroactive disenrollment.

Good Medicare HMOs can save you money and give reliable care. But never sign up on the word of a telephone or door-to-door salesperson, or through a newspaper ad. Visit the HMO, get its brochures, ask for a detailed explanation of how everything works, ask how specific illnesses are handled, ask if your doctor can prescribe the drugs you use, talk with older members, and check the HMO's ratings in the *Consumer's Guide to Health Plans* (page 375). For detailed advice, get *Managed Care: An AARP Guide* (page 369).

WAYS TO SAVE MONEY ON MEDICAL COSTS

1. Join an HMO and see only the doctors on the list.
2. If you're on Medicare, get doctors who "accept assignment." That means they charge no more than what Medicare will pay. You still pay your annual deductible and a 20 percent share of each doctor bill. But you don't have to pay any excess charges. The vast majority of doctors accept assignment today. If your doctor doesn't—and refuses when asked—ask a friend, a doctor or nurse, or a nursing home for a suggestion. The insurance company that administers Medicare is required to publish a list of participating physicians. At least one copy of that list should be in your local Social Security office—if you *have* a local Social Security office. A local senior citizens group might also have it or ask the insurer for it directly.
3. Medicare patients facing surgery should ask the surgeon whether every member of his or her team will accept assignment. Radiologists and

anesthesiologists, who rarely meet with patients, often say no. Make a stink and see what happens. Tell your surgeon to get someone else on the team.

4. In fee-for-service plans, ask your doctors to limit their fees to whatever your insurer pays. They may surprise you and say yes. That way all you'll pay is your policy's deductible.

5. Get generic drugs unless there's a good reason not to.

6. Have your old X-rays sent to a new doctor or dentist; that should save you the cost, and risk, of being X-rayed again.

7. Get advice by telephone from the doctor or nurse. It saves the cost of an office visit.

8. Check your insurance coverage before undergoing elective surgery. Your plan might not pay unless you get a second opinion. If you have any doubts about your condition, get a second opinion anyway—even if *you* have to pay.

9. Know your HMO's rules by heart. What will it cost you to see a doctor outside the plan? If you're rushed to the nearest emergency room, how soon must the HMO be notified (if your family calls too late, the HMO may not pay the bill)? If you take sick out of town, what's the procedure for getting permission to see a doctor and having the visit billed to the HMO?

10. If you're paying a portion of the doctor or hospital bill, get it itemized. Hospitals are notorious for billing for treatments that you didn't use. They list some of their services in code. Still, there are easy things to check. Were you actually in the hospital that day? Did you really use the services you were billed for? Just for sport, you might visit the billing office and ask the hospital to itemize any lump sum for "pharmacy" or "miscellaneous." You'll be surprised at what turns up—or rather, at what doesn't turn up. Don't pay for anything that can't be accounted for.

11. Get a copy of the doctor or hospital bill to see what your insurer actually paid. The insurer might have received a discount. If you owe a percentage of each bill, your percentage should be figured on the discounted amount, unless your contract specifically says otherwise. Some insurers overcharge by billing you for a percentage of the full amount.

12. If there's a 24-hour emergency clinic in your area, check its prices. It's generally cheaper than a hospital emergency room. A call to your doctor —if you can reach him or her—should be cheaper than either.

13. Learn how to take care of your illnesses yourself and follow your doctor's directions to the letter. A large percentage of the people readmitted to the hospital soon after being discharged come back only because they didn't follow doctor's orders.

14. Tell the hospital you want to use your own aspirin, sleeping pills, and other routine medications, if they don't conflict with treatment. Hospitals may charge $3 or more a pill for dispensing these drugs themselves.

15. Make a living will to avoid the extraordinary cost of futile treatments when you are terminally ill (page 124). Your instructions may be ignored, however, unless you have a surrogate there to speak for you.

16. Compare drug prices at several pharmacies. You'll find wide differences. The American Association of Retired Persons in Washington, D.C., runs a mail-order pharmacy, where prices are generally low. Many health maintenance organizations also run their own low-cost mail-order pharmacies (although they might refuse you a brand of drug you need).

17. Try store-brand over-the-counter drugs. They're cheaper than brand-name remedies and often just as effective. Or just as ineffective, as the case may be.

18. Check yourself regularly for breast cancer.

19. Don't rush to the doctor every time you feel sick. A lot of illnesses go away by themselves.

20. Lose weight. Quit smoking. Drink less. Eat right. Wear seat belts. Exercise. There is no doctor bill so cheap as the one that no one has to pay.

21. Report overbilling and other forms of Medicare fraud to the program's fraud hotline: 800-HHS-TIPS. Any money Medicare saves leaves more money in the till for beneficiaries like you.

DON'T WASTE YOUR MONEY ON . . .

One-Disease Insurance, such as coverage specifically for cancer or heart attacks. These and other limited-payment policies are increasingly turning up in "kitchen-sink" employee plans. Those are the plans where a company offers whatever list of benefits an insurance agent brings. Employees pick the ones they want and pay the cost themselves. But the odds are against your lucking into the one disease you insured against. Put your money toward broader coverage that protects your general health. If I can't talk you out of buying, check the exclusions carefully. These policies are cheap because they don't cover a lot.

Hospital Insurance. This policy pays a fixed number of dollars per day if you enter the hospital. Typical choices: $100 or $200 for the first 30 days and $200 or $400 for the next 150 days. These help pay the indirect costs of hospital stays that aren't covered by your insurance policy, such as travel or a babysitter for the children. But nowadays, you're often kicked out of the hospital in a day or two, even after major surgery. Your policy might not even pay unless you've been hospitalized for at least 2 days. So what exactly are you buying? For preexisting conditions, benefits typically won't be paid for the first 12 months.

Accident Insurance. It pays medical bills that result from an accident, not an illness. But why would you think that your biggest risk in life is falling off a ladder or being hit by a truck? Only 4.5 percent of deaths are accidental. When such deaths occur they often give rise to a lawsuit, a form of "insurance" you carry at no charge. Put your money toward comprehensive coverage that includes both accident *and* sickness.

Insurance That Blares, "You Cannot Be Turned Down!" These policies are hawked on TV by celebrities. Or they arrive unsolicited in the mail. They accept all comers, which gives some hope to people who are otherwise uninsurable. But there are long waiting periods before they'll cover any illness that you had when you signed up. If you enter the hospital, it might be 3 days before benefits start. You could be in and out without collecting a cent. Some of the policies ask rudimentary health questions, but not enough to make them attractive to people who have other options. If you buy such a policy when you're in reasonably good health, you're probably overpaying by 100 percent. The celebrities who promote them should be ashamed of themselves.

Double Coverage. An insurance agent might urge you to add a cancer policy or hospital policy to the health insurance you already have. The appeal: "This gives you an extra payment when you need it." Or, "This fills the gaps that your other policy doesn't cover." You might better say that it fills the gaps in the insurance agent's personal income. The best way to get extra money is to build up your own personal savings. Cheap hit-or-miss insurance is always a waste.

WHAT IF YOU OR A MEMBER OF YOUR FAMILY GETS A NASTY DISEASE AND IS UNINSURED?

You've got problems. A growing number of states are forcing insurers to take you, but usually not at a price you can afford. If you have no company insurance, the moral is: BUY NOW, while you and your family still have your health.

Here are your limited choices if sickness disqualifies you from regular coverage. For particulars, ask an insurance agent or your state's insurance commission.

• A handful of states require insurers to take everyone, sometimes at standard rates. These policies usually have large deductibles but will at least cover you for catastrophic costs.

• Some Blue Cross/Blue Shield plans and some HMOs have open-enrollment periods. But you're subject to the rules on preexisting conditions, which may deny coverage for your particular illness for 6 to 18 months. Some diseases may not be accepted, period. Your premium will usually be high, although some states limit how much the insurer can charge. Open enrollment at HMOs may be limited to small businesses and the self-employed.

• You or your spouse might try for a job at a company with a group policy. These plans take all comers, including dependents who are seriously ill. But you may have to wait up to 12 months before the insurer will cover those particular bills. The money available for some illnesses may be capped. Some plans exclude certain illnesses completely, not just for new employees but for everyone.

• If your illness eventually forces you to leave the job, and your company employs 20 people or more, you can stay in the group plan for 18 months at your expense. After that, you can buy individual coverage at standard rates if you can afford it. If you leave your job because you're totally disabled, you can keep the group plan for up to 29 months. If you die, your spouse can keep the plan for up to 36 months.

• The states have special programs for uninsured children from families with modest incomes. Call Medicaid or your city's social services office.

• Your doctor may know of a program for people in need of expensive prescription drugs.

• Try an independent insurance agent. You might get lucky. Some insurers are more liberal than others about accepting certain kinds of health risks.

• If your state has a health insurance pool for high risks, check it out. Unfortunately, you may have to pay 150 percent above the normal price, with a high deductible, substantial co-payments, and modest lifetime benefits. But at least you're protected from most catastrophic costs. At this writing, pools have been approved in twenty-six states. To qualify, you generally have to have lived in the state for 30 days to 12 months and been turned down by one or two private insurers. Some medical conditions, such as cancer or AIDS, let you into the pool immediately. In a few states, there are waiting lists for coverage.

• The healthy dependents of an unhealthy worker can buy their own insurance through many associations, Blue Cross/Blue Shield, or another private insurance company.

• Pray that you're 65 when illness strikes. Medicare has to take you, at no increase in price.

SPOUSES AND CHILDREN WITHOUT THEIR OWN MEDICAL COVERAGE

Everything here applies equally to men. But dependent coverage is overwhelmingly an issue for women and children.

If you are covered under your husband's employee group plan, you risk losing your health insurance if he separates from the company plan or separates from you. That can happen if he dies, if you divorce or separate legally, or if he goes onto Medicare. You can buy your own policy, as an individual or through an association, but it may be expensive. If you're in poor health, you might not find coverage at any price.

For some wives, safety nets exist. But it all depends on where your husband works and what kind of policy he has.

If Your Spouse's Company Employs 20 People or More: You're usually allowed to stay in the employee plan for up to 3 years at your expense. This is known as your COBRA benefit. You're charged the group premium plus 2 percent. The price may be higher than you'd like, but you'll probably get more coverage per dollar than individual policies offer.

To stay in the group, you must: (1) Make sure that your husband's company notifies the insurer about your eligibility. Notification has to be made within 30 days from the day your husband dies or goes onto Medicare, or within 60 days of your divorce or legal separation. Call the company yourself if you think that your husband might not. (2) Watch for a letter from the insurance company asking if you want to continue. You have 60 days to say yes. If you miss any of these deadlines, you're dropped from the plan without the right of appeal.

Your grown children can stay in the group for up to 3 years after they get too old for formal family coverage. To keep them enrolled, alert the plan within 60 days of each child's cutoff age. Some plans will keep them even after COBRA expires.

Your COBRA coverage ends as soon as you (or the child) qualify for another group plan—for example, if you get a job with employee benefits. But if you have an illness that the new plan won't cover, or won't cover right away, your old plan will keep on paying the bills.

If you haven't joined another group plan by the time your COBRA benefits end, you come under the "portability" rules (page 356). You have access to at least two individual health plans without passing a health exam and with no waiting periods for preexisting conditions, including pregnancy. These might be plans from other insurers, your COBRA plan converted to an individual policy, or a state risk pool. There is, of course, the usual hitch: you may not be able to afford the premiums.

If Your Spouse's Company Employs Fewer Than 20 People: You don't get COBRA benefits. But if you've had at least 18 months of group coverage, you have a right to buy an individual policy with no health exam and no waiting period for preexisting conditions, including pregnancy.

If Your Family Carries Its Own Individual Coverage: You can keep the policy if your husband dies. In fact, your premiums will go down because the policy now carries one less person. Many new widows don't realize this and keep on paying for health insurance at the old rate. As soon as you tell the insurer about the death, however, any overpayments should be refunded. Also, ask for a lower premium as soon as your children leave school and are no longer covered under your policy.

If your husband keeps the policy when you divorce or legally separate, you lose your personal health insurance. The children can still come under his plan as long as he agrees to it. Coverage for you might be part of the divorce agreement. If you're in poor health, however, you probably won't find a policy of your own, except perhaps in a state high-risk pool. If your husband is in good health, perhaps he'll agree to look for individual coverage, letting you keep the policy you have.

If Your Income Is Modest: Your state should have a special program for uninsured children. Call an insurance agent or your city's social services office.

HELP FOR THOSE (LIKE ME) WITH PAPERWORK PHOBIAS

And you thought the *government* was bureaucratic. Have you filled in any private-insurance claims lately? Maybe not if you're in an HMO. You face no paperwork there as long as you stick with its approved physicians. In the Medicare program, the doctors submit the claim forms for you. Sometimes they'll handle claims for Medigap coverage, too.

But you face paperwork, big time, in traditional health plans, Medigap plans that you have to handle yourself, PPOs, and point-of-service HMOs if you go to doctors outside the network. You may also have to beard Medicare if the local claims administrator incorrectly rejects a bill.

If everything works right, you fill in the insurance form, attach your doctor's medical report, and send it in. Back comes a check in the right amount. Or the doctor gets the check directly.

What can go wrong? Your doctor might put down the wrong code number for your illness, resulting in an incorrect payment or an outright denial. If you took two children to the same doctor on the same day, the insurer's computer may decide that one of the claims is in error. Forms might come back requesting more information. Forms might get detached, so write your name and policy number on every piece of paper. You might need a special form for prescription drugs. If you're dealing with two insurers—one for doctor bills, one for hospital bills—they may fight over who should cover expenses related to both. You might make a simple mistake on the form like transposing two numbers. (Tip: Fill in a blank form with care and make multiple photocopies of it. Use a copy for every claim.)

Most of all, you might lose track of your expenses. People often save medical bills at home, intending to send them all in at once as soon as they equal the plan's up-front deductible. But some might be misplaced, causing you to pay more than you should. If you submit medical bills after a year or more, they may be refused. The time limits for making a claim will be spelled out in your policy.

Instead, send in a claim for every covered bill, even though you know that you haven't yet met the plan's deductible. The insurer keeps track of those bills and knows to the penny when the deductible is reached. Another reason to send in claims that you know won't be paid: you might need your plan's official denial in order to submit the bill to another insurer or have it paid by your company medical spending account (page 355).

With just a tiny amount of patience, you can handle a few claims a year. But a serious illness can pile up so many bills that filling in claim forms becomes an overwhelming burden. Bills may not be paid because you're too sick to put in claims. A helper may not have the time to take care of a sick person and do the paperwork, too.

You may know a punctilious person who will take over the claim forms for a fee. If you have a small business, maybe your bookkeeper will do it. Alternatively, try the Yellow Pages under Insurance Claims Processing Services. Or get a reference from the National Association of Claims Assistance Professionals, 5329 S. Main St., Suite 102, Downers Grove, IL 60515 (800-660-0665). Send your name, address, phone number, and $1, and NACAP will send you the name of the member nearest you (ask for a second name if you'd like to interview more than one person). Typical fees: $30–$35 an hour in rural areas, up to $85–$90 in big cities.

Claims professionals take the mess off your shoulders. They may charge flat fees, hourly fees, a percentage of the claims collected, or some combination of the three. Besides filling in claims, they should chase payments that are overdue and correct payment errors. One thing they can't do: rescue any payments denied you when you don't follow the health plan's rules.

MEDICARE

Medicare spending is being slowed by paring payments to doctors, hospitals, and HMOs. They'll have to find more efficient ways of treating patients, and no one knows what that's going to mean. But there remains one immutable fact: people 65 and up have national health insurance, unlike those under 65 who may have to go without.

You qualify for Medicare if you've met the work requirement for Social Security benefits, or if you're on the account of someone who qualifies. The latter group includes spouses, unmarried ex-spouses whose marriages lasted at least 10 years, widows and widowers, and parents who got half their support from a Social Security–eligible child who died or became disabled.

You can go on Medicare earlier than 65 if you've been receiving Social Security disability payments for 2 years or if you have lost the use of your kidneys.

Medicare Comes in Two Parts

Part A covers hospital bills and bills for skilled nursing homes, hospice care, and a certain amount of home health care. You have already paid for this coverage in your Social Security taxes, so you get it automatically at 65, at no extra cost.

A tiny percentage of people don't qualify automatically for Part A—for example, those who haven't met Social Security's work requirement. However, you're eligible for Part B (sign up within 3 months before reaching 65). If you buy Part B you're allowed to buy Part A, which cost $311 a month in 1997. For those with official poverty-level incomes, Part A will be paid by your state Medicaid program.

Part B is optional. It carries a monthly premium, which the government deducts from your Social Security check. Your coverage includes, among other things, doctor bills, outpatient surgery, emergency-room treatment for patients not admitted to the hospital, X-rays, laboratory tests, "durable" medical equipment such as wheelchairs and hospital beds, mammograms, PAP smears, screening for diabetes and colon cancer, physical therapy, speech therapy, and some hospitalization for mental care. There's no coverage, however, for prescription drugs.

When you register for Medicare Part A, you're asked if you also want Part B. For 96 percent of you, the answer is yes—*absolutely* yes. But a few people should say no. Here's how to decide:

You Will Need Part B If . . .

• You are moving from an employee plan to a retiree group plan that is still subsidized by your employer. Your benefits stay pretty much the same. But at 65, your company plan pays only the bills that Medicare doesn't—and the plan assumes you have Part B. Some companies pay the Part B premium for you.

• You're covered under your spouse's retiree plan and you're 65 or older. You typically get the same coverage as your spouse, so you, too, will need Part B.

• You have individual (or family) health insurance. Your policies will carry you past 65 but the cost will probably soar. You're better off with Part B and perhaps a Medigap policy (page 395). You have to register for Part B and pay the premium yourself.

• You have no other health insurance. You depend entirely on Medicare to pay your covered medical bills. If you're at the official poverty level, your state Medicaid program will pay the Part B premium for you.

• You're totally disabled and have been on a company disability plan. When you qualify for Medicare, you'll typically have to take both parts. The company may supplement the coverage you get.

• You're 65 and working for a company that employs fewer than 20 people. You will usually be taken off the group health plan (if there is one) and put onto Medicare. Any additional benefits you get depend on how generous your company is. It might pay your Part B premium; it might provide a complete, supplemental Medigap plan; it might offer nothing. These same rules apply to a spouse who is covered on your plan.

• You're 65 and retired but can go on the health plan of your working spouse. There may be a medical exam and a waiting period for covering preexisting conditions. In this case, you'd want Part B. If you can enter the plan with no preconditions, however, and you're in good health, you can do without Part B—at least until your spouse retires.

• You're in a Medicare HMO. The Part B premium is part of the price you pay.

If you fall into one of these groups, sign up for Part B when you get Part A. The premiums for late enrollees go up 10 percent for every year they delay.

When you join Part B at 65, you have 6 months in which to buy Medigap insurance (page 395) at standard rates, regardless of your health. If you dally, that no-excuses opportunity is lost. If you apply later and have a health problem, most states allow you to be rejected.

Consider Taking Only Part A If . . .

• You're 65 and working for a firm that employs at least 20 people and has a good health-insurance plan; or you're 65 and have a spouse who works for such a company. Under the law, you must be allowed to stay in the plan with no reduction in benefits. Your medical bills are insured by the company, just as they were before you turned 65. So Part B may be superfluous.

But don't fail to sign up for Part A! It doesn't cost you anything and gives you extra coverage. Any hospital expenses not paid by the company's insurance (including deductibles and co-payments) can be submitted to Medicare—an ace in the hole that younger people don't have. You are subject to the usual Medicare deductibles. But after that, the government picks up any eligible bills that your health plan doesn't. (If you're seriously ill, reconsider Part B; it, too, can cover bills the company plan won't pay.)

If you skip Part B at 65, for the reasons just discussed, be sure to sign up for it as soon as you or your spouse leaves work. If you wait longer than 8 months, surcharges apply and you won't be able to join until the next Medicare open-enrollment period.

• You're 65 and working for a company that employs fewer than 20 people, but you're part of a multi-employer plan. All the employers might have agreed to keep their workers on group insurance, regardless of their age. This puts you in the same situation as the big-company employee. Sign up for Part A, but in most cases Part B won't be worth the expense.

When you finally leave the job and join Part B, you have 6 months in which to buy Medigap insurance (page 395) at standard rates, regardless of your health, even though you're older than 65.

What If You Have Two Plans to Choose From? You might have health insurance under your own retiree plan plus the option of spousal coverage under the plan of your working spouse. The spousal coverage usually isn't worth paying for. Medicare and your own plan will cover enough of your bills.

What If Your Spouse Is About to Retire, You Have No Employee Plan of Your Own, and You're Not Yet Eligible for Medicare?
There are several ways that you might be insured:

1. Your spouse's retiree plan. It might cover you fully as a dependent.

2. Your spouse's employee group health plan. You may be eligible for up to 3 years of COBRA coverage at your expense, provided that you notify the plan in time (page 386).

3. A conversion policy. Your spouse's old group policy may be convertible into an individual plan for you alone. But it's expensive. You'd buy it only if you couldn't find a cheaper plan somewhere else.

4. Your family's individual health plan, assuming you've been carrying one. It can be retooled to provide full coverage for you alone.

5. A new individual policy that you buy yourself. This suggestion is probably a pipe dream. Older people find individual coverage prohibitively expensive, if they're offered it at all.

WHEN TO SIGN UP FOR MEDICARE

If you took early Social Security retirement benefits (age 62–65): You'll be enrolled in Medicare automatically at 65. You'll get a notice when coverage starts. If you don't want Part B, check the appropriate box on the notice and send it back.

If you qualify for Social Security's disability benefits: You'll get Medicare 2 years after receiving your first disability check.

If your kidneys fail: Sign up immediately. You get benefits 3 months after the start of dialysis at a medical facility or right away if you're in a self-dialysis program. Transplant patients get benefits the very month they enter the hospital.

If you're 65 and about to retire: Sign up for Medicare when you apply for Social Security. Do it during the 3 months before your 65th birthday. That way you'll be covered from the month of your birthday on. If you sign up in your birthday month, your Part B coverage starts the first day of the following month.

If you're 65 and still working: Sign up for Part A (and Part B, if you want it) during the 3 months before your 65th birthday and no later than your birthday month. The same is true for a spouse covered under your plan.

If you worked past 65, stayed in an employer plan, and have just retired: Join Part B in the month that you retire or up to 3 months before. That way you'll be covered as of that month. If you join during the following 7 months, you are covered from the first day of the month after the month you enroll. The same rules apply to a spouse who is covered by your plan.

Don't miss your sign-up dates! If you do and get sick, here's what happens:

1. You're normally okay on your Part A bills. Anyone 65 or older who has met Social Security's work requirement can sign up without penalty at any time. If you haven't met the work requirement, you must be claiming benefits on the account of someone who has. Expenses are covered retroactively for the past 6 months. If you forget to enroll and then enter a hospital, you or your representative should fill out a statement of intent to claim Medicare benefits. That's considered an application and your bills will be insured (although a formal application must be made eventually). If no intent form is signed at the hospital and you die, Medicare won't pay.

2. There will be a gap in your Part B coverage, depending on how long you procrastinate. If you sign up within the 3 months after turning 65, you'll have to wait 2 months before your coverage starts. Any bills incurred during that period won't be paid. If 3 months pass, you won't have another chance at Part B until the next general enrollment period. That's January 1 through March 31 of each year, with coverage beginning the following July 1. Your premium will be 10 percent higher for each 12-month period when you could have been enrolled but weren't.

3. No surcharges apply if you work past 65 and join Part B within 8 months of your retirement. Otherwise, you will have to wait until the next general enrollment period and pay the 10 percent surcharge for being late.

WHAT MEDICARE DOESN'T COVER

I haven't listed in detail all the benefits Medicare provides. The government publishes dandy free booklets on the subject, which you can get from your local Social Security office. You can also find a wealth of consumer information on the Web site run by the Health Care Financing Administration, which is the government agency that oversees Medicare. Go to http://www.hcfa.gov. Or write for the excellent free booklet *Guide to Health Insurance for People with Medicare*, HCFA, 7500 Security Blvd., Baltimore, MD 21244.

It's more important that you understand the gaps in your government insurance. Most of them are small. Older people have virtually all of their medical bills insured.

1. You pay an up-front deductible when you're hospitalized. It's applied to every "benefit period," which roughly corresponds with a spell of illness and rises a little bit every year (in 1997 the deductible came to $760). Once you've paid the deductible, you're covered in full for 60 days. If the need for hospital treatment continues, you pay part of the bill ($190 a day in 1997) for the 61st through the 90th day. You requalify for 90 days of coverage again and again, as long as you return to the hospital during different "benefit periods."

2. After 90 days in the hospital during any single benefit period, you start dipping into what's called your "lifetime reserve days." You get 60 of those, which you also pay a portion of. Once they're used, they're forever gone. But hardly anyone faces this long a stay today. You'd almost certainly be moved to a skilled nursing home.

3. For doctor bills and other medical services, Medicare establishes a fee schedule that varies slightly from one part of the country to another. You pay a small deductible every year ($100). After that, Medicare pays 80 percent of the scheduled fee for that particular treatment and you pay 20 percent. To take an example, say $500 is the scheduled fee. Medicare pays $400, you pay $100. In certain hardship cases, doctors can waive your share.

Most doctors charge no more than the Medicare maximum. They're called participating doctors or doctors who "accept assignment." At your very first meeting, make sure the doctor participates. Some states require docs to abide by the Medicare fee.

A few doctors insist on billing more. If you insist on seeing them, you'll have to pay the excess charge. In traditional Medicare, however, they can't charge more than 15 percent above the scheduled amount (10 percent in New York). Using this example, a procedure that should normally cost $500 can't go above $575. Medicare's payment toward such a bill would stay at $400 (80 percent of the scheduled fee). You'd have to pay $175. Check the Explanation of Medicare Benefits form that you get after every claim to be sure that the doctor didn't charge more than the allowable amount.

A Warning: When you go to the hospital for surgery, you may think you've controlled your costs because your doctor accepts what Medicare will pay. But the radiologist or anesthesiologist may not accept it, which you won't realize until you get their super-charged bills. For these docs, you're a captive patient; they don't have to compete for your business by charging a "Medicare-reasonable" price. To me, the whole arrangement smacks of monopoly profits. The hospitals should not allow it. Your own doctor should not allow it. You should be able to assemble an entire team that accepts Medicare assignment.

Another Warning: Hospital outpatient departments are permitted to bill you for 20 percent of what they charge, which is generally much higher than the Medicare-approved amount. For example, say they bill you $600 when $350 is the approved amount. They may tell you they "accept assignment." Nevertheless, your 20 percent share of the total charge comes to $120. If your share were figured on the Medicare-approved amount, as it is everywhere else, you'd pay only $70. Medicare is gradually correcting this problem, tying your co-payment to the Medicare-approved amount. But the fix will take many years. For now, consider an ambulatory surgical center for outpatient surgery, where your co-pay will be only 20 percent of what Medicare approves.

4. Medicare pays for "appropriate" treatment that is "medically necessary." It might deny payment for treatment that it doesn't think you need. If a decision goes against you, or you think you haven't been properly reimbursed, you can and should appeal (page 395).

If your doctor anticipates a problem with the board that decides how long you should be hospitalized and how your treatment should be managed, he or she should present your case before you're even admitted, if there's time.

5. You're insured for up to 100 days in a skilled nursing home if you're there to recuperate after spending at least 3 consecutive days in a hospital. After the 20th day, however, you pay part of the cost ($95 per day in 1997).

6. You're not insured for the cost of most prescription drugs. This can be a serious problem for people with chronic illnesses. Some Medigap policies pay for drugs, but their premiums are high (page 396). You'll probably pay the least for drug coverage in a Medicare HMO (page 377).

7. Important! Medicare doesn't cover the cost of long-term custodial care for people with Alzheimer's disease or who need daily help with such things as eating, dressing, and bathing. The Medicaid program pays for patients who have no substantial income or assets. If you don't qualify for Medicaid, consider buying long-term-care insurance (page 401).

8. Among the excluded odds and ends: routine physicals, eye and hearing exams, glasses, hearing aids, private-duty nurses, medical bills you incur while traveling abroad, most immunizations, dentures, routine dental and foot care, orthopedic shoes, and homemaker services. Some of these can be covered by Medigap insurance or a Medicare HMO. Travel agents sell short-term health insurance to seniors on cruises or other foreign trips.

One of the Kindest Things Adult Children Can Do for Their Parents Is to See That the Medicare Bills Are Properly Reimbursed. If you don't have time to do it yourself, hire a Medicare claims adjuster (page 387). Sometimes Medicare turns down valid bills or doesn't pay as much as it should.

If that happens, ask your doctor to check the claim form to be sure that everything was filled in correctly. If the form shows that the doctor charged more than the amount Medicare allows, ask if he or she will waive the excess charge. In traditional Medicare, it's illegal for docs to charge more than 15 percent above the Medicare amount (10 percent in New York), although they can charge what they like for expenses not covered by Medicare.

Appealing Medicare Denials. If you disagree with the decision on a Medicare claim, you can ask for a review. Information on how to do it, and the deadlines for filing, are enclosed with the form rejecting the claim. Follow the rules to the letter, don't miss the deadlines, and don't let anyone discourage you, including personnel at the Social Security office. Thousands of people win their cases.

Part A and Part B have different appeals procedures. To win, you have to present additional information about your case, specifically rebutting the reason given for turning you down. The process takes time and paperwork, but a lot of money gets recovered.

Write to your congressperson as part of your attack. His or her office might follow up on your complaint. Check the Yellow Pages under "Senior Citizens." You may find an organization that helps older people with problems like these. Consult a lawyer if a lot of money is involved. The AARP has a free booklet, *Knowing Your Rights: Medicare Protections for Hospital Patients* (Stock #D12330), AARP, Fulfillment EEO1139, 601 E St. N.W., Washington, DC 20049. You'll also find detailed information at http://www.hcfa.gov, the Web site of the Health Care Financing Administration.

PLUGGING THE MEDIGAP

How will you cover the expenses that Medicare doesn't? Low-cost company insurance solves the problem for some lucky retirees (although their monthly premiums are going up). Medicaid pays the bills for many low-income people. Everyone else has the option of a Medicare HMO (page 377) or a Medicare-supplement policy, popularly known as Medigap insurance.

Medigap policies are sold by private insurers. You cannot be rejected for reasons of health, or even charged a higher premium, if you apply for Medigap within 6 months after turning 65 and joining Medicare Part B. Starting in July 1998, you also get guaranteed admission under two circumstances: (1) You joined a managed-care plan at 65 and, within 12 months, switched to regular Medicare plus Medigap. (2) You started out with Medicare and Medigap, switched to managed care, then switched back again within 12 months. In this case, your free pass is limited to your old Medigap plan and just a few others.

Medigap insurers can refuse to pay for preexisting conditions during the first 6 months the plan is in effect.

THE MEDIGAP STANDARDS

Only ten standard Medigap policies are on the market today, labeled A through J. Each one has a different benefit mix, but the mix doesn't change from one insurer to another. So the companies are competing solely on service, reliability, and price. All ten policies aren't available in every state or from every insurer. Three states—Massachusetts, Minnesota, and Wisconsin—have standardized policies of their own (for details, call the insurance department in the state capital).

Otherwise, here are the policies you can choose among, from the cheapest (policy A—around $400 annually) to the most expensive (policy J—around $2,000). Each insurer sets a different price, so check out several options. Every policy is guaranteed renewable unless you don't pay your premiums or materially misstate your health status on your application. All of these plans can make you wait 6 months before covering preexisting conditions.

SHOULD YOU REALLY BUY
MEDIGAP INSURANCE?

With any insurance, "first dollar" coverage is expensive, relative to what you get. "First dollar" means no deductible. The insurer picks up the bill from the very first dollar you owe—for example, the $100 annual deductible for doctor bills. One rule of insurance is that people should pay those dollars themselves. Regrettably, every Medigap plan has to offer this feature.

Another rule is that it's not worth insuring expenses likely to occur because the cost of insurance may be roughly what you'd pay anyway. As an example, take the plans that offer prescription-drug insurance. To get the full benefit from plans H and I, you'd need to spend at least $2,750 on drugs. With plan J, you'd need to spend at least $6,250. They're great buys for people who need a lot of expensive drugs to control a chronic illness. Otherwise, you might as well build your own "drug fund" with money in the bank.

BENEFITS	STANDARD PLANS									
	A	B	C	D	E	F	G	H	I	J
Basic benefits: your 20% share of each doctor bill under Part B; your co-payment for days 61–90 of a long hospital stay; your co-payment for "lifetime benefit" days; 365 extra days of hospital expenses if you exhaust Part A; 3 pints of blood a year; your 50% share of outpatient mental-health expenses	✓	✓	✓	✓	✓	✓	✓	✓	✓	✓
The Part A hospital deductible		✓	✓	✓	✓	✓	✓	✓	✓	✓
The $100 Part B deductible for doctor bills			✓			✓				✓
Your share of the cost of a stay in a skilled nursing home for days 21–100, after a 3-day hospital stay			✓	✓	✓	✓	✓	✓	✓	✓
Some emergency care abroad			✓	✓	✓	✓	✓	✓	✓	✓
Up to $1,600 annually for short-term custodial help if you're recovering at home from an illness, injury, or surgery				✓			✓		✓	✓
$120 of preventive care annually, such as physical exams and hearing tests					✓					✓
Part of what your doctor might charge in excess of the approved Medicare amount						✓			✓	✓
Basic benefit for prescription drugs: half your cost up to an annual benefit of $1,250, after you've met a $250 deductible								✓	✓	
Extended benefit for prescription drugs: half your cost up to a maximum annual benefit of $3,000, after you've met a $250 deductible										✓

Medicare SELECT—You can buy any one of these Medigap plans, but you have to see certain doctors and go to certain hospitals. Medicare pays, no matter where you go. But the Medigap portion is reimbursed only for the participating doctors. As you get older, your premium may rise. At 65, SELECT costs less than a regular Medigap policy from the same insurer but may not be the cheapest plan on the market. By 75, SELECT policies often cost more.

Yet another rule is not to insure for risks you're not going to take. Young retirees who travel abroad can buy trip medical insurance through travel agents. When you're older, you probably won't make those trips, so why have a plan that insures you permanently for medical care abroad? And why have a plan that covers excess doctor's charges (charges above the approved Medicare amount) when four doctors out of five don't bill excess charges and most of the rest will waive them if asked?

Insurance should cover dangers that are plausible but remote and would impose a terrible burden if you had to shoulder the cost yourself. But most of the holes these policies plug aren't very large. Assuming you enter retirement with a decent amount of savings, I could argue that you don't need Medigap at all.

At most, consider the basic plan. It protects against super-long hospital stays, even though they hardly ever happen today. After that, your money is probably better spent on long-term-care insurance (page 401). Long-term care is more than a gap in your Medicare coverage—it's a crater. That's the kind of risk to insure.

Pricing Medigap

Some insurers fix your premium based on your age when the policy was bought. Others charge everyone the same (state law may require it, to protect consumers against predators).

In yet other states, insurers can and do raise your premium as you age. To me, that's a form of bait and switch. You're lured with a low starting price; once you're locked in, your premiums rise steeply, especially for older people (see Medicare SELECT, page 397). When you reach your 80s, the premiums may become a serious burden. When buying Medigap insurance, ask the agent for a policy whose premium is fixed for life—and be sure that's specified in the contract. Such coverage will cost more at the start, but you'll be able to budget for it and will probably pay less over a lifetime.

Employee group Medicare supplements are often a bargain, although they're available only to a company's retired and disabled employees. Some associations offer Medigap, but compare the price with what's available elsewhere. Association insurance isn't always cheap and you're usually charged more as you age.

When Policy Shopping. Check Blue Cross/Blue Shield, the American Association of Retired Persons (AARP), and a Medicare HMO, as well as the policies your insurance agent sells. HMOs (page 377) often offer more Medigap coverage at a lower price than freestanding policies provide.

If you're in poor health and didn't sign up for Medigap during those 6 open months, some insurers (including the AARP) accept all comers for plans A through G. Also, check with your state's insurance department. Some states require the Blues and HMOs to accept all applicants during open-enrollment periods. A few states require insurers to take all comers at standard rates.

Whatever you do, buy from a company with high safety-and-soundness ratings (page 342—Weiss is the only firm that rates large numbers of HMOs). Reject any insurer whose literature implies that it's somehow connected with Medicare or Social Security. The government does not sell Medigap insurance.

Should You Switch Medigap Policies? The ten standard policies were introduced in 1992. A policy bought previously may be equally good or better, so from a benefits point of view there's generally no need to switch. But your insurer may discontinue that older line, or the price may be raised to something unaffordable. If you've purchased since 1992, you might switch to get a different mix of benefits.

Don't switch unless you must. Once you've passed 65½, you may be charged substantially more than the standard price. At this point, your best buy will doubtlessly be an HMO.

It's illegal, by the way, for an agent to sell you more than one Medigap policy. If you buy a new one, you're supposed to sign a statement saying that you plan to cancel the old one. Be sure to do so as soon as your new coverage takes effect.

When you buy a Medigap policy you have 30 days to change your mind. If you regret your move, once the salesperson walks out the door, mail back the policy and ask for a premium refund (registered mail is probably a good idea).

If Your Income Is Low. You don't have to buy your own Medigap coverage. The Medicaid program will supply it, often buying you one of the ten standard policies. Two other state-run options exist for low-income people: the Qualified Medicare Beneficiary Program, which provides free basic Medigap for the old or disabled whose incomes are at or below the poverty level; and the Specified Low-Income Medicare Beneficiary Program, for the elderly just above the poverty level.

A Little-Known Gap in Medigap. If you're under 65 and on Medicare because you're disabled or suffering from kidney failure, you're not acceptable to the sellers of Medigap coverage except in the handful of states that require insurers to take you. Ask an insurance agent or the state insurance department if yours is one of those states. Some states make coverage available in their high-risk pools.

You do qualify for Medigap at 65, at standard rates and regardless of your health, as long as you enroll within 6 months after turning that magic age. If you use a lot of prescription drugs, don't fail to buy a Medigap policy that covers them. Like other Medigap enrollees, you'll have to wait up to 6 months before being covered for preexisting conditions.

Paying Claims. Your Medicare carrier will handle both your Medicare and Medigap claims if your doctor accepts Medicare assignment (page 393) and indicates on the Medicare form that you want all the payments made directly. You'll get an Explanation of Medicare Benefits Form explaining what was paid and what you still owe.

GAMES SLEAZY AGENTS PLAY

They claim to be from Medicare when they're not, or they print "Medicare Consultant" on their business cards. Medicare doesn't sell insurance or send out consultants.

They scare you into thinking that your next illness will wipe you out. It won't. Medicare covers almost all big doctor and hospital bills.

They disparage the cheaper Medigap policies and put you into the costlier ones. Plan F (page 397) is a particular favorite because it covers doctors' charges that exceed what Medicare pays. But hardly any doctors levy excess charges today, so you're paying for a benefit you're unlikely to use. Guess whom that helps? (Tip: it's not you.)

They play bait and switch (page 363). Your policy looks cheap at the start, but ten years from now it may be so costly that you can't afford it anymore. To do some agents justice, they may not know how the policy works. (Given the choice, would you rather your agent be sleazy or dumb?) Ask them what people 75 and 85 are paying now. They can look it up.

They claim that the policy covers you for things it won't. Check this by asking for the policy outline they're supposed to give you. Send the agent away, read the outline yourself, and then decide.

They don't report all your recent illnesses if you're buying after 65½ and they fill out the application for you. That gets you a policy at an affordable price. But you only *imagine* that you're insured. When you file a claim, the insurer may refuse to pay on the ground that your application fraudulently concealed your true state of health.

They tell you your present Medigap policy is awful, in order to switch you to a new one if your health is good. That costs you another sales commission. If your health isn't good, they'll sell you unnecessary cancer or heart-attack insurance.

They sell you a Medigap policy even though you have Medicare-supplement coverage through a retiree health plan. They claim that the extra insurance will double your payment. In fact, your retiree insurance usually won't pay if you've bought a separate Medigap policy.

They sell you policies that pay $100 or $200 a day when you're in the hospital. But you're not in the hospital much nowadays. When you have Medigap or Medicaid, this stuff is unnecessary.

Think about checking an older relative's insurance to see if he or she is innocently carrying this junk.

RETIREE GROUP COVERAGE

When you retire, your group health plan may transform itself into supplemental Medicare coverage. You'll have to sign up for Medicare Parts A and B, but your company may cover most of the Part B premium cost. Your policy will probably cover the gaps in Medicare, listed on page 397, plus such extras as home care, generous payments for prescription drugs, and perhaps dental care. There are no waiting periods or exclusions for preexisting conditions.

Check the booklet that describes your costs and benefits, including those for your spouse. It will almost certainly state that the company has the right to change the plan. I call this the "maybe not" clause, as in, "I'm paying all your medical bills today, but tomorrow maybe not." Benefits can be shaved and your annual premium can be raised. Nevertheless, even at a higher cost you have much better coverage than seniors who have no company plan at all.

A company cannot cancel a benefit that was specifically promised, except in a bankruptcy or a corporate takeover. Even then, it's rare for a retiree medical plan to be withdrawn. If the worst happens, you still have Medicare and can buy your own Medigap if you want.

LONG-TERM-CARE (LTC) INSURANCE

Long-term-care policies address themselves to a brand-new insurance market: the first generation of Americans to be fearful not of dying too soon but of living too long. These policies pay for custodial care if you're no longer able to manage yourself—because of Alzheimer's, perhaps, or because you need substantial help with the simple activities of daily life. Nursing homes cost $30,000 to $80,000 or more a year. The policy might also cover adult day care, an assisted-living facility, or even approved care in your own home.

What is your chance of needing long-term care? Sales material tends to exaggerate. According to the National Association of Insurance Commissioners, only one person in 3 who turned 65 in 1990 will spend time in a nursing home, not counting the patients who stay 3 months or less. One out of 4 will stay a year. About one out of 10 will stay 5 years or more—with the risk much higher for women than men.

Who should consider LTC insurance? You're a likely candidate if you have money to spare and:

1. You could afford to pay the nursing home yourself—for a while, at least—but would rather not. You want your spouse to have the money, or you want to leave it to your kids. So instead of using your own funds to pay the bills, you buy an insurance policy that will cover most of the cost.

2. You couldn't afford the nursing-home bill unless you sold some of your assets. You don't want to do that, especially if you have a spouse to think about.

3. You have a modest income and few assets, so you'd qualify for Medicaid immediately (page 409). Financially speaking, you don't need LTC insurance. But you usually can't get into the better nursing homes if you start as a Medicaid patient (they put you on an eternal "waiting list"). You're more likely to go to a Medicaid home where the care is more bare-bones.

Nursing homes aren't supposed to discriminate, but they often feel they must. Medicaid doesn't pay enough to maintain a patient in quality circumstances. So the homes prefer you to start as a private-pay patient— for 6 months to a year, at least—before switching to Medicaid. By maintaining a mix of Medicaid and private-pay residents, the homes can keep their standards up. To assure their parents' access to these homes, children sometimes assist them with LTC premiums.

Who might not want to buy? If you have no spouse who needs your money, and your children are well provided for, why bother with LTC insurance? You may never need nursing-home care. If you do, you can pay for it yourself and go on Medicaid when your money runs out. Long-term care is one of the contingencies that you spent a lifetime saving *for*.

Should you buy through an association or employee plan? Consider it if you're offered a policy and can afford it. You typically buy at a discount (but compare it with other policies to be sure). Your premium will be based on your age when you buy but not on your state of health. At larger companies, you generally don't even have to fill in a health questionnaire. Ditto at smaller firms if enough employees participate. Otherwise, questionnaires are required and buyers charged an average price, based on their collective health. Coverage will be offered to your spouse and sometimes even to your parents, depending on their health.

But check what happens when you leave the company or the association. You want to be sure that you can take the policy with you at no increase in price. If you can't, buy your policy somewhere else. Any coverage you buy should be able to stay with you for life.

If your employer or association switches to a new LTC insurer, stay with the old one if you can. That way your premium won't go up. If you switch to the new insurance company, you'll probably have to pay more because you're older now. In some cases, however, the new insurer will let you keep paying the old rate.

If you bought your plan through your spouse's employer, and your spouse dies or splits, you're entitled to continue coverage on your own.

When should you buy LTC insurance? The younger you are the cheaper it is. If you buy at 50 and hold for 35 years (to age 85) you'll pay less than if you buy at 75 and hold for 10 years, even counting what that early money could have earned if invested elsewhere. Furthermore, you can't buy a policy unless you're in reasonably good health, so the longer you wait, the greater the risk that you won't be fully insurable.

The actual dollars you spend depend on the benefits you buy. At 50, you're probably looking at $500 to $1,000 a year for individual coverage if you're in tip-top health. At 70, it's $3,500 to $5,000 a year. In real life, young people tend to have more pressing financial worries than long-term care. So the typical buyer is 60 or 70—obviously, someone with money to spare. You might get interested in your 50s, however, if you're offered a low-cost employee policy.

What type of coverage should you have? There are two types of policies. "Disability" or "per diem" policies pay a flat daily amount, regardless of your cost of care. You might choose anything from $50 to $250 a day. No proof of expenses is required once you've qualified for benefits (although your health will be checked from time to time). "Reimbursement" policies pay a percentage of the actual cost (often 100 percent), up to the daily maximum you bought. Reimbursement plans require more medical paperwork but are generally less expensive.

Most policies limit what they'll pay for certain types of care, especially care at home.

How much LTC coverage should you buy? At minimum, estimate how much you could afford to pay for a nursing home, from your pension, savings, and Social Security. Compare that with the nursing home's actual daily cost and insure yourself for the difference. If you could pay $50 a day and the home costs $110, you'd want to be covered for $60 a day. Alternatively, if you want more income to go to your spouse, insure yourself for the full $110 a day.

Next, consider how long you're willing to wait before benefits begin. The longer the wait, the lower the monthly premium. A 100-day wait might require you to pay $10,000 or $12,000 before the policy kicked in. But your premium might be 5 percent lower than if you took a 60-day wait and 10 percent lower than if you took a 20-day wait, depending on your age. Any days you wait for home-care benefits are normally counted toward your nursing-home wait. Most new LTC policies don't pay at all unless your disability is expected to last at least 90 days.

Leaving aside short stays of 3 months or less, the average nursing-home stay appears to be somewhere around 3 years. Around 10 percent of the patients stay 5 years or longer. A 5-year benefit costs 15 to 20 percent more than a 3-year benefit. A lifetime benefit costs 25 to 50 percent more. If you buy in your 80s, you might be offered only a 2-year benefit.

Whether to buy a 5-year or lifetime benefit depends on how you want to handle your personal finances. If you enter a nursing home and outlive the policy, you'll have to spend your own money, which may be okay with you. If it's not, buy a longer-term policy. If both the insurance and your personal savings run out, the nursing home keeps you for whatever Medicaid pays.

Policies may have dollar caps rather than time limits. The higher the cap, the more you'll pay. An unlimited cap covers you for life. A $250,000 cap might last 5 years, depending on what local nursing homes charge, and costs perhaps 20 percent less than unlimited cap. Some policies have both time and dollar caps.

An important question for your agent, rarely asked: How does the LTC insurer calculate how fast you're using up your benefits? Some policies pay for a specified number of days, even if your expenses on some of those days were small. The better policies go by dollars, covering you until a specified dollar pool has been depleted.

What Should the Policy Include? Read any policy carefully before sign-ing up—and I mean the actual contract, not the short sales brochure. Some literature waffles; some salespeople misspeak. You have 30 days during which you can give the policy back and get a refund. Here's what you want to see in a long-term-care policy, in black and white:

1. *Comprehensive coverage.* Your policy should click in if you're suffer-ing from Alzheimer's or a similar brain disease, or if you're unable to perform at least two of the following activities: bathing, dressing, toileting, continence, eating, and transferring (for example, from your bed to a chair). Some policies cover only five of those activities, perhaps leaving out bath-ing. Yet the ability to bathe yourself is often the thing that goes first. Restric-tive policies may not pay until you fail three of the tests.

Check what the insurer means by "unable to perform." Some policies won't pay unless you can't perform those activities without help. Less re-strictive policies pay if you merely need supervision. If the policy is vague, benefits are easier to deny.

Also find out if you're covered for nervous or mental disorders other than those traceable to an organic disease such as Alzheimer's. Most LTC policies exclude them. They also exclude coverage for drug or alcohol addiction.

2. *Payment for care in any licensed nursing facility*—a nursing home, assisted-living facility, adult day care, or any other approved setting. Avoid policies that limit you to particular types of places. You and the insurer should be able to decide on the best venue. You should also be covered for every level of care—skilled, intermediate, custodial, medical, and thera-peutic.

3. *A home-care option.* Some nursing-home policies offer a rider for certain types of home care. The annual home-care benefit should equal at least half of the money available for a nursing home. Some policies set up one benefit for nursing homes and a separate one for home care. More flexible policies give you a pot of benefits that can be used in any qualified setting—home, community, or nursing home. The latter type of coverage is more expensive but the dollars may go further.

If your budget is limited, buy only nursing-home coverage. That's the potentially catastrophic cost. Home care is a lovely extra, but only if you can afford it.

Some people do exactly the opposite—they buy LTC policies for home care only. But you're deluding yourself if you think that your policy's limited benefits will keep you home indefinitely. Any condition that triggers home-care coverage will probably land you in a nursing home, and sooner rather than later. You'll then be stuck with paying for your care yourself.

4. *An inflation option.* This is chiefly for younger buyers. If you choose a $100 benefit at 50, what will that buy when you're 80? Sweet nothing, that's what. A typical inflation rider adds 5 percent to your benefit each

year. That can be a simple 5 percent or a compounded 5 percent. The latter costs more but is also worth more. You might also have the option of linking your benefit to the consumer price index, although at this writing it's rising more slowly than health-care costs. Some policies build in inflation costs, which raises your premium every year. Less costly policies give you the right to buy future inflation adjustments every one, two, or three years, if you can afford it. Older buyers—say, in their late 70s—may not want to bother with inflation protection.

5. *Level premiums.* If you buy at age 50, paying a "guaranteed" premium of $700 a year, you want that $700 to last for the life of the policy. In theory, it will. In practice, the insurer (with the state's permission) can raise prices on all LTC policies of that class if they're not profitable enough. Buyers should be prepared to pay more to keep their coverage in force. Some policies specify that your premiums will rise as you age, but that's a risky deal. By the time you reach 70, you may not be able to afford your coverage anymore.

6. *Waiver of premium.* You should be able to stop paying premiums when you start collecting benefits or if you've collected benefits for a limited period of time. The waiver should cover home care as well as nursing-home care.

7. *Preexisting conditions.* Most group policies accept all comers, regardless of health, but won't cover preexisting conditions right away. A preexisting condition is generally defined as an ailment you had in the 6-month period before joining the plan. After a 6-month wait, those ailments have to be covered. Some plans offer more liberal terms or even accept you with no wait at all. Individual policies, or group policies with health questionnaires, don't have waiting periods for preexisting conditions. But they may exclude coverage for certain illnesses or refuse to accept you, period.

8. *Lapse protection.* Loss of memory is a leading reason for needing nursing-home care. Unfortunately, one of the things you might have forgotten to pay is the premium on your LTC insurance. To protect yourself: (1) Ask the company to notify at least one friend or family member, and preferably three, if your policy is being canceled for nonpayment of premiums. (2) Tell those friends and relatives about the company's reinstatement rules, which will be printed in your contract. Where there's memory lapse, your insurer will usually restore your coverage if no more than 5 months have passed—assuming that your relatives get the back premiums paid. (3) Arrange for your premiums to be paid automatically through payroll deduction or from your bank account.

LTC insurance vs. Medigap. When people start Medicare at 65, they often buy a rich Medigap policy to plug the holes in their government insurance. But Medigap covers a lot of bills that you could probably pay yourself. By contrast, a stay in a nursing home could wipe you out. If money is tight, consider LTC coverage first, perhaps combined with the most basic Medigap policy. More extensive Medigap coverage should be lower on your list, if you buy it at all.

Do you want "nonforfeiture benefits"? Not in my book. They promise to pay for a limited amount of long-term care, at no extra cost, if you let the policy lapse after a certain number of years. This rider is hugely expensive, however. You're better off using the money for almost anything else.

State buying guides. Call your state insurance department in the state capital. See if it publishes a free *Buyer's Guide* to long-term-care insurance. By law, your agent should give you *A Shopper's Guide to Long-Term Care Insurance,* published by the National Association of Insurance Commissioners (NAIC).

Should You Upgrade Your Older LTC Policy? By "older," I mean policies bought prior to 1990 or so. Some of these policies have severe limitations —for example, they might exclude Alzheimer's disease or pay for custodial care only if you've recently had a 3-day hospital stay. Such limited coverage is probably a candidate for the dump. On the other hand, some older policies offer liberal benefits and should definitely be kept.

An insurance agent might try to talk you out of an older policy—even a good one—just to obtain a sales commission. Don't bite unless your coverage is truly inadequate. A new policy will cost you more, not just because of the sales commission but because you're older now.

If you need better benefits, talk to your present insurer first. Some let you supplement your old coverage, charging you higher premiums only for the benefits you add. Some will issue a new policy but at a lower price than you'd normally pay. Some, however, merely sell you new coverage priced at your present age. If you don't get a price break, shop around to see what other insurers have.

Some states prohibit insurance agents from charging new sales commissions on policies that duplicate the benefits you had before (but that assumes the agent reports the duplication; check this on your application). Don't cancel your old policy until your new one takes effect.

TAX BREAKS FOR LTC INSURANCE

• Part of your premium payment qualifies as a deductible medical expense, whether you buy employee coverage or an individual LTC policy. The size of your write-off depends on your age. In 1997, for example, a 40-year-old could deduct $200 while a 70-year-old could deduct $2,000. These write-offs rise every year to reflect increases in health-care costs. To make use of this tax break, however, you have to itemize deductions. You will also need high medical expenses. Qualified expenses can't be deducted unless they exceed 7.5 percent of your adjusted gross income.

- If your LTC policy reimburses you for your actual expenses, you get those benefits tax-free. If you're paid a flat per diem rate, regardless of the size of your actual expenses, the benefits are tax-free up to a fixed amount ($175 a day in 1997; this cap rises with health-cost inflation). Your deduction can exceed the cap if your actual medical expenses do.
- When you spend your own money on long-term care, it counts as a tax-deductible medical expense. You can write off qualified home-care and community-care expenses as well as nursing-home expenses. The size of your uninsured LTC expenses might reduce or eliminate your taxable income.
- These tax breaks apply to two types of LTC policies: those that meet the federal standards established in 1997 and policies in existence prior to January 1, 1997, whether they meet the new standards or not. Any new policy must disclose whether it's tax qualified.

CHOOSING AN LTC INSURER

Benefits vary so much that two policies cannot be compared by price. Ask your insurance agent to show you what two or three different companies offer so you can get a feel for the kinds of choices you might make. There's a place for comparing policies in the back of the NAIC *Shopper's Guide.*

Whatever you do, pick a company with top safety ratings (page 343) that's firmly committed to selling LTC insurance. This business is pretty new; companies come and go; it's not clear that the risks are properly priced. An unusually low-priced policy may be canceled after just a few years, leaving you high and dry. At this writing, companies considered committed to the business include Aegon USA, CNA, GE Capital Assurance, John Hancock, MetLife, Travelers Life & Annuity, and UNUM Life Insurance Co. of America (although not all of these insurers sell policies in all states and it's always possible that one or more will sell its book of business!).

While we're on the subject of reliability, let's deconstruct that lovely phrase "guaranteed renewable," which almost all new policies are. This means one thing: the insurer can't cancel your policy individually (unless you stop paying premiums). But it can abandon the business in your area or your state, and there goes your "guarantee." That's why it's so important that your company be devoted to LTC insurance. You need to believe that someone will say, "yes, ma'am," forty years from now when your granddaughter calls to activate your benefits.

LTC ALTERNATIVES

- Join a continuing-care or life-care community. This is LTC insurance by another name. The community provides medical care, home care, and social services. You pay a large up-front sum plus a monthly maintenance fee, which will rise as the cost of maintaining the community does. You also agree to pay other costs that may be assessed in the future. You move into a house or apartment, as you choose, and carry on your life. You're not accepted unless you can live independently.

If you start to fail, you move to more supervised quarters that include home care. If that's not enough, you move to the community's nursing home. The community will also have close ties to a nearby hospital. With some contracts, you prepay for certain amounts of nursing care; with others, you're guaranteed access to care but pay for each service that you use.

When considering these arrangements, don't judge only by the living quarters or activities. Take a good look at the home-care apartments and nursing home to see if they're really of the quality you want. Talk to some of the residents, especially the sick ones. Be sure the facility is accredited by the Continuing Care Accreditation Commission sponsored by the American Association of Homes and Services for the Aging (AAHSA). Among the other things to check: an audited financial statement (is the line labeled "fund balance" or "net assets" in the black?), written assurance from an actuary that the community is on a sound financial footing, a history of the community's rise in monthly fees (if the fees aren't keeping up with inflation, that may portend a big rise in the future), any lawsuits against the community, the occupancy rate (if the rate is falling, why?), and your financial options if you decide to leave. A lawyer should read the contract and explain it to you before you sign. Call the AAHSA (202-783-7286) for a free list of accredited communities plus a brochure on how to evaluate one. You'll also find a list of members and detailed consumer information on AAHSA's Web site, http://www.aahsa.org.

• Some insurers (UNUM is one) sell disability policies (page 429) that turn into long-term-care insurance when you retire—a pretty smart option, I'd say. The chances are small that you'd have to enter a nursing home while you're still of working age.

• Many life insurance companies let you draw on some or all of the policy's face value to help cover nursing-home bills (page 338). But this may deprive your family of funds they'll need after you die. Using Medicaid is probably a better choice.

• Take a reverse mortgage on your home (page 942) and use that to help pay your nursing-home bills.

Don't Count on Being Cared For by One of Your Adult Children, in Your Home or Theirs. What with jobs, kids, mobility, illness, and divorce, your children may not have the time, energy, or resources to take up the burden of your care. They will worry about you. They will supervise. But if you guilt-trip them into doing it all themselves, you may hurt their marriages or their health, cost them their jobs, cause them to turn down a job promotion, or spark tension between the caregiver and the rest of the siblings who pop in only on holidays. It's better to spend your savings on LTC insurance or nursing-home bills and leave the kids nothing than to leave them money in a cup of bitterness.

THE MEDICAID PLOY

If you're poor, with a modest income and few assets, the Medicaid program will cover your bills. It's taxpayer supported and administered by the states. In the case of a married couple, with one in a nursing home and one in the family home, the home and a decent income can be kept for the healthy spouse. If there's no healthy spouse, most of the assets have to be used for your nursing-home bills before Medicaid will pay. As a general rule, you can't get Medicaid right away if you give away property within 3 years of applying for benefits.

Enter the poverty makers—lawyers who teach you how to look poor on paper even when you're not. Their objective is to help you hide or sequester your assets—through hidey-holes, giveaways, and trusts—so you won't have to pay for your own long-term care. Your kids get your assets and we, the taxpayers, pick up your costs.

To my mind, this is a cynical misuse of a public program. So I'm darned if I'm going to tell you how to do it. There's nothing illegal about Medicaid planning, it's simply unethical (although, at this writing, there are criminal penalties for taking certain evasive actions). Often, the parents don't want to take this course. They're pushed into it by their kids.

Here's the ethical approach. Pay your own bills as long as you can. When your income and assets fall below a specified minimum, Medicaid will step in. You'll stay in exactly the same nursing home (although you may have to move from a single room to a double). You'll get the same care you got before. And because you started out as a private-pay patient, you'll be in a higher-quality home than if you had gone the "false poverty" route. In some cases, states give you Medicaid while you're alive, then recoup the cost from your estate after you die. Collection efforts such as these will get steadily tighter as Congress struggles to limit the growth in Medicaid spending. You can't assume that the false-poverty loophole will always exist.

Four states—California, Connecticut, Indiana, and New York—run a program called Partnership for Long-Term Care. There, you can buy a long-term-care policy that lasts a certain period of time. After that, you can go on Medicaid without having to spend any more of your personal money. Ask an insurance agent about it.

GETTING PAID

The vast majority of health-insurance claims are faithfully paid. But then there are those unhappy few.

Usually, there are claims with a problem at the edge. Maybe there's a technical question about whether the insurance applies. Maybe there's evidence that might be construed as fraud even when it's not. Maybe the company wants to improve its profits by toughing out every marginal case.

In denying marginal claims said to fall outside the plan, an insurer initially has little to lose. You might give up and go away. You might not find a lawyer willing to help, if the claim is small. If you do find a lawyer, the insurer can usually settle—and settlement might take a year or more. You might even die (although your heirs might sue).

If you have an individual or association plan, complain to the state insurance department before getting a lawyer. That *might* help settle your problem, at no cost to you. If that fails and you think your insurer is dealing in bad faith, see if you can get a lawyer interested. The law is on your side if (1) the language of the policy is unclear or (2) the terms of the policy could reasonably lead you to think you were covered and (3) you told the truth on your application. Nor will the law let you be stripped of your coverage on a technicality, like missing the date for filing the claim. (If you have an employee plan, however, you'll be bound by rules that make it almost impossible to win—page 371.)

The tragedy is that while you're arguing, a family member lies desperately ill with no one on hand to pay the bills. Without guaranteed payment, hospitals, doctors, and therapists may be reluctant to rally around.

No one can predict when an insurer might turn tough—refusing treatment or denying claims. But here are some precautions to take.

Before signing up, check what the contract says about the health problem you or a family member has. Check, too, when a treatment is in dispute. If you're covered by employee insurance, the booklet that explains the benefits is effectively your copy, although you can be ruled by a definition in a master copy that you've never seen.

When buying individual coverage, get an explanation for every single little thing you don't understand. That's one of the services that insurance agents are paid for, so spend as much time as you need. Put notes in the margin to remind yourself of what the agent said (he or she may misstate, which could be important evidence in an administrative hearing or in court). If you don't like what you see in a new policy you've bought, you have 30 days to return it and get a refund.

Pay special attention to the exclusions, including the unstated exclusions. For example, the policy may cover treatment in a "skilled nursing facility." By inference, this means no coverage in other types of nursing homes.

Check the definition of a "dependent." Are your 18-year-old children covered automatically, or will you have to prove that they haven't become independent adults? Is your college student covered even though he or she is studying part-time?

If your claim is denied, get a written explanation for why the company turned you down. Ask for specifics, not generalities. Check the reasons against the language in your policy. If the language can be read in another way, and you have an individual or association plan, you may have a case. Write to the person who heads the insurer's claims department (call the company to get the name). That sometimes stirs someone to take another look at your case. Talk to your insurance agent, who has an interest in keeping you happy. The state insurance department might also be able to help, unless you're in an employee plan (some states help with employee plans, too). Complain, complain, complain. Nothing will happen if you don't.

Keep complete records of your claim, starting with the medical bills and doctor's report. Keep copies of letters. Note the date and purpose of telephone calls, who you spoke with, and what was said. Follow up those calls with a short letter. This strengthens your hand if you have to sue. It might show bad faith on the insurer's part.

THE TRAP OF POST-CLAIMS UNDERWRITING

To "underwrite" means to evaluate you as a health risk. You want a company that checks you thoroughly—with a physical exam and by double-checking what you put on your application. If they know everything about you, and charge you accordingly, they cannot later refuse to pay on the ground that you dissembled about your state of health.

You run a risk with insurers who give you a health questionnaire and don't check it out. If you later fall ill, they'll go over your application and your health records with a magnifying glass, looking for something you failed to mention. That's called post-claims underwriting. If they find what they think is a material omission, they may reject your claim or revoke your entire policy—even if the omission has nothing to do with the illness you have now. The contract typically says that insurers cannot challenge your policy after 2 years have passed, except for fraud. But they can call a material omission fraud.

It's illegal to do post-claims underwriting on long-term-care insurance, with one exception: if you misrepresent your condition and put in a claim for it before 2 years have passed. In some states, post-claims underwriting is illegal in other cases, too. What you can do:

• Tell the whole truth on your health-insurance application. You're kidding yourself if you get health insurance under false pretenses. When you file a claim, you'll find that the policy isn't worth the paper it's written on.

• List everything—every operation, every illness, every medication you take or have taken, every physical condition, even athlete's foot. Don't listen to an insurance agent who says, "No one needs to know that." Remember, any significant medical facts may already be on file at the Medical Information Bureau (see next section).

• If the agent fills in the application, make sure he or she does it right. Some agents put "no" where they should put "yes," so that the company will accept you. If your claim is rejected later, it's no skin off the agent's nose. He or she will claim that the error was yours. It's essential that you read the application before signing it, and don't sign if it's incorrect.

• When you get your health-insurance policy, a copy of your application should be attached. Double-check it for accuracy. If you find a mistake, notify the company in writing and ask for an answer *in writing*. The agent might say over the phone that the mistake doesn't matter, but it might matter very much when you file a claim.

• If you're currently covered, don't exaggerate an illness in order to claim an insurance payment. Your doctor might agree to call a routine office visit "flu," but if you change insurers three cases of "flu" might put you into a high-risk pool. "Flu" might even be excluded from your policy altogether.

YOUR MEDICAL HISTORY

Few people have ever heard of the Medical Information Bureau (MIB). But if you've applied for individual health, life, or disability insurance, the insurer may have checked with MIB before it wrote the policy.

MIB exists, first, to catch people who falsify their insurance applications. If one insurer learns that you've had a heart attack, that information goes to MIB. If you approach another insurer and fail to mention your heart condition, MIB will tell the tale.

But the truthful may run into trouble, too. Doctors who examine you for insurance coverage send MIB any health information that they think is relevant to life expectancy. Usually, it is—but sometimes the information may mean little or nothing. A squiggle in an EKG may be well within the normal range, but the doctor may send MIB a brief, coded description of it, just in case. If you apply for more coverage, an insurer might rule out anyone with EKGs on file. You may be in perfect health, but the insurer won't take you at low, preferred rates. Instead, you'll be asked to pay the higher, standard rate.

By law, you have to be told that your MIB file influenced the adverse decision. In that case you can get a free copy, check it for accuracy, and challenge anything you believe to be mistaken. MIB contacts the insurer that submitted it; the insurer is supposed to make a "reasonable effort" to check with its medical source and "appropriate efforts" to contact medical sources you suggest. If the report turns out to be wrong or incomplete, it's deleted or amended. If the insurer stands by the report, you can add a statement of dispute. You can also ask an insurer to reexamine you and have a doctor write a letter in your behalf. If your condition has changed, your MIB file can be amended, although the original information will remain. New reports added to the system, including updates of old ones, stay in the system seven years.

MIB keeps files on about 15 million insurance applicants. Its reports show specific illnesses, overweight and underweight, high blood pressure, pertinent X-rays and lab tests, suicide attempts, occupational poisoning, psychological disorders, a family history of certain diseases, drug addiction or alcoholism (confirmed by the applicant or a medical source), and any other risk information the insurance company considers relevant to health or longevity. A nonmedical category notes reckless driving records, hazardous sports, amateur flying, and applications for much more life insurance than seems warranted. This kind of material comes from your application and from private insurance investigators (you authorize investigations and MIB searches when you sign an insurance application). Disability insurers use MIB to find out if you're carrying policies that you didn't mention on your application.

Nothing in the file is verified by MIB. That's left to the insurer and you. If you're simply checking your file, and haven't been turned down for insurance, a copy costs $8. For instructions on how to get it, call MIB at 617-426-3660.

PLAY IT SAFE

Pick an insurer with top safety ratings (page 342—only Weiss rates HMOs and doesn't cover all of them). If your health insurer fails, the results can be horrendous. All the states have guaranty funds, but state rules vary widely as to who gets protection and for what. At this writing, only some thirty-four Blue Cross/Blue Shield plans are covered. Most guaranty funds also exclude HMOs, self-insured companies (as are most large and medium-size firms today), fraternal-benefit groups, and Multiple Employer Welfare Arrangements, although some of these plans may be backed up in other ways.

Even if you're covered, the fund may pay you no more than $100,000 —sufficient for most people but a terrible problem for those currently undergoing costly treatments. Other states pay up to $500,000 for health claims and $300,000 for disability claims.

Whether you can continue your coverage without passing another medical exam depends on the type of policy you had. Sponsors of group policies will almost certainly find new insurers. You *must* be given new coverage if your policy was guaranteed renewable and noncancellable. While the mess is being sorted out, the guaranty association collects your premiums and pays out claims. If your policy wasn't guaranteed, however, you've lost it. You'll have to start hunting for coverage from scratch. Those in poor health will have to turn to state risk pools or go uninsured. Even if you find new insurance, you may lose coverage for preexisting conditions.

Fortunately, health insurers rarely fail, but prudent shoppers stick with quality, just in case.

CODA

Turn over every stone, every shingle, to get some kind of health insurance. It should top your list of necessities, after food, clothing, and shelter. Insure against major illnesses by taking big deductibles, even if you can't afford coverage for everyday care. No one wants a charity case. Hospitals may not admit you for anything but emergency care unless you have an insurance card. Even then, they may kick you out as soon as your heart is pumping again.

In financial terms, "going bare"—that is, without health insurance— endangers your personal solvency. A single serious illness could take all you have.

Of greater importance is that uninsured people often can't get any treatment at all. So going bare endangers your life.

14.

Disability—The Big Black Hole

The Risk That Everyone Forgets

You insure your house, your car, even your old couches and chairs. But you forget your single biggest asset—your earning power.

You plot. You plan. You save. You invest. Then you fall off a roof (or your spouse does), wind up in a wheelchair, and your entire financial plan falls apart. You go through your savings like a buzz saw. Your comfortable standard of living goes down the drain.

All because you forgot to insure your earning power, which is your most valuable single asset. If you're sick, you have health insurance. If you die, your family can cash in your life insurance policy. But disability falls between the cracks. You're alive—in a bed or a wheelchair—and have no money coming in. You need disability insurance, which sends you a check when you can't work.

Are you just about ready to skip this chapter because you can't afford to buy? Not so fast! There are new kinds of policies today, more reasonably priced than the old ones were. Coverage is also streaming into the workplace, where employees can buy for a third of the price of individual insurance and without passing a health exam.

For single people, not rich, disability coverage is a must. You have no spouse to support you if you can't work and no independent income.

Anyone at risk of getting AIDS should buy before the damning antibodies show up in the blood. Buy, too, if there are inheritable disabilities in your family. The expected spread of genetic testing may block you from coverage in the future.

If you're carrying life insurance and have no dependents, consider switching to disability coverage instead.

If you already have a policy, ask yourself whether it's large enough. You probably need additional coverage if your income has risen since you first bought.

Whether married people need disability coverage depends on each spouse's income and assets. If you had no paycheck, could your spouse's salary support the family, including the extra costs of your disability (special home care, perhaps)? Are you certain your spouse could keep working rather than tending to you? Alternatively, could you live on your savings for many years? If so, you don't need the insurance. If not, you need it badly. In many two-paycheck families, husband and wife should each carry a policy. ("Housewife disability" policies—for nonworking spouses—appeared briefly a few years ago, but seem to have vanished except as spouse riders on certain group policies. The benefits were too small and the price too high.)

WHAT DISABILITY INSURANCE DOES

It pays you a monthly income if, due to illness or accident, you're not able to hold a suitable job. The younger you are, the lower the premium you pay.

You insure for a specified dollar amount, such as $2,000 or $3,000 a month. The checks typically last until 65 but can stop earlier or later, depending on the policy. If you buy new coverage after 60, you're usually entitled to benefits only for 2 years or so.

Younger people should increase their coverage as their incomes rise. The price of each addition depends on your age at the time. A health check is required unless you bought a rider letting you forgo it (page 427). When looking for more coverage, check your current company first. Older policies in particular (more than 10 years old) may offer favorable rates. It's also more efficient to deal with a single company's claims department. If you're offered a much better deal by another insurer, however, take it.

When you're not in excellent health (a "rated risk"), your insurance will cost you more—if you can buy it at all. On policies bought outside the workplace, underwriting is pretty strict. Here's where there's no substitute for an experienced, energetic agent. Some insurers are less restrictive than others. The agent should try several companies to see what kind of deal you can get.

There are many variations to disability coverage, as will be explained. Shoot for coverage that—together with any other corporate or government benefits—gives you a minimally acceptable income. If you have extra money to spend, put it into savings and investments rather than super-rich disability benefits. You're more likely to retire healthy than retire sick.

YOUR AUTOMATIC COVERAGE

Almost every worker has a source of at least some disability pay:

There's Workers' Compensation, for work-related injuries. Disability payments vary widely from state to state. The maximum is 66.6 percent of your pre-disability gross wages or 80 percent of your take-home pay, up to a specified ceiling. The ceilings, however, are generally low. Employers buy workers' comp for their employees; the self-employed have to buy their own.

There's Social Security, if you worked long enough to be eligible for coverage or are eligible on your spouse's account. But you have to be so pulverized, physically or mentally, that you cannot work in any substantial job (there's a limited exception for the blind). Your checks don't start until you've been disabled for 5 consecutive months. Furthermore, your doctor has to expect your disability to last for at least a year or to lead to your death.

Social Security applies these rules strictly, sometimes too strictly. You may have to appeal (ideally, with the help of a lawyer) to collect the benefit truly due you. Two-thirds of those who apply for benefits are turned down the first time they apply, generally because they're judged fit for some kind of work. Of those who appeal, however, about two-thirds are accepted. If you carry a private disability policy, the insurance company may pay the legal costs of challenging a turndown. Anything you get from Social Security usually reduces the monthly amount that your private insurer pays.

To find out what benefit you and your dependents can expect to collect, see page 902. Beneficiaries get annual cost-of-living increases which protect their purchasing power. After 24 months on Social Security disability, you qualify for Medicare.

There's Veterans' Insurance, if you can trace your ailment to something that happened while you were on active duty with the armed forces. Low-income veterans who are totally disabled, and who served during periods designated as wartime, can get benefits even for disabilities that are not service-related.

There Are Disability Funds in Several States, including California, Hawaii, New Jersey, New York, and Rhode Island, plus Puerto Rico. They pay sickness benefits for a limited number of weeks to people disabled off the job.

There's Employer-Paid Coverage, generally limited to large and medium-size companies. You may get short-term sick pay and long-term disability pay at no cost to you, you lucky duck.

WORKPLACE POLICIES: COVERAGE YOU CAN AFFORD

Disability insurers are finally discovering America. Until recently, they sold principally to business executives and high-earning professionals. Now they're noticing everyone else: middle managers, midlevel professionals, small-business owners and employees, technicians, skilled clerical and white-collar workers, gray-collar workers in high-tech manufacturing plants —the vast middle market that needs disability coverage, too.

This new group, however, can't afford the fancy individual policies that doctors and lawyers buy. So the trend today is toward stripped-down coverage sold through the workplace, where it can be delivered at a lower cost. Your premium rises as you age. A ballpark price might be $20 to $25 a month for someone in his or her mid-30s buying a disability policy worth $1,500 a month. In your mid-40s, you might be charged $30 to $35. Women and men are charged the same. That makes it a great buy for women, who would otherwise pay much more for their coverage than men.

Workplace disability insurance, including unisex pricing, is available for groups as small as 3. There are four ways that coverage might be delivered:

1. The company pays for everything. This is usually reserved for (whom else?) the executive classes.

2. The employer gives everyone a basic benefit, regardless of health. Employees have the option of buying more. The additional coverage may or may not be portable (see page 419). To buy these supplements, you may have to pass a health exam.

3. The employer adds disability pay to a cafeteria plan. Employees receive a fixed number of credits and use them to pick the benefits they want. Some plans offer two levels of disability coverage. You can insure for either 50 or 70 percent of pay. The higher amount is available no matter how much disability coverage you have outside the company plan.

4. The employer offers the plan but employees buy the coverage themselves through payroll deduction. Everyone in a given age range is charged the same. The coverage may or may not be portable.

In big firms, there's often no health screening when you originally join the firm and sign up for disability insurance. Or the screening is rudimentary, to identify major illnesses that can interfere with your ability to work. More careful screening is applied to workers who join the plan later or to workers in very small firms. Screening identifies people who cannot be covered or illnesses that the plan will exclude.

In all these plans, you probably won't be covered immediately for preexisting conditions, defined as ailments you've known about during the past 3 or 6 months. Benefits generally don't start until you've been free of that problem for at least 12 months.

Some employers offer short-term disability ("sick pay") for 3 to 12 months. The dollars aren't large—maybe a flat amount per week or a low percentage of salary. This is meant to be "grocery money," supplementing your personal savings while you recuperate.

If you're sick longer, you qualify for long-term disability, payable until you're 65. Typically, you get a fixed percentage of salary, up to a cap of perhaps $5,000 to $6,000 a month (this calculation may or may not include your bonuses and commissions). Your disability income will be reduced by certain other payments, including Social Security, workers' compensation, and any pension your company pays. There may be partial benefits if, despite your disability, you're still able to work part-time.

Not all workplace plans offer gap-free coverage. Some, for example, will pay you to 65 after an accident but only for 2 to 5 years for a disabling illness. Some cover total disability (when you cannot work at all) but not partial disability. Some cover partial disability but only for a limited number of months. Even so, limited, affordable coverage is better than no coverage at all.

If you're relying on workplace coverage, ask what happens when you leave. Traditional group plans are generally convertible to individual coverage. But conversion policies offer limited benefits at a humongous price. You'd buy one only if you were otherwise uninsurable.

What you really want is *individual* coverage through the workplace. These policies cost more than traditional plans but they're fully portable. You can take them with you when you leave, at the same price you were paying before (or perhaps just a little bit more). This lets you continue your protection, at what's still a bargain price, often to age 65. There's no worry that your next job might not offer disability coverage; or that your next group policy might not cover you for 12 months; or that you might become uninsurable; or that you can't get coverage because you're self-employed; or that you might be unemployed for a while. Your old workplace policy will carry you through.

There are gaps in portability, too. Some policies are good only for a year after you leave the job. Some don't allow you to keep the coverage if your employer switches to another group insurer. Some terminate if you're eligible for another employer's plan, even if it's not as good as the one you have.

If your workplace plan isn't portable, or you think its benefits are poor, use the rules on page 430 to check the price of an outside policy. It will cost more but you'll have it regardless of what becomes of your job or health. You can also buy partial-disability coverage if your workplace insurance pays only when you're totally disabled. Don't fail to take the workplace coverage, however, if outside policies are too expensive.

If you're disabled, go over your plan with a magnifying glass. You don't want to lose benefits by violating some technical provision. Will the plan pay if you work part-time before switching to total disability? Will it resume payments if you return to work and find that you can no longer handle the job? What exactly is the definition of disability?

Still left out of broad disability coverage: all the traditional blue-collar jobs. Payments are low and of short duration, if they're offered at all.

ASSOCIATION INSURANCE

Another source of cut-rate disability coverage is a trade or professional association. All members under 55 are typically eligible. Some policies take everyone; others screen out only the worst risks (people with AIDS, cancer, or a history of heart attacks); others screen for additional health or working conditions. Premiums increase as you age.

How much you pay may be linked to your health when you first apply. It may also depend on whether your association offers a group or individual policy. Those in mediocre health will typically pay more for individual coverage than for group.

Ask whether the coverage is portable (see the discussion on page 419). Some contracts let you keep your policy if you leave the association; others don't.

Before buying association coverage, check its definition of disability. Sometimes the price is low because the policy doesn't offer much. Also, run through the price-shopping system on page 430. You might be able to do better with an outside plan. It's especially important to check the alternatives if your association offers coverage that isn't portable.

A plus for some associations: They may insure members who work from home and who therefore find it hard to buy coverage. Some associations, such as the Independent Business Alliance in New York City, specialize in insurance and other services for home-based entrepreneurs. (At this writing, home-worker policies are offered only by UNUM, the country's largest group insurer.) *Another plus:* Many associations offer unisex rates, which make their policies especially cheap for women. This is changing, however. In the future, more groups will be charging women a higher price.

INDIVIDUAL COVERAGE

This is coverage you buy yourself, without employer sponsorship. It might be your only coverage or it might supplement employer coverage.

Individual policies are sold by insurance agents and are generally more comprehensive than workplace or association insurance, so they're expensive. Prices vary tremendously, depending on the company and the benefits you choose. You may be looking at $25 to more than $100 a month for a man in his mid-30s buying a disability income worth $1,500 a month. In his mid-40s, he might be charged $45 to more than $120. Women in that age range might pay about one-third more. Unlike workplace insurance, however, premiums on individual policies don't rise as you age.

Until the early nineties, agents concentrated on selling cushy, Cadillac coverage to business executives and professionals. But nowadays, leaner policies are coming on line for people who don't want to spend as much.

How much you personally would pay depends not only on your age but also on your health, sex, the state you live in, the insurer you choose, the benefits you want, your smoking history, and your job. The lower your occupational risk (based on industry claims data), the lower your cost and the better your benefits may be.

The lowest prices go to people with clean-hands jobs like college professors and accountants. Their illness and accident risk is low. When disabled, they're usually eager to recover and get back to work.

Most clerical workers, by contrast, aren't offered affordable individual coverage because, when disabled, they may not be motivated to return to their jobs. Blue-collar workers have two strikes against them: presumed low motivation and the increased risk of industrial accidents.

For a general idea of how risky a client you're thought to be, check the sample classifications below. Almost all individual disability insurance is sold to Classes 5 and 4. They also get the most favorable definitions of disability and the best options. Some insurers now offer limited policies to certain workers in Class 3. For the rest, individual disability coverage is effectively unaffordable.

If you're in Class 5, you might pay as much as 20 percent less than if you landed in Class 4. So ask your agent to show you alternatives from the top companies. The agent might say that he or she has shown you the best —but verify! Different companies reach different conclusions about where a particular job belongs.

CLASS 5. Selected professionals, such as accountants, architects, lawyers, pharmacists, and college professors.

CLASS 4. Doctors, dentists, big-business executives, technicians, and selected middle management. Some insurers slot lawyers here because of their litigiousness. Some have dropped certain doctors to Class 3, especially if they practice in California or Florida, where a lot of disability claims are being made.

CLASS 3. Small-business management, white-collar and selected gray-collar workers, supervisors, skilled clerical and technical workers, real-estate agents, and teachers.

CLASS 2. Sales clerks, unskilled clerical workers, barbers, and pink- and blue-collar workers whose jobs involve some manual labor.

CLASSES A AND B. The all-but-untouchables: skilled workers in risky jobs (carpenters, bricklayers) and workers in heavy-lifting jobs (porters, baggage handlers).

If You're Self-Employed and Work at Home, it's almost impossible to get individual disability coverage. You don't have to drive to an office every day so it's hard for insurers to tell when you're truly unable to work full-time. Sometimes, however, part of your income may be insurable. For example, if you consult from home but give seminars away from home, you might get a policy that protects your seminar income.

Professional and business associations may offer coverage to members who work at home (page 420). Workers with no disability protection might want to accept the package of life and disability insurance that comes with credit cards, auto loans, personal loans, and mortgages. That coverage is pocked with exclusions (read the fine print) but it's better than nothing.

If You're Female, you're at a big disadvantage. Women make more claims than men (for example—surprise, surprise—pregnancy-related claims), so they're charged higher premiums by insurers that establish rates by sex. At 30, you might pay 50 percent more than a man of the same age; at 40, it might be 35 percent more; at 50 (post-pregnancy), 10 percent more. A few companies, however, charge unisex rates, which give women a break. Ask your insurance agent to find them. Workplace and some association plans also offer unisex pricing. (In Montana, unisex pricing is mandatory for all insurers doing business there.)

HOW MUCH COVERAGE DO YOU NEED?

You need enough insurance to feel that you and your family would be okay if you couldn't work. You're shooting for a decent standard of living —not grand but decent.

To put that into dollars and cents, go back to page 31, where you figured how much money you'd have in the kitty if you became disabled. (What? You skipped that calculation? This proves my point about needing insurance: you never know when you'll get caught.)

Estimate how much monthly income your kitty might throw off. Add that to your other sources of income, such as spouse's earnings, company-paid disability benefits, and Social Security. If that's not enough to pay your bills, including the extra expenses connected with being disabled, fill as much of the gap as you can with disability coverage from your company or an insurance agent.

Insurers won't knowingly sell you a large enough policy to replace all your income. That destroys your incentive to work. Instead, they'll restrict your coverage to a portion of what you earn. High-income people might be able to replace only 40 percent of their earnings with insurance benefits. Middle-income people might be able to replace 60 to 70 percent. Your effective income is higher, however, because these benefits aren't taxable (page 431).

What if you go for 100 percent coverage by buying individual policies from two different insurance companies? You probably won't get away with it. Insurers always ask whether you have any other coverage, so you'd have to lie. To test your truthfulness, they can run your name through the Medical Information Bureau (page 412), which keeps track of the policies you apply for. They also can telephone your employer.

What if you try to get extra coverage by overstating your income? The insurers will probably ask for your pay stubs, W-2s, or tax returns. If they catch you in any kind of lie, they'll reject you out of hand.

Some insurers check you out when you first present yourself as a client. Others wait until you make a claim, then check with the Health Claims Index, a database of claims being made and paid. If they learn that you understated your coverage, they'll reject all or part of your claim and give you that share of your premiums back. If you push, they may charge you with fraud.

What if you're currently overinsured but only because your income dropped? Your insurer probably won't pay more than 100 percent of your previous earnings. Your benefit would be scaled back and some of your premiums returned.

What if you're overinsured because you added a big workplace policy to a preexisting individual policy? In this case, the insurers should pay even if total coverage comes to more than 100 percent of your pay.

HOW TO GET THE BEST VALUE

Your budget for disability insurance is probably limited, so weigh all the following options carefully. You're not looking for bells and whistles. The objective is a policy that meets your reasonable needs—no less, no more.

Fixed Premiums vs. Rising Premiums. An excellent buy for people on a limited budget is an *annually renewable disability-income* (ARDI) policy. It works very much like term life insurance. The premium starts low and increases a little every year. By contrast, a traditional disability policy charges more when you first buy but fixes that price for the policy's entire term.

ARDI makes sense for younger professionals and business people who, in the past, may have felt that they couldn't afford disability policies. Depending on your age, you might cut 25 to 50 percent off your initial cost.

Your gamble is that, as the price of the policy rises, so will your income. That's a pretty good bet. ARDI's modest extra cost each year shouldn't be a strain. In early middle age, however, ARDI starts getting pretty expensive. You'll want to drop the policy or convert to fixed-price coverage. If you're insurable, don't convert without checking out the competition. Another insurer may offer you a better price.

A few insurers offer *step rates*—lower rates in the first few years, when your earnings are low, and higher rates later. But the steps may be big. ARDI raises the price just a little every year and is, to my mind, a better choice.

Noncancellable vs. Guaranteed-Renewable. "Noncancellable" is a comforting word. It means that your policy's benefits can't change, premiums can't rise, and the company can't cancel it. It's renewable every year on exactly the same terms.

Many companies no longer offer noncancellable insurance or offer it with more limited benefits than they used to. Instead, they're pushing "guaranteed-renewable" coverage. Here, your benefits can't change but the company can raise the premium—not on your policy individually, but on the entire policy class.

Guaranteed-renewable policies cost 10 to 20 percent less than comparable noncancellable coverage, but you're taking a price risk. If claims are higher than projected, the insurers can ask the state regulators for a premium increase—and they'd doubtlessly get it. Insurers could even manufacture the grounds for a premium increase if they wanted their older—hence riskier—policyholders to drop out (see "death spiral," page 363).

Shorter Term vs. Longer Term. Policies that pay benefits for just one or 2 years are inexpensive and will cover a lot of grief. Only around 10 percent of disabilities last longer than a year. But what if you're one of the unlucky 10 percent? You and your family need protection against the very worst that can happen, so try to arrange for payments right to age 65—at which point you'd pick up Social Security retirement pay and maybe a pension. (If you're already on Social Security disability, you switch to its retirement program at 65, with no change of benefit.)

A few insurers offer policies that pay benefits for life if you're disabled anytime up to age 65 or 70. But you pay through the nose. Lifetime benefits are strictly a luxury buy for people with high current incomes who aren't saving much of it. They'd be smarter to put their extra money toward retirement savings instead.

In real life, many people cancel their disability insurance earlier than

65. They may retire early. Or they may accumulate enough net worth to guarantee an income even if they couldn't work, which means they no longer need disability coverage.

Depending on your purse and your occupation, you might not be able to get coverage to age 65. In that case, take the longest period available or that you can afford. Even a 5-year policy is better than nothing.

Don't keep paying disability premiums after you retire. It's a waste of money. Consider long-term-care coverage instead.

If you're still working after 65 and in good health, you might be able to renew your coverage to age 70 or longer, but at a high price. It's probably not worth it.

High Benefits vs. Low Benefits. Don't save money by buying less disability income than you actually need. The policy either supports you when you can't work or it doesn't—and if it doesn't, your financial plan isn't worth a tinker's damn.

Insurers set a maximum that they'll cover you for. The more you make, the lower the percentage of income they'll provide. A person earning $50,000 a year should be able to buy at least 60 percent coverage ($2,500 a month). But a person earning $200,000 may be able to buy only 40 percent ($6,666 a month). Some companies offer higher maximums, so ask your insurance agent to shop around.

If you have a substantial income from interest, dividends, and capital gains, you won't be able to buy as much disability insurance. The rules on this point vary from company to company. Some might restrict your coverage if your unearned income reaches $1,500 to $5,000 a month; others, if your unearned income exceeds 20 percent of your earnings. The working rich can't buy disability insurance at all. They don't need it. They'll live on their capital if they have to quit going to the office.

What if you can't afford as much coverage as you need, all the way to 65? Insurers recommend that you buy the monthly benefit you require for as many years as you can.

"Own Occ" vs. "Any Occ" vs. Income Replacement. Here we come to the all-important definition of "disabled." What are the terms under which your policy pays?

Some pay if you can't perform the duties of your own occupation ("own occ"). For example, a surgeon becomes disabled if he or she loses a finger. Traditional own-occ policies pay full benefits even if you take up another line of work. A nine-fingered ex-surgeon could collect disability even while holding a full-time administrative job at an HMO. These "double-dip" policies, however, are going the way of the dodo. More common (and less costly) own-occ coverage says that, *if* you can't work in your own occupation but choose to try another, the income you earn will be considered in calculating the size of your benefit. But you aren't required to retrain if you'd rather not. To strengthen your claim to benefits, define your occupation in as much detail as you can.

Some pay only if you can't work at any occupation that reasonably fits your education, experience, and training (with a similar income level implied). If a nine-fingered surgeon is well enough to hold an administrative post at an HMO, he or she would no longer be considered disabled. The checks would stop whether or not he found a job. That's a big weakness in this type of coverage. You're subject to the judgment of the insurance company. Many policies combine these two definitions, giving you "own-occ" coverage for the first 2 to 5 years, then switching you to "any occ."

Some policies insure your income rather than your occupation. This is generally the most cost-efficient choice. You're covered for a certain level of income. If you can't work at all, you get your full insured benefit. If you can work at your own job part-time, or handle a lower-paying job for which you are reasonably suited, your policy pays the percentage difference between your lower earnings and your insured benefit. As an example, say you're earning 60 percent of what you did before. Your policy will pay 40 percent of your disability benefit. That protects the insured portion of your income, regardless of what job you hold. With an income-replacement policy, the insurer can't cut off your checks if you choose not to take up another line of work.

Income replacement won't pay a business owner whose income continues even if he or she is unable to work. On the other hand, the policy continues to pay if you're a fee-paid professional who returns to work but can't rebuild a client list immediately. (In the latter case, an own-occ policy could also help if it had good transition benefits—see page 429.)

What's the best choice? Own-occ with residual benefits (see page 427) or income replacement. If your occupation is pretty general—say, business executive—own-occ coverage may not buy you anything extra. If you can't function in your own occupation, you probably can't function at all. In that case, income replacement would be the better choice.

Long vs. Short Elimination Period. This is the waiting period before benefits begin. The longer you're willing to wait, the lower the premium you'll pay. One-month waiting periods make no sense; you'll surely be able to cover your bills over so short a period. Instead, consider any period between 3 and 12 months. A 6-month wait might cut your insurance premium by 30 percent.

Coordinate your coverage with any sick pay or short-term disability benefits that you're entitled to. If your employer will pay short-term benefits for 6 months, your personal, long-term policy could pick up from there.

If your budget requires you to choose between a higher benefit and a longer waiting period, take the longer waiting period. You can always scramble for money over the short term. It's the long term you have to worry about.

Do You Want Residual Benefits? Absolutely, with an own-occ or any-occ policy. Without "resid," these policies pay nothing if you're able to work part-time. With "resid," you're paid if you're still able to work but your illness or accident leaves you unfit for the schedule you kept before. Maybe you're working only part-time. Maybe you had to switch to a less taxing, lower-paying job. Residual benefits help fill the gap between your old, high salary and your current one.

A true resid pays a pro rata portion of what you're insured for, depending on how much money you earn. Say, for example, that your policy carried a maximum benefit of $4,000 a month. If, after a stroke, you can work part-time earning 60 percent of your previous income, you'd get 40 percent of your disability benefit, or $1,600. Resid also should pay if you never were totally disabled but were gradually overcome by an illness that put you partly out of commission.

Note that own-occ or any-occ policies plus residual benefits give you the same result as owning an income-replacement policy. They're sold as different types of coverage but they're pretty much the same.

Instead of resid, some policies pay what they call "partial" benefits. That might be 50 percent of your full disability benefit, regardless of how much you earn. But this payment usually doesn't last very long, and you may be eligible only after a spell of total disability. A few policies pay partial benefits for a period of time, then switch to residual.

Many own-occ and any-occ insurers include this coverage automatically; others sell it separately, as a rider; a few don't offer it at all. Depending on the company, you're generally considered partly disabled if, because of your health, you lose anywhere from 20 to 50 percent of your former income.

When you're on resid, you'll probably have to report your income every quarter (for those on straight salary) or perhaps every month (if your income varies), so the insurer can pay the proper percentage amount. Your insurer may also want to check your tax returns. With income-replacement policies, you also have to disclose your earnings periodically.

Some less expensive policies make fixed-dollar payments for partial disability—for example, $1,000 a month, regardless of what you can earn. But these payments usually stop after 6 or 12 months.

Do You Want the Waiver of Premium? Yes, for sure. It lets you stop paying for your insurance if you become disabled. Most policies bundle it into your basic coverage but sometimes you have to buy it separately.

In theory, you shouldn't need a waiver. Your disability income should be large enough to cover all expenses, including your insurance premiums. In practice, however, waiver of premium is a surer thing. It's especially important if you own a guaranteed-renewable policy, whose price could rise.

Do You Want Inflation Protection? Yes and no.

Yes to *pre-disability protection*—built into some policies, sold separately with others. When sold separately, it's generally an inexpensive option. Your insured amount rises by a certain percentage every year for a specified number of years. If you don't want to pay for the increased amount in any given year, you can decline it. Once you're disabled and start getting benefits, however, your payments are fixed.

No to *post-disability protection*, unless you have money to burn. This expensive rider guarantees you a rising disability check. Some insurers let you pick a fixed annual raise, like 3 percent. Others link your payment to the consumer price index. It's a nice addition but will cost you an extra 20 to 40 percent.

Do You Want a Future-Purchase Option? Only if you can afford it and expect your earnings to rise by much more than the general inflation rate. It lets you add coverage at specified times in the future, even if a change in your health status makes you otherwise uninsurable.

The right to buy more insurance without a health exam may cost 5 to 15 percent of the policy price, depending on your age and the company. Each time you exercise this option, you'll pay the premiums for your age at the time.

If you take this rider, use it. Add to your policy on a regular basis. A future-purchase option generally expires sometime between ages 46 and 52. Don't fail to update your policy in that final year.

If you don't choose this option and stay in good health, you can still increase your disability insurance as your income rises. But you'll have to pass a medical exam.

Do You Want a Reducing Term? This is a neat solution for people who need extra coverage for a specific period. Say, for example, that you're buying a business and agree to pay the owner over eight years. As security for the payments, the owner might ask you to carry both life and disability insurance. You can buy coverage that expires on a date you name, which in this case would be the date that your debt is supposed to be paid up. The policy should piggyback on a regular policy that keeps you and your family protected, too.

Other Policy Provisions. Some of these are built into your basic policy, some are sold separately. Every company is a little different. Consider all your options but don't waste your money on minor stuff.

Nonsmoker discount—if you don't smoke, look for a company that rewards you.

Rehabilitation payments—your policy will pay for rehab in order to get you back to work. It should also train you for a new job and pay for mechanical aids that help you function at the office. But it won't finance any rehabilitation if it's clear that you'll never be able to work again. Expect your disability insurer to be in close contact with your doctors and your employer.

Transition and fallback benefits—disability income normally stops when you return to work. But what if your old job turns out to be too much for you? What if it takes awhile to rebuild your former income? What if you lost a bonus by being away from work? The policy should cover any losses due to your disability, support a home-to-job transition plan, and resume paying benefits if it's clear that you'll have to train for something else.

Integration with Social Security and other plans—this sensible provision saves you quite a bit of money. If you go on disability, the insurer reduces your payment by any disability benefits you receive from Social Security, workers' compensation, the military, or a state disability fund. Your total payment doesn't change. It simply comes from different sources.

A Social Security rider—comes with policies that sell lower benefits. The rider pays you extra if you're not disabled enough to qualify for Social Security payments.

Limited "soft" coverage—a growing number of insurers limit benefits to one or 2 years for ailments that can't be measured objectively, such as back and muscle pain, headaches, repetitive stress disorders, and chronic fatigue syndrome.

Presumptive disability—a lottery ticket. You are presumed to be totally disabled if you lose the use of any two limbs, eyesight, speech, or hearing. Full payment is due even if you go back to work full-time. Generally, this isn't worth paying extra for. If you really are disabled, the basic policy will pay. If you aren't, you shouldn't collect.

Accidental death and dismemberment—another lottery ticket that hitches a bit of life insurance to your coverage. But it pays only if you die or lose a limb in an accident, not if you die after an illness (the more likely case).

Hospital income—you get a certain number of dollars per day while you're in the hospital. This provision isn't worth a lot. Modern medical practice tries to keep you out of the hospital or sharply limits your stay.

A premium refund—a way the insurer makes money by appealing to your greed. Under this rider, you get some or all of your premium back after 5 or 10 years if you've made no claims or only a small claim. The insurer might even project that you'll earn a high rate of interest on the money. But that rate vanishes if you have a period of insured disability or if your group of policies is less profitable than the insurer expected. For this dubious gamble, you might pay an extra 50 percent or more. Don't be tempted. Put that money toward strengthening some other part of your disability coverage.

New designs—insurers are trying to broaden the market for disability coverage. A UNUM Life Insurance policy, for example, can turn into a long-term care-policy when you retire. A UNUM workplace plan can insure super-risky jobs like sheriff and police officer against the need for catastrophic care, such as help with bathing, dressing, eating, and so on. A MassMutual policy replaces the pension credits you lose during years when you're totally disabled and cannot work (the money goes into a taxable trust, but you can manage the investments). Watch for other new ideas to emerge.

Don't Replace an Old Noncancellable Policy with a New One. The benefits in the older policies are better than you can buy today. If you need more coverage, add a second policy. Treat your first one as the treasure it is.

HOW TO SHOP

Companies vary widely in what their policies cover, so it's all but impossible to make true cost comparisons. Generally speaking, lower premiums signify less insurance protection, but that doesn't mean the policy is inferior. To be first-rate, all a policy has to do is meet your needs.

For fixed-premium coverage, the Consumer Federation of America suggests that you use as a benchmark the noncancellable income-replacement policy from USAA Life (800-531-8000). Get a price quote and a list of benefits. This policy is low-load, meaning it carries low sales expenses. Instead of dealing with commissioned salespeople, you deal with the company itself, by phone and mail. The policy is available to better risks (typically, white-collar professionals and businesspeople) in most states.

Next, call the Wholesale Insurance Network (WIN) in Tampa, Florida (800-808-5810), for a quote on the low-load, income-replacement policy sold by Provident Life and Accident. It's available to residents of most states, can be bought by phone, and costs 20 to 25 percent less than the similar policy sold by Provident's commissioned salespeople. If you need to consult with someone about the policy's options, WIN will refer you to an insurance adviser, who charges a fee for his or her time.

With information about these low-loads in hand, call a couple of insurance agents to see if they can find something better. Women will get lower rates at one of the few remaining companies that use unisex pricing.

If you can't afford fixed-premium coverage, get a quote on annually renewable insurance (page 423).

PREEXISTING CONDITIONS

When you fill out your application, you have to disclose all past and present illnesses. The insurance company will either (1) cover them at the policy's regular price, (2) charge you a higher price, (3) restrict your benefit, (4) refuse to cover a particular ailment, or (5) refuse to cover you at all. If any restriction is applied, ask your insurance agent to try again. Sometimes, a little pressure—or checking with some other insurers—can lead to a better result.

Don't lie about your illnesses, physical or mental. The insurer may check your health history through the Medical Information Bureau (page 412). It may also check with your doctors. If you're seeing a psychologist or psychiatrist, disclose it—even if you're there just for general enlightenment. If you're caught in a misstatement, your application will almost certainly be turned down.

Once your policy has been in effect for 2 years (3 years in some states, including California), the insurer normally shouldn't deny payment based on errors of fact in your application. If you put down the wrong age, payments will be adjusted to match your real age.

But the 2-year limit doesn't protect you if you fibbed about your health. The insurer will investigate. Your claim can be rejected on grounds of fraud if you failed to list a pertinent illness that would have affected the insurer's decision to accept you. *Warning:* Many insurers are being aggressive about this. Even trivial ailments not listed could be used to duck a claim. You might win your case in court, but who wants to go through all that? If you *are* turned down, ask the insurer to specify in writing why, exactly, your claim fails to meet the contract's terms. These decisions are often subjective. You need an answer specific enough to help a lawyer judge your case.

INCOME TAXES

You pay no tax on disability income from policies that you buy with your own after-tax money. Most workers' compensation isn't taxable, either. Nor is income from state disability funds (unless the payments are in lieu of unemployment pay). But income from employer-paid plans is fully taxed. Up to 85 percent of your Social Security disability income can also be taxed, depending on how much other income you have.

What if your employer gives you a basic disability policy and you supplement it by buying coverage through payroll deduction? If you become disabled, the company-paid portion of your benefit is taxable; the rest isn't. Fortunately, you don't have to figure this out yourself. The insurer will send you a 1099 form every year.

WHOM CAN YOU TRUST?

You're counting on this insurance company to pay you a check many years in the future. But for some companies, disability coverage has been a money loser. Whom can you trust to stick around?

The disability specialists are UNUM and Provident Life and Accident. They're committed to the market and are said to be the most consistent in handling claims.

Diversified blue-chip companies want a disability line for their agents to offer. Among the top companies: Mass Mutual and Connecticut Mutual (merged in 1996), Northwestern Mutual, and Guardian Mutual. In low-load individual coverage: USAA Life. This group of companies has a weaker commitment to the disability market but a strong tradition of giving good service to policyholders.

The leaders in employee group coverage include UNUM, Metropolitan Life, Hartford Life, and Fortis Benefits.

Many companies, especially the smaller ones or the ones with small disability portfolios, are wrestling with the question of whether to stay in the market at all. Some of them sell the policies of other insurers. Some put their names on policies that other insurers develop and manage.

If your company decides to drop its disability business, two things could happen. It could service its existing policies, although perhaps not as well as it did before. Or it could sell its policies to another insurer. In that case, keep track of when your premiums are due, just to be sure you're not lost in the shuffle. If you don't pay your premiums, for whatever reason, your policy will expire. For simplicity, you can have the premium deducted automatically from your bank account each month. The cost: just one or 2 percent more than an annual payment.

It is rare, but not unknown, for a company to "neglect" to send renewals to policyholders who had claims in the past and might again. This practice, sometimes called starring, is illegal. If you think it has happened to you, complain to the state insurance department.

Look for companies with top ratings for safety and soundness (page 430). When insurers run into financial problems, they sometimes start treating policyholders badly, denying or delaying claims. You may be pressed to accept a modest lump sum instead of years of benefits. You have a good lawsuit if the insurer didn't disclose the true value of the policy you gave up.

Follow the rules *exactly* when filing a claim. A company may turn you down just because you didn't fill out the claim form properly, or failed to follow complex claim procedures, or missed a deadline. You're especially vulnerable if you have an aggressive insurer who thinks you won't sue.

Ask your doctor to talk to you before filling in the form the insurer will send, which seeks a description of how disabled you are. The questions may be phrased to tilt the answers the insurer's way. Be sure that your doctor understands your job's physical and mental requirements so he or she can judge accurately whether you're able to perform.

If you have any trouble collecting—or one of your relatives does—call a lawyer right away. If it's a friend, he or she might help, even with a small claim. Sometimes small claims turn into class-action lawsuits. Also, write to your state's insurance department in the state capital.

Most claims are paid in good faith, but there's bad faith in the industry, too.

DON'T LEAVE HOME WITHOUT IT

If you have to work for a living and have no disability insurance, you effectively have no financial plan. Everything you own is held hostage to your continuing ability to get up in the morning and catch a bus. That's no way to live. Buy as much coverage as you need or can get. Fit it into your budget the way you do any other necessity, and get on with your life.

15.

The Driving Dream

The Search for the Best and Cheapest Auto Insurance

If you hold your car for four years or so, and have a teenage driver, it can cost you more to insure the car than it did to buy it.

Auto insurance is a toll bridge over which every honest driver has to pass. Policies cost the most in cities and suburbs. That's where most of the cars are and, as night follows day, most of the accidents. But even in the wide-open countryside, the price of insurance keeps going up.

Rates rise for a lot of reasons:

Today's cars are getting complex and expensive to repair.

Streets are more congested, so people bump into each other more often.

In some cities—Boston, especially—theft is endemic. In others, fraud seems unstoppable. Los Angeles and Philadelphia come immediately to mind.

Medical costs keep going up.

There are more lawsuits and higher settlements in injury cases.

Some badly designed no-fault laws encourage litigation rather than discourage it.

More buyers have been choosing small cars and sports cars, which generate more collision and injury claims than big cars.

By law, insurance companies are allowed to exchange price information, so they may not compete as much as they should.

New approaches to risk evaluation are reclassifying many drivers. People who once would have been "preferred risks" now are labeled "standard risks" and charged a higher premium. Many formerly standard risks are dropping down to substandard, where they must pay even more.

In some states, inept regulation has forced even good drivers into assigned-risk pools, where they're charged extra for their coverage.

The whole crazy system needs reform.

There are ways to reduce your auto insurance costs, about which more follows. But how you insure against an auto accident—and what you yourself can expect to recover—depends on where you live.

FAULT VS. NO-FAULT

If You Live in a "Fault" State and are hurt in an auto accident that is the other driver's fault, you collect from his or her insurance company. That presumes that the other driver *has* insurance, which may not be the case. Many of the country's most reckless road hogs don't bother with coverage, even in states that supposedly require it. Tens of thousands of drivers simply can't afford it. You have to buy uninsured-driver coverage to protect against this risk.

If you luck out and the other guy does have insurance, the policy might be too small to cover all of your injuries.

You can sue for a larger amount, but it won't do you any good unless the driver is rich enough to pay. Moral: make sure that you're hit only by a millionaire.

If you caused the accident, the other guy doesn't have to pay. Your own liability insurance pays for the person you hit but not for any injuries you sustained. If you're partly at fault, state law dictates to what extent each policy pays.

The fault system does produce occasional huge judgments. You can sue not only for medical costs and the wages you lost while out of work but also for "pain and suffering," which is where the big money lies. But it's a lottery. You collect only if (1) the other guy has enough insurance and personal assets to cover a judgment and (2) the accident was at least partly his fault. Many injured people get much less than they deserve or nothing at all.

Lawyers love fault laws because they make so much money on lawsuits. But fault systems probably cost you money in higher insurance premiums and can't be relied on to help you if you're truly hurt. Pure no-fault is better, but whenever it threatens to be enacted into law the lawyers spend huge sums of money to fight it. They try to persuade the voters that fault laws are good for them. When that fails, they lobby to water down no-fault so it can't achieve its goals.

If You Live in a "No-Fault" State* and are hurt in an auto accident, your own insurance company pays your medical bills and lost wages up to a certain ceiling. You collect even if the accident was entirely your fault. So everyone with auto insurance is protected, not just people who luck into the right kind of accident.

If your injuries are bad enough or your medical bills are high enough, you can also go to court and try for a pain-and-suffering award. There, fault rules apply: you don't collect unless you can prove that the other driver was at least partly at fault.

Two states—New Jersey and Pennsylvania—offer you a substantive choice: either fault or no-fault insurance. If you choose fault, however, you have to pay more for it.

One state, Michigan, pays for property damage under its no-fault rules. The rest address only bodily injury.

No-fault can save money and slow down the rise in auto insurance premiums, but only if lawsuits are restricted to serious cases, such as death, disfigurement, or severe impairment. Five states pursue no-fault seriously, in the view of Jeffrey O'Connell, the father of no-fault and professor of law at the University of Virginia: Michigan and New York, closely followed by New Jersey, then Florida and Minnesota. In the rest, even people with modest medical bills are allowed to sue. The natural result: accident victims run up their medical expenses so that they can get into court, and no-fault's potential savings don't materialize.

In Either Type of State, your insurer will investigate the case, handle the settlement negotiations, defend you in a lawsuit, and pay any judgment against you up to the limit of your policy. If the judgment is larger, you have to cover the excess amount yourself.

WHAT KIND OF COVERAGE DO YOU NEED?

Liability for Bodily Injury— absolutely essential

It protects you if you're sued for injuring someone in an accident, including pedestrians and passengers riding in your car. The policy pays the victim's medical costs, loss of earnings, and pain and suffering. You're also protected if someone is injured by a family member driving your car, a friend who is driving your car with permission, or a family member who is driving someone else's car with permission.

---

* At this writing, Colorado, Florida, Hawaii, Kansas, Kentucky, Massachusetts, Michigan, Minnesota, New Jersey, New York, North Dakota, Pennsylvania, and Utah.

How much liability coverage should you carry? That depends on how you look at it. I offer three angles of vision:

1. *Protect your assets.* That means buying enough insurance to cover your net worth, on a bet that you won't be sued for a higher amount. If you don't own much besides your car, you'd buy only the minimum that your state requires—maybe $10,000 for every person injured, up to a cap of $20,000 for the whole accident (expressed as 10/20). If you own a home, you might want $100,000 for each person injured, to a maximum of $300,000 per accident (100/300); or $300,000 per accident without regard to how many people are hurt. The wealthy might want $500,000 to $1 million worth of coverage or more.

But how good is this strategy, really? You can be sued for more than your insured amount and you're not off the hook just because the judgment exceeds your net worth. You can be ordered to pay out of future paychecks for years and years. Your earning power is an asset that needs to be protected, too.

2. *Protect yourself.* If you're hurt by a driver who's uninsured or under-insured, you can be paid by your own auto policy, even above any no-fault limit. But only a handful of states let you purchase more protection for yourself than for the other guy. A $10,000 cap for him normally means a $10,000 cap for you, too. There are pros and cons to uninsured motorist coverage (page 439). If you think you need this protection, you'll probably want to buy more than the minimum.

3. *Protect the injured.* Drivers have a social and moral obligation to everyone else on the road. If you damage a life you should pay for it. That means buying a substantial insurance policy—at least $100,000/$300,000— even if you don't have a lot of assets to protect. Higher liability limits may not even cost very much.

Liability for Property Damage—essential, and a little extra doesn't hurt

This pays for any damage you do to someone else's property. Buy at least enough to cover a car—say $20,000, or $70,000 if you're tempted to veer into BMWs. But what if you hit a bus or a storefront? Costs can climb pretty fast. Some extra protection usually doesn't cost very much.

Medical Payments—offered in fault states, but not essential

This coverage picks up the medical and funeral bills of anyone injured in your car, without regard to who caused the accident. It covers your family if they're hurt as pedestrians or while riding in another vehicle, including a taxi or a bus. It covers an elderly friend who stumbles while getting into your parked car and breaks her hip.

But it offers less protection than meets the eye. Your auto insurance will normally cover only the bills that your health insurance doesn't pay, which may not be very much. Those injured in your car may also have health insurance. If they want more money, they'll sue for it whether or not you have medical-payments insurance. Many people skip this coverage or buy $2,000 per person just to plug the deductible in a health insurance policy. If your health insurance is skimpy, beef up that policy, not this one.

In no-fault states, medical payments are tucked into your basic auto-insurance policy.

Personal-Injury Protection (PIP) — a no-fault fixture

You're covered for: (1) your own medical bills up to a stated limit; (2) part of your lost wages; (3) funeral expenses; (4) in some states, replacement services—for example, a babysitter hired while a mother is in the hospital.

How much you ultimately collect depends on your state. There may be no ceiling or one as low as $2,500. There may be a low ceiling on each doctor bill. You can usually fall back on your health insurance if no-fault doesn't pay enough of each bill, but that depends on your state. Ask if you can choose between using your no-fault and health insurance policies.

To lower the cost of your personal-injury protection, see if your medical bills and lost wages can be paid primarily by your regular health and disability insurance. If so, you can buy less PIP. It becomes no more than a backup system for expenses otherwise unpaid. Some insurers also let you save a few dollars by signing up for a PIP managed-care plan.

Collision—essential for new cars and for drivers who have a substantial auto loan; worthwhile as long as your car has a reasonable market value

This portion of your policy covers repairs to your own car, no matter who caused the accident. If the car is totaled, and was financed, you need the insurance to repay the loan.

The price of collision insurance depends on the size of the deductible. That's the amount you pay toward each repair before the insurance policy kicks in. Deductibles range from $100 to $1,000. The higher the number the less your insurance costs. If the accident wasn't your fault, your deductible may be covered by the other driver's policy.

Collision insurance is generally written to cover your particular car's fair market value, defined as its book value (as determined by standard tables), minus any unusual wear and tear, minus a charge for unusually high mileage. The insurer won't give you a penny more. So compare the premium you pay with what you'd get if the car were totaled. Drop coverage on cars so old or damaged that their value is nominal. What's nominal? Any loss that leaves you philosophical instead of sore.

Comprehensive—essential for new cars, useful for older ones

This pays for random damage to your car from fire, earthquake, flood, vandalism, hail, pets chewing the upholstery, and the odd stone thrown up from the highway. It also covers theft and perhaps the use of a rental car after a theft. (Removable tape decks, CD players, and other expensive equipment might be covered by your homeowners policy or by a special rider to that policy.) Deductibles range from $50 to $1,000; the higher the deductible, the cheaper your insurance. Windshields may be insurable separately, with no deductible.

Comprehensive insurance covers the car's fair market value, which generally declines with time. Many drivers keep their comprehensive coverage even after dropping collision because comprehensive tends to be cheaper. Still, the insurer won't pay anything more than the car is worth.

Uninsured and Underinsured Motorist— required in many states; otherwise, your call

This pays the cost of your injuries and those of the passengers in your car if you're hit by (1) an uninsured driver who's at fault, (2) an at-fault driver whose small insurance policy won't cover all your damages, or (3) a hit-and-run. It also covers lost wages. In some states, you might even be reimbursed for damage to your car. In no-fault states, uninsured-motorist coverage clicks in if you're injured badly enough to sue. You can collect from this policy on top of your no-fault, personal-injury protection.

Why bother with uninsured-motorist coverage (you might ask) if your life, health, and disability policies already protect your family, cover your injuries, and pay you an income if you're disabled and cannot work? If this truly describes you, the extra coverage won't add a lot. It merely gives you the right to sue for pain and suffering if you didn't cause the accident or were clipped by a hit-and-run. These can be rare or chancy claims. But a settlement would help with your other expenses, like extra support systems if you become disabled.

A more likely scenario is that you have life and health insurance but little or no disability coverage. You may not be able to afford disability insurance (page 415) and can't count on qualifying for Social Security. In this case, it's well worth parting with the $80 to $150 you'd have to spend on uninsured motorist protection.

What if you have insufficient life and health insurance? I'd spend the $80 to $150 beefing them up so I'd have more protection regardless of how harm came to me. Next, I'd add to the medical-payments or personal-injury portion of my auto policy. When money is this short, uninsured-motorist coverage would be last on my list.

Towing and Service/Rental Car Reimbursement—a toss-in

If you have an accident or your car breaks down, you're covered for the towing cost and the labor charges for repairs. The price: $5 or so a year. For another $20 to $30, you might get $15 to $20 a day to rent a car while yours is being repaired. Small stuff like this you can take or leave. If you belong to an auto club, leave it; these benefits probably duplicate what you have already.

Umbrella Insurance—worthwhile, if you have a substantial net worth

An umbrella policy covers liability judgments that exceed the limits of your auto and homeowners policies. Typically, you have to carry $250,000 worth of liability on your auto insurance and $100,000 or so on your home. After that, you can insure for up to $1 million or more. Umbrella insurance is generally priced according to the number of cars you own. Expect costs to range from $200 to $300 or more a year. Some companies will add a $1 million rider to auto and homeowners insurance.

Umbrella coverage may defend you not only against claims of damage or personal injury but also against libel (unless you're a professional writer or broadcaster), slander, false arrest, invasion of privacy, and similar charges that spoil your day.

MORE WAYS TO SAVE MONEY ON AUTO INSURANCE

• *Compare prices.* Here lies your single biggest shot at saving money. In any city, or any zip code, some insurers charge twice as much as others for exactly the same coverage.

Insurers don't price-advertise, so it takes some work to find those that are lower cost. No single company always has the best rates. Each one prices differently, in different places, for different kinds of customers.

The Consumer Federation of America recommends that you start with a quote from State Farm (their agents are in the Yellow Pages) and GEICO (selling by phone and mail from Washington, D.C., in all states but Massachusetts and New Jersey; 800-841-3000). Good drivers who live in California or Arizona should try 20th Century in Woodland Hills, California (800-211-SAVE). If you're 50 and up, check the American Association of Retired Persons in Washington, D.C., which offers coverage to members, spouses, and certain driving-age children through the Hartford insurance group (at late ages, you may have to pass a medical exam). Anyone connected with the United States military should try USAA in San Antonio, Texas (800-531-8080). USAA insures present and former military officers, including their spouses, widows, and widowers. Their grown children can buy from a USAA subsidiary, which charges somewhat higher rates. At this writing, USAA is gradually expanding its rolls to include active-duty enlisted personnel and their families. The expansion is proceeding a few states at a time and should be complete by the end of 1998.*

With these prices in hand, ask an independent insurance agent if he or she can do better for you. Often, the agent can turn up a lower rate, perhaps from a regional company or a company that's especially competitive for drivers of your age and sex.

Rate isn't everything, of course. You also want your claims handled promptly, fairly, and without any hassle. Amica in Providence, Rhode Island, for example, which sells by phone to better risks (800-242-6422), may not be the cheapest in your zip code but is widely considered to give excellent service. Ask your friends how they like their own insurers. Some states publish data on customer complaints.

When you find a good company that's substantially cheaper than the one you have now, consider a switch. But don't leave for penny-ante savings. Insurers often give special treatment to their longtime policyholders. For example, after an accident they may be less likely to increase your premium. Some insurers guarantee to renew your policy for life (a benefit that their customers may not realize they have). If you do switch, don't let your old policy run out until you've held the new one for 60 days. Sometimes an insurer accepts you as a policyholder, then rejects you later—perhaps after finding something on your credit report it doesn't like (page 238).

---

* For auto insurance, USAA accepts commissioned or warrant officers and their families from all of the uniformed services, including the Coast Guard, the National Oceanic and Atmospheric Administration, the Public Health Service, and the U.S. Information Agency; also, foreign service officers of the U.S. State Department, special agents of the FBI and Treasury, and officer candidates. The program for enlisted personnel includes the National Guard and Selected Reserve who have a current, active relationship with the armed forces.

• *Tell your insurance company or agent about any changes that could lower your rate.* For example, you should pay less when: (1) the young driver in your family graduates from college and leaves home; (2) you retire and stop using your car for commuting; (3) you start carpooling or move closer to your place of work; (4) you install an antitheft device; (5) you move to a city that's less accident prone or from the city to the suburbs or the country; (6) you have a birthday—some insurers reduce rates for people 55 and up who take a defensive driving course; (7) you marry; (8) you divorce and your ex-spouse (who has all the speeding tickets) stops using your car.

• *Reshop for a policy every 5 years.* Any of the changes in circumstances just listed may get you a better rate from a different company than your current one. It doesn't cost anything to check around and could save you hundreds of dollars a year.

• *Find out if your state has an auto-insurance buyer's guide.* A few consumer-minded insurance commissioners publish price guides showing what the various auto-insurance companies charge. It's a true public service —something all states should do since they have all the rates on file. To see if your state has a buyer's guide, call the insurance commissioner's office in the state capital.

• *Don't buy your collision and comprehensive coverage from the lender who finances your car, or any insurer he or she recommends.* That's going to be high-cost insurance. Count on it.

• *Raise the deductible on your collision insurance* from $250 to $500, or from $500 to $1,000. You'll pay less for the policy if you eat the smaller bills yourself. Odds are, you'll save more in premiums than you'll ever pay out of pocket in claims.

• *Drop collision insurance on an older car.* The insurer won't pay any more than the car is worth (page 438). Get an appraisal from an auto dealer.

• *Buy a car that's cheap to repair.* Your insurance agent can tell you which cars are money-eaters and which aren't. By this measure, a Ford Escort might cost $400 less to insure than a Cadillac Eldorado.

• *Don't drink or smoke.* Some insurers give discounts to clean livers.

• *Consider a body-shop "managed-care" plan.* Some insurers cut the cost of your collision insurance or cover more of your auto-repair bill if you'll have the car fixed in a designated shop. These shops work for a lower price. They may be just fine, or they may cut corners. Ask your own mechanic to double-check.

• *Earn a discount by insuring all your cars with the same company, and by buying your homeowners or tenants insurance there, too.* But shop first for the cheapest insurer. Even with a discount, high-priced policies are no bargain.

There may be additional discounts for young drivers who take driver education; teetotalers; nonsmokers; graduates of defensive-driving courses;

senior citizens; students with good grades; families whose teenage drivers go to school more than 100 miles away (so they can't get at the car!); cars parked in a garage or off the street; low-mileage cars; drivers who carpool; cars with air bags or seat belts that wrap around you automatically; cars with four-wheel, antilock braking systems; and cars with antitheft devices.

• *Describe exactly how your car is used.* A car driven for pleasure costs less to insure than a car used for everyday commuting.

• *In a no-fault state, people without jobs—for example, retirees—may be able to drop the portion of their personal-injury protection that covers loss of wages.* Keep it, however, if your spouse has a job.

• *Pay the premium all at once if you can afford it.* It costs more to pay in monthly or quarterly installments. Alternatively, set up automatic monthly payments through your bank. That should be cheaper than having to write a check once a month.

• *Share your car with your teenager (if you can stand it).* When teens have their own cars or drive your car more than half of the time, they're "principal drivers" and cost more to insure. They cost less when they're "occasional drivers," using your car less than half the time. They also cost less if they drive a safe, older car with no collision insurance.

• *Drive safely.* Your rates soar if your record shows convictions for drunk driving, "chargeable accidents" (meaning they're at least partly your fault), or a couple of speeding tickets.

• *Shop for the best risk classification you can get.* Many insurers are effectively raising premiums by rating more drivers as standard risks rather than as preferred risks. Standard risks pay anywhere from 10 to 60 percent more, depending on the company. Every insurer may rate you a little differently, however. If you have a good driving record, ask your agent to try for a company that will consider you a preferred risk. If you've been classified as substandard, look for an insurer that will take you as a standard risk.

• *If you're turned down for coverage because of your driving record, look for a better option than your state's high-risk pool.* Many companies are taking a second look at substandard drivers. You might have had a speeding ticket in the past couple of years or an accident that was partly your fault. In the old days, that could have dumped you into your state's assigned-risk pool. Now, however, you might find private coverage at a lower cost. To begin with, try State Farm, Allstate Indemnity, Dairyland, Integon, and the Progressive Insurance Corp. Progressive, in Mayfield Village, Ohio, gives quotes by phone to any insurance buyer (call 800-288-6776).

• *Reform.* If your bad driving record tags you with a higher premium or lands you in a high-risk pool, work at keeping your record squeaky clean. After 3 years shop again. A different company might take you at a better rate. Sometimes, however, it takes 7 years or more to escape your foolish past. A drunk-driving conviction may not be escapable.

• *Check on company group plans.* In Massachusetts, insurers can offer group plans, at a 5 to 10 percent discount, through employers, teachers associations, credit unions, and other organizations. Elsewhere, auto insurance may be offered through payroll deduction but not necessarily at a discount. Compare prices at other insurance companies before signing up.

• *Move.* Low insurance rates give you yet one more reason to avoid big, crowded cities. You can generally save $1,000 or more by living in a small city, a suburb, or deep in the country. Your rates may go up, however, if you move from Wyoming to a country town in Pennsylvania because Pennsylvania's rates are generally high all over.

Make All Valid Claims. Drivers often don't make small claims on their policies for fear of driving up their insurance rates. But the claim might not affect your price. For example, you're normally not held responsible for certain types of physical damage, like a windshield broken by flying gravel; accidents caused by animals; accidents that aren't your fault; and claims below a certain limit, like $300 or $600, even if you were at fault. Ask your company for a detailed statement, in writing, of which claims make your rates go up. That should ease your mind about reporting other kinds of claims.

BUY QUALITY

Not all insurance companies survive. Some go broke, sending their policyholders scrambling. The industry supports state insurance-guaranty funds, to make sure that the claims of all policyholders will eventually be paid. But they're not necessarily paid right away. A truly large bankruptcy might hold up claims for quite a while. So why tempt fate? Buy from a company highly rated for solvency (page 341).

GET IT RIGHT

Check a new policy for accuracy as soon as it arrives. A number of policies come through with mistakes: wrong amounts of coverage, a child left off the list of drivers, a discount forgotten. If you don't catch the error, you won't have the coverage you expected.

Don't Lie on Your Application! The insurer will run your name through the state motor-vehicle department to check whether you're licensed, what marks you have on your license, and how many licensed drivers live at your address. It will also check the Comprehensive Loss Underwriting Exchange (C.L.U.E.) in Atlanta or a similar service, where insurers report the claims you've made over the past 5 years. If you say you've never filed a claim but

C.L.U.E. turns up three, the door is going to be slammed in your face. The insurer can also check the claims record of every driver at your address.

If you're turned down for coverage or charged a higher rate based on information from a claims-reporting service, you have to be told and given the service's name and address. Write for a free copy of your record to be sure it's correct. The report may show claims at a given address before you lived there or for a particular vehicle before you owned it.

CAN YOU BE "FIRED" BY YOUR INSURER?

Absolutely. Every 6 months your policy normally comes up for renewal. At that time the company might blow you off or shift your policy to a related insurer that accepts higher risks. Maybe you've had a couple of speeding tickets. Maybe you've put in one claim too many. Maybe the company is withdrawing from your state. If it won't renew, see if another company will pick you up. Otherwise, you'll have to join the state's high-risk pool, where your coverage will come at a much higher rate.

When you first apply for a policy, the insurer generally has 60 days to evaluate you. After that, you can't be canceled before the policy's renewal date unless you didn't pay your premium, your driver's license was suspended or revoked, or you made a deceptive statement on your insurance application.

WHAT TO DO IF YOU HAVE AN ACCIDENT

Keep this list in the glove compartment, just in case:

1. Attend to any injuries. Have someone call an ambulance and the police.

2. Move your car to a safer place, if it can be driven, in order to prevent further damage. Warn oncoming traffic away from the wreck.

3. Get the other driver's name, address, phone number, license number, vehicle registration number, and insurance company, and give him yours. Look at his or her license to see if there are any restrictions he or she wasn't observing (wearing eyeglasses, for example). If the car is registered to someone else, get that person's name and address.

4. Get the names and addresses of witnesses, and their statements of what they saw. This is especially important if you think you weren't at fault. If they won't talk, get the license numbers of their cars. Get the names and badge numbers of the police who arrive on the scene.

5. If you think the other driver was drinking, insist that you both take a breath test.

6. Jot down your recollection of how the accident happened, including the speed you were traveling at. Note weather conditions, time of day, and any hazardous conditions. Describe the area, writing down exactly where you're located. Fresh impressions are compelling in court.

7. Don't sign anything unless required to by the police. Don't admit guilt or shared guilt. Don't say that your insurance will cover everything. Don't say how much insurance you have.

8. Ask the police whether you should report the accident yourself and, if so, how and where.

9. Call your insurance agent and tell him or her what happened. Summarize the evidence you have. Don't rely on the other driver's promise to pay; that might not last long. Report even small accidents if someone was injured. That injury might turn out to be serious. You risk losing coverage if you don't report promptly.

10. If you or any of your passengers were injured in any way, even bruised, see a doctor.

11. Cooperate with your insurance company on filling in forms and making reports. But don't make a quick, final settlement with your own company or with the other driver's. Injuries that don't seem serious at first may worsen with time.

12. If you're struck by a hit-and-run driver, tell the police within 24 hours. If you don't, you might lose your insurance coverage.

13. If you're sideswiped and worry that the other driver is trying to force you over in order to rob you, keep going, if you can, and find a police department. Call your insurer from there. Normally, you shouldn't leave the scene of the accident. But if you felt unsafe, your insurer will cut you some slack.

14. Keep records of all expenses connected with the accident, such as lost paychecks or the cost of renting a car until yours is fixed. In a no-fault state, your company might pay. In a fault state, the other person's company should reimburse you if the accident was his or her fault.

15. If the accident was serious, talk to a lawyer about what happened to get a handle on your rights and what your damages might be.

WHEN TO SEE A LAWYER

The following claims will be paid immediately without a lawyer's intercession: *in no-fault states,* your own medical bills and lost earnings, and those of everyone in the car with you; *in fault states,* only the medical bills that are paid through your own health insurer or through the medical-payments coverage you carry on your auto insurance; *in both kinds of states,* car repairs, if you carry collision insurance.

You will need a lawyer: *in no-fault states,* when the injuries are serious enough to warrant going to court; *in fault states,* when the accident was serious. You'll want an evaluation of the settlement proposed by the insurance company.

The insurance company will defend you if you're sued. But if you bring the lawsuit, you'll need a lawyer of your own. He or she should have long experience in trying personal-injury cases. At a first meeting (which might be free or might cost a flat fee), the lawyer will advise you whether the case is worth pursuing. Sometimes it is, sometimes it isn't. If you go ahead, you typically pay the lawyer nothing if you lose and a fixed percentage (usually one-third, plus expenses) if you win. If the insurance company has already made you an offer, a lawyer might be persuaded to take one-third to one-half of anything extra he or she can get.

Collision claims are usually negotiated between you and your company without legal intercession. A good insurance company inspects the car, tells you to get an estimate of what it will cost to repair, and promptly pays its share of the bill. No muss, no fuss. If you have to use the insurer's repair shop, don't sign a release until your own mechanic has examined the work. If something was overlooked, the insurer should fix it.

And then there's the other kind of insurer: a foot-dragger, a corner-cutter. Don't blindly sign a piece of paper accepting the insurer's estimate as the full cost of the repair. Get a second opinion from your own mechanic. And be sure to have your mechanic check the work. If the estimate or the repair was insufficient and the claims adjuster balks, invoke the arbitration clause contained in many auto-insurance contracts. When it's all over, find a better insurance company.

If your car is totaled or stolen, the insurer is supposed to pay fair market value. If the offer is too low, get signed statements attesting to your car's actual value from auto dealers in your area. With those statements in hand, make a pitch for more. You never get what you don't ask for.

If you think you're being taken, go on the offensive. Complain to your insurance agent, the state insurance commissioner (copy to the president of the insurance company), and your local consumer office. Ask a lawyer to write a letter on your behalf to the insurance company's president. Tell your insurance agent that you're pulling all of your policies—auto and homeowners—out of the company. Sometimes, pressure works.

If the accident was the other person's fault, your company will go after his or her insurer and collect your property-damage claim in full. You will already have been paid if you carry collision coverage, but your company will have subtracted the deductible. Once your insurer has been reimbursed, it owes you the deductible, too. Don't forget to ask for it.

RENTAL-CAR INSURANCE

When you rent a car, the rental agency offers to sell you insurance to cover accidents on your trip. In most cases, you can decline it. You get the same or better protection from your personal auto insurance or perhaps from the rental-car insurance attached to the credit card you use.

But there are holes in your personal or credit-card coverage. If you don't know the rules and decline the rental agency's trip coverage, you may be driving uninsured.

You do want to decline that coverage if you can. It's shockingly expensive. Take a package covering collision or theft of the rental car, $1 million in bodily injury coverage if you hit someone, and modest amounts of property damage and medical payments. Depending on your state, you might pay $130 to $225 for a one-week trip.

To avoid this expense, ask your auto-insurance agent whether your personal policy covers you when you drive a rental car. If the answer is yes, ask about the limitations (and double-check them in the policy itself). For example, there may be no collision or theft insurance if you don't buy it for your own car, too. You're generally not covered in foreign countries. Some policies don't cover rental cars, or cover them only when your car is being repaired. What's more, the coverage typically lasts for only 15 to 31 days. If you have an accident on day 10 but don't turn in the car until day 32, you're not insured. For long rentals, see if the rental-car agency has any special deals.

If you're driving a rented car on company business, your company probably insures you. Ask about it. The company might refuse to pay, however, if you have an accident while using the rental car for personal purposes.

If your personal or company policy doesn't cover your rental car, you have another option. Certain credit cards will protect you against damage or theft for a limited number of days if you use that card when you pay for the rental. They may also cover any deductibles under your regular auto insurance.

But again, there are limitations. At this writing, Visa covers only gold-card holders; MasterCard offers it on gold cards and a few standard cards; American Express covers all its U.S. cardholders. You're usually insured only for standard cars and minivans carrying up to 8 passengers, not luxury cars, larger vans, or sport vehicles driven off road. American Express cancels your insurance if you're 2 months behind on your bill.

If there's an accident, you risk losing your credit-card coverage unless you follow certain procedures. You must call the credit-card company—not the bank, but the card company itself—within a limited period. There's a special phone number—one for the United States, another when you call from abroad—which you should keep in your wallet.

If you don't know your car-insurance rules, call your auto insurer or credit-card company and ask for them. And check back from time to time to see if they've changed. You don't want to be caught out.

FITTING YOUR COVERAGE
INTO YOUR FINANCIAL PLAN

Spend your money on high liability coverage so that any reparations you owe will be paid by the insurance company, not by you personally. Good auto insurance protects your personal assets just as surely as a good investment plan.

16.

Fire! Theft! Wind! Flood!

Protecting Your Home and Everything in It

Without enough insurance, you're betting your savings that nothing bad will happen. I'd rather bet a few extra bucks that something might.

I have a friend whose house burned down. Luckily, he'd increased his homeowners insurance just a few months before. Unluckily, he'd made the mistake of pegging his coverage to the resale value of his house. He figured that, for insurance purposes, his house was worth what he could sell it for, minus an estimate for the price of the foundation and the land.

That's a mistake a lot of people make. The resale value of your house is often less than the cost of rebuilding it from the foundation up—and rebuilding a house is what homeowners insurance is all about. My friend's policy turned out to be too small. His error cost him plenty.

Homeowner or tenant, you're living in a dream world if your property isn't fully protected. It doesn't matter that you've drawn a nice financial plan. It doesn't matter that you're saving money and living smart. One pretty day you might come home from work and see nothing but fire engines and flames. In a few shocking hours your house is gone. And so are your savings, if you don't have enough homeowners or tenants insurance to make good the loss. You'll have to start building up capital all over again.

Some people deliberately play the odds. It's rare for a home to be totally destroyed, so they don't insure for the full rebuilding cost. Sometimes they feel they can't afford it. But a financial plan is only as sound as its backup systems. When you insure for something less than 100 percent, you are holding your savings hostage to luck. If your coverage slips below 80 percent of cost, which it easily might, even your lesser losses probably won't be fully insured (page 456).

Full insurance may not be worth it, however, if your home's market value is well below its replacement cost. Say, for example, you own a city row house worth maybe $90,000 but costing $200,000 to rebuild. If that house burned, you might not attempt to replace it. You'd buy another one instead. If this is your plan, insuring only the market value is enough.

WHAT TYPE POLICY DO YOU WANT?

Whoever said "A person's home is her or her castle" (it was said that way, right?) knew what he or she was talking about. Your home deserves "castle" coverage because it's worth that much to you.

Each insurance company has a slightly different contract, but all policies follow the same broad outlines (except in Texas, which has special forms, page 453). Buy the best you can afford and recheck your coverage every year.

Policies on the following forms will repair or replace structural losses up to your policy limit, provided that you keep your home sufficiently insured (page 455). You're covered for the cost of living in a hotel, motel, or mobile home while your own home is being rebuilt, as well as for your liability to anyone injured on your property. Your furniture, clothing, and other personal property are typically insured for half the policy's face value. So if you carry $200,000 on your home, the contents are insured for up to $100,000. (Some policies cover contents for 75 percent of the policy's face value.)

How much are you paid for each loss? Less expensive policies cover "actual cash value," which means replacement cost minus depreciation. If your house burns down, you don't get the full rebuilding cost; the insurer deducts something to account for the fact that you had an older house. Ditto for used furniture: you're paid its secondhand value, not the cost of replacing it. So you're not as well protected as you think.

If possible, upgrade your coverage to *replacement cost*. That way you'll secure the full cost of replacing your home and restocking your furniture up to the dollar limit of your policy. That will give you the money you'll need to buy things new. To get replacement-cost coverage, however, you must insure for at least 80 percent of what it would cost to rebuild (page 459).

Better yet, go for *guaranteed replacement cost* or some variant of it. This pays full replacement cost even if it exceeds your policy's face value (page 454).

The basic policy forms:

Basic Coverage (HO-1) is a dinosaur, no longer sold by some insurers and in some states. Where available, it typically covers only 11 or 12 specified risks to your home and personal property, leaving out such common happenings as burst pipes, falling tree limbs, and sudden leaks from an air-conditioning system. Some policies cut you down to 8 or 9 risks, excluding vandalism, glass breakage, and theft. The latter coverage is usually reserved for remote or one-season cottages that are uninhabited for months at a time. Buy HO-1 only if it's all you can get. It covers the actual cash value of your loss, although you might be able to upgrade to replacement cost (see above).

Broad Coverage (HO-2) insures some 16 or 18 risks to your home and personal property, ranging from fire, wind, and living in the path of a volcano to burst pipes and a short-circuited electrical system. It normally covers the actual cash value of your loss, although you usually can upgrade to replacement cost (see above).

Special Coverage (HO-3), the most widely sold, costs just a little bit more than HO-2 but is a better deal. On the house itself, you're protected from all risks except a few that are specifically excluded, such as earthquakes, floods, sewer backups, and wars. Check your policy for the exclusion list. A few insurers provide all-risk coverage for personal property, too. Usually, however, your personal property is insured for the 16 or 18 specific risks included in HO-2. HO-3 typically offers replacement-cost coverage, but lets you upgrade to guaranteed replacement cost (page 459).

Tenants Coverage (HO-4) protects against 16 or 18 risks to your personal property, although a few insurers give you all-risk protection. You can also get coverage for built-in improvements you make to the apartment, your liability to anyone injured there, and your potential liability if you negligently cause an accident that damages the landlord's or other tenants' property. For more on personal property, see page 458. Most insurers put roommates—be they lovers or just friends—on a single policy.

Condominium and Cooperative-Apartment Coverage (HO-6) protects your personal property and any part of the structure you're responsible for. You can insure against 16 or 18 specific risks, but an all-risk policy is better. Show your insurer the condo agreement, which stipulates what you're responsible for. Sometimes the condo or co-op insures the unit as it was originally built, so you only have to insure the changes (yours and those made by previous owners); sometimes you have to insure everything from the bare walls out. Normally, only 20 percent of your policy's face value can be used to make repairs on your own additions or alterations. If you've renovated your unit, consider boosting this part of your policy.

The building itself, the common areas, and the owners' common liability should be covered by insurance bought by the condo or co-op board. But consider buying your own loss-assessment coverage. It pays if your condo or co-op suffers damage or loses a lawsuit for which it was underinsured, requiring the unit owners to kick in.

Unique or Old-Home Coverage (HO-8) is for hard-to-duplicate houses such as Victorians or true Colonials. They'd be far too expensive to replace in their original form. So instead of basing your coverage on replacement cost, most policies insure only for the home's market value. In a few states, insurers have to pay actual cash value (replacement cost minus depreciation) if that comes to more than the market value. Your coverage might also be defined as "modified replacement cost"—replacing carved oak banisters, plaster walls, and fancy hardware with the simpler building materials commonly used today.

Your house is usually insured only against the limited risks commonly used for HO-1 policies. That leaves out burst pipes and faulty wiring, which older homes are especially subject to. You might not even get replacement-cost coverage (page 459) for personal property or for lesser losses, like a kitchen fire. Nor can you usually insure your personal property for more than 50 percent of the policy's face value. HO-8, in short, is mediocre, but sometimes the best that you can get.

Some insurers impose HO-8 coverage on older houses that aren't unique. This can be a sign of illegal discrimination. An old house in the suburbs might get an HO-3 while the same house in a less desirable urban area might be offered only an HO-8. HO-8s are more expensive, per $1,000 of coverage, than HO-3s, so you're paying more for less.

Mobile-Home Coverage is generally a costlier form of HO-2 or HO-3. You can cover the home for a fixed dollar amount, for replacement cost (the price of a new home), or for actual cash value (the market value of your older home).

Texas Coverage comes in three basic forms: HO-A insures against 8 classes of risk to your home and its contents, paying only their actual cash value or the cost of repair. HO-B insures against all risks to your home except those specifically excluded, and 12 risks to personal property. On the home, you get replacement-cost coverage; on contents, you get actual cash value. HO-C covers all risks to both home and personal property except those specifically excluded. Premises are covered at replacement cost or actual cash value, whichever is greater, and contents at actual cash value. With HO-B and HO-C, you can buy replacement-cost endorsements for the contents of your home. Many other endorsements are available, including—at some companies—guaranteed replacement cost. There are variants of HO-B and HO-C for tenants and condominium owners. Mobile-home owners generally buy a variant of auto insurance.

One-Form Coverage, introduced by State Farm, abolishes all the separate HOs. There's a single contract, with coverage linked to how much of your home's replacement cost you choose to insure. If you cover 100 percent, you get super-protection; in a total wipeout, payments can even exceed the policy's face value (see next section). If you cover 80 to 99 percent of replacement cost, your losses will be replaced, in full, up to the policy's face value. At less than 80 percent, your loss is repaired up to the policy's face value but with simple building materials, perhaps of lower quality than you had before. Your premium is adjusted, depending on your insurance percentage and amount.

YOUR INFLATION PROTECTION

Most policies today come with automatic inflation protection. At every renewal, your policy's face amount goes up, in line with an index of area construction costs. Naturally, your premium goes up, too. But that's better than having a major fire and finding that you're underinsured. A few insurers let you decline this inflation guard. Don't. At this writing, it raises your coverage and your premium by a modest 2 to 3 percent a year.

There's no guarantee, however, that these increases will hit the mark. Your coverage may rise too slowly, leaving you more exposed than you had thought. Or it may rise faster than local building costs, forcing you to buy more insurance than you need. So even with an inflation guard, get a replacement-cost appraisal every few years, to be sure you're still on track.

For Super Protection Against Inflation and Other Price Risks, get "guaranteed replacement-cost coverage." It promises that, if your house is destroyed, the insurer will repair or replace it in virtually every detail, even if the cost exceeds the policy's face value. If the house was custom-built for you, the insurer might even pay the same architect and interior designer to supervise the reconstruction. This coverage saves your skin if you're underinsured because you and your agent underestimated your rebuilding costs. It's especially valuable for homes that might be caught in a common disaster, such as a wildfire. When a lot of homes need rebuilding at once, builders put their prices up.

Some insurers don't offer guaranteed replacement-cost coverage on houses more than 25 years old, houses worth significantly less than the cost of rebuilding them, or unusually detailed and expensive homes. The latter might find coverage, however, through companies that cater to the carriage trade. Some insurers offer what they call "extra replacement cost" or an "increased insurance amount." Here, your payment is capped at 20 or 50 percent over the policy's face value. You may have to negotiate how much over face value the company is going to pay.

To get guaranteed replacement-cost coverage, you have to insure for 100 percent of the expected rebuilding cost. The face value (and price) of your policy will rise automatically every year, in line with the general increase in construction costs. If you improve your home in some way, you have to notify the insurer so that that extra value can be covered, too.

From time to time the insurer may reevaluate the cost to rebuild. Don't accept a big increase that seems unjustified. You're required to cover only the cost of reconstruction today. If you think the insurer overestimated costs, take your case to your insurance agent or get a replacement-cost appraisal of your own.

Warning: The local building code may have changed since your house was put up. Guaranteed replacement-cost policies typically pay for repairing your house but not for bringing it up to code. Ask about an "ordinance or law" endorsement, which covers needed code improvements, too.

HOW MUCH INSURANCE DO YOU NEED?

In my book (and this is), your policy should equal 100 percent of your home's replacement cost. You can't go by market value, which includes the land as well as the house. You need to know what it would cost to rebuild from the ground up. In super-high heat, even the foundation may be damaged.

You'll get the best answer from a builder or appraiser (tell the appraiser you want building costs, not market value). Alternatively, you could use your insurance agent's rules of thumb. If the agent steers you wrong, however, and you find out too late that you're underinsured, the problem is entirely yours.

Guaranteed replacement-cost coverage keeps you fully insured for the right amount. Second best is automatic inflation protection. Third best is to use your insurance company's worksheet every time your policy comes up for renewal to figure out how much more insurance you need to buy.

You'll probably have to increase your coverage even if housing values fall. No matter how bad the real-estate market, building costs generally rise.

• • •

What happens if you're insured for less than the full replacement cost? That depends on how much less.

If You're Covered for 80 Percent or More of Replacement Cost, your insured losses are paid in full up to the limits of your policy. Say, for example, that your home's replacement cost is $100,000 and you're insured for $80,000. If a fire in the kitchen costs you $5,000, your insurer will pay the entire bill (minus the deductible). If the house burns to the ground, you collect $80,000. (A few companies require 90 percent coverage before smaller losses will be paid in full.)

If You're Covered for Less Than 80 Percent, you will not collect in full on any loss, even a small one. On a kitchen fire that costs $5,000 to fix, you might get $4,000 or less. The exact amount will depend on the age of the house and the payment formula used.

Many homeowners don't insure for 100 percent. If you can't afford full coverage, buy as much as you can. If you can afford it but are gambling that the worst won't happen, I think you're nuts. But maybe you know more about the future than I do. At the very least, keep your policy at 90 percent of replacement cost. That assures full coverage for anything but a catastrophic loss and avoids philosophical discussions with your insurer over whether your coverage met the critical 80 percent test.

You don't have to rebuild exactly what you had before. You don't even have to rebuild in the same location. You can simply take the money (usually, the actual cash value) if you decide not to rebuild at all.

Unless you have guaranteed or extra replacement-cost coverage, however, the insurer won't pay more than the policy limit. If that's not enough to rebuild, too bad.

WHAT'S COVERED, WHAT ISN'T

Policies differ. So do state laws governing what has to be covered. The depth of your protection depends on what your policy says, but here's a general look at what it might include.

• Garages, sheds, driveways, fences, and other detached structures, typically for 10 percent of the coverage you carry on your house.

• For homeowners—trees, shrubs, and plants worth up to 5 percent of the policy's face value, with a maximum of $500 per item. For renters or condo owners, it's 10 percent up to a $500 maximum per item. They're not protected against wind or storm damage, only from theft, fire, lightning, vandalism, and so on.

- The contents of a house—typically covered for 50 percent of the policy's face value. Some insurers have raised that limit to 75 percent. You're insured for losses both at home and away from home, including things stolen from your bank safe-deposit box. For types of coverage, see page 459.

- The cost of protecting your home against further damage or loss— for example, boarding up broken windows or gaps in the wall that a fire burned through.

- Reasonable living expenses if you have to move out of your house while it's being repaired. Ditto if the authorities move you out of your house because of direct damage to a neighbor's house by a peril that your policy insures against. For example, your company would pay your hotel bill if the police or fire department prevented you from going home because your neighbor's house was on fire. You're covered only for extra expenses (restaurant meals), not expenses you'd normally incur (groceries). Reimbursement is generally limited to 20 percent of your policy's face value.

- Lost rent if you rent out part of your house and those quarters become uninhabitable because of a fire or other insured damage. But you don't get the full amount. The insurer deducts the rental-business expenses that you normally would have incurred.

- Removing debris from your property.

- Up to $500 if your town doesn't have a fire department and you contract with the firefighters of another town to pay a fee if they make a house call.

- Medical payments coverage, for the minor medical bills of visitors or employees hurt on your property or injured by your family or pets away from home. If your dog bites the window washer, you can send your insurer the doctor bill. Typically, you're insured for up to $1,000. For a few bucks more, you can raise that to $5,000.

- Up to $500 worth of damage that you accidentally do to the property of others, and another $500 or $1,000 for losses from forgery, counterfeit money, credit-card theft, or theft by a computer whiz who lifts money electronically out of your account.

- Theft or damage to the personal property of a guest or a domestic employee.

- Up to $1,000 for a loss to your condo or co-op building if your owners' association assesses you for it. You can beef up this coverage if you want.

Different Policies Have Different Exceptions. But in General, Here's What Might Be Ruled Out:

- A separate structure on the property that's used for business or rented out.

- Losses due to a power failure from a source outside your home.

- Water damage, including floods, tides, sewer backups, and seepage from groundwater. But you're covered if accidental damage to the roof lets in the rain, and from the havoc wrought by firefighters' hoses.
- Losses from neglect—for example, property that's stolen because you walked away from a partly burned home without boarding up the windows.
- Damage you deliberately do yourself.
- Earthquake, except by special endorsement.
- Ice or snow damage to awnings, fences, patios, and swimming pools.
- Vandalism to houses left vacant for more than 30 days.
- Frozen or burst pipes in a house you've left unoccupied, without maintaining the heat or draining the pipes.
- Damage from settling or cracking.
- War.
- Normal wear and tear.
- Damage done by birds, rodents, insects, or your own pets (although the policy will repair your porch if it collapses due to hidden insect damage).
- Smoke damage from nearby factories or agricultural smudging.
- Claims on policies obtained by misrepresentation or fraud. So don't lie if you're asked whether your dog bites or whether you've had any previous losses.
- A continuous leak from the plumbing, heating, or air-conditioning system (you're covered only for sudden leaks).
- Nuclear explosion—although if you're nuked, the exclusions in your homeowners policy will be the least of your troubles.

COVERING YOUR PERSONAL PROPERTY

Clothes, furniture, and other personal effects are normally insured for up to half the face value of your homeowners policy. A few companies insure them for 75 percent. With a $200,000 policy, then, you get $100,000 to $150,000 worth of personal-property protection. There are fixed maximums for special items like jewelry and furs (page 460). You can raise all these ceilings by paying a larger premium. You may also have $500 of credit-card coverage in case a crook gets your card number and it costs you some money.

If you're a renter, or own a condominium or cooperative apartment, you insure for the full value of your personal property.

Your policy covers damage or a theft reported to the police. It protects property in your home, temporarily out of your home (say, when you're carrying it in your handbag), or with one of your children at school or college. You're generally not covered, however, for personal property that you merely lose or break. There has to be vandalism, theft, or an accident that you or your family didn't cause. If you accidentally break someone else's valuable property, however, the policy should pay.

What are you covered for per item? In standard policies, less than you think.

Standard Reimbursement

When your insurer reimburses you for an item, you normally get its "actual cash value"—officially defined as its replacement cost minus depreciation. In other words, it's value as used property, not new.

Your fire-damaged living-room couch may have cost $800, but that was five years ago, before it was clawed by your cat and used as a trampoline by your kids. It's actual cash value, as priced by standard insurance formulas, might be only $450. The additional cost of a new couch comes out of your pocket.

Almost everything new loses value over the years: furniture, clothing, electronics, cameras, carpeting. Your insurer will repair the damaged item or reimburse you for its actual cash value, whichever is less. But you won't get the money you need to buy something new. To refurnish your house after an expensive loss, you need replacement-cost coverage (next section).

Good antiques, on the other hand, should increase in value as the years go by. Your basic insurance will generally cover their current appraised value, even though it's higher than when the policy was new. But you'll have to prove your claim—with a proof of purchase, a new appraisal, a picture, and other details about the items. The insurer can also decide to repair an item rather than replace it.

Replacement-Cost Reimbursement

If you can afford it, this is definitely the coverage of choice. You get whatever money you need to start over from scratch. If your $800 couch goes up in flames, you might collect $900 because that's what it costs to buy a couch of similar quality, new. The insurance company will also make repairs if the item can be restored to its original condition.

Only replacement-cost coverage can restock your closets, rooms, and china cabinets after a major wipeout. The only articles not covered are those that are obsolete and in storage (your old Schwinn bicycle) and articles not in working condition (the broken TV set in the back bedroom).

Where possible, the insurer sends you an actual replacement. If you know the make and model of your TV set, for example, the insurer will send you another one or one very similar. These goods are purchased at a discount. If you want cash instead—say, to put toward a larger-screen TV

—the insurer gives you only the discounted price. That's more than you'd get with a regular policy but less than full retail value. Where standard replacements aren't possible, however, you get the full retail price of the substitute.

Standard Limits on Valuables

In standard policies, insurers pay a fixed, maximum price for the theft or covered damage to certain items, no matter how large your total coverage is. The typical limits: $2,500 for silverware, goldware, pewterware, and gold and silver plate; $200 for all bullion coins, rare coins, cash, and gold, silver, or platinum bars; $1,000 for all securities, deeds, manuscripts (which might include rare books), tickets, letters of credit, accounts, evidence of money owed you, and stamps; $1,000 for boats and their trailers, furnishings, equipment, and motors; $1,000 for other trailers; $1,000 for grave markers; $2,000 for guns; $2,500 for business property on the premises; $250 for business property away from the premises (such as a laptop computer stolen at an airport); and $1,000 to $2,000, collectively, for the theft of jewelry, watches, gems, and furs.

These limits apply to valuables in your bank safe-deposit box as well as to property kept at home. To raise your coverage, read on.

Blanket Coverage

For a small extra payment, you can raise the limit on most of the categories just listed. For example, you might want to cover $10,000 worth of jewelry with a $2,500 limit per item. If something is stolen, you'd report the loss, substantiate its value, and collect. No proofs of ownership are required in advance, but you'll need them if you make a claim. So keep sales slips and take pictures of your valuables, just in case.

Scheduled Coverage

Particular items of special value should be individually insured. Have each one appraised and listed separately: sterling silver flatware, $5,000; mink coat, $6,000; Dream Diamond, $7 zillion. If any scheduled item is stolen or damaged, the insurer pays its scheduled value, with no deductible. You're also paid for items that you merely lose. But there may be no coverage for accidental breakage unless you buy extra coverage.

Other valuables, such as antiques, collectors' items, fine china, guns, musical instruments, or golfing equipment, don't have to be scheduled to be fully covered. You can insure them for their actual cash value (including any appreciation in value) right along with your other personal property.

Here Are the Advantages of Scheduling Your Valuables:

1. They're covered if they merely disappear. If they're not scheduled, there has to be a likelihood of theft.

2. They're protected against practically all forms of damage, not just the 16 or 18 listed in your regular policy. This includes accidental wine or ink stains on an Oriental rug.

3. If they're included in your basic policy, they might push the value of your personal possessions above the policy's maximum limit. It's often cheaper to schedule a few items than to raise the ceiling on your total coverage.

4. You won't have to haggle with the insurer over whether you really owned the items and what they were worth.

Here Are the Disadvantages of Scheduling:

1. It costs extra money.

2. You're covered for no more than the exact amount of the appraisal. If your Picasso lithograph was listed at $2,500, that's what you'll get—even if the appraisal is old and the lithograph is worth $4,000 today. Had it not been scheduled, you'd have gotten its current market value minus the policy's deductible.

3. You may wind up paying for insurance that you don't really have. Say, for example, that you scheduled your mink for $5,000. It's now three years old and worth only $3,500. If it's stolen, you'll normally get only $3,500, even though it's insured for more. Solution: Buy replacement-cost coverage for scheduled items. You'll then be paid the full value that they were insured for.

All scheduled items should be reappraised regularly so they won't be underinsured. Special items you don't schedule need to be appraised only once, and their pictures taken. If they're damaged, their value can be updated, based on the work that was done before.

Count the Risks

You're insured only against the specific risks listed in the contract—as few as 9, as many as 18. You can also buy all-risk coverage, which actually should be called almost all-risk. It leaves out things like floods, war, and wear and tear. But only all-risk coverage protects you against paint dropped on the carpet or wine stains on your pink velvet loveseat. Ask your company about cigarette burns. Some cover them under the "fire" clause in your basic policy; others pay only if you buy all-risk insurance. Also ask about breakage: What's covered, what isn't? You pay for minor damage, under your deductible.

If a guest damages your property, his or her policy might pay under the property-damage clause or the liability clause.

What May Not Be Covered

Policies vary on this point, but here are some likely examples:
- Pets.
- Damage done to your property by pets (although if your neighbor's dog knocks over your Ming vase, the neighbor's policy might pay).
- Aircraft.
- Boats, except in limited circumstances.
- Most motorized vehicles and the equipment, radios, or tape decks in them (unless they're parked on your property). But you're usually covered for off-road vehicles that service the premises, like lawn mowers, or that assist the handicapped, like motorized wheelchairs.
- The property in a room you rent regularly to someone not in your family.
- Records and data pertaining to your business.
- Theft of materials from a house under construction.
- Items that disappear, without the likelihood of theft.
- Breakage, unless it's vandalism.
- Loss of a gem from its setting.
- Marring.
- Wear and tear.

Ask about any special items in your home. A computer. A satellite dish antenna. A wine cellar. A coin collection. Ask about family members. Does the policy cover your mother who lives with you? Clarify your coverage before any damage is done.

When You Don't Replace

What if a spare camera is stolen from your house and you don't want to buy another one? At the very least, you'll be paid its current, flea-market value (replacement cost minus depreciation). If you carry replacement-cost coverage, there may or may not be limits on what you can collect. Some policies pay full cost, whether you buy or not; others pay up to a ceiling, say $1,000.

When Your Lost or Stolen Property Is Found

You can give it to the insurer and keep the money. Or you can keep the property and give back the money. Your choice.

UPPER-CRUST COVERAGE

Some policies are specifically aimed at the well-to-do. You get replacement-cost coverage on both your house and its contents. You get protection against all risks. In addition, there might be:

• Higher payments for valuable items. For example, jewelry and furs may be covered up to $5,000, silverware up to $10,000, and guns up to $5,000.

• Coverage for a power outage in your neighborhood.

• Coverage for food lost when your freezer thawed.

• A bit of liability coverage for a small, part-time business run out of your house. The policy might also pay toward replacing data lost in an accident to your personal computer.

• Coverage for damage from the backing up of a sewer or drain—not included in the average policy.

• Higher limits on your coverage for personal liability.

• Recompense, up to $500, for the cost of changing the locks when your keys are stolen.

• The additional cost of rebuilding a damaged or burned-out portion of your house to meet the standards of a new building code.

• Reimbursement for items not obviously stolen but simply missing.

• Homeowners, auto, and umbrella insurance, bundled together for a single package price.

You can get much (but not all) of this upper-crust coverage by increasing the limits on your regular policy or by buying endorsements. Which choice to make depends on what you need. Ask the insurance agent to make a list of all the extras in the higher-cost policy. Cross off the ones that aren't essential. When you've pared down the list, find out what it would cost to add those extras to a standard policy. There's no point buying more insurance than necessary.

Even with upper-crust coverage, you may have to schedule valuable items like silverware, jewelry, and furs.

LIABILITY INSURANCE

This is your "banana-peel" coverage. You're protected if someone—not a family member—slips on your banana peel, breaks a leg, and sues. You're covered for injuries on your premises. Your family members (and pets) are also covered for their actions (or bites) away from home. Some states require that you carry workers' compensation to cover domestics, painters, gardeners, and other full-time or occasional employees. You're also covered if you negligently damage someone else's property—for example, if your wheelbarrow got away from you on a slope and smashed into your neighbor's new Mercedes.

Only unintentional damage and injuries are covered unless the perpetrator is under 13. So you can't slash your neighbor's tires in a driveway dispute and expect your insurer to replace them. But it will pay in full if your small daughter hits your neighbor in the eye with a rock.

What if that same daughter, at 14, vents her emotions by deliberately setting fire to your neighbor's porch? The property damage won't be covered but injury to your neighbor might. Your lawyer (you'll need one!) will argue that although your nasty daughter meant to scorch the porch, she didn't intend to send anyone to the hospital for smoke inhalation, so the injury was unintentional—hence, insured. Right now, some policies pay if a court holds a parent financially responsible for children's evil deeds. Other policies don't.

If your dog bites the United Parcel Service driver, your insurance pays. If the dog lunches next on the driver for Federal Express, it pays again. But at that point the insurer may cancel your policy, refuse to renew it, or try to exclude the dog (I say "try to" because it's not clear that such an exclusion would stand up in court). In some states, courts can levy extra, punitive damages after a second bite—your punishment for keeping a dangerous dog. Those extra damages might not be covered by your insurance. After a dog bite, find out what your liability could be if the sweet pooch bites again.

Your basic policy probably includes $100,000 of liability coverage. That's not much, especially if you own a swimming pool. For a small additional fee, you can have $300,000 of coverage or even $500,000. Some companies take you up to $1 million.

Alternatively, you can buy "umbrella insurance," which covers losses in excess of the limits on both your homeowners and auto policies. You're required to carry certain minimums on your basic policies, maybe $250,000 on auto and $300,000 on your home. After that, the umbrella goes up. The ceiling can be $5 million or more. The insurance might also cover your liability if you're charged with invasion of privacy, false arrest, libel, or slander. Average price: $200 to $300 a year.

Not Covered Might Be:

• Employees and clients if you run a business from home. Ditto if you run a child-care service. Even that Federal Express driver bitten by your dog won't be covered if he or she was delivering something for your business. For business risks, you need separate business or child-care insurance.

• Aircraft.

• Injuries from most boats and motor vehicles (they have to be insured separately). But off-road vehicles like golf carts and dirt bikes might be covered. Ditto small boats or boats parked in your yard.

• Claims by one family member against another.

• Damage to your own property.

• Any disease that someone catches from you.

• Damage done by a leaking waterbed to an apartment you rent, unless you cover the bed with a special endorsement.

If you're sued, your insurance company not only pays the damages up to the limit of your policy; it also covers all the legal costs of reaching a settlement or going to court.

FLOOD INSURANCE

Your Policy Probably Doesn't Insure You Against Floods. In fact, there's usually not much protection against water damage of any sort. If flooding is a risk, and your community has met federal flood-prevention standards, most homeowners can insure themselves—for home and contents— through the government's National Flood Insurance Program. For information, see an insurance agent. In 1997 the most you could insure for was $250,000 on a house or condominium and $100,000 on contents. There's normally a 30-day wait before your coverage takes effect, so don't put off applying until you hear that the waters are rising. There's no waiting period, however, if you apply and pay for a policy in connection with a loan.

If you've ever received federal disaster insurance after a flood and don't buy this coverage, you won't qualify for disaster aid again.

EARTHQUAKE INSURANCE

Insurance companies may sell earthquake insurance as a separate policy or as an endorsement to your homeowners policy. Deductibles run from 2 to 20 percent of the home's insured value. In California, most policies are placed through the California Earthquake Authority (CEA), with a 15 percent deductible, no coverage for outbuildings and pools, only $1,500 for living expenses while your home is being repaired, and no more than $5,000 (above the deductible) for replacing your home's contents. Some California insurers may offer modest wraparounds to cover certain losses that CEA-approved policies don't.

Find out if you live near a geological fault (there are some in states other than California). If so, consider buying this coverage. Premiums are lowest for policies on wood-frame houses, which can sway with a quake and aren't too expensive to rebuild.

What's the very best earthquake insurance? Move to Dallas, where the earth doesn't move.

HURRICANE COVERAGE

Homeowner policies normally cover wind damage except in places where windstorms are especially bad—for example, along the Gulf and

Atlantic coasts. There you may need special beach or windstorm coverage. Beach plans, in seven states, help protect coastal properties against wind and water damage during hurricanes. Wind plans, in four states that are hurricane prone, protect only against hail and windstorm damage.

Some companies "shoreline," meaning they don't write beach policies at all. Others insist on a large deductible if you're damaged in a hurricane rather than an ordinary windstorm.

FOR REJECTNIKS

Thousands of homeowners in inner cities, high-risk coastal areas, or earthquake zones find good policies hard to get. Only a handful of companies may offer insurance at all. Those that do may provide bare-bones coverage or charge a painfully high price. Still, buy the best coverage you can. Losing your home will cost you more than paying a high premium for insurance. It's a rock-bottom rule of real estate: *never* buy a property you can't insure.

People who can't get normal homeowners or tenants coverage generally have access to risk pools organized by the state. You buy these policies through insurance agents:

Fair Access to Insurance Requirements (Fair) Plans—available in about half the states, for protection against such perils as fire, rioting, wind, hail, smoke, and theft. Some include crime insurance.

Rural Risk Plans—in two states, to protect homes against fire when no fire stations are nearby.

Plans from State Underwriting Pools—for broad-based coverage in areas where individual private insurers have pulled out.

If you run into racial discrimination, complain in writing to your state insurance department in the state capital. It may get you nothing but satisfaction, but do it anyway. You never know. Some states, such as Texas, have special programs for areas "underserved" by insurers in the past.

If one company rejects you, try another. They have different rules for accepting applicants. But you might not get coverage anywhere if you haven't paid your property taxes for a couple of years, if a past policy was canceled because you didn't pay your premiums, or if your house has been vacant for a while.

If you're switching companies, keep your old policy for a month in case your new company reneges. For example, the new company might back away because of something it sees on your credit report (page 231).

INSURANCE ON A HOME BUSINESS

More than 12 million people are believed to be working from home. A fire, a burst pipe, or a tornado could wreck not only their living quarters but also their livelihood. A lawsuit brought by an injured customer or employee could wipe them out financially. A thief might vanish with their computer or inventory.

Some self-employed people think that special business insurance will cost more than they can afford. But you might find the bare-bones coverage you need for as little as $15 to $50 a year—with the price depending on where you live, the company you insure with, and the type of business you run. A more comprehensive policy might cost around $75 to $400.

Home-business insurance is an industry in transition. The traditional coverage wasn't designed for today's consultant/telecommuter/business-service/home-based entrepreneur. New types of policies are being developed, targeted at the new workplace's special needs.

So when looking for insurance, it's important to speak with two or three different agents. Some can offer more inventive policies than others. Here's where to look for coverage:

1. *Your current homeowners or renters insurance.* You may think that your policy already covers the contents of your home office, but that's not necessarily so. It typically protects only $1,000 to $2,500 worth of business equipment and a $250 loss off-premises (for example, if a pickpocket lifts your cellular phone). The equipment is insured against the risks named in your homeowners insurance, such as fire, theft, windstorm, and so on, but not flood (that comes only under federal flood insurance) and not if your toddler dumps his spinach into your laser printer. There's no protection against business lawsuits and no income replacement if your business shuts down because of damage to your home.

Nevertheless, simple homeowners insurance may be enough for a one-person craft or service business. Read your policy to see what's covered. Strictly speaking, a business computer is often excluded. But if you also use it for games, balancing your checkbook, and other personal matters, the insurer may accept it as covered personal property.

2. *Endorsements to your homeowners or renters insurance.* You can usually raise your home-business coverage limits to protect equipment worth up to $10,000 or $15,000, and $1,000 or $1,500 off-premises. There may also be endorsements for limited types of liability, like injury to customers on premises, but not for broad business risks like false advertising or product liability. To qualify even for limited liability coverage under an endorsement, your business might have to be "incidental," meaning very small. Cost range for a simple endorsement: around $10 to $15 a year— and perhaps $40 for a package of several protections. Some insurers are

developing more comprehensive endorsements at a higher price. Liability protection for home day care is written separately.

3. *Traditional business owner's policies.* These policies cover the works: loss of equipment, inventory, computer files, business property, cash up to $5,000 or $10,000, a broad range of business-liability risks, and off-premises losses of equipment worth $15,000 or more. You get all-risk protection, meaning that you're covered for any loss not specifically excluded. If there's spinach in the laser printer, you put in a claim.

Just as important, if your business shuts down because of damage to your home, you can be reimbursed for up to 12 months of lost business income. You're also covered for the cost of setting up shop in a new location. Recent price range for a typical home-office package with a $250 deductible, anywhere from $100 to $400 a year, depending on where you live. These policies, however, may cover more than you need.

4. *Mini-business owner's coverage, specifically designed for low-risk, home-based businesses.* This coverage is quite new and not yet widely available. At this writing, a handful of insurers offer it as an endorsement to regular homeowners coverage. For stand-alone policies for low-risk home businesses, try RLI Insurance in Peoria, Illinois. Among other things, you get coverage for anywhere from $5,000 to $50,000 worth of in-home business equipment ($1,000 to $50,000 off-premises); $300,000 to $1 million worth of business liability protection, for personal injury and property damage (although there's a long list of exclusions); and loss of business income for up to 12 months if a fire or hurricane shuts down your office at home. Prices run from $150 up. Also try State Farm or ask an insurance agent.

THE INVENTORY

Make a day of it—maybe a rainy Saturday in March. Lay in plenty of film. Plenty of diet soda. Plenty of chocolate bars to keep up your energy. Photograph everything in your house. Open every drawer, every cabinet, every closet, and take pictures from a close enough range to show all the contents. Make overall views of your rooms and what's in them. Take close-ups of special items like good china, Waterford crystal, and antiques. Don't forget the cellar, attic, and garage. When it stops raining, take pictures of the outside of your house—the landscaping, driveway, sidewalks, toolshed, pool.

When the pictures come back, describe the items briefly on the back. Put down the model number and price of the more costly items, and when you bought them.

If you have a video camera, use it instead. Talk about each item as you show it, recording the model and price on tape.

The inventory is your guarantee that you'll collect all the protection you paid for. With it, you can make a full list of all of your losses. Insurers will generally accept a list you reconstruct from memory. But you'll never recall every single item, and those little things add up. Pictures also show the quality of your furniture and prove that your modest home really did contain an antique Oriental rug.

Keep the inventory—along with sales slips for the more expensive items and any appraisals or descriptive material about them—in your safe-deposit box. You'd be chagrined if these records burned in the same fire that destroyed everything else.

Tot up the rough value of everything you own. It's probably double what you thought. When buying property insurance, most people focus only on their few expensive pieces of furniture. But what drives up the price of refurnishing a house is the pencils and potholders, jackets and mittens, baseballs and houseplants. Your family's clothing alone may be worth $8,000 or more.

APPRAISALS

All special items should be separately described and appraised—furs, good jewelry, antiques, paintings, Oriental carpets, rare books, special collections, and so on. Take pictures of them in relation to other things in your home to prove they were there. To find an appraiser, ask your insurer, a local jeweler and a furrier, or look in the Yellow Pages. Keep the pictures and appraisals in your safe-deposit box.

The first appraisal is the most expensive because everything has to be written up. After that, you can coast. The only appraisals that have to be updated regularly are those for the items that are separately scheduled (see page 460). Leave everything else alone. When something is stolen or damaged, just give the insurer the description, the picture, and the original appraisal. The appraiser will update the value for you. The only reason to reappraise everything is to run a check on whether you have enough personal-property insurance to cover all of your possessions.

FINDING A GOOD, LOW-COST COMPANY

Call several sources and compare prices. In any given city, the most expensive insurer may charge 50 percent more than the least expensive for the very same policy. Many consumers don't realize this, or don't take it seriously. You might waste hundreds of dollars if you can't be bothered shopping around.

There are three sources of homeowners insurance: (1) Companies that sell by phone, such as Amica in Providence, Rhode Island (800-242-6422), specializing in better risks, and GEICO in Washington, D.C. (800-841-3000). Anyone associated with the United States military should call USAA in San Antonio, Texas (800-531-8080—page 441). (2) Companies that sell exclusively through their own agents, such as Allstate and State Farm. (3) Companies that sell through independent agents. These agents can work with several carriers, although they usually specialize in one or two. Prices vary depending on your circumstances and where you live, so the same company may not be the cheapest for everyone. Amica and some other insurers pay a dividend at the end of the year, so their true cost is lower than it seems (although dividends aren't guaranteed).

Rate isn't everything, of course. You also want your claims handled promptly, fairly, and without any hassle. Ask your friends how they like their own insurers. Some states publish data on customer complaints.

OTHER WAYS TO SAVE MONEY ON HOMEOWNERS AND TENANTS INSURANCE

1. Buy your auto, homeowners, and umbrella policies from the same company. You may get a package deal.

2. Install deadbolt locks, smoke detectors, a fire extinguisher, and burglar alarms. You get a discount if your house is protected.

3. Pay annually. It's cheaper than paying semiannually or quarterly.

4. Raise the deductible. The standard deductible is $250, meaning that you pay the first $250 of any claim. The price of your policy goes down if you take a $500 or $1,000 deductible, but the savings may be only $50 or so. Ask yourself whether such a small price cut is worth the risk.

5. Quit smoking. Many insurers give nonsmokers lower rates.

6. If you have a second home, place both homes with the same insurance company. That way you pay only once for liability coverage.

7. Retire. Many companies charge retirees less than workers because they're more likely to be home during the day.

8. Call your state insurance department. A few states help you price-shop by publishing booklets that compare what various companies charge.

9. Buy a recently built house. Discounts are often available for insurance on houses up to 7 years old.

10. Don't automatically take any coverage offered through your company's payroll-deduction plan. It's not always cheap. Compare prices before signing up.

11. Build or rebuild your house right. Some insurers give discounts to coastal homes with storm shutters, shingles that are nailed down rather than stapled, and roofs that are strapped to the walls.

12. Don't overinsure! You might be paying for more coverage than you can use. Check it out if you insured your house for its full market value or something close to it. Your purchase price covered the land as well as the house, and there's no point insuring your yard against fire and theft. Get a replacement-cost appraisal of the value of the house vs. the value of the land, and cover only the house. If you're paying your insurance premiums through your mortgage lender, you'll probably need a letter from the appraiser to reduce your homeowners coverage.

13. Don't underinsure. Lower coverage costs less up front but will leave you stranded if you have a major loss.

WHICH CLAIMS PUT YOUR PREMIUM UP?

A good insurer lets you make every weather-related claim you deserve. Your premium shouldn't go up just because you've had repeated damage. After some bad storms insurers may raise rates generally in your area, but that will happen whether you make claims or not. (Some insurers, however, do raise individual rates after two or more weather-related claims, so ask about it.)

If you have too many fires or thefts, however, your insurer might conclude that you're a careless person (or a cheater). It might raise your premium or deductible, even cancel your coverage. Ask your agent about your company's rule on this point. Many companies won't accept you if you've made several claims of this kind on other insurers.

Don't Lie. When applying for new coverage, you'll be asked about past claims. As a double check on your truthfulness, the insurer will run your name and address through the Comprehensive Loss Underwriting Exchange (C.L.U.E.) or a similar service, where insurers report the claims you've made over the past 5 years. If you "forget" to mention a claim that C.L.U.E. reports, the insurer may decide that you can't be trusted and turn you down.

If you're rejected for coverage or charged a higher rate based on information from the claims-reporting service, you have to be given the service's name and address. Write for a free copy of your record to be sure it's correct. It may list claims made from that address before you owned the house.

THE PUBLIC ADJUSTER

As you're standing in the street, staring at the smoking ruins of your house, someone may shove a card into your hand. It's a public adjuster. He or she helps you evaluate your losses and bird-dogs your insurance claim. The fee: 10 to 15 percent of what you recover.

Some people figure it's worth the price to have the adjuster round up proofs of value and handle the paperwork needed to process a claim. But you shouldn't need an adjuster to get a fair settlement.

Your insurer or agent will give you advice on filing the claim. In the normal course, you'll be paid in full without having to hire a consultant. If you don't agree with your insurer's appraisal, you can get one of your own and demand a referee. If you do decide to turn to a public adjuster, make sure he or she is licensed by your state and ask for references. Base the fee on the extra money the adjuster gets for you, beyond what you were originally offered.

WHAT TO DO AFTER A LOSS

1. After a fire or theft, board up the broken windows in your home so that the remaining property can't be stolen. Your insurer will pay for it.

2. After a theft, notify the police.

3. Call your insurance agent.

4. Make a list of everything you lost, approximately when you bought it, and what you paid for it (or smugly produce the inventory you made in advance). The insurer will help you estimate current cash value.

5. Keep a list of all your expenses.

6. Get estimates for repairs.

7. Don't sign any contract to work with a public adjuster until you've first tried working with your insurance company.

8. If anyone is injured, don't take the blame without first calling your insurance company.

BUY THE BEST

Some homeowners insurance companies have gone broke, and more will in the future. All the states have property/casualty guaranty funds to assure that policyholders don't get stuck. But the maximum recovery may be only $100,000 to $300,000, which might not be enough to cover your house. Save yourself the grief. Buy only from an insurer with high ratings for safety and soundness (page 341).

TRUST NO ONE

When you get an insurance policy—any policy—double-check it to see that you got what you ordered. Large numbers of policies come through with mistakes: wrong amounts, wrong endorsements, wrong types of coverage. When you put in a claim and find you're not covered, it's too late to argue.

STEP 4

YOUR OWN HOME

Once upon a time a big wind flattened the flimsy homes made of sticks and straw that had been ruining the neighborhood. The gentry moved in and property values went up. The third little pig—with the house of brick—grew fat and prospered. Those were the days when everyone knew that houses mattered.

Nowadays it isn't so clear. House prices are high. In most cities, real-estate values aren't moving up as fast as they used to. For this (we ask ourselves), we're cleaning the gutters, painting the shutters, paying the taxes, and feeling broke? Why not rent a house and let the landlord worry?

But Americans won't, and never will. For all the huffing and puffing of the doubters, a home of our own is still the rock on which our hopes are built. Price appreciation aside (and most houses *will* appreciate, eventually), homeownership is a state of mind. It's your piece of the earth. It's where a family's toes grow roots. It's where the flowers are yours, not God's.

17.

A House Is a
Security Blanket

Yes, Doubters, It Still Pays to Own

*Homeownership is your only hope of living "free" when you
retire. Rent goes on forever. Mortgage payments eventually
come to a stop.*

A house may not be your best investment in the decade ahead. If the
eighties and early nineties taught us anything, it's that real estate doesn't
always go up. Over the long run, the value of homes should follow the
inflation rate, but over the time that you own your particular house, its
value might rise, fall, or stall. You can't predict.

But there are reasons other than profit for owning a home. You get tax
deductions on mortgage interest and tax-free capital gains. You're landlord-
free. You know the deep contentment of holding a spot of ground that
others can enter by invitation only. You won't lose your lease. You can
renovate to suit. Your mortgage payments build a pool of usable funds that
you might not otherwise have saved. A house is collateral for a loan. House
payments often cost less than rent, after tax. Above all, you can look forward to the day when—finally–you'll live mortgage-free.

20 WAYS OF BUYING YOUR FIRST HOME

1. *Save money for a down payment.* People are doing it every day. No video toys. No dinners out. A cheaper apartment than you really could afford. A second job. A bigger savings account in place of a vacation.

2. *Visit the Mommy-and-Daddy Bank.* Many children nowadays rely on their parents to lend or give them part or all of their first down payment. A parent who's a gambler might even co-sign your mortgage loan. (The M&D Bank may have to tell the lender, in writing, that the down payment is a gift.)

3. *Move.* If you can't afford a house near Washington, D.C., or Los Angeles, think about Wisconsin or Tennessee. Think about it when you're young and looking for your first job, because that's often where you'll buy your first home.

4. *Commute.* The farther into the country you're willing to go, the cheaper the houses.

5. *Buy an older house.* It might cost 15 to 25 percent less than a newly built house for the same floor space. The down payment will be lower, too.

6. *Buy a wreck.* If you can stand living in a construction site for a year or two, and are handy with tools, you can buy a wreck cheap and fix it up. Just be sure that it's in a neighborhood worth spending money on.

7. *Lower your consumer debt.* The less debt you carry the more you can borrow toward a home.

8. *Make a deal with the seller.* Ask if he or she will lower the price by enough to cover your closing costs or let you pay part of the down payment over one to 3 years. To guarantee payment, you give the seller a second mortgage or deed of trust against the house. At the start of your house search, tell the real-estate broker that you need this kind of deal. Some sellers might even be interested in an equity share (page 500).

9. *Get a low-down-payment loan backed by private mortgage insurance.* Normally, lenders want 20 percent down, but they take much less when you qualify for private mortgage insurance, as most borrowers do. The mortgage insurer makes the payments on the loan if you default. With this guarantee, the lender may accept as little as 10 or even 5 percent down, depending on market conditions.

Your premiums are usually bundled into your monthly mortgage payment, although sometimes the first-year cost has to be paid up front. The price depends on the type of loan and how much money you put down. Some insurers charge a fixed annual rate on the loan's declining balance. Others charge roughly 0.3 to 0.9 percent for the first 10 years, then perhaps 0.2 percent in subsequent years. Once your equity reaches 20 or 25 percent, you can usually cancel your coverage (page 498).

Some lenders offer to pay the insurance premiums for you in return for charging a slightly higher mortgage rate. That's a good deal if you'll move within 5 to 10 years. Your insurance premium is effectively transformed into tax-deductible interest. The appeal fades, however, if you'll stay in the house for a long time: you'll continue to pay the extra interest long after you could have qualified for canceling your insurance coverage.

You might be offered two mortgages in lieu of mortgage insurance: a first mortgage for 80 percent of the cost of the house and a second mortgage, at a higher rate of interest, for another 10 percent of the cost. You'd pay the final 10 percent in cash. This arrangement can be less expensive than private mortgage insurance, especially if you'll pay off the second mortgage fast.

10. *Get a low-down-payment mortgage insured by the Federal Housing Administration.* You can put down as little as 3 percent of the property's first $25,000 in value, 5 percent of the next $100,000, and 10 percent of the rest (or 3 percent on a house worth $50,000 or less). At this writing, the insurance costs 2.25 percent at closing for loans lasting longer than 15 years, 2 percent for loans of 15 years or less, and 1.75 percent for first-time homeowners who take a financial counseling course. You can borrow the cost from the lender and repay over the mortgage term. An additional 0.5 percent premium is tacked onto your monthly mortgage payment, payable for various periods depending on how much money you put down.

FHA loans are offered chiefly by mortgage banks, but they're also available at some commercial banks and S&Ls. Borrowing limits are usually set county by county and cover homes that are modestly priced. Here are the maximum loans in 1997 for single-family homes: $81,548 as a standard maximum; $160,950 in high-cost areas; $241,425 in Alaska, Guam, Hawaii, and the Virgin Islands. These limits are always moving up, so check what the lenders are offering now. To find the answer on the Web, go to http://www.hud/gov/hmowbuy.html.

11. *Get one of the special low-down loans available to borrowers with modest incomes or no traditional credit histories.* Lenders all over the country are giving mortgages to people they never used to consider. For details, see page 479.

12. *Get a no-down-payment loan backed by the Department of Veterans Affairs.* You can usually borrow as much as the house is appraised for, up to certain limits imposed by the mortgage market—around $214,000 in 1997 (this number rises annually). The up-front fee for a no-down loan is 2 percent. That drops to 1.5 percent if you can afford a down payment of 5 percent or more, and 1.25 percent if you can put 10 percent down. This fee needn't be paid in cash; you can include it in the loan.

VA loans are generally made through mortgage banks, although S&Ls and commercial banks may offer them, too. Generally speaking, you qualify if you're a veteran or on active duty and have served at least 2 years. The qualification period is shorter for people who served in the Persian Gulf. At this writing, VA loans also go to people who have done 6 years in the Selected Reserve, including the National Guard. Reservists pay an extra 0.75 percent up front. Their eligibility is scheduled to expire in October 1999, but may be renewed. Check your regional VA office for details. For its number, call 800-827-1000.

13. *Sell the stocks or mutual funds you own that aren't part of your tax-deferred retirement plan.* You don't lose money by putting the proceeds into a down payment; you're just transferring the asset from one pocket to another.

14. *Borrow part of the down payment from your employee retirement-savings plan, if the plan allows it.* For details, see page 262. But lenders normally don't want the entire down payment to come from loans. You'll also need personal savings or gifts.

15. *Borrow part of the payment from your bank.* Take a loan against the credit line on your bank credit card or write a check against your overdraft checking. This choice should be desperation only, to wrap up a deal. Make sure that it won't disqualify you from getting the size loan you need.

16. *Buy from a builder in a new development.* Builders often sell on flexible terms. One example: a *buydown.* The builder might pay the lender $3,000 or so to reduce your mortgage payments for one to 3 years. On fixed-rate loans, that payment lowers the rate; on adjustable mortgages, it narrows the difference between the mortgage's index rate and what you're charged. Either way, it helps you qualify for a loan. The $3,000 is added to the price of the house. Don't waltz into this deal without asking how much more your monthly payment will be when the buydown expires. Sometimes it's a lot.

17. *Get a job with a company that helps its employees buy houses.* Some pay closing costs, buy down the mortgage rate for a few years, or make low-interest loans to help you meet the down payment.

18. *Lease with an option to buy.* You generally pay a nonrefundable fee (perhaps $3,000 to $5,000) for the right to buy the house in one to 3 years at a stated price. You move in as a tenant, paying more than the normal rent. The fee plus the extra rent is credited toward a down payment. When it comes time to buy, you get your own mortgage for the remaining money owed. For more on lease options, see page 824. To find one, ask a real-estate agent, look for lease-option ads in the newspaper, or check the classifieds under "Rentals." People renting out houses would sometimes rather sell. Don't sign a lease option without having a lawyer go over it, to be sure it's fair.

Do this deal only if your income will definitely qualify you for a sufficient mortgage—in fact, prequalify yourself with a lender (page 479). The lease option should be viewed solely as a way of accumulating a down payment. If you can't get a mortgage when the time comes to buy, your option will expire and you'll lose the extra money you paid. (You might recover something from this disaster if the option price is less than the house's fair market value. Before the option expires, advertise it for sale. An investor might respond.)

19. *Search for an equity-sharing deal.* They're hard to find in these days when there's less equity growth to share. But a friend or relative might be interested. Typically, an investor puts up most or all of the down payment, you handle the monthly payments and other expenses, and you both share in any profits from the house's appreciation. For details, see page 500.

20. *Assume a mortgage.* If the seller has a mortgage, look into taking it over instead of applying for a loan of your own. Assumptions are quicker and save you money on closing costs, even after paying the loan-assumption fee. A low-rate FHA or VA loan can be assumed by a qualified buyer at no change in terms. With conventional loans, however, you'll usually have to pay the current mortgage rate.

When you assume a mortgage, you owe the seller the difference between the value of the mortgage and what you agreed to pay for the house. Put another way, the down payment is high. If you don't have the cash, ask the seller to let you pay in installments. Just be sure that you're getting a reasonable rate of interest on the two loans, combined. If not, forget the assumption and get a loan of your own. (Urgent memo to sellers: Be sure that the lender releases you from liability on the mortgage. Otherwise, you're responsible if the person who assumed it defaults.)

HOW LARGE A MORTGAGE CAN YOU AFFORD?

First house or fifth one, here's what a lender classically wants to see:

• No more than 28 percent of your gross monthly income spent on housing expenses—mortgage payment, insurance, and taxes. On FHA loans, expenses can rise to 29 percent. "Income" is the regular income you've had for at least a year. If part of it comes in bonuses, commissions, overtime pay, alimony, or child support, lenders will want proof that this money will keep coming (mostly likely, a portion of this income won't be counted at all). If you're self-employed, they'll look at your net income after expenses. Lenders vary in how they qualify people applying for adjustable-rate loans (ARMS—page 481). Some let you meet the 28 percent test based on the loan's first-year discount interest rate; some use the probable second-year rate or the first-year rate plus the annual cap (usually 2 percent).

• Total debt payments (monthly mortgage and consumer debt) not exceeding 36 percent of your gross monthly income. Count as consumer debt any bills with at least 10 monthly payments left. You might be restricted to 33 percent of income if you're putting less than 10 percent down.

Lenders may let you exceed these limits if you have an excellent credit history, make a big down payment, make a lot of money, already spend more than 28 percent of your income on housing expenses (typical where housing costs are high), or have a lot of liquid assets. You qualify for special affordable-housing loans with monthly debts as high as 40 percent of income (page 480), and for VA loans with debts as high as 41 percent. Note that these are *guidelines*. Lenders can change them.

Before you go house shopping, use these guidelines to figure out how much you can borrow. That tells you how large a house you can afford. A number of Web sites offer mortgage calculators (four such: http://www.financenter.com, http://www.homepath.com, http://www.hsh.com, and http://www.interest.com). Real-estate agents usually have software, too. Lenders will "prequalify" you—meaning they'll estimate what you can borrow. Better yet, go for preapproval—a loan guarantee that lasts for a certain period of time. Many lenders will preapprove home shoppers at low or no cost by phone, mail, or over the Web. By loan shopping before you buy, you'll have plenty of time to find a good deal. If you wait until after you find a house, time pressure may force you to take the nearest loan at hand.

Don't Borrow to the Hilt Just Because a Banker Says You Can. Borrow no more than you feel comfortable repaying. If you buy less house than you can technically afford, you'll have money left over for other investments or for something this book sometimes forgets to mention—*fun*.

If Your Debt Levels Fall Within the Guidelines, You Might Get a Contingent Mortgage Approval Within Minutes. The lender taps into your credit history and checks your credit score (page 219). If you score above a certain level, you're an automatic yes, pending a property appraisal and a safety check to be sure that you're currently employed. If you're just below that level, you're a maybe; a loan officer will assess you and decide yes or no. Low-scoring applicants get a no, unless you've applied for a special program for people whose credit history is blotched.

Special Rules for People with Credit Problems

In the past, most mortgage bankers brushed you off if you had too much debt or your credit history showed a stain. That made you a "subprime" borrower. For loans, you relied on finance companies that impose high interest rates.

Now, many banks will take you on, and at lower rates than most finance companies charge. Still, your past indiscretions carry a price. At a time when a quality "A credit" pays a mortgage rate of 7.4 percent, a B credit might pay 9 percent, a C credit 10.5 percent, and a D credit 11.5 percent. Some lenders charge even more than that. Your rank in the credit pecking order depends on your level of debt, how many late payments your credit history shows, and whether you've endured court judgments or bankruptcy. Once your credit history improves, you can refinance at a better rate.

The lower your rank on the credit scale, the less you'll be able to borrow against a house. So subprime loans don't help cash-poor buyers or people trying to take all the money out of their homes when they refinance. They also aren't for people still in the grip of a job or credit crisis. Your problems have to be behind you. If you haven't cleaned up outstanding judgments—even if they're only over disputed medical bills—settle them and record the legal satisfaction. That might save you a couple of points in mortgage interest.

Different lenders apply different standards for determining your level of risk, so hold conversations with two or three of them. To find a subprime loan, ask a local mortgage broker or lender, check the newspaper ads, or visit the Web sites at http://www.hsh.com and http://www.interest.com.

Special Rules for People with Low-to-Moderate Incomes

Hundreds of lenders today offer affordable-housing programs that let you put little or no money down. Check 'em out, if your income is modest, your debts aren't too high, and you're steadily employed. The lender might accept you if:

• You've saved as little as 3 percent toward the house you want. You'll also need closing costs, but they can be borrowed as part of the loan. Some lenders require an additional 2 percent down, but that can come from relatives or a local agency that gives homeownership grants. With a few programs, the entire down payment can be borrowed.

• You can show that you've always paid your rent, utilities, insurance premiums, and installment debts on time, even though you have no formal credit history.

• Your monthly housing debt (mortgage payments, real-estate taxes, and homeowners insurance) won't exceed 33 percent of your gross monthly income. Your housing debt plus other debt, such as student loans, car loans, and installment payments, won't exceed 40 percent of your income.

For a free list of lenders that participate in the program backed by Fannie Mae (Federal National Mortgage Association), plus the name and phone number of a loan officer to ask for, call 800-7-FANNIE. Having the name can be important. Only one or two officers may even know about the loans. Fannie Mae also backs no-down-payment loans offered to people of modest means through the Farmers Home Administration.

A TECHNICAL PHRASE YOU CAN'T IGNORE

Negative Amortization. Negative "am," as it's called for short, is a high-tech, death-defying, money-eating system for owing *more* money every time you make a monthly mortgage payment. "Amortization" is the payment schedule by which you reduce a loan to zero. "Negative" amortization means that, instead of going down, the amount of your loan goes up.

You run into negative am whenever your monthly payments aren't large enough to cover all the interest due. As an example, say that you're paying $1,000 a month on a floating-rate mortgage whose rates go up. You now own $1,050 in interest every month, but keep paying your contractual $1,000. The missing $50 is added to your loan principal, so you now owe more than you did last month. That cost will compound because you're paying interest on interest. You run into negative am with adjustable-rate mortgages whose payments stay level for set periods of time while the loan's underlying interest rate is allowed to change (these are usually loans linked to the 11th District cost-of-funds index—page 484).

Competition is eliminating loans that lead to negative am, but ask about it. If you have such a loan, raise your payments voluntarily when rates go up, so you won't get stuck.

FINDING THE RIGHT MORTGAGE

It used to be easy. A 30-year loan. A fixed interest rate. Sign here. Now you have dozens of choices—different rates, different terms, different fees. Here's the menu:

Adjustable-Rate Mortgages (ARMs)

As a bet on the loan with the lowest total cost, I like ARMs best. The interest rate and monthly payment change periodically with the general level of rates. On an ARM with an annual adjustment, you usually start with a rate that's 2 or 3 percentage points under the cost of fixed-rate loans—a tremendous saving. Even if interest rates shoot straight up, the ARM will probably be cheaper over the next 3 or 4 years. Ask the lender to show you. An ARM would eventually cost more if rates rose and didn't fall, but rate rises rarely last longer than a couple of years. Over a full interest-rate cycle, ARMs should cost the least. For more on ARMs, see page 483.

Get an ARM If: (1) You need the lower monthly payment in the first year to buy the house you want. (2) You can handle higher payments when they come. (3) You won't panic when payments rise because you have faith that they'll fall again. (4) You expect to own the house for only 4 or 5 years (short-term owners should go for the cheapest ARM they can find). (5) You have plenty of money or plenty of confidence that your income will rise. (6) You're thinking about resale. ARMs can generally be assumed by the buyer, which eliminates his or her closing costs (page 495).

Fixed-Rate Mortgages

With these mortgages, you're safe. Your monthly payments are fixed for as long as you hold the loan. If rates rise, you've got a terrific deal. If they fall, you can refinance at the lower rate (page 497). Fixed-rate mortgages make the most economic sense when they're priced within one percentage point of an ARM's *regular* interest rate (not the discount "teaser" rate given in the ARM's first year).

Get a Fixed-Rate Loan If: (1) The size of the payment doesn't stop you from getting the house you want. (2) You want to lock in your mortgage payments because you can't count on earning a higher income in the years ahead. (3) You couldn't afford your house if your mortgage payment rose. (4) The thought of rising mortgage payments scares you stiff. (5) You think current mortgage rates are unusually low. (6) You're near retirement, at which point your income will drop.

Hybrid Mortgages

These are great loans for borrowers who are stretching their incomes to buy a house. You get a fixed rate for a specified number of years (often 3, 5, 7, or 10), then the loan converts to an adjustable rate. You pay more per month than for a straight ARM but less than for a straight fixed-rate loan. Make sure your deal is guaranteed. Some hybrids let the lender change the terms if interest rates suddenly shoot up.

Get a Hybrid Loan If: (1) You'll stay in the house for only a few years. In effect, you get a fixed-rate loan at a lower monthly cost. (2) You think mortgage rates will fall, at which point you'll refinance. In the meantime, you want a mortgage payment that's guaranteed. (3) You expect to be earning more money when the fixed term ends, so switching to an ARM won't bother you.

Two-Step Mortgages

This fixed-rate loan starts out by charging slightly less than the market rate. After 5 or 7 years it switches to slightly more than the going rate for the remaining term. You have some protection if interest rates shoot up. The lender can't charge any more than 5 or 6 percentage points more than the rate you started with.

Get a Two-Step Loan If: (1) It gives you a better start rate than a hybrid loan. (2) You know you'll move before you reach the second step.

Balloons

Balloon mortgages offer low, fixed payments for a short period of time, maybe 5 to 7 years. After that, the entire loan falls due. Some balloons convert automatically to fixed- or adjustable-rate mortgages, running another 25 or 23 years. But in most cases, lenders can decide whether or not to refinance the loan. Usually they will. You may be turned down, however, if you've fallen behind on some payments or put a second mortgage on your house. That will drive you to subprime financing at a higher rate. Before you borrow, be clear about your options at the end of the term and what fees and interest rates you might have to pay.

If you buy a house and give the seller a note for part of the down payment, that's a balloon. When it falls due, the seller will rarely extend the term. If you don't have the cash, you'll be expected to borrow the money somewhere else.

Consider a Balloon If: (1) The seller offers this loan to help with your down payment and you're sure you can pay when the term is up. (2) The bank offers a balloon with very low payments—say, only the interest for a fixed number of years. You expect to sell and repay the whole loan sometime before the balloon falls due. (3) If you don't sell, you're sure that the bank will let you refinance. They'd rather work with you than foreclose. But who can ever be truly *sure?* Balloons are a hazardous undertaking at any time.

Graduated-Payment Mortgages

There aren't a lot of these around. Where they're offered, they're aimed at first-time buyers who think their incomes will go up. Fixed payments or interest rates start low and rise over a certain number of years.

ALL ABOUT ARMS

Take this checklist with you when you go to the bank. Use it for hybrid mortgages, too, because they'll eventually turn into ARMs.

How often does the interest rate change? Annual changes are the most common, followed by changes every 6 months. Some ARMs adjust every 3 or 5 years. Generally speaking, the more frequent the adjustment, the cheaper the mortgage over an entire interest-rate cycle (including both rising and falling rates). But if you're going to own the house for just a few years, you might want an ARM that locks in your rate for that length of time.

What is the interest rate linked to? Most mortgages today are tied to indexes of Treasury securities. Six-month ARMs are tied to 6-month Treasury bills; one-year ARMs to one-year Treasury bills, and so on. Some loans adjust biannually with the London Inter Bank Offer Rate (LIBOR), which reflects Eurodollar borrowing rates for major British lenders; it tends to rise and fall in smaller increments than Treasuries of comparable terms. Some rates reflect the cost of funds for S&Ls in the Federal Home Loan Bank Board's 11th District, which covers California, Arizona, and Nevada. The cost-of-funds index changes slowly so your payments don't rise or fall a lot, even if they're adjusted once a year. But the sluggishness of the cost-of-funds index means that it may still be going up when rates in general have turned down, and vice versa. Over a whole interest-rate cycle, a mortgage linked to short-term Treasuries should cost less and is the easiest to follow in the newspapers.

What is the spread between the stated mortgage-interest rate and the underlying index? This is also called the *margin.* One lender might charge 2.25 percentage points more than the Treasury index; another might charge 3 points over. When two lenders use the identical index, the one with the narrower spread is charging less (assuming he's not making it up in higher fees). The spread may be suspended for the first year or two, to give you a bargain or teaser rate. But after that, you pay the spread for the life of the loan.

What's the teaser? ARMs usually charge bargain first-year rates called teasers. Typically, they're one to 3 points under the regular rate. Every time your rate adjusts, it will rise toward the regular rate (although the rise can't exceed the annual cap). During this short period, your payment can go up even if rates in general are coming down. Once you've used up your teaser, your payment will rise and fall with market rates.

What are the caps? You want limits on what you'll have to pay if interest rates go leaping up. Lenders generally won't allow your rate to rise by more than 2 percentage points a year, no matter what happens to the underlying index. For example, say that market rates rise by 3 percentage points and stay there. Your mortgage rate will rise 2 points the first year, then one point the second year. Alternatively, if rates rise by 3 percentage points and then fall back, your mortgage rate will rise 2 points the first year, then stay level or fall the second year, depending on how far the index drops. Over the life of the loan, your rate can't rise by more than 5 or 6 percentage points, usually measured from your low, initial teaser rate. Given two similar loans, choose the one with the lower caps.

How bad can it get? Look at the largest monthly payment the loan might require. If that dismays you, get a fixed-rate loan or shop for an ARM with a lower lifetime cap.

What happened in the past? Ask the lender to show you how a mortgage payment like yours would have fluctuated over the past 10 years. The

| | MONTHLY PAYMENT ON A: | |
INTEREST RATE*	30-YEAR LOAN	15-YEAR LOAN
5.5 percent	$568	$ 817
6.5 percent	632	871
7.5 percent	699	927
8.5 percent	769	985
9.5 percent	841	1,044
10.5 percent	915	1,105
11.5 percent	990	1,168

* On a $100,000 loan.

table above gives you a general idea, assuming a $100,000 loan. If the payment gyrations of an ARM make you uncomfortable, consider a fixed-rate loan instead.

Is there a floor? Some loans limit how far your interest rate can fall. All things being equal, look for a loan without a floor.

Is there a risk of negative amortization? Loans with "negative am" sometimes allow your monthly payments to slip below the total amount of interest due. The lender adds the unpaid interest to the loan balance. So your loan amount goes up instead of down. Not recommended. You'll find plenty of ARMs without this catch.

How often does your monthly payment change? You want it to change every time the loan's interest rate does. Otherwise, you run the risk of negative amortization.

Can I convert? Some ARMs carry the right to switch to a fixed-rate mortgage after a certain number of years without paying closing costs all over again. Lenders charge for this in various ways. Some add an up-front fee. Some tack an eighth or a quarter of a point onto your initial interest rate, or an extra half point or more to the interest rate on your future fixed-rate loan. With charges like these, nobody's giving you a bargain. Since you can't predict whether you'll want to convert, this generally isn't an option worth paying for. Compare the extra cost of a convertible ARM with your lender's normal refinancing fee. If rates drop, it may be cheaper to refinance.

Is the loan guaranteed? Ask what happens if mortgage rates climb above the lifetime caps. Is that cap guaranteed or can the lender force you to refinance? With two-step loans, do you have to pass a credit check to qualify for the second step? Ask if there's any way that the lender can force you to pay more than you currently expect if market conditions or your personal circumstances change. Take the time to read the fine print. You want a contract set in stone.

How do I check the rate? If I had one dollar for every mistake a lender made when it adjusted an ARM payment, I'd be an instant millionaire. The bank may pick the wrong index, loan balance, or adjustment date; it might round the rate up when it should have been rounded down; a new loan servicer might get your loan terms wrong; principal prepayments might not have been credited properly. Small errors compound into large ones over the years. When you take an ARM, ask when the rate will be adjusted, how it's done, and how you can track the index that underlies your loan. Verify the rate whenever a change looks too big or too small or your payment rises when interest rates in general have been going down. Pay the most attention to older loans. Small errors grow into big ones over several years. Consumers can get refunds if they were overcharged on a paid-up loan.

Several services will check your ARM rate for you, among them: American Homeowners Foundation (AHF), 6776 Little Falls Rd., Arlington, VA 22213 (800-489-7776), free unless there's a refund, in which case AHF takes half; and Loantech, Inc., P.O. Box 3635, Gaithersburg, MD 20878 (800-888-6781), $69. You'll find a free calculator at http://www.hsh.com.

After Holding Your ARM for Several Years, See If It's Still Competitive. These loans are cheap in the early years, but in later years the lenders may charge slightly more than the going interest rate. Consider refinancing with a new ARM if you can get a low teaser rate and the new loan doesn't raise your lifetime cap (page 495).

ON POINTS

In mortgagespeak, one point is one percentage point of the loan amount—for example, $1,000 on a $100,000 loan. *Discount points* are subtracted from your loan, so in this example you'd borrow $99,000 and repay $100,000.

There's a trade-off between the points you pay and the mortgage interest rate you're charged. The fewer the points the higher the rate, and vice versa. If you'll be in the house for only a few years (usually no more than 4 or 5), you'll save money by paying zero or minimal points. If this is a house you'll keep for years, it costs less in the long run to pay extra points and get a lower interest rate. Here's how to decide, assuming you take a fixed-rate loan:

1. What the points will cost	$_____
2. How much you'll save in payments each month because you pay points	$_____
3. Divide line 1 by line 2. If you'll live in the house for more than this number of months, paying points will save you money.	$_____

This estimate is squishy because it leaves out interest and taxes, but it puts you in the ballpark. Savings on ARMs are more complicated to figure. For a calculator that includes taxes and interest and deals with both ARMs and fixed-rate loans, go to http://www.financenter.com.

One last point about points: Paying them might not be the best way of using your money. If you added that cash to your down payment, for example, you might avoid the need to buy private mortgage insurance.

Lenders may also charge a one-point loan-origination fee. You can pay this in cash or add it to the loan. Adding the fee to the loan saves money up front, but you'll have to repay two or three times that amount in interest costs.

FINDING THE RIGHT MORTGAGE LENDER

It's nuts not to shop. Some lenders have sharply lower rates and fees than others do, especially for prime borrowers. One percentage point saved on a 15-year, $100,000 loan is worth $18,360. That's $102 a month.

Mortgage banks are often the cheapest. Their main business is mortgages, including those backed by the Federal Housing Administration or Department of Veterans Affairs. At this writing, the nation's three largest mortgage retailers are Norwest Mortgage (800-405-8067; http://www. norwest.com), Countrywide Home Loans (800-570-9888; http://www. countrywide.com), and Chase Manhattan Mortgage (800-678-1051; http:// www.chase.com).

Credit unions are your next-best bet, although only the larger ones are in the mortgage business. Then try savings banks or savings and loan associations, then commercial banks. Big commercial banks often have mortgage-banking subsidiaries.

For Comparative Shopping:

1. Check the newspapers. Many papers run tables of local mortgage rates, lender by lender. Low-rate banks also advertise. Those banks may compensate by charging higher fees, but you should be able to find a good deal if you check all the costs.

2. Ask the real-estate agent. He or she knows the local market and who is giving good deals. But hold off on an offer to get you a loan on the spot, through a computer link with a particular lender. The agent earns a fee for referring you, so the loan may not be the cheapest around. Note that lender's best offer, then check other rates.

3. Call a mortgage broker. Brokers know the rates currently being offered by local and national lenders and should be able to find you something good. Banks pay these brokers to handle the paperwork, so in theory

your loan shouldn't cost any more than if you had found it yourself. Even the application fee should be the same. In practice, however, some brokers tack something on. Ask what his or her total compensation will be—how much from you directly and how much from the bank. Make it clear that you don't want to pay a premium.

As in any field, some mortgage brokers are more competent and attentive than others. Look for someone whose business is at least 5 years old and ask how many local and national lenders he or she represents. Also ask for references. One weaselly practice to watch out for: the lender may pay the broker a bonus for talking you into a higher-rate loan. Check the rates in the newspaper against whatever loan the broker suggests.

4. Shop the Web. Many national and regional mortgage banks advertise rates and take applications on-line. Three sites for pots of information: Mortgage Market Information Services at http://www.interest.com, http://www.hsh.com, and http://www.financenter.com. Also check out the offers at the leading national lenders (page 487).

5. Buy the *Homebuyer's Mortgage Kit,* at this writing, $23 from HSH Associates, 1200 Rte. 23, Butler, NJ 07405 (800-873-2837 or 973-838-3330). You get a survey of the current mortgage rates offered by major lenders serving your area, with detailed descriptions of at least three loans from each, a 56-page booklet called *How to Shop for Your Mortgage,* a newsletter, and the latest ARM indexes. Subsequent surveys cost $11.

RANDOM MORTGAGE FACTS

• Don't sign an agreement to buy unless it includes a mortgage contingency clause. That makes your purchase contingent on finding a loan. If you can't borrow enough money, the deal is off and you get your deposit back.

• To compare the cost of fixed-rate loans, look at the annual percentage rate (APR). The APR includes points and certain other financing charges, and is always higher than the stated lending rate. But it doesn't include all your closing costs, so a loan that looks a tad cheaper could be a tad more expensive after everything is paid. To get the best deal, you still have to check the fees.

On adjustable loans, the APRs last only until the first interest-rate change. They're useful for comparing two loans with adjustable rates but tell you nothing about what you'll ultimately pay.

• Lenders charge an application fee to cover the cost of processing your loan. It's not refundable if you're turned down and generally runs in the $100 to $400 range.

• Here's the minimum your lender will need when you apply for a standard loan: (1) The purchase contract for the new house and the sales contract if you sold an old one. (2) Banking information—names and addresses of your banks, bank account numbers, copies of your latest statements. (3) Employment information—employer's name and phone number, proof of earnings (pay stubs, W-2 forms), your 2 most recent tax returns. (4) If you're self-employed: balance sheets for your business and 3 years of business and personal tax returns. (5) Names and addresses of all creditors and the amounts you owe (this will be checked against your credit report). (6) Proof of what you currently pay for housing, either mortgage or rental payments. (7) Proof of other assets you own such as mutual fund or brokerage house statements and retirement fund reports. (8) Proof of a cash reserve—enough for the down payment, closing costs, and the first two or three mortgage payments. (9) A Certificate of Eligibility if you're applying for a VA loan. (10) A letter from the donor if you're using a cash gift for the down payment (the bank wants to be sure it's not a loan). (11) The mortgage-application fee. There will be more requests for financial data as the loan processor checks you out. In fact, it's going to drive you nuts. But button your lip and supply the data. If the application seems stalled, keep calling to try to move it along. At a certain point, it's prudent to call a higher bank official.

• When a lender drags its tail and a deadline looms, call a mortgage broker and ask about starting all over again. Some lenders can close loans fast, efficiently, and at no extra cost.

• The lender will have the property appraised. If the value turns out to be less than you agreed to pay, that's your problem not the bank's. It will lend only on the appraised amount. You'll have to come up with more cash than you'd planned or get the seller to accept a lower price.

• As a general rule, avoid a mortgage that levies a prepayment penalty. That's a fee for repaying the loan within a certain number of years. Some lenders insist on it if you're planning to pay one point or less up front. In that case, shop for a more agreeable bank. You don't want to be stuck with extra fees if, for some reason, you have to move soon after buying.

On the other hand, some lenders make an offer that might interest you. They'll give you a lower interest rate and perhaps lower closing costs if you'll accept a penalty for refinancing during the first 3 to 5 years. Limited prepayments might be allowed, so you could add, say, an extra 20 percent to every monthly payment. Once the penalty period expires, you can refinance at will. If you take this deal and mortgage rates plunge, you'll wish you hadn't, because you're not free to refinance. Still, consider this loan if it's the cheapest one around. Prepayment penalties are more common on ARMs than on fixed-rate loans. *Never* accept a penalty that applies if you sell the house.

• When lenders are highly automated, loans can close within 20 days or less. But it might take 60 days or more if there's a buying or refinancing jam. During that time interest rates will change—usually just a little but sometimes a lot. With a "floating" loan commitment, you'll get the rate, points, and other terms that are current on the day your loan closes. They may be higher or lower than you're offered now. With a "lock-in," generally good for 30 to 45 days, you're guaranteed the terms available when you first applied. Short-term lock-ins are usually free, but to lock the rate for a longer term, you'll probably have to pay a fee. Get the rules in writing. The best contracts stop your rate from rising but will allow it to fall. Keep on the phone to be sure that your paperwork doesn't stall on someone's desk. Sometimes a lender will extend a lock-in's term, but usually not.

• If you want to close on a new house before selling your old one, your lender may give you a "bridge loan" to cover the cost. It's due in 6 months or a year, in a lump sum. If you need it extended, the lender will probably agree but at a cost.

• Some lenders make quickie, "low-documentation" loans to high-net-worth buyers who put down 25 to 30 percent of the house price. There's only a cursory check of your income and employment. The lender closes your mortgage within 14 to 30 days. You need a blue-chip credit history and may be charged an extra one-half to three-quarters of a point in interest. Why would a blue-chip borrower accept a higher mortgage rate? Maybe because your income varies a lot, or you're self-employed and your tax returns don't show how flush you really are. These loans may require mortgage insurance, despite the high down payment you made.

• When you take a mortgage, you'll usually be offered tie-in insurance —life, disability, even unemployment insurance. If you lose your job or become disabled, your mortgage payments will be made for you for a certain period of time. If you die, the policy pays off the loan. Appealing as this sounds, it is generally a poor buy (page 274). Get extra term life insurance payable to your family and let them decide how the proceeds should be used.

• Your monthly payment to the lender usually includes the cost of your homeowners insurance and real-estate tax. Those funds go into an escrow account from which the bank pays the premiums and taxes when they come due. The account may or may not earn interest, depending on state law. By federal law, lenders can collect just enough to cover the actual bills, with no more than a 2-month cushion for unanticipated expenses. If your annual statement shows extra money in your escrow account, ask for it back. Escrow is required on loans sold to Fannie Mae or Freddie Mac (the Federal Home Loan Mortgage Corporation). If your loan is larger than Fannie or Freddie will accept—around $214,600 in 1997—the lender may let you handle your own insurance and taxes.

• Jumbo or noncomforming loans—those too big for Fannie and Freddie—typically carry slightly higher interest rates. But check with a mortgage broker. Some lenders seek out these loans and charge lower rates.

• Read all the loan disclosures. Don't rely on the banker or real-estate agent to tell you how your mortgage works. Federal regulations require enough disclosure to make a mortgage contract foolproof, but nothing can make it damn-foolproof. You can't be fully protected if you won't read what you sign.

• If you're facing foreclosure and your house is worth less than the mortgage against it, try to negotiate a graceful exit. Some lenders will accept a "short sale" or "deed in lieu of foreclosure." You sign over the house; they write off the loan; the lender avoids foreclosure costs. The lender might even agree to keep the stain off your credit report if your troubles arose from illness, unemployment, or some other emergency beyond your control.

• When you pay off a mortgage, be sure the lender records that fact. If the loan still shows, you'll have to clear it before you can sell or refinance. That's no more than a nuisance if you have all the documentation. If you don't, you'll have to pursue the lender or buy an expensive bond. If you gave a second mortgage to an individual (say, the person who sold you the house), get a letter stating that the note was paid in full. If that individual went to the courthouse and formally recorded the loan, you'll have to record the payoff, too.

LARGE DOWN PAYMENT OR SMALL?

If you have a choice, is it better to sock a lot of money into your home and take a small mortgage? Or should you take a large mortgage and invest the extra cash somewhere else? Different borrowers will reach different conclusions. Here are the issues to consider:

How Much Would You Earn on a Separate Investment? To be profitable, it has to yield more than the interest you're paying on the mortgage.

How Likely Are You to Invest? If you're more apt to spend your cash than save it, chuck it into the mortgage before it gets away.

Do You Have Consumer Debt? Credit-card debt costs more than mortgage debt. You're better off with a larger mortgage, using your cash to pay other bills.

How Much Do Low Monthly Payments Matter? If you care a lot about holding down your ongoing housing costs, make the largest down payment you can muster. The more cash you put into the house, the smaller the loan you'll have to take and the less you'll pay each month. Buyers close to retirement usually put a lot of money down. Younger buyers usually can't. Stationery stores carry books of mortgage payment tables, showing monthly payments at different loan amounts and mortgage rates. Or check the Web sites on page 488.

How Much Do You Care About Mortgage Costs? The bigger your down payment, the less your lender is likely to charge. You'll pay fewer points and may even get a lower interest rate. A down payment larger than 20 percent eliminates private mortgage insurance, saving you maybe $30 to $150 a month.

How Liquid Are You? You'll need cash for the closing, the move, and anything that needs doing immediately to your new home. Set that money aside, then figure how much you have to borrow.

SHORT TERM OR LONG?

The traditional mortgage runs for 30 years. Monthly payments are low, which is what first-time buyers usually need. But in the early years, most of that payment goes for interest, not principal. Over any holding period, 30-year loans cost more in interest than loans of shorter terms.

Among the middle-aged, buyers are choosing 15-year and even 10-year terms. Monthly payments are higher, but these loans build equity faster and minimize interest costs. They're a way of ensuring that you'll own your home free and clear by the time you retire.*

How to Shorten the Term of the Loan You Have. Just send in a check for a larger amount than is actually due. That money will go toward reducing your loan, automatically. Many lenders even have a spot on the monthly bill where you can note extra principal payments. Others suggest that you send a note with every check, so the bank will know there's no mistake. A disciplined way of prepaying is to add money every month. Alternatively, send a larger check whenever you can. Every dollar counts.

With a fixed-rate mortgage, your prepayments shorten the term of the loan. If you have an adjustable mortgage, however, the bank may keep the term the same and lower the monthly payment you owe. To accelerate that mortgage, continue to pay the higher amount you did before.

Note that making prepayments doesn't give you the right to skip a month. You still owe the basic monthly payment, no matter how far ahead of schedule you are.

---

* Here's another idea for ensuring that you'll own your home free and clear. Look at how much you'll have left on your mortgage in the year you'll retire. Buy a zero-coupon bond (page 779) that matures in that year and delivers enough cash to pay it off.

For Maximum Flexibility, Take a 30-Year Loan and Repay It Faster. Be sure you get a loan without a prepayment penalty. Ask the lender how large a payment you'll have to make to get rid of the loan over 15 or 20 years, and pay at that rate. If you run into financial trouble, you can always switch to the smaller, minimum payment that the loan requires. Here's what shorter terms can save on a $150,000 loan:

Loan Term	Monthly Payment*	Total Repaid*	Savings Over a 30-Year Loan
30 years	$1,049	$377,579	N/A
25 years	1,108	332,547	$ 45,032
20 years	1,208	290,014	87,565
15 years	1,391	250,294	127,285

* At 7.5 percent interest. Numbers are rounded.
SOURCE: Mortgage Bankers Association of America.

Is It Worth Your While to Pay Off Your Mortgage Faster?

Often, yes. Faster payments will:

- Force you to save. Otherwise, that money might be frittered away.
- Reduce the amount of interest you pay over any period of time that you hold the loan.
- Give you an attractive risk-free return on your money (your return on investment equals your mortgage rate).
- Build your equity faster. By the time your children are 18, there should be enough money in your home to help cover their college tuition.
- Put you in a better position to trade up to a larger house. When you sell, you'll have more money in hand to put toward your next down payment.
- Ensure that you're mortgage-free by the time you retire.
- Get you a lower interest rate. The rate on a 15-year loan may be a quarter or half point less than the rate on a 30-year loan.
- Save you a small fortune in interest payments. One of the crazier bits of homebuyers' lore says, "Take a bigger, longer-term mortgage because it gives you more interest deductions on your tax return." You do indeed get more deductions—but only because you've paid more interest! Why would you do that if you don't have to? The majority of your interest cost comes right out of your pocket even after tax.

But it doesn't make sense to quick-pay your mortgage if:

- You're carrying credit-card debt that's costing you 12 to 20 percent. By paying it off, you get a 12 to 20 percent return on your money. First, get rid of consumer debt. Then accelerate mortgage payments.
- You'll earn more by investing your extra money somewhere else than by putting it into your mortgage. For example, you should first put the maximum into your tax-deductible retirement account.

Never pay for quick-pay.

One way to quick-pay painlessly is through a biweekly payment schedule. Instead of making monthly payments, make half a monthly payment every 2 weeks. Result: one extra full payment per year, which shortens the term of a 30-year loan to about 22 years. This is a great system if it's free but not if you have to pay (lenders may charge $300 or more for the paperwork). You achieve the same thing just by adding extra money to your payment each month.

BUYING A FORECLOSED HOUSE

Some get-rich-quick shows on radio or late-night TV sell you the dream of a bargain price on a foreclosed home with no money down. Fat chance. There's competition for the houses worth having and lenders apply their usual down-payment rules. Occasionally, you can make no-cash deals with the Federal Housing Administration or Department of Veterans Affairs. But they generally want up-front money, too.

Foreclosed homes are handled by real-estate brokers, not by some shadowy office on the edge of nowhere. They carry a market price. If their prices are lower than those of similar, occupied homes, that probably means they need more fixing up. Bargain hunters often ask about foreclosures so the better houses go. When a house attracts no interest, the bank may accept 10 or 15 percent less—but that's still a market price.

Where you might get a break is the mortgage rate, if you buy from the lender's own inventory. Ask the banker who handles your account to call the REO ("real-estate owned") division and say you'd be a serious bidder. Get a property list, to see if there's something you might be interested in. An inspection can be arranged through a real-estate agent. As part of your bid, tell the institution you need a deal on the mortgage—maybe a lower rate for the first couple of years and zero closing costs.

For a list of the local foreclosed properties owned by Fannie Mae, plus the names of the brokers handling them, write to the Fannie Mae Public Information Office, 3900 Wisconsin Avenue N.W., Washington, DC 20016. Or check out the list on the Internet: http://www.fanniemae.com. For homes owned by Freddie Mac, check out http://www.freddiemac.com (there's no place to write). The lists aren't long, however, when times are good.

Buying a house at the foreclosure sale itself is a hazardous undertaking best left to professional investors (page 827). Sales occur or get canceled at the last minute; you can rarely inspect the home's interior before buying; you need someone to check on the liens and whether the title is clear (a mistake can wipe you out); if your bid is successful, the full price has to be paid by cashier's check on the spot. Home buyers shouldn't get involved in this. Wait for the lender to take the house and put it back on the market (as usually happens, because no outside bidder will pay enough). Then you can walk through the property, buy with clear title, and get a mortgage loan.

AT THE MORTGAGE CLOSING

Bring money. The lender is required to mail you a good-faith estimate of all the closing costs within 3 business days of receiving your mortgage application. Before the closing, your lawyer, real-estate broker, or escrow agent should give you the exact figures. Expect to pay anywhere from 3 to 7 percent of the loan amount—for title search, title insurance, survey, appraisal, credit check, loan-origination fee, processing fees, legal fees, recording fees, homeowners insurance, mortgage insurance, and taxes. These amount to big bucks—often $5,000 on a $100,000 home. If you have enough money to make only the down payment, you can generally add your closing costs to the loan amount. In fact, you can get a "no cash" mortgage—no points, no fees, no closing costs—in exchange for a slightly higher mortgage rate.

When looking for a lender, compare closing costs as well as interest rates. Some banks and S&Ls extract much less from you than others. Negotiate everything on the settlement sheet. Lenders have no business charging fees for "processing" or "document preparation." That's what your loan-origination fee is supposed to cover.

WRITING IT OFF

All interest is deductible on mortgage loans up to $1 million and on home-equity loans up to $100,000. Those two loans can be bundled into a single tax-deductible first mortgage for $1.1 million.*

You can spread your deductible loan over two homes (one a personal residence, the other a vacation or secondary home), but not over three or more. The loan has to be secured by the property itself and you have to borrow within 90 days of making the purchase.

If you build a house, the interest on your construction loan is normally deductible for 2 years from the time you first break ground. This loan also must be secured by the property. You have to get the mortgage within 90 days of the finishing date.

You can deduct any up-front points you pay for a loan used to buy or

---

* Mortgages acquired on or before October 13, 1987, are still fully deductible even if they exceed the $1.1 million cap.

improve your principal home. But points paid for a mortgage on your vacation home have to be written off over the life of the loan.

You can deduct the portion of your monthly condominium maintenance fee that represents your share of the building's real-estate tax.

IT'S 9:00 P.M. DO YOU KNOW WHERE YOUR MORTGAGE IS?

Probably not. The days are long gone when your banker kept mortgages in his vault.

Nowadays, banks sell most of their mortgages to private investors. You still might mail your monthly payment to the bank you borrowed from. But the bank only "services" the loan by processing your check, paying your real-estate taxes and homeowners insurance, and sending the investor the rest of the money. For this, the bank collects a fee—but from the investor, not from you.

Your bank might also sell the right to service your mortgage. In that case, you should get two notices, one from your old servicer and one from your new one. Both notices have to give you the new servicer's name and address, the date you will start making payments there, toll-free numbers for both servicers in case you have any questions, information about any changes in the credit-insurance package, and any new procedures for handling your escrow account. The terms of the mortgage itself will remain the same.

When servicers change, keep an eye on what happens to your tax and insurance payments. The servicer normally pays them from your escrow account. But if there's a hitch in transferring the account, a payment might be missed. You'll discover it when you get a notice in the mail from your city or the homeowners insurance company. If there's a penalty for late payment, the mortgage servicer has to pay it—provided, of course, that your own monthly payments were made on time. Sometimes the new servicer finds that your escrow account is short of money, in which case your monthly payments will rise.

There's a 60-day grace period after the change, during which you won't owe a late penalty if you mistakenly send your mortgage check to the wrong servicer.

Crook alert: A letter might arrive telling you that a new servicer will handle your loan. But if you send your check to the new address, the money might vanish into the night. Look for a letter from your current servicer announcing the change. If you're suspicious, call.

WHEN TO REFINANCE

When mortgage rates skid, you can refinance at a profit. Get a new, low-rate loan and use the proceeds to pay off the loan you're carrying now. If you need extra money, you often can take a larger loan with little or no increase in the amount you have to pay each month.

Borrowers should hit the phone the moment rates look attractive. If you dally, they may rise again. Six refinancing ideas:

• Replace your current fixed-rate mortgage with a new fixed-rate loan. That's a smart move as long as your savings—in interest costs or monthly payments—will outstrip the refinancing cost during the time you'll keep the house. Paper-and-pencil jockeys should be able to figure that out. For an on-line calculator, go to http://www.financenter.com.

• If you like adjustable mortgages, exchange your current ARM for a new one and glory in its low, first-year teaser rate. You might save as much as 2 or 3 percentage points. You'll also lower the cap on how high your mortgage rate could be allowed to rise.

• Switch your adjustable mortgage to a fixed-rate loan. A new ARM would be cheaper, but you may want the security of knowing that your monthly payments cannot rise.

• Switch your 30-year loan for one with a 15-year term, perhaps at little or no increase in monthly cost. A shorter term greatly reduces your interest expense.

• Pay off a balloon loan ahead of time if you see a regular mortgage rate you can afford.

• Consolidate a first and second mortgage into a single loan if you're carrying both mortgages at a higher rate, combined.

What It Costs to Refinance. Talk to your current lender first. You can often recast your present mortgage for a low fee without going through a full-scale refinancing.

Some lenders charge zero up front if you'll pay 0.25 or 0.5 percentage points over the going rate. This offer still might cost you less than you're paying now. Also, it effectively makes your closing costs deductible.

Expenses rise, however, if you want to take a larger loan. Then you're scrutinized—and charged—as if you were borrowing from scratch. Many Web sites, including those mentioned in this chapter, offer refinancing calculators to help you decide whether the savings are worth the costs. For short-term needs, it's cheaper to get a home-equity loan that you'll pay off fast (page 249).

If your credit history isn't pristine, you won't qualify for refinancing in the regular market. But subprime lenders will take you on (page 479). You'll pay a higher interest rate, but from your point of view the deal might still make sense.

Warning: Refinancing probably won't save you money if the new mortgage lasts longer than the term remaining on your present loan. Your monthly payment might drop but you'll pay for more months, which costs more dollars in the end. Try to refinance for the term left on your loan or less.

If you take a new mortgage for a larger amount, in order to pay off credit-card debt, you are stealing a fortune from your future. You're relieved of your high monthly credit-card payments, which gets you out of a short-term bind, and the interest is tax deductible. But consumer bills that you should repay over just a few months (or a few years, at worst) are now stretched over 15 or 30 years, costing you interest every year. If you have to consolidate these bills, go for a home-equity line of credit and pay it off as fast as you can.

GET YOUR FHA INSURANCE REFUND

When you take an FHA loan, you pay the full mortgage insurance premium up front. But at some point you'll probably sell the house and repay what you own. If you terminate the loan within the first 7 years and never defaulted on a payment, you'll get part of your premium back. At this writing, you get an 80 percent refund if you repay after just 2 years. That percentage diminishes until the end of the seventh year, when a refund is no longer owed.

You should get a check automatically within 45 days. If it doesn't come, ask your mortgage company whether it told the U.S. Department of Housing and Urban Development (HUD) that your loan has been repaid. If the answer is yes, call HUD's insurance division at 703-235-8117 and ask what's up. You'll need your 10-digit FHA case number (on your copy of the canceled mortgage), the date you paid in full, and the property's address. You can also write to HUD at P.O. Box 23699, Washington, DC 20026. Include your name, daytime phone number, FHA case number, the date the loan was paid in full, and the property's address.

HUD sends checks to the address shown on the loan-termination form. If there's no address, it writes to the one shown on the mortgage, so if you move, be sure to give the post office a forwarding address. If HUD has to hunt you down, you'll have to file a refund-claim form to get your check.

You get no refund if the buyer assumes your loan. The buyer gets the refund if he or she repays within the first 7 years of the loan's original term.

HOW TO DROP YOUR MORTGAGE INSURANCE

When you buy a home with less than 20 percent down, you have to purchase mortgage insurance, paying perhaps $25 to $100 a month on a

$100,000 loan. But on most loans you can cancel the coverage when your equity reaches 20 or 25 percent. You'll have to put your request in writing. The cancellation rules depend on who currently owns your loan.

If the loan is held by Fannie Mae, you can usually drop the insurance if you've paid on time over the past 12 months and meet one of the following conditions:

1. Your mortgage is down to 80 percent of the property's value when you first bought. If the loan was a refinancing, you must have made at least 12 consecutive payments.

2. Your mortgage balance is less than 80 percent of what the house is currently worth.

You may have to pay for an appraisal, costing perhaps $200 to $500. This shows what the property is worth and helps the mortgage servicer warrant that its value is holding up. Ask the bank for the names of appraisers it accepts.

If the loan is held by Freddie Mac, you can cancel the insurance if you ask in writing, have a good payment record, and:

1. Your mortgage is down to 80 percent of the property's value when you first bought, you've held the loan for at least 2 years, and the property hasn't dropped in price. *Or . . .*

2. Your mortgage balance is 80 percent of the home's current appraised value. In addition, you've had the loan for at least 2 years and improved the property; or you've had the loan for at least 5 years. *Or . . .*

3. Your mortgage balance is 75 percent of the current appraised value and you've had the loan at least 2 years.

4. If yours is an adjustable-rate mortgage, at least 12 months must have passed since the last increase in interest rate.

If the loan is held by some other private insurer, the rules may be tougher. For example, you may not be allowed to measure your equity by the home's increased value. Only the original value may count.

Laws may change. California requires mortgage servicers to cancel your coverage automatically if the loan was made after January 1, 1998, your payments are current, and your loan has dropped to 75 percent of what the house was worth when you first bought. Several other states require that you be notified once a year about your right to cancel. At this writing, similar bills are pending in Washington. When you first buy mortgage insurance, ask your lender about your termination rights.

FHA Mortgage Insurance Effectively Cannot Be Canceled. Most of these loans go into Ginnie Mae pools, which require that insurance be kept up.

You Cannot Cancel Mortgage Insurance If the Lender Bought It for You. The price of the coverage is included in the mortgage rate you pay. To escape the cost of the insurance you will have to refinance.

With Those Exceptions, I Know of No Mortgage Insurance That Cannot Be Canceled. Don't let your mortgage servicer tell you otherwise. When you ask in writing, the servicer should tell you what the rules for cancellation are and remove the coverage if you qualify. Some servicers stonewall. That's what impelled the drive for legislation.

Don't Accept No for an Answer. When you qualify for dropping coverage and your lender resists, consider refinancing. If you get a new ARM, chances are you'll pay less than you're paying now—and the new loan won't need mortgage insurance.

EQUITY SHARING

A cashless buyer in an expensive housing market needs someone to help with the down payment. An independent investor might put up the money in return for a share in the rising value of the home. More likely, a relative will step in, or perhaps a seller desperate to unload a house without coming down any more in price.

There are many ways of cutting an equity-sharing deal. Typically, the investor/relative/seller covers the down payment and gets the tax deductions available to business properties (page 513). The occupant pays the mortgage points and closing costs, handles the monthly mortgage payments, and takes care of everyday expenses (utilities, minor repairs). You become co-owners, with both names on the property and the loan. As collateral for meeting his or her obligations, the occupant gives the investor a second mortgage or deed of trust. (Obviously, you need a tax lawyer to set up this deal properly.)

After a specified period of time—usually 5 to 7 years—the occupant has to refinance the house and buy out the seller or investor. Alternatively, the house may be sold and the profits split. A typical split is 50/50, which may be fair if the occupant put nothing down. But if the occupant helped with the down payment, he or she deserves a large piece.

It's often hard for equity sharers to find a mortgage if the occupant puts no money down. When you do get a loan, the lender may tack an extra half point onto the interest rate.

If equity sharing interests you—as occupant, seller, or investor—here are the answers to some of the questions you will have:

Where Will You Find an Investor? Look first to the owners of homes that aren't selling, then to family, then to real-estate agents who might know of interested investors. Check the real-estate pages of newspapers for ads from professional equity investors (but be clear about their fees before signing on). You might even place an ad yourself.

As an Occupant, What Are Your Risks? If housing prices fall, stay flat, or rise by only a small amount, you won't accumulate enough equity to buy out the investor when the term is up. The house will be sold and you still won't be able to finance a home entirely on your own. Even if housing prices leap, you might not earn enough to command the big mortgage you'd need to buy out your partner's share. So before getting into the deal, figure out what appreciation you'll need and whether you think it possible.

As an Investor/Seller/Relative, What Are Your Risks? If housing prices go nowhere, so does your investment. When it's time to sell the house, you might not find a buyer. The mortgage debt will show on your credit record, which might prevent you from getting other loans. If you need money before the contract ends, you're probably stuck. The occupant may not be able to buy you out at the market price. If the occupants get divorced or lose their jobs, they might be unable to pay. You'd have to take over the payments on the first mortgage or deed of trust while foreclosing on the second loan you hold. There could be a fight.

If the deal works out, however, you get an attractive return without the headaches of being a landlord. For at least a whisper of protection, ask your partner to put up part of the down payment—say, 5 percent.

Coda for Parents. Equity sharing is often praised as a way of earning profits and tax breaks while helping your children buy a home. But do you want to be on the hook for paying the first mortgage or deed of trust if they cannot? You can get off that hook by selling the house, but would you force your kids to move? Would you foreclose if they're recalcitrant? If not, don't treat aid to kids as a moneymaking opportunity. Keep things simple by lending or giving them down-payment help. Equity sharing makes sense only for parents who are experienced real-estate investors and kids who understand that business is business if the deal doesn't work.

THE GREAT CONDO QUESTION

Condominiums and townhouses are homes attached to one another. You own a unit but you and your neighbors share common areas—lobbies, central heating, landscaping, a pool. Cooperative apartments are similar, except that you own shares in the building as a whole with the right to lease a certain unit. Monthly maintenance fees are levied on each owner to keep the common areas in good repair. You're also assessed for special expenses, such as replacing an elevator.

Condos and townhouses have two big advantages: they cost less than comparable freestanding houses and require less personal upkeep. If your condo's roof starts to leak, you don't have to call the roofer or nail up shingles yourself, you have only to help pay for repairs. For the young, condominiums are often a first step into the housing market. For the old, they're a comfortable step back from the burden of caring for a house.

But check these drawbacks before you opt for condo or co-op living:

• Condominiums typically rise less in value than freestanding houses and fall much faster when market conditions are poor. You're far more likely to lose money on a condo than on a house. That's because buyers prefer new units, where they can pick the rugs and appliances themselves. To sell, you may have to slash the price. Young people ready to trade up may find that they've built little or no equity. For some owners, condos become a trap.

• The smaller the condo, the harder it is to sell for a profit. Two-bedroom units sell better than one-bedroom units, which sell better than studios (studios barely move at all on the resale market). Townhouse condos do better than two-bedroom apartment condos.

• Most lenders allow home-equity loans on condos but rarely on co-ops. Co-ops boards often limit the amount of financing you're allowed.

• The condo developer might have low-balled the monthly maintenance fee. You learn too late that it's going to cost a lot more than you thought to keep the building or development running. New condos might also have hidden flaws that will be expensive to repair.

• The condo owners might be suing the builder for shoddy construction and other sins. Check this out before you buy. Also ask if any special assessments are in the wind for improvements or major repairs.

• If owners can't sell, they may move away and turn their units into rental properties. As more renters come in, the character of the condo changes. Tenants don't treat the property as carefully as residents would. The absentee owners don't want higher maintenance fees because they can't recover the cost by raising rents. If owners can't find tenants or earn enough rent, they might not pay their maintenance fees. That could force the condo onto a bare-bones budget—reducing services, deferring maintenance, and cutting property values. There may also be special assessments on the other unit holders to cover the bills. Banks generally don't give mortgages in new developments where tenants occupy more than 30 percent of the units, or in older developments that are more than 40 percent rented, although exceptions may be granted. If tenant occupancy passes 50 percent, you can't get FHA mortgages, either. If you're an owner, that makes it tough to resell.

• Townhouse developments have long lists of "don'ts": don't paint your front door red, don't plant bushes by your front walk, don't use an outdoor clothesline, don't keep a large dog, don't, don't, don't, don't. These rules will be enforced by neighborhood posses who want to keep the grounds looking uniformly attractive. If you like red doors and large dogs, don't move in.

• Buildings converting to condo or co-op ownership may have hidden flaws. If the present owner of your building proposes that you buy it, the tenants should hire a lawyer and engineer. You need to know what's wrong with the building (will it need a new roof? new wiring? at how much per tenant?); what it will cost to run the building well; what taxes you'll pay after conversion; and whether the title is clear. Will you own the land under the building or only the building itself? If someone else owns the land, what's to prevent him or her from jacking up the rent or, worse, not renewing the lease? With conversions, an insider's price is usually low, but it's no bargain if the building needs expensive repairs or the units aren't easy to resell. Unless you feel certain that the unit is a sound investment, try to stay as a renter and let the new owners handle the headaches. Or bail out.

• Each condominium development or co-op building is governed by a board of owners. Your property values depend on how well the board members do their job. Do they enforce collections from people who don't pay their maintenance fees on time? Are they unafraid to levy higher assessments for essential maintenance? Can they settle disagreements about what amenities the building should invest in? Will they see that the building is always kept in good repair? Under an ineffectual board, a co-op or condominium can fall apart.

• If an owner doesn't pay his or her maintenance fee, the condo board generally has the right to foreclose. But even then, the condo may not get the money it's owed. The proceeds of the foreclosure sale go first to satisfy tax liens and second to repay the first mortgage. Only then can the condo collect and there may not be enough money left—especially on units that are fairly new or where condo values have declined. The remaining owners may be assessed to cover the default.

• Buyers of cooperative apartments run similar risks. You're on the line for the building's entire mortgage, tax bill, and upkeep. If your neighbors don't pay their share, you may have to kick in. A co-op, however, can generally evict an owner who doesn't pay and sell the unit on the open market. The co-op takes any money it's owed; the former owner gets whatever is left. To minimize defaults, co-op boards don't let you sell your apartment at will. The buyer's finances first have to be checked. If the board finds reason to object—personal or social as well as financial—you lose the sale.

The Trend in Townhouses Is Away from Condos. They're increasingly being built to sell as individual homes.

If You Want a Condo or Co-op, Here's Your Best Hope of Making Money on the Deal:
Find a building whose units are almost entirely occupied by owners rather than by renters. These buildings are usually better maintained. Be-

ware the condo where the sponsor couldn't persuade enough tenants to buy their own apartments.

Buy a two-bedroom condo rather than a studio. The larger units hold their value better because there are more potential buyers.

Stay away from small buildings. If a 10-unit condo needs a new roof, each owner could face a whopping cost.

Buy where condos or co-ops are the normal form of ownership, such as New York City or downtown Chicago. There, their prices behave more like those of individual houses.

Buy a well-kept, well-run older condo rather than a new one. Its price will be lower and you don't risk the new-condo problems: careless construction, unfinished amenities, and higher taxes and maintenance fees than the salespeople said. The owners' association will be functioning smoothly. There should be a sizable reserve for unexpected repairs.

Find a unit with amenities appropriate to the people who might buy from you—good schools and a playground for young families; social spaces and bus service for older people.

Don't buy where you see new condos going up or space where the builder can build new ones in the future. Most buyers choose new units when they can. You may not be able to sell unless you drastically cut the price.

Don't buy without reading all the condo documents (murky as they are), to be sure that you understand—and can live with—the bylaws, the budget, and the rules.

When checking the budget, look for a sizable reserve for repairs. If there isn't one, take a walk. It shows that the building is poorly run. Ditto if there's no reserve for the cost of collecting maintenance fees from any owners who default. Ask about the delinquency rate: What percentage of owners aren't paying their bills? What is the board doing about it? A sound building assumes a certain percentage of deadbeats and budgets for it. If the budget assumes that everyone will pay, you're going to get a nasty surprise.

Avoid a building or condo development with a lot of defaults or where more than 20 percent of the units are rented out. Outside owners default at a much higher rate than owner-occupants—and when others don't pay, you'll have to pick up the slack. A growing percentage of renters also means that the building will run down.

THE STRATEGIC RENTER

In some circumstances, it's smarter to rent than to buy.

Maybe you have a rent-controlled apartment that's unbelievably cheap. These bargains are fading from the scene, but as long as you have one, keep it and use your extra money to invest.

Maybe you expect to move within 3 or 4 years. You'd probably lose money on a house if you bought and sold in such a short period of time.

Maybe you're young and single and want to be ready to change your life in a moment. Or you're newly divorced and haven't decided what you'll do next.

Maybe you're retired and want to sell your house. You could invest the proceeds and use part of the income to pay rent.

Maybe you see house prices slipping in your area and hope to buy more cheaply if you wait a year.

But for Long-Term Occupancy, Ownership Is Best. You'll get a nice return on investment even with housing prices only crawling up. For example, take a $100,000 house that gains 3 percent—$3,000—in value. If you bought that house on $15,000 down, you've made 20 percent on your money. On a $10,000 down payment, you've made 30 percent. For some estimates of the investment value of buying vs. renting, see Appendix 4, page 1000.

On paper, there's nothing wrong with investing your money in something other than a house—as long as you really do it and add money each month, as people repaying mortgages do. But to equal what you get from a paid-up house, you'll have to build a large enough fund to cover your rent from the day you retire until the end of your life. I don't see many pots that large. Whoever first said that a house was a security blanket wasn't kidding.

18.

A Second Home for Fun and Profit

The House That Doesn't Cost You Anything (Much)

Imagine a house that helps pay for itself. While you're sitting in the sun, it's making money and lifting the mortgage from your back.

As luck would have it, I'm writing this chapter in my second home. My husband and I have had a string of them. We've built them, rented them out, sold at a profit, and built again. We've made some money and had a lot of fun. A vacation house that comes close to carrying itself is a dream property. It's always on tap for your own weeks off and the renters help you pay the bills.

But you shouldn't think of a house like this as a true investment. It's more like owning a pleasure palace at a discount price. You'll almost never get enough rent to cover your costs, let alone make a profit. A portion of the cost, especially the mortgage payment and major repairs, is going to have to come out of your pocket. If property values rise enough, the house might make money after all. But to measure up as a good investment, the sale price has to be large enough to cover your annual losses plus interest and deliver a compounded double-digit profit for each year you held. That's a tall order, rarely achieved.

Back when we built our vacation houses, the profit hurdle wasn't so high. We broke even on rentals after tax and made good money on capital gains. We got out of the game the first year we found that our costs, after tax, would exceed our rents. As a business proposition, real estate stinks if you *must* get enormous capital gains to bail you out.

The one house we kept (and still put up for rent) isn't quite at break-even. From an investment point of view, we'd do better with our money in a tax-exempt bond. But it's not much fun vacationing in a tax-exempt. It has a lousy view of the sea.

Maybe you can afford to keep a vacation home or condo without renting it out. But if you can't, renters are fabulous. They help you carry a place that you otherwise wouldn't own. You're not making money but so what? Just a look out the window—at the mountains or the beach—proves that you came out ahead.

On the Other Hand . . .

Why do you want to own a second home? Lots of people (like me) have dandy rentals on the market. We're the ones who have to worry about cash flow, customers, and repairs. If you rent the same place every year, it can feel like home and you haven't had to make a capital investment. Or you can pick the nicest and newest house each year. If you tire of that neighborhood, you can vacation somewhere else and let the owners worry about who's going to rent it next. Enjoy *my* money-losing home while putting your own cash toward reducing college debt or building up a retirement account.

One plausible reason for buying is that you're not really investing, you're planning ahead. You expect to retire in that home, so you're buying it now and getting renters to help with the mortgage. But how do you know that you'll want to live there 15 years from now? Maybe the town will change. Maybe your opinions or health status will. Maybe you'll want a house big enough for grandchildren rather than a condo on a golf course. Maybe you'll want to be close to your kids rather than close to the beach. Retirement homes are best chosen 5 years or so before you actually retire.

If you really will vacation and retire there, it's great to get renters to help with the mortgage. But consider the home's resale potential. You may want to retire in some other way.

To Buy a Place That You Plan to Rent . . .

• Buy an existing house. If it has a vacation-rental history, so much the better. You'll know what your net costs are likely to be. If there's no rental history, ask a local real-estate agent what you can charge and how long the rental season is. As a check on the agent, talk to one or two people who own rental homes nearby.

• Buy a run-down rental house and fix it up. You might be able to raise the rent and rent for a longer season than the previous owner did. I said you *might*. There's no guarantee you'll succeed.

• Buy an empty lot and pay for it as fast as you can. Once the property is yours, put a house on it. You can get a mortgage for 75 to 80 percent of the combined value of the house and land. That's usually enough to build the house and furnish it.

• Buy a condominium. Older condos are usually cheaper than new ones and often just as nice. Ask a real-estate broker to show you some places. If you refurnish, you might be able to get more renters. But condos are harder to resell than freestanding homes. They don't rise nearly as much in value and may even fall while house prices are going up. Better to view yours principally as a vacation home with renters providing a little income on the side.

New condo owners should get involved with the homeowners' association. Spend a year on the board so you'll know how the condo operates and what costs are coming down the pike. If you sense a growing resistance to paying maintenance fees, you might want to sell before the development runs down.

Your rental success depends on the right answers to these questions:

1. *Is the house or condo in a known resort or vacation spot that's easy to get to?* For a steady supply of renters, buy where vacationers already come. You need an infrastructure—advertising, rental agents, house cleaners, and service people who make quick repairs. Your home shouldn't be much more than half a day's drive from a major population center.

2. *Is the place large enough?* The rental trade leans heavily toward families. That means at least two bedrooms and preferably three. With four bedrooms or more you'll tend to attract two families vacationing together. That may or may not mean higher rents, but does create more wear and tear. You'll have extra rentals if you'll allow dogs. I do, and have never had any damage.

3. *Is the house and property something special?* Land on water—an ocean, a lake, even a lagoon—costs more than land elsewhere. But houses on water rent for a premium and rent for more weeks each season than equally good houses back from the beach. That extra income helps you cover the higher price. In slow real-estate markets, property on water sells better than those with less interesting views (provided, of course, that beach erosion hasn't reached your front door).

In ski areas, houses with picture-perfect views of the mountains do better than houses overlooking the road. Golfers like villas overlooking the golf course. Bird-watchers like marshes. Windsurfers like bays. The best-renting condo resorts have classy amenities—pool, health club, beach. Within the resort, condos surrounded by green space rent better than those that back up on the supermarket road.

Still, homes back from the beach or with no mountain view are cheaper to buy, so check the market for lower-priced rentals. If demand is steady, you can purchase a modest place and still attract enough business to cover part of your cost. Regardless of price range, look for something a little special—a garden, a good layout, quiet woods in back. To bring in extra rent, you need an edge.

4. *Is the house or condo well furnished?* Today's affluent renters won't put up with early Salvation Army furniture, lumpy mattresses, and campfire kitchens. They want comfort and will pay for it. So set up a convenient house, with modern appliances, VCRs, good chairs and beds, plenty of lamps, and, for summer homes, air-conditioning—in the bedrooms, if nowhere else. Keep the pillows and shower curtains fresh, the grime out of the bathroom, and the screens in good repair. Your renters will repay you by returning year after year. You'll also get a steady trade from rental agents, who like houses that clients don't complain about.

5. *Do you have a good rental agent?* If you have only one or two rentals a summer, maybe you can find tenants yourself. Take pictures of the house or condo, inside and out, to show your friends or put on your Web page. The Web might bring you renters from England or Japan.

To rent more often, you'll need an agent. Look for one who's well located on the main road, works at the business full-time, advertises widely, and is well known in the community. An agent keeps your house as full as its location, price, and condition allow, collects the rents, sends you the checks, cleans up between tenants, fields complaints, and arranges for small repairs. The commission: usually 15 to 25 percent of the rent, plus cleanup costs.

Some condo resorts handle rentals themselves for commissions in the 50 percent range. That's a greedy price, even if it includes cleanup costs. But you may be stuck. Unless you rent through the resort, your tenants might not be allowed to use the clubhouse, golf course, and pool.

6. *Can you rent for enough to cover most of your cash costs?* Ideally, the rents cover everything. In practice, the net rents may cover only your operating costs—utilities, routine maintenance, replacements, small repairs. You'll probably have to pay part or all of the mortgage and major repairs yourself. Before you buy, ask yourself: What can I afford to pay each month and each year? Can I really count on rentals to cover the rest?

If you *must* have extra income to maintain the house, you shouldn't buy at all. Your financial condition is too fragile for this kind of risk. If you decide to ignore that boringly good advice, don't take the salesperson's word that "rentals are no problem." Check the history of the property or properties just like it. Build in a safety margin. Could you carry the house if it rented only half as much as you expected? How long could you carry it if it were damaged by a hurricane, vandalism, fire, or a flood and you couldn't rent for a while? Your homeowners insurance will probably cover lost rents if the damage was done by a peril the policy covers you for. But you won't be paid immediately. Flood insurance doesn't cover lost rents.

You're at Risk If You Need Rental Income, or Are Buying for Investment, and You . . .

. . . Buy in a spot where few tourists come. You might love the house yourself. But don't expect to rent it much or sell it easily.

. . . Buy a house that's remote. Neither renters nor buyers will normally beat a path to your door.

. . . Buy a small, dreary house or run-down condo, even in a strong tourist town. Renters will avoid you except when everything else is full. So will real-estate agents because their clients would complain. You won't even attract many tenants by dropping your rent. No vacationer wants to be stuck in a dingy living room, with grumpy kids, when it rains.

. . . Buy a condo in an area where lots of building is going on. The number of new rental properties may exceed demand. If the development has no rental history, you don't know what income you're likely to get.

. . . Buy land or a condominium in a development that's not fully sold out. As long as it's in business, the development company will hog all the buyers who come to visit. It won't be easy to find someone to sell to. That might not matter, however, if you're sure you can hold for many years and want to be sure you get a condo on the beach.

. . . Respond to a postcard that offers "free gifts" for sitting through a sales pitch. In the enthusiasm of the moment, you might buy a time-share property that you don't really want, can't rent, and can't resell at any price. Never, *never, NEVER* respond.

Buying Country Property and Homes

Here come the city slickers, buying up country properties for a song. So how come the local yokels hum so happily when they sell? Because they know things that you don't about the hazards of making the property pay. I'll list just a few: (1) the boundaries may be uncertain; you'll have to pay to establish them (Farmer John's old "deed plot" is *not* a survey); (2) the area may not be zoned, meaning that *anything* can be built right across the road; (3) toxic agricultural chemicals may have been buried there, which you'll be responsible for removing; (4) you may have to drill a well; (5) it may cost a fortune to bring electric power to your castle in the woods or to rewire an old farmhouse for computer and fax; (6) "wetlands" rules will complicate your plans to build near a lake, stream, or marsh; (7) there may be easements across the land for logging, riding, or utility poles; (8) it may take years to get permission to subdivide.

That's just for starters. When buying country property, you need a good local lawyer and real-estate consultant to keep the yokels from giving you donkey ears.

FINANCING A SECOND HOME

My first choice is a local lender. They know the properties, have a good fix on what they're worth, and understand the needs of buyers of second homes. Next check the national lenders that give loans by phone (page 479). Trying your home bank is probably a waste of time. They usually don't lend on real estate that's out of town. Developers often offer financing for the lots, homes, or condos they have for sale. You put a small sum of money down and pay the rest over a specified number of years.

Loans on second homes are usually more expensive than those on first homes. Expect a higher interest rate and extra points. You might also have to put more money down.

INSURING A SECOND HOME

For a quote on homeowners insurance, go first to the company that insures your primary home. It may take your second home at a discount. Next, see what a local insurance agent can do. You might find a special vacation-home policy, like the one sold by The Chubb Group in around fifteen states. Chubb's policies cut prices two ways: they let you take less coverage on the contents of your vacation home (you probably keep fewer valuables there than in your principal home); they also pay less for temporary living expenses (if your vacation home burned, you wouldn't have to live in a motel while it was being rebuilt). For information, call 800-CHUBB-08. Beach or waterfront property needs flood insurance (page 465).

Whichever policy you choose, keep your liability coverage high in case a renter is injured and sues. Don't let hazards linger. Repair the front steps, replace the bad lamp cord, stick nonskid pads on the shower floor.

Don't buy a house that you cannot fully insure unless you're rich enough not to care. Theft and vandalism coverage might not be granted to remote cottages. Fancy beachfront homes might cost more to rebuild than the maximum $250,000 that flood insurance policies paid in 1997. Without insurance a lot of your equity is at risk.

THE CARETAKER

You need someone to check the house regularly for storm damage, burst pipes, vandalism, a dead furnace, and other problems. If you put up the house for rent, the rental agent may provide this service. Otherwise, ask for recommendations from other vacation-home owners in the area or a contractor you trust. Some possibilities: a neighbor who might want to make a little extra money, the handyman at a local apartment house or condo complex, or a local police officer or firefighter.

THE TAX GOD ISN'T OVERLY FOND OF SECOND HOMES

Some of the rules that apply to your principal residence apply equally to a second home (page 495). You can deduct mortgage interest, property taxes, and casualty losses.

You lose your interest deductions, however, for a third house, a fourth house, and so on up. That is, unless they're business properties, in which case they operate under different rules (page 513).

You're taxed on your profit when you sell a vacation home. One way around this, used especially by new retirees: Move into your vacation house for 2 out of the 5 years before you sell. That makes it your principal residence, which you're usually allowed to sell tax free (page 940).

BUT THE TAX GOD REALLY MESSES AROUND WITH PEOPLE WHO TAKE RENTERS

When you rent your house or condo to others, what's deductible depends on your income, your involvement with your rental property, and how much you use the house yourself. Here are the general rules:

Your Rental Home Is Treated as a Personal Residence if you use it more than 14 days a year or more than 10 percent as much time as you rent it, whichever is greater. Days you visit the home to make repairs and attend to your rental business are not counted as personal use. On the other hand, if you rent to a relative or friend at something less than the going rate, that *is* personal use.

All your expenses are allocated between business and personal use. If the house is rented 40 percent of the total number of days it's used, then 40 percent of the overhead—interest, taxes, utilities, repairs, maintenance, rental costs, depreciation—are business expenses.

When preparing your income taxes, you would normally:

1. Figure the portion of interest and taxes that applies to your personal use and deduct it along with your other itemized deductions on Schedule A.

2. Report the rental income on Schedule E. Deduct from it, first, the portion of interest and taxes that applies to the rental use of the property. After that, deduct the business portion of your insurance and maintenance costs. Finally, deduct depreciation. But your total allowable deductions cannot exceed your rental income. In most cases, that means that some expenses will go unused.

3. If the business portion of your interest and taxes exceed the rent, the remainder can be deducted with your personal expenses on Schedule A.

4. Other unused business expenses can be carried forward to future years. If you hold the property long enough to pay off the mortgage, your rents may start to exceed your current expenses. At that point, you can start deducting unused expenses from previous years.

There's a twist to the rules if you rent for fewer than 15 days. You don't report that rental income on your tax return and you don't deduct any rental expenses except those for taxes and mortgage interest.

Your Rental Home Is Treated as a Business Property if your own use amounts to no more than 14 days or 10 percent of the time as you rent it, whichever is more. You allocate expenses to personal or business use, just as you would if it were a personal residence. But in this case, you cannot deduct the mortgage interest and taxes for the short time that covers your personal use. On the other hand, you get a break when you want to sell. You can do a tax-free exchange for a different property (talk to an expert in commercial property transactions about this). If you sell at a loss, that loss is deductible from your ordinary income.

If a rental agent manages your house or condo: You can normally write off expenses only against your rental income or any income you're getting from other "passive" investments—meaning businesses where you're a silent partner. You will probably have excess expenses that can't be deducted currently. Just carry them forward. Unused expenses can be deducted from the profits on this or any other passive investment when you sell.

If you manage the property yourself or actively participate in the management: In general, this covers people who find their own renters, collect the money, and handle maintenance and repairs. You may be able to write off *all* the expenses, even if they exceed your rental income. That creates a tax shelter. Some of your ordinary earnings are protected from tax.

You qualify for this shelter if you meet one of the following tests: (1) Your adjusted gross income (not counting income and losses from other shelters) doesn't exceed $100,000. Lucky you can write off up to $25,000 in business losses, including depreciation. (2) Your income falls between $100,000 and $150,000. Over that range, the $25,000 deduction gradually phases out.

There's one exception. You will *not* qualify for tax shelter if your tenants, on average, rent your house for fewer than seven days at a time. In short, no tax break if you own a ski condo that principally attracts weekend renters.

Is It Better to Treat Your Second Home as a Personal Residence or as a Business Property? If you're entitled to the $25,000 exemption (few are), it's better to have a business property. Ditto if you plan to buy and sell because you can do a tax-free exchange. Otherwise, flunk the business test by using the home more than 14 days. That way, you get an unlimited deduction for mortgage and taxes.

ABOUT TIME BOMBS . . . OOPS, I MEAN TIME-SHARES

If you can't afford a house, and you can't afford a condominium, maybe you can afford a piece of a condominium.

That's a time-share. You generally buy the right to vacation in the same unit, for the same week, every year. If you buy a "floater," you can be put into any unit of the size you contracted for. Your basic cost might be $7,500 to $25,000. There are also monthly maintenance costs and special assessments.

The most desirable time-shares are in spiffy resort areas—on the beach, by a golf course, near Disney World. You can buy for cash or on terms. You have to pay regular maintenance fees to keep the property clean and in good repair. Some resorts find you a tenant if you can't use your regular week (you pay a rental commission of 25 to 50 percent). Or you can swap, using someone else's unit in a different resort in return for letting a stranger make use of yours.

Time-shares are sold as "prepaid vacations"—locking in today's prices for the rest of your life. But that's not quite true (these days, what is?). If you finance your purchase, the interest rate effectively pushes up the price. Your annual real-estate taxes and maintenance costs will rise. Many resorts hit you with extra assessments—in the $500 to $1,000 range—for major improvements or repairs. It might be 10 to 20 years before owning the time-share actually becomes cheaper than renting the unit every year, even projecting an annual increase in rents. Will you want to visit the time-share 21 years from now? *Really?*

If you do buy, stay away from the developer's mesmerizing (and misleading) sales pitches. See if there's a bulletin board listing resales, ask any unit owners you run into during your visit, or call a local real-estate agent. If you see a unit you like, make a low offer. You can probably buy a time-share for 50 percent of the developer's price or less. Some people who bought for $15,000 will be thrilled to get out at $3,000—and they'll let you pay in installments, too.

The So-Called Advantages:

1. A time-share is a cheap vacation, especially for a family. (But renting a time-share unit is cheaper than laying out the money to buy it.)

2. You see some of the same friends around the swimming pool every year. (But the same will be true if you always rent at the same time.)

3. You can swap for a time-share in other parts of the country, or elsewhere in the world, and get a unit of about the same quality as yours. (But renters can pick any kind of time-share they want—anywhere, anytime—without negotiating a swap.)

The Definite Disadvantages:

1. Unless you buy a good time-share—a desirable place, a desirable unit, a desirable week—you might not be able to make a good swap. You'll be stuck every year with the unit you have or a unit of indifferent quality, at an inconvenient time, in a place you might not want to be. If you own an off-season week, you generally can't swap for a week at a better time of year.

2. If the resort runs downhill in the future, you won't want to go there anymore—and neither will anyone else. If your life pattern changes and you don't use the time-share, you'll be paying for a vacation you no longer take. You cannot count on getting a renter when you're not there.

3. Monthly payments, monthly maintenance fees, and assessments keep on running, whether you visit or not.

4. You will almost certainly *not* make money. If you manage to sell, you'll take a loss—probably a huge one. There are always those rare birds that do indeed sell at a profit, but I've never met one. Count yourself lucky if you find a buyer at all.

GETTING OUT OF A TIME-SHARE

How I Sold My Time-Share would be one of the world's thinnest books. This deal is easy to get into but hard to get out of. Almost all the new buyers are grabbed by developers, not by individuals with units to resell. Here are some ideas, but don't count on any of them to work for you:

1. Ask the developer. Sometimes they handle resales, but only in popular resorts where no more new units are being built. Typical commission: 25 to 50 percent.

2. List with a local real-estate agent. Try not to hear the agent chuckle.

3. Use the Internet. You might find some sucke . . . er, *buyer,* there.

4. Print some pretty for-sale flyers showing a price well below the one the developer offers. When visiting your unit, pass them out to the happy, innocent people lounging by the pool. You have a shot if the time-share is obviously a going concern with assessments apparently under control.

How do you get out of a time-share that you haven't been able to sell?

You probably can't if you're only a year or two into the deal. If you quit paying, you'll be sued and your credit report will be wrecked. If you've paid for the unit, or almost paid, and decide to walk, you might not be sued for any remaining money due. But the default will still show up on your credit history.

Some developers will take the unit back. You get no money for the time-share, but at least you're off the hook.

Some brokers take advantage of owners desperate to resell. They'll claim they have buyers and ask you for a "listing fee" of $300 or more. You don't get a buyer and never see your money again.

Instead of Buying a Time-Share, Consider Renting a Unit In a Time-Share Building. You can get a lovely place for far less than the weekly cost of a hotel or motel. Good rental time-shares offer one to three bedrooms, a kitchen, a living room, and access to lots of amenities: swimming pool, golf course, tennis court, local entertainments. You might go every year when the children are small. But you're not tied down financially. When the kids grow up, you say ta-ta to the family vacation and try something else. You can also rent condominiums that aren't used as time-shares. Condo resorts are usually top-of-the-line. Any travel agent can find you a condo or time-share rental, or call a resort you're interested in.

Time-shares sometimes offer vacations at a discount if you'll sit through a sales pitch aimed at getting you to buy. Expect the salesperson to tell you that time-shares are a terrific investment (they're not), they "lock in today's vacation price" (not so—see page 514), and they're easy to resell (fat chance). Buy only if you know that you'll want to vacation in this resort, or others like it, for as many years as you can imagine—*and* it won't matter whether you ever sell or not.

If You Still Want to Own a Time-Share, Don't Buy from the Developer. Buy from One of the Thousands of People Trying to Resell. Resales are available through local real-estate agents. You might get a splendid unit at 50 percent or more off the developer's price.

Before signing any time-share contract, read through all the clauses and decipher the rules. What are the monthly maintenance fees? How often do they rise? What special expenses might you have to pay? What do you actually own? Can you sell to someone else (assuming you can find a buyer) or are resales prohibited? Do you get the same unit every year? If you're offered a "bonus week," when can you take it? What happens if some of your fellow owners stop paying their share of the costs? What if someone is injured in your unit? What if the developer doesn't finish the project, leaving you without some of the promised amenities? How is the property owners' association run, and what are its rules? What kind of unit can you expect in a time-share exchange? Who manages the property? (You want an independent company that's in the hospitality business, not a subsidiary of the developer.)

Don't buy from a resort that lures prospects with "free gifts." Or from salespeople who imply that you're making a good investment. Or if you're told that "today only" there's a discount price. Or without taking home the sales contract and other ownership documents to read and consider quietly.

Stick with a nationally known company, of good reputation, whose resorts you have visited and liked, and whose salespeople don't hustle you. If there is such a combination.

FITTING A SECOND HOME INTO YOUR FINANCIAL PLAN

Like a first home, a second home does double duty. It's a place to live and has elements of an investment. It forces you to save (assuming that prices hold up so that you can build equity). It costs you money as long as you own it, but you hope to sell for more than you paid. On the downside, you've made a costly purchase that probably can't be sold in a hurry. You may lose money if your resort suffers a real-estate slump.

When you own two homes, you need the protection of cash in the bank to pay the mortgages just in case your income stops. If you've tapped all your cash to buy the house, make it your top priority to build up your liquid savings again.

STEP 5
PAYING FOR COLLEGE

A friend and I were celebrating over lunch. He had just written his last tuition check. My husband and I had the end in sight.

"It's funny," my friend said. "For years, I was terrorized by the unimaginable price of college. The cost projections were appalling. How was I ever going to pay? I saved *some* money, but not enough. When my daughter started filling out applications, I lived every day with a stone-cold fear.

"Then I borrowed some money through one of those college-payment plans, and suddenly it was over. And it wasn't so bad.

"I suppose," he went on, "that if I hadn't been scared into saving some money, I couldn't have done it. But in the end, I lived."

I recount this story just to remind you that almost every child who wants to go to college gets there. And when your children graduate, life resumes.

19.

Tuition, Room, and Board

The Matterhorn of Personal Finance

Paying for college is a peak experience. No one who has stood in those chill winds ever forgets them.

College is worth it. Write that tuition check and repeat after me: College is worth it. All of today's best jobs take smarts (and most of the lesser jobs, too). Regardless of what you pay for a college degree, you—or your child—will earn it back in spades.

The burden is heavy. But it shouldn't get very much worse in the years ahead than it is right now.

Parents pale when they see college-cost projections. But as the price of a degree goes up so will your income and assets—thanks to raises, job changes, and investments. Relatively speaking, the average college should cost just about the same in the year 2008 as in 1998, especially the state colleges and universities. The price of highly selective private colleges has been rising faster than disposable incomes. But pressure from parents is forcing those schools to moderate their price increases and create more innovative payment plans.

You *will* find a way to pay for college. Everyone does. If you don't save enough, you'll have to borrow. But you'll make it.

HOW MUCH? HOW MUCH?

That depends on the school you choose. Most state colleges and universities are not unreasonably priced, especially for in-state students. Private colleges cost much more. Highly selective private colleges and universities are practically off the charts. But the top-dollar schools also have the biggest financial-aid budgets, so don't assume that you can't afford the freight. Your price isn't the sticker price, it's what you pay out of pocket after receiving any grants or student jobs you're eligible for.

The table below tells you roughly what to expect, assuming that total costs rise by 6 percent annually. The projections include tuition, fees, room, board, books, supplies, transportation, and personal expenses. Many state schools charge considerably less than what's shown here. You'll pay even less if you live at home and commute. On the other hand, the best-known private colleges cost more—in fact, at this writing, they're passing $130,000 for four years of education.

GET OUT THE SMELLING SALTS, MA, SHE'S ABOUT TO MENTION WHAT COLLEGE WILL COST*

THE YEAR YOUR CHILD STARTS SCHOOL	FOUR YEARS AT A PUBLIC COLLEGE †	FOUR YEARS AT A PRIVATE COLLEGE
1997	$ 44,743	$ 94,416
1998	47,428	100,081
1999	50,274	106,086
2000	53,290	112,451
2001	56,487	119,198
2002	59,887	126,350
2003	63,469	133,931
2004	67,277	141,967
2005	71,314	150,485
2006	75,593	159,514
2007	80,128	169,084
2008	84,936	179,229
2009	90,032	189,983
2010	95,434	201,382
2011	101,160	213,465
2012	107,230	226,273
2013	113,664	239,849
2014	120,484	254,240
2015	127,713	269,495
2016	135,375	285,665

* Tuition, room, board, books, fees, transportation, and other expenses.

† In-state residents only. Out-of-staters: add $4,738 to the cost for 1997 and multiply by 6 percent annually until you reach your matriculation year.

SOURCES: The College Board; T. Rowe Price

The good news is that a $60,000 salary will rise to $108,000 in 15 years, assuming 4 percent wage inflation. You'll earn even more if you're promoted to higher-level jobs. So you will, some way, find the money to pay—if not for a private school, then for a public one.

PRICE, QUALITY, AND PRESTIGE

Here's a tale for our times. It's about two private colleges, Dim Bulb U and Wise Guy Tech. Both were down in the dumps because enrollment had fallen off. How could they attract more students?

Dim Bulb U cut its price to make its degree more affordable. The kids stopped coming and its reputation sagged. Wise Guy Tech jacked up its price to Ivy League levels and students banged down the doors to get in. It added more services, upgraded buildings, and its prestige ballooned.

This story is true. Only the names have been changed to protect the guilty. Parents tend to equate price with quality. In the competition for students, schools have found that it pays to charge more. That's one of the reasons that private institutions cost so much—not to mention the price competition for top faculty, the need to keep the campus technologically up to date, country-club competition (lovely dorms, weight-training rooms), modern science and performing-art centers, and continuing investment in program improvements. High prices bring in extra money from well-to-do students, which can be spent, Robin Hood style, supporting students who can't pay.

Do you want to play this game? If so, keep on writing out those checks. If not:

• Consider a high-priced private college or university only if you have a personal reason for valuing that school's environment, size, location, and academic departments, and if its national reputation lives up to its cost. Do you know if it has an effective alumni network to help graduates get jobs? The school will cost less than it appears if you get a lot of student aid.

• Apply to lower-priced private colleges. Many of them do a splendid job, especially for the average student. Check out a wide range of schools to see what each offers in student aid. Many offer substantial "merit scholarships" to talented students who don't qualify for much need-based aid.

• Apply to your state university, especially if your grades are good. You'll get a top education, often at half the price. As the price gap widens between public and private education, talented students are streaming into the public universities, especially those with fine academic reputations.

• Consider state colleges, which should cost even less. They vary in quality, however. In states such as California, which underinvest in education and let their classrooms crowd up, you may have to attend for five years or more to get all the courses that a particular major requires. It may be cheaper to go to a school that you know you can graduate from in four years or less.

This Paragraph Is for Optimists Only: It's *faintly possible* that college costs will start rising more slowly than forecast. The reason: demographics. The children of the baby boom are now approaching college age—a nice little population bulge that will fill a lot of empty dorm rooms. The more students a school can cram into its present physical plant, the more slowly tuitions can rise.

Back when the baby boom crowded into college (1964–80), the tuition charged by private four-year colleges rose an average of 0.9 percent annually, after adjusting for inflation. I'm not forecasting a replay. But it's at least plausible that you won't have to borrow quite as much as you feared.

HOW MUCH OF THE PRICE WILL YOU HAVE TO PAY?

ALL OF IT, probably, if you currently make $80,000 and up.

PART OF IT if you make $50,000 or $60,000.

ONLY A SLIVER if you earn under $20,000.

These are such bald generalizations that you ought to chase me out of town. The amount of aid you actually get depends heavily on such things as the size of your family, the age of the parents, the cost of the school, the number of family members in college, the avoirdupois of your savings account, and how badly the school wants you to enroll. A student judged able to pay in full for good old State U may well qualify for financial aid in the Ivy League. Still, those income ranges give you a general feel for the landscape.

Upper-middle-class parents, just barely getting by on $90,000 a year, feel broke. They haven't got the money for the pricey private school they want. So they assume that the school will come to their rescue with a reasonable grant.

Forget it. You're telling your sad tale to a financial-aid officer who may be earning $45,000. From that perspective you don't look broke. In fact, you look like a burgher who saw college coming 18 years ago and didn't bother to save any money. Why should the school pull your chestnuts out of the fire? You might get a loan, but don't look for much free money. Aid officers save their sympathy, and their funds, for promising kids whose families earn less.

College aid is based on an eligibility calculation. There's one for federal programs (also used by most state colleges and universities) and a second one used by most private colleges. Conceptually, they work roughly like this:

1. Add up your family income and assets. The federal calculation omits the value of your home, retirement plans, and certain other assets. Most private colleges include home equity and perhaps other assets, too.

2. Subtract the money you need to live on, plus an allowance for taxes (including the education tax credit, if you qualify) and retirement savings.

3. Much of the remaining "discretionary" money has to be spent for college. That's your "expected parental contribution." This part of the calculation is determined by a standard, federal needs analysis used, with minor variations, by all schools.

4. Look up the total price of the school your child wants.

5. Subtract your parental contribution.

6. Subtract the money your child is expected to pay out of his or her income and savings.

7. The remainder shows your eligibility for aid, sometimes called financial need. *Need* is the difference between what you and your child are expected to pay and the college's total cost.

8. The college that accepts your child tries to fill your need (or most of it) with grants, loans, and student jobs.

On paper, that approach sounds reasonable. The college tries to make up the difference between what it charges and what you can afford to pay. If your family contribution is determined to be $8,000 and the college costs $12,000, you'll be eligible for $4,000 in aid. If the college costs $30,000, you'll be eligible for $22,000 in aid. Your family contribution remains the same, no matter which institution you choose. So the pricier the school, the better your chance of getting help.

But the joker lies in the calculation's second line: the amount of money you need to live on. No one cares about your actual bills. Instead, your income and assets are judged by a standard formula developed by the federal government. It assesses your need by playing a game of "let's pretend."

Let's pretend, it says, that you live on a lower-income budget (as compiled annually by the U.S. Department of Labor). That's your official living allowance. In 1997 it was $18,070 for a family of four. Anyone netting that much or less is assumed to be too broke to pay for school. But anyone with a higher net income is expected to make a contribution. If your actual living expenses are higher than the rock-bottom budget allows, tough luck. You can't expect the college to make up for the fact that you're living especially well.

When the low living allowance is subtracted from your earnings, there appears to be lots of money left over. No matter that most of that money goes for locked-in expenses like mortgage payments and real-estate taxes. The standard formula pretends that you really are living a bare-bones life. So it concludes that you have much more money to spend on college than, from your point of view, is actually the case.

Most middle- and upper-middle-income families will be shocked by the amount that the colleges expect them to pay. That's why you should start saving now. It will protect you from a lot of borrowing later. Even lower-income families will be pressed for as much as they can come up with.

THE BOTTOM LINE

The table on page 526 shows how much an average family was expected to contribute toward a college or university in 1997–98 under the federal rules. Here's how to use it:

• Look for your 1996 pretax income on the left. (What you're expected to pay for college generally depends on how much you earned in the *previous* year.)

• Read across to the column that best represents your current net worth, as the federal-aid formula counts it: the value of your savings, investments, and second home, minus your mortgage and other debts. Don't count the value of your principal home, family farm (if you live there), tax-deferred annuities, retirement plans, or life-insurance cash values. Count only 40 percent of the first $80,000 you hold in a family business.

• The figure in the crosshairs shows you roughly what the feds expect you to pay (your "EFC," or "expected family contribution"). If it covers the cost of the school that your child will attend, you can't expect any student aid. If it falls short, at least some federal aid should come your way.

• For years after 1997, guesstimate your payment this way: find your expected payment for 1997–98 and multiply that number by the subsequent growth in the consumer price index.

• When you have more than one child in college, your expected family contribution is divided among them, making each of them eligible for more aid. For example, if you have to pay $8,000 for one child, your expected contribution will be only $4,000 for each of two.

• On top of the parental contribution shown here, a contribution is expected from student earnings. There's a formula for calculating it (student earnings, minus taxes, minus $1,750, with half the remainder going toward the college bill). Other colleges expect a flat amount, such as $900 to $1,200 for the first year of school and $1,100 to $1,500 for each subsequent year.

• If your income is under $50,000 and you're eligible to file one of the two simple tax returns—the 1040EZ or 1040A—the feds don't count your assets when figuring what you're expected to pay. But private colleges probably will.

• This table is for a two-paycheck couple, with income only from employment and an allowance against net assets for two retirements. The older parent is 45. They take the standard deduction on their 1040 tax return and have two children, one of whom is in college.

THE PARENTAL CONTRIBUTION
(USE THIS AS A ROUGH GUIDE TO WHAT YOU MIGHT PAY)*

1996 INCOME	NET FAMILY ASSETS†						
	$40,000	$60,000	$80,000	$100,000	$120,000	$150,000	$200,000
$ 20,000	$ 0	$ 190	$ 718	$ 1,246	$ 1,774	$ 1,980	$ 3,507
$ 30,000	1,217	1,737	2,265	2,859	3,535	3,813	6,124
$ 40,000	2,827	3,487	4,254	5,145	6,170	6,610	9,430
$ 50,000	5,093	6,092	7,220	8,348	9,476	9,917	12,737
$ 60,000	8,089	9,200	10,328	11,456	12,584	13,040	15,860
$ 70,000	10,570	11,681	12,809	13,937	15,065	15,521	18,341
$ 80,000	13,557	14,668	15,796	16,924	18,052	18,508	21,328
$ 90,000	16,544	17,655	18,783	19,911	21,039	21,495	24,315
$100,000	19,530	20,642	21,770	22,898	24,026	24,481	27,301
$110,000	21,281	21,281	22,392	23,520	25,776	27,468	30,288
$120,000	24,181	24,181	25,292	26,420	28,676	30,068	33,188

* Federal Methodology, 1997–98. Most private schools use the Institutional Methodology, which counts more assets and generally results in a higher family contribution.
† Excluding home equity, annuities, life insurance cash values, and retirement plans.
SOURCE: The College Scholarship Service of the College Board

A one-paycheck couple with exactly the same income and assets would pay slightly more than the table shows. That's because the family doesn't have as many work-related expenses. A single parent would pay even more because he or she is presumed to have lower living expenses than a two-parent family. You'll also pay more if you're under 45 or have just one child. Older parents pay less, as do parents with more than two children.

• To estimate what some private colleges and universities will expect you to pay, take 5.6 percent of your home equity and add it to the appropriate figure in the table. Some colleges also include 5.6 percent of the value of your retirement plans, salary-deferral plan, tax-deferred annuities, and life-insurance cash values.

• Starting in 1999, these amounts will rise for people who take an education tax credit (page 527).

This table won't hit your contribution on the button, but you'll get a general idea.

For a Better Fix on What You'll Probably Have to Pay: Go to the College Board's Web site, http://www.collegeboard.org. You'll find a free calculator where you can enter your personal financial data. The earlier you start figuring your expected contribution, the better prepared you'll be when that day finally comes. For the free *EFC Formula Book* describing how your expected family contribution is calculated, write to the Federal Student Aid Information Center, P.O. Box 84, Washington, DC 20044. (Unfortunately, it isn't usually published as early as you'd like.)

HOW WILL YOU PAY?

You have five sources of funds:

Savings and Investments. This is by far the cheapest source of money. When you save in advance, you cover part of the tuition with money you earn from interest, dividends, and capital gains. To see the tremendous boost you get from starting early on college savings, see the table on page 183. Some of the savings can come from tax-favored plans (page 558).

Current Income. Spending current income reduces your standard of living for as long as the college bills last. Parents usually cut back on vacations and retirement-plan contributions. But at least it's over when it's over.

Loans. This is the most expensive source of funds because loan-interest payments hang around your neck for years. Young college graduates can probably handle the payments. They get low-interest loans and can look forward to a lifetime of rising incomes. Parents aren't so lucky. Loans mortgage their future at a time when they may not have many working years left.

Work. The work-study program is open to middle-income kids as well as the poor. It lets students earn some of their tuition by taking a job. But the income allowed under work-study may be limited. To earn more, a student will have to find a part-time job on campus or off.

Grants. Free money goes to students in the greatest need. But hardly anyone gets a totally free ride. Most eligible students get an aid package made up of low-interest loans and a work-study job, as well as a grant.

You have two types of tax credits (credits are deducted directly from your income-tax bill, dollar for dollar):

The HOPE Scholarship Credit—available during each of the first two academic years of school, to students enrolled at least half time. You get 100 percent of the first $1,000 you pay in tuition and fees and 50 percent of the second $1,000, for a total of $1,500. You can take a HOPE credit for each student in the family. Effective date: January 1, 1998. This credit puts students through many community colleges virtually free.

The Lifetime Learning Credit—available any year you're in school, for an unlimited number of years. From 1998 through 2002, you get up to $1,000 (20 percent of the first $5,000 paid in tuition and fees). Starting in 2003, you get up to $2,000 (20 percent of the first $10,000 paid in tuition and fees). This credit is available even for incidental study—say, a single course to improve your job skills. You get the same credit no matter how many students you have in school. Effective date: July 1, 1998.

The Eligibility Rules for Both of These Education Tax Credits:

• They're for you, your spouse, or your dependent child. If you're divorced and claim your child as your dependent but your spouse pays the tuition, neither of you gets the credit.

• They offset the amount you pay for tuition and eligible fees (after deducting any grants) at qualified institutions of higher learning—trade schools, community colleges, and four-year schools. You don't get credits for room and board.

• Singles get the full credit if their adjusted gross income is under $40,000. Over that amount, the credit shrinks; at $50,000, it phases out entirely. Marrieds get the full credit up to $80,000; it phases out at $100,000.

• You can't use both credits at once for the same child. But you can use different credits simultaneously for different children.

• You can't claim a tax credit for a particular child in a year you take money out of an education IRA (page 558) for that same child. Nor can you use it in a year you take Series EE bond money tax free (page 565). But you can combine the credits with withdrawals from prepaid education plans (page 567) or nondeductible IRAs and 401(k)s. You can also take a tax credit for one child and an education IRA for another.

• When you claim your child as a dependent, the credits go on your tax return, not the child's. When the student is independent, the student gets the credit if he or she also pays the tuition.

Starting in 2002, the income limits and HOPE credit amounts will be adjusted for inflation.

How to Make the Best Use of These Credits.
Students entering college in the fall might take the Lifetime Learning credit the first calendar year, use the HOPE credit the second year (for the second semester of the first academic year), use the HOPE credit the third year (the first semester of the second academic year), then go back to Lifetime Learning.

Students entering a low-tuition community college in the fall might prepay the second-semester tuition before year end. That maximizes what they spend in a calendar year, giving them the largest possible HOPE.

You don't have to pay with cash to qualify for a credit. You can pay with the proceeds of a loan.

If you have an education IRA, try to use it all at once. That way, you'll lose only one year of tax credits.

After 2002, parents with just one child in school who pay more than $7,500 in tuition and fees will do better with the Lifetime Learning credit every year, forgetting the HOPE. Parents with more than one student will do better with the HOPE.

Graduate students and adults in continuing education can use Lifetime Learning every year.

A MATTER OF FORM(S)

Check the catalogues or the Web sites of the colleges that interest you to see which financial-aid forms they want.

Every applicant has to fill in a FAFSA—a Free Application for Federal Student Aid. You'll find the forms at high schools, college financial-aid offices, or by calling 800-4-FED-AID. Or file by computer via FAFSA Express. To get FAFSA software, call 800-801-0576 or download it from the government's Web site at http://www.ed.gov. When you file electronically, you still have to mail in a signature page.

For most state colleges and universities and some private colleges, the FAFSA is enough. Many private colleges, however, also ask you to complete a Financial Aid PROFILE provided by the College Scholarship Service (ask at your high school or college; call the CSS at 800-778-6888; or check the Web site at http://www.collegeboard.org/profile.html). PROFILE covers all the FAFSA questions and goes on to ask about family assets and income that the FAFSA ignores. You pay $5 to register plus $14.50 for each school that will receive the report.

Some colleges use their own financial-aid form. Get it immediately. To delay is to lose.

Some states require separate forms for state financial-aid programs. They'll be at your high school guidance office or college-aid office.

FIVE STEPS TO COLLEGE AID

STEP ONE. Get the FAFSA (see previous section) plus whichever other financial-aid forms each college wants, fill them in (ideally, in December), keep copies for yourself, and mail or e-mail the originals as soon as possible after January 1.

Don't drag your feet! Your aid application has to go through a processing firm before it's passed on to the college. Most colleges have early deadlines for having the material in hand, like February 15. Early-decision students may have to file PROFILEs by October or November. Federal Pell Grants (the government's leading grant program, page 536) and Federal Stafford Loans (the leading loan program, page 541) are always available to qualified students. But if you apply late, the money in the other programs may be used up. A trough that was full in February may be empty by April. You want to get your nose in first.

The forms have the same grim feel as an income-tax return.

First, you give personal data about yourself and your family. Then you put down all your taxable and nontaxable income. Next you add up certain assets—bank accounts, mutual funds, family businesses, investment real estate. Then the student weighs in with his or her own income and assets. If the student is married, the spouse has to report, too.

That's for federal aid. Most private schools also ask for home equity and may even pry into retirement plans, life-insurance cash values, salary-deferral plans, and tax-deferred annuities. They may want to know if any relatives can be expected to help. You might also be asked about any unusual expenses, such as private-school tuition for younger children or unreimbursed medical bills. (If the form doesn't cover these expenses, mention them in a separate letter. Mention any other circumstances that impinge on your ability to pay—for example, that one breadwinner had to quit work to take care of an ailing grandparent, or you have a child in graduate school, or you're carrying high debts because of a previous business failure or bout of unemployment.)

Leave no questions blank unless the form specifically tells you to. If something doesn't apply to you, write 0 (zero) where the answer should go. Otherwise, the people who process the forms will have to check back with you, which holds up your paperwork. Be sure to enter the code number for every school and state-aid agency that should receive the report. If the form is illegible in spots, filled in incorrectly, or left unsigned, you'll get it back, which means that your schools might get it late.

Do your tax return early so you'll know how much you earned. That also simplifies the job of filling in the financial-aid form because many of the questions are keyed to lines on the 1040 or 1040A. (You don't actually have to file your tax return early if you don't want to; just fill it in and use the data to help you apply for college aid.)

If the W-2 form from your employer is late, don't wait for it. Make a close estimate of your income so that you can mail the aid form on time. Send the college your exact earnings later. You may be asked for your tax return as verification.

If you need help completing the form—and thousands of families do —ask for it at your high school guidance office or college financial-aid office. For toll-free help from the government, call 800-4-FED-AID. For on-line help, go to http://www.ed.gov/prog_info/SFA/FAFSA/index.html.

STEP TWO. Watch the mail. An aid-processing center is now analyzing your ability to pay. The FAFSA generates a personal Student Aid Report (SAR), used to determine what you'll get in federal grants and loans. You should receive it within four weeks (about one week if you filed electronically). If you don't, call the Federal Student Aid Information Center (800-4-FED-AID) and ask what's happening. If you filed a PROFILE you should get an acknowledgment within three weeks, along with a report showing all the data on the form.

Check the data on the SAR and the PROFILE report to be sure that the processor hasn't made any mistakes. Return the form to the processor only if there's an error or if you want the financial report sent to some colleges that weren't originally on your list. Call the schools to be sure that the data was received.

Your report will show the all-important federal "EFC"—expected family contribution—the minimum the colleges will expect you to pay. Look for it on the SAR in the upper-right-hand corner. It will say, for example, "EFC12500"—meaning that you'll have to come up with at least $12,500 this year. An asterisk next to this amount means the college will ask for verification of the income and assets you reported. If you're applying to a private college or university, the PROFILE result will probably show that you'll have to pay an even higher amount.

STEP THREE. Wait to hear. The college's own office of financial aid establishes a budget for each student, depending on whether he or she is single, married, living in a dorm, apartment, or at home, and so on. If you have extra expenses—say, medical expenses for a chronic condition—ask if the college will build them in. Some schools are generous, others stingy.

From that budget, the school subtracts the money that parents and student are expected to pay. Any gap between the student's budget and your total family contribution is your "financial need." That can be filled with grants and loans from the feds, your state, and the college's own funds. The aid office decides which resources to tap and in what order.

A few schools accept the students they want, then fill their financial needs in full. If you're $8,000 short that year, that's what you'll get in aid.

Others won't accept you unless they can afford to provide all the aid you need. At these schools, your ability to pay is one of the factors the admissions office weighs.

Many schools give full aid to some applicants while leaving others hanging. For example, a student with an $8,000 need may be offered only $5,000 worth of help. You go on a waiting list for the missing $3,000. If the money doesn't come through, you'll have to raise it yourself. The school might assume that you'll use a PLUS loan to fill the gap (page 542). If you won't or can't, you'll have to choose some other school.

Most schools offer aid to certain super-bright kids who don't officially qualify for it. For information on no-need scholarships, see page 540.

STEP FOUR. Accept, reject, or appeal. If you qualify for aid, your package will reflect how badly the school wants you. The greater its interest, the more you'll be offered in free grants. Students further down the list will be offered smaller grants and larger loans.

Telephone the school if the aid package is too small and you think that something has been overlooked. Maybe a parent died suddenly. Maybe a competing school has made a better offer and you're hoping your first-choice school will match it (if it really wants you, it will). Any change that raises your grant and lowers your loan puts money in your pocket. Often, however, the package stands. It *always* stands if your only complaint is, "I can't afford it." No one can afford it.

STEP FIVE. Return to "Go." Every year you have to suffer through this process all over again. Your eligibility for aid may change. The mix of loans and grants may change. If you filled in a FAFSA, you should get a partly preprinted Renewal FAFSA between late November and January 1. If you don't, call the college-aid office and ask for advice.

FIVE WAYS OF IMPROVING YOUR SHOT AT AID

1. Don't ask for an early-admissions decision. Early-decision students have declared themselves. They want this school and no other. The school knows you'll come even if your aid package is mediocre. So it probably will be.

2. Apply to schools in pairs—say, two similar private colleges and two similar universities. If you get a better award from your second-choice school, your first-choice school may be willing to match it—especially if the two schools are competing for the same kinds of students.

3. Apply to schools where you're in the top 25 percent academically. They'll want you more than schools that see you as marginal.

4. Athletes should apply to schools whose teams are in their ability range. You don't have to be a top athlete to get an athletic scholarship—just better than average and an asset to the team. Write to the school's coach and have your high school coach write, too, detailing your letters, victories, and value to the team. And remember: colleges need tennis and lacrosse players just as much as they need footballers.

5. See what your own state has to offer. You can often get more aid at an in-state school than you can by going out of state.

One Sure Way of Losing Aid (for Men 18 to 25). Fail to register for the Selective Service. Federal aid goes only to men who have registered (unless you're exempt and can prove it). No one is being drafted today; this law is a holdover from the riotous Vietnam era when Congress decided that draft protestors ought to be punished. Aid forms are computer-matched against selective-service lists, to catch artful dodgers. You're supposed to register within 6 months of turning 18. You can do it by checking a box on the FAFSA. Late registrants aren't being prosecuted.

FOR PARENTS ONLY

What If You're Having a Fight with Your Kid and Refuse to Pay for College or Fill in a Financial-Aid Form? The child is usually stuck. In almost all cases, the college won't award any aid without financial information from the parents. Otherwise, everyone would "fight"!

What If You're a Divorced Single Parent? If the child lives with you, he or she can apply for federal aid based on your income alone. But most colleges will want to see the other parent's income, too, before dispensing the aid they administer themselves. If the other parent won't cooperate, the child might not qualify for much.

What If You're a Stepparent? Your income is counted right along with that of the blood parent.

What If You Don't Want Your Children to Know How Much You Earn? You could fill in the form privately and simply tell your child to sign. But the Student Aid Report, showing all the financial data, comes back to the child. I suppose you could hang around the mailbox and intercept it, but your secret probably can't be kept.

What If You Don't Want to Show Anyone Your Tax Returns? You may have no option. The college might insist on seeing tax returns as a condition of granting aid.

What If You're Unemployed or About to Be? Tell the financial-aid office. Normally, colleges use last year's income when figuring what they expect you to pay. But they can use this year's projected income if you or your spouse is out of work.

FOR INDEPENDENT STUDENTS

If you're an independent student, you can apply for aid based on your own income rather than on that of your parents. The sons and daughters of the middle classes often try to "go independent" because that could qualify them for more help. By contrast, students from low-income families might get more help if they file as dependents rather than as independents.

You are generally considered independent if you'll be 24 by December 31 of the year the grant will be awarded. This is true even if you're living at home on your parents' dole and even if you're taken as a dependent on their income-tax return. (When you're living at home, however, some schools may decide to count family income as part of your financial resources. This won't affect your eligibility for federal aid but will make it harder to qualify for aid controlled directly by the college.)

If you're under 24, you're independent if:

- You're an orphan or ward of the court (or were a ward of the court until 18).
- You're a veteran of the armed forces.
- You're married.
- You're in graduate school.
- You have legal dependents other than a spouse.
- You're declared independent by a financial-aid officer because of special circumstances.

WHERE THE LOOPHOLES ARE

You can manipulate the financial-aid form in your favor. Of two families with exactly the same income and assets, one child may qualify for somewhat more assistance simply because the parents used all the available loopholes. It's unfair but not illegal. Still, I'd discourage you from trying it because—counting all the costs—the game usually isn't worth the candle. Besides, your aid package depends mainly on the size of your income rather than the value of your assets. Check it out, on the table on page 526.

Here's what parents try, and the drawbacks:

1. *Reduce the size of your reported assets.* You can do this (without lying) because the federal financial-aid form asks about some assets but not others. You have to disclose your bank accounts, stocks, bonds, mutual funds, investment real estate, and family business—but not the value of your principal home or family farm, or the money saved in tax-deferred annuities, life-insurance policies, and retirement plans (only your current year's contribution is counted). If you took $20,000 out of the bank and invested it in a tax-deferred annuity, you would suddenly look $20,000 "poorer." That might qualify you for an extra $1,120 in aid.

But—Private colleges and universities have their own questionnaires that ask about these hidden assets. So you might have bought that tax-deferred annuity for nothing. Even if the school doesn't ask, you can't be sure that you'll get more aid. Even if you do, the annuity may have cost you more than your child got in additional aid. Worst of all, by buying annuities or insurance policies, you have put your cash out of easy reach. If you need this money to help pay for tuition, you'll owe taxes and maybe penalties on the withdrawals.

2. *Low-ball the value of your house.* The private-college aid forms ask what you paid for your house and what it's worth now. It's expected to have risen in value by a certain amount, based on a national housing index. Parents may report that their house just matches the average, even if it did better.

But—you don't know exactly what the housing index calls for. Some colleges use regional indexes rather than the national one. If you guess too low, you will unleash some embarrassing questions. People caught cheating may hurt their child's chance of admission.

3. *Avoid taking capital gains from the year before college starts until your child's last year in school.* Your realized gains are reported as income, which the college will tap more heavily than it taps the value of unsold investments.

But—What if you felt that some of your stocks were overpriced, but you failed to sell lest it affect your student aid? If stock prices slump and you need the money for tuition, you'll have to sell for less.

4. *Take strategic loans.* Say you need $20,000 to buy a new car. Don't go for a regular auto loan. Instead, borrow against your home. Reducing your home equity reduces your reported assets on the aid forms of private colleges, making you look $20,000 poorer. You can also reduce your assets by buying the car for cash.

But—Shrinking your assets by $20,000 makes a negligible difference to your eligibility for student aid. With luck, you might pick up $1,120, but there's a risk you'll get no extra aid at all. Even if your aid package is indeed $1,120 heavier, the extra money might come in the form of a student loan that has to be repaid. If you need a car anyway, borrowing against home equity is often the cheapest way of financing it. But don't run up unnecessary loans just to add a few hundred dollars in college aid.

5. *Save college money in your own name, not in your child's.* Almost all of a child's savings are expected to be spent for four years of education, whereas only part of a parent's are. Assume, for example, that you put aside $18,000 for tuition. If it's in your daughter's bank account, the college will take $6,300 in the first year, or 35 percent. But if it's in your bank account, the college will take about $1,008, or 5.6 percent. This holds down the money you're forced to spend and may qualify your child for more student aid.

But—This helps only those families who are likely to get aid in the first place. If you're over the income limit, it's smarter to keep at least some assets in the child's name because the child will pay lower taxes on the earnings (page 89). If you saved in the child's name and have come to regret it, too bad. That money is the child's, not yours. You could reduce those assets, however, by using them for things the child needs—perhaps a computer or a car to take to school (although private colleges will count the car as an asset).

6. *Attend college part-time.* If a parent enrolls in a college degree–granting program at least half-time, the amount he or she is expected to contribute to the child's education at a state college or university may be cut in half. A $6,000 contribution, for example, could be reduced to only $3,000. That might qualify your child for additional federal aid—and, for that matter, the parent, too.

But—At private colleges, the aid officer normally doesn't follow this formula. Your child may get no increase in aid, leaving you saddled with two expensive tuition bills. Besides, who can afford a second tuition when you're already worried about the first?

7. *Manipulate your small-business income.* Farmers and small-business owners have a lot of holes for hiding income in.

But—Many private colleges have special small-business forms asking about dividends and assets. Financial-aid officers doubt claims that a family business isn't throwing off a living wage.

8. *Hire an accountant or financial planner to carry out all these dodges.* This one calls for a five-but answer.

But—It costs money to play asset games. You pay a fee to the accountant or planner, then pay a sales commission for the life insurance or annuity that he or she recommends. Your expenses could easily exceed what you pick up in college aid. The annuity may not even be a good investment.

But—You lose ready access to some of your money, which you may still need for college bills. For example, there's a 10 percent penalty for any funds withdrawn from a tax-deferred annuity before age 59½.

But—There's no guarantee that your efforts will yield any extra aid at all, or anything to speak of. The size of your college-aid package is driven mostly by the level of your income rather than the size of your net assets.

But—You may ruin your child's chances of getting any financial aid at all. "Every family has one opportunity to tell the complete truth," one aid officer told me. "If I catch anything, I put that application at the bottom of the heap and look at it again only if I have any money left." By contrast, aid officers can be tremendous advocates for students whose families play it straight.

But—Manipulating your assets is unfair to the spirit of the student-aid system. Whether to do so is more than a financial issue. It's a conscience call.

Tell the Truth on Your App! About 30 percent of the federal forms are selected for verification against tax returns and other data. If you're caught lying, it will ruin your chances for any discretionary aid. You can even be fined and sent to prison (you won't be, but you might as well know the very worst).

GRANT ME A GRANT

A grant is the college subsidy of choice. It's free money. You don't work for it and no one wants it back. Here's what's around:

• For undergraduates, the largest single source of grants is Uncle Sugar—most of whose money is reserved for the poor. At this writing, the government's Federal Pell Grants ran to a maximum of $3,000 for the lowest-income undergraduates. The size declines as family income rises. If your family earns $35,000 to $40,000, a Pell might provide no more than $400. Pells are generally available to full-time or half-time students at accredited academic, technical, or vocational institutions (this even includes certain correspondence courses). You apply for a Pell and all other federal aid automatically when you fill in the FAFSA (page 529).

• Federal Supplemental Educational Opportunity Grants (FSEOGs) are dispensed through college-aid offices to especially low-income people who have no hope of raising other funds. Awards run from $100 to as much as $4,000 a year, with the biggest ones going to the truly poor. Like Pells, FSEOGs go only to undergraduates.

• The Federal Work-Study Program isn't exactly free money because you have to take an approved job. But you don't have to pay anything back. Work-study, administered by the college-aid office, is often open to middle-income students as well as the poor and graduate students as well as undergraduates. You work until you've earned your full award—say, $1,000—then the job is over. To earn more money, you'll have to find a different job.

• You can volunteer for AmeriCorps, working in nonprofit and community organizations for up to 2 years. You'll earn a modest living allowance (about $7,500 a year) plus an annual $4,725 credit toward college costs (generally $2,362.50 if you work part time). That credit can be used at any college or graduate school, or to pay down federal student loans. For information, call 800-94-ACORPS.

• The states make awards, mostly to state residents going to in-state schools (although some states offer reciprocity to each other's students). A few awards are based entirely on merit. Most target financial need. For information, talk to your high school guidance office or college financial-aid office.

• Colleges make need-based grants in the form of tuition discounts. Instead of charging you, say, the $12,000 you're supposed to pay, they may settle for only $7,000. *One warning:* You'll get the most aid in your freshman year. Once you're committed, some schools will start shaving your grant, giving you a little less money every year. Before choosing a college, ask about its policy on aid renewal. If your aid package gets too small, think about transferring.

• Special grants often go to scholars, musicians, and other students with unusual talents, even when they have no financial need (page 540).

• You can sometimes give yourself a grant equivalent by:

✔ Taking Advanced Placement courses in high school. If the college gives you credit for them (check this point before applying), you might get through school in six or seven semesters rather than the traditional eight. That saves you a bundle.

✔ Using the College-Level Examination Program (CLEP). Many schools extend college credit to people who pass these proficiency exams.

For information about the program, contact CLEP at P.O. Box 6600, Princeton, NJ 08541 (609-771-7835). Ask the schools you're applying to whether they accept CLEP credits. You'll find a list of the schools at http://www.collegeboard.org/clep/html/indx001.html.

✔ Going to a junior college for two years, at a low price, then transferring to a full-term college for your last two years. Just be sure that all your course credits are transferable, so you won't have to stay an extra semester at the second school.

✔ Living more cheaply off campus than on. Or living at home for a couple of years.

✔ Taking courses in the summer for credits that can be applied to your degree. Enough of these courses might save you a whole semester.

✔ Attending a college that lets you get your bachelor's degree in three years instead of four.

✔ Getting external college credits—by mail, through public TV courses, even on the Internet. For a summary of these programs, get *College Degrees by Mail* by John Bear, $12.95 from Ten Speed Press, P.O. Box 7123, Berkeley, CA 94707 (800-841-2665); also look at three Peterson's publications (800-338-3282): *The Independent Study Catalog*, $16.25, for correspondence courses; *Distance Learning*, $24.95, for college and university programs available through television, computer, and audio or videocassette; and *Virtual College*, $9.95, a discussion of how to choose a distance learning course. (Those are all 1997 prices.)

• Computerized college scholarship services offer to tap you into a running river of private scholarships, many of them (they claim) unused. That's baloney. First, they haven't a clue how much is actually "unused." Second, most "unused" grants are those available to corporate employees, which you couldn't qualify for anyway.

You pay these phony services maybe $45 to $200 and get back a printout supposedly tailored to your personal profile. For most students, that's money down the drain. Many of the scholarships won't apply to you. Many will be too small to make much difference ($500 or so). Many you knew about anyway (like Pell Grants). Many are available only for specific colleges that you might not want to attend. The deadlines for entering may have passed. Even if you find a substantial award, it may not reduce the amount your family is expected to contribute toward your college education (see next section)! You're better off putting your time into researching colleges with good grant and loan programs.

If you insist on searching, do it yourself, by Web. Many high schools and colleges subscribe to computerized databases you can use. You'll find a free service at http://www.collegeboard.org. Another service, http://www.fastweb.com, is free at this writing, but you may have to let your name be sold to advertisers. I tried them both, in the name of a hypothetical freshman. The College Board sent more awards, but neither sent anything juicy and some of the scholarships didn't apply.

The Delusion of Private Scholarships

You see it every year: thousands of students competing for hundreds of private scholarships offered by foundations, clubs, corporations, and civic groups. The kids do science projects, enter debates, write essays on "America, My Home." They turn the pages of huge directories of scholarships or send $100 to a computer outfit to find scholarships for them. Some awards are based on merit; most take financial need into consideration.

Let's say you win one. Everyone cheers. There's a formal presentation and you get your picture in the newspaper.

Then what?

Your college may effectively take your scholarship away. One common way of doing so is to reduce your college grant, dollar for dollar, by any outside scholarship you win.

Say, for example, that your college costs $14,000, of which you're expected to pay $8,000, leaving a $6,000 gap. To plug that gap, the college offers a $4,000 grant and a $2,000 loan. You then win a $1,000 Mothers' Club scholarship. Result: The college takes $1,000 out of your grant. Your total aid package remains the same, but the college is putting up $3,000, not $4,000. What happens to the college's $1,000? It goes to some other needy student. Your efforts assisted someone else.

The colleges say it isn't their fault. Under the rules for awarding aid, all your sources of income have to be taken into account—and an outside scholarship is a source of income.

So why bother writing essays? I see several possibilities:

1. When you don't qualify for college aid. A merit award would indeed reduce the amount you have to pay yourself.

2. When a college has admitted you without giving you all the aid you need. It might let you keep any scholarship you capture privately.

3. When the college is giving you both a grant and a loan. The aid officer might reduce your loan by the amount of your outside scholarship, rather than your grant. So when you graduate, you'll be less in debt.

4. When your aid package includes work-study. The school might let you substitute the outside scholarship for the job. That would leave you more time to study (or play).

So writing essays can't hurt—*after* you've pursued all of the standard sources. At the very least, you'll get a citation and a kiss from your mother. And one of the colleges you apply to might treat you generously. If you have a favorite college, ask how it handles outside scholarships before putting yourself out.

Money for Rich Kids

Not all grants are based on financial need. Certain highly desired students can also find aid, even if they come from well-to-do families.

"No-need" scholarships are offered by colleges that want to upgrade the quality of their student bodies. They're buying brains, just as the Big Ten colleges buy quarterbacks.

You needn't be a genius to qualify. At some schools, money is available to any student with a B average, a spot in the top third of his or her high school class, and above-average scores on one of the college testing programs (for 1996, that meant more than 1,013, combined math and verbal, on the Scholastic Assessment Test or more than a composite score of 20.9 on the American College Testing program). The better schools look for B-plus or A averages, SATs exceeding 1,250, or ACT scores over 27.

Certain colleges also make no-need awards to students with special skills, like acting or music. And, of course, there are always athletic scholarships—with more offered to women than used to be the case.

Some states offer no-need awards to honor students attending a private college in state.

For a rundown of what's available at about 1,300 schools, send for *The A's and B's of Academic Scholarships,* at this writing $9.50 from Octameron Associates, P.O. Box 2748, Alexandria, VA 22301. Some are tiny grants, maybe $200 or $300. But others run to $1,000 or more, sometimes even topping $10,000.

You won't find the nation's most prestigious colleges giving no-need money. They attract all the talent they can handle. But the second-rank schools are begging for brains.

Be sure to ask if the award is renewable. Some schools pay you to come but don't pay you to stay. Also, look for schools that have special honors programs, so your brains won't go to waste.

Scholarships and Taxes

Grants for tuition, books, fees, supplies, and equipment are still tax-free for students working toward a degree. But any money you get for room and board should be reported as taxable income. Ditto for grants or tuition reductions given in return for teaching or other services to the school. Research assistantships may be tax-free, however, because you're helping only the professor, not necessarily the school.

LEND ME A LOAN

The cheapest loans go directly to students, courtesy of the state and federal governments. Students can borrow without collateral, co-signers, or credit histories. The special loans for parents carry higher interest rates and borrowers have to pass a credit check. Interest is tax deductible up to certain limits (page 544). But even nondeductible loans are interesting, because loan rates are low and repayment terms attractive.

Here are your choices:

1. The program you call student loans and the government calls Federal Stafford Loans. Staffords come in two flavors:

• Subsidized Staffords, for students whose FAFSA forms show that they're eligible for aid. The government pays the interest while you're in school and for the following 6 months. After that, you pay.

• Unsubsidized Staffords, for students whose income makes them ineligible for aid. You're responsible for the interest. You can put off making interest payments while you're in school, letting your debt compound. Or you can pay as you go (a sounder choice, financially).

Interest payments aside, these two types of loans work exactly the same way. The interest rate is variable: 3.1 percent over the rate for 91-day Treasuries, adjusted annually, with a cap of 8.25 percent. Principal repayments don't have to start until 6 months after you leave school. Once established, your monthly payment is usually fixed; changing interest rates may merely lengthen or shorten the repayment term. Usual repayment period: 5 to 10 years, although payments can be stretched over as many as 30 years.

Staffords are available through some banks, S&Ls, credit unions, state loan-guarantee agencies, or around 1,400 institutions of higher learning. (The Staffords you secure through your schools are called Direct Loans, meaning they come directly from the government without using a bank as the source of funds.) You can use student loans for trade schools as well as academic studies, although government-backed funds can't be used at schools that have had super-high loan-default rates.

Apply for a Stafford as soon as your college accepts you—either through the college (for students whose schools make Direct Loans) or through the lender you choose. You'll generally pay 4 percent in insurance and loan-origination fees. You can pay it in cash or add it to the loan amount.

Check the following table for the maximum you can borrow each year. These amounts are reduced for students attending less than full-time. You may also get less if you receive other forms of financial aid.

2. Low-income students might get a Federal Perkins Loan at only 5 percent interest. But you can't apply for it on your own. It's awarded by the college as part of a package of financial aid. Undergraduates can normally borrow as much as $3,000 a year, to a maximum of $15,000. Graduates get $5,000 a year, to a maximum of $30,000 (minus any Perkins money they took as undergraduates). At most schools, average Perkins loans are lower than the maximum, but at some schools you can borrow a bit more (up to $4,000 for undergrads and $6,000 for grads). The government pays the interest while you're in school and for the following 9 months. Then repay-

HOW MUCH UNCLE STAFFORD WILL LEND

	FRESHMEN	SOPHOMORES	JUNIORS	SENIORS	FIFTH YEAR	TOTAL
Dependent undergraduates	$2,625	$3,500	$ 5,500	$ 5,500	$ 5,500	$23,000
Independent undergraduates and dependent undergrads whose parents don't qualify for PLUS loans*	6,625	7,500	10,500	10,500	10,500	46,000
Graduate students	$18,500 each year †					138,500‡

* Typically, you're given the maximum subsidized Stafford; any additional money you borrow comes in the form of an unsubsidized Stafford.
† The first $8,500 is a subsidized Stafford; the rest is an unsubsidized Stafford.
‡ Including your undergraduate loan.

ments begin. Normally, you make payments over the next 10 years, although that period can be extended.

3. If student loans aren't enough, parents can borrow from the government, too, under a program known as PLUS—Parent Loans for Undergraduate Students. You can borrow up to the total cost of your child's education, minus any student aid awarded. You do have to pass a credit check. But the government doesn't evaluate your debt load or your ability to repay, so use this largesse with care.

PLUS loans are available from private lenders and directly through many colleges. The interest rate floats at 3.1 points over the rate for one-year Treasury bills, with a 9 percent cap. Normal loan term: 5 to 10 years, although payments can be extended. Fee: up to 4 percent. Repayments start within 60 days of the final loan disbursement for that academic year. No deferrals are normally allowed. That's just as well. No sense letting this debt build up.

4. Some states offer terrific loans at low interest rates. Out-of-state students might even qualify. The college financial-aid office will know.

5. State college-loan agencies may cut special deals with students who want to be teachers. If, after two years in the classroom, you can't stand the little darlings one moment longer, you can switch to another field without penalty.

6. If you're training for one of the health professions, Uncle Sugar really rolls out the cart. You'll find loans for doctors, nurses, dentists, optometrists, public health officers, podiatrists, veterinarians, pharmacists, physical therapists, and others. Any medical or professional school will have a full list.

7. The college may offer you a loan of its own, at low or no interest.

Or it may send you the brochures of one or more commercial lenders who offer a variety of installment plans.

8. Here are five commercial-loan sources that offer unsecured loans for both undergraduates and graduate students, either directly or through participating lenders. All give you the option of deferring principal repayments while the student is in school. (1) The Education Resources Institute, 330 Stuart St., Boston, MA 02116 (800-255-TERI); (2) University Support Services, 205 Van Buren St., Suite 200, Herndon, VA 22070 (800-GO-PLATO or http://www.uss.org/plato.htm); (3) Nellie Mae (New England Education Loan Marketing Corporation), 50 Braintree Hill Park, Braintree, MA 02184 (800-9-TUITION or http://www.nelliemae.org); (4) The College Board, with loans administered by Key Education Resources, 745 Atlantic Ave., Suite 300, Boston, MA 02111 (800-KEY-LEND or http://www.collegeboard. org)—the loan you can defer is called ExtraTime; (5) Sallie Mae (Student Loan Marketing Association), 1050 Thomas Jefferson St. N.W., Washington, DC 20007 (800-643-0040 or http://www.salliemae.com).

Most of these programs require you to pay interest currently, even though you've deferred repaying principal. TERI's program for graduate students lets you defer interest payments, too.

Compare rates and fees before signing up. Some lenders charge more than others. Also compare payback plans to see if you get a rate break for repaying on time (page 546).

Then look at what the government charges for a PLUS loan. PLUS is often the better deal. PLUS also applies looser credit standards than the private programs do.

Don't defer payments if you can possibly afford it. In fact, try to prepay. You want to get rid of this debt so that your retirement won't be encumbered.

9. Homeowners should borrow against their home equities, once they've maxed out on deductible loans at lower rates (page 248). Here, the interest is tax deductible on loans up to $100,000.

10. Your college may send you brochures for one or more commercial tuition plans. These plans convert the twice-a-year lump-sum payments required by many schools into 12 equal monthly installments. There may also be 5- to 15-year payment plans at variable interest rates. Tuition plans generally include life and disability insurance. If you die or become totally disabled, all the rest of your child's college bills will be paid in full. A leader in the field is Key Education Resources, 745 Atlantic Ave., Suite 300, Boston, MA 02111 (800-KEY-LEND).

As a homemade alternative to Key-type plans, consider this: Pay the college bill by borrowing at the lowest interest rates you can. Buy more term life insurance to guarantee your child's education if you die, and pray that you won't become disabled. (If you do become disabled, your child will qualify for much more student aid.)

What's Tax Deductible? Here are the rules:

• Interest can be deductible on loans taken for your own education, that of your spouse, or that of a dependent. Exception: you can't deduct interest on loans given by relatives.

• You get the deduction even if you don't itemize on your tax returns.

• The maximum deduction goes to singles with adjusted gross incomes under $40,000 and marrieds under $60,000. As incomes rise, the deduction declines, phasing out at $55,000 for singles and $75,000 for marrieds. After 2002, these income levels will be adjusted for inflation.

• You can deduct up to $1,000 in 1998, $1,500 in 1999, $2,000 in 2000, and $2,500 in 2001 and each year thereafter.

• You can take the deduction only for interest paid during the first five years in which payments are required. If you started repayments in 1996, for example, you get the deduction only through 2000. Don't count any months that the loan is in deferral with no interest due.

• If the student is your dependent, the deduction goes on your tax return. When students are independent and paying their own loans, however, the deduction goes on their returns.

Reduce Your Interest Rate. Several private programs will lower your rate on Stafford loans if you always pay on time. Ask about it before borrowing. The discount is offered through the following funding sources, which lend directly or will give you a lender's name.

• Nellie Mae (New England Education Loan Marketing Corporation, 50 Braintree Hill Park, Braintree, MA 02184, 800-9-TUITION or http://www.nelliemae.org) takes off 0.25 percent if you authorize monthly transfers from your bank account. If you make your first 48 payments on time, you have two further choices: (1) Ask Nellie Mae to make your last 6 monthly payments for you (the best choice for people who don't plan to prepay); or (2) ask for a 2 percent reduction in your rate for the remainder of the term (choose this if you plan to save money by prepaying your loan). These rate breaks apply to new borrowers, not to people seeking to consolidate their loans.

• Sallie Mae (Student Loan Marketing Association, 1050 Thomas Jefferson St. N.W., Washington, DC 20007, 800-643-0040 or http://www.salliemae.com) takes off 0.25 percent if you authorize monthly transfers from your bank account. If you make the first 24 payments on time, your account will earn a cash bonus. If you make the first 48 payments on time, you can lower your interest rate by 2 percentage points for the remaining term of the loan. If you consolidate your loans with Sallie Mae (page 546) and make the first 48 payments on time, your rate will drop by one percentage point. This applies to Staffords, PLUS loans, and any other government-backed education loans. Your monthly payments don't drop. Instead, you pay off the loan in a shorter period of time.

• USA Group (P.O. Box 6180, Indianapolis, IN 46206, 800-LOAN-USA or http://www.usagroup.com) takes off 0.25 percent if you authorize monthly transfers from your bank account. If you make the first 48 payments on time, your interest rate drops by 2 percentage points for the remaining term of the loan. You can use the savings either to reduce the size of your monthly payments or reduce the term of the loan.

Should You Borrow from Your Company Savings Plan?

Don't borrow from your retirement plan to pay tuition if you can possibly avoid it (page 262). Borrow against your house instead. If you don't have that option, however, your retirement plan is a source to consider. Borrow if the plan gives you better terms than you'd get from a commercial student-loan program or from a bank.

Who Should Borrow, Parent or Student?

Where there's a choice, I vote for the student. Students' debts aren't nearly as unmanageable as most people think. Two studies in California found that fewer than 5 percent of the college seniors who borrow will actually wind up in trouble. Average indebtedness remains low relative to starting salaries. As the salaries of college graduates rise, student loans get easier to repay. Defaults are high among low-income students who attend trade schools but generally not among the graduates of community colleges and four-year institutions.

When parents take on debt, they're looking at a repayment obligation lasting 5 to 10 years. That may take them right to the edge of retirement and beyond, reducing their nest egg and permanently lowering their standard of living in old age. I know that no sacrifice is too great, etcetera, etcetera. But the plain fact is that the young people are better placed than the old to eliminate debt and still build a comfortable future for themselves.

Besides, it's the students who gain the most from the education. So why shouldn't they shoulder more of the price?

Loan Consolidation: Yes or No?

Oppressed by the size of your student-loan payments? Tired of writing several checks a month to repay your various loans? There's a way out. As long as you're out of school, you can consolidate your debt.

Consolidation takes all your government-backed student loans—all your Staffords and Perkins and any loans you've taken for studies in the health professions—and packs them into a single loan with a single monthly payment. The new term is 10 to 30 years, so you lower the amount you have to pay each month. PLUS loans can be consolidated, too (except in the government's income-contingent plan, page 546). You can even "consolidate" a single loan. You don't have to put up any collateral or even pass a credit check. Consolidation loans are granted on your signature alone.

Both the government and private lenders offer consolidation plans. The government charges variable rates, capped at 8.25 percent for Staffords and 9 percent for PLUS loans. Rates at private lenders are generally fixed. There are no other fees. Private lenders may set minimums for consolidating (you need at least $7,500 in loans to go to Sallie Mae). If you're not comfortable with the repayment plan you chose, you can switch to another lender's plan. Direct Loan borrowers can consolidate only through the government's plan, but you'll be offered plenty of choices (for information, call the government's Loan Origination Center, 800-557-7392).

Your Repayment Choices:

1. *An extended repayment plan.* This reduces your monthly payments by stretching them over a longer term. How long depends on how much you owe.

2. *A graduated repayment plan.* You repay over the same length of time allowed in the extended plan. But your payments start low and rise every 2 years, on a fixed schedule. This arrangement works well if your first job pays peanuts but your income gradually goes up. If it doesn't, you can escape higher payments by switching to another plan.

3. *A standard repayment plan.* You make fixed monthly payments of at least $50, to pay off your loan in a maximum of 10 years.

4. *An income-sensitive plan,* offered by private lenders. It's for people who borrowed heavily to go to school and now work at low-income jobs. Your payments are pegged to the size of your monthly income. You can pay as little as 4 percent of what you earn and as much as 25 percent. Ask the lender what happens if your chosen payments don't cover the standard interest and principal due. The lender might lower the payment required by extending the term of the loan for a specified number of years. At minimum, you will always have to pay the interest. You will also have to document your income annually, so that payments can be reset.

5. *An income-contingent plan,* offered by the government. The size of

SIZE OF DEBT	MAXIMUM CONSOLIDATION TERM
Less than $7,500	10 years
$7,500–10,000	12 years
$10,000–$20,000	15 years
$20,000–$40,000	20 years
$40,000–$60,000	25 years
More than $60,000	30 years

your monthly payment depends on the size of your debt, your adjusted gross income (including your spouse's), and how many dependents you have. If your income is minuscule, you might pay nothing. Otherwise, payments will range from 4 to 15 percent of income. If your minimum payment isn't enough to cover the interest on your debt, that unpaid interest is added to your loan balance, increasing the sum you must repay. If you still have a balance due after 25 years of payments, the rest of your loan will be forgiven (the amount not collected will be reported as taxable income).

For information on the government's loan-consolidation plans, call 800-557-7392 or check http://www.ed.gov. For information on private plans, check with your own lender; with Nellie Mae (New England Education Loan Marketing Corporation), 50 Braintree Hill Park, Braintree, MA 02184 (800-9-TUITION or http://www.nelliemae.org); or with Sallie Mae (Student Loan Marketing Association), 1050 Thomas Jefferson St. N.W., Washington, DC 20007 (800-643-0040 or http://www.salliemae.com; its Web site includes a calculator for comparing the various payment options). See who offers you the best rates and terms. Sallie Mae cuts your rate by 0.25 percent if you authorize your bank to make automatic monthly payments, and another one percent if you make the first 48 payments on time.

Don't Stretch Out the Loan Term Unless You're Desperate. Adding extra years to your loan means extra years of interest payments. You might still be paying off the cost of your own education when it's time for your children to enter school.

The Smart Way to Consolidate. Pack all your loans into a single payment, take the shortest term possible (10 years), and save money by paying off your loan in an even shorter period of time. There's no prepayment penalty.

Loan Payments Can Be Deferred or Forgiven

When loan repayments are a burden, sometimes you can get a break. Check here to see if you're eligible for deferment, forbearance, or outright cancellation.

On Deferment. *If you received your first loan on or after July 1, 1993, payments can be temporarily deferred if you:*
- Return to school at least half-time.
- Study full time in an approved graduate or post-graduate fellowship program.

• Receive services from a rehabilitation program for the disabled, full-time.

• Can't find work, even though you're job hunting. Repayments can be deferred for up to 3 years, but you have to reapply for this deferral every 6 months.

• Face economic hardship as defined by the U.S. Department of Education. One criterion: working full-time and earning less than the minimum wage. This deferment, too, can last for up to 3 years.

• Work in a social-service job that lets you cancel your student loans (page 549; this is for Perkins borrowers only).

If you took a Stafford, Perkins, or Direct loan between August 1, 1987, and June 30, 1993, payments can be temporarily deferred if you:

• Return to school at least half-time.

• Teach in a place that the government defines as short of teachers (Stafford and Direct loans only).

• Join the armed forces, Commissioned Corps of the Public Health Service, or National Oceanic and Atmospheric Administration Corps.

• Join the Peace Corps or Vista, or participate full-time in a similar program with a tax-exempt organization.

• Have to serve an internship or residency to qualify for your profession.

• Are temporarily totally disabled.

• Have to care for a dependent who's temporarily totally disabled.

• Take a parental leave from work for up to 6 months (Stafford and Direct loans only).

• Have small children and are a working mother entering (or reentering) the workforce at a low wage.

On Forbearance. *If you don't qualify for deferment but are having financial problems, you can request forbearance. Payments can be temporarily reduced or postponed if you:*

• Can't pay owing to poor health.

• Find that your payments on certain federal student loans equal or exceed 20 percent of your monthly gross income.

• Are serving in a medical or dental internship or residency, or in a position under the National Community Service Trust Act of 1993, including AmeriCorps (Stafford and Direct loan holders only).

Plus Loans are eligible for deferral and forbearance, too, under various conditions.

On Cancellation. *Your loan can be wholly or partly canceled if you:*

• Die.

• Become totally and permanently disabled.

- Go bankrupt, if 7 years have passed since the loan came due (a loan can be wiped out earlier if a court decides that repaying it would create undue hardship). In some cases, however, your student or parent loan may not be discharged in bankruptcy.
- Enlist in the Army, Army National Guard, or Army Reserve. If you sign up for certain types of military work, the U.S. Defense Department will forgive your loan for each year you serve.
- Were cheated by a school that closed before you completed your course or falsely certified that you could benefit from the course. This generally applies to dishonest trade schools.
- Hold a Perkins loan and teach low-income or handicapped students; teach in a shortage area; work as a full-time nurse, medical technician, or law-enforcement officer; provide services to high-risk children in a low-income community; provide early-intervention services to infants and toddlers; serve in the armed forces in an "area of hostilities," or join Vista or the Peace Corps. Part of your loan is forgiven for each year you serve.

Do You Owe Interest During the Time That Loan Repayments Are Postponed? No, if you defer a subsidized Stafford or Perkins loan. Yes, if you defer an unsubsidized Stafford or PLUS. Yes, if you've been granted forbearance rather than deferral. If you owe interest, you'll have a choice: make your payments monthly (even though your principal payments are deferred) or defer the interest, too—adding it to your total debt. You'd be smart to keep paying interest monthly. Otherwise, the total amount of your debt goes up and you'll face higher payments when the deferral ends. (If those payments are burdensome, however, you can consolidate.)

Never Default!

If you do . . .

. . . You may never get any other federal student aid.

. . . A collection agent may pursue you.

. . . Your delinquency will show up on your credit report.

. . . Your wages can be garnished.

. . . If you work for the federal government, the payments may be withheld from your salary.

. . . Your income-tax refunds may be held back. If you file jointly, so might your spouse's.

. . . Your college might refuse to send out your transcripts.

. . . Perkins loan users will deprive the fund of money that could have been used for some other needy student.

. . . You'll be a dirty rat.

ADULT STUDENTS

Adults can apply for the same college-aid programs that kid students get. But there's a catch. Your application for federal aid (the FAFSA form) asks for your prior year's earnings and assumes that the same amount of money will be on tap for this year's costs. If you're quitting your job to go to school, you won't have that income anymore. Raise this problem with your school's office of financial aid. The school can ask the government to refigure your eligibility for aid, based on your projected income while you're in school. The PROFILE form adjusts for this at the time you file.

RAISING MONEY FOR GRADUATE SCHOOL

As a parent, you're financially exhausted. Child One is through college; Child Two will be finished in two years. Retirement is within sight.

Then Child One says that he or she wants to go to graduate school. No boxer could deliver a harder punch.

Most parents assume that their financial obligations stop with the undergraduate degree. If the kid wants more education, that's his or her responsibility.

But try telling that to a university. Most of them look at parental income before granting any financial aid. Parents of graduate students aren't squeezed as hard as the parents of undergraduates. Still, your expected contribution may be high. If you won't help pay, your child might not be able to go.

How much aid is available depends on what your child will study. In medicine, law, and other well-paid professions, middle-class students are expected to pay their own way. Borrow it or earn it, but don't look to the grad school for much of a grant.

Advanced science degrees, on the other hand, are heavily funded by scholarships and research assistantships, which are often awarded on merit, not need. The social sciences offer administrative assistantships, such as being a counselor. The arts may give teaching assistantships. Write for *A Selected List of Fellowship Opportunities and Aids to Advanced Education,* free from the Publications Office, National Science Foundation, 1401 Wilson Blvd., Arlington, VA 22230. An electronic version can be found at http://www.nsf.gov. It includes opportunities in the humanities as well as the sciences. For a particularly helpful book, try *Financing Graduate School* by Patricia McWade, published by Peterson's Guides, Princeton, NJ, available through bookstores for $16.95 or from Peterson's at 800-338-3282.

When hunting for a grant, talk to the head of the academic department you want to join as well as the student-aid office. That's the person who can hand out fellowships, assistantships, and departmental grants. Also, take a look at cooperative education (see below).

What if a student still comes up short? The grad schools aren't entirely flint-hearted. Some don't pursue the parents of students who have been self-supporting for 3 years. Some let stepparents off the hook. Every family should talk to the financial-aid office to see if there's any wiggle room.

THE JOB CONNECTION

Sometimes your job can lead to a grant. Employers may help pay for college courses or let you alternate between work and school. In the armed services, you can march for your money. Whatever the deal, you get an education at a fraction of the cost that other students pay. Here's what's out there:

Cooperative Education

A co-op student gets a job related to his or her field of study. Your salary pays a significant share of your college costs. Schedules vary. You might alternate semesters, one in school, one at work. You might attend classes in the morning and work in the afternoon. It may take five years to earn a baccalaureate degree. Co-op programs are also offered by two-year community colleges and some graduate schools. Around 200,000 students participate.

For the free directory, *A College Guide to Cooperative Education*, write to the National Commission for Cooperative Education, 360 Huntington Ave., Boston, MA 02115. It covers programs for both graduates and undergraduates.

The Military Budget

Military scholarships are harder to come by now that the size of the nation's armed forces has been reduced. But new officers do have to be trained, so college money is still on tap. To compete for a one- to four-year scholarship from the Reserve Officers Training Corps (ROTC), you need high grades and, usually, a tilt toward math, science, nursing, or engineering. ROTC isn't offered at every college. For information call the Army at 800-USA-ROTC, the Navy at 800-USA-NAVY, the Marines at 800-MARINES, or the Air Force at 800-423-USAF.

If you enlist, grants are available for taking courses at local colleges on your own time. The Army forgives part of your student loans if you enlist and sign up for certain types of work. At this writing, the Navy is thinking of doing the same.

You can also allocate $100 a month of your military pay toward a higher-education fund during the first 12 months you're in the service. If you do, the Department of Veterans Affairs will help pay for your education —at a college or trade school—provided that you're honorably discharged. The size of your grant generally rises each year to match inflation. At this writing, here are the rules:

If you stay in the service for less than 3 years, you'll get $12,515, payable monthly for 3 years while you're in school. For a hitch of 3 years or more, you can get $15,403. You're also eligible for the higher amount if you do 2 years active duty plus 4 years in the Selected Reserve or National Guard. Your particular branch of service may add even more if you sign up for certain lines of work. After leaving the service, you generally have up to 10 years to matriculate. If you don't go to school, you normally don't get your $1,200 contribution back.

Enlistments in the military reserve are also attractive. For a 6-year commitment, you qualify for education assistance worth up to $7,317 and get drill pay besides. Of course, you might also have to fight.

The spouses and children of veterans may qualify for education benefits if the vet dies or is permanently and totally disabled as a result of his or her service duties; dies from other causes while suffering from a service-connected disability; or has been listed for more than 90 days as missing in action, captured by an enemy, or interned by a foreign government. In 1997 the government paid $404 a month for full-time students, for up to 45 months. To qualify, children generally have to be 18 to 26. Spouses have up to 10 years to complete their training.

For a guide to military scholarships, get *Need a Lift?*, $3 from the American Legion, National Emblem Sales, P.O. Box 1050, Indianapolis, IN 46206.

The Company Perk

Some companies pay part or all of the price of courses at local undergraduate institutions or training schools. In return, you may have to agree to stay with the company for a certain number of years.

The big question is, will you be taxed on the value of the company contribution? The answer is no if the course is designed to improve your performance in your present job. But Congress goes back and forth on whether to help with courses you're taking to ready yourself for a better job or just for the fun of it. At this writing, Congress's latest decision was not to tax this sort of aid to employees starting undergraduate courses up to June 1, 2000, but to tax aid for graduate-level work. Check with your employee-benefits department for the latest information.

For More Information on Raising Money for College:*

Get the government's excellent free booklet on its own student-aid programs, *The Student Guide: Financial Aid from the U.S. Department of Education*. Call 800-4-FED-AID. At that same number, someone will answer any questions you have on federal aid. Or check the government's Web site: http://www.ed.gov. The government continually adjusts its programs, so keep in touch.

Send $10 to Octameron Associates, P.O. Box 2748, Alexandria, VA 22301, for *Don't Miss Out: An Ambitious Student's Guide to Financial Aid*, a sound, strategic guide to finding and qualifying for student aid. Octameron publishes many other booklets on specific kinds of aid. For information, go to http://www.octameron.com.

For $26.95, get Peterson's *College Money Handbook,* available through bookstores or by calling Peterson's customer service at 800-338-3282. It lists more than 1,600 institutions, their expenses, the amount of aid on tap, the no-need awards you can apply for, money-saving options (like accelerated degrees, ROTC, co-op education, guaranteed tuition plans, and off-campus living), and athletic scholarships. A helpful chart gives parents a general idea of what they'll be expected to contribute to their children's education. You also get a CD-ROM to help you estimate costs and apply directly to 300 schools. Athletes should check Peterson's *Sports Scholarships and College Athletic Programs*, $24.95.

Try the College Board's *College Costs and Financial Aid Handbook*, available through bookstores or for $16.95 from College Board Publications, Box 886, New York, NY 10101 (800-323-7155). This general guide to college aid gives you worksheets to help you fill in the financial-aid forms, the costs of more than 3,100 colleges, universities, and proprietary schools and the kinds of grants they offer, lists of schools with tuition waivers or special tuition-payment plans, as well as a table showing how much parents should expect to pay. You can get the same information free on the College Board's Web site, http://www.collegeboard.org.

Go to http://finaid.org for a superb roundup of everything you could possibly want to know about financial aid, including scholarship sources, calculators to help you figure out your expected family contribution, advice from financial-aid administrators, and links to Web pages for state-aid agencies, federal student-aid guides, and college-aid offices.

DON'T GET SCAMMED!

One day you may get a phone call or a thrilling letter in the mail. You have qualified for a scholarship! Just send $5 or $10 or $20 for processing

---

* By the time you read this, prices may be up.

costs. I guarantee that that promise is a fake. You *never* have to send money for a scholarship you've won. College aid *never* comes unsolicited.

Some other lies: The letter says, "Hurry, apply now or lose the money." It asks for your bank-account number "so the money can be wired to you directly" or your credit-card number "to verify who you are." It claims that everyone is eligible to share in this pot of cash. The envelope looks as if it came from the government.

Don't believe a word of it. It's a cheat.

WHAT'S YOUR BEST SHOT AT GETTING COLLEGE AID?

For low-income kids, the money is there—although even these families will be pressed to their limit for contributions.

Middle-income families should:

1. Check out schools with no-need scholarships.

2. Apply to schools where your academic record puts you in the top 25 percent of the applicant pool.

3. Miss no deadlines for college-aid applications, which may be as early as February 15.

4. Check all the financial data about your family when you get the aid form back from the processor, to be sure that nothing was entered wrong.

5. Go for cooperative education.

6. Go to a state school. Private schools may offer more aid but they'll also saddle you with more loans.

7. Go to a school in your home state. Or check the schools in neighboring states to see if you can study there without paying a nonresident fee.

8. Ask the student-aid officer to base your grant on your projected income rather than on last year's earnings. This is critical to families whose earnings will drop—for example, parents who lose jobs or adults who give up jobs to return to school.

9. Write a letter explaining any special circumstances that cause money to be especially tight in your family. This won't help with federal or state aid, but might improve your college grant.

10. Apply to competing colleges or universities. Their aid formulas vary. If one school offers you more aid, the other might decide to match it.

Grants are nice when you can get them. But, bottom line, you won't get through school without a lot of savings and loans.

20.

The Best College Investment Plans

How to Beat the College Inflation Rate

If you play it too safe with your college funds, you'll never raise the money you need.

Many parents blanch when I talk about putting college money into stocks. "They're too risky." "The market might fall." "I need something safe."

And, in fact, that's right. You *do* need safety—but only in the few years before your child matriculates. If you're investing when your child is young, what you need is growth. Stock-owning mutual funds have averaged 10 to 12 percent annually on money invested for at least a decade. College inflation is currently running at 6 percent. For stock buyers, college gets *cheaper* over time, because their investments rise faster than tuitions do.

In some years, stocks drop. On rare occasions, the market has gone nowhere for a decade or more. So hedge by owning some bonds or bond mutual funds. But the odds strongly favor stock-market investments. Over the long term, nothing beats them for growth.

A STRATEGY FOR COLLEGE INVESTING

What to buy depends on how old your children are. When they're young, make it stocks. If the market drops, you can afford to wait for prices to climb again. When your children are older, however, their college money should be kept in investments that are absolutely safe.

For Children Zero to 12

Save money regularly. The sooner you start, the less college will effectively cost because you'll be paying part of the bill with money that your money earns. To appreciate the astonishing value of early savings, take a look at the table on page 183.

Put your savings into a mix of U.S. and international stock-owning mutual funds with good records. Don't try to buy and sell as market conditions change; too often, you'll guess wrong. Just faithfully put your money away, month after month, in good times and bad, and reinvest the dividends. Don't worry if the market falls. It will rise again. Over 10 years or so, your stocks should far outpace certificates of deposit, Series EE Savings Bonds, zero-coupon Treasuries, or any of the other popular college-saving deals.

For Children 12 to 14

Over these years, deposit your new savings into safe havens: Series EE Savings Bonds, long-term certificates of deposit, and zero-coupon Treasuries that will mature when your child starts school. What's more, start methodically moving some of your money out of stocks. By the time your child reaches 14, 25 percent of your college savings should be earning interest in secure investments. These funds may lose some purchasing power, after taxes and inflation. But that's a small worry compared with the risk that stock prices will drop and not recover by the time college bills are due. This hoard of safe money guarantees your child's freshman year.

Keep the other 75 percent of your money in stocks, for your child's sophomore, junior, and senior years.

When Your Child Reaches 14

If any of your child's freshman-year money is still in stocks, take it out. The market beats everything in the long run, but in the short run it can kill you. In the eight declines of 15 percent or more since World War II, it has taken stock investors two years, on average, to recover the money they started with, assuming that dividends were reinvested.* So that's the time period for playing it safe. The market might not fall, but you can't take the risk.

You might move your freshman-year money into bond funds for the next couple of years (see the following section). Otherwise, choose safe

---

* Measured by Standard & Poor's 500-stock average. The longest recovery time since 1945 was 3.6 years, after the bear market that started in 1972. The shortest time: 10 months. After the Great Crash of 1929, it took investors 15.5 years to get even, a reminder that the worst does happen. Source: Ibbotson Associates

investments that will mature the month before the start of the college term. Over four years, the highest-paying safe investment, after tax, will probably be Series EE Savings Bonds. You pay only federal taxes on the interest, not state or local taxes. If your income isn't too high, the interest will be partly or fully tax exempt (page 565). Alternatively, look at short-term Treasuries —straight bonds or zeros (page 562), which also escape state and local tax. Both these investments should yield more than taxable certificates of deposit. Or see if your state has a prepaid tuition plan that makes sense for you (page 567).

The next year, when the child is 15, be sure all your sophomore-year money is out of the market and stored somewhere safe. When the child is 16, take out the junior-year money. At 17, take out the senior-year money. Your timing on these removals may vary because you won't want to sell if the market is down. But over these critical four years, move your money gradually out of harm's way.

Additional investments made in these years should also go into safety-first instruments, not into mutual funds.

If You Bought Bond Mutual Funds as a College Investment. Since 1945 it has taken bond investors an average of 1.5 years to break even after a market decline of 5 percent or more, with bond interest reinvested. The worst bond market (the one starting in 1958) lasted about two years. So you're probably okay if you keep your bond funds until your child is 16 and then move the freshman-year money out. Move out the sophomore-year money at 17, the junior-year money at 18, the senior-year money at 19.

If You Don't Start Saving Until Your Child Is 13 or 14

You've missed the safest part of your personal stock-market curve. To buy stocks now is too great a risk. Consider bond mutual funds instead.

Parents who start saving *very* late and won't qualify for much college aid may have to borrow so much money for college that they can't afford to retire when they planned. Ditto for divorced men who remarry and start second families and women who have children in their late 30s or early 40s. Most likely, your children will have to shoulder much of the college cost.

Should You Sell Your Stocks If They're Doing Great? Say you have a whiz of a mutual fund that did 18 percent last year. Why not leave the money there, use PLUS loans for college, defer the principal payments until your child is out of school, then repay the whole amount out of the profits you've made.

Sounds like a great idea to me if (1) you're willing to gamble that your stocks will keep going up and (2) you can afford the loan repayments if your mutual fund winds up in the tank. On the whole, this is a risk that only higher-income people can afford.

TAX-FAVORED WAYS TO SAVE

1. *Start an education Individual Retirement Account.* If you qualify, you can put up to $500 every year in an IRA opened for a child under 18. You can't deduct your contribution, but the earnings are entirely tax free if used for higher education. This isn't big money. Still, any tax-free account is better than a taxable one. If the child doesn't use all the money for school, the account can be transferred to another one of your children or grandchildren. If the beneficiary reaches 30, any remaining money is distributed and taxed. A 10 percent tax penalty would be due as well.

You cannot contribute to an education IRA and a state prepaid tuition plan in the same year. Tuition plans accept larger contributions and, unlike IRAs, generally match the rise in in-state college costs. But there are restrictions on how the money can be used (page 567).

Singles qualify for a full education IRA contribution with adjusted gross incomes as high as $95,000. If you earn more, your allowable contribution shrinks, phasing out at $110,000. Marrieds get a full contribution with incomes as high as $150,000, phasing out at $160,000.

You can't use an education IRA in a year you also claim a HOPE or Lifetime Learning tax credit (page 527). So IRAs make sense only if (1) you don't qualify for a credit or (2) the child is so young that the IRA's potential long-term earnings will exceed the size of the credit.

2. *Start a regular Individual Retirement Account with after-tax dollars.* The earnings accumulate tax free. When you take money out to pay for higher education—for yourself or for a spouse, child, or grandchild—you'll owe income tax but no 10 percent tax penalty if you're under 59½. The same rules apply to withdrawals from Roth IRAs or IRAs funded with pretax dollars, but those are best left alone until retirement.

WHAT IF YOU CAN'T SAVE AS MUCH AS YOU NEED?

Save less. Try to acquire one-third to one-half of the money you're going to need. With that as a base, you can manage the rest through tax credits, borrowing, money pinched from current income, and money that your child earns.

Start saving a small amount each month and raise it every time your income goes up. Or tell your child from an early age that he or she will have to contribute part of the cost.

Aim for an in-state college or university even if you yourself went to a private school. Many state schools are terrific. Private and out-of-state public schools can potentially offer you more student aid (they cost more so you may qualify for extra help). But they're apt to leave you with large debts.

HOW TO SAVE FOR COLLEGE AND RETIREMENT AT THE SAME TIME

Ideally, you fund your retirement plan in full and start a separate college-savings plan. But what if you can't afford them both? Here's a surprising answer to a question you might think unanswerable. *Don't* specifically save for college. Instead:

1. Buy a house. Build equity by adding extra dollars to your payment every month, to reduce the mortgage as fast as you can. You are creating a savings pool with money you otherwise might spend. Your payments are earning a risk-free return equal to your mortgage interest rate.

2. Don't open a home-equity line of credit. If you already have one, clean it up. Clean up your credit-card bills, too.

3. Set up a tax-deferred retirement-savings plan (Chapter 29). Sock every penny into it you can. Retirement plans are wonderful ways to save because your contributions are pretax. In company plans, your employer often matches part of your contribution. That's *free money,* not to be missed! What's more, the accumulated value of retirement plans isn't counted as personal wealth on the federal financial-aid application, which might help you qualify for a grant or subsidized student loan.

4. When your child goes to college, apply for college aid. Your child should take (and expect to repay) the maximum student loan. You can take PLUS loans (just large enough to get the maximum deduction for education-loan interest), then home-equity loans (whose interest is fully deductible, on loans up to $100,000).

5. Keep contributing to your company plan, for the employer match (if any), the tax deduction, and tax deferral. If you can't contribute and make loan repayments, too, you've chosen a college that's too expensive. If you want to make the sacrifice, reduce your retirement contribution and put the money toward tuition instead. But don't make any withdrawals from your retirement plan. Leave the money there to grow.

6. When your children are through college, use the income that formerly went for tuition to pay off your loans.

7. All during the financially tight college years, your retirement fund will continue to accumulate even if you can't afford fresh contributions. As

soon as possible, however, resume putting money into your plan in order to collect those matching funds from your employer.

8. If you do have a little spare money, save it for college in a tax-favored plan—first an education IRA, then a nondeductible IRA or 401(k).

What Can Go Wrong? You might not accumulate enough home equity to support a sizable home-equity loan. Or your income might not be large enough to qualify you for the loan you need. As a fallback, however, you could take a PLUS.

What Else Can Go Wrong? You might be forced to retire early and couldn't afford to take on college debt. But in this case, even people with savings intended for college accounts may have to take that money for their own retirement needs. Your children will probably have to pay most of the college bills themselves. But colleges give more aid to students whose parents have retired.

IF YOU HAVE A SEPARATE COLLEGE FUND, WHO SHOULD OWN IT?

Keep the savings (or part of them) in your child's name if you don't expect to qualify for student aid (page 535). Kids get a tax break on their income from savings. So the money is worth more in their account than in yours as long as you don't run afoul of the kiddie tax (page 89).

But if you expect to collect college aid, keep the savings in your own account. The college-aid formula generally considers only 5.6 percent of a parent's countable savings when deciding how much the family should pay (page 535). But it takes 35 percent of the child's savings every year. With the savings in your name, you'll pay a little more in income taxes (unless those savings are in a tax-deferred retirement account). But you should be rewarded with a little extra college aid.

The Downside to Giving the Funds to Your Child:
1. You probably can't get the money back if you should need it.
2. A dependent child with unearned income over $500 has to pay income taxes on it.
3. The child gets the money at 18 even if immature (21 to 25 in many states if you use the Uniform Gifts, or Transfers, to Minors Act).
4. Having unearned income requires a child to pay a bit more tax on his or her earned income.
5. Unearned income over $1,300 is taxed at the parents' rate until the child is 14.

The Downside to Keeping the Money Yourself:

1. You pay income taxes on the earnings, probably at a higher rate than your child would.

2. You might not get student aid, because your income turned out to be higher than you originally expected.

3. If you get extra aid, it might not be enough to compensate for the extra income taxes you paid over the years.

4. The money is part of your estate, which matters if you're wealthy enough to owe estate taxes.

5. Congress might change the law, nicking student assets for less.

So go figure.

Some planners recommend a "minority trust" as a way around the kiddie tax. It's for children under 14 who have a lot of money in their names. But the costs associated with setting up and managing the trust may wipe out any tax advantage.

If you buy Series EE Savings Bonds for college, you should own them yourself. That's the only way of getting the tax break, as long as your income isn't too high to qualify. For more on using EE bonds for higher education, see page 565.

FOUR SMART INVESTMENT MOVES

You'll find the scoop on the following investments in other parts of this book. Here, just a word about how to use them for college savings.

1. *Stock-owning mutual funds*—the best buy when the children are small. Make regular contributions to a mix of U.S. and international stock-owning mutual funds in good markets and bad. Invest any birthday or holiday money, and inheritances, too.

As college approaches, don't sell the shares yourself. Give them to your child and let the child sell them when he or she reaches 18. That way, the gain will be taxed in the child's super-low bracket. You can give your child shares worth up to $10,000 a year gift-tax-free ($20,000, if the gift is made jointly with your spouse). Those amounts rise with inflation, from 1999 on.

2. *Home equities*—accelerate your mortgage payments, to build equity faster. You'll then have more tax-deductible borrowing power when the time comes for a college loan. If you currently have a home-equity loan, start paying it off.

3. *Series EE Savings Bonds*—better than certificates of deposit in the 4 years before tuition is due. Taxes on the interest are deferred; when paid, you owe only federal tax, not state or local taxes; if you meet the income qualifications, the interest might be fully or partly tax exempt (page 565). But don't buy them when your children are young. As long-term investments, they're subpar.

4. *Education IRAs*—better than Series EE bonds for people who don't get a tuition tax credit (page 527), because the earnings are tax free.

IF NOT STOCKS, WHAT?

Some parents worry about buying stocks for young children's college accounts. They feel safer with bonds and real estate. If you go that route, here's what you can expect:

1. *Bond mutual funds:* Not as risky as stocks but not safe, either. You'll make some money when interest rates fall but take some losses when interest rates rise (for more on bonds, see Chapter 25). Your after-tax return probably won't keep up with the rising cost of college; on the other hand, it might not miss by very much. You might prefer to borrow the shortfall rather than live with stock-market risk. If you do buy bond funds, sell them two years before you're going to need the money and put the proceeds somewhere safe. You don't want to risk market losses during that final stretch.

2. *Individual intermediate-term bonds*—taxable or tax-free—maturing when college begins: Your principal is safe but your net interest will probably not keep up with the rise in college costs. You'll receive semiannual interest payments which you'll have to reinvest at even lower rates. If you buy Treasuries, go with zeros, which reinvest the interest at the same rate you're earning on the bond. You'll pay tax on the interest as it accrues, but your nest egg will come pretty close to matching the rise in college costs.

3. *Zero-coupon bonds*—consider putting 10 to 20 percent of a young child's college savings into zero-coupon bonds that will mature when college starts. Over 10-year holding periods there's a tiny risk that stocks won't yield their usual gains. Bonds are your hedge.

Zeros can also be good, safe investments for the 4-year period before tuition is due. For the details on these bonds, see pages 193 and 779. Here's how to use zeros for college investing:

• Buy zeros that will mature just before you'll need the money. This is the best advice on zeros you'll ever get! Stagger your maturities so a zero bond falls due in each of the 4 years that your child will be in school. Too many fond grandparents buy their grandchildren 20- or 30-year zeros that will have to be sold before maturity. An early sale exposes your money to market risk. If interest rates rise, the value of your zeros will plunge and you can kiss part of your savings goodbye. Also, small amounts of zeros don't fetch a good price—another reason not to sell before they mature.

• Try for newly issued zeros, not older zeros that are up for resale through brokerage firms. You don't get such good prices on resales and the tax complications of buying them are disheartening (page 780). But older zeros may be all you can get if you're buying for periods of three or four years.

- Buy zero Treasuries, not zero tax exempts, for the following reasons: (1) If you're looking for new issues in 4-year maturities, you're more likely to find them in Treasuries than in tax-exempt municipal bonds. (2) If you have to sell before maturity, Treasuries fetch better prices. Small issues of munis may effectively be unsalable. (3) Most Treasuries cannot be called away from you before maturity, whereas a municipal might be called after just 10 years—a consideration if you're buying longer-term zeros.

- Alternatively, consider American Century–Benham Target Maturities funds—taxable zero-coupon mutual funds that mature in various years from 2000 on (call 800-321-8321). Mutual funds are especially good for smaller purchases. Minimum initial investment: $1,000.

Federal taxes are owed on Treasury-bond interest, but not state and local taxes. Income on zeros held in the child's name will be taxed at a lower rate if the child doesn't have much other unearned income or if the child is 14 or older (page 89).

4. *Real estate:* Some families invest in a one- or two-family home and rent it out as a way of building savings for college. In the year before the child matriculates, they plan to sell the house, put the equity in the bank, and draw on the money as tuition bills come due.

But many rental houses are mediocre deals (page 820). The rent is often too low to cover all your expenses, so it may cost money to run the property every year. To make up those losses and earn a profit, you'll need substantial appreciation after tax. Gains like that are unusual these days.

Financial planners love to talk about buying a house in the town where your child goes to school, renting rooms to students to cover part of the mortgage, and paying the child a deductible salary to manage the building. That's neat on paper, but not too many of us have junior Donald Trumps sprawled on our living-room floors.

5. *Series EE Savings Bonds:* Better than bank CDs if they'll be all or partly tax free for college (page 565). They make sense for savers who can't stomach any risk at all, even though they probably won't keep up with the rise in college costs. A better choice is a prepaid tuition plan if your state has one and your child will go to an in-state school. Or use an education IRA if you're starting to save when the child is very young.

HOW ABOUT LIFE INSURANCE?

Don't Buy It If Your Primary Goal Is Saving Money for College.

The pitch sounds convincing: "Buy a universal policy as a college investment. The cash in the policy builds up tax deferred. At college time you can withdraw, tax free, a sum equal to the premiums you paid. Or you can borrow against the cash value. Regular premium payments are a disciplined way of building savings tax deferred and there's money for college if you die."

But how large a pot of savings do you build? After you pay the insurance premium and the sales commission, there's not much left for your cash account, especially in the early years (page 302). Broker-sold insurance policies typically don't yield competitive net returns on investment until the 15th year or so—not too helpful if your child is 5 or 10. If cash for college is your prime interest, you'll do better with any other investment.

That's for straight universal life. What about variable universal life whose cash values can be invested in stocks? For college savings, that's even worse. Variable policies carry higher internal charges. To overcome them, you need high returns on stock investments over a long period of time—15 years or more. But college savers ought to switch out of stocks in the 3 or 4 years before the tuition is due, which curtails your investment too soon. Worse, in order to keep your money safe, you'd have to switch into the policy's money market account, where expenses will eat up most of your modest yield. Check page 306 to see what can happen to a variable policy with an average return from stocks of 10.2 percent. After 10 years your net return might be only 4.8 percent.

What If You Need More Insurance as Well as College Savings? Buy cheap term insurance and devote the rest of your money to growth investments, including investments in education IRAs and nondeductible IRAs. Even term plus Series EE bonds would be better than most life insurance savings, especially if the EE bond interest is fully or partly tax exempt.

What If You Already Own Universal Life Insurance? In this case, it's a good way for conservative savers to build a college fund. You're already paying the premiums, so any money you add will earn the policy's crediting rate, tax deferred. You'll generally get the equivalent of a short- to intermediate-bond return. When college rolls around, you can withdraw that money tax free, although you may pay a surrender charge. Variable universal policies invested in stock are still problematic, however. You'll get subpar returns when you switch to the policy's money fund in the 3 or 4 years before you're going to need the cash. You should have been in the stock account for many years prior to that, to allow your savings to build.

Bottom line: don't *buy* life insurance if college savings are your primary need. But use the tax deferral to save in a universal policy that you already have.

Whatever You Do, Resist Buying Life Insurance on a Child in Order to Build College Funds. It's a total waste of money. A good part of each payment goes for insurance, which the child doesn't need. Take a policy paying 5.7 percent. If you bought one for your 5-year-old boy, depositing

$100 a month, you'd have around $19,000 when he reached 18. If you put that same money into Series EE bonds at 5.7 percent, you'd have nearly $23,000. A 10 percent mutual fund would double that.

No reputable agent will sell a "college" policy on a child. If you already own one (hence have paid the expenses), it might be a decent long-term investment as long as you have other money to use toward a college account. Check this out with the Consumer Federation of America (page 313). If you don't have other money, cancel the policy, cancel your agent, and put the proceeds into a better investment.

PLANS DESIGNED FOR COLLEGE SAVINGS

In terms of potential total return, none of these plans are as good as plain old stock-owning mutual funds held for the long term. But each one might interest nervous savers who don't want to risk any principal.

Series EE Savings Bonds

Series EE bonds are hung like a Christmas tree with income-tax breaks. For all buyers, the interest can be tax deferred until redemption. If you put those earnings toward tuition—at a college, university, technical school, or qualified vocational school—the interest is partly or entirely tax free. You escape at least some tax if you meet *all* of the following conditions:

• You bought the EE bond anytime since January 1, 1990. The tax break doesn't apply to bonds bought before that date.

• At the time of the purchase, you were at least 24 years old.

• The bond is owned in your name or co-owned with your spouse. It cannot be carried in your child's name or co-owned with your child.

• You redeem the EE bond in a year you have to pay fees and tuition for yourself, your spouse, or your child (but not your grandchild), or roll the money into a state prepaid tuition plan. If grandparents want to help, they should give money to the parents and let them buy the EE bond (or use some other strategy—page 569).

• The proceeds are not used for room, board, books, or other higher-education expenses. In other words, don't cash in bonds worth more than the school's tuition and fees.

• You meet an income test in the year the bonds are redeemed. The following table shows the rules for 1997. These amounts are indexed to inflation and are high enough so that most parents qualify for at least a partial exemption. In the income range labeled "partly tax free," the deduction is gradually phased out.

• You did not take an education tax credit for the child that year.

WHEN YOUR EE-BOND INTEREST IS TAX-FREE FOR EDUCATION

YOU'RE SINGLE AND YOUR INCOME* IS:	YOUR EE-BOND INTEREST IS:
Less than $50,850	Fully tax free
$50,850 to $65,850	Partly tax free
More than $65,850	Not tax free

YOU'RE MARRIED AND YOUR INCOME* IS:	
Less than $76,250	Fully tax free
$76,250 to $106,250	Partly tax free
More than $106,250	Not tax free

* Adjusted gross income, 1997. Indexed to inflation.

Warning: Even if your income doesn't appear to exceed the ceiling, your tax break may be smaller than you expect. Here's why. In the year you redeem some EE bonds, your reported income will be enlarged by the EE-bond interest you just collected. The higher your reported income, the harder it is to get the full tax break.

Say, for example, that you're a single parent with an income of $49,000 in 1997 dollars. You pick up an extra $4,000 in interest by cashing in some Series EE bonds. Your total income is now $53,000—putting you $2,150 over the limit for collecting EE-bond interest entirely tax free. Part of your interest will be tax exempt, but not all of it.

What to Do: (1) Buy EE bonds in relatively small denominations so you won't have to redeem in higher amounts than you actually need. That helps keep taxes to a minimum. (2) Redeem bonds that have accumulated the smallest amount of interest (for more on EE bonds, see page 196).

EE bonds carry a variable interest rate, so you have some protection if rates rise. That's a clear advantage over fixed-rate college-savings bonds.

Before settling on an EE bond, check the high-rate certificates of deposit (page 66). They may pay more after tax, and can also be used in the same year you take an education tax credit (page 527).

College-Savings Bonds

These are tax-exempt zero-coupon bonds sold by a few states expressly for college savings. You invest a small amount of money which grows to a fixed sum by the time your child matriculates. Some states have college trusts that pay a variable rate. In either case, the state might add a kicker to the yield, or maybe a cash bonus, if your child chooses an in-state school.

Wherever college bonds are offered, small savers line up to buy them. But you may earn more from Series EE bonds if you qualify for a substantial tax break. Compare the net yields on EEs with the yields on college bonds and buy the one that pays the most. Lean toward the college bonds if you think that your income will be too high to use the tax exemption on Series EEs.

If you do buy a college-savings bond, be sure it matures when you're going to need the money. If you have to sell early, you may take a loss.

State Prepaid Education Plans

Several states* have education-prepayment plans, with others on the way. Parents or grandparents put up money for a particular child. The state guarantees that this sum will cover a fixed portion of the tuition or a certain number of college credits when the child goes to school. Between now and then, tuition might rise 20, 50, or 100 percent, maybe 5 zillion percent. No matter. If you prepaid one-half of the tuition, you'll owe only the other half. The state pays the rest. Florida also has a prepaid plan for room or board, which other states may copy.

These plans vary from state to state. Most peg your payments to average tuition costs at in-state public colleges. Most (but not all) let you transfer the money to private or out-of-state schools. Massachusetts lets out-of-state parents participate in its plan, which includes many of the state's private colleges. You can pay monthly, annually, or in a lump sum. Your effective return on investment will generally depend on how fast state-college costs increase (although states may use other formulas). If your child doesn't go to college, the account can generally be passed to certain other family members. If not, or if you drop out of the plan, you'll get your principal back, sometimes with interest, sometimes without. When your child withdraws the money for college, the plan's increase in value is taxed at his or her income-tax rate.

Should you buy into these state plans?

Yes if you're sure that your child will attend an in-state public school (or in Massachusetts, a participating school). That's where your prepaid dollars will buy the most. And *yes,* if you're a conservative investor who wants a tuition guarantee. Prepaid education plans are convenient and safe.

But *no* if there's a good chance your child will want a private or out-of-state school; your prepaid plan might cover a disappointing percentage of the cost. And *no* if you're a savvy investor. That same money invested in stock-owning mutual funds for 10 years or more should cover tuition with something left over for the other college costs. And yet again *no* if you have to borrow money to participate. You'll probably pay more in loan interest

---

* At this writing, Alabama, Alaska, Colorado, Florida, Georgia, Massachusetts, Michigan, Missouri, Ohio, Pennsylvania, Tennessee, Texas, Virginia, Wisconsin, and Wyoming. Some plans may not be open to new sales.

than the rate of increase in college costs. Put the equivalent of the loan payments into Series EE bonds instead.

For a list of state prepaid education plans, check the Web at http://www.finaid.org/finaid/ptp.html#state_programs.

Prepaid State Plans vs. Education IRAs: You can't fund both in the same year. The plusses for state plans: They generally guarantee to match the rise in in-state tuition costs. They also accept more money, so you can accumulate more for children who will attend state schools. The plusses for IRAs: The gains are tax free and can be used at any school.

College Prepaid Education Plans

Some colleges invite alumni and others to register their young children and prepay 4 years of school—either tuition only or tuition, room, and board. For a relatively small sum of money now, you're guaranteed that the giant bill of the future will always be fully paid. Furthermore, this effort gives your child an edge with the admissions office since the school won't want to lose both the money and your goodwill. But what if your babe grows up and doesn't like your school? I see quarrels in my crystal ball—and penalties if the child won't go. I say, don't ask for trouble. Pass this idea by.

Some colleges offer not to raise your costs for 4 years if, when your child matriculates, you pay 4 years' tuition in advance. Prepayment gives you a risk-free, tax-free return on investment equal to the college's current inflation rate. Some schools accept partial prepayments. But don't borrow the money to pay in advance if the loan interest rate is higher than tuition inflation. And ask how much money you'll get back if your child drops out.

Bank Prepaid Education Plans

The granddaddy is the CollegeSure certificate of deposit, created by the College Savings Bank at 5 Vaughn Dr., Princeton, NJ 08540. You deposit a lump sum into a federally insured CD or start making regular installment payments. Your guaranteed return on investment falls one or 1.5 percentage points under the college inflation rate, depending on how much you put up. You have to deposit relatively more money than college costs today. By investing that excess, the College Savings Bank guarantees that the growth in your total deposit will match the average private-college inflation rate. You owe income taxes each year on the interest earned and pay stiff penalties for withdrawing before your child reaches college age.

Is this a good buy? Not today, because the yields are so low (minimum: 4 percent). CollegeSure's chief appeal is its guarantee. If college inflation runs higher than it is today, this CD should meet it. But a tax-deferred Series

EE bond will probably serve you better, especially if you get some tax exemption on the interest. EE-bond rates also rise with inflation.

Other banks have looser college-savings programs. For example, they might show you how much you have to deposit each month to cover the cost of the college you want. When costs rise, the bank recomputes the payments so you know you're always meeting the school's inflation rate.

BUM INVESTMENTS FOR COLLEGE

1. Tax-deferred annuities. There's a 10 percent tax penalty for withdrawing money before 59½. The insurer may charge withdrawal penalties even past 59½.

2. Any bonds, including zero-coupon bonds, that will have to be sold before maturity. You risk taking a beating on the price.

3. Life-insurance policies on children.

4. Life-insurance policies on adults, because of their slow cash build-ups (although it may be worth investing in a universal life policy that you already have).

5. Money market mutual funds, because the after-tax return is so low.

6. Income-paying real estate, unless that's your primary business. It's hard for amateurs to make money; there's the hassle factor of managing property; and you may not be able to liquidate at the price you want in the year you want to sell.

7. Unit trusts (page 793). You periodically get small payments that have to be reinvested, usually at a low interest rate. You might lose some of your capital if you have to sell before maturity.

8. Index options, gold coins, options on oil futures, penny stocks, new issues, football games, lottery tickets, racehorses. Well, maybe not racehorses. I knew a horse once named Rutland Road . . .

LET'S HEAR IT FOR GRANDPARENTS!

A grandparent can pay any amount at all for college, with no gift-tax consequences, as long as the money goes directly to the school and is used to help cover tuition and fees.

A grandparent—and anyone else, for that matter—can also make a tax-free gift of up to $10,000 a year to each child (that amount rises with inflation starting in 1999). Gifts to kids are generally made through state Uniform Gifts (or Transfers) to Minors Acts (page 90).

But *don't* make gifts to the children or, for that matter, to their parents. Such gifts reduce the amount of college aid they'll get. Instead, grandparents should keep the money in their own accounts, then ride to the rescue when the tuition actually falls due. The exception to this rule: families that know they won't get college aid. In this case, the taxes on the savings will probably be lower if they're kept in the child's name (page 89). If you're raising cash by selling appreciated stock, give the stock to the child and let the child sell.

ARE YOU A SUCKER TO SAVE?

No, you're not. It's a myth among struggling college savers that they may be making a mistake. The more you save, they say, the greater your assets, so the less you'll get in college aid. The aid formulas penalize savers and reward spendthrifts.

There is some truth to that statement, but not much.

It's true that the greater your assets, the less student aid you'll get. But the size of your student-aid package is based mostly on income. Your assets don't make a whole lot of difference. Furthermore, every aid package contains loans. By saving less, you wind up having to borrow more.

Spendthrift, low-asset families might pick up an extra $1,000 in grants and subsidized student loans. And then what are they going to do? They'll still owe a huge sum of money and they won't have the savings to cover it. They'll be up to their necklaces in debts.

Truly, savers win the day.

THE BEST-GUESS COLLEGE PLANNER (SHORT FORM)

How much should you be saving for college? Here's a down-and-dirty way of estimating what to put away each month.

But use this quick calculation only if: (1) You have no other college savings. (2) You are comfortable with targeting the average college cost rather than the cost of a particular school. (3) You are willing to assume that college expenses will rise by 6 percent annually. (4) You are willing to guess that your college-investment portfolio will earn 8 percent pre-tax. Otherwise, skip to the Best-Guess College Planner (Long Form) in Appendix 5. That allows for more options when figuring out how much to save.

In truth, I'd rather have every reader use the Long Form because it gives you a better answer. The Short Form, like most conventional college planners, advises you to save a fixed sum of money—for example, $500 a month. But that's unrealistic. Right now, $500 a month might be more than you can afford. Ten years from now, it might be pocket change.

The Long Form, by contrast, figures out what percentage of your income should be saved every year. If you settle on a fixed percentage—such as 5 percent a year—your college contributions can start low and rise as your salary does.

But for Short Form addicts, here's the easiest way, courtesy of the mutual fund company T. Rowe Price.

Short Form

1. Add up the number of years from now that your child will start school. Count the current year. A 10-year-old will matriculate in 9 years—this year plus 8 years more.

Number of years until school starts: _____

2. Enter the average 4-year cost of the type of college that your child will attend. See the table below and choose a private or public school.

College cost: _____

3. On the following table, look down the left-hand column to the number of years before college starts. Read across to the proper column. That's how much you have to save each month to meet the average college cost.

	MONTHLY INVESTMENT*	
YEARS TO COLLEGE	PUBLIC	PRIVATE
1	$3,570	$7,533
2	1,817	3,834
3	1,232	2,600
4	939	1,982
5	764	1,612
6	646	1,364
7	562	1,187
8	499	1,053
9	450	950
10	410	866
11	378	798
12	351	740
13	328	692
14	308	649
15	290	613
16	275	580
17	261	552
18	249	526
19	238	503
20	228	482

* Assumes an 8 percent pretax return on investments with no additional investments once the child starts school.

SOURCE: T. Rowe Price

CONQUERING YOUR FEAR OF FLYING

When savings are hard to come by and the objective is so important, it can be scary to put money in stocks. Who will forget the stunning Crash of 1987? Who can feel safe from another crash? Who can deny that a ghastly bear market, lasting a couple of years or more, can cut the value of stocks in half?

On the other hand, if you don't buy stocks (assuming you'll hold 5 years or more), your college fund may lose purchasing power rather than gain it.

So . . . take a look at the 10-year performance of stocks on page 577. It should comfort you. Think about the rest of the data I present in Chapter 21. Check the lists of mutual funds with good records in Chapter 24 and consider a couple.

You needn't put all your money in stock funds if investing worries you. Go with half your money and promise yourself to quit reading the papers when stock prices fall. Keep making investments through thick and thin, holding on to the faith that stocks will always rise again. Stow the other half of your money in Series EE bonds or similar safeholes.

You'll be okay.

When college finally starts, I'll wager that your stocks have won the day.

STEP 6

UNDER-STANDING INVESTING

There is a secret to investing that cuts a path directly to the profits that you're looking for. The secret is simplicity. The more elementary your investment style, the more confident you can be of making money in the long run.

This insight isn't easy for investors to accept. Wall Street resembles nothing so much as an Oriental souk, whose subtle vendors bow and beckon, urging this purchase and that. The goods are colorful and varied. The more intricate the investment package, the stronger the spell it casts. But it's stuffed with risks you couldn't even begin to imagine. This glittering merchandise almost always profits the vendors more than you.

And you don't need it! You can rack up a superb lifetime investment record with just three or four good stock-owning mutual funds, maybe a bond fund, and some Treasury securities or tax exempts. That's all you really need to know. Investing is easy if you buy the simple things and buy them well.

21.

Drawing Up
Your Battle Plan

Which Kinds of Investments
Serve You Best?

*When you start, the jigsaw puzzle that's your personal
money lies in dozens of pieces, all jumbled up. When you
finish, the picture will be clear.*

For investment success, you need a concept, a framework on which to
hang all the thoughts and suggestions that are constantly coming your way.
Should you buy this mutual fund or that one? How do you choose between
stocks and bonds? Which risks make sense and which don't?

There are logical answers to these questions, but only if you start with
a sensible investment plan. Once you've drawn that plan, the mysteries
of money will become clearer. You'll see exactly the kinds of investments
you ought to make. Just as important, you'll know which investments to
avoid.

Your plan will not make you rich tomorrow. You're not betting the farm
on the pipe dream of doubling your money overnight. Instead, you're using
your common sense to map a steady strategy for building wealth.

YOU CAN ONLY GET POOR QUICKLY;
GETTING RICH IS SLOW

I would write a get-rich-quick book if I could. Everyone (me included)
dreams of learning how to beat Wall Street in three easy lessons and with

no risk. But the schemes behind such books are usually a ticket to the poorhouse.

There are no easy ways to beat Wall Street! That's not even an intelligent goal. Thoughtful people buy the kinds of investments that will yield the combination of safety, income, and growth they need. At the end of the road, they will look back and see that they did well.

FIRST PRINCIPLES OF INVESTING

Before you draw up your own battle plan, you need to know what has worked in the past. These are the lessons that history teaches:

1. *For building capital long term, buy stocks.* You are taking only a modest risk. Over 10-year periods, stocks have almost always outperformed bonds and have left simple bank accounts in the dust.

2. *Buy stock-owning mutual funds, not stocks themselves.* Good mutual funds give you professional money management, full time. The managers diversify your investments and balance your risks. Picking stocks individually is a fascinating game but for dedicated hobbyists only.

3. *Diversify.* Although stocks win the race in the long term, you and I live in the short term. That means we need buffers—investments that give our capital some protection in a year when the economy falls apart and stocks decline. You also need different types of stocks because they perform differently at different times. So think "portfolio"—your portfolio being every investment, piece of real estate (including your home), savings account, and retirement account you own. Stocks for growth; money market mutual funds for ready savings; bonds and high-dividend stocks for steady compounding of interest; your home as an inflation hedge.

4. *Keep it simple.* Plain-vanilla stocks and bonds will do the job. All the other stuff—options, commodities, limited partnerships—usually leave you wiser but poorer.

5. *Have the courage to hold your mutual funds for the long term.* Successful investors check the charts showing long-term stock-market performance (up, down, up, up) and believe them. When the occasional downturn occurs, they roll into a fetal position until the market comes back.*

6. *Reinvest your dividends.* If I do no more than make you appreciate dividends, this chapter will have done its job. An investor who put $100 into the Standard & Poor's 500-stock average on the last day of 1925, held until January 1, 1996—and spent all the dividends—would have earned $5,807. If that investor reinvested all dividends, he or she would have had $137,095! Compounding interest and dividends is the investment world's strongest, surest force.†

---

* A bull market *rises*. A bear market *falls*.

† Thank you, Ibbotson Associates, Chicago.

7. *Ignore market timing.* Market timers try to sell when the stock market nears its peak and buy again when stocks bottom out. As if they knew. This game isn't worth the candle because you are so often wrong. On a percentage basis, stocks rise much further than they fall. So the odds are on the side of the people who stay invested all the time.

A study done by the University of Michigan for Towneley Capital Management in New York makes this point perfectly. The researchers looked at the 31 years from 1963 to 1993. They found that if you were out of the stock market during the 90 best days—just 90 days out of 31 years—you'd have missed an amazing 95 percent of all the market's gains. Those magic days were scattered randomly over the entire period. One dollar invested in 1963 and not touched would have grown to $24.30. But if you missed those 90 days, your dollar would have grown to only $2.10—less than you'd have earned from Treasury bills.

If you'd been on the sidelines during the market's worst 90 days, your dollar would have multiplied to a breathtaking $345.40. But if you think you can pluck those days out of a 31-year period, I'd say you'd been spending too much time in the hot sun.

So stay invested, collect your dividends, and reinvest them. Your protection against temporary declines is diversification—having some of your money invested somewhere else.

8. *Invest regularly.* Use a portion of every paycheck to invest in mutual funds. Don't worry about "bad" markets. They are good buys for long-term investors because stock prices are so low.

9. *Stick to your investment strategy.* One year you'll make money. One year you'll lose money. But time is on your side. Don't let impulse investing or sudden market changes shake you out of your long-term plan.

10. *Have patience, patience, patience, patience.* The urge for quick returns hurls you into lunatic investments—the financial equivalent of lottery tickets, with just about the same odds. A successful investor hitches a ride on private industry's long-term growth.

HOW RISKY ARE STOCKS, REALLY?

Having made such a strong pitch for buying stocks, I can hear the echoes coming back—"Yeah, but what about the '87 Crash? What about the '90 Crashette? What about all the other times that stocks have fallen (maybe even as you read!)?"

Well, what about it? Those drops are temporary. No one knows what stocks will do tomorrow, but the evidence is clear as to how they'll probably perform over 10 or 20 years. They will almost certainly go up. A lot.

The following table shows your odds of making money over various holding periods—one year, 5 years, 10 years, and 20 years—since 1926. Four things stand out:

YOUR ODDS OF MAKING MONEY IN STOCKS

HOLDING PERIOD	YOUR CHANCE OF EARNING*			YOUR CHANCE OF LOSING
	0–10%	10–20%	OVER 20%	
1 year	16%	18%	38%	28%
5 years	30	51	9	10
10 years	47	48	2	3
20 years	38	62	0	0

* Compounded annually. Computed in April 1997 by Chicago's Ibbotson Associates. All dividends reinvested.

1. In any one-year period, stocks are dicey. You get the biggest gains if you hit them right. But you also risk the biggest losses.

2. Over 5-year holding periods, your chance of loss is small. Over 10-year periods, it is negligible. Over 20-year periods, zero.

3. The longer you hold stocks, the stronger the likelihood that you'll earn compound annual returns in the area of 10 to 20 percent (but it's much closer to 10 percent than 20 percent).

4. You probably won't earn more than 20 percent long-term, despite the historic bull-market run that started in 1983.

One Further Fact That Every Investor Should Know: Since 1926, stocks have outperformed inflation by roughly 7.5 percent annually. That's a far better average real return than you'll get from any other financial investment.

Yes, but . . .

What about Murphy's Law, which says that if anything can go wrong it will? Or Quinn's Law, which says that Murphy was an optimist? In living memory, stocks have had two especially bad patches, so far.

First, they were trounced by bonds during the early, and deflationary, 1930s. (The reincarnated among us will remember that bonds also rolled over stocks during the deeply deflationary 1870s.)

Second, in the inflationary 1970s, stocks finished just a whisker behind both corporate bonds and Treasury bills. Stocks hate super-high inflation just as they hate severe deflation.

In every other decade, however, stocks finished first, usually by a mile. They can do just fine during modest inflation as long as it isn't accelerating over 4 percent. And they're just as happy during modest deflations (although you have to go back to the nineteenth century for proof). That's why smart investors emphasize stocks, with a prudent diversification into bonds just in case.

But just because stocks usually beat bonds doesn't mean that stocks themselves will always pay great gains. Look at the deadly 17 years after the Dow Jones industrial average first hit 1,000 in February 1966. It fell back, then rose to 1,000 again, then fell back, then rose again to 1,000, then fell back. It didn't definitively charge above the 1,000 mark until January 1983. During that period investors who bought and held big-company stocks gained 7 percent annually, all of it from compounded dividends. After inflation, they earned only 1.2 percent. (During that same period long-term bond investors earned 4.3 percent a year but lost money after adjusting for inflation.)

Here's something you *really* don't want to hear: in the 10 years from 1965 to 1974 the Dow earned only 1.2 percent annually—an entire decade when it didn't pay to buy and hold the nation's leading stocks. (Small stocks and internationals did better. That's why you diversify.)

HOW TO LIMIT ALL YOUR RISKS

Some investors stay out of stocks in order to keep their money "safe." But they don't know what "safety" means. Bonds and bank accounts carry hazards that you haven't even thought about. A fixed-income investment can eat up your future just as surely as if you had fed it to sharks. You have to understand your whole range of risks in order to make good investment decisions.

Of all risks, the most familiar is *market risk*—the risk of losing money in a bad investment.

Adjust for this by (1) diversifying your investments so that a single loss (even though temporary) doesn't leave a hole in your wealth, (2) buying only the boring old standbys like diversified mutual funds, and (3) skipping the dizzy investment ideas that only a novice or maniac could love. If you can't resist "diz," give yourself a small mad-money fund to play with. I'll wager that your boring investments come out ahead.

Everyone also endures *economic risk*—the hit you take when the economy turns down.

Adjust for this risk by minimizing investments that get bashed in recessions such as junk bonds and aggressive growth mutual funds. Those investments soar in good times and may give you better long-term returns. But you have to be willing to suffer larger-than-usual losses when business profits sag.

Less understood is *inflation risk*—the risk of losing the purchasing power of your capital. This is the monster that eats fixed-income investors for lunch. After inflation and taxes, a certificate of deposit, zero-coupon bond, or Treasury security—even an inflation-adjusted security—yields very little. You preserve the purchasing power of the cash you put up, which is important, but your money doesn't really grow. After years and years of investing, you come out with a pittance in real terms.

Adjust for inflation risk by (1) not keeping large, permanent sums of cash in money market mutual funds and similar short-term investments; (2) avoiding an all-bond portfolio, even in retirement, and (3) putting at least some of your money into stocks for real growth. Here's how well (or how poorly) all the common investments survive inflation.

AVERAGE COMPOUNDED RETURNS AFTER INFLATION

	1926–96*	1946–96†
30-day U.S. Treasury bills	0.6%	0.5%
20-year U.S. Treasury bonds	1.9	0.9
5-year U.S. Treasury bonds	2.0	1.4
Common stocks (S&P 500)	7.4	7.5
Small-company stocks	9.2	9.1

* Average inflation for the period, 3.1 percent a year.
† Average inflation for the period, 4.3 percent a year.
Dividends reinvested but not adjusted for income taxes.
SOURCE: Ibbotson Associates, Chicago

The consistency of long-term common-stock yields over inflation is nothing short of astonishing. Consider the following measurements by Jack W. Wilson and Charles P. Jones of North Carolina State University and Richard Sylla of New York University: From 1926 to 1996, stockholders earned 7 percent annually after inflation. (The professors' result for the 1926–96 period is a tiny bit different from Ibbotson's because of a different methodology.) From 1871 to 1925 stocks earned 6.63 percent—almost exactly the same. So no matter what's happening to stocks today, it is reasonable to expect that, 20 or 30 years from now, you'll show a 7 percent real return over inflation, whatever that may be. With occasional exceptions, of course, such as 1966–83. In the stock market there are always exceptions.

Bond investors face *interest-rate risk*—the risk that interest rates will rise. When that happens, the value of your bonds (or bond mutual funds) falls and you lose money. Furthermore, the income you're earning may no longer beat inflation and taxes.

Adjust for interest-rate risk by owning short- to medium-term bonds (maturing in maybe 2 to 10 years). When rates rise, these bonds don't fall as much in price as 20- or 30-year bonds.

Fixed-income investors also face *reinvestment risk*. Say that interest rates are rising and you have to choose between a one-year CD at 6 percent and a 5-year CD at 5.5 percent. You decide on the higher rate. But when that CD matures, one-year rates may be down to 5 percent. That 5.5 percent you spurned last year is no longer available. You'd have made more money by going for the 5-year CD originally.

Adjust for reinvestment risk by "laddering" your fixed-income investments. For example, you might own CDs or bonds maturing in one year, 2 years, 3 years, 4 years, 5 years, and all the way up to 10 years. Every year a CD or bond matures. If interest rates rise, you can reinvest the proceeds of that bond at a higher rate. If interest rates fall, you'll still be getting high interest income from your longer-term investments. For more on laddering see page 67.

If you hold a "callable" bond, you also face reinvestment risk (a bond is callable if the issuer can call it in before maturity). Take a 30-year tax-free municipal that's supposed to pay 5.8 percent interest for another 20 years. If interest rates fall, the municipality will call in the bond after 5 or 10 years, and you can kiss that income goodbye. Adjust for this risk by buying only noncallable Treasury bonds.

Then there's *liquidity risk*. A "liquid" investment can be sold immediately, at market price, if you suddenly find that you need the money. An "illiquid" investment can't be sold fast except at a discount. Not all of your investments have to be liquid, but enough of them do to assure you quick cash if you ever need it, without having to take a loss. So what's liquid?

• A money market mutual fund is liquid. You can get your cash at any time.

• A certificate of deposit is relatively liquid, but not perfectly so. You can always get the money, but it may cost you an early-withdrawal penalty.

• Mutual fund shares are normally liquid. You can sell at any time, at current market value. Occasionally, however, a fund's liquidity may be impaired. If scads of investors all want out at the same time—as has happened during panics in the junk-bond and municipal-bond markets—selling pressure can push down the market price. The fund also has the right to suspend telephone redemptions or delay mailing your check for up to 7 days.

• Individual stocks are liquid as long as they trade on the major stock exchanges. Small stocks sold over the counter (page 711), however, may cost you a lot if you have to sell.

• Gold bullion coins are liquid anywhere in the world.

• Retirement accounts are superficially liquid in that you can usually cash them in. But I count them illiquid because of the tax cost and penalty of breaking into them too soon.

• Small amounts of tax-exempt bonds are often illiquid. No one wants to buy them except at a discount.

• Precious gems are hugely illiquid. They're salable but the dealer may not offer you anything close to what you think they're worth.

• Real estate is generally illiquid. It can take months to sell and even then you might have to mark down the property's price.

• Your own business is illiquid.

• Units in most limited partnerships are so illiquid that there may be no market for them at all (raising the question, are these investments or wallpaper?).

Adjust for liquidity risk by balancing illiquid assets with liquid ones. Anytime you buy something, ask: What happens if I want to sell? Can I get my money fast? Can I sell at market price without taking a discount or paying a penalty? If not, how long might I have to wait for my money? You should have enough liquid assets to carry you for a year, even if no other money is coming in.

The final risk is one almost no one thinks of. It's *holding-period risk*— the chance that you'll have to sell an investment at a time when it's worth less than you paid.

Say, for example, that you've been saving for a down payment on a house and are keeping it all in a stock-owning mutual fund. Two weeks before you'll close on the house, the stock market drops. You lose 25 percent of your down payment, can't buy the house, and your marriage breaks up. That's holding-period risk.

Or say that you bought a 30-year zero-coupon bond (page 779) for your child's college education. When college begins, the bond still has 15 years to run. You have to sell it to pay the tuition, but the market is down, no one wants a single bond unless you'll chop the price, and you're stuck. That, too, is holding-period risk.

I like stocks if the holding period will last for at least 4 or 5 years. I love stocks for holding periods of 10 years or more. But I hate and fear stocks for shorter periods because you cannot count on getting your capital out.

I fear 30-year bonds for any purpose but speculation on falling interest rates (page 759). I hate any bonds that will mature well past the date when I know that I'm going to need the money.

To adjust for holding-period risk, match your investments to how soon you're going to want the funds.

• Cash you'll need within one to 2 years belongs in a safe place. Two possibilities: money market mutual funds and shorter-term Treasury bills (page 188). Both preserve your capital while offering some inflation protection. (On money funds, your inflation protection is the fact that interest rates can rise. On 3- or 6-month Treasuries, you can roll over your investments at a higher rate.)

• Cash you'll need in 3 or 4 years might be okay in an intermediate-bond fund. But for true security, I'd keep this in money markets, too.

• Cash you won't need for more than 4 years should be invested for income and growth.

Finally, there's *investment-book risk.* All the investment returns you see here are averaged over calendar years. The same is true for most articles in personal-finance magazines. But there are zillions of possible holding periods, which may produce higher or lower returns. Sophisticated financial planners use something called a "Monte Carlo simulation." It looks at thousands of random possibilities to help you assess the chance of achieving average, above-average, or below-average results. If you see a planner (Chapter 32), he or she should have this capability.

THE RIGHT SHOE FOR THE RIGHT FOOT

You cannot escape taking *some* kind of risk, so the next thing to ask is whether your current range of risks supports or undermines your purpose. Here's a general guide.

Use safe savings, with no market risk, for:
A cash reserve equal to 3 or 6 months' pay.
Accumulating a down payment on a house.
Saving for a big vacation.
College savings that are needed within one to 4 years.
Protecting capital when you've lost your job.
A parking place for money waiting to be invested elsewhere.
Preserving any sum you dare not put at the slightest risk.
Use stocks for:
Accumulating college tuition while your child is young.
Building a retirement fund.
Generating an income out of dividends and capital gains.
Use medium-term bonds for:
Adding to your income, from interest earnings.
Adding some price stability to a stock portfolio.
A deflation hedge.
Use long-term bonds for:
Speculating on falling interest rates.
A deflation hedge.
Use investment real estate for:
Building retirement savings over 10 years or more.
An inflation hedge.

To find out if you're carrying the right investments to support your personal goals, fill in the table on the following page.

First, list all your savings and investments, both inside and outside your retirement plan. Divide them into short term and long term. Then list your short- and long-term goals. Note that "growth" isn't a goal, it's a strategy. "Early retirement" and "college tuition" are goals.

The table may show a mishmash of investments acquired without thinking what goals they should serve. The money you're saving for a down payment might be in a bond fund instead of cash; your retirement savings may be in certificates of deposit. Later chapters will help you straighten all this out.

DO YOUR CURRENT INVESTMENTS MATCH YOUR GOALS?

Your Short-Term* Goals	Your Current Short-Term* Investments	Appropriate Investments
$_____	_____	Money market mutual funds
$_____	_____	Certificates of deposit
$_____	_____	Short-term Treasuries
$_____	_____	Series EE Savings Bonds

Your Medium-Term† Goals	Your Current Medium-Term† Investments	Appropriate Investments
$_____	_____	Short- and intermediate-term bonds and bond mutual funds
$_____	_____	Conservative stock-owning mutual funds
$_____	_____	Individual blue-chip stocks

Your Long-Term‡ Goals	Your Current Long-Term‡ Investments	Appropriate Investments
$_____	_____	Stock-owning mutual funds, including aggressive funds
$_____	_____	Intermediate-term bonds
$_____	_____	Intermediate- and long-term bond funds
$_____	_____	Individual stocks
$_____	_____	Real estate

* Maturing in 3 to 4 years or less.
† Maturing in 3 to 10 years.
‡ Maturing in more than 10 years.

SHOOTING CRAPS

"But where's the fun?" you ask. "Where are the kicks, the highs, the joys of the chase? I want to have some sport with my money!"

And why not? So do I. Over the years I have fallen in love with one oil well (dry), one new venture (bankrupt), one glamour stock (down 80 percent, which is when I learned about stop-loss orders), and one of the worst mutual funds in history. I did make some money on some of my fliers (including that mutual fund, which I dumped before it went too far down). But that's not the point. What matters is that I was gambling with play money, not with the bulk of my assets. My basic holdings were, and are, in a suitable range of sober investments for my old age.

I want you to get all the pleasure you can from the money you've earned. If that means rolling dice in a Wall Street crap game, so be it. Just don't throw around your kid's college-tuition account or the life insurance proceeds meant to see you through widowhood. Fund your serious needs seriously. If there's anything left over, do whatever you want with it.

ASSET ALLOCATION: HOW TO DO IT, WHY IT WORKS

So far we've been matching appropriate investments and levels of risk with a whole range of personal objectives, short term and long. Now it's time to consider pure long-term investing, such as parlaying your savings into enough to live on when you retire. Here, other kinds of matching schemes come into play. You are asking the question: What return do I need from my long-term investments? How much risk am I willing to swallow in order to get it?

Enter the concept of "asset allocation." To explain it, let me start with a tale of two investors, as told by Marshall Blume, professor of finance at the Wharton School in Philadelphia.

Fighter Jock puts $100 into stocks in August 1929, just before the Great Crash. Measured by the Dow Jones industrial average, with dividends reinvested, it takes him almost 16 years to get his money back.

Savvy Sal also has $100, but she puts $50 into stocks and $50 into bonds and maintains that 50/50 split. When her bonds are worth more than 50 percent of her capital, she sells some and buys stocks. When her stocks are worth more, she sells some and buys bonds. She does this every month (Blume is measuring by the market averages here), always seeking to keep half of her money in each investment. In just 6 years, she recovers her original stake.

Notice what Sal did *not* do:

She did not sell all her stocks at the bottom and give up the market for ever and ever.

She did not try to guess when the market would rise or fall again. She just followed her investment formula.

She did not let herself be swayed by the news of the day. Instead, she invested for the long term.

She did not fail. She beat Fighter Jock, who bought stocks and held them. And she beat the investors who fled the market and put their money in the bank.

Sal practiced asset allocation—which, simply put, means dividing your money among stocks, bonds, cash, and other kinds of investments and keeping it there. People don't pay a lot of attention to asset allocation, *but it's the key decision that determines your investment success,* not how smart (or dumb) you are at picking stocks or mutual funds.

"But wait," you say, "Sal was just lucky. What would have happened had stocks bounced right back after 1929?"

In that case, Fighter Jock would have done somewhat better. But from time to time he'd have taken a big loss.

Sal would also have taken occasional losses on her stocks as well as her bonds. But because she owned both, her total portfolio of investments would never have dropped as far as Jock's. Her long-term results would still have been fine, without as much fear along the way.

But the fact remains that stocks didn't bounce back after 1929. And Sal was positioned to handle that risk.

TIME OUT FOR THEORY

Even if you know that you're supposed to diversify your investments, maybe you don't know why. A lot of study has established several things:

1. Different types of investments tend to move in different cycles. Some may go up while others go down. Some go in the same direction, but not at the same time or at the same speed. Some move by larger percentages than others. Owning different types of investments protects you from big losses in your total portfolio and can improve your returns. *Something* you own is usually going up (or at least not going down as fast). You are less exposed to risk.

2. *When* you buy isn't nearly as important as what types of assets you buy and how much you own of them. You can be all wrong on your market timing and still do well if you are properly diversified.

3. "Market timing" (which means buying before the market goes up and selling before the market goes down, ha-ha) is extraordinarily hard to do. The average investor won't guess right often enough to beat the investor who buys and holds. Most professional investors don't do much better. The Forecaster's Hall of Fame is an empty room.

4. Almost no one, including investment professionals, can "beat the market" over the long term. It's a waste of time to set that kind of standard for yourself.

5. You cannot predict which types of investments—known as asset classes—will do better over the next 5-year period. U.S. stocks? European stocks? Emerging markets? Bonds? Treasury bills? Who knows?

These findings lead to the conclusion that you shouldn't break your head trying to predict what will happen to stocks, interest rates, or the economy. Don't seek truth in the financial press. Don't consult gurus. Don't be stampeded into the market, or out of it.

Instead, focus on what you're investing *for* (page 582). Then split your money among the types of investments most likely to achieve that goal. And stick with them. Amen.

HOW TO MIX 'N' MATCH

To minimize risk, you need a mix of asset classes that rise and fall at different times or at different speeds. In the real world, no investments counter each other quite that neatly. Nor do they maintain their relationships consistently. For example, long-term bonds are behaving more like stocks than they used to. U.S. and European stocks are also moving more in tandem. In general, however, here's how the various assets move in relation to each other:

• Stocks behave differently from Treasury bills.

• Long-term bonds behave differently from short-term bonds.

• Gold stocks behave differently from other stocks.

• Foreign stocks and bonds behave differently from U.S. stocks and bonds over the long term, although not necessarily over the short term.

• Real estate often behaves differently from stocks and bonds, although in specific regions of the country they can all behave alike.

Here's how to choose which assets to own:

• In case of unanticipated inflation, you want real estate, inflation-adjusted Treasuries, gold, or money market mutual funds.

• For anticipated (but moderate) inflation and economic growth, you want U.S. and foreign stocks. You also want stocks during periods when consumer price increases are gradually slowing down (disinflation); and perhaps even when prices are falling somewhat (deflation), depending on what the economy does. To diversify among U.S. stocks, you need mutual funds dedicated to small companies, large companies, value stocks (low-priced and unloved), and growth stocks (earnings rising rapidly). For more on value vs. growth, see page 696.

• In case of economic slowdowns and severe deflation, you want high-quality, noncallable long-term bonds—which means Treasuries.

• To stabilize the value of a portfolio, you want cash equivalents (money market mutual funds, short-term Treasuries) and short- to medium-term bonds.

• To prevent weight gain, hair loss, acne, and wrinkles—and to confront an unknown future—you want a stake in all of these investments. The exact mix, however, has to be matched to your personal needs and will change over time.

• To keep it simple, you want to own many of these investments through mutual funds.

You have *not* diversified if you own 10 stocks. It takes a minimum of 15, spread carefully over 15 different industries, to approach a proper mix.

You have *not* diversified if you own 3 growth mutual funds. Those managers all pick the same kinds of stocks and they'll rise or fall in tandem.

You have *not* diversified if you own all stocks.

Nor have you diversified if you buy a bond fund, a Ginnie Mae fund, and some certificates of deposit. These, too, are much alike.

At minimum, you need a mix of U.S. stocks and medium-term bonds. An investor with more money will add international and emerging-market stocks. Real estate also belongs in the pot. Beyond your own house, consider real-estate investment trusts or owning another piece of property.

Just to Make It a Little Harder: Selecting an appropriate level of risk means more than choosing among stocks and bonds. Within any class of investment, some types of securities carry more risk than others.

Say, for example, that you're buying stocks to help fund a college education for your kids. A conservative investment would be a mutual fund that buys blue-chip, dividend-paying companies. An aggressive choice would be a fund that buys the stocks of small companies or companies in Southeast Asia.

If you want bonds, a conservative choice would be Treasuries, an aggressive choice would be junk bonds.

So you really have two decisions to make: (1) What mix of investments best suits your needs? (2) Within each investment class, how much risk do you want to take?

A FIXED MIX VS. A FLEXIBLE MIX

Within the church of asset allocation, two theologies are at war. One says: fix your portfolio at whatever mix of assets is right for you and stay there until circumstances change (which is my view). The other says: keep changing the amount you hold of each type of asset, to focus on whichever market you think is the strongest.

With a *fixed mix,* you might own, say, 55 percent U.S. stocks, 15 percent foreign stocks, and 30 percent bonds. From time to time you'd check your portfolio to see if it needed "rebalancing." That means bringing everything back to the percentages that you started with. In general, you rebalance when your investment mix gets out of line by 5 to 10 percent.

To rebalance, you add up the value of all your investments. If your U.S. stocks are now worth, say, 65 percent of your portfolio, you would sell enough to bring the percentage back to the 55 percent you started with. You'd reinvest the proceeds in a class of assets that had underperformed. For example, say your international stock funds had dwindled to only 10 percent of your holdings. You'd buy enough shares to bring that segment back up to 15 percent.

Why rebalance? Two reasons: (1) To maintain a steady level of risk. If your money is 70 percent in stocks, you're more vulnerable to bear markets than if you're only 60 percent in stocks. By rebalancing, you limit your losses when prices head south. (2) To cash in on profits. Rebalancing forces you to take profits out of assets whose prices have gone up and reinvest that money in assets that are cheap. Miracle of miracles, you are selling high and buying low, just as the market magicians say you ought (the average investor buys high and sells low, then wonders why he or she loses money). Rebalancing may or may not improve your total return, depending on market conditions. But it puts you in a position to gain when underperforming assets start moving up again.

With a *flexible mix,* you might decide that U.S. stocks will make up, say, 30 to 70 percent of your portfolio. When times look good, you'll put in 70 percent; when you get worried, you cut back to 30 percent.

In other words, you try to time the market, guessing when it will rise or fall. And not just one market but perhaps four or five of them, depending on how diverse your portfolio is. To me, this is a gambler's game. It adds greatly to your chance of loss.

It's Not Always Practical to Rebalance. Rebalancing acts are principally for mutual-fund investors, who can easily sell shares in one fund and move to another. It doesn't work well when you own a portfolio of individual stocks. Rebalancing also requires a tax-deferred account. If you have to pay taxes on your profits each time you sell, your portfolio will lose velocity. Investors with taxable accounts are better off leaving their current investments alone. To rebalance, put all new investment funds into the lagging asset—not only your new contributions from income but also the distributions from your other assets.

YOUR REWARD, AT LAST

The tables on pages 590 and 591 take some of the guesswork out of allocating assets among U.S. stocks, bonds, and cash. They help you decide how much risk you are willing to tolerate in order to earn a desirable return. The first table, covering stocks and long-term Treasury bonds, was prepared by Towneley Capital Management, an investment advisory firm in New York City and manager of the Eclipse funds. The second table, for stocks, medium-term Treasuries, and cash, comes from the mutual fund company T. Rowe Price. Here's how to use the data:*

Read down the columns headed "The average return." That shows the average long-term return you can expect if you hold the indicated mix of investments. Stocks are measured by Standard & Poor's 500-stock average,

---

* The returns on these tables don't match because they use different methodologies. Towneley rebalances the portfolio monthly and calculates 12-month periods from the start of every month. T. Rowe Price rebalances annually and uses calendar years.

medium-term bonds by 5-year Treasuries (Table Two), long-term bonds by Treasuries maturing in more than 10 years (Table One), and cash by 30-day Treasury bills.

When you see a return that looks good to you, read across to the last column. There, you'll find the largest percentage loss that that particular mix of investments has ever had in a single year. In Table One, for example, the portfolio with a 12.2 percent return once lost as much as −31.7 percent. You recover those losses in later years but must be prepared to suffer through.

If the loss looks too scary, read on down the column until you find a one-year loss that seems tolerable. Then look back to the first column to see what mix of investments you've chosen and what your average return is likely to be. If that return looks too low, rethink the size of the one-year loss that you're willing to risk (remembering that these losses are temporary).

That's investing, in a nutshell. You are looking for the highest possible return commensurate with the risk you're willing to take.

The middle column, by the way, is strictly for fun. It shows the kind of luck you might have in a superior year, in both stocks and bonds. But it shouldn't enter into your investment decision. Long-term investors won't earn the single highest return; they will earn something closer to the average return.

These tables are pretax, so they're for people who are investing retirement accounts. Your returns will vary if you're investing after tax. The higher your bracket, the less you'll net from bonds.

The Risk/Reward Tables Carry Some Home Truths:

To minimize risk and maximize gain, don't choose an all-bond portfolio. For proof, look at Table One and compare the portfolio fully invested in long-term bonds with the one that contains 80 percent bonds and 20 percent stocks. The mixed portfolio had a smaller maximum one-year loss yet a higher average return.

Table Two shows that adding cash to the mix will cushion your loss in declining years but greatly reduce your average return. You don't need cash in a retirement portfolio that you won't touch for many years. Your cash belongs in regular, taxable accounts and needn't exceed an amount you'll need for expenses in the next two to four years.

Adding a modest amount of bonds to an all-stock portfolio, and rebalancing every year (Table Two), gives you about the same return that you get from stocks, with a little less risk.

For maximum growth potential, choose all stocks—at least, for that portion of your money available for long-term investment. Stocks show the highest risk of loss in a single year but the biggest average gain over time.

If you want solid growth but with some protection against market drops, choose a mix of stocks and bonds. Younger people should tip toward higher returns because they have time for their stocks to recover

FINDING YOUR CENTER: RISK VS. REWARD

TABLE ONE

If You Own	The Average Return*	The Single Largest One-Year Gain	The Single Largest One-Year Loss
100% stocks† No bonds	13.6%	61.2%	−38.9%
90% stocks 10% bonds‡	12.9	58.4	−35.4
80% stocks 20% bonds	12.2	55.5	−31.7
70% stocks 30% bonds	11.4	52.7	−28.3
60% stocks 40% bonds	10.7	49.9	−24.8
50% stocks 50% bonds	9.9	47.1	−21.3
40% stocks 60% bonds	9.2	47.8	−17.7
30% stocks 70% bonds	8.6	49.5	−14.2
20% stocks 80% bonds	7.7	51.1	−10.6
10% stocks 90% bonds	7.0	52.8	−11.4
No stocks 100% bonds	6.2	54.5	−13.4

* From 1950 through 1996, compounded annually, dividends reinvested, portfolio rebalanced to the original investment mix at the start of every month.

† Measured by Standard & Poor's 500-stock average.

‡ Long-term U.S. government bonds.

SOURCES: Towneley Capital Management, New York City; Standard & Poor's Corporation; Crandall, Pierce and Company, Libertyville, Illinois.

from any drop. If you're following Table One, consider a stocks-to-bonds ratio of 90/10 or 80/20. Middle-aged people and young retirees should look at 70/30 or 60/40 splits. Much older retirees might move to 30/70 or 20/80 allocations of stocks to bonds, but never to 100 percent bonds. That is, if you're interested in growth.

MAKING YOU WHOLE

There's one more thing you might want to know about investment risk—namely, your break-even time. Say you hold stocks or bonds at a bull-market peak and then a bear-market slide sets in. How long will it take

FINDING YOUR CENTER: RISK VS. REWARD

TABLE TWO

If You Own	The Average Return*	The Single Largest One-Year Gain	The Single Largest One-Year Loss
100% stocks†	12.8%	52.6%	−26.5%
80% stocks 20% bonds‡	12.6	41.3	−20.5
60% stocks 30% bonds 10% cash**	10.2	30.5	−14.1
40% stocks 40% bonds 20% cash	8.8	22.5	−7.5
25% stocks 40% bonds 35% cash	7.6	20.8	−2.1
100% cash	6.9	14.7	0.9§

* From 1950 through 1996, compounded annually, dividends reinvested, and rebalanced to the original investment mix at the start of every year.
† Measured by Standard & Poor's 500-stock average.
‡ Medium-term U.S. government bonds.
** Thirty-day Treasury bills.
§ Small gain.
SOURCE: T. Rowe Price, Ibbotson Associates

before you get your money back? The following table gives you the answer, for every 15 percent decline in stocks and every 5 percent decline in intermediate-term Treasuries. One column assumes you reinvest all dividends; the other assumes you spend the dividends rather than reinvest them.

Three points to note: (1) The 1930s don't seem relevant to modern times. You never know, of course, but I draw my personal risk assessments from the period since World War II. (2) Reinvesting dividends and interest gives you an enormous payback, especially in long bear markets, and most especially when you invest in bonds. (3) When you live off bond interest instead of reinvesting it, half a generation can pass before average bond values rise again. To be sure of getting your principal back, buy individual bonds and hold them to maturity.

CONSTRUCTING YOUR PORTFOLIO

You need to take a total-portfolio approach. Put all your assets in a pot, then divide them into the types of investments that serve your personal

HOW LONG DOES IT TAKE TO GET YOUR MONEY BACK?

IN STOCKS*

MONTH THE BEAR† MARKET STARTED	NUMBER OF MONTHS BEFORE YOU BROKE EVEN (DIVIDENDS REINVESTED)	NUMBER OF MONTHS BEFORE YOU BROKE EVEN (DIVIDENDS NOT REINVESTED)
August 1929	186	304
July 1957	13	16
December 1961	17	22
January 1966	15	16
November 1968	29	43
December 1972	43	92
November 1980	24	26
August 1987	22	24
May 1990	10	10
Average	42.5	61.4
Average Since World War II	24.6	31.1

* Standard & Poor's 500-stock average.
† Prices down 15 percent.
SOURCE: Ibbotson Associates

IN BONDS*

MONTH THE BEAR† MARKET STARTED	NUMBER OF MONTHS BEFORE YOU BROKE EVEN (INTEREST REINVESTED)	NUMBER OF MONTHS BEFORE YOU BROKE EVEN (INTEREST NOT REINVESTED)
January 1928	—	26
May 1931	14	28
June 1954	—	470
February 1958	—	423
May 1958	25	—
March 1967	—	296
July 1972	—	168
April 1973	—	42
December 1976	—	116
January 1979	—	81
June 1979	10	—
May 1980	18	—
April 1983	—	25
October 1986	—	59
January 1994	17	—‡
Average	16.8	157.6
Average Since 1980, When the Post–World War II Inflation Spiral Ended	17.5	42.0

* Five-year Treasuries.
† Prices down 5 percent. Whether they reach this mark depends on when dividends were reinvested.
‡ As of this writing, still not recovered.
SOURCE: Ibbotson Associates, 1997.

time horizon and control your risk. You'll find specifics on all these investments in later chapters. Here, you're constructing a battle plan. These are examples, not gospel! Every investor is a little bit different as to wealth, health, income, expectations, needs, and financial responsibilities. Every investment adviser will have different ideas about how portfolios should be constructed. Every time period is marked by different tax laws, interest rates, and market conditions—all of which influence portfolio choices. But these are reasonable frameworks to start with.

When tracking your progress, don't look at just one of your investments. Your stocks might slide by, say, 10 percent. But if your bonds slide by less than 10 percent and you have some cash, your total portfolio might be down by only 2 or 3 percent. That's the measure to go by.

A Young Single Person

1. Cash reserve—in a bank or money market fund.
2. Retirement account—as heavily into stock funds as you can stand. Consider stock-index funds, value funds, growth funds, internationals, and emerging markets.

A Young Married Couple with Small Children

1. Cash reserve—in a bank or money market fund.
2. Inflation hedge—a house and the stock funds in your college and retirement accounts.
3. College account—as heavily into stock funds as you can stand. As your child approaches the teenage years, switch to a mix reflecting the medium-term portfolio on page 595.
4. Retirement account—as heavily into stocks as you can stand. Consider stock-index funds, value funds, growth funds, internationals, and emerging markets.
5. Deflation hedge—the bonds in your tax-deferred retirement account, as long as they're noncallable Treasury bonds.

A Middle-Aged Couple with Small Children

1. Cash reserve—in a bank or money market fund.
2. Inflation hedge—a house, maybe a vacation house, the stock funds in your college and retirement accounts, and some inflation-protection Treasury bonds.
3. College account—as heavily into stocks as you can stand. Consider stock-index funds, value funds, growth funds, growth-and-income funds, internationals. As your child approaches the teenage years, switch to a mix in the medium-term portfolio on page 595.

4. Retirement account—consider a long-term mix of medium risk rather than high risk. For stocks, choose the usual suspects: international funds, emerging markets, stock-index, and growth-and-income, but perhaps with more emphasis on the latter.

5. Deflation hedge—the bonds in your tax-deferred retirement fund, as long as they're noncallable Treasury bonds.

A Middle-Aged Couple with Children in College

1. Cash reserve—a paid-up credit card. (All your cash is in the hands of the college bursar! Your only emergency money is your credit line.)

2. Inflation hedge—a house, maybe a vacation house, the stock funds in your retirement account, and some inflation-protection Treasury bonds.

3. College account—in Series EE Savings Bonds; alternatively, in Treasuries or bank CDs timed to mature when semesters begin.

4. Retirement account—consider a long-term mix of medium risk (page 595) rather than high risk. For stocks, it's international funds, emerging markets, stock-index, and growth-and-income, but perhaps with more emphasis on the last.

5. Deflation hedge—the bonds in your tax-deferred retirement fund, as long as they're noncallable Treasury bonds.

A Young Retiree (55 to 65)

1. Cash reserve—enough money in a bank or money market mutual fund to cover 12 months of expenses not paid by your pension and other regular income.

2. Inflation hedge—a house, maybe a summer house, your common stock funds, and some inflation-protection Treasury bonds.

3. Retirement account—a long-term allocation of moderate risk (page 595). Consider stock-index funds, growth-and-income funds, value funds, growth funds, and internationals. Buy intermediate and short-term bond funds or individual bonds.

4. Deflation hedge—your bonds are noncallable Treasury bonds.

An Older Retiree (65 to 75)

1. Cash reserve—enough money in a bank or money market fund to cover 12 months of expenses not paid by your pension, Social Security, and other regular income.

2. Inflation hedge—a house, maybe a vacation house, stock funds, and inflation-protection Treasuries.

3. Retirement account—a long-term allocation of moderate risk (below). Consider stock-index funds, growth-and-income funds, value funds, growth funds, and internationals. Buy intermediate and short-term bond funds, or buy individual bonds and ladder them (page 755).

4. Deflation hedge—your bonds are noncallable Treasury bonds.

An Even Older Retiree (75 and Up)

1. Cash reserve—enough money in a bank or money market fund to cover for one or 2 years of expenses not paid by your regular retirement income. Also, a firm determination to spend your principal as well as your income, if that's what it takes to live comfortably.

2. Inflation hedge—a house, stock funds, and inflation-protection Treasuries. You've sold your vacation house and reinvested the proceeds for income and some growth. Why growth? Because you could easily live for another 20 years or more.

3. Retirement account—a mix of medium risk, if you have enough pension and investment income to live on. Concentrate on funds that pay high dividends, such as stock-index and equity-income funds. Buy intermediate and short-term bond funds, or buy individual bonds and ladder them (page 755). Choose a low-risk portfolio from the box, below, if your current income is insufficient and you're dipping into principal to pay the bills.

4. Deflation hedge—your bonds are noncallable Treasuries.

PICK YOUR POISON: HIGH, MEDIUM, OR LOW RISK

SHORT-TERM PORTFOLIO, for money needed within 2 years: 100% in cash—money-market mutual funds, Series EE bonds, one-month Treasuries, or bank CDs.

SHORT- TO MEDIUM-TERM PORTFOLIO, for money you'll want within 3 to 5 years: *low risk*—35% cash, 40% bonds, 25% stocks; *medium risk*—20% cash, 40% bonds, 40% stocks; *high risk*—10% cash, 30% bonds, 60% stocks.

MEDIUM-TERM PORTFOLIO, for money you'll want within 6 to 10 years: *low risk*—20% cash, 40% bonds, 40% stocks; *medium risk*—10% cash, 30% bonds, 60% stocks; *high risk*—20% bonds, 80% stocks.

LONG-TERM PORTFOLIO, for money you won't touch for more than 10 years: *low risk*—60% stocks, 30% bonds, 10% cash; *medium risk*—80% stocks, 20% bonds; *high risk*—100% stocks.

SOURCE: T. Rowe Price

What If All Your Retirement Money Is in Company Plans That Don't Allow the Investment Choices Suggested in the Sample Portfolios? Your plan should at least have a stock fund and a fixed-income fund. Given these choices, younger people should put every nickel into stocks—especially an index fund, if you're offered one. It doesn't matter that you might leave the company in five years; you can roll that money into an Individual Retirement Account and keep it invested in stocks. In early middle age (say, 40 to 50), you might want 70 percent of your money in stocks. After 50, your stock allocation might drop to 60 percent. These are only examples, but they indicate a direction.

Don't Make the Mistake of Diversifying Your Retirement Savings Separately from Your Other Savings. Conceptually, you possess a single sum of money, some of it in the retirement account, some of it not. Your diversification plan should be tailored to that sum of money as a whole. The investments outside your retirement plan can fill in the pieces that the plan doesn't offer.

For example, your 401(k) plan might restrict your stock investments to U.S. mutual funds, so use your outside money to diversify into a foreign-stock fund. Alternatively, allocate higher investment risks to your pension plan (because you won't touch that money for 20 years or more) and choose lower risks for the savings you keep outside the plan (because that's Junior's college money, which you'll need 5 years from now).

You get the idea. Count all of your money when deciding whether you're properly diversified. Married couples should consider both spouses' portfolios as a unit. You may run your money separately but you're going to retire together and your standard of living will depend on what's in the common pot.

HOW TO GET MONEY TO INVEST

It's no mystery.
Save money.
Buy shares in a mutual fund every month.
Month after month after month after month.
After month.
If that doesn't work, inherit.

THE ENEMIES OF GOOD INVESTING

Don't look in the stars, look in yourself, as the great playwright wrote. You read all this stuff about steady investing and nod your head. But in a bear market, you may forget your good intentions. Our attitudes and emotions tend to undermine the strategy we set. Mastering these attitudes is just as important as mastering an investment discipline. Here are the most common mental errors, according to Jim Sullivan, a principal of the consulting firm Arthur Andersen:

1. *Fear of loss.* We're more alarmed by a minor loss than we're cheered by a major gain. To prevent these temporary losses, we invest more conservatively than we should. *Antidote:* Check out the market's past performance. See how little you get from conservative income investments, after taxes and inflation.

2. *Short-term focus.* If the mutual fund in your 401(k) loses money in one or two quarters, you might sell it and shift to something "safe." Conversely, you might leap into a fund that currently tops the performance list. *Antidote:* Check out a series of quarterly performance lists. A fund that's hot for six months often cools in the next six months (right after you buy!), and vice versa. Once you've chosen a fund for good reasons (Chapter 22), stick with it for 2 or 3 years unless the fund's management and objectives or your circumstances change.

3. *Fear of making the wrong decision.* With so many investments to choose from, some investors freeze. They leave their money in the bank or the fixed-income account in their retirement plan. They leave it in mutual funds they know are unsuitable. They might hand it over to someone to manage without knowing much about the person they've handed it to. *Antidote:* This book, of course! Keeping your money in its usual place is a decision, too—and often the wrongest one of all.

4. *Fear of regret.* You're afraid that you'll hate yourself in the morning. You *should* have bought that East Asian fund that rose 25 percent instead of the balanced fund that did only 10 percent. You *should* have switched to a money fund this year because stocks went down. Self-recrimination produces one of two effects. You do nothing, so you won't have to kick yourself around. Or you desperately try to catch up by jumping into that East Asian fund (too late). *Antidote:* Check out the long-term growth of conservative funds—balanced funds, equity-income funds, index funds. Simple and steady gets you where you want to go.

5. *Exaggerated hopes of gain.* At bull-market peaks, participants tend to believe that huge gains will continue indefinitely. They quit diversifying into bond funds and rush entirely into stocks. Then stocks collapse. *Antidote:* The table on page 577. Do you have the conviction to hold if your stocks drop by 40 percent or more? What if two bad years occur back to back? Diversified portfolios are easier to live with.

HOW TO HANDLE
INVESTMENTS AFTER . . .

Marriage. If you have two paychecks and agree on an investment approach, pool your money into a joint portfolio. Or keep two portfolios with similar kinds of investments.

If you don't agree, set up separate portfolios shaped to the risks that each of you wants to take. Draw up an overall mix for your mutual assets. Then dole out the higher risks to the more adventuresome partner and the lower risks to the other. (But even the spouse with the lower risks should own some stock funds. Why get stuck with the poorer yields if you divorce?)

If you both work in the same industry and have been buying your company's stock (maybe because you get a special deal on the price), you are overexposed to that industry's risk. Periodically, sell some company stock, if the plan allows it, and diversify into something else. If your company gives you stock as part of your 401(k), direct your personal investments elsewhere.

If you both have employee retirement-savings plans, coordinate your investments. See what each company's plan has to offer, then decide where to put your money. Together, your retirement plans should reflect the mix of stock and fixed-interest vehicles that you find appropriate as a couple.

A New Baby. Keep up with your retirement investing (Chapter 29). Any separate college fund should be in stock-owning mutual funds.

An Inheritance. Don't keep a stock just because Daddy loved it or because its price is up (or down). Maybe Daddy was holding a rotten stock. Maybe it yields income when you need growth. Maybe it was his company's stock and he was sentimentally attached to it. Keep only those assets that fit your own investment plan. Everything else should be replaced.

A Divorce. Investments made jointly aren't necessarily right for singles. So rethink your portfolio from the ground up. You may have to live on some of the money that you took from the marriage, which means keeping a larger cash reserve.

A New Job. If you get a lump-sum payout from your former company's pension plan, roll it into an Individual Retirement Account or, if allowed, into the retirement plan of your new employer. That preserves its tax deferral. Divvy up the money among the same types of investments that you had before. Or use the IRA for investments not included in your new company plan—say, international or emerging-market funds.

Unemployment. Roll a lump-sum payout from your pension plan into an Individual Retirement Account in order to preserve its tax-deferred status. Invest the IRA in a money-market mutual fund or money-market deposit account at a bank. Draw on this cash only as a last resort. Withdrawals will cost you income taxes plus a 10 percent penalty if you're under 59½ (for a way of avoiding the penalty, see page 876).

If you have other investments, sell them (or sell the ones that won't generate a big tax bill) and put the proceeds into a money market fund. This preserves your capital. You may need to draw on this money and can't run the risk of losing it in a market decline.

Live on your cash reserve (you have one, right? In cash or a nice clean home-equity line of credit?) and your taxable investments. If you don't find a job right away and your money runs low, make IRA withdrawals as needed.

When you get a job, use any remaining taxable savings to clean up debt. Anything left in your IRA can now go back into stocks.

Retirement. Don't shift all your money into bonds and money market funds. You will probably live another 20 or 30 years and, during that time, even modest inflation can decimate fixed incomes. You need a substantial stake in stocks in order to grow enough capital for your later years.

A Windfall. Maybe it's a lottery ticket. Maybe a big royalty check. Maybe the proceeds of selling your house. First, put the money in a bank or money-market mutual fund while you think about what to do. Second, ask an accountant what portion of your windfall you will have to pay in tax (keep that in the bank until next April 15). Third, attend to your obligations, like paying off debts or setting up a college fund. Finally, study up on investments. Don't talk to a stockbroker or financial planner until you have a good idea of what you want. Salespeople can mislead the uninformed.

If your windfall is from an upcoming lump-sum pension distribution, don't lay a finger on the money until you've talked to an accountant. The size of your net proceeds will depend on the tax choice you make.

WHEN—AND WHEN NOT— TO BE AN AVERAGING INVESTOR

You already know that you ought to invest part of every paycheck— for the good of your soul, for your future, and because your mother told you so. Steady investing keeps you from plunging too heavily when prices are high. And it disciplines you to keep on buying when stocks decline. Low markets are the equivalent of a bargain-basement sale.

In a seesawing market, monthly investing can make you more money than periodically investing lump sums. That's because you are "dollar-cost averaging." Your fixed-dollar purchase buys more shares when prices are low and fewer shares when prices are high. Result: a lower average cost per share. Dollar-cost averaging worked especially well in the late 1960s and 1970s, when stock prices rose and fell and rose and fell, never exceeding 1,000 on the Dow Jones industrial average.

But this technique is a loser in bull markets like those of the 1980s and early 1990s. When prices are moving steadily up, monthly investing gives you a higher average cost per share than if you'd been able to invest all your money at once.

When you're making retirement contributions through a payroll-deduction plan, you have no choice but to buy stocks periodically. Reinvesting all dividends is another form of automatic dollar-cost averaging.

But say that you have a lump sum of money—from a retirement payout, an inheritance, or a life insurance policy. You have a choice: invest it all at once or dollar-cost average by investing it gradually over a year.

In most cases, you'll do better investing your money all at once. Stocks rise more often than they fall. The chances are two out of three that lump-sum investing will outperform dollar-cost averaging.

But then there's that fatal, final, one-third of the time when stocks will drop soon after you invest.

I think of dollar-cost averaging not as a way of making extra money but as a way of limiting risk. A lump sum invested gradually over 12 months saves you from being badly hurt if you happen to start investing just before a market drop. If you worry more about losing money than making it, this technique is for you.

Dollar-cost averaging is better done with diversified mutual funds than with individual stocks. The broad market always recovers but certain stocks might not. If you choose a rotten stock, buying more shares on the way down would be throwing good money after bad.

MEMO TO THE NERVOUS

Maybe you quake more easily than others. You know in your heart that stocks are the best investment in the long run, but the thought of owning them scares you stiff.

Obviously, I'd like to change your mind. So try this: Put just a little money into a diversified, stock-owning mutual fund—maybe 20 percent of your savings. Pick a simple fund, like an index fund (page 701), and invest a modest sum every month for the next 12 months. Then forget about it. Pretend it isn't there. Five years from now, take a look at what you've got. The result ought to make you feel pretty good, good enough to put even more money in stocks. If I can divert even a small portion of your long-term retirement savings into the stock market, this book will have done its job.

But you have to promise to leave that investment alone. If you'll panic and sell the first time stocks drop, forget it. You don't belong in the market just yet. But do keep on reading, to learn more about how investing works. Willingness to accept stock-market risk isn't necessarily a function of your personality. It may be a function of your knowledge. The more you learn, the more you'll come to understand that long-term stockholdings aren't as risky as you thought.

MEMO TO THE NERVELESS

Some investors are fearless. They're not happy unless they're buying options on futures and borrowing against their house to do it. A reader once asked me what I thought about investing his son's college fund in a single junk bond. I said, "Not much." And he said, "But mutual funds are no fun." For him and his kin, this book will have helped if they speculate wildly with only part of their money (preferably a small part).

I'm not asking you to give up your habit. But for your family's sake, balance your high-wire act with investments that are reliably dull. Learning not to take stupid risks is equally a function of knowledge and experience. With luck, you'll learn your lesson while you still have some money left.

THE OUTLOOK

Breathtaking bull markets—like the one that started in the early 1980s —are rare. Stocks will continue to move higher, with dips and pauses every now and then. But the gains may take on a more normal look—maybe 8 or 9 percent annually, down from 16.5 percent from 1983 through 1996. But the market works its will in any number of ways. So let me suggest some possibilities and how to handle them.

We Might Have a Sideways Market for a While—with stocks rising and falling but not making much of a net advance. Dollar-cost averaging does well in a crab-walking market. So does a "fixed-mix" portfolio (page 587) that you continually rebalance—taking profits on the upside and rein-vesting in assets that are underpriced. Buy-and-hold isn't much of a thrill. Bonds might do as well as stocks. Long-term stockholders have to look past the sideways years to the next true market rise.

Our Hopes Might Be Briefly Interrupted by a Terrible Market—with stocks and bonds both falling and interest rates spiking up. That's why money you'll need within 2 years should always be kept in safe investments like certificates of deposit, Treasury bills and notes, or money-market mu-tual funds. Money you'll need within 2 to 4 years could be in bond funds but should be safely out of stocks.

Nothing truly prepares you for the hot, nasty breath of the bear other than the certain knowledge that this too will pass—probably in no more than a year or two. Your portfolio is defended if you own some bear hedges: noncallable Treasury bonds and notes, some shorter-term bond funds, maybe gold-stock mutual funds, and, of course, cash. But keep on buying stocks. You are locking them up at bargain prices. They will earn you good money when the market turns around.

We Might Have a Deflationary 1930s Market—the market of your deepest dread. I can't make a case for it. But as long as you own cash and Treasury bonds, they'd be your safety nets. Incidentally, there were two bull markets in stocks during the 1930s for anyone who had the money to play. (Really. Check it out.)

We Might Have an Inflationary Depression—with business down while consumer prices spiral up. Your defense would be gold stocks, money-market mutual funds invested in Treasuries, inflation-protection Treasury bonds, and, as a hedge against a dollar collapse, foreign-currency bonds or bank accounts. I rate this possibility virtually nil.

We Might Wind Up with a Terrific Twenty-first Century—with interest rates down and stocks and bonds pushing higher, both in America and abroad. This case rests on continued international growth, low inflation and interest rates, increased savings by the baby-boom generation, expanded world trade, no serious shortages of energy long term, and the continuing spread of the free-market faith.

This is not just my favorite forecast, it is also the most likely one. Long term, the world has always gotten richer and stocks have always trended up. On a percentage basis, history says that you might as well invest for success.

WHAT MAKES A GOOD INVESTOR?

To handle money well, you need a certain resilience of spirit. Peter Lynch, former manager of the Fidelity Magellan Fund, looks for these qualities:

Patience
Humility
Flexibility
Persistence
Detachment
Self-reliance
Common sense
Open-mindedness
Tolerance for pain
Ability to admit mistakes
Ability to do your own research
Ability to ignore a general panic
Ability to make decisions on incomplete information
Ability to ignore gut feelings because gut feelings are usually
wrong.

22.

How to Pick a Mutual Fund

Every Investor's Bedrock Buy

*I love mutual funds. Left alone to compound, they're the
surest way to wealth—but only if you're sophisticated
enough to keep them simple.*

There are two ways of investing: directly, by buying your own securities
from a stockbroker, and indirectly, by buying shares in a mutual fund.

I'm for mutual funds, especially for stock investments. Bonds are a little
trickier; sometimes you should go for individual bonds instead. But for
long-term growth, a stock fund will serve you better than any other financial
investment.

MUTUAL FUNDS DEFINED

A mutual fund is a shared investment. Many people send in money; a
manager invests it in the kinds of securities promised in the sales literature.
You own a pro rata share of all the securities the manager buys. So instead
of buying an individual stock or bond, you've bought a share in a basket of
them. You'll find stock funds, bond funds, money-market funds, international funds, real-estate funds—literally, something for everyone (page
605). There are even funds for people who don't want to bother picking
funds.

SEVEN REASONS TO LOVE
MUTUAL FUNDS

1. You get full-time money management from the person who runs the fund. You don't get that from stockbrokers. A broker's job is to sell stuff, not to worry about the overall shape of your portfolio.

2. You can pick the level of market risk you want to take (page 605). By contrast, when you buy your own stocks, you generally have no idea how risky your total investment position is.

3. In an index fund, your investments are guaranteed to do just about as well as the market, a promise no other investment can make.

4. You share in the fortunes of a large number of securities rather than owning just a few.

5. You can check a fund's past performance record.

6. You can participate in the stock market's long-term gains without having to think of which particular stock to buy or sell. Your mutual fund manager does that for you.

7. You can automatically reinvest your dividends and capital gains. Steady compounding doubles and redoubles your returns.

But What About the Big Killings That Are Made in Individual Stocks?

What about them? Your neighbors who buy stocks would be lucky if they made a killing one time out of 20. In some years, they've probably done it more often—but everyone is a genius when the market is steaming up. Even in good years, your neighbors accumulate losers and mediocrities (which they don't mention). Counting losers as well as winners, I'll bet that they don't do as well as the average mutual fund, especially if they don't reinvest all their dividends and capital gains.

There are arguments for buying stocks directly (page 708). But I'd buy mutual funds first. And even if I played around with stocks, I'd use funds for my central holdings. In fact, I do.

OPEN-END MUTUAL FUNDS

These are the traditional mutual funds that we all know and love. You invest in a pool of money that belongs to many different people. You can add money to the pool or cash out of it anytime you want. That's why the fund is called *open-end*. A *managed* or *actively managed* fund is run by someone who picks the fund's securities. An index fund, by contrast, is described as *unmanaged* or *passively managed* because it owns only the securities contained in a particular market index.

Your shares are priced at their *net asset value* (NAV). That's the total market value of all the fund's securities, minus liabilities, divided by the number of shares outstanding. Share prices rise or fall every business day, reflecting what happens to the fund's investments.

Every year you receive a pro rata share of the dividends, as well as any net profits from the sale of securities. This income can be taken in cash or reinvested automatically in more fund shares. Payouts are called *distributions* and may be paid monthly, quarterly, or annually. (Fixed-income funds may declare distributions daily, even though they pay out on monthly or quarterly schedules.)

Open-end funds have prospectuses, usually updated annually, that tell you how the fund invests. The fund's managers also send their shareholders semiannual and annual performance reports (some also send quarterly reports).

UP THE LADDER OF RISK

Here's a summary of the kinds of open-end funds available, what they invest in, and what they purport to do. I've started with the funds that carry the least market risk and, roughly speaking, advanced to those that carry the most risk. Use this list as a quick reference to check on the funds you read about. For a more detailed discussion of how to use stock and bond funds to advance your personal goals, see Chapters 24 and 25.

TYPE OF FUND	RISK LEVEL	INVESTMENTS*	OBJECTIVE
Money market	Low	Commercial paper, certificates of deposit, Treasuries, etc.	Keep capital safe; earn current short-term interest rates.
Tax-exempt money market	Low	Very short term municipals	Keep capital safe; earn current short-term, tax-exempt interest rates.
International money market	Mid–low	Foreign CDs, governments, and other short-term paper	Hope for higher returns than in U.S. money funds; reap gains when the dollar falls and losses when it rises.
Short-term bond, taxable or tax exempt	Mid–low	Government, corporate, or tax-exempt bonds, one- to 5-year maturities.	Keep capital fairly safe; earn a slightly higher taxable or tax-exempt income than money markets pay; small risk of loss.
Intermediate-term bond, taxable or tax exempt	Mid–low	Government, corporate, or tax-exempt bonds, 5- to 10-year maturities	Earn a higher taxable or tax-exempt income than on shorter-term bonds; accept more gains and losses of principal; expect solid total returns long term.

(*continued*)

Type of Fund	Risk Level	Investments*	Objective
Long-term taxable bond	Middle	Government or corporate bonds, 15- to 30-year maturities	Earn high current income, speculate on declines in interest rates; accept the risk of higher losses in hopes of getting higher total returns.
Long-term tax-exempt bond	Middle	Tax-exempt municipals, 15- to 30-year maturities	Earn high tax-exempt income in return for more risk of loss if bonds are sold before maturity.
Ginnie Mae	Middle	Securities backed by a pool of government-insured home mortgages; uncertain maturities, usually not more than 12 years	Earn good income; get a periodic return of capital; accept risk of loss if interest rates rise.
Global bond	Middle	Bonds of U.S. and foreign companies and countries	Go for high bond income; win gains when the dollar falls but risk losses when the dollar rises; U.S. bonds cushion the currency risk.
International bond	Middle	Bonds of foreign companies and countries	Go for high bond income; greater gains when the dollar falls, but greater losses when it rises.
Income	Middle	Emphasis on bonds and dividend-paying stocks	Emphasize income, but get more growth than bond funds offer; limited losses when the stock market falls.
Balanced	Middle	Part stocks, part bonds and preferred stocks	Earn reasonable income; get reasonable growth; limited losses when market falls.
Zero-coupon bond	Middle	Discount bonds paying no current interest	Accrue high bond income; dividends reinvested at the same rate paid by the bond itself; a lucrative speculation on falling interest rates, but big losses when rates rise. Safe if held to maturity.
Equity income	Mid–high	Stocks that pay high dividends, like blue chips and utilities	Earn modest income; get good growth; risk of average loss when the stock market falls.
Growth and income	Mid–high	Stocks that pay high dividends and also show good growth	A little more growth and a little less income than equity-income funds pay; average risk of loss when the market falls.

TYPE OF FUND	RISK LEVEL	INVESTMENTS*	OBJECTIVE
Asset allocation (fixed portfolio)	Mid–high	A mix of assets: cash, stocks, bonds, foreign stocks, etc.	Seek good growth and limited losses in any market.
Asset allocation (flexible portfolio)	Mid–high	A constantly changing portfolio mix, trying to emphasize the best markets at any given time	Seek good growth and limited losses in any market; risk of being in the wrong market at the wrong time.
Lifestyle	Mid–high	A mix of assets: stocks, bonds, cash	Create an asset allocation suitable to people of different ages and temperaments.
Convertible	Mid–high	Preferred stocks and bonds, convertible into common stocks	Earn higher yields than on common stocks but less than on bonds; hope for limited losses; less growth than in pure stock funds.
Fund of funds	Mid–high	Shares of other mutual funds	Earn average stock-market gains and losses; big risk of paying too much in management fees.
Stock index	Mid–high	Stocks picked to match the performance of a specific market as a whole	Earn average stock-market gains and losses.
Large-size companies (known as big caps)	Mid–high	Major U.S. and multinational firms	Buy the largest and best corporations that perform reliably over time.
Medium-size companies (known as mid caps)	Higher	Companies of medium size	Earn better returns than big-company stocks.
Real estate	Mid–high	Stocks in real-estate companies	An inflation hedge; risk of loss when this industry falters.
Conscience	Higher	Stocks in "moral" companies—no nuclear, no pollution, no tobacco, etc.	Earn average growth; bigger risk of subpar gains and higher losses because of the limits on investment.
High-yield bond, taxable or tax-free	Higher	Low-rated and unrated (junk) bonds; municipals or corporates	Higher income than other bond funds pay; good performance in economic upturns; higher risk of defaults; poor performance in recessions.

(continued)

Type of Fund	Risk Level	Investments*	Objective
Global equity	Higher	Stocks of U.S. and foreign companies	Earn worldwide capital gains and losses.
Growth	Higher	Stocks whose earnings usually rise fast	Earn above-average market returns (one hopes); accept larger losses when the market falls.
Value	Higher	Unloved companies whose stocks are down	Buy stocks cheap and wait for them to recover; higher dividends than growth stocks pay.
International equity	Higher	Stocks of foreign companies	Earn international capital gains; bigger gains when the dollar falls; bigger losses when it rises.
Aggressive growth (capital appreciation)	High	Shooting for the moon, with high-growth stocks, options, new issues, etc.	Earn above-average gains at the risk of above-average losses; minimal dividend income.
Asset allocation (globally flexible)	High	A constantly changing portfolio mix, focusing on several U.S. and international markets	Seek good growth and limited losses in any national or international market; a risk that the manager will bet wrong.
Sector	High	Stocks of one particular industry	For market timers, who hope to catch an industry's rising trend, then sell before stocks decline; not for investors who buy and hold; big risk of loss.
Small-company growth; small-company value	High	Stocks in the smaller companies traded on stock exchanges or over the counter	Achieve superior long-term gains relative to other growth or value funds; risk that high gains will be followed by periods of slower gains; above-average risk of loss; minimal dividend income.
Microcap	High	Teeny-tiny companies	Earn higher returns than the average small-stock fund—but be prepared to hold for a decade and endure a wild ride.
Gold and precious metals	High	Stocks of gold and precious-metal mines	A hedge against war, monetary turmoil, and, usually, unexpected inflation; gold stocks often go up when other stocks fall; big risk of loss.

* Some funds in these categories invest differently, but this is the general expectation.

DO YOU REALLY NEED ACTIVELY MANAGED FUNDS?

Most mutual fund managers don't beat the market indexes over time, so why would you bother investing with them? For people who buy bonds or the stocks of larger companies, index funds (page 701) are proven winners. They're competitive in the small-stock and international arena, too.

A handful of managers have indeed outperformed the indexes over various time periods, suggesting that they might be able to do it again. But finding them is *hard*. The 12-step program outlined here is not for the faint of heart. You're looking for a wizard touched with rare skill or amazing luck. You can't just pluck a name out of a magazine or best-buy chart.

Many people pay financial planners one percent or so to pick funds for them. Good planners are better at finding winners than you and I, but there's no guarantee that they'll beat the indexers, either. In fact, most of them probably don't.

Admittedly, index investing is boring. No heart-pounding thrills in a super year; no night sweats when a fund goes south. But I invest for profit, not thrills. To get the heart pounding, there's always love . . . or bungee jumping.

A 12-STEP PROGRAM FOR PICKING MUTUAL FUNDS

Let's say you've bought my story and will use index funds for your core investing. But you want to invest at least some of your money with those rare wizards who might outperform. Here's how you go about finding them:

1. READ UP. Get some specialized books on fund investing that will carry you past what you're learning here. One I've always found useful is *Sheldon Jacobs' Guide to Successful No-Load Fund Investing,* at this writing $25 from the No-Load Fund Investor, P.O. Box 318, Irvington-on-Hudson, NY 10533 (800-252-2042). ("No-load" means no up-front sales charge.) Jacobs also publishes the annual *Handbook for No-Load Fund Investors* ($45), a compendium of performance and other data on 2,200 funds.

For a clear-eyed discussion of mutual funds that barbecues herds of sacred cows, pick up *Bogle on Mutual Funds* by John Bogle, the brilliant founder of the Vanguard funds (Dell paperback, $13.95).

A Commonsense Guide to Mutual Funds by Mary Rowland (Bloomberg Press, $19.95) gives you a quick, short roundup of investment tips.

Mutual Fund Mastery (Times Books, $20) shows you a systematic way of screening for funds that might beat the market indexes. It's by money managers Kurt Brouwer and Steve Janachowski, who chose the funds named in Chapters 24 and 25 (disclosure: I was interviewed for the book but you can skip that part). In an especially valuable section, the authors show you how to use the Morningstar pages discussed in the following section to identify the few managers worth their pay.

2. SETTLE ON A SUITABLE ASSET ALLOCATION. Decide how to diversify your assets, based on what you concluded from Chapter 21. Start with large U.S. stocks (index funds, natch), add an international fund, then fill in with small U.S. stocks, growth stocks, value stocks, and bonds. For an explanation of growth and value, see pages 697 and 698. You have *not* diversified if you buy five aggressive-growth funds. They may own different companies, but they'll all soar or plunge together. Quantity doesn't mean you're diversified, either; you may own thirty funds, three-quarters of them much alike. Thirty funds is way too many, anyway. You can cover all the bases mentioned in this paragraph with just six funds. Ten would be plenty. As you will see, even ten good managers can be hard to find.

3. DISCOVER THE MANY RESEARCH TOOLS THAT ARE READILY AT HAND. Here's where you start developing short lists of potential buys—three or four funds in each asset category you're aiming for. Good information sources include:

• *Barron's* magazine and *The Wall Street Journal* for fund performance data, published quarterly.

• The performance and "best-buy" lists found in the following magazines: *Forbes* (second August issue, with an update early in February), *Business Week* (three consecutive weekly issues, starting the third week of January), *Kiplinger's Personal Finance Magazine* (August or September, with a separate mutual funds issue every February), and *Money* (February and August). These magazines present different best-buy lists because they evaluate funds differently. But any of these lists will do. If you don't subscribe, you can find back issues in your library.

• Morningstar is the leading source of information for retail investors. While developing your fund portfolio, you might take a three-month, $45 trial subscription to the monthly *Morningstar No-Load Funds*. You'll get reams of data on nearly 700 no-load and low-load mutual funds, making it easy to check out any fund that comes to your attention. For $5, you can get a detailed, one-page report on a single fund. Serious hobbyists might subscribe to the newsletter *Morningstar Investor*, $79 a year; it offers general-interest articles and performance data on 500 leading load and no-load funds. Alternatively, try *The Value Line No-Load Advisor*, containing general articles plus performance data on 600 no-load and low-load funds; $29 for a two-month trial. The biweekly *Value Line Mutual Fund Survey* also provides detailed fund reports. A three-month trial subscription costs $49.

Both Morningstar and Value Line offer software and access to their full databases on-line. Contact Morningstar at 225 West Wacker Dr., Chicago, IL

60606 (800-735-0700) or Value Line Publishing at 220 E. 42nd St., New York, NY 10017 (800-577-4566).

• The Net is stuffed with money sites, as any surfer will discover. For fund investors, here are some good starting points:

America Online subscribers can use the keyword "Morningstar" for limited access to Morningstar data, including lists of top-performing funds. Funds can be screened by performance rating or investment objective.

At http://www.networth.galt.com, you'll find short versions of Value Line's mutual fund profiles as well as those for Morningstar, price graphs of funds compared with standard price indexes, and other goodies.

Morningstar's own Web site at http://www.morningstar.net—free at this writing—offers good information about individual funds, although not all the details you will find on its $5 fund pages.

You might explore *Kiplinger* magazine's site (http://www.kiplinger. com), which offers general information plus fund performance lists.

Mutual Funds Magazine Online, at http://www.mfmag.com, offers articles, a research database, and fund-screening tools.

At http://www.investools.com, you can buy a wide variety of research reports, including the $5 Morningstar pages.

Finally, don't miss the Mutual Funds Home Page (http://www.brill. com)—jammed with mutual fund stuff, including manager interviews, fund 800 numbers and Web sites, news, and links to other financial sites.

• Ask the mutual fund for any recent reports the manager may have written. Check your library or the Net for articles or interviews. If you find some, skip the stuff about the manager's kids and dogs and concentrate on his or her investment approach. Is there a clear investment system? Do you understand it? Does it make sense for someone like you?

• Don't ignore the ads in newspapers and magazines. Fund companies put their advertising dollars into their better-performing funds. The money these ads generate gives managers fresh cash to work with, so they can pursue new ideas. Too much cash all at once can hinder a manager's performance, but a steady flow of money into a shop with good ideas lifts a fund faster than otherwise would be the case. (Be cautious, however, about the advertised "5-star" funds—page 615.)

• For a directory of more than 200 true no-load mutual funds, send $5 to the 100% No-Load Mutual Fund Council, 1501 Broadway, Suite 1809, New York, NY 10036. For each member fund, the directory lists the address, phone number, size, age, investment objectives, minimum investment, and shareholder services.

4. GO NO-LOAD. When you're picking funds yourself, stick with those without sales charges—no front load, back load, or level load (page 619). It's worth buying a load fund if you get truly superior performance; the fund lists in Chapters 24 and 25 even suggest some. All things being equal, however, you'll do better in no-loads because none of your money goes for

sales commissions. No-loads also tend to have lower annual expenses than load funds do. For a list of the leading no-load fund families, see Appendix 12, page 1027.

If you're working with a financial planner who takes only fees, you'll get no-loads, too. There are two ways of paying: a flat fee for investment suggestions that you will implement yourself or an annual fee of 0.5 to one percent of assets a year for the planner to manage your money for you (some planners charge 1.5 percent on small accounts—yet another reason to use index funds).

Stockbrokers and financial planners who take commissions recommend load funds. That's how they're paid for their advice. Some brokers take wrap fees in lieu of commissions (page 667), usually in the 2.5 to 3.5 percent range.

5. LOOK FOR FUNDS WITH LOW ANNUAL EXPENSES. You'll find a full discussion of expenses on page 619, including the surprising bite that a "mere" 1.5 percent a year subtracts from your investment gains (hint: you lose a lot more than 1.5 percent). Index funds have the lowest costs. To earn his or her fee, any fund manager has to deliver an investment return high enough to cover expenses *and* outperform an index fund, not just for a year or two but over a long period of time. That's a tall order, especially if the fees exceed the averages shown on page 623.

6. LOOK FOR MANAGERS WHO HAVE BEEN IN PLACE FOR AT LEAST 5 YEARS. Managed mutual funds are run by *people,* not computers, and you need to know who those people are. When the top stock picker leaves a fund, it effectively has no record until the new manager shows what he or she can do. The fund should tell you who the manager is and how long he or she has been there.

If a true wizard starts a new fund or takes over an existing one, he or she is worth a flier. But over time, most well-known names prove to be more lucky than skilled.

A few excellent funds are run by teams who have been wizard-trained. In this case, a change in lead manager may not matter much, as long as he or she has been with the group a long time. When a fund claims to have team management, however, read that section of the prospectus with care. The investment method used by the fund should be clearly spelled out and most of the team's major players should have been on board awhile.

Some funds falsely claim team management, to keep you from knowing when the real shot caller leaves. In general, you should stick with funds whose lead managers are specifically identified. *One tip:* Check the fund's page in Morningstar or Value Line, to see who was interviewed about the fund's current direction. That's probably the manager.

7. LOOK FOR SUPERIOR PRIOR PERFORMANCE. Previous good records aren't predictive by themselves, but the list of superior performers will include those few managers who have skill as well as luck.

Your quarry is always a *manager,* not a particular fund. So the fund's performance is relevant only if that manager is still there and his or her methods haven't changed. Otherwise, the testing period has to start all over again.

The manager's record (lasting 5 years or more) should outperform the market index closest to his or her investment style. Big-stock funds should be doing better than Standard & Poor's 500-stock index; small-stock funds, better than the Russell 2000; international funds, better than the EAFE index (Europe, Australia, and Far East); bond funds, better than a matching bond index—say, Lehman Brothers Aggregate Bond Index or the Lehman Municipal Bond Index. You want substantial outperformance—say, 2 percentage points a year. For a measly 0.5 percent, it's not worth taking the risk that the manager isn't a wizard after all. Remember: most managers *don't* beat the index over time.

Once you've checked the cumulative record, deconstruct it. See how the fund performed every year against the relevant market index. A skillful manager ought to be beating the index about half the time. The rest of the time he or she shouldn't miss by much. Testing annual performance is one of the secrets of smart fund selection. Managers with one great year are merely lucky. Two great years and three lousy ones don't show talent, either. You're looking for consistency. Evaluate only what the manager has done with mutual funds. Don't count previous records drawn from running money for insurance companies, banks, or individual accounts.

Where do you learn how a manager has performed year after year, compared with a standard market index? You get a glimpse in the fund's most recent annual report to shareholders, where a graph shows how the fund and the index have performed over the past ten years (or the life of the fund, if less). But that doesn't lay out each year's performance separately. For that you need *The Value Line Mutual Fund Survey, Morningstar No-Load Funds,* or Morningstar's separate $5 pages. Or call the fund's 800 number. Its customer service people should have the data.

8. COMPARE THE FUND WITH ITS PEER GROUP. It should outperform its peer group as well as a general market average. A growth fund, for example, should outdo the average growth fund at least half the time and cumulatively over the period. You'll find this data in Morningstar and Value Line, too. You can also find each fund group's average returns in the mutual fund roundups prepared by *Barron's, The Wall Street Journal,* and various magazines (page 610).

9. CHECK FOR CONSISTENCY OF INVESTMENT STYLE. A fund's style is defined by the kinds of stocks it invests in. Your best source is Morningstar. It prepares "style boxes" for each fund, defining the way the fund behaves. Is it invested primarily in large, medium-size, or small companies? Does its manager lean toward value stocks, growth stocks, or a blend? You want to see consistency (Morningstar shows prior-year style boxes at the top of

each fund's detailed report). If the fund has drifted out of small stocks and into larger ones, pass it by. That's probably a fund with more new cash from investors than it knows what to do with. Small-stock managers often drop to the middle of the pack once they're pushed toward the big-stock arena.

Warning: Funds don't always stick to their charters when they invest. Take the manager of a mediocre big-stock fund. If he or she buys some smaller stocks when that sector is hot, they might propel the fund onto some top-ten lists. But that's underhanded. The fund is outperforming other big-stock funds only by adding stocks that don't belong and, incidentally, by exposing you to extra risk. Morningstar tries to classify funds based on the way their securities behave rather than by the types of funds they say they are. Funds sometimes dispute their Morningstar classifications, but these guides are the best that investors can get.

10. CONSIDER THE FUND'S SIZE. Its size should be congruent with its investment goals. Small-company funds tend to lose their character once they've passed $1 billion in size. Mid-size-company funds can generally handle up to $5 billion. Big-company funds can be any size. As for bond funds, the bigger the better.

Managers sometimes announce that they're going to close their funds. That's no time to buy. You've effectively been told that the fund has attracted more new money than it can handle, which means that performance may fall off. Reconsider the fund when it opens again, provided that its larger size hasn't forced the manager to change his or her investment style.

11. CHECK THE FUND'S PERFORMANCE IN DOWN MARKETS. At this writing, that means the Crash of 1987, the Crashette of 1990, and the dip in 1994. Yet more downers lie ahead.

In a bear market, some funds drop further than the general market average, then spring back—growth funds, for example. Others go down less but may not turn up as fast—more descriptive of value funds. Think about which type of fund would make you happier. Daring investors love volatility; down markets let them buy good funds cheap. But conservative investors hate excessive drops in price; they might be scared into selling at the bottom, losing their chance to recover their loss. The fund's prospectus shows annual performance in each of the past ten years (or the life of the fund, if it's younger than that). For earlier years, ask the salesperson or call the fund. For comparison, Standard & Poor's 500-stock average rose 5.1 percent in the Crash year of 1987 (big price gains earlier in the year cushioned the big losses that came later). During the 1990 Crashette, the S&P lost 3.1 percent.

12. CHECK THE MINIMUM INVESTMENT. A few funds let you start with as little as $250 to $500, but most want $1,000 to $3,000. A few hold out for $10,000 and up. When you open an Individual Retirement Account, however, you usually need no more than $250 to $500. Some high-minimum funds are available for less through certain discount brokerage houses

(page 647). Once you've become a shareholder, funds might accept additional investments of as little as $50 to $100.

Very Few Managers Will Make It Through This Screen. If you put your present funds through it, you might find they're subpar. Indexing is the easiest and most reliable choice. Finding wizards takes work.

Don't Let Stars Get in Your Eyes. Morningstar awards stars to most mutual funds that have 3-year records. They get anywhere from one star (bottom rung) to 5 stars (tops), and the top funds trumpet their wins in ads. But these ratings merely show past performance adjusted for risk; they're not a reliable guide to the future. One study of Morningstar's 5-star funds found that more than half of them showed below-average results in the following 12 months. The flip side of that finding, of course, is that nearly half recorded above-average results. In short, when you go by stars alone, your odds of picking a winner are probably just about even. Ditto for Morningstar's "category ratings," marking the top funds in each of 44 special categories.

Other ranking systems fare no better. Take the weekly mutual fund performance lists published by Lipper Analytical Services in New York. You often see mutual fund ads bragging, "We're #1," based on the latest Lipper survey. But that, too, doesn't nail the future. The firm's president, Michael Lipper, says he has tried to find a predictive device in his data but without success.

Why such seesaw performance for so many leading, diversified funds? One reason is that they may not be nearly as diversified as you think. The bulk of their assets may be crammed into a single hot sector, like technology, making them sector funds in disguise. When the yen for that sector fades, these funds fade, too.

A Contrarian's Starting Place. Hunt for managers who have had good records in the past but aren't currently burning up the charts. They're on Morningstar's 2- or 3-star list or Lipper's list of laggard funds published daily in *The Wall Street Journal*. The stocks they buy have been out of favor for a while and might be ready to come back.

Don't Be Driven by Fund Envy. Every month the personal finance magazines heap praises on the Fabuloso Funds of the Moment. Unfortunately, they're almost never funds you own. If you buy them, they usually shine for a while, then fall off. That's because it's not skill that puts most of these fund managers on top. Their stocks or investment style just happen to be in vogue. When styles change, their stars will dim and the magazines will fall in love with another set of funds. Screen a Fabuloso Fund just the way you'd screen any other. Magazine editors don't know any more about the future than you do.

BUYING A NEWLY ISSUED FUND

Why would you bother? A new fund is a risk. Its manager may have hit home runs at his or her last fund, but these are new conditions and who knows how long it will take for the portfolio to shake down?

There are some possible advantages. A new stock fund starts small, so its winning picks will have more impact than they would on a bigger fund (ditto its losing picks, of course). The manager will be working with passion to make the fund shine. The fund has a flow of fresh cash to leverage the manager's best ideas. In bull markets, these funds often have pretty good opening months.

Still, performance is a question mark. Unless you've screened the manager at his or her last position and think you have a wizard, stick with funds whose long-term record is spread out for all to see.

BUYING A MUTUAL FUND AT A BANK

Screen it as carefully as you would any other fund. Bank funds aren't safer or better. They are *not* government insured. They're not cheaper or smarter or more attuned to small investors. You can lose money; these are *not* CDs. They're just mutual funds with sales charges, competing for your money along with all the rest.

FOR PEOPLE WHO THINK THAT THE SEARCH FOR SUPERIOR MANAGERS IS A DELUSION OF CROWDS

To find a wizard, you have to love running barefoot through statistics —and even then, you might be wrong. My personal choice is to keep things simple, which is a synonym for *boring*. Boring investing also has a remarkable record of success. Here are two ways of snoozing your way to wealth:

1. Buy index funds, which copy the market as a whole. There's a shelf full of bond-index and stock-index funds—enough to create a well-diversified portfolio for people in every financial circumstance. The granddaddy of indexing is the Vanguard Group in Valley Forge, Pennsylvania (800-662-7447). For more about index funds, see page 701.

2. Buy a simple, well-defined, no-load asset-allocation fund. This is one-stop shopping. You pick the mix of investments you want and the fund that delivers it. T. Rowe Price in Baltimore, for example, offers three Per-

sonal Strategy Funds: the Income Fund (40 percent stocks, 40 percent bonds, 20 percent money markets); the Balanced Fund (60 percent stocks, 30 percent bonds, 10 percent money markets); and the Growth Fund (80 percent stocks, 20 percent bonds and money markets). These funds diversify over every range of risk, including foreign securities and high-yield bonds, so you own a slice of everything. Vanguard does something similar with its four LifeStrategy Funds—Growth, Moderate Growth, Conservative Growth, and Income.

When you buy an asset-allocation fund, ask how much the advisers can change the allocation. The T. Rowe Price mix isn't supposed to vary by more than 10 percent above or below the designated levels—a good rule. Avoid funds whose managers can drastically change the mix. They're market timers by another name and their records show it.

VETTING THE FUND PROSPECTUS

Read the prospectus before you buy! Sales literature is fine, but it takes a prospectus to clue you in to the fund's costs and risks. When investing, there's no avoiding risks, but you should understand the ones that you're about to take.

Many fund prospectuses today are reasonably simple and written in plain English, especially those for no-load funds that investors pick themselves. A complex prospectus implies some complex investment techniques that may entail more risk than you care to take. If you have questions, call the fund's 800 number (for a no-load) or ask the salesperson to investigate. If you don't understand the explanation, you aren't yet ready to invest.

Some funds send abbreviated prospectuses of only a couple of pages. These short profiles explain the fund, lay out its past performance, disclose its costs, and describe the type of investor it seeks. They can't replace the 12-step screening system described on page 609. But if you won't screen, the profiles will at least guide you to appropriate funds. Before investing, I'd still crack the long prospectus, to check on the manager and the risks.

Obsessives might also ask for the Statement of Additional Information (SAI). It's Part B of the prospectus, sent only on request. Most of the data there is probably not your cup of tea. But you might be interested in the list of directors and officers, and their compensation.

Keep the prospectus permanently on file. It includes information you're going to need about how to manage your fund investment.

The One Chart That Tells You the Most About Performance Isn't Usually in the Prospectus. It's in the fund's most recent annual report to shareholders. Get it, without fail. The chart shows how well the fund has performed relative to a standard market index for the past 10 years or the life of the fund, whichever is less. You'll see at a glance whether it's keeping up with funds of its type. Why would you purchase a fund that missed?

Two warnings: The manager who produced that record may no longer be there. Also, you don't get year-by-year performance, so you can't tell if the fund has been slowing down. Still, this graph sheds some light in a particularly dark corner.

The annual report also discusses and explains the fund's performance during the previous year—something else you should check before investing. The best managers are very explicit about this. I'd suspect a fund that gave me fog or boilerplate.

When you read a prospectus, here's what you're looking for:

The Fund's Objectives

Read this section with great attention. What you see is (usually) what you get. I remember a guy who was horrified by the losses he took in the junk-bond crash of 1989. It had never dawned on him, poor soul, that that's what his "high-yield" bond fund invested in. I suppose I ought to have felt sorry for him, but I didn't.

Study the fund's objectives in light of the ideal portfolio you have designed for yourself. Will this fund fit in? Does it buy small stocks, invest for growth, emphasize income? Does the manager try to time the market and is that what you want? If the fund has two objectives—say, income and growth—it won't maximize either one of them. But that mixed objective may be exactly what you want.

Some prospectuses speak for several funds, each with a different investment objective. Make sure you sign up for the one you want.

What the Fund Invests In

This section should tell you exactly how the fund expects to meet its goals. What will it buy? Just as important, what won't it buy? Some funds stuff everything into this section, to leave its manager free to go in any direction he or she chooses. That's not a good sign. Your intent is to buy a particular type of investment, not give its manager a blank check. A good fund defines itself and stays within those limits.

To help you understand its investments, the fund may include little primers on such things as how the bond markets work and what options are. Small growth funds often get their kick from high-risk initial public offerings.

Don't Assume You Understand the Fund Just by Knowing Its Name. Among the disasters of recent years: a "government income" fund up to its neck in risky derivatives; an "asset allocation" fund 25 percent invested in the no-man's-land of emerging markets; a "blue-chip growth" fund heavily invested in new issues; a "dividend growth" fund with practically no dividends (the prospectus explained it was looking for companies that would pay dividends in the future).

Special Risks

On the front of the prospectus, READ ANY SENTENCES SET IN CAPITAL LETTERS. That's usually a red alert. Maybe the fund is buying especially risky securities. Maybe its expenses are unusually high. Or whatever. A SENTENCE IN CAPITAL LETTERS TELLS YOU THERE MIGHT BE TROUBLE. The risks will be covered in greater detail inside the prospectus—a section you shouldn't fail to read. If you lose money and complain, you can count on the lawyers for the fund to say, "We told you so."

What Mutual Funds Cost

There are four types of costs—direct sales commissions, marketing charges, money-management fees, and overhead expenses. You pay sales commissions, or "loads," only when you buy from a stockbroker or commission-paid financial planner. These broker- and planner-sold funds may also levy substantial marketing charges.

"No-load" funds charge no sales commissions and usually no marketing fees (although occasionally there's a small fee of 0.25 percent). You buy them directly from the fund company or through a mutual fund supermarket (page 632).

Both types of funds—the loads and the no-loads—charge annual overhead and money-management expenses. These costs plus the marketing fees (but not the sales commission) make up a fund's "expense ratio" (the ratio of costs to total net assets). Every investor pays a pro rata share. On average, no-load funds charge lower fees than load funds do, hence have lower expense ratios (page 622).

Mysteriously, most investors don't pay much attention to expense ratios, so the average fund has greedily been raising its take. The fees seem small because they're quoted as a percentage of your total investment. But when measured against your investment gain, they actually take an enormous bite. As the following table shows, the 2.5 percent you might pay for a brokerage-house wrap account can only be called confiscatory. Even a 1.5 percent fee burdens your returns. In a slow-growing market, only a low-cost fund—charging 0.5 percent or less—keeps you alive. Bond funds need low fees to make any headway at all. For a calculator that shows you the effects of fees on your return, go to http://www.financenter.com. All other things being equal, low-cost funds will net you more than high-cost funds.

COST OF A $10,000 INVESTMENT
AT 2.5 PERCENT OF TOTAL ASSETS A YEAR

WHEN THE MARKET RISES	YOU EARN	YOU PAY*	PERCENTAGE OF GAIN PAID IN FEES
20%	$2,000	$275	13.8%
15	1,500	269	17.9
10	1,000	263	26.3
5	500	258	51.6
1	100	251	*Tilt†*

COST OF A $10,000 INVESTMENT
AT 1.5 PERCENT OF TOTAL ASSETS A YEAR

WHEN THE MARKET RISES	YOU EARN	YOU PAY*	PERCENTAGE OF GAIN PAID IN FEES
20%	$2,000	$165	8.2%
15	1,500	161	10.7
10	1,000	158	15.8
5	500	154	30.8
1	100	151	*Tilt†*

COST OF A $10,000 INVESTMENT
AT 0.5 PERCENT OF TOTAL ASSETS A YEAR

WHEN THE MARKET RISES	YOU EARN	YOU PAY*	PERCENTAGE OF GAIN PAID IN FEES
20%	$2,000	$55	2.8%
15	1,500	54	3.6
10	1,000	53	5.3
5	500	51	10.2
1	100	50	50.0

* Fee assessed on principal plus earnings.
† You paid more than you earned.
SOURCE: The Vanguard Group

You'll find the fund's loads and expenses in a fee table in the front of the prospectus. If you look at nothing else, look here. How many of the following costs will you have to pay?

A Front-End Load—an up-front commission paid to the salesperson. It's assessed on what the fund calls its *A shares* and typically ranges from 4.5 to 6.5 percent. That's $45 to $65 for every $1,000 you put up, leaving you $955 to $935 to invest. High-load funds charge 8.5 percent; low-load funds, around 2 or 3 percent. At any commission level, you get a discount for investing a lot of money at once. If you're going to put up, say, $10,000, but in stages, see if you can file a "letter of intent," giving you a reduced commission right from the start.

A Contingent Deferred Sales Load—an exit fee, charged if you drop your fund within a specified number of years. For example, you might pay 6 percent if you sell the first year, 5 percent the second year, and so on. Six full years would have to pass before you could sell your shares without paying a penalty. Some funds assess the exit fee against your original investment. Others assess it against whatever the fund is currently worth, which raises your cost if the market goes up.

Shares with exit fees are generally known as the fund's *B shares*. Some salespeople tell B-share customers that they're buying a no-load because there's no sales charge up front. That's a lie. The broker always gets a commission. You simply pay it in other ways—including higher 12b-1 fees (described further on). Before buying, be sure you understand how long you're going to be locked in.

A Level Load—an annual charge for sales commission and money management combined. Typically it's 2 percent of the value of the account, divided between the broker and the mutual fund manager. There may also be a one percent front-end or back-end fee. Brokers usually call these *C shares*.

A Trailing Load—an annual fee paid to the broker every year for making the original sale. It usually runs around 0.25 or 0.5 percent.

A 12b-1 Fee—an annual fee paid to cover sales expenses, principally the salesperson's commission but also advertising, marketing, and distribution fees. The maximum fee: one percent on broker-sold funds and up to 1.25 percent on other funds. It's usually levied every year, eternally. Some firms, however, reduce it after 5 or 6 years. Load funds are the heaviest users of 12b-1 fees. By definition, a no-load can't charge a 12b-1 of more than 0.25 percent. A majority of no-loads don't levy this fee at all.

An Exchange Fee—levied by many fund families when you sell one fund and buy another within the group. It runs between $5 and $25 and is usually the only charge.

A Money-Management Fee—charged by every mutual fund, load and no-load, to compensate the managers who run the money.

Transaction Costs—the price of buying and selling securities. Index funds cost the least to run. Next lowest in cost should be U.S. bond funds, then U.S. funds that buy large company stocks. Funds that buy smaller U.S.

companies incur higher transaction expenses because those markets are less efficient. Global and international funds, especially those in emerging markets, carry the highest costs of all. Transaction costs don't show in the funds' published list of fees and expenses. They're paid out of assets as a regular cost of doing business.

Other Fees—shareholder accounting, franchise tax, start-up fees, account maintenance fees, legal and audit fees, printing and postage, you name it, someone is charging it.

Waived Fees—Some funds, especially newer ones, raise their yield and hold down reported costs by temporarily waiving some of their fees. Only the asterisk tells the tale. Say, for example, the prospectus shows an expense ratio of "1.25%*." Under the asterisk, you might learn that the full fee is 1.8 percent but the fund is taking less for a certain period of time. As the fund's assets rise, the potential expense ratio will gradually fall. But when making a buying decision, go by the higher cost. You might eventually have to pay it.

Redemption Fees—penalties charged by some no-load funds, especially index funds, for withdrawing money within the first 3 to 6 months of opening the account. The fee usually runs between 0.5 and one percent, and is meant to deter you from using the fund for short-term trading. Traders add to fund costs and can make it hard for managers to execute their long-term strategies.

Hypothetical Costs in Dollars and Cents—a table in the prospectus discloses what you might pay over one, 3, 5, and 10 years, in dollars and cents, for every $1,000 invested, assuming a modest investment gain of 5 percent a year. Stated this way, the expenses look too small to worry about— another reason high-cost funds get away with noncompetitive charges. Sneak another peek at the table on page 620 to remind yourself what you're really paying. At this writing, the Securities and Exchange Commission is considering changing this table to show the cost incurred on $10,000 invested.

Most Published Performance Data Make Load Funds Look Better Than They Really Are. That's because the measuring services—be they magazines or Morningstar—usually compute performance without deducting the upfront or back-end sales charge. You may have to hold for many years before a superior load fund will outperform a lesser-yielding no-load fund.

Choosing a Sensible Way to Pay. (1) Buy a no-load. (2) Buy a no-load (yep, I repeated myself). (3) If you're dealing with a broker or commissioned planner, here's how to choose among the loads:

• Pay a front-end load ("A shares") if you intend to hold the fund for many years. This method of payment gives you the lowest annual fee (see the table below). Over time, what you save on fees should more than cover the cost of your up-front load.

• Consider the deferred sales load only if you plan to hold for many years *and,* in 5 or 6 years, your annual 12b-1 fee will drop to the level that "A-share" investors pay. Otherwise, "B shares" will cost more. "B shares" may also cost more if your fund rises steeply in value. If you sell early, you'll be stuck with an exit fee; if you hang on, you'll pay that high 12b-1 forever.

• If you don't plan to hold for many years, the best deal is the level load—"C shares"—with no front-end or back-end fee.

YOUR GUIDE TO AVERAGE FUND EXPENSES

Here is the average annual percentage of assets you pay for various types of funds. These "expense ratios" include all money-management and overhead costs, but not front- and back-end sales charges. Smart investors stay away from funds with above-average annual fees.

	Average Annual Fees Charged by Pure No-Loads	Average Annual Fees Charged by Funds with Front-End Loads	Average Annual Fees Charged by Funds with Back-End Loads
Stock funds			
Index	0.54%	0.73%	1.57%
Growth and income	0.81	1.12	1.89
Equity income	1.00	1.20	1.92
Growth	1.04	1.37	2.07
Small company	1.16	1.50	2.19
Real estate	1.16	1.54	2.39
International	1.27	1.77	2.48
Emerging market	1.57	2.26	2.93
Balanced funds			
Stocks and bonds	0.93	1.20	2.02
Bond funds			
Tax-free municipal	0.62	0.85	1.53
General corporate	0.67	0.91	1.64
General government	0.71	1.05	1.72
High yield	0.81	1.12	1.83

source: Morningstar, 1997

The Portfolio Turnover Rate

This tells you how fast the fund manager buys and sells. An 80 percent turnover rate means that 80 percent of the portfolio's average value changed in a single year. Generally speaking, 40 percent is low turnover for stock portfolios, 80 percent about average, and 120 percent, high. Rapidly traded funds have high transaction costs. To compensate, they need superior returns. Among funds that make high-risk investments, a high rate of turnover might help. Among lower-risk funds, it generally hurts.

The Financial Results

The financial tables show the fund's results per share, in dollars and cents, for up to the past 10 years. Some parts of the table won't interest you, but there are some nuggets here—especially the bottom line. Here's what to look for:

"Net Investment Income (Loss)"—shows what the fund is earning in interest and dividends, after expenses. Income funds will show larger dividends; aggressive growth funds, smaller ones. The fund has to pay out at least 98 percent of what it earns.

"Dividends from Net Investment Income"—your dividends per share. Income investors can look back to see how reliably the fund has paid. You can take this distribution in cash or reinvest it in more fund shares.

"Net Realized and Unrealized Gains (Losses)"—shows how the securities are performing. Aggressive growth funds may show larger capital gains; income funds will show smaller ones. Realized gains are distributed to investors as taxable income. Unrealized gains represent potential taxable income in the future.

"Distributions from Realized Capital Gains"—your share of the taxable capital gains. The fund has to distribute at least 98 percent of its net capital gains (after deducting losses). You can take this distribution in cash or reinvest it in more fund shares.

"Net Asset Value, Start of the Year" and **"Net Asset Value, End of the Year"**—show the value of each share at the start and end of each year, after distributing income and capital gains. A common investor mistake is to think that the change in the net asset value equals the total return. To figure your total return, you have to include the distributions, too. If they're reinvested automatically in new fund shares, multiply the number of shares you now own by the net asset value. That shows you what your investment is currently worth. Do this at the end of each year to see how your investment has progressed.

"Ratio of Expenses to Average Daily Net Assets"—gives you a figure for operating expenses. This ratio should fall when net asset values rise. If it stays level or rises, too, the fund isn't managing its expenses well.

"Total Return"—the payoff line. This tells you what percentage return the fund earned (or lost) in every fiscal year. Look back at the record. Does the fund bounce around a lot—a great year followed by a lousy year—or is it reasonably consistent? How high has it gone in a good year and how low in a bad year, and is the low okay with you? If the fund changed managers, can you spot a difference in the annual returns? Even if it didn't change managers, do the recent returns suggest that the investment method might have changed? *One warning:* you can't use these returns to compare the performance of two different funds. Funds have different fiscal years, so their returns may be shown over different time periods.

For the Fund's Return Compared with a Standard Market Index, see the annual shareholders' report. Sometimes it's in the prospectus, but usually not.

The Name of the Manager

Most funds are led by an individual money manager. In 1993, the Securities and Exchange Commission ordered the funds to disclose that manager's name and how long he or she has been there. For a manager with a short tenure you also get a sketch of his or her business career for the past 5 years.

If the manager leaves, you must be informed. The change can be shown in the prospectus (check this when you get your new prospectus every year), or you might get a notice in your midyear or quarterly report.

If your fund is run by a team of managers, however, it doesn't have to note when one of them departs. As you might expect, a growing number of funds have suddenly decided that they're team-managed. But except for index funds and money-market funds (which don't have to disclose a manager's name), there's almost always a single shot-caller. Check for manager tenure, to try to judge whether the team has changed.

Here's What You're Still Missing

You know from the annual report how the fund performed, but you don't know how *you* performed. Your total return will be different from the fund's if you added money during the year (for example, by reinvesting dividends) or took money out. Maybe you earned more than the fund because you invested or withdrew at a lucky time. Maybe you earned less. If you track your investments by computer—on software or the Internet— you can calculate your true return yourself. Financial planners will report it if they're managing your money. But the funds ought to tell you, too. It's not a big deal to develop the software and give you a personalized report. How can you plan for the future if you're only guessing at what rate your money is building up?

THE PROPAGANDA

With the prospectus comes sales literature. It shows you "the mountain" —the amount by which your investment would have grown had you been in the fund for many years. But each fund's mountain shows a different time period, so you can't compare one with another. Nor does the mountain show each year's percentage gain or help you spot the years when the fund didn't do as well as the general market average. In short, the mountain is there to impress, not inform. For better performance data, check the literature for the fund's one-, 3-, and 5-year average annual returns (not adjusted for sales loads). Returns are computed in a standard way and can be compared with those of other funds.

The propaganda will also explain the fund's investment objectives and investor services. It's a good place to start, provided that you go on from there.

THE FUND'S REGULAR REPORTS

Read every communication from your fund's manager. This normally isn't boilerplate; it's serious stuff. All funds have to report semiannually; some report quarterly, too.

These reports include financial statements, for numbers mavens who understand them. And they list what securities the fund held on the reporting date, for shareholders in a position to analyze them. That list data isn't current. Many of those securities will have been sold before the report even got in the mail. But you can see if your manager really diversifies or if he or she makes big bets on certain industries.

The annual report *must* show you how the fund performed relative to a standard market index. Some funds skip this step in the semiannual report, which gives their managers 6 months to string you on.

HOW FUND DISTRIBUTIONS WORK

A "distribution" is money paid out by a mutual fund to its investors. An *income distribution* (known as a dividend) comes from the interest and dividends earned on a fund's securities. A *capital gains distribution* is the net profit realized by selling securities that rose in price (after subtracting any losses). Common-stock funds generally make distributions once a year.

Before buying a fund, check its distribution date. If you buy just before a distribution (usually in December), you're buying yourself an extra tax. Say, for example, that a fund is selling for $10 a share. The planned distribution is $1 a share. After the distribution the fund will sell for $9—reflecting that $1 was paid to shareholders. *Your fund has not lost money!* Investors still have $10, but only $9 remains part of the fund's net asset value. The other $1 is in your pocket or reinvested in additional fund shares. If it's reinvested, the value of your fund account will be back to $10. Still, that $1 distribution is a taxable dividend. When you buy just before the distribution, you get that year's tax without profiting from the fund's gains. The best time to buy is right after the annual distribution date.

Stock-and-bond funds often make distributions quarterly. Bond funds may declare dividends daily and pay them monthly, so timing your purchase isn't an issue. Money market mutual funds credit interest daily.

Even on stock funds, the distribution date doesn't matter if you own the fund in a tax-deferred retirement plan.

There Are Three Ways of Handling Distributions:

1. Reinvest everything in more fund shares (the right option for anyone trying to lay a nest egg).

2. Reinvest enough of the distribution to preserve your capital's purchasing power (the right option for people who need income but will be living on their capital for many years). The rest can be withdrawn and spent.

3. Receive everything in cash (the right option for anyone eating up a nest egg—usually in late old age).

AUTOMATIC MONTHLY INVESTMENTS

If I had my investment life to live over again, here's what I'd do: From the very first day I got a steady paycheck, I'd put money away regularly. If I couldn't do it through payroll deduction, I'd do it automatically through a mutual fund. Almost any fund will arrange it. You sign the papers; the papers go to your bank; your bank takes a fixed sum per month out of your checking or savings account and sends it to the fund. There's usually a small fee for each transfer—more, if the money is moved by wire; less, if you use a preauthorized check. Some funds let you start an automatic monthly investment plan with as little as $50 plus additions of only $25 a month. If you're eligible, your investment can go into a tax-deductible retirement plan. Otherwise, it goes into a regular, taxable account. If you have a retirement plan at work, use your outside mutual fund account to buy types of investments your company plan does not include.

I sure wish I'd done it. I got smart too late.

MUTUAL FUNDS AND RETIREMENT PLANS

Almost all funds offer Individual Retirement Accounts, Simplified Employee Pensions, 403(b) plans, and Keogh plans. You can transfer money from your current plan to a new one at the fund without paying any taxes on it. The mutual fund will tell you how.

But taxes may be due when you switch money out of a regular mutual fund account and into a retirement account. Your shares are first sold (for a taxable gain or loss), then reinvested in the retirement plan.

MANAGING YOUR ACCOUNT BY PHONE

Once you've made the arrangements, you'll be able to sell shares or switch from one fund to another just by picking up the phone. When you sell by phone, you get the very next price that the fund computes—usually its price at the end of that day.

Normally, the money is mailed (or wired) right away to your home address or a predesignated bank. But the fund has the right to put off sending the money for up to 7 days (as it might in a market panic).

For security reasons, you normally can't use the phone to change the bank the money is wired to. Changes have to be made by mail, over a signature guarantee (page 629). But you can probably change your address, provided you give enough identifying information.

An alternative way of selling fund shares: Switch by telephone into a money market fund. Then write a check against the fund.

MANAGING YOUR ACCOUNT BY MODEM

Most funds now have electronic links, of varying functionality. At the very least, you should be able to check current performance—yields, dividends, net asset value; and the status of your account—its total value and any recent transactions. You may also be able to buy and sell by modem (money for new investments would be transferred from your bank account). If your fund isn't there yet, it will be soon.

MANAGING YOUR ACCOUNT BY MAIL

Don't just write a letter asking the fund to cash some of your shares. First check the prospectus (you kept it, of course) to see what the drill is. Maybe a simple letter will do. On the other hand, maybe the system is more complicated. Writing that letter may delay things.

There are two ways of redeeming fund shares or switching from one fund to another:

On Your Signature Only—offered by many funds (but not all of them), even if you hold the account with another person. Signature redemptions are good for sums up to a certain limit, often $50,000. The money has to be switched into another fund at the group or paid to the account holder at the address of record or a predesignated bank.

With a Signature Guarantee—which means taking each sell order to a bank, stock-exchange member, credit union, or S&L, where someone can guarantee that the signature is yours. On joint accounts, you'll need guarantees for both signatures. (Having your signature notarized isn't enough. Notaries merely check your identity and attest to the fact that they saw you sign it. Guarantors ensure that you're the person you claim to be. If you're not, the guarantor makes good the loss.)

A few funds require signature guarantees for all transactions. Some let you choose between guarantees and plain signatures. Normally, money-market funds accept one-signature checks on joint accounts, up to the maximum set by the fund. It is possible, however, to set up the account so that both signatures are required.

The signature-only option is the easiest and, for most people, sufficiently safe. If someone forges your name, the fund (or its transfer agent) bears the responsibility. If the fund sends a check to your address, and someone forges your signature and cashes it, the responsibility shifts to the bank that took the check.

If you want to keep a single joint owner from making withdrawals from the account, however, go for two-signature accounts with the added protection of a signature guarantee.

What If You and Your Spouse Hold a Fund Jointly and One of You Decides to Split? Or One of You Fears That the Other Will Split? Notify the fund by certified mail that both signatures will be required to withdraw or transfer money. This order can be entered by either spouse. If you can prove that the fund made an error in letting your spouse withdraw the money, the fund has to make good.

What If Your Spouse Forges Your Name, Gets the Joint Check, Forges Your Signature on the Check, and Cashes It? Your bank is responsible for restoring your half of the money. But you'll have to prove your signature was forged (not easy, given the ease with which many husbands and wives sign each other's names). Your best defense is to notify the bank that you won't be signing any joint checks.

READ YOUR MUTUAL FUND STATEMENTS

Increasingly, mutual fund statements are turning into planning tools. They may tell you how you've allocated your assets (big stocks, small stocks, internationals, and so on). A couple show the percentage change in your personal account, not just the change in the net asset value of the fund (your personal performance depends on when you bought or sold your shares). They may contain tax information. Use what you learn from these statements to make yourself a better investor.

AUTOMATIC WITHDRAWAL PLANS

These are wonderful arrangements. They let you live off your capital while still keeping it invested for growth. Not all funds offer withdrawal plans, but the majority do.

When you're on such a plan, your fund sends you a check of a certain size every month or every quarter. You still have your dividends reinvested automatically. The fund simply cashes in enough shares to pay the regular income you want. If your check this month exceeds what the fund has earned, your withdrawal reduces your principal. If not, your withdrawal comes out of earnings. You can stop the checks or change the amount anytime you want. In a rising market, you get a regular income and a rising nest egg, too.

To start a withdrawal plan, you usually need at least $10,000 invested, although some funds will go with as little as $5,000. There's a minimum withdrawal and a small fee per check. Withdrawals might be made in one of three ways:

1. You can receive a fixed number of dollars—say, $250 a month. More shares will have to be sold when the market dips and fewer when the market rises.

2. You can receive the proceeds from the sale of a fixed number of shares—say 20 shares a month. You'll get less money when the market dips and more when it rises.

3. You can sometimes receive a fixed percentage of your fund investment—say, monthly checks paid at the rate of 6 percent of capital a year.

You'll get less money when the market dips and more when the market rises.

Withdrawal plans that send monthly checks, handy as they are, sometimes add to your miseries at tax time because calculating capital gains can be such a pain (page 635). But it's no problem if you're in a fund that tells you your average cost per share. If not, make a single lump-sum withdrawal each year, put the cash in a bank or money-market fund, and make your monthly withdrawals from there.

These plans aren't suitable for volatile funds. Apply them to more stable investments, such as balanced funds or equity-income funds. For a sense of how much it's prudent to withdraw, see page 913.

SHOULD YOU SWITCH-HIT?

This is a game played by market timers. They buy a stock fund in a no-load fund family. When they think the market is going to fall, they sell the fund (by telephone or modem) and move the proceeds into a money market fund. When they think stocks will improve, they move the money back. Often they're not thinking at all—they're just following a newsletter guru. There may be a switching fee ($5 to $25), but some funds make no charge at all.

As a long-term strategy, fund switching is a lousy idea, for several reasons:

First, because few investors can time the market well (page 706).

Second, because selling shares may trigger a capital gains tax. Switching can't even pretend to be viable except in a tax-deferred account.

Third, because the newsletters that advertise their timing prowess may not be telling you the whole story. They can weed out their poor calls and highlight the better ones by choosing the time period they show.

Some mutual funds limit the number of switches you can make. A few won't accept telephone switches at all.

ONE-STOP SHOPPING

How do you put together an intelligent mutual fund portfolio without being overrun by paperwork? Two ways:

Be a Groupie. Buy all your funds from a single no-load mutual fund family. Not many are large enough to provide enough good funds for a decent asset allocation. But you could certainly make a good mix at Fidelity, Vanguard, T. Rowe Price, INVESCO, Scudder, and Strong (800 numbers on page 1027).

Just don't be a brokerage-house groupie. Brokers have a sufficient variety of funds, but most broker-brand funds are mediocre. You can buy better funds through wrap accounts, but the cost of the wrap wrecks your returns (page 667).

Shop the Supermarkets. At this writing, around 50 discount brokerage firms offer mutual fund supermarkets. You have hundreds of no-load funds to choose from, all of which can be handled through a single brokerage account. You can even find funds that are normally purchased only through financial advisers, such as those from MAS, Brinson, Compass, and Dimensional Fund Advisors. There is typically no transaction fee. You may not even be charged for opening the account.

Each supermarket has a different set of funds, so check to be sure it offers the ones you want to buy. Those not on the no-fee list may still be available for a fee, usually in the $25 to $50 range. You can use the same account to buy stocks, bonds, load funds, and any other investment the discounter handles.

Jack White & Co. in San Diego (800-233-3411) runs the nation's largest supermarket, the NoFee Network, with 1,200 funds from 185 no-load groups. Charles Schwab's popular OneSource (800-435-4000) lists 800 no-fee funds from 100 groups—and provides a wealth of information services, besides.

Fidelity FundsNetwork in Boston (800-544-9697) is the only place where Fidelity's no-load funds are offered without a fee. At this writing, its list also includes about 820 other funds from 113 no-load families. To buy Vanguard funds at no fee, you have to call Vanguard (800-662-7447); it runs a small supermarket—the FundAccess program, with 485 funds from 25 families. For T. Rowe Price funds at no fee, you need T. Rowe Price's mutual fund division (800-638-5660); its Discount Brokerage (800-225-7720) also offers 415 no-fee funds from 49 groups.

There's a downside to supermarkets. Because trading is free, it's easy to try to time the market by buying and selling shares when you think conditions will change. But that deprives you of mutual funds' unique advantage: the broad participation they give you in worldwide economic growth, compounded over time. When you treat your funds like trading cards, you mess that up.

I just said trading was free, but it isn't, quite. No-load funds have to pay the supermarkets for shelf space; many pass along that cost to you in the form of higher annual fees.

FOLLOWING THE PRICE OF YOUR FUND

There's an 800 phone number you can call—or probably a Web site to dial—to get your fund's net asset value. Or you can follow its price in the daily newspaper listings. The newspaper table typically shows you the net asset value (NAV), the percent change from the day before, and the total return so far this year. Funds that are very small and new aren't included in the fund performance tables distributed by the National Association of Securities Dealers. Some newspapers publish the results only of the largest funds.

The Best Tip on This Page: *Don't* follow the daily changes in price. That might make you nervous. Ideally, you will pick a handful of funds and vow fidelity. You won't flip through magazines hunting for younger, prettier funds. You won't sneak peaks at quarterly reports. You'll turn off the TV whenever anyone threatens to tell you about the Dow. From this point on, you'll think about each fund once a year, when you get its annual report, read what its manager has to say, and check its progress against the market and similar funds. Change it only if you run into one of the problems listed on page 634. Otherwise, file the reports and do something more useful than checking how the market did. Making money is fine, but it's not a life.

HOW SAFE IS YOUR FUND?

A mutual fund can't go broke the way mismanaged businesses can. It's hard to loot because the securities are held by a third-party custodian, usually a bank. A fund company's creditors cannot attach your assets. You can lose money in a bad market; you can be charged outrageous fees; your investment can be returned in the form of securities rather than cash; redemptions may even be temporarily suspended. But your sell order is always priced on the day it comes in. The fund cannot delay mailing your check for more than 7 days.

When a fund becomes unprofitable to run, it is generally merged with a larger fund. If no one wants it, the securities will be liquidated and the proceeds distributed to investors. Fraud is possible in any business, but people with access to mutual fund money must be insured. To my knowledge, no fundholder has ever been told, "Sorry, the money walked out the door."

WHEN TO SELL A MUTUAL FUND

Sometimes your fund won't do as well as its peer group does. But if you chose the manager carefully, why be in a hurry to sell? Every manager goes through periods when his or her stocks are out of style. If nothing appears to have changed in the fund or the way the manager makes decisions, hold on—or buy more—and wait for its quality to show.

But patience isn't always a virtue. Consider selling when:

The Lead Manager Leaves the Fund. Sometimes a superb replacement is on hand, trained by the former manager. But that's the exception, not the rule. The new manager may have had a good record somewhere else, but you don't know whether it can be duplicated here. What's more, he or she may drastically change the types of stocks the fund invests in. In most cases, you should leave when the old manager does.

The Fund Lags the Average of Similar Funds for More Than Two Years. Read the shareholders' report to see what the manager thinks went wrong. Sometimes there's an interesting reason to hang on to stocks that haven't been doing well. If that reason makes sense, you might decide to stick. If I thought I had a wizard, I'd probably stick for 3 years or more. If the annual report read like an annual excuse, however, I'd bail. Maybe the manager's passion for stock picking has cooled. Maybe he or she is running too many funds or has taken on too many administrative duties. Call and ask how many funds the manager runs or oversees, compared with what he or she was doing when you originally bought.

The Fund's Investment Style Changes. It's important that managers play their own game. If they switch from small stocks to larger ones, or from U.S. stocks to internationals, a caution light should flash. If performance slows, the new game isn't working and you should start looking for a new fund. Once a year get your funds' Morningstar pages so you can follow the style box (page 613). If the manager wants to try something different, let someone else be the guinea pig.

Your Investment Style Changes. Something happens in your life to change the amount of investment risk you want to take.

You Invested for a Specific Purpose and Now That Purpose Is Behind You. Say, for example, you bought growth funds to help fund a young child's college education. College is now four years away. At this point, it's risky to hold stocks (page 556), so you'd sell and invest in something safe.

P.S. *Don't dump a fund just because it hasn't done as well as the S&P 500.* The type of stocks your mutual fund buys may simply be out of style for the moment. Growth funds or value funds sometimes lag the S&P for a couple of years. Alternatively, your fund might have some other investment objective—for example, high income or limited risk. You should worry only if your fund lags other funds of its type. If your objective is keeping up with the S&P, buy an S&P index fund or hunt for a wizard who can beat it.

HOW YOUR FUND IS (GULP) TAXED

Every April 15, I wish I had never heard of mutual funds. Figuring the income tax is a pain in the neck—especially if you don't keep orderly records. So (read my lips) keep orderly records. You'll hate yourself if you toss all your statements into a file and don't sort them out until tax time comes. Here are the rules:

Reporting Dividends and Capital Gains. This is the easy part. In January, your fund will tell you how much you got last year (on a 1099-DIV form— one copy to you, one copy to the IRS). You simply enter that income on your tax return. You owe taxes on the income even if it was automatically reinvested in new fund shares and even if the value of your fund went down. If the fund sends you any other tax information, read it gratefully. Tax-exempt bond funds will tell you whether any of your dividends are taxable in your state.

Reporting Capital Gains and Losses. This is the hard part. You owe taxes when you make a profit by selling fund shares for more than they cost. When you sell for less, you have a deductible loss. The cost of each share is what you paid for it (including the sales commission if it's a load fund). But different shares carry different costs because they were bought at different times. Your regular monthly statement will tell you what price you paid for any new shares, including shares bought with reinvested dividends.

As time goes by, you will collect a huge pile of shares, acquired at a wide range of costs. When you sell a share, which one have you sold? Which cost do you use when figuring your gain or loss?

There are two ways to figure it—a (ha-ha) simpler way, known as *average cost basis* and a (truly) complicated way, known as *cost basis*. Why would you choose the complicated way? Because you're a masochist who wants to defer some taxes.

Many Mutual Funds Give You a Hand. They mail you a statement showing your average cost basis for recent years, so you won't have to figure it yourself. They may also mail you a booklet explaining how to compute your tax.

Some funds don't bother, however, and I don't know of any whose average cost data goes back very far. If you've had your account for many years, the best your fund can do is supply you with records that you may have lost (but ask for them early; there's always a rush).

Tax Records: The (Ha-Ha) Simpler Way

To figure your average cost yourself, keep a Mutual Fund Notebook. Across the top of the page, enter the headings you see on the following

TAX RECORDS: AVERAGE COST BASIS

Date	Kind of Transaction	Amount	Number of Shares	Price per Share	Cumulative Cost Basis	Average Cost per Share*
12/31/95	New investment†	$10,000.00	535.3	$18.68	$10,000.00	—
1/20/96	Dividend reinvested	267.87	15.1	17.74	10,267.87	—
1/20/96	Capital gains distribution reinvested	455.92	25.7	17.74	10,723.79	—
3/31/96	New investment	1,000.00	51.3	19.48	11,723.79	—
4/30/96	New investment	1,000.00	49.9	20.03	12,723.79	—
TOTAL			677.3		12,723.79	$18.79
6/12/96	Sale of shares*	$ 2,500.00	(125.6)‡	$19.90	(2,360.02)§	—
NEW TOTAL			551.7		10,363.77	$18.79

CAPITAL GAIN PER SHARE: $1.11 (selling price of $19.90 minus the average cost of $18.79).

TOTAL TAXABLE CAPITAL GAIN: $139.42 (the $1.11 capital gain per share times 125.6 shares sold).

* No need to figure the average cost until you sell some shares.
† Including sales charge and exit fee, if any.
‡ Figures in parentheses are reductions.
§ This is your tax cost. See the explanation under *"Important"* on page 639. Not all the numbers match exactly, because of rounding.
SOURCE: T. Rowe Price

table, titled *Tax Records: Average Cost Basis.* Start a separate page for each fund. Every time you get a statement from one of your funds showing purchases and sales (including purchases from the automatic reinvestment of dividends and capital gains), enter the information in your notebook. Do the same thing for older statements if you're bringing past records up to date.

Whenever You Sell, Figure Your Average Cost Per Share. To do that:

1. Add up the cost of all the shares you have ever bought, including those bought with reinvested dividends and capital gains distributions. On the following table, that's the "Cumulative Cost Basis"—of which you should keep a running tally. (As you will find out later, this is your tax cost, even if not your actual cost.)

2. Divide by the number of shares you own. On the table, get this number by adding up what you've entered in the "Number of Shares" column.

3. The result is the "Average Cost per Share." Always keep a tally of the cumulative cost of your shares and how many you own, so you won't have to go back to the beginning each time you sell.

4. Compare the average cost with the sale price. In the table, the average cost is $18.79 and the sale price is $19.90. So there's a $1.11 capital gain per share.

That's the end of the easy part. From now on, it's no more Mr. Nice Guy.

To prepare yourself for figuring your *next* capital gain or loss, you have to determine your new cumulative cost. To do that, you calculate the *tax basis* of the transaction—which is the number of shares you sold multiplied by your average cost. On the table, you would multiply 125.6 (number of shares) by $18.79 a share (average cost) to get a tax cost of $2,360.02. Subtracting that from your previous cumulative cost gives you $10,363.77. For tax purposes, that is your new cumulative cost. (Note that none of this has anything to do with the actual money you received for your shares, but that's life in the tax trench.)

You have to specify on your tax return that you're cost averaging. Once you start with this system, you have to continue it for that particular fund. You can't change your cost-reporting method without permission from the IRS.

You also have to specify that you're using either the "single-category method," which means averaging all of your shares together, or the "double-category method," which means averaging all the short-term shares (held for a year or less) and separately averaging all the long-term shares (held for more than a year). In most cases, it's not worth the bother—and saves you no money—to go to the effort of separate categories. Investors generally specify a single category and move on.

At the end of the year, you'll have the full record to use for preparing your income tax.

If you're reconstructing past records, you'll have to start with the oldest year and work forward. Would I do that? No way. Some things are not worth the aggravation. I'd see an accountant and do whatever he or she says.

Tax Records: The (Truly) Complicated Way

Why would you want to keep more complicated records? Because they let you control the size of any capital gain you report to the IRS. Normally, you will want to reduce the gain in order to minimize your current tax.

So get a Mutual Fund Notebook and across the top put the headings you see on the table on page 638 titled *Tax Records: Cost Basis.* Enter all purchases, just as you did for the previous table, including the shares you bought when your dividends and capital gains were reinvested.

Before every sale (it must be before), decide exactly which shares you want to sell and specify them in a dated letter to the mutual fund. Using the example given on the following page, you might write "Redeem 50 of the March 31, 1996, shares that I purchased at a cost of $19.48 per share." Keep a copy of the letter.

TAX RECORDS: COST BASIS

Date	Kind of Transaction	Purchase Price	Sale Price	Number of Shares	Cost Basis	Per Share Gain (Loss)	Total Taxable Gain (Loss)
12/31/95	Investment*	$18.68	N/A†	535.3	$10,000.00	N/A	N/A
1/20/96	Dividend reinvested	17.74	N/A	15.1	267.87	N/A	N/A
1/20/96	Capital gains distribution reinvested	17.74	N/A	25.7	455.92	N/A	N/A
3/31/96	Investment*	19.48	N/A	51.3	1,000.00	N/A	N/A
4/30/96	Investment*	20.03	N/A	49.9	1,000.00	N/A	N/A
6/12/96	Sale of shares bought* on 3/31/96	19.48	$19.90	(50.0)‡	($974.00)§	$0.42	$21
TOTAL				627.3	11,749.79		

At this point, go back and cross off the shares you bought on 3/31/96. Subtract the number of shares you sold, and make the following note of what remains:

6/12/96	Remaining shares purchased on 3/31/96	19.48	N/A	1.3	25.32§	N/A	N/A

* Including sales load and exit fee, if any.
† Not applicable.
‡ Figures in parentheses are reductions.
§ This is your tax cost. See the explanation under *"Important"* on page 639. Not all numbers match because of rounding.
SOURCE: T. Rowe Price

Assume you sell those 50 shares for $19.90. If you sell them against an average cost of $18.79, your gain is $1.11 a share. But if you sell the specific shares you bought on March 31 at $19.48, your gain is only 42 cents a share. So you pay less tax. If you sell the shares you bought on April 30 at $20.03, you'll have a deductible loss of 13 cents a share, even though the fund has been profitable for you overall.

The complicated method of tax reporting is terrific for deferring your tax. But the bookkeeping is horrendous. You have to keep track, perpetually, of which shares you own and which ones you've sold. In the example shown on the table, you sold 50 of the shares bought on March 31. To adjust your records, you would cross off the 51.3 shares bought on that date, subtract the 50 you sold, and indicate that you still have 1.3 of those particular March shares left.

Some mutual fund statements show you the cost basis of each batch of shares. Let's hope it's the start of a trend.

Important: To get the proper cost basis when you sell shares, you multiply the number of shares sold by the price you paid for them. In the example, you'd multiply the 50 shares sold by the $19.48 you originally paid. To get the cost basis of the remaining shares, you'd multiply 1.3 shares by $19.48.

If you didn't designate which shares to sell, you have to assume that the fund sold the shares you held the longest. Use their cost in figuring your gain or loss. In the table, you'd have sold 50 of the shares you bought on 12/31/95.

In any year when you sell shares, your fund will send you a 1099-B form for tax purposes. This form shows the total amount you received for your shares. It does not indicate your net gain or loss. Don't accidentally pay taxes on the whole 1099-B amount!

Keep all of your statements and transaction records. At tax time, mutual funds are swamped with requests for duplicates from shareholders who need them to compute their taxes. You can usually get duplicate records for 5 to 7 years back for a small fee. But why get caught in the crush? Set up a file for original records and keep them.

If You Own an International Fund or a U.S. Fund That Also Buys Foreign Securities, you face the same tax rules that govern any other mutual fund. Then the IRS kicks you again.

The year-end statement from the fund will show your share of any foreign taxes paid. You're entitled to either a tax credit or an itemized deduction for that amount. The credit is worth more, but trying to figure it out is a waste of a nice spring day. Take the tax deduction instead.

The Government Is Here to Help You. For the IRS's official word on how mutual fund holders should handle their taxes, call 800-TAX-FORM for the free IRS Publication 564, *Mutual Fund Distributions.*

Computers Were Born to Help. You can get software programs, or find sites on-line, that keep track of your investment portfolio and automatically compute your tax basis. All you do is enter the data. The little green men who live inside your computer do the actual work.

You Don't Have to Worry About Any of This Stuff If You're Taking Money Out of a Tax-Deferred Retirement Account. All withdrawals are taxed as ordinary income, regardless of their source.

Some Funds Are Designed to Minimize Taxable Distributions. The manager buys shares and holds them rather than selling and taking capital gains. When selling seems prudent, gains are generally sheltered by realizing capital losses. But large untaxed gains build up inside the fund. If investors ever flee and the fund has to liquidate some stocks, you could face a pretty big taxable distribution.

Tax efficiency is nice, but it's not a good enough reason to select a fund. Fund rankings don't always change by much, after tax. Superior performance overwhelms all.

CLOSED-END MUTUAL FUNDS

A closed-end mutual fund normally raises money only once. It sells a fixed number of shares and invests the proceeds. The fund is then listed on a stock exchange or Nasdaq, just like any other public company. If you want to own shares, you buy through a discount or full-service stockbroker, paying regular brokerage commissions.

The prospectus normally comes out only once, when the fund is first offered to the public. After that, buyers get regular shareholder reports.

There are closed-end funds for practically every kind of security. But they're concentrated in bonds, narrow sectors of the U.S. economy, and international investments. Most of the single-country funds are closed-ends.

WHAT A CLOSED-END FUND IS WORTH

Closed-end funds have two relevant measures of value: (1) the current net asset value (NAV) of all the securities in the portfolio, and (2) the share price of the fund on the stock exchange.

Typically, closed-end funds sell at something less than net asset value —known as a *discount*. Take, for example, the Skyrocket Fund, owner of securities worth $10 a share. You can probably buy it for $9 a share, a discount of 10 percent.

Sometimes, however, investors fall in love with a particular closed-end fund and bid up its price to something more than net asset value—known as a *premium*. If you bought the Skyrocket Fund at $11, it would be selling at a 10 percent premium.

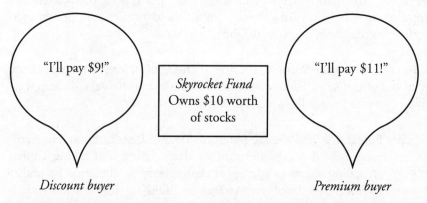

"I'll pay $9!"

Skyrocket Fund
Owns $10 worth
of stocks

"I'll pay $11!"

Discount buyer   *Premium buyer*

Premiums rarely last. When a fund sells for more than its net asset value, it is usually way overpriced. If you buy, your odds of losing money are high.

HERE'S HOW TO PLAY
THE CLOSED-ENDS

First, check the listing of closed-end funds that appears in *The Wall Street Journal* on Mondays. You'll see each fund's net asset value and premium or discount. Make a list of the funds with the largest discounts.

Research those funds just the way you'd research a stock—for example, by getting its annual report, data from the *Value Line Investment Survey*, Web stories, best-buy lists from financial publications (page 610), and so on. Screen out funds with new managers, high expenses, suspect yields (if they're bond funds, see next section), and political risk (if they're single-country funds). Then check each fund's price history—through library research (back issues of the *Journal* will do), a stockbroker's help, or membership in a Web site that provides statistical information. You want to know its typical price range relative to net asset value. As an example, take the Skyrocket Fund again. You might discover that every time it sells for 15 percent below its net asset value it rebounds to about 5 percent below. You'd buy whenever its discount was deep and hold for appreciation.

Long-term buying and holding isn't typical of closed-end investors. More likely, they trade. They buy when the discount is deep enough—usually, 10 to 15 percent or more, which usually occurs in lousy markets. When the discount shrinks to 5 percent or so, they sell. They buy back when the discount widens again.

Not all deeply discounted funds are good buys. The fund might own chancy or illiquid enterprises, past performance may be poor, or the dividend might be ripe for cutting. Many funds deserve their low price.

With Closed-End Bond Funds, You Really Have to Keep Your Wits About You. These funds often mesmerize investors by paying especially high dividends. Sometimes that's legitimate; a fund's yield will rise if its price goes to a discount. But sometimes the dividends are phony. Your big check may come partly from option income or the fund's own capital. This flimflam hurts investors three ways: First, you are being deceived about the fund's actual yield. Second, a payout of capital means that the net asset value is being eroded, which will drive the share price down. Third, when part of the "dividend" comes from sources other than bond interest, the payment is unlikely to last. Eventually, the dividend will be cut and the fund's share price will decline. Always check on the source of the dividend payments before you invest.

With Closed-End Funds, You Have Three Ways of Making Money:

1. The value of its securities can rise. Example: The Skyrocket Fund, with a net asset value of $10 a share, goes to $12 a share because the stocks it owns went up in price. You bought it at a 10 percent discount ($9) and, in the market, that discount still holds. Your shares are now worth $10.80 (the new $12 price less 10 percent). Both the net asset value and the share price have risen 20 percent.

2. The discount can shrink. Example: The Skyrocket Fund stays at $10 a share, but investors get interested in its prospects and bid the price up from a 10 percent discount to a 5 percent discount. The $9 price rises to $9.50. The net asset value went nowhere, but investors gained 5.5 percent. Sometimes, a discount even rises to a premium. Occasionally, a closed-end fund switches to open-end, which eliminates the discount.

3. The value of the securities can rise *and* the discount can shrink—the best of all possible worlds. Example: The $10 Skyrocket Fund goes to a $12 net asset value and the discount shrinks from 10 percent to 5 percent. You bought at $9; now the shares are worth $11.40 (the $12 net asset value minus 5 percent). The net asset value rose 20 percent, but your share value rose 26.6 percent.

Needless to Say, There Are Also Three Ways of Losing Money: The net asset value can drop, the discount can deepen (or a premium can drop to a discount), or both of those things can happen at once. The last is the worst of all possible worlds.

You could lose money even when the net asset value is going up. Take the Skyrocket Fund yet again, with a NAV of $10. Due to investor optimism, it's selling at $12, a 20 percent premium. Stock prices rise and Skyrocket's NAV goes to $11. But sensing an end to the party, investors bail out. The market resets Skyrocket's price at a 10 percent discount. Your $12 shares are now worth only $9.90 (the $11 NAV minus 10 percent). So the NAV rose by 10 percent, but you lost 17.5 percent.

That's especially apt to happen to a fund selling at a premium, so smarties avoid premiums. Smarties are also familiar with the discounts at which their favorite closed-end funds usually trade. You can make money in closed-ends but not by blundering around. You have to be disciplined, buying funds from good managers only at steep discounts. If market prices are high and the discounts shrink, bide your time.

CLOSED-ENDS ARE FOR . . .

1. Anyone who loves stock-market action, because a closed-end is really a stock. You analyze it just as you would an individual company and speculate on its price.

2. Stock investors interested in betting on a specific foreign country. Single-country open-end mutual funds generally don't exist.

3. Bond investors who find high yields among funds selling at a discount. With this caveat: you have to investigate the yield to find out whether it's for real (page 641).

BUYING A NEW CLOSED-END FUND

There's one simple rule for buying newly issued closed-end funds: Don't. Ever. Never ever.

The offering price of a closed-end fund includes the cost of the offering as well as the commissions paid to the brokers who sell the shares. Buyers pay perhaps 8 percent over the fund's net asset value. The syndicate supports the price while all the shares are being distributed. Then they let it go.

The selling brokers always claim that *this* time, *this* fund will stay at a premium price—which is what persuades their customers to buy. But the price almost always drops. Moral: Buying a closed-end fund on the opening is usually buying into a loss. If you like the fund, wait for it to go to a discount. If it doesn't, forget it and buy something else.

FOLLOWING YOUR CLOSED-END

The funds' net asset values, share prices, and latest discounts or premiums are reported every Monday in *The Wall Street Journal,* in the financial pages of some other newspapers, and in *Barron's* magazine. A leading newsletter in the field is *The Investor's Guide to Closed-End Funds,* P.O. Box 161465, Miami, FL 33116. Price at this writing: $75 for a two-month trial subscription or $365 a year.

A FINAL SUGGESTION

Here's a strategy for people who crave both wealth and action from their mutual funds:

1. Put your long-term faith in open-end index mutual funds. Make regular investments and leave the money alone. Don't switch in and out in hope of outguessing the market because you usually won't. Index funds are no-brainers and, for busy people, that's what investing should be. Eventually, this strategy can make you rich.

2. Use actively managed open-end funds and the occasional closed-end fund to satisfy your urge to play. Try to beat the market with open-ends. Buy promising closed-ends at deep discounts. Learn more about investing as you go along. Have yourself a ball. If your picks don't do as well as your index funds . . . well, you know what to do.

23.

Working with a Stockbroker

Where It Helps and Where It Hurts

A stockbroker can make you or—quite literally—break you.
The less you know about investing,
the more breakable you are.

What do you need a stockbroker for? Only if you want advice on buying individual stocks, bonds, and other securities. The broker pitches investment ideas and finds information about securities you suggest. When you decide to buy or sell, he or she will handle the order.

You can trade without a personal broker by using a discount brokerage house (page 646). There, you're talking to order-takers who execute whatever you've decided to do.

Either way, the brokerage house is the gatekeeper to the wider market. You can buy mutual funds, Treasury securities, and a limited number of stocks yourself (page 687), but you need a broker for everything else.

Brokers are also moving into personal planning, or an imitation of it. They'll talk about your retirement objectives, when your kids will go to college, and how you'll manage to pay for it all. You may fill in a form disclosing your assets and evaluating your tolerance for risk. The firm will respond with a strategy for investing and asset allocation (page 660). Some brokers do allocations themselves. Either way, they'll select specific investments to implement the strategy. Or they'll advise you to invest with certain money managers (wrap accounts, page 667). Financial planners sell this service, too (Chapter 32).

A conscientious broker should propose commonsense, long-term investments tailored to your goals and financial position. But let's face it, lots of brokers aren't conscientious. They'll ask, "What's the commish?" (meaning, "How big is the sales commission?"), before hitting the phones to call their clients. They push the riskier products that pay them more, yet may tell you there's virtually no risk at all. Between the conscientious and the unscrupulous, there's a group that's simply not too bright.

All brokers, even the conscientious, can be prisoners of their firms. If the firm wants something sold, it will scramble the sales force to sell it.

You can make a lot of money without ever having a stockbroker's name in your Rolodex, but if you want individual stocks, a good broker is helpful. Much of your success may depend on his or her competence and honesty, as well as how professionally you deal with the relationship.

First, You Have to Decide What Kind of Brokerage Firm You Need.

The most common is the traditional full-service broker. Some are huge, national firms—known as wirehouses—such as Merrill Lynch, PaineWebber, Dean Witter Reynolds, A.G. Edwards, Smith Barney, and Lehman Brothers. They offer every service and sell every financial product possible. Or you might prefer a regional firm that offers special expertise in the stocks of its geographical area—say, Robert W. Baird in Milwaukee, Piper Jaffray in Minneapolis, and Sutro & Co. in San Francisco.

The only reason to choose a full-service broker—be it a wirehouse or a regional firm—is for investment advice. Your broker will call you with buying and selling ideas, send you the firm's securities research, handle your orders, keep up with the news about the companies you've bought, schmooze with you about the market, and help you make investment decisions. For this, you generally pay the full sales commission on products you buy. Investors with large, active accounts might get discounts of up to 25 percent. Small investors, however, may be nickeled and dimed with extra charges, like $30 annually for accounts that aren't very active.

If you design your own strategy and pick your own stocks, you don't need a full-service firm. Instead, give your business to a discount broker. Discounters generally provide no stock research and offer no investment advice. Their principal job is to execute your orders to buy and sell. For this, they charge lower commissions than a full-service broker does.

Discounters come in two main varieties, which one might call "business class" and "coach." In the business class are the Big Three: Charles Schwab & Co., headquartered in San Francisco; Fidelity Investments in Boston, and Quick & Reilly in New York City, all with offices around the country. In terms of the products and services they offer, they are practically indistinguishable from full-service brokers, with one main difference: they don't advise you on which stocks to buy.

Back in coach are the deep discounters—beloved of all dedicated stock traders and serious long-term investors. They may offer some useful investor services, but they're principally bare-bones order-takers.

Here's How Their Prices Compare:

1. The Big Three charge an average of 58 percent less than the full-service firms (although on some trades they may be only 20 to 30 percent cheaper). You get the same range of savings from banks that offer discount brokerage services.

2. The deep discounters—true bargain shops—charge an average of 76 percent below the full-service firms and 43 percent less than the Big Three, according to a 1996 survey by Mercer, Inc., in New York City, which reports on discount brokerage firms.

Here's How to Decide Which Type of Broker to Use:

Call a deep discounter for executing one-time trades—for example, if you want to sell all the securities you inherited.

Call a deep discounter if you make your own investment choices and want nothing from a broker except fast service at a low commission.

Call one of the Big Three if you want extra customer service, such as access to a long list of no-load mutual funds or stock reports.

Call a full-service broker if you want access to a firm's stock-research department, financial planning advice, and someone to advise you when to buy and sell. Some investors keep two accounts: one with a discounter, for his or her own ideas; one with a full-service broker as a resource for other ideas. (It's not kosher to pick your stockbroker's brains, then place the order with a discounter. Give credit where it's due.)

Don't call a stockbroker at all if you don't know anything about picking stocks or other investments. Instead, keep your money in a bank, read about no-load mutual funds (Chapter 22), and then buy a fund of your own. Naive investors risk losing a lot of money if they fall into the hands of a manipulative salesperson. Deal with a stockbroker only if you know enough to judge the value of his or her advice.

SHOPPING THE DISCOUNT FIRMS

Each discounter has a different pricing schedule. Some are cheaper for large-volume trades, others are cheaper for trades in high dollar amounts. Fee schedules vary for listed stocks, bonds, options, and other securities. All charge a minimum commission, generally in the area of $18 to $39.

A few discounters charge flat fees rather than commissions. National Discount Brokers in New York, for example, charges a flat rate of $25 for all over-the-counter stocks (stocks not traded on a major exchange) and $33 for the first 5,000 shares of a listed stock. Sometimes that's rock-bottom, sometimes other discounters can beat it.

To find the 30 cheapest firms for 22 typical trades, send for *The Dis-*

count Brokerage Survey, Mercer, Inc., 379 West Broadway, Suite 400, New York, NY 10012, or call 800-582-9854. Special price for readers of this book: $29.95. You'll also get the names and addresses of 83 discount brokers, along with price comparisons of the discount-brokerage arms of 37 banks. To see a sample page of the survey, visit Mercer's Web site at http:// www.mercer-inc.com.

The broker you pick, incidentally, doesn't have to be in your hometown. You can handle all your business by phone, fax, and mail. Some brokers take orders by computer.

The following table shows you how much money you can save:

WHAT A STOCKBROKER CHARGES FOR BUYING YOU:*

	100 SHARES AT $30 A SHARE	500 SHARES AT $30 A SHARE	1,000 SHARES AT $30 A SHARE
Typical full-commission broker	$81	$206	$309
The big three:			
Charles Schwab	55	106.60	127
Fidelity Investments	54	106.10	126.50
Quick & Reilly	49	81.50	96.50
Deep discounters:			
Ceres Securities, Omaha	18	18	18
Wall Street Equities, NYC	24	24	24
Aufhauser & Co., NYC	27.49	27.49	36.50
Freedom Investments, Omaha	28	28	28
Washington Discount Brokerage, NYC	28	28	28
National Discount Brokers, NYC	33	33	33

  * Includes shipping-and-handling fees and transaction costs. Special discounts and account restrictions may apply.
  SOURCE: *The Discount Brokerage Survey,* 1996

CHOOSING A DISCOUNTER

Take a look at the kinds of trades you make: what securities you buy, how often, and how much. Think about the services you want: Do you buy on margin? Do you trade by computer? Call some of the firms that interest you and get their brochures, or check their Web sites if they're on-line. You're looking for answers to the following questions:

1. What securities does the firm trade? Most handle stocks, corporate bonds, and options. Some also trade U.S. Treasury securities, tax-free bonds, Ginnie Maes, and mutual funds. Some discounters offer mutual fund supermarkets that let you choose among the funds of different fund families.

2. What commissions are charged for the kinds of trades you usually make? If you become a steady customer, you might get a deeper discount if you ask for it. One firm, New York City–based Muriel Siebert & Co., offers individuals the same rock-bottom commissions it gives institutions that trade thousands of shares.

3. Are there fees for buying no-load mutual funds? If so, skedaddle. You can buy at no charge from the fund company directly. Several broker-age firms also charge no fees for buying or selling a selected list of no-loads, including Bull & Bear Securities in New York City (800-262-5800); Charles Schwab, with offices nationwide (800-435-4000); Fidelity Investments in Boston (800-544-3902); Jack White & Co. in San Diego (800-233-3411); Muriel Siebert & Co. in New York City (800-USA-0711); and T. Rowe Price Discount Brokerage in Baltimore (800-225-7720). For more on fund super-markets, see page 632.

4. Is there a minimum starting balance? And must you do a minimum number of trades per year in order to maintain an account? (Even if the answer is yes, the firm will usually take a one-time order—for example, when you're selling inherited securities.)

5. Do you have to deposit the money or the securities into your account before the broker will accept an order to buy or sell? Or can you settle within 3 business days?

6. If there's cash in your brokerage account, will it be swept into a money market account to earn interest?

7. Can you place orders by personal computer or Touch-Tone phone? Will you get an additional discount for doing so? Schwab charges a flat $29.95 commission on any stock trade of up to 1,000 shares, if you'll agree to do most of your business electronically. At Freedom Investments, trades that size cost a flat $25 if done by computer or Touch-Tone phone.

8. Is there an asset-management account (page 660)?

HANDLING YOUR ACCOUNT ON-LINE

If you've been wondering whether to invest by computer, the answer is absolutely yes. Financial transactions are cheaper on the Internet for investors who buy products that carry sales commissions. Trading is suffi-ciently secure and the systems are generally pretty simple. You can place orders and check your investments 24 hours a day.

Some brokers maintain their own proprietary networks that you ac-cess with special software. But increasingly they are choosing to open "offices" on the Internet. To reach a virtual stockbroker, all you need is a modem, which links your computer to a telephone line, and a Web connection.

Once you're on the Web, you can browse from broker to broker, checking the prices and services. At this writing, only discount brokers let you trade on-line, but full-service brokers will get there, too.

If you're a mutual fund investor, you can assemble a portfolio of no-load (no-sales-charge) funds on-line. Among the leading discounters:

• Jack White, with more than 1,100 no-fee funds, at www.jackwhiteco.com (800-233-3411).

• Charles Schwab, with some 800 no-fee funds, at www.eschwab.com (800-435-4000).

• Accutrade, with some 700 no-fee funds, at www.accutrade.com. (800-494-8939).

Before opening an account, check for ancillary costs, such as annual maintenance fees or fees for selling a fund within a short period of time. To buy some no-load funds, you have to pay a $25 to $45 commission.

On-line discount brokerage firms also sell stocks, bonds, load funds (which carry sales charges), and other securities. Among the discounters selling stocks at rock-bottom transaction costs:

• Datek—www.datek.com (212-514-7531); minimum commission at this writing, $9.99.

• Waterhouse—www.waterhouse.com (800-555-3875); minimum commission, $12.

• E*Trade—www.etrade.com (800-786-2575); minimum commission, $14.95.

Each on-line broker has its little quirks. For example, it might charge extra for letting you talk to a human broker or for providing current stock-market quotes (quotes usually come with a 15- or 20-minute time lag).

Before opening an account, find out how you can place an order if your computer crashes. Some firms connect you by Touch-Tone phone, but you'll want to be able to reach a human broker, too.

For privacy, your monthly statements will be e-mailed over an encrypted line. For security, some firms don't let you make cash withdrawals on-line.

Your account is insured by the Securities Investor Protection Corporation for up to $500,000, just as traditional accounts are. On-line firms typically carry additional private insurance.

THE FULL-SERVICE BROKER

Stockbrokers (or "investment brokers" or "financial consultants," as they're calling themselves these days) are salespeople. Period. They may or may not have training in financial planning and risk management—most often not. They're trained in sales. Their job is to push financial products.

Even if they yearn to be serious students of the stock market, they haven't the time. Within three years of joining a major firm, a stockbroker is generally expected to handle $10 million to $30 million a year in buy-and-sell transactions. To do that, he or she must bring in $40,000 to $120,000 in trades every working day. And to do *that,* the broker has to spend every minute on the telephone, pitching current customers and bringing in new ones.

"They chain you to your desk in the morning and they're not going to release you until a certain quota has been reached," one broker said in a focus group for the National Endowment for Financial Education in Denver.

Most stockbrokers sincerely want you to do well. Good brokers will think about your long-term objectives and look specifically for investments to match.

But their primary focus is sales commissions. That's what wins them awards and vice presidencies. When a broker asks a colleague, "How are you doing?" he's not asking, "Have your recommendations made money?" All he wants to know is, "How much have you sold and what commissions have you racked up?" The more high-commission products a broker can induce you to buy, the more the broker earns—for himself and for his firm.

The firm, incidentally, is a hard taskmaster. It demands certain levels of commission income. It may circulate each broker's "production" throughout the office to keep up the pressure for higher sales. It fires brokers if they don't bring in enough accounts or squeeze enough commission income out of the accounts they have. Since production is often reported on a monthly basis, some brokers push through as much business as they can at the end of the month in order to make the grade.

SO HOW DO YOU FIND A GOOD STOCKBROKER?

I have emphasized the conflicts of interest so that you'll know what you're up against. It's important to know that, kindly and lovely as a broker may be, deep down he or she is not your friend. To shop for a full-service broker:

1. Gather recommendations from associates whose investment objectives are similar to yours.

2. Call the office managers of the brokerage houses that interest you. Say that you're looking for an experienced stockbroker who entered the business not later than 1985. (That guarantees that he or she will have seen two bad markets—although, at this writing, no one since 1972 has seen a prolonged bear.) Give a brief summary of your resources and your investment objectives and ask for a recommendation. Tell the manager that you want a "good fit," not just the "broker-of-the-day." The B-O-T-D is the one in line for the next walk-in customer. Often, it's a new broker or one of the office's less successful brokers.

3. Stick with firms that belong to the New York Stock Exchange (NYSE) and have been in business for at least 25 years. Firms born of the Great Bull Market may not have staying power. Firms that specialize in issues not listed on the NYSE may be manipulating penny stocks (page 792).

4. Telephone the brokers on your list, explain that you're looking for someone to help with your investments, and make appointments to interview them by telephone. During the interview ask (and write down) how long they've been in business, what colleges they went to and when they graduated, where and when they earned their professional credentials, what other brokerage firms they've worked for, and why they left. Ask what kinds of investments they know best and which ones they're weak on. Ask what most of their clients buy. An income investor belongs with someone who buys a lot of bonds; a speculator needs a broker who loves new issues and hot stocks. A broker may claim that he or she is good at everything, but that's not possible. Brokers generally recommend the types of investment that, in their hearts, appeal to them the most. For that reason, you may find it helpful to have a broker whose way of life is similar to your own.

Tell the brokers about yourself, how much money you'll invest, and what your financial circumstances are. Ask what general kinds of investments they'd suggest for someone like you. Talk about how much risk you are willing to take with your money. Take notes. If you feel that a broker is talking nonsense, or not taking you seriously, or not connecting with your needs, or showing off, or sounding impatient, cross him or her off your list. Also cross off any kids—first, because they still believe the stuff they learned in training school about the virtues of all the firm's financial products; and second, because you don't want a neophyte learning his or her lessons on your money.* Kids on the fast track, with a big mortgage, a new BMW, and total faith in what they're selling, may push you toward risky investments that pay high commissions. Kids on the slow track may be so nervous about their new job that they don't advise you well.

5. Ask each broker for the names of three satisfied customers with whom he or she has worked for at least three years. The broker may say, "That's confidential." You say, "Please get their permission to give out their names." Don't accept excuses or be intimidated by a broker who says that he or she doesn't give referrals. A broker who can't produce happy clients for you to call may not have any. When you talk to the clients, check what the broker has told you against their personal experience. Ask what they think the broker has done for them.

6. Check on the brokers you're interested in. Ask their colleges whether they graduated; find out whether they told the truth about their professional

---

* An old joke says that brokerage firms pay $100,000 to train a new stockbroker and customers pay $1 million.

credentials. Call your state securities office to get their CRD report (page 655). It will show you how long they've been registered as stockbrokers, what firms they've worked for, and whether any of their customers filed complaints against them.

All this checking may sound obsessive, but it isn't. You'd be astonished by how many lies are told, even by brokers at famous firms. Here's a story from ex-stockbroker Mary Calhoun of Watertown, Massachusetts, who now acts as an arbitrator and an expert witness in arbitrations between investors and brokers. She says that when she started, a Merrill Lynch superbroker advised her, "Mary, never tell anyone you've been in business less than seven years!" If you find that a broker has misled you in any way, cross that name off. Anyone willing to tell you a small lie will tell you a whopper, too.

7. Once you've finished with the phone work, pare down your list to two or three finalists. Set up personal interviews to see how you like them one-on-one. Answer all the questions that the broker is likely to have about you. Discuss how you might best work together. Get more specific about what the broker would recommend. Ask for written proposals. If you have a substantial sum of money, consider opening accounts with two brokers, not just one. A broker might give a client slightly better prices on, say, bonds, if he or she knows that there's competition. Also, ask whether the broker offers discounts on sales commissions. Many do if your orders are large enough, especially if you came up with the investment idea. The broker knows you can always take it to a discounter.

8. If you'll be asking the broker to check your own stock ideas, see how much help he or she is prepared to give. Some will just funnel you research reports from the firm's own analysts. Others will send basic information even on stocks the firm doesn't follow. You might get Value Line assessments of the companies you're interested in, information about them from Standard & Poor's, annual reports, the 10K financial disclosure statements that the companies file every year with the Securities and Exchange Commission, and other data that's easy for a brokerage firm to obtain. Spend some time talking to the broker about this, if getting stock information is important to you.

9. Ask what the broker will send you about stocks you already own. You should get updated research reports, newspaper clippings, company announcements, and the company's annual and quarterly reports. Computerized investors can also pull information from the Net.

10. Ask about commission rates, annual fees, transaction costs, and any other expenses. No fee should show up on any of your account statements that you haven't been told about in advance.

11. After interviewing two or three brokers, discuss their written proposals with someone you trust. Do their portfolio strategies make sense for you? Does the advice sound honest and intelligent? *Money* magazine has found in surveys that brokers are apt to take female clients less seriously,

spend less time with them, recommend fewer investment options, and offer them more conservative advice. If you have an inkling that your prospective broker is being sexist, he probably is (or *she* is—women can be sexist, too). Always remember that the broker isn't doing you any favors; you're doing the broker a favor by becoming a client. Walk away from anyone who seems to be talking down.

12. All this takes time and it should. You want a long-term relationship with a broker and shouldn't blindly stab at the first one who comes along. If you're not happy with one of the brokers after the personal interviews, keep looking. You have nothing to lose by leaving your money in the bank or a money market mutual fund—even if the market is going up. Stocks, it is said, are like buses. If you miss one, another one will be by in just a few minutes and it will be going the same way.

I know that in the real world you bump into a broker on the golf course, at a dinner party, or at your church or temple and say, "Sure, you can handle my account." But you won't have a clue whether your new best friend is really competent or will listen to what you say about the kinds of investments you want.

No matter how you find your broker, start the account with only a portion of the money you have to invest. See what the broker does with it and how well you work together.

To Replace a Broker You Already Have. Maybe you're uncomfortable with the advice you're getting but not with the firm. In that case, tell the broker—politely—that the relationship isn't working. Call the office manager and ask to work with someone else (but don't accept a rookie). Interview the new broker just as you did (or should have done) before and be candid about why the other one didn't work out. Your original broker shouldn't take offense. This sort of thing happens all the time.

Alternatively, you might want to move to another firm. How to make the switch depends on who's holding your securities. If you hold them yourself, just tell the old broker bye-bye and start dealing with your new one. If your securities are at your old firm, fill in the account-transfer form that your new broker will give you and he or she will move the securities for you. You can sell them even if they're still in the old broker's hands.

Individual Retirement Accounts may be slower to move than other securities, if you need to change the custodian.

Leaving may even cost you money if you're holding your old firm's name-brand mutual funds or investment trusts. Your new firm can't accept them so you have to sell, perhaps for an exit fee of up to 6 percent. If you leave them with your old firm, you may be charged an inactive-account fee of $30 or so every year. These are good reasons to stay clear of broker-brand products in the first place.

Don't ask the old firm to ship securities directly to you. That might take weeks of "misunderstandings," arguments, and tears.

When changing brokers, add four questions to the interview list: Which securities in my present portfolio would you sell? Why? What would you replace them with? Why? An investor who switches brokers can be easy pickings. You're not happy with the service you had before, so it's easy to convince you that you're holding rotten stocks. The more the broker can get you to sell, the higher the commissions he or she will earn. But maybe you're holding a lot of good securities. Maybe the problem with your old broker was chemistry, not advice. If the new broker wants to replace what you have with substantially similar securities, suspect the worst.

COLD CALLS

The phone rings at dinnertime. "Hello, I'm from Famous Brokers, Inc. You've heard of us, of course." Or (a secretary's voice), "Please hold the phone for Mr. von Patter, our vice president."

You're getting a cold call. A stockbroker has your number and is hoping to hook you before you hang up. "Would you be interested in a rare opportunity? No? How about something medium-rare? How about conservative municipal bonds? You should buy now. This market is good."

Hang up. Say no thanks and goodbye. Don't even wait to hear the spiel. You've just read about how to find a broker. Don't settle for one who picked your number from a pack of cards.

DISHING THE DIRT ON YOUR BROKER

Never start an association with a stockbroker and a brokerage house without first checking up on them. Do it even if you're dealing with a well-known firm. Big firms hire hyenas, just as small firms do. A hyena who's a "big producer" (producing huge sales commissions) may be welcome almost everywhere, even though he or she eventually wipes the customers out.

You can learn a tremendous amount about your broker—at no cost— by tapping into the computerized Central Registration Depository (CRD) jointly maintained by the state divisions of securities regulation and the National Association of Securities Dealers (NASD).

The CRD contains the broker's history for the past ten or more years— what firms he or she worked for, the reason for leaving, and any years of self-employment or unemployment. It reveals black marks on the record— gambling convictions, crimes involving money and securities, fraud, bankruptcies, and unsatisfied judgments. You'll also find arbitration awards and court judgments; arbitration and customer-complaint settlements of $10,000 or more; complaints alleging forgery, theft, or misappropriations within the past two years, losses of $5,000 or more; pending consumer complaints alleging sales practice violations; and disciplinary actions for violating the rules of various regulatory bodies and exchanges. Similar information is recorded about the brokerage firm and its principals. These forms are supposed to be updated anytime there's new information—for example, an arbitration decision against the broker, a new complaint, or a change of employment.

To Get All This Information, Call Your State Securities Commission. For the phone number, ask the information operator in your state capital or call the North American Securities Administrators Association in Washington, D.C. (202-737-0900). Say that you're planning to open a brokerage account and want background on the broker (and also the firm, if it's a small one). Most states give out information by phone and will follow up with copies of the full CRD. Other states require a written request.

At this writing, only the states tell all. The National Association of Securities Dealers gives out an expurgated version, ignoring any bankruptcies or outstanding liens, pending customer complaints, and even settled complaints. Sometime in 1997 or 1998, however, it is supposed to start disclosing the same information you get from the states. Call the NASD at 800-289-9999 for a free report or e-mail your request to http://www.nasdr.com. A helpful Web site: http://www.investorprotection.org.

Most people ask only for the disciplinary record (if any). But you should also get the broker's personal and employment history. If the firm is small, ask for the files on all of its principals. Here's what you're looking for:

• Has the broker hopped around from one firm to another? Maybe he or she churns through a book of customers and starts over somewhere else. If the broker goes from one small firm to another, maybe you're dealing with a specialist in penny stocks (page 792).

• Did the broker leave his or her last firm during or after an arbitration award or disciplinary hearing? That's not a good sign.

• Is the broker enmeshed in personal troubles—judgments, bankruptcies, lawsuits? At best, they will be distracting. At worst, the broker will feel pressed to sell the highest-commission products in order to dig out of the hole.

• How long has he or she been selling? Rookie brokers may fudge on this point. You want someone who has been through both bad times and good and has some perspective. You also want someone who is truthful about his or her length of service.

• What kinds of firms has the broker worked for? You'll probably recognize the big national or regional names. But if you see a lot of firms you never heard of, maybe this broker isn't so hot. Ask your state securities office about the firms. They may peddle penny stocks.

• What is the firm's disciplinary record? Even minor violations, if there are a lot of them, suggest that the firm encourages brokers to abuse accounts.

• What is the broker's disciplinary record? The vast majority of brokers don't have one. That's the kind you want.

Warning: The broker may have had troubles that don't appear on the CRD. That's because firms may not report complaints as the regulations require. One state official told me about visiting a firm and finding hundreds of complaints just stuffed in a file. If you have a major problem with a broker, complain in writing both to the firm and to the proper regulatory authority—both your state securities office and the National Association of Securities Dealers (call the NASD at 800-289-9999 for the number of your local office). Wait a couple of months and then pull the broker's CRD. If it's not on the record, tell the regulators about it.

YOUR BASIC BROKERAGE ACCOUNT

When you open an account, a full-service broker will ask for your full financial profile: savings, investments, liabilities, net worth, investment goals. Don't mislead the broker. He or she needs good information in order to give you good advice. The broker may run a credit check on you (and on your spouse, if you live in a community property state).

Check the form for accuracy and insist on a copy. The broker will include a simple statement of your objectives but feel free to add to it if you wish. You might write, "I want to keep my money safe and earn some income. I'd like some growth, but I don't want to take much risk." Or, "My long-term objective is to compound my money at an annual average of 10 percent. I am willing to take prudent risks, but not highly speculative ones." Or, "This is a retirement account. I am aiming for growth of 12 percent and understand that involves a high degree of risk." Or, "This is my daughter's college account and I'll need the money when she's 18." Ask the broker to initial the statement. No offense should be taken as long as you're friendly and businesslike. The suitability of the broker's recommendations will be measured against your objectives and the financial profile you present.

If you're making a small purchase or sale, a discount broker may ask only for your name, address, and credit references. But if larger trades will go through your account, the discounter may want the same net-worth information that full-service brokers gather.

A *cash account* is for customers who don't want to get fancy. You plan to buy stocks or bonds and pay in cash by the settlement date (within 3 business days of making the trade). When you sell, you receive your money. That's all. Cash-account agreements often preserve your ability to sue if you think your broker did you wrong. (Some agreements, however, require arbitration—page 680.)

A *margin account* is for people who expect to borrow money from their stockbrokers in order to buy securities. Margin accounts also let you sell short (page 722) and trade a wider variety of securities, like options.

Don't sign a margin-account agreement unless you really intend to borrow or invest exotically. Once you have the account, you may be talked into buying on margin even though you didn't mean to. Most margin agreements also compel you to take complaints to arbitration rather than to court. If you start with a cash account and subsequently open a margin account, you may find that the latter's arbitration clause embraces the cash account as well.

Tip: The account form will probably limit you to arbitration forums run by the brokerage industry. Add, in writing, the American Arbitration Association (page 680) and initial it. If the broker accepts the form and does business on that basis, and problems arise, your lawyer may be able to get your complaint to AAA, where you have a better shot at getting neutral arbitrators, says attorney Robert Dyer of Orlando, Florida. Customers who are obviously interviewing several brokers have a better shot at getting this accepted than customers who aren't. Some discount brokers and regional firms drop compulsory or industry arbitration, to make themselves more attractive to clients.

A *discretionary account* lets the broker buy and sell without getting your permission. It's an open invitation for him or her to earn extra commissions by stepping up trading in your account. Don't give a broker discretion! If you'll be out of the country for a while, give your broker your phone and fax number.

A *joint account*—say for husband and wife—allows each of you, separately, to give the stockbroker buy and sell directions. But any check issued from the account will be cut in both your names. If you're into a marital slugfest, your lawyer should notify your broker that any withdrawals from your account must have both signatures on the check. Find out what other steps should be taken to protect your half of the investments.

Disclosure statements, signed when you open a new account, should outline all the risks you face—with options, commodities, stocks, and any other securities tradable through the account. Read everything. Get explanations for anything you don't understand. If you later complain that you were led down the garden path, the broker will whip out this statement to argue that you knew exactly what you were doing. (But even though you signed the statement, you can still pursue a legitimate claim. You can say that you didn't understand the danger of a particular investment or that the investment was too risky for someone in your circumstances—page 673.)

A *confirmation slip* shows each buy and sell order—the security, the price, and the broker's commission. Sometimes the commission reads "zero" when, in fact, the broker has been paid (page 665). Brokers are paid for selling you everything except money-market mutual funds.

It's important to keep the record straight as to who initiates each order. You place an *unsolicited order* when you pick a stock and ask your broker to buy it for you. An order is *solicited* when the broker calls you to recommend it. Your confirmation slip will show one or the other. Object immediately and in writing if a solicited order is erroneously marked "unsolicited." That's often the mark of a broker trying to slip you a stock that's too risky for you. A 72-year-old widow might have a good case against a broker who led her into penny gold-mining stocks—but not if the broker alleges that the widow is a smart, retired businessperson and the stocks were her idea. Insist that your record be corrected. If your broker blames the mistake on "computer glitches" more than once, switch brokers.

Be sure that your brokerage-house account is covered by the Securities Investor Protection Corporation (SIPC). If a firm fails and can't make all of its customers whole, SIPC steps in. It protects securities accounts worth up to $500,000 (including up to $100,000 in cash). Most brokerage houses buy private insurance that covers even larger amounts.

After a failure, all accounts are usually moved to another firm within a week or two. There's hardly any break. If some of your securities are missing because of the firm's tangled record-keeping, SIPC will usually replace them for you. You retain the continuing gains or losses in market value, just as if the securities had never been lost. If buying replacements is impractical, however, SIPC cashes you out for the value of your securities on the day of the failure.

Where Should You Keep Your Securities? Keep them at the brokerage firm if you continually buy and sell. When you sell, your broker needs those securities within 3 business days in order to complete the transaction. If you're holding them yourself, you'll have to hand-deliver or overnight mail them immediately. If they don't reach the broker in time, the firm may: (1) hold the trade open for one or 2 days at no extra cost, (2) levy a fee on your account, or (3) cancel the trade and charge you for any losses sustained. Simple convenience plus potential for loss dictates that you keep the securities where your broker can get them easily.

The brokerage house will register your securities in the firm's own name, known as its *street name*. Its records, however, will show that those shares are yours. The companies whose stocks or bonds you own will send the broker all your mail—dividend or interest checks, proxies, annual reports, tender offers. The broker put the checks in your account and sends the mail on to you. Occasionally, you can arrange to get quarterly and annual reports from the company directly. The dividends paid in street names can be automatically reinvested in new shares of the company, although you may pay a fee. The broker should monitor your account for calls on your bonds (page 746) or tender offers to buy your stock.

You also need to pay in 3 business days when you place an order to buy. For this reason, investors usually keep cash from previous sales in their broker's money market fund. That way it's right at hand. Alternatively, you can overnight mail a check or arrange to send funds from your bank account electronically. You often have to pay before you receive official confirmation of your order, so always take notes when you talk with your broker. If the "confirm" differs from what you expected, ask for a correction —immediately and in writing.

If you trade rarely you may prefer to hold your securities yourself. That avoids any broker's fees for having an inactive account. You'll need a stock or bond certificate, which might cost $15 or so. The securities will be registered in your name; the dividend checks and other company mail will come directly to you. Keep the securities in a safe-deposit box. If you want to sell, follow the broker's instructions for signing the certificates and sending them back.

Companies with dividend-reinvestment plans reinvest your dividends at no charge (page 687). To stay in the plan, you may need to hold at least one share in your own name.

One Risk to Holding Securities Personally Is That You Might Lose Them, and lost securities can be expensive to replace. Why the high price? Because the issuer has to buy insurance against the risk that you, or someone else, might find the securities and sell them. It's especially costly to lose "bearer bonds," whose coupons anyone can clip.

Replacement takes several weeks to several months. If a lost certificate turns up within a year, however, you might get some of your money back. Fast, free replacements are possible only if you place an order, have the securities mailed to you, and they never arrive.

You May Not Be Able to Hold Your Securities Personally, Even If You'd Like To. Engraved stock and bond certificates are going the way of the passenger pigeon. Instead, your purchase may be registered by computer in a system known as book entry. Already, all Treasuries and some municipal and corporate bonds are issued only in book-entry form. Your confirmation slip is your proof of ownership—so guard it carefully, just in case your broker's computers go haywire.

THE ASSET-MANAGEMENT ACCOUNT

Most full-service brokers, some discounters, some large banks, a few insurance companies, and several mutual-fund families offer asset-management accounts. Regular investors love them. These accounts gather up most of your financial transactions and report them to you on a single statement.

You open this account with a minimum deposit, in cash and securities, of anywhere from $5,000 at Schwab to $20,000 at Merrill Lynch. The cash usually goes into a money market mutual fund, either taxable or tax exempt.

Different firms offer different ranges of services. Some offer two or three levels of service, for different fees. Annual fees run from zero to $200. In general, you can use this account as:

• A ready-savings account, earning money market interest rates. Any interest or dividends earned on your investments and any proceeds from the sale of securities are automatically swept into this account—sometimes weekly, sometimes daily—where they will immediately start earning more interest.

• An interest-paying checking account. You can write checks against the cash or securities you hold. You might even be able to pay a merchant by debit card (page 225).

• A source of instant loans, accessed by a credit card.

• A central record keeper. Once a month you get a statement summarizing all your transactions: purchases and sales of securities, interest and dividends earned, purchases made by check or credit card against your account, and the current value of all your investments. At year-end you get a cumulative statement for tax purposes. Some asset-management accounts let you code the checks you write so you can sort them instantly into deductible and nondeductible expenses.

These Accounts Do Carry One Particular Risk for Investors Who Don't Understand How They Work. At brokerage firms, asset-management accounts are generally margin accounts. That means you can borrow against your securities—probably up to 50 percent against the value of your stocks, convertible bonds, and certain mutual funds; 70 percent against corporate bonds; and 85 to 95 percent against your Treasuries, depending on the broker. You pay a variable rate of interest.

The amount you can borrow is usually featured right at the top of your monthly statement. You draw on that credit line by writing a check, buying more securities without putting up cash, or putting down your credit card and not repaying the balance in full. You may have more borrowing power at your brokerage firm than you could get at a prudent bank.

But what happens if you borrow against your securities and their price declines substantially? You'll get a "margin call," asking you to put up more cash. If you can't, some of your securities will be sold and the money used to repay the debt.

In short, these are not like bank loans—something borrowers may not understand. Margin loans might be called in for payment at any time.

Don't borrow against your securities for consumer purchases. When that happens, you dissipate the net worth you are struggling to build. Borrow against securities only to make other investments—and then very carefully. (For more on margin loans, see page 259.)

HOW TO BE A SMARTER CUSTOMER

The more you know about investing, the better ideas you'll get from your broker and the smarter decisions you'll make about your own account. Brokers won't teach you. You're responsible for reaching a minimum level of competence yourself. Here are some ways to teach yourself about stocks and bonds:

Read. Four good, classic books on securities analysis are *The Intelligent Investor* by Benjamin Graham (HarperCollins), *The Battle for Investment Survival* by Gerald M. Loeb (Fraser Publishing), *Stock Market Primer* by Claude N. Rosenberg Jr. (Warner Books), and *Stocks for the Long Run* by Jeremy Siegel (Irwin). For a fascinating peek at the mind of a stock picker at work, try *One Up on Wall Street* (Penguin) by Peter Lynch, former manager of the Fidelity Magellan Fund (but don't buy his tall tale that investing is as easy as buying stock in the products that fly off the supermarket shelves). For a broad discussion of all kinds of investments, get *Dun & Bradstreet Guide to $Your Investments$* by Nancy Dunnan (HarperCollins). Prowl your library and bookstore for others.

Subscribe. For business news, get *The Wall Street Journal, Business Week,* and *Forbes.* For news and features directed at investors, don't miss *Barron's* magazine. For news and information about all aspects of personal finance, take *Kiplinger's Personal Finance Magazine, Money* magazine, and *Smart Money.* (But read them for general principles. Don't be seduced away from your sensible long-term plan by hopping onto every hot fund of the month!)

Serious students of long-term stock investing need the weekly *Value Line Investment Survey,* a guide to public companies, their financial data, and the outlook for their stocks. You can get it by mail ($570 for a one-year subscription, call 800-833-0046); or on CD-ROM for Windows ($595, with disks mailed monthly and weekly updates available on-line; call 800-535-9648). Or write to Value Line at 220 East 42nd St., New York, NY 10017.

Join. Try the American Association of Individual Investors (625 North Michigan Ave., Suite 1900, Chicago, IL 60611 [800-428-2244]). For $49 a year, members get the monthly *AAII Journal,* other investment information, and access to seminars on investing and financial planning. Or subscribe to AAII's *Computerized Investing* ($40), a bimonthly publication on how to manage your investments by computer. If you join AAII *and* subscribe to *Computerized Investing,* you pay a total of only $79. Web Site: http://www.aaii.org.

Try The National Association of Investors Corp. (P.O. Box 220, Royal

Oak, MI 48067 [248-583-6242]), which helps people form investment clubs. Learning in a group is more fun and often more effective than learning on your own. An NAIC membership costs $39 a year and includes a subscription to the association's magazine, *Better Investing*. You can also ask for a free copy of the NAIC's book, *Starting and Running a Profitable Investment Club*. That book is also available in bookstores; a purchase earns you $10 off your NAIC dues. You'll find information on its Web site at http://www.better-investing.org.

Study. Some schools and colleges offer adult-education courses. But take care when you're studying with a stockbroker or financial planner whose "courses" are indirect pitches for his or her services. Learn what you can from the course but don't take it as gospel—especially if your "professor" is "teaching" a marvelously "safe, high-yield" investment.

Surf. You'll find pots of investment information on the Web. A good place to start is (are you ready?) a *book: The Savvy Investor's Internet Resource* (IDG Books Worldwide) by Bryan Pfaffenberger and Claire Mencke. They translate both computer and investment jargon into standard English. The guide also includes a Web directory of investment resources. Some good sites to start with:

- For free stock-market quotes (delayed 15 to 20 minutes), plus other stock data and investment information: NETworth Quote Server (http://quotes.galt.com), Quote.com (http://www.quote.com), and Stock Smart (http://www.stocksmart.com).

- For the American Association of Individual Investors, an excellent source of information on personal finance and investing, including computerized investing: http://www.aaii.org.

- For finding other sites: http://www.infomanage.com/investment.

- For the news, subscribe to *The Wall Street Journal Interactive Edition* (http://www.wsj.com). You'll get current and recent *Journal* articles, access to *Barron's* investment magazine, and a slew of company news and global market data. Cost: $49 ($29 for subscribers to the *Journal*'s print edition).

Beware investment chatlines. They're pocked with stock hypes posted by dishonest brokers and investors who hope to manipulate you to their profit. It takes an experienced investor to find the forums for good ideas.

Experiment. Start a "learning account" with real cash and use it to invest. Try out the ideas that you've read about in books and magazines. See if your stocks go up and, if they don't, how it feels to lose. Test your ability to make good decisions in the face of rapidly changing conditions. You can't learn on paper. You have to put real money at risk.

SALES COMMISSIONS:
THE GHOST IN THE CLOSET

Now you have a good broker (you hope). You have a brokerage account and you're starting to trade.

The broker has a long-term incentive for you to succeed—not only to keep you as a client but also to gain the accounts of your family and friends. But he or she has a short-term incentive to harvest commissions. Brokers' earnings usually derive from how often and how much you buy and sell, not from your investment success. The firm may reward your broker for superior "performance" even though your account is going down the tubes. An ethical broker tries to earn commissions without shoving too much down your throat. By contrast, a callous broker may tempt you to:

• Trade stocks instead of holding them for the long term, even when that wasn't your original intent. For example, shortly after selling you shares in GrandSlam, Inc., your broker may advise that "it's time to take profits." That's three commissions—one for buying you GrandSlam, another for selling it, yet another for buying you something else. There's always the chance the broker is right; maybe you should be taking profits. On the other hand, maybe the broker is telling other clients to *buy* GrandSlam. Anyway, if you're investing for the long run, the broker shouldn't be selling you stocks you have to trade.

• Buy stocks on margin (page 259). That's risky for you but can raise your broker's commission by 100 percent.

• Buy into investment ideas that require frequent trades, like stock-index options (page 801). The odds of your losing money are high but your broker can make a fortune.

• Buy certain stocks, bonds, mutual funds, or other investments that bring extra profits into the firm. To move this merchandise, branch supervisors may be offered higher commissions, bonuses, or points toward a Hawaiian vacation. So the brokers hit the phones and call you up. The analysts who produce research reports may also get bonuses if you buy the stocks they recommend.

• Buy high-commission products. Instead of selling you plain-vanilla stocks, brokers might push "packaged" products—loaded mutual funds, unit trusts, and annuities.

• Trade, trade, trade, so the broker can show impressive commission numbers.

But, you say, how can these brokers succeed if they're burning their clients all the time? Some clients don't know it, or don't know it right away. And there are always new suckers—er, customers—coming along. It would seem smarter to cultivate long-term relationships, which careful brokers do. But when you drop a stockbroker, where do you go? To another stockbroker, natch. And the broker you left gets some other broker's unhappy customer. So it's just one big shuffle.

I should add that a broker needn't be venal or self-interested to burn up your money. He might just be dumb. Here's the comment of a broker who lost an Oklahoma farm couple $200,000 by selling their municipal bonds and putting the money into options trading. "Hey, I'm sorry," he said. "I didn't know what I was doing."

Here's a test for any new broker whom you're considering, suggested by former stockbroker Mary Calhoun. Tell the broker that you want to buy a $10,000 Treasury bill (brokerage commission: $25). If he or she says, "Sure," you've probably got a straight shooter. But if the response is, "Why don't you buy our Federal Securities Trust, it's even better," then say good-bye. The broker was trying to switch you to an investment that paid a commission of $300 to $490. The trust is better only for the broker, not for you.

COMMISSIONS UNVEILED

Ever wonder why so many apparently blameless investors wind up buying so much awful stuff? It's because the commission structure is skewed. Salespeople earn the most by selling the riskiest investments.

For proof, just look at the table on page 666 and imagine that you have $10,000 to invest. That money may generate sales commissions of as little as a few dollars and as much as $1,000 or more, depending on what the broker recommends—and zero to $1,000 when you sell. The table shows the "ladder of temptation."

These Lopsided Commissions Explain a Lot of Things. For example, why might a broker urge you to buy a brand-new mutual fund with no track record when you can choose among hundreds of good, seasoned funds already on the market? Answer: He or she earns a bonus by selling the new one.

And why isn't your broker urging you to save state and local income taxes by buying Treasury securities? I don't have to bother writing that answer down.

Your broker earns a commission on almost anything he or she sells. Depending on the investment, there are up-front commissions, commissions spread out for as long as you hold the product, or both. So don't be misled if the confirmation slip (confirming your buy or sell order) shows that the broker earned "zero." In many transactions, the compensation to the broker isn't disclosed. This could happen when you buy (1) new-issue stocks and bonds, where the commission is paid by the issuing company;

WHAT A BROKER CAN EARN BY INVESTING
$10,000 OF YOUR MONEY

IF THE BROKER CHOOSES	THE BROKERAGE FIRM WILL EARN
An options program	$250 to $1,000-plus*
A loaded, newly issued mutual fund	$450 to $575†‡
A loaded existing mutual fund	$450 to $500†
Annuities or life insurance	$400 to $5,000
Newly issued common stock	$350 to $850
A unit investment trust	$300 to $490
Stock bought on margin**	$200 to $1,000
Long-term bonds	$100 to $600
A closed-end mutual fund	$100 to $500
Stock on the New York Stock Exchange	$100 to $500
Short-term bonds	$38 to $150
U.S. government securities	$25 to $150
Bank certificates of deposit	$10 to $150
A no-load mutual fund	zero
A money market account	zero

* Options trade often, so these high commissions are paid over and over again.
† Front- or back-end load.
‡ The mutual fund company may kick back its portion of the commission to the brokerage firm, resulting in an even higher commission.
** "Margin" means bought with money borrowed from the brokerage house.

(2) stocks or bonds bought out of the company's own inventory; and (3) mutual funds that carry high, annual 12b-1 fees (including ongoing, "trailing" commissions for brokers) and exit fees in lieu of an up-front sales charge. Brokers may earn more on these "zero-commission" sales than by selling seasoned stocks or mutual funds.

Fee-Based Accounts. Some brokerage firms offer accounts with no commissions. Instead, you pay a fixed percentage of assets every year in return for which you get a certain number of trades. At Merrill Lynch, for example, accounts worth $100,000 to $250,000 are charged 1.5 percent of assets, entitling you to 17 transactions in the first year and 12 each year after that. Larger accounts pay lower fees and get more transactions. At PaineWebber, you can choose to pay anywhere from 0.75 to 2.5 percent, depending on the size of your account and the number of transactions you expect to make (trades of mutual funds, unit trusts, and annuities are excluded).

These fees presumably remove the brokers' incentive to sell high-commission products. They get paid regardless of what you buy and their income rises only if your assets do. The firm, however, may still pay its brokers bonuses to sell the new issues they underwrite. What's more, the average customer doesn't trade nearly as much as these programs allow, especially after the first year. For buy-and-hold investors, paying commissions is usually cheaper than paying annual fees. Paying 2.5 percent a year, whether in commissions or fees, is financial bloodletting (page 620).

Wrap Accounts. With a wrap, both you and the broker quit trying to manage your money. Instead, the two of you—or perhaps an "investment committee"—examine your finances and goals and put your money with an array of appropriate institutional money managers. For a minimum of $100,000 to $200,000, these wraps give you entree to managers whose normal minimum might be $1 million or more.

For this you pay a percentage of assets—between 2.5 and 3.5 percent (financial bloodletting, part 2). Fees are lower on all-bond accounts. There's no sales commissions on trades and you get a consolidated statement showing how all the managers do.

If you can't meet the $100,000 minimum, you might be offered a mutual fund wrap. The broker takes $25,000 or $50,000 accounts, spreads the money over several funds, and charges around 1.5 percent. On top of that, you pay the fund's money-management fees, which again brings your total to 2.5 or 3.5 percent.

I hate wrap accounts because the fee is too high. A broker can send you directly to a money manager for around 1.75 percent, including custodial fees and commissions. You'd pay about the same if you found a manager through a friend or business adviser.

As for mutual fund wraps, why pay 1.5 percent of your assets to get the names of mutual funds? You have several better options: (1) Read the fund-selection and asset-allocation portions of this book and do it yourself; (2) use the free asset-allocation suggestions offered by many no-load mutual fund families; (3) consider the asset-allocation funds run by the mutual fund companies T. Rowe Price, Vanguard, and Fidelity, which make fund selections for you; (4) work through a fee-only planner, who will manage your wrap for one percent or less; (5) if you seek the advice of a broker or commission planner, and will hold your investment for more than 5 years, buy the funds directly (at a 4.5 percent sales charge) and don't add the layer of "wrap." Starting in the sixth year, you'll net more than if you were paying 1.5 percent year after year after year after . . .

THE RESEARCH DEPARTMENT

Okay, so the broker is driven by commissions. But what about the Famous Brokerage Firm's research department? These workaholics slave night and day over financial reports and computer screens to dope out what's happening to the companies they follow. They know a good buy from a bad one—or think they do.

But the analysts have their necessities, too. They're an arm of the selling organization. They might earn special bonuses if their stocks rise in price, which helps keep the favorable mentions coming.

Worse, they're hostage to their firm's investment-banking clients. For example, say their firm is wooing an airline company for its banking business. The analyst may be pressured to issue a favorable report on the stock. If the firm takes a private company public by offering its shares for sale (an "initial public offering," or IPO), the firm's own analysts virtually have to recommend it, even if they privately think it's a dog.

An academic study of 1990–91 IPOs gives damning evidence of the analysts' conflicts of interest. It compared the performance of new issues touted *only* by analysts at the underwriting firm (the firm that managed the offering) with new issues also recommended by outside analysts. Those that only the underwriters liked trailed the market by 8 percentage points one year later, and trailed the other IPOs by 21 percentage points. After the second year their record was even worse.

The moral: If your broker offers you a new issue, ask who's recommending it. If he or she can find studies only by the firm's own analysts, give it a pass. But give it a look if outsiders like it, too.

Even so, give it a *careful* look. The best IPOs go to the big institutions first—for example, aggressive growth mutual funds (that's why their share prices sometimes jump so high). Major individual investors come next in line. Everyone else gets mere slivers of good stocks or the dogs that the big boys didn't want.

Some analysts are afraid to issue negative reports. If they do, their sources in that company might dry up, which could hurt their careers. The company might even try to harm their reputations, or worse.

Take Marvin Roffman, formerly of the regional brokerage firm Janney Montgomery Scott in Philadelphia. He once said, in a voice above a whisper, that Donald Trump's Atlantic City casino, the Taj Mahal, wouldn't earn enough money to cover its debt. Trump threatened to sue and the firm ordered Roffman to recant. When he didn't, he was fired. Janney Montgomery couldn't have cared less that Roffman was telling the public the truth.

In a 1990 survey of leading analysts done by *Institutional Investor* magazine, 61 percent said they'd been pressured to pull their punches at least once in their careers. And 39 percent did indeed tone down their opinion in their written reports, which go to the little guys like you and me. Meanwhile, they hinted at their true opinions over the phone to major clients.

Here's a quick guide to analysts' recommendations: *Strong buy*—accumulate the stock. *Buy*—the stock isn't collapsing yet, but watch it. *Hold* —sell as fast as you can. *Sell*—the company failed last week. As Lily Tomlin has said, "No matter how cynical you become, it's never enough to keep up."

GUILTY MANAGEMENT

Brokers take the heat but managers often light the fire. Even a well-meaning broker can be driven to rogue practices by a firm that insists on high sales at any cost. New brokers and less successful brokers are especially vulnerable to this kind of pressure. Management might: (1) set quotas which brokers have to meet to keep their jobs; (2) raise quotas unreasonably, which tempts brokers to churn accounts; (3) offer incentives for selling mediocre products, such as extra pay or fancy vacations; (4) pass out misleading sales information (it's marked "for internal use only," so it doesn't have to be vetted by regulators); (5) create a climate of callousness by passing out perks and vice presidencies to big producers no matter how dirty their techniques.

TWELVE WAYS TO KEEP YOUR BROKER FLYING RIGHT

1. Talk to the broker about your investment goals and how best to balance income, growth, and risk. These objectives should be written down on the new-account form, in words that satisfy you, on your first visit as a customer. Get a copy of the form and keep it with your records.

If the broker doesn't fill out a new-account form, or if you would like to be more specific, set down your objectives in a letter, ask the broker to initial it, and keep a copy. Those are his or her marching orders. If your letter says, "Prudent growth investments for my daughter's college education 10 years from now," and your broker puts you into stock-index options, you have proof that the investment wasn't suitable. Don't be afraid to present this letter. A good broker finds it helpful to know what your expectations are.

2. Read every word of the account agreement before signing it and get explanations for everything you don't understand. Refuse a margin account if you don't plan to buy on borrowed money. No point being tempted.

3. Confirm every verbal buy or sell order in writing so there's no mistake (and keep a copy). Your letter to the broker should include your understanding of the investment's goals. If the broker has told you that this oil-well deal is "safe for someone who needs income," repeat that promise in your letter. If the hole comes up dry, the letter could help you win a settlement or an arbitration case. (Remember: A broker, when challenged, will usually say that he or she explained all the risks and you understood them. Your letter shows exactly what you thought you were buying. If more of these letters were written, more brokers would settle without giving you a hard time.)

4. Write down the following magic questions and keep them near the telephone. Ask each one of them every time your broker recommends an investment:

- Why are you suggesting this?
- How does it meet the goals I outlined?
- What is the investment's past performance?
- If it's a stock, how high is the price/earnings ratio, compared with its historical range (page 715)? What is the expected return on the investment and how was that expectation reached?
- How long do you recommend that I hold it?
- Can I sell whenever I want? Are penalties involved?
- What research data are you sending me?
- On a scale of one to 10, how would you rate the market risk?
- What are the commissions and other transaction costs (each sell order typically carries a small fee as well as a sales commission)?
- What can go wrong? (There is no investment that can't go wrong.)
- If I don't choose this investment, what alternatives might you suggest?

The answers should help weed out investments that are inappropriate for you. If you're interested, get the backup material and think about it for a day or two. Never tumble when a broker says, "It's now or never." First, that's rarely true. Second, if it is, say never. Smart investors never buy sight unseen. On the other hand, don't take a week to decide. By then the price may be higher than you ought to pay.

5. Check every slip that confirms a trade. Mistakes are sometimes made in writing up orders. The broker might enter the wrong stock symbol or write "buy" instead of "sell." If you don't catch the error right away (and didn't confirm your order in writing), the broker may claim that there was no error and it could be hard for you to prove otherwise.

6. Check your statements to make sure checks are deposited in the correct account and in a timely manner.

7. When you call your broker about a mistake, follow up with a letter. If the error isn't straightened out, call the firm's office manager and ask why. Send the manager a copy of the letter you wrote to the broker. Any broker who is slow to correct a "mistake" may be covering something up.

8. Call (and write) immediately if an investment pitched as "safe" starts to go down or if you suddenly, and unexpectedly, take a loss that you can't afford. The broker might have misrepresented the purchase. (Tip: It's not true that options are safe because "you make money no matter which way the market goes." You don't.) Don't dally to see if the price will rise. Too tardy a complaint makes it look as if you're sore only because the speculation failed.

You'll normally need some evidence to prove your case, such as the instructions on your new-account form or a letter you wrote to the broker confirming your understanding of the purchase.

9. Keep written notes of every conversation with your broker, date them, and put them in a file. This is the best advice on this page! If the broker ever claims that you gave permission for a trade when you didn't, or argues, falsely, that he or she fully explained a risky investment, your notes will prove otherwise. Good arbitrators give a lot of weight to contemporaneous notes, faithfully kept.

Incidentally, let the broker know that you're taking notes—as in, 'Just a minute, I'm writing this down." Stockbrokers tend to highlight the promise in any investment and glide over the risks—which might happen less often if they know that their comments are on the record.

10. Keep all paperwork: your new-account agreement, confirmations of trades, monthly statements, copies of the letters you write to your broker, notes of conversations, literature about your investments. You never know what will help you win a settlement if you think you've been misled.

11. Keep track of the fees and commissions you pay. They're on each confirmation slip, but brokerage firms (being no dopes) don't normally aggregate them on your monthly statements. Only your broker has the tally —and should send it to you if you ask.

12. Go for periodic portfolio reviews. Discuss the big picture to be sure that you and your broker still agree on your goals. Then ask the broker to show you your percentage return for the year (adjusted for purchases, sales, dividends, and commissions) and your average annual return since your relationship began. Only a few firms disclose this routinely, probably for good reason, but you should insist. How else can you hold your broker accountable or see how good your own investment ideas really were? The data you need is right there on the broker's computer.

If your broker can't or won't compute your average annual returns, do it yourself on a home computer. For a review of the many different types of investment-management software on the market, get *The Individual Investor's Guide to Computerized Investing,* $24.95 from the American Association of Individual Investors (page 663). The guide is also on CD-ROM ($19.95), which lets you check out the products interactively.

If you think you may have a major problem, or just want to check on your broker or bank trust officer, call Stock Broker Analysis (SBA), 576 14th Ave. South, Naples, FL 34102 (941-261-9106). For a flat $375, the firm will analyze your portfolio to unearth your total investment gains, total costs, and net percentage returns, compared with what you could have earned had your money been invested in a pure stock or bond index. In the rare event that the project takes more than 5 hours, you'll be notified. The charge is $75 for each additional hour. SBA has found excessive commissions not just in stock accounts but also in accounts made up primarily of bonds or unit trusts.

Another source of help: GreenTrak, 60 E. 42nd St., New York, NY 10165 (800-815-3434). GreenTrak charges $300 to show you how well your account has performed historically. The study also shows how much you've paid in commissions and fees.

If your broker makes more than 3 percent of your average account balance in any year, he or she is trading too much.

TO FLY RIGHT YOURSELF . . .

. . . Stick to your investment program. By saying yes to what fits and no to what doesn't, you blaze a clear trail for your broker to follow.

. . . Take responsibility for understanding everything you buy. If, after two explanations, you still don't get it, skip it. No investment is so special it's worth buying blind. Besides, if the broker can't explain it maybe he or she doesn't understand it, either.

. . . Don't whine, complain, or chew over opportunities lost. Let the market bury its dead. This is always the first day of the rest of your investing life.

. . . Don't deceive your broker about the size of your assets, where they're invested, and what other brokerage accounts you keep. A good broker will make better recommendations if he or she knows the whole picture.

. . . Take your losses like a man—er, person. After the crash of 1987 hundreds of speculators tried to walk away from legitimate debts they owed their brokers, forcing the brokers to go to court or arbitration to try to collect. Resist only if you were genuinely misled.

. . . Don't succumb to fantasies. You know in your heart that no investment is risk-free. You know in your gut that no one can guarantee an extra-high return.

. . . Be honest about your own investment results. Most investors remember their winners, forget their losers and never average the two together. So they haven't a clue how well they've actually performed. For paper-and-pencil information on how to find out, see page 1009. For easier tracking, get a good computer program—maybe *Quicken* or *Managing Your Money*. If you discover that you're underperforming the average mutual fund (which wouldn't be surprising), take the hint.

WHEN BROKERS ARE LIABLE FOR YOUR LOSSES

When you lose money based on what a broker advised, you can sometimes force the brokerage firm to give it back. To collect, however, you have to be able to show that the broker handled your money in a way that's specifically illegal (stupidity is not a recompensible offense). Here's a list of the cardinal sins:

1. *Unsuitable investments*. The broker buys securities that contravene your stated goals or are too risky for someone in your position. Say, for example, that you tell the broker that all you have in the world is $50,000, which you need to live on. The broker says, "Sure," and puts you into an array of speculative or non-dividend-paying stocks. If you take major losses, the broker should be liable. It makes no difference that you approved the purchases. The broker should never have recommended them in the first place. (What's speculative? Among other things, I'd list small companies, companies with prices under $5, companies that don't score B+ or better in Standard & Poor's *Stock Guide,* and companies not rated there. It was also wrong for the broker not to have put some money into bonds.)

It's also unsuitable for a broker to concentrate most of your money in two or three stocks, talk you into buying on margin, or buy you aggressive growth stocks if you're a widow needing income.

2. *Churning*. You're being churned when securities are constantly bought and sold for your account solely to generate sales commissions. Sometimes, so much money is siphoned off that it's almost impossible for you to come out ahead. There's no specific rule on how much trading is too much. What's fair in a speculator's account is excessive for novices with a limited amount of funds. To find out what your broker is doing, add up the fees and commissions and any margin interest you paid over the past 12 months; using your monthly statements, find your average account value over the same 12 months; then divide your costs by the average value (if you bought on a margin, count only the equity in the account). The result is the percentage return you have to earn just to cover your costs. If it's higher than 3 percent, you are probably being churned.

You can also look at the turnover ratio in your account. This is the total equity value of all purchases for the year divided by the average equity in your account. Three times is considered a red flag, although two times is too much for conservative investors. You occasionally find churning in bank trust accounts, too.

3. *Unauthorized trading*. The broker buys and sells without your prior permission. This happens more often than you might think and is one strong reason for keeping notes of your conversations. A broker may claim you gave permission when you didn't.

4. *Misrepresentation*. A broker lies about an investment, conceals pertinent information, or plays down known risks. For example, say that your latest monthly statement shows a drop in the value of your account. Your broker might say, falsely, "That's a mistake, you're really making money. It's just that some of your options profits aren't posted yet." Another example: The broker may whisper that Red, Inc., is about to merge and advise you to load up on it. He neglects to mention that the Justice Department is opposing the takeover. When you see that in the newspapers, he says that he has a friend at Justice who heard that the government will drop its

case. That turns out to be a lie. The deal blows apart and your stock heads south.

If you can prove any concealments or lies (ideally, from those notes you keep of your conversations with your broker), you may be able to recover your loss.

5. *Overleverage.* You're induced to borrow more against your securities than is consistent with your investment goals. Your broker may not have fully disclosed the risk of buying securities on margin or taken the time to see if you truly understood. If you didn't grasp the fact that a margin call could cost you some of your stocks, maybe you have a case. Margin buying is almost never consistent with conservative investment goals (page 260).

6. *Falsification of documents.* A broker notes on your new-account form or options agreement that you're richer than you really are. This can happen with brokers who peddle high-risk investments. To trade options, the firm might require you to have a net worth of $100,000, not counting your house. If you're worth less, the broker might put down $100,000 anyway and later claim that you supplied the false amount. Never sign a brokerage agreement that contains false numbers or blanks that a broker can fill in later.

Brokers have also been known to forge client signatures, which, of course, is illegal. The forgery may go undetected unless you pay close attention to your account statements. Look for any trading, checks, or cash releases to third parties that you didn't authorize.

7. *Theft.* A broker may actually lift money from your account. For example, your statement might say that your brokerage firm sent you $3,000 from your asset-management account, but you never got the check. Or you might find that you suddenly own just 400 shares of AT&T when last month you owned 500 shares. A good brokerage firm will always restore losses from theft, but first you have to notice them. Untold millions of dollars are probably lost each year by people who don't read their brokerage-house statements or don't understand what they read. (Adult children of elderly parents, take note.)

8. *Unregistered securities or an unregistered broker or brokerage firm.* You can recover your losses if your broker sells a stock, partnership, or any other security not registered for sale in your state, unless an exemption has been filed. Unregistered securities are typically over-the-counter stocks selling for $5 or less a share. By statute, most states entitle you to get all of your money back, plus interest and attorney's fees. Firms and brokers must also be registered to do business in your state.

9. *Negligence.* If your broker fails to act with due care—for instance, carrying through your orders to buy or sell—he or she may be liable for negligence. A broker may also be negligent for failing to tell you the bad news about a security.

The deadliest sin is incompetence, but it's hard to collect on. If your broker offered muddled advice and you took it, you may have to pay. It's not illegal to be dumb.

IF YOU'VE BEEN CHEATED, DON'T MAKE THESE MISTAKES

Don't blame yourself. The fault doesn't lie in your personal greed or innocence, nor is your loss a "lesson" or just one of investing's unlucky breaks. The broker has a duty to offer you securities that suit your needs and tolerance for risk, and to describe them honestly. If he or she cheats, you have a right to be outraged. You have to accept investment risk, but acceptable risks don't include deception, fraud, and abuse.

Don't walk away. Demand reparations—from the broker, the broker's office manager, and the president of the brokerage firm. Sometimes that works. If you get a form letter claiming that you knew the risks, your course of action will depend on how much you lost. A small loss might not be worth trying to collect, alas. For a larger loss, go to arbitration (page 680) or mediation (page 678). The more noise you make, the more willing a firm might be to settle your case quickly, if it suspects it's in the wrong.

Don't let the clock run out. Industry arbitration forums generally don't accept claims based on transactions that are more than 6 years old. This is called the "subject matter" limit. It's different from statutes of limitations, which can be much shorter. The statutes limit the time you have for alleging specific violations, and although arbitration panels don't have to follow them, they usually do. Claims under federal law have to be challenged within one year from the date of discovery and no more than 3 years from the date of the transaction. State laws may give you a little longer. Nevertheless, any delay may jeopardize your claim. Boston attorney David Shellenberger says there's also a psychological statute of limitations. Arbitrators may hold it against you if you don't bring a claim immediately.

Many people are so nice that they don't want to offend their broker by complaining too much or closing their account. That's how the broker gets to abuse you some more.

HOW TO GET ACTION ON YOUR COMPLAINT

Act Immediately. Call your broker the moment anything feels wrong. If you let a problem linger, your complaint may lose its credibility. This is especially important if a broker makes a transaction you didn't authorize. If you don't object immediately you may be deemed to have ratified the transaction.

Don't Yell. Ask the broker for an explanation and take notes. Ask for his or her explanation in writing. Tell the broker exactly how you want the problem corrected ("sell that stock and restore my money"). Send a letter stating why the investment was unsuitable and reiterating your view of what should be done. If you don't get a written explanation from the broker, it's likely that his or her excuse won't wash. When brokers duck you, it's always for a reason.

Follow Up. If 2 weeks pass, nothing has changed, and the written explanation hasn't arrived, write a short, polite letter to the branch office manager (call the office and ask for the person's name). Include a copy of the letter you sent to your broker and copies of records that prove your point. These might include monthly account statements, order confirmations, notes to your broker, and the written investment objectives that your broker started out with. State the rule that you think has been violated ("An unsuitable investment for someone in my position . . . " "Misled me as to the risks in options . . . "). Ask for a specific remedy ("Restore my purchase price of $12,000 plus interest lost since 11/13/96 . . . " "Mark on the statement that this trade was solicited, not unsolicited . . . "). Make it clear that you are prepared to take this case further.

If another 2 weeks pass and still nothing happens, repeat the entire exercise with the president of the brokerage house.

The regrettable truth is that letter writing almost never works. I advise it only because sometimes the firm responds favorably, which would save you a lot of trouble. If it rejects your complaint in writing, the letter might support your complaint that the firm doesn't properly supervise its brokers. You might get a letter from the firm's lawyer falsely stating that if you go to arbitration and lose, you'll be liable for the broker's enormous legal fees. You won't, assuming you haven't brought a frivolous case. The firm is trying to scare you off and should be called on it. Proof of attempted intimidation might win you sympathy from an arbitration panel.

Call the Cops. If you get a letter from the firm's lawyer saying that you're wrong, the broker is right, and your claim is denied, don't fold your tent. Write a letter to the consumer-protection office of your state's division of securities. You should also write if the broker simply fails to respond. Enclose copies of your letters to the broker and copies of the records that prove your claim. Sometimes your state's enforcers can solve your problem, usually within a few weeks. To get the telephone number of your state securities commission, call the North American Securities Administrators Association in Washington, DC, at 202-737-0900.

You can also write to the Office of Investor Education and Assistance at the Securities and Exchange Commission, 450 Fifth St. N.W., Washington, DC 20549 (202-942-7040). This is mostly a form-letter office—sending inquiries to firms that investors complain about and forwarding your broker's response. Nevertheless, it's important to write. Several complaints about a particular broker or firm can trigger an investigation. For personal help, however, your best shot is your state securities office.

BRINGING UP THE BIG GUNS

When a broker does you wrong and the state securities office can't help, you normally go to arbitration (page 680). Unfortunately, many panels are biased against individual investors. Even if your broker obviously screwed you, they may say it's your fault for not understanding what was going on.

At this writing, an effort is under way to get better, more neutral arbitrators. And fortunately, the current system can also produce judgments that are fair. So go ahead with arbitration. Just don't be surprised if your case isn't treated with the respect it deserves.

In arbitration, you don't necessarily need a lawyer by your side. You do have to tell what happened in a clear, orderly, and well-organized way, starting with the day you opened the account. You should bring any relevant witnesses and documents to support your case. You can't win just by showing up and saying your broker did you wrong. The broker will say that the risks were fully explained and you understood them.

But investors without lawyers don't fare as well. They win cases less often than investors with lawyers do, and when they win, they get smaller amounts. There's also a catch-22 at work: If you put on a good, solid legal case all by yourself, the arbitrators might decide that you're such a smart cookie, you should have known better than to make such a dumb investment, and rule against you. The process is, well, *arbitrary*.

By all means get legal advice when a lot of money is at stake. Arbitrations increasingly look like mini-lawsuits rather than informal courts of equity—except that you don't get the full protection of the securities laws. The brokerage firm will hire lawyers adept in total war. They'll drag their feet, paper you with motions, try to hold the hearing far away from where you live, fail to produce documents that are crucial to your case, and twist what you say when you testify. You need a lawyer to hammer them.

The lawyer should specialize in securities arbitration. Otherwise, he or she won't know what documents the firm may be holding that could help you prove your case. If you have a family lawyer, ask him or her to find you someone. Alternatively, get a referral from your state's bar association or the Public Investors Arbitration Bar Association (call 888-621-7484) or your state's bar association. You can also get names from the Securities

Arbitration Commentator's *Advocate Record, Investor's Edition* (P.O. Box 112, Maplewood, NJ 07040 [201-761-5880]). SAC will send you a list of all the lawyers who've handled cases in the past year in the nearest city where arbitrations are heard, the sum they sought, and the actual award. Cost: $25, $50, or $75, depending on the size of your area's list (10 percent off if you cite this book as a reference).

Lawyers generally charge a fee of one-third to 40 percent of your recovery and nothing if you lose. Some want $5,000 or $10,000 up front, not refundable if you lose. You'll also have to cover expenses, which can be substantial. If the claim is for $25,000 or less, the lawyer may tell you it's not worth his or her time.

There are also a handful of arbitration services, especially in California and Florida. These are small firms of non-lawyer experts and perhaps a securities lawyer, too. They're of varying competence. Like lawyers, they work on a straight contingency fee, also one-third to 40 percent of the award. Look for them in the Yellow Pages.

At a preliminary meeting (which usually costs little or nothing), the lawyer or expert will discuss the relevant legal issues and tell you whether your case appears strong or weak. If you decide to go ahead and your claim is too small to make it worthwhile to hire a lawyer full-time, arrange for regular consultations—probably at $100 to $300 an hour—to help you develop the case on your own. Experienced advisers can spot complaints that you didn't even know you had. For example, you might have charged that you were given an unsuitable investment without noticing that the broker was also churning your account. Or you might not think to ask for the brokerage firm's research reports on the stock you bought; maybe the broker went off on his or her own rather than following the firm's opinion. Good preparation—a lawyer's specialty—is critical. Once your "paper case" is firmly in hand, you can go to the hearing and speak for yourself.

A lawsuit might be possible, depending on the nature of your brokerage agreement. But it's not worth the time and expense unless really big bucks are involved. The cases that normally go to court are class actions involving many claimants at once.

Don't Be Intimidated. Your accountant might tell you that your broker has been churning your account. When you talk to your broker, he or she may act outraged. "What, you listen to that bean counter? When I'm the one knocking myself out to make money for you?" That's a standard ploy and a sure sign that your accountant is right. Don't fold your tent.

MEDIATION—
THE WAVE OF THE FUTURE?

Mediation can be a fast and simple way of pursuing a settlement. It helps especially when your case is morally strong but legally flawed, the other side is liable but the damages are unclear, there's bad blood between the parties, or a pigheaded lawyer or client presses for more than the case is worth. As a neutral third party, the mediator can assess each side's strengths and weaknesses and serve as a reality check.

You have to agree to mediate, meaning (in most cases) that you'll have to give something up. Here's how the process works:

Both sides agree on a mediator, chosen from a list of experienced people whose professional backgrounds are disclosed. You'll want someone who understands the industry.

The proceeding starts with a general meeting where the adversaries and their lawyers present their evidence and their views. Each side then retires to a separate room. The mediator speaks privately to each. He or she explains the relative merits of your case, probes for the kind of settlement you'd accept, and conveys (with permission) the irreducible needs of the other side.

Settlement offers and counteroffers are then carried back and forth. The mediator gradually moves the discussion forward and may lean on one side more than the other. But he or she can't dictate a deal. The parties reach a compromise themselves—typically during the mediation or just after.

There's no written award, only a voluntary settlement document which the mediator may or may not see. Unless you agree, mediation isn't binding. If you don't like the final offer, you're free to walk.

The National Association of Securities Dealers runs the industry's mediation program. For the free brochure, *NASD Mediation,* call 212-858-4400. For a one-day mediation, you pay a $150 administrative fee (if you haven't already filed an arbitration case), roughly $600 for the first four hours, and $150 per hour thereafter. The latter cost is split with the brokerage firm. Small cases may cost more in mediation than arbitration, but you aren't exposed to the risk of an unfair arbitration award.

A coalition of financial-planning organizations endorses mediation through the American Arbitration Association (212-484-4000), which is independent of the financial industry. At the AAA, your filing fee is $300 if no arbitration case has been filed, and $700 to $1,000 per day for the mediator, split with the brokerage firm.

You don't have to have a lawyer but you should at least talk to one in advance. Consider hiring representation if your case is for more than $10,000 and you are unfamiliar with securities law.

You can ask for mediation without filing an arbitration claim. But that makes it harder to gather evidence you may need. Many investors file for arbitration, wrestle documents from the other side, then go to mediation with evidence in hand. If mediation doesn't work, arbitration can proceed.

ARBITRATION:
HOW TO TAKE YOUR BEST SHOT

Arbitration is binding. You lay your case before a panel and abide by the result. About half the investors get an award. It's rare to get all your money back, however, and even rarer to win punitive damages against a dirty-dealing broker. Although many arbitrators are fair-minded, others are biased toward the industry; awards are inconsistent and sometimes capricious, and the arbitrators usually don't publish the reasoning behind their decisions. Nevertheless, when you signed the customer agreement with your broker, you most likely agreed to settle disputes in arbitration, which, for all its horrors, is better than going to court. And you might even win! Here's how to give it your best shot:

Choose the Best Arbitration Forum. Arbitration is run by the various securities and commodities exchanges as well as the independent American Arbitration Association (AAA). AAA has a better record for siding with investors, but few customer agreements allow you to have a hearing there. For a way of wedging the AAA into your customer agreement, see page 658.

AAA arbitrations are worth the effort. Consider the 10,000 awards dating from May 1989 to June 1995, analyzed by the Securities Arbitration Commentator: Investors using a panel run by the National Association of Securities Dealers (NASD) won 58 percent of the time; at the New York Stock Exchange (NYSE), 52 percent of the time; at the AAA, a startling 70 percent of the time. That's why most brokers bar you from going! The AAA is more apt to listen to your side of the story. It also take cases older than 6 years.

If you can't get access to the AAA, you can choose which industry panel to use. Here's where an experienced lawyer or securities-arbitration expert can help. The panels' reputation for bias varies from city to city. In some places, the NASD is preferred, but in others it's the NYSE.

The NASD charges filing fees on a sliding scale: $15 if you're asking for $1,000 or less, $300 for claims in the $100,000 to $500,000 range, and a maximum of $850 for claims topping $10 million. There's a fee for a pre-hearing conference, then a hearing-session deposit fee ranging from $25 to $2,750 (refundable if you settle in advance). At the end of the case, the arbitrators assess a total forum fee. They also decide who has to pay—sometimes the side with the weaker case, sometimes a 50/50 split. If the panel decides in your favor and thinks that the broker should bear your costs, you should get your deposit back. If you lose, you could be told to pay the fees for the entire hearing, although the panel generally doesn't go that far.

The NYSE has similar filing fees and hearing deposits. At the AAA, filing fees are $300 for cases with claims up to $25,000, $1,000 for claims in the $50,000 to $250,000 range, and a maximum of $4,000 for claims over $5 million. Hearings are $200 per day and the arbitrator receives $400 per day, split equally by both parties.

For information on arbitration involving commodities accounts, see page 685.

Try to Find Impartial Arbitrators. At this writing, the industry is being pressed to develop a better (read: fairer) way of choosing arbitrators. I'll describe the system of 1997–98, then explain the type of system the industry says it's moving toward.

Under the traditional system, an industry forum picks arbitrators to hear your case. At the NASD, you get three for cases of $30,000 or more—one industry arbitrator and two supposedly representing the public. For smaller cases you get one, although you can ask for three if your case is large enough. At the NYSE you get three for claims of $10,000 or more.

You're given the arbitrators' names and backgrounds. You can strike one "for cause," although that's hard to do. You get one "free" strike, which lawyers use on arbitrators who have shown exceptional bias in the past. That person is replaced by another appointee—who could be even worse than the one you got rid of.

The AAA has a better system, which the industry may adopt. It gives both sides a list of several arbitrators and information about their backgrounds. You can reject as many as you want. The rest are ranked in your order of choice. A panel of three is then assembled. If properly run, a list system stops the industry from using its favorite, biased arbitrators over and over again.

If asked, the NASD and NYSE will fax you the previous awards made by the chosen arbitrators. You'll get the most recent data at no cost; if you want more, there may be a modest fee. The data will cover only awards made in their forum.

Securities-arbitration lawyers may have their own databases of the awards each arbitrator makes. For a list of all of your arbitrators' awards in any forum dating back to May 1989, contact the Securities Arbitration Commentator (P.O. Box 112, Maplewood, NJ 07040 [201-761-5880]). It charges $10 per arbitrator and $2 per award. Mention this book to receive a 10 percent discount. If you're in an AAA arbitration, SAC will check the record of up to fifteen arbitrators for a flat $45 fee.

Do get these records! Your opponents know which arbitrators tend to favor the industry and will try to get them appointed. If you innocently accept them, you may lose your case before it starts.

Selecting arbitrators is another area where a lawyer or expert might help. A so-called public arbitrator, for example, might be a retired securities attorney who once represented the industry. Even "neutral" arbitrators know that they may not be invited back if they find against the industry too often. If the arbitrator is in the securities business, pull his or her CRD (page 655), to see if there are any complaints of customer abuse. Also pull the CRD for his or her firm, if it's small. It might be in the business of hustling penny stocks. That could be a reason to challenge the arbitrator for cause.

Gather the Information Needed to Prove Your Case. Arbitrators hear plenty of cases where it's the broker's evidence (even if flaky) against little more than the customer's word. Usually, the broker is going to win such a contest by default. Even cases presented by a lawyer (if not an experienced arbitration lawyer) may not marshal enough facts.

For starters, you need the complete history of your account: the new-account agreement showing your objectives and financial situation, monthly and annual statements, and all the order confirmations. If you've misplaced any of these documents, the brokerage firm is supposed to supply them. You'll be in an especially good position if you kept a running record of your dealings with the broker, including contemporaneous notes of what the broker told you about each investment and copies of all your written instructions.

Ask for the firm's research on the securities in dispute. Did your broker misrepresent the investment? Ask for any information it distributed to brokers that described the investment and how to sell it. Brokers may rely on internal sales documents that don't explain the risks.

Ask for the broker's personnel file. Ask for copies of any other complaints against the broker. Get the broker's full CRD file from your state, not the summary from the NASD (page 655), which will disclose any prior disciplinary actions. Ask for any tapes of telephone conversations between your broker and you.

Also ask for the parts of the firm's compliance and supervision manuals that relate to your situation. You need it to figure out whether your broker violated the firm's own rules. Do the rules say, "Don't concentrate a client's money in just two or three securities"? Do they say, "Recommend only the stocks that we do research reports on"? If your broker strayed off the reservation, this will help your case. The supervision manual will instruct the office manager on how brokers should be managed—instructions that, in your case, were probably not followed.

The brokerage firm is supposed to meet your reasonable requests for information. If it resists (and it almost always does), ask for help from your arbitrators. File a motion to compel. Write a letter to the NASD to forward to the arbitrators, even if they haven't been named yet—not that you can count on the NASD to help. It often takes months to appoint the arbitrators, during which time the brokerage firm can ignore you with impunity. In theory, you're entitled to get the documents before the hearing, so you can study them. In practice, documents may be produced, literally, at the hearing-room door—by which time it's too late for you to analyze them. It's an extraordinary abuse of process which—at this writing—the NASD hasn't done much to fix.

While the broker's lawyers are stonewalling, they will demand that you produce documents for them—for example, personal financial information and your investment history with any other brokerage firm. They'll be trying to prove that you're a sophisticated investor who knew exactly what you were doing.

If you think your case is complicated and may take more than one day in arbitration, write on your original claim form that you'd like the hearing to take place on consecutive days or within a short period of time. Otherwise the hearings might be scheduled weeks or months apart, giving the arbitrators time to forget the facts about your case. When you are contacted to schedule hearings, remind the caller that you asked for consecutive days.

Line Up Witnesses. Maybe you know other customers whom the broker similarly misled. Maybe you have another broker who can testify that you always asked only for conservative investments. Maybe someone at work overheard you discussing the investment with your broker and repeating the broker's claim that there was "no risk." If this witness cannot be available in person, ask the arbitrators in advance for approval to put the person on a speakerphone during the hearing (and make sure there's a speakerphone available). An affidavit from the witness is less helpful and sometimes not permitted because he or she cannot be cross-examined.

If you want to call the firm's office manager or compliance officer as a witness and the firm refuses, ask your arbitrator to order it. A grandmother living on her income might want to ask these officers what they were doing while her broker sold her stock-index options. The firm's compliance manual doubtless says that they shouldn't have let such a sale stand.

Try to Settle the Case. The NASD reports that roughly 80 percent of its arbitration cases are settled by the parties. At the NYSE, it's 70 percent. The stronger your evidence, the more likely the other side will make a deal, so it helps if you have at least a minimal "paper case." Ask for full damages: your losses covered, compensation for the money you lost while your funds were tied up in this lousy investment (those are called opportunity costs), attorney's fees, the cost of filing the case, and interest from the day you filed the claim. But be prepared to compromise. Accepting a known sum usually beats the risk of going through arbitration and perhaps ending up with a slim or mediocre award. Settlements commonly range from 20 to 80 cents on the dollar.

In your dealings with the brokerage house, don't shout, don't weep, don't accuse, don't tremble. Lay out your demands in a businesslike way and stick to them.

Ask for a Hearing in a Convenient Place. Hearings should be held in a large city near where you lived when you opened the account, since most of the evidence and witnesses will be there. If there are extenuating circumstances—for example, you're retired in Florida and cannot travel easily—ask to have the hearing near where you live now.

Ordinary cases take a day, maybe two. But complicated cases may stretch over several months, making them almost as troublesome as a lawsuit to pursue.

If your damages come to $10,000 or less, you don't get a hearing unless you specifically ask for it. (This limit is expected to rise to $25,000 in 1998.) You can prosecute your case just by sending a written claim plus statements from witnesses and supporting evidence. You'll get the decision in the mail. An "on-the-papers" case usually has better results if a lawyer helps you prepare it.

Organize Your Narrative in Advance and Practice Telling It. Arbitrators are accustomed to hearing clients present their own cases and will generally do their best to help you along. Tell your story in an orderly way, starting with when you opened the account. Organize your presentation around the specific points of law you think the broker violated. Be as clear and forceful as you possibly can.

Typically, each side makes a brief opening statement. Then you present evidence and witnesses. The brokerage firm (which will always have a lawyer) will do the same. Each side will cross-examine the other. The arbitrators question both of you and listen to your closing arguments.

In general, investors complain that their broker soft-soaped them into thinking that a risky investment was safe or didn't act on their orders to sell an investment that subsequently declined. The broker replies that the customer knew exactly what he or she was doing and is sore only because the investment failed. The wealthier you are and the better established in your profession, the tougher it is to argue that you're a Wall Street innocent, even when you are. That's why notes of your conversations with your broker can be so important. They establish what you and the broker said to each other at the time.

In cases of flagrant abuse, you can ask for punitive damages. These are assessed when the broker's behavior is so outrageous that conscience recoils from merely requiring that he or she give the money back. You don't stand much of a chance of winning punitives when your claim is small. But they were awarded in nearly 7 percent of cases claiming $1 million or more, according to a Securities Arbitration Commentator survey in 1996.

About 4 to 12 weeks after the hearing, you get a decision in the mail. Arbitrators go by what they think is fair, not just by legal precedents. You usually cannot appeal.

Bring In a Court Reporter. That gives you a record of what everyone said—a positive incentive to keep the arbitrators polite and restrict the number of whoppers your broker is prepared to tell. In the rare instance that you might want to appeal, you can have a transcript made. Tapes are made of all arbitrations, but they're often inaudible, hence unusable to prove perjury or other misconduct.

FOR MORE INFORMATION . . .

The arbitration forums publish consumer guides explaining exactly how to pursue a claim. For information, write to the Director of Arbitration at:

The National Association of Securities Dealers Arbitration, 33 Whitehall St., New York, NY 10004, (212-858-4400). Ask for their arbitration-information packet or *NASD Mediation* booklet. For information by Web, go to http://www.nasdr.com.

The New York Stock Exchange, 11 Wall St., New York, NY 10005 (212-656-3000).

The American Arbitration Association, 140 West 51st St., New York, NY 10020. Call 212-484-4000 or look them up on the Web at http://www.adr.org.

For complaints against commodity brokers, the government-sponsored Commodity Futures Trading Commission (CFTC) runs a reparations program that is quick, cheap, and designed for investors to use without a lawyer. Rather than an arbitrator, the CFTC employs administrative law judges for cases over $30,000 and judgment officers for smaller cases. It costs only $50 to $225 to file, depending on the size of the case. The hearing may be conducted by telephone. Common complaints concern unauthorized trading, churning, and failure to disclose risk. For more information call 202-418-5250, write to the CFTC Office of Proceedings, 1155 21st St. N.W., 3 Lafayette Center, Washington, DC 20581, or go to the Web at http://www.cftc.gov.

The National Futures Association, 200 West Madison St., Suite 1600, Chicago, IL 60606, runs an arbitration program for complaints against commodity brokers. But lawyers say that if the firm is a member of the NASD, you'd be better off filing there. NFA has a small panel of arbitrators, which are felt to be biased toward the industry. The NFA also assigns arbitrators and does not allow peremptory challenges. Call 800-572-9400 or pull information off the Web: http://www.nfa.futures.org. The filing fee ranges from $50 for claims up to $2,500 to $1,550 for claims over $150,000. The NFA also offers mediation.

TRUTH BREAKS OUT

A couple of years ago I got a letter from a stockbroker that made a strong impression. I had written some newspaper columns that criticized certain shoddy sales practices and mail from furious brokers was raining down on me. But this letter was different.

I have been employed as a broker for the past 15 years. Most of those years have been with a major [brokerage] house. I must admit that at first your columns angered me as much as anyone who has ever had their lucrative employment threatened by an "outsider." But upon reflection, I am convinced you are right. . . .

The first thing a securities salesman learns is to gain the confidence of his customer. This enables the salesman to more easily sell the customer the products that pay the salesman the highest commission. All securities firms have different commission schedules for different investment products. Most firms will respond that their brokers are free to sell their customers any investment product they wish. But in practice, the broker-salesman is "encouraged" to sell the product most profitable to the firm and do it often. All securities firms also have formulas that indicate how often customer's money should turn over, and these are considered minimums. . . .

When I first entered the business, our firm had a broker who can truly be considered a "customer's man." He had the most clients, and the most money of his clients under his control, that I had ever heard of to that point. The firm's management took the view that he was not producing enough commissions. The broker said that we were in the middle of a bear market (this was 1974), and he was not going to squander his clients' money to produce commissions for the firm. The firm finally pressured the broker so much that he resigned.

We younger, hungrier brokers fell upon his book of clients like a pack of hungry wolves, and tried everything to keep that book and generate commissions. But I don't think we kept a single one. . . .

I don't want you to conclude from what I have written that I am like that broker—far from it. I, too, have fallen prey to the siren's song of wealth and glamour that has been and is Wall Street. I have overtraded customer accounts, and bought for them "investments" that made more sense for me than them. I guess I wrote [to you] as a catharsis, and to clear my head and that of my colleagues of the siren's song.

The letter was signed "Anonymous Vice President, Investments, Major Investment Firm," with an invitation to write if I wanted the writer to disclose his name. How tragic to feel that your whole life has been built upon a fraud.

BUYING STOCKS WITHOUT
SALES COMMISSIONS:
THE NEW NO-LOAD WORLD

You can buy many individual stocks through the company itself without going through a stockbroker. There's no sales commission and often no fees. At this writing, some 1,000 companies offer this service, including some of the bluest of chips: General Electric, General Motors, AT&T, Coca-Cola, Texaco. You have to buy one or more shares through a broker or other share-buying service and register it in your name. After that, you can purchase broker-free.

Some 150 companies take no-load buying one step further: you don't have to buy even one share from an outside source. These programs are called *direct purchase*. Well-known companies with free direct-purchase plans include Dial, Exxon, Mobil, and Barnett Banks. Those with fees include Amoco, Enron, Home Depot, McDonald's, Procter & Gamble, and Wal-Mart. Fees generally run $5 to $15 on signing plus small service fees when you buy—a fraction of what the brokerage commission would be. A few companies, however, charge $15 a year. For super-small investors, that's too much.

Once you've made your initial purchase, you enroll in the company's dividend-reinvestment plan (DRIP). All your dividends are reinvested automatically in additional shares. Most of the traditional plans and all the direct-purchase plans let you buy extra shares for cash and add them to the plan. You can put in as little as $10 and as much as $10,000 per month, depending on the company. You're generally charged the current market price, although some firms (mostly utilities) sell the shares at a discount, usually 3 to 5 percent.

Dividend reinvestment is a terrific deal. If you get small dividend payments by check, you'll probably fritter them away. But reinvested, they add up to real money. As an example, say you bought 100 shares of McDonald's on the last day of 1986, at a cost of $6,113. Had you spent the dividends, your account 10 years later would have been worth $27,225. But with dividend reinvestment, you'd have picked up an extra 61 shares, raising your total to $30,029.

These plans are strictly for investors who want to buy regularly and hold. You normally don't buy on the day that you place your order. Instead, the company buys a block of shares weekly or monthly for all the investors who sent in their money during that time. Selling is slow, too. A few companies let you put in an order to sell by phone; otherwise you have to write or fax written instructions. To get your money might take as long as 10 business days. Sales fee: zero to $10, depending on the plan. Alternatively, you can request a free stock certificate, which the firm is supposed to deliver to you within 72 hours. You can take that to a local discount broker to sell. If speed is an issue, check the company's redemption policy in the prospectus before you buy.

A few DRIPs and direct-purchase plans offer special services, such as Individual Retirement Accounts, automatic investment plans (they'll deduct as little as $25 a month from your bank account and use it to purchase shares), and loans against your shares.

You can get a free list of the direct-purchase plans, plus their investment requirements, from (1) The Moneypaper, 1010 Mamaroneck Ave., Mamaroneck, NY 10543 (800-388-9993). Or (2) the DRIP Investor, 7412 Calumet Ave., Suite 200, Hammond, IN 46324 (800-711-7969). To invest, call the companies for the prospectus. Alternatively, call the DRIP Investor's clearinghouse (800-774-4117), which provides free prospectuses and application forms for some of the plans. You can get the same service by Web at http://www.netstockdirect.com or http://www.dripinvestor.com. The DRIP Investor also runs http://www.noloadstocks.com, through which you can ask for free notification by e-mail whenever a new no-load program starts up.

Both companies also offer guides to all the traditional DRIPs plus information on how to use them. At this writing, the DRIP Investor's *Directory of Dividend Reinvestment Plans* costs $15.95; The Moneypaper's *Guide to Dividend Reinvestment Plans* costs $27.

If you own shares in a company with a DRIP, you can arrange to make future purchases, including dividend reinvestments, through the plan rather than through a brokerage house.

If a company whose DRIP you want to join requires that you own at least one share, you can buy it from a stockbroker (minimum commission, $25 to $40); from The Moneypayer ($36 membership plus a stock-purchase fee of $15 to $20), or from the National Association of Investors Corp. ($35 membership fee plus a $5 stock-purchase fee—see page 662).

Tax alert: If you buy shares at a discount, the discount is generally taxed as income that year (although in 1994 private-letter ruling from the IRS has encouraged some companies to treat the discount as part of your capital gain when you sell). You're taxed on any commissions and fees that the company pays on your behalf (commissions are charged at institutional rates and might run 5 to 10 cents a share). Reinvested dividends are taxable, just as they are in mutual funds. You'll get a 1099 form at the end of each year.

If you sell just part of your DRIP account, it can be the very devil to figure out your income taxes. Every dividend you received was used to buy shares, or fractions of shares, at a different price, and you'll have to work out the gains you made on all of them. Fortunately, there's a way around this, says the DRIP Investor's Charles Carlson. Sell your entire account at once. You then figure your cost by adding up the amount of your initial purchase, all the dividends that were reinvested, and any additional investments you made in cash. That data is easy to find on the year-end statements the company sent. You saved every single statement of course. Mmmmm, you didn't? Call the company to see if it can pull your chestnuts out of the fire.

STRIKING GOLD IN OLD
STOCKS AND BONDS

Maybe you own some mystery securities—stocks or bonds you inherited or bought years ago, whose prices aren't listed in the newspaper. Some of these companies have expired, others may be too small to make your newspaper's daily stock listings, yet others may have been reborn as divisions of larger companies. Here's how to find out if your securities have any value:

• Call the information operator in the city where you last knew the corporation to be. It may still be operating at the same old stand. When you get the telephone number, call the company and ask for its share price.

• Write to the company at its last known address, search for its address in your public library, or troll the Internet. One library source: Dun & Bradstreet's *Million Dollar Directory,* which lists 160,000 U.S. corporations with a tangible net worth of more than $500,000. If you find the address, write to the treasurer, who will know what your securities are worth.

• Ask your stockbroker, if you have one. He or she might find the company in the reference book *National Stock Summary* or the Pink Sheets, which list thousands of small public companies whose names can't be found in the newspaper stock quotations. Your broker can also check with the firm's company-reorganization department.

• Send photocopies of the certificates to R.M. Smythe & Co., 26 Broadway, Suite 271, New York, NY 10004, with a self-addressed, stamped envelope. Smythe will find out whether each security has value. The search takes 2 to 3 weeks. Cost: $75 for each company.

• Don't throw out old stock or bond certificates until you've learned that the company formally went out of business. Even moribund firms are sometimes brought to life again.

INVESTMENT NEWSLETTERS

To add to your knowledge of investing, you might subscribe to a range of newsletters. You can buy almost any view on the market that appeals to you. There are market-timing letters. Growth-stock letters. Psychic-advisory letters. Mutual fund letters. Bond letters. Insider-buying letters. Asset-allocation letters. Technical-analysis letters. Precious-metal letters. College-professor letters. End-of-the-world letters. Letters that channel the spirit of Bernard Baruch. To publish a newsletter, you don't even have to register as an investment adviser.

Legitimate letters genuinely try to be good stock pickers for their customers. Others don't. The baddies may buy small-company stocks, then try to run up the price. They may have "consulting" relationships with the companies they tout (in other words, they're paid to promote). Newsletter editors aren't required to disclose these conflicts of interest explicitly, so you'll probably never know about them.

Because of their quirky unevenness, newsletters aren't for stock-market innocents. You have to be able to tell the sound from the wacky, the honest from the spurious, the smart from the ordinary. Some letters are promoted with bogus claims. You might laugh off a writer who trumpets "874 percent on your money in eight months!" But what about one who claims 45 percent? Is that true or false?

A 1995 study of 237 investment letters done for the National Bureau of Economic Research found that less than a quarter of them beat the appropriate market index. What's more, they were lousy at market timing (just as I was saying on page 576, yada yada yada). Other studies have found only 20 percent or 12 percent beating the market over a decade.

Some letters with big reputations trade stocks furiously or make big-money bets on stock-index options. If you don't do the same, you won't match their investment returns. In general, letters tend to do well only in one kind of market environment, and you have to know which.

But if you're savvy about securities and want fresh sources of ideas, letters can make interesting reading. Here's how to find some:

Buy the monthly *Hulbert Financial Digest* newsletter, $59 the first year, from Hulbert Financial Digest, 316 Commerce St., Alexandria, VA 22314. Each month it highlights five market letters; twice a year you get performance data for the 160 newsletters in the Hulbert database. New subscribers get a newsletter directory and the latest performance data free.

What's especially good about Hulbert's data is that it's compiled in a uniform way. The publicity that the newsletters put out themselves covers various time periods (carefully chosen) and is generally unaudited, so investors can't compare these periods unaided. Hulbert ranks them over identical periods of time. Hulbert also deducts brokerage commissions, which gives a more realistic picture of what a market letter might do for you.

You want a letter with a good 7-year performance. Hulbert says. And you probably don't want to have to call a daily hot line for advice. When reading a new letter, think about whether you're willing to take the kinds of risks it recommends. If you plan to follow its model portfolio, test to see whether you can afford it. Some require multimillion-dollar investments.

Most require at least $100,000. If you have less than that, Hulbert thinks you should look for a mutual fund letter instead. (Mutual funds are smart buys for bigger portfolios, too.)

One drawback to letters: To hold their subscribers' interest, they have to keep finding new things to buy and sell. That's not the approach that long-term investors should take.

Another drawback: The editors can't time the market or pick stocks reliably. You're dreaming if you think that a good newsletter will make you rich.

PERSONAL MONEY MANAGERS

If you have a large sum of money to invest, maybe you'll want a personal adviser. Some advisers handle as little as $50,000 or $100,000, but most set minimums of $250,000 or $500,000.

People with smaller accounts go to financial planners, who manage money and handle other personal-finance matters, too (Chapter 32). They usually put you into no-load mutual funds, for an advisory fee of 0.5 to 1.5 percent, but can also find you individual money managers.

In the $1 million range, investors tend to seek advisers who only manage money and will buy you a portfolio of stocks and bonds. But ask yourself whether this is merely a vanity play. Some of this country's best investment brains run no-load mutual funds and charge maybe one percent of assets per year. A personal manager probably won't do any better and may cost 2 or 3 percent, including commissions and custodial fees. What's more, you'll get that manager's standard stock or bond portfolio for people with your investment goals, which isn't much different from being in a fund.

A planner or money manager makes economic sense only if:

• You face a lot of family complications and need a good mind to lead your money through the minefields.

• You have no time to think about money management and don't want to.

• You don't feel sure enough of yourself to pick good mutual funds (although, after reading Chapter 22, I don't know why not!).

• You have a truly large pot of money, like $10 million and up, and want someone to think continuously about how it should be deployed.

Most planners and managers are acquired through personal recommendations. A stockbroker may also be a source; he or she can send you directly to a manager who, in turn, gives the broker your trades. (This should be a direct referral, not through an expensive wrap account.) Be sure to check the adviser's background, as disclosed on Form ADV (page 957).

A free directory of the larger independent money-management firms (but not those associated with broker-dealers or firms that have only one principal) can be had from the Investment Counsel Association of America, 1050 17th St. N.W., Suite 725, Washington, DC 20036. But don't even ask for the directory unless you have at least $500,000. Only a handful of the 215 advisers that ICA lists accept accounts smaller than that.

A few consultants specialize in finding money managers for you. One such: Michael Stolper, Stolper & Co, 525 B St., Suite 630, San Diego, CA 92101. His minimum fee is $3,000, but it often runs higher. Stolper's managers accept accounts only in the $1 million range.

If you use a consultant to find an adviser, pay a flat fee, not a percentage of assets. Specify that you want a proven, stable firm whose principals have been there for at least 3 years and preferably 5. Ask the firm to certify that it's independent of the referring consultant.

Don't believe the performance numbers you read in the adviser's marketing literature. They're often exaggerated. Ask for audited 10-year numbers, and if you can't get them, walk. If the firm splits your money among several managers, get performance data for all of them.

Many middle-monied people who seek personal investment attention head for bank or brokerage-house trust departments. Some are mediocre. Some hit you with fees at every turn—fees for the trusts, brokerage fees, annual fees charged by the bank's own mutual funds. A trust officer can churn an account just as readily as a stockbroker can—perhaps more easily if the account belongs to an orphan or to someone who's old and no longer paying a lot of attention.

But some play fair and have reasonable investment records. To tell which is which, compare the performance of the bank's own pooled funds with standard stock or bond indexes (the bank should provide them for you) and the average stock or bond fund (their performance is published quarterly in leading newspapers—page 610). Ask for a written list of all fees and transaction charges, including brokerage charges. Don't sign any trust documents until they've been read by a lawyer of your own. Your biggest question: Is there any impediment to quitting this deal if I or my heirs don't like the results? You shouldn't be locked in. The bank or brokerage firm should always be earning the right to keep your money.

A FINAL WORD

Who really needs a stockbroker? To me, the conventional answer is all wrong.

You're advised to find a broker if you're a new investor, if you're inexperienced, or if you need a lot of help in reaching your investment decisions. Yet these are the very people least able to tell a good broker from a bad one, and the most susceptible to bad advice.

I'd say: If you're a new or inexperienced investor, don't look for a stockbroker at all! You can't afford the learning experience. Start with a couple of no-load mutual funds and relax. Only a savvy investor can pick what's choice from a broker's patter and blow off the rest.

Like the SAT tests for college admissions, there ought to be an admissions tests for opening a brokerage account. If you don't score above "innocent" on the Verbal and Math, a kindly investor-protection angel would tell you that a stockbroker isn't for you.

24.

Stocking Up

Your Ticket to the Future

*Over the long term, stocks beat the tar out of other financial
investments. If you haven't yet noticed my preference for
stock-owning mutual funds, you've been using this book
as a doorstop.*

You need two main things from your investments, and stocks offer both.
(1) *Real growth*—so that after inflation and taxes you will have more money
than you started with. Over the long term, stocks have run 7.4 percentage
points over the inflation rate. By contrast, long-term Treasury bonds have
run only 1.9 percentage points over inflation, so after taxes bonds just
barely keep up. (2) *Income*—in case you need to live off your capital.
Stocks pay dividends, whether you own them individually or in mutual
funds. You can reinvest those dividends or take the money in cash. If you
buy a stock-owing mutual fund, the fund will send you a regular check for
whatever sum you like (page 630).

WHAT MAKES STOCK PRICES RISE?

Plain old supply and demand. Prices rise when more people want to
buy a stock than want to sell it.
Over the short term, prices rise because:
1. Investors believe that the company's earnings will improve—because of a strong economy, a new product, new management, a new
business strategy, and so on.

2. The market in general is moving up, creating enthusiasm for all kinds of shares.

3. Interest rates drop, which makes stocks more attractive relative to bonds. (However, if it's early in what turns out to be a recession, stock prices might drop when interest rates do—for a while, at least. In the investing game, there are no guarantees.)

4. There's a takeover offer for the company, or the hope of one.

A reversal of these conditions leads more people to sell the stock than buy it, which makes the price fall.

Over the long term, prices rise because of fundamental economic factors. Government and business make capital investments, in technology, infrastructure, and human skills. As a consequence, the economy grows, creating more and more national wealth. That's what makes it possible to be a long-term stock investor.

So what do I think stock prices will do over the short-term? Beats me. In the 1991 edition of this book, I guessed that since we'd never had two stunning decades back-to-back, the market would probably deliver average or subnormal returns in the 1990s. Some prediction. In the early and middle nineties, stocks dazzled the eye, thanks to stupendous profits from business restructuring, low interest rates and inflation, new technologies, an expanding global market, and a river of boomer retirement money flowing in.

Nevertheless, trees don't grow to the sky. Stocks rise in most decades, but not always at the same rate of speed. After big booms, markets usually flatten out for a while—although no one can guess when that time will come. Even if prices slow, however, equities usually beat the competition. Every investor—even a retiree seeking income—needs part of his or her portfolio there.

There are two ways of buying stocks. You can pick individual issues or you can buy mutual funds.

BUYING STOCK-OWNING MUTUAL FUNDS

Classic, diversified mutual funds are dull, dull, dull. That's why I like them. You can make lots of money by buying and forgetting them, and getting on with the rest of your life. Rightly used, mutual funds have almost no entertainment value. For thrills, I go to the racetrack. For my retirement, I buy boring mutual funds.

Even if you love the blood sport of buying individual stocks, use diversified mutual funds for your core holdings (if you need to be reminded of why this is such a good idea, see page 604).

Regrettably, many investors are treating their funds as if they were stocks. These investors track the market daily, follow quarterly performance reports, zap into funds they buy on tips or because they were featured in a magazine, then zap out again if the fund price drops a little bit. But this traduces mutual funds' very reason for being. Only the money manager is supposed to trade. You're supposed to buy and hold. Jumping in and out of funds raises your cost of investing, increases the risk of buying and selling at the wrong time, and makes it almost impossible to keep up with the general stock market over time. It also drives you into the arms of investment advisers who help you trade, which is another expense.

Do yourself a favor and simplify your life. Accumulate no more than 6 or 7 *well-diversified* funds, allocate them over different types of investments, invest in them regularly, then sit back and wait. *That's* how to become a mutual fund millionaire.

In the major U.S. markets, your best long-term choice is a low-cost index fund whose price matches that of the market average (page 701). At the very least, make this fund your core holding. Choose one that follows Standard & Poor's 500-stock index, which would make it a big-company growth-and-income fund. Most active fund managers find S&P funds hard to beat (for a discussion of active vs. passive management, see page 604).

Next, add funds that buy smaller stocks and international stocks. Consider indexing here, too, although in these areas managers have a better shot at outperforming the index.

For the money you put with active fund managers, half might be in a "growth" fund, which owns companies whose earnings appear to be accelerating, and half in a "value" fund, for out-of-favor stocks that are available cheap. As your net worth increases, add a fund invested in foreign stocks—in lots of countries, not just one. After that, move on to a fund that spreads its money over many different emerging markets: Asia, Latin America, Africa, and Eastern Europe.

Some investors allocate their stock portfolios this way: big-stock growth, big-stock value, small stock-growth, small-stock value, international, and emerging market.

However you do it, your objective is to own well-diversified funds with different kinds of investment strategies, so you'll own a piece of whatever portion of the market does the best.

In the next few pages, I've listed the main types of mutual funds, what they do, for whom they're designed, and the risks they run. You'll also find the names of some funds in each category, chosen in 1997 by Brouwer & Janachowski, Inc., of Tiburon, California, which invests $500 million of its clients' money in no-load mutual funds (minimum account, $1 million). It's hard to beat the market, but these funds are thought to have a good chance. Brouwer & Janachowski also looked at how the funds performed in poor markets. If you can do reasonably well when stock prices rise and minimize losses when prices fall, you should get good results over time.

The suggestions include no-load funds, which you buy yourself, and load funds sold through stockbrokers and financial planners. Obviously, no stock-fund recommendations last forever. But these are all worth a look, for money you've chosen not to put in index funds.

1. Growth Funds invest in companies, mostly big or middle-size, whose earnings are believed to be accelerating. Dividends are a low priority.

If all goes well: You get excellent long-term performance. They're at their best when the market is zipping up. Most of your returns come from capital gains, with very little from dividends.

What to worry about: Bear* markets are bad for their health. And yours, too.

Who should buy: Long-term, performance-minded investors who can stomach larger-than-average market drops but don't want to run the higher risk of investing in small-company funds.

Some good-looking funds: No-loads: Brandywine Fund (Greenville, Delaware, 800-656-3017); Founders Growth Fund (Denver, Colorado, 800-525-2440); Harbor Capital Appreciation Fund (Toledo, Ohio, 800-422-1050); Mairs & Power Growth Fund (St. Paul, Minnesota, 800-304-7404—at this writing, concentrating on Minnesota companies); Papp America-Abroad Fund (Phoenix, Arizona, 800-421-4004); Vanguard Primecap (Valley Forge, Pennsylvania, 800-662-7447). Load funds: Enterprise Growth Portfolio; Fidelity Advisor Growth Opportunity Fund; Franklin California Growth Fund (concentrated in California companies); Guardian Park Avenue Fund; Merrill Lynch Growth Fund.

2. Aggressive Growth Funds and their cousins, "emerging growth," buy hot new issues (page 701) and small companies whose earnings have been rising fast. These funds are a blur of buy and sell, hopping onto stocks that are going up, hopping off stocks whose prices stall. Expenses are high and dividends slim.

If all goes well: Aggressive growth funds shine in strongly rising markets, especially when a lot of new issues are being offered. They usually bounce back strongly after a stock market drop.

What to worry about: They get creamed when markets fall or when the bubble bursts in a sector where stock performance has been the dizziest. The damage could be drastic if the fund owns stock in very small firms and has to sell to raise cash to meet shareholder redemptions. The fund's own selling could drive a stock price down. Investors have to be prepared to suffer.

Who should buy: Deluded market timers who think they know how to catch the upswings without being buried when stocks go down. Investors with nerve. Long-term investors who are gambling with 5 to 10 percent of

---

* Bear markets fall; bull markets rise.

their money and can ignore market drops. Over their holding period, they might get higher returns.

Some good-looking funds: No-loads: American Century–Twentieth Century Ultra Fund (Kansas City, Missouri, 800-345-2021); Kaufman Fund (New York City, 800-261-0555). Load fund: Putnam New Opportunities Fund.

3. Value Funds buy good companies that are temporarily unwanted and unloved on a long-term bet that their stocks will turn around. They follow the classic approach of legendary investor John Templeton, who says, "In selecting investments, look for the points of maximum pessimism." Buy what everyone else is selling or is afraid to touch.

If all goes well: You'll have a strong investment. Value stocks don't perform as well as growth stocks do when the market soars. But over full market cycles, they've matched or outperformed growth stocks historically. They also have higher dividend yields. On average, one-third of your return will probably come from dividends, with the rest from capital gains.

What to worry about: Bear markets, of course. But good value funds don't decline as much as growth funds do.

Who should buy: Long-term, performance-minded investors who want decent dividends, too. Whether they're stock pickers or indexers, some of the country's finest investors take a value approach.

Some good-looking funds: No-loads: Clipper Fund (Beverly Hills, California, 800-776-5033); Oakmark Fund (Chicago, 800-625-6275); Torray Fund (Bethesda, Maryland, 800-443-3036). Load fund: Davis New York Venture.

4. Small-Company Funds specialize in "small-capitalization"* stocks. Generally speaking, a stock is "small-cap" when its share price, multiplied by the number of shares outstanding, comes to less than $500 million (some managers set higher caps, up to $1 billion). Funds may specialize in small growth stocks, small value stocks, or buy some of both. When small-cap funds start attracting a lot of money and can't find enough small stocks to buy, they start adding middle-size ("mid-cap") companies, too.

If all goes well: Historically, small caps have done better than big caps, over long time periods. But it costs more to buy and sell small stocks, so beating the big-stock averages isn't guaranteed.

What to worry about: They're hammered in bad markets and may do worse than big-cap funds for several years in a row. For example, they pooped out in the second half of the 1980s, saw some great years in the early 1990s, then faded again (the subsequent move should be up, if the cycle holds).

---

* A stock's capitalization is its market price multiplied by the number of shares outstanding. Put another way, it's the value the market puts on the company as a whole at a given point in time.

Who should buy: Long-term, performance-minded investors who don't scare easily and will hold for at least 5 years. It's not unreasonable to make small caps one-fifth or one-quarter of your portfolio.

Some good-looking funds: Acorn Fund (Chicago, 800-922-6769); Baron Asset Fund (New York City, 800-442-3814); Columbia Special Fund (Portland, Oregon, 800-547-1707); RSI Retirement Trust Emerging Growth Equity Fund (New York City, 800-772-3615)—for tax-deferred retirement plans: defined-benefit plans, SEPs, IRAs, Keoghs, 403(b)s. Load funds: Fidelity Low-Priced Stock Fund; Franklin Small Cap Growth Fund.

5. Growth-and-Income Funds emphasize blue-chip companies that grow steadily, sometimes splendidly, and pay good dividends. An index fund (page 701) is a growth-and-income fund.

If all goes well: You get more current income than growth funds pay, plus the potential for solid price appreciation. In some years, these funds have outdone the growth funds, thanks to the compounding effect of reinvested dividends.

What to worry about: What can I say? They're still stock funds, which means they go down when the market does, although generally not by as much as the growth funds do. The dividends help cushion the drop.

Who should buy: Investors who like blue chips, want some income from their stocks, and don't demand aggressive performance in rising markets. They're an excellent choice for novice or conservative stock investors, investors who will hold only one fund, or investors who hold more aggressive funds and want to diversify.

Some good-looking funds: Dodge & Cox Stock Fund (San Francisco, 880-621-3979); Selected American Shares (Santa Fe, New Mexico, 800-243-1575). Load funds: Fundamental Investors; Kemper-Dreman High Return Fund; United Income Fund. Through certain discount brokers only: MAS Funds Value Portfolio—Institution Class (try the brokerage firms Jack White and Charles Schwab).

6. Equity-Income Funds and Income Funds concentrate on companies that pay high dividends even if they don't show terrific growth. Good examples would be certain electric utilities, some telephone companies, and real-estate investment trusts.

If all goes well: You get somewhat more income than growth-and-income funds provide and somewhat less growth. In declining markets, your losses shouldn't be as bad. Your income should keep up with inflation because these kinds of companies keep raising their dividends.

What to worry about: That some of your companies will quit raising their dividends, which would hurt the price of your fund. The electrical-power industry is deregulating, so those stocks aren't the solid workhorses they used to be.

Who should buy: Conservative investors who want more income from their money while staying invested for modest growth.

Just one suggested fund: T. Rowe Price Equity Income Fund (Baltimore, 800-638-5660).

7. Balanced Funds buy common stocks, preferred stocks (which pay higher dividends than the common), and bonds. They may allocate fixed percentages of their money to stocks and bonds—say, 60 percent stocks, 40 percent bonds. If that's the allocation you want, it's simple to let the fund do it for you.

If all goes well: Your fund emphasizes income without abandoning growth. When interest rates fall, balanced funds can grow smartly because both their stocks and their bonds should rise. In a bear market, their interest and dividends help support the price of the shares.

What to worry about: You're in trouble when interest rates rise. The value of your bonds will drop and your stock might, too.

Who should buy: Income investors who don't want to foreclose on their chances for some capital growth.

Some good-looking funds: No-loads: Dodge & Cox Balanced Fund (San Francisco, 800-621-3979); Vanguard Wellington Fund (Valley Forge, Pennsylvania, 800-662-7447); CGM Mutual Fund (Boston, 800-345-4048—more volatile than the others).

8. Sector Funds specialize in the stocks of a particular industry. Each one buys only housing stocks, airline stocks, health-care stocks, biotechnology stocks, financial stocks—the sector list goes on and on. A fund will typically move up strongly when its industry gets hot, then stagnate or fall as buying interest moves to some other market sector. Sector stocks move differently from the market as a whole.

If all goes well: You will pick exactly the sector that's about to move up and sell before it peters out. Then you'll hop to another sector that's about to move up. You'll do this successfully, over and over (pinch me, I'm dreaming).

What to worry about: You'll buy a fund after its big move up. As soon as you buy, it will go limp. You might catch the losses but not the gains.

Who should buy: Highly experienced investors who understand how various industries respond to changes in the economy and who have a good track record for picking individual stocks.

Some funds with good records: Forget it. These funds fluctuate too much. Areas to consider as long-term holds (especially after a scare that drives their prices down) are technology and health care for growth, energy as an inflation hedge, and utilities for income (trusting the manager to handle the risk of electric-utility deregulation).

9. International Funds—for foreign stocks. Every investor should consider them (see Chapter 27).

Some good-looking funds: No-loads: Artisan International Fund (Milwaukee, 800-344-1770); Hotchkis and Wiley International Fund (Los Angeles, 800-236-4479); Janus Overseas Fund (Denver, 800-525-3713; T. Rowe Price International Stock Fund (Baltimore, 800-638-5660); Vanguard International Growth Portfolio (Valley Forge, Pennsylvania, 800-662-7447). Load Funds: EuroPacific Growth Fund; GAM International Fund; Templeton Foreign Fund.

10. Emerging-Markets Funds—the aggressive growth funds of the international world (see Chapter 27). Volatile, high-risk, but well worth 5 percent of your portfolio.

Some funds to try: No-loads: Vanguard International Equity Index Fund —Emerging Markets Portfolio (Valley Forge, Pennsylvania, 800-662-7447); Warburg, Pincus Emerging Markets Fund (New York City, 800-927-2874—at this writing, pretty new, so watch it). Load funds: Merrill Lynch Developing Capital Markets Fund; Templeton Developing Markets Trust.

KEEP IT SIMPLE: BUY AN INDEX FUND

You can win at the stock-picking game by deciding not to play at all. Do it by buying an *index fund.* Indexers don't try to beat the market. They don't break their heads on stock analysis or economic trends. They simply buy the stocks (or a representative selection of the stocks) that make up a particular market index, such as Standard & Poor's 500. Come what may, good markets or bad, a fund matched to the S&P will follow that index, minus the fund's own management costs. Market-index returns are exactly what everyone praises when they point out how well stocks do over time. During the 10 years ending December 31, 1996, the Vanguard Group's Index Trust—500 Portfolio, which follows the S&P, outperformed more than four-fifths of all other stock-owning funds. It's usually in the top third and rarely falls out of the top half.

At this point, you may feel disappointed. Index funds sound profitable but dull, dull, dull. The thrill of investing is to find a fund that beats the market, not matches it.

Ah, yes . . . but easier said than done. In the 1980s and 1990s, the majority of mutual fund managers, including the stars you see on the covers of magazines, fell behind the major market averages.

How come so many hotshot stock pickers couldn't keep up? "It's sort of like par golf," an executive of the Vanguard Group once said (Vanguard specializes in index funds). "Par is what you're shooting for, but how many golfers actually beat it?"

Active fund managers stumble into sand traps that the indexers don't. First, they hold a cash cushion, which means that not all their money is invested. Second, they have a massive burden to overcome—namely, their fees. A no-load (no-sales-charge) fund may levy a management fee of around one percent. It costs 2.5 percent in transaction fees to buy and sell securities and more if the fund does a lot of trading. So the manager may have to do at least 3.5 percentage points better than the market just to cover his or her expenses. Throw in an up-front sales charge plus annual 12b-1 fees and the manager has to produce even more. Some of these so-called actively managed funds may hold superior stocks. But you pay so much in expenses that high performance gradually melts away.

Third and most important, it's not clear that fund-picking wizardry actually exists. To explain what I mean, let's take a superstar manager of a major mutual fund. He will own some stocks that are part of the S&P 500 but will also buy many smaller stocks. In a year when the S&P index rises higher than his fund, he'll say, "That's luck. The market is favoring big stocks." In a year when he beats the S&P (because his smaller stocks did well), he'll brag, "That's genius, I can pick stocks that are going up."

But if he has such foresight, how come he didn't pick big stocks during their better year and then switch to smaller stocks? Was he stupid that year and then suddenly got smart? I don't think so. The market simply cycled from one type of stock to another. When his type came up, he took credit for foresight when it was merely happenstance.

Study after study has shown that it hardly matters which particular stocks you own. Your long-term performance depends mainly on the type of investments you make—big stocks or small ones, growth or value. U.S. or international. In other words, how your money is allocated over the market as a whole.

When you're buying big American companies, low-cost index funds outperform most of the active managers over time. So here's the question: *If active managers can't beat the market on a regular basis, after expenses, why should you pay them to miss?* Buy index funds instead. Or put half your money in index funds that buy large and midsize companies and spread the rest over actively managed funds of varying types—perhaps the funds suggested earlier in this chapter. Keep comparing the managed funds to the index funds to see which wins. Out of the thousands of people who manage money, a few will outperform the market over your holding period. But no one—even professional fund pickers like Brouwer & Janachowski —knows for sure who they're going to be.

What if the economy sours? Index funds will tank, but so will their competitors. Some managed funds may not drop as far, while others will plunge; they'll have different recovery rates, too. Over a full market cycle, however, index funds should still produce above-average returns. And they don't need regular monitoring the way managed funds do. The manager won't change; the investment committee won't make a disastrous asset-allocation decision. They're the perfect funds to buy and hold.

Still not convinced? Here are the clinchers: They don't make a lot of trades the way the managed funds do, so investors don't face high (and taxable) capital-gains distributions at the end of the year. If you have both a tax-deferred retirement account and a regular account, hold your managed stock funds in the former and your index funds in the latter. Minimal trading also holds down transaction costs, a tremendous advantage in international and emerging markets, where trading expenses are very high.

Evaluating Indexing, Sector by Sector

It's a no-brainer to index investments in large and midsize American companies. Only the most skilled (or luckiest) managers will beat the S&P 500 over time.

But battles still rage over specialty funds—small stocks, internationals, and emerging markets. Is indexing equally valid there or do stock-pickers have an edge? I'll tell you what's known, judging by the performance of Vanguard's index funds—the funds with the longest records.

Small-Stock Funds: Most studies suggests that you have a 50/50 chance of picking a managed fund that will beat Vanguard's small-stock index fund. Pure chance, but interesting. Vanguard mimics the Russell 2000 index, which contains smaller stocks than are held by the typical small-stock managed fund. You might divide your small-stock money between Vanguard and a managed fund that invests in both small- and mid-cap stocks.

International Funds: Here, index funds lack the long history that U.S. funds have, so they can't be evaluated yet. At this writing (1997), Vanguard's European index fund has a 6-year record that beats the average managed European fund. Expenses account for much of its success. Vanguard charges 0.35 percent a year vs. 1.9 percent for the managed funds.

But Vanguard's Pacific fund is another story. It's 70 to 80 percent invested in Japan, due to the structure of the index it copies. So it's not diversified; you might better describe it as "Japan plus."* If you want to diversity over the Pacific Rim, you'll be better served with a managed fund.

For your first (or only) international fund, you should buy one that invests worldwide, not in a single area. Vanguard's Total International Portfolio would fill that bill—giving you Europe, the Pacific ("Japan plus"), and emerging markets rolled up together. Diversified managed funds have a

---

* Vanguard might divide this fund into two portfolios—one for Japan, one for the rest of the Pacific Rim. But then you'd have to decide for yourself how much Japan you want to own—and betting on specific countries isn't what indexers want to do.

50/50 chance of beating this combo. Again, you might divide your money between Vanguard and a managed fund.

Emerging-Market Funds: Vanguard introduced one in 1994, so it's far too new to talk about. But it's well diversified, owns many of the stocks its competitors do, and pays less in transaction costs.

Single-Country Funds: Morgan Stanley runs index funds for particular countries. They're known as World Equity Benchmark Shares (WEBS) and share some of the characteristics of closed-end funds (page 640). Expenses are in the one percent range. But buying them is more like picking stocks than investing in diversified mutual funds. They're for specialists who actually know what's going on in Australia, Malaysia, or France (I sure don't).

Choosing an Index Fund

When you buy an index fund, only three things matter: What does it cost, which index does it mimic, and how closely does its past performance mimic the index it's following?

You Want the Cheapest Possible Fund. The less that's taken out in fees, the better an index fund performs. Never pay a sales load; the biggest and best are all no-loads. At this writing, do-it-yourselfers can get the widest selection of index funds, at the lowest cost, from the Vanguard Group in Valley Forge, Pennsylvania (800-662-7447). Its S&P fund charges a miniscule 0.2 percent a year. Investors can create suitable asset-allocation plans using Vanguard funds alone. Another low-cost group of funds, from Dimensional Fund Advisors (DFA) in Santa Monica, California, is available only through investment advisers and financial planners who manage money for a fee.

"Enhanced" index funds try to tart up their performance by writing options or playing other nonindex games. Naturally, they charge more for this "service," which may or may not make you any money. Give these "index-plus" funds a pass. They contravene the very concept of indexing by adding the fallible judgment of a manager to the mix.

A fund's past performance should mimic its index minus the management fee you pay. If the fund falls short, something else is at work. It may be offering low fees but making extra money in brokerage costs.

Banks and some other mutual fund groups offer index funds, too. But check their costs against Vanguard and DFA before buying. Where costs are lower, see if that's temporary (because fees are being waived) or permanent. In indexing, only the lowest-cost players make any sense. *Never* buy an index fund that carries an upfront or backend sales load.

You Want the Most Suitable Index for Your Investment Goals. If you're interested in blue chips, you'll probably choose a fund linked to Standard & Poor's 500-stock average. Less popular are the Major Market Index funds that copy the Dow Jones industrial average.

To match the entire stock market, consider Vanguard's Total Stock Market Portfolio. It mimics the Wilshire 5000 index, which includes all regularly traded U.S. stocks, large and small.

For bets on smaller companies, Vanguard offers two choices. Its Extended Market Portfolio mirrors the Wilshire 4500 index, which includes both small and midsize stocks. Its Small Capitalization Stock Portfolio mirrors the Russell 2000 index of small stocks with average market caps of around $600 to $700 million.

For fans of growth or value stocks (page 698), S&P/BARRA has made two indexes out of the S&P 500. Its Growth Index covers the S&P firms with growing sales and earnings, above-average price-to-book ratios, and below-average dividend yields. Its Value Index takes the firms with below-average price-to-book ratios and above-average dividend yields. Using these indexes, Vanguard offers a Growth index fund and a Value index fund.

For foreign stocks, performance in the developed countries is measured by Morgan Stanley Capital International's Europe, Australia, and Far East (EAFE) index. Vanguard has split the EAFE in two, creating a Europe fund and a Pacific fund. Both focus on the larger markets and larger stocks. The Pacific index is dominated by Japan.

In emerging markets, Vanguard's Emerging Markets Fund captures the growth of fourteen developing nations, as tracked by Morgan Stanley's Select Emerging Markets Index. You can buy the EAFE and emerging markets as a package through Vanguard's Total International fund.

For income investors, bond funds copy standard measures like the Lehman Brothers Aggregate Bond Index. Vanguard breaks up that index to create short-, intermediate-, and long-term funds. Actively managed bond funds, by the way, tend to rise and fall when the index funds do, especially when they buy quality bonds. That's because bond performance doesn't vary as widely as stock performance does. In the bond world, index funds are even more attractive because of their lower management costs.

A newer Vanguard entry offers income and growth: an index fund for real-estate investment trusts (REITs), which is tied to the Morgan Stanley REIT index. For more on REITs, see page 836.

For classic asset allocation, Vanguard's Balanced Index fund offers 60 percent stocks (Total Market) and 40 percent bonds (Lehman Brothers Aggregate Bond Index). Alternatively, you can make up your own allocation. Remember to rebalance from time to time (page 587) to keep the allocation that you originally intended.

Like Vanguard, Dimensional Fund Advisors has a wide assortment of well-regarded funds. They all lean to value stocks, not growth, and are available exclusively through investment advisers. The menu includes U.S. and international stock funds invested in both large and small companies, some regional and one-country funds, an emerging markets fund, and some bond funds.

Timing the Market

Timers try to get into the market by buying stocks ahead of an upswing or during its early stages. They'll take their profits just before the market drops down.

That's the dream; here's the reality. In almost all cases, you'll miss the turns. Succeeding once doesn't mean that you'll succeed again. You'll sell too soon. You'll sell too late. Ditto when you buy. For more trashing of market timing, see page 576.

Aha, you say, even though *I* can't do it my market-timing newsletter or adviser can. Not in my opinion. When letter writers get it right, it's luck not science, which means they won't reliably get it right again. For example, here's what 114 market letters advised in August 1987, with the market topped out and the Crash just two months away, as reported by *Hulbert Financial Digest:* 42 percent were fully invested or even buying stocks on margin. Half were 90 percent invested or better. Only 20 percent had less than half of their model portfolios in stocks. A mere 2.6 percent had gone fully into cash or were recommending short sales (page 722). And these are supposed to be the experts! Many letters got less aggressive in the following two months as the market started to wobble down, but were those the letters you subscribed to and, if so, did you act fast enough? I wonder if the writers themselves followed their own advice in time.

Be skeptical of the glorious records that many market timers publish. They're usually not audited. They ignore the effect of commissions and taxes. They may not be real (a three-year-old newsletter may present twenty years of results to "prove" how well its system would have worked in the past—but systems developed in hindsight often stumble in real time). They may make false comparisons, such as setting their own investment record, including dividends, against the Dow Jones industrial average without dividends—something you wouldn't know from the ad. Finally, you don't know how well the results compare with those of investors who bought and held, which would be the only fair test.

Even if a newsletter tells you to sell at just the right time, it may miss the moment when you should have bought back in. There's no point selling at $10, feeling like a genius as the market drops to $8, then not rebuying until the price has run up to $11. That turns you from genius into goat. You didn't rebuy because you kept thinking prices were going to fall back and the market faked you out ("whipsawed" is the word). Remember: To make money, every timer has to make three right calls. You have to get in, then out, then in again.

But say you subscribe to a newsletter that you or your buddies still believe in. Ask yourself whether you'll really follow every call. If you'll pick and choose among the buy/sell recommendations, forget it. That's no system at all. You'll *never* make money in taxable accounts, where you have to give the government part of every profit you take.

As an experiment, devote a small part of your money to following a market timer while leaving the rest in a well-allocated selection of mutual funds. After two or three market turns, ask yourself: Do the gains on my good calls outweigh the losses on my bad ones? What's the effect on my long-term return of subtracting any commissions paid or taxes owed on capital gains? If your market-timed account isn't markedly higher than the funds you bought and held, timing isn't worth the risk.

Still, some of you can't resist it. So I offer here a few simple ideas that shouldn't get you in too much trouble. They can work, although not consistently. They apply to the stock market overall, not to the shares of specific companies. Everybody knows these ideas, of course, so by the time you buy or sell, there may be no value left. (Another reason why timing strategies are a crock.) Anyway . . .

• *Buy during recessions.* That's when stocks are at their cheapest. But you have to buy early in the recession, if you can identify it; economists often can't. Toward the middle and end of a business downturn, stocks are already leaping up. (The best time to sell, on average, comes about four months before a recession starts, so remember to count.)

• *Buy after a major stock-market crash—defined as a fast and sudden drop.* The 1980s saw a crash (down 22.6 percent in a day) and a crashette (down 7 percent). After such an embarrassment, stocks typically bounce back by 50 percent. Where they go from there is anybody's guess.

• *If a smaller market crashes, buy that, too.* Latin American markets toppled in 1995 during the Mexican peso collapse but later came roaring back. In 1997, currency crises hacked away at Southeast Asia—another buying opportunity. You may have to hold for a while in order to get your reward, but you'll have bought relatively cheap.

• *Buy when the Federal Reserve has cut the discount rate twice in a row over a 3-month period.* (The discount rate is what banks pay for short-term loans from the Federal Reserve.) Falling rates depress money-market yields, so investors switch their cash into stocks.

• *Buy when the volume of rising shares greatly outnumbers the volume of falling shares.* "Volume" means the number of shares traded. Watch the daily volume on the New York Stock Exchange, reported in *Barron's, The Wall Street Journal,* or your local newspaper. When "up" volume exceeds "down" volume by at least nine to one (not counting the stocks that remain unchanged), it's often a buy. Market timer Martin Zweig says that two such days within three months is especially good news.

• *Sell when there's an inverted yield curve.* That's when short-term interest rates rise higher than long-term interest rates. When the curve is inverted for only a month or two, there may be no bear market. But if short rates keep climbing, stocks will probably fall.

• *Sell when interest rates get too high.* Thanks a bunch. If I knew what "too high" was I'd believe in market timing. But it's indubitably true that, at a certain point, rising interest rates pull money out of stocks and the market falls. One common clue: The Federal Reserve has raised the discount rate three times in a row (although sometimes it takes four). When interest rates rise, bond prices fall; when there's a big rise, they fall a lot. If you had sold after the bond-market crash of April 1987, you wouldn't have been trampled in the stock-market crash the following October. (But would you have bought back in in time?)

• *Sell when dividends get too low.* What's "too low"? I don't know that, either. When I first wrote this book in 1991, everyone "knew" that you ought to sell when the average dividend paid by the companies in Standard & Poor's 500-stock index fell below 3 percent. But at this writing (1997), it has been under 3 percent for 5 years while the stock market has been rushing up. I mention this to show (again) why market timing is so hard. A rule of thumb may work for a while, then suddenly not work—and no one posts a notice that it's going to change. The obverse of that S&P rule, by the way, is that stocks are a buy when the dividend yield rises to 5 or 6 percent. I haven't a clue if that's still operative or not. You can get the dividend yield from a stockbroker or by checking the table called "Indexes' P/Es & Yields" in *Barron's* every issue.

It remains my opinion that staying invested in mutual funds with good long-term records, and reinvesting dividends, will bring far better long-term results than chasing market turns.

Research has proven beyond all doubt that your asset allocation accounts for almost all of your returns, with only a tiny role played by which stocks you bought and when you bought them.

BUYING INDIVIDUAL SHARES

Broadly speaking, individual shares move with the market, up and down. But they also have their own separate cycles. A stock might suddenly rise, or stall, or wander down in price while the rest of the stocks in its industry are doing something else entirely.

All this means that picking stocks is more demanding of your time, knowledge, and persistence than picking mutual funds. Successful investors subscribe to investment publications, read company reports, analyze industries, and study market valuations. They devote many hours to study and research. They keep their eyes open to what's going on around them, how the world is changing, what neighborhoods and nations need.

Picking stocks is a serious business but it's also an endless and colorful entertainment. A competitive sport. You are pitting your brains and foresight against the collective judgment of millions of other investors, all—like you—seeking an edge. Next to horse racing, investing is the world's most exacting wager. (I put the stock market second to horse racing only because a stock can come around a second time.)

For people willing to do the work and with enough money to diversify (say, $75,000), stocks are also a highly efficient investment. You have no annual expenses, as you do with mutual funds—only the brokerage commission and you can use a discount broker. You choose when to sell and pay the capital gains tax (fund investors pay taxes when the fund manager takes net gains). You can buy and hold stocks without ever selling at all. Top candidates for holding: brand-name blue chips with proven ability to grow and a history of increasing dividends every year. Some of these stocks can be bought directly from the company, allowing you to skip the brokerage commission entirely (page 687).

Don't Count Yourself a Stock Picker If You Merely Buy Stocks on the Advice of a Broker. Stockbrokers (or their firms' research departments) may have good ideas. But if you just nod and say, "Yes, yes," you aren't an investor, you're a sheep. You need to develop a mind of your own.

The following pages are mere hints for new investors. You'll have to dig far deeper than this if you're going to be any good. For starters, see the book list on page 662.

Some Definitions

When you buy the *common stock* of a corporation you are buying an ownership share. A tiny slice of the company belongs to you and you are owed a tiny slice of its dividends. Your interest in the company is known as *equity*. Stockholders are also referred to as equity investors.

The company's executives (who run the show) take one of two attitudes toward your profits: They might pay them out to you in quarterly dividends. Or they might keep the profits and reinvest them in the business. Most companies do some of both.

When you buy a *growth stock,* you aren't expecting dividends. You're expecting rapidly rising earnings (15 percent a year or more) and a higher stock price. When you buy a *blue chip,* you expect dividend increases as well as steady share-price growth. An *income stock* leans more toward dividends and offers less growth. Traditional utilities and real-estate investment trusts are income stocks.

In general, the higher the dividend, the less the share price tends to fall in bear markets and the more slowly it tends to rise when markets go up. You usually have to trade income for growth.

Your bottom line is *total return*—your dividends plus your gain or loss on the price of the stock. Say, for example, that you bought a stock for $50 and saw it rise by $5 over the next 12 months, to $55. You also earned $2 in dividends. Your total return was $7, or 14 percent on your original $50 investment. On a total-return basis, an income investor with high enough dividend earnings might do better than someone who gambles solely on growth.

When economic growth slows down, you hear a lot about *defensive stocks*. They're supposed to fall less in bear markets than other stocks do. Food stocks and pharmaceuticals are good examples. But they still go down. When growth turns up, you hear a lot about *cyclical stocks,* whose earnings tend to rise (and fall) when the economy does. Steel, housing, automobiles, and airlines are cyclical industries.

You need to think about whether you want to buy *speculative stocks,* which behave very differently from blue chips. As an example, consider what happens when management reports an unexpected earnings drop. The stock price will fall, but a blue chip may not fall very far. Many people follow the stock—analysts, brokers, shareholders—and they'll move in to buy if it looks cheap. But there aren't mobs of people waiting to buy a lesser-known stock. The price may plummet on bad news. Conversely, it may soar on good news (sharp ups and downs constitute *volatility*). Many naive investors don't know they hold speculative stocks until the market suddenly shows them.

Shares trading at around $5 or less are called *penny stocks*. They'll reduce your $5 to pennies—count on it (page 792).

A Mini-Tour of the Markets

The biggest markets are the most liquid, the best regulated, and the least subject to price manipulation. As markets and company size get smaller, prices get flakier and crooks find it easier to play games.

The New York Stock Exchange—also known as the Big Board. Here's where most of the biggest and best-known companies trade. It's an "auction market," where prices are set on the trading-room floor by the competing bids of buyers and sellers.

The American Stock Exchange—also known as the Amex, where more medium-size and speculative stocks are traded. This is also an auction market.

Regional Stock Exchanges—small exchanges found in Boston, Philadelphia, Cincinnati, Spokane, and Chicago (the Midwest Stock Exchange). The Pacific Stock Exchange in San Francisco and Los Angeles is also a regional exchange. They list local stocks as well as some stocks that are traded on other exchanges. Being listed is supposedly a guide to quality, but don't count on it. It's easier to manipulate stocks on the regional exchanges than on the big national ones.

The Over-the-Counter Market—also known as the OTC. This isn't an auction market. Instead, one or more dealers will "make a market" in a particular company. That means they'll buy its shares as they come up for sale, at prices they determine, and sell shares to other dealers at whatever markup they can get. These markets are open to collusion and manipulation. Your buying price might be set higher than a true auction market would allow, and your selling price might be lower. This can happen especially with companies that are *thinly traded*, meaning they have only a small number of shares outstanding. The difference between the buying and selling price is called the *spread*. Always ask about the spread. If your buying price is 10 percent higher than the selling price would be at that particular moment, your stock must rise by 10 percent just for you to break even. That's a lousy deal.

Some well-established companies trade OTC. But this market is better known for its newer issues, which may not even file financial statements.

Nasdaq (the National Association of Securities Dealers Automated Quotations System)—where you'll find the better-known and more actively traded OTC shares. Most OTC companies are said to be *unlisted* because they're not on a formal exchange. If they're on Nasdaq's National Market or Small Cap Market, however, they're generally considered *listed*.

To make it to Nasdaq a stock has to have at least two market makers. Most of them have several. They post firm buy and sell prices on an electronic network, which—in theory—encourages price competition. In practice, however, firms have colluded to keep the spreads artificially wide. In 1997, twenty-four major Nasdaq dealers settled charges of price-rigging and manipulation with the Justice Department. Collusion isn't supposed to be happening anymore, but once you leave the auction markets of the major exchanges, you never know.

Nasdaq's Bulletin Board—which gives prices electronically or by phone for more than 14,000 OTC stocks. Prices are also distributed daily in a volume of Pink Sheets. Some of the Bulletin Board prices are firm; others are soggy (meaning that when you ask a dealer for a published price, he or she may suddenly change it); still others are blatantly manipulated. A few large companies trade on the Bulletin Board, including the American Depositary Receipts (page 817) of some large foreign companies that don't want to make the financial disclosures required for listing on an exchange. Most of the companies, however, are small.

A Mini-Tour of Buying and Selling

An order to buy or sell a stock is placed with a stockbroker. Individuals generally give *market orders,* telling the broker to execute the order at the best price available at the time. A professional investor may give a *limit order,* telling the broker to stay within a certain price, as in, "Don't pay over $25 for that stock."

The *spread* is the difference between the *asked price* (what you pay when you buy) and the *bid price* (what you get when you sell). For example, a stock might be quoted at $10 asked and $9.75 bid, for a 25-cent spread. Actively traded shares have narrow spreads, maybe "an eighth" (12.5 cents) or "a quarter" (25 cents) a share.* Thinly traded shares have much wider spreads, especially if they're over the counter. The wider the spread, the greater the gain you need in order to make a profit. There has to be an awfully good reason to buy OTC stock with a wide spread (offhand, I can't think of one).

A *round lot* is 100 shares of stock, which is the ideal minimum order. Anything less is an *odd lot.* Odd-lot orders can be pooled before the stock exchanges open for the day and executed at the regular price. If you insist on buying or selling odd lots later in the day, you'll pay a surcharge.

Learn to invest by degrees. When you find a stock you like, buy 100 shares. If the company continues to do well, buy another 100 shares. Step into it gradually. If something bad happens, you can quit right there. With this system, you don't have to make an all-or-nothing buy decision, which helps investors who feel unsure. And it dollar-averages your cost (page 599).

In many cases, it's also smart to sell by degrees: 100 shares this week, 100 shares next week, and so on. When prices have been rising sharply, spaced sales are a way of taking profits without getting out of the stock entirely. You can reinvest in a company whose price may have more room to run. Spaced sales also save you from making an all-or-nothing sell decision about a stock whose price has stalled. You can sell a bit, then quit selling if you see a reason to hold the company longer.

As a general rule, you should think about selling any stock that drops 10 percent from its peak price. If the stock is volatile—meaning it typically shows steep drops and gains—you might not sell until its slide reaches 15 percent. Investors who like to buy and hold might not sell at all if they

---

* These spreads should shrink if, as expected, the exchanges start quoting share prices in decimals rather than eighths or sixteenths.

think the company is sound. In fact, they might buy more. But if your stock drops 10 percent when the rest of the market doesn't, at least take a look at what's going on.

To force yourself not to hang on to a deteriorating stock, enter a *stop-loss* order. That tells your broker to sell the stock automatically if it drops to a certain price. If the stock moves up, set a new stop-loss order at 10 percent below the new, higher price. Stops can be made on stocks listed on the New York, American, and Nasdaq stock exchanges.

A stop-loss isn't a guarantee. In a free-falling market, your order may not be executed at the price you set. Normally, however, your broker will come pretty close.

Constant trading—buying and selling stock—costs a lot of money. Even with a discount broker your commissions may come to one or 2 percent. If you turn over all of your stocks once a year, you might pay up to 4 percent. That means you'd have to gross 14 percent on your investments to net 10 percent, pretax. So the less you trade, the better your chance of making money.

If you're trading in a taxable account, there's even more incentive to buy and hold. That way your profits won't be taxed. Profits on stocks held for 18 months or less are called *short-term capital gains* and taxed in your highest marginal bracket. *Long-term capital gains*, on stocks held for more than 18 months, are much more lightly taxed.

Just because you buy doesn't mean you have to sell. A good company's stock price may stall for a while while other stocks move up. But that's why you diversify. America's major corporations, with their global reach, are stocks to hold for years and years.

Sad Stories I Have Heard (or, What It Takes to Break Even)

You bought a stock and it's a dog. As soon as you bought it, the price started down. But you haven't sold because you don't want to take the loss. You will wait until the price comes back.

You Are Cherishing Four Illusions:

1. You think that the price will come back soon because you couldn't have been so wrong. (In fact, the price could stay down for years.)

2. You think that as long as you don't sell you don't have a loss. (But a "paper" loss is just as real as the other kind. The stock is worth less than you paid for it. Period.)

3. You think that there's only one way of earning back the money you lost: by holding on to the stock you lost it in. (But you might earn your money back faster by selling the stock and reinvesting in something else.)

4. You think that gains come just as easily as losses.

The falsity of this last point needs an illustration. When a stock drops from $50 to $25, you lose 50 percent of your money. To recover, however, your stock has to climb from $25 back up to $50—a rise of 100 percent. How many stocks do you buy expecting a 100 percent increase in price? Not very many.

That's why it's so important to cut your losses before they get too deep. The farther your stock falls, the harder it becomes to earn the money back.

If You're Holding a Loser, Consider Selling for the Tax Loss. Capital losses are deductible in full against realized capital gains, and deductible at the rate of $3,000 a year against your ordinary income. If you still like the stock, you can buy it back after 30 days—perhaps at a lower price if the market is going down. If you rebuy before the 31st day, you can't take the tax loss. And that's all you'll hear from me about taxes and stock portfolios. If God had wanted me to be J. K. Lasser, He or She would have arranged it.

A Short List of Stock-Picking Points to Give You a Glimpse of What It Takes

Every stock picker has a system but it can't be packaged and delivered. You start by trying this and that, and pretty soon you've cleared a path. Since there are thousands of stocks that rise in the long run, one path may work just as well as another. In that eclectic spirit, I offer some ways of helping stock pickers get started. But the sooner you open your own path, the clearer your view of the market will become.*

You might start by attaching yourself to a major trend. Maybe something political, like the opening of Eastern Europe. Maybe something economic, like the odds of rising or falling interest rates. Maybe something demographic, like the growing need for health care for the elderly. Maybe something technological, like the growth of the Internet for commercial use. Conversely, you might say, "All these big-picture trends are overpriced. What other industries are coming along?" Think about the industry you work in. What developments there are going to influence profit growth?

Once you've found a possible industry, ask: Is it growing? Can it raise its prices without setting off price wars? Are profit margins sustainable? Can it keep its labor costs under control? Can competitors easily enter this industry, or will the leaders keep their franchise for a while? Does it have any political troubles? Is it a steady grower, even during general recessions?

If you like the answers you get, start looking for promising companies

---

* Financial planner Lynn Hopewell of Fairfax, Virginia, comments: "Mostly useless, Jane! Laymen can't pick stocks. Their choices wind up being all emotion." He's right, but you'll have to learn that yourself.

WHEN A STOCK DROPS BY	THE GAIN YOU NEED TO BREAK EVEN IS
5%	5%*
10%	11%
15%	18%
20%	25%
25%	33%
30%	43%
35%	54%
40%	66%
45%	82%
50%	100%
55%	122%
60%	150%
65%	186%
70%	233%
75%	300%
80%	400%
85%	566%
90%	900%
95%	1,900%
99%	9,900%

* Rounded down from 5.2%. Even small losses require greater percentage gains in order to win your money back.
SOURCE: The American Association of Individual Investors

within that industry. Ask: Is the company an industry leader? Does it control a unique product or service? Does it dominate a profitable market? Does it have some new products coming along? Has management done a good job of raising the company's earnings and profit margins?

This is what analysts call a top-down approach. You start with a big thought, then narrow your focus to companies that embody it. Investors who start by screening stocks for certain financial characteristics are said to be working bottom-up.

Once you've got a likely company, ask: How popular has this company already become with investors? One measure is its *price/earnings (P/E) ratio*. When a company carries a high P/E, its earnings have usually risen rapidly and investors are betting that growth will accelerate some more. At companies with low P/Es, profits have grown more slowly or are in a slump. One popular theory of investing says: pick low-P/E stocks. They're out of favor, which means they have more room to rise.

To calculate a price/earnings ratio, you divide the current market price by the company's earnings per share for the past 12 months. Or save yourself the trouble and look up the ratio in the stock tables printed in most newspapers. At this writing, P/Es in the 20 to 25 range and higher are generally considered rich. P/Es under 10 are considered low—and perhaps a good buy if the company is sound. P/Es under 5 suggest a company in trouble or facing serious business risks. That could be a buying opportunity if you see improvement down the road. At this writing, Eastern Europe sells at P/Es of 4 to 5.

Every stock has its own P/E range. You should study its history and the P/Es of other stocks in the industry before deciding whether it's selling at an attractive price.

The P/E is also known as a *multiple*. At a 15 P/E, a company is said to be selling at a multiple of 15 times earnings. Stock analysts may also refer to "a multiple of 15 times estimated earnings," meaning that they're judging the stock price by what they think the company will earn in the current year.

One important point about P/E ratios: The concept of high or low is a floating one. The current value of any investment depends on what competing investments have to offer. Stocks sell at somewhat lower P/Es when interest rates are high (because bonds are attractive alternative investments) and at higher P/Es when interest rates are low.

Many stock pickers also use P/Es to guess if this is a good time to buy. If the P/E is lower than the company's growth rate, the stock might be cheap. If the P/E is higher than the company's growth rate, the stock might be overpriced. (Note that I said *might*.)

What is the company's *dividend yield?* To calculate it, divide the annual dividend by the stock's current market value. Income investors look for dividends in the 5 percent range in industries that typically pay high yields, such as traditional utilities and real-estate investment trusts. High dividends also can mean that a company's stock price has dropped, which appeals to "value" investors. But value investors have to distinguish between companies whose troubles are temporary (say, they need to be reorganized but new management has a plan) and those that will stay in the pits for a while (they face serious problems with no visible way out). A super-high dividend might be cut.

One much-touted way of trying to get ahead of the market is called the Dow dividend strategy. You buy equal dollar amounts of the 10 highest-yielding stocks in the Dow Jones industrial average and hold them 12 months. Then you switch to the newest top 10. Historically, this strategy has beaten the average significantly, not counting taxes and transaction costs. But as of this writing, all is not well among the Dow-dividend faithful. In a number of years in the early 1990s, the 10 *lowest* yielders were better buys. By the time you read this, maybe that will be the game.

Dividends become less important in fast-rising markets. Growth investors aren't interested in them at all. But in flat markets, dividends make up a substantial portion of your total return. (For more on dividends, see page 718.)

Growth investors look for companies whose earnings are growing faster than 15 percent a year. They're especially fond of smaller companies —"smaller" meaning sales in the $50 million to $500 million range, not penny stocks (page 792). Historically, such companies have grown faster than the giants; when they're good, they're very, very good. But giants can be growth stocks, too. In the late eighties, they trounced the smalls.

Momentum has been a favorite game of growth-stock investors. You look at how fast a stock is rising relative to its previous pace or to an independent index. A stock whose price rise has picked up speed is expected to have a further run. Like any other system, this one will work until it doesn't.

Technical investors ("chartists") take their buying and selling clues from changes in the stock price, without regard for what the company does. *Fundamental* investors inspect the industry and company, seeking good news. One place to look for news is the *annual report* (page 729). You want to see widening profit margins. An especially good bet is a company whose low profit margins appear to be improving. Another friendly number is operating income, which tells you whether revenues from the company's basic business have grown.

The annual report also tells you the *earnings per share.* That's the company's total earnings divided by the number of shares outstanding. Investors like to see earnings per share heading steadily up (and plenty of companies "manage" their reports to show exactly that). Stocks jump when earnings turn out to be markedly better than analysts expected. The new expectation is that those stocks will do better yet.

Don't automatically write off a stock whose earnings per share are down. In some cases, that's good news, too. For example, the company might have made a major capital investment that will produce higher earnings in the future. Or maybe a new, improved management group is writing off the mistakes of the old regime. You always have to know what the company is up to.

Some investors pick companies whose own officers are buying stock. Insiders tend to buy more than usual before large price rises in the stock and may sell more than usual before large price declines. Buying is generally a better signal than selling (executives sell for personal as well as investment reasons). But one or two purchases don't mean much. It's more significant if three or more insiders buy within a 3-month period and no insider sells, opines market timer Martin Zweig. The best price gains come in the first 6 months after insiders start to purchase, with the biggest punch packed into the first month. So copycats have to move fast. Conversely, when insider selling turns out to have been a signal, the price decline tends to be gradual (except in cases of deception or fraud when insiders bail in advance of a shocking earnings drop).

Here are two newsletters that follow company insiders: *The Insiders,* ($49 a year; call 800-442-9000 or write to 2200 SW 10th St., Deerfield Beach, FL 33442); and *Vickers Weekly Insider Report* ($137 a year plus $39 postage and handling. Call 800-645-5043 or write to 226 New York Ave., Huntington, NY 11743).

What about *buybacks,* when companies announce major purchases of their own shares? One camp says that's good. Top management thinks the stock is cheap relative to the company's prospects. Another camp says that's bad. Top management isn't clever enough to invest that money in ways that will make the company grow.

What about *spin-offs?* Sometimes a big company sets up one of its businesses as an independent firm. All current shareholders automatically get a piece. Those who don't want it tend to sell within the first month, so the price of the spin-off might go down. If you think that the business is sound, that's a good time to buy.

Beginners should start with no more than 25 percent of their money. (Actually, they should start with index funds and add individual stocks only after they've accumulated a substantial sum et cetera, et cetera, and so forth.) Stick with leading companies whose management keeps on showing good results. Remember demography: senior markets are growing while the number of young adults is shrinking. Avoid OTC stocks until you've learned a lot more about markets, prices, and values. You're not looking just for a stock, you're looking for a *company* whose prospects you think are strong. When good, farsighted management creates a good, farsighted strategy to grow a good company or rescue a troubled one, you've got a winner.

A Word About Inherited Stock. You didn't pick it, it was chosen for someone else—probably someone with very different goals from yours. It may be from Daddy's beloved company, but sell it if it doesn't fit. At the very least, sell enough so the stock makes up no more than 5 percent of your assets. If the company falters, you don't want your retirement to falter, too.

Remember This About Any Stock Price!

The stock market *anticipates.* The current price generally contains all that investors know, or can reasonably guess, about a company's prospects over a reasonable holding period. On the day you buy, you have paid in full for the expected value of any new product or service that the company has announced. For the stock price to rise, prospects for that company have to *improve* beyond what investors can now foresee. Fortunately, prospects often do.

Dividends

A dividend is your cut of any profits that the company distributes to shareholders. It's declared and usually paid quarterly.

Rapidly growing companies pay low dividends or none at all. Profits are reinvested in the business to help shareholder value grow. This pleases growth investors who seek high capital gains.

Slower-growing companies, on the other hand, don't get the same high returns by reinvesting in their basic businesses. Sometimes they use their profits to buy other companies (for good or ill). But they also pay dividends to shareholders. This pleases investors who want income as well as reasonable growth.

If you're an income investor, look for companies that have paid dividends for 10 years or more and whose dividends usually rise every year—because rising dividends help pull the stock price up. Stagnating dividends suggest that the company isn't going anywhere.

Even growth investors should think about owning some dividend-paying stocks, for two reasons. First, they normally don't drop as far as growth stocks do when bear markets strike. That helps stabilize your portfolio. Second, dividend-paying stocks may deliver higher total returns (dividends plus capital gains) than growth stocks do. One smart use of dividends is to buy more of the company's stock. For companies with dividend-reinvestment plans, see page 688.

Consider selling your shares, however, if your high-dividend company takes on a lot of debt. Dividends may be cut, so the company can make its payments. Dividends also get cut when a company or industry restructures, as will happen to many electric utilities, or when dividend yields are unusually high.

When timing your purchases and sales, watch out for stocks selling *ex-dividend*. That is the 5-day period before a dividend is paid. If you buy during those days, you will not be recorded as a shareholder on the company's books, so you won't receive the dividend. If you sell any shares, however, the dividend follows you because you are still the owner of record.

When a stock goes ex-dividend, the amount of the dividend is subtracted from the price, so the market price should fall. If it doesn't, that means that the value of the stock has actually gone up.

All things being equal, you might as well buy when you can collect the dividend. A stock that's ex-dividend has an *x* next to its name in the stock tables published in the newspaper. Some companies pay part of their dividends in the form of new stock rather than cash.

The Truth About Stock Splits

Nouveau investors think that stock splits make their shares worth more. Wrong, wrong, wrong. After a stock split, a company is worth exactly the same as it was before. Your $120 stock might be split into two $60 shares or three $40 shares but the total value remains $120. In a reverse split, four shares worth $5 each may be combined into a single $20 share. After a split, all prior financial information will be restated to reflect the changed number of shares outstanding.

So the news that "they're splitting the stock" should not be a clarion call to buy. On the other hand, the stock is definitely worth a look. Companies with high share prices usually don't split their stocks unless they expect stronger growth and higher dividends. If that indeed happens, the stock price will rise. Studies show that a stock that has split tends to outperform the market for up to 3 years.

Sometimes, however, the company is just trying to drum up interest in the stock. Individual investors are more comfortable with share prices in the $50 range than in the $100 range. So they may be willing to buy a bit more if the stock splits down to a level they like. But all you get out of a ploy like this is a short market flurry. The price won't rise if the company's prospects remain unchanged.

Beware of a Low-Priced Company That Splits Its Stock. There's no reason for a $30 stock to split into two $15 pieces, except to hype itself to the innocent.

New Issues: For Rich Gamblers Only

Stock markets will careen from the heights of greed to the pits of fear and back again until the last syllable of recorded time. And whenever the Greedometer hits new highs, new issues come pouring out.

A new issue is a private company whose shares are being sold to the public for the first time. It's often called an IPO, which means—depending on your view of these things—Initial Public Offering or It's Probably Overpriced.

Some IPOs are genuine businesses with real earnings and honest prospects. These are the only ones to entertain. Some are businesses with promise but launched at too rich a price. Some use the money they raise from the public merely to buy out the founder—and why would you, as an investor, want to do that? On the fringes of this market are the start-ups—two guys and an idea. The idea may be great but there's no proof that they can turn it into a business. Beyond the fringe are the "blind pools": an entrepreneur raises money in order to buy (he assures you) a profitable business but you don't know what that business is going to be. Don't just walk away from a blind pool. Run.

New issues bubble up on hope and hype. Speculators dream of copping a $10 stock that will be worth $20 within the week. The odds are better than even that an IPO will show a profit over the first 30 days. But the biggest gains come on offering day, and what's your personal chance of getting your hands on such a hot stock? High if you're a big player, trade through a firm that's part of the underwriting syndicate, and give your broker a lot of business. Otherwise, low. The average Joe and Joan are there to take the mediocrities off the broker's hands. And even high fliers may tank within a very few months.

In recent years IPOs have shown mixed returns. The class of 1994 had a median one-year gain of 2.5 percent, according to Securities Data Co. in Newark, New Jersey. The class of 1995 had a median gain of a sizzling 50.3 percent

—but, as always, with a catch. There were 491 new issues that year. Their one-year returns ranged from a gain of 881 percent to a loss of 97.5 percent.

It's fun to believe the new-issue hype, which is often stirred by the underwriters' own analysts (page 667). But longer-range studies consistently show that new issues do worse, on average, than Standard & Poor's 500-stock average. And that doesn't even count the trash issues offered at less than $5 a share.

So . . . don't buy IPOs. If one interests you, get the prospectus and watch the stock. If the company is real, with audited earnings increases, a reasonable P/E ratio, and genuine prospects, buy it later. You'll probably get it at less than the offering price. Genentech flew from $35 to $89 on its birthday in late 1980, but by 1982 it was selling at $26 a share. Apple Computer's first day took it from $22 to $36, but it bottomed out later at $10.75. Hot companies that go public at super-high price/earnings ratios (100 times earnings isn't unusual) are unrealized losses just waiting to happen.

If you cannot resist trying your hand at an IPO, look for a "senior issue" —a company that has been in business for three or four years, with palpable markets and rising earnings. The new money should be used for expansion, not for paying off bank debt or enriching the founders by buying their shares. If you can't get any shares at the opening, don't chase the price up. Wait for it to drop. If it doesn't, forget it. Another stock will come along.

The prospectus—the legal document that accompanies the new issue of any stock, bond, or mutual fund—is chock-full of pertinent information about the company and is, unfortunately, the least read publication in America. Even *Undertaker's Weekly* has more fans.

Secondaries. You can also buy newly issued stocks from companies that are already public. For well-established companies, they're called *secondary offerings*. For new companies that went public a year or more ago, they're called *follow-ons*. Analyze them the way you'd look at ongoing companies, with particular reference to how they intend to use the new money they're raising.

Preferred Stocks: Old Dogs Don't Learn New Tricks

Preferred stocks sound tempting. They pay a fixed, high dividend, sometimes more than the same company's bonds. If common-stock prices rise, the preferreds will rise a little, too. So you get a good income plus some hope of capital growth.

But a lot more is wrong with preferreds than right:

1. If you're interested in growth, you'll get far, far more of it from the common stock. The common may also pay dividends, and unlike the preferred, the common's dividend can rise.

2. If you're interested in income, bonds are safer. Preferreds have excellent payment records, but in a pinch the company could cancel your dividends for a while. With *cumulative* preferreds, the dividends must be made up; with *noncumulative* preferreds, they don't.

3. If you're interested in preserving your principal, bonds are safer, too. Preferreds fluctuate more in price and they don't "mature," so there's never a point when you can expect your capital back (or they mature in 49 years, with no guarantee of principal if you sell prematurely).

4. The moment a preferred succeeds—when prices are up and you're reveling in your high dividend payments—the corporation may call in the shares. Not only will you lose the stock but the call price may be at something less than market price.

5. When you sell, you may have to take a discount on the price. There's not a big market for preferreds.

There are angles to preferreds. Some have adjustable dividend payments that fluctuate with interest rates. *Participating preferreds* earn a portion of the company's profits in addition to the dividend. These gimmicks may or may not be to your advantage. You need a broker whose research department really understands preferreds.

They're generally bought by conservative investors for their retirement accounts or by people looking for high current income, especially low-income retirees. If you're interested, buy only companies with high-rated bonds (A or better) so you'll have some assurance that the dividend will be paid.

Convertible Preferreds: A Gambler's Game

These preferreds can be converted into common stock at a specified, higher price. While you hold them, you earn a fixed dividend—less than you'd get from bonds or regular preferreds but more than the common pays. If the stock price rises above the conversion price, you get an attractive capital gain. If the price of the common falls, however, your convertible is "hung." You can wait it out, but the company may call in your shares. You might be forced to convert at a loss. If what you want is a safe, high income why would you run this risk? These stocks are for fun, not for real.

Selling Short: For Sophisticates Only

To "short" a stock is to make a bet that the price will fall.

Here's the Ideal Transaction.

1. You borrow 100 shares of stock from your broker and sell it at today's price—say, $50. As collateral, you put up 50 to 100 percent of the

stock's current market value, typically using your own cash plus a loan from your broker.

2. Over the following four weeks, the stock price plunges to $10.

3. At that point you "cover" your short by buying 100 shares at $10 and returning them to your broker. Your gross profit is $40 a share.

4. From that you subtract your buying and selling commissions; any dividends paid by the stock during the time you held it, which you owe to the owner; and the interest you owe on any money borrowed from the broker (known as a margin loan). Occasionally, the broker charges a premium for making the loan.

Here's What Can Go Wrong:

1. The stock price can rise instead of fall. If you have to buy back the shares at $60 you'll lose $10 a share, plus commissions, plus interest on the margin loan. The higher the stock rises, the more money you lose.

2. If you put up only part of the price and the stock goes up instead of down, you might be asked for more collateral. That's known as a margin call. If you don't comply, part or all of your position will be sold, leaving you liable for any losses, plus commissions and loan interest. Note, too, that no short sale pays dividends.

The average investor can't stand the tension of having a short sale run the wrong way. It's different from owning a stock outright. When your own stock falls, you can comfort yourself with the thought that it will rise again. But when a stock rises, you can't feel sure that it will fall. You need a lot of experience (plus a fundamentally dark view of life) to get a kick out of a short sell.

The riskiest shorts* are popular companies that are overpriced. Happy campers may drive those prices higher still. The safest shorts are stocks that already appear to be moving down.

To protect yourself, set a stop-loss limit. Tell your broker to close out your position if the stock rises by a certain amount, say 10 percent.

Remember: Short sellers potentially have more to lose than other investors. If you buy a $10 company that goes bankrupt, you cannot be out any more than 100 percent of your investment, or $10. But say that you short a $10 stock and the price goes to $30 before you cover. You've lost $20, which is 200 percent of your investment.

Free Money: Use It or Lose It

Some securities are like lottery tickets. For some special reason your number comes up and you get a payoff you didn't expect. You get it, that

---

* A friend who read this said that the riskiest shorts are short shorts, but then he's sexist through and through.

is, if you're truly watching your investment (or your broker is). If not, you may lose money that should have been yours. For example:

Warrants. When you buy certain securities—such as new issues or the preferred stocks or bonds of speculative companies—they might come with "warrants." They're a sweetener, to get you to buy an issue that otherwise looks like a dog. (It could still be a dog, but the warrants make it look like a more valuable dog.) Warrants give you the right to buy a certain number of the company's common shares at a specified, higher price.

Say, for example, you buy the low-rated bonds of Mongrel, Inc. They come with a warrant giving you the right to buy shares in Mongrel at $5 anytime over the next five years. The current market price is $4. Those warrants are worth money. If the underlying stock moves up, they're worth more money. If the stock price exceeds $5, your warrants are said to be "in the money."

You can sell the warrants through a stockbroker if you don't want to use them to buy the stock, but they generally have an expiration date. If you do nothing, warrants eventually become worthless. And that's just what happens when people don't pay attention. They forget about their warrants and let them expire, unsold and unused.

Warning: The modern, predatory company might cut the ground from under its warrant holders. Just when the stock is moving up nicely and you're expecting jackpot gains, the company will call in the warrants at, say, 5 cents each. You have 30 days either to sell the warrants at the current, higher price or exercise them and buy the stock. You won't lose money on this transaction but you'll lose the future gains that, as a warrant holder, you expected and deserved.

If you don't hear about the redemption (by reading your company mail or getting a call from your stockbroker), you'll wind up with warrants worth only a nickel apiece. It's a dirty trick. Those warrants were your reward for taking extra risk. The company breaks faith with you by taking them away. Moral: Don't bother buying new issues with warrants. The company may not allow you to reap the gains you gambled for.

For speculators: Suppose that you own no warrants. You can still speculate in them by buying them through a broker. If the stock moves up smartly, you'll earn a higher percentage profit from the warrants than from the stock. If you're wrong, of course, you'll also swallow a larger loss. If you buy and the company suddenly decides to redeem, you could lose money on the transaction, even if you were smart enough to buy a warrant that should have been worth a lot.

Spin-offs. A company may designate a subsidiary as a separate corporation and give it away to its shareholders. Your stock certificate will arrive automatically by mail. But to know that you're now a shareholder in this new entity, you have to open your company mail. Unknown numbers of stock certificates get thrown away by people who simply aren't paying attention.

You don't run this risk if your stocks are held by your broker in a street name. The certificate goes to the broker, who will report its arrival on your monthly statement.

What if you don't tell your company that you've moved and your stock is mailed to an old address? The company should get it back. After 3 to 7 years or more, depending on state law, the certificate should be turned over to the state as unclaimed property. You can retrieve it at any time. If you do so before it's turned over to the state, you receive any dividends and appreciation that the spin-off earned. When the state gets the shares, however, they're normally sold. From that point on, you can claim only the original value the state received.

Convertibles. A company in trouble may give its current bondholders some convertible preferreds to encourage them to hang on. The converts can be turned in for common stock at a fixed, higher price. If the company does well, so do you. But many investors never realize that they have this right and lose that extra capital gain.

Calls. A company "calls" a preferred stock or bond by ordering investors to turn it in for cash. If you don't get the word, you will lose money. You'll discover the call eventually because you'll stop getting dividends or interest. When you contact the company, you'll receive the securities' call value, but lose the money you could have earned by turning in the securities earlier and reinvesting the proceeds.

You might lose even more if you ignore a call on convertible bonds or convertible preferred stocks. The call value may be considerably lower than the value of the underlying common stock. If you don't convert into the common stock by the call date, or sell your security to someone else, all that extra value will go down the drain.

Class Actions. Sometimes the price of a stock suddenly collapses and it turns out that management has been fudging. Maybe the financial statements mixed some fiction with the facts. That lapse will almost certainly trigger a class-action lawsuit on behalf of everyone who owned shares at the time. You'll get a notice about the lawsuit (keep it). You'll get another notice if there's a settlement or judgment in your favor. To collect your money, you'll have to make a phone call, fill in a form, and—sometimes— follow up to be sure that you get the check. People who don't open their company mail, or can't be bothered filling out forms, are giving up found money.

Stock Rights. When a company sells new shares, it might give first dibs to its current stockholders. As an incentive to get you to buy, you'll be offered a discount on the price. This deal is offered to you by mail; the piece of paper guaranteeing you a discount price is called a *right*.

Say, for example, that your stock sells at $10 and you're offered the right to buy more at $9. If you exercise that right, you'll save $1 per share —the difference between your discounted buying price and the market price. If you don't want to buy any more stock, you can sell that right— probably for slightly less than $1, after commissions.

Either way you have to act within a specified number of weeks or the right will expire. If you throw out your company mail without reading it, your rights will vanish into a landfill. You may actually lose money because, once the period for exercising the right expires, the company's share price may fall by the value of the rights that were issued. You have to exercise (or sell) your rights just to stay even.

Children can do their elderly parents a great kindness by keeping track of all these matters. Arrange for all company mail to come to you. A forget-ful investor can easily lose substantial sums.

The firm may handle your securities in your best interest—for example, by selling rights or warrants that would otherwise expire worthless—even if you give no instructions to do so. The profits go into your account. However, you cannot count on your broker's picking up every single offer. You have to pay attention, too.

If you're not prepared to follow your investments closely enough to keep track of such things as tenders, spin-offs, and warrants, sell your shares and buy mutual funds.

Mergers and Buyouts

Every year thousands of shareholders lose money because they don't respond to a tender offer for their stock. Shareholder Communications Corporation in New York City estimates, conservatively, that in the 1980s and 1990s mergers alone produced $150 million to $300 million annually in tender-offer payments that haven't been claimed. Shareholders can retrieve this money after the fact but will lose all the dividends and appreciation they could have earned in the meantime.

If you're dragged into one of these corporate circuses, you'll need some definitions:

A *merger* is the voluntary combination of two companies under a new corporate name. Usually, the shareholders of both companies turn in their old shares for those of the new entity.

A *takeover* is the friendly purchase of one company by another. The dominant company offers cash and/or securities to the shareholders of the company it buys.

A *hostile takeover* is an offer from a group that your company's management objects to. The company may counter with a higher bid of its own. It may restructure, sometimes offering you a big dividend. Or it may ask a more acceptable partner—a "white knight"—to bid for the company shares.

A *management buyout* is an offer from management to buy most or all of the company's common shares. Management borrows the money to make the offer, which is why these deals are called leveraged buyouts. When you use debt you are using leverage. Managements were buying out companies left and right in the 1980s, but in the early and middle 1990s this business quieted down.

Tender Offers

These come from anyone who wants to buy some or all of your shares, usually at a higher price than you could get in the open market. You are being asked to *tender* (surrender) your shares.

Tender offers drive up the price of your shares, although not necessarily quite as high as the tender price. For example, a tender at $33.50 for a share that's selling for $25 might push the market price up to $32. The discount allows for the risk that the deal might fall through. The greater the risk, the larger the discount.

In some cases, however, the share price might jump higher than the offer—say to $35. That shows that the pros expect a second bidder with a higher offer.

You have three ways of responding to a tender offer:

1. Sell your shares in the open market for a quick and easy profit. This is the surest way of making money. You'll get your profit even if, in the end, the tender fails.

2. If it's a hostile takeover, consider holding on to your shares for a while. You're betting that more offers will be made and the stock price will go even higher. Then you can sell. This, of course, is a gamble that you might lose.

3. Tender to the would-be buyer. The offer will probably be higher than the stock price. In a partial tender, where the buyer wants, say, only 50 percent of the shares, you'll have to respond within ten days to ensure that at least some of your shares will be taken.

There are good arguments against tendering. First, if the deal fails, you'll get your stock back and will have lost all the gains you could have made by selling your shares in the open market. Second, the value of the offer may not be firm. It might be announced at, say, $33.50 per share. But if that price includes preferred stock and bonds with payment gimmicks, the package may be cheaper than the bidder claims. Third, even if it's a good offer the payout may take months to accomplish. That's why, after all the bidding has stopped, a quick sale in the open market often looks more attractive.

After a merger or takeover, the stock price of the enlarged company usually goes nowhere for a while, or falls. So you might want to sell any shares you own and look around for a better stock. This is particularly true if the buying group loaded up your company with debt.

What If You Fail to Sell or Tender Your Shares? This can happen if: you don't read the financial news; you ignore the mail you get from your company; you moved and never gave your company your new address; you (or your elderly parent) have forgotten that you own the shares; your broker, who is holding the shares, neglected to inform you; or you've been asleep for twenty years.

In a partial tender, your untendered shares still have value in the open market. But if the buyout or takeover was for all the shares, there will no longer be a public market for the shares you kept.

The ultimate value of those untendered shares will depend on the deal. Companies that make all-cash offers will set aside that money for you. It won't earn any interest, so its value will be demolished by inflation. But it's there, somewhere, if you suddenly wake up and claim it.

You may be luckier if the tender offer included securities. Those unclaimed securities will stay in your name, gaining or losing value as the market changes. Dividends will accrue (although the dividends won't earn interest). If you call up the company in a couple of years and ask about your shares, you may find them worth a handsome sum.

But your company isn't a permanent lost-property office. After 3 to 7 years (longer, in some states), the money and securities due on untendered shares are turned over to the state as unclaimed property. You can get them back, but your securities will probably have been sold and from that point on you'll have earned no interest on the money.

When a brokerage firm holds your stocks, you may or may not be informed of tenders or impending expirations or redemption dates. A good firm will do so, but it's not required. Ask about this when you open an account.

Buying on Margin

You buy securities "on margin" when you borrow some of the money from your stockbroker. Why do it? Because a lucky margin buyer will make a bigger profit than someone who buys the same stock for cash.

Suppose that you're interested in a $50 stock. For $5,000 cash, you'll get 100 shares. If you borrow another $5,000 from your broker, you'll get 200 shares.

If that stock rises $5 in price, the cash buyer earns $500—a 10 percent return on his investment. But the margin buyer earns $1,000—a 20 percent return on his own $5,000. He also earns double the dividends because he owns double the number of shares.

That's called *leverage*—increasing your profit by buying an asset with borrowed money. For stocks listed on the leading exchanges, and certain major over-the-counter stocks, you can borrow up to 50 percent of the cost, depending on the broker. Smaller loans, or none at all, may be allowed against over-the-counter stocks.

Unfortunately, a successful margin investor does not get to take all the profits home. Besides sales commissions, you have to repay the loan plus interest. Brokers charge around 0.5 to 2.5 percentage points over the "broker call rate," which is the interest the broker pays on money borrowed from the bank. The interest expense compounds in your brokerage account and you generally pay it when the securities are sold. (That amount is deductible against investment income earned from your various securities.)

On the downside, margin loans can kill you. If the share price drops by $5, the cash investor loses 10 percent while the margin investor loses 20 percent. If the price drops by $12 a share, the cash investor is merely holding on to a loser. The margin buyer may have to put up more money or be partly sold out.

For the details on margin loans, see page 259. I want to restate only two points here:

1. Interest charges and sales commissions can easily eat up the profits on securities held on margin for many months. Margin buyers make money only on securities whose price moves up fast.

2. If your stock drops too far in price, the broker will ask for more collateral in the form of cash or securities. That's what's known as a margin call. If you don't have the money, some of your securities will be sold to cover the debt. You usually get a margin call if the value of your interest in all the securities in your account, net of the debt, shrinks to 30 or 25 percent of market value. To make margin calls less likely, borrow less than the maximum 50 percent.

Reading an Annual Report

Where do you start? Not at the front. At the back.

Turn to the report of the certified public accountant (CPA). This third-party auditor will tell you right off the bat if the report fairly represents the company's financial condition, according to "generally accepted accounting principles."

CPAs have been known to let some real howlers get by. But the auditors are the only numbers police an investor has, so you might as well see what they have to say. If the CPA qualifies his or her opinion in any way, or calls the report clean only if you take the company's word about a particular piece of business (which the CPA clearly didn't want to do), watch out. Doubts like these are usually settled behind closed doors, before the annual report is published. When they make it into print, it suggests that the company is a riskier investment than you might want.

Now go to the front, to the letter from the chairman. Usually addressed "to our stockholders," it reflects both the character and the well-being of the company. Is it stuffy or friendly? Straightforward or obfuscating? Proud or defensive? This letter should tell you how the business fared this year—its failures as well as its successes. Most important, it should tell you why. Candor builds confidence. Beware of sentences that start with phrases like "Except for" and "Despite the." They're clues to problems. Think about selling any stock whose chairman barely mentions that earnings fell.

On the positive side, the chairman's letter should give you some insight into the company's future and its stance on the economic and political trends that affect its business. You want a savvy letter, not a lot of boring double-talk.

While you're up front, look for what's new in each line of business. Is management getting the company in good shape to weather the tough and competitive twenty-first century?

Next go to the footnotes of the financial reports. These are worth a try even if you're not a numbers person because they explain so much. A number that looks bad in the report itself may actually be good because of some special circumstance. A number that looks good may actually be bad.

For example, are earnings down? If it's only because of a change in accounting methods, that may be good. The company owes less tax and has more money in its pocket. Are earnings up? Maybe that's bad. There may have been a special windfall—like the sale of a business—that won't happen again next year. Does the company own shares in another company? The balance sheet may list those shares at original cost while the footnote says they're worth twenty times that amount. Does the company have a huge deferred tax or pension liability? That means that the earnings aren't on as sound a footing as you might have thought. You need the footnotes to tell you whether the numbers in the main report present a fair picture of the company's finances.

If you're going to be a real stock picker, you can't avoid being a numbers person for very long. The key to a company's performance lies in its financial data, not in its press releases.

Start with the *balance sheet*. It's a snapshot of where the company stands at a single point in time. On the left are *assets*—everything the company owns. Things that can quickly be turned into cash are *current assets*. On the right are *liabilities*—everything the company owes. *Current liabilities* are the debts due in one year, which are paid out of current assets.

The right-hand side of the balance sheet also shows you the *stockhold-*

er's equity. That's the difference between total assets and total liabilities. It is the presumed dollar value of what stockholders own. You want it to grow from year to year.

The difference between current assets and current liabilities is *working capital*. You want to see a nice cushion here. It says that a company can pay its bills. Some analysts apply rules of thumb to the ratio between current assets and current liabilities—for example, that assets should be twice liabilities. That's known as a *current ratio*.

But holding that much working capital may not be a terrific idea. Why leave money sitting around that could be earning 20 or 30 percent if invested in the business? I raise this point to show you that "traditional" ratios aren't gospel. On the other hand, the stocks of companies with small amounts of working capital may be risky. What will management do if business contracts? They need a clear strategy for paying their bills.

One important number to crunch is the company's *debt-to-equity ratio,* including its preferred stocks. You get it by dividing long-term liabilities by stockholder's equity.

A high ratio means that the company borrows a lot of money to spark its growth. That's okay if the company is in a stable industry with reasonably predictable earnings—enough to cover debt service. One example would be a regulated utility. But high debt-to-equity ratios can bury a company that is vulnerable to cycles of boom and bust, like brokerage firms, retailers, or steel companies. The boom years are fine. It's the bust years that kill you. In general, analysts worry if the debt of an industrial company amounts to more than 25 to 30 percent of equity.

The second basic source of numbers is the *income statement,* or *statement of profit and loss*. It shows how much money the company made or lost over the year. Formerly, this statement always came with a brief analysis by management called a *review of operations*. Since 1997, alas, companies have been allowed to leave the written analysis out. So you're often on your own.

Most investors look first at the bottom-line number: *net earnings per share*. But it can fool you. The company's management might have boosted earnings by selling off a plant, changing the depreciation rules, or cutting the budget for research and advertising. (See the footnotes!) So don't get smug about net earnings until you've found out how they happened. This much-watched figure is often manipulated to make companies look better or worse than they really are.

The 5-year *summary of operations* gives you more perspective. Look for *net sales* or *operating revenues*. This is the primary source of money received by the company.

Ask yourself: Are net sales or operating revenues going up at a faster rate from year to year? If not, is the company reducing the rate of rise in its costs? When costs rise faster than sales, profits may get mushy. Also ask: Are sales going up faster than inflation? If not, the company's real unit sales are falling behind. And ask again: Have sales gone down because the company is selling off a losing business? If so, profits may be soaring—which is great! And one time more: What's happening to *operating income* (income from the business, excluding unusual gains or losses)? Is it rising faster than *operating costs?* If so, *net profit margins* are widening—and that's usually Investor Heaven. Falling profit margins are not. Some companies help with this analysis by breaking out net profit margins for you.

As a savvy investor, however, you have to be sensitive to the many other variables that affect profit margins. Say, for example, that margins are rising because the company raised prices. "Great," you say, and hold on to the stock. Then the stock price falls and you wonder why. It turns out that your company's competitors held prices level. So your own company's sales and profits fell. Professional investors anticipated that the price increase wouldn't take and promptly drove the stock price down. (I never promised you that analyzing a company was going to be easy.)

One way of following dividends is to divide them by the company's total earnings. What percentage is being paid out to shareholders? You should get a fairly stable percentage payout over the business cycle, with dividends rising as earnings improve.

That brings up the most important thing of all. One annual report, one chairman's letter, one ratio won't tell you much. You have to compare. Is the company's debt-to-equity ratio better or worse than it used to be? Better or worse than industry norms or your company's major competitors? Better or worse at this point in the economic cycle than it was last time? Are liabilities growing or shrinking? How do this year's footnotes and audit letter compare with last year's on the same topics? In company-watching, comparisons are all. They tell you if management is staying on top of things.

Financial analysts work out many other ratios to tell them how the company is doing. You can learn more from specialized books on the subject. The Web is a font of information about corporations. You can check the financial reports the company files with the Securities and Exchange Commission on the SEC's Edgar database (http://www.sec.gov).

One thing you will never learn from an annual report is how much to pay for a company's stock. The company may be running well—but if investors expected it to be running better, the stock might fall. Or the company might be slumping badly—but if investors see better days ahead, the stock could rise.

You study the report to learn how well the company is handling its problems and opportunities and whether it appears to know the difference. You study the market to get a feel for its price.

When to Sell a Stock

You can hold a good mutual fund forever. You can also find good blue chips that get bluer every year. But many stocks should be sold from time to time as their potential peters out. Sometimes a whole industry gets into trouble because of competition or unfavorable market trends. Sometimes an individual company comes under pressure because of a crippling legal liability or a misjudged merger. Sometimes a stock just dies in the water while other industries pass it by.

In the Long Run, It Is More Important to Avoid Bad or Tuckered-Out Stocks Than to Pick Good Ones! Since the bias of the stock market is up, eliminating losers will, of itself, improve your performance.

The most amateurish of all mistakes is to hold on to a stinker because (you think) you couldn't have guessed so horribly wrong. Oh yes you could. But there's nothing wrong with making mistakes. That happens all the time in professional investing. The error lies in not correcting your mistake, by selling the stock while your loss is still small. Small losses can be canceled by small gains. Big losses drag down your performance for years (page 714).

Consider Selling When:
• The reason for buying the company has passed and no new reason is in sight. (The decision to hold a stock is virtually the same as a decision to buy. Does this company look better to you than other companies you might own?)

• Your stock did just fine for two or three years but its gains are now slowing. It's not doing as well as other stocks you own or other stocks in the same industry.

• Your company's industry will be hurt by a fundamental economic change. For example, many utility stocks are coming under pressure, due to deregulation. (Any such companies become a buy again when conditions change or when they adjust their business to the new realities.)

• The financial reports aren't looking quite so good. This quarter's earnings are lower than last year's, or lower than expected for two quarters running. Profit margins have stopped widening and started to narrow. One piece of bad news is usually followed by more bad news.

• The stock price is down by 10 to 15 percent.

• In the annual letter from your company's chairman, he or she makes excuses for failing to reach last year's goals and you see no plan for pulling out of the slump.

• Something odd is happening to the price. Perhaps it jumped 20 percent soon after you bought it, with no apparent explanation—in which case, you might want to take your lucky profits and run. Or perhaps the price suddenly dropped by 8 percent. Maybe someone knows something you don't.

• You think that prices are too high for stocks in general (see market timing, page 706) and the stock isn't something that you want to hold forever. Furthermore, your stock's price/earnings ratio has ballooned to a much higher level than normal.

Please note that I said "consider" selling. Some of these stocks may still be good long-term holds. So do your selling slowly, to see what happens—dropping 100 shares this week, 100 shares next week, taking some profits and watching the price. You might decide to sell half and hold the rest—*unless* you're investing with taxable money. It may cost more to sell and pay the tax than to hold through a market drop (unless the loss can shelter a capital gain you took on another stock).

Don't Sell a Stock Just Because It Has Risen a Few Points and You Don't Want to Lose the Profit. Maybe it will keep on going up. "Let your profits run," the old saw says.

Conversely, don't panic if the stock drops 5 points. That might be temporary. Consider selling if it drops by 10 to 15 percent (or if you have some other good reason to dump it). Short of that, sit back and wait. Or buy more. If you believe in the company, this is your chance to get more shares at a better price.

One Final Point

Smart shoppers will drive 50 miles to a factory outlet to buy a new coat at 40 percent off. But when stocks go on sale at a big discount (because the stock market has gone down), many shoppers shy away. They feel safer buying stocks when they're expensive rather than when they're cheap. And then they wonder why they don't make any money.

Buying stocks cheap is the only way to capture the superior performance that the market delivers over time. So look at bear markets as if they were half-price sales and buy.

25.

How to Use Bonds

Income Investing—The Right Way and the Wrong Way

Seeking safe investments, people drop stocks and buy bonds.
Out of the frying pan into the fire.

Properly used, bonds are safe and solid investments. They pay regular income and protect wealth. But more often than not, they're improperly used. Investors seeking income may find themselves eaten up by inflation and taxes. Investors seeking safety may suffer capital losses. Our sense that bonds or bond funds are secure has not caught up with the truth of the marketplace. Often they ride the same crazy roller coaster as stocks. Between 1993 and 1997 long-term bond prices fluctuated more than 30 percent, either up or down, in a single year.

Bonds are enormously useful to almost any investment plan. But you have to know how to play them right.

A BOND IS . . .

. . . a loan. You lend money to a government or corporation and earn interest on the funds. After a certain period of time the borrower pays the money back. When you "buy" a bond (through a discount broker, full-service stockbroker, or sometimes a bank), you are accepting an IOU. If the borrower repays at the end of the loan's full term, the bond is said to have "matured." If the borrower decides to prepay the loan, the bond is said to have been "called." Bonds come in four main types: Treasuries, issued by the U.S. Government; corporates, issued by corporations; tax-exempt municipals, issued by cities, states, and other municipal authorities; and asset-backed securities, issued to help finance auto, credit-card, mortgage, and other loans. Those backed by mortgages are called mortgage securities.

A BOND IS NOT . . .

. . . a higher-rate certificate of deposit. Bond investors shoulder some risk. Usually, your principal and interest are paid on time—but they might not be if the issuer goes bad. Furthermore, the bond's underlying value goes up and down as market conditions change. If you sell a bond before maturity, you might get less (or more) than you paid. A CD's value, by contrast, always remains the same.

A BOND MUTUAL FUND IS NOT . . .

. . . like a bond. You can hold a bond until maturity or until it's called and get all your money back. But there's no special date when a mutual fund will return your original investment. The market value of the fund changes every day—sometimes rising, sometimes falling. How much you get when you sell your shares depends on market conditions at the time. Because of this uncertainty, bond mutual funds can make investors more nervous than holding individual bonds.

WHY NOT STICK WITH A BANK CD INSTEAD OF BUYING A BOND?

Why not, indeed? Certificates of deposit are the very best choice for people who want total simplicity, no fees, and guaranteed principal at all times.

But bonds have some advantages. Some are fully or partly tax free, whereas CDs are fully taxable. And they usually (although not always) yield higher returns than comparable CDs.

WHAT ARE BONDS GOOD FOR?

Use bonds to:

1. *Preserve your purchasing power.* For this you want intermediate-term bonds (maturing in roughly 5 to 7 years), with all the income rein-

vested in money market mutual funds. Your money won't grow very much, after taxes and inflation. But you'll hold on to the value of what you have. For details, see page 758.

2. *Reduce the risk of owning stocks.* Although the riskier types of bonds can be almost as volatile as stocks, others live milder lives. What's more, bond prices tend to rise and fall at different times than stocks, and at different rates of speed. So if you own both stocks and bonds and 'average their performance together, you have a more stable portfolio than if you owned only one of them.

3. *Provide income to live on.* But exactly how to invest for income isn't as clear-cut as you might think (page 756). You might want a mutual-fund withdrawal plan (page 630) as well as interest income from bonds.

4. *Improve the yield on money you'd otherwise keep in cash.* Prudent investors hedge against the risk of suddenly needing money. You don't want to have to sell stocks when the market is down, in order to raise enough money to fix the car. Treasury bills, money market funds, or bank CDs are the safest places for your "prudence fund." But you can pick up a couple of percentage points in yield by switching to short-term (2-year) bond funds.

When stocks tumble, short-term bond prices may also decline. But the drop may be small, provided that the fund is managed conservatively. If you have no emergency need for cash, you can hold your short-term bond fund until it recovers and earn perhaps 25 percent more than if you had stuck with money market funds. If an emergency does overtake you at a time when bond prices are down, selling your short-term fund should result in only a modest loss.

I specified a *conservatively managed* fund because some short-term funds—including those with "government income" in their names—hold highly speculative securities (derivatives—page 749). In a poor market they could dive 20 percent or more in price. For that matter, long-term bonds can dive, too.

How to Avoid High-Risk Bonds and Bond Funds. Bond expert Theresa Havell of Havell Capital Management in New York City asks four questions about any bond she buys:

What's the credit quality? You're shopping in the triple-A to single-A range (page 762). Ask a bond fund what its average credit quality is.

What's the duration? For a full explanation of duration, see page 746. Short durations shield you from too much risk; long durations expose you to wild and risky price swings and explain the sudden losses that can occur in government bond funds when interest rates go up. An optimal duration is 3 to 3.5 years, Havell says. At that point on the spectrum, you've increased your yield without adding too much extra risk. A speculative duration is 6 years or longer.

What's the volatility? This one is trickier. A fund may appear to have a short duration, but if interest rates drop, the duration may lengthen. The fund's price may plunge further than you believed it could. That's because the fund buys risky derivatives (page 749), the bond market's toxic waste. You can guess that they're present if the fund yields markedly more than its peers. You can also guess that the manager is irresponsible, because risky derivatives don't belong in retail "government" funds. Fund investors buy governments for stability, not thrills. (Mortgage-backed securities like Ginnie Maes have changing durations, but those particular investments can't work any other way. You simply have to be prepared—page 765.)

What's the currency? Stick with dollar-denominated bonds. Foreign-currency bonds will go bad if the value of the dollar rises (page 814).

Try to evaluate all four risks. Alternatively, stick with Vanguard bond funds (page 784), which don't take hidden risks and behave as expected in the market.

How to Get High Yields on Bonds. Flip the advice in the previous paragraphs. Look at bonds of lower credit quality, longer durations, more volatility, or denominated in other currencies. You take on more risk, which may or may not be rewarded over your holding period. You will never get high yields *and* certainty in the same bond or bond fund.

BONDS VS. BOND MUTUAL FUNDS

Whether to buy a bond or a bond fund is often a tough call. Whereas stock investors clearly belong in mutual funds, many bond investors may be better off owning bonds individually. Here are the issues. You decide.

The Case for Buying Individual Bonds:

1. *You can stack the deck so you won't lose money.* For example, you might buy Treasuries that will mature when you'll need the funds. That spares you the risk of selling early and guarantees that you'll get your principal back. Or you might buy top-quality municipals with 5- to 10-year terms—again, presuming that you hold to maturity. It's extremely rare for such a bond to slide into default.

By contrast, most mutual funds don't offer you a maturity date, so you aren't guaranteed a fixed return. You can't even be sure that, on the day you sell, you'll get all your principal back. Everything depends on the fund's market value at the time.

2. *It's cheaper to buy individual bonds than mutual funds as long as you stick with bonds that are newly issued.* With new bonds you get the same price that the big institutions pay and the issuer swallows the sales

commission. At maturity or when the bond is called, you can redeem it through the issuer's paying agent at no fee.

With mutual funds, on the other hand, you pay up front or annual fees (often both), the amount depending on the fund you choose. These fees reduce your investment returns.

One warning: Your costs go up if you buy older bonds out of a stockbroker's inventory. The broker will be eager to sell because these bonds carry lucrative price markups—up to 5 percent and sometimes more. But mutual funds get much better prices on older bonds than you ever will. You have an edge only if you stick with new-issue bonds.

3. *You probably can't afford much diversification when you buy individual bonds.* But that doesn't matter if you invest in Treasury securities. You should also be okay with municipals rated A or better that mature within 10 years or less; there's only a minuscule risk that munis won't pay on time. Ditto when you buy the bonds of America's leading companies.

When you buy individual bonds of any sort, your main concern, after quality, is holding period. You should feel sure that you won't have to sell the bond before maturity. Small holdings can't be sold early at a decent price. To test your certainty, ask yourself this: Could I afford to keep this bond even if I lost my job? Or even if the value of all my other investments dropped?

The minimum investment on individual bonds is generally $5,000 for corporates and municipals, $5,000 on shorter-term Treasury notes, and $1,000 on longer-term Treasury notes and bonds.

Conclusion: Buy individual bonds if: (1) you'll buy new issues; (2) you'll buy Treasuries or other top-quality bonds, so default won't be an issue; (3) you'll hold the bonds until maturity; (4) you want fixed interest to live on; (5) you'll reinvest every penny if you don't need to live on the interest. Otherwise, the purchasing power of your capital will steadily decline. (With zero-coupon bonds, your interest is reinvested automatically— page 779).

The Case for Buying Bond Mutual Funds:

1. *Your dividends can be reinvested automatically, earning the same yield that the bond fund pays.* To get a similar result with individual bonds, you have to buy zero-coupons. (Reinvestment options aren't material, however, if you plan to live on the income from your bonds.)

2. *You can invest small sums.* The initial purchase may be $1,000 to $3,000, after which you can make small, regular contributions. Even smaller contributions are accepted in an Individual Retirement Account or 401(k).

3. *If you think you can hold for several years but might need the money earlier, a mutual fund is a safer buy.* Fund shares can be redeemed at a better price than you'd get for individual bonds that you're forced to sell before maturity.

You can minimize costs by buying no-load (no-sales-charge) funds. Funds containing similar kinds of bonds perform very much alike, so the lowest-cost players should win the day.

4. *A short-term bond fund may yield more than short-term Treasuries, even after fees.* That's because the fund contains some corporate securities, which deliver higher returns.

5. *Funds make sense for investors who want to speculate on a decline in interest rates.* When interest rates fall, bond values rise and you could sell your fund shares for a capital gain. The value of individual bonds would increase, too, but you wouldn't get as good a price if you tried to sell. Speculators should buy only no-loads; gains melt away when you have to pay front-end or back-end sales commissions.

6. *You get a lot of diversification for a small amount of money.* This is critical to investors attracted by the higher yields on medium- to low-grade bonds. Some of the lower-grade bonds may default. To minimize that potential loss, you need to own a piece of many different issues.

Conclusion: You should buy bond funds if: (1) you are guessing that interest rates will fall (good luck!); (2) you have only a modest amount of money (less than $10,000) and don't want to buy Treasuries or high-grade municipals; (3) you want to make regular, small contributions; (4) you aren't sure of your holding period and want to be able to sell at current market value at any time; (5) you want to speculate in lower-quality bonds and therefore need broad diversification; (6) you want the discipline of automatic dividend reinvestment; (7) your investment will be short-term.

To me, the answer to the question "bonds or funds?" turns on these points: (1) Do you demand, to a high degree of certainty, that by a specific date you will get all your capital back, in addition to all the interest you've earned? If so, buy high-quality bonds, not funds. (2) Do you need a lot of flexibility, to sell intermittently and invest small amounts of money? If so, buy bond mutual funds.

Is there a case for buying bonds in a unit trust? I'm skeptical, although unit trusts are widely sold for this purpose. (Read more about them, starting on page 793.)

The Case for Buying No Bonds at All. Buy stocks for growth. Make your other investment cash, not bonds, and keep it to a minimum. When stock prices rise, you'll be holding a higher percentage of your assets there, so the riskiness of your total portfolio will increase. When the market falls, you'll suffer sharper, temporary losses than if you also held some bonds. But your gains should be greater in the long run.

Alternatively, you can keep your market risk at the level you started with. Do this by selling stock when the market rises and adding the proceeds to your cash reserve. When stocks fall, use your cash to buy. Hold your cash in a money market mutual fund or Treasury bills. This kind of portfolio can outperform a mixed portfolio of stocks and bonds, and with less risk when the market drops.

The Case for Owning a Higher Percentage of Bonds Than You Probably Do, Even If You're Young. Over 5-year periods you don't know which type of asset will perform the best—stocks, bonds, or cash. A particularly good time to buy bonds has been when stock dividends are low. Historically, that has yielded competitive returns for bond investors over the following 10 years, compared with stocks (although let me read you every investor's Miranda warning: past performance doesn't guarantee future results). At this writing, the dividends paid by the stocks in the S&P 500 are the puniest ever—just 1.7 percent (a high dividend ratio would be 5 or 6 percent). In these circumstances, bonds show the same or greater potential for gain than stocks and a smaller potential for loss—*if* history repeats.

THREE ABSOLUTELY WRONG THINGS TO DO WITH BONDS

1. Do not—repeat, NOT—invest most or all of your pension-plan money in bonds when you're young or middle-aged. This is a waste of your precious youth. Adjusted for inflation (and, eventually, taxes if you're using retirement money), bonds give you only modest growth. Younger and middle-aged people need significant holdings of stocks. You still need stocks in retirement, too,

2. You should not—repeat, NOT—assume that tax-free bonds are always the best for that portion of your portfolio devoted to bonds. Tax-free municipals yield less than taxable bonds. To profit, you have to be in the 28 percent federal tax bracket and up. (For more on this point, see page 775.) If you're in a lower bracket or are investing tax-deferred retirement money, go for taxable bonds. In retirement accounts, corporates outperform Treasuries because of their higher yields. Outside retirement accounts, where your interest is taxable every year, Treasuries beat corporates in most states. That's because Treasuries are exempt from state and local income taxes.

3. You should not—repeat NOT—put most or all of your money into long-term bonds and CDs at retirement in order to live on the income. This advice may startle you because buying more bonds or bond funds is the first thing many new retirees do. But they're typically only 60 to 65. The value of their bond income will wilt even with low inflation rates. By age 70, you will be poorer and won't be able to restore the value of your capital. That won't matter if your life span is short—but who can tell? You normally shouldn't tip toward bonds until your mid-70s. (For more on investing at retirement, see page 936.)

You should not—repeat NOT—pay any attention to this particular piece of advice if you're scared of stocks, don't know anything about them, and can live on your pension, Social Security, and interest income. In this instance, you might not even want a bond mutual fund because it will occasionally show a loss. You especially don't want a bond investment that pays a higher-than-normal yield (it also carries a higher-than-normal risk).

People unwilling to tolerate occasional losses are candidates for Treasuries and bank CDs. As the value of the fixed portion of your income shrinks, you can compensate by dipping into capital (the longer you live, the fewer years you have left and the less capital you will need for future expenses).

Financial advisers can yammer away about optimal returns until they're blue in the face. What you deserve from your money—more than anything else—is the sense that you're *secure*.

For an explanation of how best to use bonds for income, jump to page 755. But you'll understand the strategy if you first learn how bonds work.

THE BOND BUYER'S MANTRA

Repeat after me:

Falling interest rates are good. When interest rates fall, bond prices rise. If you hold a bond mutual fund, its share price will go up.

Rising interest rates are bad. When interest rates rise, bond prices fall. If you hold a bond mutual fund, its share price will decline.

These basic principles of bond investing inform every paragraph of this chapter, so remember them.

If you buy individual bonds and hold to maturity, changes in market price don't matter. When the bond matures, you will get your money back. If you buy bond mutual funds and hold for more than 10 years, you may also make money even if interest rates go up. That's because the fund keeps buying new bonds at those higher rates, and the extra interest eventually overcomes your loss of principal. But you do have to stick with the fund for a good long time—longer than many investors are willing, or able, to wait.

WHAT'S A BOND WORTH?

Bonds have several values:

The Principal. When you put up $1,000 for a new bond, you will get $1,000 back on the day the bond matures. That's your principal. The bond's face value is known as *par*.

The Price. When you read that a bond costs 100, that means $1,000. It's "100 percent of the par value." When you read that a bond costs 95.25, that means $952.50, or 95.2 percent of the par value. To get the dollar price, you add a zero to the quote.

The Interest. Most bonds pay interest semiannually on your money. This is called the *coupon*. A $1,000 bond paying $70 a year ($35 semiannually) has a coupon interest rate of 7 percent.

The Market Price. If you want to sell your bond before maturity, the price will depend on market conditions. Remember your mantra. If interest rates have risen since your bond was issued, your bond is worth less than it was when you bought it. If interest rates have fallen, your bond is worth more. This is the most critical fact about bond investing and the least understood. The interest payments you get from your bond remain the same. But the market price continually adjusts, so your bond always yields the return that investors currently demand. This makes no difference if you plan to hold your bond until maturity. But it makes a big difference if you want to sell ahead of time.

The table on page 744 shows how the bond market works. The left-hand column shows how interest rates might change. The right-hand column shows the effect of these changes on the price of a particular bond.

KEEPING IT SIMPLE

When you buy individual bonds, always buy new issues. These are bonds newly offered to the public by government bodies or corporations. The issuer pays the broker's commission. You get a prospectus explaining what the money is being raised for and what is backing your interest and principal payments.

New-issue bonds come at an honest market price. No one can monkey around with the stated yield. On the whole, new-issue transactions are simple, sweet, and clean.

This is really all you need to know about buying individual bonds.

MESSING IT UP

What gets you into trouble is buying older bonds. Dealers have huge inventories of these bonds, so one can be found that exactly serves your purpose. Older bonds are part of the so-called secondary market.

What's wrong with buying older bonds? In a word, price. All things

HOW BOND PRICES CHANGE

What happens in the market	What happens to your bond
You buy a new 30-year bond. You pay its par value and earn a 6 percent coupon.	Your $1,000 bond, at 6 percent interest, pays you $60 a year.
Immediately, market conditions change. Newly issued bonds now have to pay 6.5 percent in order to attract investors.	The market value of your $1,000 bond drops to $934.* Its fixed $60 interest payment now produces a 6.4 percent current yield. You have an unrealized loss on your investment of $66. The bond is said to be priced at a *discount.*
Immediately, market conditions change again. Newly issued bonds now have to pay only 5.5 percent in order to attract investors.	The market value of your $1,000 bond rises to $1,073.* Its fixed $60 interest payment now produces a 5.6 percent current yield. You have earned $73 on your original investment. The bond is said to be priced at a *premium.*
Thirty *(zzzz)* years later . . .	You have collected a total of $1,800 in interest payments ($60 a year). The market value of your bond might have dropped to $900 in some years and risen to $1,100 in others. When the value was high you could have sold for a profit. If you didn't, you'll redeem it for $1,000— the 6 percent return you bargained for.

* I'm rounding these numbers.
SOURCE: Ian MacKinnon, The Vanguard Group, Valley Forge, Pennsylvania

being equal, an older bond costs more than a new one because of the dealer's markup—the additional sum that is added to the wholesale price. Sometimes these markups are excessive.

The biggest markups (and sales commissions) are usually on longer-term and zero-coupon bonds (page 779). There are also big markups on all the firm's garbage—bonds of poor credit quality or oddball bonds with virtually no resale market. Those are the bonds that many brokers push. Incidentally, these markups don't show on your confirmation statement. Any sales commission disclosed will represent only a portion of the real price you paid.

Many firms do enforce honest markups. In general, says former stockbroker Mary Calhoun, you are being overcharged if any retail markup or broker's commission exceeds 2 points ($20) per bond on long-term bonds or one point ($10) on intermediate-term bonds. According to industry guidelines, firms are not supposed to clip you for more than 5 percent. Naive investors have been charged 6 to 10 percent—and double that, if they both sell and buy. Some dealers have been caught adding 15 percent markups to zero-coupon bonds. By contrast, institutional investors pay $2.50 to $5.

If, for some reason, you can't wait for the right kind of new-issue bond and are forced to buy an older one in the secondary market (where I would go only at gunpoint), try these strategies for uncovering the markup:

1. Ask your broker. He or she is supposed to disclose the markup if the bond came out of the firm's own inventory, and reputable brokers always will. If you don't trust your broker, ask to see the inventory list where markups are disclosed. They're written in code, so ask for the codebook.

2. If the bonds come from another broker's inventory, they will be listed in the daily Blue List of bonds for sale. Ask your broker for a photocopy of the page. (But those prices are "indication only." They drop when a sophisticated investor presses for better terms.)

3. Write down your broker's price quote. Then call a second broker (maybe a discount broker) and ask what you could sell that bond for today. The difference between that day's buying price and selling price is the first broker's markup. If the first broker is overcharging, confront him or her and demand a better price. Or ask the second broker to find you a more competitively priced bond. (Investors with large accounts should work with two brokers routinely. You want them to compete for your business with the best prices and ideas.)

4. Besides the markup, ask your broker for the bond's current yield, the yield to maturity, and the yield to first call (these terms are all explained in the following section). With a new issue, all these yields are roughly the same. But they may all be different when you buy on the secondary market. An unscrupulous broker may quote you only the highest one.

5. When asked about markups, some brokers will pull a how-dare-you-mistrust-me act. Ignore it. Tell them it's just business. If they object, you have the wrong broker. Incidentally, your broker should be told that you always shop around for price.

THE BOND-BUYING BUZZWORDS

Once you stray off the straight-and-narrow path of new-issue bonds, you land in a briar patch. A few of the terms listed here apply to every bond. But most of them describe the pricing of older bonds that are selling for more, or less, than their face value. To explain these terms, I'll use the examples I gave in the table on page 744, starting with a $1,000, 30-year bond paying 6 percent interest.

Coupon. The fixed interest payment made on each bond. A $1,000 bond paying $60 a year has a $60 coupon. Put another way, its "coupon rate" is 6 percent. It is typically paid semiannually—$30 every 6 months.

Current Yield. The coupon interest payment divided by the bond's price. A new-issue, $1,000 bond paying $60 a year has a current yield of 6 percent. If the price of the bond dropped to $934, the current yield—still based on a $60 interest payment—would rise to 6.4 percent. (Remember your bondspeak: at $934, the price would be quoted at 93.4.)

Premium. The amount by which the bond's market value exceeds its par value. A $1,000 bond selling at $1,073 carries a $73 premium. Bond prices can go to premiums when interest rates fall.

Discount. The amount by which the bond's market value has fallen below the par value. A $1,000 bond selling at $934 is at a $66 discount. Bonds go to discounts when interest rates rise.

Call. When the issuer decides to redeem a bond before its maturity date. For example, a bond maturing in January 2010 might be "called" in September 2000 and you'd have no choice but to surrender it. The earliest possible call date is usually specified in the bond contract. Some bonds are callable at any time. The "call price" is usually the par value plus a sweetener.

Term. Generally speaking, short-term bonds run for under 3 years. Intermediate-term bonds run up to 10 years. Long-term bonds go longer than that.

Duration. Duration doesn't affect you if you buy individual bonds and hold to maturity. It's a sophisticated measure for two groups of people: (1) investors who speculate in bonds—buying in hope of a price increase so they can sell at a profit, and (2) bond-fund investors wondering which of two similar funds carries the higher risk.

By "risk," I mean how far the fund's price might drop when interest rates rise and bond prices decline. A general measure is the fund's maturity. Long-term bonds and bond funds swing more in price than short-term bonds and bond funds do (page 743). But what about two funds of the same maturity? One might be riskier than the other because of the kinds of investments it makes.

That's where duration comes in. It estimates how violently a bond or bond fund will react to a change in interest rates. The shorter the duration the less price change you can expect.

As an example, take two 30-year bonds—one a zero bond, which pays all its interest at maturity; the other a bond that pays interest twice a year. The zero has a duration of 30 years; the other bond has a duration of 12. Put another way, the zero behaves like a 30-year bond while the other behaves like a 12-year bond. A 12-year bond will decline less in price than a 30-year bond when interest rates rise, so it carries less market risk.

When you're looking at two bond funds with similar credit ratings, maturities, and yields, ask about duration (most funds can tell you their duration over the phone). If one has a noticeably higher duration, it carries more market risk. When you take higher risks, you should be rewarded with higher yields. Some bond funds have changing durations (see "volatility," page 738). They shouldn't be offered to individual investors in the first place (except for funds that invest in mortgages).

Yield to Maturity. What your bond would earn if you held it to maturity and reinvested each interest payment at the same yield paid by the bond itself. For example, if the broker says that your yield to maturity is 6.2 percent, that assumes that every single interest payment is reinvested at 6.2 percent. If you spend your interest income or reinvest it at a lower rate, you will earn less. That's not a big deal if you buy the bond at par ($1,000). If you reinvest at less than the bond interest rate, or not at all, your true yield to maturity will be only slightly less than the original quote (you'll have to trust me on this; that's how the professionals calculate). But if you buy an older bond, there may be a marked difference between the current yield and the yield to maturity. Because of this difference, you might be flim-flammed into buying a bond that yields less than you think.

For example, say that new 10-year bonds are selling at 5.4 percent yields. Your broker calls you up one day and says, "Hey, I have this nice little number at 6 percent." "Great," you say. "Buy." You think that the bond is beating the market. But your broker doesn't mention that the bond costs $1,046, a $46 premium. At maturity, you will redeem the bond for $1,000, taking a $46 capital loss. Your yield to maturity, counting that loss, should be 5.4 percent. So you're getting less than your broker claimed. If the bond is called before maturity (as bonds selling at premiums often are), you might get less than 5.4 percent. You'd also get less if the broker charged you more than $1,046 for the bond.

The reverse is true when you buy a bond selling for less than its face value. Say you pay $946 for a $1,000 bond. At maturity, you'll have a $54 capital gain. Counting that gain, the bond's yield to maturity will be higher than its current yield. Why would you deliberately buy a bond reporting a lower current yield? Because the issuer isn't likely to call it early. You accept less current income in hope of hanging on to the bond's high yield to maturity, including its built-in capital gain. (I say "in hope" because this strategy doesn't always work. If interest rates fall far enough, these bonds, too, may rise to premiums and be subject to a call.)

Yield to First Call. This is what a bond will yield if the issuer calls it (repays it) at the earliest date the contract allows. It's also the yield you will most likely get if you buy a bond that's selling at a premium (that is, over $1,000). In the previous section I showed what the yield to maturity might be for a premium bond—that is, a bond selling for more than its $1,000 face value. But that was just an academic exercise. In real life, the issuer won't let you keep those bonds until maturity. They pay high current rates of interest, and the issuer will want to replace them with bonds paying lower rates. So the information you really need is the yield to the first date that these bonds can be called. That's your likeliest yield and holding period.

Continuing the example used in the previous section: If you paid $1,046 for the bonds and they were called the following year, your actual yield would be only 1.4 percent because of that $46 capital loss. That's something your broker probably forgot to mention. Anytime a broker offers you a bond with a high current yield, ask: (1) Is the bond selling above par (above $1,000), and if so, what is its yield to first call, or (2) is it a junk bond (page 770)? Most Treasuries cannot be called.

Total Return. Ultimately, this is the only calculation that matters! It's all the money you earn on the bond or bond fund and it comes in two parts: (1) the annual interest and (2) the gain or loss in market value, if any.

For example, take a $1,000 bond with a $60 coupon and assume that bond prices go up. If you sell that bond for $1,050, your total return that year (before brokerage commissions) is $110, or 11 percent—$60 from interest and $50 from the gain in the market price.

Or suppose that you pay $1,050 for a $1,000 bond with a $60 coupon, for a current yield of 5.7 percent. If you sell that bond one year later for only $1,000, you'll have taken a $50 loss. Your total return is $10, or 1.0 percent—$60 from the bond interest minus the $50 loss.

Out of all these yields, brokers have created so many sophisticated fiddles that I couldn't begin to understand them all. Nor would I want to. Just give me a nice new-issue bond and leave me alone. If you do buy an older bond from a broker, the only way to know what you're getting is to ask for the current yield, the yield to maturity, and the yield to first call.

MUTUAL FUND YIELDS

Many bond mutual fund managers fiddle, too, to make you think that you're earning more than is actually the case. Because of their sorry abuse of the public, the Securities and Exchange Commission (SEC) wrote a rule dictating how yields must be disclosed.

These rules cover advertising material and automated-quote services on telephone lines but not what you're told in person by a stockbroker or financial planner. So ask the broker or fund salesperson specifically for the "SEC yields." Any other yields may be misleading.

Here's what the rules say you should get: (1) the current yield for the past 30 days; (2) the yield to average maturity, which is the average maturity of all the bonds in the fund's portfolio; (3) the yield to average call, if there's a good chance that the bonds will be called before maturity; (4) the fund's total return for the latest one-, 5-, and 10-year* periods. Funds with shorter life spans have to disclose their performance from the day they began. "Total return" is their interest income plus or minus any gains or losses in the value of their shares.

You Cannot Compute Your Actual Yield from Your Dividend Check. The check might not contain every penny of this term's interest income (some of it might be in your next check). It might also include income from writing options or capital gains distributions from bonds that were sold at a profit. You have to rely on the fund to tell you what it's yielding.

HOW RISKY ARE BONDS?

In certain ways they are nearly as risky as stocks—especially the longer-term bonds. Bond risk comes in several forms.

Market Risk (part one)

The market value of your bonds will rise and fall as interest rates go down and up. If you sell, you might get more than you originally paid or you might get less, just as would happen if you sold a stock. This matters only if (1) you sell your bonds before maturity or (2) you own a bond mutual fund. Anytime you sell a mutual fund, the price is set by market rates.

Short-term bonds are safest (if they're conservatively invested) because they fluctuate the least in price. They also pay the lowest rates. Intermediate-term bonds come next. Long-term bonds fluctuate the most.

To minimize market risk: Buy a "ladder" of short- to intermediate-term bonds, as explained on page 755.

Market Risk (part two)

Two apparently similar bond funds can behave differently when interest rates change. A rise in rates may hurt one fund's price just a little bit while hurting another fund a lot. The difference may depend on how each fund uses *derivatives*—complex securities where the price of one asset depends on the price change in another asset. Some derivatives increase a

---

* Ask for the 3-year yield, too. The 10-year yield is useless unless the fund's manager has remained the same.

fund's market risk, other derivatives lower it. A fund yielding more than its peer group may be using derivatives in a speculative way. To estimate a fund's riskiness, use the Havell approach (page 737).

Holding-Period Risk

The longer it takes for your bond to reach maturity, the greater the chance that you'll have to sell ahead of time. You risk losing money when you sell early because market prices might be down.

To minimize holding-period risk, don't buy 20- and 30-year bonds. The odds of your holding that long are small. The average income investor should buy short- to intermediate-term bonds (no more than 10 years). If you're buying an intermediate bond fund, plan on holding it for at least 2 years. That's how long it took investors to recover from the worst bond market in the twentieth century (starting in May 1958).

Inflation Risk

As prices rise, both your principal and interest lose purchasing power. Take that $1,000 bond with a coupon of $60 a year. After just 5 years of 3 percent inflation, your $1,000 principal will have a purchasing power of only $862 while your $60 interest check will buy only $52 worth of goods. Your standard of living has dropped by 14 percent. And what will happen over the next 5 years, and the 5 years after that if inflation persists?

To minimize inflation risk, don't spend all the interest if you can avoid it. Instead, reinvest enough to counter the inflation rate. For example, suppose that you own a $1,000 bond and inflation is running at 3 percent. In order to maintain its purchasing power, your $1,000 principal needs to rise in value by $30. If you're earning $60 in interest, you should reinvest $30 (to bring your principal up to $1,030), pay the taxes due, and live on what's left. In a bond mutual fund, reinvestment is easy. If you own individual bonds, put that $30 into a bank or money market fund.

Call Risk

If interest rates fall, corporations and municipalities will "call in" their older, high-interest bonds and issue new ones at lower rates. Typically, you get 5 to 10 years' call protection from both corporations and municipalities. The call may come at par ($1,000) or par plus a small premium. But that's not much consolation. You will have been earning a high rate of interest. After the call you'll have to reinvest at a lower rate.

Most bonds are called through a refunding—the company issues lower-rate bonds and uses the proceeds to retire its higher-rate debt. You may also be parted from some of your bonds by a sinking fund—a lottery system for retiring a certain number of bonds each year (in which case, no sweetener is paid). A special or extraordinary redemption can occur in specified circumstances, such as changes in the economics of a project that make it unworkable.

Calls used to be one of the normal hazards of bond investing that you could hedge against successfully. Now, it's guerrilla war out there. Bond issuers tuck weasel words into the finest of print to deceive you and your broker about how early a call could come. One reason not to be a bond-holder (or to buy a mutual fund and let the fund manager worry about it) is that so many corporations and municipalities are playing fast and loose with your call protection.

What do you lose when your bonds are called? If you bought at par, your principal is returned intact (sometimes with a little sweetener). But you lose the capital gain you earned when the bond's value rose. If you paid more than the call price, you suffer an early capital loss. When a convertible bond is called, you'll lose the higher price it might have been selling for in the open market. Calls also deprive you of high bond income that would have kept you sitting pretty for many years.

To eliminate call risk, buy newly issued U.S. Treasury notes and bonds, paying current dividends. They are almost always call-proof (or not callable until 25 years have passed, which, by me, is the same thing). Plenty of intermediate-term corporate and municipal bonds are also noncallable.

If you buy in the secondary market, buy bonds with low interest payments, selling at discounts from par value. Your yield to maturity will equal that of higher-coupon bonds but your investment isn't as likely to be called. Or buy zeros that are callable only at par. If they're callable at their "accreted value" they're no better than garden-variety bonds.

Default Risk

The issuer might not pay the bond's principal and interest on time. For example, the company might go bankrupt or its loans might have to be restructured. U.S. Government bonds have no default risk. Higher-quality municipals and corporates stumble only rarely. Low-rated bonds are the ones most likely to descend into default. Most of them are corporates.

To minimize default risk, buy only higher-quality stuff. You will sacrifice some yield. A 10-year AAA bond might yield 0.5 percentage points less than a BBB-rated bond, depending on the market at the time. That's a pretty small price to pay, compared with the risk of losing money. You can also buy insured muni bonds, giving up maybe 0.15 to 0.3 percent of the yield.

The two most common bond-rating systems, from Standard & Poor's and Moody's, are shown on page 752. Admittedly, these systems aren't perfect. Companies occasionally default while they're rated A. But on the whole, the bond raters have done well at identifying winners and losers.

	Risk	Standard & Poor's*	Moody's†
Investment-Grade Bonds	Champagne, roses	AAA	Aaa
	Good enough even for the Queen	AA	Aa
	Probably fine, but down in class for a conservative investor	A	A
	Okay for now, but a daring buy for people who normally choose quality bonds	BBB	Baa
Junk Bonds*	Junk with pretensions, or "junque"	BB	Ba
	The real stuff, and risky as heck	B	B
	Junk that's showing its true colors	CCC	Caa
	Junk that smells like old fish heads	CC	Ca
	Junk that isn't paying interest anymore: on life support	C	C
	Defaulted bonds: brain dead	D	C
	Unrated bonds: bonds that neither of the major rating services have touched; probably low junk, although some small municipalities may be of high quality.		

* A plus (+) or minus (−) from S&P indicates that, within its category, the bond is relatively strong or weak. Moody's designates a strong bond with the numeral 1.

† Buying individual junk bonds is much too risky for the average investor. Instead, buy them in junk (high-yield) bond funds. Use this explanation of the ratings to check the fund's portfolio, to see how much of its assets are invested at various quality grades.

Credit Risk

If a company starts racking up losses or a municipality admits to budget deficits, the credit rating on its bonds will fall. As long as you hold those bonds, your interest payments stay the same (provided the issuer doesn't default). But if you have to sell before maturity, you'll take a beating on the price. When a company's or municipality's finances improve, its credit rating rises and so does the price of its bonds.

To minimize credit risk, check your bond's current safety rating and whether that rating is likely to change. Both Standard & Poor's and Moody's publish credit-watch lists of companies that might be downgraded or upgraded. These reports are carried regularly in the financial press. To find an issue's current rating and whether it's on a watch list, call the ratings desk at Moody's Information Center (212-553-0377) or the credit division of Standard & Poor's (212-208-1527), both in New York City.

Deception Risk

There are several ways of making you think you're earning more than is actually the case. Two examples:

1. A broker or planner may tell you that your fund's current yield (from interest and other income) is 7 percent. But that's only part of the story. If interest rates rose last year, your fund may have dropped in value—say, by 4 percent. So its total return—7 percent in income minus 4 percent in market losses—was actually only 3 percent. Quite a difference.

2. A unit trust might buy a 3-year, A-rated $1,000 bond with an 8 percent coupon interest rate that has only one year left to run. It's selling at a current yield of 7.8 percent, compared with only 5.5 percent on newly issued one-year bonds. The trust buys that bond in order to jack up its current yield. But it has to pay a fat $1,024 for it. When the bond is redeemed, the trust will take a $24 loss. The bond's actual yield to maturity is only 5.5 percent. Thus are customers duped. Salespeople are supposed to give you the current yield plus the yield to maturity, which would show what you'll really earn. Good ones do. Would that everyone were good.

To minimize deception risk: Check the prospectus for the SEC yields and the annual total returns (page 748). You can use these yields to compare one fund with another.*

Name Risk

Names can be another way of deceiving investors. Analyst Catherine Gillis of Morningstar in Chicago, which tracks mutual funds, once found 55 closed-end municipal bond funds whose names included the phrases "investment grade," "investment quality," "insured," or "quality income." Only 17 had 3-year records. Of those, 16 showed *higher*-than-average risk. Two other descriptions that can be deceptive: "short-term" and "government income."

Takeover Risk

Management, old or new, may trample on the bondholders. Suppose, for example, that you're a conservative investor who buys only quality

---

* Unfortunately, you can't compare bond-fund returns with the rates on bank certificates of deposit. The calculations don't mesh.

bonds. One day a raider attacks your company, or the company's own management does, and loads it up with debt. Your AA bond might drop to a junk rating overnight and lose value in the marketplace. To put it technically, you have been screwed. If you can hold to maturity, you will still get the principal and interest you bargained for. Your only question is whether the bonds will last until maturity.

To minimize takeover risk, consider selling the bonds of any company mentioned as a hostile takeover candidate (although you will probably take a loss). At this writing, hostile takeovers are rare.

A BOND STRATEGY
FOR INCOME INVESTORS

You are an income investor if you expect to live on the monthly checks that your capital produces. You don't reinvest your dividends and interest, you take the money and spend it. For bond buyers, there's a right way and wrong way to go about this.

The Wrong Way to Get Income from Your Bonds

The wrong way, in my view, is to buy a lot of long-term bonds. This conclusion may surprise you because "long bonds" usually pay the highest interest rates. The year you buy them, you'll earn some real spending money, even after inflation and taxes.

So you love Year One. Year Two, however, isn't quite so terrific. Both your capital and your income lose purchasing power. By Year Three you are barely breaking even, after taxes and inflation. By Year Four, you are probably in the hole. Each subsequent year your bond income buys you less and less. How much less depends on the inflation rate.

• If inflation holds steady or declines, you'll get poorer slowly, losing a modest amount of purchasing power every year. For extra money, you may have to sell some bonds before maturity. If interest rates have fallen the sale might yield a modest profit, but you'll take a loss if interest rates are up. Small amounts of municipal bonds may be virtually unsalable. Your money may still stretch over your lifetime, but you can't be sure. If your savings are small, the diminished real value of your bonds may force you to reduce your standard of living in later years.

• If the rate of inflation rises, the purchasing power of both your capital and your income will take a devastating hit. You will have to use up your money at a much faster rate than you had planned or cut back sharply on expenses.

• Only if average consumer prices drop and soon—in other words, the country enters true deflation—will you be glad you're collecting income from long-term bonds. In that case, your purchasing power would rise (provided that you owned noncallable Treasury bonds; corporates or municipals would be called by their issuers, robbing you of your high-interest income). But deflation is an outside bet. Americans lived through bouts of deflation in the 1870s, parts of the 1880s and 1890s, and the 1930s, but not since.

Why take any of these risks when you can pursue a sensible income strategy with intermediate-term bonds instead? The extra yield you get from long bonds may be in the 0.5 percent range. That's a pretty skinny bonus for putting your money at such hazard.

The Right Way to Get Income from Your Bonds

Buy a mixture of intermediate- and shorter-term bonds. Here's why:

• They pay a reasonable income. It's less than you'd get from a portfolio of long-term bonds, but usually just a tiny bit less.

• They give you inflation protection. If interest rates rise, your maturing short-term bonds can be reinvested at a higher interest rate. That will preserve some of your purchasing power. Unlike the owners of long-term bonds, you're not chained to a fixed check.

• They protect you against the need to sell bonds before maturity, perhaps at a loss. With the right mix of bonds, you always have some that are reaching their maturity date. That gives you fresh cash to use.

• Historically, the total return on intermediate bonds—changes in principal plus interest—has been just as good as that on long-term bonds. Intermediates do a little better when inflation rises; long bonds do a little better when inflation falls. But the differences even out. So you can pursue this strategy without feeling that you're losing capital on the deal.

Here's how to carry this strategy out:

Buy bonds with maturities of one, 2, 3, 4, and 5 years—all the way up to 10 years. That's called laddering your investments. Altogether, your income might equal what you'd get from a 7-year bond. People with substantial assets will choose a ladder of municipals or Treasury securities (including zero-coupon Treasuries). It's generally assembled with the help of a stockbroker or other financial adviser. People with fewer assets can build this same ladder with bank certificates of deposit (page 66).

When your one-year bond (or CD) matures, you have a choice. If short-term interest rates are uncommonly high, you can increase your income by reinvesting for another one-year term. Alternatively (and this is the usual case), long-term rates will be higher. So you'd increase your income by reinvesting in a 10-year bond. This helps offset the hole that inflation has left in your purchasing power.

The following year your 2-year bond will come due. You'll again have a choice about where to reinvest for better returns—probably by buying another 10-year bond. Or you might fill in a particular bond maturity that's missing.

Eventually, you will have a "ladder" of 10-year bonds, some of which are maturing every year. Result: a decent income plus some inflation protection. Every year you will have fresh cash in hand. If you need money, it's there to spend. You won't be forced to raise it by selling bonds before maturity, perhaps at a loss. If you don't need money right now, you can reinvest for higher income if rates are up.

What can go wrong?

Being no dope, you have already spotted the crack in my ladder. If interest rates decline steeply, you lose. Every time one of your bonds matures, you might have to reinvest at a lower interest rate. In that case, you'd have been better off putting all your money in intermediate- or long-term bonds. But that's strictly hindsight. Standing here today, you don't know where interest rates will go. You have to be ready for anything. The ladder gives you liquidity and choice.

Even if interest rates do decline, bond ladders don't have to lower your income right away. In the first year, for example, you would reinvest the proceeds of your one-year bond in a 10-year bond. Assuming that 10-year rates are higher, your income might rise, even if rates in general are coming down. The risk of reinvesting at lower rates may not arise until most of your bonds are in the 7- to 10-year range.

You might include some long-term bonds to hedge against the risk of declining rates. Hold them for the rest of your life. If they have to be sold at a loss before maturity, let your heirs do it. For them, it's free money anyway.

Two Critical Backstops for Income Investors

1. Don't put all of your money in bonds, regardless of their maturity. Going back to the table on page 744, you can see that adding stocks improves your returns while reducing risk. You might keep 70 to 80 percent of your money in bonds, for the interest they produce, and put the remainder in stocks.

Which kinds of stocks? Income investors will probably go for equity-income funds or blue-chip stocks with a history of dividend increases. But looking only at dividends is taking too narrow a view of how one can get income from stocks. Capital growth is a source of income, too. As your stocks rise in value over time, sell some of the shares and spend the money. It makes sense to supplement bond interest with cash withdrawals from stock-owning mutual funds (page 630).

2. You might add some zero-coupon bonds (page 779) to the mix. The financial adviser who figured out the strategy I'm about to explain calls it his "nursing-home bailout program." Pretend you're the client, and think about it this way.

"I'm 60, I own my house, and statistics say I have 22 years to live. I want to live well.

"I'll divide my capital into money to spend and money to save. The spending money will be deployed partly in short- and intermediate-term bonds and partly in conservative dividend-paying, stock-owning, no-load mutual funds. My savings will go into 22-year zero-coupon bonds and a small amount of stock-owning mutual funds.

"Over the next 22 years, I will consume every dime in my spending account—all the bonds and all the mutual funds. I'll tap the funds through annual cash withdrawals. I'll spend a certain percentage of my bonds as they mature. I have figured out a spending rate that gives me a reasonable chance of maintaining a steady standard of living.

"If I'm still breathing after 22 years, I will turn to my savings stash. There, my stocks will have gained and my zeros will have matured. That gives me a fresh pot of capital to sustain the remainder of my life. If I have to enter a nursing home, my stocks, my zeros, and the value of my house should pay for quality care."

That's what I call a creative use of bonds!

Mutual Funds for Income Investors. Can you "ladder" with bond mutual funds? No, because most bond funds have no maturity date. For true ladders, you need individual bonds or bank CDs.

But you get a similar effect by owning a combination of short- and intermediate-term funds. Leave all your dividends in the funds to be reinvested. For the income you need, make regular, fixed withdrawals from each—once a year or on a monthly cash-withdrawal plan. (Mutual fund cash-withdrawal plans are enormously useful to income investors and insufficiently understood—page 630.)

Here are some no-load mutual fund groups that offer both short- and intermediate-term funds: American Century–Benham in Kansas City, Missouri; the Dreyfus Corporation in Uniondale, New York; the Fidelity group in Boston; T. Rowe Price in Baltimore, and Vanguard in Valley Forge, Pennsylvania. Minimum investments are $1,000 to $3,000. You can buy the funds of different groups through one of the mutual fund supermarkets (page 632). One-stop shoppers should consider T. Rowe Price's Spectrum Income Fund, which diversifies your investment over bonds of a variety of maturities, credit quality, and countries.

A BOND STRATEGY FOR
PRESERVING PURCHASING POWER

If you don't need to live on the income from your bonds, you can use that money to maintain the purchasing power of your capital. Here's how:

Buy individual, high-quality, intermediate-term bonds—perhaps 5- to 10-year Treasuries. They're safe and you owe no state or local income taxes on the interest. If you buy zero-coupon bonds, your interest will be reinvested automatically at the same rate of interest you earn on the bond itself (page 779). If you don't buy zeros, reinvest every dime that you earn —in Treasury notes if you earn enough, or else in a money market mutual fund. You might pick a money fund fully invested in Treasuries, so state and local taxes won't be due on those dividends either.

In you're in the 28 percent bracket or higher and investing outside a retirement plan, consider tax-free municipal bonds instead.

Don't buy your securities all at once. Buy some next year, too, so you'll cover a range of interest rates. Your money won't grow much in real terms but your purchasing power will be preserved.

Can You Do It with Mutual Funds? Yes, but only if your holding period is long enough. You'll succeed with ease if interest rates stay roughly level or decline. But if interest rates rise, the value of your fund will drop and you may have to hold many years to catch up. So you run a risk.

But mutual funds have an ace in the hole. You can reinvest small dividend payments at the same yield as the mutual fund returns, which is better than you'd get from a money market fund.

A BOND STRATEGY FOR
TOTAL-RETURN INVESTORS

Total-return investors want capital growth. They don't care if it comes from stocks, bonds, dividends, interest, or capital gains. They just want to make money after taxes and inflation.

You might think that bonds could be the ticket, especially some long-term bonds. If interest rates fall significantly, bond prices will rise, producing a handsome capital gain.

But if interest rates fall, stocks will probably rise even faster than bonds. There's more risk in stocks. Still, they're the main chance for anyone going for maximum returns.

Bonds normally play a supporting role. Use them to preserve part of your capital so you'll always have something to fall back on. That means owning some bonds or bond funds of intermediate terms and reinvesting all the interest. With Treasuries or high-quality tax-exempts in your back pocket, you can feel more confident about braving the near-term risks of stocks.

A BOND STRATEGY FOR INTEREST-RATE SPECULATORS

Here's where long-term bonds come in. They're a terrific speculation on the direction of interest rates.

Suppose you're convinced that interest rates are going to drop. Remember your mantra: Falling interest rates are good. Falling interest rates mean profits. When interest rates fall, bond prices rise. To your mantra, add this corollary (no modern mantra is without its corollary): the longer the term of the bond, the bigger the profit when interest rates decline.

The following table shows exactly how much bigger. If you put $10,000 into Treasuries and interest rates dropped one percentage point over 12 months, you'd pick up only $97 on a one-year bill—a gain of less than one percent. But you'd get $1,637 on a 30-year bond, for a 16.4 percent gain. The potential gain on a 30-year zero-coupon bond is a huge 34 percent. Conversely, if interest rates rose, the longer-term bonds would lose the most.

The nerviest speculators buy Treasury bonds on margin, putting up 10 percent of the cost and borrowing 90 percent. They go for zeros, where the price swings are biggest. You can make huge profits if your timing is right and take huge losses if it isn't.

Take the 30-year zero shown in the table. Assume you bought it on 90 percent margin, putting up 10 percent of the cost and borrowing 90 percent from your broker. If, over the next year, interest rates fell by one percentage point, you'd earn a 277 percent profit before interest charges and commis-

| | THE GAIN OR LOSS ON A $10,000 INVESTMENT WHEN INTEREST RATES: | |
TREASURY SECURITY	FALL BY 1%*	RISE BY 1%*
1-year	$ 97	$ −95
5-year	443	−421
10-year	798	−729
20-year	1,310	−1,110
30-year	1,637	−1,312
30-year zero	3,400	−2,527

* Assuming a 5.5 percent yield on all issues.
SOURCE: Ian MacKinnon, The Vanguard Group, Valley Forge, Pennsylvania

sions—big-time leverage! But if rates rose one percent, you could poten-tially suffer as much as a 316 percent loss (in the real world, you'd get margin calls and would probably bail out).

Speculators should buy only Treasury bonds. Unlike corporates or mu-nicipals, most Treasuries cannot be called away from you if interest rates decline. They will pay today's rates for 25 years or more.

Can You Do This with Mutual Funds? Yes, by buying shares in any low-cost Treasury-bond fund (interest-rate speculation is the *only* reason for buying Treasuries in funds). To get the most bang for your buck, choose the zero-coupon bond funds run by the American Century Funds (Kansas City, Missouri). If you go through certain discount brokers, you can even buy them on margin.

In a typical market cycle, bond prices rise before stock prices do. A speculator would swing first into long-term Treasuries and then into stocks.

A BOND STRATEGY FOR HISTORIANS

Some investors get scared every time rates pop up, for fear they portend a drift back to double-digit price increases. But that's not likely. From 1791 to 1996, U.S. prices rose at an annual compound rate of only 1.45 percent, and that included three periods of inflation greater than those we experi-enced in 1980.*

Inflationary spasms are usually followed by periods of zero inflation or even deflation, when prices fall. Here's the record of American price changes:

U.S. PRICES, 1792–1996*

RATE OF PRICE CHANGE	HOW OFTEN THOSE CHANGES TOOK PLACE
Over 1%	54% of the time
Under 1%	20% of the time
Stability	26% of the time

* Annual compound rate.
SOURCE: The Leuthold Group, Minneapolis

In stable periods, long-term U.S. Treasury bonds yield around 5 per-cent. When rates are higher than that, they have room to fall.

---

* Those periods were the 1790s, 1860s, and 1910s, computed on a moving-average basis. For this data, my thanks to investment adviser Steven Leuthold, who, in 1980, published an insightful book, *The Myths of Inflation and Investing.* Among its little treasures was a 1,000-year history of consumer prices in the Western world. He found that prices rose about 61 percent of the time and fell about 39 percent of the time. The annual compound inflation rate ran at less than one percent —suggesting that, over time (sometimes over a lot of time), market economies stabilize themselves.

A BOND STRATEGY FOR LOSERS

Not *real* losers, just losers this year. If interest rates rise and your bonds show a substantial loss, you can do a tax swap that actually leaves you better off. Here's how:

1. Sell the bonds to realize the loss.

2. Use the proceeds to buy other bonds at the market's current, lower prices. The swap extends the maturity of the investment and your yield to maturity drops a bit (that's the price of the transaction). But you wind up with roughly the same interest income you had before.

3. Use the loss in bonds to tax-shelter any capital gains you took this year or to offset $3,000 of your ordinary income. Carry any additional losses forward and use them on future tax returns.

4. Be sure not to buy exactly the same bonds. If you do so within 30 days, you can't claim the loss.

Tax-loss swapping doesn't work as neatly with mutual funds as it does with bonds. After selling fund shares, you'd park your money for 30 days, then buy the shares back. Alternatively, you could switch into another fund. This works only with no-load mutual funds because they have no sales charges. Paying front-end or rear-end sales charges may erase any tax you save.

Before hustling to sell a fund, find out if you really have a loss. If you bought several years ago and reinvested the dividends, you may still be ahead.

Warning: If you buy bonds for less than their face value and eventually realize a profit, that profit is taxed as ordinary income, not a capital gain. So what you save in taxes today might be repaid in taxes tomorrow.

THE BOTTOM LINE ON BONDS

Speculators should buy long-term bonds and bond funds, especially zero bonds. They're a bet on the direction of interest rates, just as stocks are a bet on dividends and profits. If interest rates fall, long-term bonds will yield high returns. If interest rates rise, however, long-term bonds will tank.

Income investors should look to a ladder of intermediate- and short-term bonds or CDs, or cash-withdrawal plans from intermediate- and short-term bond funds backed up by dividend-paying stocks.

For investors still building their long-term retirement savings, bond investments have a single purpose: to preserve the purchasing power of that portion of your capital that you want to keep safe (say, 10 to 30 percent of your money). By buying 5- to 10-year Treasuries or other intermediate-term bonds and reinvesting the dividends, you provide yourself with a rock to stand on while the rest of your money is deployed for growth.

A bond mutual fund is *not* a bond—a point essential for any bond investor to grasp! With a bond, you always get your principal and interest at maturity (as long as the issuer doesn't default). With a bond fund, you can't be certain of what you'll earn over your holding period because your fund's value fluctuates. When you sell, you may get more than your original investment, plus the interest it earned. Or you may get less, depending on market conditions at the time.

DECISION TIME: WHICH BONDS TO BUY? HOW TO BUY THEM?

You now have (I hope) a theory of bonds. You know why you want them and how you'll use them. The next step is to choose the bonds that will serve you best.

When buying individual bonds, always look to the credit rating (page 752). AAA and AA are top quality, while A might be called a "business risk." BBB is on the very cusp of investment quality. One slip and it's junk. If you'd buy the stock, why wouldn't you buy the bond? Because bonds aren't as easily sold in small amounts. Individual bonds are bought through discount brokers, full-service stockbrokers, and some banks. Treasury bonds can also be bought directly from the Federal Reserve.

When choosing an open-ended mutual fund, go through the selection process outlined in Chapter 22. Also, take a look at the funds that are named here. They were picked in 1997 by the firm of Brouwer & Janachowski, Inc., in Tiburon, California, which invests $500 million of its clients' money in no-load mutual funds (minimum account, $1 million). The list includes both no-load funds that you buy yourself and load funds sold through stockbrokers and financial planners. For especially good value, look at the MAS and PIMCO institutional funds, available only through certain discount brokers (try Jack White at 800-233-3411 or Charles Schwab at 800-435-4000). For some tips on choosing closed-end bond funds, see page 641.

Treasury Bonds

No bond is safer than a Treasury. Other bonds pay higher interest rates. But Treasuries' strong advantages may matter more.

Treasuries, Defined:

Medium-term Treasuries run from 2 to 10 years and are called *notes*. Minimum investment for new issues: $5,000 for 2- and 3-year notes; $1,000 for longer terms. Long-term Treasuries, called *bonds,* are issued today at 30-year maturities, with a minimum investment of $1,000. You can buy them from the Federal Reserve or through a stockbroker or bank. (Treasuries of one year or less, called *bills,* are generally for savers, not investors; see page 192.)

When I say that Treasuries are "safe," I mean only that the interest and principal payments will always be made on time. Treasuries are exposed to the same market risk as any other bonds. If you sell before maturity, you might get more or less than you paid, depending on market conditions at the time. You have to hold to maturity to be sure of getting all your capital back.

Treasuries don't pay as much income as other bonds of comparable maturities, but the interest is taxed only at the federal level, not by states and cities. So the net difference in income isn't as large as it seems. For people in high state tax brackets, Treasuries may yield more.

Most Treasuries pay fixed interest rates, but some are indexed to inflation.

Why You Might Want a Treasury:

1. You might want a bond with no credit risk. Treasuries will never be downgraded or default.

2. Treasury bonds are noncallable, at least for the first 25 years. If you're speculating on declining interest rates and win your bet, these are the only high-rate bonds that you'll be able to hang on to. Corporate and municipal bonds will be called away (page 750).

3. Treasuries are liquid. If you have to sell before maturity, you get better prices on them than on other kinds of bonds.

4. You can buy Treasuries from the Federal Reserve, paying no brokerage commission (page 203).

The Drawbacks:

1. In return for their safety and liquidity, Treasuries yield less than other bonds of comparable maturities.

2. Taxpayers in top brackets net a lower current income from Treasuries than they would from tax-exempt bonds. But you might not care, in view of Treasuries' other advantages, especially their immunity to call.

Inflation-Protection Treasuries

These securities guarantee that inflation won't erode your purchasing power. Whether inflation goes up or down, you get a fixed, real return. Here's how that works:

When an issue of inflation-protection Treasuries is sold, the market sets a basic interest rate. The government credits additional interest, equal to the rise in the consumer price index. The inflation adjustment accrues semiannually. Your total return is that basic rate plus the inflation rate, no matter how high inflation runs.

As an example, say that new Treasuries pay 3 percent. If inflation is running at 3.5 percent, your total return would be 6.5 percent. If inflation is running at 5 percent, your total return would be 8 percent. After inflation, you're always left with that real return of 3 percent.

If the consumer price index ever dropped, your bond's principal would drop, too—but never below the bond's face value. So you also get a bit of protection against deflation.

There are just two little hitches: (1) Only the basic rate is paid semiannually in cash. You don't get the inflation adjustment until you sell the bond or it matures. (2) Even though you don't get the inflation adjustment in current cash, you're taxed every year as if you did.

Who should buy: Conservative savers with tax-deferred retirement accounts.

Who should not buy: People living on the income from their investments. Too little interest is paid out currently.

Products to watch for: At this writing, inflation-adjusted Treasuries are new. As the market develops, financial firms are expected to create annuities whose payments rise with inflation (of interest to retirees) and inflation-adjusted zero-coupon bonds (of interest to people saving for specific goals, such as a college education).

If you choose a Treasury, would you buy . . .

Individual Bonds? Absolutely yes. You don't need to diversify because Treasuries carry no credit risk. So there's no point paying a mutual fund's annual management fee. You can buy your Treasuries directly from a Federal Reserve branch or bank, paying no sales commission (page 203). If you buy through a broker or commercial bank, you'll be charged their normal bond commissions.

You can also redeem your bond through the Fed at maturity, but not before. If you want to sell early, the Fed would have to transfer your Treasury to something called the commercial book-entry system to make it accessible to stockbrokers. Anyone who expects to sell before maturity should buy through a broker or bank (for details, see page 203).

Always buy newly issued Treasuries if you can get the maturity you want. When you buy existing bonds, the bank or broker who sells them will mark up the price—perhaps to more than you should pay (to get a fair price, see page 745). Treasuries are ideal for the "ladder" suggested on page 756. If you don't need current income, reinvest all the interest you earn in order to maintain the purchasing power of your capital.

A Mutual Fund? No. You'll net more money, more securely, by buying Treasuries individually. If you want a mutual fund invested in government-insured securities, go for one with higher yields, like a mutual fund that buys Ginnie Maes. The only reason to buy Treasury funds is to speculate on a decline in interest rates, expecting to sell for a profit after a limited period of time.

Don't fall for the funds that call themselves Treasury "Plus." They try for higher yields by pursuing fancy options programs (selling calls—page 801) but they're usually at the bottom of the performance lists. If ever there were a plain-vanilla investment, it's a Treasury bond.

If you insist on a Treasury fund: Go for the lowest possible cost. That's the no-load Vanguard Fixed Income–Intermediate-Term U.S. Treasury Portfolio, Valley Forge, Pennsylvania (800-662-7447).

Ginnie Maes

A Ginnie Mae is a black-box investment whose workings you and I will never see. It's a fine, conservative bond with an appealing yield. But you have to treat it carefully. Very carefully.

Ginnie Maes, Defined:

Ginnie Mae is short for Government National Mortgage Association. It's the highest-yielding government-backed security that you can get. New Ginnie Maes often yield 0.5 to one percentage point more than Treasuries of comparable maturities—and they're guaranteed by the full faith and credit of the U.S. Government. Unfortunately, it takes at least $25,000 to buy a new issue. That's why so many investors buy their Ginnie Maes in the form of mutual funds or unit trusts (page 793).

A Ginnie Mae is a pool of individual mortgages insured by the Federal Housing Administration or guaranteed by the Department of Veterans Affairs. Your own mortgage might be in a Ginnie Mae. Every time you make a monthly mortgage payment, your bank might subtract a small processing fee and pass the remainder to the investors in that pool.

Each investor gets a pro rata share of every homeowner's mortgage payment. When a homeowner prepays a mortgage, the investors get a pro rata share of that, too.

Important! Ginnie Maes work differently from bonds. When you buy a bond, each semiannual check you get is pure interest income. At maturity you get your capital back. But with a Ginnie Mae, each monthly check is a combination of (1) interest earned and (2) a payback of some of the principal that you originally invested. At the end of the term, you'll get no capital back. It will have been paid to you already, over the life of your investment.

Suppose, for example, that you get a check for $237. Of that amount, $229 might be interest; $8 might be principal. That's an $8 bit of your original investment, returned to you. If you're living on the income from your investments, what should you do with this check? You can spend up to $229 of it because that's interest income. But you must save the remaining $8. If you spend that $8, you are consuming your principal, which is something few Ginnie Mae investors understand. The statement that comes with your check will tell you how much is interest and how much is principal.

Each month the amount of principal in your check will be a speck higher and the amount of interest a speck less. Over the term of the Ginnie Mae, you will gradually receive all your principal back. If you spend every check you get, all your principal will be gone. Conversely, if you save every check, including the interest, you will preserve the purchasing power of your capital, after taxes and inflation.

Also Important! If a broker says the fund is "government guaranteed," that means only "guaranteed against default." Principal and interest payments will always be made on time. But the feds don't insure your investment result. How much money you make on a Ginnie Mae, or a Ginnie Mae fund or unit trust, depends on investment conditions and how wisely you buy.

Why You Might Want a Ginnie Mae:

1. You like its high current yield and its government-backed proof against default. Unlike Treasuries, Ginnie Maes are fully taxable by state and local governments as well as by the federal government. So you might choose them for the "safe" portion of your tax-deferred retirement fund. They're also worthwhile in states that have no income tax.

2. If you're living on your savings, Ginnie Maes deliver attractive income to people in low tax brackets—for example, retirees with modest incomes.

The Drawbacks for investors in individual Ginnie Mae bonds and unit trusts. (The following list of risks is formidable, but plunge on. It has a happy ending.)

1. The size of your check varies every month, depending on how fast the mortgages are prepaid. This can disconcert an income investor. Some months you get more, some months you get less.

2. You have to keep track of how much of your check is interest and how much is principal. When the principal payment is small, the best way to reinvest it at a decent rate of return is to stow it in a money-market mutual fund. (A Ginnie Mae mutual fund will reinvest it for you.)

3. You may be deceived by your Ginnie Mae's high current rate of interest. A unit trust, for example, might be paying 9 percent because it is packed with older, high-rate mortgages for which the trust paid more than face value. But when those homeowners refinance, the trust will take a loss. What you thought was an 8-year 9 percent investment might turn into a 3-year 6 percent investment. *Sic transit* truth. Just as bad, you may never

realize how small your return actually was because yields on Ginnie Maes are so tough to calculate.

4. Any yield that's promised on a Ginnie Mae is only an estimate. Not until all the mortgages are finally paid can it be said with certainty what you earned. And no one will bother doing that calculation for you. So you'll never know.

5. If you have to sell your Ginnie Mae before maturity, the odds are that you'll lose money. These securities tend to rise very little in good markets and to plunge in bad ones. You might get lucky, but you never know.

6. The happy ending: you can get around most of these problems by buying Ginnie Maes in mutual funds.

If you choose a Ginnie Mae, would you buy. . .

An Individual Security? After that long list of drawbacks, how could I recommend an individual Ginnie Mae? In fact, I don't. Nor do I like the unit trusts (page 793). If you do buy an individual security, buy only a newly issued Ginnie Mae, for sale at face value. Then you can't be jerked around by a broker quoting a phony yield. Avoid at all costs a high-interest Ginnie Mae that sells for more than its face value. Its true yield, after all the mortgage prepayments, will be much lower.

Sometimes older Ginnie Maes are good deals—and they sell for less than $25,000 because some of their mortgage principal has already been repaid. But you can't easily tell the good deals from the bad, so the safest thing is to stay away.

A Mutual Fund? In my view, this is the only way of buying Ginnie Maes. Leave it to the fund manager to worry about whether he or she is getting the right price. All your principal is reinvested for you, even those $8 bits. You can reinvest the income, too. You get semiannual and annual reports of how well your fund is doing. Minimum investments are often $1,000 or so. As with any other mutual fund, however, share prices rise and fall. You risk losing money if interest rates rise. Check the prospectus to see if the fund buys any mortgages that don't carry a government guarantee.

Some Ginnie Mae funds: No-loads: Dreyfus Basic GNMA (Uniondale, New York, 800-782-6620), Vanguard Fixed Income–GNMA Portfolio (Valley Forge, Pennsylvania, 800-662-7447). A load fund: Smith Breeden Intermediate Duration U.S. Government Series.

Other Government Securities

There's an alphabet soup of government agencies that raise money from the public. Among the notes and bonds that are exempt from state and local taxes: those issued by the Federal Farm Credit System, which makes farm loans ($1,000 minimum investment), and the Federal Home Loan Banks, which make short-term loans to savings and loan associations ($10,000 minimum investment). Other securities are fully taxable. Check an agency's tax status before you buy.

Agency bonds aren't backed by the full faith and credit of the federal government, but they'd probably be bailed out in a pinch. Many agency securities have a credit line with the Treasury. They yield a hair more than Treasuries—maybe an extra 0.25 or 0.35 percent. That's $25 to $35 a year on a $10,000 investment. If you're sure that you'll hold the note to term, maybe that extra fraction is worth it. But it's not if you might have to sell before maturity. You won't get as good a price for agency notes as you would for Treasuries because the resale market isn't as broad.

How to Get the Right Price on Government Securities. In the past, it has been difficult for individual investors and their brokers to find and get the best price on government bonds. It took a lot of calling around. But now the American Stock Exchange has a special program for small investors (that means people investing $5,000 to less than $1 million). The Amex system displays complete price information for government notes and bonds, so a broker can give you a proper quote.

Corporate Bonds

Corporates pay higher interest than Treasuries. That's because they're riskier. Business conditions may cause their quality ratings to drop. Some corporate bonds default.

Corporates, Defined:

These bonds represent loans made to corporations and come in a wide range of maturities. You need at least $5,000 to invest (that's five bonds at $1,000 each). You'll get the best price if you buy bonds newly issued to the public. You could easily be overcharged if you buy older bonds out of a stockbroker's inventory (page 743). Some corporate bonds are backed by some sort of collateral, like equipment or real estate—although, in a bankruptcy, that collateral can be tough for bondholders to get their hands on. Most corporates are debentures, meaning that they're secured only by the executives' smiles.

Why You Might Want a Corporate:

1. You're investing with tax-deferred money in your retirement plan and want more interest than Treasuries pay. Corporates are fully taxable, by federal, state, and local governments.

2. You're in the 15 percent federal tax bracket. At that level, you will normally net more, after tax, from taxable corporate bonds than from tax-exempts.

3. You want higher yields than Treasuries pay and you're willing to bet that if you choose short or intermediate bonds from large, highly rated companies, they will pay interest and principal on time.

WARNING TO HOLDERS OF UTILITY BONDS: They've been the corporate of choice, for their high and reliable interest payments. But the electric utility industry is being deregulated. Some companies will continue high interest payments while others won't. Some companies with high credit ratings will suffer downgrades. These bonds aren't easy pickings anymore.

The Drawbacks:

1. You usually get only 5-year call protection on utility and telephone bonds, so if interest rates decline you won't enjoy your high interest rates for very long. Industrial bonds may offer 10-year protection.

2. The interest on corporate bonds is taxed by every government in sight—federal, state, and local. That's why corporates are principally for low-bracket investors or tax-deferred pension plans.

3. Corporates are hard to sell before maturity at a decent price. If you buy, you should plan on holding them until maturity.

4. The bond's credit rating could be cut, which would lower its market value. This matters principally to investors who might have to sell before maturity. Among the things that could hurt your bond's credit rating: business goes bad, a takeover stuffs the company's balance sheet with debt, a regulatory commission doesn't let the utility raise its rates.

5. The company might default.

If you choose a corporate, would you buy. . .

An Individual Bond? Probably, from a chip so blue you felt it would never disappoint *and* if you're buying for a short or intermediate term.

Otherwise, corporate bonds can be riskier than they seem. A merger or takeover may reduce their quality rating. In a crisis, the managers may save cash for the stockholders (including themselves) while trying to dragoon the bondholders into taking less than they're owed. When corporates are compared with Treasuries, corporates don't stand up so well. Treasuries can be bought without a sales commission and the interest they pay is free of state and local income taxes. After tax, quality corporates may yield no more than Treasuries and might even yield less. So why bother?

A Mutual Fund? Absolutely yes. If you're going for corporates, a well-managed, diversified fund is an intelligent buy. Look for a no-load (no-sales-charge) fund with a portfolio made up largely of blue chips. It will probably include some of the higher-yielding government-backed securities, like Ginnie Maes. It may also own some slightly lower-rated bonds to enhance your return and help cover its own expenses.

Some good-looking, diversified taxable bond funds—primarily invested in quality corporates but may include high-yield, government, mortgage-backed, international, and other fixed-income securities: No-loads: Dodge & Cox Income Fund (San Francisco, 800-621-3979), Harbor Bond Fund (Toledo, Ohio, 800-422-1050), Warburg Pincus Fixed Income Fund (New York City, 800-927-2874). A load fund: FPA New Income. Through discount brokers: MAS Domestic Fixed-income Portfolio, PIMCO Total Return Fund—Institutional Shares.

High-Yield (Junk) Bonds

These bonds—munis or corporates rated BB or lower—act more like stocks. Their price responds to changes in interest rates, but they also rise and fall as the economy does. They're a reasonable bet for a small portion of your portfolio if you're prepared to hold for the long term and can stomach occasional big drops in price.

Junk Bonds, Defined:

I'm always astonished by the readers who tell me they wouldn't touch junk with an eleven-foot pole (which is the pole they reserve for investments they wouldn't touch with a ten-foot pole). Then they ask what I think of their high-yield bond fund.

They're so blinded by the emotional power of words ("junk" sounding bad, "high-yield" sounding good) that they can't accept that the two are one and the same. But the higher the yield to maturity, the junkier the credit rating. In the bond markets, there is no free lunch.

Corporate junk comes from companies with poor credit ratings or none at all. The reasons vary. Some were great businesses once but have lost their touch. Some are smaller firms with good potential but not yet ready for prime time. Some were mauled by takeover artists—if not raiders, then their own management—and are now buried under debt. Some are true basket cases.

Municipal bonds get junk ratings if the project the bonds financed (such as a hospital or bridge) isn't earning enough revenue to cover the debt reliably. Cities and states with intractable budget deficits may also wind up in the junk heap.

International junk comes from countries whose financial supports are as mysterious to them as to everyone else.

Why You Might Want Junk Bonds:

For the high yield, why else? When bought in good economic times, the average junk bonds pays around 2 percentage points more than quality bonds. One problem: that's probably not enough to compensate you for the risk that the economy might sour, in which case your junk fund will drop in price—sometimes precipitously. Ideally, you'd buy junk in more skeptical times when the average bond yields 3 or 4 percentage points more.

The Drawbacks:

1. If the company or project does badly, the bond will default and you'll lose your high interest income. In reorganization, you'd be lucky to get 40 percent of your principal back. You might be forced to exchange your bonds for preferred stocks, whose value may sink so low that you'll lose even more of your money.

2. If the company or project does well, the issuer will call in its junk bonds and refinance the debt at a lower rate of interest. So you don't get to keep those lovely high yields. You endure all the risks, then are robbed of some of the rewards. Heads they win, tails you lose.

3. If you want to sell a small number of junk bonds before maturity, it is almost impossible to get a decent price. Many junkers aren't salable at all.

4. They have what Brian Mattes of the Vanguard Group of mutual funds calls "media risk." When a single junk-bond issue goes into default, the media hammer the story. Investors panic and junk-fund prices drop. But that's a terrific time to buy.

If you choose junk bonds, would you buy . . .

An Individual Bond? No, no, a thousand times no. Junk is too risky. If you're bold enough to buy these bonds at all, you need to be able to afford a portfolio of them, in the hope that your winners will cover your losers. You also need a terrific bond analyst to buy them for you. (A friend of mine sent his kids to college on a handful of well-chosen junk bonds. I mention this only as a reminder that someone can make money in anything—although not necessarily you and I.)

A Mutual Fund? For the average investor, it's the only way to go. You are gambling that, with good management, the fund's high income will more than make up for the capital you'll lose through defaults or loss of market value, especially in recessions. Junk funds are investments for people with long holding periods, not for people seeking income. You need to reinvest dividends to make up for the losses your fund will take on its underlying capital. If you spend the income, you're consuming your profits and leaving your losses to build up.

Some high-yield funds: A load fund: American High-Income Trust, Fidelity Advisor High-Yield Fund. Through discount brokers: PIMCO High Yield Fund—Institutional, MAS High-Yield Securities—Institutional.

Municipal Bonds

If you're in one of the higher tax brackets, munis net you more income than you'd earn from taxable bonds. Check the cost of diversifying. It's usually wise to own the bonds of issuers in more than one state.

Municipals, Defined:

Municipal bonds are issued by cities, states, counties, or local government entities. Munis pay less interest than taxable bonds but are exempt from federal tax. If you live in the state where the bond was issued, you're normally exempt from state taxes, too. No state taxes the bonds of Puerto Rico, Guam, and the Virgin Islands, but most of them tax the interest on bonds issued by other states. If you own an out-of-state bond in a mutual fund, that portion of your dividends will be state-taxed. In a few states, Treasuries are a better choice—either because interest income generally passes untaxed or because your munis are taxable, too.

Munis come in the same short, medium, and long maturities as any other bonds. The minimum investment is $5,000, but brokers may not accept less than $20,000. You should be able to get 10-year call protection, although some munis sneak in calls after 5 years or less.

The Case for Owning Only Your Own State's Bonds and Bond Funds.

Munis rarely default, so you probably aren't going to lose any money by owning only bonds issued in your own state. With $25,000 to invest, you'd diversify over five different issues and avoid all tax. In cities that levy income taxes, you might buy city bonds and duck local taxes, too.

The Case for Diversifying into the Bonds of Other States.

At this writing, states and cities are flush. The economy has been kind and tax revenues are flowing in. But things won't be so ducky during the next downturn, especially given the holes being poked in the social safety net. Welfare needs could overwhelm state budgets, causing credit ratings to fall.

You may not care that an issuer's credit rating slips if you own individual bonds that you plan to hold to maturity. In almost all cases, high-rated issuers pay. But occasionally they don't, and for unexpected reasons. Remember Orange County, California, rated AA, whose default arose entirely from imprudent investing.

If you own tax-exempt bond mutual funds, however, credit ratings matter a lot. A cut in an issuer's safety rating lowers the value of its bonds and reduces the share price of any fund that owns them. If your fund has a lot of that issuer's bonds, your investment could take a substantial hit.

Where state and local taxes are super-high, investors usually swallow the risk of owning only local bonds. Where taxes aren't so bad, however, check what diversification would cost. Your state will probably tax the income from out-of-state bonds—but how much is that, really, in dollar terms? A multi-state bond fund might even yield more than your one-state fund, helping to offset the tax. For the calculation you need to compare multi-state with one-state funds, see Appendix 7 (page 1013).

Bearer Bonds. If you own any munis issued before 1983, they might be *bearer bonds* without your name on them. When interest is due, you clip off the interest coupon and take it to the paying bank, which will probably charge up to $10 or so for giving you your money.

Keep those bearer bonds in a safe place! If lost they are difficult, even impossible, to replace. Anyone who finds the bonds can clip the coupons and collect the interest.

Another problem with bearer bonds: If the bond is called, you may not get the word on time. Your broker is supposed to alert you if you keep your bonds at the brokerage firm, but he or she may not notice. If you keep the bonds yourself, you're unlikely to spot the call in the newspaper listings. It will probably be printed, in flyspeck type, in a journal so obscure that not even the publisher's mother reads it. *The Wall Street Journal* and other papers print the major calls, but you might not read those, either. You'll learn about the call eventually, when you present your semiannual interest coupon at the bank and the paying agent laughs. When you turn in the bond, you'll get the principal you're owed. But once the call date has passed, your money will not have earned any interest. Virtually every bearer bond is callable now.

Since 1983 all munis have been issued in registered form, either in your name or the street name of your brokerage house. You might not get a certificate; your bond is often only a blip in a computer. If it's in your name, the interest is mailed to you directly. For bonds in street names, the interest goes to your brokerage firm, which puts the money in your account.

Munis may be sold as serial bonds, with a portion of the issue coming due every year. It's important to buy munis that will mature exactly when you'll want the money. If you try to sell before maturity, odds are you'll be offered an awful price.

When you buy, go for newly issued bonds. You'll pay the same price that the big, institutional buyers do. When you buy older bonds, you pay a higher price. Some brokers, in fact, sell older bonds at abusive markups or rook you by offering too low a price when you sell.

Municipals Come in Several Types:

1. *General obligation (GO) bonds*—backed by the taxes raised by the state or municipality. They are issued for public purposes like building schools and waste-treatment plants. GOs are the very safest munis. They rarely default. Even so, a GO's credit rating may drop if the issuer's finances weaken. That won't matter to people holding GOs to maturity as long as the issuer doesn't default. But it lowers the value of any tax-exempt mutual funds holding that issuer's bonds.

2. *Revenue bonds*—backed by revenues from the projects they were issued to finance. Some revenue bonds are of the highest quality, especially when they're issued for essential services. If the proceeds of the bond are used to build a water main, for example, the bond interest may be covered by the very money that residents pay to use the water. But revenue bonds used for hospitals, low-income housing, nursing homes, and retirement developments can be the bond world's equivalent of the Irish Sweepstakes.

3. *Industrial-development and pollution-control bonds*—a form of revenue bond used to finance buildings and equipment that will be leased to private companies. The bonds have to be for a public purpose. Revenues from the leases pay the bond interest, so their success depends on how well the private companies do. Defaults have been low so far, but these munis carry a higher degree of risk.

Some municipalities have been caught issuing "tax-exempts" to raise money for purely private purposes. The feds reclassify them as taxable. Don't buy any bonds that aren't clearly for the public good.

4. *Taxable municipals*—revenue bonds issued principally for private purposes such as stadiums and shopping centers. They may be exempt from state and local taxes, but not from federal tax. Individuals should handle them with care. They're often lower rated and won't pay off unless the enterprise succeeds.

5. *Prerefunded municipals*—higher-coupon bonds that, for complicated reasons, are effectively backed by U.S. Treasury securities. At the call date, these munis will be redeemed. If you own a muni that the issuer decides to prerefund, its credit quality and price will rise. At that point, you might want to sell the bond. If you hold to maturity, you will lose your capital gain. Alternatively, if the interest rate is rich enough, you might want to keep on collecting it for as long as you can.

6. *"Black-box" bonds*—a shorthand term for bonds issued by state and local agencies to get around state debt-limit laws. They're called black box because no one, including the brokers who sell them, is exactly sure how reliably all these bonds are backed. In a budget crunch, would the issuing agencies have the authority to pay? Who knows? Because of these uncertainties, black-box bonds sell at higher yields than other munis. They're living proof that debt-limit laws make great applause lines for politicians, but fundamentally don't work. When a government needs money, it will usually

find ways to raise it. Individuals should avoid black boxes. Stick with old-fashioned general obligation bonds and soundly backed revenue bonds.

7. *Zero-coupon municipals*—see page 779.

Are You in the Right Bracket for Tax-Free Municipals?

For a tax-free bond to make any sense, you generally have to be in the 28 percent federal bracket or higher. Occasionally, interest rates are high enough, relative to taxable bonds, to interest even those in the 15 percent bracket.

Not so the tax-free money market mutual funds. Often, these funds yield so little that they make sense only for those taxed at 31 percent and up.

In a kind of financial flag burning, some low-bracket investors buy tax-exempts purely to do the government out of a check. They don't care that their spite is costing them money. But that's chuckleheaded. Buy tax-frees only if they yield more than you'd get, after tax, from a taxable bond of the same credit quality and maturity. (And even then, you might prefer taxable Treasuries for their call protection—see page 763.)

Here's a quick-check table for finding out whether tax-free or taxable bonds make more sense for you. When making comparisons, always use bonds or bond mutual funds of equivalent maturities and credit quality. Otherwise, you might make the wrong choice.

To use this table, look down the left-hand column to find the yield of the tax-exempt bond or fund you're considering. Then read across to the column under your federal income-tax bracket. That shows the taxable yield you'd need to match the return from the tax-exempt.

Note that this table works only for Treasury securities, where no state and local taxes are owed. If you're considering a corporate bond, your breakeven yield will be a little higher. A short calculation in Appendix 7 (page 1013) shows you what a corporate would have to earn.

That appendix also provides calculations for (1) working backward from a taxable security to see what tax-exempt yield you'd need to beat it; (2) checking the taxable equivalent of tax-exempt securities whose yields don't show on this table; (3) finding tax equivalents for higher brackets than those shown here; and (4) finding out whether you'd net more from a mutual fund that owns only your own state's bonds or a higher-yielding fund containing the bonds of several states.

Some Municipal Bonds and Bond Funds Carry Insurance. If the issuer defaults, the insurance company will make all the interest and principal payments. Sometimes banks give the guarantee by issuing a letter of credit. Most insured bonds are of single A quality. Thanks to the guarantee, however, they're classified as AAA.

... THIS IS THE MINIMUM YIELD YOU NEED FROM A TREASURY SECURITY TO EQUAL A TAX-EXEMPT, IN THE FOLLOWING TAX BRACKETS

IF A TAX-EXEMPT BOND YIELDS . . .	15%	28%	31%	33%	36%	39.6%
3.0	3.5	4.2	4.3	4.5	4.7	5.0
3.5	4.1	4.9	5.1	5.2	5.5	5.8
4.0	4.7	5.6	5.8	6.0	6.3	6.6
4.5	5.3	6.3	6.5	6.7	7.0	7.5
5.0	5.9	6.9	7.2	7.5	7.8	8.3
5.5	6.5	7.6	8.0	8.2	8.6	9.1
6.0	7.1	8.3	8.7	9.0	9.4	9.9
6.5	7.7	9.0	9.4	9.7	10.2	10.8
7.0	8.2	9.7	10.1	10.4	10.9	11.6
7.5	8.8	10.4	10.9	11.2	11.7	12.4
8.0	9.4	11.1	11.6	11.9	12.5	13.2
8.5	10.0	11.8	12.3	12.7	13.3	14.1
9.0	10.6	12.5	13.0	13.4	14.1	14.9

SOURCE: David Kahn, Goldstein Golub Kessler & Co., New York City

The insurance costs investors anywhere from 0.15 to 0.3 percentage points in yield. But even though rated AAA, insured bonds may yield a bit more than their uninsured AAA counterparts. That's because investors don't quite trust the insurance companies. In a couple of cases, the insurer's own credit rating has dropped, which brought down the ratings of the bonds it backed. Insured bonds also tend to rise and fall more in price than top-rated uninsured bonds, so they carry more daily market risk.

Note that the insurer does not guarantee the bond's market value. You are not reimbursed if you sell before maturity and lose money because the bond's rating is down. You're protected only against nonpayment of interest and principal.

Some municipal-bond mutual funds and unit trusts insure their whole portfolios. Ten years ago that smelled like nothing more than a marketing gimmick. Since the Great Depression only around one percent of all munis are said to have failed. But in recent years there have been a few spectacular defaults. The collapse of the Washington Public Power Supply System's bonds, which carried an investment-grade rating of Baa at default, turned investors especially queasy. I still think muni-bond insurance is a marketing gimmick. But nowadays, maybe it's worth paying for both belt and suspenders.

Why You Might Want a Tax-Free Bond:

Why else but to earn a safe and steady tax-free income? If you don't need this income to live on, reinvest every interest payment in other bonds or money market mutual funds. Otherwise, your capital will lose purchasing power. If you expect to drop to a low tax bracket in retirement, time your munis to expire by retirement day.

For the good of your nerves, pick high-grade, general obligation munis. Low-grade issues pay more and hardly ever default, but might cause you a lot of worry in the next recession when government budgets come under pressure. Munis can be high-performance investments in the hands of a competent analyst. But normally, they're for the no-worry portion of your portfolio. Save your risk-taking for stocks, where the rewards are generally higher. If you insist on speculating in low-rated munis, take a look at the states and cities mired in the most serious credit problems. That's where you'll make the most money, assuming that the bonds are paid.

The Drawbacks:

1. The liquidity is awful on individual municipal bonds. If you try to sell a $5,000 bond before maturity, you'll probably have to accept a discount ("haircut") of 2 to 3 percent. On a $10,000 bond, the haircut might run one to 1.5 percent. That's on top of brokerage commissions. In short, selling early wrecks your total return.

2. If you live in a state with budget problems, your risks are compounded. Your bonds' credit ratings might be downgraded, which would lower their price. You'd wind up with a low return or even a loss if you had to sell before maturity. For gamblers, lower-grade munis are probably worth a flier. If they don't default, they'll pay spectacular yields. For safety, however, don't buy a lot of them.

3. Unlike Treasuries, munis can be called, generally after 10 years. So you might get your principal back early. If interest rates have fallen, you will have to reinvest at a lower rate, which will lower the yield you earn on your capital.

4. If you're subject to the alternative minimum tax, tell your broker about it. The AMT taxes certain types of municipals, such as student-loan bonds and some industrial-development bonds. Luckily for me, advanced tax advice is outside the mission of this book. See an accountant.

5. Municipalities are exempt from many of the laws on financial disclosure that rule corporations. Since 1995, however, they've been required to tell investors about changes in their financial condition—for better or worse. These disclosures are zapped to depositories where brokers can check them. It's the issuers' obligation to report and the broker's obligation to check, so you won't unknowingly buy from an issuer in financial trouble. But it takes time and money to make these reports. Smaller issuers, in particular, may not have the staff to keep on top of things. In short, you may *not* have the latest information. But at least you now have someone to sue.

How to Get a Good Price on Older Bonds: Newly issued bonds sell at par ($1,000 a bond). But older issues trade at more or less than par, depending on the market at the time. Sometimes brokers add extravagant markups when you buy and pay shameless, below-market prices when you sell.

To check whether a broker's price is fair, call the Municipal Bond Service (800-BOND-INFO), run by Standard & Poor's and the Public Securities Association. It provides the approximate buy/sell prices that institutional investors pay. You're given a market price if the bond traded more than four times that day (the vast majority don't). Otherwise, you will get an "evaluated price"—what its evaluators think the bond is worth. You also get its safety rating and current yield. When you call, be prepared with the bond's CUSIP number or the issuer's name, issue date, series number, coupon, and maturity date. Cost: $9.95 plus tax for 25 price quotes.

If you choose a municipal bond, would you buy . . .

An Individual Bond? Absolutely, as long as you can afford to diversify over four or five issues and intend to hold until maturity. You pay no sales commission if you buy a new issue, and escape the sales charges and continuing fees charged by mutual funds and unit trusts. At maturity, you will get all your capital back (assuming no defaults). That's a promise that mutual funds can't make because they have no maturity date.

But when you buy an individual muni, it should generally pass the following tests: (1) It's blue-chip quality—AAA or AA. (2) It doesn't yield more than other AAA or AA issues, which would indicate a special risk. (3) It's a general obligation bond, or a revenue bond for an essential municipal service. (4) It matures within 10 years, so you're pretty sure of holding for the full term (which is not so likely with 30-year bonds). Alternatively, it is targeted to mature in exactly the year that you know you're going to want the money. (5) It doesn't have an early call date. (6) It's a new issue, so you get the same price that the professionals pay. If only an older bond fits the maturity you need, ferret out the markup to see if the price is fair (page 745). Don't buy a low-rated or unrated muni under the illusion that, since it's a "government issue," it's safe. It isn't.

New at this writing: Inflation-protection municipals, modeled after inflation-protection Treasuries (page 763). There's a low base interest rate paid in cash plus an inflation adjustment, payable at maturity. Because these are municipals, you owe no taxes on the interest that accrues.

For help in buying individual munis and judging whether the price is fair, try a $99 introductory annual subscription to the *Lynch Municipal Bond Advisory,* P.O. Box 20476, New York, NY 10025 (212-663-5552). Regular annual subscription: $350. You also get help with muni funds.

A Mutual Fund? Yes, if you: (1) Have only small amounts of money to invest. (2) Need monthly income. (3) Aren't sure exactly when you might need to tap your principal. Fund shares can be sold at any time, at a better price than individual bonds would bring if you had to liquidate before maturity (although, in either case, you could lose some of your principal if interest rates have risen). (4) Believe that interest rates won't rise long term, so your bond shares won't lose value. If rates do rise, the value of your fund will fall—and there's no date certain when you know that your principal will be returned. (5) Understand the market risk. Some funds keep a high percentage of their money in high-quality bonds. Others concentrate on lower-quality A and BBB bonds. The latter yield more but could run into heavy weather if the market is roiled by rising interest rates or falling credit quality. Some of their bonds might slip from BBB down to junk, at great loss to their shareholders. These bonds would still be making interest payments, but their market price would fall. (6) Choose a no-load (no-sales-charge) fund with low expenses, so your yield doesn't go through a meat grinder.

Whenever there's a major default—as happened in Orange County, California, in 1995—prices on muni funds usually sag. That's almost always a buying opportunity.

Some intermediate-term multi-state muni fund: No-loads: Vanguard Municipal Bond Fund—Limited Term Portfolio (short term), Vanguard Municipal Bond Fund—Intermediate-term Portfolio (Valley Forge, Pennsylvania, 800-662-7447). A load fund: Morgan Grenfell Municipal Bond Fund.

Zero-Coupon Bonds

Zeros are for extremists. You're either a wild speculator, hoping for a quick capital gain, or a careful planner who wants to lock in a fixed sum of money by a certain date.

Zeros, Defined:

A zero bond has no current "coupon" or interest payment. Instead, you buy the bond at a fraction of its face value and wait. The interest accumulates within the bond itself, usually compounded semiannually. At maturity, the bond is redeemed for its face value.

For example, suppose that in June 1997 you buy a 10-year, $1,000 Treasury zero yielding 6.75 percent. You'd have paid $517.50. The following year the bond would be worth $553, thanks to accumulated interest. The year after that you'd have $591. And so on up. (The bond's value also rises and falls in response to market conditions, but that's another story.) In June 2007 you'll redeem that zero for $1,000.

Most people who buy zeros go for Treasury bonds, although you might also be interested in municipal zeros. Corporate zeros are bought chiefly by institutions.

All the interest you earn will compound at the bond's own, internal interest rate—in the previous example, 6.75 percent. A regular bond can't do that for you. With regular bonds, you get a dividend check every 6 months and have to reinvest the money as best you can (for example, in a money market fund).

Zeros sold under acronyms like TIGRs and CATS are brokerage-house promises-to-pay that are secured by Treasuries. I have no reason to believe that arrangement isn't safe. But for a direct participation in a Treasury itself, buy the zeros known as STRIPs, which are the most widely traded. You have to buy through a stockbroker; STRIPs aren't available directly from the Federal Reserve. (STRIP means "separate trading of registered interest and principal" securities. Aren't you sorry you asked?) The zeros known as LYONs are zero-coupon convertible bonds (page 782). Zeros can even be backed by mortgage securities such as Ginnie Maes.

There are two ways of buying zeros. You can get them when they're newly issued or you can turn to the secondary market and buy an older zero out of a brokerage firm's inventory. New issues are best. New-issue Treasuries can generally be had in a wide variety of maturities. Among tax-exempts, however, your choice will be more limited.

If you buy older zeros from a broker, take care that you're getting a fair price. Check the price services for Treasuries (page 784) or municipals (page 778). If you use two brokers, get competitive quotes. *Warning:* Older zeros complicate your tax return. In the year you buy the zero, only part of the taxable interest belongs to you. You'll need an accountant to sort it out.

Don't be so dazzled by the zero's apparent "low price" that you neglect two crucial strategic questions:

First, "What's the yield, net after commissions?" It's no big deal to turn $520 into $1,000 in 10 years. That's 6.75 percent, compounded annually. If you can get more than 6.75 percent in another investment, that is the better choice.

Second, "What will $1,000 be worth in 10 years?" After inflation and taxes, it might buy just a bit more than $520 did in 1997. Zero bonds can maintain the purchasing power of your capital, but your money doesn't grow by much.

Why You Might Want a Zero:

1. You want to guarantee that you'll have a fixed sum of money in a certain year. By paying $520 in June 1997, for example, you knew for sure that you'd have $1,000 in July 2007. Zeros are commonly used to accumulate money for college (you don't keep ahead of college inflation but you come pretty close—see Chapter 20). They're perfect for covering fixed-

dollar obligations, such as paying off your mortgage on the day you retire, repaying a balloon loan, paying the tax on a large capital gain, or guaranteeing a future cash payout negotiated as part of a divorce. You'll generally get a better return than if you had saved for the payment in a money market fund.

2. You are speculating on falling interest rates. Recite your mantra: Falling interest rates are good. When interest rates fall, bond prices rise. When rates decline, zeros move up faster in price than any other kind of bond. So they're the gambler's chip of choice.

3. You want to lock in a tax-exempt interest rate. Most Treasury and many muni zeros cannot be called prior to maturity. That's the only kind to buy. Noncallable munis yield a little less than callable ones do, but callable zeros may foil your investment goal.

The Drawbacks:

1. If interest rates rise instead of fall, you'll lose more value in zeros than you would in other bonds if you have to sell before maturity. For proof, see the table on page 759. So buy only zeros that you're sure you can hold to term. If your child will be off to college in 15 years, buy a 15-year zero, not a 30-year zero that you'll have to sell (if, indeed, you want zeros at all).

2. You'll have to comparison shop, to be sure that you're not over-charged. Stockbrokers tent to talk prices, not yields. For just $266.50, your broker might say, you'll have $1,000 in 20 years. What's the yield? On the surface, 6.75 percent—which might sound just fine. But if the commission is $25 per STRIP, your net yield drops to 6.28 percent. Another broker might charge you $266.50 plus only $10 per STRIP, for a fatter net yield of 6.55 percent. So always ask about yield to maturity *after* commissions (the net yield should show on your confirmation slip). And call more than one broker, including a discount broker. I went through this exercise a few years ago and found a difference of $34 per $1,000 between the highest and lowest offers. That's a difference in yield of 3.4 percent—not chicken feed.

3. Income taxes are owed every year on the interest buildup inside a zero-coupon Treasury. But your bond doesn't pay any cash to help cover the tax. To avoid paying taxes on phantom income, put Treasury zeros into tax-deferred retirement plans or into the accounts of children who owe no tax. Otherwise, consider using tax-free municipal zeros.

4. Some zeros are callable. Your bonds might be snatched away after 5 or 10 years when you had planned on holding them for 15. Early calls are doubly painful because a zero's big payoff comes during the final third of the bond's life. If a broker sold you a zero municipal priced at more than its current principal and interest value (it happens), you could lose principal on an early call.

5. As with any other bond, zeros will probably not be as good a long-term buy as stocks. They serve some financial-planning purposes but aren't the key to real growth.

If you choose a zero, would you buy . . .

An Individual Bond? Yes, if you plan to hold until maturity. It's the cheapest way of buying these bonds, assuming that you get a good price. With zero-coupon Treasuries you don't have to diversify. Most brokers' commissions run $5 to $10 per bond.

A Mutual Fund? In most cases, no. The funds levy annual management fees, which reduce your yield. Buy a fund only if you're speculating on falling interest rates. It's cheaper to trade no-load mutual fund shares than to buy and sell zeros directly, and you'll get a fairer price on the bonds.

Unlike other bond mutual funds, zero-coupon funds have fixed maturity dates—for example, 2000, 2005, 2010, 2015, 2020, or 2025. On maturity day, all the bonds are redeemed and the investors paid. The further away the maturity date, the bigger your profit if interest rates fall and you sell before maturity. Conversely, the bigger your market losses if interest rates rise. But you suffer no loss if you hold the fund to maturity.

The no-load fund with the largest number of maturities to choose from: American Century–Benham Target Maturities Trust, Kansas City, Missouri (800-4-SAFETY).

International and Emerging-Market Bonds.
See Chapter 27.

International bond funds to try: Load funds: Global Total Return, IDS Global Bond Fund. Through discount brokers: PIMCO Foreign Bond Fund —Institutional Shares.

An emerging-markets bond fund to try: The no-load Scudder Emerging Markets Income Fund (Boston, 800-225-2470).

Closed-End Bond Funds. See Chapter 22.

Convertible Bonds

Convertible bonds are widely marketed to conservative investors, especially retirees, as a "safer" way of participating in stock-market growth. But they carry more risks than many buyers realize.

Convertibles, Defined:
These bonds can be converted into a fixed number of the company's common shares. You can make the exchange when the common shares have

risen to a certain price. While you're waiting, you earn interest, although not as much as you'd earn from that company's regular bonds.

When the stock price rises, the price of the convertible normally goes up, too, although not as much. You can sell your converts at a profit if you'd rather not make the switch to stocks.

When the stock price falls, converts normally don't drop as far as the underlying stock. Like a bondholder, you can sit tight and collect a regular income.

Why You Might Want a Convertible:

They pay higher dividends than the underlying stock. There's potential growth if the stock appreciates and somewhat less risk if the market falls. But not as much less risk as you think. In the 1987 crash, converts dropped almost as precipitously as stocks. They went down again with stocks and bonds in 1994.

WHAT THEY DON'T TELL YOU: Many converts come from smaller, low-rated companies. When the market drops, the convertibles don't decline as far as the underlying stock, but that may not be saying much. They may lose more value than blue-chip stocks. What's "safe" about that?

Furthermore, the convertibles market isn't as liquid as the market for bonds and stocks. If a lot of people want to sell, prices will drop more quickly than they would for other investments. That's another reason why converts don't give you as much bear-market protection as you might expect.

The Drawbacks:

1. They pay less income than you'd get from regular bonds and offer less appreciation than you could get from stocks. Conservative investors will accept that in return for offsetting gains. But you may not know about the other risks.

2. A convert costs more than the underlying stock is currently worth. So you're making a bet that the stock price will rise substantially. In the mid-1990s, you won that bet—but the dice can roll against you, too. Pricing convertibles is a science too complex for the average investor. If you overpay, it might take years to make the money you expected. Your bond might even be called by the company before you've had time to earn a profit.

3. Let's assume that you get lucky and the company's stock is running well. Your convert is moving up in price and you're collecting nice interest payments. Suddenly, the bond might be called. That forces you to sell or convert to the stock, like it or not. If you weren't following your investment and heard about the call too late, you'll still get the call value of the bond but will lose the extra value that the bond had gained in the marketplace.

4 If your company is taken over, the tender offer could potentially eliminate your conversion rights.

• • •

If you choose a convertible bond, would you buy . . .

An Individual Bond? No. You don't know how much to pay for it and the risk is high because so many converts are issued by companies with poor credit ratings.

A Mutual Fund? Yes, if you absolutely must. Buy why not buy a balanced stock-and-bond fund rather than muddle along with a mediocre hybrid? Or why not a high-yield bond fund, since so many converts are from lower-quality companies, too? As a class, high-yield funds tend to outperform converts.

DO YOU WANT AN INDEX FUND?

The Vanguard Group in Valley Forge, Pennsylvania, offers a cornucopia of low-cost funds—taxable and tax-exempt, short-, intermediate-, and long-term, broadly or narrowly invested in the bonds of your choice. They follow standard indexes such as the Lehman Brothers Aggregate Bond Index. Index funds outdo comparable managed funds, thanks to their lower fees (at Vanguard, around 0.3 percent a year). Pure index funds—not "enhanced" funds (page 704)—also contain no hidden risks. A "short-term government income fund" won't include emerging-market bonds that could blow up in your face, as happens with some managed funds.

Managed funds, by contrast, diversify over a wide range of investments. In the same fund, you'll get a mix of corporates, governments, internationals, and high-yields. If you get a good manager (always the challenge) he or she has a shot at outdoing the index fund. But, of course, you're taking extra risk. If you don't want that risk, index funds are the way to go.

FOLLOWING YOUR BONDS

Daily bond prices don't matter to investors who plan to hold until maturity. But speculators can follow the major bonds in *The Wall Street Journal, Investor's Daily, Barron's,* and the financial sections of many newspapers. You'll see, in abbreviated form, the company's name, the bond's coupon interest rate, the maturity date, the current yield (coupon divided by price), the number of bonds that traded that day (small, compared with stocks), the day's price action, and the change from the previous day.

The listings for Treasury securities show the coupon rate, the maturity date, the "bid price" (what investors would get if they sold their bonds), the "asked" price (what investors would pay to buy bonds that day), any change from the previous day, and the current yield based on the asking price. But these are wholesale prices for large purchasers like mutual funds. As an individual buyer, you'll pay more than the newspaper shows; as a seller, you'll get less.

The prices of bond mutual funds, for both open-end and closed-end funds, are carried in the same tables as those for stock-owning mutual funds.

HEY, JANE, YOU FORGOT TO MENTION MONEY FUNDS...

No I didn't. Money market mutual funds are not investments, they're variable-rate savings accounts. I love them for your ready cash (page 188). They're terrific parking places for funds awaiting investment somewhere else. They're ballast for a portfolio with too much risk, but they are not long-term investments in themselves.

When you stash most of your assets in a money fund, you are robbing yourself of growth. You'll appear to stay even with inflation but, after tax, your purchasing power will slowly shrink. The investment alternative to money funds is a short-term, one- or 2-year bond fund. It pays a slightly higher yield with small risk to your ready cash, provided that the fund also has a short duration (page 746).

...AND TAX-DEFERRED ANNUITIES

Check them out on page 886, along with all the other tax-deferred investment vehicles.

VIATICALS

Here's a rising investment, pitched to investors seeking high returns: "viatical" life insurance deals. The word comes from viaticum, the communion given to Christians who are dying or in danger of death. The investment looks interesting for the well-to-do who can afford to tie up money for several years. But there's some fraud out there, which could cost you every dime you put up.

Viatical deals are struck with people who are terminally ill. Mostly, that means people with full-blown AIDS or end-stage cancer. To raise money for treatment and other bills, they sell part or all of their individual or group life insurance policies—generally for 50 to 80 cents on the dollar.

Increasingly, these policies are being bought by institutions, like banks and life insurance companies. They hold them until the seller dies and then collect the policy's face value. Individual investors are pitched by a network of brokers and planners. Typically, you join a group that buys a particular policy; the viatical company does the paperwork; when the person who sold the policy dies, you get a pro rata share of the payoff. To the living, this may sound too macabre to consider. To many who are dying, however, it's cash in their pockets when they need it most.

Your exact return on this investment can't be predicted in advance. If a group of investors pays $80,000 for a $100,000 policy and the person dies in a year, they earn 25 percent. If the person lives 2 years, the return is 12.5 percent. After 3 years, it's 8.3 percent. The industry puts the average annual return at 15 to 20 percent, although I can't verify that. (Of the $80,000 you pay, by the way, the sick person may get $65,000. The remaining $15,000 goes for sales commissions and fees.)

What makes this investment so safe, the brokers say, is that the patient *will* die and you *will* collect—probably soon. But they earn big commissions for selling this product, usually 5 to 6 percent of the policy's face value, so they may ignore the following risks:

Treatment. The patient may live much longer than anticipated. New drugs for AIDS, for example, have lengthened the lives of people who never expected reprieve. Great for the patient, bad for the investor. Even without new treatments, patients may be hardier than their doctors thought.

Additional payments. The money you put up was intended to pay the insurance premiums over the patient's life expectancy. If the patient lives longer, you'll have to put up additional funds.

Fraud. Some companies take your money and run. In 1995 a Florida firm sold an estimated $3.5 million worth of policies that didn't exist. An Arizona firm sold more than $7 million worth of high-interest bonds said to be backed by viaticals, but weren't. Some patients leave the country, making it hard for investors to collect on the policies.

Overpromising. A firm might offer "guaranteed" 3-year returns of 42 percent. But no one can guarantee that investors will get that sort of annual yield. Walk away from a company or salesperson who makes any promises about what you might earn.

Ownership. The policy you buy may not be put into your name. The owner becomes the viatical company, which names a trust company as beneficiary. To get paid, you have to depend on both. That may be your only option if you're buying just a piece of a policy. If you buy a whole policy, it should be put into your name directly.

If You're Interested in Buying Viaticals, discuss all these risks with the salesperson—especially the size of any extra payments you might have to make—and be prepared to wait longer than you thought. You can get a free list of the companies that sell or broker policies from The National Viatical Association (NVA) in Washington, D.C. (800-741-9465). Working through members diminishes the risk of fraud. (If you want to sell a policy see page 339).

THE DIALOGUE OF STOCKS AND BONDS

Investors often act as if stocks and bonds live in separate worlds—one on Neptune, one on Mars, with orbits that will never cross. In fact, they are two sides of the same financial marketplace, always adjusting to each other's prices. Investors who follow their dialogue have a better feel for what's going on.

Stock and bond prices rise and fall approximately in tandem. If stock prices are booming while bonds are fading, something's wrong. Either bonds will perk up or stocks will turn down. Stock and bond prices do move in opposite directions for short periods of time. But they're never happy until they're once again on parallel tracks.

Bonds usually (but not always) lead stocks, which is why investors should pay attention to what the bond markets are doing. A spectacular example came in 1987. The bond market crashed in April and May while stock investors were still reaching for the stars. Then, in October, stocks crashed, too.

The mediator between stocks and bonds is interest rates. Their influence on the market cycle is crystal clear.

At the start of a typical cycle, interest rates rise and bond prices gradually decline. For a while stock investors pay no attention. But eventually, rates get so high that investors can't resist them. They move money out of stocks and into various fixed-income vehicles. Stocks start to fall. ("Usually," says Roy Neuberger of the investment firm Neuberger & Berman, "when both short-term and long-term rates start rising they tell the stock investor one story: run for the hills.")

High interest rates also put a damper on business. The economy slinks into recession and demand for new credit slows way down.

This is when the cycle turns. Slow credit demand means that interest rates have room to fall, which causes bond prices to rise. Pretty soon, professional investors switch some of their money out of interest-rate investments and back into stocks. Stock prices bottom out and move sharply up. Bonds have led stocks once again.

Typically, however, market-timing investors don't yet believe that anything has changed. They sit through the first 30 or 40 percent of the rise in stocks without lifting a finger to invest, thus losing some of the market's fastest gains.

Why do investors wait so long to buy? Usually because the economy is in the pits. They forget that markets *anticipate*. Falling interest rates signal easier credit, which paves the way for recovery. Investors should anticipate, too, or else (my choice) stay in the market all the time.

Stocks and bonds have one more important relationship. They define the risks you choose to take and what your returns are likely to be. If you think you've been setting your investment sights too low, you'll reduce the percentage of bonds and other fixed-income investments you hold and raise your long-term commitment to stocks. If you think you've been taking unreasonable risks, you'll buy fewer stocks (or different ones), lower your holdings of long-term bonds, and move into shorter- and intermediate-term bonds. Either way, the balance you strike between stocks and bonds will determine the size of the nest egg you'll have when you come to the end of your working life.

26.

The Call of the Wild

Some Absolutely Awful Investments

Wall Streeter Ray DeVoe calls it The Crack of Doom. It's the point when you know, for sure, not only that you are going to lose money, but that you are going to lose a lot more money than you can afford.

Quinn's First Law of Investing is never to buy anything whose price you can't follow in the newspapers. An investment without a public marketplace attracts the fabulists the way picnics attract ants. Stockbrokers and financial planners can tell you anything they want because no one really knows what's true.

The First Corollary to Quinn's First Law says that, even when the price is in the newspapers, you shouldn't buy anything too complex to explain to the average 12-year-old.

These rules proscribe some of Wall Street's most popular investments. They're "popular" not because you've been dying to own them but because brokers and planners press them upon you. Not coincidentally, they all carry higher sales commissions than surer, simpler investments do. I wouldn't touch any of them myself—and hope that you'll avoid them, too.

I won't even offer you "how-to" lists for finding gems among the dreck. Some gems exist, but they're not worth the time it takes to do the research or the risk that your broker will talk you into buying something that you shouldn't.

LIMITED PARTNERSHIPS: WHERE DID ALL THE MONEY GO?

The competition for "worst investment" is pretty stiff. But limited partnerships make the final cut. A limited partner is best defined as someone who gets a limited amount of his or her money back (if that). Thousands of people are holding partnership units they bought in the 1980s and can't get rid of. If you're able to sell, you'll get only a fraction of your money back.

The textbook definition of a limited partner is someone who makes a passive investment in oil, real estate, nursing homes, cable TV, equipment leasing, or any other venture. You're "passive" in that you make none of the business decisions. A general partner runs the business and accepts liability for any lawsuits. The limited partners get a pro rata share of the profits or losses. There are supposed to be cash distributions along the way (a lot of these deals are called "income" partnerships) plus some tax deductions. After a specified number of years the investment is supposed to be sold (at a vast profit, you're led to believe) and the proceeds distributed. What proceeds? Years later, people who paid $1,000 a pop are still hoping that maybe someone will offer them $198.

A few partnership deals are still being sold (the name has been sanitized: they're now "direct investments"). But it's a waste of my time and yours to try analyzing them. If they're tax deals, they probably just defer the tax and you might lose some money along the way. If they're income-and-growth deals, you're unlikely to see much of either. When a small "tax-free" check arrives in the mail, it feels like a profit but is merely a bit of your own, original capital back (cherish it; the rest is slipping away). The partnership sponsor may pocket 15 percent of your money off the top plus another healthy slice each year. The broker may get 8 percent.

Some people buy these deals anyway. As the great man said, you can fool some of the people all the time. But none of those people are reading this book.

So-o-o-o-o, the only important question about partnership investments is how to get rid of these dogs if you're still holding them or if you inherit them.

What Are Your Partnership Units Worth?

Who knows? In many cases, not even the sponsor does. Here are your sources of information, flimsy as they are:

Your Brokerage-House Statement. A purported value for your units may be printed on your statement, but that "value" is probably a fantasy (I'm being kind). It's common to show your investment at its original cost, even though it's unsalable. Pressure the broker to change this, especially if the units are in your retirement plan. If they're overvalued, they'll force you to make larger-than-necessary withdrawals when you reach 70$^1/_2$. Overvaluations also trigger higher taxes in large estates.

The Partnership Sponsor. It's probably the sponsor who's giving those phony valuations to your broker. Many partnerships refuse to compute a value at all. Some can't even be found (although *someone* keeps earning management fees each year).

The Secondary Market. Around a dozen firms buy and sell units of existing partnerships. Some participate in the on-line Central Trading Facility, developed by Cantor Fitzgerald in New York City. Your stockbroker can check that market to see how large a bid (if any) your units will attract. A competitor, the Chicago Partnership Board, posts free information on the Web: http://www.cpboard.com. That site shows units for sale, recent prices, and other data. You can also call the board at 800-272-6273.

A Research Service. Robert A Stanger & Co. of Shrewsbury, New Jersey, offers information on private and publicly registered partnerships—where the sponsors are located (if known), what's happening to distributions (if any), whether those distributions represent real earnings or are just a payback of your original capital, the partnership's cumulative returns, and what the sponsors say the units are worth. Phone: 908-389-3600. Cost: $5. For an extra charge, Stanger will send a printed report.

The Stock Markets. You get truly accurate information only if your partnership shares are publicly traded. Open markets tell all.

How to Get Out of a Rotten Partnership (Maybe)

Try Selling Through the Secondary Market. Seek competing bids on the Central Trading Facility and the Chicago Partnership Board. You'll be shocked at how little buyers will pay. Still, one firm may offer a better deal than the others do. Always ask if the price is firm and how long it will take to close. Some bidders may play around with you for a while, then name a lower price. Your units are probably unsalable, however, if they haven't been generating income.

Look into Abandoning the Deal—a potential solution for people in so-called income partnerships who never took big tax deductions. You can generally abandon a property whenever you want just by telling a third party what you're doing. The clearest way: Send a certified letter to the general partner, saying something like "I hereby irrevocably abandon my interest. Do with it what you wish." You can write off a capital loss on your tax return. But see an accountant before you act. Bailing out of a loser sometimes triggers an income tax.

Die. A drastic solution but, hey, we're talking long-term plans. Any taxes you might have owed will be buried with you. Your heirs can sell or abandon the units, whichever works. If they keep your dog and the deal is eventually liquidated at a loss, they can write off the loss on their tax returns.

Why You Might Not Want to Sell, Even If You Can

Since the early 1990s real-estate prices have been improving. So have the prices offered for the better real-estate partnership units, even though they're low relative to what you paid. A number of savvy investors cruise the secondary markets. If you're holding a partnership someone else is willing to pay for, it's probably worth keeping. Some oil-and-gas partnerships have a potential future, too.

If you do sell, you risk bringing a tax bill down on your head. You'll have to give back any partnership tax deductions you took that exceeded your investment. Sometimes that's big bucks. You're better off holding a zombie investment—a deal that's one of the living dead—than paying the price of burying it.

PENNY STOCKS: FOR SUCKERS ONLY

Penny stocks come from mystery companies, with an untested business, that sell for $5 or less per share. Not all cheap stocks are bad. But almost all the really rotten issues are cheap. They're peddled, by phone, by Hole-in-the-Wall Gangs who transfix their victims with the claim that the investment "cannot lose." With automatic dialing, a penny-stock broker can place two hundred calls a day.

If you're ever tempted by the pitch, here's what will happen. You'll buy the stock and, lo and behold, the price will rise. So you'll buy another stock and that will rise, too. It feels like luck (you genius, you), but actually the broker manipulates the price. You keep getting good news while the broker milks you for all the money he or she thinks you've got.

Then things change. Suddenly, one of your stocks goes down. You want to sell, but discover you can't. In penny-stock schemes, the brokers will not process your order unless you use your "profits" to buy another stock. They keep rolling your money into other ventures until they finally wipe you out.

Some penny-stock hustles are "blank checks" or "blind pools." (One state securities commissioner calls them "deaf pools," as in: "Give me your money and you'll never hear from me again.") You buy shares in a hollow company or "shell" that does no business of its own. When it gets your money, it goes looking for small, private companies to buy. Some of these companies are legitimate, like a printer or a bakery. Others are frauds.

When there's a business—real or apparent—publicists send out lyrical reports predicting a brilliant and profitable future. Brokers hit the telephones and start pushing the stock. They create excitement by quoting higher and higher prices which are literally plucked out of thin air. The insiders make money by selling their shares to all the deluded innocents who think that the company is real. Some of these stock scams are run by organized crime.

As soon as the scamsters have scored their gains, they drop the stock and switch to another one. The price collapses to its true value, which may be only a few cents a share.

In certain circumstances a penny-stock broker is supposed to get proof that you, the investor, are financially able to shoulder the hazard of buying these shares. You'll be asked about your income and net worth and will have to sign a "suitability statement." New investors also have to sign a purchase order; you can't be held to an okay that you gave by phone. But brokers may tell you that the forms are "just paperwork," "routine," and "not worth reading." If you believe them, it's your loss. The forms alert you to the risk.

You don't even have to sign these forms if you've bought penny stocks before, you initiated the purchase (the broker my falsely claim you did), the broker doesn't make a market in the stock (meaning that the broker doesn't control the price), or it's listed on a national or regional exchange. These loopholes help keep penny-stock scams in business.

If you're called by a penny-stock broker who strong-arms you to buy, hang up. Stay away from stocks that don't trade on a major exchange (the exchanges set financial requirements for the stocks they list). Ignore the touts on the Internet. If this advice comes too late, tell your broker to sell your shares and send you the cash. If he or she won't, threaten to call the state securities commissioner. That sometimes works. And carry through with the threat (for where to get the phone number, see page 656). Your complaint might help shut that boiler room down.

UNIT TRUSTS: THE MYSTERY DEALS

Imagine a house with an elephant in the basement. It's been said that the animal holds up the house. Grateful for the constant support, the householders feed their elephant lavishly. But they never go down with a flashlight to see if the beast is as big as they thought.

That pretty much defines the bizarre faith engendered by unit investment trusts, a multi-billion-dollar industry directed especially to conservative municipal-bond investors. You buy unit trusts for their "steady income" and "locked-in yields." Stockbrokers like to claim, based on no independent evidence, that the trusts do better than comparable mutual funds.

But no one has ever gone down with a flashlight to look. I know of no other major investment for which so little performance data is available. It's impossible to tell whether unit trusts are better than, or even as good as, competing mutual funds. I do know, however, that some of the claims made for unit trusts are simply not true.

A unit trust is a fixed portfolio of securities—usually municipal bonds or Ginnie Maes but sometimes corporate bonds or stocks. A package of securities is assembled. You buy an interest in the package for a minimum of $1,000. The trust is held, virtually unchanged, for anywhere from 6 months to 30 years. Securities are occasionally sold out of the trust but no new ones are added. The sales commission runs in the area of one to 5 percent and the trustee's fee, up to 0.2 percent annually. Most trusts run on automatic pilot, so there's no management fee. Some, however, charge 1.75 percent a year for no discernible reason.

You get a pro rata share of the trust's interest or dividends, mailed to you monthly, quarterly, or semiannually. As the securities mature, you'll also receive a pro rata share of the proceeds. For example, take a $20,000 investment in a municipal-bond unit trust. Initially, you might earn $90 a month in bond interest. Five years later a block of those bonds may mature. You'd receive a $2,000 check, representing your share of the proceeds. That $2,000 is a return of some of the capital you invested. After that, your monthly check might drop to $82 because there are fewer bonds in the trust. Each check specifies how much is interest and how much is principal.

Ginnie Mae unit trusts are a little more complicated. They invest in mortgages, so every check you get is a combination of mortgage interest and principal—the latter being a partial return of your own capital. Every time a homeowner prepays a mortgage, the proceeds are distributed to the trust's investors (for more on Ginnie Maes, see page 765).

Trusts invested in stocks pay out dividends. When the trust expires the stocks are sold and the proceeds divided.

The distributions you receive from unit trusts cannot be reinvested in the trust itself. But the sponsor may arrange for them to be reinvested in a money market mutual fund.

In theory, a bond-holding trust remains in existence until the last one matures. In practice, the sponsor often sells the remaining securities and distributes the proceeds when the trust's principal value has shrunk to perhaps 25 or 20 percent of its opening value. That shag-end sale may bring a profit or a loss, depending on market conditions at the time.

You can usually sell your shares back to the unit trust sponsor before maturity. If the sponsor won't buy them, you may be able to redeem the shares directly through the trustee. Depending on the state of the market, you might get more or less for the units than you originally paid. But you'll take a discount from market price.

The Question for Bond Trust Investors Is Whether They Will Really Earn Those Lovely Yields They Read About in the Sales Literature. There is no way of telling. No independent service tracks the performance of unit trusts to find out what they actually pay. Any investment whose claims can't be checked invites abuse. I find the following soft spots in bond unit trusts.

Their Allegedly Superior Returns Aren't Proven. Unit trusts claim that they outperform comparable mutual funds because they charge no management fees. More of your money is supposedly left in the trust to compound.

But you pay a sales load up front, which you don't with a no-load mutual fund. And because unit trust portfolios are more or less fixed, the sponsors may not weed out investment mistakes. You should disregard this performance claim until someone starts charting the trusts' performance relative to bond mutual funds, especially the low-cost index funds that charge only 0.3 percent a year. They may be the better buy.

You Might Lose Money If Your Trust Doesn't Last Until Its Stated Maturity Date. Trusts have the right to cash you out early if calls and redemptions shrink their assets by a specified amount. But if the remaining bonds are sold, what price will they bring? Some unit trusts have been dumping grounds for bonds that the sponsors otherwise couldn't sell. At liquidation, investors in these trusts would almost certainly take a loss.

The Income Isn't Steady. Bond unit trusts are most often bought for their alleged "steady stream of income." The payments, your broker may say, are "fixed." But payments are not fixed. They might stay the same for a couple of years, but then your trust could start melting at the edges.

Here are four ways that your income might shrink:

SHRINKER ONE: Some higher-interest bonds will probably be called before maturity or retired through a sinking fund. This usually lowers your final yield. During the early 1990s huge numbers of securities in municipal-bond unit trusts were called—to the shock of the people living on that income. The trusts try for call protection on their bonds of at least 5 years and sometimes 10. But that's a far cry from a "steady stream of income" on a 30-year trust. If long-term, guaranteed income is your objective, buy noncallable Treasury bonds instead.

SHRINKER TWO: Some securities will be sold out of the trust in order to cover early redemptions. If the amount of bonds sold exceeds the sum redeemed (as sometimes happens), the leftover money will be distributed to investors—returning a small share of their principal whether they want it or not. In choosing which securities to sell, the trusts try to hold your yield steady. Sometimes they can; sometimes they can't.

SHRINKER THREE: The credit quality of some bonds will slide. If a bad bond has to be sold out of the portfolio, you lose some of your principal. If a bond defaults, you lose interest and, generally, part of your principal (although some residual value will remain). Says former stockbroker Mary Calhoun, "There are fantastic safety problems with certain unit trusts. . . . Some of the sponsors put in poorer-quality bonds because they're desperate to get the yields up."

Junk-bond unit trusts are double trouble. Their better-quality bonds get called (because those issuers will be able to borrow at lower rates). The poorer bonds remain in the trust. After the calls, you lose some of your "steady" income and you're stuck with the issues most likely to default.

SHRINKER FOUR: Some trusts are smoke and mirrors. They pay a higher income than you'd get from other bond investments, which makes you think you're earning a superior yield. But, in fact, you're earning a normal yield and are running an abnormal risk of loss.

Here's how that happens: The trust buys a lot of older municipal bonds that carry higher interest rates than are available today. So investors get more current income—say, 7 percent tax-free. But to get those irresistible rates the trust had to pay a premium—say, $1,130 for each $1,000 bond. Those bonds will almost certainly be called before maturity at their $1,000 value, leaving the trust with a $130 loss per bond. After the call, your actual yield might be 5.5 percent—vastly less than you thought you were earning.

But that's only Step One in the deception. Step Two is to disguise the loss. The trust does that by buying zero-coupon bonds. Zeros pay no current income; each year's interest is added to the value of the bond itself. The gains from the zeros are supposed to balance the losses you take on the bonds that are called.

That's the theory, anyway. In practice, these trusts are time bombs. Follow what is going to happen: (1) You will lose a lot of your tax-free income when your high-rate bonds are called. (2) You will take a capital loss on the money used to buy those bonds. (3) The zeros will eventually cover that loss, but you'll have to wait until they mature 20 years from now. (4) If you sell early you'll probably lose money. To be sure of coming out whole, you have to wait for the trust to liquidate. So much for the "high-yield" unit trust that was supposed to pay a steady income!

Shares in older unit trusts, which some stockbrokers peddle, can run you into a similar trap. You're attracted by the high current income. But when those bonds are called, your income will drop and you'll be left with a capital loss.

Yields on Bond Unit Trusts Can Be Checked Before You Buy, thanks to disclosures required by the Securities and Exchange Commission (SEC).

On new unit trusts, the prospectus and sales material have to disclose two things: the current return, which tells you what the trust is yielding now; and the estimated long-term return, if it's materially different. It won't be, for trusts that buy new bonds at par. But the long-term return might be lower, if the trust sponsor packed it with older higher-rate bonds. (Neither of these yields deduct sales commissions, so they're both overstated a bit.)

If you're offered shares in older trusts, the broker is required to disclose both the current and long-term return. Some brokers may "forget," ahem, so you'll have to remind them.

If a broker offers you a unit trust that apparently yields markedly more than the new bonds coming to market, laugh hysterically and change the subject. "If you want a high yield real bad, that's what you'll get," a friend of mine says. "A real bad high yield."

You Will Never Know What Your Bond Trust Actually Earned. You'll get a check when the trust is cashed out but no information on what your yield turned out to be. The sponsors say that the brokers have the tools to compute it if you ask. So ask—but who knows if your broker can actually figure it out? The sponsors should disclose it as a matter of course, but maybe they'd rather you didn't know.

Sophisticated Investors in Tax-Free Securities Rarely Buy Unit Trusts. They buy high-quality, new-issue, intermediate-term bonds instead. There's no up-front sales commission on these bonds, some are noncallable, you pay no annual management fee, and the income really is steady. Unit trusts, with their misleading yields, are pitched to smaller investors who know less about how the bond market works.

A unit trust invested in Treasury bonds (as some are) is a pure con. You're paying a 3 to 5 percent sales commission to buy securities that you can get yourself, commission-free, from the nearest Federal Reserve bank (page 204).

The Yields on Equity Unit Trusts. Your returns depend on what happens to the price of a fixed group of stocks over a fixed period of time. If your trust matures during a downturn, tough luck. You don't have the option of holding on. One popular series of trusts buys "the dogs of the Dow"—the ten highest-yielding stocks in the Dow Jones industrial average. At the end of each year, the old trust is sold and a new one begun. At this writing, the dogs have been doing reasonably well, but time will tell. They have a lot of sales and management expenses to overcome. You also have to pay taxes on your annual gains, unless you hold the dogs in a tax-deferred account.

You Can Be Misled as to How an Equity Unit Trust Is Likely to Behave. Sponsors put together baskets of stocks that, *in hindsight,* shot the moon. Then they advertise that performance as if it will be achieved by the trust you're about to buy. That's fakery. Looking backward, analysts can find all kinds of investment systems that apparently worked (that's called "backtesting"). But those outcomes could have been random chance. Stock-picking systems need to be tested in real time—going forward in good markets and bad—before you can say how well they work.

COMMODITIES: A LOSER'S GAME

For those of you eager to lose money on commodities, let me count the ways.

Commodities Funds

Public commodities funds are limited partnerships. They buy and sell tangible investments like metals and agricultural products; they also trade foreign currencies as a hedge against the dollar. Typically, it costs no more than $2,000 to $5,000 to buy in. Sponsors may hold out the hope of gains as high as 90 percent a year.

But that's a joke, as studies of the public commodity funds have found. On average, they have yielded lousy returns for their investors—on the order of 4 to 10 percent annually, depending on the time period and the fund. And they've been a poor hedge against inflation. (These conclusions come from work by Professors Edwin Elton and Martin Gruber of New York University and Joel Rentzler of Baruch College.)

There are two worms in the commodities apple:

1. *Costly mistakes.* Fund managers trade furiously, trying to catch quick changes in trends. They "go long" some commodities, betting that prices will rise, and "go short" others, betting that prices will fall. So inflation itself is no guarantee of profit. Your manager has to be on the right side of each bet.

2. *Kleptomanical fees.* If one counts management fees, performance fees, and brokerage commissions, investors in commodity funds have paid an average of 19 percent a year just to have their money managed, as opposed to around one percent in stock-owning mutual funds. So even when your manager rides the price trends right, the fees leave large portions of the profits sticking to his or her fingers rather than yours.

During various time periods some funds do show sensational gains. But there's no reliable way of identifying them in advance. A manager's performance this year says nothing about how well he or she is going to do next year.

On new funds offered to the public, the managers' past performances look consistently superb. The money they made for previous clients may be reported at 50, 60, even 70 percent a year. But those astonishing track records are a clever form of fiction. They're not wrong exactly, but they're biased and misleading.

There are two slugs in the performance cabbage:

1. *Luck.* The law of averages says that, in any period, some of the country's 2,000 commodity managers will do spectacularly well for their private clients. They're not geniuses; they've just hit a hot streak. At the height of their streak, they're picked to run a public commodities fund. But soon their performance reverts to average and their funds poop out.

2. *Guile.* In the prospectus, managers are required to show their track record for at least the past 3 years. But they can show more if they want to. That allows them to pick the time period that creates the most attractive record.

Fighting their bad reputation, the commodities funds have come up with a gimmick. It's a performance guarantee—a no-risk offer, safe even for my sainted grandmother. At the end of 5 years or so, the brokers say, you will get back at least as much as you invested, and much, much more if the fund succeeds.

How is this miracle achieved? Part of your money buys a zero-coupon bond; the remainder goes into commodities. After 5 years the zero is worth your original investment. (Some funds use bank letters of credit for this guarantee.)

But the price of security comes high. Just to net 8 percent, your "guaranteed" fund might need gross returns on its commodity investments of anywhere from 15 to 23 percent a year to cover its expenses and offset the money invested in the zero. If your investment earns less (and it probably will) it's a bust.

Besides, what's the big deal about getting your money back after 5 years? It will have earned no interest. At 3 percent inflation, your purchasing power will be down by 14 percent.

Commodities Futures

Many an innocent has lost his or her life savings by hearing or seeing an infomercial touting commodity futures. If winter is coming, the pitch is for oil ("prices will rise!"). When floods come to the farm belt, it's for wheat ("prices will rise!"). These soulless opportunists seize the weather, the season, or the news and use it to separate unsophisticates from their money.

Those are the innocents. What shall I say about the guilty—experienced investors who open commodity futures accounts in the nutty belief they can beat the game? They're on the road to learning Quinn's Second Rule of Investing: never buy anything that trades in a pit.

The "pits" are the arenas where future contracts are bought and sold: a contract on June gold; a contract on December wheat; a contract on March soybeans. You put up perhaps 5 or 10 percent of the cost of the contract to bet on the price of a specific commodity on a specific date. Prices are moved by rumor, politics, war, scientific discoveries, business announcements, economic developments, and international weather and crop reports, and they move fast. You can "go long" (a gamble that prices will rise) or "go short" (a gamble that prices will fall). Winners may earn many times their investment. But if prices run against you, you can lose far more money than you put up—perhaps tens of thousands of dollars more. In fact, you are liable for up to the contract's full value. Fortunes can be lost or made within a few days or even a few hours.

End of lesson. The only other thing you need to know is that an estimated 75 percent of commodities speculators lose money. I would bet that 99.9 percent of *amateur* commodities speculators lose money.

The record is probably no better for plungers who buy options on futures. A *call option* gives the holder the right to buy the underlying futures contract at a specified price within a specified time; it's a bet that the price will rise. A *put option* gives the holder the right to sell and is a bet that the price will fall. If you pay, say, $1,000 to buy an option and prices move in your direction, the value of your option will rise. But if prices run against you, you can never lose more than the $1,000 you put up.

There are two main differences between options on futures and futures themselves:

1. When you buy or sell a future, you are contracting to buy or sell the actual commodity. If you don't close out a purchase (at a profit, you hope) before the contract's delivery date, you'll literally have bought the farm. You'll own warehouse receipts for a silo full of soybeans or wheat. By contrast, when you buy an option on a future, you are buying the right to the contract's change in value over a limited period of time. If you don't sell or exercise your option, it will expire worthless.

2. With futures, you can lose much more than the money you put up. The same is true if you sell an option. Both carry unlimited risk. If you buy an option, however, your losses can't exceed your original investment. For this reason, brokers say that buying options is "safer," although the risk of losing 100 percent of my investment isn't on my comfort list. (Any kind of options trading is terrific for brokers. They earn $250 to $1,000 every time you buy and again when you sell. How are you going to beat costs like that?)

You don't have a prayer of winning if you buy through the slickies who tout options on get-rich-quick radio and TV shows. (For information, call 800-555-GYPP.) The investments they sell are real enough but their prices are grossly inflated. As much as 40 percent of your "investment" may be sliced off the top in sales commissions and hidden costs. Any price moves in your commodity would have to be huge to cover these expenses and yield a profit.

Any customer with a modest income and few assets who was fast-talked into buying options on futures has a good chance of winning a reparations case against the broker. There's no way these investments are suitable for anyone with a low net worth. For reparations and arbitration procedures, see page 675.

STOCK-INDEX OPTIONS AND FUTURES

You can book bets on stocks without ever owning one by buying and selling stock options and futures. They're a speculation on the future prices of some of the major market averages. If you think you know where the Standard & Poor's 500-stock index will be next month, here's the place to make your fortune.

During the early years of the Great Bull Market options players made astonishing profits on very small amounts of cash. But the morning after the '87 Crash those same investors woke up to learn that they'd lost many times their original stake. An Indiana teacher who thought he was risking only $5,000 found himself $100,000 in debt (the firm settled this case in arbitration). A stockbroker in Oklahoma, after losing a large arbitration case, admitted to his clients that options confused him. "I never should have messed with them," he said. A Florida broker who suffered huge losses in his own account took his brokerage firm to arbitration, arguing that he was in over his head and his boss should have realized it.

If the brokers didn't understand what they were doing, you can imagine where their customers stood. Yet as I write, in mid-1997, that same game is being played again. Here's a glimpse of the complexities of stock-index trading, just to show you what you're up against.

Stock-Index Options, Defined: When you buy or sell these options, you're hoping to profit from the changing price of stocks. You're betting that a specific stock index will rise or fall by a specified amount within a limited period—typically one to 4 months. The cost of the option is known as its *premium*. You also have to pay brokerage commissions.

Buying a call is betting that the index will rise by at least a certain amount. Buying a put is betting that the index will fall by a certain amount. When you buy an option, your risk is limited to the money you put up.

When you *sell* an option, however, your risk is unlimited. Many investors and brokers fail to grasp this crucial difference. So, in their innocence, they hit on what seems like a "safer" way of playing a strong market than buying calls. They decide to sell puts, which are a bet that stocks won't fall over a specified period of time. But if you're wrong, you can lose far more than you put up. Many unlucky players were selling puts on the eve of the 1987 Crash, which explains why their losses were so big.

A winning option can be held until maturity and settled for cash or it can be sold at a profit ahead of time. To cut your losses on a losing option, try to dispose of it before it expires. If you don't, or can't, that money is gone. Options are offered on a variety of stock-market indexes, but the most popular is the Standard & Poor's 100 (100 blue-chip stocks).

If you don't want a 3-month speculation, you might consider LEAPS (page 803). They're available for certain individual stocks as well as for the market index as a whole. But remember: If you buy the stock directly and the price goes down, you still own its remaining value. If you buy an option and lose your bet, not a single dime remains.

Stock Futures, Defined: When you buy or sell futures, you are contracting to buy a particular commodity. In this case, the commodity is a stock-market index, the most popular being the S&P 500-stock index. You put up about 10 percent of the contract as collateral. If stock prices move in the right direction (either up or down, depending on your bet), you can sell the contract at a profit. Or you can take a cash settlement at the end of the contract's term. Either way, you get your collateral back. If the market runs against you, you will be asked for more collateral. Your losses could be substantially more than you put up.

Options on Stock Futures, Defined: Here, you're betting on whether the price of a stock futures contract will rise or fall. You can buy or sell either puts or calls. Either way, you will own a piece of paper that speculates on the changing worth of another piece of paper. (If you're not with me, that's proof that you shouldn't be with an options broker, either.)

The prices of options on futures swing more widely and wildly than the prices of options on the stock indexes themselves. So of these three super-risky investments, buying futures options combines the highest potential for gain with "limited" losses (*only* 100 percent of your investment could go down the drain).

A Conservative Use of Stock-Index Options Is to Hedge Against an Anticipated Market Drop. If you own a large and diversified stock portfolio, but don't want to sell for tax or other reasons, you can buy puts on an index that resembles your holdings. In a market decline, you'll lose on your stocks but make money on your puts. Your losses may not be fully covered by your gains, but at least you'll have limited the shock. If the market doesn't fall, however, you'll have paid a pretty penny for peace of mind.

A Speculative Use of Stock-Index Options Is to Bet on Which Way the Market Will Move. Minor changes in the index produce big percentage gains or losses on the money you put up. But to win this game you have to get three things right: (1) the market has to move in the right direction; (2)

the index has to rise or fall by more than enough to cover your costs; and (3) the change has to come within a short and specified period. That's market timing with a vengeance. It shouldn't surprise you to hear that the majority of options buyers lose. But their brokers win. At a full-service firm, your combined buying and selling commissions generally run in the area of 5 to 8 percent of your invested capital, although they can go both lower and higher.

Just as you can speculate in puts and calls on the market as a whole, you can do so on individual stocks, such as General Electric or IBM.

A conservative use of options is to sell calls against blue-chip stocks you own—an action known as writing covered calls. If you own IBM, for example, you can sell someone the right to buy it from you at a specified higher price (the "strike price"). The money you collect is called a premium. If IBM doesn't rise above the strike price, you keep the premium and the stock—so you eat your cake and have it, too. If the price does go up, your IBM stock will be called away, costing you the capital gain. So you earn extra income by writing options but will give up a lot of stock profits, over time. Speculators soon lose interest in covered calls.

A hugely high-risk use of options is to sell them against stocks you don't own, a strategy known as writing naked calls. Suppose that you write such a call against General Electric. As long as the price of GE doesn't rise above the strike price, you win. If it does, you lose. You would have to buy GE in the open market, whatever its price, to deliver to the person who bought the call. Alternatively, you might write naked puts. As long as the stock doesn't drop below the strike price, you win. If it does, you will have to buy the stock for something more than its market price.

Some speculators substitute options for stocks. If you feel in your gut that IBM will go up pretty soon, it's cheaper (and potentially more profitable) to buy a 3-month call on the stock than to buy the stock itself. If the price rises enough, you win. If your gut was just registering indigestion, however, you'll be out the money. One popular game: buying calls on companies that announce stock splits, in hope the stock will jump in price.

To give your loot more time to work, you might consider buying LEAPS —long-term equity anticipation securities. These are options that can last for up to 3 years, giving you more time for the stock price to move your way. Longer-term options cost more than the short-term kind.

When the speculators are Wall Street pros, I couldn't care less. Professional investors are action junkies and options are an easy fix. Ditto for economists and other interest-rate experts who often gamble on Treasury-bond futures. But no individual seriously trying to build net worth should use options, period. Even if you win at the start you will lose in the end.

CHICKEN FUNDS:
THE ULTIMATE PLUCKING MACHINE

Chicken funds (mostly unit trusts) flourish after any stock-market scare. Sponsors package a "safe" zero-coupon bond with a speculative or growth investment like stocks or real estate. Part of your money buys the zero, which returns your original investment after a specified period of time. The rest goes into the riskier side of the package. The pitch is: "Come back to the market, my dear departed ones. I'm positive that your money will grow. To calm your nerves, I will guarantee that, whatever happens, you will get your money back."

Salespeople call chicken funds "balanced investments." I call them humbug. The zeros don't lower your investment risk.

Here's what's wrong with chicken funds:

Over 5 to 8 years the zero will mature—eventually repaying the money you originally put in. But it will have lost a lot of purchasing power. Also, you may have paid taxes every year on the interest building inside the bond. To keep up with inflation and taxes and earn a real return on your money, you are counting on the other part of your investment—the stocks or the real estate—to succeed. So the zero hasn't shielded you from risk at all.

You're at double jeopardy if you want to sell. You'll lose money unless both parts of your packaged investment did well. Had you held, say, your stocks and your zeros separately, you'd be able to sell just one or the other, as market conditions dictate.

Markets Are Not "Safe." Zeros Will Not Make Them So. When you buy a zero combined with any other kind of investment, you are really making a three-part bet: that your growth investments will succeed; that you will hold to maturity; or that interest rates will fall, so that if you sell before maturity, the zero will show a profit, not a loss. That's a lot of ifs. Furthermore, you pay a higher commission to buy zeros packaged with growth investments than you would if you bought them separately through a mutual fund or discount broker.

COLLATERALIZED MORTGAGE
OBLIGATIONS (CMOs)

CMOs are touted to people who might otherwise buy Ginnie Maes. They're packages of AAA-rated mortgages, either government or privately insured. They offer higher rates of interest than Ginnie Maes and are supposed to pay out in a certain number of years.

But how fast you get your money back depends on how fast people repay the mortgages you've invested in. If rates fall, people will prepay. Instead of having, say, a 7-year investment, you might be repaid over just 2 years. That lowers your yield. You're also forced to reinvest at a time when interest rates are down, so you get less income from your money than you did before. By contrast, if interest rates rise people might repay their mortgages more slowly. What you thought was a 7-year investment might last 20 years or more. Can you afford to wait that long? It's hard to sell CMOs before maturity at a decent price.

If you're tempted by a CMO, ask the broker to show you what happens to the investment's payout rate and yield if interest rates rise or fall by one, 2, and 3 percentage points. The results may astonish you. A type of CMO called a planned amortization class (PAC) is supposed to repay in the period originally promised, but in bad markets that hasn't worked out.

Personally, I'm skeptical of fancy new ways of holding investments that worked okay the old way. You'll be happier in the long run with a Ginnie Mae mutual fund.

A FEW MORE THINGS YOU MAY REGRET IN THE MORNING

1. Any new investment touted as "safe" with a higher-than-normal yield. This field is so jammed with hopefuls that I had trouble picking just one to tell you about. Anyway, for your delectation, here's the story on adjustable-rate mortgages (ARM) or adjustable-rate securities funds:

These often are sold as higher-yielding substitutes for safe investments —"almost a CD" or "like a money market mutual fund with a higher yield." But CDs are safe and money funds safe enough. Not ARM funds. The value of their principal fluctuates—perhaps just a little, perhaps a lot, as interest rates rise and fall. The securities in ARM funds are backed by adjustable-rate mortgages and collateralized mortgage obligations (page 804), some of which are riskier than others. The higher the return relative to CDs and money market funds, the more your fund is apt to fall when interest rates rise. In the bad bond market of 1994, returns on ARM funds ranged from a happy 4.3 percent to a shocking − 20.6 percent.

There's nothing wrong with ARM funds per se. But you can't be sure how big a risk you're taking and the salesperson doesn't know, either. If you hold for 2 or 3 years you should net more than you would from CDs, but that's not a sure thing. ARM funds are no place for money that you're trying to keep absolutely safe.

2. Any mutual fund calling itself Something Plus—as in Government Plus. Such a name implies high yields at no increase in risk. That's never true. There is always risk. "Plus" means "We'll try to squeeze out some

extra money by hedging with index options, zloty futures, and puts on Imelda Marcos's shoe collection." That might work. Then again, it might not. Mark these funds a minus. Ditto any fund calling itself *enhanced*.

3. Anything hyped on late-night, get-rich-quick TV shows. No-money-down real-estate deals. Options on grain or oil futures. Penny stocks. Investment tapes and books of any kind.

4. Anything hyped by phone, by a salesperson you don't know. Even if the firm is honest, this is no way to pick an investment. If the firm is dishonest, you're being set up to lose serious money. The bigger the profit the broker promises, and the greater the pressure to make a decision, the worse the investment is going to be.

5. Diamonds and other precious gems. Wholesale prices are rigged. Markups are huge, as are discounts when you try to sell. Published price indexes are unreliable. The price of any individual stone depends on subjective judgments about its "quality grade," which is an invitation to cheat. Even if the dealers all agree on a stone's grading and it's backed by a certificate from the Gemological Institute of America, you could still get burned by paying too much. True investment-grade stones are kept in their own soft bags, in vaults. Stones made into jewelry generally are of lesser grade and don't fluctuate so much in price. By the time a stone is set, it may retail for more than double the value of the gem itself.

6. Smaller stocks that trade over the counter in limited amounts. Brokers may take huge markups on these issues. You may need a 20 percent increase in price just to cover the overt and hidden costs. Buy a smaller OTC stock only for a sound, fundamental reason, and plan to hold it a long, long time.

7. Rare, or "numismatic," coins. These are strictly for specialists. Among coin collectors, the condition of a coin is critical and you're in no position to judge. Two coins of the same apparent grade could sell for different prices, depending on who graded them. A coin might be graded up when you buy in order to make it more expensive. When you sell, a different dealer might grade it down, which lowers its price. Even the price of an 'MS65" (MS meaning "mint state"), which is just about tops, will vary according to who certified it. Some quite ordinary coins are sold to the credulous at excessive prices. To buy well, you have to know your way around.

By all means collect rare coins as a hobby. Start visiting dealers and auctions. Subscribe to *Coin World,* published in Sidney, Ohio, which has reasonably good coin-price indexes. If you really get smart about your hobby, your passion could become your investment. Otherwise, it's a waste of money.

8. Collectibles of all kinds—stamps, art, porcelain, rare books, maps, antiques, rare wines, Oriental rugs, baseball cards, Mickey Mouse ears. None is worth a moment of your time. They yield their treasure only to

dedicated collectors, who study them, admire them, and understand their value. Buy a lithograph because you love it, not because you think it will make you rich.

GOLD: THE ULTIMATE WORRY BEAD

For some, it's a trauma defense. Let the Middle East mushroom into darkest night, let Russia flame into civil war, there will be gold.

For others, it's the supreme inflation hedge. If the U.S. dollar is ever carted off in wheelbarrows, there will be gold.

But in practice, gold doesn't always work out so well. Take the trauma defense. Back when Lebanon first fell apart, rich people rushed to their banks to retrieve their gold, only to be robbed of it by gunmen at the door. The gold hoards of many Kuwaitis were similarly seized by Iraqi troops.

Gold is also a bust as an ordinary inflation hedge. In 1974, with gold at $200 an ounce, it became legal again for Americans to own it. Since then, there has been a huge run-up in price followed by a collapse. Over the whole period, gold has fallen well behind the inflation rate.

Gold will protect you against a hyperinflation or currency collapse. But those risks are remote, hence not worth the average investor's time and money. You need to grow your assets for college tuition and retirement. You cannot afford to prepare yourself for Armageddon, too. For everyday inflation protection, you are well enough hedged by owning your own home, common stocks, and short-term or inflation-protection Treasury securities (page 763).

For ordinary investors, gold is like any other sector—sometimes good, sometimes not.

What moves gold prices? Who knows? Demand may suddenly explode for a wide variety of geopolitical reasons, none of them predictable. But surprises aside, gold is thought to move up on the expectation of higher inflation ahead and move down on the expectation of level to lower inflation—that is, unless there's a competing inflation investment that looks even better. Lately, investors have been perfectly happy in short-term government securities rather than gold.

If you're still interested in owning gold, here are the various ways to buy:

Gold-Mining Stocks and Mutual Funds. There are two ways of using these funds, one aggressive, one conservative:

Gunslingers swing into mutual funds when they think that gold prices are going to rise. The stocks of gold-mining companies move up faster and higher than gold itself. Conversely, the stocks suffer faster and deeper losses when gold prices drop, so speculators may not own them long.

Conservative buyers might own a gold mutual fund for diversification. Gold stocks often go up when the rest of the market is going down, and vice versa. And unlike gold itself, the stocks pay dividends. To avoid the funds' roller-coaster price risks, invest a fixed amount of money regularly, every month, for several years. You'll wind up with a long-term precious-metals position at a reasonable average cost.

Gold Bullion Coins and Bars. These are for trauma strategists, who hold gold against the risk of some frightful (but not unthinkable) disaster. "Bullion" coins have no numismatic interest. They're traded on the basis of their gold content plus a small premium to cover distribution, manufacturing costs, and profits. Premiums depend on the weight of your coin and the size of your order. For a small order of one-ounce coins, you might pay 3.5 to 6 percent over the gold price, depending on the dealer, plus a one percent sales commission. There may also be a shipping charge.

Investors stick with one-ounce coins. The smaller coins (half-ounce, quarter-ounce, and so on) are more heavily freighted with sales and manufacturing expenses, making it hard for buyers to earn a profit. You'll see small coins in jewelry, not in safe-deposit boxes. Of the many bullion coins now on the market, the most widely sold are the U.S.-minted American Eagle, the Canadian Maple Leaf, the Australian Nugget, and the Chinese Panda.

Here are some cost data to help you gauge the fairness of the prices you're offered on a purchase of 5 to 10 gold coins: The U.S. and Canadian mints sell coins to primary wholesale dealers for the current auction price of gold plus 3 percent. The primary wholesalers mark up the price by about half a percentage point and sell to retailers. The lowest-cost retailers add another half point, so their coins sell at the price of gold plus 4 percent. Other retailers price up from there. So gold prices have to rise by 4 percent or more for you to break even after costs.

Costs are typically higher if you buy just one coin and lower on a larger order. You may owe sales taxes unless you can legally store your gold hoard out of state.

When you resell a coin, you might be offered 2 to 3 percentage points over the auction-market price minus a one percent sales commission—but bids vary, so shop around.

The best way to compare prices is to call several dealers and ask for "the market"—both the buying price and selling price for an order of the size you're interested in—plus the commission, shipping charges, and any other fees. Don't tip your hand in advance by indicating whether you mean to buy or sell.

Bullion bars are generally fabricated for wealthy investors who buy their gold in major league amounts. Small bars are poured, too, but sometimes by little-known companies whose bars may or may not be readily accepted for resale. To protect your investment, stick with the majors. The dominant small bars traded in the United States are made by Crédit Suisse and Pamp SA, sealed in plastic and sold with a certificate of authenticity. One-ounce bars sell for the gold price plus premiums of $7 to $10.

Silver Doesn't Carry the Same Cachet as Gold. The price may indeed go up in times of rising inflation and high political risk. But silver more often trades as an industrial metal, responsive to changes in the photography, dentistry, and electronics industries. The coin of choice for silver investors is the one-ounce American Eagle. It sells at about 1.25 to 1.5 percent over the price of silver, plus a one percent sales commission, for lots of 100 to 400 coins. Investors can also buy silver bars.

Platinum coins have a modest following. Like silver, platinum is used primarily in jewelry and for industrial purposes (especially in auto antipollution devices). Prices jump around a lot. The jury is out on whether this metal will ever be considered a store of value. The commonest platinum coin is the Canadian Mint. In 1997 the U.S. Congress passed a bill allowing an American coin.

THE IMPOSSIBLE TRIPLE PLAY

The bad investments pretend to be all things to all people. "Buy me," they whisper, "and you'll get your three wishes—high growth, high income, and no risk." Some throw in a fourth wish, tax avoidance, just for spice.

But no single investment fulfills all those hopes. Each one leans in one direction, at the expense of the others. When you go for high income, you give up some safety and growth. When you go for high growth, you give up some safety and income. When you go for safety, you lose growth and income. Any investment that promises all three is a fraud of some sort.

The financial press is loaded with warnings from saddened investors who fell for one slick promise too many. Study their stories. Better an object lesson than a learning experience.

27.

Aimez-Vous Growth?

The Case for Putting Some Money Abroad

The question is no longer whether Americans should invest
abroad. It's only what to buy and how much.

With the twenty-first century upon us, Americans should be investing abroad as comfortably as they do at home. Thousands of you do already. But to many investors, foreign markets still feel like too much of a gamble.

I'd like to change your mind.

There are four strong reasons for putting some of your money abroad:

1. *To invest in some of the world's most powerful economic trends.* These include the rebuilding of Eastern Europe, the consolidation and restructuring of Western Europe, Latin America's new appetite for private investment, the growth of consumer markets in Asia as its armies of workers rise to the middle class, the spread of sophisticated global communication, and the rapid growth of any low-wage country whose government encourages private capital. Two-thirds of the world's investment opportunities are now offshore.

2. *To catch other countries' business cycles.* Over the long term, leading international companies do as well as similar companies in the United States. But over the short term, their stocks rise and fall at different times and at different rates of speed. Potentially, you can improve your returns by having a piece of the action, wherever it is.

3. *To invest in currencies other than greenbacks.* When you buy foreign stocks, you're exchanging dollars for foreign currencies. Sometimes dollar-based investments give you the best international returns, sometimes foreign currencies do. Owning both is a way of spreading risk.

4. *To reduce the risk to your investments overall.* This surprises many investors, who assume that foreign stocks carry greater risks. Individually, they may, but not in combination with U.S. stocks. Foreign markets may be strong when U.S. markets are weak, and vice versa. When one market declines, another may rise. During major U.S. market drops, such as the Crash of '87, foreign markets usually drop in synch. But over time, the diversification thesis holds. Even if U.S. and foreign markets yield similar long-term results, a global portfolio carries less downside risk.

What's a Good International Asset Allocation? Advisers suggest that you commit 20 to 30 percent of your portfolio. Put the bulk of it into a well-diversified stock-owning mutual fund, with perhaps 5 percent in emerging markets and 5 percent in an international small-company fund.

THE DOLLAR CONNECTION

When you buy foreign securities, two factors influence how much money you'll make or lose: (1) How well those particular foreign markets perform. Do stocks rise or fall? Are bond interest rates going up or down? Is the political or economic climate good or bad? These concepts are familiar to anybody who invests. (2) Which way the U.S. dollar moves. This is the unfamiliar part. The dollar connection leaves a lot of investors confused.

Sometimes the Dollar Declines on Certain International Markets. American currency is worth less while foreign currency is worth more. The result: Foreign securities *rise* in value, in dollar terms. As an example, take a $100 Japanese stock whose price in Japan remains unchanged. If the dollar drops by 5 percent against the Japanese yen, the dollar price of that stock rises to $105. You have made money solely because of the currency change.

Sometimes the Dollar Rises on Certain Foreign Markets. American currency is worth more while foreign currency is worth less. Result: Foreign securities *fall* in value, in dollar terms. If you buy a $100 Japanese stock and the dollar rises 5 percent against the yen, your stock will be worth $95. Your loss came from the currency, not from any weakness in the underlying stock.

The dollar may rise against one currency while it's falling against another, depending on such things as comparative rates of inflation and whether each country's interest rates are moving up or down. Some countries peg their currencies to the dollar, but that doesn't free you from risk. These countries might suddenly devalue their currency and repeg it at a lower rate.

Generally speaking, your foreign investments are helped by a falling dollar and hurt by a rising dollar. A country's bourse may be flying in local-currency terms but look depressed to a U.S. investor because the dollar is going up. When the dollar moves down again, U.S. investors will show much better returns.

But the relationship between currency and investment performance isn't exact. When the dollar rises against a national currency, that country's products get relatively cheaper for American consumers. Its exports, corporate profits, and stock prices usually go up, which offset your losses from the unfavorable currency change. The reverse may happen when the dollar declines. That country's exports get more expensive, so its exports, profits, and stocks go down. Economic change offsets the effect of currency change.

Now you understand (I hope) why international investing needs to be a long-term proposition. Over the short term, currency change may dominate. Over the long term, however, the effects of currency cycles roughly cancel each other out—especially in well-diversified funds that invest in major markets. Long-term investors are hitched to international growth. Your capital gains will far outweigh the effects of short-term currency shifts.

It's quite another story, however, for people in single-country funds—especially in volatile emerging markets. There, a government-sponsored currency devaluation could hurt your returns for a considerable period of time.

Investors in foreign bonds also shoulder a big risk. Your long-term returns are lower than you'll earn from stocks, so a negative currency change eats up proportionately more of your gain. In some years, your entire gain or loss comes entirely from currency fluctuation. Foreign bonds should be thought of as pure currency diversification—a bet against the dollar that should earn a competitive return over a *long* holding period.

Every investment gain or loss in foreign markets come in two parts—changes in the market itself and changes in currency values, if any. Both contribute to your total return. The following table shows how that worked in various stock markets for the 12 months ending in December 1996.

DO YOURSELF A FAVOR: BUY MUTUAL FUNDS

It's hard to pick foreign stocks and bonds successfully. To do so, you have to follow foreign economies, politics, tax laws, financial news, and interest rates; the outlook for each foreign currency relative to the dollar; each company's growth, profitability, and prospects; and the vagaries of each foreign stock market.

IF YOU INVESTED IN	THE PRICE INDEX* ROSE (FELL) BY	THE LOCAL CURRENCY ROSE (FELL) BY†	AMERICAN INVESTORS GAINED (LOST)‡
Spain	50.2%	−6.7%	40.0%
Finland	42.2	−5.8	33.9
Ireland	25.0	5.6	32.0
United Kingdom	15.6	10.2	27.4
United States	23.2	0	23.2
Australia	9.1	6.8	16.5
Germany	22.3	−7.1	13.6
Italy	7.9	4.3	12.6
Austria	12.5	−7.1	4.5
Switzerland	19.4	−14.3	2.3
Singapore	−7.9	1.1	−6.9
Japan	−4.9	−11.1	−15.5

* The Morgan Stanley Capital International index of local stocks.
† Against the dollar.
‡ The percentage change in U.S. dollars is not directly equivalent to the percentage change in the local index plus or minus the change in currency values.
SOURCE: Morgan Stanley Capital International

That's a lot. What's more, you have to do your research without access to as much financial information or stock-market data as is available in the United States. You're more dependent on investment-advisory services and the recommendations put out by the research departments of brokerage firms. There's less investor protection, more stock manipulation, and more government interference abroad than American markets tolerate.

Or you could buy mutual funds.

If ever there is an argument for mutual funds, it's for buyers of international securities. Sit back, relax, and leave the driving to them.

WHICH TYPE OF STOCK FUND?

International funds buy securities everywhere but the United States. For your first (or sole) foreign investment, this is the kind to own. Look for a big, diversified fund. It leans toward larger companies in the industrialized countries but usually allocates some money to emerging markets and smaller stocks, too. With this investment, you stay in control of the portion of your total assets that you keep abroad. You also share in every type of international growth.

A growing number of international funds specialize in smaller stocks. They're more volatile than big, diversified funds but ought to deliver higher capital gains, long term.

Global funds buy stocks worldwide. As much as one-third of their assets could be invested in the United States. They'll beat the pure international funds when the American market is strong and underperform them when it's weak. At various times, you'll have different portions of your money invested abroad, depending on what the manager decides to buy.

Regional funds stick to a local group of countries, such as Europe or the Pacific Rim. They're bets on a particular part of the world, for those who think they know which part of the world is going to do the best. Some Pacific funds specifically exclude Japan, so they look good when Japan is in a funk. But they may trail when the Japanese stock prices march up.

Emerging-markets funds buy stocks in less developed markets around the world: Eastern Europe, Asia, Latin America, Africa, the Near East—you name it, these funds have it. They're wildly volatile and subject to enormous economic, political, and currency risk. You wouldn't want to put a lot of money here. On the other hand, the countries they invest in tend to be the fastest growing in the world. The big international fund you own may invest in emerging markets for you. If not, buy one of these funds, shut your eyes to the rough years, and plan to hold for a *very* long time.

International index funds have had mixed success. For a discussion, see page 703.

Single-country funds are generally closed-end (page 641). That frees their managers to invest in small stocks, private placements, and illiquid issues—commonplace in very small markets—without worrying about how to pay off investors who want to cash out. If these funds had to be prepared to sell shares to meet sudden waves of redemptions, they'd have a more limited investment palette. Their selling might also drive share prices down, especially in countries where the stock market is small.

Like any other closed-end fund, these should generally be bought only when they trade at a deep discount to the value of the securities in the fund's portfolio (say, a discount of 10 to 15 percent or more). If you buy at a premium over the net asset value, you are usually setting yourself up for a loss. Ditto if you buy when the fund is first being offered to investors.

Even at a discount, any single-country fund carries extra risk. If that country's market or currency hits a downdraft, so does your investment—and the manager can't shift his or her money to a more profitable part of the globe. If a new closed-end fund for that particular country is introduced, investors may lose interest in the older fund, causing its price to drop.

Closed-ends are for people who want to roll the dice on a particular country. Don't even think about it unless you know that country well, and have taken the time to study how its fund price moves.

Foreign-Bond Funds

Unsuspecting investors buy foreign-bond funds in hope of securing a higher-than-normal income. They don't understand the currency risk (page

811). You'll get a fine yield if the dollar stays level or declines, but your income or total return will shrink if the value of the dollar goes up.

There's no free lunch in the interest-rate market. If a bond is paying 12 percent in U.S. dollar terms, when similar American bonds are at 7 percent, it means that the market expects a 5 percent rise in the dollar against that particular currency, to equalize yields. You'll make extra money only if the market guessed wrong and the dollar doesn't rise that far. The market may indeed guess wrong but you can't count on it.

International bond funds vary in how they handle currency shifts. Some adjust your dividends up and down as the dollar falls and rises. If you're living on this income, you'll find that your periodic payouts gyrate a lot. Other funds pay the full dividend and adjust for currency changes in other ways—maybe in the fund's net asset value or maybe in your individual tax basis (page 637). These changes aren't as noticeable if you're reinvesting dividends.

The funds may try to stabilize their dividend payouts by hedging currencies and placing other arcane bets. The cost of hedging normally makes only a minor difference to a fund's net asset value. On the other hand, one reason you invest abroad is for currency diversification and hedging takes some or all of that away. If you haven't diversified against the dollar, why have an international fund at all?

Some advisers tout global bond funds instead of international funds because global funds include U.S. bonds. This limits your currency risk but also reduces your diversification.

Over the long term, international diversification lowers the downside risk in a fixed-income portfolio. That's because bond prices rise and fall in different countries at different times, so you're usually getting good performance from at least part of your portfolio. But for the average investor who owns stocks and bonds, the reduction in risk may be negligible. Owning international stocks is important, but as you allocate your assets, international bonds should be one of the last things you buy—if you buy them at all.

There's an interesting argument, however, for tossing some money at bond funds invested in developing-country debt. They're wildly speculative. One year you'll be creamed, the next year you'll have sensational gains. But assuming that these fast-growing countries gradually improve their credit ratings, you could get superior returns over the very long term. Play with a *small* amount of money (in your retirement account, if you have the option), and only if you're an experienced investor. Then hang on for the roller-coaster ride.

If you depend on your capital for a steady income, homegrown bonds are generally best. If you do choose a foreign-bond fund, make it a no-load (because you don't want sales charges cutting into your total return) or a closed-end fund selling at a decent discount.

Foreign-Currency Mutual Funds

Take care. Some advertise themselves as money market funds because they buy foreign money market instruments, such as short-term government securities and certificates of deposit. But the value of your shares isn't fixed at one dollar, as is the case with real money market funds. Instead, your investment will fluctuate with changes in the dollar value of foreign currencies.

Although these mutual funds earn interest, they're almost entirely currency plays. Some buy just a single currency, some buy several. They'll do moderately well when the dollar declines and badly when it rises. Their expenses are high, which takes a big bite out of their potential yield. To me, there are plenty of better places to put my money. Like, almost anywhere.

Warning: It costs more to buy foreign securities than American securities. You pay for currency conversion and face much higher expenses for completing transactions. There are often big markups on securities prices, especially in emerging markets. As a result, global and international funds charge higher annual fees than domestic funds.

For how to account for foreign taxes paid by your fund, see page 639.

Many U.S. Mutual Funds Invest a Small Portion of Their Money Abroad. Check your prospectus to see if your funds have the right to do so. Then check your semiannual reports to see if any foreign shares have actually been bought.

If all your funds together routinely keep around 20 percent of their assets in foreign stocks, you don't have to buy an international fund in order to diversify. Your American funds have done it for you.

But, but, but. One or two of your funds may change their minds and sell part of their positions. You'd then have less foreign diversification than you'd intended. Furthermore, U.S.-based managers may not have as much success with foreign stocks. If things go badly for the countries they bought, they may cut and run rather than prowl the world for other opportunities. Your fund should be working with research firms that are located abroad. Check for this in the prospectus and annual report.

For better control of your asset allocation, consider splitting your money between pure U.S. funds and pure international funds. Separate funds also make it easier to measure your managers' relative performance. An all-U.S. fund can be cleanly compared with a U.S. fund index. If it also contains international stocks, it's harder to judge how good your manager actually is.

SOME OTHER WAYS
TO JOIN THE PARADE

If you're willing and able to do your own securities and currency research, there are several other roads to foreign investing:

U.S. Multinational Corporations—an armchair way for your money to travel. Look for major U.S. companies that earn a large percentage of their profits abroad. Just a few examples: IBM, Coca-Cola, Minnesota Mining & Manufacturing, Microsoft, Procter & Gamble, and McDonald's. Owning them gives you a stake in international growth as well as a minor currency play. Their foreign earnings are worth more when the dollar declines and less when the dollar rises. On the other hand, U.S. companies pretty much rise and fall with the S&P 500-stock index, so you aren't truly diversifying your overall investment risk.

Foreign Stocks Trading in the United States—on the major exchanges or over the counter. Almost all of them are Canadian shares. Canada's markets track American stock indexes pretty closely, so you don't get much diversification there. If you buy Canadian mining shares, you're in your own universe, not mine.

American Depositary Receipts (ADRs)—an indirect way of buying individual company stock. ADRs represent foreign shares that are held in the vaults of a custodian bank. You buy and sell them as if they were the stocks themselves. At this writing, more than 1,300 ADRs are offered to retail investors. Some are listed on the New York or American Stock Exchanges or on Nasdaq. Many trade through the Pink Sheets (page 711). You can also get some through dividend-reinvestment plans (page 688).

More than one-fourth of the ADRs are "sponsored" by the companies themselves. They give you American-style financial information (although not as quickly) and pick up the cost of administering the securities. The remaining ADRs are "unsponsored," meaning that they're managed by a bank without company involvement. With unsponsored ADRs, you usually get no financial reports. The administrative cost (maybe 2 to 4 cents a share) is deducted from your dividends. The ADRs of some well-known companies are unsponsored, including, at this writing, Mitsubishi Electric, Club Méditerranée, and Olivetti. Many ADRs represent one share each, but some represent bundles of five or ten shares or fractions of a single share. The Nestlé ADR, for example, is one-twentieth of a Swiss share.

Many of the listed ADRs attract a lot of buyers. But Pink Sheet issues are often illiquid. When you sell them, you're apt to take a haircut on the price. Generally speaking, investors should stick with sponsored ADRs that are listed on Nasdaq or the exchanges and trade actively all the time.

Foreign Ordinary Shares—direct investments in individual stocks on foreign stock exchanges. You have access to thousands of shares that have no ADRs—for example, the small British company that made headlines after cloning Dolly the sheep. The discount broker Charles Schwab offers a global investing service, although the costs are much higher than for speculations in U.S. shares.

Individual Foreign Bonds—absolutely not for the average buyer. They carry high minimum investments—often $25,000 to $50,000 or more. And it's tough to make money on them after paying all the costs—currency conversion, brokerage commissions, transaction fees, and the profit that brokerage houses tack on to the price. Bond lovers should buy mutual funds, instead.

Foreign-Currency Bank Accounts—offered by a small number of banks. You can get interest-paying money market funds and certificates of deposit denominated in Japanese yen, German marks, Canadian or Australian dollars, French or Swiss francs, British pounds, the Euro, if it materializes, and other currencies. Interest is paid in those currencies, and so are the fees charged.

At present, these accounts are used principally by companies that do business abroad and by travelers locking up the cost of their foreign vacations. For example, if you're going to Germany six months from now and buy a 6-month, mark-denominated certificate of deposit, your vacation fund will be insulated from any changes in the value of the dollar. If you care.

A Contrarian Case. Rex Sinquefield, co-chair of Dimensional Fund Advisors (page 705), thinks that the typical international mutual fund isn't giving Americans much diversification. His research shows that the leading international growth stocks behave pretty much like comparable stocks in the United States. So they don't materially enhance your investment returns or decrease your risks. Your best shot at adding value internationally, he thinks, is by buying foreign funds that emphasize smaller stocks and "value" stocks (page 698).

At this writing, big-company stocks are whomping smaller stocks, both at home and abroad. So Sinquefield's thesis doesn't look so good. But markets are supposed to reward risk, so over the long term he might be right. At minimum, this is an argument for splitting your international money between a big-stock and small-stock fund.

FOLLOW THE GROWTH

Countries the world over are learning from the American economic model: deregulate industries, downsize the public sector, open trade, reduce public debt, reorganize the corporate sector, and hold inflation and interest rates low. If these trends persist, with no shock to the global political or economic system, they prefigure the same long-term growth in foreign markets as the 1980s and 1990s gave us here.

28.

Real Estate—The New Winning Systems

Finding the Properties That Pay

*Everyone said, "You can't lose money in real estate because
they're not making any more of it." Hmmmm. Where did
everyone go wrong?*

To make money in real estate today you need a system. Any one of a score of systems will do. Successful investors are following their fortunes along more tracks than I have the space to write about. You'll find 17 of their strategies starting on page 823. Unsuccessful investors are mostly on one of two tracks, both of them so popular that I want to dismiss them before getting down to serious business.

HOW TO LOSE MONEY IN REAL ESTATE

The most desired loser today is the single-family rental house. I'm speaking of houses that are rented for less than their carrying cost. You dip into your pocket to help cover the expenses, but you believe that you'll more than earn that money back when you finally sell. This strategy worked fine in the 1970s and part of the 1980s, when speculation and the baby boomers lit a firecracker under housing values. But those great gains have fizzled out. Even if prices drift gently up—say, at 4 percent a year—most rental houses aren't good deals. After expenses, you'd probably do better with nice, quiet tax-free bonds. And tax-free bonds never call to complain that the windows leak or the bulb in the back hall burned out.

Investors in rental condominiums are doing even worse. Condos are chronically overbuilt, which holds down their rents and resale values.

The other popular strategy in trouble is the "cosmetic" fixer-upper. You buy a house with a few minor problems and put some money into repairs. A few months later you try to resell at a higher price. But *everyone* wants that perfect little fixer-upper, so it's not cheap. The price you need to make a profit will probably exceed the property's value after the makeover. So, for a year or more, no one will buy. To pick up some money, you'll take a tenant whose rent won't cover your carrying costs. That brings you back to the failed strategy I mentioned first.

You May Not Even Realize That You're Losing Money on the Property! As long as you sell for more than you paid, you might think that you came out ahead. You'll then be encouraged to get yourself into another terrible real-estate deal. So do yourself a favor and find out the truth. Determine what you made or lost on any venture you tried in the past, counting all expenses and stating your profits as an annual compounded rate of return. And don't buy into anything new without a businesslike projection of what it will take to make a profit.

HOW TO MAKE MONEY IN REAL ESTATE

Active real-estate investing is a part-time or full-time job. You're a deal maker, an entrepreneur. You're running your own small business. The successful investor will:

• Work up a personal investment system. (For some overlooked approaches, see page 823.)

• Spend a lot of time looking at properties. You might do one deal for every 50, or 100, or 1,000 you consider. You won't actually visit 1,000 properties, but you might look at 1,000 deeds in the courthouse. If even reading this sentence bores you, forget active real-estate investing. Buy real-estate investment trusts instead (page 836).

• Nail all the operating costs—not just mortgage, taxes, and insurance but also advertising for tenants, repairs, utilities, trash hauling, maintenance of all kinds, reserves for repainting and replacements, fix-up costs between renters, loss of rent during those periods, and a dozen other things. You'll need to improve the property after you buy it, but by just enough to maintain its value and make it rentable.

• Develop strict financial criteria to identify properties worth buying. For example, you should have rules for how much you'll pay for a property —*any* property—relative to its fix-up costs, rents, and expenses (page 833), and rules for the minimum projected profit you'll accept. Investors who fail either lack sound criteria or lack the discipline to follow them. It does no good to buy the best property you can find if it doesn't meet your financial criteria. You should be looking somewhere else.

• Learn how to project a property's probable compounded annual rate of return. It's not enough to say, "Wow, I'll net $3,000 a month." That might come to only a 3 percent return on the capital you invested. At that rate, you might as well keep your money in the bank.

• Have a large enough line of credit to carry a good investment through a bad market or a period when it cannot be rented. Otherwise, you may be forced to sell at a giveaway price.

• Look for properties that my friend Jack Reed* calls lepers. Neither the seller nor other potential buyers see much value in them. But thanks to your X-ray vision, you might. Some leper strategies follow. One of your criteria: Buy only properties that you can get for at least 20 percent below what you believe is their true market value. That's not an easy job, but real-estate investing isn't easy anymore.

TOMORROW IS YESTERDAY— AND A GOOD THING, TOO

To discover how rental real estate will be played in the '90s and '00s, put away all your books by Donald Trump. Have a chat with your grandfather instead. For people who plan to hold properties for the long term, real-estate investing has reverted to an older style. You stand or fall by the annual income you get from rents, rather than making money mainly on tax deductions and capital gains. A good rental investment has to generate real cash. Every year. Year in, year out.

Investors in single-family rental homes won't find many deals that meet this test. The price of the average house is too high, relative to the rent you can get. But in some cities and neighborhoods, it still pays to be a landlord. You can also pump value out of unorthodox properties that other investors might not even bid on.

JACK REED'S RULES FOR INVESTING IN RENTAL PROPERTY, IN BRIEF:

• Buy for at least 20 percent less than market value.

• Buy only property that can be upgraded profitably (zoning change, subdividing, renovation).

• Buy only in regions of the country where the normal deal is cheap enough to provide positive cash flow (more money coming in each month than going out). These are usually cities that are off the beaten path.

---

* Jack tracks down profitable investing strategies for his newsletter, the *Real Estate Investor's Monthly* ($99; 342 Bryan Dr., Danville, CA 94526). Send him a self-addressed, stamped, business-size envelope and he'll send you a free copy. To learn how to invest, get his invaluable *Residential Property Acquisition Handbook,* $39.95.

- Don't rely on market-wide appreciation for profit. If prices rise, fine. If they don't, you can still make money thanks to your bargain purchase, upgrading, or positive cash flow.

Alternatively, forget about rentals and look for properties that—for one reason or another—can be had at a bargain price. You buy low, solve the property's problem (if there is one), then resell immediately at fair market value. But be warned that these flips don't always work out. You may misjudge the property and overpay. When the property is vacant, vandals may strike. A buried heating-oil tank in the yard may have sprung a leak, socking you with a cleanup cost. And that's just the start of the stories I've heard. Many properties are indeed bought and sold on short schedules. But you should always be prepared for a longer haul.

HOW TO FIND RENTAL PROPERTIES THAT PAY

A property "pays" if its rents cover all your costs plus 5 to 10 percent. That extra money is both profit and cushion against the risk of unexpected costs. Here are 7 strategies to try:

Luck Into Living in a Low-Priced City. If you don't, scope out those cities for property investments. In a few neighborhoods, you can still buy a well-kept house through a real-estate agent and rent it profitably. But this tends to happen only during a temporary loss of confidence in the neighborhood's real-estate values, perhaps due to a plant closing or a recession. When owners feel optimistic again, prices are generally too high for investors to make a go of it.

Buy in Working-Class Neighborhoods. Homes and apartment houses there are far less likely to be overpriced than they are in the classier sections of town. And working-class homes rise just as much in value, maybe even more.

Buy a House with a Problem That Traumatizes the Seller. Maybe asbestos was blown onto the ceiling. Maybe the foundation has dropped four inches and the floors tip. Whatever the problem, investigate the cost of solving it, then offer a low enough price to make the repair and guarantee yourself a substantial profit. The seller may accept, just to get the monster off his or her hands. (This strategy, incidentally, is a variant on buying a house that needs only cosmetic repairs. By going beyond cosmetics, you may truly get a bargain price.)

Buy a One-Bedroom House (a freestanding house, not a condominium). There aren't many of these left, but they're dandy investments. They sell cheaply because hardly anyone wants to own one. And they rent dear because they appeal to single people and childless couples. If the house has an enclosed space that you can turn into a second bedroom inexpensively—an attic, a breakfast room, a sun porch, an attached garage—you have a real winner. But check out the neighborhood before converting the garage. In some areas, houses without garages are tough to resell. And be sure you get the required permits.

Buy Two Houses on One Lot—one of them in the other's backyard. Few homeowners want them, so the second house goes for about two-thirds off. But most tenants don't mind proximity. You get normal rents and a fine cash flow. You might also take a look at the profit potential in moving one of the houses to a lot of its own.

Rent Your House with an Option to Buy. This strategy works especially well when rents are sagging and real-estate prices are going nowhere. It has made investors a lot of money but there are some legal risks. First, the good part:

You put an ad in the paper reading "$4,000 moves you in" or "Buy a house, no money down," depending on how much money (if any) you want up front. Usually, it's one to 3 percent of the purchase price. You then strike a deal that will let the tenant buy the property at a fixed price, probably within one to three years. The tenant pays the monthly rent plus something more, which is credited toward his or her down payment. If the normal rent is $800 a month, the lease-option rent might be $1,200, with $400 put toward the purchase price. Part of the up-front payment might also go toward the price. At the end of the term the tenant can buy at the specified price, although he or she isn't required to.

You and your tenant/buyer sign a rental agreement and an option agreement. If the contract lasts longer than a year, consider annual increases for both the rent and the house price. Your local apartment association can supply a lease but there are no standard forms for the option sale. You'll need a lawyer to draw it up.

Lease options greatly improve your cash flow by paying you more than you'd get from rents. They bring you tenants who take especially good care of the house. And you often can set a purchase price at the high end of the going range. If the tenant ultimately can't buy, you get to keep all the extra money.

Fairness demands that you work with tenants who will have a good shot at making the down payment and qualifying for a mortgage. It's dirty pool to take lease-option money from people who obviously won't be able to buy. Nevertheless, more tenants probably pass on the option than take it up.

Now the bad part: A lease option amounts to a land-contract sale. Sales can lead to tax reassessments. They trigger the due-on-sale clause in your mortgage, giving the lender the option of ordering you to pay off the loan (lenders rarely hear or care about lease options, but they might). As a practical matter, these and similar risks are rarely encountered. Still, you should know they're there.

If Your House Has Some Extra Land—a little more than the zoning requires but not enough to subdivide into a separate building lot. Sell that extra eighth or quarter of an acre to a neighbor for a garage, a swimming pool, or a green space for planting shrubs and trees. You'll still have to go through a formal subdivision, but the extra money you get from the sale can turn a breakeven property into a winner.

PROPERTIES JUST WAITING TO BE SQUEEZED FOR CASH

Here are some properties that can be "flipped"—bought at a low price and sold pretty quickly for a profit:

A Teardown. Buy a house or a duplex that is going to be torn down. Don't pay any more than $1,000 for it. Hire a house mover to take it to another lot. You can generally sell the property for twice the money that you have in it, if you do it right.

Absentee Owners. Do some research at the county records office. Write to everyone who owns land locally but lives somewhere else. Ask what they would sell their property for. Maybe one out of 200 will name a price that's half the real value because he or she doesn't know the going price of property in your town. That one you buy. (The flip side of this advice: if you ever get such a letter, don't answer it before calling a local real-estate agent to find out what the property is worth.)

Tax-Sale Redemptions. In some states, former owners have a right of redemption if their homes were seized for nonpayment of property taxes and sold at auction. Call or write such people if their houses sold for substantially less than market price. They usually have several months to redeem their homes for the sale price plus interest. If that's utterly beyond their means, you might make a deal. Put the redemption money into an escrow account; let the former owner use the account to redeem the house and sell it to you at the same low price; pay the former owner a reasonable premium, and resell the house at full market value. (There is no flip side to this advice. For the former owner, it's all found money. He or she might even advertise for someone to do this deal with.)

Houses sold at IRS seized-property sales carry redemption rights all over the country. But each state has its own rules for local tax or foreclosure sales. Some states don't allow ex-owners to redeem.

Expiring Options. Look for people who are renting a house with an option to buy at something less than the current market value, but who haven't the money to do the deal. You can buy their option, take over the house at the low option price, and resell for a higher price. Valuable real-estate options are expiring all the time, unused. Where do you find them? Advertise—"We buy options to purchase real estate." Or write to the tenants of any real-estate investor who does a lot of lease-option deals. Or write to tenants against whom eviction notices have been filed to see if they had an option on the house they're quitting. Or see if any lease-option memoranda have been filed with the county clerk. Some investors buy valuable options and resell them to someone else rather than taking title to the property (because of the environmental risks—page 831).

Tenancies in Common. A person who owns property as a tenant in common (page 85) may want out. But the other owners might refuse to sell and decline to buy the defector's interest. That person can sometimes start a lawsuit to require a sale. But he or she may be constrained by personal considerations, or else may want the money fast. In this situation, an investor can often buy the defector's interest at a low price, then force a buyout or sale or wait until the other owner decides to sell voluntarily. You can advertise for these investments—"We buy the interests of tenants in common"—or go through deed records and compile a mailing list of tenants in common. Opportunities often arise when Great Uncle Garrett leaves a plot of land to all three of his nephews, who hold different views on what should be done with it.

Probate Sales. Estates will sometimes (not often) sell real estate at a low price to buyers who pay cash. This usually happens when heirs are pressing for their money and aren't using a real-estate agent. To find these properties, send a letter to the executors of every estate filed for probate. You might send out hundreds of letters a month, leading to one deal every three months on the terms you want.

Clouded Titles. Attorneys, paralegals, and specialists in title searches, in particular, might invest in properties with clouded titles. The owners may be glad to sell at almost any price. Buy only when you can cure the title and resell the property for full market value. (But don't buy if you've been advising the owner and have a fiduciary relationship, unless the owner gives up on the property. In that case, get a signed waiver releasing you from your duties.)

Houses Going to Foreclosure. Send a letter every 10 days to people whose houses are scheduled for foreclosure. Offer to buy immediately for cash. Not many people respond at first because they're still hoping to save their homes. But they become more interested once they accept the inevitability of the loss. Foreclosures often result from divorce. Anger, spite, and a shortage of cash may have stopped the mortgage from being paid. With an offer in hand, the couple may decide that selling the house is the best way out. Have a thorough title search done before going through with the deal. The house may be encumbered by liens. The records don't always show how much is currently owed on the liens, so work with the owner to find out.

One advantage of buying from the owner is that you usually get a low price. One risk is that the owner may go bankrupt, which could tie up the house in court. Some states have laws regulating preforeclosure sales, so check them out.

Foreclosure Sales. Foreclosure or trustee sales are a lot trickier than people think. You normally can't inspect the house in advance, so you have no idea what shape it's in. The house has to be worth at least 30 percent more than the mortgage against it to make your risk worthwhile. And you'll need to check the title to be sure you're not buying into a financial wipeout. What if the title isn't clear? What if there are other mortgages on the property that the buyer will have to pay? What if there are liens? Unless you're an expert, you'll have to pay someone to do a *careful* search, and quickly. A sale sometimes takes place on a few hours' notice.

Sales normally occur on the courthouse steps. You need a cashier's check in the exact amount of your bid. You shouldn't pay any more than 70 percent of the fair market value, as best you've been able to determine it, and preferably less. Get-rich-quick books often tout the bargains in foreclosure sales, but professionals say a good house is hard to find. Maybe one deal in twenty makes any sense. New investors should generally buy after a foreclosure, or before.

Foreclosed Houses Held by a Bank. By following foreclosure sales, you'll learn which lenders have bought particular properties that interest you. Call the bank officer in charge. Make an offer on the property that's at least 25 percent below market value. The bank will generally say no. Call the following week with the same offer. The bank will keep saying no and no. But if the property doesn't sell, and you persist, one day the bank may suddenly say yes. Investors get perhaps one out of every 25 properties they pursue this way, but that house will be a bargain. Incidentally, if the bank says a property has been sold, ask if the deal has actually closed. If not, keep calling. Sometimes sales fall through.

HOW MUCH LEVERAGE SHOULD YOU RISK?

Real-estate profits are greatly magnified by *leverage,* defined as the amount of debt you carry relative to your investment. Take a $100,000 house which rises $3,000 in value. If you bought the house for cash (no leverage), you made only 3 percent on your money. If you bought with a $20,000 down payment (average leverage), you made 15 percent. With a $5,000 down payment (high leverage), you made 60 percent. Conversely, if prices fall, the higher your leverage the larger your percentage loss.

But it's not the wipeout I worry about as much as the cash flow, which is the income you get from the property, after expenses. The lower your down payment, the bigger your mortgage and the larger your monthly payments. With big payments, it's impossible to cover all your costs with rents. You'll have negative cash flow. You'll be reaching into your pocket each month to help support your investing habit. What happens if you lose your job or are forced into early retirement? If your salary was supporting your real-estate investment, you may have to sell the property fast, maybe for 10 to 15 percent less than its actual value. When you have a big mortgage to repay, your profits may evaporate.

The wise investor arranges for rents to cover his or her costs. Working backward, that generally means getting the house at a bargain price.

HAVE YOU THE NERVE TO BE A LANDLORD?

Before buying any rental property—a single-family home, a duplex, a fourplex—ask yourself: Do I have the guts to evict? To demand the rent on time? To demand the rent at all if someone gives me a sob story? Can I throw out an illegal pet? A sweet mutt just saved from extinction at the pound? A mutt adored by a crippled 4-year-old?

If you can't answer all these questions with a hard-boiled yes, don't even try to be a landlord. In this game, nice guys get their clocks cleaned. You may set out to be the first decent landlord in history and discover, too late, that you were merely incompetent. Buying any sad story, from any tenant, could cost you not only your profit but your principal.

I don't mean to be harsh on tenants, having once been one myself.

Most tenants are fine. They take care of your property and pay on time. Other tenants start out fine, then turn into monsters. They bounce checks. Make excuses. Break rules. When it becomes clear that you're going to evict, they may sell your stove and refrigerator, break all the windows, and punch holes in the walls.

Before even getting into this business, get up to speed on your local eviction procedures. Find out how fast you're allowed to act and how easy or hard it is to protect your property. Send an eviction notice if the rent is even one day late. A good tenant may be furious, but will pay on time from that day forward. Bad tenants you want out sooner, not later.

Never take tenants without checking them out: a credit check, personal calls to the tenants' past two employers, and personal calls to the past two landlords, asking if they'd rent to these people again (the current landlord might lie, just to get rid of them). Insist on cash or money orders for the security deposit and the first month's rent (that gets rid of people who give bum checks and will hold the apartment until you can evict them). If bad tenants slip through your screen, move against them decisively. Enforce all rules to the letter. Demand cash or money orders from anyone who ever bounced a rent check. Evict anyone who violates the lease. Grrrrr.

THE ACCIDENTAL LANDLORD

Some homeowners try to sell and can't (or can't sell for any price they will accept). So they move to a new house and find tenants for the old one. What happens?

If you have a recent mortgage, you probably can't charge enough rent to cover your expenses. So the house may keep on leaking money. You get a small tax break: All rental expenses can be written off against rental income and, in many cases, against other income, too (page 835). When you finally sell, you may be able to treat the property as a "temporary rental," which lets you avoid any tax on the profit.

Don't let the house become a permanent rental! If that happens, you will owe a capital gains tax on the property when you sell. How do you hang on to the status of "temporary" landlord? Keep offering the house for sale, don't give a lease, and pray that you won't have to rent it for very long. Best advice: (1) Don't get into this box in the first place. Owning two homes can be Bankruptcy City. Sell your own house before buying another. If you take a new job in another city, live in a rented room until your house is sold, even if it means leaving your family behind. It's the lesser misery. (2) Sell on a lease option (page 826). You can usually strike a fair deal with an individual buyer, who will pay a fair rent plus something extra toward the down payment. A professional real-estate investor, however, who's aware of your anxiety, might offer only rent and demand that the entire payment go toward the purchase. Whatever you decide, try not to let the option run for more than a year or two. Never sign a lease-option contract without the advice of an attorney who specializes in real estate. (3) Slash the price on your unsold house, just to get rid of it. It might be worth selling for less than its mortgage value if you can arrange with the bank to refinance the remaining debt.

THE HUGE RISKS IN RAW LAND

Generally speaking, it's not smart to buy land and sit on it, waiting passively for its price to rise. Prices may rise slowly, and in the meantime empty land devours money. You'll owe real-estate taxes and maybe loan interest if you financed your purchase with the seller.

Raw-land owners also face enormous political risks. For example, your town might decide that it's growing too fast and downzone your land from commercial to residential, or from multi-family to single-family use, or to a greenspace. That sharply reduces your property's value. Or a new town environmental officer may declare part of your property a wetland, which virtually prevents its use as a building lot. In some parts of the country, you may be unable to get water rights. *Anything* can happen to a piece of raw land, and most of what can happen is bad.

When a land deal is good, however, it often is very, very good. Consider investing when:

• You have reason to believe that you can, within a reasonable period, make the land more valuable. For example, you might subdivide it into building lots, get its zoning raised from residential to commercial, or get a road approved for a plot that was previously inaccessible. Any of these changes will raise the land's value.

• You believe that you have some inside information about where roads will go or where a major company plans to move. In real estate, it is usually legal to trade on such tips. Your risk is that the tip was wrong or that, though right, it didn't affect the value of your property.

• You can buy on an option. With an option, you pay the owner for the right to purchase the land, at a stated price, within a certain number of months or years. During that period, you do the rezoning or subdividing and line up a buyer. Then you take possession of the land and flip it to your buyer on the same day. If your plans don't work out, however, your option will expire. The landowner gets to keep both the property and your option money.

When You Do a Raw-Land Deal: The checklist is long. Can the property be built on? What are the town's environmental rules? What's the present zoning? How will water and electricity get to the site? Where will the town allow roads to be built? What about sewage systems? Can foundations be dug or will a developer have to blast? Where does the town stand on development, politically? How fast does the planning board act on proposals brought before it? Arm yourself with a good, local real-estate lawyer. If you plunge into raw-land development, you are going to need one.

THE HUGE NEW ENVIRONMENTAL RISKS

Any real-estate investor—from the owner of a single-family house to a major-league developer—faces extraordinary liabilities under the rapidly changing laws on environmental protection. You may say, "I have no problem with my property." But a year from now a new substance may be found to cause cancer and be added to the government's "horribles" list. Surprise! That substance may be found in your roof. Unless you replace the roof, your investment may go down the tubes.

You think this far-fetched? Consider the retired California couple who invested in a mortgage on a pear orchard. The borrower defaulted and they foreclosed. Two fuel tanks were found buried on the property. To start, they had to pay $30,000 toward the cleanup and the state could force them to spend $100,000 more. And consider the Indiana homeowners who lived near an area where the state stored road salt. The salt got into the groundwater and contaminated the wells. The water was drinkable but the homeowners' pipes and appliances corroded. Their property values plunged.

And consider that nice piece of land you just bought. Fifty years ago it might have been the site of a factory that left toxic chemicals in the soil. Or tomorrow night two guys in dark clothes may use it as a dump for leaky drums of industrial waste, leaving you responsible for the cleanup. You're also in trouble if you own a building that's found to have asbestos in it. The law may not force you to remove it, but few people will buy or finance the building as long as the asbestos is there, so your investment has been damaged.

Professional investors won't buy a property anymore without first getting an environmental audit. The auditor tests the property for buried oil tanks, chemicals, pesticide residues, asbestos, and other substances that impair its value. Individuals should get audits, too, especially if you're buying open land, land next to an old gas station, a commercial or industrial property, farmland, or an apartment building. In fact, your lender may require it. Probable price range for small investors: $500 to $30,000, depending on the property. Before rejecting the expense of an audit out of hand, think what you'd lose if you bought a contaminated piece of real estate that had to be cleaned up.

Three other reasons to check for toxic waste: (1) If you buy a property and waste crops up later, you may not be forced to pay for the cleanup as long as you made "all appropriate inquiry" before buying. "Appropriate" hasn't been defined, but an audit should do it. (2) Even if the government has to pay for cleaning up your property, it might not do the job for years. In the meantime you're holding a worthless investment. (3) Anyone who buys your property will probably subject it to an environmental audit. If wastes are found, it may kill the deal and will certainly reduce its price.

In short, the risks of investing in real estate have risen sharply. The average investor has not yet caught up with these new environmental dangers, which wreck any deal you do.

WHAT IT TAKES FOR SUCCESS IN HIGH-RISK CONDITIONS

Total Awareness, All the Time. You should follow real estate constantly, tracking the ever-changing political and financial risks. The new environmental hazards, for example, might persuade you to lean toward the shorter-term investing ideas. Some investors don't even want their names on a chain of title, lest they get hit for part of a property's cleanup costs. So they're finding ways to trade property interests without ever owning the real estate themselves. One idea: options. You can trade them without taking title to anything.

Patience. You may have to look at dozens of properties in person, and hundreds on paper, to find one that meets your investment specifications. Many a seller is lying in wait for an idiot who will overpay.

Tough-Mindedness. You have to be firm with tenants, firm with buyers, firm with sellers. Not mean, but firm. Real estate is a deal-making business with fewer rules than the average consumer is used to. That's why your investment criteria are so important, as is your discipline in following through.

Flexibility. A truly superior investor brings his or her technical knowledge of real-estate contracts and finance to bear on a single critical point: the special needs of the person on the other side of the deal. What can you give him or her to secure the terms you want? If there's no way to reach your minimum criteria, bow out.

Quick Decision Making. When you first think about real estate, take a lot of time to study up. Read some books on real-estate finance. Learn about local property values. Analyze your area's economy: Are jobs and people moving in or out? Check the environmental hazards. Choose some investment niches to investigate. Set some yardsticks for yourself (see below). But once you step into the arena, be prepared to move quickly. No one leaves money lying on the table for very long. If you have to think and think and think and *think* about it, someone else will buy.

An Iron Gut. In almost every deal, something goes wrong. Price estimates are bad. Somebody dies. The town passes new laws that change the rules. Your lender drops out. The seller tries to change the terms. A tenant sets fire to an apartment. Most of the problems can be worked through. But it will take time, your nerves will fray, and you might not make as much money as you thought. That's how real-estate investing goes. If you can't handle pain, buy Treasury bills.

Time. Direct investing in real estate is a part-time or full-time business. To make money, you have to be personally involved: inspecting properties, evaluating prices, negotiating, arranging for tenants, seeing to repairs, going to zoning hearings, lining up financing, living your deal in a dozen ways. If you don't have the time, don't even think about trying to buy.

Clear Financial Yardsticks. Before you begin your real-estate investment career, draw up some yardsticks for yourself. Measure every opportunity against them. If they fit, follow up. If they don't, move on. Find out quickly if a deal falls within your financial parameters so you won't waste your time on something that can't produce a large enough return. These yardsticks will change as you gain experience, but they should always be written clearly on your cuff. They act as a discipline against the all-too-human tendency to buy that pretty house or lot just because it's there.

SOME RULES OF THE ROAD

No set of financial parameters fits every investment or every investor. But here are some guidelines to start with:

• Don't make improvements to a house or building you own unless you can get $1.50 of increased market value out of every $1 you spend. You need to fix up a fixer-upper, but by just enough.

• A rental property is worth its risk when its rents run 5 to 10 percent over all your known costs. Fifteen percent is even nicer. This cushion is for profit, unexpected expenses, or an unexpectedly high vacancy rate. When you follow this rule, you'll forgo most traditional rental properties today, but the ones you buy should be profitable.

• On rental properties that you plan to hold, focus on the "capitalization rate," which is the rate of return on your invested capital. You have a 10 percent cap rate if your net operating income comes to 10 percent of the price of the property. (Net operating income is the rental income from the property minus expenses such as insurance and repairs but before mortgage payments.) Many buyers go with low, 4 or 5 percent cap rates, counting, for their profit, on the property's rise in value. But those are poor investments. Tougher-minded buyers won't accept cap rates lower than 10 percent.

• Given all the risks in rental real estate, you should be shooting for a combined annual return of 25 percent, in appreciation, amortization, cash flow, and tax savings. To calculate a one-year rate of return, add the dollar amounts of those four items and divide by the money you invested. There are fancier ways of calculating returns, but for individuals this will do.

• Another way to figure: You want a current cash return on your investment of at least 10 to 15 percent. In the first year, your cash return is your net operating income (rents minus operating expenses), minus your mortgage payments, divided by your down payment and closing costs. In later years, divide by your current equity, which is the property's value minus the mortgage balance.

• Bargains are measured by the discount you can get from current market value. Professionals demand discounts of at least 20 percent. If they can't get that price on a particular deal, they move to the next one. When they buy a property they expect to resell almost immediately.

• All things being equal, invest close to home, in neighborhoods you know—but only if prices are reasonable there. If they're not, you have two choices: Forget about real estate or buy in another part of the state or the country where you think you can make a profit. Long-distance rental-property ownership is no big deal as long as you have some local help. Bargain purchasing—buying a teardown, for example—can be done anywhere. Foreclosure buying, however, requires a close understanding of state law.

• Consider assuming the seller's mortgage if the lender will allow it. Sometimes the mortgage carries a low fixed interest rate. Sometimes it's an adjustable loan with a low lifetime cap. In either case, it's cheaper to take over a mortgage than to get a new one because you don't pay points and closing costs. If you're the seller, make sure that the buyer assumes all responsibility for your mortgage and that the lender releases you from liability, in writing. You don't want to find yourself back on the hook if the buyer defaults. If the lender won't release you (and many won't), you may not want to allow the assumption unless the buyer puts so much money into the property that you feel sure he or she won't walk away.

AS LITTLE AS POSSIBLE ABOUT TAXES

You Can Deduct Your Rental Costs, including depreciation, against your rental income from this and similar projects. Any excess expense can tax-shelter some of your regular income if you meet the income limits explained on page 513. If you don't, all your unused tax deductions are allowed to accumulate. You can use them against rental income in future years, or to reduce the size of your taxable profit when you finally sell this or another investment property.

Investors in Raw Land Get Virtually No Tax Breaks because land isn't depreciable. If you borrowed money to buy the land, you might not even be able to write off the interest. Such interest can normally be deducted only against income from other investments, such as stock dividends. (The loan interest becomes deductible, however, if you borrowed on a home-equity line of credit.)

You Can Defer Paying Taxes When You Dispose of an Investment Property by doing a "1031" tax-free exchange. Instead of selling the property, you exchange it for another one. You don't even have to do a direct, two-way swap. You can set up a three-cornered trade (or more). For example, suppose you want Cindy's property, Cindy wants Sally's, and Sally wants Sam's. You can each deed the house to the proper person, noting that the agreement is part of an overall plan to accomplish an exchange. Get help from a professional to do this right.

If You Don't Do a Tax-Free Exchange, You May Have a Taxable Gain Even If You Sell at a Nominal Loss. The depreciation deductions reduce your *adjusted basis* in the property (your adjusted basis amounts to your cost, for tax purposes). You have a gain if you sell for more than your adjusted basis, even if it's less than you originally paid.

CAN YOU GET RICH BUYING
SECOND MORTGAGES?

A second mortgage is a second loan against a home. It makes a tempting income investment because it pays a lovely yield. And it normally doesn't require property management, as direct real-estate investing does. But you face huge risks if the borrower defaults.

When you buy a second mortgage, you are betting that that borrower is going to make his or her payments on time—and, in fact, most do. You advertise for these loans ("We buy second mortgages") or find them through real-estate brokers and lawyers. They are usually bought at a discount from face value in order to increase your yield.

Before buying, put the borrower through a credit and employment check (don't count on the broker to do it for you). Some of these borrowers are perfectly sound but others are flakes whom normal lenders wouldn't touch.

You want a loan that comes due within a short period—say, 2 or 3 years. It should be collateralized by real estate, usually by the property itself. The borrower should have substantial equity in the property and a history of making all payments on time. In general, the house should be worth at least 30 percent more than all the loans against it. Raw land should be worth at least 60 percent more because of the risk. Many investors won't buy second mortgages against raw land.

If the borrower defaults, he or she will probably default on the first mortgage, too. If the first mortgagor forecloses, your interest will probably be entirely wiped out. You might have to make the first mortgage payments for a while, or bid on the house at the foreclosure auction, in order to salvage your investment. Talk about these risks with a real-estate attorney before getting into second mortgages. Buyers of second mortgages should have a substantial personal income, or a large pool of assets, to support their investment if something goes wrong.

Can You Get Rich by Listening to Seminar Gurus? In most cases, no—you can only get poor. Poor, by spending your hard-earned money on the windy books and tapes they flog. Poor, if you try to follow their half-baked schemes, which will cost you money with small chance of reward. Really poor, if you can't afford the deals you get into. They set you up for default, personal bankruptcy, and maybe even jail. After the end of the 1980s real-estate boom, many of these "geniuses" wound up broke and in bankruptcy court.

I studied a group of guru TV programs once, talked to the gurus, and got their materials. I found them misleading, fantastical, false, and, in some cases, flatly illegal. The dream they sell—that you can buy profitable property with no credit, no job, no experience, even with a bankruptcy behind you—shouldn't pass anyone's first-round BS test.

FOR THE PASSIVE INVESTOR

If dealing with tenants or bidding at auction is harder work than you had in mind, consider a real-estate investment trust (REIT—pronounced *reet*). It's for potatoes who want to own properties without leaving their couches.

REITs do your investing for you. They're real-estate management companies that buy, own, and manage properties that they intend to hold for the long term.

REITs trade on a stock exchange. That means you can buy and sell at will. You're not locked in, as would be the case in a real-estate limited partnership. You invest through a discount or full-service stockbroker, paying normal brokerage commissions. The price of a REIT will rise and fall in line with its management success, dividend payouts, property values, and broader stock-market trends.

REITs earn income from rents, leases, and the occasional capital gain. By law (and to avoid being taxed), they have to pay out most of their earnings to their investors every year. As a result, their current yields are relatively high—often a magnet for income investors. An especially high yield, however, is always suspect. It means that the REIT has dropped in price—maybe because some of its properties are failing or because its dividend may be cut.

REITs are considered safe-ish havens when the general stock market drops. Their high dividends attract defensive investors and also offset their decline in price. When property values are moving up and management is competent, REITs may become growth stocks, with earnings gains in the 12 to 15 percent range.

On the other hand, there are fewer buyers for REITs than for better-known stocks. So a modest wave of selling or a rash of new REIT stock coming to market may depress the industry's collective price. You're also closely tied to real estate. If property values sag, REITs will, too.

But REITs can reduce the risk in your overall investment portfolio, for two reasons: (1) They typically hold up better in bear markets than other kinds of stocks. (2) In recent years, REITs have followed a price path that's somewhat different from other stocks. If this continues, putting some money into REITs will add valuable diversification to your total investment portfolio.

REITS COME IN THREE TYPES, BUT ONLY ONE OF THEM MATTERS

Equity REITs are the principal object of desire—your best long-term bet for dividends and growth. They own apartment buildings, hotels, community shopping centers, regional malls, outlet centers, industrial parks, office buildings, self-storage buildings, nursing homes, mobile-home parks, and other properties. Some are regional, others are nationwide—but most specialize in certain types of properties. Speculative REITs raise money for unusual types of properties, like private prisons, or properties they haven't even purchased yet. Blue-chip REITs are major real-estate companies, with long histories of superior management, rising dividends, and increasing profits.

REITs are tough for individuals to analyze. The key number is *funds from operations (FFO)*—generally defined as income after operating expenses and before depreciation and amortization. You want the FFO to grow. Nearly all REITs disclose FFOs on their shareholder reports. You shouldn't invest in those that don't.

To check how the market assesses a REIT, compare its FFO to earnings. A high FFO-to-earnings ratio says the REIT is expected to keep on growing at a high rate; a low ratio says it's in trouble (although it could improve). Different types of REITs carry different ranges of ratios and you need to know where yours fits in.

Another question: Where are the dividends coming from? Are they fully covered by FFO or is the REIT paying its investors by selling properties or dipping into reserves? If the latter, avoid it; the dividends may not be sustainable.

Not that you can always tell what's going on with FFO. Some REITs fudge that number or structure themselves to benefit their sponsors more than their shareholders.

Mortgage REITs haven't as good a performance history as equity REITs. Instead of buying properties they invest in mortgages and, sometimes, construction loans. They may have some sort of equity participation, so they're not necessarily straight income investments. Still, they behave more like bonds than stocks, doing their best when interest rates are stable. If you want to diversify into real estate, mortgage REITs don't cut it.

Hybrid REITs combine equity and mortgage REITs. But for real-estate participation, the equity side is the only one that counts.

Initial Public Offerings (IPOs) are always risky. Untested real-estate companies will try to raise money for properties they haven't even bought yet. Well-established companies are more promising, although—like other IPOs —they might come to market overpriced. Best bet: don't chase a new REIT stock. See if its price settles back after a few months and consider it then.

Consider Secondary Offerings—new issues of stock from REITs that are public already. They're generally raising money to purchase more property. Their history tells you something about their likely success.

Watch Out for REITs with Conflicts of Interest! A mortgage REIT that lends to its sponsor has its sponsor's needs in mind, not yours. An equity REIT "advised" by a developer may be paying too high an advisory fee, lending money to the developer, or buying his or her properties at too high a price. REITs that invest in nursing homes may be controlled by the operators of the homes. Look for these interlocking relationships in the REIT's prospectus, proxy statement, and annual reports (you get them all from your broker before investing, natch). You want an independent REIT, preferably one whose management owns a significant portion of the stock (that's in the proxy statement, too). Owner/managers are investing with you, not against you.

The Best Way to Buy REITs: Let a smart money manager buy them for you. At this writing, the two largest real-estate mutual funds are substantially devoted to REITs: Cohen & Steers Realty Shares in New York City (800-437-9912) and Fidelity Real Estate Investment Portfolio in Boston (800-544-8888). In 1996 the Vanguard Group in Valley Forge, Pennsylvania, started the industry's first index fund, Vanguard's REIT Index Portfolio (800-662-7447). It's tied to Morgan Stanley's index of REITs, but whether it can beat managed funds remains to be seen. Check the expense ratio on any fund you consider. When you're investing for income, it's especially important to choose a fund that has low costs.

BUYING MORTGAGES

Some investors buy second mortgages or deeds of trust from people who don't want to hold them anymore. For example, take a homeowner who sells a house and takes back a note for part of the down payment. The buyer/borrower promises to pay over the next three or five years. After a while, however, the homeseller wishes that he or she had cash instead. Enter an investor, who buys the note at a discount from its face value. Assuming that the borrower pays on time, these notes can yield a high rate of return.

Personally, I rank mortgages as my twenty-first favorite investment—roughly between unsecured loans to horseplayers and Chinese Railway bonds. Here's what you face:

1. These borrowers aren't first-rate risks. If they were, they'd have had enough cash for the down payment or enough credit at the bank. Don't invest without running a credit check, to be sure that the borrower always pays all of his or her loans on time. Don't invest if the borrower put little or no money down on the home.

2. If you hold a second mortgage and the first mortgage goes into default, you'll probably have to make the first-mortgage payments yourself, for a while at least. Don't invest unless you can afford it. Otherwise, the property will fall into the hands of the bank.

3. If the first mortgage goes into default and you don't make the payments, the bank may foreclose and sell the house. The sale price may cover the first mortgage but not your second mortgage, too. To protect your investment, you'd have to buy the house yourself. As a safety cushion, don't

invest unless the house is worth at least 30 percent more than all the loans against it—and get your own appraisal to prove it.

4. If the mortgage you're holding goes into default and you want to foreclose, it will trigger foreclosure on the first mortgage, too. Check the foreclosure procedures in your state before putting up a dime.

5. A property that looks good now will lose a lot of value if the economy sours or a local plant shuts down. You limit these risks by buying notes with no more than 2 or 3 years to run.

6. The best yields come from mortgages or deeds of trust on properties that would be tough to dispose of if the borrower didn't pay: raw land, cooperative apartments, vacation lots, mobile homes. In these cases, don't invest unless the property's appraised value is at least 50 percent more than the loans against it.

The mortgage business is full of brokers who try to match investors with sellers in return for a finder's fee. A broker may assure you that he or she has checked out the deal thoroughly—which may be false. Either do all the checking yourself or invest with a well-established broker known for dotting the *i*s and crossing the *t*s. Lawyers are especially suited for making mortgage investments because they're not daunted by the idea (or price) of going to court. If a court fight would worry you, let me suggest a few peaceful Chinese Railway bonds.

WHY BUY REAL PROPERTY AT ALL?

Investors buy real estate to make a buck. They study the market, see an advantage, and go for it. But it's riskier than, say, a no-load, stock-owning mutual fund. Real estate *in general* may do well, eventually. But if your particular property comes a cropper—because of an environmental hazard, a lawsuit, a difficult tenant, a change of zoning—your loss can be huge. You can't easily trade out of it, the way you can a stock. That's what makes REITs more attractive than, say, raw land.

The classic argument for owning property is diversification. Real-estate prices may go up at a time when stocks are going down. Carefully chosen real estate is a better inflation hedge than stocks.

But if diversification is the only draw, the average investor needn't bother. You may own your own home. You may also own a vacation home. Odds are that a substantial percentage of your net worth is tied up in these properties. Your next logical step would be stocks rather than another piece of property.

The lure of real estate, however, isn't always logical. A devoted investor becomes obsessed by properties—tromping through them, judging them, reshaping them, haggling over them. They're not like mutual funds that you can buy and forget. You have to give real estate your soul.

STEP 7

RETIRE- MENT PLANNING

Nowadays, a retirement plan is critical even for the young. It didn't used to be. When I came up, you thought about it later. You had children in your 20s and by your early 50s you had written your last tuition check. That left you 10 or more good years, at the peak of your earning power, to put aside money for yourself.

But the world today is a different place. Couples are waiting until their 30s to start having children. That means they'll be writing tuition checks in their early 60s. They'll have no time left to save money for themselves. The same is true for people who divorce, remarry, and start second families. Adding to the pressure is the corporate push for early retirement. Older parents may lose their paychecks while their children are still young.

This change in pattern calls for a brand-new plan of attack. You should save for retirement in small bites, over *all* your life.

29.

How to Retire in Style

The Tax-Deferred Route to Easy Street

*It's daring and challenging to be young and poor, but never
to be old and poor. Whatever resources of good health,
character, and fortitude you bring to retirement, remember,
also, to bring money.*

Are you old enough to remember Harvey? Harvey was America's most
famous rabbit, a giant of his kind, a star of his own eponymous movie. He
was invisible. Only his co-star, Jimmy Stewart, could see him. But despite
Harvey's handicap, his performance was so riveting that he stole the show.

You might wonder what this has to do with a chapter on retirement
savings, other than the fact that only gray-hares will remember the film at
all. But I think of today's inflation as Harvey. It's always there (in the 3
percent area, as I write), yet workers treat it as invisible. *Only* 3 percent
inflation; nothing much. I've seen some retirement-savings guides that
barely mention inflation at all.

For a comfortable income in retirement, you traditionally aim for 80
percent of your preretirement earnings. That's in the first year. In the second
year, your purchasing power will have shrunk a bit and so will the value of
fixed capital. In the third year, you'll start to notice it, and more so in the
fourth. At 3 percent inflation, every $100 you have now will be worth $74
in 10 years, so by then you'll be living on something around three-quarters
of your preretirement income. If the inflation rate goes up, things get worse.
At 5 percent inflation, for example, that $100 would be worth only $60 in
10 years. In the following decade, your standard of living could drop by
another half. That's Harvey for you. Invisible but riveting.

HOW MUCH MONEY WILL YOU
REALLY NEED?

Plenty.

Social Security benefits (yes, doubters, you *will* get Social Security—see page 901) rise with the consumer price index, as do many government pensions.* But private pensions are usually fixed. So is the income from most annuities and the interest on bonds and certificates of deposit. You have to be clever to stare down inflation in retirement.

Still, you can do it. Here's how:

• *Save enough money before retirement to offset your pension's annual loss of purchasing power.* As a pensioner, you will then be free to dip into your capital every year for money to cover the higher prices you have to pay. Acquiring extra savings may be less of a struggle than you think. To find out how to do it, sharpen your pencil and fill in the worksheet, "How Much Should You Save for Retirement? (Long Form)," in Appendix 2 (page 984).

• *Take advantage of every tax-deductible, tax-deferred corporate or individual retirement plan that comes your way.* Put in every dollar you're allowed. Company savings plans often match at least part of the money you put in. That's like finding gold in the street. All you have to do is bend over and pick it up.

• *If you're saving for retirement and college for your kids, put retirement first.* Thanks to the tax deferral, retirement plans earn money faster than anything else—even without an employer match. Start a college account with the money you have left (if you have anything left). Most company plans permit borrowing if you can't rustle up the college money anywhere else (page 545). For a strategy that combines college and retirement savings, see page 559.

• *Own your own home.* A house stabilizes your living costs and gives you inflation protection over long periods of time. In old age, a paid-up home gives you extra equity to live on. For example, you might sell the house, buy something smaller, and bank the surplus. Or you might use a reverse-mortgage plan (page 942).

• *Don't kid yourself about early retirement.* It takes a fortune to quit at 50 and keep yourself going for another 40 years. Maybe you have a fortune, thanks to Silicon Valley stock options or a lifetime of maximizing your 401(k)—in which case, bon voyage. Otherwise, you are likely to want some part-time earnings, even if you quit at 60.

• *Invest a substantial portion of your long-term retirement savings for growth.* That generally means stock-owning mutual funds. Bonds have a

---

* The reported consumer price index probably overstates inflation, although it's not clear by how much.

place, but you're wasting your youth (by which I mean all the years under 65) if you keep a large portion of your retirement plan in fixed-income investments.

• *Even after retirement, keep a portion of your capital invested for growth*—say, in equity-income or growth-and-income mutual funds. For asset-allocation suggestions, see page 582. If you switch all your money into fixed-income investments at 60 or 65 and live on the interest, Harvey at any size will gradually eat you up.

WHERE YOUR RETIREMENT FUNDS WILL COME FROM

Your retirement security generally stands on three legs: a pension, Social Security, and personal savings.

Pensions are paid to employees by most big companies, many mid-size companies, and various government entities. The size of your retirement benefit typically depends on your income, age, and the number of years you worked there. Either way, the longer you stick with a company, the larger your benefit should be (page 848).

But pensions are changing, even for "lifers." The benefit may stay, but its relative importance may shrink. You'll be expected to contribute to a separate savings plan yourself. If you don't, your retirement income will fall short.

If your company is reorganized or taken over, your pension might be frozen in its tracks and replaced with a plan that offers less. Pensions remain critical to retirement planning, but you can't be dead sure they will always pay as planned.

Social Security will be with us always. But even with cost-of-living increases, the monthly checks mailed in the twenty-first century may not replace as much of a beneficiary's working income as the checks do that are mailed today—especially for higher-income people.

Personal Savings are growing more critical to your security in old age. With both Social Security and your employer edging back, you're much more dependent on what you put aside yourself.

The best way to build a retirement fund is through automatic-payment plans. You want money to slip out of every paycheck into tax-favored retirement accounts without your even seeing it.

Many employees can use payroll deduction to roll pretax dollars into 401(k) plans or 403(b) tax-sheltered annuities or mutual funds. Some corporate plans accept extra, after-tax contributions, whose earnings will then grow tax deferred.

You can also arrange to make automatic monthly contributions from your bank account to a tax-favored plan offered by a mutual fund group. Nothing could be simpler. All you have to say is yes. Funds offer Individual Retirement Accounts, Keoghs, 403(b)s, and Simplified Employee Pensions.

WHAT YOU SHOULD BE SAVING NOW

For a down-and-dirty estimate of the percentage of salary you should save, take a look at the Short Form retirement planner on page 846. These aren't the numbers you actually need. They're meant as a wake-up call, to get you moving. I'll explain in a minute how to find out exactly what to save. But first, let me tell you what the Short Form can do for you.

It's a quick-check savings target for workers with two types of retirement plans: (1) a traditional pension, if they stay at the same company for life; (2) a 401(k) plan in lieu of a pension. At each age on the table, these workers are assumed to have no personal savings—they're starting from scratch. They get annual 5 percent raises, won't withdraw money from their plans during their working years, qualify for Social Security, stay with the same employer (if they qualify for a pension), and want to retire at 65 on 80 percent of their preretirement earnings. I've assumed a half-point reduction in their Social Security benefits—which may not occur but is certainly worth planning for.

Three facts stand out: First, the older you are before you start saving, the tougher it is to acquire the money you want. At some point, you'll have to change your retirement plans. Second, workers with company-funded pensions are a heck of a lot better off than workers without. Third, if you wait too long, it's not enough to have a tax-deferred retirement plan; you'll have to build outside savings, too. Where there's need for double savings, the numbers appear on the table in boldface.

The Short Form makes no allowance for the Harvey Effect—the inflation that will steadily nibble down your income. On the other hand, neither does it account for investments you already have. If you've started on a retirement plan, you'll need to save less than what's shown here.

For a clear fix on what you, personally, should be putting away, turn to Appendix 2, "How Much Should You Save for Retirement? (Long Form)" (page 984), where you'll find some worksheets. Fill them in. As far as personal planning is concerned, that may be the most profitable hour you will ever spend. The worksheets tell you exactly what percentage of income to save, not only for yourself but for Harvey, too.

To encourage you to use it, I'd have moved the Long Form right to this page if it weren't so, well, *long*. Alternatively, try using retirement-planning

HOW MUCH TO SAVE FOR RETIREMENT
(SHORT FORM)

| Earnings | To Retire at 65, Save This Percentage of Salary Starting at* | | | |
	Age 25	35	45	55
$30,000				
With pension and COLA†	2.6%	2.6%	1.7%	0%#
With pension, no COLA‡	5.7	7.3	9.5	13.7
With 401(k), company match§	4.8	7.8	13.5	46.6**
With 401(k), no company match ¶	9.7	15.9**	30.0**	60.0**
$60,000				
With pension and COLA†	3.8	4.9	6.4	8.9
With pension, no COLA‡	6.9	9.6	14.2	25.9
With 401(k), company match§	5.3	8.7	16.7**	59.2**
With 401(k), no company match ¶	10.6	19.0**	35.2**	73.0**
$100,000				
With pension and COLA†	5.0	7.0	10.6	20.0
With pension, no COLA‡	8.0	11.6	18.4	36.9
With 401(k), company match§	5.7	9.5	22.1**	69.8**
With 401(k), no company match ¶	11.4	21.5**	39.5**	82.0**
$150,000				
With pension and COLA†	5.5	8.0	12.7	25.2
With pension, no COLA‡	8.6	12.6	20.5	42.4
With 401(k), company match§	5.9	10.0	24.9**	77.6**
With 401(k), no company match ¶	11.8	22.6**	42.6**	91.3**

* The table assumes that, at each age, you start with zero personal savings. You have 3.5 percent inflation, a 7.5 percent after-tax return on investments, and Social Security at 0.5 percent less than inflation.
† Traditional pension at 50% of final salary with cost-of-living increase.
‡ Traditional pension at 50% of final salary with no cost-of-living increase.
§ Assuming full funding with a dollar-for-dollar company match.
¶ Assuming full funding.
** Numbers printed in boldface show higher percentage savings than can be put into a 401(k). To meet these goals, you'll need outside savings, too.
# Pension and Social Security cover your expenses in full.
SOURCE: Financial planner Harold Evensky, Evensky, Brown, Katz & Levitt, Coral Gables, Florida.

software. The *Quicken Financial Planner*, a program I worked on (plug, plug), tells you roughly whether your current savings and investments will be enough—and if not, how to set things right. You'll find Web planners at http://www.quicken.com and http://www.financenter.com.

But "enough" is a slippery goal. No plan can get everything just right because none of us knows what's going to happen. Everything changes— jobs, markets, lives. Things we assume to be true today will turn out to be only partly true and we don't know which part or how serious the error will be. For this reason, sophisticated financial planners use what's called Monte Carlo simulations. They run your retirement options through thousands of randomly generated scenarios—changing the value of such things as inflation, interest rates, and stock prices—so you'll have a feel not only for the most likely outcome but also the worst case. That helps you think about fallback positions. We all follow our hopes but it's dangerous to kid ourselves.

Before you can tell what to save for yourself, you have to know what is being saved for you. That's where your company pension comes in.

YOUR PENSION: THE EMPLOYER'S PART

You *must* understand your corporate plan. If you don't know how much retirement income is guaranteed and how much isn't, you won't have a clue as to what you ought to be saving now. You're entitled to an Individual Benefit Statement once a year, showing the size of your pension credit (ask for the statement in writing if you don't get it automatically). Don't burst out laughing when it comes. Pension credits always start small. To understand how these credits build, drop by the employee-benefits office for a full-dress explanation.

Corporate plans come in two basic types: defined-benefit plans and defined-contribution plans.

Defined-Benefit Plans

These are the classic, old-fashioned pensions. At retirement, you get a fixed lifetime income, the amount generally depending on how long you worked and how much you earned. Typically, you pay nothing into the plan. It is financed entirely by your employer. But inflation will probably erode this income. In 1995 only about one-quarter of the plans included a formal cost-of-living adjustment, according to the consulting firm KPMG Peat Marwick. Government plans are an exception—most of them do offer automatic cost of living adjustments, although they may be something less than the inflation rate.

Regrettably, many companies are cutting back their classic plans. New payment formulas are reducing the relative size of pensions given to long-term employees, especially those in the middle and upper-middle salary ranges.

Some plans are terminated. When that happens, your benefits to date are replaced with an insurance company annuity. But that's not nearly as good. Pension credits build faster as you move toward retirement, whereas annuity payments are fixed. What's more, an annuity's safety depends on the solvency of the insurance company. You're not covered by the employer-funded pension-insurance plan (page 850).

How to get the most from a defined-benefit plan:

1. Don't job-hop too readily. Traditional defined-benefit pensions pay the most to workers with the longest service.

You may think it's okay to quit the company after only a few years because you're vested in the plan (you "vest" when the money in your pension account becomes yours to keep). Full vesting may come in one to 7 years, depending on the plan. But in that short period, what are you vested in? Only a peanut payment. You have to stay 20 or 30 years before you are looking at real money.

What if you move through three or four different companies, earning a vested benefit each time? All things being equal, they will not add up to the same size pension you'd get by staying with a single employer.

This fact shows up clearly in the following table. I've shown you two brothers, earning the same starting salaries ($30,000), getting 5 percent raises, and working for companies with exactly the same pension rules. Itchy Brown worked for four different companies, 10 years each. His brother, Boring, spent 40 years in the same place. Boring's pension is nearly twice as large. Plans with different rules might produce a narrower (or wider) difference, but the principle is the same.

THE JOB SWITCHER'S RISK

	ITCHY BROWN	BORING BROWN
First-job pension	$ 5,289	$91,438
Second-job pension	8,616	N/A
Third-job pension	14,034	N/A
Fourth-job pension	22,860	N/A
Total annual pension	$50,799	$91,438

SOURCE: KPMG Peat Marwick

I'm not arguing that you should chain yourself to the first desk you ever occupy. But be aware that when companies pay traditional pensions, job changing carries a price. Your new offer has to be markedly better before it's financially smart to quit. Had Itchy Brown earned a lot more money at his subsequent jobs, or received stock options that turned out to be lucrative, he'd have beaten Boring Brown hands down.

The closer you come to middle age, the more critical this risk-reward analysis becomes. What will your new salary be? What salary increases lie ahead? What level of benefits and what vesting does the new pension carry? Will the company pay you a "signing bonus" to cover the future credits you're losing by leaving your old pension plan too soon? Are you being offered stock options instead of a pension, and are they worth the risk?

2. If you do quit the company, take care not to forget about your vested benefit. Often, your pension is frozen at its current level, payable at retirement age. If it's worth $800 a month at 65, that's what you'll get—even though, in that distant year, the purchasing power of the money may have dropped significantly. Still, in retirement every dollar counts. Keep a note in your personal files so you won't forget any small pensions due from previous employers.

You're entitled to vested benefits even if a company terminates the plan, merges, or goes out of business. The Pension Benefit Guaranty Corporation keeps a list of people who haven't claimed pensions due them from failed plans. At the end of 1996, some $10 million was owed to nearly 3,000 people. If you might be one, check the "Pension Search Directory" on the Web at http://search.pbgc.gov.

Sometimes you can choose between waiting for payment until 65 or taking your money in a lump sum and rolling it into an Individual Retirement Account. You might also be able to roll it into your new employer's pension plan.

But your lump sum will be "discounted"—that is, reduced—by a certain interest rate, also known as a discount rate. You will have to invest your money to yield at least that percentage amount per year, for as long as you live, simply to get as much monthly income as the pension plan would pay! Ask the employee-benefits office what discount rate it uses. If you're sure you can earn more, take the lump sum; otherwise, leave it with your old employer, if the plan allows and if fully insured by the PBGC. (For more on this, see page 850.) Do not take this money and spend it. You will never make it up.

3. If you hate your new job and return to the company you left, find out what happens when you rejoin the pension plan. You can pick up old pension and vesting credits as long as you weren't away for too many years.

What if you quit for a short period of time to have (or adopt) a child? You'll get credit for up to 501 hours of service while on maternity or paternity leave. You accrue no new benefits during the time you're gone, but the credits help you hang onto the pension level you've already earned.

4. Know what all your benefits are. As you approach middle age (or if you're thinking about a new job), ask the employee-benefits office to estimate what your actual pension is likely to be. Walk through the calculation step-by-step and check the assumptions the company is using. It's not unusual for pension administrators to make mistakes (page 881).

5. Find out to what extent your company "integrates" its plan with Social Security. With integration, your pension check is partly reduced by your Social Security benefit. Lower-paid workers feel this cut more than the higher-paid. You need guidance on what your combined benefit is likely to be, so you'll know how much extra you have to save.

6. Don't let your spouse lose any benefits due under your company plan. As long as you're partly or fully vested, and have reached early-

retirement age, your spouse can usually get something out of your pension, even if you die before actually retiring. Ask the company for its Survivor Coverage Data, which will explain it all. For more on spouse protection, see page 921.

7. **If you divorce, your spouse is entitled to part of your pension or an equivalent sum.** See page 150.

8. **Don't worry about the safety of your pension plan if you earn an average salary.** The industry-funded Pension Benefit Guaranty Corporation (PBGC) insures the basic pensions owed by defined-benefit plans that fail. Both you and your survivor are covered. The 1997 ceiling: $2,761.36 a month for a single worker who retired at 65. Younger retirees receive less, as do married retirees with joint-and-survivor pensions. The maximum payment for workers in newly failed plans goes up each year.

But the PBGC doesn't cover every company benefit. If your pension plan failed, you'd lose the amount of your pension that exceeded the PBGC ceiling as well as any collateral benefits, such as life and health insurance, severance pay, disability pay, and recent improvements in the plan.

There's no coverage at all for the defined-benefit plans of government entities; some plans run by churches and fraternal organizations; the plans of professional-service employers (for example, doctors and lawyers) that haven't covered any more than 25 active workers at any time, and workers' compensation or unemployment insurance. Nor does the PBGC insure defined-contribution plans (page 851).

9. **Check into what stands behind your pension if you're higher paid.** Your monthly benefit may exceed the amount the PBGC insures. It may not even be fully contained in your company's qualified pension plan. A significant portion might be in a supplemental plan backed by nothing but your company's good health. If the company fails, part of your pension might be uncollectible.

Top-level executives usually know how much of their pension is guaranteed and how much isn't. Their excess benefits are often kept in trust, guarded against all contingencies except the company's inability to pay. But employees with upper-middle incomes may not know that they're in a supplemental plan.

To find out exactly where you stand, ask your employee-benefits office: (1) What percentage of the pension plan is "funded"—meaning, what portion of all benefits could the company afford to pay today? A strong plan is 100 percent funded, or nearly so. (2) How much of your retirement fund is in the regular pension plan and how much, if any, is in a supplemental plan? If your plan permits lump-sum withdrawals when employees leave, would any of your current payment come from the supplemental plan? (3) If you're in the supplemental plan, are the payments protected by any sort of trust? If you have only your company's promise to pay, and leave to take another job, you might want to take your pension benefit in a lump sum. Just in case.

New-Style Defined-Benefit Plans. These plans calculate your benefits in a slightly different way. Instead of piling up most of your pension credits in your later years, they spread out the credits more evenly. This helps the Itchy Browns, who don't stay with one firm long enough to acquire a decent retirement income. Your statement generally shows the lump sum you've accrued to date. If you leave the company, you can often take it with you, rolling it into an Individual Retirement Account. At this writing, the following versions are the most popular:

1. *Cash balance plans.* The company credits a certain percentage of each year's pay to your pension account, plus interest on the entire sum. That's great for the average younger worker. Nothing is lost if he or she quits in order to take another job. But longtime workers with above-average raises won't get as much as they would have under a traditional defined-benefit plan.

2. *Pension equity plans.* They also credit your pension account with a percentage of pay plus interest, but they make adjustments for age and your salary level when you retire. This approach works better for workers who rise to higher-level jobs and people hired in mid-career.

Like traditional pensions, these are generally fully funded by your employer. You can turn them into a lifetime income at retirement. If the plan fails, you're covered by the Pension Benefit Guaranty Corporation. The bad news is that these plans pay lower lifetime benefits than traditional pensions do. Younger workers get more portability, but longtime workers often retire on less.

Defined-Contribution Plans

The number of these plans is exploding because, for employers, they're no-risk deals. Instead of promising you a specific lifetime pension, the company promises only to contribute a certain sum toward your retirement savings every year. It takes no responsibility for the size of the pension you ultimately get. Defined-contribution plans include all forms of profit-sharing —401(k)s, stock-bonus plans, Employee Stock Ownership Plans, employee Keogh plans, and Simplified Employee Pensions.

The company's contribution might be in cash or in stock. It might be a fixed and guaranteed percentage of your salary (known as a money-purchase plan) or an optional contribution based on a percentage of salary or profits (known as a profit-sharing plan). The company might also match any contributions you make to a savings plan. Most retirement plans are held in trust. If the company fails, all your money should still be there (barring fraud, from which no private plan is ever perfectly secure—page 883).

The money in these plans is all invested—sometimes at the company's discretion, sometimes at yours. By retirement, you can accumulate a sizable sum. You can generally take the money in a single check, leave it with the company to manage for you, or turn it into a fixed monthly income for life.

How large will your retirement income be? Who knows? The size of your check depends on how much was contributed each year, how well those funds were invested, and the state of the markets at the time you leave the job. You bear all the risk. Maybe you'll retire on more than a defined-benefit plan would have paid. On the other hand, maybe you'll get less—and with a shocking suddenness. Think of what happened to people who retired late in 1987. After the October stock-market crash, the money in their retirement plans might have been chopped by 30 percent.

Defined-contribution plans don't come with cost-of-living raises. You have to create your own inflation hedges by investing well. The plans also have much higher money-management expenses than traditional pension plans do, which cut into their investment returns.

How to get the most from a defined-contribution plan:

1. Some companies perch a defined-contribution plan on top of a defined-benefit plan. You have to understand both plans and how they work together. Typically, the defined-benefit part will carry less and less of the load in the years ahead. The responsibility for producing a decent income for retirees will be shifted toward the riskier defined-contribution plan. Both plans carry the same vesting schedule. Check the details, including the current size of your benefit, in the plan documents: the Summary Plan Description and the Individual Benefit Statement. The company is required to give them to you (page 884).

2. It's less costly to job-hop when you're backed by defined-contribution plans. Your new employer may not cover you for the first year, but after that you'll participate in full. All things being equal, 40 years of work under defined-contribution plans should net you only a slightly smaller sum from a series of employers than you'd get if you stayed with a single one, assuming that you worked for each company long enough for the benefits to vest.

3. If you want to quit, find out your "escape date"—the earliest you can leave the job with your full retirement account in hand. Your own contributions, plus the money they earn, are always yours for the taking. But you usually have to have worked for a while before you're vested in any matching money your employer gives. (Some companies, however, vest you in their contributions immediately.)

4. Job switchers should reinvest their lump-sum retirement-plan payouts in an Individual Retirement Account (or their new employer's pension plan, if that's allowed). If you spend the money, that chunk of your pension savings is permanently gone. You will never make it up. Besides losing that nest egg and the value of years of tax deferral, you will owe income taxes on the payout plus a 10 percent penalty if you're under 59½. Spending even a dime of an early lump-sum payout is just nuts.

5. Don't fail to contribute to these plans when they're offered (page 854). Major employers plan for their pensions to cover a certain percentage of your retirement pay, expecting the rest to come from Social Security and your 401(k) account. They assume you'll contribute the maximum. If you don't, your nest egg will fall short.

6. You *must* learn something about investing—a new responsibility that many savers haven't accepted yet. Professionally run pension funds invest heavily in stocks because, over time, they produce the largest returns. Yet many individuals still go for lower-yielding fixed-income investments. If you put all your 401(k) money into bonds, the size of your pension will disappoint you. (For more on investing 401(k) money, see page 878.)

Employee Stock Ownership Plans (ESOPs)

Of all the defined-contribution plans that you might be offered, an ESOP is by far the riskiest. Its name is wonderfully evocative, suggesting a company bursting with zeal, eager to spread the wealth. The better the company does, the richer its stock-owning employees get. And, in fact, if your little company grows big, you could strike it rich. But some companies go bankrupt, taking their ESOPs—and your retirement savings—with them. ESOPs are not insured by the Pension Benefit Guaranty Corporation.

Some ESOPs diversify a bit. However, most are made up entirely of the company's own stock. Each employee holds an ESOP account, to which stock is added periodically. But those shares are frozen; you cannot sell them. You get the stock's value—in shares or cash—when you leave the company or retire.

If the shares trade publicly, you at least know exactly what they're worth. But if your company is privately held, the shares are worth what an appraiser says they are—and who knows if the price is right?

Dozens of new ESOPs are set up each year not because employees are clamoring for them but because they offer management so much. ESOPs provide companies with special tax breaks; they're a captive buyer for a retiring owner's personal shares; and they can sometimes help defend management against a takeover.

It's unfair for a company to construct its only (or major) pension plan as an ESOP. No employee should be asked to stake his or her entire future on whether, at retirement, the company's stock will be up or down. You should also be offered a defined-benefit pension plan or broadly diversified defined-contribution plan. If there is one, use it.

If you are stuck with only an ESOP, use it and keep your fingers crossed. Jump at another good job if it comes along. In the meantime, make superhuman efforts to save money for yourself—for example, by funding an Individual Retirement Account (page 853). If your company fails or flags, that personal money may be your major retirement fund.

Even if you take a new job, you may be stuck in the ESOP for years. Companies often take 2 or 3 years to distribute your funds. By law, they can dribble it out over 5 to 10 years.

If you stay with the company, take full advantage of two escape hatches that your ESOP is forced to offer by law:

1. When you reach 55 or older and have been in the plan for at least 10 years, you can demand that 25 percent of your ESOP be invested in other assets. This switch can be made all at once or over 5 years. Do it even if the company's stock is going up. You might retire early, and who knows where the stock price will be then? You need a more diversified portfolio.

2. In the sixth year (you'll usually be 60 or 61), you can order that half of your money be switched out of your company's stock into a broader range of investments (that's 50 percent of the ESOP minus the percentage you took out before).

If your company offers a good defined-contribution plan, you can put the money there. Alternatively, tell the ESOP to roll your payout into an Individual Retirement Account, where you can invest it yourself. Either way, diversify to the fullest. It's the safest thing to do.

Top-Heavy Plans

This phrase refers to small-company plans that disproportionately benefit the highest-paid people, usually the owners. A lot of law has been written to force them to offer their workers a fairer shake. Advice on handling these plans is a job for your friendly certified public accountant, not me. I mention them only to remind the top-heavies that they might lose their tax benefits if their plans don't follow 5 zillion rules.

YOUR PENSION: THE DO-IT-YOURSELF PART

Those defined-contribution plans I just mentioned expect a contribution from *you*. Savings aren't optional if you hope to escape genteel poverty in old age.

The earlier you start saving the better. A dollar today is always worth more than a dollar tomorrow, thanks to the unflagging power of interest, dividends, and profits left alone to compound. Compounding is a true perpetual money machine. No force (except early withdrawals!) can ever stand in its way.

401(k) Savings Plans: For Employees, the Best Deal in Town

You'll find these wonderful 401(k) salary-deferral plans at almost every large company and many smaller ones. Details differ from firm to firm. But at bottom, they are all the same unbeatable deal.

Many young people avoid these plans because they "can't afford" them. But you gain so much in tax savings and, usually, free employer contributions that it's crazy not to join. If you don't, you'll look back ten years later and kick yourself. (A possible alternative for $2,000 of your money: a Roth IRA, page 868—but *only* if your employer doesn't contribute to your 401(k).)

Your 401(k) questions answered:

How Does the Plan Work? You agree that part of your salary will be set aside every year for your retirement. That money is exempt from current federal income taxes (although not from Social Security taxes and, sometimes, local income taxes). The earnings on your contributions—interest, dividends, and capital gains—accumulate tax deferred. You are taxed only when you withdraw the funds.

Your plan may also allow for after-tax contributions. You get no deduction for saving this money, but the earnings will accumulate tax deferred.

How Do I Contribute? By payroll deduction, which is doubtless why 401(k) plans work so well. These dollars slip into the plan without your seeing them go. You live on the net paycheck you receive, forgetting the portion that was set aside. Left alone, your 401(k) money sits there peaceably and grows.

How Much Can I Put In? Your own maximum pretax contribution is some percentage of salary (set by your company) up to a legal ceiling that rises with inflation every year. In 1997 it was $9,500.* After-tax contributions go on top of that.

The maximum annual contribution to all of your company savings plans, including any after-tax dollars and what your employer puts up, is 25 percent of your salary, up to a ceiling of $30,000.

Higher-paid employees, however, may not be able to fill their plans up to the top. They're not allowed to save a substantially higher percentage of pay than lower-paid employees do. So although you were theoretically allowed $9,500 in 1997, your real-life limit might have been lower than that —and lower ever since.

---

* This is your total, annual pretax contribution, even if you work two jobs with two 401(k) plans. If the plan is a SIMPLE 401(k), your maximum pretax contribution in 1997 was $6,000 (page 861), also indexed to inflation.

Whatever your ceiling, fund these plans to the absolute maximum of your ability. Start small, if you must, and step up your commitment every year. If you change jobs several times in your life, this may be the only significant pool of retirement money you'll ever have.

Does My Employer Contribute? Usually yes. You might get 25 or 50 cents—sometimes even $1 or $1.10—for every pretax dollar you put in, up to a certain percentage of pay. Some companies match after-tax contributions, too. Often, the match is made with company stock instead of cash. This is free money, even if the stock goes down. Any employee who doesn't contribute is throwing a huge profit away.

What Happens to the Money? Most plans allow you to pick from two or more investment vehicles chosen by the company. These might include stock-owning mutual funds, bond funds or fixed-interest contracts, money market mutual funds, and the company's own stock. The trend is toward a larger number of choices. (For more on retirement-plan investments, see page 878.)

Can I Switch from One Investment to Another? Absolutely. When you can make the change depends on the rules of the plan. Some plans set fixed dates—for example, quarterly or annually. Some allow a fixed number of switches per year that you can use whenever you want. Some permit daily switches by phone. But constant tinkering is dumb. Your best strategy is to decide what percentage to keep in stocks and stick with it. Any change should depend on your personal goals, not what you think the market is going to do.

When Is My Money Invested? Your employer has to put the money in the plan within 15 business days after the end of the month that your contribution was taken out of your paycheck.

How Do I Know How My Investments Are Doing? Once a year you should get a written report on the status of your account. If you don't, ask for it in writing; your employer is required to give it to you. Big-company plans or the mutual funds they offer may distribute monthly or quarterly reports. There may even be an 800 number that gives you updates every day. (My advice: Don't dial. Following daily fluctuations tempts you to trade, which will almost certainly depress your long-term returns.)

Can I Make Cash Withdrawals from the Plan While I'm Still at Work? As a practical matter, no, if you're under 59½. Most (but not all) plans allow withdrawals in cases of genuine hardship. But you have to prove an "immediate and heavy financial need" with no prospect of getting the money anywhere else. Once over that hurdle, you face other rules: limits on how much can be withdrawn; restrictions on when you can start making contributions again; taxes and penalties on the money you take out. Withdrawals are easier after 59½. At that point few companies continue the hardship rule, and although you owe income taxes no penalty is imposed.

But why would you want to take money out? If you need cash, borrow it instead.

Can I Borrow from the Plan? At most companies, yes. There is normally no credit check. You can borrow your own contribution plus the money it earned. You may also be able to borrow your employer's contribution, plus earnings, too. Some plans allow loans for any purpose; others restrict them to value-added purposes, such as buying a house or paying tuition; a few permit no loans at all. For the pros and cons of borrowing against your retirement plan rather than from another source, see page 262. *Never* borrow just because you want something and the money is there.

How Much Can I Borrow? The size of your loan depends on the value of the account. On accounts of $20,000 or less, you can get up to $10,000. With larger accounts, you can borrow 50 percent of the value, up to a legal maximum of $50,000. (Some plans impose lower maximums.) If you already have one or more loans against your plan, your further borrowing is reduced. Your account must be loan-free for a full 12 months before you can borrow the maximum again.

Does My Spouse Have to Agree to the Loan? At this writing, no, not if your plan meets the no-consent rules outlined on page 922.

What Are the Loan Terms? You pay market interest rates, probably equal to the bank prime lending rate plus one or 2 percent. The interest usually isn't tax deductible. Most loans have to be repaid within 5 years, although longer periods (10 to 30 years) may be allowed for loans taken out to buy a principal residence. Repayments are usually made by payroll deduction.

You might be able to deduct the interest if (1) you borrow against your employer's contribution and the money it earned or your own after-tax contributions *and* (2) use the money to make investments (for the rules on deducting investment interest, see page 264). You might also get an interest deduction if you borrow to buy a principal residence and secure the loan with your mortgage or deed of trust. As a practical matter, however, the plan may not segregate the employer's contribution, so you can't identify it for borrowing purposes. And many plans won't accept your mortgage as security. Interest is never tax deductible if you're a "key employee," partner, or shareholder in an S corporation.

What If I Still Have a Loan When I Leave My Job? You generally have to repay it—right away or within 3 months. A few companies give you a year or more. Sometimes new retirees repay over the loan's full life. If you cannot repay (say, by getting a bank loan), the loan is treated as a withdrawal. You'll owe income taxes on the money and a 10 percent penalty if you're younger than 55.*

Can I Take All My Money from the Plan If I Leave? You can take every dime you contributed plus all the income you earned.

If your company added money, too, how much you get depends on the plan. Some companies give you everything regardless of how long you worked. Others give you nothing unless you stayed in the plan 5 years, or vest you gradually from the third year on. In all cases, however, you will be fully vested after 7 years. To avoid paying taxes on your 401(k) and to keep your cache intact, roll it into a traditional Individual Retirement Account or your new employer's retirement plan, if that's allowed. (Roth IRAs don't accept rollovers from employee plans.)

You can leave your 401(k) in your old company's plan if you like its investment choices and your account is worth more than $5,000. This is usually a terrific option. Your money is kept away from financial predators. If you've made after-tax contributions, they can continue to grow tax deferred.

But ask what the rules and limitations are. Can you switch your investments around? Can you take out the money whenever you want? If you don't like the answers, switch to the IRA. Also ask yourself whether you trust your company. If financial problems arise or a merger looms, switch to an IRA just in case the plan gets changed.

How Long Does It Take to Get My Money When I Leave? Legally, the plan can hang on to your money until you're 65 or have been in the plan for 10 years, whichever is later (but not past 70½). In real life, it depends on the company. Sometimes you have to wait until the end of the following calendar quarter, when the administrator officially values the plan. Sometimes the money comes within weeks. Some plans don't pay you for several years. In the meantime, your money stays in the plan in whatever investments you chose. Ask about the rules in advance so you won't go nuts waiting.

Am I Taxed When I Leave the Plan? You are not, as long as you roll the money into an Individual Retirement Account or the qualified plan of your

---

* Starting at 55, there's no tax penalty for 401(k) withdrawals if you leave your job for any reason, be it retirement or quitting to take a new job. IRA withdrawals, by contrast, cost you a 10 percent penalty until you reach 59½.

next employer, if that's allowed. But unless you're careful, you can get stuck with taxes and penalties by accident! Here's how to avoid them:

Pick the IRA that you want before effecting the rollover. Fill in the forms and ask the IRA representative how the check should be made out. Once that's done, tell your plan to send the check to the IRA directly. Result: no muss, no fuss, no tax. It's okay to receive the check yourself as long as it's made out to the IRA trustee. You just pass the check along.

Do not have the check made out to you personally. If you do, here's what happens: (1) Your company usually withholds 20 percent for income taxes. (2) You deposit the remaining 80 percent into your new IRA account, but you're 20 percent short. (3) You have to find an equivalent sum to add to the IRA within 60 days. (4) If you don't, the missing amount will be treated as a withdrawal. You'll owe taxes on the money plus a 10 percent penalty if you're under 55. (5) If you spend part of the 80 percent, that's taxed as a withdrawal, too. You preserve your tax shelter only on money switched to the IRA within 60 days.

There are two ways out of this mess: Either borrow the money to top up your IRA, claim the 20 percent as a refund, then use it to repay the loan. Or don't let it happen in the first place.

Which Individual Retirement Account Should I Roll My 401(k) Money Into? For future investment, put the money in one of two places: (1) A mutual fund group that offers a diversified list of well-regarded stock and bond funds. You might start by depositing everything into the group's money market fund. Let it sit there in safety while you study other investments. Later, you can transfer the cash into the stock and bond funds you want. (2) A self-directed IRA at a full-service or discount brokerage house. These IRAs let you buy individual stocks and bonds as well as mutual funds. They can also receive any company stock coming out of your plan. If you go with a discount brokerage house that runs a mutual-fund supermarket (page 632), you can buy funds from different mutual-fund groups through a single account. That saves a lot of paperwork.

If you're planning on finding another job, don't roll your lump-sum distribution into a preexisting IRA. Keep this sum in a separate IRA of its own. That allows you to switch it into a new employer's retirement plan if the plan accepts rollovers and you like its investment choices or want to borrow against the money. Retirement money that has been mixed with other funds can't go into employer plans.

If you're retiring and want to turn your IRA into a lifetime income, roll it into an immediate-pay annuity at an insurance company (page 925).

Should I Roll the Money into an IRA If I'm Going to Need It Pretty Soon? That depends on how old you are. If you're 55 or older when you leave your job, withdrawals from your 401(k) are penalty-free. If you roll that money into an IRA, withdrawals won't be penalty-free until you're 59½. Logical conclusion (I think): Those over 59½ should switch to an IRA, taking out money later, as needed. Those 55 to 59 should take cash they're going to need up front and put the rest into an IRA.

What Happens to My Money When I Retire? You get it all. For your payout options, see page 913.

What If I Divorce? Your spouse is entitled to a share. See page 921.

What If I Die? Your spouse gets the money unless he or she has waived the right (page 921). If you're unmarried, the money goes to the beneficiaries you name.

How to get the most from a 401(k) plan:
1. Make the maximum contribution or as close to it as you can. A 401(k) with a company match is the richest deal you'll ever find. Contributions are excludable from income, up to a cap; the earnings are all tax deferred, and the plan usually offers several investment choices. In an emergency, you can usually borrow some of the funds. I'd fund to the max even in plans where no loans are allowed.
2. Invest a good part of your money in the plan's stock-owning mutual funds rather than in income investments. Over the long term, stocks yield the best return by far. If you stick to bonds or fixed-interest contracts, your plan will deliver less retirement income than traditional pensions pay.
3. Don't invest much of your 401(k) in your company's stock. Don't buy any if the company uses stock to match your contribution. You don't want your job *and* your retirement riding on a single firm, even a wonderful firm. You never know when things might change.
Some companies match your full contribution only when you buy company stock. Otherwise, they match only half your contribution. That takes unfair advantage of you. A 401(k) should be structured to help you diversify.
4. Although 401(k)s are designed for retirement, they're also worthwhile for college savings as long as there's a loan provision. That's better than saving outside the plan, if you get an employer match. A loan from your plan does not deplete your retirement savings as long as the interest you pay is no less than the plan was earning on its other investments. The odds are that you'll find better sources of college money (page 540)—student loans, PLUS loans, tax-deductible home-equity loans. But a 401(k) loan may be preferable to an unsecured loan from a bank.
5. Ask your employer what you're paying for the plan. The cost of administering traditional pension plans usually runs under 0.5 percent a year. But costs are much higher for 401(k)s—typically up to 1.5 percent or more. Small-company 401(k)s tend to be the worst. Employees may pay

outrageous fees and commissions, especially if an insurance agent or stockbroker set them up. You're generally better off in plans run through discount brokers or no-load mutual fund groups.

Nothing requires your employer to disclose the full cost of your 401(k). You can find out the cost of any registered mutual fund that's in the plan, along with any commissions you pay to buy and sell. But that's about it. The plan's total administrative expenses show on the summary annual report—given every year to workers in plans with 100 people or more and every 3 years to workers in smaller plans. But you can't sort out what this means for your individual account.

That's something Congress should fix. A 401(k) plan ought to disclose an expense table, just as stock and mutual fund prospectuses do. A 2 or 3 percent charge each year makes an enormous difference to your retirement nest egg over time.

Should I Make After-Tax Contributions If the Plan Allows It? That depends on the tax laws, your tax bracket, how you plan to invest the money, and whether your employer will match what you put in. An employer match is free money you won't want to lose. All of the money in the plan will accumulate tax deferred.

If there's no employer match, fund a Roth IRA first (page 868). If you still have money to spare, where you save it will depend on how you plan to invest.

For buying taxable bonds or bond mutual funds, use after-tax contributions to your 401(k) (assuming its bond-investment choices are attractive). The 401(k) keeps the earnings tax deferred. If you're buying stock, however, it's a closer call. Stock profits in a 401(k) are taxed as ordinary income when withdrawn, whereas outside the plan they get the favorable rate on capital gains. Generally speaking, you'd use a 401(k) only if you trade stocks or mutual funds a lot and want to protect your realized profits from current tax. If you buy stocks and hold them, or get only modest capital-gains distributions from your mutual funds, invest your after-tax money outside the 401(k).

Don't consider an after-tax 401(k) if the investment choices are poor and there's no employer match. Ditto if you can't withdraw the funds at will. And note: if you leave the company, all the earnings will be taxed.

IS YOURS A "SIMPLE" PLAN?

Firms with fewer than 100 employees might offer SIMPLE plans—short for Savings Incentive Match Plan for Employees. They can be either 401(k)s or Individual Retirement Accounts (page 867) and follow most of the rules for each. In 1997 qualified employees could contribute up to $6,000 a year (indexed to inflation and rising in $500 increments). The company contributes, too. It might match your contribution up to 3 percent of your total pay (with the option of dropping to one percent in 2 out of any 5 years). Or it might contribute a flat 2 percent for all qualified workers, whether they've funded their plans or not. The self-employed who are modestly paid can put more into a SIMPLE IRA than into a traditional one.

You're immediately vested in the money the company puts up, meaning that it's irrevocably yours. But if you withdraw money from a SIMPLE IRA during the first 2 years, you'll owe taxes on it plus a 25 percent penalty. After that, the penalty drops to 10 percent if you're under 59½. (SIMPLE 401(k)s may offer loans but not withdrawals.)

SEPs for the Self-Employed: the New First Choice?

For years, people with self-employment income have thought of Keogh plans first (page 863). But if you can save more than a SIMPLE IRA allows, I'd look at Simplified Employee Pensions (SEPs) first. They're handled as Individual Retirement Accounts, which makes them cheaper and easier to administer than Keogh plans. There's zero government paperwork and oversight.

The obvious SEP candidates are people who work for themselves full time: consultants, artists, professionals, writers, or owners of unincorporated businesses. Less obvious are employees who moonlight. Suppose, for example, that you work for a company that has a pension plan. None of that income is SEP-eligible. But what if you give piano lessons on the side? That's self-employment income, a portion of which can be whisked into a SEP. A partnership can also set up a SEP but only in the name of the partnership, not for the partners individually.

SEPs let you invest and tax-deduct the same annual dollar amount that profit-sharing Keoghs do: up to 13.04 percent of your self-employment earnings, minus one-half of your self-employment (Social Security) tax. The maximum contribution rises with inflation and worked out to $24,000 in 1997. (See page 864 for instructions on how to figure your personal maximum.) You can add to your SEP every year or not, depending on what you can afford.

SEPs, Keoghs, and Individual Retirement Accounts have similar withdrawal rules: a 10 percent penalty for withdrawals before 59½ and mandatory withdrawals starting at 70½. For free IRS booklets on these plans, call 800-TAX-FORM. For SEPs and Keoghs, ask for *Retirement Plans for the Self-Employed,* Publication 560; for IRAs, *Individual Retirement Arrangements,* Publication 590.

Where you establish the SEP will depend on how you want to invest. They're available from mutual fund groups, full-service and discount stockbrokers, financial advisers, and banking institutions. Don't put a tax-deferred variable annuity inside your SEP. In this context, it's merely a more expensive way of buying stocks and bonds. If, in retirement, you want to turn your nest egg into a lifetime income, you can use your SEP proceeds to buy an annuity then.

SEPs differ from Keoghs in three minor ways and two major ones. *What's minor:* You get no special tax break on lump-sum withdrawals. You can't put life insurance products into the plan (which is probably just as well). You can't roll your SEP into an employer's retirement plan. *What's major:* You can't borrow against a SEP if you should need the money. And your maximum contribution is less than certain types of Keoghs allow. But for those making average contributions, a SEP's simplicity beats all.

SEPs are easier than Keoghs for small businesses with a few employees, too. But Keoghs make it possible to exclude part-time and occasional employees if you're of a mind to do so. If you have employees, don't start any retirement plan before discussing the options with an accountant.

If you die or divorce, SEPs follow the IRA rules.

How to get the most from your SEP:

1. Hold down your paperwork by having just one plan. It might be with a mutual fund family you like, or with a full-service or discount brokerage house where you can buy stocks and bonds as well as mutual funds. Keep two plans at most, one of each type.

2. Arrange for automatic deposits into your SEP—a guaranteed easy way to save. A fixed amount of money can be withdrawn from your bank account each month. Anytime you get a windfall, add a piece of it to your SEP.

3. You can start or add to a personal SEP right up to the due date of your tax return (including extensions) and still take a current deduction for the contribution.

Keogh Plans for the Self-Employed: Best for the Well-Paid

The self-employed should choose either a SEP or a Keogh, without fail. No Kindly Big Corporation is going to send you a check at 65. Even if you have a corporate job and pension, use a SEP or Keogh for any moonlighting income. You'll be amazed at how much it's worth when you retire.

Keoghs require more paperwork than SEPs but they offer more options and let you set more money aside. So which Keogh? Here's what they're called and who might want them:

• *A profit-sharing Keogh.* This is the one that's like a SEP and is usually the plan to start with. There's a ceiling on contributions, but below that limit you can put in whatever you can spare. In a year when you're broke, you don't have to contribute anything at all.

There are two ways of establishing the ceiling: (1) Punt, by asking an accountant. (2) Figure it out yourself. I'm a punter myself, but for those who are cleverer than I, here's the second way:

Begin by taking 15 percent of your self-employment earnings. Reduce that by half of your self-employment (Social Security) tax and also by the amount you'll contribute to the plan.

Because you're clever, you'll have noticed a little problem there. To figure your maximum contribution, you first have to know what your contribution is going to be. Fortunately, we have computers in our lives and they know how to crack the code. You take your self-employment earnings, reduce it by half of your self-employment tax, and multiply by 13.043 percent. Here's an example:

Earnings: $100,000
Minus Social Security: −5,227
Subtotal: 94,773
Multiplied by 0.13043: $ 12,361
$12,361 is your maximum contribution

Now for the next step (ha-ha, I'll bet you thought we were through). There's a limit to the amount of earnings you can use for the calculation. In 1997 that limit was $160,000—a figure that's indexed to inflation. To find the maximum contribution for people who earn big bucks, multiply the current year's earning limit by 15 percent. In 1997 you couldn't put in any more than $24,000 ($160,000 multiplied by 0.15). The future, permanent ceiling: $30,000.

Use this same calculation to figure out how much you can put in a SEP.

• *A money-purchase Keogh.* This plan is for higher-income people who are sure the money will keep rolling in. You can put away more than profit-sharing Keoghs allow. But you have to pick a percentage of income that you'll contribute every year and stick with it. You'll owe a penalty if you can't make the specified payment. The IRS might allow you to change your percentage contribution, if you plead bad business conditions. But anyone struggling to make payments should probably bag the plan and roll the money into an Individual Retirement Account.

The maximum you can put in a money-purchase Keogh is 25 percent of your self-employment earnings, after reducing those earnings by one-half of your self-employment tax and the sum that's going into the Keogh. Another circular calculation. To find the answer, reduce your self-employment earnings by your self-employment tax and multiply by 20 percent. Using the preceding example, your maximum contribution would come to $18,955—about $6,500 more than you could contribute to a profit-sharing Keogh. High earners can't contribute any more than $30,000.

Earnings: $100,000
Minus Social Security: −5,227
Subtotal: 94,773
Multiplied by 0.20: $ 18,955
$18,955 is your maximum contribution

• *A combination Keogh.* You use both of the plans I've just mentioned. I'm not going to slog through calculations (*now* will you see an accountant?). The bottom line is this: You set your mandatory investment in the money-purchase Keogh at a level you're sure you can always afford. You use the profit-sharing Keogh for extra money in years you're flush. The combo can give you the maximum allowed for a money-purchase Keogh ($30,000) without being committed to it every year. People often start with a profit-sharing Keogh, then add a money-purchase plan.

• *A defined-benefit Keogh.* This plan gives you a fixed annual income at retirement. It's for high-income people 50 or older with a fondness for hanging around actuaries. You pick the annual pension you want, then contribute (and tax-deduct) whatever sums are needed to reach that goal. Your contributions could be quite large. In 1997 you were allowed to build a kitty big enough to yield a pension as high as $125,000, starting at age 65. That figure is indexed to inflation.

Each year your plan has to be checked by an actuary. He or she will update it for any changes in the law, tell you how large a contribution you should make, and send you a bill—and the service isn't cheap. If your income drops, a defined-benefit Keogh can be stopped in its tracks and the money rolled into an Individual Retirement Account.

If you have employees, they have to be included in your Keogh, too. In a profit-sharing plan, you contribute up to 15 percent of their compensation; in a money-purchase plan, up to 25 percent. Yes, that's right. Higher contribution levels than yours, because your employees' compensation isn't reduced by the sum that's going into the plan. Anyone with employees should have a chat with an accountant before starting any pension plan.

As with the SEP, where you set up your Keogh will depend on how you want to invest. They're available from mutual fund groups, full-service and discount stockbrokers, financial advisers, and banking institutions.

If you die or divorce, defined-benefit Keoghs follow the pension rules; all the others follow the 401(k) rules.

How to get the most from your Keogh:

1. Pick the plan that will give you the largest deduction you can afford.

2. If you don't now have a Keogh plan, start one by the end of the year, even if you put only $100 into it. As long as the paperwork is done by year-end, you can make tax-deductible contributions all the way up to the due date of your tax return (including extensions). You cannot *start* a Keogh after the first of the year and still get a deduction for the previous year, as you can with a SEP.

3. If you'll want to take loans from your Keogh, be sure the plan document allows it. Loans aren't allowed if you own more than 10 percent of the business.

4. Centralize your plan and arrange for automatic contributions, just as you would for a SEP (page 862).

5. Suitable investments for Keoghs are stocks, bonds, mutual funds, and certificates of deposit. Don't put a variable annuity in your plan. In this context, it's merely a more expensive way of buying stocks and bonds. If, in retirement, you want to turn your nest egg into a lifetime income, you can use your Keogh proceeds to buy an annuity then.

6. Evaluate whether to put $2,000 into a Roth IRA, even if that limits what you can put in your Keogh each year (page 868).

Other Retirement Plans Not to Be Missed

403(b) Plans—tax-deferred plans for employees of religious, charitable, or educational organizations. Most of them are funded with insurance annuities, but a few organizations offer a couple of mutual funds, too. Your annual, tax-deductible contributions are subject to ceilings so complicated that I wouldn't dream of trying to explain them here. Suffice it to say that the maximum is usually the lower of $9,500 or 25 percent of pay, reduced by contributions to other plans. The maximum can rise to $12,500 if you've worked for a qualified organization at least 15 years. You contribute through an automatic payroll-deduction plan. Employer matches aren't as common as they are in 401(k)s. Loans against the plans are usually allowed. If you leave your job, you may be able to take the 403(b) with you; alternatively, roll the money into an Individual Retirement Account.

There's an escape hatch if you don't like the investments you're offered. The plan administrator might not tell you about it or even know. But you're entitled to shift your money out of the plan's annuity and into a 403(b)(7) custodial account at the mutual fund group of your choice, tax-free. The fund will tell you how it's done.

When you quit a 403(b) annuity, you may owe an early-withdrawal penalty, so balance that against the mutual fund's potential for higher growth. Sometimes, early-withdrawal penalties are waived. Even if they're not, you can usually transfer 10 percent of the money each year, penalty-free.

Alas, the 403(b) rules will probably require that your regular contributions keep going into that unwanted annuity. You might leave the dollars there a few years to reduce the early-withdrawal fee or bite the bullet and switch right away. Form a committee of employees to see if you can get your employer to change the rules. One difference between the two types of plans: loans aren't allowed against the mutual funds' 403(b)(7) plans.

If you die or divorce, 403(b)s follow the 401(k) rules.

Federal Thrift Savings Plan—for federal government employees. It works the same as a 401(k).

Section 457 Plans—offered to state and local government employees. The contribution limits are complex. At best, they're the lesser of $7,500 or one-third of includable compensation. The $7,500 limit increases with inflation in $500 increments, and rises to as much as $15,000 in the 3 years before retirement, to help you catch up with any missed contributions in earlier years. There's rarely an employer match and no loans are allowed against the plan. If you leave the government, the money has to stay in the plan or be cashed out (whereupon taxes will be due). You can't roll it into an Individual Retirement Account.

The employer usually manages the money. In the past, 457s weren't kept in a separate trust—but then Orange County, California, went broke and its plan took a haircut. Now, new 457 plans have to be fully funded and protected. Starting in 1999, older plans are also supposed to be funded and in trust.

If you die or divorce, 457s follow the 401(k) rules.

INDIVIDUAL RETIREMENT ACCOUNTS

As investments, traditional Individual Retirement Accounts (IRAs) are modest but valuable additions to an old-age savings plan. They're fully tax deductible for millions of savers and partly deductible for millions more. Even if not deductible, they accumulate money tax deferred.

Roth IRAs aren't deductible but can accumulate earnings entirely tax free. For long-term savers, that's better than traditional IRAs, municipal bonds, or tax-deferred annuities.

IRAs also receive rollovers from other retirement accounts. When you get a lump-sum payout from a pension or profit-sharing plan and shift the money to an IRA, your lovely tax shelter is preserved.

Your IRA Questions Answered

How Much Can I Contribute? Individuals can put away up to $2,000 a year out of earnings or alimony. Two-income couples can save up to $4,000

—$2,000 for each. One-income couples can also save up to $2,000 each, if they file joint returns. But both IRAs must be funded with earnings, not interest or dividends. If your earnings as a couple are nominal, one or both IRAs might have to be smaller than $2,000.

By the way, I mean it when I say that you can contribute *up to* $2,000. You don't need the full $2,000, as some savers believe. You can contribute a lesser amount. You can even skip a year (although that would be a pity). If you earn less than $2,000, you can contribute all of it to your IRA (net of expenses, if you're self-employed).

You can contribute to more than one IRA in a single year. But the $2,000 limit ($4,000 for couples) applies to all your IRAs combined.

The rules are different when you're rolling over a lump-sum payout from a retirement plan. There's no ceiling on the size of the rollover. But you can transfer the money only into a traditional IRA, not into a Roth.

Should I Choose a Roth IRA? Go for it, if you qualify. It has lots of possibilities, for your personal savings and for your kids.

You can fund a full Roth IRA if you're single with an adjusted gross income under $95,000, or married under $150,000. If your income exceeds those levels, the amount you're allowed to contribute gradually declines, phasing out for singles at $110,000 and couples at $160,000. Effective date for the Roth IRA: January 1, 1998.

The Roth IRA Rules:

1. You get no tax deduction for the contribution. A Roth is funded with after-tax dollars.

2. When the IRA is 5 years old, you can take out your profits entirely tax free, under one of the following four circumstances:

- You're over 59½. This makes the Roth a terrific vehicle for long-term retirement investing.

- You want to use up to $10,000 of your IRA earnings to buy or build a first home for yourself, your spouse, your child, your grandchild, or your parents. A first-time home buyer is defined as someone who hasn't owned a home during the past two years (if married, the spouse can't have owned one either). This $10,000 is a lifetime draw; you can take it all at once or in bits and pieces.

- You're disabled.

- You've died and your beneficiaries are receiving the money.

3. At any time and for any purpose, you can withdraw the amount you contributed tax free. So your annual investments are always available, at no cost. That gives you tremendous flexibility. Withdrawals exceeding your contributions are subject to income taxes if they don't meet one of the

conditions listed above. They're also subject to a 10 percent penalty if you're under 59½.

4. As with other IRAs, you can make a contribution just before filing your tax return and apply it to the previous year. So $2,000 contributed in April 1999 can be counted in 1998. Your 5-year holding period would then start in December 1998. That jumps you toward the time you can start taking money out tax free.

5. You can keep contributing for as long as you like, even past 70½ (the cutoff date for other IRAs). You can also leave the money untouched, to accumulate for heirs. There's no date when withdrawals have to start.

6. You can roll your money from one Roth IRA into another Roth IRA tax free, if you want to change the institution that holds the account.

7. You cannot make a tax-free rollover from a traditional IRA into a Roth. Nor can you do a rollover from an employee plan.

8. You're allowed to roll a traditional IRA into a Roth if (1) you're willing to pay taxes on the accumulated profits *and* (2) your adjusted gross income is less than $100,000. No tax penalty will be owed. If you act in 1998, the tax can be stretched over four years. For rollovers made in 1999 and later, the tax is due in the current year. (One hitch: that $100,000 includes the amount you'll withdraw from your traditional IRA, so to qualify, your actual earnings have to be lower than that.)

If you meet the income test, consider the rollover if: (1) you have a nondeductible IRA; (2) you have a deductible IRA whose tax is small; *and* (3) you will hold the Roth for many years. If you'll owe a big tax, however, leave your traditional IRA alone. Put new contributions into a Roth.

Should My Kids Use a Roth IRA? Great idea, if your family can afford to use it as a tax-planning device. Roths have to be funded out of earnings. But if your kids earn $2,000 over the summer or even doing chores at home, they could put the money into a Roth and you could return the cash to them with a $2,000 gift. They'd have to file a tax return but would probably owe no tax. When they grow up, or 5 years after starting the Roth, they'd be able to buy a home, using up to $10,000 of their IRA earnings plus their own contributions, tax free.

They could also tap a Roth for higher education, drawing out their own contributions tax free. If they take any more to help pay tuition that additional money is taxed, but no 10 percent penalty is due.

If they just leave their Roth money alone, it should grow to a mighty big sum by the time they retire.

Should I Contribute to a Tax-Deductible IRA Instead of a Roth? Generally no. Traditional, deductible IRAs are better only in limited circumstances.

Among them: (1) You need the tax deduction in order to make the full IRA contribution. (2) You're contributing in your 50s and will withdraw the money at 59½. Over short holding periods—say, less than 10 years—the traditional IRA's tax deduction will probably be worth more than the Roth IRA's tax-free gains (but check it out). (3) You will soon retire, and will be in a low or zero tax bracket. (4) Your income is too high for a Roth and the company you work for doesn't have a retirement plan.

Who's Eligible for a Traditional, Tax-Deductible IRA? You can deduct a full $2,000 if you don't participate in a company retirement plan. Mostly, that means people whose companies have no plans. If your spouse also has no plan (perhaps because he or she is a homemaker), you can deduct a second $2,000.

If your company has only a defined-contribution plan (page 851), you don't "participate" until money goes into the plan on your behalf. That may not occur during your first year on the job—in which case you'd be able to make a deductible IRA contribution. If your company has a defined-benefit plan, however, you participate even if you're not vested yet.

People who participate in company plans can have deductible IRAs if their adjusted gross incomes don't exceed a specified ceiling. The ceiling in 1997: $25,000 for singles and $40,000 for marrieds. Above those levels, the IRA write-off phases out.

The ceiling for deductible IRAs is scheduled to rise each year, topping out in 2005 at $50,000 for singles and $65,000 for couples. (The phase-out: $60,000 for singles and $75,000 for marrieds.)

What if your spouse participates in a retirement plan and you don't? You can deduct a full $2,000 IRA for yourself if your combined incomes don't exceed $150,000. This deduction phases out at $160,000.

How Does a Tax-Deductible IRA Compare with Other Tax-Deductible Investments?
1. Company 401(k) plans almost always beat IRAs for employees with modest earnings who are eligible for both. The 401(k) permits larger contributions and usually allows loans. What's more, the employer often matches the money you put in. If you won't save more than $2,000, however, an IRA is better than a 401(k) with poor investment choices and no employer match. IRAs also maintain their tax shelter if you leave the company.

2. Keogh plans and SEPs usually beat IRAs, too, because you can put more money into them. The IRA wins, however, if your earnings are small. Every penny of an annual paycheck of $2,000 or less can be stashed in an IRA to accumulate tax deferred, whereas only a portion of it could be put into a Keogh or SEP.

Should I Contribute to a 401(k) Instead of a Roth IRA? Yes, if the company matches some percentage of your contribution. Yes, if payroll deduction is the only way you'll save. Yes, if you want to be able to borrow against your plan. Money taken from a 401(k)—say, a college loan—can be replaced with interest. Money taken from an IRA never can be replaced.

But if your employer doesn't contribute, you don't plan to borrow, and you can't afford to fund both a 401(k) and a Roth, put the first $2,000 into the Roth. In the long run, the tax-free compounding is going to be worth more. You can make Roth contributions automatic by having money deducted from your bank account.

The same applies to savers with 403(b)s and other tax-deductible retirement accounts.

What if Congress changes its mind and takes away the Roth someday? Trust that current Roth-holders will be grandfathered. There will probably be enough of you to keep the tax break you bargained for.

Who Should Make After-Tax IRA Contributions? *Anyone* can contribute $2,000 to a nondeductible IRA, regardless of income. Do so if you earn too much to qualify for a Roth or a deductible IRA. You're using after-tax dollars, but the money accumulates tax deferred. Taxes aren't owed until you take the money out.

Nondeductible IRAs are good places for fixed-income investments. Wherever you hold them, they're taxed at ordinary-income rates, and in IRAs that tax will be deferred. IRAs also make sense for people who like to trade stocks or mutual funds, because you can buy and sell without paying capital gains taxes every time.

The downside is that these IRAs complicate your tax returns. Every withdrawal becomes a mix of taxable and nontaxable money. (But that's not your problem if an accountant prepares your returns.)

How Do I Set Up an IRA? Decide where you want to invest your retirement fund, then ask an appropriate institution for its IRA account forms. Fill out the papers, send in the money, and you're up and running.

For certificates of deposit, you'd go to a bank, S&L, or credit union. For a diversified portfolio of mutual funds, you'd choose a mutual fund group or discount brokerage house that runs a mutual fund supermarket (page 632). If you want individual stocks and bonds as well as mutual funds, use a discount brokerage house or a full-service broker. If you want real estate, you'll need an independent pension administrator (page 879). If you want a variable annuity . . . but why would you? In this context, they're merely a more expensive way of buying stocks and bonds. If you're into hard assets, IRAs can hold American Eagle gold, silver, and platinum coins (if a platinum coin is minted), coins issued by a state, or gold, silver, platinum, and palladium bullion bars. But no art, and no collectibles. (IRAs that let you choose among many different types of investments are known as self-directed IRAs.)

At banking institutions and no-load mutual fund groups, setup fees are usually minimal or zero. There may be small, annual maintenance fees. Brokerage firms charge a setup fee plus an annual maintenance fee payable separately and deductible as part of your miscellaneous tax deductions. Brokerage commissions, however, are subtracted from your IRA money.

You're allowed to have as many IRAs as you want—for example, one at a bank, one at a mutual fund group, one at a brokerage firm. But whether you have one IRA or ten, your total annual contribution can't exceed your $2,000 ceiling (except for rollovers, page 876, plus an extra $500 for an education IRA, page 558).

Do not, incidentally, use your IRA to buy municipal bonds or muni funds. You don't need tax deferral for these investments because they're tax exempt already. What's more, if you put them in a regular IRA, their interest becomes taxable at withdrawal.

How Do I Roll a Retirement-Plan Distribution into an IRA? Maybe you retired early. Maybe you quit your job to take another one. Either way, you might be entitled to a lump-sum distribution from your employer's qualified plan.

If you're happy with the plan, consider leaving your money there (page 858). You might want its fixed pension or approve of its choice of investments for your 401(k). Alternatively, you can take your money and still preserve its tax shelter by rolling it into an IRA.*

You can take the rollover in one of two ways:

1. *The good way.* This is the "direct rollover." It's paid directly into your new IRA (or into your new employer's qualified plan, if that's an option you want). Sometimes you never see the check; sometimes you receive it but it's made out to the trustee of the new IRA or plan. All employers have to offer you this option.

2. *The bad way.* The check is made out to you personally and you deposit it in the new IRA. This triggers the withholding-tax mess explained on page 859. If you take the check personally by mistake, be sure it gets into your new IRA within 60 days. If it's mailed on the 61st day, it will be treated as a withdrawal. You'll have to take the money out, pay taxes on the whole amount, and pay a 10 percent penalty if you're under 59½.

With smaller checks, a rollover sometimes doesn't seem worth it. But $1,500, at an untaxed 8 percent a year, grows to $7,000 in 20 years and $15,500 in 30 years, without your having to lift a finger. That's worth it.

---

* You can roll it only into a tax-deferred IRA. Rollovers into Roth IRAs aren't allowed.

Some distributions cannot be rolled over into IRAs. Excluded are:
- Any after-tax contributions you made to the retirement plan.
- Any amount you're required to withdraw because you've reached age 70½.
- Any sums you've arranged to receive in installment or annuity payments. These are defined as roughly equal payments, made at least once a year and scheduled to last for your lifetime, life expectancy, the lifetime or life expectancy of you and a beneficiary, or 10 years or more.

Three rollover hints:

1. You can roll over all of the money or some of it as you choose. What's not rolled over is subject to tax (and penalties, if you're under 59½).
- You have to roll over the very same assets that came out of your old pension plan, with two exceptions. You can sell an asset (stock, for example) and roll over the cash instead. Or you can spend some of the cash you took from the plan and replace it with other cash.
- Don't add your rollover funds to an existing IRA. Segregate this money in an IRA of its own. Rollover money in a segregated account can be rolled into a new employer's retirement plan, if you ever choose to do so. Funds from commingled IRAs can't. (But go ahead and commingle if you've retired for good.)

Can I Change My IRA Investments? Yes indeed. You can switch from one investment to another within the same institution or to another institution entirely.

Within the same institution, switching can be as easy as picking up the phone. To switch to another institution, you can either: (1) request a direct IRA-to-IRA transfer, which can be done as often as you want; (2) have a check made out to you, which you must roll into the new IRA within 60 days. Done this way, each IRA can be rolled over just once a year.

Sometimes you're thwarted by the institution you leave behind. It may drag its heels on transferring your investments. It may charge an exit fee. A few brokerage firms can actually prevent you from leaving because the agreement you originally signed locks your money up. Moral: Don't open an IRA without first checking your escape routes. And get a list of all the fees.

Can I Make Early Withdrawals from an IRA? Yes, if you're willing to pay the price. First come income taxes. Second, there's usually a 10 percent penalty if you're under 59½. Third, if your IRA is in a bank certificate of deposit or annuity, you may owe an early-withdrawal penalty.

How Long Can I Contribute? For tax-deferred IRAs—as long as you have earnings, up to the year before you reach 70½. Then you have to stop. But you can keep on depositing up to $2,000 a year for an at-home spouse who is under 70½. For Roth IRAs—you can contribute as long as you want.

Can I Borrow from, or against, an IRA? No dice. But if you have a truly short-term need for money—for example, a bridge loan while waiting for a mortgage to come through—you could tap your IRA through the rollover rule. No taxes are due if you take money out of your IRA, use it, then replace it within 60 days. You're allowed to do this once a year, with each of your IRAs, including Roths.

What If I Divorce? As part of the divorce agreement, some or all of the IRA money may go to your former spouse. Anything taken out of the account can be rolled into an IRA for your ex. The funds must be shifted to the new IRA within 60 days or taxes and penalties will be due.

What If I Inherit a Traditional IRA? If you're the spouse of the person who died, you inherit the IRA estate–tax-free. Spouses also have two special options. You can treat the IRA as your own (call the trustee to change the name) or roll the money into another IRA, tax-free. Rollovers are the most flexible and can probably be done at the bank or investment firm that held the original IRA. All the investments can even be left intact, if that's your choice. Name new beneficiaries. You can take money at any time, although withdrawals aren't mandatory until you reach 70½. Over 70½, withdrawals can be based on your age plus the age of your oldest beneficiary.

If you need money immediately and are younger than 59½, withdraw the funds directly from your late spouse's IRA. You'll pay taxes but not the 10 percent penalty for being underage.

If you inherit from someone other than your spouse, you can't roll the money into an IRA of your own. You have two ways of taking the funds: (1) withdraw all the money over five years, on whatever schedule you like, paying income taxes when the money is received; (2) defer the tax by setting up an annual withdrawal schedule based on your life expectancy. If you're young, the required withdrawals might be quite small, which keeps the tax low (although you can take larger sums if you want). If the IRA names more than one beneficiary, however, you have to use the life expectancy of the eldest.

What If I Inherit a Roth IRA? A spouse can keep the IRA intact— treating it as his or her own (call the trustee to change the name) or rolling it into another Roth IRA, tax free. You should name new beneficiaries. You can take the money whenever you want or let it build up in the IRA and leave it for your heirs, income-tax free.

If you inherit from someone other than your spouse, you can take the funds over 5 years or based on your life expectancy, as explained above. There's one wonderful difference: any withdrawals you make are tax free.

What If I Leave a Roth to a Young Child or Grandchild? When minors are beneficiaries, think custodian, special language, maybe an irrevocable trust. This is lawyersville. But a minor can let investments accumulate over a lifetime, then take the profits tax free. For a gain like that, lawyers are worth it. Tip: If you have more than one beneficiary, set up a Roth IRA for each of them. That lets each beneficiary take the money on the schedule that works best.

How to get the most from an IRA:

1. Put yourself on a regular monthly contribution plan with a bank or mutual fund. That should guarantee you the maximum $2,000 deposit every year. Savers who wait until the last minute may come up short. It's okay to deposit less, but that lost amount can never be made up.

2. If you didn't make monthly contributions, all is not lost. You can open an IRA on the very eve of the day that your tax return is due (not including extensions), deposit up to $2,000, and still deduct it for the previous year.

3. If you have a scattering of IRAs at many different institutions, consolidate them. They add to your paperwork and maybe to your maintenance fees. Better to have all the money under one roof—with a mutual fund group or in a self-directed IRA at a brokerage firm. You might also wring a higher return from a single lump sum than from a clutch of separate, disorganized accounts. Or two lump sums. Roth IRAs have to be separated from tax-deferred IRAs. If you keep your IRA money in the bank, make sure that all your retirement accounts at any one financial institution don't exceed the federal deposit insurance limit (page 74).

4. If you're a TWOI-some—two workers, one income—use a spousal IRA to build up the assets of the at-home spouse.

5. As a general rule, you shouldn't tap your IRA until retirement. If you're a homeowner and need money, take a home-equity loan, instead. You will probably earn more on your IRA than you will pay for the home-equity loan, after tax. But if you're in serious need of cash and under 59½, take a look at Loophole Nine on page 877. It's a way of using your IRA funds without paying the 10 percent early-withdrawal penalty.

6. If you want to move your IRA from one institution to another, there are two different ways of getting the job done: transfers or rollovers. Which you choose will depend on your character and your needs.

A transfer is the sure and easy way. The new institution does most of the work and every dime of your money is reinvested. The drawback is that transfers sometimes take weeks. That's damaging only when you want to make a particular investment right away. (Tip: Ask your old institution if there's an exit fee and pay it promptly. That sometimes pushes things along.)

A rollover is the quicker way. Ask the old institution to close your account, which should be accomplished within 5 days. You get the check, then hand the money to the new institution. No tax money is withheld. (The withholding rule, which you may recall from page 872, applies only to distributions from qualified employer plans, not from IRAs.) The success of any rollover, however, depends on your self-discipline. You may be tempted to spend a few bucks while the money passes through your hands, so your IRA may not be reinvested intact. Furthermore, you have to complete the rollover within 60 days. If you miss the deadline, you'll have made a permanent withdrawal on which taxes and maybe penalties are due.

7. If you're moving to a mutual fund group and aren't yet sure which funds you want, put your IRA into its money fund and choose investments later. If you dither around trying to pick a stock or bond fund, the 60-day deadline might get by.

GETTING AWAY WITH IT

Whether you have a 401(k), SEP, Keogh, 403(b), or Individual Retirement Account, it usually costs you an extra 10 percent to withdraw your money if you're younger than 59½. But loopholes dot any government rule. The penalty may be waived in the following circumstances:

1. You're totally disabled.

2. You're dead, and the money is going to your beneficiary.

3. You've left your job and are at least 55. This particular loophole works for all plans but IRAs and SEPs.

4. The money is going to a divorced spouse pursuant to a court decree. To avoid penalties on IRAs and SEPs, transfer the funds into a new IRA.

5. You need the money for deductible medical expenses that exceed 7.5 percent of your adjusted gross income. But in this case, there's a catch. Taking money out of your pension plan raises your income, which reduces the size of the medical deduction you can take. Thank you, Uncle Sam.

6. You're withdrawing from a deductible or nondeductible IRA (but not a Roth) because you've been unemployed for more than 12 weeks and need money to pay for health insurance for yourself and your family.

7. You're paying for qualified higher-education expenses.

8. You're withdrawing up to $10,000 from any IRA for a first home (page 868). If it's a Roth, you have to have held the IRA for at least five years.

9. You set up a payment schedule for withdrawing the money over the rest of your life.

Loophole Nine sounds restrictive on the surface, but it is, in fact, the most flexible one of all. It applies to IRAs as well as to all the other retirement plans.

Loophole Nine. This escape route is so useful that I want to spend a few paragraphs telling you about it. It lets you avoid the 10 percent early-withdrawal penalty if you're under 59½. You just set up a regular withdrawal schedule that, if followed faithfully, would lead to "substantially equal" periodic payments for the rest of your life (or for the joint life expectancies of you and your spouse or another beneficiary).

Here's the beauty part: The payments *don't* have to last for life if your need for money is short term. Once you start withdrawing, you must keep to the schedule for at least 5 years and until you reach 59½. After that, you can change your mind. You might decide on larger withdrawals or smaller ones. Or you might take no more money at all. Mandatory withdrawal rules don't begin again until you pass 70½, except for Roth IRAs, which can be kept for as long as you want.

I can think of several problems that Loophole Nine might solve. For example, you might tap the fund to help pay for your child's college degree. Once those bills are behind you (and 5 years have passed and you're 59½), you can stop the withdrawals and let your remaining money grow. Or you might have lost your executive job and replaced it with a job paying less. A withdrawal plan could provide the extra income you need. It might also be a way of paying alimony.

This loophole works best for the middle-aged who may not have to use it for more than 5 years or so. Young people should forget it. Their monthly payments would be small. And, once started, withdrawals must continue at least until they reach 59½. That would pretty much run down the fund.

There Is One Immutable Law of Financial Planning That This Little Game Runs Up Against. God punishes anyone who uses loopholes. In this case, your trials are actuarial.

There is more than one way of calculating "substantially equal" payments and the method chosen makes a huge difference to the size of your income. I ran one example for a 55-year-old woman. She had a Keogh worth $150,000 that was earning a 9 percent rate of return. Depending on which calculation she chose, her first-year payment could have been as little as $5,245 or as much as $15,490. Alternatively, she could have divided her money into two separate $75,000 Individual Retirement Accounts, drawn $7,735 a year from one of them and left the other one alone. Or she could have split the IRAs into different sizes. The possibilities are endless.

The IRS's free Publication 590, *Individual Retirement Arrangements,* leads you through all the numbers. If you find them too complicated (most people do), ask an accountant for advice. If you get the size of your "substantially equal" withdrawals wrong, tax penalties may be due.

WHICH FINANCIAL INVESTMENTS BUILD THE BEST RETIREMENT FUND?

That's easy. A preponderance of well-diversified stocks or stock-owning mutual funds, held for the long term. No financial investment does better than stocks or so soundly outperforms inflation. When stocks are down, people treat them like lepers. But, in fact, that's the very best time to buy.

Bonds and money-market funds take the edge off your losses during those months (or years) when stocks decline. So it's worth owning some of them, too. But stocks provide the most long-term growth. For a full explanation of this position, see Chapter 21. The young and middle-aged who invest their retirement money in well-chosen stock-owning mutual funds will wind up much wealthier than those who don't.

By the mid-1990s, that message had finally gotten through, thanks largely to the extravagant bull market that started in 1991. At this writing, a majority of 401(k) money is going into equity funds—quite a difference from just a few years ago, when fixed-income investment contracts dominated retirement funds.

Over long periods (which is an appropriate measure for retirement funds), stocks run about 7.4 percent ahead of inflation, compounded annually, while intermediate-term government bonds run 2 percent ahead, reports Ibbotson Associates in Chicago. After taxes, you make money on stocks but practically nothing at all on bonds. There are periods when bonds do as well or better than stocks, which is why you should own some. But for 20-year money, stocks are impossible to beat.

The only exception to my enthusiasm for stocks is stock in the company you work for. Life is long and bad things happen even to good companies. I'd hate to stake my entire financial life—my retirement fund as well as my income and health plan—on the fortunes of a single firm. If your company is contributing stock to your retirement account, don't buy a single share more. If it's not, follow the mutual fund rule: no more than 5 percent of your assets should be committed to a single stock.

What about real estate as a retirement-plan option? Okay, if you're buying funds invested in real estate investment trusts (page 836). They're easy to sell if you want to switch to something else. Not okay if they're shares in illiquid real-estate partnerships. Your money might be stuck there for years.

When investing retirement-plan money, don't look at it in a vacuum.

I've heard people say, "I divide my money half and half, between stocks and fixed-income investments." That sounds reasonable until you see what's really going on. Their retirement funds might indeed be divided as they said. But when you look at all their other savings—their money market fund, the Series EE bonds in their children's college account, the utility bonds their grandfather left them—it turns out that, at age 35 or 40, only 25 percent of their total available assets are invested for growth.

Please, folks. Line up *all* your investments before deciding what to do about any one or two of them. Set a single, total risk level for yourself (page 589) and spread it over every savings and investment account you own. Put the higher-risk investments (stocks) in your retirement plan because this is money you'll leave alone for 10 to 30 years. Put lower-risk investments (bonds, CDs) in accounts you may have to tap sooner.

Would I write these same words if I knew in advance that, when you read them, the stock market would be in a tailspin? You bet I would. That's what stocks do from time to time. You buy low markets and wait them out —even if it takes years. You'll never get the market's superior gains unless you have the nerve to buy during serious downturns when Wall Street reluctantly throws a half-price sale.

Nor would I say anything different if, when you read this, stocks were roaring up. Long-term investors shouldn't give a thought to where stock prices will be next week. Your horizon is 20 years, by which standard prices today are cheap.

WHAT CAN GO WRONG?

Not much goes wrong, I'm pleased to say. As a way of investing, retirement plans carry little risk. Abuses occur, but not a lot. The biggest danger is that you won't invest enough or won't invest well enough.

Nevertheless, there are some weaknesses in the system that you need to know about:

Individual Retirement Accounts, Keoghs, and SEPs

• You might put your account with a dishonest pension-plan administrator, who introduces you to fraudulent investments or embezzles your money.

By law, you need a third party to make transactions in your retirement plan. Usually, your administrator is the mutual fund or brokerage house where you keep your plan. But you might also choose an independent administrator. The independents handle a wider range of investments, including real estate and venture-capital deals. Administrators also prepare your retirement plan's financial reports.

Crooks find an opening here because *anyone* can enter the field. It's entirely unregulated. Pension administrators handle hundreds of millions of dollars, yet they're neither licensed nor audited. Even better, from embezzlers' points of view, they're dealing with people who might not want money from the account for 20 or 30 years.

Most administrators do a reliable job. But a few attract business by promoting unusual or illiquid investments—things like real estate, jukebox deals, technology partnerships, wireless cable, and ostrich farms. These investments may initially pay—or appear to pay—super-high returns. But they're often fraudulent. When the scheme unravels, your administrator may go broke or to Brazil, taking your retirement money along.

To avoid disasters, keep your retirement money with large, well-known pension administrators: banks, trust companies, mutual funds, insurance companies, and full-service or discount brokerage houses. They're all regulated by various government entities and let you hold a wide range of securities, including stocks, bonds, and mutual funds.

A bank trust department might also accept real estate if your account is large enough. Otherwise, those who put real estate in retirement plans will have to use an independent administrator. *Do not* use one associated with a hard-selling investment firm that does a lot of illiquid, supposedly high-yield deals. Those are calamities you ought to see coming.

Traditional Pensions

• Your pension payout is insured by the Pension Benefit Guaranty Corporation (PBGC) up to a certain amount per month (page 850). But if the plan fails, you lose collateral benefits such as life and health insurance.

• Your company can terminate its pension plan and put all your benefits to date into an insurance company annuity. There's no PBGC protection if the insurer fails. Your state insurance-guaranty funds may or may not cover pension annuities. Your employer, however, is required to make a prudent choice. Employees might successfully sue an employer that chose a risky insurer, especially if some conflict of interest was involved. But the court battle will be expensive and long.

Profit-Sharing Plans and 401(k)s

• Your company can give you poor investment choices. As you know from Chapter 21, you need a proper asset allocation to gain your ends. But some 401(k)s offer dumb choices—a blend of the most conservative investments (money funds, fixed-income contracts) and the riskiest (the company's own stock).

• Very small plans may be run by the boss as a personal perk. He might buy speculative stocks, toy with options, and chase initial public offerings—none of them appropriate for the average employee in the plan. Or maybe he's into ego "investments"—classic cars which he just happens to drive; art which happens to hang on his walls. He might also take a flier (with your money) on his brother's new restaurant, despite its slim odds of success. If you leave your job, you may not be able to cash out of the plan. If you do, there's no telling whether you actually got a fair price (probably not). This boss isn't necessarily malign, but he's stupid and you pay the price.

• Your boss may be malign. Small plans, in particular, can be subject to fraud. The owner of the company—also the pension fund's trustee—may take illegal loans from the fund, deduct money from your paycheck but fail to deposit it in your account, or siphon off money into his or her personal account. If the company goes bankrupt, there's little or no hope of getting your money back. Your boss might also use 401(k) funds to start other businesses and they might fail, too.

If you stop getting regular reports on your plan (page 883) and can't find out anything from the plan administrator, you ought to report that to the government (page 885) and stop putting money in. The PBGC doesn't cover losses in 401(k)s.

• Even in larger companies, you may not be able to choose your investments yourself. The company may handle the money in its own best interest, not yours. In two celebrated bankruptcy cases in the early 1990s, one firm's 401(k) was invested entirely in company stock, the other one almost entirely in company-owned retail stores. Starting in 1999, however, the company can't put any more than 10 percent of your contribution into its own stock or other assets, unless you agree. Don't agree.

403(b)s

• Your plan may offer you annuities that carry too high a cost. But there's often a way around this problem (page 866).

• I can't think of anything else. By law, 403(b) accounts can be invested only in insurance company annuities and mutual funds. You're protected from crooks and from yourself. Other plan holders should be so lucky.

Mistakes in Calculating Company Retirement Checks

Mistakes are getting more common because retirement plans are so complex. Traditional pension payouts are checked by an outside auditor, but 401(k) payouts might be figured by payroll clerks who aren't up to speed on your plan's finer points.

Three bright yellow flags should warn you that something might be wrong: (1) Your retirement-plan payout is inexplicably less than your colleagues got. (2) The money seems low for the number of years you worked. (3) Your company merged or got a new pension-plan administrator, often the start of a royal muck-up. Where do mistakes originate? Let me count the ways:

• If you have a 401(k): A clerk might not post a contribution. Over time, that will grow to a major loss.

• If you have a profit-sharing plan: You might receive the wrong percentage contribution. When you leave the company, your account might not be valued on the proper day.

• If you worked past normal retirement age: the extra months or years might not be figured in your benefit.

• If you started out in a union plan and then moved to management: Your union credits might be forgotten. The same thing can happen to a worker moving from one division of a company to another, when the divisions have separate plans.

• If your plan counts "all" compensation toward your pension: it might forget to include your bonuses, overtime, and commissions.

• If your pension is based on your 5 highest earning years: the computer might assume that those are the last 5 years you worked, which isn't always the case.

• If you ever worked part-time: Those years might be dropped from your pension calculation. You're generally covered if you work more than 1,000 hours a year. But some companies accept 500 hours or less, so check it out, says pension attorney Ronald Dean of Palisades Park, California.

• If you've been in and out of the workforce and your plan has a Social Security offset: The company might overestimate your Social Security earnings, which reduces your pension check. Get a copy of your Social Security earnings history (page 902), then ask the company what it assumed when it figured your check. If its assumptions were incorrect, show proof of your earnings. The company will refigure your pension, giving you a larger check.

• If you leave with a lump sum: all the errors that affect the calculation of monthly pension checks affect you, too.

• If the pension laws have changed: Your company may still be running by the old rules. For example, it may use an outdated interest-rate table to calculate how much money you're owed.

Catching the Error. It's impossible for employees to find most of these mistakes unaided. But a few show up, in black and white, on the regular plan reports you get (you read them, right?). Two things to look for:

On the annual statement showing the value of your profit-sharing or 401(k) plan, make sure that your full contribution was credited. Some employers are lax about this. Also make sure that you got the proper employer match.

On the annual statement showing how much your traditional pension benefit has grown, check that the company counted all your earnings and hours. What? You don't know the hours you worked? That's why you should keep all your W-2 forms. They help prove your work history, which might get lost if your company is sold. W-2s also show what you put into 401(k)s and similar plans. If you catch a mistake, assemble your proof and ask the plan administrator to correct it.

If you suspect that your retirement check is wrong, query the plan administrator. Don't do it by phone. If you haven't asked in writing, you haven't asked. Request all the factors used to calculate your payout, such as your earnings, the benefit formula, and the number of years you worked. The wrong birth date or hire date can make a big difference to what you get.

If you see nothing obviously wrong but still feel uncomfortable, call the National Center for Retirement Benefits in Northbrook, Illinois (800-666-1000). It charges nothing to check out your pension, profit-sharing, or 401(k) payment, but takes 30 percent of any money it recovers. The fee drops to 25 percent of the recovery for handling 10 or more people from the same company, and 25 percent or less if you had no pension and it secures you one. This firm doesn't handle union or government plans.

An actuary can also tell you if you've been properly paid. A typical fee: a few hundred dollars for traditional plans and more for 401(k)s. The trouble is, hardly anyone has ever seen an actuary. Try your library for the *Enrolled Actuaries Directory*. But you'll have to call a string of them to find one who takes individual cases.

If you want to sue, the Pension Rights Center (202-296-3776) or the American Association of Retired Persons (202-434-2277), both in Washington, D.C., will send you the names of pension lawyers in your state. Lawyers typically charge one-third of the money you recover, plus expenses.

Don't delay if you suspect you've been underpaid. You don't want a statute of limitations to cut off your claim.

Hiding Your Plan's Financial Condition

This is rarely a problem with big-company plans. But some small plans refuse to issue government-mandated reports and those are the plans most likely to misuse your money. Even if they do report, they don't have to be specific about what's going on. Remember the bankrupt company I mentioned, which put most of its workers' 401(k) money into its own retail stores? The "investments" section of the report requires the plan to report only the percentage of money in stocks, bonds, and real estate—which it could answer without disclosing how concentrated its real-estate investment was.

Here are the reports you're supposed to get and what they say. Keep all these documents as well as any updates that come your way.

• Summary Plan Description—free when you join the plan. You can get one at other times if you ask the plan administrator in writing, but you might be charged a modest fee. This is more colloquially known as your Plan Handbook.

What you'll learn: Your plan's rules, explained in a simple way. How you qualify for coverage and how you get your money out. If you want to read the entire plan document, you can get a copy or peruse it wherever it's kept, but it's written in cuneiform.

• Summary of Material Modifications—free, within 210 days after the end of the plan year when the change was made.

What you'll learn: Any change in rules, although this is pretty late to be notified. Good companies usually announce changes right away.

• Summary Annual Report—free once a year, if your plan covers 100 people or more. Free once every 3 years for smaller plans, with no reports required in the interim (although some plans report anyway).

What you'll learn: How much money the plan gained or lost on its total investments last year. It's expressed in dollars, however, not as a percentage return. The report also gives a figure for administrative expenses paid by the plan and should show any financial transactions between the plan and people close to it.

Several problems with this report: (1) The investments can be described so generally that you don't have a clue what the plan really buys. (2) It's often out-of-date. It needn't be filed until 7 months after the end of the plan year. (3) Lots of expenses are left out. (4) It doesn't disclose the plan's percentage gain or loss. (5) Reports from small plans provide less detail and aren't audited. So who really knows? (6) You might discover that the plan is overweighted in, say, real estate. But there's nothing much you can do about it, in plans that don't allow you to choose your own investments. You can complain, of course, and spread the word around the office—that might help. Otherwise, your choices are to take the risk or not be in the plan at all.

• Individual Benefit Statement—free once every 12 months. Some plans send it automatically and perhaps even quarterly. Others give it only to those who ask for it in writing.

What you'll learn: In 401(k)s, how your individual account is performing. In pension plans, how large a benefit you have accrued so far. In profit-sharing plans, what the value of your share is worth.

It's essential to get this report and check it carefully for mistakes. The pension-plan report shows your wages earned and hours worked, which translates into benefits. The 401(k) report shows investments, contributions, withdrawals, and loans. If you don't pick your own investments, you'll be told only that you own a share of "stocks, bonds, and real estate," with no further particulars. But you can write to the plan administrator and ask for them.

- Funding Disclosure Notice—for traditional pension plans.

What you'll learn: Whether your plan contains less than 90 percent of the money needed to pay benefits. You get no disclosure if it's more than 90 percent funded.

What If Your Boss Refuses to Distribute Reports? This is not uncommon in small plans where most of the money belongs to the honcho anyway. On paper, you're told to write the plan administrator—but that may be the boss, who could also be the plan's trustee.

You can get the annual report (Form 5500) from the U.S. Department of Labor, Pension & Welfare Benefits Administration (PWBA), Public Disclosure Facility, 200 Constitution Ave. N.W., Washington, DC 20210 (202-219-8771). You'll be charged only a copying fee.

But you can't get an Individual Benefit Statement except from the plan administrator.* If he or she balks, or you think that money is being misappropriated, call the PWBA at 800-998-7542. An operator will refer you to the Labor Department office that handles complaints in your area. Try to get other employees to call, too. PWBA doesn't have enough people to follow up on every complaint, but it does get money restored to some plans.

When PWBA writes to a company, it doesn't reveal who complained, but in offices with two doctors, a nurse, and a receptionist, it's not hard to figure out. Workers may put up with pension abuse for fear of losing their jobs.

Even if you get the report, it may be couched in language that conceals what's really going on. Outside trustees or recordkeepers may know that something's wrong (for example, the plan may not receive a contribution that's due), but—astonishingly—no law requires them to tell. One would think that's what trustees were *for.*

Bottom line: 401(k)s pretty much run on the honor system today. At the very least, plans should have outside trustees with a duty to tell if something's wrong.

Publications: PWBA has a good book, *Protect Your Pension,* free by calling 800-998-7542. Among other things, it tells you how to decipher a Form 5500 (the annual report) and how to calculate the plan's investment return. This and other publications are also available on PWBA's Web site: http://www.dol.gov/dol/pwba.

---

* Congress plans to make the summary plan description and summary of modifications available only from the administrator, too, except in unusual circumstances. At this writing, however, you can also get them from the PWBA.

AUNT JANE'S SINGLE MOST IMPORTANT SECRET FOR ACCUMULATING HUGE POTS OF MONEY FOR YOUR RETIREMENT, REVEALED HERE FOR THE FIRST TIME

When you're due a payout from any retirement plan, and you haven't yet retired, leave the money where it is or roll it into another plan. Don't spend it. Don't even think of spending it. Don't think even of spending part of it. Give it a kiss and forget about it.

The sum that you want to spend may seem small. But it's not just the loss of that money that hurts. It's the loss of all the money that that money would have earned over the next umpty-ump years, plus the loss of the shelter that protected that money from tax.

Steady deposits in tax-favored retirement plans are only the beginning of wisdom. You also have to leave that money alone.

TAX-DEFERRED ANNUITIES

So potent are the words "tax deferral" that, in their presence, otherwise strong minds turn to pudding. Analysis flies out the window. Of all the unexamined premises of financial planning, one of the most dangerous is that tax deferral is always smart.

Which brings me to tax-deferred annuities.

I am not speaking here of tax-deductible annuities bought by teachers and others for their 403(b) retirement-savings plans. They're as valid a vehicle as any other retirement plan (if you have good investment choices and low costs) and should be funded to the maximum.

The subject before us is retail tax-deferred annuities, bought by conservative savers with after-tax dollars. In certain limited circumstances, they make sense. But a lot of hogwash accompanies their sale. You need to know how to step around it.

All retail annuities have three things in common: (1) You get no tax deduction for the money you put up. (2) Inside the annuity, your money compounds tax deferred. (3) At withdrawal, the earnings are taxed as ordinary income.

Beyond that, each annuity has its own cost structure, gimmicks, and rate of return. You buy one from banks, stockbrokers, financial planners, insurance agents, or mutual funds. But regardless of who makes the sale, an annuity is always backed by an insurance company.

Here's what the industry has to offer:

An *immediate annuity* pays you an income over your lifetime or for a fixed number of years, starting now (for the scoop on immediate annuities,

see page 925). A *tax-deferred annuity*—the type that concerns us here—
accumulates money for the future. Some retirees buy both kinds (a deal
known as split funding)—an immediate annuity for current income and a
deferred annuity to build more capital for later years.

Deferred annuities come in three types, depending on how you want
to invest: A *fixed annuity* pays an interest rate that isn't fixed at all; it may
change on a predetermined schedule. But it's still a straight interest-rate
investment. An *equity-indexed annuity* is linked to the stock market's rise
and fall, but with a guarantee that you'll always earn a fixed minimum rate.
A *variable annuity* offers you "subaccounts" that are invested in stocks and
bonds. They get real popular when the stock market goes go up.

A *single-premium annuity* is bought with a single sum of money. Minimum purchase: $2,000 to $10,000, although buyers typically put up much
larger sums. A *flexible-premium annuity* takes smaller or irregular amounts.
You might pay $100 a month, or dump in $1,000 every now and then.

When you decide to quit accumulating money and start spending it,
annuities offer another range of choice. You can take monthly payments
for the rest of your life. You can make periodic withdrawals. You can take
the money in a lump sum. You can roll your savings into another annuity
tax-free (for more information on withdrawals, see page 927).

You Don't Date Annuities, You Marry Them

An annuity isn't a mutual fund that you buy today and sell tomorrow.
Nor is it a certificate of deposit, ready for any new use at maturity. When
you buy an annuity, you are making (or ought to be making) a 20- or
25-year commitment, at minimum. You might move your money from one
annuity to another (a kind of serial marriage). But it's expensive to quit the
investment altogether. How expensive? Read on.

The Best Way to Use an Annuity: Buy it by your early 40s; use it to
accumulate money; well after the start of your retirement, convert it into an
income payable for life (that's called *annuitizing*). If you don't plan to
annuitize, a deferred annuity may be a subpar investment for you.

*When you take money out of a retail annuity, there are IRS rules and
penalties and insurance-company rules and penalties.*

The IRS Saith:

1. Income taxes are owed on your tax-deferred earnings whenever you
take the money out.

2. There is normally a 10 percent penalty on earnings withdrawn before 59½. So this isn't a short-term savings vehicle for the young. The
penalty is waived only in limited circumstances, among which are death

and disability. You can also dodge the penalty by setting up a lifetime withdrawal schedule.

3. If you make regular, periodic withdrawals (say, in monthly payments over your lifetime), part of each withdrawal is treated as taxable income. The rest is the nontaxable return of your own capital.

4. If you make occasional withdrawals, subject to no particular schedule, the entire withdrawal is treated as taxable income. Taxes are levied until you have taken all of the money earned on the principal you put up. After that, you can start withdrawing your original investment, tax-free.

The Insurance Company Saith:

1. You usually have to pay a surrender fee for quitting the annuity too soon. The first year it's often 7 percent of the money withdrawn. In the second year it's 6 percent, and so on until, after 7 years, the penalty finally dribbles away. Some start at 7 percent, then level off at 5 percent. A few companies charge a surrender fee if you leave anytime within 10 or even 20 years. With flexible annuities, new surrender fees may be attached to every deposit you make. Drawn-out exit fees are designed to lock customers in.

At the other end of the scale, a few annuities release you after only one year, with a penalty of 6 months' interest for leaving any earlier.

2. An annuity with a long-term lock-in doesn't cut you off from your cash entirely. Usually, you can withdraw a portion of the policy's value every year (say, 10 percent) without paying a surrender fee. But you'll still owe income taxes on money you take out and maybe a 10 percent penalty, too. If you think you might need to retrieve some funds, you shouldn't be buying a tax-deferred annuity in the first place.

3. A handful of insurers let you draw out money, without penalty, to cover the costs of a nursing home, terminal illness, or unemployment.

FIXED ANNUITIES

These investments pay about the same as short- to medium-term bonds —*if* you get a good one. Your problem is guessing which is a good one in advance. Of those at the top of the list today, fewer than one-third may still be there 10 years from now.

A fixed annuity guarantees you a fixed rate of interest for a certain period of time—often one year but sometimes as much as 10 years. After that, the insurer can raise or lower your rate at specified periods of time. The size of the rate change depends on market trends, company profits, and how the insurer treats its existing customers. Some give their older customers attractive rates; others save their best rates for the new customers at the door. If you're unhappy, it may be expensive to move your money somewhere else. You'll owe early-withdrawal penalties for at least 5 to 7 years and sometimes much longer. The insurers do guarantee you a certain minimum rate—usually around 3 percent. You can keep the annuity until you're 85 or 90, if you're so inclined.

A variant on the traditional product is a *fixed-term annuity with market value adjustment*. You get a guaranteed interest rate for a specified number of years—often 5. At the end of the term, you can take your money without penalty or renew for another fixed term. If you withdraw early, your earnings will be adjusted. If interest rates have dropped since you purchased the plan, your cash value will go up; if rates have risen, your cash value drops. In either case, you may pay a surrender penalty, too. Every time you re-up the surrender period usually starts all over again.

Some annuities offer a *bailout*—a downside guarantee that's higher than the minimum rate. You're allowed to quit without paying the surrender charge if your current rate drops a certain percentage below your starting rate. Annuities with bailouts typically pay less interest than annuities without—say, 5.75 percent when others are paying 6.5 percent. Bailouts aren't much used when interest rates are low because there's so little room between the initial rate and the guaranteed minimum rate.

An annuity might also be *two-tier*—or, as I'd rather spell it, "two-tear," as in weep. You're offered an extra-high first-year interest rate—maybe 11 or 12 percent when other annuities are at 6 or 7 percent. After that, you start getting market rates or less. If you cancel the annuity—*ever in your life* —you lose that high initial rate. The insurer will recalculate your earnings at a mediocre rate, even if you've held the investment for 30 years. You can see why this deal makes me cry.

Annuities might also offer a *bonus rate*—an extra one or 2 percent in the first year, to make itself look good. After that your rate will probably drop, even if general interest rates rise. Bonus-rate annuities often charge surrender fees for longer-than-average periods of time. After a while they're apt to start paying low, noncompetitive rates. Even if they don't, their bonuses sometimes have minimal long-term effects.

Surrender fees are often handled as *rolling loads*. Every dollar you put in has to stay there for the full surrender period. For example, say you make periodic payments over 10 years into an annuity with a 7-year rolling load, then withdraw the money. You can retrieve your older payments penalty-free but your newer payments will carry a surrender charge.

Before buying a fixed-rate annuity, ask if any of these angles apply. A plain-vanilla annuity from a well-regarded company should suit you best.

The Big Fakeroo

Certain kinds of annuities work just fine for certain financial-planning purposes. I am troubled, however, by the way these investments are so often sold. You may be misled about what they are likely to yield.

The typical brochure extols the glories of tax deferral. On a slick little chart, you'll see a fat line zipping up to Heaven. That represents how fast your money grows untaxed. Inching up from the very bottom of the chart is a thin, unhappy line. That supposedly shows the pitiful returns earned by simps who let their investments be taxed every year.

But those pretty charts may greatly exaggerate what annuities actually yield. Often, they "forget" the tax you owe when you cash in the annuity. So they're comparing apples and oranges: annuity returns pretax vs. the after-tax return of a bond or certificate of deposit. Once taxes are subtracted, the annuity doesn't look nearly as good.

Many salespeople argue that there's no point showing the annuity's value after tax because that's not the way to take the money. Instead of cashing out all at once, you should stretch your income—and your taxes— over a lifetime. That may be true, but historically, a majority of investors haven't. Even for those who will, the sales brochure is wrong because it doesn't account for the taxes they owe on the income they receive. After tax, your yield drops. You need a long holding period to make fixed annuities pay.

Where Costs Are Low: A few companies sell low-load fixed annuities, often through financial planners who charge fees for their time. For annuities sold directly, call USAA Life in San Antonio, Texas (800-531-8000), Fee For Service (800-874-5662), or Lincoln Benefit (800-LBL-WATS; Lincoln Benefit also has an agent-sold version that pays a lower interest rate, so be sure you ask about the low-load). There's a low-load annuity on the Web sold by Independence Life & Annuity: http://www.websaver.com.

WHO MIGHT WANT A FIXED ANNUITY?

This investment works for people who put safety first, are satisfied with the tax-deferred interest rate, and buy from a company that treats its older customers as well as its new ones (page 891). A likely buyer might be:

• A conservative person in early middle age, saving for retirement, who doesn't need current income from his or her capital, doesn't care that fixed-income investments don't show much growth after taxes and inflation, and plans to keep the annuity virtually for life. You're treating this as "safety" money for your late old age. You won't make withdrawals until you absolutely have to.

• A saver with plenty of growth investments who wants a safe interest-rate hedge and plans not to touch the money for many years.

• A saver who normally won't budge out of certificates of deposit. A fixed annuity may pay more interest and it's tax deferred. Good fixed annuities even make sense for Individual Retirement Accounts or Keogh plans if the interest rate is higher than you'd get from other investments. You're wasting the annuity's tax shelter but getting a better yield.

• A saver who intends to turn the annuity into an income for life. That way your money remains tax deferred, not only while it's building up but also during the years you are gradually drawing it out. This is the surest way of making an annuity pay.

• Someone who's allergic to taxes, at all costs. But look first at municipal bonds. Their current yield may be a little less than annuities pay. But that yield is good until maturity, whereas the interest rate on annuities will change. Furthermore, you'll eventually owe taxes on your annuity savings while munis are permanently tax exempt. After tax, it will take a deferred annuity many, many years to equal the net income you'd get from a muni bond.

Don't Sit Tight in a Lousy Annuity that started out well but now pays a subpar interest rate. Look for a better company (page 893) and make a tax-free exchange.

Before Even Considering an Annuity, put every nickel you can into tax-deductible savings and investments: 401(k) plans, SEPs, Keoghs, 401(b)s, and deductible Individual Retirement Accounts. *Any* tax-deductible investment is worth more, in the long run, than investments that are merely tax deferred. A Roth IRA (page 868) is better than an annuity, too.

How to lower the risk of getting a poor annuity:

1. Beware of annuities whose interest rates are markedly above average. Those headliner rates are likely to drop, probably to subnormal levels. Why would an agent tout you onto such an annuity? Probably because it's paying an extra-high sales commission. Buy a high-rate annuity only if the agent can prove that the company has a long history of treating longtime customers fairly.

2. Never buy from a company whose exit fees are unreasonably high. A standard surrender charge in the industry starts at 5 or 7 percent and declines by one percentage point every year. The baddies charge fees for 10 years or more.

3. Ask the salesperson the following questions: What interest rate did the company pay on this particular annuity (or one similar to it) 6 years ago? When the annuity's interest-rate guarantee ran out, what renewal rates did the customers get in each subsequent year? During those same years what interest rates were paid to brand-new buyers of annuities like this?

You are looking for: (1) a company that pays both its old and new customers the same rate, or (2) a company that pays old customers no more than 0.75 percentage points less than new ones (assuming that interest rates remained unchanged), or (3) a company that, in an unchanging interest-rate environment, drops the second-year interest rates on its annuities by no more than 0.3 percentage points (ignoring any first-year bonus). That would constitute fair treatment in the opinion of Timothy Pfeifer, a consulting actuary at Milliman & Robertson in Chicago.

What you don't want to see: (1) an annuity that paid 10 percent for the first two years, then rapidly dropped to 6 percent, or (2) a company paying new customers 9 percent while renewing old customers at 5 percent. That tells you that only new customers ride in the golden coach. Older customers get demoted to scullery maid. Why walk into a deal like that?

If you are buying a flexible-premium annuity, ask what rate was paid on new deposits as opposed to the rate paid on old deposits over the past 6 years.

The rates paid on old deposits are readily available. In the course of researching this chapter, I spoke to two insurance-company actuaries, both of whom pressed a button and called up all the rates on their computer screens. If the agent or insurer won't supply the information you asked for, or claims it's too difficult to get, assume the worst. If your agent says that your particular annuity hasn't been sold for the past 5 years, ask for the rates on a similar contract. If the agent still says no, you say no, too.

Do you think that getting all these rates is too much trouble? Here's what one actuary said to me: *"Tell your readers to make their agents disclose the annuity's past interest-rate history. Many agents won't bother as long as their customers don't insist. And because of that, a lot of bad annuities get sold. But agents are a dime a dozen. If more people quit doing business with uncooperative agents, maybe this industry would start telling more truths."* Amen.

4. At this writing, I can't recommend the computerized illustrations that agents use to show how annuities grow over 20 years. Among other sins, they project current interest rates, which are not guaranteed. They may include undisclosed "bonus" rates which you'll get only if you stay with the company for 20 years. If you're in the clutches of a two-tier company (page 889), the agent may show you only the rate you'll get if you turn the annuity into an income for life. Some of these gimmicks may be mentioned in the footnotes, but probably in language that won't mean anything to you. The state insurance regulators are discussing ways of improving disclosure. Until that happens, you'll be hard put to tell the good illustrations from the bad ones.

5. Don't buy annuities with two-tier payouts. If you ever cash out of the annuity or transfer your money to a better-paying insurance company, you'll get a lower interest rate from the first day you bought—even if you've been with that insurer for 30 years. The difference can be huge: say 8 percent for stayers but only 5.5 percent for people who take their money

somewhere else. You're tied to the company even if its rates aren't as good as they used to be (and why should it bother being competitive, since it knows that you can't leave?). *Always* ask the agent whether he or she is recommending a two-tier company and if so, end the conversation.

Why not buy from such a company if it's paying a high rate and you plan to turn your annuity savings into an income for life? First, you don't know that it will always pay high rates. Second, if you want a lifetime annuity income at retirement, you might get a higher payout from a different insurer. Third, your plans may change.

6. Look for a company that seems committed to the annuity business. One measure: it should write at least $100 million in new annuities per year. An insurer that's only dabbling in annuities is more likely to write contracts that start with a high rate, then drop you to a lower one.

7. Annuities guarantee a floor below which your interest rate won't fall. At this writing, the standard is around 3 percent. If you need a tie-breaker between two competing annuities, choose the one with the higher floor.

8. Make sure that your annual statement will show your annuity's yield as a percentage rate. Some statements show only dollars earned, which can conceal many sins. If you see only dollars, ask your agent for a letter from the company disclosing the true yield. You're entitled to know.

9. Don't buy an annuity paying less interest than you can earn on a similar investment outside the annuity. The agent may assure you that, thanks to the tax deferral, the annuity will win. Maybe so—but not in your lifetime. As an example, consider a tax-deferred annuity paying 5 percent vs. a taxable investment at 6 percent. It takes *30 years* for the annuity to pull ahead, says financial planner Lynn Hopewell of the Monitor Group in Fairfax, Virginia, if you're in a combined state and federal tax bracket of 35 percent.

10. Never buy without checking the competition. An insurance agent may say, "My Best Super American Plan pays the highest rate in the country," and that could be pure BS. How do you check? Read on.

HOW TO SHOP FOR A FIXED ANNUITY

Check out comparative rates in the *Annuity & Life Insurance Shopper,* $14, from United States Annuities, Heritage Chase-Talmadge #8, Monroe Township, NJ 08831 (800-872-6684). This quarterly catalogue lists some 1,800 annuities of all types—fixed and variable, deferred and immediate-pay—from some 60 leading insurance companies. For each company, you get the most recent interest rate prior to press time, the guarantee period, two previous interest rates, the bonus and bailout rates if any, the guaranteed minimum rate, the surrender charge, and the safety-and-soundness ratings from all five of the rating companies. The catalogue also lists the maximum protection given to annuities by each state's insurance guaranty fund. You can call for more information about an annuity, including the current rate, and buy it from USA by phone. Or use these rates as a benchmark when talking with an insurance agent or financial planner.

Another source for rates: the *Comparative Annuity Reports Newsletter,* P.O. Box 1268, Fair Oaks, CA 95628, which monitors 100 fixed annuities. For $20, you get two successive monthly issues ranking the annuities by rate. The first issue also shows each company's "accumulation values"— meaning the amount of money that might be built up over 10 years, based on current rates. You'll see that some apparently high-rate companies rank low in the number of actual dollars they might deliver—chiefly because their "bonus" rates aren't worth what they seem. The second issue shows the "withdrawal values"—what you'd get if you quit after 10 years. That shows the effect of surrender charges. Long-lasting surrender charges knock a company down in the rankings, especially a company that sells two-tier annuities (page 889).

But remember, both the *Shopper* and the *Newsletter* tell you only about rates today. No one knows how much each annuity will pay in the long run. These publications help in two ways: (1) they show you where general market rates are, so a salesperson can't talk you into an annuity that's subpar from the start; (2) they identify the two-tier and first-year bonus programs that might not work out.

Neither publication shows all the low-load annuities, so check them yourself—page 312.

When you buy from an agent, he or she will receive a sales commission. Four to 5 percent is pretty standard for a classic single-premium deferred annuity, with a trailing commission of maybe 0.25 percent every year you stay in the plan. There's another one or 2 percent for the wholesaler. On short-term annuities, the commission may be one percent plus another one percent each time you renew. The commissions on indexed annuities are running from 5 to 7 percent. No knowledgeable customer will deal with agents who collect 10 or 11 percent commissions. They're selling junk annuities that will benefit them, not you.

Beware the agent who claims that he or she is earning no commission. There is always a commission, except at low-load companies like USAA that sell through salaried agents by phone. But annuity commissions don't come out of your cash investment, as is the case with loaded mutual funds or cash-value life insurance. All the dollars you put up go directly into your annuity. Commissions are paid from the difference between what the insurer earns on its investments and the interest rate it pays to you, as well as from the surrender charge if you leave early.

Buy fixed annuities only from an insurance company with decent safety-and-soundness ratings from at least three of the five insurance-rating companies: A+ or better from A.M. Best, AAq or better from Standard & Poor's, Aa3 or better from Moody's, AA+ or better from Duff & Phelps, B or better from Weiss (page 342). An annuity may be a lifetime commitment. You can't afford anything less than the very best. Many of the most aggressive companies, tempting you with the highest first-year rates, have mediocre ratings. They might as well raise a flag reading, "We can't afford to pay high interest very long."

If you want to invest a lot of money, split it into more than one annuity, each one comfortably below the amount that your state guaranty association insures. Most state guaranty funds specifically cover tax-deferred annuities if an insurer goes broke but others have left their coverage vague. In most states, the maximum payment is $100,000. A handful will pay $300,000 or $500,000. The industry *might* cover more, as a public relations gesture.

EQUITY-INDEXED ANNUITIES

Indexed annuities are children of the great bull market of the 1980s and 1990s. Whether they'll survive a prolonged bear market or a boring go-nowhere market is anyone's guess.

They're sold to people who normally buy interest-rate investments, such as fixed annuities or bank CDs. These conservative investors would love to earn higher, stock-market returns but wouldn't dream of putting any money at risk.

An indexed annuity is their grail. It combines the potential for stock- or bond-market gains with little risk of principal loss. The value of your investment is linked to changes in a market index—most commonly, Standard & Poor's 500-stock average. If the market doesn't rise, you're guaranteed a minimal return.

But although the concept can be stated simply, these products have many moving parts. Salespeople may show you how great they are over periods when markets do well, while glossing over how little you'll earn if stocks cool down. You're highly unlikely to equal the stock market's full return. You give up some gain in exchange for never having to bear a loss.

If indexed annuities interest you, here's what to ask about:

1. What is the annuity's term? Generally, you commit to holding for 5 to 10 years. The shorter the term, the greater the risk that the stock market won't perform well over your holding period. A one-year indexed annuity is a roll of the dice.

2. What do you earn when the market goes up? You're credited with anywhere from 60 to 100 percent of the price gain of the S&P 500 (or some other average), excluding dividends. Some insurers can change that percentage from year to year, so you're never sure how much you'll get.

The loss of dividends is significant. At this writing, they're low—averaging under 2 percent. Since 1926, however, they've accounted for 43 percent of the S&P's compounded gains.

3. At the end of the term, how does the insurer figure your gain? Some use the market price on the day the annuity matures. Some look at each policy anniversary date and pick the highest one. Some average the price over your annuity's final 12 months. Some credit a portion of each year's market gains, if any. Some give you 100 percent of the gain but deduct one percent for expenses. And there are other systems. There's no way of knowing in advance which one will pay the most. Everything depends on how the market does over your particular holding period.

4. Are there caps? Some annuities cap the rate they'll credit you with in a single year. For example, if stocks go up 20 percent you might get only 14 percent. The insurer might change the cap from year to year.

5. What if stock prices drop? You'll be credited with zero that year—and sometimes a loss, if you give up and quit. If stock prices rise the following year but remain below the previous peak, some annuities credit you with a gain but others don't. So stocks can rise while your annuity earns nothing (the reverse can happen with certain types of annuities).

6. What if you want to quit the annuity early? Some insurers pay you only the guaranteed minimum return. Some credit you with all or part of your earnings to date but impose a surrender charge. You might lose money if you withdraw ahead of time. Some annuities let you take 10 percent of your money a year, penalty-free. Others don't.

7. What if everything crashes? Your indexed annuity carries a minimum guarantee. It's typically quoted as "3 percent," but 3 percent of what? Often, 3 percent of 90 percent of your capital. For 5- to 10-year holding periods, that works out to just 0.85 to 1.9 percent a year. Assuming 3 percent inflation, you *do* have a loss—not in nominal capital but in purchasing power.

There's one risk here that I don't know how to evaluate. Insurers usually back these annuities with a combination of bonds and call options on stocks. In unusual markets, options can behave in unusual ways. Any unexpected losses will adhere to the insurer, not you. But the insurer may recoup by reducing the percentage of stock-market growth that it credits your contract with. So be very clear about your minimum guarantee.

An Alternative to Indexed Annuities. Consider putting 70 percent of your money in a traditional fixed annuity and 30 percent in a variable annuity invested in stocks (page 897). You might also allocate your money within a single, variable annuity—70 percent in the fixed account, 30 percent in the stock-market account—if you find a low-load variable annuity with an attractive fixed account. There's a good chance that this combination will pay more than an indexed annuity *and* give you more protection when stock prices drop.

VARIABLE ANNUITIES

On the surface, variable annuities seem Heaven-sent to anyone who buys mutual funds. You start the annuity with anywhere from $1,000 to $10,000, depending on the company. That money is invested in "subaccounts" which amount to mutual funds and accumulate tax deferred. There's a range of investment choices: U.S. stocks, international stocks, bonds, a balanced stock-and-bond portfolio, a fixed-income account. You pick your own mix and can typically switch whenever the spirit moves you. Or you can ask the company to allocate your assets for you.

But it costs more to buy mutual funds through annuities. Diversified U.S. stock funds often charge one percent or less. Most variable annuities charge 2 percent or more. Sales expenses and profits account for most of the extra cost. The rest is insurance. You pay for the built-in option to convert your annuity into a monthly lifetime income. You're also given a guarantee that, if you die, your heirs will collect at least as much money as you originally invested.

These extra costs lower your investment return. Annuity investors may wind up with less money after tax than if they had bought those same mutual funds outside the annuity. All annuity withdrawals are taxed as ordinary income. If you invest your annuity in stocks, you get no advantage from the low tax on capital gains.

When deciding between variable annuities and taxable mutual funds, there's one major question to ask: How long does it take for the value of the annuity's tax deferral to overcome the burden of its higher cost and higher tax rate at withdrawal? Exact answers will vary with your assumptions on capital gains taxes, annuity costs, investment returns, your age at purchase, and the portion of the investment that can be taxed as a capital gain. But here are some general thoughts, based on sample calculations by the annuity and mutual fund company T. Rowe Price, using a capital gains rate of 20 percent.*

• *If you plan to cash out of your investment around the time you retire and your tax bracket doesn't change:* Low-cost variable annuities (with sales and insurance charges under one percent) might take more than 20 years to equal comparable no-load mutual funds, assuming 9 percent returns. With the higher-cost annuities sold by banks, stockbrokers, and many financial planners (sales and insurance charges averaging 1.25 percent), it might take 25 years or more. That's pretty long to wait.

• *If you plan to build up a nest egg, then make steady withdrawals over your life expectancy, starting at 65:* When you buy at 55, the annuity never delivers more cumulative income than you'd get from a mutual fund,

---

* These examples assume a conservative investment in equity-income funds, for an investor in a combined state and federal tax bracket of 38 percent before and after retirement.

assuming that, when you retire, your tax bracket doesn't drop. If you buy at 45, the annuity just barely edges ahead.

If your tax bracket drops in retirement, the annuity looks better for 45-year-olds and is marginal for those who buy at 55.

• *The younger you start, the better your chance that the annuity will work out, especially if you plan to hold for your life expectancy.* For example, take a parent or grandparent making a gift to a child or young adult. Instead of giving $10,000 in cash, give a variable annuity invested in stocks. It might not be touched for 40 years or more, and *then* it should beat the mutual fund. Annuities are also good buys for thirtysomethings and, depending on your tax bracket, people in their early 40s.

But although annuities might be good for younger investors, they're the ones least apt to buy. The typical customer is someone in later middle age who doesn't realize how many years it takes to make annuities pay. These buyers defer their tax but get less for their money in the end.

• *The higher your tax bracket and the more you invest in stock, the less attractive annuities become when the capital gains rate is low.* If you buy annuities at all, low-loads are the best way to go (page 312).

• *Annuities invested at fixed interest rates are problematic, too.* As an example, say that you're fully invested in short-term bonds at 6 percent. It would take a low-cost annuity more than 20 years to outperform a 6 percent bond mutual fund. A high-cost annuity could take more than 30 years. Why would you bother?

• *If you have only a small sum to invest— $2,500 to $5,000—variable annuities are a waste.* Insurers levy $20 or $30 annual fees that chop 0.5 to one percent off your returns.

• *If you already have a variable annuity, you generally shouldn't cash it in.* You've paid the price; stick around for the investment gain. Start withdrawals as late as you can and take the money over several years to keep the tax deferral running longer.

• *If you plan to save money in an annuity, then turn it into a guaranteed income for life:* In this situation, any annuity—high cost or low cost—will beat a mutual fund investment *if* you exceed your life expectancy. So it's potentially a good buy for people in good health who will make the lifetime-income choice.

To decide whether you should buy mutual funds or variable annuities, call 800-341-0790 for T. Rowe Price's free IBM-compatible software program, the *Variable Annuity Analyzer*. It builds in the low insurance cost of Price's annuity but you can vary your tax rate, fund cost, and investment return. Three other mutual-fund groups also sell low-cost annuities—meaning no sales charge, no exit fee, and low annual insurance fees: Janus in Denver, Scudder in Boston, and Vanguard in Valley Forge, Pennyslvania (the cheapest). The discount brokers Charles Schwab and Jack White are in the market, too, and offer wide investment choices. Also check Ameritas (page 312) and Fee For Service (page 890).

Before buying a variable annuity, look at every one of its "subaccounts" —annuityspeak for the mutual funds the insurer offers. That's your range of investment choice. The salesperson may tout one of the funds that has a red-hot record this year, but what are your alternatives if that fund fades? Many annuity funds have records that are distinctly subpar. Also, check out all the fees. Variable annuities often charge "rolling back end loads"— meaning that each investment you add has to stay put for 7 years or so; otherwise, you'll owe an exit fee when you take that money out.

Another point: Don't let your choice turn on the annuity's death-benefit guarantee. That's the clause that says if you die your heirs will get at least all the money you invested, even if the market has dropped. Some annuities compete by raising the guaranteed amount from time to time or promising a fixed return on principal. But these enhancements raise your costs and make it even less likely that your annuity will yield more than an outside mutual fund.

Unlike fixed annuities, variables are held in a separate account. They're not endangered if your insurance company fails.

At Low Capital Gains Rates, It's Hard to Justify a Variable Annuity. Even low-cost annuities don't look as good as plain vanilla mutual funds, over any reasonable holding period.

You shouldn't even think about buying a variable annuity unless you can answer all of the following questions "yes":

• Have you put the maximum into your tax-deferred retirement plan? That comes first because those contributions can be deducted from tax. You might also want to add any after-tax money that your plan accepts.

• Have you funded a Roth IRA if you're eligible?

• Will you invest the money in stocks or high-yielding bonds? You need big gains to overcome the annuity's price. Investments in ordinary bond funds, fixed-interest accounts, or money market funds will never do as well inside the annuity as they do on the outside.

• Will you leave the annuity alone until you reach 59½? Prior withdrawals will cost you a 10 percent tax penalty.

• Will you start young enough to make the tax deferral pay—no later than your early 40s? Older investors should generally buy mutual funds instead of variable annuities.

• Is this investment for you rather than for your heirs? If not, your heirs would rather you bought straight mutual funds. They'll owe income taxes on the deferred gains in inherited annuities but they can receive unrealized gains in mutual funds income-tax free. (Actually, your heirs might prefer you to buy single-premium life insurance—see page 901.)

• Is your tax bracket high? In low brackets, variable annuities may never outperform mutual funds.

• Is the capital gains rate unusually low? Unless you will turn your annuity into a lifetime income, *forgeddaboudit.*

WHO MIGHT WANT A VARIABLE ANNUITY?

An investor who:
1. Has a substantial sum on hand—at least $25,000.
2. Is in a high income-tax bracket where tax deferral matters more.
3. Will keep all of his or her money in subaccounts devoted to stocks. Only stocks have a chance of growing by enough to cover the fees and still return a decent profit.
4. Will stick with the annuity for at least 20 years.

SHOULD YOU SWITCH ANNUITIES?

Yes, if you're in a fixed-rate annuity and the insurer is stiffing you with a truly rotten rate—say, 4.5 percent in a 6 percent world. But don't switch before checking how well your new insurer treats longtime customers (page 891).

Yes, if your own insurer offers a fixed annuity at a higher interest rate than you're earning now *and* you're willing to stay until the new surrender period expires.

Yes, if you're in a fixed annuity and would prefer the choice of investments that variable annuities offer. But the switch might not pay unless you keep your money in its stock account. Your investment has to do well enough to overcome the variable annuity's higher costs.

Probably, if you're in a variable annuity but keep all your money in its bond and fixed-income accounts. You might net more from a fixed annuity.

No, if you're in a fixed annuity, like the rate, and aren't a risk taker. Stay where you are. There's nothing in a variable annuity that you really want. Don't switch to a new fixed annuity, either, just for a high first-year bonus rate. That bonus may raise your yield by only a minuscule amount over a 10-year holding period. What's more, insurers with eye-popping first-year rates often drop your rate into the cellar once they've got you in their clutches.

No, if you're being offered a two-tier annuity (page 889) or the surrender period is exceptionally long.

No, if the agent pitches you on the variable annuity without explaining the costs and risks that this chapter talks about. I've spoken in generalities; the agent should lay out everything in dollars and cents. Also *no* if the agent has switched you before and proposes to do it again. You're being churned. That means your money is being turned over to earn the agent a commission, not to get you a better deal.

There's a lot of churning going on in annuity sales today. The insurers that encourage it offer gorgeous interest rates, so it seems to make sense to switch. But they'll be quick to lower your rate once they've locked you up. Not coincidentally, you'll be paying super-high sales commissions (8 percent or more), which is why the agent keeps pestering you to switch.

If You Do Switch Annuities: Do a 1035 tax-free exchange. Your agent will handle the paperwork.

SHOULD YOU BUY SINGLE-PREMIUM LIFE INSURANCE INSTEAD OF A VARIABLE ANNUITY?

This is a question for older people with plenty of money.

Suppose you have an investment that you never touch and can be liquidated without triggering capital gains taxes. Maybe a big certificate of deposit that you keep rolling over. You intend that the money pass to your children. If you put the CD into an annuity, all the interest would accumulate tax deferred.

But it might be smarter to buy single-premium life insurance instead (page 316), despite the policy's high cost. Your children will net extra money from the insurance proceeds. And they don't pay taxes on it, as they would if they inherited a deferred annuity. If you need any money during your lifetime, you can always borrow against the policy (although with a 10 percent penalty if you're under $59\frac{1}{2}$). The loans would be treated partly as taxable income, but so what? So would occasional withdrawals from a tax-deferred annuity. The insurance is expensive, but in this particular circumstance it might be the better choice.

SOCIAL SECURITY

You *will* get a Social Security check when you retire. If you doubt me, just look around and count the votes. How many among us would vote to abolish Social Security's safety net? What is the future of any politician who tried? There's a good deal of talk about privatizing Social Security, leaving beneficiaries to invest for themselves. But I wouldn't take bets on that.

Nevertheless, Social Security probably won't be worth as much in the future as it was in the past. The benefits you get may replace a smaller percentage of your working income. More of the money is apt to be taxed. And today's young people will have to work up to two more years (to age 67) before they can retire on their full Social Security check. At this writing, retirees get full benefits at 65.

That's why it's so important to save more money for yourself. You won't get as much out of Social Security as your parents and grandparents did.

The next chapter—on deploying your money at retirement—tells you how and when to claim Social Security benefits. The question here is how to create the largest benefit you can.

Here's How to Get the Most from Your Social Security Account

1. *Pay your tax!* Kids who float from job to job may think it's clever to work "off the books." But, like everyone else, they will eventually knock at Social Security's door. When figuring your benefit, Social Security looks at how many (or how few) years you officially held a job during the years you were old enough to work. If your record shows several years of zero participation, your retirement check will be dragged down. It's sometimes fun to be young and poor but never to be old and poor. So pay the tax.

2. *Make sure that your account shows all the Social Security earnings you have to date.* More often than you realize, payment records go awry. Your employer might err when reporting your earnings to Social Security or fail to report them at all. Social Security might err in transferring that record to your account. You might err when giving your Social Security number. In 1995 the Social Security Administration was sitting on a cumulative $250 billion* worth of reported wages, some of it dating back to 1937, whose owners have never been identified.

Here's how to make sure that you'll get every dime that's coming to you. Check your Social Security record. Call toll-free 800-772-1213 and ask for Form SSA-7004—a Personal Earnings and Benefit Estimate Statement (PEBES)—or order by Web: http://www.ssa.gov. Fill it in and mail it to Social Security.

Within 4 to 6 weeks, you'll get a statement showing how much was credited to your Social Security account each year. You may see a zero in the most recent year because Social Security hasn't posted your current wages yet. But if there are zeros in earlier years and shouldn't be, call Social Security right away. Maybe it can correct the error without specific information from you. All the same, look for old tax returns and W-2 forms to prove that you really did pay taxes that year. If your old company is still in business, ask it for a letter confirming that year's salary. (Starting in 1999, a Social Security statement will be mailed to you automatically, once a year.)

3. *Find out if you qualify for Social Security benefits at all, and if not, how close you've come.* The Social Security statement also shows how many work credits you need in order to earn a check. A woman who worked many years ago, then dropped out to have children or take care of an elderly parent, may find that—with just a couple more years of full- or part-time work—she'll qualify for a Social Security benefit. Having your

---

* That's a big number, but it represented only 0.5 percent of all posted wages.

own account may not matter to someone who can collect on the account of a present or former spouse (page 933). But it matters a lot if you don't have that to fall back on.

4. *Make your personal planning decisions in light of what Social Security is likely to pay.* Here, too, the answers you get from the PEBES form will help. Your Social Security statement discloses: (1) your estimated monthly retirement benefit (in today's dollars) when you reach 62, full retirement age (currently 65), and 70; (2) the likely survivors' benefits for your family if you die in the current year; and (3) what you might get in disability pay if you become totally and permanently disabled. Starting in 1998, you'll be able to get this information through Social Security's Web site as well as by mail.

The deeper you move into middle age, the more critical this information becomes. Once you know how much income you can count on, you'll get a better fix on how much more you have to save.

5. *Keep on truckin'.* You can file for benefits as early as 62. But that permanently reduces your Social Security check—currently, by 20 percent. The older you are when you retire, the higher your benefits will be. At this writing, you get full benefits at 65.* Bonuses are paid for every additional year you delay retirement, up to age 70.

Looked at one way, early retirement makes sense. You collect a lot of money in those years between 62 and 65. If you wait until 65 you retire with a bigger check, but 12 years may pass before you make up for the three years of early-retirement pay you did without.

Looked at another way, however, early retirement makes no sense at all unless you're bored, ill, or can't find work. On the job, you are earning more than your retired colleagues get, and your paychecks are adding to the size of your future Social Security benefit. Assuming a normal life span, retiring at 65 will bring you more benefits overall.

6. *After the turn of the century, plan on collecting a double income. Stay on the job and file for Social Security, too.* At 65 through 69, every $3 you earn above a certain income ceiling costs you $1 in Social Security benefits. But that ceiling is rising (page 935). In 1997, it was $13,500. By 2002, it will reach $30,000. Most workers who stay on the job will find that it pays to file for Social Security at their full retirement age—collecting benefits and a salary at the same time. Even with above-average earnings, this strategy may net you more than the bonus you'd get by waiting until 70 to collect. You'd need a longer-than-average lifetime—meaning many extra Social Security checks—for a delayed retirement to pay.

7. *Don't retire at 62 if there's any chance that you'll have to return to*

---

* Starting in 2000, the age for getting full retirement benefits starts creeping up. For example, I won't qualify until I reach age 65 and four months. If you were born in 1960 or later, full benefits won't be payable until you reach 67. You will still be allowed to claim Social Security as early as 62 but your check will be cut by 30 percent.

a serious part-time job. At 62 through 64, every $2 you earn above a certain income ceiling costs you $1 in Social Security benefits. In 1997, retirees that age could earn only $8,640 free and clear (the ceiling rises with inflation every year). It wouldn't take much to cut your Social Security check in half, if you had to take a job.

If you do retire early, then return to work, then retire again, your benefit will be refigured. Your check will be larger than it was when you first filed. But collecting any benefits early holds down the size of your final check. (For more on this point, see page 931.)

Would you be better off dropping out of Social Security?

Many people imagine that they'd have more money if they could ditch Social Security. "Just give me my contribution and my employer's and I could invest for a higher income," they say. I wonder. To begin with, you probably wouldn't invest it all. You'd spend some. Some would be thrown away on bad investments. Some might be invested too conservatively. In the end, you might fail to build the enormous sum needed to pay yourself a Social Security–equivalent income that kept up with the inflation rate for the rest of your life. And if you failed, what then?

Even if you could amass this money, many of your fellow citizens couldn't (fewer than half of us currently invest in stocks). You might be okay but a large group of seniors would be broke—just as they were before Social Security began. Welfare payments would soar.

Without the program, you'd also lose life insurance benefits.

Several Social Security reform proposals are on the table. All involve higher taxes in some form; all trim benefits in some way, and all involve putting some of Social Security's money into stocks, with either you or the trust fund directing the investments. But some proposals take away much of the safety net.

I'm for the net. Compulsory Social Security protects part of everyone's old-age income against the hazards of life and judgment, and we should be grateful for it. Without it, many more of our elderly would live poor.

30.

Making It Last

Still Living Rich, at 99

If you ever needed a plan for your money, you need it now.
You earned it. You saved it. Now it's time to spend it well.

Here you are, at the very lip of retirement or beyond. You have pretty much defined your standard of living by the pension you earned and the money you saved and invested years ago. But it's not over yet! You still have plans to lay and choices to make. How you handle your pension and investments will make a huge difference to your comfort for years to come.

EARLY RETIREMENT: THE AMERICAN DREAM

You may have no choice about when you retire. Your job may be reorganized right out from under you.

Or you may have an apparent choice. An early-retirement bonus may be offered to anyone willing to take the leap (page 908). If you say no, your job may continue as usual. But then again, it may not.

Or you may jump yourself, without being pushed. Some people point their entire savings and investment programs toward bailing out of the workforce at 50 or 55.

The Truth Is, You Can't Retire at 50

Correction: you *probably* can't.

It takes a tremendous amount of money to be able to quit early—far more than you think. Until you sit down with a calculator (or accountant or financial planner), you won't appreciate how much capital you're going to need, especially when future inflation is factored in.

If you have no children to educate, own your home free and clear, have savings and investments worth $500,000 or more, live modestly, and will collect a pension at some point in the future in addition to Social Security, maybe you can do it. Especially if you expect an inheritance.

Short of that, you should figure on staying at work. Even if you retire on an inflation-indexed government pension, you will probably need another job.

The very earliest that most employees can even consider shaking loose is 55. You will probably get a company pension (half the size or less of what you'd receive at 65). You will get penalty-free access to many of your own retirement plans, such as 401(k)s, 403(b)s, and employee Keoghs. You can tap your IRA at an even earlier age (see page 876).

But will this money really last for the rest of your life?

To Retire Early . . .

Here's what you need for the life of leisure you intend:

1. *Health insurance,* to carry you to 65 and Medicare. Corporations may provide health plans for retirees. If not, you can usually stay in the group plan, at your expense, for up to 18 months (page 355). After that, however, you will have to find your own individual plan.

2. *A pension.* If early retirement is your overriding goal, there are two possible strategies: First, luck into working for one of those young technology companies that give their employees stock options whose value soars. Roll everything into an Individual Retirement Account, diversify, and create an income that will last for the rest of your life. Second, luck into staying with the same large employer all of your working life—collecting a pension and a well-diversified 401(k). Job hoppers can lose significant pension benefits (page 848). A government pension would serve you best, thanks to its cost-of-living increases. Corporate pensions usually come in fixed dollars that erode from the day you start collecting.

Social Security can start at 62. But if you stop working several years earlier than that, your monthly benefits will be lower than if you had stayed on the job.

3. *A major nest egg.* There are two ways of counting how much you'd need.

First, assume that you'll live on the total return you get from your retirement investments. To keep the purchasing power of your savings intact, you'd have to reinvest enough each year to offset inflation. By this rule, what sounds like plenty might turn out to be paltry.

Suppose, for example, that you have $225,000 in an IRA and feel rich. Your money yields 8 percent pretax but inflation is running at 3 percent annually. You're single, with a small pension and an average annual state and federal tax rate of 15 percent.* Here's your situation.

Your $225,000 is earning $18,000. To preserve your IRA's purchasing power, you must let it grow by 3 percent, or $6,750, bringing it up to $231,750. After withdrawing the rest of the earnings and paying your tax, you're left with just $9,563 to spend. You'll have even less, if all or part of your nest egg is in a taxable account.

Alternatively, assume that you'll gradually use up your nest egg. To find out how long your capital will last, look at the table on page 914. It shows you how much of your capital you can afford to spend each year to make your money last a lifetime (instructions for using the table are on page 913). If your $225,000 is invested at 8 percent and has to support you for 35 years, you can take around $13,000 the first year you retire. Each subsequent year you'd take 3 percent more, to keep up with inflation.

That might work if you have an early-retirement pension, too. At 62, Social Security would kick in. Still, $250,000, though a big slug of money, doesn't put you on Easy Street.

4. *No kids at home.* All the expenses of raising and educating your children should be behind you.

5. *Life insurance* if you're married. Your spouse may not be able to live on the reduced pension and Social Security left behind if you die first, especially if you're forced to eat into your capital.

6. *Low housing expenses.* Sell your house, buy a smaller one or a condominium, and invest the proceeds that remain. Or move to a low-cost part of the country. Or move to Mexico or Costa Rica. One money-making idea, if you think you'd be a successful landlord: buy a two-family house, live in one half, and rent out the other half (but check the laws on rent control and eviction first—and see page 829).

7. *Low living expenses.* Early retirees need simple tastes. Cheap entertainments. Only one car (or no car at all—use taxis and buses). Life in the country where real-estate taxes are low. I don't mean to make this sound like a downer, but you have to be very clear in your mind that—without stock options—quitting work means keeping to a slender budget.

8. *A job.* Forget "early retirement" in its classic, freebooting sense. Think about earning enough money to fill the gap between your pension income and your expenses so you can leave your capital alone to grow. Some companies rehire their own retirees for temporary work on specific projects. Many senior-citizen centers keep lists of companies that seek older

---

* When projecting a retirement budget, don't use your marginal tax rate (which is the rate applied to the highest portion of your income). Use your average rate (see page 912).

people for occasional work. If the job is covered by Social Security, so much the better. That beefs up the retirement benefit that you'll get at 62.

9. *A spending and investment plan* worked out with an accountant or financial planner. Don't try to doodle this by yourself on a yellow pad. Taxes, inflation, interest rates, the size of your savings, and the sources of your income all have a bearing on whether you can afford to retire. If you do quit work, you need to know quite specifically what your savings must yield to keep you afloat, how much you have to earn, and what you can afford to spend. That's a job for a professional. If you spend too much in your early-retirement years, you'll eventually descend into genteel poverty.

A Dangerous Complacency

People who dream of retiring early are dangerously complacent about inflation. They shrug off 3 percent increases as if they were zero. But at 3 percent inflation, you'll need $1,344 worth of income 10 years from now for every $1,000 you have today, just to preserve your standard of living. In 20 years, you'll need $1,806 for every $1,000 you have today. Where are you going to get that kind of money? Especially if you're living off capital rather than adding to it?

The Golden Boot

Not all early retirees have a choice.

You may arrive at work one morning to learn that your company has opened an early-retirement window for everyone 50 and up. Typically, you have 30 to 90 days to jump out the window (or be politely shoved). If you leave, you'll get bonuses not normally available. Should you take the offer?

As you sit at your desk, with your heart beating a little faster, ask yourself the following three questions:

Question One: Do I really want to retire (or at least leave this job)? If the answer is yes, see an accountant and work out the arithmetic. This window may fit perfectly with your plans. If the answer is no . . .

Question Two: What happens if I stay? In the bosses' minds, all employees are divided into "greenwood" and "deadwood." Some of you they want to keep; others they want to sweep away. But they can't walk down the hall saying, "You, you, and you, retire early," without running afoul of the age-discrimination law. So it's up to you to guess their intent.

Take it for granted that deals have been offered indirectly to particular employees ("congratulations, you're due for a double bonus next year and a vice presidency will be opening up"). If nothing like that has come your way, drop by your boss's office for a chat. What's the future of your department? Is your job subject to reorganization? What's your next promotion? Is your boss going to stay or go? If the vibes say "stay," you might want to chance it. Someone has to keep the shop open. If the vibes say "go," don't hesitate. You may lose your job anyway and without a goodbye bonus. To collect your bonus, you may have to sign an agreement not to sue under the Age Discrimination in Employment Act. Asking you to sign is legal.

Question Three: Where do I get advice? Don't try to figure out the finances yourself. Your company's employee-benefits office may have an explainer on the staff. Alternatively, see an accountant or a true financial planner (not a salesperson—page 910) who is capable of analyzing the offer objectively and has the computer capacity to do so. You may have to choose between taking a higher pension or taking severance pay, and only savvy calculating will reveal the better offer. You may have to choose between taking a lump sum and investing it yourself or letting the company invest it for you. Often, it's better to leave it with the company (page 916).

Anyone given the Golden Boot might be offered several incentives. Typically, they include a higher pension than you've actually earned; a cash bonus to help you make the transition to civilian life; a supplemental monthly income of maybe $400 to $500, paid until 62 when Social Security starts; a modest life-insurance policy; and health insurance until you're eligible for Medicare.

Despite all these goodies, an early retiree gets the short end of the money stick. Even if you're 60 and are offered the pension of a 65-year-old, you've lost five years of salary, which would have paid a lot more than the pension does. But a Golden Boot is a leg up for anyone with other work in mind. Taking this income as a base, you can write a book, start a business, or accept a lower-paying job that offers you more satisfaction.

YOUR RETIREMENT SPENDING PLAN

Early retirement or late, you now face the ultimate reality test. Your capital and life circumstances are pretty much known. What can be squeezed out of your resources? How much can you afford to spend each year so that you won't run out of money?

These simple questions involve some extraordinary choices, which will affect your personal comfort for the rest of your life. You have to decide:

• What's the best way of taking money out of your various retirement plans—in annuity payments or in a lump sum?

• When should you swallow the income taxes on your tax-deferred investments?

• How should your retirement savings be invested?

- Who should invest those savings for you?
- Should you keep your present house or sell it?
- What rate of inflation should you assume?

None of these questions has just one answer. You need to test one set of possibilities against another to see how the alternatives play out. When you have only a couple of choices, you can often make the right decision yourself. But for complex and multiple choices, I don't recommend flying solo. God hasn't made enough erasers and yellow pads for you to work this out alone.

Fortunately, God has made more than enough certified public accountants (CPAs), who practice in every town in the country. Go see one. Ask for advice. A CPA can lay out each and every choice: What net income you'd get from various types of pension-plan distributions. How much capital you can round up to invest. What yield you will need from your capital in order to support your standard of living. Whether it pays to sell your house. What inflation will do to your purchasing power. Don't begrudge the expense of the analysis. At this stage of life, it's the best investment you could make. Some financial planners can help you, too. Look for a planner who charges flat fees for his or her time. Ideally, you want an adviser who has the software to do a Monte Carlo simulation (page 581).

Do not bring these questions to a CPA or financial planner who earns commissions by selling financial products. Salespeople are biased toward lump-sum withdrawals from pension plans because that gives you money to buy the investments they sell. But what if those investments fail? Can you afford to take the risk? Your best choice may be to leave your money right there in the pension plan for the company to manage for you.

Once you've nailed down your income and assets, you have to shape a budget to match. Chapter 8 should help you go about it. When listing your outlays, don't look back at your old life, look ahead to your new one. The differences are going to surprise you.

Retirement spending is totally unlike workaday spending. Your house may be paid for. Your children are gone (one devoutly hopes). The fires may no longer burn in your breast for classier furniture, show-off cars, or drop-dead parties. You no longer need disability insurance if you have no earnings to replace. With sufficient savings (or no dependents), you don't need term life insurance, either—which saves you the price of the insurance premiums (although you may want to keep cash-value life—page 296). You'll buy more sneakers and sweatshirts and fewer dresses and suits. Instead of keeping two cars, you may drop to one.

Celebrating their freedom, the newly retired often travel. But after a while, that impulse usually quiets down. One critical expense is good health insurance, the cost of which will escalate even if your employer is paying part of the tab. Nevertheless, your real expenses, after inflation, will gradually fall. The older you get, the less purchasing power you are likely to need. So your capital will last longer than you might think.

Once you have assembled all your resources and all your expenses, ask an accountant or qualified planner the following question: "Assuming a reasonable investment return on my savings, and assuming that I want my income to keep up with inflation every year, how long will my present resources last?"

The news might be good.

"Ms. Certain," your accountant might say, "assuming that your savings earn 7 percent and assuming that you want to maintain the purchasing power of a $35,000 income, including pension and Social Security, your money will easily last until your death with a nice chunk left over for your heirs."

With that comforting knowledge, what might Ms. Certain do?

- She might feel free to donate some money to charity.
- She might roll her lump-sum pension distribution into an IRA and leave it alone to grow.
- She might travel, throw parties, and live it up.
- She will most certainly relax. She knows for sure that, at life's end, she won't be a bag lady on the streets. If she has to enter a nursing home, she has enough money to pay the bill. Medicaid will carry her if her savings run dry.

On the other hand, the news may be bad.

"Mr. Hopeful," your accountant might say, "assuming that your savings earn 7 percent and assuming that you want to maintain the purchasing power of a $35,000 income, you will run out of money in 14 years." That will startle Mr. Hopeful, whose life expectancy might be 24 years. But at least he knows his situation and can start to adjust.

- He might try to increase his return on investment by holding less money in passbook savings and more in bond funds and equity-income funds.
- He might take part-time work.
- He might reduce his expenses and live on, say, $25,000 a year.
- He might sell his house, buy something smaller, and use the remaining equity to build up his nest egg.
- He might accept his son's invitation to move into the small apartment over the son's garage—if not now, then maybe 10 years from now.
- If he has a choice, he might change his mind about retiring and stay at work a little longer

Knowing the limits of your savings gives you tremendous power over your future. You'll know what to do in order to make your retirement work.

For Do-It Yourselfers

If your finances are pretty simple, you can work out the budget yourself. The table on page 912 shows how (I've given an example on the right). All calculations are pretax.

YOUR RETIREMENT SPENDING PLAN

		EXAMPLE
1. Retirement income		
Social Security	$ _____	$ 8,000*
Pension	$ _____	$ 19,000
Lifetime annuity	$ _____	0
Earnings	$ _____	$ 2,800
Other income†	$ _____	0
Total income	$ _____	$ 29,800
2. First-year retirement expenses, including taxes	$ _____	$ 37,000
3. Gap between income and expenses‡	$ _____	$ 7,200
4. Total savings, in banks, retirement plans, mutual funds, and so on	$ _____	$120,000
5. Percent of total savings needed to fill the gap between this year's income and this year's expenses	_____	6%
6. The return on investment that your savings are earning	_____	8%
7. Using the table on page 914,§ find out how long your savings will last.	_____	31 years

    * Social Security benefits rise with inflation, so this calculation has a small spending cushion built in.
    † Don't count income from your savings. That is included later.
    ‡ If there isn't a gap, you're fine. Go read a murder mystery.
    § Assumes an annual 3 percent inflation rate. For other rates, see page 1015.

Get Real About Your Options! Preretirees keep saying, "I need such-and-such amount of income from my investments," says investment adviser Lynn Hopewell of the Monitor Group in Fairfax, Virginia. But if they take what they want in the early years, they may run out of money later. The right question is, "Given a certain investment fund, how much can I spend each year and still maintain the purchasing power of my capital?" To answer that question, you need a realistic view of investment returns, taxes, inflation, and how long you're likely to live.

The experience of the mid-1990s—with the major U.S. stock-market averages up by an average of nearly 20 percent a year—is not life. Since 1926, stocks have averaged 10.7 percent; since 1946, 12.2 percent. And remember, those are *averages*. Future returns might exceed the average. On the other hand, they might fall below—and what good is a financial plan that leaves you broke if stocks flounder for a while? Your personal portfolio won't even equal the stock market's gains because part of your money is probably invested in bond funds or money market funds. Hopewell suggests that you assume an 8 percent return pretax.

When figuring your taxes, apply your *average* rate. That's the total tax you pay—federal, state, and local income taxes and Social Security taxes, if any, divided by your total income. It's lower than the marginal rate you're used to thinking about (the marginal rate is the tax you pay on every additional dollar earned). But it tells you more about how much disposable income you'll have to live on in retirement.

As a general rule, you will have to hold more stocks in retirement, and withdraw less from your capital each year, than you probably expect.

HOW MUCH OF YOUR CAPITAL CAN YOU AFFORD TO USE EVERY YEAR?

The table on page 914 shows how long your savings are likely to last in a world of 3 percent inflation. It assumes that you'll maintain your purchasing power by drawing enough extra money out of your savings to match the annual rise in prices. For example for every $1,000 you take in the first year, you'll take $1,030 in the second year, $1,060.90 in the third year, and so on. In Appendix 8, starting on page 1015, you'll find tables with different inflation rates.

To use this table, add all the capital that you are free to draw on: bank accounts, retirement plans, and other investments. Decide what percentage of your capital you will need this year and find that percentage in the left-hand column. Read across that line to the column showing the average rate of return your money is earning. That shows how many years your capital will last.

As an example, use the retirement spending plan shown in the preceding table and assume that the $120,000 nest egg earns an average of 8 percent pretax. You need $7,200 to meet your expenses, or 6 percent of your total capital. At an initial 6 percent withdrawal rate, and allowing for a 3 percent average annual increase in the price of everything you buy, your capital will last for 31 years. If your withdrawal rate shows that your capital won't last as long as you will, you'll have to redo your retirement spending plan. You've hit the wall. It's too late to kid yourself.

HOW TO TAKE MONEY OUT OF YOUR RETIREMENT PLANS

Given a fixed and final retirement sum, the size of your income will depend on two things: (1) the kind of pension plan you have and (2) the system you choose for taking money out. Some plans are easy; they offer you no choice at all. More likely, you will have several choices—some of them better for you than others. Here's how to get the most from your pension, taking it plan by plan:

THE 3 PERCENT SOLUTION

PERCENT OF CAPITAL WITHDRAWN IN THE FIRST YEAR*	WILL LAST THIS MANY YEARS, IF THE ORIGINAL WITHDRAWAL RISES BY 3 PERCENT ANNUALLY AND YOUR MONEY IS INVESTED AT THE FOLLOWING AVERAGE RATES OF RETURN										
	4%	5%	6%	7%	8%	9%	10%	11%	12%	13%	14%
2%	68	158	#	#	#	#	#	#	#	#	#
3%	40	52	100	#	#	#	#	#	#	#	#
4%	28	34	43	72	#	#	#	#	#	#	#
5%	22	25	29	36	55	#	#	#	#	#	#
6%	18	20	22	26	31	44	#	#	#	#	#
7%	15	17	18	20	23	27	36	#	#	#	#
8%	13	14	15	17	18	21	24	31	#	#	#
9%	12	12	13	14	15	17	19	22	27	44	#
10%	10	11	12	12	13	14	15	17	19	23	33
11%	9	10	10	11	12	12	13	14	16	18	21
12%	9	9	9	10	10	11	11	12	13	14	16
13%	8	8	9	9	9	10	10	11	11	12	13
14%	7	8	8	8	8	9	9	10	10	11	12
15%	7	7	7	8	8	8	8	9	9	10	10

* Assumes a single withdrawal at the start of the year. All the numbers are rounded.
SOURCE: John Allen of Allen-Warren, Arvada, Colorado.

Notes to the table
1. Look up your probable life expectancy on the table in Appendix 11 (page 1025). Think about how long your parents and grandparents lived. Pick a likely life span for yourself. That's the period over which you need your money to stretch.
2. The average rate of return on your nest egg assumes that some investments earn more and some less. Over time, for example, your stock investments may earn 10 percent, your bond investments 7 percent, and your money market mutual funds, 5 percent. Keep the money you need for each year's living expenses stashed in a money fund. Invest the rest of your nest egg for longer terms.
3. Recalculate as inflation changes, based on the current value of your nest egg and the amount you need for expenses. Appendix 8 contains tables for inflation rates from zero to 7 percent.
4. What if it appears that your savings will run out before you do? You can lower your living expenses, raise the returns you're getting from your investment (a plausible answer for anyone holding every dime in cash), or try to earn more money.

Your Defined-Benefit Plan

This is the classic pension plan. You get a taxable, monthly income for the rest of your life. Corporate pensions are usually fixed. At retirement, your payment looks generous (or adequate, or stingy, as the case may be). Ten years later it looks worse because price increases have eroded its purchasing power. Occasionally, corporations cough up a cost-of-living benefit for retirees. But not often. Anyone tied to a corporate defined-benefit plan had better come armed with a separate pool of savings and investments, to make up for your pension's unstoppable losses to inflation. Government pensions, by contrast, often have an annual cost-of-living adjustment, although the increase may be something less than the inflation rate.

Before you get your first check, there may be two choices you have to make:

1. *Should the pension cover you alone or you and your spouse?* You get a larger monthly check if you take the pension for your lifetime only. But at your death, the pension stops and your spouse gets nothing. That's okay as long as your spouse doesn't need your pension or if you have good reason to believe that your spouse will die first. But if your spouse will depend on that money, it should cover both your lives. A two-life pension (joint and survivor) isn't as big, but at least your spouse won't be left empty-handed.

If you do opt for spousal protection, you generally face another choice. Should you leave your spouse the same size check you get as a couple or a smaller check? If this income is critical to your spouse's welfare, take the largest check your spouse can get. (For more on this issue, see page 921.)

2. *Should you take your pension as a monthly income or in a lump sum?* Generally, monthly payments are your only choice. But some employers offer the option of lump sums. If you doubt that your company is sound, take the lump sum, unless your pension is fully insured by the Pension Benefit Guaranty Corporation (page 850). Otherwise, here's how to decide which choice is best:

• If you're highly dependent on this money, take the monthly pension. A pension lasts for life, even though it's eroded by inflation. If you take the lump sum and invest it, you might not be able to make it last.

• If you're an inexperienced investor, take the monthly pension. A financial planner might show you, on paper, that you'd get a higher income by investing the lump sum. But what if the planner's investments fail? You lack the knowledge to judge whether you're getting good advice. And sometimes, even good advice doesn't work out.

• If you're a terrific investor, consider the lump sum. But first, ask what "discount rate" of interest the company uses to decide how large your lump sum should be. This rate is critical! You'll have to invest your entire lump sum at that same rate *for life* just to match what you'd get from the company. To improve your income, you'd have to invest at a higher rate. Unless you're firmly convinced that you can beat the discount rate, you're better off with the monthly pension.

• If you have other sources of income, take the lump sum. You can roll that money into a tax-deferred Individual Retirement Account and let it accumulate for your older age. That gives you inflation protection.

• If you're rich enough not to need a pension, take the lump sum. Roll it into an IRA and leave it to your kids.

• If your health is so poor that you don't expect to live very long, take the lump sum. You can tap it for larger payments than you'd get from a pension because it doesn't have to cover a full life expectancy.

For ways of handling a lump sum, if you choose it, see page 917.

You may decide on a lump sum solely because you need some quick money—maybe to repay debts or buy an RV for retirement travel. You'll put the rest of the cash in an IRA, where it may or may not be invested well. An alternative, if your company allows it, is to take part of your pension in cash and the rest in monthly checks for the rest of your life.

Double-check the size of your pension if it is "integrated" with Social Security. Integration means that it's partly reduced by the size of your Social Security benefit. When making that reduction, companies estimate what your benefit will be. If they estimate too high, they wind up paying you too little. (For more on the errors made when calculating pensions, see page 881.)

Your Defined-Contribution Plan

At retirement, you're owed a lump sum of money. Period. No promises have been made about the size of this sum or how long it will last. Maybe it will see you through a comfortable retirement. Then again, maybe it won't. These plans include profit-sharing, 401(k)s, stock-bonus plans, and Employee Stock Ownership Plans. There are various ways of taking this money:

You Might Choose a Lifetime Annuity—a fixed monthly pension covering you alone or you and your spouse (or another beneficiary). Your employer buys the annuity from a commercial insurer. Check out the insurer's safety-and-soundness ratings and how much it will pay each month. Then check what other high-rated insurers pay (page 342). You might get a higher monthly income by rolling the money into a different annuity. *The risk:* Every year your fixed payment will buy less and less. In general, annuities are smarter for the old-old than for the young-old.

You Might Choose Periodic Payments—an income that lasts a specified number of years. You get higher payments than you would from a lifetime annuity. But at the end of the period, those payments stop. *The risk:* When payments stop, your other income may not be enough to live on. Periodic payments suit someone who expects another source of income (like a payout from a trust fund), someone with a comfortable nest egg that can be tapped when these payments stop, or someone in poor health who doesn't expect to live very long. If you die before collecting all the money in your retirement fund, the remainder goes to a beneficiary.

You Might Leave Some or All of Your Money in the Company Plan—a terrific idea for people who won't need the income right away. You get professional money management at no extra charge and can make withdrawals as you need them (at times specified by the plan). It also makes sense to stay in the plan if you're 55 to 59½. At those ages you can make penalty-free withdrawals from a 401(k), provided you've left the company. In IRAs, you're not penalty-free until you pass 59½. To stay with the company, however, your total retirement account must be worth at least $5,000. Otherwise, you'll be cashed out. *The risk:* The pension-fund manager might produce mediocre investment returns. But he or she will almost certainly outinvest the average retiree.

You Might Roll the Money into an Individual Retirement Account—so you can invest it yourself. For how to do it without tax complications, see page 872. Penalties apply if you withdraw IRA money before 59½ unless you meet one of the exceptions on page 876. *The risk:* You might invest the money badly.

If your company has both a defined-benefit plan and a defined-contribution plan, play it this way:

1. Leave the money in the defined-contribution plan to grow tax deferred.

2. Live on your monthly defined-benefit pension, Social Security, and other savings for as long as you reasonably can.

3. When inflation has eroded your fixed pension so much that you're feeling the pinch, start using the money in your defined-contribution plan. That fund may have gained enough in value to restore or increase your purchasing power.

The Lump-Sum Withdrawal

When you take all the money out of your pension or profit-sharing account, there are three things you can do with it:

1. *Have the plan trustee roll some or all of the funds directly into an Individual Retirement Account.* (Tax-qualified plans are required to offer you this option.) You can leave the money alone to build tax deferred. No withdrawals are required until you pass age 70½. Or you can tap the IRA as needed for living expenses, paying income taxes on the money you take. There is usually a 10 percent penalty on withdrawals prior to age 59½ unless you go for Loophole Nine (page 877). Note that rollover IRAs are only for money that you or your employer contributed pretax, plus all of the money you earned tax deferred. You cannot roll over any after-tax contributions that you might have made to the company plan. If you want a tax-favored investment for this money, too, consider a Roth IRA or municipal bonds.

2. *Have the plan pay out the funds to you, then roll the money into an IRA yourself.* To avoid being taxed, you have to complete the rollover within 60 days. But why would you make this choice? When a 401(k) plan is paid directly to you, your employer generally has to withhold 20 percent

for income taxes. That 20 percent will be treated as a taxable withdrawal unless you replace it with other money within 60 days (page 859).

You might be considering this option because of a short-term need for cash. You plan to make temporary use of the plan distribution, then scoot it into an IRA before 60 days are up. Here's a better way of accomplishing that end: Have the plan trustee roll your distribution directly into an IRA, take cash from the IRA to cover your short-term needs, then return it to the IRA within 60 days. That way you won't have 20 percent withheld. If you have a permanent need for cash, take that from the IRA, too.

3. *Ask if the company will give you some of the money in cash and roll the rest into an IRA.* This gives a payout that doesn't have to go back to the IRA—and with no tax penalty if you're at least 55 (although 20 percent will be withheld for income taxes). What you don't take in cash glides into the IRA untouched.

4. *Take all the money as straight income, pay taxes currently, and invest the remainder.* If you go this route and you're at least 59½, you may be able to use a special tax calculation called 5-year averaging. It reduces your tax by treating the payment as if it were spread over 5 years. But that's relevant only when full withdrawals make sense in the first place. Usually, it's smarter to defer the tax by rolling the money into an IRA. In any case, 5-year averaging will no longer be available after 1999.

If you were born before 1936, you can use 10-year averaging (based on 1986 tax rates). Any part of the payment coming from the plan contributions made prior to 1974 can be taxed as a long-term capital gain, at 20 percent.

Your Keogh Plan

With a profit-sharing or money-purchase Keogh (page 863), follow the rules that I just laid out for defined-contribution plans. You can tap the Keogh, or not tap it, at any rate you like. Or you can take a lump sum. No withdrawals are required until you pass 70½. Defined-benefit Keoghs, by contrast, work like any other defined-benefit plan. You either take the monthly pension you planned on or roll the cash into an Individual Retirement Account if the plan allows lump-sum distributions.

Your IRA or
Simplified Employee Pension (SEP)

This money is normally available starting at age 59½, or earlier if you use Loophole Nine (page 877). When you pass age 70½, withdrawals become compulsory. IRA and SEP holders cannot use 5-year tax averaging if they take all their money in a lump sum. But you probably wouldn't choose lump-sum withdrawals, anyway.

After That Magic Age . . .

For most of us, 70½ is the witching age. You have to set up a lifetime plan for removing all the money from your corporate and personal retirement accounts. Only Roth IRAs can go on forever.

Your first withdrawal from your employer's plan generally must occur by April 1 of the year following the later of (1) the year you reach 70½ or (2) the year you retire. The rule is slightly different for withdrawals from IRAs or from employer plans when you own more than 5 percent of the company. In those cases, you have to start taking money no later than April 1 of the year following the year you reach 70½, whether or not you're retired.

After that, each year's required amount must be taken no later than the close of the calendar year. That could give you two payments the first year —one after reaching 70½, which you can defer until April of the following year; and one for 71, which must be completed by the end of December. (If you take both payments in one year, you might be pushed into a higher bracket—check this out.)

If you're still working, you can keep on contributing to Keoghs and 401(k)s after 70½, but not to tax-deferred IRAs or SEPs. You can contribute to Roth IRAs, however, as long as you want.

How Much Do You Have to Take Out Each Year? Enough so that, if you continued at that rate, you would empty all your retirement plans over (1) your lifetime, (2) the joint lifetimes of you and your spouse, (3) the joint lifetimes of you and a designated beneficiary, or (4) any shorter period you designate. If the beneficiary is not your spouse and is young, the payments are figured as if he or she were no more than 10 years younger than you are (if you die during the term, the payout rate can flip to the beneficiary's actual age). If your spouse is the beneficiary, however, you use his or her actual age.

As to life expectancy, you have two choices. You can calculate it once and use that lifespan for all subsequent withdrawals. That pulls more of your income into the earlier years. Or you can recalculate your life expectancy (and that of your spouse) every year. That pushes more income into the later years, where it might benefit a surviving spouse (or raise your estate tax, depending on your situation). Once you decide to recalculate annually, you aren't allowed to change your mind.

Here's an interesting reason to calculate just once. If you do so, and you and your spouse die in a common accident, your beneficiaries can choose to continue the lifetime withdrawal schedule you set up. If you're recalculating every year, however, your beneficiaries will have to withdraw all the money from the IRA at once. That could create a horrendous tax.

How do you figure your withdrawals? It's easy—and I say this as one who's allergic to arithmetic. The steps are:

1. What was the balance in your IRA last December 31? (Look at the December 31 before you turned 70½, if this is your first withdrawal.)

2. What is your life expectancy or the combined life expectancy of you and a beneficiary? You'll find the single-life table in Appendix 11 (page 1025). For joint lives, consult the IRS's free Publication 590, *Individual Retirement Arrangements,* an indispensable guide to how these plans are taxed.

3. Divide the balance of the IRA by the life expectancy. That gives you the minimum withdrawal.

4. Do this for each IRA you have (always excepting the Roth). Add up the results. That's the amount that must be withdrawn. You can take it from one IRA or from several as long as the total dollar amount is met.

5. Go through the same steps for each Keogh or other retirement plan you own. With these plans, the proper amount must be taken from each plan separately. You can't use extra withdrawals from one Keogh to cover money that ought to come out of another, as you can with IRAs. This argues for combining all your Keoghs into a single plan—in a mutual fund or self-directed Keogh held at a brokerage firm. Then you can cash in whichever investments seem the most appropriate.

If you can't figure out the proper withdrawals yourself, the trustee for your retirement plan might help. Or ask an accountant or qualified financial planner. Some savers buy an immediate-pay annuity (page 925) to put their withdrawals on automatic pilot.

It is Critical That You Take the Right Amount Each Year. If you withdraw too little, you'll be socked with a 50 percent penalty on the sum that you should have take but didn't (unless you can convince the IRS that it was an accident; you were just all thumbs with the life-expectancy tables).

What If I Die While I'm Making Withdrawals from My Plan?

• *If you have a regular pension, defined-benefit Keogh, 401(k), 403(b), or 457, converted into a lifetime annuity.* The pension dies with you, if you arranged to have it last for your lifetime only. If there's a beneficiary, he or she receives whatever payments you provided for.

• *If you have a tax-deferred IRA or SEP.* Your spouse steps into your shoes, which gives him or her a full range of options (page 921). Other beneficiaries will be constrained by what you've already done. If you based your withdrawals on a one-time calculation of life expectancy, those same payments can go to your beneficiaries until the money is exhausted. If you were recalculating your life expectancy each year, or if you die before starting regular, scheduled payments, they'll have to take all the money within 5 years. They cannot roll their inheritance into an IRA of their own.

• *If you have a Roth IRA.* As with a regular IRA, your spouse can treat the Roth as his or her own (page 874). Other beneficiaries have two choices:

(1) withdraw all the money within 5 years or (2) starting in the year after your death, make annual withdrawals calculated to last over the beneficiary's lifetime. All withdrawals from Roths come entirely tax free.

• *If you have some other retirement plan.* Beneficiaries follow rules similar to those for a tax-deferred IRA or SEP, with one exception: Your spouse cannot treat your plan as his or her own. All beneficiaries are treated alike.

SPOUSE PROTECTION

The law worries a lot about widows, and so it should. Wives usually live longer than their husbands and generally wind up with far lower incomes. So an automatic "survivor annuity" has been written into all defined-benefit pension plans and the lifetime-payout option offered by defined-contribution plans. It protects men as well as women, but as a practical matter women need it more. Here are the spouse-protection rules for the various kinds of plans:

With All Defined-Benefit Plans and Defined-Contribution Plans Where the Employer Has to Put In a Fixed Percentage of Your Salary Each Year— the plan must offer a "preretirement survivor's annuity." If you die in harness, your spouse will receive a lifetime income. It's worth half of what your own benefit would have been if you had chosen to retire early.

Your spouse can waive this right, however. If he or she does and you live to retire, you'll have a larger pension check. But if you die, "the pension goes right into the box with you," says Peter Elinsky, a partner in the consulting firm KPMG Peat Marwick. The spouse gets no pension from the company, ever.

I once got a sad letter from a widow. She waived her preretirement benefit thinking that it covered only the years before her husband retired—and indeed, the company's form letter was none too clear on this point. When he died unexpectedly, she was horrified to learn that she had lost his "postretirement" pension, too. Don't waive the preretirement benefit if you'll need your spouse's pension to live on. If you've waived it and changed your mind, it can be reinstated (provided that your spouse is still alive).

Pension plans offer yet another form of spouse protection. If you live to retire and then die, your spouse automatically gets a lifetime income worth at least 50 percent of what you were getting (and up to 100 percent, if that's what you want and your plan allows it). That's called a joint-and-survivor payout.

Your spouse can waive this benefit, too, which would give you a larger check each month. But when you die, the pension stops and your spouse gets nothing. That's okay as long as your spouse has an adequate income. If not, a single-life pension is usually a mistake. (Nevertheless, some insurance agents urge this choice upon you. "Take the larger pension," they say, "and protect your spouse with an insurance policy instead." That is almost always a bad idea. For the reasons, see page 923.)

Some pension plans let you take your benefit in a single lump-sum payout. Again, your spouse has to agree.

The protection here is absolute. In one case, a female executive was retiring and wanted to take the maximum pension lasting for her life alone. Her husband was in jail for assaulting her. She had to visit him to ask if he'd forgo his joint-and-survivor check and he refused. Solution: divorce.

With Profit-Sharing Plans, Including Employee Stock Ownership Plans, 403(b)s, and 401(k)s—spouses get some protection, but not as much as they would under a defined-benefit plan.

If you die before retirement and you're married, all vested benefits in profit-sharing accounts normally have to go to your spouse. Your spouse can waive the benefit, however. This might be an issue for single parents. You probably named your children as beneficiaries of your 401(k). If you remarry, your new spouse becomes the beneficiary, no matter what the plan says. If you still want your children to get part or all of the money, your spouse has to waive his or her right to it. Ask your employer how to do this. The waiver *must* be made through the plan.

If at retirement you decide to convert your plan into a lifetime income, your spouse still is protected. The annuity has to cover you both unless the spouse specifically agrees that the payments will cover your life only.

There's no spouse protection, however, if you take all your money in a lump sum. You can spend it any way you want.

With Plans You Set Up Yourself—IRAs and SEPs offer no specific spouse protection. You're not required to create a survivor annuity. The assets in the plan can be left to any beneficiary you name.

Keoghs mimic corporate plans. With a defined-benefit or money-purchase Keogh, spouse protection is required. With a profit-sharing Keogh, you follow the rules for corporate profit-sharing plans.

A Spouse Can Sign Away His or Her Right to Your Pension. In some cases, this makes sense. A pension for a surviving spouse may not matter if: (1) your spouse has a good pension of his or her own; (2) your spouse is gravely ill and not likely to outlive you; (3) you have so much money that your spouse doesn't need the pension to live on. The consent has to be in writing and notarized, so the company knows it's real. Think carefully before going ahead, because waiving the benefit at retirement is an irrevocable choice. Once a spouse says bye-bye to his or her share of the pension, it's gone forever.

BEWARE PENSION MAX

One of the tragedies of our time is that so many spouses are being talked out of their pension protection by an army of insurance agents and financial planners. These salespeople believe—incorrectly—that they've found a better way. They call their product "pension maximization," pension max for short.

They advise you, the worker, to take the higher, single-life pension. You use that extra income to buy a life insurance policy. If you die first, your pension ends but the proceeds of the policy will create an income for your spouse. If your spouse dies first, you cancel the insurance and have that higher pension for the rest of your life.

Sounds neat—especially when it's laid out in a slick, computer-generated presentation. But many such presentations mislead. After paying for the policy, the couple may have less to live on, after taxes, than if they had taken the joint-and-survivor pension. More distressingly, if the husband dies, the insurance policy may not be large enough to provide the promised income for the wife.

After I aired this opinion in a newspaper column, angry insurance reps peppered me with dissenting letters. I invited them to prove the glories of a pension-max program started at retirement age. Ten of them took up the challenge; their work was analyzed by two financial planners using two different systems.

Only one proposal worked passably well, and it turned out to be a ringer. It was constructed by a computer-software company, using an Ameritas life-insurance policy that carried a minimal sales commission (page 312). All the proposals sent in by insurance agents were off the mark. Some ignored taxes, to make the couple's income look higher than would actually be the case. Some lowballed the amount of insurance needed, which gambled with the widow's income. Some suggested policies that cost more than the couple would gain in extra pension benefits. Some started the program well before retirement but didn't include those early costs in their "proof" of how well the idea worked.

A luckless client is not likely to find the holes in pension max proposals. I couldn't have found them either without expert help. Many a widow will discover the error only on learning she won't have all the income she'd counted on. (If this happens to you, consider suing the insurance agent and insurance company; that may be the only way of sending the industry a message.)

• • •

Even if a pension max proposal appears to work mathematically, the widow is taking a long list of other risks:

Income Risk. Inflation or unexpected expenses may eat away at your retirement income. At some point, you may no longer be able to afford the premium on the life insurance. The widow will lose the protection she had counted on.

Inflation Risk. Many government pensions and some private ones provide regular cost-of-living adjustments. Pension-max proposals rarely offer enough life insurance to cover all that extra income. So the widow is shortchanged.

Interest-Rate Risk. Pension max is usually funded with universal life insurance, which is linked to changes in interest rates. If rates fall, you may have to pay more for the coverage or accept a lower death benefit. If the former, your current disposable income will be pinched; if the latter, the widow might get less income than she expected.

Longevity Risk. Even if the insurance isn't enough to replace the husband's pension in full, pension max will work out if the husband lives long enough. After a few years that smaller policy will be okay, because the widow herself has fewer years to live. But you're taking an awful risk. If the husband is hit by a truck the day after retirement, the widow's income will come up short.

Annuity Risk. Today, a $200,000 life-insurance policy might buy a 70-year-old woman a lifetime income of $1,532 a month. But if interest rates fall, that sum will buy a widow something less. So you cannot be sure that the insurance policy will provide the income needed.

Marital Risk. If the husband owns the policy and the marriage goes bad, he might cut off the wife by canceling the insurance or changing the beneficiary.

Management Risk. If the widow gets a lump sum, she may not have the knowledge and experience to manage it well. Instead of buying an annuity, she might be persuaded to put it into investments that cost her some of the money.

Health Insurance Risk. A widow who leaves her husband's pension plan may lose company health coverage. It is particularly risky to leave public-sector pension plans, like those for teachers and other state employees, because benefits are often added later.

• • •

My bottom line: At retirement, no widow who will need the income should gamble on pension max. The presentation she and her husband get from the planner or insurance agent probably doesn't tell the whole story. To check what the agent is saying, turn to Appendix 9 (page 1019). There, you'll find a list of additional risks plus a worksheet that will tell you the truth about any proposal you get. Never buy pension max without running it through this calculation. Odds are that the proposal either lowers your after-tax income as a couple or provides too little insurance protection for the wife, or both.

IMMEDIATE-PAY ANNUITIES— CREATING AN INCOME FOR LIFE

If you enter retirement with a lump sum of money, there are two ways of turning it into a regular income. You can do it yourself—say, by drawing periodic checks from mutual funds, cashing certificates of deposit, or living on the interest from bonds. Or you can buy an immediate annuity from an insurance company. These annuities start paying you now and guarantee you an income for life.

You may own an annuity already—a tax-deferred annuity, bought to build your savings up. You can convert that money, tax free, to an immediate annuity at any insurance company you want. Don't automatically stick with the insurer you have. Shop for the one that pays the most.

Here are the ways that annuities pay. For how these various withdrawal methods are taxed, see page 927.

Straight-Life Annuity. You get a fixed monthly, quarterly, or annual income guaranteed to last for as long as you live. This arrangement pays you the highest possible monthly check. If you die before reaching your life expectancy, the insurer keeps the extra money. If you outlive your life expectancy, the insurer swallows the extra cost.

Annuity for "Life or Period Certain." Your income covers your lifetime or a fixed number of years, whichever is more. A typical choice is "life or ten years certain." Under this arrangement, the insurer makes regular payments for at least 10 years—to you if you're alive, or to a beneficiary if you die. If you die in the eleventh year, your beneficiary gets nothing. But you yourself get payments for as long as you live. "Period certain" arrangements cost money. You get a smaller income than from straight-life annuities. The longer the period, the smaller your monthly checks.

Most people who buy annuities choose "periods certain." It galls them to think that they might drop dead the day after buying, leaving everything to the insurer. But so what? Once dead, why care? Assuming you live for the "period certain," your heirs get nothing anyway. Consider providing separately for your heirs (say, by leaving them the house or putting part of your money in trust), then buying a straight-life annuity for yourself alone.

Two variants on "periods certain" are the "cash refund" annuity and the "installment refund" annuity—both of which guarantee enough payments, to you or a beneficiary, to match your full, original investment. The former pays your beneficiary in a lump sum, the latter makes installment payments. Either way the contracts lower the size of your monthly income.

Installment Payments. You sign up for a fixed number of payments— level or rising—over a period of your choice (but not exceeding your life expectancy). You may outlive this income so you'll need a source of support to fall back on. But if you die before getting all the money, the remainder goes to your heirs rather than to the insurance company. This can be a good alternative to a straight-life annuity.

Joint-and-Survivor Annuity. Your fixed monthly income lasts for your lifetime and the lifetime of a named beneficiary, such as your spouse. The size of your check depends on what your beneficiary will receive after your death. Half your check? Two-thirds of your check? The same size check? The more you leave, the smaller your income while you're still alive, and vice versa.

Occasional Payments. You withdraw money from time to time, as it suits you. Normally, the company lets you do this until age 85. Then you may have to set up a withdrawal plan. If you die, all the money left in your account goes to a beneficiary.

Hybrid. You allocate part of your money to lifetime payments. The rest can be left to accumulate or be tapped for occasional payments.

Variable Payments. You link your monthly income to a variable annuity (page 897), which ideally should be invested in stocks. This produces higher payments in some months and lower payments in others. Over time you have a good shot at getting more total income than a straight annuity would pay. But you might not. This is for people who have other sources of income and can afford the risk. To limit your risk, consider an equity-indexed payout annuity. It lets your payments rise to a higher, fixed level if the stock market rises, with no reduction if the market drops. But payments in general are less than you'd get with a straight variable annuity.

Lump Sum. You take the money and run. The usual reason is to switch to an annuity sold by another insurance company because it pays more than your present annuity does (page 929). In this case, you'd do a 1035 tax-free exchange into the new annuity. But first find out if you're in a "two-tier" company (page 889). If so, and you leave, the interest you've earned on your annuity over the years will be reduced sharply. Two-tier deals are a disgrace, but once you're hooked it generally makes sense to stay.

Systematic Withdrawals. Instead of receiving a straight-life annuity, you establish an income based on your life expectancy. At 65, for example, you will—on average—reach 85. So you draw on the annuity as if you had 20 years to live. By 75, your life expectancy will have lengthened to 87, which changes the size of your monthly payment.

With this system, your income is being adjusted annually to provide you with substantially equal payments over a *lengthening* life expectancy. If the annuity also covers your spouse, payments can be jiggered to reflect your changing joint life expectancy. You can take extra payments from time to time. If you die, the account generally goes to a beneficiary, not to the insurance company. If at any time you decide that you want a level income for life, you can usually switch to a straight annuity.

Systematic withdrawals have a lot of uses. They're especially dandy for people using Loophole Nine (page 877) or who have reached age 70½ and have to start taking minimum withdrawals from their tax-deferred retirement plans.

Two points about systematic withdrawals: (1) Your interest rate isn't locked in. If you're using a fixed annuity, your rate will change from year to year. If you're using a variable annuity, you'll get whatever the contract earns. (2) You start out with a smaller monthly income than a straight-life annuity would pay. But over the years your income should rise, assuming no sharp drop in interest rates (and depending on the system you use for calculating life expectancy). Rising payments help you offset inflation.

Not all insurers offer automatic withdrawals calculated this way. But you're always free to figure out this rate of withdrawal on your own.

How Annuity Payouts Are Taxed

When You Buy an Immediate-Pay Annuity with a Lump Sum of Money:

• *If the money was rolled over from a qualified retirement plan:* No taxes are due on the rollover. Instead, you'll be fully taxed on every check you get.

• *If you bought the annuity with an after-tax lump sum:* Each payment is a mix of taxable income and a tax-free return of your original capital. At the end of the year, the insurer will tell you how much taxable income you received. The portion that's taxable is established by the IRS.

When You're Holding a Tax-Deferred Annuity and Switch to Immediate-Pay:

• *If you take a lifetime annuity or payments over a fixed period:* Each payment is a mix of taxable income and a tax-free return of your original capital. At the end of the year, the insurer will tell you how much taxable income you received. If you started these payouts before reaching 59½ and they're projected to last for your lifetime, you're not subject to the 10 percent tax penalty on early withdrawals.

• *If you take a lump-sum withdrawal:* You're taxed all at once, on all of your earnings over the years. There's also a 10 percent penalty if you're under 59½. Not a smart move.

• *If you roll your lump sum into another insurer's annuity:* You can use a tax-free 1035 exchange. Your insurance agent will show you how.

• *If you make occasional withdrawals:* They are treated entirely as taxable income until you have taken out all the money that your investment ever earned. Any further withdrawals are a tax-free return of your original principal.

• *If you die:* The tax depends on the type of annuity and its status.

1. If you're collecting income from a straight-life annuity and die before recovering all the money you paid in, the loss is reported on your final tax return. (If you recover more than your original investment, it is taxable as received.)

2. If you're collecting income from an annuity designed to last for your lifetime or a "period certain," die before the period expires, and leave the payments to a beneficiary, the beneficiary pays taxes on the income received.

3. If you're still accumulating money in the annuity and die, it passes to a beneficiary. The beneficiary normally has two choices: take the money as a lifetime income or withdraw it within 5 years. A married couple, however, can arrange for a joint annuity that continues to grow tax deferred even if one spouse dies. Do it this way: Designate one spouse the owner and annuitant (the annuitant is the person who will receive the money); designate the other spouse as the contingent owner and beneficiary. If either spouse dies, the other can keep the contract growing.

How to Get the Most from Annuity Payouts

1. If you have a tax-deferred annuity, leave it alone as long as you can. Spend your after-tax savings first.

2. If you have a pot of after-tax money, wait as long as you can before turning it into a lifetime annuity. The older you are the higher your monthly

payout will be. At 65, $100,000 might buy a woman $729 a month; at 75, it buys her $966. What's more, any fixed income will be shaved by inflation every year. The fewer years inflation has at you, the stronger your finances will be. If your health gets worse, you'll also be glad that you didn't buy too early.

3. Don't buy a straight annuity if you're not well. These products are for healthy people who worry about outliving their savings. But consider an "impaired-risk" immediate-pay annuity, which some companies offer. They assume shorter life spans, so your money will buy you a higher income per month. As with any immediate annuity, you are betting against the insurance company. It's betting you'll die; you're betting you'll live.

4. Consider installment payments or a systematic withdrawal program if you hope to leave some of your annuity money to heirs. But you get smaller payments than if you had chosen an income for life.

5. Don't expect to get a higher lifetime income by taking the money, investing it yourself, and making regular withdrawals. You might beat the payout you'd get from the insurance company, after tax—but then again, you might not. And there's no guarantee that your money will last as long as you do.

6. You can often get a higher income just by switching your money to a better-paying insurance company. The differences can be truly amazing. As I write, I am looking at a price list for 38 companies. With $100,000 in after-tax cash, a 70-year-old man can buy an income as small as $809 a month or as large as $935 a month, depending on the company he chooses. For a woman, the range is $692 to $851. Some companies offer unisex rates, which are generally better for women.

7. Once you choose your company, you are usually locked in for life —so take the time to choose carefully. A few insurers, however, let you stop payments in midstream and take some or all of the remaining money in cash. That will probably be the trend.

How to Buy the Very Best Immediate-Pay Annuity

This is one of the easiest jobs in personal finance. First you buy the right publication and dial the right phone number. After that, the process takes five steps and five minutes:

1. The right publication is the *Annuity & Life Insurance Shopper,* $14, from the brokerage firm United States Annuities (page 893). At this writing, it shows single-life prices from 38 insurance companies for men and women 60, 65, 70, and 75, as well as some unisex rates. You can buy the annuity directly through United States Annuities, which will answer your questions and handle your order by phone. Or use the list as a benchmark when talking to your insurance agent or financial planner.

A second source: *Comparative Annuity Reports Immediate Annuity Newsletter* (page 894), $10. It shows single-life rates with 10 years certain from 50 insurers, for men and women 70 and 75.

The right phone number is 800-874-5662. That's Fee For Service, which can give you a quote on low-load immediate-pay annuities. It often has the best rates in the marketplace. You won't find all these annuities on other lists.

Prices are quoted in terms of monthly incomes. A price of $8.51, for example, means that for every $1,000 you give the insurance company, it will pay you $8.51 a month for life. If you have $100,000, that's $851 a month (100 multiplied by $8.51), or $10,212 a year. If you have $250,000, that's $2,127.50 a month, or $25,530 a year.

2. With the *Shopper* in hand, check the companies that pay the five highest monthly incomes per $1,000 invested and compare them with the best low-loads you get from Fee For Service.

3. Starting from the top of your list, find out if that company has good ratings from at least three of the five main insurance-rating services (page 342—ratings are in the *Shopper*). To date, almost all immediate-pay annuities have been honored when an insurer failed, so you don't necessarily have to stick with triple-A companies. But for comfort, there should be an A in each rating somewhere. If the insurer with the highest monthly payout also meets your quality standards, go no further.

4. If you've been saving money in a tax-deferred annuity at a top-rated insurance company, ask that company for its quote on immediate-pay annuities. Insurers often give current customers better rates than they offer to customers buying in from the outside.

5. To spread your risk, you might buy annuities from two or more companies. Or you might buy one fixed-pay and one variable-pay.

The Charitable Alternative

Here's a way of earning an income from your money while serving others, too. Forget about buying an annuity from a life insurance company and letting the insurer walk away with anything left over. Give that money to a charitable organization instead. A college. A hospital. A museum. A church. Many such organizations stand ready to pay you a lifetime income in return for cash and other types of gifts. You get a tax deduction, too. If you give appreciated property, you'll save on capital gains taxes. For details, see page 125. You won't get as large an income as insurance companies pay. But you'll have the pleasure of knowing that you've done some good.

Penguins and Predators

My husband and I visited Antarctica years ago. I remember watching penguins who had to enter the water to feed. One by one they'd gather at the water's edge, forming a dithery little crowd, hesitating for long minutes before plunging in. On land they were safe; in the water were leopard seals who ate penguins for lunch.

New retirees are penguins. Awaiting them in the retirement waters are leopard seals: financial salespeople, who want to lunch on their lump-sum retirement payouts. As the boomer generation retires in larger numbers, more money will vanish into their waiting jaws. Some employers become accomplices. They refer retirees to specific planners or invite a planner to give a preretirement course. But on what basis are these "teachers" chosen? Some may give good advice indeed. Others are hustlers in disguise.

One danger of the 401(k) retirement system is that employees won't put aside enough money for themselves. Another is that, once they've saved it, a leopard seal will snatch it away. You must take great care to protect your lump sum. If you don't leave your money with your company, roll it into an IRA at a bank or money-market mutual fund. Take a long time to test advisers or examine mutual funds, before deciding what to do with the money next.

WHEN SHOULD YOU START DRAWING SOCIAL SECURITY?

That decision isn't always obvious. You have several choices, especially when you're married. Go over all the options with a Social Security representative (page 934) before deciding exactly when to claim your check.

If you're single, you have only one question to consider: At what age should you retire, assuming that you have a choice? If you're married, consider age along with other issues.

Social Security will tell you how much you'll get if you retire at various ages, starting at 62. From 62 to 70, benefits ratchet up each year. Starting at 70, however, you get no further credit for waiting. Here are some reasons for picking a particular age:

Retire at 62 if you can afford it and your health is poor. Your benefit will be lower than if you had waited until your full retirement age (at this writing, 65). But early benefits provide larger total payments to anyone who doesn't expect to live for many more years. How many years? Until about 75.

Retire from your main job at 65, switch to a part-time job, and collect Social Security, too. The amount of money you can earn between 65 and 69 and still get a full Social Security benefit is going to rise steeply over the next few years (page 935). In 2002, you'll be allowed a paycheck as high as $30,000.

Retire later than 65 if you're earning a good income and like your job or have a younger spouse who will probably outlive you. Your salary is much higher than a Social Security check would be and your earnings add to the size of your final Social Security benefit. For every year after 65 that you put off claiming benefits, your Social Security check goes up. At this writing, the increase is 5 percent a year for people 65 or 66; it rises to 8 percent a year for people reaching 62 in 2005 and later.

Work an extra 2 or 3 years if that's what's needed to claim a Social Security benefit.

If you're married, the optimal retirement age depends on your health, your respective ages, your income, your expected life spans, and the size of each spouse's Social Security account.

Here are the basic rules:

If only one spouse works and has a Social Security work record, the other is entitled to benefits as a result of that record. You get up to 50 percent of your working spouse's benefit while you're both living and up to 100 percent after your spouse dies, depending on what age each of you retired.

If both spouses work and have separate Social Security records, you each get your own separate benefit. But when your own benefit is less than you would collect as a spouse, you get an extra payment to bring you up to the spousal level.

You can retire on your own account whenever you want. But you cannot retire on your spouse's account unless your spouse has also retired. Exception: an eligible divorced spouse can collect on his or her ex's account even if the ex has not retired (page 155).

Here are the various ways that this game can play out:

- *When the wife* has no significant benefit of her own:*

1. The husband may retire as early as 62 on a reduced benefit. At 62 the wife may also take a reduced benefit. She gets 37.5 percent of whatever her husband would have gotten at full retirement age. If he dies and she is at least 65, she gets 100 percent of whatever benefit he was receiving.

2. The husband can retire as early as 62 while the wife waits until 65. That gives the wife 50 percent of what her husband would have gotten at full retirement age. You may decide, however, that the dollar difference isn't worth the wait.

3. The longer the husband waits to retire, the larger his benefit may be and the more his spouse can collect. That's especially important to a younger spouse.

- *When the wife has a benefit of her own, but it's less than her spousal benefit:*

1. She can retire as early as 62, using her own benefit, even though her husband is still working.

---

* These rules are the same for a husband with little or no Social Security earnings who applies for benefits on his wife's account. But using "wife" as "spouse" tells the story in its most typical way. I could use the word "spouse" everywhere, but you'd never figure out which spouse I was talking about. Try it and see!

2. When her husband retires, she can also receive her spousal benefit, to raise her Social Security income to a higher level. Her check will be higher at 65 than if she takes it earlier—but maybe not by much. Ask Social Security what the difference would be.

3. If her husband retires first and then she retires, she gets the spousal benefit for her age at the time. She doesn't have the option of waiting until 65.

• *When the worker dies and the widow has a widow's benefit as well as a separate Social Security record of her own:*

1. She can start her widow's benefit as early as 60. As early as 62, she can switch to her own Social Security benefit, if it will be higher. She'll get even more if she can wait until 65.

2. She can take the widow's benefit and keep it if that will always be the higher amount. If she can afford it, it may pay to wait for the benefit until 65.

• *When the wife has a benefit of her own and it's better than her spousal benefit:*

1. She can retire on it at any time, from 62 on, and will keep it. She will never switch to a spousal benefit.

2. If her husband's benefit is small, he may get more money by claiming a spousal benefit on his wife's account.

• *When one spouse has a government pension, and also qualifies for Social Security benefits on the account of the other spouse:* Don't expect to collect much Social Security, if any. You generally get only the amount of your Social Security benefit that exceeds two-thirds of your government pension. That is usually zero.

• *When you have an eligible child at home:* Your family is entitled to additional Social Security benefits. But you're subject to a maximum monthly benefit, no matter how many eligible members are in your family.

How Much Can Widows, Widowers, and Spouses Earn and Still Get Benefits?

All Social Security benefits are subject to the retirement test explained on page 935. Whether you receive benefits as a retiree, spouse, widow, widower, or child, your check goes down if you exceed the earnings limit. A 62-year-old widow, employed at good wages, may find that she earns too much to collect much of a widow's benefit. In that case, she'd be smarter not to claim it. Let it build up until she actually retires, when the check will be larger.

Can You Unretire?

Sure. If you quit work, start getting Social Security, and then take a job again, you can simply withdraw your claim.

Two things could happen.

1. You could repay all the Social Security money you've already received. That cancels any reduction you took for retiring earlier than 65. You are treated as if you never retired at all.

2. You can simply report that you've returned to work. Depending on the size of your income, your benefit will be reduced or stopped. When you retire again, your retirement age will be refigured, based on the number of Social Security checks you previously received. For example, if you retire at 62, receive the equivalent of six full checks, return to work, suspend benefits, then retire again at 65, you'll be treated as having retired at 64 and six months. Checks for re-retirees aren't refigured until 65, so if you re-retire earlier you will have to wait.

Applying for Social Security Benefits

You can apply as early as 3 months before you want your benefits to start. Otherwise, benefits generally start in the month when application is made. If you apply after 65, you can—if you want—claim back payments for up to 6 months (but because of your late filing, you might lose a month of Medicare protection—see page 391).

Before okaying your benefits, the government will want your Social Security number, originals or certified copies of your birth certificate and the birth certificates of anyone else applying for benefits (no photocopies allowed), and proof of how much money you made last year. If you don't have all these documents and can't get them, don't worry. Social Security will suggest some acceptable substitutes. All Social Security benefits are indexed to the inflation rate.* You get your higher checks each January.

How to Get Paid

Your Social Security check can be mailed to your address. Or—easier and faster—you can have the money sent directly to your bank. Social Security wires it to your checking account or savings account, as you prefer. Starting in 1999, direct deposit becomes mandatory.

How to Talk to Social Security

If you like to deal in person, check the Yellow Pages under U.S. Government to see if one of Social Security's 1,300 offices is anywhere near you. Unfortunately, budget cuts have all but eliminated the staffers who visited shut-ins, set up shop once a week at senior-citizen centers, and circuit-rode to rural areas. For good, general information, check the Web

---

* At this writing, there's talk of reducing the inflation adjustment.

site at http://www.ssa.gov. You can telephone Social Security toll-free (800-234-5772), Monday through Friday, from 7:00 a.m. to 7:00 p.m.

How Much Can You Earn and Still Get a Full Social Security Benefit?

In 1997 retirees 62 through 64 could earn $8,640 free and clear. Over that amount, every $2 in earnings cut $1 off their Social Security checks. This earnings limit rises with average wage increases every year.

Retirees 65 through 69 could earn up to $13,500 but were docked $1 for every addition $3 in earnings. For this age group, however, the amount of "free" earnings increases steeply. Here's what the law allows:

Year	Amount You Can Earn at 65 through 69 Before Your Social Security Payment Will Be Docked*
1998	$14,500
1999	15,500
2000	17,000
2001	25,000
2002	30,000†

* Above these amounts, you lose $1 for every additional $3 in earnings.
† Indexed to wage inflation in subsequent years.
SOURCE: Social Security Administration

What If You Earn Over the Social Security Limit?

When you file your tax returns, Social Security gets a report of what you earned. That's checked electronically against the benefits you got. If your benefit turns out to have been too high, Social Security will ask for some money back. You can write a check or pay in installments by having your subsequent Social Security checks reduced.

Alternatively, you can report at the start of the year that you expect to exceed the earnings limit. Estimate how much extra you're likely to make. Your monthly check will be adjusted accordingly—then readjusted when Social Security gets your tax returns. If you earn less money than you originally thought, Social Security will restore any benefits due.

How Your Social Security Benefits Are Taxed

Retirees with middle incomes and up will owe federal income taxes on part of their Social Security benefits. There are two levels of tax. At the first level (incomes of $25,000–$34,000 for singles or $32,000–$44,000 for marrieds filing jointly), up to 50 percent of your benefits are subject to tax. At the second level (above $34,000 for singles or $44,000 for marrieds filing joint returns), you'll owe tax on up to 85 percent of your Social Security benefits. That doesn't mean your tax rate is 85 percent—only that up to 85 percent of your benefits are taxed in your regular bracket. Some states also tax Social Security income, but most don't.

At year-end, you'll be mailed a Social Security Benefit Statement, showing how much money you received. Use that to figure out whether any taxes are owed. When adding up your income, include half your Social Security benefits, municipal-bond interest, and certain other nontaxable items.

HOW SHOULD YOU INVEST FOR RETIREMENT?

The investment rules in Chapter 21 are as good at 65 as at 35. But there are several points that retirees, in particular, should think about:

1. *You are not dead!* You will probably live for another 25 years or more, during which time inflation will nibble or chomp at any fixed income you receive. You may impoverish yourself if you put all your money in bonds, certificates of deposit, money market mutual funds, or other fixed-income investments. You *must* keep some portion of your capital invested for growth—for example, in equity-income mutual funds.

2. *"Safe" investments aren't!* Take the person who insists on owning only 7 percent government bonds. In 15 years (when he or she will almost surely still be alive), and assuming 3 percent inflation, the purchasing power of those bonds will have been cut in half. How "safe" is that?

3. *Paying taxes won't kill you!* When investing, pursue an appropriate total return and pay your taxes as they fall. If you look at the tax angle first and the investment angle second, you are going to make some lousy decisions. For example, if you're a low-bracket investor, municipal bonds will yield you almost nothing, after inflation.

4. *It's too late to start over!* Hordes of entrepreneurs troll for early retirees who dream of beginning another life. They'll hold out a dream of riches if you'll just invest your severance pay or lump-sum pension payout in their guinea-hen farms or solar go-carts. Don't do it. You are holding the only serious money that you will ever have. If you want to start another business, grow it yourself, out of personal experience and the contacts you have.

5. *There's more than one way to skin a cat!* "Income investors" usually focus on interest income—from bonds or certificates of deposit. But stock dividends are income, too. With a portion of your money in dividend-paying stocks, you're getting income *and* some growth. Furthermore,

growth in the value of your stocks is income, too. Whether you're getting 7 percent from the interest on a $10,000 bond or by selling 70 shares of a $10 stock, you're collecting $700 to spend.

An Investment Program to Consider:

1. *Invest part of your money for growth.* Put it in conservative mutual funds that buy dividend-paying stocks. Reinvest all your dividends. Every year withdraw as much money as you're going to need for expenses or set up an automatic monthly withdrawal plan—see page 630. Increase your withdrawals once a year to keep your purchasing power level with inflation. Ten years later, you may still have the same amount of capital you started with, or not very much less, thanks to your mutual fund's increase in value.

2. *Invest part of your money in a collection of short- and intermediate-term bonds.* Spend the income and reinvest the principal as your bonds fall due. Or spend the principal, if you need it. Alternatively, buy short- and intermediate-term bond mutual funds and reinvest the dividends. Set up an annual (or monthly) withdrawal plan, just as you did for your mutual funds invested in stocks.

What If You're Afraid of Stocks?

Ignore all the previous advice. Some people haven't the temperament for stocks, don't care about the market, and would be scared stiff if they took a loss. The last thing in the world I want you to do is hand your money to a planner who invests in ways that alarm or confuse you. Leave your money in the bank and live on whatever you have. Millions of people do exactly that. At this point in life, your personal sense of security matters most.

When Should Retirees Give Up Stocks?

Never, if you're mentally active, well-to-do, and can afford to outwait the market's cyclical declines. You probably won't have to use all your money during your lifetime, so you can risk keeping some of your capital invested for growth. You may not get all the benefit but your heirs will.

The advice changes if you expect to spend most of your capital during your lifetime. During early retirement you still need stocks to increase the value of your capital and stay ahead of inflation. In late retirement, however, you can't afford the risk of a prolonged market downturn.

So take a look at your own statistical life expectancy in Appendix 11 (page 1025) and modify it by your own state of health and the age your parents died. Roughly five years before, consider selling your remaining stock-owning mutual funds and moving entirely to fixed-income investments. Sell stocks even earlier if your health is poor. Keep twelve months' worth of living expenses in a money market mutual fund. With the rest of your capital, build a ladder of short- and intermediate-term bonds or certificates of deposit (page 755). Spend all of the income from your bonds or CDs and as much principal as you need from each bond or CD that matures. The table on page 914 will help you determine how long your capital can last. If you own a house, you can always release that capital, too—by taking a reverse mortgage or selling and moving into an apartment or senior-citizen complex.

Near the end of your life, you shouldn't be saving money anymore. It's time to spend. These are the years you accumulated all those savings *for.*

31.

Retiring on the House

How to Tap the Equity You've Built

Your home is your piggy bank. You have only to shake it and money will fall out.

A lot of money rides on your house. It's usually your biggest asset. When you retire, should you pull out that money or leave it alone? If you pull it out, what's the best thing to do next?

These questions focus on where you'll live and how much debt you'll want to carry. The decision may ultimately be swung by things that have nothing to do with money: your health, community ties, the weather, where your kids live, and your feelings about the house you're in. But the money issue has sharpened now that so many people have seen housing prices fall for a period of time. Should you sell right now, while you know what your equity is worth? Or should you hang tight? Suddenly, in retirement, you've become a housing speculator.

SHOULD YOU MOVE?

Don't Move if you're happy in your house, can afford to keep it, and don't care if its value rises or falls. The money you have in home equities is not material to your welfare, at least not now. If you run short of cash sometime in the future, you can think of selling then.

But Move Sooner Rather Than Later if you want to live somewhere else and depend on the current value of your house to buy the new house or condo you want. Maybe your house will be worth more next year—but then again, maybe it won't. Move, too, if you know that you'll want to age in a smaller place. It's easier to clean out a big house while you still have your health.

Here's How to Make Money on a Move:

1. Go to a lower-cost part of the country. Not only will a new house or condominium cost less, but your other living expenses will usually be lower, too. That leaves you more money to invest for a higher retirement income.

2. Stay in your community but trade down to a smaller place. You'll pay less for taxes, insurance, and upkeep, and will have money left over to invest. Why be house-poor in retirement? Shake loose that cash and enjoy it, instead.

3. Sell your house and rent. Homeownership is generally best for long-term capital appreciation, but at this point in life that may not be your goal. If you're older, you might cash out of your house and invest the equity. It can probably cover rising rent for the rest of your life and leave you with extra money to live on.

4. Move to a lower-cost part of the world. Even when the dollar declines, it can be cheaper to live in certain countries abroad. Your pension and Social Security checks will follow you, but Medicare won't. So check the local health services and whether Blue Cross or another private policy will cover you both at home and abroad. Three other issues critical to expatriates are taxes (U.S. and foreign), the inheritance rules in the country you've moved to, and investments that hedge against a dollar decline.

5. If you're looking at continuing-care communities, see page 407.

The Government Practically Pays You to Move

Locked up in your house lies a beautiful pot of money, all of it reachable only if you decide to move. It's everything you paid into the house plus all of your gains over the years. Married couples can take up to $500,000 in profits untaxed; singles get up to $250,000.

In some states, counter–tax breaks may encourage you to stay. In California, for example, people who don't move pay lower property taxes than people who do. But that's the exception. For the majority of Americans, moving pays.

YOUR ALTERNATIVES TO MOVING

For many retirees, trading down to a less expensive house or condominium is so practical that it should top their list of retirement solutions. But if you want to hang on to your house despite the fact that money is short, you have several alternatives:

• You might take in a roommate or a boarder. A house too costly for one to maintain might be duck soup for two. Some mortgage lenders make special loans available to homeowners who want to add a senior-citizen apartment. But don't make a move without checking the following points: (1) Does your zoning allow you to take in boarders? (2) Are you subject to rent control, or are rent control laws on your town's agenda? If so, your tenant might gain the right to occupy that apartment forever, at a fixed or slowly rising rent. (3) Is the boarder covered by your liability insurance? (4) Have you taken a lesson in how business properties are taxed? For example, if you sell, you're taxed on the profit on the portion of your house that was used as a rental apartment. (5) Have you a written lease? Without one, you may have no grounds for evicting a bad tenant. (6) Do you have the temperament to be a landlord (page 828)?

• You might sell the home to one or more of your children and lease it back from them for life. Here's how that deal works: (1) The children give you a 10 or 20 percent down payment. (2) You give them a mortgage for the rest of the money they owe. (3) The children send you a mortgage payment every month. (4) You pay your children a monthly rent, which, at the start, is smaller than the mortgage payment you receive. So holding the mortgage adds to your income. (5) The children pay the insurance and taxes. For them, the house is a rental property, so the mortgage interest, taxes, insurance, and depreciation are all deductible business expenses. These deductions shelter their rental income and possibly some of their ordinary income, depending on how much money they make (see page 513). (6) The children see to maintenance and repairs, which for them are also tax deductible. You usually pay the utility bills.

Work out this transaction with a lawyer. The house price, mortgage interest rate, and current and future rent must all be set at fair market value or your children will lose their tax deductions. You have some risks with a sale/leaseback. What if your child gets a divorce and has to sell the house as part of a property settlement? What if you and your child have a fight and he or she tries to drive you into a nursing home? Remember King Lear. You can also do a sale/leaseback with an outside investor, but that's even riskier. Outsiders could push you hard if they wanted their money out.

• You might reduce expenses by using local programs available to low-income homeowners. For example, you may be able to defer your real-estate taxes or get a home-repair loan that needn't be repaid until your house is sold. Ask about these and other forms of financial assistance at your local senior-citizen center.

• If you own your house free and clear, you might give it to a charity or an educational institution. Talk to the charity about the kinds of arrangements it will make. You'll get an immediate tax deduction and the right to live in the house for life. You pay the real-estate taxes, insurance, and maintenance. At your death (and the death of your spouse, if the gift covers both of you), the house passes to the charity. This solution pays the most if you're older and your tax bracket is high.

• You might take a reverse mortgage.

Reverse Mortgages: Money from Home

Reverse mortgages (also known as home-equity conversions) have been a long time coming, but now you generally have a choice between at least two programs and sometimes more.* Don't buy from a salesperson who shows you only one. You might get a much better deal somewhere else.

Reverse Mortgages, Defined:

These loans let you tap most of the cash you've invested in your house, without having to move. They're for older people—typically 75 and up—with small incomes and a life more pinched than it ought to be. Different lenders offer different programs, but generally speaking, the deal works like this:

1. A lender agrees to make you a loan against the value of your house. How much you can borrow has nothing to do with your income or credit history. It depends entirely on your age, the age of your spouse, how much equity you have in your house, and which reverse-mortgage program you choose.

For example, say you're a 75-year-old widow. Your paid-up home is worth $100,000 and the loan interest rate is 7.5 percent. A loan backed by a Federal Housing Administration (FHA) lender might give you $350 a month for as long as you live in the house. If you took out the loan at 85, you might get $580 a month.

2. You can take the money in one of several ways: a check a month, a fixed number of checks, a lump sum, or a credit line that you can draw against at will. Borrowers especially like the credit line because it lets them use money as needed.

3. When you choose monthly checks, you'll usually get them for as long as you live in the house. So how much you borrow is dictated by how long you stay there. Some plans will pay you an income for life no matter where you live.

---

* In Texas, they'll carry more restrictions than in other states.

4. You pay little or no cash up front. All closing and insurance costs are included in the loan.

5. You pay no interest currently on the money you borrow. The interest compounds, to be paid off when the loan is settled.

6. When you die or leave your house, the loan comes due. Depending on the mortgage terms, the lenders might also be owed a piece of the home's appreciation or current value. Typically, the money is raised by selling the house. When the mortgage is paid, anything left over goes to you or your heirs.

7. You might get so many checks that you wind up owing more than the house is worth. In that case, the lender normally swallows the loss (but ask about this before signing up).

Each check looks and feels like income. But it isn't income, it's a loan. So it doesn't raise your income tax or reduce the size of your Social Security check. Nor will it hinder your access to programs for the low-income elderly in most states, as long as you borrow only enough to cover your expenses each month.

The Rewards:

- With most reverse mortgages, you can stay in your home as long as you're able, thanks to the income they supply.
- The checks help you finance home health care, which may keep you out of a nursing home.
- The money also helps you keep the house in good repair.

The Risks:

- A reverse mortgage may seduce you into keeping your house when you shouldn't. It might be wiser to sell your house and move to an apartment, condominium, or senior-citizen home. Consider these options first and a reverse mortgage second.
- You pay huge effective rates of interest if you leave your house soon after taking out the loan. That's because you pay closing costs and other fees up front while receiving the loan balance gradually, over time. Even over time, this loan is relatively expensive.
- When you quit the house, you may have little or no equity left. How will you finance new housing or home health expenses? So as not to lose everything, consider a credit line and draw on it lightly.
- For young retirees, the monthly checks are far too small. Don't even consider this loan until you're 75 or older.
- Some lenders offer fixed-term loans lasting anywhere from 3 to 10 years. Such loans may make sense if you're already wait-listed for a senior-citizen apartment, will move in with a child, or believe you won't outlive the loan. If these expectations fail, however, you'll be forced from your

home before you're ready. In general, you should stick with loans of indefinite term.

• You may misunderstand the loan's permanence. A "lifetime" loan doesn't necessarily last a lifetime. It lasts only as long as you stay in your home. The contract defines the end of that term and you should study its every nuance. Can you spend three months in a nursing home and then return? Can you be evicted if the lender believes that the property isn't being well kept?

Reverse Mortgages When You Move

You can buy a new home, pay for part of it in cash, and take a reverse mortgage for the rest of the price. That preserves some of your personal savings and lets you live without mortgage payments. The reverse loan doesn't come due until you leave the house. As I write, this loan is available only from lenders working with Fannie Mae (the Federal National Mortgage Association); eventually, others may offer it, too. Borrowers have to be at least 62, but the loan makes more financial sense for people who are older than that. Skip the loan, however, if you think you'll sell this house and move to another one. Reverse mortgages cost too much if they're held for only a few years.

How to Get the Best Deal:

1. Be sure to compare at least two programs—one from the FHA and one backed by Fannie Mae. On straight loans, FHA lenders usually pay the most. Fannie Mae lenders pay more, however, if you'll surrender up to 10 percent of the value of your home. Other programs lend larger amounts to people who have expensive homes. By choosing the right lender, you can get tens of thousands of dollars more.

2. When comparing reverse mortgages, look at the Total Annual Loan Cost (TALC)—your true, effective rate of interest. It includes every single fee you pay and all the lenders supposedly calculate it in an identical way. TALC rates are important because other ways of comparing these loans don't tell you a lot. For example, FHA loans carry an up-front insurance fee, which makes them look more expensive than the credit lines offered by private lenders. But credit lines typically carry higher interest rates, which make them more costly in the end. The TALC will tell.

3. If you want a credit line, consider the FHA program. Its credit line increases until you use it up. TransAmerica's line increases, too, but not as fast.

4. Think about whether you really need to borrow this money. Under federal law, you have to be counseled first and the counselor is required to show you alternatives. If you need money only for home repairs, a local program may provide it. You may be better off selling your house and moving to something smaller.

5. Beware of insurance agents who urge you to borrow a large lump sum and use the money to buy the lifetime annuities they sell. If you need a monthly income, you can get it from the mortgage alone, as long as you live in the house. If you want monthly payments that last for life, consider the annuity sold by The Hartford in conjunction with the FHA and Fannie Mae programs. All its terms, conditions, and costs are spelled out. It's also figured into the TALC rate so you can judge the total cost of your decision (broker-sold annuities should also be put in the TALC rate, but aren't). Other reverse-mortgage lenders may offer annuities of their own.

Some heartless insurance agents sell seniors on the reverse-mortgage concept, then charge them 8 to 10 percent of the loan amount for disclosing a lender's name. The agent might also go with you to the required counseling session. That's to ensure that you choose the lump-sum payout, so you'll have enough cash to buy the annuity. To try to stop this disreputable practice, most lenders won't deal with the clients these agents bring in.

HOW TO FIND A
REVERSE-MORTGAGE LENDER

• Write to the nonprofit National Center for Home Equity Conversion, Suite 115, 7373 147 St. W, Apple Valley, MN 55121. Send $1 and a stamped, self-addressed, business-size envelope and ask for NCHEC Preferred. You'll get a list of all the reverse-mortgage lenders and counselors who have agreed to abide by the NCHEC's code of ethics. That includes showing you every available program to see which suits you best and refusing to deal with any referrer who charges outrageous fees.

• Call the U.S. Department of Housing and Urban Development toll-free at 888-HOME-4-US. It will send a free list of approved reverse-mortgage counselors and the names of lenders who offer the Home Equity Conversion Mortgage, the loan insured by the FHA. How much you can borrow depends on the value of your home and what part of the country you live in. In 1997 the maximum home equity used to determine the loan ranged from $81,584 to $160,950.

• Call 800-7-FANNIE. It will send you the names of lenders who use Fannie Mae's Home Keeper Mortgage. Maximum home equity used in 1997: $214,600. At this writing, it's available in all but a handful of states. Fannie's most popular program is the "equity share," because it gives you the largest amount of money. But on the first day of the third year, your loan balance rises by 10 percent of the value of your house. That makes for an expensive loan, unless you stay in your house beyond your life expectancy.

• Three other programs are available in a limited number of states. They'll lend even more than Fannie Mae if your house is worth it, but the fees and TALC rates are generally higher. Call Household Senior Services,

800-414-3837; Transamerica HomeFirst, 800-538-5569; or Financial Freedom, 888-500-5151 (at this writing, in California only).

• A few states make limited-term reverse mortgages, lasting perhaps 7 to 12 years. When the term is up, your loan has to be repaid—generally meaning that you'll have to sell the house. These loans cost less than the other plans and are helpful in limited circumstances: for example, if you need home health care while waiting for a place in a nursing home. Some public-housing agencies also offer limited-term loans, usually to low-income homeowners for specific purposes such as paying taxes or keeping the house in good repair.

For an excellent free booklet explaining reverse mortgages, send for *Home-Made Money, a Consumer's Guide to Home Equity Conversion* (Stock #D12894, from the American Association of Retired Persons, Fulfillment EE01153, 601 E St., N.W., Washington, DC 20049).

CONTEMPLATING THE PAID-UP HOUSE

If you have enough cash to pay off the mortgage, should you or shouldn't you? This is one of those questions that can only be answered, "It depends."

If you're rolling in money, pay off the loan. A paid-up house stabilizes your living costs, saves you interest payments, and makes you feel secure. You don't give a hoot about locking up capital because you have all the income you need.

If the money you're rolling in happens to earn more than your mortgage interest rate, you might decide to keep the loan. But even in these situations, you might pay off your mortgage just for the pleasure of it.

If you are definitely *not* rolling in money, hang on to your mortgage. If you pay off the loan, your precious liquidity will be lost. You'll be house rich but cash poor. You might even be forced to sell the house just to get your capital back out. For you, paying interest on a mortgage is the price of financial flexibility.

If you paid off the mortgage and regret it, you can (1) try for a home-equity credit line from your bank (hard to get, however, if your income is small); (2) sell your house, buy something smaller, and add the extra capital to your bank account; (3) consider a reverse mortgage.

SHOULD YOU RENT OR OWN?

When you retire, security is what matters most. You want an easy style of life you can afford. If your present house is eating up too much of your income, you have two choices: (1) Trade down to something smaller, perhaps in a cheaper part of the country. That will free up spending money. (2) Sell your house, invest the proceeds for a higher retirement income, and rent an apartment.

To figure out which way is best, estimate the net sum of money you'd have on hand if you sold your present house. Count your current savings and investments, plus the proceeds of the home sale. Call that your kitty. Then make the following comparisons.

If You Buy a New House:

1. Reduce your kitty by the amount you'd invest in the house. Do this calculation two ways—once assuming a mortgage and once assuming that you paid cash. Estimate how much income you would get from your remaining kitty, after tax.

2. Add up your monthly housing expenses—principally mortgage (if any), taxes, insurance, utilities, and a reserve for repairs. If you itemize on your tax return, subtract the value of the deduction for mortgage interest and real-estate taxes. These are your net housing expenses.

3. Subtract your net housing expenses from the monthly income your kitty throws off. If the kitty won't cover all your costs, subtract the remaining expenses from the rest of your after-tax retirement income (Social Security, pension). What's left is the net you have to live on without dipping into capital.

If You Rent:

1. Estimate how much income you would get from your kitty, after tax.

2. Add up your monthly housing expenses—principally rent, utilities, and insurance.

3. Subtract your expenses from the income the kitty throws off. If it won't cover your housing costs, subtract the remaining expenses from the rest of your after-tax retirement income. What's left is the net you have to live on.

Other Considerations:

This rough comparison tells you which choice will give you a higher income right now. But it leaves things out. On the homeowning side of the ledger, your house might rise in value, which would provide more equity for your later years. Young retirees might want to own; older retirees might want to rent. Furthermore, homeowners' costs are pretty stable. Real-estate taxes may rise, but that increase is small compared with the potential rise in rents.

On the renter's side of the ledger lies a much larger pool of capital, thanks to all the money that was liberated from the house. With wise investing, that capital might gain more in value than if it were still tied up in home equities. Rents will probably rise every year or so. But you can cover them with your investment gains or with that extra capital you have on tap.

So the question of renting vs. owning also gets answered: "It depends." Work out the numbers and see how you feel about it.

THE PIGGY BANK

Older people count themselves lucky if they enter retirement with a home, especially a paid-up home. It's worth the effort when you're young if it points you toward freedom as you age.

STEP 8

MAKING IT WORK

This book, I hope, has been moving you to pick up the phone and make decisions. First you have to study and learn, but then you have to follow up. A plan that stays in your head is a daydream. What adds to your wealth are the actions you take and whether you manage to take them in time.

At the end of this chapter, you'll find the broad principles that give shape to financial plans. Tackle them one after the other. Flesh them out with safe and sane financial products (many of which I've named in this book). You'll get more ideas as you go along.

Occasionally, your goals will change, as successes and mistakes refine your knowledge of yourself. But having made one plan, you can easily make more and better ones. No activity is more comforting than drawing a circle around your finances and pronouncing them sound.

32.

Be Your Own Planner

The Secret, Revealed

You've been waiting for thirty-one chapters for the secret to handling money well. Here it is. Use common sense. The simplest choices are the best ones. Impulse is your enemy, time your friend.

Most of us don't need professional financial planners. We don't even need a full-scale plan. Conservative money management isn't hard! To be your own guru, you need only a list of objectives, a few simple financial products, realistic investment expectations, a time frame that gives your investments time to work out, and a well-tempered humbug detector, to keep you from falling for rascally sales pitches. Don't put off decisions for fear you're not making the best choice in every circumstance. Often, there isn't a "best" choice. Any one of several will work.

Occasionally, however, you do want an expert opinion—usually to address a narrow question. I can think of a handful of circumstances when you might seek help from an accountant or professional planner.

1. You earn good wages but cannot manage to save a dime. You need a reality check. Someone has to show you—in dollars and cents—how little you'll have when you retire unless you shape up. Most of us shape ourselves up. But if you can't, get help.

2. You face a question that can't be answered without some technical expertise. For example, your company may have made a general early-retirement offer and you want to examine your alternatives. Or you're

retiring and have several choices about how to handle the money in your retirement plan. That's a one-time decision with many tax and personal ramifications, and you want to get it right.

3. You're following your own plan—for savings, investments, and insurance—and wonder if an expert can improve it. Arrange for a meeting at an hourly fee. Make it clear that you want to talk about strategies and concepts, not sit through a sales pitch for financial products. Make no decisions until you've gone home and thought about it.

4. You have a substantial amount of money and lack the time to manage it yourself.

A talk with a planner will have one of three results: (1) You'll find a wonderful adviser who makes suggestions you're grateful for and whom you'll decide to work with. (2) You'll feel more confident that your personal decisions have been good ones and will continue managing your affairs yourself. (3) You'll run into a planner who makes you doubt your competence while urging you to rely on his or her advice. In that last case, turn up the volume on your humbug detector. You may need to be saved from buying the high-cost products the planner is poised to sell.

Don't go near a planner if you've just come into a lot of money (an inheritance, an insurance settlement, a lump-sum retirement payout) and don't know what to do with it. Clients with loose cash and weak convictions are fresh meat, ready for roasting. A self-interested planner may urge you to buy high-commission investments that serve his or her objectives better than yours. Because you don't know much about investing, you won't know what's going on.

Before you set foot in the office of a stockbroker, insurance agent, or financial planner, learn the basics yourself. Sock your money into bank certificates of deposit or a money market fund, then study up. Read books. Join an investment club. Take all the time you need to understand the tried-and-true principles of successful investing. Six months, one year, the wait doesn't matter. During that time your money will quietly earn interest with no risk of loss. The only expert that a novice can safely visit is a certified public accountant who doesn't sell financial products. The accountant can advise you on taxes, answer technical questions about budgets and finance, and make some general suggestions as to how to allocate your money. Should you pay off debt? Raise your standard of living? Set aside a college fund?

When you're ready to invest, try it yourself—a little in this mutual fund, a little in that one. Give it a year, see how it feels, then invest some more. You'll make better decisions by taking pains.

Once you've had some experience with investing, consider shopping for a financial adviser. You now know the language. You should be able to tell the difference between good and poor advice. That's what this long apprenticeship was for: to develop your ability to judge.

The Best Thing a Planner Can Do for You: Help you set realistic objectives for spending, saving, and investing. Picking mutual funds is incidental compared with designing the framework that achieves your ends.

WHICH KIND OF PROFESSIONAL TO SEE

See A Certified Public Accountant—for tax planning, budget planning, small-business planning advice, and long-term income and savings projections. Some CPAs have expanded their practice into personal financial planning (page 959). *Enrolled agents,* who are licensed to represent you before the IRS, and licensed *public accountants* also have tax practices.

See a Tax Attorney—for wills and estate planning.

See an Insurance Agent or Fee-Only Life-Insurance Planner—for an insurance policy, although some life-insurance policies you can buy yourself. A Chartered Life Underwriter (CLU) knows more about insurance than the average agent. Your attorney and insurance planner should work together if you want a policy to help pay estate taxes or buy your share of a closely held business.

See a Stockbroker or Call a Discount Broker—to buy stocks and bonds. Mutual funds you can buy yourself, although brokers do this, too. Many brokerage firms will also find you an investment adviser (typically, for sums of $200,000 and up). The fee will be stiffer than if you found the adviser yourself (page 955).

See a Financial Planner—for advice on how your finances fit together: budgeting, saving, taxes, insurance, investing, and retirement planning. Some planners also manage your money for a fee, usually investing it in no-load mutual funds. To qualify for money-management services, you'll probably need an investment account in the $100,000 to $200,000 range. You can manage smaller sums youself, based on your personal reading and suggestions from planners who charge by the hour.

See an Investment Adviser—for help with managing a large sum of money. Most advisers specialize in investing and set minimums in the $250,000 to $500,000 range. Unlike planners, they don't handle other aspects of personal finance. Some planners are capable investment advisers, many others aren't.

See a Bank Trust Department—for handling a trust for dependents after your death, but go there only if you have no other choice. A few trust departments have stellar investment records, but many are mediocre, with customer service I'd call languid, at best. Believe it or not, banks may not even provide true performance reports. Your annual report will show where your money is located. But it may not disclose your trust's percentage gain or loss compared with standard stock and bond indexes. Look at a sample report before signing up. Minimum trust: in the $100,000 to $200,000 range, depending on the institution. Big brokerage firms are bidding for trust business, too.

See the Materials Offered by the Major No-Load Mutual Fund Groups —for useful advice about allocating assets. They often have newsletters explaining different kinds of investments and helping do-it-yourselfers with college or retirement planning.

See What's Around in Financial Software—for developing a financial plan yourself. One such that I worked on: *Quicken Financial Planner.*

Don't Look for a Universal Expert. No one can handle every aspect of financial planning well. A good planner helps you decide what to do, supplies whatever piece of the plan falls under his or her expertise, then directs you to specialists for the rest.

WHAT ABOUT "THE PLAN"?

Among most financial planners, The Plan is out of style. In theory, it's your starting point: a comprehensive tome—part personalized, part boilerplate—that analyzes everything you've done so far and points to additions and changes that you ought to make. In professional hands, true plans cost a lot of money—typically $2,000 to $6,000. Clients haven't wanted to pay.

So most plans today amount to sales tools, promoted by stockbrokers, insurance agents, and planners who primarily sell products. The cost: anywhere from $250 to $1,500. You fill in a questionnaire about your finances; back comes a computer-generated program telling you what you lack. The analysis may well produce some good ideas. On the other hand, GIGO often rules—garbage in, garbage out. The program is designed to sell, not to explore alternatives. The questionnaire might not even consider your best investment options—for example, adding more money to your tax-deductible 401(k). The broker would rather you spent the money on products he or she has for sale.

As an experiment, I once purchased several of these commercial plans. My question to each salesperson was, "How much should I be saving for retirement?" The plans came up with radically different answers. You simply cannot trust them to provide the guidance you need.

What if you pay $500 or $1,000 for what turns out to be an unsuitable plan? Some clients execute it anyway (or at least part of it) because they don't want to "waste" the money they've already spent. That attitude plays into the planner's hands. I say: Walk away. You're lucky that you've lost only the fee you paid up front and not all the rest of the money that might have followed.

When you work with a genuine planner, not a salesperson in disguise, a plan will probably evolve. Initially, you may get a mini-plan addressing the question you came to ask—for example, "Am I saving enough for retirement?" or "What should I do with the money I've inherited?" If you keep working with that planner, you'll gradually address other issues and a full-fledged blueprint will emerge. Some planners still urge you to start with a blueprint. Such a plan may include a year of consulting on any financial issue that comes along.

If your finances don't yet require this level of service, do your own plan, using computer software or your trusty yellow pad. You'll find plenty of guidelines in the earlier chapters of this book. Define your financial objectives, spending options, strategy for debt repayment, fallback positions, and investment goals. Work out how much you ought to be saving for retirement and implement your program with suitable mutual funds. It's important to write everything down. In your head, a plan is only a vague hope that things will turn out well. On paper, it's an action project that can be tested against your progress every year.

THE PLANNER PROBLEM

In theory, a financial planner is a one-stop money pro. This paragon knows a little something about everything. He or she will uncover your past financial crimes, help you formulate new goals, and draw a map to get you there. Under a planner's loving care, your scattered savings and investments will blend miraculously into a blueprint for a prosperous future (background music: trumpets, crashing cymbals, tonic chords).

Sometimes that even happens.

More often it doesn't. There's a lot of bad advice out there.

The majority of planners are delivery systems for prepackaged financial products. They make their living selling insurance policies, tax-deferred annuities, unit trusts, loaded mutual funds, and other high-commission investments. They may give you very good advice. On the other hand, they cannot escape the taint of bias. Most planners have to sell or starve.

Horror stories abound: life insurance policies sold on 2-year-olds, limited partnerships sold to elderly retirees, "pension maximization" plans that will backfire on widows. All the caveats that I've written about stockbrokers also apply to financial planners, and in spades.

Planners who charge fees instead of commissions have no compulsion to sell. But that doesn't guarantee that they'll give you good advice. And they sure would like to manage your money, whether they're skilled enough or not.

Conflicts of interest lie everywhere. Nevertheless, there are lots of white hats in this profession who can make good suggestions and turn your messy finances into a model of organization. The trick is to find them.

HOW FINANCIAL PLANNERS ARE PAID

There are five ways for planners to make a living:

1. *Commission only.* These planners don't make a cent unless they sell you something that carries a sales commission. They lean toward high-commission products (page 665), which presents a tremendous conflict of interest.

2. *Fee and commission.* This is probably the most common arrangement. The planner charges a fee for certain services—for example, for drawing a simple plan—and also earns commissions on any products you buy. Commissions may or may not be deducted from the planning fees.

But make no mistake about it: Sales commissions are the driving force and produce the same biases you see in commission-only planners. About half the planners disclose their commissions to clients, according to a study by the Securities and Exchange Commission. The rest leave you in the dark unless you press for information.

You can get wise advice from a competent fee-and-commission planner. But in judging any proposed investment, keep in mind that it serves the planner's needs as well as yours. The bias toward high-commission products is easy to spot. More subtle is the bias to sell you *something* in cases where nothing would have served.

3. *Fee offset.* These planners set a fixed fee for their advice. You might pay by the hour, the job, or the month. If the planner manages your money, you'll pay a fixed percentage of assets. The products can be either load or no-load, but any sales commissions earned are subtracted from your fee. So in theory the planner has no incentive to lean toward high-commission stuff. Either way, you pay the same. (But he or she might slip in load products if you grumble about the fees.)

4. *Fee only.* These planners charge only for their advice, accepting no other form of remuneration. As with fee-offset planners, their fee structures vary—hourly charges, monthly or quarterly retainers, fees per job, or a percentage of the money they have under management. The products they sell are entirely no-load—meaning that no sales commissions are attached. Of all the financial-consulting arrangements, this is the cleanest.

But fee-only planners have conflicts of interest, too. Say, for example, that you're leaving your job and have money invested in the company's

401(k). You can leave it there or roll it into an Individual Retirement Account. Often, it's best to leave the money where it is. But if the planner can persuade you to switch to the IRA, he or she will probably get the money to manage, at a fee of perhaps one to 1.5 percent a year. You have to be on your toes when evaluating *any* planner's advice.

Some fee-only planners, especially certified public accountants, sell no products at all. They give you advice, then turn you loose. That's not too helpful, unless you can implement the plan yourself. Otherwise, you'll pay double: once for the plan and again for the services of a stockbroker or insurance agent (who may change the plan).

5. *Salary and bonus (or commission).* This is more typical for planners who work at banks. They may also act as agents for insurance companies. In either case, they generally sell commissionable mutual funds and tax-deferred annuities.

Incidentally, fees charged for tax and investment advice can be written off on your income-tax return. They're part of that bagful of miscellaneous expenses that are deductible to the extent that they exceed 2 percent of your adjusted gross income. Sales commissions, however, are not deductible up front; they're used to reduce your taxable profits when you sell.

Some Planners Claim to Be Fee-Only When They Aren't. They'll offer certain services for a fee, such as money management or a financial plan. But they'll also sell commission products, which can bias their advice. Check their ADVs (page 957) or state registration forms. If they sell commission products, it will say.

Which type of planner is more expensive—one who charges sales commissions or one who charges fees?

Superficially, straight-fee or fee-offset planners seem more expensive. You pay more for The Plan, if you want one. You pay hourly fees for analysis and advice (usually in the $75 to $200 range) or maybe quarterly retainers. Often, you're charged a fixed percentage of the money the planner manages for you (commonly 0.5 to one percent a year, with a top of 1.5 percent). What you don't pay are sales commissions. Any products that the planner buys will be no-load (no-sales-charge).

By contrast, fee-and-commission planners might charge $250 to $1,500 for The Plan, if they bother with one at all. That's often the only payment you will make out of pocket. The rest of the planner's compensation is indirect: from sales charges or charges subtracted from your investments. Because you don't write separate checks to pay the commissions, you may not realize how large they are. Ask the planner how much he or she will earn on every product sold. When you add them together, you may discover that commission planners are actually more expensive than planners who charge only fees. They're especially expensive if they sell you products you don't really need.

Nothing is free, even services that look free. If you want financial advice, you'll have to pay for it. But different systems of payment carry different incentives. Commissions encourage people to sell. Fees encourage people to be good enough to persuade you their advice has value.

When shopping for a planner, try first for one with a fee-only or fee-offset practice who works on specific problems for a flat fee or hourly rate. The National Association of Personal Financial Advisors (NAPFA) has names (page 962). But some of those planners work only with wealthier clients, so you may have to call around. If you can't find a satisfactory NAPFA member, try the International Association for Financial Planning (IAFP— page 962); most of its members work for commissions but some work for fees.

If you choose a fee-and-commission planner, discuss what you need, ask for a flat fee or hourly rate, and suggest that if you buy any products, the planner deduct the commission from the fee. That way, the planner gets paid for his or her time, whether you buy anything or not. If the commission will obviously exceed the fee, however, the planner will still be motivated to find products for you to buy. Ask what the commissions are. *Every* planner, fee- or commission-paid, should be willing to disclose.

Whoever you work with, accept only advice that makes sense to you. If you're not sure about the investments the planner presents, you have only to mumble and hesitate until the session is over. Don't say yes when you're undecided. Never say yes under pressure, even of the most jovial sort. If you think you'd like to work with a particular planner but are a cautious type, start small. Add to your investment as you gain confidence in the planner's M.O.

THE BACKGROUND CHECK

At this writing, the public disclosure that's required of planners is a mixed bag. Here are the rules for planners who give investment advice:
- *Firms that handle $25 million or more in assets* have to register with the Securities and Exchange Commission (SEC).
- *Firms that handle less than $25 million* normally register with the states. In states that don't require it (at this writing, Colorado, Ohio, Iowa, and Wyoming), they register with the SEC.
- *Individual planners* are regulated by the states, including planners working for the larger firms. At this writing, just 31 states require them to register. But their firms are all registered somewhere—either with the SEC or with the state. If the principal planner *is* the business, the firm's own registration tells you what you need to know.
- *What registration means.* The planning firm has to make various

disclosures. Firms filing with the SEC fill in Form ADV (for "adviser"), Parts 1 and 2. Part 1 is for the regulators. Part 2 is for the public. It lists the planning firm's services and investment methods, the education and business background of the principals, and the way customers are charged. At this writing, it's being expanded to include arbitrations and customer complaints. New customers have to be given a copy of the ADV Part 2 or a brochure containing the same information. Ongoing clients have to receive an updated copy every year.

Planning firms also file a Schedule D for each individual adviser, giving the details of his or her background and disciplinary history, if any. The firm doesn't have to give you the Schedule D. By law, it has only to tell you about any disciplinary actions taken against your planner. But I wouldn't do business with a firm that didn't release the Schedule Ds.

Most states have an equivalent ADV form with similar disclosures for the firms they regulate. The 31 states that register planners require them to demonstrate some minimal knowledge, such as an acquaintance with state and federal securities laws. The states may also have some operating requirements, such as bonding, minimum amounts of net capital, and rules on maintaining books and records.

Check what's checkable on the ADV (education, prior employment), to see if the planner is on the square. The regulators have no idea whether these documents tell the truth.

If the planner has no state or federal ADV and is giving you investment advice, he or she is breaking the law. That's not someone you should be working with.

• *The black holes.* There are three. (1) States may not have the budget or the will to enforce their own securities laws. (2) In the 19 states that don't license planners, anyone can enter the field without demonstrating even minimal knowledge. (3) When states license a planner, they have no easy way of discovering whether he or she has a disciplinary record in another state.

At this writing, both the states and the SEC are working on ways of setting up hot line and Web connections to give regulators and consumers easy access to state and federal ADVs. The states that license planners may eventually require each of them to have a full CRD (page 655). If that happens, you'll be able to check a list of planners without making a lot of telephone calls.

SIXTEEN WAYS OF LOOKING FOR A PLANNER

There's no easy way of finding a good planner. As in any other field, competence ranges from brilliant to dim. You can probably spot the dim, but working with mediocrities is risky, too. They may steer you wrong because they don't see all the angles of the questions you pose or understand the risks in some of the products they sell so enthusiastically.

Here are some ways of finding a planner who's really good:

1. Turn back to page 651, where I list ways of finding a stockbroker. Most of those rules will also help you find a good financial planner, so I won't repeat them here.

2. In the initial phone call, tell the planner why you're seeking help and what services you need. For money management, ask about the minimum account. If there seems to be a fit, ask for written material about the firm, including the state or federal ADV. Read it before deciding to set up an interview. Don't settle for just the firm's brochure. Say you want to see the real ADV.

3. In the written material, check out the planner's educational background. Here's what you want to see:

• *Higher education.* A college degree is a reasonable proxy for a mind that can tackle complex issues.

• *Evidence of planning expertise.* Some schools give certificates in financial planning, most notably the College for Financial Planning in Denver (the Certified Financial Planner designation, or CFP) and the American Institute of Certified Public Accountants (the Personal Financial Specialist designation, or PFS). A number of colleges and universities give finance or financial-planning degrees. The American College in Bryn Mawr, Pennsylvania, gives a Chartered Financial Consultant designation, or ChFC. It identifies insurance agents who have studied financial planning with an emphasis on using life insurance products.

All these diplomas attest that the planner has passed a number of exams in such areas as taxes, insurance, investments, and estate planning. But degrees and certificates are only a starting point. They don't say whether a particular planner is any good.

• *No kidding around.* If the business card says "financial planner," look for the CFP or PFS designation. If they're not there, you could be dealing with anyone: a stockbroker in hiding, an insurance agent with pretensions. You can tell who they are by the products they advise you to buy. People calling themselves "retirement planners" often are insurance agents. "Financial consultant," "registered representative," or "investment broker" means stockbroker. None of these salespeople are planners in the sense you seek.

4. Call your state securities commission to see if your planner has a record at the Central Registration Depository (CRD—page 655). If so, get a copy. It will show the planner's past employment, reasons for leaving every job, infractions of various sorts, and any customer complaints. For the number of the state commission, call the North American Securities Administrators Association, 202-737-0900. At this writing, the states that license

advisers plan to require them all to report to the CRD, or a similar entity, at some point in the future.

One hitch: Firms don't always forward customer complaints to the CRD, as the rules require. If you make a complaint, send a copy to your state securities commission and the National Association of Securities Dealers, if the adviser is a member. They'll see that it's filed properly.

5. Draw up a short list of planners to speak with in person. The opening interview should be free. Take a financial statement with you, showing your assets and liabilities, to give the planner a general idea of what he or she will have to do.

6. Ask about the planner's professional background. The basics should have been in the written material, but ask about previous employers and occupations. You want someone who has been practicing financial planning for 10 years or more, preferably at the same firm. Skip any new kids on the block, including career switchers who have been practicing for only a couple of years. Also skip any planner who hops around from firm to firm.

7. Ask what kinds of clients the planner has. Firms often specialize— in doctors, entrepreneurs, entertainers, teachers, or young, upper-middle-income families. The more experience the planner has with people like you, the better.

8. What are the planner's special areas of expertise? Which lawyers, accountants, or other specialists are on tap, and will they all give you a discount? If the planner will manage your money, how did he or she acquire the skill? How are investments chosen and followed? There are a lot of amateurs running money today.

9. Think about what the planner asks *you*. He or she should inquire not only into your finances but also your family, feelings about money, general knowledge of investments, personal goals, and way of life. Since you can't do everything, what are your priorities? If you're married, your spouse should attend at least the initial meeting and the planner should elicit his or her feelings, too. Planners who don't seem interested in you won't give you the best advice. You might take a list of objectives to the initial meeting and ask how the planner would approach them, one by one.

10. Think about how the planner answers the questions you pose. Does he or she seem open, straightforward, comfortable with issues, friendly, willing to explain? If the chemistry isn't right, the relationship won't work, no matter how bright the planner is. If you have any reservations, raise them on the spot, to see what the planner has to say.

11. Ask for the names of 5 clients you can speak with, who have been with the planner for at least 3 years. If you're refused, take your business somewhere else. When offered the names, don't fail to call. Ask how the planner is to work with, any problems they see, and how much better off they are, thanks to what the planner did.

12. If the planner will manage your money, discuss investment philosophy and approach. Also look at the performance reports that clients get. They should show the period's total, annualized return, net of all fees and expenses, compared with several standard indexes: Standard & Poor's 500-stock index, the Russell 2000 index of smaller stocks, the Lehman Brothers Aggregate Bond Index, 90-day Treasury bills, and consumer price inflation. That helps investors keep track of their progress relative to the rest of the world. Younger people might want to try to keep up with the S&P. Older people might be content with double the inflation rate.

13. Don't pick a planner just because he or she is quoted in the newspapers. Reporters are looking for quotes and comment and rarely check on whether the planners are any good. Courting the press is one way planners advertise.

14. Don't pick a planner just because he or she gives investment seminars. That's advertising, too. A San Francisco planner, Lawrence Krause, once told his trade secrets to the magazine *CALUnderwriter:* "You don't have to know as much as you think you have to know in running a seminar. All you have to know is more than your audience, and your audience doesn't know your subject. . . . You also have to remember that you're not there to educate. You're there to sell. The purpose of a seminar is twofold: one, to confuse your audience; and two, to create dependence. . . . As long as you are going to confuse them, do a good job of it. Then you ask for the order, so that they'll come to see you afterward."

Now you know.

15. Ask the planner, "How are you paid?" This question is critical. A planner should hand over a schedule that discloses his or her compensation in full. Planning fees, hourly fees, quarterly retainers, the sales commissions on various products (front-, middle-, back-end, and renewal commissions), continuing fees from the firms that package the financial products the planner sells, fees from the lawyers or accountants he or she refers you to, fees for managing money.

Ask specifically what percentage of the firm's income comes from commissions on insurance products and annuities; how much from stocks, bonds, and mutual funds; how much from direct fees. That tells you where the planner's interests lie. If 60 percent of the income comes from insurance products, for example, you have an insurance agent.

If the planner claims not to know where all the income comes from, he or she is either fibbing or running a lousy business. Either way, you don't want to deal.

16. Get a written list of the services you'll get and what they're likely to cost. You might not be given this on the spot. The planner may want to think about it. Also find out how you terminate the relationship. You should be free to quit at any time, with nothing owed beyond the end of the current month.

For the Names of Local Planners to Interview to add to any personal recommendations you already have, plus assorted advice on choosing a planner, contact:

• The National Association of Personal Financial Advisors (NAPFA), 355 West Dundee Rd., Suite 200, Buffalo Grove, IL 60089 (800-FEE-ONLY or http://www.napfa.org). All members charge straight fees, taking no commissions or kickbacks for business referrals. They work solely with no-load products.

• The American Institute of Certified Public Accountants' Personal Financial Planning Division, 1211 Avenue of the Americas, New York, NY 10036 (800-862-4272). Ask for product G00616, a free list of CPAs who have taken the courses needed to become a Personal Financial Specialist. Most PFSs charge only fees, but some earn sales commissions on products they sell. So ask about it.

• The International Association for Financial Planning (IAFP), Suite B-300, 5775 Glenridge Drive NE, Atlanta, GA 30328 (toll-free 888-806-PLAN or http://www.iafp.org). Most of its members charge sales commissions, but you can request the names of planners who will work on a fee basis (they're not true fee planners, however, unless they charge only fees). You can also ask for planners who specialize in certain areas, such as estate planning or investments.

• The Institute of Certified Financial Planners, 3801 E. Florida Ave., #708, Denver, CO 80231 (800-282-PLAN or http://www.icfp.org). It gives you the names of planners with CFP designations. A majority charge sales commissions, but some work on a fee basis or charge only fees.

Whatever the source, follow the same rule: check 'em out, check 'em out, check 'em all out!

If You Have a Quick Question: Call Money Minds (800-275-2272), a firm that sells no financial products but answers tax and planning questions by phone for a fee of $3.95 a minute (calls typically run for 4 to 12 minutes). I once tested this service and got helpful answers to the everyday questions I posed. For investment advice that requires research, you're charged $125 an hour.

For a Character Check Beyond the CRD: Call the National Financial Fraud Exchange in Reston, Virginia (800-822-0416). For $39, NAFEX will run the name of the adviser you're considering through its database of people with dubious records. The names are collected from some 100 government and private watchdogs, and include both real-estate and financial transactions. This check might pick up an infraction in another state that your own state securities commission doesn't know about. There are two gaps in NAFEX: it doesn't cover insurance agents or track court cases unless they're reported by a government agency.

WHEN A PLANNER DOES YOU WRONG

In the largely unregulated industry of financial planning, no formal body sets the rules and punishes rule breakers. You can complain to the International Association for Financial Planning in Atlanta or to the schools that grant the financial-planner designations (page 959). But all they can do is yank the offender's professional certification or membership—hardly an onerous penalty, since he or she can go on practicing without it. Furthermore, these groups may not lift a finger until a planner has been found liable in another forum, such as a stock-exchange arbitration.

Here's a sampling of the complaints typically brought against financial planners:

* Failing to tell the truth about how large a fee the planner earned.
* Failing to diversify a client's investments to minimize risk.
* Putting clients into investments unsuitable for someone of their age and circumstances, such as stock-index options.
* Exaggerating an investment's likely yield, while failing to disclose the risks.
* Selling "rare" coins at hugely inflated values.
* Roping clients into outright frauds: nonexistent investments, Ponzi schemes, misrepresentations of every sort.
* Misrepresenting the tax benefits and investment outlook for limited partnerships.
* Giving bad tax advice.
* Failing to disclose that the planner had a financial interest in the investment being sold.
* Failing to process a client's investments or insurance properly, leading to financial loss.
* Ignoring a client's specific investment instructions and goals.

If you think you have grounds for suing your planner, start by trying to work out a settlement. Sometimes, a letter from a lawyer helps. If you're stonewalled, complain to the appropriate state regulator. For recalcitrant investment advisers, stockbrokers, or insurance agents who sell variable annuities or variable life, call your state's securities commission (get the phone number from the information operator in your state's capital or the North American Securities Administrators Association, 202-737-0900). For other insurance agents, call the state insurance commission (also in the state capital). Occasionally they can help.

Some planners may have required you to sign an arbitration agreement, which generally requires your case to be heard in a forum dictated by the securities industry (page 658). Other planners may be open to mediation through the American Arbitration Association (page 680)—a program backed by the three financial-planning associations. If the deal was a fraud to begin with, however, there may be nothing left to recover.

TO PROTECT YOURSELF

When doing business with a planner, proceed in the same orderly way that you would with a stockbroker (page 669)—with written goals, notes of conversations, and so on. In a confrontation, you might find that the planner kept his or her own notes, which a court or arbitration board might consider more credible than your memory.

If the planner tells you that a specific investment carries little risk, ask for a letter confirming it. This sort of paper trail supports a winning claim. It may also encourage your planner to proceed with caution and exactitude. If your planner makes a move that differs from what you thought you'd agreed on, telephone immediately. If you don't like the explanation, send a letter reiterating how you want your money handled.

AUNT JANE'S LAST RECIPE: A DO-IT-YOURSELF FINANCIAL PLAN

Over the next eight weeks, take the following eight steps to success:

Make a List of Specific Objectives.

The list might read: "A college education for Lynn and Kate, a down payment on a house, graduate school for Brian, hockey camp for Howard next year, Temma's wedding, two weeks in France year after next, a retirement income worth $50,000 a year." Put down exactly what you want. Your objectives will change as your life does, but you should always know what you're working toward.

Draw Up a Spending Plan.

This isn't a big deal. You've known about budgets all your life, and if you've forgotten, there's always Chapter 8.

Calculate What You Have to Save.

This isn't a big deal either, once you've specified what you're aiming for. Ask yourself, "How much will each objective cost?" and "When am I going to need the money?" Then point your savings toward those goals. In the Appendix, you'll find tables for figuring how much to save for education and retirement. Plot short-term savings in your head. You want to go to France year after next? Take this year's price, divide by 24, and put away that much per month. Nothing complicated about it.

You'll have to coordinate your savings with your spending plan, which is the hard part. But if you didn't intend to try, you never would have bought this book. (You say that your mother bought this book for you? Oh, well. Try anyway.)

Secure What You Have.

This is your safety net: life, health, disability, homeowners, and auto insurance. I've steered you toward inexpensive coverage, where it exists. Do-it-yourselfers can buy some policies by phone.

Develop a Risk Plan.

Decide on a prudent level of investment risk for someone of your age, goals, and circumstances. On this point, Chapter 21 should help.

Follow Through with an Investment Plan.

You will do splendidly with a few no-load mutual funds, chosen yourself and held long term, plus some Treasury securities, tax-exempts, or certificates of deposit.

Check Out a Tax Plan.

For most of us, tax planning isn't the gold mine that it used to be, now that so many deductions have been eliminated. Chiefly, you need a tax-deductible retirement plan (Chapter 29) and, if you're in a high bracket, some municipal bonds. What could be easier? If you have a high net worth, however, you'll have to deal with estate taxes, trusts, executive-compensation contracts, and all the other tax entanglements that wealth is heir to. *That's* when you need professional help—and only the most experienced planners will do. Your outriders will include a clutch of specialized professionals: tax lawyer, accountant, actuary, investment adviser.

And a Retirement Plan.

For how much to save, see Chapter 29 and Appendix 2 (page 984). When retirement day comes, however, you often need professional help. Chapter 30 gives you a look at the landscape. Then ask an accountant or competent planner to lay out the consequences of your various tax and pension choices. You can't afford to make a mistake. The adviser can also project a spending and investment plan to carry you through the rest of your life. Or use the tables in this book to do that job yourself.

And that's it. The planning process from first sharpened pencil to final phone call. A project you can handle, step-by-step, just by applying some basic, down-home common sense.

For generations, most Americans have managed their money themselves and done a pretty good job of it. And they still can. The trick is to turn your back on today's insanely complex financial marketplace and buy the simple things that you can analyze yourself. Trust me on this one. In the world of money, one or two clear and strong ideas, persisted in, will make you richer in the end.

Afterword

Many people contributed to this book. My special thanks to Louise Nameth, who cheerfully and tirelessly checked fact after fact *after fact* as these chapters rolled along. The excellent Amy Eskind and her husband, Nashville stockbroker Billy Eskind, updated the chapters on stocks, bonds, and (yes) stockbrokers. Kate O'Brien Ahlers tackled the minutiae of mortgages while juggling work for my newspaper column. Peter Elinsky, a partner in KPMG Peat Marwick, and senior manager Denis Yurkovik overhauled the two retirement chapters. Lynn Kane of *Newsweek* kept my office and professional life together against great odds.

The chapters were read and commented on by many experts in many fields. I greatly appreciate the time they spent and the pains they took to set me straight.

To the following collaborators, a toast:

John Allen of Allen-Warren, Inc., Arvada, Colorado, a financial planner who loves precision and accuracy above all things; Theodore Benna, 401(k) Association, Langhorne, Pennsylvania; money managers Kurt Brouwer and Steve Janachowski of Brouwer & Janachowski, Tiburon, California, authors of *Mutual Fund Mastery;* attorney William P. Cantwell; Martin Cohen, Cohen & Steers Capital Management, New York City, one of *the* experts on REITs; Mark Coler, president of Mercer, Inc., in New York City, and tracker of discount brokerage firms; attorney Charles A. Collier Jr., Irell & Manella in Los Angeles, who checked the estate-planning chapters both for general issues and community property matters; Larry Costello, marketing manager for PNC Mortgage Corp. of America; the public relations staff at Countrywide Home Loans; Glenn Daily, fee-only life insurance consultant in New York City and author of *The Individual Investor's Guide to Low-Load Insurance Products,* who contributed to every page where life insurance and annuities are found; Frank Doyle, special assistant to the director of the Health Care Financing Administration; securities arbitration attorney Robert Dyer of Allen Dyer Doppelp Milbrath & Gilchrist in Orlando, Florida; Dennis Fassuliotis, publisher of the *Auction & Foreclosure Investor* in Charleston, South Carolina; attorneys Marcia Fidis and Anne

"Jan" White of Pasternak & Fidis in Bethesda, Maryland, who tackled divorce issues; James Floyd, senior research analyst for the Leuthold Group in Minneapolis.

Also, bond expert Theresa Havell of Havell Capital Management in New York City, who took great pains to clarify the many difficult issues facing bond investors; Jack Harris, research economist at the Real Estate Center, Texas A&M University; from the Health Insurance Association of America: Jane Galvin, director of managed care, Marianne Miller, director of policy development, and assistant vice president Harvie E. Raymond (Harvie's thumbprints are on every health-insurance page; he didn't agree with all my opinions but checked facts again and again to get things right); Thomas J. Herzfeld, head of Thomas J. Herzfeld Associates, Inc., a Miami investment firm specializing in closed-end mutual funds; Judy Hole, a producer for CBS News, who found the story line in a couple of chapters when I'd lost it; Lynn Hopewell, a certified financial planner in Fairfax, Virginia, and one of the industry's gurus; from HSH Associates, the mortgage experts in Butler, New Jersey: vice presidents Paul Havemann and Keith Gumbinger; actuary James Hunt, insurance and annuity consultant to the Consumer Federation of America, who pressed me to think and rethink several critical issues; from the Insurance Information Institute in New York City: senior vice president Sean Mooney and Jeanne Salvatore, director of public relations and consumer affairs; Sheldon Jacobs, publisher of *The No-Load Fund Investor,* Irvington-on-Hudson, New York; John Joyce, manager of information and training services for the College Scholarship Service, The College Board, New York City.

Also, David Kahn, partner in the New York City accounting firm of Goldstein Golub Kessler & Co.; from the Kwasha Lipton Group of Coopers & Lybrand, an employee-benefits consulting firm in Fort Lee, New Jersey: Mary Case, principal, Harry Gross, partner, and Will Applegate, consultant; from the consulting firm KPMG Peat Marwick: John Gabel and Ross Konigsburg, senior managers, who checked the health insurance chapter; Charles Lanigan, disability insurance expert; Anna Leider, head of Octameron Associates, Alexandria, Virginia, which publishes excellent books on student aid; attorney Ira Lurvey of Lurvey & Shapiro in Los Angeles, who checked the divorce section for community property issues; James Lynch of the *Lynch Municipal Advisory Letter* in New York City; Charles Mandelstam, attorney for Dornbush Mensch Mandelstam & Schaeffer, New York City; John Markese, director of research for the American Association of Individual Investors in Chicago; David Martin, director of John Hancock's contracts & legal division; Wesley G. McCain, chairman of Eclipse Financial Asset Trust and Towneley Capital Management, Inc., in New York City, managers of institutional, individual, and mutual fund accounts, and Towneley's Mimi Eng of client servicing; Randall McCathren, vice president and general counsel for Bank Lease Consultants in Nashville,

Tennessee, who knows everything there is to know about auto leasing; Drs. Richard W. McEnally and Richard J. Rendleman Jr., professors of finance at the University of North Carolina's Business School at Chapel Hill, specialists in securities options and futures; Robert McKinley, president and editor of RAM Research in Frederick, Maryland; Alexander Miller, president, Shareholder Communications Corp., New York City; Anna Moretti, consultant to Choice in Dying in New York City; from the Mortgage Bankers Association of America: assistant director Brian Carey, associate director of public affairs Desiree French, and senior director Steve O'Connor.

Also, Richard L.D. Morse, professor emeritus, Kansas State University, who can see beneath the surface of any advertised interest rate; the staff of the National Association of Insurance Commissioners; Thomas Ochsenschlager, a partner in the consulting firm Grant Thornton, who answered many tax questions; Jeffrey O'Connell, one of the fathers of no-fault auto insurance and a professor of law at the University of Virginia School of Law; attorney Marjorie O'Connell of O'Connell & Associates in Washington, D.C., on divorce issues; Daniel Pederson, president of the Savings Bond Informer in Detroit and author of *U.S. Savings Bonds*; Timothy Pfeifer, consulting actuary for Milliman & Robertson in Chicago, who straightened me out on annuities; John T. Reed, editor of the *Real Estate Investor's Monthly,* Danville, California, primary architect of the theories of real-estate investing presented here; from T. Rowe Price in Baltimore: William "Chip" Wendler, vice president of Rowe Price–Fleming International, and Steve Norwitz, vice president, T. Rowe Price Associates, who tirelessly read chapters and produced tables; from Sallie Mae, the student loan organization in Washington, D.C.: Gisela Vallandigham, assistant vice president, and Josh Dare, director of corporate communications; securities arbitration attorney David E. Schellenberger in Boston.

Also, Kenneth Scholen, head of the National Center for Home Equity Conversion in Apple Valley, Minnesota, and author of *Your New Retirement Nest Egg: A Consumer Guide to the New Reverse Mortgages;* Muriel Siebert, president and chair of the discount brokerage firm of Muriel Siebert & Co. in New York City; Harold Skipper, professor of risk management and insurance at Georgia State University; Diane Spinner, senior vice president, Fleet Investment Services in New York City; from State Farm Fire and Casualty: John Robinson and David Harris, vice presidents—underwriting; attorney Marilyn Sullivan of Larkspur, California, author of *The New Home Buying Strategy;* John Trollinger of the Social Security Administration; from the UNUM health insurance organization in Portland, Maine: Guy Bertsch, manager of long-term-care macro risk, Eric Helsley, vice president of the long-term disability product center group, Jay Menario, vice president of product development, Theodore Merrill, vice president of association/affinity operations, and Tracy Sherman, director of public relations; from USAA in San Antonio, Texas: Kenneth McClure, senior vice president for marketing, King and Cathy Mawhinney, health product managers, Jack Marvin Green, director of risk underwriting for the USAA group, and members of the USAA property and casualty underwriting department; Don White, manager of media affairs for the American Association of Health Plans in Washington, D.C.; from the Vanguard Group of no-load mutual funds, in Valley Forge, Pennsylvania: Jeremy Duffield, managing director of Vanguard Investments of Australia, Ltd., Ian MacKinnon, senior vice president and head of the fixed-income group (I stole some of Ian's jokes), and Brian Mattes, principal and vice president of corporate communications; Lawrence Waggoner, professor of law at the University of Michigan Law School in Ann Arbor, Michigan; estate-planning attorney William Zabel of Schulte Roth & Zabel in New York City and author of *The Rich Die Richer and You Can, Too.*

My special thanks to Heather Fabian, public affairs manager for Ibbotson Associates, a market research firm in Chicago, and Ibbotson vice president and chief economist Paul Kaplan, for the tables and data they produced. Dozens of other specialists—regrettably too many to name—talked me through knotty problems and helped me put issues in perspective. Errors of fact and opinion are my own.

Making this book happen were Mort Janklow, who truly deserves the sobriquet Superagent, and Alice Mayhew, my wizard editor at Simon & Schuster, whose patience *does* know an end. My old friend Edward Engberg suggested the title. My husband, David, read everything and made suggestions. My wonderful friends let me bore them with my troubles, murmured sympathetically (not saying, "What, you're still working on *that?*"), and took David out to dinner during the months when I clapped myself into book jail to get the final chapters out.

Warmest thanks to all.

Appendixes

1. THE BEST LIFE INSURANCE PLANNER YOU WILL EVER FIND

Here's the professional way of establishing how much life insurance you need. All it demands of you is blind obedience. Follow the directions and you'll get the right answer.

You'll be doing a "present value" calculation, which accounts for the fact that a dollar received or spent right now is worth more than a dollar received or spent in the future. In professional lingo, you will be "discounting" future income and expenses to find out what that money is worth today.

The easiest way to explain this concept is with an example.

Assume that you owe your landlord $1,000 tomorrow. To make that payment, you need $1,000 in hand right now.

But if that $1,000 payment isn't due until next year, you need only $943.40 today, invested at 6 percent. If the payment isn't due until 10 years from now, you need only $558.39, also invested at 6 percent. That's what "discounting" means. That's the "present value" of a future $1,000 payment.

What if inflation is running at 3 percent, so that 10 years from now your $1,000 rent will have grown to $1,344? Present value analysis can handle that, too. In this case, you'd need $750.44, invested at 6 percent.

To do the calculations, you need a yellow pad, a sharp pencil, a hand-held calculator, and a trusting heart. Your reward is knowing that the size of your life-insurance policy will be exactly right.

All credit for this presentation goes to financial planner John Allen, J.D., of Allen-Warren, P.O. Box 740035, Arvada, Colorado, (303) 650-1267. He offered me the method and then fussed with my prose until we got it right.

Step One

Pick an After-Tax Rate of Return That You Think You Can Probably Earn on Your Money. Keep it reasonable. For 1997, a good number is 6 to 7 percent. I'd call 8 percent aggressive and 5 percent conservative. You will use this rate of return at key points in the following calculation. It is also known as the discount rate.

After-tax rate of return or discount rate	_____%

Step Two

What Sources of Money Would Your Survivors Have If You Died Today?

List all available income and savings. Don't include the value of your house if your spouse will continue to live there. Home equity should be counted only if your spouse would sell the house and live on the net proceeds.

SOUCES OF MONEY AFTER YOUR DEATH	CURRENT DOLLARS
• Your spouse's annual wages.	$_____
• Annual Social Security "family benefits" (payable to your spouse and children until the youngest child reaches age 16).*	$_____
• Social Security "survivor's benefits," payable to your spouse from your Social Security account, usually starting when your spouse reaches age 60.†	$_____
OR	
Your spouse's own "retirement benefit," payable annually from his or her own Social Security account, starting as early as age 62.‡	$_____
• Any portion of a pension you are currently receiving that would be paid annually to your spouse.	$_____
• Any pension due your spouse from his or her own earnings.	$_____
• The value of your cash savings.	$_____
• The value of your investments.	$_____
• Life insurance proceeds.	$_____
• Other lump-sum payments.	$_____
• Other usable assets, such as real estate.	$_____

* To find this payment, see page 903. Your unmarried children are due their own Social Security payments up to age 18 (19, if they're still in high school, and perhaps for life if they're disabled). I've left these extra years of payments off the chart, just to make your life a little simpler.

† To find this payment, see page 903. Younger spouses can get payments if they're disabled or if they're caring for eligible children.

‡ To find these payments, see page 903.

Step Three

How Soon Does Your Family Get This Money, and How Long Do They Have It?

For each of the money sources in Step Two, list: (1) the likely annual payment they will get; (2) the probable rate of growth, which can be different for each item; (3) the net discount rate;* (4) the number of

---

* The net discount rate equals the discount rate chosen in Step One, minus the rate of growth selected for this item in the table. For example, if your discount rate is 6 percent and your rate of growth is 5 percent, your net discount rate is one percent.

years they have to wait before the money becomes available;* (5) the number of years over which the money will be paid.† Following this table, you'll find instructions on how to fill it in. I've given examples for each major money source.

Here's where you learn how to enter your various sources of money onto the table. As an example, I've taken a husband seeking the right amount of coverage for a surviving wife age 45, with two college-bound children age 15 and 18.

MONEY SOURCE	CURRENT PAYMENT	RATE OF GROWTH	NET DIS- COUNT RATE	HOW SOON AVAILABLE	HOW LONG PAID
1._____	$_____	___%	___%	_____	_____
2._____	$_____	___%	___%	_____	_____
3._____	$_____	___%	___%	_____	_____
4._____	$_____	___%	___%	_____	_____
5._____	$_____	___%	___%	_____	_____
6._____	$_____	___%	___%	_____	_____
7._____	$_____	___%	___%	_____	_____
8._____	$_____	___%	___%	_____	_____
9._____	$_____	___%	___%	_____	_____
10._____	$_____	___%	___%	_____	_____

The net discount rate is the discount rate chosen in Step One—for this example, 6 percent—minus the rate of growth you choose for each particular item. (For the life expectancy table, see page 1025.) I haven't illustrated every money source; just enough of them to give you the idea.

1. WAGES. *Current payment*—your spouse's current income after tax. *Rate of growth*—the annual raises your spouse expects (say, 5 percent). *How soon available*—put down 1, because wages are payable currently. *How long paid*—until your spouse will quit or retire, say until age 62 (which means through age 61). That's 17 years. (Use this same method for figuring the value of any pension you are currently receiving that would be payable to your spouse.)

---

* The first year your spouse will receive the money. Use 1 for any funds available within a year of your death. Use 2 for money payable the year after your death. For example, if you die in 1998 and a certificate of deposit is payable in 1999, the answer to "How Soon Available" is 2. If you die in 1998, and your spouse will get Social Security in 2008, that money becomes available in year 11—the year of your death plus 10 years.

† The number of years your spouse will receive the money. Begin with the year the payment starts. For lifetime payments, use the spouse's life expectancy (tables on page 1025) plus a cushion. I've used 3 extra years, but your personal cushion should depend on your family history.

Money Source	Current Payment	Rate of Growth	Net Dis- count Rate	How Soon Available	How Long Paid
Wages	$30,000	5%	1%	1	17

2. SOCIAL SECURITY FAMILY BENEFITS. *Current payment*—what your family would receive this year, in spouse's and children's benefits. *Rate of growth* —Social Security normally rises by the inflation rate, so say 3 percent. *How soon available*—put down 1, because payments would begin immediately. *How long paid*—until the youngest child reaches age 18 (meaning through the 17th year). That's three years more.

Money Source	Current Payment	Rate of Growth	Net Dis- count Rate	How Soon Available	How Long Paid
Social Security family benefits	$13,000	3%	3%	1	3

3. SOCIAL SECURITY RETIREMENT BENEFIT. *Current payment*—the amount your spouse will receive when benefits start. *Rate of growth*—Social Security normally rises by the inflation rate, so say 3 percent. *How soon available* —the year your spouse will retire, say at age 62. *How long paid*—starting in the retirement year and lasting until life expectancy, plus, say, three years. For a 45-year-old woman, life expectancy is 85; adding three years brings you to age 88. That means payments *through* the 87th year, stopping when the 88th year begins—for a total of 26 years of payments.

Money Source	Current Payment	Rate of Growth	Net Dis- count Rate	How Soon Available	How Long Paid
Social Security retirement benefit	$9,000	3%	3%	18	26

4A. SPOUSE'S PENSION, PAYABLE IN THE FUTURE, WITH NO COST-OF-LIVING AD-JUSTMENT. *Current payment*—the estimated size of your spouse's pension in the first year. Your spouse's employer can help make the estimate. *Rate of growth*—enter zero. *How soon available*—the year your spouse will retire, say age 62—18 years away. *How long paid*—starting in the retire-ment year and lasting until life expectancy. For a 45-year-old woman, life expectancy is 85; adding three years brings you to age 88. That means payments *through* the 87th year, stopping when the 88th year begins—for a total of 26 years of payments.

Money Source	Current Payment	Rate of Growth	Net Discount Rate	How Soon Available	How Long Paid
Pension	$12,000	0	6%	18	26

4B. SPOUSE'S PENSION, PAYABLE IN THE FUTURE, WITH A COST-OF-LIVING AD-JUSTMENT. Apologies. This one is a little more complicated. Fortunately, you don't have to understand it. Just fill in the blanks and it will come out okay.

First, find out from your spouse's employer what he or she is likely to receive at retirement and what the cost-of-living adjustment is. Then enter here: *First-year pension payment: _____. The number of years before it will be paid: _____. The cost-of-living adjustment: _____.*

Then go to the Accumulated Capital Table (page 992). Go down the left-hand column until you reach the number of years before the pension will be paid. Follow across the row to the percentage representing the cost-of-living adjustment, and enter here the factor you find there. *Factor: _____.* Divide the first-year pension payment by the factor, and enter the result: $_____. This is today's deflated value of that first-year pension payment.

Example. Assume a $24,000 pension, starting in the 18th year with a 3 percent cost-of-living adjustment. The factor from the Accumulated Capital Table is 1.65. Divided into the pension, you get $14,520.

Now you're ready to fill in the table on page 972. *Current payment*—the deflated value of your future pension payment, as just calculated. *Rate of growth*—the cost-of-living adjustment. *How soon available*—the year your spouse will retire, say age 62, 18 years away. *How long paid*—starting in the retirement year and lasting until life expectancy. For a 45-year-old woman, life expectancy is 85; adding three years brings you to age 88. That means payments *through* the 87th year, for a total of 26 years of payments.

Money Source	Current Payment	Rate of Growth	Net Discount Rate	How Soon Available	How Long Paid
Pension	$14,520	3%	3%	18	26

4C. SPOUSE'S PENSION, PAYABLE CURRENTLY, WITH A COST-OF-LIVING ADJUST-MENT. This is for couples who have already retired. *Current payment*—the first-year amount your spouse will get after your death (from the spouse's own pension, or the survivor benefit payable from your pension, or both). *Rate of growth*—the cost-of-living adjustment (say, 2 percent). *How soon available*—immediately, so enter 1. *How long paid*—life expectancy plus a cushion. If the wife is 69, life expectancy is 18 years. That's to age 87. Adding a three-year cushion brings you to 90. So payments continue through the 89th year, stopping in the 90th—for a total of 21 years of payments.

Money Source	Current Payment	Rate of Growth	Net Dis- count Rate	How Soon Available	How Long Paid
Pension	$12,000	2%	4%	1	21

5. FIVE-YEAR CERTIFICATE OF DEPOSIT. *Current payment*—the full amount of the CD at maturity. *Rate of growth*—the net the CD is earning, *after tax* (say, 4.5 percent). *How soon available*—when the certificate matures. *How long paid*—enter 1, because it is paid all at once.

Money Source	Current Payment	Rate of Growth	Net Dis- count Rate	How Soon Available	How Long Paid
Five-year CD	$20,000	4.5%	−1.5%	5	1

6. MUTUAL FUNDS. *Current payment*—the current value of all your funds. *Rate of growth*—consider using the discount rate (after-tax rate of return) that you chose in Step One, even if your funds are, at the moment, growing at a higher rate. You chose the discount rate for long-term planning purposes. *How soon available*—right away, so enter 1. *How long paid*— the money is available all at once, so enter 1.

Money Source	Current Payment	Rate of Growth	Net Dis- count Rate	How Soon Available	How Long Paid
Mutual funds	$30,000	6%	0%	1	1

7. LIFE INSURANCE PROCEEDS. *Current payment*—the proceeds of the policy if you died tomorrow. *Rate of growth*—use the discount rate (rate of return) that you chose in Step One, which is the after-tax rate your investments are expected to earn. *How soon available*—right away, so enter 1. *How long paid*—the money is available all at once, so enter 1.

Money Source	Current Payment	Rate of Growth	Net Dis- count Rate	How Soon Available	How Long Paid
Life insurance	$150,000	6%	0%	1	1

Step Four

What Is the Value of Each Money Source in Today's Dollars? To find out, you do a present value calculation. It shows you what all your resources—

income, savings, wages, investments, Social Security benefits, and future pension—would be worth today if you had all the money to finance them in a single lump sum.

To get the right answer, you'll have to consult the table you filled in on page 972 and punch up a few numbers on a hand-held calculator. On the left, below, I show you the steps. On the right, an example.

The example calculates the present value of your spouse's earnings over the next 15 years. I've assumed that the spouse is currently earning $30,000 after tax, and will get 5 percent raises every year. The discount rate (from Step One) is 6 percent. The net discount rate (6 percent minus your spouse's 5 percent raises) is one percent.

This isn't hard! Just follow the bouncing ball.

Run through this calculation for each source of money on your table. (Time-saving tip: Anything available immediately and payable all at once is worth exactly its current value. If your mutual funds are worth $30,000, put that down. If your life insurance is worth $150,000, put that down. Ditto for savings accounts, money-market mutual funds, and stock portfolios.)

Add everything up. You'll get a single lump sum, representing the present value of all of the resources you expect to have in the future.

THE BOUNCING BALL		THE EXAMPLE
A. Go to the first source of income on your table (in Step Three).	$	$30,000
B. Take the net discount rate.	%	1%
C. Take the number of years over which the money will be paid.		17
D. Go to the Discount Table on page 996. Read across the top to find the net discount rate. Read down the left-hand side to find the number of years over which the money will be paid. Enter the factor you find where these two lines intersect.		15.72
E. Multiply the current payment by that factor.	$	$30,000
	×	×15.72
	$	$471,600
F. Stop. Do some deep knee bends. Get a glass of beer. Stare out the window.		
G. Take the net discount rate again.	%	1%
H. Look at how soon the money will be available.		1
I. Go to the Accumulated Capital Table on page 992. Read across the top to find the net discount rate. Read down the left-hand side to find the year the money will be available. Enter the factor you find where these two lines intersect.		1.00
J. Enter the number you got in E above.	$	$471,600
Divide by the factor you got in I.	÷	÷1.00
Present value:	$	$471,600

MONEY SOURCE	PRESENT VALUE
1. _____	$_____
2. _____	$_____
3. _____	$_____
4. _____	$_____
5. _____	$_____
6. _____	$_____
7. _____	$_____
8. _____	$_____
9. _____	$_____
10. _____	$_____
Total	$_____

Step Five

What Would It Cost Your Family to Live After Your Death? Go back to your spending plan (page 166) and eliminate any expenses related to you. If you count yourself in the middle class, your survivors should be able to pay their daily bills with 75 to 80 percent of your current after-tax income (but check it out).

On separate lines, enter any temporary or unusual expenses, such as your funeral and your kids' college. For college, use the current one-year cost of the kind of school you want each child to attend: tuition, room, board, books, transportation, and incidentals.

Throw in a contingency fund to cover the accidents of life. A good figure might be 10 percent of your income. This sum does double duty. It provides more principal for your spouse to live on. At the spouse's death, it becomes a legacy for your children.

EXPENSES AFTER YOUR DEATH	CURRENT DOLLARS
• Annual expenses while the children are young.	$_____
• Annual expenses after the last child leaves home.	$_____
• The mortgage.	$_____
• Other expenses.	$_____
• The cost of your funeral and other final expenses.	$_____
• First-year college expenses for Child One.*	$_____
• First-year college expenses for Child Two.	$_____
• Other lump sums owed, such as estate taxes.	$_____
• A contingency fund.	$_____
• A legacy for your children.	$_____

* Enter each child separately. They will attend school at different times, so their expenses carry different weights.

Step Six

When Will These Dollars Be Needed, and for How Long? For each expense, put down: (1) The total one-year cost, today; (2) the rate at which you expect that particular price to rise; (3) the net discount rate;* (4) the number of years before the expense begins;† (5) the number of years the expense will continue.‡ Following this table, you'll find instructions on how to fill it in. I've given examples for each expense.

EXPENSE	CURRENT COST	INFLATION RATE	NET DIS- COUNT RATE	STARTING YEAR	HOW LONG PAID
1._____	$____	___%	___%	_____	_____
2._____	$____	___%	___%	_____	_____
3._____	$____	___%	___%	_____	_____
4._____	$____	___%	___%	_____	_____
5._____	$____	___%	___%	_____	_____
6._____	$____	___%	___%	_____	_____
7._____	$____	___%	___%	_____	_____
8._____	$____	___%	___%	_____	_____
9._____	$____	___%	___%	_____	_____
10._____	$____	___%	___%	_____	_____

Here's how to enter your various sources of money onto the table. I've assumed a surviving wife age 45, with two college-bound children age 15 and 18.

The net discount rate is the discount rate chosen in Step One—for this example, 6 percent—minus the rate of growth you choose for each particular item. For life expectancy tables, see page 1025.

1. DAILY EXPENSES WHILE THE CHILDREN ARE YOUNG. *Expense*—the annual cost of living for your spouse and children until the last child gets out of school. *Current cost*—75 to 80 percent of what you budget today. *Inflation rate*—pick a likely average rate (say, 3.5 percent). *Starting year*—these expenses start now, so put down 1. *How long paid*—through the youngest

---

* The net discount rate equals the discount rate chosen in Step One, minus the rate of growth selected for this item in the table. For example, if your discount rate is 6 percent and your inflation rate is 3 percent, your net discount rate is 3 percent.

† The first year this bill will have to be paid. Use 1 for any expenses that start immediately or within a year of your death. Use 2 for expenses that start the year after your death. For example, if you die in 1998 and your child starts college in 1999, the "Starting Year" is 2. If you die in 1998 and college won't begin until 2008, that cost arrives in year 11—the year of your death plus 10 years.

‡ Begin with the year the payment starts. For lifetime payments, use the spouse's life expectancy (tables on page 1025) plus a cushion of 3 years or so.

child's 21st year. For a 15-year-old, that's the current year plus 6 years, 7 in all.

Expense	Current Cost	Inflation Rate	Net Dis-count Rate	Starting Year	How Long Paid
Daily expenses while the children are young	$39,000	3.5%	2.5%	1	7

2. DAILY EXPENSES AFTER THE LAST CHILD LEAVES HOME. *Expense*—the annual cost of living for your spouse alone. *Current cost*—often, one-third less than the family expenses when the children were home. *Inflation rate* —pick a likely average rate (say 3 percent). You can assume a lower (or higher) inflation rate in your future than you picked for the years that the children were small. *Starting year*—these expenses start in the year the last child leaves home; for this example, in the 8th year from now, when the spouse is 52. *How long paid*—for the rest of the spouse's life. Figure life expectancy plus a cushion of three years or so. For a 45-year-old woman, life expectancy is 85; adding the cushion brings you to 88. So these expenses will last *through* the 87th year, stopping when the 88th year begins. That's 36 years of costs, from age 52 through age 87.

Expense	Current Cost	Inflation Rate	Net Dis-count Rate	Starting Year	How Long Paid
Daily expenses after the last child leaves home	$26,000	3%	3%	8	36

3. MORTGAGE. *Expense*—the annual mortgage payment. *Current cost*— how much you pay each year. *Inflation rate*—zero for a fixed-rate mortgage. For simplicity's sake, use zero for an adjustable-rate mortgage; even though payments rise in one year they may fall the next. *Starting year*—1, because payments have to be made right now. *How long paid*—the number of years until the loan is paid off.

Expense	Current Cost	Inflation Rate	Net Dis-count Rate	Starting Year	How Long Paid
Mortgage	$17,500	0%	6%	1	12

4. FUNERAL AND FINAL EXPENSES. *Expense*—the cost of the funeral and settling the estate. *Current cost*—funeral home, lawyer's fees. *Inflation rate* —zero, because these costs are paid immediately. *Starting year* and *how*

long paid—both 1, because all the expenses fall within the first year. Estate taxes are handled the same way.

Expense	Current Cost	Inflation Rate	Net Discount Rate	Starting Year	How Long Paid
Funeral and final expenses	$7,000	0%	6%	1	1

5A. COLLEGE EXPENSES FOR CHILD ONE. *Expense*—the full cost of one year at college today (tuition, room, board, books, transportation, incidentals). *Current cost*—if you expect no college aid, put down the full amount for the school your child will attend. If your family will qualify for college aid, turn to page 525 to calculate how much of the college bill you might have to pay. *Inflation rate*—college costs are rising faster than other costs; for this example, I used 6 percent. *Starting year*—if the child will start school this year, or is in school already, put down 1. Otherwise put down the number of years before the first tuition bill is due. *How long paid*—put down the number of years until the child graduates: up to four years for undergraduates; more, if you want to finance graduate school.

Expense	Current Cost	Inflation Rate	Net Discount Rate	Starting Year	How Long Paid
College expenses for Child One	$14,000	6%	0%	1	4

5B. COLLEGE EXPENSES FOR CHILD TWO. *Expense*—the full cost of one year at college today (tuition, room, board, books, transportation, incidentals). *Current cost*—if you expect no college aid, put down the full amount for the school your child will attend. If your child will qualify for college aid, turn to page 525 to calculate how much of the college bill you might have to pay. *Inflation rate*—college costs are rising faster than other costs; for this example, I used 6 percent and put the second child at a state school. *Starting year*—the number of years before the first tuition bill is due. *How long paid*—put down the number of years the child will be in school: up to four years for undergraduates; more, if you want to finance graduate school.

Expense	Current Cost	Inflation Rate	Net Discount Rate	Starting Year	How Long Paid
College expenses for Child Two	6,000	6%	0%	3	4

6. A CONTINGENCY FUND. *Expense*—your cushion, in case expenses are higher than you figured. *Current cost*—put down any sum that seems reasonable. *Inflation rate*—zero. This sum is treated as if it were paid all at once. *Starting year*—now, or 1. *How long paid*—immediately, or 1.

EXPENSE	CURRENT COST	INFLATION RATE	NET DIS- COUNT RATE	STARTING YEAR	HOW LONG PAID
Contingency fund	$10,000	0%	6%	1	1

7. LEGACY. *Expense*—the sum you would like to leave to your children. Your spouse can live on the income from this sum during his or her lifetime. *Current cost*—whatever you want to leave. *Inflation rate*—zero, because it's treated as paid all at once. *Starting year*—the year your spouse will probably die, which means life expectancy plus the cushion you have been using. In this example, the 45-year-old spouse will die after 43 years, so the legacy will be paid in the 44th year. *How long paid*—all at once, or 1.

EXPENSE	CURRENT COST	INFLATION RATE	NET DIS- COUNT RATE	STARTING YEAR	HOW LONG PAID
Legacy	$100,000	0%	6%	44	1

Step Seven

What Is the Value of All Your Expenses, in Today's Dollars?
Bad news.

You have to follow Step Four all over again. So I'm restating it here.

The example on the right in the following table shows how to figure the present value of a 45-year-old widow's $26,000 in annual living expenses, growing at the rate of 3 percent a year. She needs this money from the time her last child leaves home (in the 8th year from now, when she's 52) until her death (upon reaching age 88, after 36 years have passed).

Run through this calculation for each expense on your table. Add everything up. Result: A single lump sum, representing the present value of all the expenses you expect to have in the future.

Step Eight

Do You Already Have Enough Money? Compare the present value of all of your sources of money (Total, Step Four) with the present value of all your future expenses (Total, Step Seven).

A. Go to the first expense on your table in Step Six. $_____ $ 26,000
B. Take the net discount rate.   _____ %   3%
C. Take the number of years the expense will run.   _____   36
D. Go to the Discount Table on page 996. Read across
   the top to find the net discount rate. Read down the
   left-hand side to find the number of years before the
   money will be paid. Enter the factor you find where
   these two lines intersect.   _____   22.49
E. Multiply the current payment by that factor. $_____ $26,000
                                                                           ×_____   × 22.49
                                                                           _____ $584,740

F. Stop. Watch a soap opera. Make some waffles with
   maple syrup. Jog around the block.
G. Take the net discount rate again.   _____ %   3%
H. Enter the number of years before the expenses start.   _____   8
I. Go to the Accumulated Capital Table on page 992.
   Read across the top to find the net discount rate.
   Read down the left-hand side to find the number of
   years before the expenses start. Enter the factor you
   find where those two lines intersect.   _____   1.23
J. Enter the number you got in E above.   _____ $584,740
   Divide by the factor you got in I.   ÷_____   ÷ 1.23
                                              Present value: $_____ $475,398

EXPENSE	PRESENT VALUE
1. _____	$_____
2. _____	$_____
3. _____	$_____
4. _____	$_____
5. _____	$_____
6. _____	$_____
7. _____	$_____
8. _____	$_____
9. _____	$_____
10. _____	$_____
Total	$_____

Present value of all resources $_____
Minus: Present value of all expenses $_____
Difference (plus or minus) $_____

If your family's resources are greater than their expenses, throw away your worksheets and pour yourself another beer. You're in great shape. You don't need any more life insurance.

If your family's expenses will be greater than their resources, you do indeed need life insurance. So go on to . . .

Step Nine

How Much More Life Insurance Do You Need? Buy enough to cover the total deficit shown in Step Eight. If you're $150,000 short, buy a $150,000 life insurance policy.

Your immediate needs can probably be covered by inexpensive term insurance (page 285). Redo this calculation every 3 to 5 years to see how you're doing.

If, at middle age, you decide that you'll want to carry life insurance into older age, start converting some of your term insurance into a cash-value policy (page 296).

Notes to This Calculation

• I've assumed that the surviving spouse will use up all the money you left behind. Principal will be tapped for college expenses and other lump sums listed in Step Five, as well as for daily living expenses. If you want your spouse to live mostly on the income from principal, you will have to provide extra money—under "legacy," Step Six. This objective will probably have to be funded with additional life insurance.

• Assume a good salary for the widow only if she is already employed. If she starts work after her husband's death, her salary will probably be low.

• The trickiest part of this calculation is knowing how many years to count because the answer isn't obvious. How many years before a particular benefit will begin? How many years will it be paid? There are two points to remember: First, *count the current year.* If your child is 15 and will be at home until graduating from college at age 21, that's 7 years from now: this year (your child's 15th), plus 6 years. Second, when finding the number of years you have to wait for a benefit, don't count the year that a benefit begins. Suppose you're 45 and will retire at age 62. You have 17 years to go—the current year plus 16 years, taking you through age 61. Age 62 isn't counted. What's the easiest way to count the years? Use your fingers. And toes.

• When both spouses work outside the home, the life insurance has to be done twice (two yellow pads) to find out how large a policy each of you needs. Do it once assuming that the husband dies first, and again assuming the wife dies first.

• Recheck your insurance every 3 to 5 years, or when something changes in your life—a new baby, an inheritance, or divorce. Maybe you'll need more coverage, maybe you'll need less.

2. HOW MUCH SHOULD YOU SAVE
FOR RETIREMENT? (LONG FORM)

This mini-workbook answers three critical questions: (1) How much money will you need for a comfortable retirement? (2) How much have you got already, counting pension, Social Security, and personal savings? (3) How much more will you need to save, starting today?

I chose this particular retirement planner because—unlike so many others that I studied—its feet are planted in the real world. For example, it faces the fact that fixed pensions don't carry you very far in an inflationary time. You need enough savings to overcome your income's gradual loss of purchasing power. This workbook also reminds you that your home equities can add to your retirement standard of living, and counts the value of any inheritance you're due.

Most usefully, it doesn't project a flat amount per month that you ought to save (although you can calculate one if you want). Flat amounts are unrealistic. In today's dollars, they are much too large—probably more than you can afford. In the dollars of 2010, however, they are much too small.

A savvier approach is to figure out what percentage of gross income you ought to be putting away each month. Your retirement savings will then rise right along with your income, in order to produce the sum you'll need.

To use this mini-workbook, you will first have to round up some basic financial information (all good stuff that you ought to know). (1) Get a projection of your probable Social Security retirement benefit (available free, see page 902). (2) Get your projected pension benefit, available from your company's employee-benefits office. Ask whether your pension has an annual inflation adjustment after retirement, and how much your employer contributed last year to your pension or profit-sharing plan. (3) Get the amount of money in your current tax-deferred retirement-savings plans, such as 401(k)s, profit-sharing plans, Keogh plans, SEPs, and Individual Retirement Accounts.

This worksheet was developed jointly by the accounting firm Coopers & Lybrand and the no-load mutual fund group T. Rowe Price in Baltimore. Although the reasoning is sophisticated, the actual steps are easy to follow. To help you, I've shown a specific example on the right. The whole exercise should take you just about an hour.

For a free copy of T. Rowe Price's excellent *Retirement Planning Kit,* which includes investment suggestions as well as this do-it-yourself financial planner, call T. Rowe Price at 800-638-5660. Tell them Jane sent you.

Step One

YOUR WORKING ASSUMPTIONS

GENERAL ASSUMPTIONS		EXAMPLE
1. The average rate of inflation you expect.	_____	4%
2. The annual rate of return you expect on your investments, pretax.	_____	9%

ASSUMPTIONS FOR YOUR WORKING YEARS

3. The inflation-adjusted rate of return on your investments (subtract line 1 from line 2).	_____	5%
4. Your federal, state, and local income-tax bracket.*	_____	33%
5. Your after-tax bracket (subtract line 4 from 1.00).†	_____	67%
6. The after-tax rate of return on your investments (multiply line 2 by line 5).	_____	6.03%
7. Your inflation-adjusted after-tax rate of return (subtract line 1 from line 6).	_____	2.03%
8. Number of years to retirement.‡	_____	20

ASSUMPTIONS AFTER YOU RETIRE§

9. Your federal, state, and local income tax rate.	_____	20%
10. The percentage of income you keep after tax (subtract line 9 from 1.00).	_____	80%
11. The after-tax rate of return on your investments (multiply line 2 by line 10).	_____	7.2%
12. Your inflation-adjusted after-tax rate of return (subtract line 1 from line 11).	_____	3.2%
13. The number of years you expect to be retired (life expectancy, page 1025, plus a few extra years—you pick the number).	_____	25

* Married couple. The working-years tax rate is your marginal bracket—the tax you pay on every additional dollar earned.

† All calculations use the decimal. For example, 0.33 subtracted from 1.00 leaves 0.67.

‡ Use 1 if this is the retirement year, 2 if you'll retire next year, and so on. In other words, the number of years to retirement plus one.

§ In retirement, this calculation uses your average tax rate. That's the total tax you pay—federal, state, and local income taxes divided by your total income. It's lower than your marginal bracket and tells you more about how much disposable income you'll have to live on in retirement.

Step Two

LINING UP THE FACTORS*

14. *Factor A:* Use the Accumulated Capital Table on page 992. In the left-hand column, find the number of years to your retirement (line 8). Read across to your assumed inflation rate (line 1). Enter the factor you find there.	_____	2.19

* You will need these factors for making all your calculations. Once you've lined them up, you can simply slip them in where needed.

LINING UP THE FACTORS (*cont.*) *

15. *Factor B:* Use the Accumulated Capital Table on page 992. In the left-hand column, find the number of years to your retirement (line 8). Read across to the assumed rate of return on your investments (line 2). Enter the factor you find there.   5.6

16. *Factor C:* Use the Accumulated Capital Table on page 992. In the left-hand column, find the number of years to your retirement (line 8). Read across to the after-tax rate of return you expect from your investments during your working years (line 6). If you don't see your exact rate of return, round down to the closest one. Enter the factor you find there.   3.21

17. *Factor D:* Use the Discount Table † on page 996. In the left-hand column, find the number of years you expect to be retired (line 13). Read across to the after-tax rate of return you expect from your investments in retirement (line 11). If you don't see your exact rate of return, round down to the closest one. Enter the factor you find there.   12.47

18. *Factor E:* Use the Discount Table on page 996. In the left-hand column, find the number of years you expect to be retired (line 13). Read across to the inflation-adjusted after-tax rate of return you expect from your investments in retirement (line 12). If you don't see your exact rate of return, round down to the closest one. Enter the factor you find there.   17.94

19. *Factor F:* Use the Discount Table on page 996. In the left-hand column, find the number of years to your retirement (line 8). Read across to the inflation-adjusted after-tax rate of return you expect to achieve during your working years (line 7). If you don't see your exact rate of return, round down to the closest one. Enter the factor you find there.   16.68

20. *Factor G:* Use the Discount Table on page 996. In the left-hand column, find the number of years to your retirement (line 8). Read across to the after-tax rate of return you expect to achieve during your working years (line 6). If you don't see your exact rate of return, round down to the closest one. Enter the factor you find there.   12.16

21. *Factor H:* Use the Discount Table on page 996. In the left-hand column, find the number of years to your retirement (line 8). Read across to the inflation-adjusted rate of return you expect to achieve during your working years (line 3). Enter the factor you find there.   13.09

† Use year 1 if this is the retirement year, year 2 if you'll retire next year, and so on.

Step Three

YOUR RETIREMENT COST OF LIVING

22. *The easy way*—and the best one for younger workers. Enter 80 percent of your current *after-tax* income. That's an estimate of what it will take to maintain your present standard of living. _____ $40,000

23. *The more accurate way*—best for people nearing retirement. Look at the spending plan on page 166 and redo it for your likely expenses in retirement. Enter your probable annual expenses, in today's dollars. _____ $42,880

Step Four

YOUR ANNUAL INCOME IN RETIREMENT

YOUR NET SOCIAL SECURITY INCOME

24. Enter your projected Social Security retirement benefit.* _____ $19,000

25. If your Social Security income will be taxable (page 935), enter one of the following tax rates:
    • If your state taxes your Social Security benefits: multiply your average tax rate (line 9) by the amount of Social Security benefits taxed (50 or 85 percent) and subtract from 1. In this example, 50 percent of the benefits are taxed (0.20 × 0.50 subtracted from 1). _____ 0.9
    • If your state doesn't tax Social Security benefits: figure out your average federal tax, multiply it by the amount of Social Security benefits taxed (50 or 80 percent), and subtract from 1. _____ _____

26. Multiply your Social Security retirement benefit (line 24) by the tax rate (line 25). The result is your net Social Security income. _____ $17,100

YOUR NET PENSION

27. Enter the projected annual benefit from your defined-benefit plan (not a defined-contribution plan, profit-sharing, or 401(k)). If you don't have a defined-benefit plan, enter zero. _____ $24,000

28. Enter the percentage of income you keep after tax (line 10). _____ 80%

29. Multiply line 27 by line 28. This is your pension income after tax. _____ $19,200

YOUR ANNUAL INCOME IN RETIREMENT (*cont.*)

ANY OTHER INCOME

30. Enter any other sources of income, such as earnings, royalties, and trust-fund income, but not income from savings. If there will be none, enter a zero here and on line 32.   0

31. Enter the percentage of income you keep after tax (line 10).   80%

32. Multiply line 30 by line 31. This is your other income after tax.   0

33. Add lines 26, 29, and 32. This is your basic after-tax retirement income. $36,300

* See page 902 for how to get your free estimate. Couples using a joint benefit should remember that that income will drop when one of you dies.

Step Five

IS YOUR BASIC RETIREMENT INCOME ENOUGH?

34. Enter your retirement expenses, from line 22 or 23. $42,880

35. Enter your basic retirement income, from line 33. $36,300

36. Subtract line 34 from line 35. This is your current annual current (shortfall) or surplus.*   ($6,580)

37. Enter Factor A from line 14.   × 2.19

38. Multiply line 36 by line 37. This is your gross annual (shortfall) or surplus at retirement, taking future inflation into consideration.   ($14,410)

39. Enter any income that you will get from a fixed annuity at retirement. If there will be none, enter a zero here and on line 41.   0

40. Enter the percentage of income you keep after tax (line 10).   80%

41. Multiply line 39 by line 40. This is your annuity income after tax.   0

42. Subtract line 41 from line 38. This is your net annual income (shortfall) or surplus in retirement.   ($14,410)

43. Enter Factor E from line 18.   × 17.94

44. Multiply line 42 by line 43. This is the amount of capital you will need at retirement to meet your annual income shortfall. $258,515†

* If you show a surplus, skip down to line 44 and enter a zero. But complete this worksheet anyway. You may not have a lifetime surplus if your pension income isn't indexed annually to inflation.

† Depending on your situation, this can look like a very big number indeed. But remember that it's expressed in future dollars at retirement, so it's never as bad as it seems.

Step Six

THE VALUE OF YOUR SAVINGS AT RETIREMENT

THE VALUE OF YOUR TAX-DEFERRED SAVINGS PLANS

45. Enter the current value of all your tax-deferred savings: 401(k)s, IRAs, Keoghs, SEPs, profit-sharing, and other company plans. _____ $20,000

46. Enter Factor B from line 15. _____ × 5.6

47. Multiply line 45 by line 46. This is the pretax value of your tax-deferred savings at retirement. _____ $112,000

48. Enter the sum you expect your employer to contribute to your defined-contribution retirement plan this year (Exclude your own contributions, if any, and any money your employer puts up to match those contributions.) _____ $4,800

49. Enter Factor H from line 21. _____ × 13.09

50. Multiply line 48 by line 49. _____ $62,832

51. Enter Factor B from line 15. _____ × 5.6

52. Multiply line 50 by line 51. _____ $351,859

53. Add lines 47 and 52. _____ $463,859

54. Enter your working-years after-tax bracket (line 5). _____ 67%

55. Multiply line 53 by line 54. This is the potential value of your tax-deferred savings, after tax.* _____ $310,786

THE VALUE OF YOUR AFTER-TAX SAVINGS

56. Enter the current value of all of your taxable savings and investments. Use the after-tax value of mutual funds, stocks, investment real estate, and other assets on which you'd owe capital gains taxes if you sold today. Exclude fixed annuities, which were covered on line 39. _____ $15,000

57. Enter Factor C from line 16. _____ × 3.21

58. Multiply line 56 by line 57. _____ $48,150

THE VALUE OF YOUR TOTAL SAVINGS

59. Add lines 55 and 58. This is what you can expect to realize from all of the retirement savings you hold today. _____ $358,936

---

* This assumes that you take a lump-sum distribution and pay taxes on it. It's a conservative assumption. You will more likely defer taxes by leaving at least some of the money in the plan or by rolling it into an IRA.

Step Seven

HOW MUCH CAPITAL WILL YOU NEED AT RETIREMENT?

60. Enter the amount of capital needed from line 44. _____ $258,515

IF YOUR COMPANY PENSION IS NOT INDEXED TO INFLATION *

61. Enter your annual after-tax pension (line 29). _____ $19,200

62. Enter Factor A from line 14. _____ × 2.19

63. Multiply line 61 by line 62. _____ $42,048

64. Enter Factor E from line 18. _____ × 17.94

65. Multiply line 63 by line 64. _____ $754,341

66. Enter the value from line 63. _____ $42,048

67. Enter Factor D from line 17. _____ × 12.47

68. Multiply line 66 by line 67. _____ $524,339

69. Subtract line 68 from line 65. This is the extra money you'll need at retirement to maintain the purchasing power of your fixed pension income. _____ $230,002

TO PAY OFF YOUR MORTGAGE AND OTHER DEBTS†

70. Enter the mortgage balance you will still be carrying at retirement, as well as other long-term loans you are likely to have. _____ $45,000

TO COVER ANY OTHER CAPITAL NEEDS

71. Enter a lump sum, in today's dollars, to cover any other financial responsibilities you will have in retirement: tuition for a grandchild, funeral expenses, an emergency fund for yourself. _____ $50,000

72. Enter Factor A from line 14. _____ × 2.19

73. Multiply line 71 by line 72 to determine the future value of these lump sums at retirement. _____ $109,500

YOUR TOTAL CAPITAL NEEDS AT RETIREMENT

74. Add lines 60, 69, 70, and 73. This is the sum you will need to achieve all the purposes you have in mind. _____ $643,017

THE CAPITAL YOU HAVE ALREADY

75. Enter the value of your current retirement savings from line 59. _____ $358,936

76. Enter, in today's dollars, any other sources of capital. You might be due an inheritance. Or you might plan on selling your house at retirement, investing some of the proceeds and moving into a smaller place. _____ 0

77. Enter Factor A from line 14. _____ × 2.19

78. Multiply line 76 by line 77. _____ 0

* If you have an indexed pension, enter zero on line 69 and go on to line 70. This calculation does not include upward adjustments that are less than the inflation rate.
† This plan tries to take you into retirement debt-free.

79. Add lines 75 and 78. This is the future value of all of the capital you have amassed so far. _____ $358,936

80. Subtract line 79 (what you already have) from line 74 (what you will need). The answer shows how much you still have to accumulate. If you get a negative number (a number with a minus sign in front of it), you already have more than you need. But check on it periodically to be sure you're not falling behind. _____ $284,081

Step Eight

HOW MUCH MORE DO YOU NEED TO SAVE?

81. Enter the shortfall from line 80. _____ $284,081

82. Enter Factor C from line 16. _____ ÷ 3.21

83. Divide line 81 by line 82. This is the current value, in today's dollars, of the extra capital you need. _____ $88,499

84. Enter Factor F from line 19. _____ ÷ 16.68

85. Divide line 83 by line 84. This is how much you should invest this year to reach your goal. _____ $5,306

86. Enter your current gross income. _____ $80,000

87. Divide line 85 by line 86. This is the percentage of your gross annual income that has to be invested annually to meet your retirement goal, assuming that your income keeps pace with inflation. Adjust your savings every year to keep up with this percentage amount.* _____ 6.6%

IF YOU WOULD RATHER SAVE A FIXED AMOUNT EACH YEAR

88. Enter the sum on line 83. _____ $88.499

89. Enter Factor G from line 20. _____ ÷ 12.16

90. Divide line 88 by line 89. This is the fixed sum of money you would have to save every year to meet your goal. _____ $7,278†

---

* To be conservative, we assumed that this money went into after-tax savings where the earnings are taxed every year.

† This shows how much harder it is to follow a fixed-sum savings program. In the first year, you would have to save $1,998 more than if you saved a fixed percentage of your annual income.

3. THE ACCUMULATED CAPITAL AND DISCOUNT TABLES

ACCUMULATED CAPITAL (in percentages)

BEGINNING OF YEAR	−3.00	−2.50	−2.00	−1.50	−1.00	−0.50	0.00	0.50
1	1.00	1.00	1.00	1.00	1.00	1.00	1.00	1.00
2	0.97	0.98	0.98	0.99	0.99	1.00	1.00	1.01
3	0.94	0.95	0.96	0.97	0.98	0.99	1.00	1.01
4	0.91	0.93	0.94	0.96	0.97	0.99	1.00	1.02
5	0.89	0.90	0.92	0.94	0.96	0.98	1.00	1.02
6	0.86	0.88	0.90	0.93	0.95	0.98	1.00	1.03
7	0.83	0.86	0.89	0.91	0.94	0.97	1.00	1.03
8	0.81	0.84	0.87	0.90	0.93	0.97	1.00	1.04
9	0.78	0.82	0.85	0.89	0.92	0.96	1.00	1.04
10	0.76	0.80	0.83	0.87	0.91	0.96	1.00	1.05
11	0.74	0.78	0.82	0.86	0.90	0.95	1.00	1.05
12	0.72	0.76	0.80	0.85	0.90	0.95	1.00	1.06
13	0.69	0.74	0.78	0.83	0.89	0.94	1.00	1.06
14	0.67	0.72	0.77	0.82	0.88	0.94	1.00	1.07
15	0.65	0.70	0.75	0.81	0.87	0.93	1.00	1.07
16	0.63	0.68	0.74	0.80	0.86	0.93	1.00	1.08
17	0.61	0.67	0.72	0.79	0.85	0.92	1.00	1.08
18	0.60	0.65	0.71	0.77	0.84	0.92	1.00	1.09
19	0.58	0.63	0.70	0.76	0.83	0.91	1.00	1.09
20	0.56	0.62	0.68	0.75	0.83	0.91	1.00	1.10
21	0.54	0.60	0.67	0.74	0.82	0.90	1.00	1.10
22	0.53	0.59	0.65	0.73	0.81	0.90	1.00	1.11
23	0.51	0.57	0.64	0.72	0.80	0.90	1.00	1.12
24	0.50	0.56	0.63	0.71	0.79	0.89	1.00	1.12
25	0.48	0.54	0.62	0.70	0.79	0.89	1.00	1.13
26	0.47	0.53	0.60	0.69	0.78	0.88	1.00	1.13
27	0.45	0.52	0.59	0.68	0.77	0.88	1.00	1.14
28	0.44	0.50	0.58	0.66	0.76	0.87	1.00	1.14
29	0.43	0.49	0.57	0.65	0.75	0.87	1.00	1.15
30	0.41	0.48	0.56	0.65	0.75	0.86	1.00	1.16
31	0.40	0.47	0.55	0.64	0.74	0.86	1.00	1.16
32	0.39	0.46	0.53	0.63	0.73	0.85	1.00	1.17
33	0.38	0.44	0.52	0.62	0.72	0.85	1.00	1.17
34	0.37	0.43	0.51	0.61	0.72	0.85	1.00	1.18
35	0.36	0.42	0.50	0.60	0.71	0.84	1.00	1.18
36	0.34	0.41	0.49	0.59	0.70	0.84	1.00	1.19

1.00	1.50	2.00	2.50	3.00	3.50	4.00	4.50
1.00	1.00	1.00	1.00	1.00	1.00	1.00	1.00
1.01	1.02	1.02	1.03	1.03	1.04	1.04	1.05
1.02	1.03	1.04	1.05	1.06	1.07	1.08	1.09
1.03	1:05	1.06	1.08	1.09	1.11	1.12	1.14
1.04	1.06	1.08	1.10	1.13	1.15	1.17	1.19
1.05	1.08	1.10	1.13	1.16	1.19	1.22	1.25
1.06	1.09	1.13	1.16	1.19	1.23	1.27	1.30
1.07	1.11	1.15	1.19	1.23	1.27	1.32	1.36
1.08	1.13	1.17	1.22	1.27	1.32	1.37	1.42
1.09	1.14	1.20	1.25	1.30	1.36	1.42	1.49
1.10	1.16	1.22	1.28	1.34	1.41	1.48	1.55
1.12	1.18	1.24	1.31	1.38	1.46	1.54	1.62
1.13	1.20	1.27	1.34	1.43	1.51	1.60	1.70
1.14	1.21	1.29	1.38	1.47	1.56	1.67	1.77
1.15	1.23	1.32	1.41	1.51	1.62	1.73	1.85
1.16	1.25	1.35	1.45	1.56	1.68	1.80	1.94
1.17	1.27	1.37	1.48	1.60	1.73	1.87	2.02
1.18	1.29	1.40	1.52	1.65	1.79	1.95	2.11
1.20	1.31	1.43	1.56	1.70	1.86	2.03	2.21
1.21	1.33	1.46	1.60	1.75	1.92	2.11	2.31
1.22	1.35	1.49	1.64	1.81	1.99	2.19	2.41
1.23	1.37	1.52	1.68	1.86	2.06	2.28	2.52
1.24	1.39	1.55	1.72	1.92	2.13	2.37	2.63
1.26	1.41	1.58	1.76	1.97	2.21	2.46	2.75
1.27	1.43	1.61	1.81	2.03	2.28	2.56	2.88
1.28	1.45	1.64	1.85	2.09	2.36	2.67	3.01
1.30	1.47	1.67	1.90	2.16	2.45	2.77	3.14
1.31	1.49	1.71	1.95	2.22	2.53	2.88	3.28
1.32	1.52	1.74	2.00	2.29	2.62	3.00	3.43
1.33	1.54	1.78	2.05	2.36	2.71	3.12	3.58
1.35	1.56	1.81	2.10	2.43	2.81	3.24	3.75
1.36	1.59	1.85	2.15	2.50	2.91	3.37	3.91
1.37	1.61	1.88	2.20	2.58	3.01	3.51	4.09
1.39	1.63	1.92	2.26	2.65	3.11	3.65	4.27
1.40	1.66	1.95	2.32	2.73	3.22	3.79	4.47
1.42	1.68	2.00	2.37	2.81	3.33	3.95	4.67

(continued on page 994)

ACCUMULATED CAPITAL (in percentages)
(continued from page 993)

BEGINNING OF YEAR	5.00	5.50	6.00	6.50	7.00	7.50	8.00
1	1.00	1.00	1.00	1.00	1.00	1.00	1.00
2	1.05	1.06	1.06	1.07	1.07	1.08	1.08
3	1.10	1.11	1.12	1.13	1.14	1.16	1.17
4	1.16	1.17	1.19	1.21	1.23	1.24	1.26
5	1.22	1.24	1.26	1.29	1.31	1.34	1.36
6	1.28	1.31	1.34	1.37	1.40	1.44	1.47
7	1.34	1.38	1.42	1.46	1.50	1.54	1.59
8	1.41	1.45	1.50	1.55	1.61	1.66	1.71
9	1.48	1.53	1.59	1.65	1.72	1.78	1.85
10	1.55	1.62	1.69	1.76	1.84	1.92	2.00
11	1.63	1.71	1.79	1.88	1.97	2.06	2.16
12	1.71	1.80	1.90	2.00	2.10	2.22	2.33
13	1.80	1.90	2.01	2.13	2.25	2.38	2.52
14	1.89	2.01	2.13	2.27	2.41	2.56	2.72
15	1.98	2.12	2.26	2.41	2.58	2.75	2.94
16	2.08	2.23	2.40	2.57	2.76	2.96	3.17
17	2.18	2.36	2.54	2.74	2.95	3.18	3.43
18	2.29	2.48	2.69	2.92	3.16	3.42	3.70
19	2.41	2.62	2.85	3.11	3.38	3.68	4.00
20	2.53	2.77	3.03	3.31	3.62	3.95	4.32
21	2.65	2.92	3.21	3.52	3.87	4.25	4.66
22	2.79	3.08	3.40	3.75	4.14	4.57	5.03
23	2.93	3.25	3.60	4.00	4.43	4.91	5.44
24	3.07	3.43	3.82	4.26	4.74	5.28	5.87
25	3.23	3.61	4.05	4.53	5.07	5.67	6.34
26	3.39	3.81	4.29	4.83	5.43	6.10	6.85
27	3.56	4.02	4.55	5.14	5.81	6.56	7.40
28	3.73	4.24	4.82	5.48	6.21	7.05	7.99
29	3.92	4.48	5.11	5.83	6.65	7.58	8.63
30	4.12	4.72	5.42	6.21	7.11	8.14	9.32
31	4.32	4.98	5.74	6.61	7.61	8.75	10.06
32	4.54	5.26	6.09	7.04	8.15	9.41	10.87
33	4.76	5.55	6.45	7.50	8.72	10.12	11.74
34	5.00	5.85	6.84	7.99	9.33	10.88	12.68
35	5.25	6.17	7.25	8.51	9.98	11.69	13.69
36	5.52	6.51	7.69	9.06	10.68	12.57	14.79

8.50	9.00	9.50	10.00	10.50	11.00	11.50	12.00
1.00	1.00	1.00	1.00	1.00	1.00	1.00	1.00
1.09	1.09	1.10	1.10	1.11	1.11	1.12	1.12
1.18	1.19	1.20	1.21	1.22	1.23	1.24	1.25
1.28	1.30	1.31	1.33	1.35	1.37	1.39	1.40
1.39	1.41	1.44	1.46	1.49	1.52	1.55	1.57
1.50	1.54	1.57	1.61	1.65	1.69	1.72	1.76
1.63	1.68	1.72	1.77	1.82	1.87	1.92	1.97
1.77	1.83	1.89	1.95	2.01	2.08	2.14	2.21
1.92	1.99	2.07	2.14	2.22	2.30	2.39	2.48
2.08	2.17	2.26	2.36	2.46	2.56	2.66	2.77
2.26	2.37	2.48	2.59	2.71	2.84	2.97	3.11
2.45	2.58	2.71	2.85	3.00	3.15	3.31	3.48
2.66	2.81	2.97	3.14	3.31	3.50	3.69	3.90
2.89	3.07	3.25	3.45	3.66	3.88	4.12	4.36
3.13	3.34	3.56	3.80	4.05	4.31	4.59	4.89
3.40	3.64	3.90	4.18	4.47	4.78	5.12	5.47
3.69	3.97	4.27	4.59	4.94	5.31	5.71	6.13
4.00	4.33	4.68	5.05	5.46	5.90	6.36	6.87
4.34	4.72	5.12	5.56	6.03	6.54	7.09	7.69
4.71	5.14	5.61	6.12	6.67	7.26	7.91	8.61
5.11	5.60	6.14	6.73	7.37	8.06	8.82	9.65
5.55	6.11	6.73	7.40	8.14	8.95	9.83	10.80
6.02	6.66	7.36	8.14	8.99	9.93	10.97	12.10
6.53	7.26	8.06	8.95	9.94	11.03	12.23	13.55
7.08	7.91	8.83	9.85	10.98	12.24	13.63	15.18
7.69	8.62	9.67	10.83	12.14	13.59	15.20	17.00
8.34	9.40	10.59	11.92	13.41	15.08	16.95	19.04
9.05	10.25	11.59	13.11	14.82	16.74	18.90	21.32
9.82	11.17	12.69	14.42	16.37	18.58	21.07	23.88
10.65	12.17	13.90	15.86	18.09	20.62	23.49	26.75
11.56	13.27	15.22	17.45	19.99	22.89	26.20	29.96
12.54	14.46	16.67	19.19	22.09	25.41	29.21	33.56
13.61	15.76	18.25	21.11	24.41	28.21	32.57	37.58
14.76	17.18	19.98	23.23	26.97	31.31	36.31	42.09
16.02	18.73	21.88	25.55	29.81	34.75	40.49	47.14
17.38	20.41	23.96	28.10	32.94	38.57	45.15	52.80

DISCOUNT TABLE (in percentages)

Payment Period	−3.00	−2.50	−2.00	−1.50	−1.00	−0.50	0.00
1	1.00	1.00	1.00	1.00	1.00	1.00	1.00
2	2.03	2.03	2.02	2.02	2.01	2.01	2.00
3	3.09	3.08	3.06	3.05	3.03	3.02	3.00
4	4.19	4.16	4.12	4.09	4.06	4.03	4.00
5	5.32	5.26	5.21	5.15	5.10	5.05	5.00
6	6.48	6.40	6.31	6.23	6.15	6.08	6.00
7	7.68	7.56	7.44	7.33	7.22	7.11	7.00
8	8.92	8.76	8.60	8.44	8.29	8.14	8.00
9	10.20	9.98	9.77	9.57	9.37	9.18	9.00
10	11.51	11.24	10.97	10.71	10.47	10.23	10.00
11	12.87	12.52	12.19	11.88	11.57	11.28	11.00
12	14.27	13.85	13.44	13.06	12.69	12.34	12.00
13	15.71	15.20	14.72	14.26	13.82	13.40	13.00
14	17.19	16.59	16.02	15.47	14.96	14.47	14.00
15	18.73	18.02	17.34	16.71	16.11	15.54	15.00
16	20.31	19.48	18.70	17.96	17.27	16.62	16.00
17	21.93	20.98	20.08	19.24	18.45	17.70	17.00
18	23.61	22.52	21.49	20.53	19.63	18.79	18.00
19	25.34	24.09	22.93	21.84	20.83	19.88	19.00
20	27.13	25.71	24.40	23.18	22.04	20.98	20.00
21	28.96	27.37	25.89	24.53	23.26	22.09	21.00
22	30.86	29.07	27.42	25.90	24.50	23.20	22.00
23	32.81	30.82	28.98	27.30	25.75	24.32	23.00
24	34.83	32.61	30.57	28.71	27.01	25.44	24.00
25	36.91	34.44	32.20	30.15	28.28	26.57	25.00
26	39.05	36.33	33.85	31.61	29.56	27.70	26.00
27	41.26	38.26	35.55	33.09	30.85	28.84	27.00
28	43.53	40.24	37.27	34.59	32.17	29.98	28.00
29	45.88	42.27	39.03	36.12	33.50	31.14	29.00
30	48.30	44.35	40.83	37.67	34.94	32.29	30.00
31	50.79	46.49	42.66	39.24	36.19	33.45	31.00
32	53.36	48.68	44.53	40.84	37.56	34.52	32.00
33	56.01	50.93	46.44	42.46	38.93	35.80	33.00
34	58.74	53.24	48.39	44.11	40.33	36.98	34.00
35	61.56	55.60	50.38	45.78	41.74	38.16	35.00
36	64.47	58.03	52.40	47.48	43.16	39.35	36.00
37	67.46	60.52	54.47	49.20	44.59	40.55	37.00
38	70.55	63.07	56.59	50.95	46.04	41.76	38.00
39	73.73	65.69	58.74	52.73	47.51	42.97	39.00
40	77.01	68.37	60.94	54.53	48.99	44.18	40.00

0.50	1.00	1.50	2.00	2.50	3.00	3.50
1.00	1.00	1.00	1.00	1.00	1.00	1.00
2.00	1.99	1.99	1.98	1.98	1.97	1.97
2.99	2.97	2.96	2.94	2.93	2.91	2.90
3.97	3.94	3.91	3.88	3.86	3.83	3.80
4.95	4.90	4.85	4.81	4.76	4.72	4.67
5.93	5.85	5.78	5.71	5.65	5.58	5.52
6.90	6.80	6.70	6.60	6.51	6.42	6.33
7.86	7.73	7.60	7.47	7.35	7.23	7.11
8.82	8.65	8.49	8.33	8.17	8.02	7.87
9.78	9.57	9.36	9.16	8.97	8.79	8.61
10.73	10.47	10.22	9.98	9.75	9.53	9.32
11.68	11.37	11.07	10.79	10.51	10.25	10.00
12.62	12.26	11.91	11.58	11.26	10.95	10.66
13.56	13.13	12.73	12.35	11.98	11.63	11.30
14.49	14.00	13.54	13.11	12.69	12.30	11.92
15.42	14.87	14.34	13.85	13.38	12.94	12.52
16.34	15.72	15.13	14.58	14.06	13.56	13.09
17.26	16.56	15.91	15.29	14.71	14.17	13.65
18.17	17.40	16.67	15.99	15.35	14.75	14.19
19.08	18.23	17.43	16.68	15.98	15.32	14.71
19.99	19.05	18.17	17.35	16.59	15.88	15.21
20.89	19.86	18.90	18.01	17.18	16.42	15.70
21.78	20.66	19.62	18.66	17.77	16.94	16.17
22.68	21.46	20.33	19.29	18.33	17.44	16.62
23.56	22.24	21.03	19.91	18.88	17.94	17.06
24.45	23.02	21.72	20.52	19.42	18.41	17.48
25.32	23.80	22.40	21.12	19.95	18.88	17.89
26.20	24.56	23.07	21.71	20.46	19.33	18.29
27.07	25.32	23.73	22.28	20.96	19.76	18.67
27.93	26.07	24.38	22.84	21.45	20.19	19.04
28.79	26.81	25.02	23.40	21.93	20.60	19.39
29.65	27.54	25.65	23.94	22.40	21.00	19.74
30.50	28.27	26.27	24.47	22.85	21.39	20.07
31.35	28.99	26.88	24.99	23.29	21.77	20.39
32.20	29.70	27.48	25.50	23.72	22.13	20.70
33.04	30.41	28.08	26.00	24.15	22.49	21.00
33.87	31.11	28.66	26.49	24.56	22.83	21.29
34.70	31.80	29.24	26.97	24.96	23.17	21.57
35.53	32.48	29.81	27.44	25.35	23.49	21.84
36.35	33.16	30.35	27.90	25.73	23.81	22.10

(continued on page 998)

DISCOUNT TABLE (in percentages)

(continued from page 997)

PAYMENT PERIOD	4.00	4.50	5.00	5.50	6.00	6.50
1	1.00	1.00	1.00	1.00	1.00	1.00
2	1.96	1.96	1.95	1.95	1.94	1.94
3	2.89	2.87	2.86	2.85	2.83	2.82
4	3.78	3.75	3.72	3.70	3.67	3.65
5	4.63	4.59	4.55	4.51	4.47	4.43
6	5.45	5.39	5.33	5.27	5.21	5.16
7	6.24	6.16	6.08	6.00	5.92	5.84
8	7.00	6.89	6.79	6.68	6.58	6.48
9	7.73	7.60	7.46	7.33	7.21	7.09
10	8.44	8.27	8.11	7.95	7.80	7.66
11	9.11	8.91	8.72	8.54	8.36	8.19
12	9.76	9.53	9.31	9.09	8.89	8.69
13	10.39	10.12	9.86	9.62	9.38	9.16
14	10.99	10.68	10.39	10.12	9.85	9.60
15	11.56	11.22	10.90	10.59	10.29	10.01
16	12.12	11.74	11.38	11.04	10.71	10.40
17	12.65	12.23	11.84	11.46	11.11	10.77
18	13.17	12.71	12.27	11.86	11.48	11.11
19	13.66	13.16	12.69	12.25	11.83	11.43
20	14.13	13.59	13.09	12.61	12.16	11.73
21	14.59	14.01	13.46	12.95	12.47	12.02
22	15.03	14.40	13.82	13.28	12.76	12.28
23	15.45	14.78	14.16	13.58	13.04	12.54
24	15.86	15.15	14.49	13.88	13.30	12.77
25	16.25	15.50	14.80	14.15	13.55	12.99
26	16.62	15.83	15.09	14.41	13.78	13.20
27	16.98	16.15	15.38	14.66	14.00	13.39
28	17.33	16.45	15.64	14.90	14.21	13.57
29	17.66	16.74	15.90	15.12	14.41	13.75
30	17.98	17.02	16.14	15.33	14.59	13.91
31	18.29	17.29	16.37	15.53	14.76	14.06
32	18.59	17.54	16.59	15.72	14.93	14.20
33	18.87	17.79	16.80	15.90	15.08	14.33
34	19.15	18.02	17.00	16.08	15.23	14.46
35	19.41	18.25	17.19	16.24	15.37	14.58
36	19.66	18.46	17.37	16.39	15.50	14.69
37	19.91	18.67	17.55	16.54	15.62	14.79
38	20.14	18.96	17.71	16.67	15.74	14.89
39	20.37	19.05	17.87	16.80	15.85	14.98
40	20.58	19.23	18.02	16.93	15.95	15.06

7.00	7.50	8.00	8.50	9.00	9.50	10.00
1.00	1.00	1.00	1.00	1.00	1.00	1.00
1.93	1.93	1.93	1.92	1.92	1.91	1.91
2.81	2.80	2.78	2.77	2.76	2.75	2.74
3.62	3.60	3.58	3.55	3.53	3.51	3.49
4.39	4.35	4.31	4.28	4.24	4.20	4.17
5.10	5.05	4.99	4.94	4.89	4.84	4.79
5.77	5.69	5.62	5.55	5.49	5.42	5.36
6.39	6.30	6.21	6.12	6.03	5.95	5.87
6.97	6.86	6.75	6.64	6.53	6.43	6.33
7.52	7.38	7.25	7.12	7.00	6.88	6.76
8.02	7.86	7.71	7.56	7.42	7.28	7.14
8.50	8.32	8.14	7.97	7.81	7.65	7.50
8.94	8.74	8.54	8.34	8.16	7.98	7.81
9.36	9.13	8.90	8.69	8.49	8.29	8.10
9.75	9.49	9.24	9.01	8.79	8.57	8.37
10.11	9.83	9.56	9.30	9.06	8.83	8.61
10.45	10.14	9.85	9.58	9.31	9.06	8.82
10.76	10.43	10.12	9.83	9.54	9.28	9.02
11.06	10.71	10.37	10.06	9.76	9.47	9.20
11.34	10.96	10.60	10.27	9.95	9.65	9.36
11.59	11.19	10.82	10.46	10.13	9.81	9.51
11.84	11.41	11.02	10.64	10.29	9.96	9.65
12.06	11.62	11.20	10.81	10.44	10.10	9.77
12.27	11.81	11.37	10.96	10.58	10.22	9.88
12.47	11.98	11.53	11.10	10.71	10.33	9.98
12.65	12.15	11.67	11.23	10.82	10.44	10.08
12.83	12.30	11.81	11.35	10.93	10.53	10.16
12.99	12.44	11.94	11.46	11.03	10.62	10.24
13.14	12.57	12.05	11.57	11.12	10.70	10.31
13.28	12.70	12.16	11.66	11.20	10.77	10.37
13.41	12.81	12.26	11.75	11.27	10.83	10.43
13.53	12.92	12.35	11.83	11.34	10.89	10.48
13.65	13.02	12.43	11.90	11.41	10.95	10.53
13.75	13.11	12.51	11.97	11.46	11.00	10.57
13.85	13.19	12.59	12.03	11.51	11.05	10.61
13.95	13.27	12.65	12.09	11.52	11.09	10.64
14.04	13.35	12.72	12.14	11.55	11.19	10.69
14.12	13.42	12.78	12.19	11.57	11.22	10.71
14.19	13.48	12.83	12.23	11.69	11.63	10.73
14.26	13.54	12.88	12.28	11.73	11.65	10.76

4. SHOULD YOU BUY OR RENT?

Which is more profitable: To buy a $100,000 house for $20,000 down and hold for 7 years?* Or rent instead, investing your down payment and other up-front costs in 7-year Treasury bonds?† To decide, go to the table that's closer to your marginal tax bracket and pick a likely rent from the column on the left. Then read across to the column representing the rate you think the house might increase in value every year. Where those lines intersect you'll find the compound annual rate of return that you'll earn on your equity—in excess of the Treasury rate—if you buy instead of rent. Rents are assumed to rise at the same rate house prices do.

In summary, here's what the analysis concludes:

1. When mortgage rates are relatively low (7 to 8 percent), renting isn't worthwhile financially unless you get an incredible bargain. Your monthly rent would have to be less than one percent of the price of a comparable home. Even then, you are betting that property values won't increase. If the house gains in value, owning would be a much better deal. If the house loses value you're still better off buying, as long as your monthly rent exceeds one percent of the price of a comparable home.

2. In general, you should rent if you think you might move within a few years, owing to the high cost of buying and selling. The table assumes a 7-year holding period, which gives you time to recover those costs. You need high rates of real-estate appreciation to recover your costs over a shorter period of time.

3. Even at modest rates of housing appreciation homeowners earn big gains on their money, thanks to the value of their tax deductions and the amazing power of leverage. A small increase in the price of your house translates into a major return on the 20 percent you put down. The higher your tax bracket, the greater your return.

4. You can use this table to evaluate housing situations other than the one specifically analyzed. For example, say you buy a $150,000 house which would rent at $1,050 a month—0.7 percent of market value. The equivalent 0.7 percent for the $100,000 house on the table is $700 a month, so use that line as a general guide. You will get a slightly higher yield because the house is more expensive. On a house costing less than $100,000, you would get a slightly lower yield. On down payments smaller than 20 percent, your potential for profit or loss is much greater than the table shows, so if the return looks positive, you'd be more inclined to buy than rent. A mortgage rate higher than 8 percent might shift the decision toward renting, instead.

---

* A 30-year mortgage at 8 percent interest and 1 discount point; $3,454 in net closing costs; local real-estate taxes at 2 percent of value per year; hazard insurance at 0.5 percent per year.
   † Treasury bonds yielding 6.65 percent.

IN THE 28 PERCENT FEDERAL BRACKET

| Monthly Rent | A Home Buyer's Profit or Loss If Rents and Real-Estate Values Changed by ‡ | | | | | |
	−4%	−2%	0%	2%	4%	6%
$ 700	loss	loss	loss	2.1	8.7	13.8
$ 800	loss	loss	loss	7.1	13.0	17.8
$ 900	loss	loss	4.7	12.0	17.4	21.8
$1,000	loss	0.5	10.5	17.0	21.9	26.0
$1,100	loss	8.2	16.3	21.9	26.4	30.2
$1,200	3.8	15.3	22.0	26.9	31.0	34.5
$1,300	13.7	21.9	27.5	31.9	35.6	38.9
$1,400	21.9	28.2	33.0	36.9	40.3	43.3

IN THE 39.6 PERCENT FEDERAL BRACKET

| Monthly Rent | A Home Buyer's Profit or Loss If Rents and Real-Estate Values Changed by ‡ | | | | | |
	−4%	−2%	0%	2%	4%	6%
$ 700	loss	loss	loss	5.9	11.9	16.6
$ 800	loss	loss	3.4	10.8	16.3	20.7
$ 900	loss	loss	9.3	15.8	20.8	24.8
$1,000	loss	7.0	15.1	20.8	25.2	29.0
$1,100	2.2	14.1	20.8	25.8	29.8	33.4
$1,200	12.4	20.8	26.4	30.8	34.5	37.7
$1,300	20.7	27.1	31.9	35.8	39.2	42.2
$1,400	28.0	33.2	37.3	40.8	43.4	46.7

‡ Compounded monthly for 7 years.
SOURCE: Jack Harris, Real Estate Center at Texas A&M University, College Station, Texas

5. THE BEST-GUESS COLLEGE PLANNER (LONG FORM)

Who knows exactly what college will cost in the future? Who knows what you'll be earning when the axe falls on your bank account? You have to make guesses—good guesses—to set up a reasonable college investment plan.

That's what this worksheet is all about. It's a four-step system for figuring out how much you ought to save each month, courtesy of the T. Rowe Price mutual fund company. The answer isn't guaranteed to provide every penny you need, but it's close enough.

What I like about this worksheet is that it tells you what *percentage* of your after-tax income you should be saving every year. Conventional college planners (including the Short Form on page 571) advise you to save fixed sums—for example, $500 a month. That's unrealistic. Right now, $500 a month might be much more than you can afford. Ten years from now, however, it might be pocket change. If you save a fixed percentage of income—for example, 5 percent a year—your college contributions can start low and rise as your salary does.

Go through the calculations separately for each child. If you save all this money, you'll win a silver cup for the Best-Prepared Parent in the class.

Step One

What Will College Cost When Your Child Finally Goes?

THE EASY WAY: Check the table on page 521, which gives you a four-year estimate for the average school. All costs are included: tuition, room, board, books, supplies, transportation, and spending money.

Total Average College Cost $____

THE BETTER WAY: Take the current one-year cost for the exact school, or type of school, that you expect your child to attend. Include everything: tuition, fees, room, board, books, supplies, transportation, spending money. *College cost: $____.*

Pick a plausible college inflation rate (at this writing, 6 percent). *Inflation rate: ____%.*

Put down the number of years from now that your child will start school. Count the current year as one. For example, an 8-year-old who will start at age 18 has 11 years to go—this year plus 10 years. *Number of years to matriculation: ____.*

Put down the number of years until your child's sophomore, junior, and senior years. If your 8-year-old starts school in 11 years, the next three years would be numbered 12, 13, and 14. *Years to the child's sophomore, junior, and senior years:* ____, ____, ____.

Then go to the MiracleGrow table on page 1006. Look down the left-hand column to find the number of years from now that college starts. Read across to the college-inflation rate you chose. Where those lines intersect, you'll find a "compounding factor." *Compounding factor:* ____. Multiply the college cost by that factor. The result is the likely cost of your child's freshman year.

Go to the next number down the column, representing your child's sophomore year, and do the same. Ditto for the junior and senior years. Add those four numbers together for the total college cost.

Freshman year	$____
Sophomore year	$____
Junior year	$____
Senior year	$____
TOTAL COLLEGE COST	$____

If you have no college savings to speak of and expect no student aid, jump directly to Step Four. I'm sorry that you're broke but you've saved yourself a lot of calculating.

Step Two

How Much Have You Saved Already? Put down the size of your current college-savings fund (plenty, right?), then go to the MiracleGrow table on page 1006. Go down the left-hand column to find the number of years to matriculation day.* Read across to the row that best represents the return you think your money will earn pretax.† For reference, the long-term return from stocks since World War II has been about 12 percent (although the roaring eighties and middle nineties saw as much as 20 percent).

Where those lines intersect, you will find a "compounding factor." Multiply your savings by that factor. The result: what your current savings will be worth when college starts. Subtract this amount from the total college cost to find out how much money you're still missing.

If you have no college savings at all, put a zero here, clear your throat, and move on.

---

*Include the current year in your count. A 10-year-old child who will start school at age 18 has nine years to wait—this year plus eight years.

† This calculation assumes that you pay any taxes due on your college fund from other income, not from the fund itself.

The savings you have now	$_____
Multiplied by the compounding factor	×_____
Gives you: the future value of your savings	$_____
Your total college cost	$_____
Minus the future value of your savings	$_____
Gives you: the missing money	$_____

Step Three

How Much Student Aid Can You Expect? If your income falls in the $80,000 to $90,000 range, you'll probably get no help. If you're earning around $60,000, you'll get help at an expensive private college but maybe not at a state university. Anyone who expects no substantial aid should skip to Step Four.

If you think you might qualify for student aid, here's a very, *very* rough guide.

1. Pick a likely college for your child and put down its total cost in 1997–98.

2. Go to the Parental Contribution table on page 526 and figure out about how much you'd have had to pay that year. Add $900 if the student is a freshman and $1,100 if he or she is a sophomore, junior, or senior. Add 20 percent, just to be conservative. That's your total family contribution. Subtract it from the college's cost.

3. Divide the result by the same 1997–98 college cost that you started with. That gives you the percentage of the bill that you can hope for in college aid. Use this as a proxy for the aid you might get in the future.

Cost of college in 1997–98	$_____
Minus your estimated parental contribution	$_____
Gives you: aid you might get	$_____
Divided by the cost of college in 1997–98	$_____
Gives you: the percentage of the cost you might get in aid	_____%

4. Enter the total college cost you found in Step One and multiply it by the percentage of the cost that might be covered by student aid. Subtract that sum (plus any gifts you expect) from the missing money that you calculated in Step Two.

Total college cost	$_____
Multiplied by the percent covered by student aid	×_____%
Gives you: hoped-for student aid	$_____
The missing money	$_____
Minus hoped-for student aid	$_____
Minus anything Grandma will kick in	$_____
Gives you: what you have to save	$_____

Step Four

How Much More Will You Have to Save to Meet Your Child's College Bills? Here's how to figure the percentage of income you should set aside.

Estimate the general rate of inflation you expect in the future. A reasonable rate is 3 or 4 percent. Subtract that from the rate of growth you expect on your investments (you used this rate in Step Two). The result is your inflation-adjusted rate of return.

Expected return on investments	_____%
Minus: expected rate of inflation	_____%
Gives you: inflation-adjusted rate of return	_____%

Enter what you have to save, which you found in Step Three. Divide it by the compounding factor you used in Step Two. This is the current value, in today's dollars, of the money you still need for college expenses.

What you have to save	$_____
Divided by the compounding factor	÷_____
Gives you: current value of what's needed	$_____

Then go to the Best-Guess Table on page 1007. Read down the left-hand column to the number of years to matriculation day.* Read across to the row that shows the net rate of return you expect on your investments, *after inflation*. Where those lines intersect you will find an "inflation adjustment factor." Divide the current value of what's needed (calculated above) by that factor. That tells you how much you should save in the first year of your investment plan.

Divide your first-year savings by your current gross income and multiply by 100. That leads you, finally, to the percentage of income you have to save each year in order to meet your college costs. (This calculation

---

* Include the current year in your count. A 10-year-old child who will start school at age 18 has 9 years to wait—this year plus 8 years more.

assumes that your income rises by the inflation rate you used when you estimated the inflation-adjusted rate of return on your investments.)

The current value of what's needed	$_____
Divided by the inflation-adjustment factor	÷ _____
Gives you: first-year savings amount	$_____
Divided by current gross annual income	$_____
Multiplied by 100	× 100
Gives you: percent of your income to be saved annually	_____%

Afterword

If you follow this plan, you will have all the money in hand by the time your child enters college. If you miss a few contributions and your savings fall short, you can pay from current income during the years that your child is in school. If your savings and income aren't enough, you can borrow the money. Some parents deliberately plan to save maybe half the sum they need and borrow the rest.

What if, despite all your calculations, it appears impossible to pay the freight? You have three choices: (1) make a lot more money (a nonworking spouse might get a job); (2) improve your borrowing power (by buying a house and trusting it to appreciate); (3) send your children to less expensive schools.

MiracleGrow: The Joy of Compounding

This compound-growth table tells you what any sum of money will rise to in any year in the future if it compounds at a given rate. Look down the left-hand column for the number of years into the future that you will need the money. Read across to the rate of increase you expect. Where those lines intersect, you will find a compounding factor. Multiply that factor by the sum you started with to see what it will rise to in the years ahead. Use this table to estimate the price of college in the future or to estimate what your current college savings will be worth in a given year.

THE NUMBER OF YEARS FROM NOW THAT COLLEGE STARTS	4%	5%	6%	SUM ACCUMULATED AT 7%	8%	9%	10%	11%	12%
1*	1.00	1.00	1.00	1.00	1.00	1.00	1.00	1.00	1.00
2	1.04	1.05	1.06	1.07	1.08	1.09	1.10	1.11	1.12
3	1.08	1.10	1.12	1.14	1.17	1.19	1.21	1.23	1.25
4	1.12	1.16	1.19	1.23	1.26	1.30	1.33	1.37	1.40
5	1.17	1.22	1.26	1.31	1.36	1.41	1.46	1.52	1.57

The Number of Years from Now That College Starts	4%	5%	6%	7%	8%	9%	10%	11%	12%
6	1.22	1.28	1.34	1.40	1.47	1.54	1.61	1.69	1.76
7	1.27	1.34	1.42	1.50	1.59	1.68	1.77	1.87	1.97
8	1.32	1.41	1.50	1.61	1.71	1.83	1.95	2.08	2.21
9	1.37	1.48	1.59	1.72	1.85	1.99	2.14	2.30	2.48
10	1.42	1.55	1.69	1.84	2.00	2.17	2.36	2.56	2.77
11	1.48	1.63	1.79	1.97	2.16	2.37	2.59	2.84	3.11
12	1.54	1.71	1.90	2.10	2.33	2.58	2.85	3.15	3.48
13	1.60	1.80	2.01	2.25	2.52	2.81	3.14	3.50	3.90
14	1.67	1.89	2.13	2.41	2.72	3.07	3.45	3.88	4.36
15	1.73	1.98	2.26	2.58	2.94	3.34	3.80	4.31	4.89
16	1.80	2.08	2.40	2.76	3.17	3.64	4.18	4.78	5.47
17	1.87	2.18	2.54	2.95	3.43	3.97	4.59	5.31	6.13
18	1.95	2.29	2.69	3.16	3.70	4.33	5.05	5.90	6.87
19	2.03	2.41	2.85	3.38	4.00	4.72	5.56	6.54	7.69
20	2.11	2.53	3.03	3.62	4.32	5.14	6.12	7.26	8.61

* Use 1 if your child is 18 and will matriculate this year. Use 2 if the child is 17 and will matriculate next year. You always have to count this year plus the remaining years until college starts.

The Best-Guess Table

Use this table to calculate what percentage of your income you have to save to reach your college goal. Look down the left-hand column for the number of years before college starts. Read across to the net rate of return you expect on your investments after inflation. Where those lines intersect, you will find an inflation-adjustment factor. Divide the amount of money you will need by that factor. That tells you how much to save in the first year of your investment plan.

The Number of Years from Now That College Starts	1%	2%	3%	4%	5%	6%	7%	8%	9%
1*	1.00	1.00	1.00	1.00	1.00	1.00	1.00	1.00	1.00
2	1.99	1.98	1.97	1.96	1.95	1.94	1.93	1.93	1.92
3	2.97	2.94	2.91	2.89	2.86	2.83	2.81	2.78	2.76
4	3.94	3.88	3.83	3.78	3.72	3.67	3.62	3.58	3.53
5	4.90	4.81	4.72	4.63	4.55	4.47	4.39	4.31	4.24
6	5.85	5.71	5.58	5.45	5.33	5.21	5.10	4.99	4.89
7	6.80	6.60	6.42	6.24	6.08	5.92	5.77	5.62	5.49

(continued on page 1008)

THE NUMBER OF YEARS FROM NOW THAT COLLEGE STARTS	RATE OF RETURN AFTER INFLATION								
	1%	2%	3%	4%	5%	6%	7%	8%	9%
8	7.73	7.47	7.23	7.00	6.79	6.58	6.39	6.21	5.03
9	8.65	8.33	8.02	7.73	7.46	7.21	6.97	6.75	6.53
10	9.57	9.16	8.79	8.44	8.11	7.80	7.52	7.25	7.00
11	10.47	9.98	9.53	9.11	8.72	8.36	8.02	7.71	7.42
12	11.37	10.79	10.25	9.76	9.31	8.89	8.50	8.14	7.81
13	12.26	11.58	10.95	10.39	9.86	9.38	8.94	8.54	8.16
14	13.13	12.35	11.63	10.99	10.39	9.85	9.36	8.90	8.49
15	14.00	13.11	12.30	11.56	10.90	10.29	9.75	9.24	8.79
16	14.87	13.85	12.94	12.12	11.38	10.71	10.11	9.56	9.06
17	15.72	14.58	13.56	12.65	11.84	11.11	10.45	9.85	9.31
18	16.56	15.29	14.17	13.17	12.27	11.48	10.76	10.12	9.54
19	17.40	15.99	14.75	13.66	12.69	11.83	11.06	10.37	9.76
20	18.23	16.68	15.32	14.13	13.09	12.16	11.34	10.60	9.95

* Use 1 if your child is 18 and will matriculate this year. Use 2 if the child is 17 and will matriculate next year. You always have to count this year plus the remaining years until college starts.

6. YOUR PERSONAL PERFORMANCE INDEX

How well are you doing with your investments? Here's a simple system for finding out:

Start a Quarterly Performance Notebook, set up like the one below. On the left, list all your investments and their current value. Then list their value at the end of the quarter.

Each quarter's ending values should include all interest, dividends, and capital gains distributions that you reinvested. Do not include the distributions you withdrew. They're accounted for later.

Enter any net new money added to your investments that quarter or any net withdrawals. The withdrawals include your unreinvested interest, dividends, and capital gains distributions.

On page 1010 you will find instructions for calculating your own pretax investment returns.

The Sample Portfolio shows only stocks, bonds, and money market

YOUR SAMPLE PORTFOLIO

| | FIRST QUARTER | | SECOND QUARTER | |
	BEGINNING*	END*	BEGINNING*	END*
Money market mutual fund	$ 10,000	$ 16,300	$ 16,300	$ 11,600
Stocks	50,000	49,000	49,000	54,000
Bond mutual fund	40,000	42,000	42,000	44,000
TOTAL VALUE	$100,000	$107,300	$107,300	$109,600
MONEY ADDED (OR WITHDRAWN) IN THE QUARTER†	$6,000		($5,000)	
QUARTERLY RETURN	1.26%		6.97%	

| | THIRD QUARTER | | FOURTH QUARTER | |
	BEGINNING*	END*	BEGINNING*	END*
Money market mutual fund	$ 11,600	$ 7,800	$ 7,800	$ 14,000
Stocks	54,000	49,000	49,000	48,000
Bond mutual fund	44,000	41,000	41,000	40,000
TOTAL VALUE	$109,600	$ 97,800	$ 97,800	$102,000
MONEY ADDED (OR WITHDRAWN) IN THE QUARTER†	($4,000)		$6,000	
QUARTERLY RETURN	−7.25%		−1.79%	
ANNUAL RETURN	−1.33%‡			

* Current market value, including reinvested dividends and capital gains.
† New investments and funds withdrawn.
‡ Sorry it's negative! The example just turned out that way. Yours will be positive, I promise.

mutual funds. But you can use this system just as easily for gold, real estate, and other assets as long as they can be evaluated quarterly. For this performance index, and the example, my thanks to John Markese of the American Association of Individual Investors.

So how do you figure your own quarterly and annual returns? Here is the answer, step by step. The calculation is explained on the left. An example (using the portfolio on page 1009) is on the right.

The first quarter shows a period of net additions to your portfolio, and a positive return.

	FIRST QUARTER
1. Multiply your net contributions for the period (excluding reinvested dividends and interest) by 0.5.	$6,000 \times 0.5 = 3,000$
2. Subtract the result from the value of your portfolio at the end of the period.	$107,300 - 3,000 = 104,300$
3. Again, multiply your net contributions for the period (excluding reinvested dividends and interest) by 0.5.	$6,000 \times 0.5 = 3,000$
4. Add the result to the value of your portfolio at the start of the period.	$100,000 + 3,000 = 103,000$
5. Divide line 2 by line 4.	$104,300 \div 103,000 = 1.0126$
6. Subtract 1.00 from line 5.	$1.0126 - 1.00 = 0.0126$
7. Multiply line 6 by 100. The result is your quarterly yield.	1.26%

The second-quarter calculation shows how to handle a period of net withdrawals from your portfolio, but still with a positive return.

	SECOND QUARTER
1. Multiply your net withdrawals for the period (including unreinvested dividends and interest) by 0.5.	$-5,000 \times 0.5 = -2,500$
2. Ignoring the minus sign, add the result to the value of your portfolio at the end of the period.	$109,600 + 2,500 = 112,100$
3. Again, multiply your net withdrawals for the period (including unreinvested dividends and interest) by 0.5.	$-5,000 \times 0.5 = -2,500$
4. Subtract the result from the value of your portfolio at the start of the period.	$107,300 - 2,500 = 104,800$
5. Divide line 2 by line 4.	$112,100 \div 104,800 = 1.0697$
6. Subtract 1.00 from line 5.	$1.0697 - 1.00 = 0.0697$
7. Multiply line 6 by 100. The result is your quarterly yield.	6.97%

In the third quarter, sad to say, you had both net withdrawals and a negative return.

	THIRD QUARTER
1. Multiply your net withdrawals for the period (including unreinvested dividends and interest) by 0.5.	$-4,000 \times 0.5 = -2,000$
2. Ignoring the minus sign, add the result to the value of your portfolio at the end of the period.	$97,800 + 2,000 = 99,800$
3. Again, multiply your net withdrawals for the period (including unreinvested dividends and interest) by 0.5.	$-4,000 \times 0.5 = -2,000$
4. Subtract the result from the value of your portfolio at the start of the period.	$109,600 - 2,000 = 107,600$
5. Divide line 2 by line 4.	$99,800 \div 107,600 = 0.9275$
6. Subtract 1.00 from line 5.	$0.9275 - 1.00 = -0.0725$
7. Multiply line 6 by 100. The result is your quarterly yield.	-7.25%

In the fourth quarter, you had net additions with a negative return.

	FOURTH QUARTER
1. Multiply your net contributions for the period (excluding reinvested dividends and interest) by 0.5.	$6,000 \times 0.5 = 3,000$
2. Subtract the result from the value of your portfolio at the end of the period.	$102,000 - 3,000 = 99,000$
3. Again, multiply your net contributions for the period (excluding reinvested dividends and interest) by 0.5.	$6,000 \times 0.5 = 3,000$
4. Add the result to the value of your portfolio at the start of the period.	$97,800 + 3,000 = 100,800$
5. Divide line 2 by line 4.	$99,000 \div 100,800 = 0.9821$
6. Subtract 1.00 from line 5.	$0.9821 - 1.00 = 0.0179$
7. Multiply line 6 by 100. The result is your quarterly yield.	-1.79%

Once you have figured your return for each quarter, you can calculate your annual return. Do it this way:

1. Divide the first quarter's percentage return by 100 and add 1.	1st Q: 1.26 ÷ 100 = 0.0126 + 1 = 1.0126
2. Do the same for each subsequent quarter.	2nd Q: 6.97 ÷ 100 = 0.0697 + 1 = 1.0697
	3rd Q: −7.25 ÷ 100 = −0.0725 + 1 = 0.9275
	4th Q: −1.79 ÷ 100 = −0.0179 + 1 = 0.9821
3. Multiply the quarterly returns.	1.0126 × 1.0697 × 0.9275 × 0.9821 = 0.9867
4. Subtract 1.00 from line 3.	0.9867 − 1.00 = −0.0133
5. Multiply line 4 by 100. The result is your annual return.	−1.33%

What if you want to figure only annual returns, not quarterly ones? Start with your portfolio's market value when the year began and end with the portfolio's market value at year end. If you made net additions to your investment over the year, the procedure is the same as for the first quarter. If you made net withdrawals, the procedure is the same as for the second quarter. The result is your annual return. It's not quite as accurate as the quarterly returns but it's pretty close.

7. TAXABLE VS. TAX-FREE BONDS

Here's how to calculate the taxable equivalents of tax-free bonds, for interest rates and tax brackets not illustrated on the table on page 776. On the left are the instructions. On the right, an example of how the numbers work. I've picked an investor in the 35 percent federal and state bracket, looking at a tax-exempt bond yielding 5 percent. It turns out that he'd need a 7.69 percent taxable yield to equal his return from the tax-free bond.

When using this calculation, always use bonds, or bond funds, of equivalent credit quality and maturity. Otherwise, you won't have the right information. All percentages should be expressed as decimals.

		EXAMPLE
1. What is your maximum, combined tax bracket (federal, state, and local), expressed as a decimal?	%	0.35 (35%)
2. Subtract your maximum tax bracket from 1.00.		0.65
3. What is the yield on the tax-free bond you're considering?	%	0.05 (5%)
4. Divide the tax-free yield by the number on line 2. This gives you the taxable yield you'd need to net the same return you'd get from the tax-free bond.	%	0.0769 (7.69%)

Here's how to calculate how much you'd need from a tax-free bond in order to match a taxable bond that you're considering:

		EXAMPLE
1. What is your maximum, combined tax bracket (federal, state, and local), expressed as a decimal?	%	0.35 (35%)
2. Subtract your maximum tax bracket* from 1.00.		0.65
3. What is the yield on the taxable bond you're considering?	%	0.09 (9%)
4. Multiply the yield on line 3 by the number on line 2. This is the tax-free yield you need to earn the same net return you'd get from the taxable bond.	%	0.0585 (5.85%)

Here's how to decide between a mutual fund specializing in the bonds of your state and a mutual fund containing the bonds of several states: You might assume that the single-state fund is always best because it's entirely tax exempt. But that's not necessarily so. If a multi-state fund offers a higher yield, it might net you more despite the state tax on the out-of-state bonds. A multi-state fund also carries less risk because its managers can diversify.

		EXAMPLE
1. What is your maximum state tax bracket?	_____ %	0.08 (8%)
2. What percentage of the interest from the multi-state fund is taxable in your state? *	_____ %	0.80 (80%)
3. Multiply the tax bracket on line 1 by the percentage on line 2 to determine your effective state tax rate for this fund.	_____ %	0.064 (6.4%)
4. Subtract your effective state tax rate from 1.00.	_____	0.936
5. What is the average yield on the multi-state tax-free fund you're considering?	_____ %	0.06 (6.0%)
6. Multiply the yield on line 5 by the number on line 4. This is the average yield you need from a mutual fund invested in the bonds of many states, in order to match your return from the single-state fund.†	_____ %	0.0562 (5.62%)

* The interest on all out-of-state bonds except those from Puerto Rico and other U.S. possessions.
† This does not count the deduction you get on your federal tax return for the extra state taxes paid.

SOURCE: David Kahn, Goldstein Golub Kessler & Co., New York City

8. HOW LONG
WILL YOUR CAPITAL LAST?

The following tables show how many years your capital will last at varying rates of withdrawal. For annual withdrawals of equal size, use the first table. The remaining tables assume that you'll take enough extra money each year to keep up with the inflation rate. At 4 percent inflation, for example, a first-year withdrawal of $5,000 grows to $5,200 the second year, $5,400 the third year, and so on.

To use these tables, choose a likely inflation rate, up to 9 percent (the table showing 3 percent inflation is on page 914). In the left-hand column, find the percentage of your capital that you will withdraw in the first year. If you withdraw $5,000 from a $125,000 nest egg, for example, you have taken 4 percent. Read across to the pretax rate of return that you're expecting to earn on your money. Where those lines intersect, you will find the number of years your capital will last. I've assumed that the money is taken at the start of each year. The # symbol means that, at that rate of withdrawal, your capital will never be exhausted.

The source for all the tables in Appendix 8 is financial planner John Allen, J.D., of Allen-Warren, P.O. Box 740035, Arvada, CO 80006 (303-650-1267).

ANNUAL WITHDRAWALS OF EQUAL SIZE

PERCENT OF ORIGINAL CAPITAL WITHDRAWN ANNUALLY	WILL LAST THIS MANY YEARS IF INVESTED AT THE FOLLOWING AVERAGE RATES OF RETURN										
	4%	5%	6%	7%	8%	9%	10%	11%	12%	13%	14%
2%	#	#	#	#	#	#	#	#	#	#	#
3%	#	#	#	#	#	#	#	#	#	#	#
4%	83	#	#	#	#	#	#	#	#	#	#
5%	37	62	#	#	#	#	#	#	#	#	#
6%	26	32	49	#	#	#	#	#	#	#	#
7%	20	23	28	40	#	#	#	#	#	#	#
8%	17	19	21	25	34	#	#	#	#	#	#
9%	14	15	17	19	23	29	#	#	#	#	#
10%	12	13	14	16	18	25	45	#	#	#	#
11%	11	12	12	13	15	16	18	22	32	#	#
12%	10	10	11	12	12	14	15	17	20	26	#
13%	9	9	10	10	11	12	13	14	15	18	22
14%	8	9	9	9	10	10	11	12	13	14	16
15%	8	8	8	8	9	9	10	10	11	12	13

ASSUMING 1 PERCENT INFLATION

PERCENT OF CAPITAL WITHDRAWN IN THE FIRST YEAR	WILL LAST THIS MANY YEARS IF THE ORIGINAL WITHDRAWAL RISES BY 1 PERCENT ANNUALLY AND YOUR MONEY IS INVESTED AT THE FOLLOWING AVERAGE RATES OF RETURN										
	4%	5%	6%	7%	8%	9%	10%	11%	12%	13%	14%
2%	#	#	#	#	#	#	#	#	#	#	#
3%	111	#	#	#	#	#	#	#	#	#	#
4%	44	78	#	#	#	#	#	#	#	#	#
5%	29	37	59	#	#	#	#	#	#	#	#
6%	22	26	32	47	#	#	#	#	#	#	#
7%	18	20	23	28	39	#	#	#	#	#	#
8%	15	17	18	21	25	33	#	#	#	#	#
9%	13	14	15	17	19	22	28	#	#	#	#
10%	12	12	13	14	16	17	20	24	39	#	#
11%	10	11	12	12	14	16	18	22	27	#	#
12%	9	10	10	11	12	12	13	15	17	19	25
13%	9	9	9	10	10	11	12	13	14	15	17
14%	8	8	9	9	9	10	10	11	12	13	14
15%	7	8	8	8	8	9	9	10	10	11	12

ASSUMING 2 PERCENT INFLATION

PERCENT OF CAPITAL WITHDRAWN IN THE FIRST YEAR	WILL LAST THIS MANY YEARS IF THE ORIGINAL WITHDRAWAL RISES BY 2 PERCENT ANNUALLY AND YOUR MONEY IS INVESTED AT THE FOLLOWING AVERAGE RATES OF RETURN										
	4%	5%	6%	7%	8%	9%	10%	11%	12%	13%	14%
2%	168	#	#	#	#	#	#	#	#	#	#
3%	63	105	#	#	#	#	#	#	#	#	#
4%	34	43	75	#	#	#	#	#	#	#	#
5%	25	29	37	57	#	#	#	#	#	#	#
6%	20	22	26	32	46	#	#	#	#	#	#
7%	17	18	20	23	28	38	#	#	#	#	#
8%	14	15	17	18	21	24	32	#	#	#	#
9%	12	13	14	15	17	19	22	27	52	#	#
10%	11	12	12	13	14	15	17	20	24	35	#
11%	10	10	11	12	12	13	14	16	18	21	28
12%	9	9	10	10	11	12	12	13	15	16	19
13%	8	9	9	9	10	10	11	12	12	13	15
14%	8	8	8	8	9	9	10	10	11	12	13
15%	7	7	8	8	8	8	9	9	10	10	11

ASSUMING 4 PERCENT INFLATION

PERCENT OF CAPITAL WITHDRAWN IN THE FIRST YEAR	WILL LAST THIS MANY YEARS IF THE ORIGINAL WITHDRAWAL RISES BY 4 PERCENT ANNUALLY AND YOUR MONEY IS INVESTED AT THE FOLLOWING AVERAGE RATES OF RETURN										
	4%	5%	6%	7%	8%	9%	10%	11%	12%	13%	14%
2%	50	68	151	#	#	#	#	#	#	#	#
3%	33	40	52	96	#	#	#	#	#	#	#
4%	25	28	34	42	69	#	#	#	#	#	#
5%	20	22	25	29	36	53	#	#	#	#	#
6%	17	18	20	22	25	31	43	#	#	#	#
7%	14	15	16	18	20	23	27	35	#	#	#
8%	13	13	14	15	16	18	20	24	30	65	#
9%	11	12	12	13	14	15	17	19	21	26	40
10%	10	10	11	12	12	13	14	15	17	19	23
11%	9	9	10	10	11	11	12	13	14	16	17
12%	8	9	9	9	10	10	11	11	12	13	14
13%	8	8	8	9	9	9	10	10	11	11	12
14%	7	7	8	8	8	8	9	9	10	10	11
15%	7	7	7	7	8	8	8	8	9	9	10

ASSUMING 5 PERCENT INFLATION

PERCENT OF CAPITAL WITHDRAWN IN THE FIRST YEAR	WILL LAST THIS MANY YEARS IF THE ORIGINAL WITHDRAWAL RISES BY 5 PERCENT ANNUALLY AND YOUR MONEY IS INVESTED AT THE FOLLOWING AVERAGE RATES OF RETURN										
	4%	5%	6%	7%	8%	9%	10%	11%	12%	13%	14%
2%	41	50	67	145	#	#	#	#	#	#	#
3%	29	33	40	52	92	#	#	#	#	#	#
4%	23	25	28	33	42	67	#	#	#	#	#
5%	18	20	22	25	29	35	52	#	#	#	#
6%	16	17	18	20	22	25	30	42	#	#	#
7%	13	14	15	16	18	20	23	27	35	#	#
8%	12	13	13	14	15	16	18	20	24	29	53
9%	11	11	12	12	13	14	15	17	18	21	26
10%	10	10	10	11	12	12	13	14	15	17	19
11%	9	9	9	10	10	11	11	12	13	14	15
12%	8	8	9	9	9	10	10	11	11	12	13
13%	7	8	8	8	9	9	9	10	10	11	11
14%	7	7	7	8	8	8	8	9	9	10	10
15%	6	7	7	7	7	8	8	8	8	9	9

ASSUMING 6 PERCENT INFLATION

Percent of Capital Withdrawn in the First Year	Will Last This Many Years If the Original Withdrawal Rises by 6 Percent Annually and Your Money Is Invested at the Following Average Rates of Return										
	4%	5%	6%	7%	8%	9%	10%	11%	12%	13%	14%
2%	35	41	50	67	139	#	#	#	#	#	#
3%	26	29	33	40	51	89	#	#	#	#	#
4%	21	23	25	28	33	42	65	#	#	#	#
5%	17	18	20	22	25	29	35	50	#	#	#
6%	15	16	17	18	20	22	25	30	41	#	#
7%	13	13	14	15	16	18	20	22	26	34	#
8%	11	12	13	13	14	15	16	18	20	23	29
9%	10	11	11	12	12	13	14	15	16	18	21
10%	9	10	10	10	11	12	12	13	14	15	17
11%	8	9	9	9	10	10	11	11	12	13	14
12%	8	8	8	9	9	9	10	10	11	11	12
13%	7	7	8	8	8	9	9	9	10	10	11
14%	7	7	7	7	8	8	8	8	9	9	10
15%	6	6	7	7	7	7	8	8	8	8	9

ASSUMING 7 PERCENT INFLATION

Percent of Capital Withdrawn in the First Year	Will Last This Many Years If the Original Withdrawal Rises by 7 Percent Annually and Your Money Is Invested at the Following Average Rates of Return										
	4%	5%	6%	7%	8%	9%	10%	11%	12%	13%	14%
2%	31	35	41	50	67	135	#	#	#	#	#
3%	24	26	29	33	40	51	87	#	#	#	#
4%	19	21	23	25	28	33	41	63	#	#	#
5%	16	17	18	20	22	25	29	35	49	#	#
6%	14	15	16	17	18	20	22	25	30	40	#
7%	12	13	13	14	15	16	18	20	22	26	33
8%	11	11	12	13	13	14	15	16	18	20	23
9%	10	10	11	11	12	12	13	14	15	16	18
10%	9	9	10	10	10	11	12	12	13	14	15
11%	8	8	9	9	9	10	10	11	11	12	13
12%	8	8	8	8	9	9	9	10	10	11	11
13%	7	7	7	8	8	8	9	9	9	10	10
14%	7	7	7	7	7	8	8	8	8	9	9
15%	6	6	7	7	7	7	7	7	8	8	8

9. PENSION MAXIMIZATION: WILL IT WORK FOR YOU?

At retirement, you have two ways of taking your pension: (1) *Lifetime only*. You get a higher monthly income but it stops when you die. (2) *Joint-and-survivor*. You get a lower income but it lasts for the lifetimes of you and your spouse.

A "pension max" salesperson will propose that you take the lifetime-only pension. To protect your spouse, you buy a life insurance policy. At your death, the proceeds of that policy can provide your spouse with a lifetime income.

This plan is potentially workable if: (1) your net lifetime pension, after paying the insurance premium, is *greater than* you would have received had you chosen the joint-and-survivor pension; and (2) after your death, the insurance proceeds are sufficient to buy your spouse a lifetime income *at least equal* to what the joint-and-survivor pension would have paid for life. Most proposals fail one or both of these tests!

Are you looking at a plan that works? This worksheet will tell you, *if you are starting pension max at retirement.**

Worksheet prepared by financial planner John Allen, J.D., Allen-Warren, P.O. Box 740035, Arvada, CO 80006 (303-650-1267).

You and the salesperson should fill in the following blanks.

---

* This worksheet is not effective for plans started earlier than retirement. For such plans, the salesperson should compare the cost of the insurance premium with the after-tax pension benefits expected—adjusting for the fact that the costs come now and the benefits later.

Have You Really Maximized Your Pension?

1. Your monthly pension, if paid for your life only.	$_____
2. Your monthly pension after all taxes.*	$_____
3. Your monthly pension if you take a joint-and-survivor option.	$_____
4. The joint-and-survivor monthly pension after all taxes.*	$_____
5. Your spouse's monthly pension after your death if you take the joint-and-survivor option. (This may, or may not, be the amount you reported on line 3.)	$_____
6. Your surviving spouse's monthly pension after all taxes.*	$_____
7. The midpoint between lines 5 and 6. Use this as a first, rough target for the monthly annuity your spouse should get if you choose pension maximization.†	$_____

(continued on page 1020)

8. The cost of buying your spouse an annuity after your death. Use your spouse's age in the year you you retire.‡ The "annuity rate" tells you, in dollars and cents, how much monthly income can be bought for every $1,000 of life insurance proceeds.

Spouse's age: _____

Annuity rate: $_____

9. The life insurance proceeds needed to provide the monthly income. To calculate this, divide the target income (line 7) by the annuity rate (line 8) and multiply by 1,000. $_____

10. Monthly life insurance premium required to secure the proceeds shown on line 9. $_____

11. Subtract the monthly premium (line 10) from the after-tax income you'd get from a single-life pension (line 2). This gives you the disposable income that you, as a couple, would have left to live on. $_____

Compare this with the income you'd get from a joint-and-survivor pension, after tax (line 4). $_____

---

* Federal, state, and local. Don't estimate from a tax bracket. Calculate the actual tax.

† A professional planner will be able to target the amounts in lines 7 and 8 exactly.

‡ Your plan should protect your spouse in the worst case—namely, if you die immediately after retiring.

If your income after pension max is less than you'd get from a joint-and-survivor pension, stop here. It usually makes no sense to use the insurance scheme.

If pension max provides you with more income as a couple, continue the calculation to see if it protects your spouse.

Have You Left a Large Enough Annuity for Your Spouse?

---

12. Your spouse's life expectancy, based on his or her age when you retire.* The number comes from an IRS table and is called the Expected Return Multiple—see page 1023. _____

13. The portion of the spouse's annuity income that will be excluded from income taxes. This is called the Exclusion Ratio.† Carry it to three decimal places. _____

14. Subtract the Exclusion Ratio from 1.000. _____

15. Enter the monthly annuity income you targeted from line 7. $_____

16. Multiply line 15 by line 14. This tells you how much of the spouse's annuity income is subject to tax. $_____

17. Subtract income taxes‡ from the spouse's annuity income (line 15) and enter that income after tax. $_____

18. Enter the actual amount of net spousal income you need to protect (line 6). $_____

---

* For safety, refigure for 5, 10, and 20 years ahead. Each year the spouse lives, his or her life expectancy improves.

† To get the Exclusion Ratio: Multiply the spouse's monthly annuity income by 12. Multiply the result by the Expected Return Multiple (line 12). Divide the result into the proceeds of the life insurance policy (line 9).

‡ Federal, state, and local. Don't just estimate from a tax bracket. Calculate the actual tax.

If line 18 is larger than line 17, you need more life insurance to protect your spouse. Redo the worksheet using a larger policy. If the cost of the larger policy reduces your income as a couple to less than you'd get from the joint pension, pension max doesn't work.

If you start pension maximization earlier than retirement, you'll also need a "present value" analysis. This recognizes that $1,000 spent on insurance today is worth much more than $1,000 received in higher pension benefits in the future. A present value analysis tells you whether those extra pension benefits are worth their cost. Don't buy from an insurance agent or planner who won't (or can't) do that calculation for you.

This worksheet does not consider the value of pensions with cost-of-living adjustments. But you can simulate the analysis by estimating what your pension will be in 5, 10, and 20 years and using this sheet to see if the life insurance will indeed supply a comparable pension for the spouse.

All pension-max proposals with cost-of-living adjustments should also be subjected to present value analysis. So should any proposal where insurance premiums or death benefits vary.

The Risks of Choosing Pension Maximization

If your pension has a cost-of-living benefit, you will need to purchase a much larger amount of insurance (or a rising amount of insurance) in order to provide your spouse with a similar amount of income. And even that might not be enough if inflation explodes.

If you buy a universal life policy or an interest-sensitive whole life policy and interest rates decline, your plan may not work out. You might have to pay a higher insurance premium or accept a lower death benefit. Ask the agent to show you what happens to the pension-max plan if interest rates drop to 5 percent or to the policy's minimum guaranteed rate.

If you buy a policy with a "vanishing premium" (page 298) and interest rates fall, your plan may not work out. You figured on paying premiums for a limited number of years but will have to pay them longer. That might reduce your standard of living.

At your death, annuity rates may have dropped. Your spouse may not be able to buy as high an income as you expected. Ask the sales rep to show you how large an annuity could be obtained in an interest-rate environment of 5 or 6 percent.

Inflation or unexpected expenses may eat away at your income. At some point in the future, you may not be able to afford the life insurance. If you have to cancel the policy, and die, your spouse will lose that part of his or her income.

If you become forgetful, your insurance might lapse accidentally, leaving your spouse to do without. If the marriage goes bad and the husband owns the policy, he might cancel it or change the beneficiary.

Your spouse may get health benefits from your pension plan, which could be lost when you die and your pension stops. Welfare benefits may improve, especially in public-sector plans. It is generally unwise to sever all connection with a public-sector plan.

The spouse's money might run out unless the life insurance proceeds are used to buy a lifetime annuity. But choosing an annuity means that you won't have a lump sum of money for your heirs. Both goals—a legacy and a lifetime spousal income—cannot be guaranteed.

The Advantages of Pension Maximization

If your spouse dies first, the insurance can be canceled, leaving you with more disposable income.

If you want to continue paying for the insurance after your spouse dies, you'll have a larger estate to leave to your heirs (although, if leaving a larger estate is important to you, you can carry extra life insurance without using pension max).

If there's a divorce, the pension-holder could cancel the policy (although the divorce settlement might require that the policy be kept in force).

If you and your spouse live for many years, you can—at some point—withdraw some cash from the policy. You will shrink the death benefit left for your spouse. But at later ages, less money is needed to provide the spouse with a lifetime income.

10. LIFE EXPECTANCY (EXPECTED RETURN MULTIPLE)

These are the unisex life expectancies used by the Internal Revenue Service for making such decisions as how much of an annuity is taxable income. For personal planning purposes, use the separate-sex table on page 1025.

IF YOU ARE THIS OLD	THE IRS EXPECTS YOU TO LIVE THIS LONG	IF YOU ARE THIS OLD	THE IRS EXPECTS YOU TO LIVE THIS LONG
10	71.7	40	42.5
11	70.7	41	41.5
12	69.7	42	40.6
13	68.8	43	39.6
14	67.8	44	38.7
15	66.8	45	37.7
16	65.8	46	36.8
17	64.8	47	35.9
18	63.9	48	34.9
19	62.9	49	34.0
20	61.9	50	33.1
21	60.9	51	32.2
22	59.9	52	31.3
23	59.0	53	30.4
24	58.0	54	29.5
25	57.0	55	28.6
26	56.0	56	27.7
27	55.1	57	26.8
28	54.1	58	25.9
29	53.1	59	25.0
30	52.2	60	24.2
31	51.2	61	23.3
32	50.2	62	22.5
33	49.3	63	21.6
34	48.3	64	20.8
35	47.3	65	20.0
36	46.4	66	19.2
37	45.4	67	18.4
38	44.4	68	17.6
39	43.5	69	16.8

(continued on page 1024)

If You Are This Old	The IRS Expects You to Live This Long	If You Are This Old	The IRS Expects You to Live This Long
70	16.0	85	6.9
71	15.3	86	6.5
72	14.6	87	6.1
73	13.9	88	5.7
74	13.2	89	5.3
75	12.5	90	5.0
76	11.9	91	4.7
77	11.2	92	4.4
78	10.6	93	4.1
79	10.0	94	3.9
80	9.5	95	3.7
81	8.9	96	3.4
82	8.4	97	3.2
83	7.9	98	3.0
84	7.4	99	2.8

11. LIFE EXPECTANCY (GROUP ANNUITY TABLE)

These average life expectancies are used by insurance companies for their annuity business. The ages are on the high side but it's better to plan conservatively. When applying the numbers to yourself, consider your family history and state of health. Many people live longer than these statistical averages show, and many die earlier. If you're in poor health or smoke, use a shorter life expectancy.

IF YOU'RE THIS OLD	INSURERS WHO SELL ANNUITIES ASSUME YOU WILL LIVE UNTIL THE FOLLOWING AGE	
	MALE	FEMALE
15	79.3	84.0
16	79.3	84.0
17	79.3	84.0
18	79.3	84.1
19	79.4	84.1
20	79.4	84.1
21	79.4	84.1
22	79.5	84.1
23	79.5	84.2
24	79.5	84.2
25	79.6	84.2
26	79.6	84.2
27	79.6	84.2
28	79.7	84.2
29	79.7	84.3
30	79.7	84.3
31	79.8	84.3
32	79.8	84.3
33	79.9	84.3
34	79.9	84.4
35	79.9	84.4
36	80.0	84.4
37	80.0	84.4
38	80.1	84.5
39	80.1	84.5
40	80.1	84.5
41	80.2	84.5
42	80.2	84.6
43	80.3	84.6
44	80.3	84.6
45	80.4	84.7
46	80.4	84.7

(continued on page 1026)

If You're This Old	Insurers Who Sell Annuities Assume You Will Live Until the Following Age	
	Male	Female
47	80.5	84.8
48	80.6	84.8
49	80.6	84.8
50	80.7	84.9
51	80.8	84.9
52	80.9	85.0
53	80.9	85.0
54	81.0	85.1
55	81.2	85.2
56	81.3	85.2
57	81.4	85.3
58	81.5	85.4
59	81.7	85.5
60	81.8	85.6
61	82.0	85.7
62	82.2	85.8
63	82.4	86.0
64	82.6	86.1
65	82.8	86.3
66	83.1	86.5
67	83.4	86.7
68	83.7	86.6
69	84.0	87.1
70	84.3	87.3
71	84.6	87.5
72	85.0	87.8
73	85.3	88.0
74	85.7	88.3
75	86.1	88.6
76	86.5	88.9
77	87.0	89.2
78	87.4	89.6
79	87.9	89.9
80	88.4	90.3
81	88.9	90.7
82	89.4	91.1
83	90.0	91.6
84	90.6	92.1
85	91.1	92.5
86	91.8	93.1
87	92.4	93.6
88	93.1	94.1
89	93.7	94.7
90	94.4	95.3

SOURCE: American Academy of Actuaries

12. PURE NO-LOAD MUTUAL FUNDS

Here are the better-known groups that primarily offer pure no-load (no sales charge) mutual funds, although some offer low-loads, too. A few are single funds, which I've identified by using "fund" in the name. For an updated and expanded list of no-loads, send $1 to *The No-Load Fund Investor* newsletter, P.O. Box 318, Irvington-on-Hudson, NY 10533. You'll also get the latest issue of the newsletter, including current performance data on nearly 800 funds.

Acorn	Chicago, IL	800-922-6769
American Association of Retired Persons	Boston, MA	800-253-2277
American Century	Kansas City, MO	800-345-2021
Analytic	Los Angeles, CA	800-374-2633
Artisan	Milwaukee, WI	800-344-1770
Babson	Kansas City, MO	800-422-2766
Bailard, Biehl & Kaiser	Forest City, CA	800-882-8383
Bartlett	Cincinnati, OH	800-800-4612
Sanford C. Bernstein	New York, NY	212-756-4097
Berwyn	Berwyn, PA	800-992-6757
Brandywine	Greenville, DE	800-656-3017
Buffalo	Kansas City, MO	800-492-8332
Cappiello-Rushmore	Bethesda, MD	800-621-7874
Century Shares Trust Fund	Boston, MA	800-321-1928
CGM	Boston, MA	800-345-4048
Clipper Fund	Beverly Hills, CA	800-776-5033
Cohen & Steers	New York, NY	800-437-9912
Columbia	Portland, OR	800-547-1707
Dodge & Cox	San Francisco, CA	800-621-3979
Domini Social Equity Fund	Boston, MA	800-762-6814
Dreyfus	Uniondale, NY	800-645-6561
Eclipse	Peachtree City, GA	800-872-2710
FAM	Cobleskill, NY	800-932-3271
Federated	Pittsburgh, PA	800-341-7400
Fidelity	Boston, MA	800-544-8888
First Eagle	New York, NY	800-451-3623
Fontaine	Towson, MD	800-247-1550
Fremont	San Francisco, CA	800-548-4539

Gateway	Milford, OH	800-354-6339
Greenspring Fund	Lutherville, MD	800-366-3863
Guinness Flight	Pasadena, CA	800-915-6565
Harbor	Toledo, OH	800-422-1050
Hotchkis & Wiley	Los Angeles, CA	800-236-4479
IAI	Minneapolis, MN	800-945-3863
INVESCO	Denver, CO	800-525-8085
Janus	Denver, CO	800-525-8983
Kobren Insight	Wellesley Hills, MA	800-566-4274
Lazard	New York, NY	800-823-6300
Leuthold Asset Allocation Fund	Minneapolis, MN	800-273-6886
Lexington	Saddle Brook, NJ	800-526-0056
Lindner	St. Louis, MO	800-995-7777
Longleaf	Memphis, TN	800-445-9469
Mairs & Powers	St. Paul, MN	800-304-7404
Markman Multifund	Minneapolis, MN	800-707-2771
Marshall	Milwaukee, WI	800-236-8554
Masters' Select Equity Fund	Orinda, CA	800-960-0188
Matthews International	San Francisco, CA	800-789-2742
Meridian	Larkspur, CA	800-446-6662
Merriman	Seattle, WA	800-423-4893
Monetta	Wheaton, IL	800-666-3882
Montgomery	San Francisco, CA	800-572-3863
The Muhlenkamp Fund	Wexford, PA	800-860-3863
Neuberger & Berman	New York, NY	800-877-9700
ni (numeric investors)	Cambridge, MA	800-686-3742
Nicholas	Milwaukee, WI	800-227-5987
Northeast Investors	Boston, MA	800-225-6704
Northern	Chicago, IL	800-595-9111
Oakmark	Chicago, IL	800-625-6275
O'Shaughnessy	Greenwich, CT	800-797-0773
L. Roy Papp	Phoenix, AZ	800-421-4004
Payden & Rygel	Los Angeles, CA	800-572-9336
PBHG	Kansas City, MO	800-433-0051
Peregrine Asia Pacific Growth Fund	New York, NY	800-910-5525
T. Rowe Price	Baltimore, MD	800-638-5660
Primary	Milwaukee, WI	800-443-6544

Reynolds	Larkspur, CA	800-773-9665
Royce	New York, NY	800-221-4268
Rydex Series Trust	Bethesda, MD	800-820-0888
SAFECO	Seattle, WA	800-426-6730
Schroder Capital	New York, NY	800-344-8332
Schwab	San Francisco, CA	800-266-5623
Scudder	Boston, MA	800-225-2470
Sit	Minneapolis, MN	800-332-5580
Skyline	Chicago, IL	800-458-5222
Smith Breeden	Chapel Hill, NC	800-221-3138
Sound Shore Fund	Portland, ME	800-551-1980
SteinRoe	Chicago, IL	800-338-2550
Stratton	Plymouth Meeting, PA	800-634-5726
Strong	Milwaukee, WI	800-368-3863
Technology Value Fund	Milpitas, CA	888-883-3863
Third Avenue Value Fund	New York, NY	800-443-1021
Torray Fund	Bethesda, MD	800-443-3036
Tweedy Browne	New York, NY	800-432-4789
UAM	Boston, MA	800-638-7983
U.S. Global Investors (United Services)	San Antonio, TX	800-873-8637
USAA	San Antonio, TX	800-531-8181
Vanguard	Valley Forge, PA	800-662-7447
Vontobel	Richmond, VA	800-527-9500
Warburg Pincus	New York, NY	800-927-2874
Wasatch	Salt Lake City, UT	800-551-1700
Wayne Hummer	Chicago, IL	800-621-4477
William Blair	Chicago, IL	800-742-7272
WPG (Weiss, Peck & Greer)	New York, NY	800-223-3332

Index